TENNESSEE

MARGARET LITTMAN

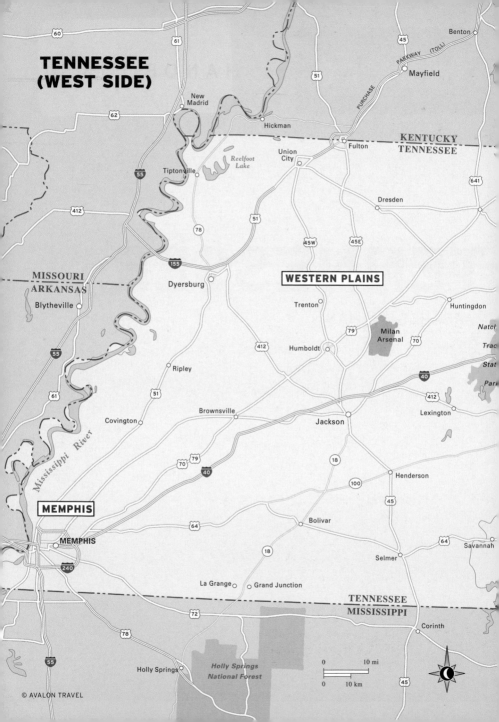

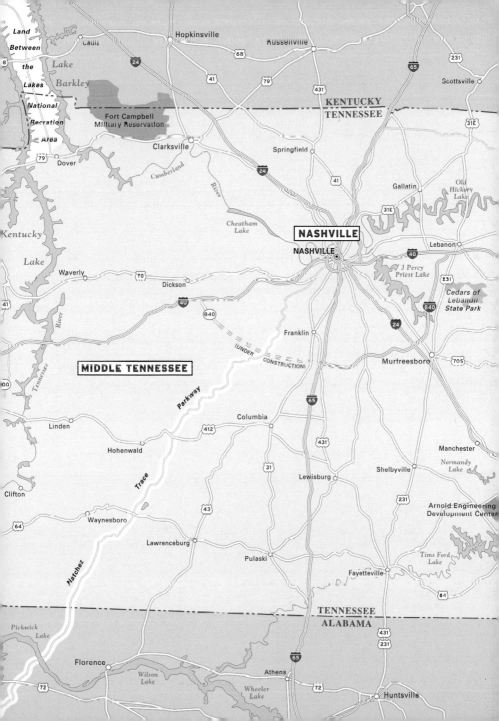

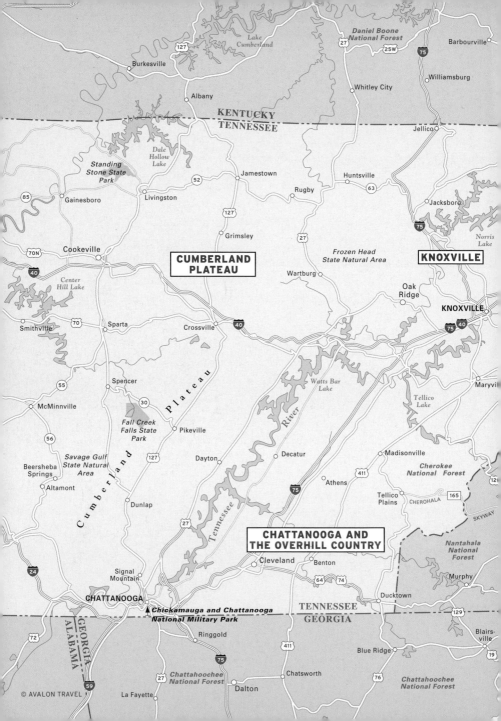

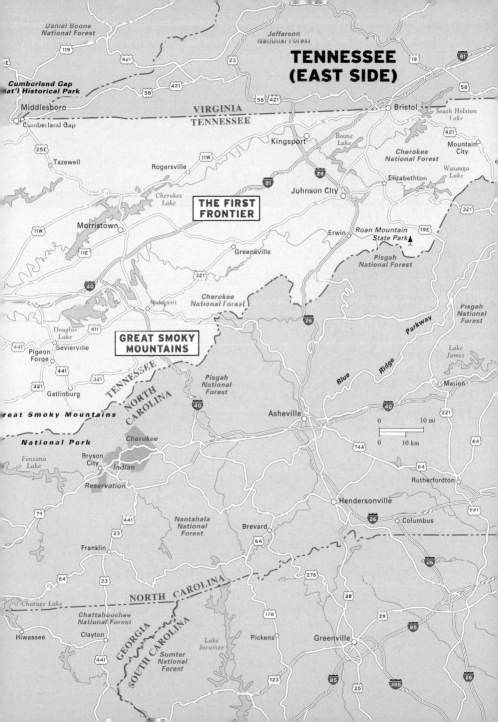

Contents

Discover Tennessee

My first visit to Tennessee was when I was a teenager. Back then I wasn't able to articulate what drew me to this Southern wonderland. But in the years since, I've moved away and come back, and now realize I have become quite verbose when it comes to the state where I make my home.

Tennessee offers a suggestion for every season, every mood, and every personality. It's the cradle of country music and the birthplace of the blues. It's produced Nobel laureates, Pulitzer Prize winners, and history-making statesmen. Creativity of all kinds seems to flow in the rivers and in the veins of the folks who call the Volunteer State home.

That creativity is evident even to visitors just passing through. It fosters an entrepreneurial energy that results in funky, offbeat music clubs for jamming, quirky boutiques for shopping, and one-of-a-kind roadside eateries for… well, eating. Allow us to introduce you to bluegrass, to Appalachian and African American quilts, to meat and three, hot chicken, and barbecue. You will soon become well acquainted with them all.

The creative spirit seems to inhabit the landscape as well. East Tennessee has mountains—*real* mountains that climb up to cloud-covered peaks, and plunge down into valleys. Moving west through the state, the mountains become the rolling hills of Middle Tennessee and then the plains toward Memphis and the mighty Mississippi, Father of Waters.

Come to explore, to eat, to drink, to distill, to study, to shop, to hike and climb, to fish and run rivers, to hear music, to *play* music... it doesn't matter. No matter what brings you here, Southern hospitality assures that you'll feel at home minutes after your arrival. Just as Tennessee's geography, its arts, its history, and its people guarantee that you will never be bored.

Planning Your Trip

▶ WHERE TO GO

Tennessee is a long state: From tip to tip, the Volunteer State stretches 432 miles. That's eight hours on the interstate highway, though I recommend you get off the interstate and explore. Cultural and historical differences help define the state's three basic geographical regions: East, Middle, and West Tennessee. Here's an overview from west to east.

Memphis

Memphis may owe its physical existence to the mighty Mississippi, but it is music that gives this city its soul. The blues were born in Memphis, and they still call Memphis home in nightclubs on Beale Street and juke joints around the city. But the Bluff City isn't just the blues. It's gospel, Elvis Presley, Soulsville, Rev. Al Green, Isaac Hayes, and Sun Studio. And it's more than music. Memphis is an urban center with fine dining, parks, and art museums. It is a city where you can unwind by watching the ducks get the red-carpet treatment at the Peabody Hotel or fuel up with a plate of barbecue.

Western Plains

Look for bald eagles and wild turkeys amid the knob-kneed cypress trees at Reelfoot Lake. Hike and camp along the shores of Kentucky Lake at the Land Between the Lakes. Along the Tennessee River is the state's only pearl farm, the charming river town of Savannah, and Shiloh, the site of an epic Civil War battle. Don't miss outsider art masterpiece Billy Tripp's Mindfield.

Even the campsites have great views at Land Between the Lakes.

IF YOU HAVE . . .

W. C. Handy Home and Museum, on Beale Street in Memphis

the Sunsphere in Knoxville

- **JUST ONE WEEKEND:** Visit Nashville, Memphis, or Chattanooga.

- **ONE WEEK:** From Nashville or Memphis add Middle Tennessee; from Chattanooga add the Cumberland Plateau.

- **TWO WEEKS:** Add Oak Ridge, Knoxville, and the Great Smoky Mountains.

- **A MONTH:** Add the Western Plains and the First Frontier.

Nashville

Nashville is a city that will never lose its quirkiness. Nashville is the epicenter of country music. It is home of the Grand Ole Opry, the Country Music Hall of Fame, and dozens of recording studios. It is the place where thousands of musicians and songwriters come to make it, and the city's nightlife is all the richer for it. Grand antebellum homes, fine arts, and excellent dining appeal to sophisticates. Museums, historic sites, and the grand Tennessee capitol recall the city's history, while expansive parks invite recreation in this leafy, livable city.

Middle Tennessee

Tennessee's midsection is a road trip waiting to happen. The landscape is rural and pure relaxation. This is Walking Horse Country, where picturesque horse farms dot the landscape and Tennessee sipping whiskey is made. In Amish country black buggies and old-fashioned homesteads litter the back roads. The Natchez Trace is a scenic highway that marks one of the oldest overland routes between New Orleans and Nashville. Explore the heartland in search of perfectly fried chicken, the world's largest Moon Pie, and exciting summertime festivals. Don't forget to sip some of that Lynchburg lemonade.

Cumberland Plateau

The Cumberland Plateau is a breathtaking landscape of caves, waterfalls, gorges, and mountains. It is home to some of the state's best parks: the Big South Fork and Pickett State Park in the north, Fall Creek Falls State Park in the center, and Savage Gulf in the south. Come here for outdoor recreation, including hiking, biking, horseback riding, camping, and kayaking. The plateau offers destinations with fascinating history: the lost English colony of Rugby, the idealistic experiment of Cumberland Homesteads, and the Children's Holocaust Memorial at Whitwell.

Chattanooga and the Overhill Country

Nestled in a bend of the Tennessee River and surrounded by the Cumberland Plateau and foothills of the Appalachian Mountains, Chattanooga is not called the Scenic City for nothing. It is a great place to bring the kids thanks to its excellent aquarium, children's museum, parks, zoo, caves, and other family-friendly attractions. East of the city lies the southern Cherokee National Forest and the Ocoee River—a destination for those interested in white-water rafting and other outdoor pursuits. No other region offers a better glimpse at the legacy of the Cherokee Indians, who once populated the hills and valleys of this Overhill land.

Knoxville

Like the better-known Memphis and Nashville, Knoxville is emerging as a center for live music and the arts. Galleries, restaurants, nightclubs, and theaters on Gay Street, Market Square, and the Old City are funky, unpretentious, and fun. Sports fans have been coming to Knoxville for years to watch the University of Tennessee Volunteers play football and basketball, and to tour the Women's Basketball Hall of Fame. Attractions such as the East Tennessee History Center and the reopened gold-plated Sunsphere add to the city's draw.

Chattanooga is set on the scenic Tennessee River.

Great Smoky Mountains National Park

Great Smoky Mountains

Tennessee's most picturesque wilderness is the Great Smoky Mountains. It is the vistas that first draw you in: the soft-edged peaks, enveloped by wispy white "smoke," touched by brilliant red and orange at sunset, and crowned by crisp white snow in winter. Hike through old-growth forest and mysterious mountain balds. Camp next to a mountain stream. Hunt for wildflowers. Bicycle the Cades Cove loop to see historic cabins and churches. Outside the boundary of the park are gateway communities offering everything from the Dollywood theme park to quiet rural retreats.

The First Frontier

It was to the eastern mountains of northeast Tennessee that early settlers moved in the 1770s. More than 150 years later the descendants of these mountain folks brought forth modern country music during the Bristol Sessions. This region of Tennessee is more closely linked to Appalachia than any other; this is a landscape of hills and hollers, small towns, and traditional ways. Jonesborough is the first city of storytelling, and the Tri-Cities draw race fans to Bristol Motor Speedway.

wildflowers in the Great Smoky Mountains

▶ WHEN TO GO

Summer is the peak travel season for Tennessee. This is the season of hot weather and crowds at many popular sites. Avoid the crowds and the heat: Spring and fall are the best times to explore Tennessee. During spring, the weather is mild, flora is in bloom, and you can enjoy springtime festivals. During the fall, the trees change color and temperatures drop.

Visitors in winter may encounter cold weather and snow. If you're a skier, head to Gatlinburg. In other parts of the state, some attractions close or cut back hours November–February, but the cool months can also be a nice time to tour as you'll have many attractions to yourself.

▶ BEFORE YOU GO

Transportation
While visitors making a getaway to Memphis or Nashville may be able to subsist on public transportation and taxis, all others will need wheels to see this state. A car is essential if you are traveling in Tennessee. If it's practical, bring your own car. If you're flying in, arrange a rental car ahead of time to save money and ease hassles. A good road map or GPS is helpful to have before you set out.

If you are flying to Tennessee, your airport will depend on your end destination. Nashville and Memphis have international airports and generally the best airfare deals. Knoxville, Chattanooga, and the Tri-Cities regional airports are convenient if you're headed to East Tennessee.

What to Take
Take a calling card that will work at pay phones and hotels, particularly if you are

snowfall along Little Pigeon River, in Great Smoky Mountains National Park

likely to get off the interstate and out of the range of cell phone signals.

Since your trip is likely to include a fair amount of driving, download a mess of tunes. Depending on your destination, pick up some classic country, bluegrass, blues, or Elvis albums to get you in the mood.

If you're planning on spending time in the Great Smoky Mountains, be sure to pack rain gear and several layers of clothes, including a jacket or sweater—even in the summer. If you think you may do some hiking, bring good boots, a backpack, and a trail map. Cowboy boots and a cowboy hat aren't required, but they're certainly always appropriate.

Explore Tennessee

▶ DOWNTOWN AND THE DELTA: MEMPHIS AND WEST TENNESSEE

Follow in the footsteps of Elvis, eat real Memphis barbecue, and explore the delta landscape that gave rise to the blues. Travel along the Tennessee River, stopping at a pearl farm, river towns, and the site of one of the bloodiest Civil War battles in Tennessee.

A Long Weekend in Memphis

DAY 1

Arrive in Memphis and check into a downtown hotel, such as the Peabody or Talbot Heirs. Grab some Gus's World Famous Fried Chicken and stroll down to Beale Street in the evening.

DAY 2

Take the Beale Street Walking Tour in the morning, stopping at the W. C. Handy Home and Museum. Take your picture with the Elvis statue, and go treasure hunting at A. Schwab. Eat lunch at the Little Tea Shop downtown, and then head over to Mud Island for the afternoon. Explore the Mississippi River Museum and the River Walk. Eat dinner in Harbor Town on Mud Island.

DAY 3

Go to the National Civil Rights Museum in the morning, eat lunch along South Main, and then go to the Stax Museum of American Soul Music in the afternoon. Head to The Majestic Grill for dinner.

Options

DAY 4

Make it Elvis Day. Start early at Graceland to avoid the crowds, and then visit Sun Studio,

downtown Memphis from Mud Island River Park

where Elvis recorded his first hit. Eat a burger at Dyers on Beale Street in memory of the King.

DAY 5

Start out at Elmwood Cemetery with the audio tour, and then drive east. Visit the Memphis Brooks Museum of Art and lounge in Overton Park. Tour The Dixon and eat dinner at the Beauty Shop in Cooper-Young.

Excursions

MASON AND HENNING

Leave Memphis, driving northeast along Highway 70. Stop in Mason to pick up some of Gus's World Famous Fried Chicken for the road. Visit the Alex Haley House Museum in Henning, and then push on to Reelfoot Lake. Check into the Airpark Inn.

REELFOOT LAKE

Explore Reelfoot Lake State Park. Take a boat cruise or hike along the lakeshore. Eat fried catfish at Boyette's.

LAND BETWEEN THE LAKES

Drive east to Land Between the Lakes. Visit The Homeplace to see frontier life re-created and watch a celestial show at the Golden Pond Visitor Center and Planetarium. Overnight in a log cabin at Leatherwood Resort in Dover.

SAVANNAH

Drive south to historic Savannah, which you can enjoy on foot. Then tour the Shiloh National Military Park. Take the audio tour or hike to the Shiloh Indian Mounds. Overnight at the hotel at Pickwick Landing State Resort Park and eat dinner at the Broken Spoke.

PINSON MOUNDS AND JACKSON

Go to Pinson Mounds State Archaeological Park to stretch your legs and tour mysterious Indian mounds. Eat lunch in Jackson at Dixie Castle, see the Mindfield art installation, and then return to Memphis on the interstate.

Graceland

Sun Studio

TOP FESTIVALS

In a state with nearly 1,000 annual festivals, how do you choose? One strategy: Start with a cross section of gatherings across the state and year, and then try some more.

- **National Cornbread Festival** (South Pittsburg, in April): A celebration of the iconic Southern side dish includes bluegrass music, cook-offs, and lots and lots of corn bread.
- **Bonnaroo** (Manchester, in June): What started as a jam-band festival on a Tennessee farm has grown into one

of the most diverse and well-organized (albeit crowded) music festivals in the United States.

- **Elvis Week** (Memphis, in August): Elvis mania always exists in Memphis, but it reaches a fever pitch during the annual remembrance of the King's death.
- **RiverRocks** (Chattanooga, in October): All things outdoors are celebrated during this nine-day music and sports extravaganza in the Tennessee Valley.

► NASHVILLE AND MIDDLE TENNESSEE

Start out in the state's capital, and then strike out through Tennessee's heartland to old railroad towns and quiet parks. See the stars on the Grand Ole Opry and make a pilgrimage to Lynchburg, home of that most famous Tennessee whiskey. Tour the sites of Civil War battles and hear the stories of those who fought and those who died.

A Week in Nashville

DAY 1

Arrive in Nashville. Check into a downtown hotel, such as the Hermitage or Union Station. Cross the bridge into East Nashville and dine at Holland House Bar and Refuge. Come back and stroll Lower Broadway and the District on your first night in town.

DAY 2

Visit the Country Music Hall of Fame in the morning and the Ryman Auditorium in the afternoon. Have lunch at Jack's Bar-b-que on Broadway and grab an afternoon drink at Tootsie's Orchid Lounge. See the Grand Ole Opry in the evening.

DAY 3

Head toward West Nashville. Drive through Music Row on your way to Centennial Park and The Parthenon. Eat lunch at Martha's at the Plantation at Belle Meade, and then spend

Ryman Auditorium

A model of Greece's Parthenon sits in Nashville's Centennial Park.

the afternoon checking out the museum and gardens at Cheekwood. Eat dinner at the Capitol Grille downtown.

DAY 4

Go uptown to the Tennessee State Capitol and the Civil Rights Room at the Nashville Public Library. Then head west along Jefferson to eat soul food at Swett's and visit Fisk University in the afternoon. Catch the show at The Bluebird Cafe over dinner.

DAY 5

Drive east to Old Hickory and spend the day at The Hermitage. Explore the home and the grounds of this estate belonging to Andrew Jackson. Grab takeout from Prince's Hot Chicken Shack on your way home and enjoy a quiet night in.

Excursions

CLARKSVILLE

Take a day trip to Clarksville. Tour the RiverWalk park along the Cumberland and find the statue of Wilma Rudolph. Eat lunch at Silke's Old World Breads and explore Dunbar Cave in the afternoon. Return to Nashville for the night.

FRANKLIN

Depart Nashville. Drive south to Franklin and visit the Carnton Plantation, epicenter of the Battle of Franklin. Eat lunch at Puckett's Grocery and Restaurant, and then spend the afternoon shopping downtown and at The Factory. Eat dinner at Saffire and overnight in Franklin.

NORMANDY

Drive to Normandy and visit the George Dickel Distillery. Eat dinner at the Bell Buckle Cafe and overnight at the Walking Horse Hotel in Wartrace. This can be your home base for three nights.

SHELBYVILLE AND LYNCHBURG

Drive to Shelbyville for the Tennessee Walking Horse National Celebration and eat

Cheekwood

Carnton Plantation

lunch at The Coffee Break. If it's not celebration season, then head to Lynchburg to tour the Tennessee Walking Horse Museum and the Jack Daniel's Distillery.

MURFREESBORO

Drive back to Nashville, stopping in Murfreesboro to visit Stones River National Battlefield on the way.

▶ KNOXVILLE AND THE SMOKIES

Start in Knoxville, and then head into the wilderness of the Great Smoky Mountains. Explore the rural reaches of the Cumberland Plateau and find the tallest waterfall east of the Rockies. Wind up in Chattanooga to tour the state's best aquarium and see Rock City, the South's most iconic attraction.

Knoxville

DAY 1

Arrive in Knoxville, and check into the Oliver Hotel downtown. Grab lunch to go from the Tomato Head, and listen to live music at the WDVX Blue Plate Special over the lunch hour. Visit the World's Fair Park and climb to the top of the Sunsphere. Eat dinner in South Knoxville at King Tut Grill.

DAY 2

Drive to Oak Ridge and see the sights related to the Oak Ridge National Laboratory. Eat a Myrtle Burger at the Jefferson Soda Fountain at lunch and enjoy dinner with a view at Riverside Grille.

Great Smokies Road Trip

DAY 3

Head to the Great Smoky Mountains. Drive to Gatlinburg and check into the Buckhorn Lodge or the Gatlinburg Inn. Drive to the top of Newfound Gap and enjoy the mountain views and cool air.

DAY 4

Get up early and take a picnic lunch to Cades

Rhododendrons bloom on the Appalachian Trail along Roan Mountain.

Cove before the crowds strike. Look at old farmhouses and churches, and spy deer and cottontails. Hike to Abrams Falls.

DAY 5

Head north to the Cherokee National Forest and drive to the top of Roan Mountain. Take a stroll along the Appalachian Trail and look for the wild rhododendron. Overnight in Erwin.

DAY 6

Drive to Historic Rugby on the Cumberland Plateau and tour the Victorian English village. Stay in one of the historic bed-and-breakfasts and dine on authentic English fare at Rugby's restaurant.

DAY 7

Drive south to Fall Creek Falls State Park and hike to the falls, the tallest east of the Rockies. Visit the nature center and stay overnight in the park inn.

DAY 8

Drive down the Sequatchie Valley, stopping in

Dayton to see the site of the Scopes Monkey Trial and Whitwell to visit the Children's Holocaust Memorial. Press on to Chattanooga, and check in to the Sheraton Read House Hotel or another downtown lodging.

spring morning in Cades Cove

BEST PARKS

Few spots in the state can rival the beauty of Reelfoot Lake.

From the purple mountain majesty of the Smokies in the east to the dark mystery of Reelfoot Lake in the west, Tennessee is a land of surprising beauty. Wherever you are in Tennessee, you don't have to look hard for exceptional places to experience the outdoors.

· **Great Smoky Mountains National Park** (Gatlinburg): The most-visited national park in the United States offers lovely mountain vistas, miles of hiking trails, and hundreds of campsites.

· **Reelfoot Lake State Park** (Tiptonville): Formed during a massive earthquake, Reelfoot Lake is an unexpected landscape of knob-kneed cypress trees and flowering lily pads, with bald eagles flying overhead.

· **Land Between the Lakes** (Dover): You get two lakes for the price of one, plus bison, hiking, history, and more at this extensive recreation area.

· **Grundy Lakes State Park** (Tracy City): This small park is home to the remarkable vistas of the Fiery Gizzard Trail and the 60-foot drop of Foster Falls.

DAY 9

Visit the Tennessee Aquarium in the morning. If the skies are clear, drive to Lookout Mountain and tour Rock City and Point Park. Watch the sun set over Chattanooga. If the weather doesn't cooperate, visit the Hunter Museum of American Art. Eat dinner at The Blue Plate.

DAY 10

Have breakfast at the Bluegrass Grill. Make your way back to Knoxville, stopping in Vonore on the way to tour a replica of the British Fort Loudoun and visit the Sequoyah Birthplace Museum.

the Stax Museum of American Soul Music

► FROM BLUEGRASS TO THE BLUES: A MUSICAL JOURNEY

Music is what many visitors to Tennessee want to experience more than anything else, and thanks to the broad spectrum of musical genres present in the state—bluegrass to the blues—music fans don't have to stick to what they know and love. Take a listen to something different; you're likely discover a new favorite. At the very least, you will come to see the connections that exist between even the most varied musical forms.

Memphis

Beale Street is still the place to start if you want to find the birthplace of the blues. Visit the W. C. Handy Home and Museum to see where the father of the blues lived while he was in Memphis. After dark, stroll Beale Street to hear live blues and jazz at clubs like the King's Palace and B. B. King's.

The single best musical museum in Memphis is the Stax Museum of American Soul Music. Here you will learn not only about the remarkable story of Stax, but also soul's musical roots in gospel and country music.

No place in Memphis is more important to American musical history than Graceland, home of Elvis Presley. Here the King lived with his parents, wife, extended family, and his buddies, the Memphis Mafia. See his remarkable taste in decor and pay your respects over his grave in the Meditation Garden.

Sun Studio is where early blues records were made, where Elvis recorded his first hit, and where the likes of Jerry Lee Lewis and Johnny Cash laid down tracks. It's hallowed ground in musical history.

Any of Memphis's juke joints get kicking late on Friday and Saturday nights.

Western Plains

It was the landscape and hardship of country living that really gave birth to the blues. Drive the rural routes in Haywood County to breathe in the delta air. Stop in Nutbush, the childhood home of Tina Turner. Then stop in Brownsville at the West Tennessee Delta Heritage Center for exhibits about the music and culture of this region.

The International Rock-a-Billy Hall of Fame in Jackson has exhibits and tours, but the best deal is to come on Monday or Saturday night for the live music and dancing lessons. Rockabilly never sounded so good!

Nashville

No part of Nashville says country music quite like Lower Broadway. It's one of the places both locals and visitors go, and colorful honky-tonks offer live music beginning at 10 A.M. daily. For the more serious of mind, start at the Country Music Hall of Fame for an introduction to all things country. Visit the Ryman Auditorium, buy your new boots at one of the half dozen clothiers on Lower Broadway, and stock up on CDs at Ernest Tubb's, Admire the hardware at Gruhn Guitars and buy a retro-print poster at Hatch Show Print.

Then for something completely different, don your best duds (still with those boots) and enjoy a night at the Nashville Symphony Orchestra. The delightful sounds of one of the South's best symphonies will ease the mind and cleanse the musical palate.

Explore wax museums, souvenir shops, and the Opryland Hotel by day in Music Valley. Spend your evening at the Grand Ole Opry and your late-night at Ernest Tubb's Midnite Jamboree, still going strong.

Sandwiched between downtown and Hillsboro Village is Music Row, the business center of Nashville. While you're unlikely to see a star here, it's still worth the gamble. Take a stroll, and then grab a sweet treat at Fido for more star-watching. At night check out The Bluebird Cafe for the next big songwriter.

Country music's biggest stars – and even bigger fans – flock to Nashville.

The Ryman Auditorium is considered the Mother Church of Country Music.

Knoxville

Listen to live music over lunch at the WDVX Blue Plate Special, and then take a walking tour of Knoxville's musical history. See the site of the last hotel where Hank Williams ever slept. Catch a live band in the Old City or on Market Square, or a concert in the historic Tennessee Theatre. Listen to modern roots music at the Laurel Theater in historic Fort Sanders.

Head out to Clinton and the Museum of Appalachia to tour its music room, with exhibits about Uncle Dave Macon and Roy Acuff.

Great Smoky Mountains

Experience the kitschy side of music in Pigeon Forge. Visit Dollywood, a theme park owned and designed by Tennessee native Dolly Parton. Get a ticket to the Dixie Stampede for a night of over-the-top entertainment, or catch an Elvis tribute show.

The First Frontier

Visit Bristol, the Birthplace of Country Music and the site of the historic Bristol Sessions. Visit the Mountain Music Museum and the home of Tennessee Ernie Ford. Head to The Carter Family Memorial Music Center for a Saturday-night concert.

In Johnson City, check in at the Down Home for bluegrass, folk, and country music. This venerable club has been nurturing music fans in upper East Tennessee since 1976.

MEMPHIS

Take away its music, and Memphis would lose its soul. Memphis may owe its existence to the mighty Mississippi, but it is music that has defined this Southern metropolis. Memphis music started with the spirituals and work songs of poor Mississippi Delta cotton farmers who came to Memphis and created a new sound: the Memphis blues. The blues then spawned its own offspring: soul, R&B, country, and, of course, rock 'n' roll as sung by a poor truck driver from Tupelo, Mississippi, named Elvis Presley.

On any given night you can find juke joints where the music flows as freely as the booze, and sitting still is not an option. On Beale Street, music wafts from inside smoky bars out onto the street, inviting you to come inside for a spell. And on Sundays, the sounds of old fashioned spirituals and new gospel music can be heard at churches throughout the city.

Memphis music is the backbeat of any visit to the city, but it certainly is not the only reason to come. For as rich as Memphis's history is, this is a city that does not live in its past. Since the 1990s, Memphis has gone through a rebirth, giving new life to the region as a tourist destination. An NBA franchise (the Grizzlies) arrived, the National Civil Rights Museum opened on the grounds of the historic Lorraine Motel, a fantastic AAA baseball field opened downtown, and Memphis made its mark with films such as *Hustle & Flow, Forty Shades of*

HIGHLIGHTS

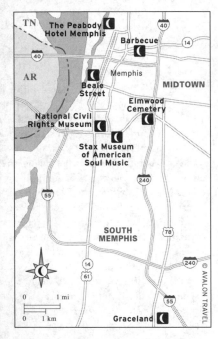

years the Lorraine Motel merely represented the tragic assassination of Martin Luther King Jr. Today, it tells the story of the African American struggle for civil rights, from before the Civil War to the present day (page 33).

◖ **The Peabody Hotel Memphis:** Even the ducks in the fountain get the red-carpet treatment at this landmark hotel. The lobby is a must-visit, even for those who are not hotel guests (page 34).

◖ **Stax Museum of American Soul Music:** Irresistible soul music is what made Stax famous in the 1960s, and it is what makes the Stax museum sweet today. Exhibits bring to life the work of Otis Redding, the Staple Singers, Isaac Hayes, and more (page 41).

◖ **Graceland:** The Elvis phenomenon is alive and well, even if the King himself is not. Presley's south Memphis mansion is a testament not only to the King's music, but also his fans (page 41).

◖ **Elmwood Cemetery:** Perhaps the most surprising attraction in Memphis, Elmwood is the final resting place of dozens of Memphis characters: madames, blues singers, mayors, and pioneers of all types (page 44).

◖ **Beale Street:** The street that gave birth to the Memphis blues celebrates its legacy every single night of the week (page 29).

◖ **National Civil Rights Museum:** For

◖ **Barbecue:** Tangy, juicy, and just a little sweet, Memphis barbecue at places like the **Cozy Corner** is the stuff of dreams (page 67).

Blue, and *Black Snake Moan.* In 2011, more than 10 million people visited Memphis.

While you're here, you can sustain yourself on the city's world-famous barbecue, its fried chicken and catfish, and its homemade plate lunches, not to mention nouveau Southern eats. Eating may not be why you come, but it will be why you stay.

Memphis is a city of the South. More than just the largest city in Tennessee, Memphis is a hub for the entire Mid-South, which stretches from West Tennessee all the way down into Mississippi

and Arkansas. As such, the city is a melting pot of cultural, musical, culinary, and economic influences from the entire Mississippi River delta.

PLANNING YOUR TIME

You can knock out Memphis's main attractions in a weekend, but it takes a bit longer to soak up the city's special mojo: the music, food, and laid-back attitude. In fact, if you want more than just a taste of Memphis's famous blues, its legendary barbecue, or its rich history, plan to stay at least a week.

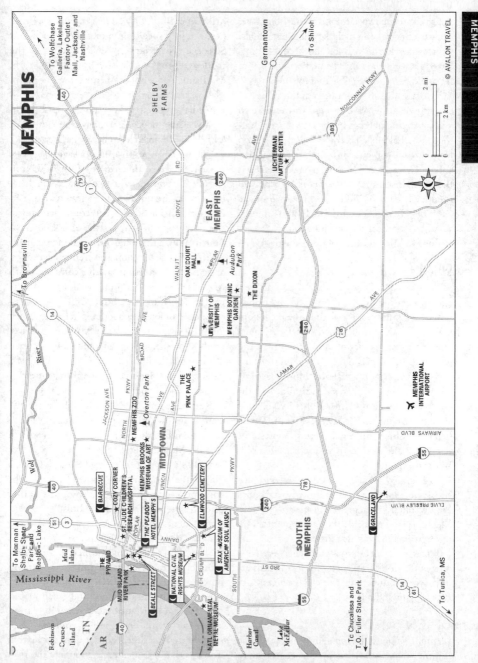

MEMPHIS

To Wolfchase Galleria, Lakeland Factory Outlet Mall, Jackson, and Nashville

SHELBY FARMS

Germantown

To Shiloh

Noconnah Pkwy

2 mi

2 km

© AVALON TRAVEL

LICHTERMAN NATURE CENTER

EAST MEMPHIS

OAK COURT MALL

Audubon Park

THE DIXON

UNIVERSITY OF MEMPHIS

MEMPHIS BOTANIC GARDEN

MEMPHIS INTERNATIONAL AIRPORT

THE PINK PALACE

LAMAR

AIRWAYS BLVD

To Brownsville

River

Wolf

To Meeman Shelby State Park and Reelfoot Lake

Mud Island

Memphis Zoo

Overton Park

MIDTOWN

BARBECUE

COZY CORNER

ST. JUDE CHILDREN'S RESEARCH HOSPITAL

MEMPHIS BROOKS MUSEUM OF ART

THE PEABODY HOTEL MEMPHIS

ELMWOOD CEMETERY

GRACELAND

ELVIS PRESLEY BLVD

THE PYRAMID

Robinson Crusoe Island

Mud Island River Park

Mississippi River

TN
AR

BEALE STREET

NATIONAL CIVIL RIGHTS MUSEUM

NATL ORNAMENTAL METAL MUSEUM

STAX MUSEUM OF AMERICAN SOUL MUSIC

SOUTH MEMPHIS

To Chucalissa and T.O. Fuller State Park

Lake McKellar

Harbor Island

To Tunica, MS

Choose downtown Memphis as your home base. The city center is home to the best bars, restaurants, sports venues, live music clubs, and, of course, Beale Street. Downtown is also the liveliest, and one of the safest, parts of Memphis after the sun sets.

While a lot of Memphis's attractions are downtown, others are located in the eastern and southern stretches of the city. A free shuttle is available to Graceland and Sun Studio from downtown, but for other attractions like the Stax Museum of American Soul Music and the Memphis Brooks Museum of Art, you will need a car or taxi. Take note that two of the city's best barbecue joints (a Memphis must), as well as its most famous juke joints, are not within walking distance of downtown.

When to Go

Memphis is a city with four seasons. The average temperature in January is 41°F, and in July it hits 81°F. Summer is certainly the most popular season for visiting—Elvis Week in August sees the most visitors of all—but the humid Memphis summer is not for the faint of heart.

The best time to visit Memphis is May, when summer is still fresh and mild, and the city puts on its annual Memphis in May celebration. Memphis in May includes the World Championship Barbeque Cooking Contest, the Beale Street Music Festival, and the Memphis International Festival.

Fall is also a good choice. The Memphis Music and Heritage Festival held over Labor Day weekend is a great reason to come to Memphis, and probably the best choice for fans of traditional Memphis music.

But if you can't come when the weather is temperate, don't fret. Memphis attractions are open year-round, and the city continues to rock, day in and day out.

ORIENTATION

Memphis is perched atop a low bluff overlooking the majestic Mississippi River (hence its nickname, Bluff City). The center city district lies, roughly speaking, along the river. Main Street, a pedestrian-only mall (except for the trolleys) runs north–south, while Union, Madison, and Poplar Avenues are the main east–west thoroughfares.

While not compact, central Memphis is entirely walkable for people willing to use a little shoe leather. The Main Street trolley makes it easy to see downtown and uptown attractions without a car.

In this guide, locations south of Union Avenue are considered **downtown,** while locations north are **uptown.** Downtown's main attraction is Beale Street. Also contained within the downtown district is the area known as **South Main,** a three-block strip along southern Main Street that is home to trendy boutiques, art galleries, restaurants, and condos. South Main is about a 15-minute walk or 5-minute trolley ride from Beale Street.

Another unique neighborhood in the city center is **The Pinch,** located along North Main Street past the I-40 overpass. Originally settled by German immigrants, the Pinch is now a hub of restaurants and nightlife. It is also the gateway to gentrifying residential neighborhoods farther north.

Restaurants in the Pinch have been categorized as uptown in this guide. You can walk to the Pinch, but the best way to get there is to ride the Main Street Trolley.

In 1989, developers created **Harbor Town,** a New Urban community on Mud Island. The concept was to create a city community that offered amenities such as schools, gyms, entertainment, and restaurants within walking distance of each other. It was also designed to promote a sense of community; homes were built close together with low fences, front porches, and small yards, so that residents would use community parks and green spaces.

In 2007, a boutique hotel opened in Harbor Town, putting the area on the accommodations map for the first time. A major draw for Harbor Town is that it is located right across the river from downtown Memphis but feels like a tight-knit residential community.

Memphis sprawls south, east, and north from the river. Head east from downtown, and you are in **midtown,** a district of strip malls, aging suburbs, and the city's best park and art museum. Poplar Avenue is the main artery of midtown, and it's a good point of reference when exploring by car (which is really the only way to get around midtown). The city's original suburb, midtown now seems positively urban compared to the sprawling burbs that creep farther eastward every year.

Located within midtown is **Cooper-Young,** a redeveloping residential and commercial neighborhood that lies around the intersection of Cooper Street and Young Avenue. Since the 1970s, residents of this neighborhood have fought the tide of urban decay by encouraging

investment, good schools, and amenities like parks, art galleries, and independent restaurants, and generally fostering a sense of pride in the area. The result is a neighborhood where you'll find lots of restaurants, a great used-book store, record shops, and other attractions that draw the city's young and young at heart.

East Memphis is where you will find large shopping malls, major hospitals, the University of Memphis, and lots of traffic jams. There are also a few attractions out here, the Dixon and the Memphis Botanic Gardens among them.

Generally speaking, **north and south Memphis** are the most economically depressed areas of the city. Visitors beat a path to attractions like Graceland and Stax in southern Memphis during the day but tend to avoid those areas at night, at least unless they are with a local who knows the way around.

Sights

DOWNTOWN

Downtown refers to the area south of Union Avenue in the city center. It is the heart of Memphis's tourist district.

C Beale Street

If you want to delve into the history and character of Memphis music, your starting point should be Beale Street, home of the blues.

A combination of forces led Beale Street to its place in musical history and popular culture. Named in the 1840s after a war hero, Beale Street was originally part of South Memphis, a separate city that rivaled Memphis during the 1840s.

Beginning in the 1850s, and continuing in greater numbers during and after the Civil War, African Americans began to settle along the western part of Beale Street. By the 1880s and 1890s, a middle class of black professionals began to emerge, and Beale Street became the center of commerce, entertainment, and life

for many of them. Together with black-owned businesses on Beale Street were laundries, bars, restaurants, pawn shops, and more operated by immigrants from eastern Europe, Ireland, China, Greece, and Germany.

From the 1880s until the 1960s, Beale Street was the epicenter of African American life, not just for Memphians but also for the entire Mid-South region. It was here that blacks felt free from many of society's restrictions.

Beale Street's decline began in the mid-20th century, and by the 1970s it was a shadow of its former self. Investment during the 1980s and '90s led to the street's rebirth as a destination for tourists and source of pride for residents, who could now show off the street that gave birth to the blues.

Today, Beale Street has two distinct personalities. During the day it is a laid-back place for families or adults to stroll, buy souvenirs, and eat. You can also stop at one of several museums and attractions located on the street. At night, Beale Street is a strip of nightclubs and restaurants, a great place to people-watch, and the best place in the state, if not the country, to catch live blues seven nights a week.

W. C. Handy Home and Museum

The story of Beale Street cannot be told without mentioning William Christopher Handy, whose Memphis home sits at the corner of Beale Street and 4th Avenue. The building was originally located at 659 Jeanette Street, but it was moved to Beale Street in 1985. Now the W. C. Handy Home and Museum (352 Beale St., 901/527-3427, wchandymemphis.org, summer Tues.–Sat. 10 A.M.–5 P.M., winter Tues.–Sat. 11 A.M.–4 P.M., adults $4, children $3) is dedicated to telling the story of Handy's life. It was Handy who famously wrote, in his "Beale Street Blues": "If Beale Street could talk, married men would have to take their beds and walk, except one or two who never drink booze, and the blind

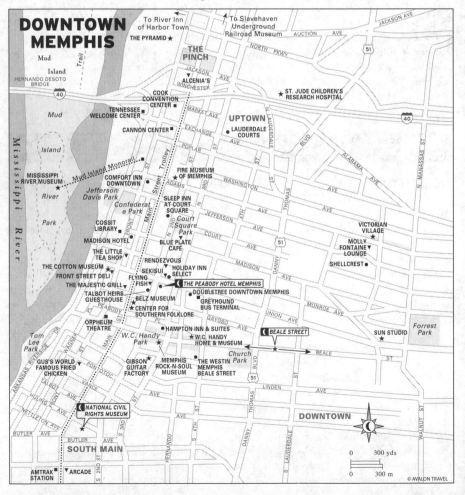

BEALE STREET WALKING TOUR

Beale Street runs from the Mississippi River to Manassas Street in midtown Memphis, but it is the three blocks between 2nd and 4th Streets that really matter. In its heyday, the Beale Street commercial and entertainment district extended farther east and west, but today, it has been condensed into the half dozen blocks from Main Street to 4th Street. This walking tour begins at the intersection of Beale and Main Streets, and heads eastward.

Near the corner of Beale and Main Streets is the **Orpheum Theatre** (203 S. Main St., 901/525-7800, www.orpheum-memphis.com). This site has been used for entertainment since 1890, when the Grand Opera House opened there with a production of *Les Huguenots*. Later, the opera house presented vaudeville shows and theater. Fire destroyed it in 1923, but in 1928 it reopened as the Orpheum, a movie theater and performing arts venue for the likes of Duke Ellington, Cab Calloway, Bob Hope, and Mae West. The Orpheum remains one of the city's premier venues for the performing arts, with Broadway productions, mainstream musical artists, and movies.

A block east of the Orpheum is a statue of Memphis's most famous native son, Elvis Presley. Depicting the King during his early career, the statue sits in **Elvis Presley Plaza.**

A. Schwab (163 Beale St., 901/523-9782, Mon.-Fri. 9 A.M.-5 P.M.) has served Memphis residents for more than 130 years, although it focuses now on odd, out-of-date, and hard-to-find items rather than general store necessities. Stop in for a souvenir or to visit the A. Schwab "museum," a collection of old-fashioned household tools and implements.

A few doors down from A. Schwab, at the Irish pub Silky O'Sullivan's, you can see what remains of one of Beale Street's most magnificent old buildings. The facade of what was once the **Gallina Building** is held up by six steel girders. From the 1860s until 1914, this facade kept watch on the business empire of Squire Charles Gallina, who operated a saloon, restaurant, and 20-room hotel, as well as a gambling room.

Beyond 3rd Street is **Handy Park,** named for famous blues composer and musician W. C. Handy. Beale Street's market house was torn down in 1930 to build the park. Since it opened,

Handy Park has been a popular place for street musicians, peddlers, concerts, and community events, all of which are presided over by the life-size statue of W.C. Handy.

About midway up the southern side of the next block of Beale Street is the **Daisy Theater** (329 Beale St.), built in 1917 as a movie house. Much of the original interior remains today. The theater is closed to the public but may be rented for private events. Contact the Beale Street Development Corporation (866/406-5986) for information.

Across the street from the Daisy Theater is the **New Daisy Theater,** built in 1941 as another movie house. The New Daisy is one of Memphis's prime live music venues, and it books rock and alternative acts from around the country.

Stately and old, the **First Baptist Beale Street Church** (379 Beale St.) was built between 1868 and 1885 and is home to one of the oldest African American congregations in Memphis. In the 1860s, the congregation started to meet under brush arbors at the present location, and the first temporary structure was erected in 1865. The cornerstone was laid for the present building in 1871. The First Baptist Beale Street Church was an important force in Memphis's African American history. It was here that black Memphians published their first newspapers, the *Memphis Watchman* and the *Memphis Free Speech and Headlight*.

Today, **Church Park** is a relatively nondescript city park with benches and some paved walks. But in 1899, when Robert Church built Church Park and Auditorium at the eastern end of the Beale Street commercial district, the park was something truly special. Church, the mixed-race son of a white steamboat captain, is said to have been the first black millionaire in the South. He was troubled that there were no public parks expressly for Memphis's African American residents, so in 1899 he opened Church Park and Auditorium on six acres of land along Beale Street. The park was beautifully landscaped and manicured, with bright flowers, tropical trees, and peacocks. The auditorium was a venue for black performers and speakers. Church Park remains a venue for community events, particularly the annual Africa in April event every spring.

man on the corner singing 'Beale Street Blues.' I'd rather be there than anyplace I know."

The Handy museum houses photographs of Handy's family, one of his band uniforms, and memorabilia of the recording company that he founded. You can also hear samples of Handy's music.

A. Schwab

During Beale Street's dark days of the 1970s and '80s, when the clubs and restaurants closed and the pawn shops opened, one mainstay remained: A. Schwab (163 Beale St., 901/523-9782, Mon.–Wed. 10 A.M.–8 P.M., Thurs.–Sat. 10 A.M.–10 P.M., Sun. noon–8 P.M.). This landmark general store opened in 1876 and was owned and operated by the same family until 2011. Originally the source for household necessities for thousands of Delta residents, A. Schwab remains a treasure trove of goods. Here you will find practical things like underwear, hats, umbrellas, cookware, and tools, as well as novelties like old-fashioned candy, incense, and actual cans of Tennessee whoop-ass. Upstairs is the A. Schwab museum, a hodgepodge of old-time tools, clothes, and memorabilia of the store's 130-plus-year history.

The new owners, who purchased the store from the Schwab family in late 2011, plan to restore the exterior facade, expand the eclectic inventory, improve the second-floor museum, and add a soda fountain.

Memphis Rock 'n' Soul Museum

Music fans should plan to spend several hours at the Memphis Rock 'n' Soul Museum (191 Beale St., 901/205-2533, www.memphis-rocknsoul.org, daily 10 A.M.–7 P.M., adults $11, children 5–17 $8), located right next to FedEx Forum off Beale Street. An affiliate of the Smithsonian Institution, this museum tells the story of Memphis music from the Delta blues to *Shaft*. Start with a short video documentary, and then follow the exhibits with your personal audio guide, which includes recordings of dozens of Memphis-influenced artists from B. B. King to Elvis. Exhibits are dedicated to Memphis radio stations; the influence of the Victrola, Sam Phillips, and Sun Studio; and, of course, all things Elvis, among others. It takes several hours to study all the exhibits in detail and to listen to all (or even most) of the music, so plan accordingly.

There is a free shuttle that runs between the Rock 'n' Soul Museum, Graceland, and Sun Studio. Look for the black van with the Sun label's distinctive yellow sun on the side.

Gibson Guitar Factory

Across the street from the Rock 'n' Soul Museum is the Gibson Guitar Factory (145 Lt. George Lee Ave., 901/544-7998, ext. 4075, www.gibson.com, tours Mon.–Sat. every hour on the hour 11 A.M.–4 P.M., Sun. noon–4 P.M.,

---

W. C. HANDY

W. C. Handy was born in a log cabin in Florence, Alabama, in 1873. The son and grandson of African Methodist Episcopal ministers, Handy was exposed to music as a child in his father's church. Handy was also drawn to the music of the black laborers of the area, and when he moved to Memphis in the early 20th century, he recognized the wealth of the blues music he heard in bars, on street corners, and in back alleys around Beale Street.

Handy was a trained musician, so he was able to set down on paper the music that had, up until then, been passed from one musician to another.

In 1909 Handy composed Memphis mayor Ed Crump's campaign song, "Mr. Crump," which he later published as the "Memphis Blues." But he is most famous for his composition "St. Louis Blues," published in 1914. Handy also created the "Yellow Dog Blues," "Joe Turner Blues," and "Beale Street Blues." Known as the Father of the Blues, Handy passed away in 1958.

© WAYNE HSIEH

The Lorraine Motel, where Dr. Martin Luther King Jr. was assassinated, now houses the National Civil Rights Museum.

ages five and up $10), one of three in the United States. The Memphis plant specializes in the semi-hollow-bodied guitar, and a wide range of models are on sale in Gibson's retail shop. On the hour-long tour of the factory floor you can see guitars being made, from the shaping of the rim and panels to the painting and buffing of the finished product. Tours sell out, so reservations are recommended, particularly during the busier summer months. Most factory workers leave by 3 P.M. and have the weekends off, so plan ahead if you want to see the factory floor in full swing.

◖ National Civil Rights Museum

If you do nothing else while you are in Memphis, or, frankly, the state, visit the National Civil Rights Museum (450 Mulberry St., 901/521-9699, www.civilrightsmuseum.

org, Mon. and Wed.–Sat. 9 A.M.–5 P.M., Sun. 1–5 P.M., adults $13, students and seniors $11, children 4–17 $9.50). Built on the Lorraine Motel site where Dr. Martin Luther King Jr. was assassinated on April 4, 1968, the museum makes a thorough examination of the American civil rights movement from slavery to the present day. Exhibits display original letters, audio recordings, photos, and newspaper clippings from events including the Montgomery bus boycott, *Brown v. Board of Education*, Freedom Summer, and the march from Selma to Montgomery. Original and re-created artifacts, such as the bus where Rosa Parks made her stand in 1955 and the cell where Dr. King wrote his famous *Letter from a Birmingham Jail*, help to illustrate the story of civil rights.

When Dr. King visited Memphis in March and then again in April 1968, the Lorraine Motel was one of the handful of downtown hotels that welcomed African Americans. The room (and balcony and parking lot) where he spent his final hours has been carefully re-created, and narration by those who were with him tell the shocking story of his death. Across Mulberry Street, in the building that was once the boardinghouse from where James Earl Ray is believed to have fired his sniper shot, exhibits probe various theories about the assassination, as well as the worldwide legacy of the civil rights movement.

Visitors to the museum can pay an extra $2 for an audio guide—a worthwhile investment. You are asked not to take flash photography inside the museum. This is a large museum, and it is overflowing with information, so visitors who want to give the displays their due attention should plan on spending 3–4 hours here. A good way to visit would be to tour the Lorraine Motel exhibits first, take a break for lunch, and then go across the street for the second half of the museum when you are refreshed.

Spending half a day here is a powerful experience, and one that raises many thoughts about civil rights. Expect interesting conversations with your travel companions after coming here. The gift shop offers books and videos for more reading on the topic.

Admission is free on Monday after 3 p.m. to Tennessee residents. In June, July, and August the museum stays open until 6 p.m.

Belz Museum of Asian and Judaic Art

The Belz Museum of Asian and Judaic Art (119 S. Main St., 901/523-2787, www.belzmuseum. org, Tues.–Fri. 10 a.m.–5:30 p.m., Sat.–Sun. noon–5 p.m., adults $6, seniors $5, children $4), formerly Peabody Place Museum, houses one of the largest collections of artwork from the Q'ing dynasty. Forged from the private collection of Memphis developers Jack and Marilyn Belz, owners of the Peabody Hotel and the now shuttered Peabody Place mall, the museum features some 1,000 objects, including an array of jade, tapestries, paintings, furniture, carvings, and other artifacts. The museum is also home to the largest U.S. collection of work by Israeli artist Daniel Kafri.

UPTOWN

Uptown refers to locations along Union Avenue and points north in the center city district. Here downtown workers are more common than tourists, and tall office buildings rise above the city blocks.

The Cotton Museum

The Cotton Museum at the Memphis Cotton Exchange (65 Union Ave., 901/531-7826, www.memphiscottonmuseum.org, Mon.–Sat. 10 a.m.–5 p.m., Sun. noon–5 p.m., adults $10, seniors $9.50, students $9, children 6–12 $8) is located in the broad rectangular room that once was the nerve center of the Mid-South's cotton trade. The Cotton Exchange was established in 1873, and it was here that buyers and sellers of the South's most important cash crop met, and where fortunes were made and lost. Located just steps away from the Mississippi River, the Exchange was the trading floor of Cotton Row, the area of town that was defined by the cotton industry.

The Cotton Museum is home to exhibits about cotton's history, its uses, and the culture that its cultivation gave rise to in Memphis and the Mississippi Delta. There are several videos you can watch, as well as a live Internet feed of today's cotton exchange—now conducted entirely electronically. The nicest thing about the museum, however, is seeing the chalkboard where the prices of cotton around the world were written by hand. There is also a replica of the Western Union office where buyers and sellers sent telegrams using an intricate system of abbreviations known only to the cotton trade. The museum expanded in 2010, with more hands-on exhibits and an educational wing.

◖ The Peabody Hotel Memphis

The Peabody Hotel Memphis (149 Union Ave., 901/529-4000, www.peabodymemphis.com) is the city's most famous hotel. Founded in 1869, the Peabody was one of the first grand hotels of the South, a place as well known for its elegant balls and big-band concerts as for the colorful characters who sipped cocktails at its famous lounge. Named in memory of the philanthropist George Peabody, the original hotel was located at the corner of Main and Monroe. It closed in 1923, and a new Peabody opened two years later in its present location on Union Avenue. It remained the place to see and be seen for generations of Memphians and Delta residents. It was David Cohn who famously wrote in 1935 that "the Mississippi Delta begins in the lobby of The Peabody Hotel."

Even if you don't stay here, you must stop by the elegant hotel lobby to see the twice-daily march of the Peabody ducks. They live on the roof of the hotel and make the journey—by elevator—to the lobby fountain every morning

© THE PEABODY MUSEUM/MEMPHIS VISITORS BUREAU

Ducks get the literal red-carpet treatment at the Peabody Hotel Memphis.

at 11 A.M. At 5 P.M. they march out of the fountain, back onto the elevator, and up to their accommodations on the roof.

The hotel employs a duck master who takes care of the ducks and supervises their daily trip downstairs. Watching the ducks is free, frenzied, and undeniably fun. It is also one of the most popular activities among visitors to Memphis, so be sure to get there early and secure a good vantage point along the red carpet to watch the duck march.

Mud Island

In Memphis, it is sometimes easy to forget that you are just steps away from the great Mississippi River. A trip to Mud Island will cure this misperception once and for all. A narrow band of land in the river, Mud Island is home to the **Mud Island River Park and Museum** (125 N. Front St., 901/576-7241, www.mudisland. com, Apr.–Oct. Tues.–Sun. 10 A.M.–5 P.M., adults $10, seniors $9, children $7), which has

exhibits about early uses of the river, steam- and paddleboats, floods, and much more.

The park's **Mississippi River Museum** begins with a refresher course on European exploration of this region—de Soto, La Salle, and Marquette and Joliet—followed by information about early settlement. The highlight is being able to explore a replica of a 1870s steamboat. In the Riverfolk Gallery there are wax depictions of Mark Twain, riverboat gambler George Devol, and steamship entertainers. The museum also remembers the numerous river disasters that have taken place along the Mississippi.

Admission to the museum includes the **River Walk** at the Mud Island River Park, a five-block scale model of the entire Mississippi River—from Minnesota to the Gulf of Mexico. Walk along the model to see scale representations of cities along the river's path, and read placards about the river's history. On a hot day, wear your bathing suit so you can swim in the pool at the end.

The river park is also home to an outdoor amphitheater, which in summer hosts big-name concerts, a snack bar, outdoor tables, and restrooms. You can rent canoes, kayaks, and pedal boats to use in the still waters around the Mud Island harbor. Bike rental is also available. Mud Island is the site of the annual Duncan–Williams Dragon Boat Races.

Admission to the river park is free. You cay pay $4 round-trip to ride the monorail to Mud Island, or you can walk across the monorail bridge for free. The monorail station is on Front Street at Adams Avenue.

Slavehaven Underground Railroad Museum

The legend of the Burkle Estate, a modest white clapboard house on North 2nd Street, has given rise to the Slavehaven Underground Railroad Museum (826 N. 2nd St., 901/527-3427, summer Mon.–Sat. 10 A.M.–4 P.M., winter Wed.–Sat. 10 A.M.–4 P.M., adults $6, youth $4). The museum here tells the story of slavery and the legendary Underground Railroad, which helped thousands of slaves escape to freedom in the North (and, after the 1850 Fugitive Slave Act, to Canada). Jacob Burkle, a German immigrant and owner of the Memphis stockyard, is said to have built the Burkle Estate around 1850. Escaping slaves would have hidden in a root cellar beneath the house before making the 1,500-foot trip to the banks of the Mississippi, where they made a further journey north.

Skeptics say that there is no evidence of this story and even point to documents that show that Burkle may not have purchased the property until 1871, well after the end of slavery. Advocates for the Underground Railroad story say that it was the nature of the railroad to be secret, so there is nothing unusual about a lack of concrete evidence.

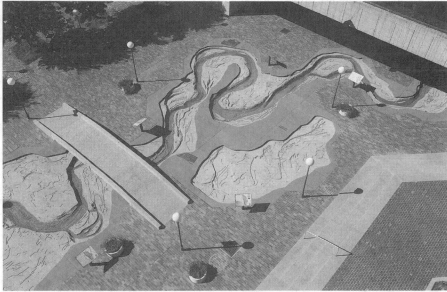

The River Walk on Mud Island is a maze of fun.

THE BIRTH OF MUD ISLAND

Mud Island rose from the Mississippi River as a result of two seemingly small events. In 1876, the river shifted slightly about 20 miles south of Memphis, causing the currents that flowed past the city to alter course. And then, in 1910, the U.S. Navy gunboat *Amphitrite* anchored at the mouth of the Wolf River for almost two years, causing a further change in silt patterns. When the ship left in 1912, the sandbar continued to grow, and Mud Island was born.

Residents initially disliked the island, since it was ugly and proved to be a danger to river navigation.

Beginning in the 1930s, poor Memphians squatted on Mud Island in ramshackle homes built of scrap metal and wood. Between 200 and 500 people lived on the island during this time.

In 1959, a downtown airport was built on the island, but the airport was closed in 1970 when the DeSoto Bridge was built. In 1974, plans were developed for what is the present day Mud Island River Park, which includes a full-scale replica of a riverboat, a monorail to the island, and the signature 2,000-foot flowing replica of the Mississippi River.

Visitors today need not be too concerned with the details of the debate; the Slavehaven museum does a good job of highlighting the brutality of the slave trade and slavery, and the ingenuity and bravery it took for slaves to escape. Perhaps the most interesting part of the exhibit are the quilts that demonstrate the way that slaves used quilting patterns to send messages to one another. Other displays show advertisements for Memphis slave auctions and images from the early 20th century that depict damaging racial stereotypes.

The museum is operated by Heritage Tours of Memphis, and staff are available to conduct guided tours of the property.

Fire Museum of Memphis

The Fire Museum of Memphis (118 Adams Ave., 901/320-5650, www.firemuseum.com, Mon.–Sat. 9 A.M.–5 P.M., adults $6, seniors $4, children $5) is a good place to take children. There is a huge display of fire-engine toys, lots of firefighting paraphernalia, and a "fire room" that presents important lessons on fire safety. You can also see old-fashioned fire engines, and youngsters will enjoy playing in the kid-friendly fire truck. The museum is located in the old Fire Station No. 1 in downtown Memphis. Admission is two-for-one on Tuesday.

St. Jude Children's Research Hospital

The sprawling complex of St. Jude Children's Research Hospital on uptown's northern fringe has been saving lives and bringing hope to children and their families since 1962. St. Jude was founded by entertainer Danny Thomas in fulfillment of his promise to God to give back to those in need. Over the years and thanks to the success of its fundraising arm—the American Lebanese Syrian Associated Charities—St. Jude has expanded many times over and now leads the world in research and treatment of catastrophic childhood diseases, especially pediatric cancers. The hospital never turns anyone away due to inability to pay, and it never makes families without insurance pay for their treatment.

Visitors can tour a small museum about Danny Thomas and St. Jude in the **Danny Thomas ALSAC Pavilion** (332 N. Lauderdale St., 901/495-4414, www.stjude.org, Sun.–Fri. 8:30 A.M.–4:30 P.M., Sat. 10 A.M.–4 P.M., free), located inside a golden dome on the hospital grounds. Just outside are the graves of Danny Thomas and his wife, Rose Marie.

The Pyramid

The Memphis Pyramid is the most physically dominating feature of the northern city skyline. Memphis's affiliation with all things Egypt began with its name and continued in 1897,

MEMPHIS

© WAYNE HSIEH

Memphis's Pyramid may be in flux, but it is still an icon on the skyline.

when a large-scale replica of a pyramid was built to represent Memphis at the Tennessee Centennial Exhibition in Nashville. Pyramids were popular symbols on Memphis paraphernalia for many years.

The first serious proposal for a life-size pyramid to be built in Memphis was written in the 1970s, but the idea did not take off until the 1980s, when the city and county governments agreed to fund it. Denver developer Sidney Shlenker promoted the plan and promised restaurants, tourist attractions, and lots of revenue for the city. The 321-foot pyramid was built and opened in 1991, minus the money-making engines that Shlenker promised. Today, the $63 million "Great American Pyramid" sits empty. Plans are in the works to turn the former Pyramid Arena into a retail center by August 2013.

MIDTOWN

You'll need a car to explore the attractions in midtown, which sprawls along Union, Poplar, and Madison Avenues as they head eastward from the city center.

Sun Studio

It is well worth your time to drop by the famous Sun Studio (706 Union Ave., 800/441-6249, www.sunstudio.com, daily 10 A.M.–6 P.M., $12), where Elvis Presley recorded his first hit, "That's All Right," and where dozens of blues, rock, and country musicians were recorded during the 1950s. Founded by radio man and audio engineer Sam Phillips and his wife, Becky, the studio recorded weddings, funerals, events, and, of course, music. Phillips was interested in the blues, and his first recordings were of yet-unknown artists such as Rufus Thomas and Howlin' Wolf. In 1953, Elvis Presley came into the studio on his lunch break to record a $3 record of himself singing "My Happiness" for his mother. Phillips was not impressed with the performance, and it was not for another year—and thanks to the prodding of Phillips's

© WAYNE HSIEH

Sam Phillips made music history from the Sun Studio front office.

Lauderdale Courts

The least-known Elvis attraction in Memphis is Lauderdale Courts (252 N. Lauderdale St., 901/523-8662, www.lauderdalecourts.com), the public housing complex where Presley lived with his parents from 1949 to 1953 before his rise to fame. The handsome brick building was saved from the wrecking ball in the 1990s thanks to its history with the King, and the apartment where the Presleys lived has been restored to its 1950s glory. Most of the year, the Lauderdale Courts Elvis suite is rented out as a hotel room, but during Elvis's Birthday Week in January and Elvis Week in August it is open for public tours.

Victorian Village

Set on a tree-lined block of Adams Avenue near Orleans Street is Victorian Village, where a half dozen elegant Victorian-era homes escaped the "urban renewal" fate of other historic Memphis homes.

Visitors can tour the **Woodruff-Fontaine House** (680 Adams Ave., 901/526-1469, www.woodruff-fontaine.com, Wed.–Sun. noon–4 P.M., adults $10), one of the street's most magnificent buildings. Built starting in 1870 for the Woodruff family and sold to the Fontaines in the 1880s, the house was occupied through 1930, when it became part of the James Lee Art Academy, a precursor to the Memphis Academy of Art. When the academy moved in 1959, the building became city property and stood vacant. Beginning in 1961, city residents raised funds to restore and refurnish the house with period furniture and accessories, and it opened as a museum in 1964. This was during the period of urban renewal that saw to the demolition of many of Memphis's other old homes, and some of the house's furnishings were taken from homes that were later demolished. Visitors to the house are given a guided tour of the 1st floor and can explore the 2nd and 3rd floors on their own. This is a good stop if you are interested in antiques.

assistant, Marion Keisker—that Phillips called Presley in to record some more. When Phillips heard Elvis's version of the blues tune "That's All Right," he knew he had a hit. And he did.

But the story of Elvis's discovery is just one of many that took place in the modest homemade Sun Studio, and this attraction is not just for Elvis fans. The one-hour tour of the studio leaves every hour on the half hour, and while you are waiting you can order a real fountain drink from the snack bar or browse the shop's collection of recordings and paraphernalia. The studio is still in business; you can record here for $75 an hour at night, and dozens of top-notch performers have, including Grace Potter, Beck, and Matchbox 20.

Tours start every half hour during business hours and take approximately 90 minutes. Children under the age of five are not permitted on the tours. There are free shuttles from Graceland and the Rock 'n' Soul Museum to Sun Studio.

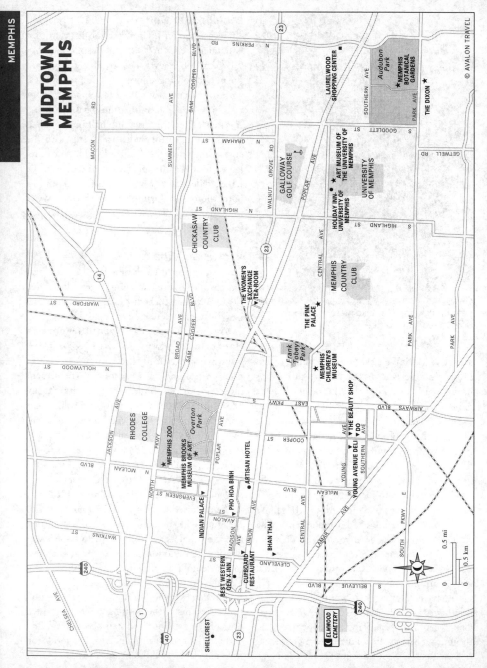

MIDTOWN MEMPHIS

© AVALON TRAVEL

The **Magevney House** (198 Adams Ave., 901/526-1484) and the **Mallory-Neely House** (652 Adams Ave., 901/523-1484) are two other historical homes in the district. The Magevney House is the oldest middle-class residence still standing in Memphis. It was built in 1836 by an Irish immigrant to the city, Eugene Magevney. The Mallory-Neely House is of the same vintage and is notable for the fact that it was not refurnished in more than 100 years and so remains remarkably true to the era in which it was built.

The Magevney and Mallory-Neely Houses are owned by the City of Memphis, and due to budget cuts the interiors have been closed to the public. Call to find out if they have been reopened or just walk by to see the exteriors.

Memphis Brooks Museum of Art

Memphis's foremost art museum is located in Overton Park in midtown, a short drive from downtown. Memphis Brooks Museum of Art (1934 Poplar Ave., 901/544-6200, www.brooks-museum.org, Wed. and Fri. 10 A.M.–4 P.M., Thurs. 10 A.M.–8 P.M., Sat. 10 A.M.–5 P.M., Sun. 11 A.M.–5 P.M., adults $7, seniors $6, students $3) is the largest fine-art museum in Tennessee, and its permanent collection includes 8,000 works of art. This includes ancient African and Asian art, as well as European, American, and contemporary art. There are 29 galleries at the Brooks, and special exhibitions have focused on the work of Annie Leibovitz, men's fashion in Africa, and the silver work of Paul de Lamerie. There is also a museum shop and restaurant, as well as an auditorium often used to screen films.

The Memphis Zoo

The Memphis Zoo (2000 Prentiss Pl., 901/333-6500, www.memphiszoo.org, Mar.–Oct. daily 9 A.M.–5 P.M., Nov.–Feb. daily 9 A.M.–4 P.M., adults $15, children $10) has been expanding and is now the proud steward of two giant pandas, Le Le and Ya Ya; large cats; penguins; lions; tropical birds; and 3,500 other animal species. More hippos have been born here than at any other zoo. Its butterfly exhibit, open May–October, is a popular favorite, and camel rides are available in the spring. The zoo is located on the grounds of Overton Park. Parking is an additional $5.

SOUTH MEMPHIS
◖ Stax Museum of American Soul Music

There is no place in Memphis that better tells the story of the city's legendary soul music than the Stax Museum of American Soul Music (926 E. McLemore Ave., 901/946-7685, www.stax-museum.com, Tues.–Sat. 10 A.M.–5 P.M. and Sun. 1–5 P.M., additionally, Apr.–Oct. Mon. 1–5 P.M., adults $12, seniors, students, and military $11, children 9–12 $9).

The museum tour starts with a short toe-tapping video that sets the scene for the musical magic that took place here during the 1960s. Exhibits include the sanctuary of an old clapboard Delta church, which illustrates the connection between soul and gospel music. You can also see Booker T. Jones's original organ, Otis Redding's favorite suede leather jacket, and Isaac Hayes's 1972 peacock-blue gold-trimmed Cadillac Eldorado, Superfly.

The museum also takes you through the studio's control room and into the studio itself, slanted floors and all. If you want to try your hand, there is a karaoke machine, and a dance floor in case you can't help but move to the music. The Stax museum is a must-see for music enthusiasts but also an educational journey for those who don't know the story behind some of America's most famous songs. It sits next door to the Stax Music Academy, a present-day music school that reaches out to neighborhood youth.

◖ Graceland

Drive south from downtown on Elvis Presley Boulevard to reach the King's most famous

SOULSVILLE

A lucky convergence of people, talents, and social forces led to one of Memphis's – and America's – most distinctive musical stories. Stax Records was founded in 1960 by Jim Stewart, an aspiring country fiddler, and his sister, Estelle Axton. The first two letters of the brother and sister's surnames came together to form Stax, a name now synonymous with the raw Memphis sound of performers like Rufus and Carla Thomas, Otis Redding, Sam and Dave, Isaac Hayes, Eddie Floyd, the Mar-Keys, the Staple Singers, and Booker T. & the MGs.

Jim Stewart chose a closed movie theater in a working-class South Memphis neighborhood for his recording studio. He was on a tight budget, so he didn't bother to fix the sloped theater floor or angled walls, and the room's reverberating acoustics came to define the Memphis sound.

Motown was known as "Hitsville" for its smooth and palatable sound, so the artists at Stax began to call their neighborhood "Soulsville," a name that still refers to the area of South Memphis where Stax is located. The soul music that Stax recorded was raw and inventive, influenced by country, blues, gospel, and jazz.

The label's first hit was with WDIA-AM disc jockey Rufus Thomas and his daughter, Carla Thomas, who came in one day and recorded "Cause I Love You." The song became an overnight sensation.

Stax tapped into the talent of the neighborhood, and particularly the African American Booker T. Washington High School, which graduated such greats as the members of the Soul Children and the Mad Lads. As the Stax reputation developed, artists came from out of town to record, including a 21-year-old Otis Redding, who drove up from Georgia in hopes of making a record and made a career instead.

Stax also operated Satellite Records right next door to the studio, and here Estelle Axton was able to quickly test-market new recordings on the neighborhood youngsters who came in for the latest music. Wayne Jackson, a member of the studio's house band, the Memphis Horns, recalls that Estelle and Jim would invite hundreds of young people from the neighborhood into the studio to listen to their newest recording. Based on the group's response, they would choose the single.

Stax was unique for its time as an integrated organization, where the love of music trumped racial differences. As the civil rights movement evolved, Stax artists turned to serious social themes in their music. In 1972 Stax artists organized WattStax, an outdoor black music festival in Los Angeles.

Between 1960 and 1975, when the Stax magic ran out, the studio produced 800 singles and 300 albums, including 243 Top 100 and 14 number-one R&B hits. Isaac Hayes's theme from the movie *Shaft* was the fastest-selling album in Stax history, and one of three Stax songs went to number one on the pop charts. Other big Stax hits were Otis Redding's "(Sittin' on) The Dock of the Bay," the Staples Singers' "Respect Yourself," and Sam and Dave's "Soul Man."

Sadly, Stax was destroyed financially by a bad distribution deal with CBS Records in 1975, and the studio was closed. Its rare master tapes were sold at auction, and the studio where soul was born was demolished.

Thankfully, the story of Stax has not been forgotten. In 2001 ground was broken for a new Stax story, one that grew into the present-day music academy and the Stax Museum of American Soul Music.

home, Graceland (3717 Elvis Presley Blvd., 901/332-3322 or 800/238-2000, www.elvis.com, Mar.–Oct. Mon.–Sat. 9 A.M.–5 P.M., Sun. 10 A.M.–4 P.M., Nov. daily 10 A.M.–4 P.M., Dec.–Feb. Wed.–Mon. 10 A.M.–4 P.M., adults $32, seniors and students $28.80, children 7–12 $14, children 6 and under free). There is plenty of parking.

Visitors can choose from three tour packages: The mansion-only tour takes about an hour and costs $32; the platinum tour includes the automobile museum, Elvis's two airplanes, and other special perks for $36. Enthusiasts can choose the VIP package for $70, which gives you "front of the line" access, an all-day pass, keepsakes, and access to exclusive exhibits, such as one that features Elvis's first-ever professional photographs, taken in 1955.

The Graceland complex blends into the strip malls and fast-food joints that line the boulevard in this part of Memphis. The ticket counter, shops, and restaurants are located on the west side of the boulevard, and here you board a shuttle van that drives across the highway and up the curved drive to the Graceland mansion. Graceland managers may have taken full advantage of the commercial opportunities presented by the home that Elvis left behind, but they have not overdone it. The operation is laid-back, leaving the spotlight on Elvis and, of course, his fans, who travel to Memphis from around the world to visit.

The mansion tour is conducted by audio guide. It includes the ground floor of the mansion (the upstairs remains closed to the public) and several outbuildings that now house exhibits about Elvis's life and career.

High points include watching the press conference Elvis gave after leaving the army, witnessing firsthand his audacious taste in decor, and visiting the meditation garden where Elvis, his parents, and his grandmother are buried. There is also a plaque in memory of Elvis's lost twin, Jesse Garon. The audio tour plays many of Elvis's songs, family stories remembered by Lisa Marie Presley, and several clips of Elvis speaking. In 2008, Graceland opened two new exhibits: "Private Presley" focuses on the King's service in the army, and "Elvis '68" is about the year 1968 in Presley's life and musical career.

The exhibits gloss over some of the challenges Elvis faced in his life—his addiction to prescription drugs, his womanizing and failed marriage, and his unsettling affinity for firearms among them. But they showcase Elvis's generosity, his dedication to family, and his fun-loving character. The portrait

It's a jungle in there: Graceland's Jungle Room.

that emerges is sympathetic and remarkably human for a man who is so often portrayed as larger than life.

The automobile museum features 33 vehicles, including his pink Cadillac, motorcycles, and a red MG from *Blue Hawaii,* as well as some of his favorite motorized toys, including a go-kart and dune buggy. His private planes include the *Lisa Marie,* which Elvis customized with gold-plated seat belts, suede chairs, and gold-flecked sinks. Other special Graceland exhibits include "Sincerely Elvis," which chronicles Elvis's life in 1956, and "Elvis After Dark," which describes some of Elvis's late-night passions, like roller skating.

The Graceland mansion was declared a National Historic Site in 2006. It attracts more than 650,000 visitors annually.

◖ Elmwood Cemetery

Elmwood Cemetery (824 S. Dudley St., 901/774-3212, www.elmwoodcemetery.org, daily 8 A.M.–4:30 P.M.), an 88-acre cemetery southwest of the city center, is the resting place of 70,000 Memphians—ordinary citizens and some of the city's most prominent leaders. It was founded in 1852 by 50 gentlemen who wanted the cemetery to be a park for the living as well as a resting place for the dead. They invested in tree planting and winding carriage paths so that the cemetery today is a pleasant, peaceful place to spend a few hours.

The cemetery is the resting place of Memphians like Annie Cook, a well-known madame who died during the yellow fever epidemic of 1878; Marion Scudder Griffen, a pioneering female lawyer and suffragette; and musician Sister Thea Bowman. Thousands of anonymous victims of the yellow fever epidemic were buried here, as were both Confederate and Union casualties of the Civil War. Prominent citizens including Robert Church Sr., Edward Hull Crump, and Shelby Foote are also buried at Elmwood.

Visitors to the cemetery may simply drive or walk through on their own. But it is best to rent the one-hour audio guide ($10) of the cemetery, which takes you on a driving tour and highlights 50 people buried in the cemetery. Thanks to a well-written and well-presented narration, the cemetery tour comes closer than any other single Memphis attraction to bringing Memphis's diverse history and people to life.

The cemetery offers occasional lectures and docent-guided tours for $15. Call ahead or check the website to find out if any are scheduled during your visit. To find Elmwood, drive east along E. H. Crump Boulevard, turning south (right) onto Dudley, which dead-ends at the single-lane bridge that marks the entrance to the cemetery.

Church of the Full Gospel Tabernacle

A native of Arkansas and longtime resident of Michigan, Al Green first made his name as one of history's greatest soul singers with hits like "Let's Stay Together," "Take Me to the River," and "Love and Happiness." Following a religious conversion in 1979, he dedicated his considerable talents to God and founded the Church of the Full Gospel Tabernacle (787 Hale Rd., 901/396-9192, www.algreenmusic. com) in Memphis, where his Sunday sermons dripped with soulful gospel.

For almost 11 years, the Reverend Al Green left secular music, dedicating himself to God's music. He began his return to secular music in 1988 and in 1995 Green released the first of three new secular albums on Blue Note Records.

According to his official biography, Rev. Green faced some criticism when he returned to the secular scene. "I've got people in the church saying, 'That's a secular song,' and I'm saying, 'Yeah, but you've got Monday, Tuesday, Wednesday, Thursday, Friday, and Saturday to be anything other than spiritual. You've got to live those days, too!'" Rev. Green says he has not neglected his duty to God. "The music is the message, the message is the music. So that's my

© ANDREA ZUCKER/M: MPHIS VISITORS BUREAU

An angel watches over 70,000 Memphians in Elmwood Cemetery.

little ministry that the Big Man upstairs gave to me—a little ministry called love and happiness."

Despite his rebirth as a secular soul performer, Al Green, now a bishop, still makes time for his church. He preaches regularly, but not every Sunday, and continues to sing the praises of God. The Sunday service at his Memphis church begins at 11:30 A.M. Visitors are welcome, and you can come—within reason—as you are. Please show respect, though, by being quiet when that's called for and throwing a few bucks in the offering plate when it comes around. And don't forget that the church is a place of worship and not a tourist attraction. If you're not in town on Sunday, you can catch the weekly choir rehearsal on Thursday at 7 P.M.

National Ornamental Metal Museum

An unusual delight, the National Ornamental

Metal Museum (374 Metal Museum Dr., 901/774-6380, www.metalmuseum.org, Tues.–Sat. 10 A.M.–5 P.M., Sun. noon–5 P.M., adults $6, seniors $5, students and children $4) is dedicated to preserving and displaying fine metalwork. Its permanent collection numbers more than 3,000 objects and ranges from contemporary American sculpture to works up to 500 years old. The museum hosts special exhibits several times a year, showcasing various aspects of metalwork. There is also a working metalwork studio, and the museum grounds on the bluff overlooking the Mississippi are an attraction in themselves. This is reputed to be the site where Hernando de Soto and his men camped when they passed through the area in 1542.

C. H. Nash Museum Chucalissa

A group of platform and ridge mounds along the Mississippi River are the main attraction at **Chucalissa Archaeological Site** (T. O. Fuller State Park, 901/678-2000, Tues.–Sat. 9 A.M.–5 P.M., adults $5, seniors and children $3). The mounds were once part of a Chocraw Indian community that existed A.D. 1000–1550. The village was empty when Europeans arrived, and the name Chucalissa means abandoned house.

The largest mound would have been where the chief and his family lived. The present-day museum, operated by the University of Memphis, consists of an exhibit about the Native Americans of the area and self-guided tour around the mounds and courtyard area, where games and meetings would have been held. There is also a half-mile nature trail along the bluff overlooking the river.

EAST MEMPHIS

East Memphis is home to old suburbs, gracious homes, and some excellent parks and other attractions.

The Dixon Gallery and Gardens

The Dixon Gallery and Gardens (4339 Park

Ave., 901/761-5250, www.dixon.org, Tues.–Fri. 10 A.M.–4 P.M., Sat. 10 A.M.–5 P.M., Sun. 1–5 P.M., adults $7, seniors $5, children $3), an art museum housed inside a stately Georgian-style home, has an impressive permanent collection of more than 2,000 paintings, many of them French impressionist and postimpressionist style, including works by Monet, Renoir, Degas, and Cézanne. It also mounts a half dozen special exhibits each year; previous ones have showcased the art of George Rodrigue and David Macaulay.

The Dixon is an easy place to spend several hours, immersed first in art and then in walking the paths that explore the house's 17 acres of beautifully tended gardens. There is a cutting garden, woodland garden, and formal gardens, among others.

Admission to the Dixon is free on Saturday 10 A.M.–noon and pay what you wish on Tuesday.

Memphis Botanic Garden

The 100-acre Memphis Botanic Garden (750 Cherry Rd., 901/636-4100, www.memphisbotanicgarden.com, summer daily 9 A.M.–6 P.M., winter daily 9 A.M.–4:30 P.M., adults $8, seniors $6.50, children $5) is home to more than 140 different species of trees and more than two dozen specialty gardens, including a Sculpture Garden, Azalea Trail, and Iris Garden. Trails meander through the gardens, but for the greatest fun buy a handful of fish food and feed the fish and ducks that inhabit the pond at the Japanese Garden. The garden puts on a number of events, including blockbuster concerts, workshops, plant sales, and programs for children.

The Pink Palace

A good destination for families, the Pink Palace (3050 Central Ave., 901/636-2362, www.memphismuseums.org, Mon.–Sat. 9 A.M.–5 P.M., Sun. noon–5 P.M.) is a group of attractions rolled into one. The **Pink Palace Museum** (adults $9.75, seniors $9.25, children $6.25) is a museum about Memphis, with exhibits about the natural history of the Mid-South

region and the city's development. There is a full-scale replica of the first Piggly Wiggly grocery market, plus an exhibit about how health care became such a large part of the Memphis economy. The museum is housed within the Pink Palace Mansion, the Memphis home of Piggly Wiggly founder Clarence Saunders.

The Pink Palace is also home to the **Sharpe Planetarium** (Tues.–Sat., adults $4.50, seniors and children $4) and an IMAX movie theater (adults $8.25, seniors $7.50, children $6.50), which shows movies daily. Special package tickets are available for all the Pink Palace attractions.

Art Museum of the University of Memphis

The Art Museum of the University of Memphis (142 CFA Building, 901/678-2224, www.memphis.edu/amum, Mon.–Sat. 9 A.M.–5 P.M., free) houses excellent but small exhibits of ancient Egyptian and African art and artifacts, and a noteworthy print gallery. There are frequent special exhibitions. The museum is closed during university holidays and in between temporary exhibits.

Children's Museum of Memphis

You will know the Children's Museum of Memphis (2525 Central Ave., 901/458-2678, www.cmom.com, daily 9 A.M.–5 P.M., $12) by the large alphabet blocks outside spelling its acronym, CMOM. Bring children here for constructive and educational play: They can sit in a flight simulator and real airplane cockpit, climb through the arteries of a model heart, climb a skyscraper, and more. The museum has 26 permanent exhibits and several traveling exhibits.

Lichterman Nature Center

Lichterman Nature Center (5992 Quince Rd., 901/767-7322, Tues.–Thurs. 10 A.M.–3 P.M., Fri.–Sat. 10 A.M.–4 P.M., adults $6, children $4.50) is dedicated to generating interest and enthusiasm for the Mid-South's nature. The park encompasses some 65 acres, and visitors will enjoy seeing native trees and flowers, including dogwood, lotus, and pine. There is a museum about the local environment, picnic facilities, and pleasant trails. Environmental education is the center's mission, and this certified arboretum is a popular destination for families and school groups.

TOURS
History Tours

Heritage Tours Memphis (901/527-3427, adults $33, youth 12–17 $25, children under 11 $23) is the city's only tour company dedicated to presenting Memphis's African American history. Operated by Memphians Elaine Turner and Joan Nelson, Heritage Tours offers black heritage, musical heritage, civil rights, and Beale Street walking tours. They can also ar range out-of-town tours to area attractions, such as the Alex Haley home in Henning, Tennessee. Most local tours cost $25 and last about three hours.

The black heritage tour starts at the W. C. Handy Home and Museum and includes a stop at the Slavehaven Underground Railroad Museum, plus narration that tells the story of black Memphians such as Ida B. Wells, Robert Church, and Tom Lee, and the events leading up to the assassination of Dr. Martin Luther King Jr. You will drive past the Mason Temple Church of God in Christ at 930 Mason Street, where Dr. King gave his famous "mountaintop" speech the night before his death.

River Tours

The *Memphis Queen Riverboat Tours* (901/527-2628, www.memphisriverboats.net, adults $20, seniors, college students, military children 13–17 $17, children 4–12 $10, toddlers $5) leave daily at 2:30 P.M. from the Port of Memphis, located at the foot of Monroe Avenue on the riverfront. The afternoon tour lasts 90 minutes and takes you a few miles south of the city before turning around. Commentary tells some of the most famous tales of the river, but the biggest attraction of the tour is simply being on Old Man River. The views of the Memphis skyline from the water are impressive. Concessions are available onboard. The riverboats also offer dinner cruises at 7:30 P.M. with live music for about $45 per person. See website to check dates and times.

Music Tours

Memphis just looks better from the passenger window of a 1955 Cadillac. That's as good a reason as any to call Tad Pierson for one of his **American Dream Safari** (901/527-8870, www. americandreamsafari.com, $40 with five passengers) tours of Memphis. Pierson offers tours with a difference—he does not just do sightseeing; he promises experiences and memories for his guests. His tours include juke joints of Memphis, gospel churches, a Mississippi Delta day trip, a special tour for photographers, plus much more. Pierson really gets the unique appeal of Memphis, and he wants to share it with his guests.

Music-themed tours are the specialty at **Backbeat Tours** (800/979-3370, www. backbeattours.com, $13–45, tickets must be reserved in advance). You will travel on a reconditioned 1959 transit bus and be serenaded by live musicians. Tours include the Memphis Mojo Tour (adults $33, students $31, children 12–17 $19), which takes you to Memphis music landmarks like Sun Studio and the Stax Museum, and the Hound Dog tour, which follows in Elvis Presley's Memphis footsteps. Backbeat can also take you to Graceland and offers two walking tours of Memphis—a Memphis Ghost Tour ($20) and "The Dark Side of Memphis" ($13) which explores the bloody and creepy side of history—on Wednesday through Sunday evenings.

Entertainment and Events

Memphis's vibrant, diverse personality is reflected in its entertainment scene. Blues, rap, R&B, and gospel are just some of the types of music you can hear on any given weekend. Alternative and indie rock finds a receptive audience in Memphis, as does opera, Broadway productions, and the symphony. There's always a good excuse to go out.

LIVE MUSIC AND CLUBS

Memphis may be the birthplace of the blues, but there's a lot more to the music scene than that. It's true that you can catch live blues at a Beale Street nightclub or in a city juke joint. But you can also find hard-edge rock, jazz, and acoustic music most nights of the week. The best resource for up-to-date entertainment listings is the free weekly *Memphis Flyer* (www.memphisflyer.com), which comes out on Wednesday morning and includes a detailed listing of club dates and concerts.

Keep in mind that big-name artists often perform at casinos in Tunica, just over the state line in Mississippi. Many of these shows are advertised in Memphis media outlets, or check out the upcoming events on the Tunica Convention and Visitors Bureau website, www.tunicamiss.com.

Blues

One of the first things you should do when you get to Memphis is to find out if the **Center for Southern Folklore** (119 S. Main St., 901/525-3655, www.southernfolklore.com, Mon.–Fri. 11 A.M.–5 P.M., Sat. 11 A.M.–6 P.M.) has any concerts or activities planned during your visit. The center has been documenting and preserving traditional Memphis and Delta blues music since the 1970s. They put on concerts and lectures, produce documentaries, offer group tours and educational programs, and organize the annual Memphis Music and Heritage Festival over Labor Day weekend. They often have live blues on Friday afternoon and offer a variety of special shows. This is one of the best places to hear authentic blues. The center has a 250-seat dining room and performance space in Peabody Place, as well as a folklore store that sells folk art, books, CDs, and hot peach cobbler, among other things. A sign stating "Be Nice or Leave" sets the tone as soon as you step into this colorful and eclectic shop, one of the best gift shops in the city. The center is a nonprofit organization and well worth supporting.

Beale Street is ground zero for Memphis's blues music scene. While some people lament that Beale has become a sad tourist trap, it can still be a worthwhile place to spend your evening. Indeed, no other part of Memphis has as much music and entertainment packed into such a small area. On a typical night, Beale Street is packed with a diverse crowd strolling from one bar to the next. Beer seems to run a close second to music as the street's prime attraction, with many bars selling directly onto the street through concession windows. The "Big Ass Beer" cups used by many establishments say it all.

Nearly all Beale Street bars have live music, but one of the most popular is **B. B. King's Blues Club** (143 Beale St., 901/524-5464, cover $5–7), owned by the legend himself. B. B. King performs here two or three times a year—keep your ear to the ground since the shows are not usually advertised. On other evenings, local acts and some nationally known performers take the stage. B. B. King's draws a mostly tourist crowd, and it is a chain, but with the blues on full throttle, you probably won't care too much.

Also on Beale Street, **Blues City Cafe** (138 Beale St., 901/526-3637, cover $3–5) books blues, plus a variety of other acts including

MEMPHIS JUKE JOINTS

In Memphis, there are only two reasons to go to a juke joint full of blues: because you feel good or because you feel bad. Beale Street is a reliable source seven nights a week, and your visit to Memphis wouldn't be complete without checking out its scene. But if you want to sneak away from the tourist crowd and catch some homegrown talent, check out a real Memphis juke joint. Live music is typical on Friday and Saturday nights and sometimes Sunday, but it gets scarce during the week. Generally music starts late (11 P.M.) and finishes early (3 A.M.). Don't be surprised if the person you've engaged in conversation sitting next to you gets called to the stage sometime during the evening and delivers a beautiful song.

Remember that it's in the nature of things for these clubs to come and go. The following listings were current as of this writing, but they are always subject to change.

- **Wild Bill's** (1580 Vollentine St., 901/726-5473): A legendary club in Memphis. The Patriarch himself passed away in the summer of 2007, but what he established will still carry on. The quintessential juke joint. Small, intimate, an open kitchen serving chicken wings, and ice-cold beer served in 40-ounce bottles. Home to Ms. Nikki and the Memphis Soul Survivors.

- **CC's Blues Club** (1427 Thomas St., 901/526-5566): More upscale. More mirrors. But a great dance floor, and don't you dare come underdressed. Security guards patrol the parking lot.

- **Mr. Handy's Blues Hall** (182 Beale St., 901/528-0150): New Orleans has Preservation Hall. Memphis has Handy's Blues Hall. Everyone bad-raps Beale Street and its jangly tourism scene, but if you catch it on a good night when Dr. Feelgood warms up his harmonica and you look around the room at the memorabilia on the walls, you could be in a joint at the end of a country road in Mississippi.

- **The Blue Worm** (1405 Airways Dr., 901/327-7947): When a legendary juke joint band gets old and disintegrates, this is where it ends up. The Fieldstones have been *the* band in Memphis since the early '60s. Now it's down to Wilroy Sanders, the Last Living Bluesman. The house band can get behind anybody and make them a superstar, for one glorious song.

- **Big S Bar and Grill** (1179 Dunnavant Ave., 901/775-9127): They say blues is a feeling. The Big S doesn't have live music, but if you want to sink into the atmosphere of a bar that's dark with mystery and history plus the warmest vibe in town, come on home. Blues DJ on Sunday nights, and the jukebox is a veritable encyclopedia of blues.

- **The Boss** (912 Jackson Ave., 901/522-8883): Thursday nights only. Ever heard the overused phrase "best-kept secret in town"? Jesse Dotson on piano. Leroy Hodges on bass. Roy Cunningham on drums. An array of singers like Preacher Man, Bill Coday, O. T. Sykes. Now you don't have to wait for the weekend.

---

doo-wop, zydeco, R&B, funk, and "high impact rockabilly." The café-restaurant is one of the most popular on Beale Street, and its nightclub, **Rum Boogie Cafe** (rumboogie.com, cover $3-5), has an award-winning house band, James Covan and the Boogie Blues Band, that performs most evenings.

Jazz

If you want a break from the blues, **King's Palace Cafe** (162 Beale St., 901/521-1851, www.kingspalacecafe.com) specializes in jazz. Lots of wood paneling and red paint make the bar and Cajun restaurant warm and welcoming. This is an unpretentious place to have a meal or listen to live music. There is a $1 per person entertainment charge when you sit at a table.

On South Main, **Café Soul** (492 S. Main St., 901/859-0557, cover varies) has live jazz, gospel, or soul most nights of the week, good for a relaxing evening after browsing the galleries.

Rock

Still on Beale Street, **Alfred's** (197 Beale St., 901/525-3711, www.alfredsonbeale.com, cover $5 Fri. and Sat.) has rock acts five nights a week. On Sunday evening, the 17-piece Memphis Jazz Orchestra takes the stage. The dance floor at Alfred's is one of the best on Beale Street.

One of Beale Street's most historic night-clubs, **The New Daisy** (330 Beale St., 901/525-8979, cover $5 and up) books rock 'n' roll, independent, and a few R&B acts. There are shows most nights of the week; call ahead or check the entertainment listings for a schedule. The Daisy is an all-ages club, and many shows attract a young audience.

Off Beale Street, the **Hi-Tone Cafe** (1913 Poplar Ave., 901/278-8663, www.hitone-memphis.com, cover varies) is probably the best place to see live music in town. The Hi-Tone books all kinds of acts, from high-energy rockers to soulful acoustic acts. They are re-ally committed to bringing good live music to Memphis. The cover charge for local shows is a few bucks, but tickets for bigger-name acts can run $20 and more. The bar serves respectable burgers and finger foods, excellent martinis, and lots of beer.

Also in midtown, **The Buccaneer** (1368 Monroe, 901/278-0909, cover varies) books rock acts most days a week. Cover charge rarely tops $5.

BARS
Downtown

You can head to Beale Street for a night out, regardless of whether or not you sing the blues.

The best place to grab a beer downtown is the **Beale Street Tap Room** (168 Beale St., 901/527-4392). With more than 30 beers on tap, this is a great choice for beer lovers. The service is friendly and low-key, and regulars have their own mug.

Off Beale Street, **The Peabody Hotel Memphis** (149 Union Ave., 901/529-4000, www.peabodymemphis.com) may be the best place to enjoy a relaxing drink. The lobby bar offers good service, comfortable seats, and an unrivaled atmosphere.

In Peabody Place about a block from Beale Street, **The Flying Saucer Draught Emporium** (130 Peabody Pl., 901/523-8536, www.beer-knurd.com) draws a lively happy-hour crowd. The bar offers more than 75 draft beers, plus cocktails and wine. Grab a seat along the windows and watch downtown Memphis come alive as the sun sets.

In the South Main district, **Ernestine and Hazel's** (531 S. Main St., 901/523-9754) is one of Memphis's most celebrated pit stops for cold drinks and a night out. Once a brothel, Ernestine and Hazel's now has one of the best jukeboxes in town. Take a seat upstairs in one of the old brothel rooms and watch South Main Street below. Rumor is the joint is haunted, but folks come here for the jukebox, not the spirits.

Midtown

The **Young Avenue Deli** (2119 Young Ave., 901/278-3123, www.youngavenuedeli.com) is a friendly neighborhood bar that books occasional live acts. Located in the hip Cooper-Young neighborhood, Young Avenue Deli has hundreds of different beers on tap or in bottles. The bar attracts a diverse crowd, from young hipsters to older neighborhood denizens.

A favorite place for music, pool, and a night out in midtown is the **Blue Monkey** (2012 Madison Ave., 901/272-2583, www.bluemonkeymemphis.com). Grab a pizza and a beer, shoot some pool, and then rock out to the live band.

Murphy's (1589 Madison Ave., 901/726-4193) is a neighborhood bar with a nice patio.

Perfect for a business date or after-work pit stop, **The Grove Grill** (4550 Poplar Ave., 901/818-9951, www.thegrovegrill.com) is popular with businesspeople and office workers.

Two of Memphis's best sports bars are found in the eastern reaches of the city. **Brookhaven Pub & Grill** (695 W. Brookhaven

© HENRYK SADURA/123RF.COM

The Orpheum Theatre at Main and Beale is one of the city's major arts venues.

Cir., 901/680-8118, www.brookhavenpuband-grill.com) has big-screen plasma televisions, great beer on tap, and lots of fans. Tuesday night is quiz night. **Gill's Bar & Grill** (551 S. Highland, 901/458-2787), near the University of Memphis, specializes in cold beers and sports, and has a great happy hour.

GAY AND LESBIAN NIGHTLIFE

Many Memphis gay and lesbian clubs don't get going until late night, after other clubs have closed.

Metro Memphis (1349 Autumn Ave., 901/274-8010, cover varies) is a gay bar and dance club that attracts both gay and straight patrons.

The city's largest dance floor may be found at **Backstreet Memphis** (2018 Court Ave., 901/276-5522, cover varies), a midtown club that has light shows, drag shows, karaoke, and other high-energy entertainment.

A nightclub institution in midtown, **J Wags Bar** (1268 Madison Ave., 901/278-4313, cover varies) doesn't usually get going until the wee

hours, after other mainstream clubs have closed. It claims to be Memphis's oldest gay and lesbian bar.

THE ARTS

Memphis has a growing arts scene. The **Greater Memphis Arts Council** (901/578-2787, www.artsmemphis.org) provides funding for more than 20 local arts groups and is a good source of information about upcoming events.

Major arts venues include the **Cannon Center for the Performing Arts** (255 N. Main St., 901/576-1200, www.thecannoncenter.com) and the **Orpheum Theatre** (Main and Beale Sts., 901/525-3000, www.orpheum-memphis.com). They regularly book major artists and Broadway performances.

Theater

For theater, check out **Playhouse on the Square** (66 S. Cooper St., 901/726-4656, www.play-houseonthesquare.org). This dynamic Memphis institution serves as home to several of the city's acting companies and puts on 15–20 different performances every year. It also offers theater classes, school performances, and pay-what-you-can shows. The playhouse also screens classic movies on the first Sunday of each month.

Theatre Memphis (630 Perkins Ext., 901/682-8323, www.theatrememphis.org) is a community theater company that has been in existence since the 1920s. They stage about 12 shows annually at their theater in midtown.

TheatreWorks (2085 Monroe Ave., 901/274-7139, www.theatreworksmemphis.org) encourages nontraditional and new theater with organizations including Our Own Voice Theatre Troupe, the Memphis Black Repertory Theatre, and the Playwright's Forum.

Music

The **Memphis Symphony Orchestra** (585 S. Mendenhall Rd., 901/537-2525, www.memphissymphony.org) performs on a varied calendar of works year-round in its home at the Cannon Center for the Performing Arts at 2155 North Main Street. The symphony was founded in 1952 and today has more than 850 musicians, staff, and volunteers.

Opera

Opera Memphis (6745 Wolf River Blvd., 901/257-3100, www.operamemphis.org) performs traditional opera at a variety of venues around town, including the historic Orpheum Theatre on Beale Street and the Germantown Performing Arts Centre.

Dance

Ballet Memphis (901/737-7322, www.balletmemphis.org) performs classical dance at the Playhouse on the Square and other venues throughout the city. The **New Ballet Ensemble** (901/726-9225, www.newballet.org) puts on performances around the city with "dancers in do-rags as well as tights," in the words of the *Commercial Appeal*.

Project Motion (TheatreWorks, 2085 Monroe Ave., 901/274-7139, www.projectmotiondance.org) is a contemporary dance collective that performs innovative works.

Cinemas

There are a half dozen multiscreen movie theaters in and around Memphis. For independent movies, try **Malco's Paradiso** (584 S. Mendenhall Rd., 901/682-1754, www.malco.com) or **Studio on the Square** (2105 Court St., 901/725-7151, www.malco.com). In the summer, check out the **Orpheum** (203 S. Main St., 901/525-3000) for classic movies, and the **Malco Summer 4 Drive-In** (5310 Summer Ave., 901/681-2020) for a drive-in experience.

FESTIVALS AND EVENTS
Spring

Memphians celebrate their African heritage over a long weekend in mid-April. **Africa in April** (901/947-2133, www.africainapril.org) honors a specific country in Africa each year; activities include cooking, storytelling, music, and a parade. The festival takes place at Church Park on the east end of Beale Street.

In early May, the Memphis-based Blues Foundation hosts the annual **Handy Awards** (www.blues.org), the Grammys of the blues world.

Memphis in May (www.memphisinmay.org), the city's largest annual event, is really three major festivals rolled into one. The **Beale Street Music Festival,** which takes place at Tom Lee Park on the river during the first weekend of May, kicks things off with a celebration of Memphis music. Expect a lot of wow performers, plus many more up-and-coming talents. The festival has grown over the years, and it is now a three-day event with four stages of music going simultaneously. In addition to music, the festival offers excellent people-watching, lots of barbecue, cold beer, and festivity. You can buy daily tickets or a three-day pass for the whole weekend.

In mid-May, attention turns to the **World Championship Barbeque Cooking Contest,** a celebration of pork, pigs, and barbecue that takes place in Tom Lee Park. In addition to the barbecue judging, there is entertainment, hog-calling contests, and other piggy antics. If you're not part of a competing team (or friends with one), you can buy barbecue from vendors who set up in the park.

Finally, at the end of the month, there is the **Memphis International Festival,** which pays tribute to a different country each year with presentations about its music, food, culture, and history.

Book your hotel rooms early for Memphis in May, since many hotels, particularly those downtown, sell out.

Summer

Carnival Memphis (901/458-2500, www.carnivalmemphis.org) takes place in June. The Carnival features a parade and fireworks. This festival, once called Cotton Carnival, was segregated for decades, but since the mid-1980s has been racially integrated.

The annual candlelight vigil at Graceland on August 15, the anniversary of Elvis's death, has grown into a whole week of Elvis-centric activities throughout Memphis. More than 30,000 people visit Graceland during **Elvis Week** (www.elvisweek.com), and during the vigil his most adoring fans walk solemnly up the Graceland drive to pay their respects at his grave. Special concerts, tribute shows, and movies are shown during the week as the city celebrates its most famous export even more than usual.

Fall

Organized by the Center for Southern Folklore, the **Memphis Music and Heritage Festival** (901/525-3655, www.southernfolklore.com), held over Labor Day weekend, sticks close to the roots of Memphis music. Performers include gospel singers, bona fide bluesmen and women, rockabilly superstars, and much more.

Performances take place in the center's shop and concert hall on Main Street, making them more intimate than other blockbuster music festivals.

End-of-summer fairs are a tradition for Southern and rural communities all over the United States. The 10-day **Mid-South Fair** (www.midsouthfair.org) in September is a bonanza of attractions: livestock shows, rodeos, agricultural judging, concerts, beauty pageants, exhibitions, carnival rides, funnel cakes, and cotton candy. In 2008 it moved from the Mid-South Fairgrounds in southeast Memphis to a 150-acre site across the road from the Tunica, Mississippi, Welcome Center, about 30 miles from Memphis.

In mid-September, the Cooper Young neighborhood throws its annual jamboree at the **Cooper-Young Festival** (www.cooperyoungfestival.com). There is an arts and crafts fair, live music, and food vendors at this street carnival.

The annual **Southern Heritage Classic** (www.southernheritageclassic.com) is one of the South's big football games. But the match of two historically black college rivals, Jackson State University and Tennessee State University, is more than just a game; it is a serious city-wide festival.

Forty-six-foot long boats with dragon heads and tails race at Mud Island River Park each September during the **Duncan-Williams Dragon Boat Races** (www.memphis.racedragonboats.com).

Winter

The colder weather welcomes a number of sporting events, including the **St. Jude Marathon and Half Marathon** (www.stjudemarathon.org, 800/565-5112) in December, which is a qualifying race for the Boston Marathon. The **AutoZone Liberty Bowl** (www.libertybowl.org, 901/795-7700) typically welcomes two of the NCAA's best football teams to town on New Year's Eve.

Taking place over the weekend closest to Elvis Presley's January 8 birthday, the **Elvis**

MEMPHIS

Birthday Celebration (www.elvis.com) draws Elvis fans with special performances, dance parties, and a ceremony at Graceland proclaiming Elvis Presley Day.

The two-day **Beale Street Zydeco Music Festival** (901/619-5865) takes place over the last weekend in February and features more than 20 bands paying tribute to Cajun music.

Shopping

GIFTS AND SOUVENIRS

Any of the half dozen gift shops along Beale Street sell gifts and souvenirs of the city. **Memphis Music** (149 Beale St., 901/526-5047) has a good selection of CDs and DVDs for music fans. For a unique gift or something practical for yourself, **A. Schwab** (163 Beale St., 901/523-9782) is your best choice, and lots of fun to boot.

Another good place for gift shopping is the **Center for Southern Folklore** (123 S. Main St., 901/525-3655), which has books, art, and music focusing on the region. All of the city's museums have good gift shops, including the

National Civil Rights Museum, Stax Museum of American Soul Music, and **Sun Studio,** where everything is emblazoned with the distinctive yellow Sun label.

If you have a car, head out to **Shangri-La Records** (1916 Madison Ave., 901/274-1916, www.shangri.com), one of the city's best record stores, which specializes in Memphis music. **Goner Records** (2152 Young Ave., 901/722-0095, www.goner-records.com) is both a record store and a record label.

If the gift recipient in your life is a fashion maven, head to **Thigh High Jeans** (525 N.

© DAN BALL/MEMPHIS VISITORS BUREAU

Nab a soul souvenir at the Stax Museum of American Soul Music.

Main, www.thighhighjeans.com) where you can buy embroidered skirts and newly remade jeans created from recycled denim. A percentage of each purchase is donated to the charity of the shopper's choice.

ART

For art boutiques and galleries, head south to the South Main arts district, where you will find galleries including **D'Edge Art and Unique Treasures** (550 S. Main St., 901/521-0054), which has contemporary folk art, and **Robinson Gallery/Archives** (44 Huling Ave., 901/619-4478, www.robinsongallery.com), a photography gallery that houses the work of *Vogue* photographer Jack Robinson Jr.

On the last Friday of each month the trolleys are free, the galleries stay open, and hundreds of arts-minded Memphians head to South Main to mingle into the night. For a directory of all South Main galleries, contact the **South Main Association** (901/578-7262, www.south-mainmemphis.net).

Since 2003 the **Wings Gallery** (100 N. Humphreys Blvd., 901/322-2984) has shown the work of artists whose lives have been impacted by cancer. Exhibitions change every six weeks.

ANTIQUES

Head out Central Avenue, to the area between Cooper and East Parkway, for the greatest concentration of antiques stores. **Flashback** (2304 Central Ave., 901/272-2304, www.flashback-memphis.com) sells both vintage furniture and clothes, including a whole lot of Levi's jeans. Another good choice is **Toad Hall Antiques** (2129 Central Ave., 901/726-0755, www.toadhallmemphis.com), easy to find because of a brightly painted mural on the outside of the building.

THRIFT STORES

In a city where vintage never went out of style, you can expect excellent thrift stores. The biggest and best is **AmVets** (2526 Elvis Presley

Blvd., 901/775-5018). You can also try the Junior League of Memphis's **Repeat Boutique Thrift Store** (3586 Summer Ave., 901/327-4777).

In a city of characters, the most colorful shopping experience in Memphis is found at **The Memphis Flea Market—The Big One** (in the AgriCenter, 7777 Walnut Grove Rd., 901/752-8441, www.memphisfleamarket.com), which takes place the third weekend of each month at the Mid-South Fairgrounds. Between 800 and 1,000 vendors turn up each month with housewares, clothing, computers, jewelry, antiques, yard art, and so much more. Between 20,000 and 25,000 people come to shop. Admission is $3 for adults, free for kids. Parking is free.

SHOPPING MALLS

The most upscale shopping mall in the Memphis area is **Wolfchase Galleria** (2760 N. Germantown Pkwy., 901/372-9409). Located in Cordova, an east-lying suburb now consumed by Memphis sprawl, the galleria celebrated its 10th anniversary in 2007. It is aging gracefully, with national retailers including Brooks Brothers, Abercrombie & Fitch, and Sephora. Department stores at the mall include Macy's, Dillard's, Sears, and JCPenney. You can take either exit 16 or 18 off I-40 to get to Wolfchase Galleria.

Also in Germantown, the swanky **Shops of Saddle Creek** (7509 Poplar Ave., 901/753-4264) has Williams-Sonoma, Banana Republic, and an Apple computer store, among others.

Closer to the city center, **Oak Court Mall** (4465 Poplar Ave., 901/682-8928) was the location of the very first Starbucks in Tennessee. It is also consistently voted Memphians' favorite mall, no doubt because it offers a good selection of stores in a pleasant atmosphere, and it's relatively close to town. Department stores at Oak Court include Macy's and Dillard's; the mall also has Aveda, Jos A. Bank, Banana Republic, and dozens more stores.

And if that's not enough for you, head across the road to **Laurelwood Shopping Center** (Poplar Ave. at Perkins Ext., 901/794-6022), where you'll find specialty clothing and shoe boutiques, as well special events like free yoga classes.

In South Memphis, **Southland Mall** (1215 Southland Mall, 901/346-7664) is Memphis's oldest mall. Built in 1966, Southland soldiers on. There is a Sears, as well as specialty shops including Radio Shack and Bath & Body Works.

OUTLET SHOPPING

You can buy directly from name-brand retailers at rock-bottom prices at the **Lakeland Factory Outlet Mall** (3536 Canada Rd., 901/388-5707). Located at the Canada Road exit off I-40, the mall boasts a number of national retailers, including Bass, Van Heusen, Dress Barn, Toy Liquidators, and Old Time Pottery, which sells discounted dinnerware, garden goods, and other housewares.

Sports and Recreation

With a professional basketball team, excellent downtown baseball club, and lots of city parks, Memphis is a great city in which to both watch sports and get active yourself.

PARKS
Downtown

Named for the legendary blues composer, **Handy Park,** on Beale Street, between 3rd Street and Rufus Thomas Boulevard, seems a tad out of place among Beale's nightclubs and restaurants. But the park is a site of historical importance, if only because of the statue of its namesake that guards its gates. The park hosts occasional outdoor concerts and festivals, and at other times you will find places to sit and a handful of vendors.

Uptown

Tom Lee Park, a long, narrow grassy park that overlooks the Mississippi, is a popular venue for summertime festivals and events. It is also used year-round for walking and jogging, and by people who simply want to look out at the giant river. The park is named for Tom Lee, an African American man who saved the lives of 32 people when the steamboat they were on sank in the river in 1925. Lee, who pulled people out of the river and into his boat, "Zev," could not even swim. An outmoded monument erected at the park in 1954 calls Lee "a very worthy negro."

Located on the northern side of downtown Memphis, **Court Square,** three blocks from the waterfront along Court Avenue, is a pleasant city park surrounded by historic buildings. Court Square is one of four parks that was included when the city was first planned in 1819. There are benches and trees, and it is a wireless Internet hot spot.

Confederate Park, located on Front Street between Court and Jefferson Streets, commemorates Confederate soldiers who died in the Battle of Memphis, as well as other war dead. There is a statue of Jefferson Davis in the center of the park. This is where many Memphians gathered to watch the Battle of Memphis in 1862, and it remains a good place to view the river below.

Midtown

Located in midtown Memphis, **Overton Park** (1928 Poplar Ave.) is one of the best all-around parks the city has to offer. This 342-acre park has a nine-hole golf course, nature trails through the woods, bike trails, an outdoor amphitheater now called the Levitt Shell, and lots of green, open spaces. The park shares space with the Memphis Zoo and the Memphis Brooks Museum of Art, making the area a popular destination for city residents and visitors.

The Madison Avenue trolley passes **Forrest Park,** along Madison Avenue, between North

Manassas and North Dunlap Streets, an ample city park dedicated to the memory of the controversial Nathan Bedford Forrest. Forrest, a slave trader, Confederate, and the first grand wizard of the Ku Klux Klan, has an uncomfortable position of prominence in Memphis and the whole of western Tennessee. Both he and his wife are buried in the park.

South Memphis

Southwest of the city center, about 15 minutes' drive from the airport, is **T. O. Fuller State Park** (1500 Mitchell Rd., 901/543-7581). The visitors center here is open weekdays 8 A.M.–sunset. Amenities at the 1,138-acre park include sheltered picnic areas, tennis courts, a golf course, swimming pool ($3), basketball courts, softball field, six miles of hiking trails, and camping facilities. T. O. Fuller State Park was the first state park east of the Mississippi River open to African Americans, and the second in the nation.

East Memphis

Located near the University of Memphis and Oak Court Mall, **Audubon Park** (4161 Park Ave.) has a golf course, tennis courts, walking trails, and other sports facilities. The Memphis Botanic Garden is located here.

Memphians celebrate the fact that their largest city park, **Shelby Farms** (www.shelbyfarmspark.org), is five times the size of New York's Central Park. But the fact is that Shelby Farms is underused, because most of its 4,500 acres are pleasantly undeveloped. There are plans to improve the park by adding more recreational facilities. However, more than 500,000 people come here annually to go mountain biking, horseback riding, inline skating, walking, or running along some of the many trails. You can also fish, raft, canoe, or sail on any of the park's six lakes. There is a wheelchair-accessible trail, areas for picnicking, and a shooting range. Shelby Farms was originally set aside to

be the county penal farm, and although it was not used in this way, the county jail is found on the western edge of the park. Shelby Farms is located on the eastern side of the city, just outside the I-40/I-240 loop that circles Memphis. It is easily accessible from exits 12 and 14 off I-40, and exit 13 off I-240. Or follow Walnut Grove Road from midtown.

BIKING

Most cyclists in the city bike as a form of recreation, rather than transportation. The City of Memphis has established five bike routes that circle the city and various neighborhoods. These routes are marked and have designated parking and restroom facilities at the start. They are not bike paths—you share the road with cars—and normal safety measures are necessary.

The **Memphis Hightailers Bicycle Club** (www.memphishightailers.com) organizes frequent rides for various levels, with distances ranging 20–100 miles. In addition, there are rides leaving every Saturday and Sunday at 8 A.M. from the Super-Lo parking lot at Southern Avenue and Colonial Street.

For bike rentals, gear, and advice about riding in and around the city, go to **Peddler Bike Shop** (575 S. Highland, 901/327-4833, www.peddlerbikeshop.com), where owner Hal Mabray will happily help you get geared up to ride. A used-bike rental will cost about $35 for a half day, $50 per day. Go for a long weekend for $100. There are also bikes for rent at Mud Island.

There are a number of parks near Memphis that are bike friendly. **Meeman-Shelby Forest State Park,** north of the city, has five miles of paved bike paths, and cyclists use the main park roads for more extensive riding. Bicyclists will also find trails at **Shelby Farms.**

It is also noteworthy that the **Mississippi River Trail,** a bicycle route that will eventually run from the headwaters of the Mississippi River in Minnesota to the Gulf of Mexico, runs from Reelfoot Lake in northeastern Tennessee, through

Memphis, and on to Mississippi. For maps and details, go to www.mississippirivertrail.org.

GOLF

The City of Memphis operates award-winning 18-hole golf courses at **Audubon Park** (4160 Park Ave., 901/683-6941), with gently rolling hills; **Fox Meadows** (3064 Clarke Rd., 901/362-0232), which is easy to walk but has several challenging holes; **Galloway Park** (3815 Walnut Grove, 901/685-7805); **Davy Crockett Golf Course** (4380 Rangeline Rd., 901/358-3375); and **Pine Hill Park** (1005 Alice Ave., 901/775-9434), a great course for walkers.

There are two public nine-hole courses: one at **Riverside Park** (465 S. Parkway W., 901/576-4296) and one at **Overton Park** (2080 Poplar Ave., 901/725-9905). Greens fees on the public courses are under $20.

One of the best-kept golf secrets in town is the 18-hole par 71 course at **T.O. Fuller State Park** (1500 W. Mitchell Rd., 901/543-7771), south of downtown. The semiprivate **Mirimichi** (6195 Woodstock Cuba Rd., 901/259-3800, www.mirimichi.com) in Millington is part-owned by heartthrob Justin Timberlake, a former Memphian. Millington is about a 30-minute drive from downtown.

TENNIS

The city operates public tennis courts at several parks, including **Bert Ferguson Park** (8505 Trinity), **Gaisman Park** (4223 Macon), **Glenview** (1141 Barksdale), **Martin Luther King Jr. Park** (South Pkwy. at Riverside Dr.), and **University Park** (University at Edward).

There are also four public indoor/outdoor tennis complexes: **Bellevue** (1239 Orgill Rd., 901/774-7199); **Leftwich** (4145 Southern, 901/685-7907); **Whitehaven,** also called Eldon Roark (1500 Finley Rd., 901/332-0546); and **Wolbrecht** (1645 Ridgeway, 901/767-2889). Fees vary per facility; call in advance for information and court reservations.

SWIMMING

The City of Memphis operates a dozen outdoor pools that are open June–August, and several indoor pools open year-round. Public outdoor pools are open Tuesday–Saturday 1–6 P.M., and admission is free. The outdoor pools include **L. E. Brown Pool** (617 S. Orleans, 901/527-3620), in southeastern Memphis; **Lester Pool** (317 Tillman Rd., 901/323-2261), in eastern Memphis; **Riverview Pool** (182 Joubert Rd., 901/948-7609), at Kansas Park in south Memphis; and **Willow Pool** (4777 Willow Rd., 901/763-2917). Expect crowds; Memphis gets hot in the summer.

Two indoor pools are open to the general public: the **Bickford Aquatic Center** (235 Henry Ave., 901/578-3732, Mon.–Fri. 10 A.M.–6 P.M.) and **Hickory Hill Aquatic Center** (3910 Ridgeway Rd., 901/566-9685, Mon., Wed., and Fri. 9 A.M.–8 P.M., Tues. and Thurs. 6–9 A.M. and noon–8 P.M., Sat. 9 A.M.–1 P.M.).

GYMS

Out-of-towners can get a day pass to the **Louis T. Fogelman Downtown YMCA** (245 Madison Ave., 901/527-9622, Mon.–Thurs. 5 A.M.–10 P.M., Fri. 5 A.M.–9 P.M., Sat. 8 A.M.–6 P.M., Sun. noon–6 P.M., day pass $10) and use the indoor pool and track, and extensive gym facilities. City residents can buy one of the membership packages.

SPECTATOR SPORTS
Basketball

In 2001, Memphis realized the dream of many in the Mid-South when the Vancouver Grizzlies announced they would be moving south. The NBA team played its first two seasons in Memphis at the Pyramid before the massive $250 million FedEx Forum opened for the 2004–2005 season. The arena is one of the largest in the NBA and hosts frequent concerts and performances by major artists.

The **Grizzlies** have yet to achieve any major

titles, but they went to the finals and play-offs in 2010–2011 and 2011–2012. Ticket prices range from under $20 to several hundred dollars. For ticket information, contact the **FedEx Forum box office** (191 Beale St., 901/205-2640, www.fedexforum.com, Mon.–Fri. 10 A.M.–5:30 P.M.). The NBA season runs October–April.

The **University of Memphis Tigers** surprised many in 2008 by making it all the way to the NCAA Championship. The team's remarkable 38–2 season brought new energy and excitement to the university's basketball program.

You can watch Tigers basketball November–April at FedEx Forum. Tickets are available from the FedEx Forum box office, or contact University of Memphis Athletics (www.gotigersgo.com) for more information.

Baseball

From April to October, the **Memphis Redbirds** (901/721-6000, www.memphisredbirds.com, $6–26) play AAA ball at the striking **AutoZone Park** in downtown Memphis. The stadium is bounded by Union Avenue, Madison Avenue, and 3rd Street, and is convenient to dozens of downtown hotels and restaurants. The Redbirds are an affiliate of the St. Louis Cardinals. Cheap tickets ($6) buy you a seat on the grassy berm, or you can pay a little more for seats in the stadium or boxes.

The Redbirds are owned by a nonprofit organization that also operates a number of community and youth programs in the city.

Racing

The **Memphis International Raceway** (550 Victory Ln., 901/969-7223, www.racemir.com) is located a short drive from downtown Memphis in Millington, northeast of the city center. The park includes a 0.75-mile

Root, root, root for the Redbirds at AutoZone Park.

NASCAR oval, a 0.25-mile drag racing strip, and a 1.77-mile road course. It hosts more than 200 race events every year, including a stop in the annual Busch Series races.

Millington is located about 30 minutes' drive north of Memphis.

Ice Hockey

The **Riverkings** (662/342-1755, www.riverkings.com, $16–27) play minor-league ice hockey at the **DeSoto Civic Center** (4650 Venture Dr., Southaven, MS), about 20 miles south of Memphis.

Accommodations

There are thousands of cookie-cutter hotel rooms in Memphis, but travelers would be wise to look past major chains. If you can afford it, choose to stay in downtown Memphis. With the city at your doorstep, you'll have a better experience both day and night. Downtown is also where you'll find the most distinctive accommodations, including fine luxury hotels, charming inns, and an antebellum guest home.

Budget travelers have their pick of major chain hotels; the farther from the city center, the cheaper the room. Beware very good deals, however, since you may find yourself in sketchy neighborhoods. There is a campground with tent and RV sites within a 15-minute drive of downtown at T. O. Fuller State Park.

DOWNTOWN
$150-200

The C **Talbot Heirs Guesthouse** (99 S. 2nd St., 901/527-9772, www.talbotheirs.com, $130–275), in the heart of downtown, offers a winning balance of comfort and sophistication. Each of the inn's nine rooms has its own unique decor—from cheerful red walls to black-and-white chic. All rooms are thoughtfully outfitted with a full kitchen and modern bathroom, television, radio and CD player, sitting area, desk, and high-speed Internet. Little extras like the refrigerator stocked for breakfast go a long way, as does the cheerful yet efficient welcome provided by proprietors Tom and Sandy Franck. Book early since the Talbot Heirs is often full, especially during peak summer months.

Over $200

In 2007, Memphis welcomed the **Westin Memphis Beale Street** (170 George W. Lee Ave., 901/334-5900, $199–369), located across the street from FedEx Forum and one block from Beale Street. The hotel's 203 guest rooms are plush and modern, each with a work desk, high-speed Internet, MP3-player docking station, and super-comfortable beds. The location can be noisy when Beale Street is in full swing.

The **Hampton Inn & Suites** (175 Peabody Pl., 901/260-4000, www.bealestreetsuites. hamptoninn.com, $199–275) is less than a block from Beale Street. The Hampton has 144 standard rooms with high-speed Internet and standard hotel accommodations. The 30 suites ($250) have kitchens and separate living quarters. The entire hotel is nonsmoking.

Plans were afoot for a Hyatt Regency hotel at One Beale (www.onebeale.2dimes.com), a $175 million mixed-use development that would sit on the riverfront at the head of Beale Street. The stalled economy put things on hold. If condo sales and other financing come through, then this may be Memphis's most luxurious hotel.

UPTOWN
$100-150

The most affordable downtown accommodations are in chain hotels. One of the best choices is the **Sleep Inn at Court Square** (40 N. Front St., 901/522-9700, $119–299), with 124 simple but clean and well-maintained rooms. Guests have access to a small fitness room, free parking, and a free continental breakfast. For those with a bigger appetite, the excellent Blue Plate Café is just across the square. It's a five block walk to Beale Street from Court Square, but the trolley runs right past the front door of the hotel.

Even closer to the action is the 71-room **Comfort Inn Downtown** (100 N. Front St., 901/526-0583, $119–149). This hotel is within easy walking distance of all the city-center attractions. Rooms aren't anything special, but the staff are often quite friendly; guests get free breakfast, Internet access, and indoor parking; and there's an outdoor pool. Ask for a room facing west, and you'll have a nice view of the Mississippi River. Parking is $8.

$150-200

Near AutoZone Park and a lot of restaurants is **Doubletree Downtown Memphis** (185 Union Ave., 901/528-1800, $134–299). A 272-room hotel set in the restored Tennessee Hotel, the Doubletree maintains a touch of the old grandeur of the 1929 hotel from which it was crafted. Rooms are large, and there's an outdoor swimming pool and fitness room. Valet parking is $22 or more per night.

If you want to be in the middle of things but can't afford to stay at the swanky Peabody, consider the **Holiday Inn Select** (160 Union Ave., 901/525-5491, www.hisdowntownmemphis.com, $139–199). Located across the street from the Peabody and near AutoZone Park, this Holiday Inn routinely gets good reviews from travelers.

Over $200

 The Peabody Memphis (149 Union Ave., 901/529-4000 or 800/732-2639, www.peabodymemphis.com, $230–2,500 for a presidential suite) is the city's signature hotel. Founded in 1869, the Peabody was the grand hotel of the South, and the hotel has preserved some of its traditional Southern charm. Tuxedoed bellhops greet you at the door, and all guests receive a complimentary shoeshine. Rooms are nicely appointed with plantation-style furniture, free wireless Internet, and in-room safes, as well as all the amenities typical of an upper-tier hotel. Several fine restaurants are located on the ground floor, including the lobby bar, which is the gathering place for the twice-daily red carpet march of the famous Peabody ducks.

One of Memphis's newer hotels is the **River Inn of Harbor Town** (50 Harbor Town Sq., 901/260-3333, www.riverinnmemphis.com, $176–599). A 28-room boutique hotel on Mud Island, the River Inn offers great river views and a unique location that is just minutes from downtown. Set in the mixed residential and commercial New Urban community of Harbor Town, the River Inn provides guests with super amenities like a fitness center, reading rooms, free wireless Internet, free parking, modern decor and furniture, two restaurants, a 1.5-mile walking trail, and spa. Even the most modest rooms have luxurious extras like 32-inch flat-screen televisions, chocolate truffle turndown service, and full gourmet breakfast at Currents, one of two restaurants on the property. The River Inn offers the best of both worlds—a relaxing and quiet getaway that is uniquely convenient to the center of Memphis.

Seeking to be the finest hotel in Memphis, the **Madison Hotel** (79 Madison Ave., 901/333-1200, www.madisonhotelmemphis.com, $200–2,500) is appropriately upscale. The decor is modern, with a touch of art deco. Guests enjoy every perk you can imagine, from valet parking to room service from one of the city's finest restaurants, Grill 83. The daily continental breakfast and afternoon happy hour are an opportunity to enjoy the view from the top floor of the old bank building that houses the hotel. The 110 rooms have wet bars, Internet access, and luxurious bathrooms.

MIDTOWN

Midtown hotels are cheaper than those in downtown. If you have a car, they are convenient to city-center attractions as well as those in midtown itself.

Under $100

There are a few budget hotels within trolley distance of downtown. The **Union Express** (42 S. Camilla St., 901/526-1050, $60–80) is about two blocks from the Madison Avenue trolley and has a dismal, but free, breakfast. The **Motel 6** (210 S. Pauline St., 901/528-0650, $45–59) is about three blocks from the trolley. These choices are certainly not ritzy, but they're acceptable and welcome a large number of budget travelers.

$100-150

The **Best Western Gen X Inn** (1177 Madison Ave., 901/692-9136, $89–180) straddles downtown and midtown Memphis. Located about two miles from the city center along the Madison Avenue trolley line, Gen Xers can get downtown on the trolley in about 15 minutes with a little luck. The hotel, which has free parking and breakfast, is also accessible to the city's expansive medical center and the attractions around Overton Park. These rooms are standard hotel style, enhanced with bright colors, flat-panel plasma TVs, and a general aura of youthfulness. The whole hotel is non-smoking, and guests enjoy a good continental breakfast and a special partnership with the downtown YMCA for gym use. This is a good choice for travelers who want to be near downtown but are on a budget, particularly those with a car. No pets are permitted here.

$150-200

If you want to cook some of your own meals and have comforts like on-site laundry facilities, **Shellcrest** (669 Jefferson Ave., 901/277-0223, www.shellcrest.com, $175 per night, $1,700 per month) is a good choice. This handsome redbrick town house is about six blocks east of downtown. It is designed to be an extended-stay hotel—most leases are for at least

one month. But if they have a vacancy and you are looking to stay for at least three nights, the owners will accommodate short-term guests at a rate of $175 per night. You get a lot for your money: The accommodations are in spacious one-bedroom apartments with a parlor, sunroom, and study, as well as a gourmet kitchen where you can cook your own meals.

The **Holiday Inn-University of Memphis** (3700 Central Ave., 901/678-8200, $119–160) is part of the university's hospitality school. All rooms are suites, with a wet bar and microwave, sitting room, and spacious bathrooms. The lobby contains an exhibit on Kemmons Wilson, the Memphis-born founder of Holiday Inn, who is credited with inventing the modern hotel industry. It is located about six miles from downtown Memphis.

Over $200

You can sleep where Elvis slept at **Lauderdale Courts** (185 Winchester, 901/523-8662, www.lauderdalecourts.com, $250). The onetime housing project where Elvis and his parents lived after they moved to Memphis from Mississippi is now a neat midtown apartment complex. The rooms where the Presleys lived have been restored to their 1950s greatness, and guests can use the working 1951 Frigidaire. The rooms are decorated with Presley family photographs and other Elvis memorabilia. You can rent Lauderdale Courts No. 328 for up to six nights. It sleeps up to four adults. The rooms are not rented during Elvis Week in August or his birthday week in January, when the suite is open for public viewing for $10 per person.

SOUTH MEMPHIS

There are two reasons to stay in south Memphis: the airport and Graceland. But even if you are keenly interested in either of these places, you should think twice about staying in this part of town. You will need a car, as some

Affordable doesn't mean lackluster at the Clarion Memphis Airport/Graceland hotel.

of these neighborhoods are seedy. A car is also a must as south Memphis is not in walking distance of anything of interest.

Under $100

If you need a place to stay near the airport, you can't get any closer than the **Regency Inn & Suites Memphis Airport** (2411 Winchester Rd., 901/332-2370, $69–109), which is right next door. In addition to offering a pool and fitness center, this hotel will shuttle you to the airport terminal for free. Another airport option is the **Memphis Airport Hotel & Conference Center** (2240 Democrat Rd., 901/332-1130, $80–130), which caters to business travelers. There is a guest laundry, free airport shuttle, room service, business center, and good fitness room.

You can't sleep much closer to Graceland than the **Days Inn at Graceland** (3839 Elvis Presley Blvd., 901/346-5500, $70–110), one of the most well-worn properties in the venerable Days Inn chain. The hotel has amped up

the Elvis kitsch; you can tune into free nonstop Elvis movies or swim in a guitar-shaped pool. There is a free continental breakfast. Book early for Elvis Week.

The totally renovated **Clarion Memphis Airport/Graceland** (1471 E. Brooks Rd., 901/332-3500, www.cedarstreethospitality. com/thecedarhotel.php, $89–124) is now a tidy, safe oasis in an otherwise unappealing part of town. Before its remodel, being close to Graceland and the airport were the only draws of this budget hotel. It remains affordable, but now it has the added perk of being clean, with updated rooms and bathrooms, plus a new restaurant and bar. There's a nice outdoor pool, a small fitness room, and a lovely lobby. Book early for Elvis Week.

$100-150

For the most Elvis-y Graceland digs, why not give in and stay at the **Elvis Presley Heartbreak Hotel** (3677 Elvis Presley Blvd.,

901/332-1000, www.heartbreakhotel.net, $115–153)? This 128-room hotel has special Elvis-themed suites ($555–601), and the lobby and common areas have a special Elvis flair. Elvis enthusiasts should check out special package deals with the hotel and Graceland.

CAMPING

You can pitch your tent or park your RV just 15 minutes' drive from downtown Memphis at **T. O. Fuller State Park** (1500 Mitchell Rd., 901/543-7581). The park has 45 tent and RV sites, each with a picnic table, fire ring, grill, lantern hanger, and electrical and water hookups. Sites are allocated on a first-come,

first-served basis; reservations are not accepted. Rates are $20 a night per site.

On the north side of Memphis, **Meeman-Shelby Forest State Park** (910 Riddick Rd., Millington, 901/876-5215) is a half-hour drive from downtown. Stay in one of six lakeside cabins, which you can reserve up to one year in advance; book at least one month in advance to avoid being shut out. The two-bedroom cabins can sleep up to six people. Rates are $80–100 per night, depending on the season and day of the week. There are also 49 tent/RV sites, each with electrical and water hookups, picnic tables, grills, and fire rings. The bathhouse has hot showers. Campsite rates are $20 per night.

Food

Eating may be the best thing about visiting Memphis. The city's culinary specialties start—but don't end—with barbecue. Plate-lunch diners around the city offer delectable corn bread, fried chicken, greens, fried green tomatoes, peach cobbler, and dozens of other Southern specialties on a daily basis. And to make it even better, such down-home restaurants are easy on your wallet. For those seeking a departure from home-style fare, Memphis has dozens of fine restaurants, some old established eateries and others newcomers that are as trendy as those in any major American city.

CAFÉS AND DINERS
Downtown

You can order deli sandwiches, breakfast plates, and a limited variety of plate lunches at the **Front Street Deli** (77 S. Front St., 901/522-8943, Mon.–Fri. 7 A.M.–2 P.M., $4–9). The deli, which claims to be Memphis's oldest, serves breakfast and lunch on weekdays only. One of its claims to fame is that scenes from *The Firm* were filmed here.

For the best burgers on Beale Street, go to

Dyers (205 Beale St., 901/527-3937, www.dyersonbeale.com, Sun.–Thurs. 11 A.M.–1 A.M., Fri.–Sat. 11 A.M.–5 A.M., $7–12). The legend is that Dyers's secret is that it has been using the same grease (strained daily) since it opened in 1912. Only in Tennessee could century-old grease be a selling point. True or not, the burgers here are especially juicy. Dyers also serves wings, hot dogs, milk shakes, and a full array of fried sides.

For coffee, pastries, and fruit smoothies, **Bluff City Coffee** (505 S. Main St., 901/405-4399, www.bluffcitycoffee.com, Mon.–Sat. 6:30 A.M.–6 P.M., Sun. 8 A.M.–6 P.M., $2–5) is your best bet in this part of the city. Located in the South Main district of galleries and condos, the shop is decorated with large prints of vintage Memphis photographs, and it is also a wireless Internet hot spot.

Midtown

No restaurant has a larger or more loyal following in midtown than **Young Avenue Deli** (2119 Young Ave., 901/278-0034, www.youngavenuedeli.com, Mon.–Sat. 11 A.M.–3 A.M., Sun. noon–3 A.M., $4–8), which serves a dozen different specialty sandwiches, grill fare including burgers and chicken sandwiches, plus salads and sides. The Bren—smoked turkey, mushrooms, onions, and cream cheese in a steamed pita—is a deli favorite. The food is certainly good, but it's the atmosphere at this homey yet hip Cooper-Young institution that really pulls in the crowds. There is live music most weekends, and the bar serves a kaleidoscope of domestic and imported beer, including lots of hard-to-find microbrews. The deli serves lunch and dinner daily.

For a good cup of coffee in the Cooper-Young neighborhood, head to **Java Cabana** (2170 Young Ave., 901/272-7210, www.javacabanacoffeehouse.com, Tues.–Thurs. 6:30 A.M.–10 P.M., Fri.–Sat. 9 A.M.–midnight, Sun. noon–10 P.M., $4–10). Java Cabana serves light breakfast fare, including pancakes and omelets, all day. For lunch or later, you can order simple sandwiches or munchies like apple slices and peanut butter, potato chips, or Pop Tarts.

For a cold treat during the long, hot Memphis summer, head to **Wiles-Smith Drug Store** (1635 Union Ave., 901/278-6416, Mon.–Wed. 9 A.M.–5 P.M., Thurs. 9 A.M.–2 P.M., Sat. 10 A.M.–3 P.M.) for a milk shake. The lunch counter at this old-fashioned drugstore also serves sandwiches and snacks, but it is the milk shakes that draw the biggest crowd. They come in chocolate, vanilla, strawberry, and cherry, and customers get to pour the cool, frothy treat into their own glass.

SOUTHERN
Downtown

Tucked inside an unassuming storefront across from the valet entrance to the Peabody Hotel is **Flying Fish** (105 S. 2nd St., 901/522-8228, daily 11 A.M.–10 P.M., $5–14), your first stop for authentic fried catfish in Memphis. If catfish isn't your thing, try the grilled or boiled shrimp, fish tacos, frog legs, or oysters. The baskets of fried seafood come with fries and

hush puppies, and the grilled plates come with grilled veggies, rice, and beans. The tangy coleslaw is a must. The atmosphere here is laid-back; place your order at the window and come and get it when the coaster they give you starts to vibrate. The checkered tables are well stocked with hot sauce and saltines.

It would be a grave mistake to visit Memphis and not stop at **Gus's World Famous Fried Chicken** (310 Front St., 901/527-4877, Mon.–Thurs. and Sun. 11 A.M.–9 P.M., Fri.–Sat. 11 A.M.–10:30 P.M., $6–12) for some of their delicious fried bird. The downtown location is a franchise of the original Gus's, which is a half-hour drive northeast out of town along U.S. 70, in Mason. It is no exaggeration to say that Gus's cooks up some of the best fried chicken out there. It is spicy, juicy, and hot. It's served casually wrapped in brown paper. Sides include coleslaw, baked beans, and fried pickles. They also serve grilled-cheese sandwiches. The service in this hole-in-the-wall establishment is slow but friendly, so come in with a smile on.

The **Arcade** (540 S. Main St., 901/526-5757, www.arcaderestaurant.com, daily 7 A.M.–3 P.M., $5–10) is said to be Memphis's oldest restaurant. Founded in 1919 and still operated by the same family (with lots of the same decor), this restaurant feels like a throwback to an earlier time. The menu is diverse, with pizzas, sandwiches, plate-lunch specials during the week, and breakfast served anytime. The chicken spaghetti is a stick-to-your-ribs favorite.

Uptown

The Little Tea Shop (69 Monroe, 901/525-6000, Mon.–Fri. 11 A.M.–2 P.M., $4.95–7.50) serves traditional plate lunches through the week. Choose from daily specials like fried catfish, chicken potpie, and meat loaf with your choice of vegetable and side dishes by ticking off check boxes on the menu. Every meal (except sandwiches) comes with fresh, hot corn bread that might well be the star of the show.

This is stick-to-your-ribs Southern cooking at its best, so come hungry. If you have room, try the peach cobbler or pecan ball for dessert. The staff's welcoming yet efficient style makes this perfect for a quick lunch. Not to be missed.

The Blue Plate Cafe (113 Court Square S., 901/523-2050, Mon.–Sat. 6 A.M.–8:30 P.M., $4–10) serves hearty breakfasts, plate lunches, and traditional home-style cooking. Its newsprint menu imparts wisdom ("Rule of Life No. 1: Wake up. Show up. Pay attention.") and declares that every day should begin with a great breakfast. It's not hard to comply at the Blue Plate. Eggs come with homemade biscuits and gravy, and your choice of grits, hash browns, or pancakes. For lunch, try a meat-and-three or vegetable plate, slow-cooked white-bean soup, or a grilled peanut butter and banana sandwich. Locals swear by the fried green tomatoes. There are three Blue Plate Cafes in Memphis; the other two are at 2921 Kirby Whitten Road in Bartlett (901/213-1066) and at 5469 Poplar Avenue in an old house in midtown (901/761-9696).

Alcenia's (317 N. Main St., 901/523-0200, www.alcenias.com, Tues.–Fri. 11 A.M.–5 P.M., Sat. 9 A.M.–3 P.M., $4–10), located in the Pinch district, is among Memphis's best Southern-style restaurants. Known for its plate lunches, fried chicken, and pastries, Alcenia's has a style unlike any other Memphis eatery, witnessed in its offbeat decor of '60s-style beads, folk art, and wedding lace. Proprietor B. J. Chester-Tamayo is all love, and she pours her devotion into some of the city's best soul food. Try the spicy cabbage and deep-fried chicken, and save room for Alcenia's famous bread pudding for dessert. Chicken and waffles is the Saturday-morning specialty.

Midtown

Just follow the crowds to the **Cupboard Restaurant** (1400 Union Ave., 901/276-8015, daily 7 A.M.–8 P.M., $6–9), one of Memphians' favorite stops for plate lunches. The Cupboard moved from its downtown location to an old Shoney's about a mile outside of town to accommodate the throngs who stop here for authentic home-style cooking. The Cupboard gets only the freshest vegetables for its dishes like okra and tomatoes, rutabaga turnips, steamed cabbage, and green beans. The meat specials change daily but include things like fried chicken, chicken and dumplings, hamburger steak with onions, and beef tips with noodles. The corn bread "coins" are exceptionally buttery, and the bread is baked fresh daily. For dessert, try the lemon icebox pie.

The Women's Exchange Tea Room (88 Racine St., 901/327-5681, www.womans-exchange.com, Mon.–Fri. 11:30 A.M.–1:45 P.M., $10) feels like a throwback to an earlier era. Located one block east of the Poplar Street viaduct, the Women's Exchange has been serving lunch since 1936, and the menu has not changed much over the years. The special changes daily and always includes a choice of two entrées, or a four-vegetable plate. Classics like chicken salad, salmon loaf, beef tenderloin, and seafood gumbo are favorites, and all lunches come with a drink and dessert. The dining room looks out onto a green garden, and the atmosphere is homey—not stuffy. The Exchange also sells gifts, housewares, and other knickknacks.

In the Cooper-Young neighborhood, **Soul Fish** (862 S. Cooper St., 901/725-0722, Mon.–Sat. 11 A.M.–10 P.M., Sun. 11 A.M.–9 P.M., $6–15) offers traditional plate lunches, vegetable plates, and several varieties of catfish. You can get the fish breaded and fried, or blackened with a potent spice mix. Soul Fish is owned in part by Tiger Bryant, owner of the venerable Young Avenue Deli, and it has the hallmarks of a well-conceived eatery. The atmosphere is open and cheerful, with a few touches of subtle sophistication. In this case, the main attraction is good food at a good price—a combination that can be hard to find elsewhere in Cooper-Young.

South Memphis

Gay Hawk Restaurant (685 Danny Thomas

Blvd., 901/947-1464, Mon.–Fri. 11 A.M.–3 P.M., Sat.–Sun. noon–5 P.M., $6–10) serves country-style food that sticks to your ribs and warms your soul. Chef Bobo declares that his specialty is "home-cooked food," and it really is as simple as that. The best thing about Gay Hawk is the luncheon buffet, which lets newcomers to Southern cooking survey the choices and try a little bit of everything. The Sunday lunch buffet practically sags with specialties like fried chicken, grilled fish, macaroni and cheese, greens, and much, much more. Save room for peach cobbler.

BARBECUE

Barbecue is serious business in Memphis, unlike anywhere else in the state. On the northern fringe of downtown Memphis is one of the city's most famous and well-loved barbecue joints: **Cozy Corner** (745 N. Parkway, 901/527-9158, www.cozycornerbbq.com, Tues.–Sat. 11 A.M.–9 P.M., $4–16). Cozy Corner is tucked into a storefront in an otherwise abandoned strip mall; you'll smell it before you see it. Step inside to order barbecue pork, sausage, or bologna sandwiches. Or get a two-bone, four-bone, or six-bone rib dinner plate, which comes with your choice of baked beans, coleslaw, or barbecue spaghetti, plus slices of Wonder bread to sop up the juices. One of Cozy Corner's specialties is its barbecued Cornish hens—a preparation that is surprising but delicious. Sweet tea goes perfectly with the tangy and spicy barbecue.

Jim Neely's **Interstate Bar-B-Que** (2265 S. 3rd St., 901/775-2304, www.interstatebarbecue.com, Mon.–Thurs. 11 A.M.–11 P.M., Fri.–Sat. 11 A.M.–midnight, $5–18) was once ranked the second-best barbecue in the nation, but the proprietors have not let it go to their heads; this is still a down-to-earth, no-frills eatery. Large appetites can order a whole slab of pork or beef ribs, but most people will be satisfied with a chopped pork sandwich, which comes topped with coleslaw and smothered with barbecue

sauce. Families can get the fixings for 6, 8, or 10 sandwiches sent out family style. For an adventure, try the barbecue spaghetti or barbecue bologna sandwich. If you're in a hurry, the Interstate has a drive-up window, too, and if you are really smitten, you can order pork, sauce, and seasoning in bulk to be frozen and shipped to your home.

Although aficionados will remind you that the ribs served at the **Rendezvous** (52 S. 2nd St., 901/523-2746, www.hogsfly.com, Tues.–Thurs. 4:30–10:30 P.M., Fri. 11 A.M.–11 P.M., Sat. 11:30 A.M.–11 P.M., $8–16) are not technically barbecue, they are one of the biggest barbecue stories in town. Covered in a dry rub of spices and broiled until the meat falls off the bones, these ribs will knock your socks off. If you prefer, you can choose Charlie Vergos's dry rub chicken or boneless pork loin. Orders come with baked beans and coleslaw, but beer is really the essential accompaniment to any Vergos meal. The door to Rendezvous is tucked in an alley off Monroe Avenue. The smoky interior, decorated with antiques and yellowing business cards, is low key, noisy, and lots of fun.

A Memphis chain, **Gridley's** (6842 Stage Rd., 901/377-8055, Mon. and Wed.–Fri. 11 A.M.–8 P.M., Sat. 11 A.M.–9 P.M., $4–18) serves wet-style barbecue ribs, pork shoulder plates and sandwiches, plus spicy grilled shrimp. The shrimp is served with a buttery and delicious dipping sauce. Try the half pork, half shrimp plate for a real treat. Meals here come with baked beans, slaw, and hot fresh bread.

CONTEMPORARY
Downtown

The Majestic Grill (145 S. Main St., 901/522-8555, www.majesticgrille.com, Mon.–Thurs. 11 A.M.–10 P.M., Fri.–Sat. 11 A.M.–11 P.M., Sun. 11 A.M.–9 P.M., $6–34) serves a remarkably affordable yet upscale menu at lunch and dinner. Located in what was once the Majestic Theater, the restaurant's white tablecloths and apron-clad waiters lend an aura of refinement. But with main courses starting at just $6, this can be a bargain. Flatbread pizzas feature asparagus, spicy shrimp, and smoked sausage, and sandwiches include burgers and clubs. Specialties include pasta, barbecue ribs, grilled salmon, and steaks. Don't pass on dessert, served in individual shot glasses, such as chocolate mousse, key lime pie, and carrot cake, among others.

It is impossible to pigeonhole **Automatic Slim's Tonga Club** (83 S. 2nd St., 901/525-7948, Mon.–Fri. 11 A.M.–midnight, Sat.–Sun. 10 A.M.–10 P.M., $12–20), except to say that this Memphis institution consistently offers fresh, spirited, and original fare. Named after a character from an old blues tune, Automatic Slim's uses lots of strong flavors to create its eclectic menu; Caribbean and Southwestern influences are the most apparent. Take a seat, and in two shakes you'll be presented with soft, fresh bread and pesto-seasoned olive oil for dipping. The Caribbean shrimp are a favorite of many diners. A meal at Automatic Slim's would not be complete without a famous Tonga Martini or one of the kitchen's delectable desserts: Pecan tart and chocolate cake are good choices. Automatic Slim's is a welcome departure from barbecue and Southern food when you're ready. Its atmosphere is relaxed, and there's often a crowd at the bar, especially on weekends when there's live music on tap.

Long the standard-bearer of fine French cuisine, **Chez Philippe** (149 Union Ave., 901/529-4000, Wed.–Sat. 6–10 P.M., afternoon tea Wed.–Sun., $78–100), located in the Peabody Hotel, now offers French-Asian fusion cuisine. The Asian influences are noticeable in the ingredients, but the preparation of most dishes at Chez Philippe remains traditional French. Entrées include grouper, bass, pork chop, and venison. Chez Philippe offers a prix fixe menu: Three courses is $78, and five courses is $88. Or opt for a seven-course tasting menu for $100; wine pairings are an additional $48 per person.

Midtown

In 2007, Memphis's foremost restaurateur, Karen Blockman Carrier, closed her fine-dining restaurant Cielo in Victorian Village, redecorated, and reopened it as the **Molly Fontaine Lounge** (679 Adams Ave., 901/524-1886, Wed.–Sat. 5 P.M.–2:30 A.M., $12–24). Carrier's vision was an old-fashioned club where guests can order upscale cocktails, relax with live music, and eat tasty Mediterranean- and Middle Eastern–inspired tapas. The restaurant has an upmarket but cozy atmosphere, with equal measures of funky and fine. The live piano jazz is the perfect backdrop for the restaurant's artistic small plates.

Surprisingly good for a bookstore café, **Bronte** (387 Perkins Ext., 901/374-0881, Mon.–Thurs. 8 A.M.–9 P.M., Fri.–Sat. 8 A.M.–10 P.M., Sun. 9 A.M.–8 P.M., $8–12), inside Davis-Kidd Booksellers, offers salads, soups, and sandwiches, as well as daily meat and fish specials. The soup-and-sandwich combo is filling and good. Breakfast may well be the best meal on offer, however. The morning menu features specials designed by celebrity chefs, including omelets, baked goods, and crepes.

One of Memphis's most distinctive restaurant settings is an old beauty shop in the Cooper-Young neighborhood. **◖ The Beauty Shop** (966 S. Cooper St., 901/272-7111, www.thebeautyshoprestaurant.com, Mon.–Sat. 11 A.M.–2 P.M., Mon.–Thurs. 5–10 P.M., Fri.–Sat. 5–11 P.M., Sun. 10 A.M.–3 P.M., $8–32) takes advantage of the vintage beauty parlor decor to create a great talking point for patrons and food writers alike. The domed hair dryers remain, and the restaurant has put the shampooing sinks to work as beer coolers. At lunch, the Beauty Shop offers a casual menu of sandwiches and salads. For dinner, the imaginative cuisine of Memphis restaurateur Karen Blockman Carrier, who also owns Molly Fontaine Lounge and Automatic Slim's Tonga Club, takes over.

At The Beauty Shop in the Cooper-Young neighborhood, you'll dine in an old – you guessed it – beauty parlor.

Right next to the Beauty Shop is **Do** (964 S. Cooper St., 901/272-0830, Mon.–Thurs. 5–10 P.M., Fri.–Sat. 5–11 P.M., Sun. 5–9 P.M., $6–15), a trendy sushi restaurant that also offers tempura, soups, and salads.

If you enjoy your beer as much or more than your meal, then head straight for **Boscos Squared** (2120 Madison Ave., 901/432-2222, www.boscosbeer.com, Mon.–Thurs. 11 A.M.–2 A.M., Fri.–Sat. 11 A.M.–3 A.M., Sun. 10:30 A.M.–2 A.M., $12–22). Boscos is a brewpub with fresh seafood, steak, and pizza. Their beer menu is among the best in the city, and many of the brews are made on the premises. Boscos also has locations in Franklin and Nashville.

East Memphis

To many minds, Memphis dining gets no better than **❰ Erling Jensen, The Restaurant** (1044 S. Yates Rd., 901/763-3700, www. ejensen.com, daily 5–10 P.M., $30–50).

Danish-born Erling Jensen is the mastermind of this fine-dining restaurant that has consistently earned marks as Memphians' favorite restaurant. Understated decor and friendly service are the backdrop to Jensen's dishes, which are works of art. The menu changes with the seasons and based upon availability, but usually it includes about six different seafood dishes and as many meat and game choices. Black Angus beef, elk loin, and buffalo tenderloin are some of the favorites. Meals at Jensen's restaurant should begin with an appetizer, salad, or soup—or all three. The jumbo chunk crab cakes with smoked red-pepper sauce are excellent. Reservations are a good idea at Erling Jensen, and so are jackets for men. Expect to spend upwards of $80 for a four-course meal here; $60 for two courses. Add more for wine.

Memphis's premier steak house is **Folk's Folly** (551 S. Mendenhall Rd.,

MEMPHIS

PIGGLY WIGGLY

Memphian Clarence Saunders opened the first Piggly Wiggly at 79 Jefferson Street in 1916, thus giving birth to the modern American supermarket. Until then, shoppers went to small storefront shops where they would ask the counter clerk for what they needed: a pound of flour, a half dozen pickles, a block of cheese. The clerk went to the bulk storage area at the rear of the store and measured out what the customer needed.

Saunders's big idea was self-service. At the Piggly Wiggly, customers entered the store, carried a basket, and were able to pick out prepackaged and priced containers of food, which they paid for at the payment station on their way out.

Suffice to say, the Piggly Wiggly idea took off, and by 1923 there were 1,268 Piggly Wiggly franchises around the country. Saunders used some of his profits to build a massive mansion east of the city out of pink Georgia limestone, but he was never to live in the Pink Palace, which he lost as a result of a complex stock loss.

Today, Saunders's Pink Palace is home to the Pink Palace Museum, which includes, among other things, a replica of the original Piggly Wiggly supermarket.

901/762-8200, www.folksfolly.com, Mon.–Sat. 5:30–10 P.M., Sun. 5:30–9 P.M., $30–70), located just east of Audubon Park. Diners flock here for prime aged steaks and seafood favorites. For small appetites, try the 8-ounce filet mignon for $32; large appetites can gorge on the 28-ounce porterhouse for $60. Seafood includes lobster, crab legs, and wild salmon. The atmosphere is classic steak house: The lighting is low, and there's a piano bar on the property.

Some say **Acre Restaurant** (690 S. Perkins, 901/818-2273, www.acrememphis.com, Mon.–Fri. 11 A.M.–2 P.M., Mon.–Sat. 5–10 P.M., $25–80) is Memphis's best. Certainly, it has one of the best wine lists in town. The menu combines Southern and Asian traditions with locally grown and raised ingredients in a modern setting.

Where else in the world can you enjoy the offbeat combination that is **Jerry's Sno-Cone and Car Wash** (1657 Wells Station Rd., 901/767-2659, Mon.–Sat. 11 A.M.–7 P.M.)?

INTERNATIONAL
Downtown
For sushi, try **Sekisui** (Union at 2nd Ave., 901/523-0001, www.sekisuiusa.com, Mon.–Sun. noon–3 P.M. and 6–11 P.M.), where a roll costs $2.50–8, and a filling combo plate will run you about $15. The downtown restaurant is located on the ground floor of the Holiday Inn Select. Sekisui is a Memphis chain, and there are other locations in midtown and the suburbs, as well as in Chattanooga.

Midtown
The **India Palace** (1720 Poplar Ave., 901/278-1199, www.indiapalaceinc.com, daily 11 A.M.–3 P.M. and 5–10 P.M., $7–17) is a regular winner in reader's choice polls for Indian food in Memphis. The lunchtime buffet is filling and economical, and the dinner menu features vegetarian, chicken, and seafood dishes. The dinner platters are generous and tasty.

Pho Hoa Binh (1615 Madison, 901/276-0006, Mon.–Fri. 11 A.M.–9 P.M., Sat. noon–9 P.M., $4–9) is one of the most popular Vietnamese restaurants in town. You can't beat the value of the lunch buffet, or you can order from the dizzying array of Chinese and Vietnamese dishes, including spring rolls, vermicelli noodle bowls, rice, and meat dishes. There are a lot of vegetarian options here.

The atmosphere at **Bhan Thai** (1324 Peabody Ave., 901/272-1538, www.bhanthairestaurant.com, Tues.–Fri. 11 A.M.–2:30 P.M., Sun.–Thurs. 5–9:30 P.M., Fri.–Sat. 5–10:30 P.M., $10–19) in midtown is almost as appealing as the excellent Thai food served there. Set in an elegant 1912 home, Bhan Thai makes the most of the house's space, and seating is spread throughout several colorful rooms and on the back patio. Choose from dishes like red snapper, masaman curry, and roasted duck curry. The Bhan Thai salad is popular, with creamy peanut dressing and crisp vegetables.

It's the regulars who are happy at the **Happy Mexican Restaurant and Cantina** (385 S. 2nd St., 901/529-9991, www.happymexican. com, Sun.–Thurs. 11 A.M.–10 P.M., Fri.–Sat. 11 A.M.–11 P.M., $7–15). Serving generous portions of homemade Mexican food for lunch and dinner, Happy Mexican is destined to become a downtown favorite. The service is efficient and friendly, and the decor is cheerful but not over the top. It's located just a few blocks south of the National Civil Rights Museum. There are three other locations in the greater Memphis area.

MARKETS

The only downtown grocery store is the **Easy-Way** (80 N. Main St., 901/523-1323, Mon.–Sat. 7 A.M.–6 P.M.), on the corner of Main Street and Jefferson Avenue. For liquor and wine, go to **The Corkscrew** (511 S. Front St., 901/523-9389).

The closest gourmet grocery is located in Harbor Town, the residential community on Mud Island, where **Miss Cordelia's** (737 Harbor Bend, 901/526-4772, www.misscordelias.com, daily 7 A.M.–10 P.M.) sells fresh produce, bakery goods, and staples. A deli in the back serves soups, salads, sandwiches, and a wide variety of prepared foods.

For a full-service grocery store in midtown, look for the **Kroger** at the corner of Cleveland and Poplar.

The **Memphis Farmer's Market** (901/575-0580, www.memphisfarmersmarket.com, Apr.–Oct. Sat. 7 A.M.–1 P.M., rain or shine) takes place in the pavilion opposite Central Station in the South Main part of town.

Information and Services

INFORMATION
Visitors Centers

The city's visitors center is the **Tennessee Welcome Center** (119 Riverside Dr., 901/543-6757), located on the Tennessee side of the I-40 bridge. The center has lots of brochures and free maps and staff who can answer your questions. It is open 24 hours a day, seven days a week. The center assists more than 350,000 travelers annually.

Although it is not designed to be a visitors center per se, the **Memphis Convention and Visitors Bureau** (47 Union Ave., 901/543-5300, www.memphistravel.com, Apr.–Sept. daily 9 A.M.–6 P.M., Oct.–Mar. Mon.–Fri 9 A.M.–5 P.M.) is a resource for visitors. You can collect maps and ask questions here. The bureau also produces videos highlighting city

attractions and restaurants, which are available on many hotel televisions.

Maps

Hand-out maps that highlight key attractions are available from visitors centers in Memphis. If you are only interested in Beale Street, Graceland, and the interstates, these will be fine. The free maps provided at the concierge desk of the Peabody Hotel are particularly well marked and useful.

If you want to explore further, or if you plan to drive yourself around the city, it is wise to get a proper city map or GPS. Rand McNally publishes a detailed Memphis city map, which you can buy from bookstores or convenience marts in downtown.

Media

The daily *Commercial Appeal* (www.

commercialappeal.com) is Memphis's major newspaper, available all over the city. The *Memphis Flyer* (www.memphisflyer.com) is a free alternative weekly, published on Wednesday with the best entertainment listings.

Memphis magazine (www.memphismagazine.com) is published monthly and includes historical anecdotes, restaurant reviews, features on high-profile residents, and lots of advertising aimed at residents and would-be residents.

There are two independent radio stations of note: **WEVL 89.9 FM** is a community radio station that plays blues, country, and other Memphis music. **WDIA 1070 AM,** the historical Memphis station that made the blues famous, still rocks today. Another station of note is **WRBO 103.5 FM,** which plays soul and R&B.

SERVICES
Fax and Internet
Send a fax at **FedEx Office** (50 N. Front St., 901/521-0261), located across from the Peabody's valet entrance.

Most of the major hotels and attractions have wireless Internet access.

Postal Service
There is a postal retail center, which sells stamps and offers limited postal services, at 100 Peabody Place (800/275-8777, Mon.–Fri. 8:30 A.M.–5 P.M.).

Emergency Services
Dial 911 in an emergency for fire, ambulance, or police. The downtown police department is the **South Main Station** (545 S. Main St., 901/636-4099). Police patrol downtown by car, on bike, and on foot.

Several agencies operate hotlines for those needing help. They include: Alcoholics Anonymous (901/726-6750), the Better Business Bureau (901/759-1300), Emergency Mental Health Services (855/274-7471), Deaf Interpreting (901/577-3783), Rape Crisis/

Sexual Assault Hotline (901/272-2020), and Poison Emergencies (901/528-6048).

Hospitals
Memphis is chockablock with hospitals. Midtown Memphis is also referred to as Medical Center for the number of hospitals and medical facilities there. Here you will find the **Regional Medical Center at Memphis** (877 Jefferson Ave., 901/545-7100), a 620-bed teaching hospital affiliated with the University of Tennessee; and the **Methodist University Hospital** (1211 Union Ave., 901/516-7000), the 669-bed flagship hospital for Methodist Healthcare.

In East Memphis, **Baptist Memorial Hospital** (6019 Walnut Grove Rd., 901/226-5000) is the cornerstone of the huge Baptist Memorial Health Care System, with 771 beds.

Laundry
Try any of these three laundries, which are located near downtown: **Metro Plaza Laundry** (805 S. Danny Thomas Blvd., 901/948-1673), **Crump Laundry Mat and Dry Cleaning** (756 E. Ed Crump Blvd., 901/948-7008), or **Jackson Coin Laundry** (1216 Jackson Ave., 901/274-3536).

Libraries
Memphis has 19 public libraries. The city's main library is **Hooks Public Library** (3030 Poplar Ave., 901/415-2700, Mon.–Thurs. 10 A.M.–8 P.M., Fri.–Sat. 10 A.M.–5 P.M., Sun. 1–5 P.M.), a modern, new public library with 119 public computers, an extensive collection, community programs, meeting rooms, a lecture series, and more. The central library is located on a busy thoroughfare in midtown and would be a challenge to visit without a car.

The downtown branch library, **Cossit Library** (33 S. Front St., 901/415-2766, Mon.–Fri. 10 A.M.–5 P.M.), has a good collection of new releases, and staff there are happy to help visitors looking for information about Memphis. The current building was constructed in 1959.

Getting There and Around

GETTING THERE
By Air
Memphis International Airport (MEM; 901/922-8000, www.mscaa.com) is located 13 miles south of downtown Memphis. There are two popular routes to Memphis from the airport. Take I-240 north to arrive in midtown. To reach downtown, take I-55 north and exit on Riverside Drive. The drive takes 20–30 minutes.

The airport's main international travel insurance and business services center (901/922-8090) is located in ticket lobby B and opens daily. Here you can exchange foreign currency, buy travel insurance, conduct money transfers, send faxes and make photocopies, and buy money orders and travelers checks. A smaller kiosk near the international arrivals and departures area at gate B-36 is open daily and offers foreign currency exchange and travel insurance.

There is wireless Internet service in the airport, but it is not free.

AIRPORT SHUTTLE
TennCo Express (901/645-3726, www.tenncoexpress.com) provides an hourly shuttle service from the airport to many downtown hotels. Tickets are $20 one-way and $30 roundtrip. Look for the shuttle parked in the third lane near column number 14 outside the airport terminal. Shuttles depart every half hour 7:30 A.M.–9:30 P.M. For a hotel pickup, call at least a day in advance.

By Car
Memphis is located at the intersection of two major interstate highways: I-40, which runs east–west across the United States, and I-55, which runs south from St. Louis to New Orleans.

Many people who visit Memphis drive here in their own cars. The city is 300 miles from St. Louis, 380 miles from Atlanta, 410 miles from New Orleans, 450 miles from Dallas, 480 miles from Cincinnati and Oklahoma City, and 560 miles from Chicago.

By Bus
Greyhound (800/231-2222, www.greyhound.com) runs daily buses to Memphis from around the United States. Direct service is available to Memphis from a number of surrounding cities, including Jackson and Nashville, Tennessee; Tupelo and Jackson, Mississippi; Little Rock and Jonesboro, Arkansas; and St. Louis. The Greyhound station (3033 Airways Blvd., 901/395-8770) is open 24 hours a day.

By Train
Amtrak (800/872-7245, www.amtrak.com) runs the City of New Orleans train daily between Chicago and New Orleans, stopping in Memphis on the way. The southbound train arrives daily at Memphis's Central Station at 6:27 A.M., leaving about half an hour later. The northbound train arrives at 10 P.M. every day. It is an 11-hour ride between Memphis and Chicago, and about 8 hours between Memphis and New Orleans.

The Amtrak station (901/526-0052) is located in Central Station at 545 South Main Street in the South Main district of downtown. Ticket and baggage service is available at the station daily 5:45 A.M.–11:15 P.M.

GETTING AROUND
Driving
Driving is the most popular and easiest way to get around Memphis. Downtown parking is plentiful if you are prepared to pay; an all-day pass in one of the many downtown parking garages costs about $10. Traffic congestion peaks, predictably, at rush hours and is worst in the eastern parts of the city and along the

interstates. But traffic isn't the problem it is in Nashville; Memphis commutes are considered more reasonable.

Public Transportation

BUSES

The **Memphis Area Transit Authority** (901/274-6282, www.matatransit.com) operates dozens of buses that travel through the greater Memphis area. For information on routes, call or stop by the North End Terminal on North Main Street for help planning your trip. The bus system is not used frequently by tourists.

TROLLEYS

Public trolleys run for about two miles along Main Street in Memphis from the Pinch district in the north to Central Station in the south, and circle up on a parallel route along Riverfront Drive. Another trolley line runs about two miles east on Madison Avenue, connecting the city's medical center with downtown. The Main Street trolleys run every 10 minutes at most times, but the Madison Avenue trolleys run less often on weekends and evenings after 6 P.M.

Fares are $1 per ride. You can buy an all-day pass for $3.50, a three-day pass for $9, or a monthlong pass for $25. All passes must be purchased at the North End Terminal at the northern end of the Main Street route.

The trolley system is useful, especially if your hotel is on either the northern or southern end of downtown, or along Madison Avenue. Brochures with details on the routes and fares are available all over town, or you can download one at www.matatransit.com. The trolleys are simple to understand and use; if you have a question, just ask your driver.

SUN STUDIO FREE SHUTTLE BUS

Sun Studio runs a free shuttle between Sun Studio, the Rock 'n' Soul Museum at Beale Street, and Graceland. The first run stops at the Graceland Heartbreak Hotel at 9:55 A.M., Graceland at 10 A.M., Sun Studio at 10:15 A.M., and the Rock 'n' Soul Museum at 10:30 A.M. Runs continue throughout the day on an hourly schedule. The last run picks up at Heartbreak Hotel at 5:55 P.M., Graceland Plaza at 6 P.M., and Sun Studio at 6:15 P.M.

The shuttle is a 12-passenger black van painted with the Sun Studio logo. The ride is free, but it's nice to tip your driver. The published schedule is a loose approximation, so it's a good idea to get to the pickup point early in case the van is running ahead. You can call 901/521-0664 for more information.

Taxis

Memphis has a number of taxi companies, and you will usually find available cabs along Beale Street and waiting at the airport. Otherwise, you will need to call for a taxi. Some of the largest companies are **Yellow Cab** (901/577-7777), **City Wide Cab** (901/722-8294), and **Arrow Transportation Company** (901/332-7769).

Expect to pay $25–35 for a trip from the airport to downtown; most fares around town are under $10. Taxis accept credit cards.

WESTERN PLAINS

From the Tennessee River to the Mississippi, Tennessee's western plains are perhaps more like the Deep South than other parts of the state. The landscape is spare; in the heart of the delta all you see for mile upon mile are cotton fields—flat with neat rows of the bushy plants. In the south, near the Mississippi state line, piney woods give rise to the state's largest timber industry. Along the Tennessee River, man-made lakes present unmatched opportunities to fish, boat, or simply relax.

Of course, life here was not always peaceful or idyllic. West Tennessee had the largest plantations and the greatest number of slaves before the Civil War. This was Confederate territory. The war touched just about every town in Tennessee's western plains, but none more than the quiet, rural community of Shiloh along the Tennessee River. On April 6 and 7, 1862, an estimated 24,000 men were killed or wounded on this bloody battlefield. Emancipation brought freedom, but not justice to thousands of African Americans who now struggled as sharecroppers and remained the victims of discrimination and worse.

Out of the hardship of life in the Tennessee delta emerged some of the state's most gifted musicians, including "Sleepy" John Estes, Tina Turner, and Carl Perkins.

The knobby knees of Reelfoot Lake and cypress swamps of other natural areas, including Big Hill Pond and the Ghost River, are a

© MARGARET LITTMAN

WESTERN PLAINS

HIGHLIGHTS

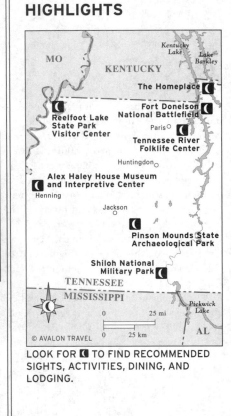

LOOK FOR 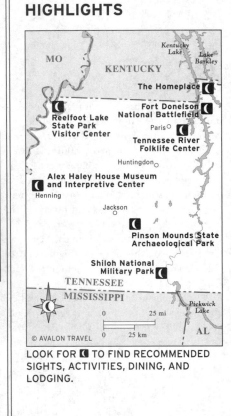 TO FIND RECOMMENDED SIGHTS, ACTIVITIES, DINING, AND LODGING.

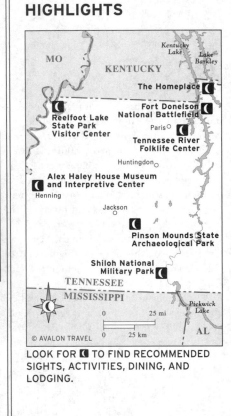 **Alex Haley House Museum and Interpretive Center:** One of the country's most celebrated writers grew up in the humble sawmill town of Henning. See the home where Alex Haley first imagined his ancestors (page 81).

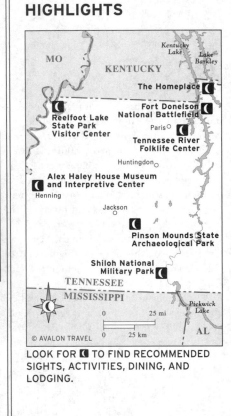 **Reelfoot Lake State Park Visitor Center:** Knob-kneed cypress trees, abundant wildlife, including bald eagles, and fresh air are elixir for those who come to this quiet corner of the delta (page 85).

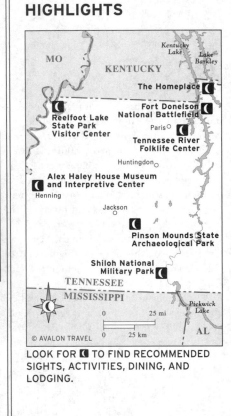 **Tennessee River Folklife Center:** Explore the forgotten past of Tennessee River pearls, steamships, and houseboats at this museum, located at Nathan Bedford Forrest State Park (page 93).

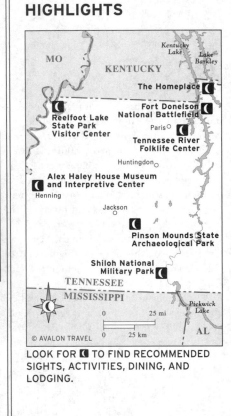 **Fort Donelson National Battlefield:** The scene of one of the Civil War's most significant battles is also a picturesque park (page 97).

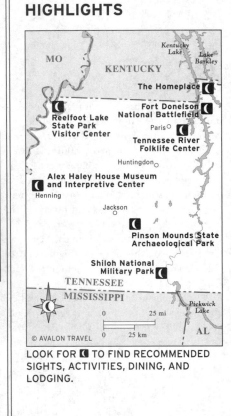 **The Homeplace:** Located in beautiful Land Between the Lakes, this living-history museum depicts the farmer's way of life at the midpoint of the 19th century (page 101).

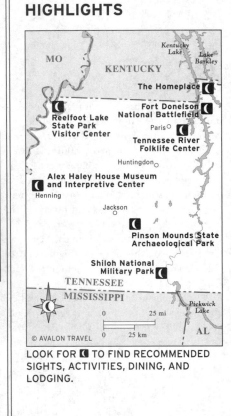 **Pinson Mounds State Archaeological Park:** The sprawling and mysterious mounds at Pinson are a reminder of those who lived here before (page 110).

 Shiloh National Military Park: See one of the state's best Civil War landmarks (page 114).

landscape unseen in other parts of Tennessee, if not the United States. These habitats give rise to exceptional bird-watching, fishing, and hunting. Come in the spring or fall to see the area at its best (and avoid the worst of summer's heat). Late summer is the season of county fairs and other festivals, and the time when the people of West Tennessee retreat to the nearest lake, river, or stream to cool off.

PLANNING YOUR TIME

A road trip is the best way to experience the western plains; get off the interstate and give

small-town restaurants and inns a try. Fresh catfish from the nearby rivers and lakes are served in traditional style—dusted with cornmeal and deep fried. Sample the varieties of hush puppies between Reelfoot Lake and Shiloh. Campers will find numerous options for shelter in state parks.

The western plains can be toured in about a week, although outdoors enthusiasts often want to budget more time to hike or fish. If you are interested in the cultural and musical attractions of the region, choose Jackson or Brownsville as your home base. If you are

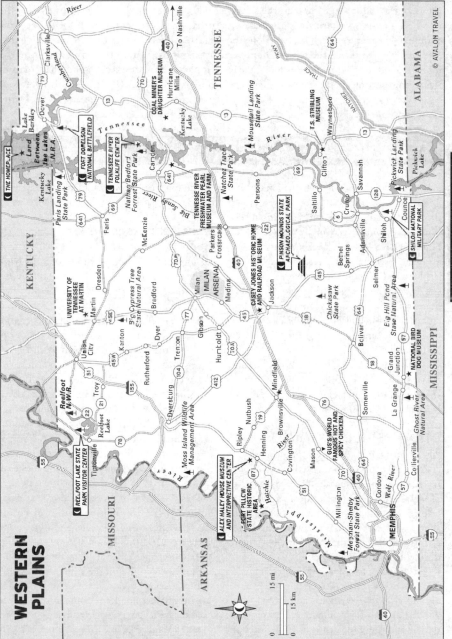

WESTERN PLAINS

WESTERN PLAINS

TENNESSEE

KENTUCKY

MISSOURI

ARKANSAS

MISSISSIPPI

ALABAMA

© AVALON TRAVEL

◀ THE HOMEPLACE

Land Between the Lakes N.R.A.

Lake Barkley

Kentucky Lake

Clarksville

Dover

To Nashville

COAL MINER'S DAUGHTER MUSEUM

Hurricane Mills

Mousetail Landing State Park

T.S. STRIBLING MUSEUM

Waynesboro

Pickwick Landing State Park

Pickwick Lake

◀ FORT DONELSON NATIONAL BATTLEFIELD

TENNESSEE RIVER FOLKLIFE CENTER

Tennessee River

Paris Landing State Park

Camden

Kentucky Lake

Nathan Bedford Forrest State Park

TENNESSEE RIVER FRESHWATER PEARL MUSEUM AND FARM

Natchez Trace State Park

Parsons

Clifton

Saltillo

Savannah

Crump

Counce

SHILOH NATIONAL MILITARY PARK

Shiloh

Paris

Big Sandy River

McKenzie

Parkers Crossroads

◀ PINSON MOUNDS STATE ARCHAEOLOGICAL PARK

Bethel Springs

Adamsville

UNIVERSITY OF TENNESSEE AT MARTIN

Dresden

Big Cypress Tree State Natural Area

Bradford

Milan

MILAN ARSENAL

Medina

CASEY JONES HISTORIC HOME AND RAILROAD MUSEUM

Jackson

Chickasaw State Park

Selmer

Bolivar

Eagle Hill Pond State Natural Area

Martin

Kenton

Dyer

Gibson

Humboldt

Trenton

Bells

NATIONAL BIRD DOG MUSEUM

Union City

Rutherford

Dyersburg

Brownsville

Grand Junction

MISSISSIPPI

Reelfoot N.W.R.

Troy

Reelfoot Lake

REELFOOT LAKE STATE PARK VISITOR CENTER ◀

Tiptonville

Moss Island Wildlife Management Area

Ripley

Nutbush

Henning

Somerville

La Grange

Ghost River Natural Area

Mississippi River

ALEX HALEY HOUSE MUSEUM AND INTERPRETIVE CENTER ◀

FORT PILLOW STATE HISTORIC AREA

Covington

Mason

GUS'S WORLD FAMOUS HOT AND SPICY CHICKEN

Cordova

Collierville

Hatchie River

Millington

Meeman-Shelby Forest State Park

MEMPHIS

Wolf River

0 15 mi

0 15 km

interested in Shiloh and the natural attractions along the southern Tennessee River, Savannah is a good choice. For a tour along the Mississippi River, the best accommodations are found around the picturesque Reelfoot Lake in the northwest corner of the state. Paris Landing State Park is a good home base for exploring the Kentucky Lakes region.

Driving is the best—honestly, the only—way to get around the western plains. Even in the largest city, Jackson, attractions, restaurants, and accommodations are spread out. A good road map or updated GPS is all you need to find your way around, and residents are friendly and helpful if you get lost.

The Delta

Flat, spare, and rural, the delta region of West Tennessee was, and still is, the state's largest producer of cotton. Cotton fields in cultivation spread out between small towns and farmhouses. Drive through these areas in the fall, and you'll see fields of silvery white blowing in the wind. County seats of the delta have stately courthouses, enclosed by classic courthouse squares. While the region is home to the cities of Jackson and Brownsville, the delta remains rural, and the way of life is laid-back and traditional.

The delta countryside is fertile soil not only for farming, but for music, too. Blues musicians "Sleepy" John Estes, Hammie Nixon, and Yank Rachell are from Brownsville.

BROWNSVILLE

The county seat of the largest cotton-producing county in Tennessee, Brownsville was founded in 1824 and quickly became the home to many of West Tennessee's most affluent settlers. Early leaders carefully mapped out the city lots, and they were sold to doctors, lawyers, and merchants who helped the town develop quickly during its first decades.

Brownsville's first newspaper was founded in 1837, its first bank in 1869, and in its heyday it also boasted an opera house and several hotels and restaurants. It lost hundreds of its residents to the yellow fever epidemic of 1878, and hundreds more fled to avoid becoming ill. A marker in the town's Oakwood Cemetery designates the resting place of the yellow fever victims.

West Tennessee Delta Heritage Center

Half welcome center, half museum, the West Tennessee Delta Heritage Center (121 Sunny Hill Cove, 731/779-9000, www.westtnheritage.com, Mon.–Sat. 9 A.M.–5 P.M., Sun. 1–5 P.M., free) is your best stop for understanding the special music, culture, and history of the delta region. The exhibits in its three museums—the West Tennessee Cotton Museum, the West Tennessee Music Museum, and the Hatchie River Museum—examine the musical heritage of the region, the ecology of the nearby Hatchie River, and cotton, the region's most important crop.

The cotton exhibit illustrates the process from cultivation to baling. A huge basket of picked cotton is there for you to touch, as well as the cotton both before and after being ginned. After driving past miles of cotton fields, visitors will welcome the illustration and explanations.

The heritage center also has displays about each of the counties in the region, with visitor information on each. There is also a gift shop stocked with some local-made goods. If you need to check your messages, this is a good place to take advantage of free wireless Internet access.

Right next to the heritage center's museums

is the **"Sleepy" John Estes Home,** a faded clapboard home that was relocated here so tourists could see where the blues legend was living when he died in 1977.

Estes was born in Ripley, Tennessee, in 1904 but lived most of his life in Brownsville. A blues guitarist and vocalist, Estes had a distinctive "crying" vocal style and sounded like an old man, even on his early recordings. Estes made his recording debut in Memphis in 1929, and he recorded regularly until the United States joined World War II in 1941. Estes spent the end of his life blind and living in poverty.

The Heritage Center is located at exit 56 off I-40.

Historic Brownsville

It is pleasant to drive or walk around historic Brownsville, a leafy area of antebellum homes and buildings. Each home is marked with a brown-and-white sign in the yard that is visible from the road and gives the approximate date of construction. For a more detailed guide, visit the Brownsville-Haywood Chamber of Commerce for a copy of their historical guidebook of Haywood County, which includes a walking tour of Brownsville.

Two of the city's most noteworthy old homes are the **Tripp Home** at 420 Main Street, a two-story Greek Revival home built in 1824, and the **Christ Episcopal Church** at the corner of West College and North Washington, organized in 1832. Brownsville is also home to the oldest Jewish temple in continuous service in Tennessee, the **Temple of Adas Israel** at 18 North Court Street, built in 1882.

Historic Brownsville surrounds the College Hill Center, where you will find the **Haywood County Museum** (127 N. Grade Ave., 731/772-4883, Sun. 2–4 P.M., free), housed in the old Brownsville Baptist Female College. This museum is home to a remarkable collection of Abraham Lincoln artifacts and papers, donated by Brownsville native Morton Felsenthal. The museum is open limited hours, so plan

accordingly or call ahead to inquire whether someone can open it for you.

The attractive redbrick College Hill Center, which houses the museum, was built in 1851 as the Brownsville Baptist Female College. After 1900 it became the Ogilvie Training School for boys, and later it was the Haywood County High School from 1911 to 1970.

Mindfield

Tucked next to a payday-loan storefront and quickmart near downtown Brownsville is the unexpected *Mindfield,* a collection of steel sculptures created by local artist Billy Tripp. At first glance it looks like an electrical transformer station, but this acre of creations is a remarkable work of outsider art. Begun in 1989, the sculptures will continue to grow and change until Tripp's death, at which point the site will be his place of internment. Tripp works on the piece more in the summer than the rest of the year.

Today it stands seven stories tall in places and includes messages of optimism and open-mindedness from the artist. There's an opportunity to leave comments about your impressions of the works, which are largely made from reclaimed steel and other materials. Find the *Mindfield* off U.S. 70, one block away from the town square.

Hatchie River National Wildlife Area

Just south of Brownsville is the Hatchie River National Wildlife Area (731/772-0501), a 12,000-acre preserve along the Hatchie River. Established to protect the more than 200 species of birds that winter or migrate on the Hatchie, the wildlife area presents excellent opportunities for bird-watching. You can also fish in many areas. Camping is not allowed. For more information, contact the Refuge Office located at the intersection of Highway 76 and I-40.

Festivals and Events

Brownsville hosts the **Brownsville Blues Fall Festival** (http://brownsvilleblues.homestead.

com) in late September or early October, which celebrates blues and the culture of the delta. Come to hear some of the best Delta blues outside Memphis, and enjoy barbecue, regional crafts, and sports activities. The blues festival is followed the third Saturday in October by the **Hatchie Fall Festival** (www.hatchiefallfest.com) on the courthouse square in Brownsville, which offers more live music and family-oriented fun.

Accommodations

Brownsville has the greatest concentration of hotels in this part of Tennessee. Most of these are located along I-40, a five-minute drive from downtown Brownsville, some even within walking distance of the West Tennessee Delta Heritage Center and fast-food restaurants. Chain hotels located here include **Econo Lodge** (2600 Anderson Ave., 731/772-4082, $50–60) and **Days Inn** (2530 Anderson Ave., 731/772-3297, $50–60). An independent option is the spartan **Sunrise Inn** (328 Main St., 731/772-1483, $45).

In the historic downtown, try **Lilies' Bed and Breakfast** (508 W. Main St., 731/772-9078, $100). Gail Carver has two rooms in this elegant 1855 home, each with its own private bath.

Food

If you are in town on Friday or Saturday, then don't miss the weekly fish fry at (**City Fish Market** (223 S. Washington Ave., 731/772-9952, Fri. 10 A.M.–5:30 P.M., Sat. 10 A.M.–4:30 P.M., $5–12), on a side street in the old downtown area. Watch the catfish being cleaned and cut up, and deep fried before your eyes. Dinner plates are served with hush puppies and slaw, and you can douse your fish with vinegary hot sauce. Fried catfish, a Southern specialty, does not get much fresher or better than this.

Otherwise, Brownsville has fast-food restaurants, a few barbecue joints, a classic Italian joint, and several Mexican restaurants. **Las Palmas** (27 S. Lafayette, 731/772-8004, daily 10 A.M.–9 P.M., $8–15) is on the courthouse square and serves combination plates, fajitas, and grilled seafood.

Information and Services

The **West Tennessee Delta Heritage Center** (121 Sunny Hill Cove, 731/779-9000, Tues.–Sat. 9 A.M.–4 P.M.) near the interstate at Brownsville has comprehensive information about visiting not only Brownsville, but all the counties in West Tennessee. Make this your first stop for information about the area. There is also a better-than-average gift shop and free public Internet access.

The **Brownsville-Haywood Chamber of Commerce** (121 W. Main St., 731/772-2193, www.haywoodcountybrownsville.com) can also help with information about the region.

NUTBUSH

This rural farming community would be a mere speck on the map were it not thanks to R&B superstar Tina Turner, who was raised in and around Nutbush from her birth in 1936 until she moved to St. Louis at age 16. Turner penned the semiautobiographical tune "Nutbush City Limits" in 1973, which gave rise to a popular line dance called the Nutbush. Turner rereleased the song in 1991.

Reality is that Nutbush is too small to even have city limits; it feels much like a ghost town today. But the lone business, the Nutbush Grocery and Deli on State Highway 19 (renamed in 2001 the Tina Turner Highway), proclaims its association with the R&B megastar with a sign. But the home where Tina Turner once lived in Nutbush was torn down long ago, the lumber used to build a barn elsewhere in town.

HENNING

The tiny sawmill town of Henning is a half-hour drive through the cotton fields from Brownsville. It would be unremarkable except for the fact that it nurtured one of Tennessee's greatest writers, Alex Haley.

◖ Alex Haley House Museum and Interpretive Center

The Alex Haley House Museum and Interpretive Center (200 S. Church, 731/738-2240, www.alexhaleymuseum.com, Tues.–Sat. 10 A.M.–5 P.M., Sun. 1–5 P.M., $6) illustrates the early childhood of the Pulitzer Prize–winning author Alex Haley. This is where Haley spent his first 10 years, and he later returned here during the summers to stay with his maternal grandparents, Will and Cynthia Palmer.

Visitors tour the kitchen where Cynthia Palmer told Haley stories of her ancestors, which he later used as inspiration for his masterwork, *Roots*. The museum has artifacts of the period, as well as family pictures and heirlooms. You also hear a recording of Haley describing Sunday dinners served in the family dining room.

The museum was established with Haley's help, and he was buried here on his death in 1991.

FORT PILLOW STATE HISTORIC PARK

The drive along Highway 87 to Fort Pillow State Historic Park (3122 Park Rd., 731/738-5581) takes you through almost 20 miles of rolling cotton fields and past the West Tennessee State Penitentiary, making it unlike any other wilderness area where you might choose to camp or hike. The park, which perches atop a bluff overlooking the Mississippi River, offers group, tent, and RV camping; picnic areas; 15 miles of hiking trails; wildlife viewing; and fishing in Fort Pillow Lake. There is also a **museum** (daily 8 A.M.–4 P.M., free) that tells the controversial story of the 1864 Battle of Fort Pillow, which many historians say is more aptly referred to as the Fort Pillow Massacre for the brutality displayed by Southern troops under the command of Nathan Bedford Forrest.

There's a boat ramp on a no-wake lake, but no boat rentals, so you must bring your own. Get a state fishing license to try to catch bass, bream, and crappie.

Visitors to modern-day Fort Pillow can hike to the remains of the fort itself and see the area where the battle took place. The museum's exhibits and a short video are dated, but an interested visitor will find a great deal of information contained in them. There are reenactments of the battle in April and November. The Mississippi River Bike Trail passes through the park.

HUMBOLDT

Humboldt was chartered in 1866 at the site where the Louisville and Nashville Railroad and the North–South Mobile and Ohio Railroad crossed. It was named for German naturalist and explorer Baron Alexander von Humboldt. Farmers around Humboldt grew cotton and after the 1870s diversified into strawberries, rhubarb, tomatoes, cabbage, lettuce, sweet potatoes, and other crops. Agriculture remains an important industry, but manufacturing is increasingly important. Companies including Wilson Sporting Goods, CON-AGRA, and American Woodmark have plants in Humboldt.

Sights

The **West Tennessee Regional Art Center** (1200 Main St., 731/784-1787, www.wtrac.tn.org, Mon.–Fri. 9 A.M.–4:30 P.M., $2) is located in the city's restored city hall building. It houses the Caldwell Collection of oil paintings, sculpture, watercolors, prints, and lithographs—the only permanent fine-art museum between Nashville and Memphis. The downstairs gallery is free; the upstairs gallery charges admission. The center also showcases memorabilia from the West Tennessee Strawberry Festival, and staff can answer your questions about the area.

Humboldt's **Main Street** is home to barber shops, real estate agents, banks, and a Mexican grocery. It also has a downtown movie theater, **The Plaza** (1408 Main St., 731/784-7469, www.plazatheater.net).

Festivals and Events

Humboldt is best known for the annual **West**

REMEMBER FORT PILLOW

The earthworks at Fort Pillow along the Mississippi River were built by the Confederates in 1861, but the fort was soon abandoned so that the rebels could consolidate their troops farther south. Union forces occupied the fort for several years, owing mainly to its strategic position at a sharp bend in the Mississippi River. On April 12, 1864, there were some 600 Union troops stationed at Fort Pillow—200 of them were newly freed African Americans who had volunteered to join the Union cause.

By 1864 it was clear to many, if not most, that the South would lose the war, so when legendary Confederate general Nathan Bedford Forrest attacked Fort Pillow on April 12, it was not a battle of strategic importance but instead a fight for supplies and pride.

Accounts are that the Confederates quickly overcame the fort by land, but that an inexperienced Union commander, Maj. William Bradford, twice declined to surrender. Whether he finally surrendered or not is a matter of debate. Regardless of whether the Union formally surrendered, there was never any question which force would prevail. Forrest had more men and the advantage of surprise. With such a clear-cut victory at hand, it is no wonder that as news of the massive Union casualties emerged, the immediate cry was of massacre.

Forrest reported that a mere 14 Union men were killed in the battle, but Union records say that 300 men lost their lives, 200 of whom were black. Even Confederate soldiers writing home described the events as "butchery" and told of savagery so great that Forrest himself rode through the ranks and threatened to shoot any Confederate who stopped killing.

The U.S. Congress immediately ordered an investigation, and after reviewing a number of accounts and interviewing witnesses, declared the battle a massacre. The Confederates dismissed this as propaganda and blamed the heavy bloodletting on poor command. The precise nature of what happened at Fort Pillow remains a matter of debate.

For Union soldiers, and particularly African American soldiers, there was no ambiguity in their minds over what took place at Fort Pillow. Recognizing that official retribution may never come, black soldiers used Fort Pillow as a rallying cry in battle. "Remember Fort Pillow," they yelled on advance.

Poet Paul Laurence Dunbar immortalized the incident in his poem "The Unsung Heroes," which reads in part: "Pillow knew their blood, That poured on a nation's altar, a sacrificial flood."

Tennessee Strawberry Festival, which celebrates one of this region's sweetest crops. Established in 1934 to encourage the growing, packing, and consumption of strawberries, the festival takes place in early May at the height of the strawberry harvest. It includes a parade, car show, foot races, beauty pageants, cooking contests, and good old-fashioned fireworks. For details and specific dates, contact the Humboldt Chamber of Commerce (1200 Main St., 731/784-1842, www.humboldttnchamber.org).

Accommodations

The pet-friendly **Deerfield Inn** (590 Hwy. 45 Bypass, 731/824-4770, $55) is a standard roadside motel, with single and double rooms, cable TV, and in-room refrigerators.

Information

The **Humboldt Chamber of Commerce** (1200 Main St., 731/784-1842, www.humboldttnchamber.org) can help with information about the town.

DYERSBURG

This town of 20,000 people was mentioned in the Arrested Development song "Tennessee":

Outta the country and into more country
Past Dyersburg into Ripley
Where the ghost of my childhood haunts me

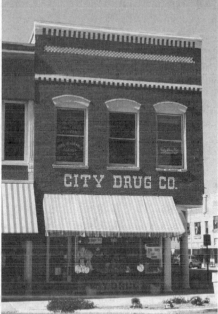

©BRENT MOORE

Much of the town of Dyersburg harkens back to the early 1900s.

Walk the roads my forefathers walked
Climbed the trees my forefathers hung from.

The county seat of Dyer County, Dyersburg has a handsome redbrick-and-white courthouse, built in 1912. The courthouse square is home to several antiques shops, professional services, and the **Downtown Dyersburg Development Association** (111 W. Market St., 731/285-3433, Mon.–Fri. 8 A.M.–noon), which promotes downtown and can provide visitor information.

You may not need any farming implements, vegetable plants, or fertilizer, particularly while traveling, but you may still want to check out **Pennington Seed and Supply** (214 S. Main, 731/285-1031, Mon.–Sat. 7 A.M.–5 P.M.) for its pecans and vintage look.

Accommodations

Dyersburg has a handful of chain hotels in the delta, outside of Brownsville. They include a **Best Western** (770 Hwy. 51 Bypass, 731/285-8601, $75–85) and **Days Inn** (2600 Lake Rd., 731/287-0888, $80–90).

Food

For a meal in Dyersburg, head to **Cozy Kitchen** (107A W. Market St., 731/285-1054, Mon.–Fri. 5:30 A.M.–1:30 P.M., $5–10), which serves breakfast and lunch on weekdays.

Information

The **Downtown Dyersburg Development Association** (111 W. Market St., 731/285-3433, Mon.–Fri. 8 A.M.–noon) is the best source of information about the town.

ALAMO

The county seat of Crockett County, Alamo was named for the Alamo Mission in Texas where Davy Crockett died. Its population is about 2,500.

You can see exotic animals including zebras, wildebeest, oryx, and water buffalo at the **Tennessee Safari Park at Hillcrest** (Hwy. 412, 731/696-4423, www.tennesseesafaripark. com, open daily early spring–late fall, cars admitted Mon.–Sat. 10:30 A.M.–4:30 P.M. and Sun. noon–4:30 P.M., call for appointment to visit in winter, adults $12, children $8) just outside of town. The park is the creation of the Conley family, who have been collecting and raising exotic animals on their farm since 1963. The farm has more than 250 animals, and visitors can drive a two-mile loop through the farm safari-style. Free-roaming animals come up to your car window to visit. At the barn there is a petting zoo where you can feed and touch more animals. While the Conleys have been raising exotic animals for decades, the park has been open to the public since 2007. The park is 16 miles up Highway 412 from I-40 at exit 78.

Old West Tennessee has been lovingly re-created at **Green Frog Village** (Hwy. 412, 731/663-3319, www.greenfrogtn.org,

Tues.–Sat. 10 A.M.–5 P.M., free), located between Alamo and Bells, just north of I-40. The village includes an antique cotton gin, 1830s rural church, antique log cabin, one-room schoolhouse, and country store. It is also an arboretum. The mission of the village is to preserve the rural culture of the Tennessee delta, and it has been the life's work of emergency-room doctor John Freeman and his wife, Nancy. It is open from April until "it is too cold to be out in the elements."

CHICKASAW NATIONAL WILDLIFE REFUGE

More than 130,000 people visit the 25,000-acre Chickasaw National Wildlife Refuge (731/635-7621) annually. The refuge, located 10 miles north of Ripley along the Mississippi River, is home to dozens of species of birds, including bald eagles. The refuge is a popular area for hunting and fishing—the fall squirrel hunt is one of the largest. You can also bike or hike along the reserve's 20 miles of paved and gravel roads, looking at acres of hardwood trees. The refuge was established in 1985 and occupies land once owned by a private timber company.

Find the refuge by driving nine miles north of Ripley on Highway 51. Turn left on Hobe Webb Road for 1.25 miles, and then right onto Sand Bluff Road for half a mile.

BIG CYPRESS TREE STATE NATURAL AREA

You won't find *the* namesake tree at Big Cypress Tree State Natural Area (295 Big Cypress Rd., Greenfield, 731/235-2700, summer 8 A.M.–sunset, winter 8 A.M.–4:30 P.M.); the 1,350-year-old tree, which measured 13 feet in diameter, was struck by lightning and died in 1976. But there are bald cypress and other flora and fauna here. A short hiking trail has signage that identifies many of the trees.

The 330-acre park, which is near Greenfield, is for day-use only and has a picnic area, covered pavilion, and a short nature trail. There's a lovely arts and crafts festival each October.

RIPLEY

Ripley's famous tomatoes take center stage at the annual **Lauderdale County Tomato Festival,** which takes place the weekend after July 4 every year. In addition to tomato tasting, cooking contests, and exhibitions, there is live music, a carnival, and a beauty contest. The event is organized by the Lauderdale County Chamber of Commerce (731/635-9541, www.lauderdalecountytn.org).

HALLS

American Pickers fans will be delighted with interesting antiques at a number of stores tucked away in small towns in this part of Tennessee. Perhaps the most interesting is **Murray Hudson's Antiquarian Books and Maps** (109 S. Church St., 731/836-5418, www.murrayhudson.com, Mon.–Sat. 9 A.M.–5 P.M.). Hudson has been collecting for more than 25 years and has a remarkable collection of old globes, some of them dating back to the early 1700s. He also sells old maps, books, and historic prints.

MASON

Along Highway 70 near Mason, one landmark restaurant attracts not only Memphians and residents of the delta, but also visitors statewide. **◖ Gus's World Famous Hot and Spicy Chicken** (520 Hwy. 70, 901/294-2028, Mon.–Sat. 11 A.M.–9 P.M., $8–12) has been heralded by the likes of *GQ* magazine and celebrity chef Emeril as *the* place for good fried chicken. Gus's is set in an old frame house, modified over the years to accommodate the thousands of loyal patrons who can't get enough of Gus's hot and spicy fried chicken. Coated in batter and a special seasoning paste, Gus's chicken is fried so that the crust is crispy, the meat juicy, and the taste just spicy enough to be perfect with a cold beer. Just when you think it can't get any better, someone drops a quarter in the old jukebox and the blues fill the air. Wise diners get two orders: one to eat now and one to eat on the way home. Don't miss the quirky signage and ambience.

Reelfoot Lake

Tennessee's "earthquake lake" is a hauntingly beautiful landscape of knob-kneed cypress trees, gently rippling water, and open spaces. It is a flooded forest, eerie looking and peaceful. With some 13,000 acres of water, the lake is also a sportsman's dream: 54 species of fish live in Reelfoot, including bream, crappie, catfish, and bass. From January to March—the best fishing season—the lake sees a steady stream of visitors who come to troll its waters. The cypress tint the water a clear but dark color, contributing to the magical feel of the place.

Reelfoot Lake is home to thousands of wintering and migratory birds. Visitors cannot help but notice the daily symphony of bird calls, not to mention the sight of ducks, herons, wild turkeys, eagles, and geese around the lake. Bird-watchers have identified some 238 species of birds in Reelfoot Lake, and the April turkey hunt in the area is excellent.

Bald eagles are the most iconic of the bird species that winter at the lake, and spotting these majestic creatures is a popular pursuit January–March. Normally, the winter eagle population on the lake numbers 100–200 birds. Bald eagles had virtually disappeared from the area in the 1960s due to the effects of DDT contamination of their nesting grounds, but thanks to a nesting project started in 1988, they have returned.

Orientation

Reelfoot Lake sits in the extreme northwestern corner of Tennessee, which makes it a little bit hard to get to. Its northernmost finger nearly touches the Kentucky state line, and the Mississippi River is only a mile to the west. Two-lane state highways circle the lake; the entire loop is about 35 miles. The southern portion of Reelfoot is a state park, and the northern half of the lake is a U.S. national wildlife refuge. Several thousand residents live in lakefront communities that dot the area.

The closest town to the lake, Tiptonville is a cluster of homes and businesses at the southwestern corner of Reelfoot. The boyhood home of Carl Perkins is found here; look for a sign on Highway 78 south of town to find it.

Most accommodations, restaurants, and provisioning locales are found along the southern shore, just a few minutes' drive from Tiptonville. The state park's Air Park Inn, along with one or two private camps and inns, are set on the lake's western shore, about 10 miles from Tiptonville. The trails and visitors center maintained by the U.S. Fish and Wildlife Service are located on the more isolated northern shore of the waters.

SIGHTS
◖ Reelfoot Lake State Park Visitor Center

The State Park Visitor Center (3120 State Rd. 213, 731/253-7756 or 731/253-8003, Mon.–Fri. 8 A.M.–4:30 P.M., free) provides the best introduction to the lake, with exhibits on its history, wildlife, legends, and ecology. You can see a traditional Reelfoot Lake boat and read the story of the local vigilantes who took matters into their own hands when the lake was threatened with development. This is also the place to sign up for popular lake cruises, guided canoe trips, and sightseeing tours.

Outside the museum are a couple of mesh cages where you can see bald eagles, owls, and red-tailed hawks. A half-mile boardwalk trail

WESTERN PLAINS

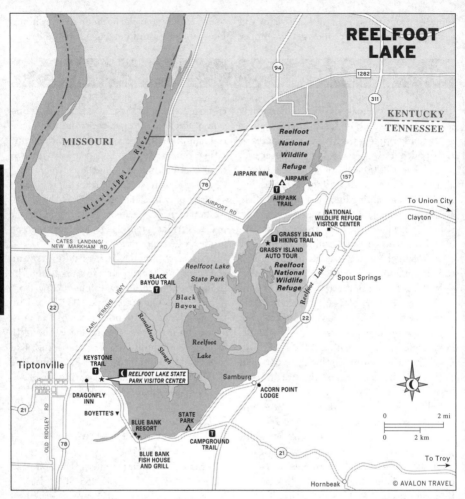

extends out over the lake at the rear of the visitors center and is a must for anyone who wants to experience the special beauty of the lake.

Reelfoot Lake National Wildlife Refuge

On the northern side of Reelfoot, near the intersections of State Highways 22 and 157, is the **National Wildlife Refuge Visitor Center** (4343 Hwy. 157, 731/538-2481, daily 8 A.M.–4 P.M., free). Here you can see exhibits about the lake,

with a special focus on the flora and fauna of the area. Take note that the Reelfoot National Wildlife Refuge, which is, essentially, the northern half of the lake, is only open to the public for fishing and wildlife observation March 15– November 15 every year, although the visitors center remains open year-round. Contact the visitors center for specific rules about fishing, hunting, and public access to the refuge.

The wildlife refuge maintains the **Grassy Island Auto Tour,** a three-mile self-guided auto

WESTERN PLAINS

SEASONAL WILDLIFE

There are distinct variations in the type of wildlife you will see in and around Reelfoot Lake throughout the year.

In January and February, the wintering eagle and Canada goose populations peak, and cold water crappie fishing is good. In March, the eagles begin their northward migration, while osprey return from South America. Wild turkeys are often visible in March.

Spring comes to the lake in April and May, with wildflowers in abundance and the best season for bird-watching. This is also the best season to listen for frogs. By June, you may see deer fawns, and the floating aquatic plants are in bloom.

July and August are the hottest months at Reelfoot Lake, and therefore the season of mosquitoes and deerflies. By September, it has cooled off. Fall fishing for crappie and bass begins.

During the fall, migrating and wintering birds begin to return. Short raccoon and archery deer hunting seasons take place in October; the deer gun hunt takes place in November. December is one of the best months to view ducks, geese, and eagles.

tour, year-round. The tour leads to an observation tower overlooking the Grassy Island part of the lake and is worth the detour required to reach it.

SPORTS AND RECREATION
Boating

If you can do only one thing when you visit Reelfoot Lake, get out on the dark, lily-pad-filled water in a boat. The best cruises are provided by the state park. The **three-hour cruises** (731/253-7756, adults $9, children 5–15 $6, under 5 free) take place May–September and depart daily at 9 A.M. from the visitors center on the southern side of the lake. Your guide will point out fish, birds, and other distinctive features of the lake. It is a good idea to bring drinks (a cooler with ice is provided) and snacks.

In March and April, the park offers a deep-swamp canoe float that departs on weekends at 8 A.M. and 1 P.M. The cost is $20. From January to March, special bald eagle tours are offered daily at 10 A.M.

Fishing

Fishing is the most popular recreation activity at Reelfoot Lake. With 13,000 acres of water and an average depth of just over five feet, the lake is a natural fish hatchery. An estimated 54 species of fish live in the lake. The most common fish are bream, crappie, catfish, and bass. The fishing season generally runs March–July, although some species are plentiful into the fall.

Because Reelfoot Lake is so shallow, and because of the cypress knees that lurk below the surface, most anglers use a specially designed Reelfoot Lake boat. If it's your first time, sign up with a local guide, who can help make arrangements for a boat rental and will share local fishing knowledge. Experienced guides include Jeff Riddle (731/446-7554), Craig Vancleave (731/592-2223), and Mark Pierce (731/538-2323). For a complete and current listing of local guides, check with the visitors center or tourist council. Boat rentals usually cost $50 and up per day, and guides charge $150 and up per day.

Several hotels catering to anglers offer special packages that include room, a boat and motor, bait, ice, and fuel for as little as $120 per night.

Hiking

Campground Trail: This half-mile trail begins in the spillway area and ends at the state park campground on the southern tip of the lake. The trailhead is located on Highway 21/22.

Keystone Trail: This 1.5-mile path skirts the edge of the lake along part of its southern shore. Hikers should wear shoes or boots that can withstand the sometimes-muddy path. Birds are common. The trailhead is located off Highway 21/22 and is adjacent to a large picnic area.

the Reelfoot Lake State Park Visitor Center boardwalk

Black Bayou Trail: This two-mile walk through the cypress swamp follows the Black Bayou Slough. The trailhead is located along Highway 78 on the western shore of the lake.

The Airpark Trail: This 1.5-mile trail winds through cypress and hardwood forest as well as open fields. The trailhead is next to the old Airpark Inn site off Highway 78.

Grassy Island Hiking Trail: Part of the national wildlife refuge at Grassy Island, this half-mile path cuts through lowland forest and over swampy wetlands. A portion follows the paved auto-tour road through Grassy Island.

Biking

The terrain around Reelfoot Lake is flat, and traffic is relatively light. Biking is a good way to get around and explore what the lake has to offer. Bring your own bike, however, since no rentals are available.

ACCOMMODATIONS

The **Blue Bank Resort** (3330 State Hwy. 21 E., 731/253-8976, www.bluebankresort.com, $70–100) has a traditional motel as well as cabins that stand over the lake, with expansive decks and a 12-person hot tub. The cabins can sleep 3–16. All rooms have a lot of exposed wood, giving the resort the feeling of a hunting lodge. The Blue Bank offers fishing packages that cost $200–300 per person for up to four nights and include gear—boat, motor, bait, and ice—for fishing. If you're just interested in a room without the add-ons, call at the last minute to find out if they have a vacancy.

The **Acorn Point Lodge** (Hwy. 22 and 1685 Lake Dr., Samburg, 731/538-9800, www.acornpointlodge.com, $59–89) has 12 rooms, half of which have lake views. Rates vary according to season and include breakfast. There are packages for hunters and groups.

For the most intimate accommodations at Reelfoot Lake, try **Dragonfly Inn** (365 Sunkist Beach Rd., 731/442-0750, www.dragonflyinnreelfootlake.com, $60), formerly Miss Pauline's Bed and Breakfast. Set in an old farmhouse, this friendly bed-and-breakfast is just one mile from Reelfoot Lake but feels removed from the crowds that exist during peak season. The four rooms are homey, and each has a private bath, individual heating and air-conditioning, and a queen-size bed. Host Marianne serves a full breakfast and accommodates anglers with early breakfasts, freezer space, and lots of boat parking in the driveway. Rates are higher during the October arts and crafts festival.

Camping

Reelfoot Lake State Park (2595 State Route 21E, Tiptonville, 731/253-9652) runs two campgrounds for RVs and tents. A small campground is located next to the old Airpark Inn

THE NEW MADRID QUAKE

A series of powerful earthquakes struck the central United States between December 1811 and February 1812. At the time there was no way of measuring magnitude, but modern scientists now say that at least three of these temblors exceeded magnitude 8.0.

The first major quake struck on December 16, 1811, and caused the ground to split open around New Madrid, Missouri. A sulfurous gas filled the air, and witnesses saw thousands of birds flying away from the area. On this day the *New Orleans*, one of the nation's first steamboats, was voyaging down the Mississippi River. The crew was no doubt alarmed to find that as they entered the earthquake-stricken area, riverbanks were shaking and waves were rocking the boat. The steamboat weathered the effects of temblors on December 19, and on December 21 the crew woke to find that the mooring that they had cast the night before was no longer secure because the very island they had anchored to had disappeared under the water.

The final quake struck on February 7, 1812, and gave birth to what is now Reelfoot Lake. The most violent of all the quakes, it caused dishes to shake in Montreal, Canada, and rang bells in Boston. The Mississippi riverbed rose and sank; boats capsized or were sucked into fissures that appeared suddenly in the earth. The quake was so powerful that it caused the Mississippi River to flow northward for a period, and it diverted a large amount of water onto once-dry land, creating Reelfoot Lake.

FOOD

Catfish and other lake fish are the food du jour around Reelfoot Lake. **Boyette's** (Hwy. 21, 731/253-7307, daily 11 A.M.–9 P.M., $10–18) is located across the road from the Reelfoot Lake State Park Visitor Center. The catfish platter is the specialty here, and it comes with generous portions of french fries, onion rings, hush puppies, coleslaw, and green beans. If you've worked up an appetite after a day of fishing, go for the all-you-can-eat catfish dinner, a steal at $16. You can also get frog legs, steaks, and burgers.

A little bit farther east along the lakeshore road you will find **Blue Bank Fish House and Grill** (813 Lake Dr., 731/253-8976, daily 11 A.M.–9 P.M., $6–20). The Blue Bank menu is sure to have something that will please anyone. In addition to all you can eat catfish, fried quail, and country ham, you can choose from pasta, shrimp, steak, loaded potatoes, and burgers. The dinner menu is $8–20, and lunchtime entrées are $6–14. They also serve breakfast. The kitchen closes 2–4 P.M. on weekdays.

For a break from the rustic, drive the 20 miles east to Troy, where you'll find **White House** (106 College St., 731/536-2000, Thurs.–Sat. 11 A.M.–2 P.M. and 5–9 P.M., $14–27), open for lunch and dinner. Set in a gracious old boardinghouse, the restaurant serves uncommonly good food in a welcoming environment. The handsome white building on the town square has a lawn and adjoining gift shop, and it is a popular venue for weddings and special events. The menu includes a half dozen different steaks, pork chops, shrimp, salmon, and chicken. At lunch, choose from sandwiches, salads, and pasta.

INFORMATION

Stop at the **State Park Visitor Center** (Hwy. 21, 731/253-7756, daily 8 A.M.–4:30 P.M.) or the **Reelfoot Lake Tourism Council** (4575 Hwy. 21 E., 731/253-6516, www.reelfoottourism.com,

site on the northwest coast of the lake. A larger campground is on the southern shore near the visitors center. Rates at both campgrounds are $20 for an RV site and $8 for a tent site. Sites are given on a first-come, first-served basis; no reservations are accepted.

Mon. 8 A.M.–5 P.M., Thurs. 9 A.M.–5 P.M., Fri.–Sat. 9 A.M.–6 P.M., Sun. 1–6 P.M.) for visitor information. The Reelfoot Lake State Park Auto Tour guide, a single-sheet handout available at any of these offices, is the most useful map of the area.

Kentucky Lake

The part of the Tennessee River that runs from the striking Land Between the Lakes region near the Kentucky-Tennessee line to Decatur County is commonly referred to as Kentucky Lake. The name reflects the river's breadth and its lakelike calmness, thanks to river dams built in the 1930s and '40s.

The lake provides opportunities for recreation and is home to a one-of-a-kind pearl farm. Off the water, this region includes Fort Donelson National Battlefield, a significant and picturesque Civil War site, and Hurricane Mills, the town known as the home of country music superstar Loretta Lynn.

HURRICANE MILLS

Loretta Lynn, the mega country music star, recalls going for a Sunday drive in the countryside west of Nashville in the early 1960s. That was when she and her late husband, Oliver Lynn, also known as "Doolittle" or "Doo," first saw the 1817 plantation home where they would eventually raise their family. "I looked up on this big ole hill and said, 'I want that house right there,'" she is reported to have said.

Lynn, who moved to Tennessee in 1960 at the beginning of her music career, is one of the most influential female artists in the genre. During the height of her career in the 1970s, she published her autobiography, *Coal Miner's Daughter,* later made into a film. In 1979 she was named Artist of the Decade by the Country Music Association. With the help of hipster/music guru Jack White, her music was introduced to a new generation with 2004's "Van Lear Rose."

The mansion that Lynn bought in 1966 is now just one of a half dozen Lynn-inspired attractions in **Hurricane Mills** (931/296-7700, www.lorettalynnranch.net), a town that time would have forgotten were it not for Loretta Lynn. First buying just the mansion, Lynn now owns the whole shebang: Even the U.S. Postal Service rents the Hurricane Mills Post Office from Lynn.

The town is located seven miles north of I-40, along Highway 13. Waverly and Dickson are the closest large towns.

Sights

Visitors to Hurricane Mills can tour the antebellum mansion Lynn bought in 1966, as well as a replica of her childhood home in Butcher Holler, Kentucky, and a simulated coal mine, made to look like the one in which her father worked. Guided tours, which cost $12 for adults and $6 for children 6–12, last about an hour and depart daily at 9:30 A.M., 10:30 A.M., 11:30 A.M., 1 P.M., 2 P.M., 3 P.M., and 4 P.M.

The **Coal Miner's Daughter Museum** (931/296-1840, daily 9 A.M.–4 P.M., adults $10, children 6–12 $5) is an 18,000-square-foot exhibit hall packed with items from Lynn's personal and professional life. Opened in 2001, the museum includes her tour bus, pictures, clothing, portraits, and gifts from celebrity friends. There is also the **Loretta Doll and Fan Museum** (free), located in a beautiful red 1896 gristmill.

The museums and plantation tours are open April–October and are generally closed during the winter. Call ahead to confirm.

Practicalities

The **Loretta Lynn Ranch** (44 Hurricane Mills Rd., 931/296-7700, www.lorettalynnranch.net) has an RV park, campground, and cabin

KENTUCKY LAKE

Eddyville

WENDALL H. FORD
WESTERN KENTUCKY
PKWY

24

NORTH
WELCOME
CENTER

Land Lake

Between Barkley

45

HILLMAN FERRY

THE TRACE

WOODLANDS
NATURE STATION

The

Benton

ENERGY
LAKE

Cadiz

Lakes

68

ELK AND BISON
PRAIRIE

80 402

TURKEY BAY
OFF-HIGHWAY
VEHICLE AREA

GOLDEN POND
VISITOR CENTER

National

WRANGLERS

Kentucky

THE HOMEPLACE

641

Lake

SOUTH BISON RANGE

Recreation

GREAT WESTERN
IRON FURNACE

Area

SOUTH
WELCOME
CENTER

PINEY

KENTUCKY

TENNESSEE

FORT HENRY

Dover

76

Oak Hill

FORT DONELSON
NATIONAL BATTLEFIELD

79

Paris Landing
State Park

To Clarksville

Tennessee

National

Wildlife

Tennessee (Kentucky)

Refuge

Paris

River (Kentucky Lake)

641

TENNESSEE RIVER
FOLKLIFE CENTER

Nathan Bedford
Forrest State Park

0   5 mi

0   5 km

Camden

70

To
Hurricane
Mills

TENNESSEE RIVER
FRESHWATER PEARL
MUSEUM AND FARM

© AVALON TRAVEL

---

rentals. There are also canoe rentals, paddle-boats, and occasional concerts by Lynn herself. For something a little different, book a night on Lynn's old tour bus. For $125–150 per night, up to four people can sleep tour-bus-style, with television, a microwave, refrigerator, and cof-feemaker. The ranch is open April–October.

For food, entertainment, and shopping, head to **Cissie Lynn's Country Store and Music Barn** (8000 Hwy. 13 S., 931/296-2275, daily 6 A.M.–6 P.M.). Operated by Loretta Lynn's daughter Cissie, the restaurant and music hall serves sandwiches and country-style food ($7–15). In the evenings there are writer's nights, live music, and special events.

Closer to the mansion, **Rock-a-Billy Cafe** (Stage Coach Hill, 931/296-1840, Fri.–Sun. 9 A.M.–5 P.M.) is a casual restaurant located in the old gristmill.

MOUSETAIL LANDING STATE PARK

Located on land once occupied by an epony-mous river town, Mousetail Landing State Park (Linden, 731/847-0841) is one of Tennessee's newer state parks. Dedicated in 1986, this 1,247-acre park lies on the east bank of the Tennessee River in the rural and picturesque Western Valley. The town acquired its name from the large number of rodents that once took shelter in the town's tanning factories. Tanned hides were shipped northward to mar-kets up the river, including Paducah, Louisville, and St. Louis.

The park contains several ruins from the his-toric era, including the original pier, a black-smith shop, and the old community cemetery.

Recreation

There is a three-mile day-use hiking trail through the woods, as well as an eight-mile loop with two overnight shelters along the way. The shelters are well maintained and provide lovely protection from the elements. The hike

WESTERN PLAINS

is relatively easy; you could complete the entire loop in a day and camp at the park campground.

One half-mile south of the main entrance to the park there is a boat launch and courtesy pier. Fishing is popular and permitted anywhere in the park. Bass, bream, crappie, striper, and catfish are among the most frequent catches.

Also near the boat dock is a small swimming beach. There is no lifeguard on duty. A small, cold creek near the entrance to the park is ideal for wading and exploration.

Kids enjoy the playgrounds, archery range, horseshoes, basketball, and volleyball court.

Camping

There are two campgrounds at **Mousetail Landing** (Rt. 3, Linden, 731/847-0841). Rates are $16 per site. The main campground, located in a woodland forest, has 24 sites, including 19 with electricity and water. There is a modern bathhouse and laundry facilities, plus picnic tables and grills. There is also a dump station.

Spring Creek Campground has 21 sites along the banks of the Tennessee River, located at the public boat dock.

NATCHEZ TRACE STATE PARK AND FOREST

Named for the famous old road from Natchez to Nashville, this is one of the largest state parks in Tennessee. The park (24845 Natchez Trace Rd., Wildersville, 731/968-3742, www.tn.gov/environment/parks/NatchezTrace, park office Mon.–Fri. 8 A.M.–4:30 P.M.) has four lakes, including Pin Oak Lake, which offers fishing, boating, and swimming. Historically the Natchez Trace has offered horseback riding through the **Natchez Trace Equestrian Center** (731/967-5340, Mar.–Memorial Day and Labor Day–late Nov. Fri.–Sat. 9 A.M.–5 P.M., Sun. 1–5 P.M., Memorial Day–Labor Day Tues.–Sat. 9 A.M.–5 P.M., Sun. 1–5 P.M.) for adults and children as young as three years. An hour's guided ride costs $24. The center was closed for much of 2012, so call ahead.

There are 13.5 miles of hiking trails at the park, as well as a museum about the natural history and wildlife of the area. Tennis courts, baseball fields, basketball course, and an archery and shooting range round out the facilities.

The park also has cabins, a campground, a resort inn, and group lodge.

CAMDEN

The town of Camden is the seat of Benton County, whose eastern edge is bounded by the Tennessee River.

Patsy Cline Memorial

Country music star Patsy Cline, together with Hawkshaw Hawkins, Cowboy Copas, and Randy Hughes, died in an airplane crash about three miles northwest of Camden on March 5, 1963. The Grand Ole Opry stars were heading back to Nashville after playing a benefit concert in Kansas City. The Piper Comanche airplane that they were in stopped in Dyersburg to refuel and took off shortly after 6 P.M., despite high winds and inclement weather. The plane crashed at 6:20 P.M. in a forest west of Camden, just 90 miles from Nashville. Cline was 30 years old.

The site of the plane crash remains a memorial to Patsy Cline, maintained over the years by her loyal fans. There is a memorial stone, bulletin board, and mailbox where fans can leave their personal sentiments about the star. The memorial is located 2.8 miles northwest of town along Mount Carmel Road.

Near Camden

North America's only freshwater pearl–culturing farm is located a few miles south of Camden on Birdsong Creek, an inlet of the Tennessee River. The **Tennessee River Freshwater Pearl Museum and Farm** (255 Marina Rd., 731/584-7880, www.tennesseeriverpearls.com, Mon.–Sat. 8 A.M.–5 P.M., Sun. 1–4 P.M., free) is the unlikely result of one family's passion for which is also a favorite place for boaters and anglers, as well as group getaways. There are dozens of cabins, 50 campsites, a marina, catering facilities, and a pool.

NATHAN BEDFORD FORREST STATE PARK

Dedicated in 1929 to Nathan Bedford Forrest, the controversial Confederate Civil War hero, this 2,500-acre state park offers camping, cabins, hiking, swimming, group pavilions, and fishing. There are seven cabins, each of which can sleep up to eight people, plus a group lodge that accommodates up to 64 people. The campground can accommodate tents or RVs.

There are more than 30 miles of hiking trails, ranging from easy to rugged. Swimming is good at Eva Beach, a rough sandy beach on Kentucky Lake.

The **park office** (1825 Pilot Knob Rd., Eva, 731/584-1841, www.tn.gov/environment/parks/NBForrest) is open daily 8 A.M.–4:30 P.M.

(Tennessee River Folklife Center

Located at Pilot Knob overlooking the Tennessee River, the Tennessee River Folklife Center (1825 Pilot Knob Rd., 731/584-2128, daily 8–11 A.M. and noon–4:30 P.M., free) lovingly depicts the traditional ways of river folk. The centerpiece of the museum is *Old Betsy*, a traditional riverboat built from old farm equipment in the 1960s by T. J. Whitfield. Exhibits include photographs of a houseboat family and displays about river mussels, the pearl industry, and traditional foods and music. The museum is comprehensive but not too large to be overwhelming.

Just steps from the doors to the folklife center is a monument to Nathan Bedford Forrest and his cavalry, which defeated a federal supply depot at Old Johnsonville, near the park, in 1984. There are impressive views of the Tennessee River from the porch outside the museum, including several manufacturing plants that emit distinctly industrial smells at certain times of the day.

© DG STRONG

Even in winter, Nathan Bedford Forrest State Park is an oasis.

WESTERN PLAINS

pearls. John and Chessie Latrendressee founded the farm in 1979 and made their first successful harvest in 1984. Wild pearls were harvested from mussels fished from the bottom of the Tennessee River for years, but the Latrendressees were the first to successfully farm the gem.

The small museum explains the culturing process, the history of the Tennessee River pearl farm, and the history of pearls. You can also watch a *CBS Sunday Morning* segment produced about the Tennessee River Pearl Farm. There is a gift shop that sells some of the homegrown pearls; others are exported around the world. For a more detailed look, sign up for one of the farm's tour packages. The full tour ($55) includes lunch and a visit to the farm itself, where you can see the phases of pearl culturing. Tours require at least 15 people, but small groups can often add onto tours that have already been booked. Call ahead to check the schedule.

The pearl farm is located at Birdsong Resort,

THE LEGACY OF NATHAN BEDFORD FORREST

Nathan Bedford Forrest is both one of the most celebrated and reviled historical figures in Tennessee. An accomplished Confederate cavalry commander and the first grand wizard of the Ku Klux Klan, Forrest has come to symbolize the Old South.

Forrest was born in 1821 in Chapel Hill, a small town in Marshall County in Middle Tennessee. At the age of 16, Forrest's blacksmith father died, and the young man became the head of his family. He had a mere six months of formal education in his lifetime, yet he became a successful businessman, primarily as a plantation owner and slave trader.

Forrest was a staunch believer in the Southern cause, and when Tennessee seceded from the Union in 1861, he enlisted as a private in the Tennessee Mounted Rifles, together with his younger brother and 15-year-old son.

In a peculiar twist, Forrest offered freedom to his 44 slaves at the outbreak of the Civil War, if they would fight for the Confederacy. All agreed, and 43 reportedly served faithfully until the end of the war.

Forrest was daring on the battlefield, often taking great risks to avoid capture and defeat. Historian Brian S. Wills wrote: "His ferocity as a warrior was almost legendary.... Forrest understood, perhaps better than most, the basic premise of war: 'War means fighting and fighting means killing.'"

Forrest was involved in dozens of battles—small and large—during the war. In February 1862 he led his men out of Fort Donelson rather than surrender. He was wounded at Shiloh and fought at Chickamauga. In May 1863, he outmaneuvered a stronger Union force in northern Alabama by fooling Col. Abel Streight into believing that Forrest had more men than he did.

Forrest's victory at Fort Pillow in April 1864 was tarnished by the deaths of so many black Union soldiers, allegedly killed after they surrendered.

His victory at Brice's Cross Roads, in Mississippi, where Forrest defeated a much larger force of Union infantry and cavalry in June 1864, is believed by many to be his greatest success.

Forrest ended the Civil War as lieutenant general in command of cavalry in Alabama, Mississippi, and east Louisiana. His last battle at Gainsville, Alabama, in May 1865 ended in surrender.

Following the war, Forrest struggled to adapt to the changes it had brought. He supported the Ku Klux Klan in hopes of restoring the conservative white power structure that existed prior to the war and served as the Klan's first grand wizard.

His business dealings floundered. Forrest lost a fortune in the railroad industry, and he spent his remaining years running a prison farm and living in a log cabin.

In his last years, Forrest seemed to reconsider many of his views on racial equality. In 1875 he spoke to a local group of freedmen, saying, "I came to meet you as friends, and welcome you to the white people. I want you to come nearer to us. When I can serve you I will do so. We have but one flag, one country; let us stand together. We may differ in color, but not in sentiment." Forrest kissed the cheek of an African American woman who handed him a bouquet of flowers, a gesture of intimacy unknown in that era.

Forrest died in Memphis in October 1877. He was buried at Elmwood Cemetery but later reinterred at Forrest Park, built in his honor, in midtown Memphis.

In the years since the civil rights movement, many people have questioned Forrest's legacy. In 2005, there was an effort to move the statue over Forrest's grave and rename Forrest Park, and others have tried to get a bust of Forrest removed from the Tennessee House of Representatives chamber: Both efforts failed.

© VIC SMITH

The Tennessee River Folklife Center is located at Pilot Knob, one of the highest elevations in the western part of the state.

TENNESSEE NATIONAL WILDLIFE REFUGE

The Tennessee National Wildlife Refuge encompasses more than 51,000 acres along the Kentucky Lake, divided into three units. The Big Sandy Unit is just south of Paris Landing State Park; the Duck River Unit is farther south, near Eagle Creek and where I-40 crosses the river; the Busseltown unit is farther south still, near Perryville and Mousetail Landing State Park.

The refuge was established in 1945 as a safe haven for waterfowl. Today it consists of several different habitats, including open water, bottomland hardwoods, upland forests, freshwater marshes, and agricultural lands. As a refuge, the first priority is to protect animal species rather than provide a space for human recreation.

Fishing and hunting are allowed in certain parts of the refuge at certain times of the year. There is an observation deck at the entrance to the Duck River "bottoms" area, where you can see a variety of waterfowl, especially in fall and winter. There is another observation deck at the V. L. Childs Overlook at the Big Sandy Unit off Swamp Creek Road. There is a 2.5-mile hiking trail here, too.

The **refuge headquarters** (3006 Dinkins Ln., 731/642-2091, Mon.–Fri. 7 A.M.– 3:30 P.M.) is just east of Paris off Highway 79.

JOHNSONVILLE STATE HISTORIC AREA

This 600-acre park (90 Nell Beard Rd., New Johnsonville, 931/535-2789, www.tn.gov/environment/parks/Johnsonville) is the site of Johnsonville before the creation of the Kentucky Lake, and this is where the battle of Johnsonville took place during the Civil War. The November 4, 1864, battle is noteworthy because it was the first time that a naval force was engaged and defeated by a cavalry.

The park has picnic pavilions, playgrounds, and six miles of hiking trails.

PARIS

Paris, the largest town in the Kentucky Lake region, was founded in 1823 and named after the French capital in honor of the Marquis de Lafayette. Not long after, tourists were traveling to this Paris to drink and soak in a nearby sulfur well, which was believed to have health benefits. The well was submerged by Kentucky Lake in 1944 when TVA dammed the Tennessee River.

In keeping with its name, Paris has a model of the Eiffel Tower, donated to the city in 1992 by Christian Brothers University of Memphis. Located in Memorial Park on the outskirts of the city, the model tower is surrounded by a playground, ball field, and walking trails. Don't expect to see it towering over the town, however, as the model is only 60 feet tall.

To learn about the history of Paris and Henry County, visit the **Paris-Henry**

County Heritage Center (614 N. Poplar St., 731/642-1030, www.phchc.com, Tues.–Fri. 10 A.M.–4 P.M., Sat. 10 A.M.–2 P.M.), located in the Cavitt Place, a 1916 Italian Renaissance–style two-story home. The center houses exhibits about the history of Henry County and can provide an audio walking guide to historic Paris. There is also a gift shop.

Festivals and Events

More than 12,500 pounds of catfish are served at the **World's Biggest Fish Fry** (www.worldsbiggestfishfry.com), which takes place in Paris in late April every year. The tradition evolved from the annual Mule Day, when farmers traveled to the town to trade their mules and other farm equipment ahead of the summer growing season. In 1953, the fish fry was established, and it has grown in popularity every year, once the organizers started using local fish. Today, the fish fry is a weeklong event with rodeos, races, a parade, and four days of fish dinners, available for $10 a plate at the Bobby Cox Memorial Fish Tent.

Accommodations

In Paris, there are several serviceable chain hotels, but the option that allows you to really experience the area at its best is to choose from the many cabins and lakeside resorts nearby.

On U.S. 641 one mile outside of Paris, the **Terrace Woods Lodge** (1190 N. Market St., 731/642-2642, www.terracewoodslodge.com, $40) is not as rustic as it sounds, with free wireless Internet, flat-screen televisions, and views of the woods. This is a standard motel, but the rooms are clean and the service acceptable.

Food

Knott's Landing (209 N. Poplar St., 731/642-4718, Mon.–Tues. 6 A.M.–2 P.M., Wed.–Sat. 6 A.M.–8:30 P.M., $4–11) specializes in pond-raised catfish served with hot rolls, hush puppies, coleslaw, and more. You can also get a traditional plate lunch or sandwich, steak, or burger. They also serve breakfast.

Paris distinguishes itself as one of the few small Tennessee towns with a stellar (albeit small) health-food store. **Healthy Thyme** (803 E. Wood St., 731/642-9528, Mon.–Fri. 10 A.M.–5:30 P.M., Sat. 10 A.M.–2 P.M., $3–4) serves fruit smoothies, vegetarian and chicken salads, and sandwiches.

Downtown Paris has a bona fide coffee shop, with espresso, cappuccino, latte, and other specialty coffee drinks. **Jack's Java** (118 N. Market St., 731/642-5251, Mon.–Fri. 7 A.M.–5 P.M., Sat. 9 A.M.–noon) doubles as a bookstore and florist, and has a creative touch with its drink names.

For a sit-down dinner, try **Sepanto Steak House** (1305 E. Wood St., 731/641-1791, Mon.–Sat. 11 A.M.–9 P.M., $10–24), where you can get seafood, pasta, and chicken as well as steaks.

Information and Services

Get visitor information from the **Paris-Henry County Chamber of Commerce** (2508 E. Wood St., 731/642-3431, www.paristnchamber.com) in Paris.

Also in Paris, the **W.G. Rhea Public Library** (400 W. Washington St., 731/642-1220, Mon.–Sat. 9 A.M.–5 P.M.) has 22,000 volumes as well as computers with Internet access. The library is open until 7 P.M. on Tuesday and Thursday evenings.

Near Paris

The most laid-back accommodations in the area are found at **Mammy and Pappy's B&B** (7615 Elkhorn Rd., Springville, 731/642-8129, www.mammy-pappysbb.com, $95), a 1900-era farmhouse in Springville. Located about 13 miles from Paris in rural countryside, this is a real getaway. Dannie and Katie Williams manage this family property, which has been lovingly cared for over the years. Each of the four bedrooms has hardwood floors and private baths. Breakfasts include homemade biscuits, and guests are also provided an evening snack. Additional nights' stays are $80 (rather than the initial $95).

PARIS LANDING STATE PARK

One of Tennessee's "resort parks," Paris Landing (16055 Highway 79 N., Buchanan, 731/642-4311) is an 841-acre park on the banks of Kentucky Lake. The 130-room park inn is located next to a large conference center and dining room, all with views of the lake. There is also an award-winning public golf course and swimming pool.

Day-trippers gravitate to the lake itself. Fishing is the most popular activity; catfish, crappie, bass, sauger, walleye, bluegill, and striper are some of the most common catches. The park maintains two fishing piers and one launch ramp for public use. There are also more than 200 open and covered slips for rent.

The park has a public swimming beach, hiking trails, tennis, basketball and baseball facilities, and pavilions for picnics and parties.

Accommodations

For accommodations on the lake, you cannot beat **Paris Landing State Resort Park** (16055 Hwy. 79 N., 731/641-4465), which has hotel rooms, cabins, and campground facilities on the water. The 130-room inn ($60–100) looks like a concrete goliath, but the rooms are comfortable, and all have beautiful views of the lake. The three-bedroom cabins ($155–175) can sleep up to 10 people and are set on a secluded point overlooking the lake. The campground ($14.50–17.50) has both RV and tent sites, a laundry, bathhouse, and dump station.

As its name suggests, **The Reel Inn** (2155 Hwy. 119 N., Buchanan, 731/232-8227, $99) caters to anglers. The lakeside offerings here include two-bedroom cabins with washer/dryers, daily maid service, full-size kitchen appliances, and other comforts of home.

Buchanan Resort (Hwy. 79, west of Paris Landing State Park, 731/642-2828, www.buchananresort.com, $69–210) has a place to rest your head, no matter what your preference. Choices include a motel, lodges that accommodate up to 20 people, and waterfront suites and cottages.

There is no shortage of welcoming resorts with lakeside cabins in the area. Another good option includes **Mansard Island Resort and Marina** (60 Mansard Island Dr., Springville, 731/642-5590, www.mansardisland.com, $68–98), which has town houses and cottages for lakegoers, and lots of amenities including a swimming pool. There are discounted rates for extended stays. Pets are not permitted.

◖ FORT DONELSON NATIONAL BATTLEFIELD

On Valentine's Day in 1862, Union forces attacked the Confederate Fort Donelson on the banks of the Cumberland River. Fort Donelson National Battlefield (Hwy. 79, 931/232-5706, www.nps.gov/fodo) is now a national park, making this site a good choice for both history buffs and those who are more interested in the great outdoors. A visitors center with an exhibit, gift shop, and information boards is open daily 8 A.M.–4:30 P.M. The 15-minute video does a good job describing the battle and its importance in the Civil War.

A driving tour takes visitors to Fort Donelson, which overlooks the Cumberland River and may be one of the most picturesque forts in Tennessee. The earthen fort was built by Confederate soldiers and slaves over a period of about seven months.

You are also guided to the **Dover Hotel** (Petty St., 931/232-5706, Sat.–Sun. noon–4 P.M. Memorial Day–Labor Day), which was used as the Confederate headquarters during the battle. The hotel, built between 1851 and 1853, is a handsome wood structure and has been restored to look as it did during the battle. It is located a few blocks away from downtown Dover.

The **National Cemetery,** established after the

The outcome of the Civil War was determined at Fort Donelson National Battlefield.

war, was built on grounds where escaped slaves lived in a so-called contraband camp during the Civil War. The camp was established by the Union army to accommodate slaves who fled behind Union lines during the war. The freedmen and women worked for the Union army, often without pay. It was not until 1862 that the Union army allowed blacks to join as soldiers.

There are more than five miles of hiking trails at Fort Donelson National Battlefield, including the three-mile River Circle Trail and four-mile Donelson Trail. Both hikes begin at the visitors center. Picnic tables are located next to the river near the old fort.

DOVER

A small town set at the southern shore of the Cumberland River, Dover is Tennessee's major gateway to the Land Between the Lakes. It is also the place where Gen. Ulysses S. Grant earned the nickname "Unconditional Surrender" during the Civil War.

Dover has a reputation for being a speed trap, so obey posted speed limits when driving here.

Accommodations

Just west of the entrance to Land Between the Lakes, the **Dover Inn Motel** (1545 Donelson Pkwy., 931/232-5556, $60–70) has both traditional motel rooms and modern cabins with full kitchens. All rooms have telephones, cable TV, air-conditioning, and coffeemakers. They cater to hunters and anglers who are going to Land Between the Lakes but don't want to camp. There is a swimming pool on the property.

Choose from a private campground or log cabins at **Leatherwood Resort** (753 Leatherwood Bay Rd., 931/232-5137, www.leatherwoodresort.com, $35 campground, $104–210 cabins). The cabins have a minimum four-night stay. Leashed pets are permitted, and there are discounts for weekly rates.

Food

As one of the last stops before entering Land Between the Lakes, Dover is chock-full of fast-food. But folks make a special trip to stop at **Cindy's Catfish Kitchen** (2148 Donelson Pkwy., 931/232-4817, Mon.–Sat. 7 A.M.–9 P.M., $12–20) for the namesake dish, not to mention other Southern specialties including sweet and mashed potatoes and hush puppies. For something entirely different, head to the **B&M Dairy Freeze** (610 Donelson Pkwy., 931/232-5927, daily 10:30 A.M.–7 P.M., $4–8), a casual restaurant serving burgers, hot dogs, and ice cream that's located just west of downtown Dover.

Located downtown, **The Dover Grille** (310 Donelson Pkwy., 931/232-7919, daily 7 A.M.–9 P.M., $5–12) serves burgers, dinner plates, Southwestern platters, pasta, and salads.

Several miles east of the town is the **Log Cabin Cafe** (1394 Hwy. 79, 931/232-0220, Mon.–Sat. 6 A.M.–9 P.M., Sun. 6 A.M.–3 P.M., $6–12). The café serves traditional Southern

UNCONDITIONAL SURRENDER

It was the day after Valentine's Day 1862, and things were bleak for the Confederate army at Fort Donelson. The fort, located on the banks of the Cumberland River, was under attack from Federal forces, and generals feared a siege.

Southern generals Floyd and Pillow slipped away overnight, leaving General Buckner, a former friend and schoolmate of General Grant, in command. On the morning of February 16, Buckner wrote to Grant asking for the terms of surrender.

In Grant's famous reply, he said no terms other than "unconditional and immediate" surrender would be accepted. Buckner surrendered, and 13,000 Confederate men were taken prisoner. The path to the heart of the Confederacy was now open, and Grant earned a new nickname: "Unconditional Surrender" Grant.

food in a modern log cabin. It is a popular pit stop for workmen; the café's breakfast will fuel you all day long.

Information

The **Stewart County Chamber of Commerce** (117 Visitor Center Ln., 931/232-8290, www.stewartcountychamberofcommerce.com) provides visitor information.

CROSS CREEKS NATIONAL WILDLIFE REFUGE

Four miles east of Dover is the 8,862-acre Cross Creeks National Wildlife Refuge (643 Wildlife Rd., 931/232-7477, refuge Mar. 16–Nov. 14 daily daylight hours, visitors center year-round Mon.–Fri. 7 A.M.–3:30 P.M.). Established in 1962, the refuge includes 12.5 miles of bottomlands along the Cumberland River, plus nearby rocky bluffs and rolling hills. There is also marsh, brush, and farmland. The refuge is an important habitat for geese, ducks, raptors, shorebirds, wading birds, and neotropical migratory birds. In January, when the bird population is at its peak, as many as 60,000 birds may be in the refuge. Mallard ducks make up the majority. American bald eagles and golden eagles also live in the refuge, along with great blue herons, wild turkeys, muskrats, coyotes, and bobcats. Farms within the refuge grow corn, soybeans, grain sorghum, and wheat; a portion of each harvest is left in the field for wildlife to consume.

A network of paved and gravel roads along the southern shore of the Cumberland are the best places to view the refuge. Rattlesnake Trail is a one-mile hiking path through the refuge. While hunting is allowed at certain times of year, camping and campfires are prohibited.

To find Cross Creeks, drive about four miles east of Dover on Highway 49. Look for Wildlife Drive on your left.

WESTERN PLAINS

Land Between the Lakes

This narrow finger of land that lies between the Cumberland and Tennessee Rivers is a natural wonderland. Comprising 170,000 acres of land and wrapped by 300 miles of undeveloped river shoreline, the **Land Between the Lakes National Recreation Area** (100 Van Morgan Dr., Golden Pond, 270/924-2000, www.lbl.org) has become one of the most popular natural areas in this region of the country. Split between Tennessee and Kentucky, the area provides unrivaled opportunities to camp, hike, boat, play, or just simply drive through quiet wilderness.

The area lies between what is now called Kentucky Lake (the Tennessee River) and Lake Barkley (the Cumberland River). At its narrowest point, the distance between these two bodies of water is only one mile. The drive from north to south is 43 miles. About one-third of the park is in Tennessee; the rest is in Kentucky. It is managed by the U.S. Forest Service, an agency of the U.S. Department of Agriculture.

History

Land Between the Lakes was not always a natural and recreational area. Native Americans settled here, drawn to the fertile soil, proximity to the rivers, and gentle terrain. European settlers followed, and between about 1800 and the 1960s the area, then called Between the Rivers, saw thriving small settlements. Residents farmed and traded along the rivers, which were served by steamboats.

In many respects, settlers in Between the Rivers were even more isolated than those in other parts of what was then the western frontier of the United States. They did not necessarily associate with one state or another, instead forming a distinct identity of their own. During the Civil War, it was necessary to finally determine the border between Tennessee and Kentucky, since this line also marked the border between the Union and the Confederacy.

It was during another period of upheaval in the United States that the future of the Between the Rivers region changed forever. In the midst of the Great Depression, Congress created the Tennessee Valley Authority, which improved soil conditions, eased flooding, brought electricity, and created jobs in Tennessee. One of TVA's projects was the Kentucky Dam, which was built between 1938 and 1944 and impounded the Tennessee River. In 1957, work began on Barkley Dam, which impounded the Cumberland River and put an end to floods that damaged crops and destroyed property along the river.

About 25 years later, president John F. Kennedy announced that the U.S. government would buy out residents of the land between the Cumberland and Tennessee Rivers to create a new park, which would serve as an example of environmental management and recreational use. The project was to bring much-needed economic development to the area by attracting visitors to the park.

The project was not without opponents, who objected to the government's use of eminent domain to take over lands that were privately owned. Residents lamented the loss of unique communities in the lake region. More than 2,300 people were removed to create Land Between the Lakes (LBL). In all, 96,000 of the 170,000 acres that make up LBL were purchased or taken from private hands.

Over time, however, the controversy of the creation of the park has faded, and the Land Between the Lakes has become well loved. It is the third most-visited park in Tennessee, behind only the Smoky Mountains and Cherokee National Forest.

Planning Your Time

Some of the best attractions at Land Between the Lakes charge admission. If you are planning to visit all or most of them, consider one of the packages offered by the Forest Service. The discount package allows you to visit each attraction once over a seven-day period at a 25 percent discount. Another option is the $30 LBL Fun Card, which gives you 10 admissions to any of three attractions. It does not expire. You can buy packages at either the north (Kentucky) or south (Tennessee) welcome station or the Golden Pond Visitor Center.

During certain summer weekends there are free two-hour tours of Lake Barkley's **Power Plant and Navigation Lock** (270/362-4236). You must call in advance to reserve a spot and complete a registration form.

SIGHTS

Driving south to north along the scenic main road, or trace, that runs along the middle of the park, you will find the major attractions within Land Between the Lakes.

Great Western Iron Furnace

About 11 miles inside the park is the Great Western Iron Furnace, built by Brian, Newell, and Company in 1854. If you have traveled around this part of Tennessee much, you will have come to recognize the distinctive shape of the old iron furnaces, which dot the landscape in the counties between Nashville and the Tennessee River. Like the Great Western Furnace, these plants were used to create high-quality iron from iron ore deposits in the earth.

The Great Western Furnace operated for less than two years. By 1856 panic over reported slave uprisings and the coming of the Civil War caused the plant to shut down. It would never make iron again.

◖ The Homeplace

Just beyond the furnace is The Homeplace (Mar. and Nov. Wed.–Sat. 9 A.M.–5 P.M., Sun. 10 A.M.–5 P.M., Apr.–Oct. Mon.–Sat. 9 A.M.–5 P.M., Sun. 10 A.M.–5 P.M., ages 13 and up $4, children 4 and under free), a living-history museum that depicts life in Between the Rivers in about 1850. At the middle of the 19th century, Between the Rivers was home to an iron ore industry and hundreds of farmers. These farmers raised crops and livestock for their own use, as well as to sell where they could. In 1850, about 10,000 people lived in Between the Rivers, including 2,500 slaves and 125 free blacks.

The Homeplace re-creates an 1850 farmstead. Staff dress in period clothes and perform the labors that settlers would have done: They sow seeds in the spring, harvest in the summer and fall, and prepare the fields for the next year in the winter. The farm includes a dogtrot cabin, where you can see how settlers would have lived, cooked, and slept. Out back there is a small garden, a plot of tobacco, pigs, sheep, oxen, and a barn. You may see farmers splitting shingles, working oxen, sewing quilts, making candles, or any other of the dozens of tasks that settlers performed on a regular basis.

The Homeplace publishes a schedule that announces when certain activities will take place, such as canning, sheering of sheep, or harvesting tobacco. Even if you come when there is no special program, you will be able to see staff taking on everyday tasks, and you can ask them about any facet of life on the frontier.

Elk and Bison Prairie

Archaeological evidence shows that elk and bison once grazed in Tennessee and Kentucky, including the area between the rivers. Settlers quickly destroyed these herds, however. Both bison and elk were easy to hunt, and they were desirable for their meat and skins. By 1800, bison had been killed off, and about 50 years later elk were gone, too.

When Land Between the Lakes was created, elk and bison were reintroduced to the area. The South Bison Range across the road from the Homeplace is one of the places where bison now live. The bison herd that roams on about 160 acres here can sometimes be seen from the main road, or from side roads bordering the range.

You can see both bison and elk at the Elk and Bison Prairie, a 700-acre restoration project located near the midpoint of the Land Between the Lakes. In 1996, 39 bison were relocated from the south prairie here, and 29 elk were transported from Canada. Since then, the population of both animals has grown.

Visitors may drive through the range along a one-mile loop. Admission is $5 per vehicle. You are advised to take your time, roll down your windows, and keep your eyes peeled for a sign of the animals. The best time to view elk and bison is in the early morning or late afternoon. At other times of day, you may just enjoy the sights and sounds of the grassland. Pay attention to the road as well as the animals, as the car in front of you may slow to take photos of one of these magnificent creatures. You may also see some bison from the trace en route.

WESTERN PLAINS

© MARGARET LITTMAN

See Tennessee as it was in the 19th century at The Homeplace.

Golden Pond Visitor Center and Planetarium

For the best overview of the history, nature, and significance of the Land Between the Lakes, stop at the Golden Pond Visitor Center and Planetarium (Natchez Trace and US Hwy. 68/80, 270/924-2000, daily 9 A.M.–5 P.M., visitors center free, planetarium shows ages 13 and up $4, children 5–12 $2, children 4 and under free). The visitors center is home to a small museum about the park, where you can also watch a video about the elk that have been restored on the Elk and Bison Prairie. There is also a gift shop, restrooms, and picnic area.

The planetarium screens at least four programs daily about astronomy and nature, with more during the holidays. On Saturday and Sunday at 1 P.M. you can get a sneak peak at the night sky above.

Golden Pond was the name of Land Between the Lakes's largest town before the park was created. Golden Pond, also called Fungo, was a vibrant town that, at its peak, had a hotel, bank, restaurants, and other retail outlets. During Prohibition, farmers made moonshine in the woods and sold it in Golden Pond. Golden Pond whiskey was sought after in back alley saloons as far away as Chicago. When Land Between the Lakes was created in 1963, Golden Pond had a population of about 200 people. Families moved their homes and relocated to communities outside the park. In 1970, when the historic society unveiled a marker at the site of Golden Pond, the strains of "Taps" rang out over the hills.

You can visit the site of Golden Pond by driving a few miles east of the visitors center on Highway 80. There is a picnic area.

Woodlands Nature Station

The final major attraction in Land Between the Lakes is the Woodlands Nature Station (north of the visitors center on the Trace, 270/924-2020, Apr.–Oct. Mon.–Sat. 9 A.M.–5 P.M. and Sun. 10 A.M.–5 P.M., Mar. and Nov. Wed.–Sat.

9 A.M.–5 P.M. and Sun. 10 A.M.–5 P.M., closed Dec.–Feb., ages 13 and up $4, children 5–12 $2, children 4 and under free). Geared to children, the nature station introduces visitors to animals including bald eagles, coyotes, opossum, and deer. There are also opportunities for staff-led hiking trips. Special events and activities take place nearly every weekend, and during the week in summertime.

Center Furnace

You can see the ruins of what was once the largest iron furnace in the Land Between the Lakes along the Center Furnace Trail. Along the short (0.3 mile) walk you will see signs that describe the process of making iron and explain why it was practiced Between the Rivers.

Center Furnace was built between 1844 and 1846. It continued to operate until 1912, much longer than any other furnace in the area.

RECREATION

Promoting outdoor recreation is one of the objectives of Land Between the Lakes. Visitors can enjoy hiking, biking, paddling, or horseback riding; hunting and fishing; and camping. There is even an area specially designated for all-terrain vehicles.

Trails

There are 200 miles of hiking trails in Land Between the Lakes. Some of these are also open for mountain biking and horseback riding.

The **Fort Henry Trails** are a network of 29.3 miles of trails near the southern entrance to the park, some of which follow the shoreline of the Kentucky Lake. The intricate network of trails allows hikers to choose from a three-mile loop to something much longer.

Access the trails from the south welcome station, or from the Fort Henry Trails parking area, at the end of Fort Henry Road. These trails crisscross the grounds once occupied by the Confederate Fort Henry. They are for hikers only.

The **North-South Trail** treks the entire length of the Land Between the Lakes. From start to finish, it is 58.6 miles. Three backcountry camping shelters are available along the way for backpackers. The trail crosses the main road in several locations. Portions of the trail are open to horseback riders. The portion from the Golden Pond Visitor Center to the northern end is also open to mountain bikers.

The 2.2-mile **Honker Lake Loop Trail** begins at the Woodlands Nature Station. This trail is open to hikers only. Sightings of fallow deer and giant Canada geese are common along this trail. The banks of nearby Hematite Lake are littered with bits of blue stone, remnants of slag from Center Iron Furnace.

Finally, at the northern end of the park are the **Canal Loop Trails,** a network of hike/bike trails that depart from the north welcome station. These trails meander along the shores of both Kentucky Lake and Lake Barkley. The entire loop is 14.2 miles, but connector trails enable you to fashion a shorter hike or ride if you want.

A detailed map showing all hiking, biking, and horseback trails can be picked up at any of the park visitors centers. You can rent bikes at Hillman Ferry and Piney Campgrounds.

Off-Highway Vehicles

There are more than 100 miles of trail for off-highway vehicles (OHVs). OHV permits are available for $15 for one to three days, $30 for seven days, and $60 for an annual pass; passes may be purchased at any Land Between the Lakes visitors center. Call 270/924-2000 in advance to find out if any of the trails are closed due to bad weather or poor conditions.

Fishing and Boating

Land Between the Lakes offers excellent fishing. The best season for fishing is spring, April–June, when fish move to shallow waters to spawn. Crappie, largemouth bass, and a variety of sunfish may be caught at this time.

WESTERN PLAINS

Summer and fall offer good fishing, while winter is fair. A fishing license from the state in which you will be fishing is required; these may be purchased from businesses outside the park. Specific size requirements and open dates may be found at any of the visitors centers.

There are 19 different lake access points where you can put in a boat. Canoe rentals are available at the Energy Lake Campground, which is over the border in Kentucky. Energy Lake is a no-wake lake.

Hunting

Controlled hunting is one of the tools that the Forest Service uses to manage populations of wild animals in Land Between the Lakes. Hunting also draws thousands of visitors each year. The annual spring turkey hunt and fall deer hunts are the most popular.

Specific rules govern each hunt, and in many cases hunters must apply in advance for a permit. Hunters must also have a $20 LBL Hunter Use Permit, as well as the applicable state licenses. For details on hunting regulations, call the park at 270/924-2065.

CAMPING

There are nine campgrounds at Land Between the Lakes. All campgrounds have facilities for tent or trailer camping.

Most campgrounds are open March 1–November 1, although some are open year-round. There's a complicated formula for figuring out the price of campsites, based on which campground it is, the day or the week, and the month of the year. In general costs range $12–13 per night; RV sites range $6–32, depending on whether there is access to electricity, water, and sewer services.

Reservations are accepted for select campsites at Piney, Energy Lake, Hillman Ferry, and Wrangler Campgrounds up to six months in advance. Call the LBL headquarters in Kentucky at 270/924-2000 or visit the website at www.lbl.org to make a reservation.

Piney Campground

Located on the southern tip of Land Between the Lakes, Piney Campground is convenient to visitors arriving from the Tennessee side of the park, and, as a result, can be one of the most crowded campgrounds in LBL. Piney has more than 300 campsites; 281 have electricity; 44 have electricity, water, and sewer; and 59 are primitive tent sites.

There are also nine rustic one-bedroom camping shelters with a ceiling fan, table and chairs, electric outlets, and large porch. Sleeping accommodations are one double bed and a bunk bed. Outside there is a picnic table and fire ring. There are no bathrooms; shelter guests use the same bathhouses as other campers. Camp shelters cost $35–37 per night and sleep up to four people.

Piney's amenities include a camp store, bike rental, archery range, playground, swimming beach, boat ramp, and fishing pier.

Energy Lake Campground

Near the midpoint of Land Between the Lakes, Energy Lake Campground has tent and trailer campsites, electric sites, and group camp facilities. It tends to be less crowded than some of the other campground and has nice lake-side sites, with a swimming area, volleyball, and other kid-friendly activities.

Hillman Ferry Campground

Located near the northern end of Land Between the Lakes, Hillman Ferry has 380 tent and RV campsites. It is nestled on the shores of Kentucky Lake, between Moss Creek and Pisgah Bay.

Electric and nonelectric sites are available. There is a dumping station, bathhouses with showers and flush toilets, drinking water, a camp store, swimming area, coin-operated laundry, and bike rentals.

Boat and Horse Camping

In addition to the campgrounds already listed,

Land Between the Lakes operates five lakeside camping areas that are designed for boaters who want to spend the night. Rushing Creek/Jones Creek is the most developed of these camping areas; it has 40 tent or RV sites and a bathhouse with showers and flush toilets. Other campsites, including Birmingham Ferry/Smith Bay, Cravens Bay, Fenton, and Gatlin Point, have chemical toilets, tent camping sites, and grills.

LBL also has Wrangler's Campground, designed for horseback riders. In addition to tent and RV sites, there are camping shelters and horse stalls. Amenities include a camp store, bathhouses, coin laundry, and playground.

Backcountry Camping

Backcountry camping is allowed year-round in Land Between the Lakes. All you need is a backcountry permit and the right gear to enjoy unlimited choices of campsites along the shoreline or in the woodlands.

FOOD

There are no restaurants in Land Between the Lakes. There are vending machines with snacks and sodas at the Homeplace, Golden Pond Visitor Center, and the Woodlands Nature Station. Picnic facilities abound.

There is a McDonald's at the southern entrance to the park. Dover, five miles east, has a number of fast-food and local eateries. Twenty miles to the west, Paris has dozens of different restaurants.

INFORMATION AND SERVICES

The Forest Service maintains a useful website about Land Between the Lakes at www.lbl.org. You can also call 270/924-2000 to request maps and information sheets. The park headquarters is located at the Golden Pond Visitor Center.

When you arrive, stop at the nearest welcome or visitors center for up-to-date advisories and activity schedules. Each of the welcome centers and the visitors center are open daily 9 A.M.–5 P.M.

The **Land Between the Lakes Association** (800/455-5897, www.friendsoflbl.org) organizes volunteer opportunities and publishes a detailed tour guide to the park, which includes historical and natural anecdotes.

Jackson

The largest city between Nashville and Memphis, Jackson is the center of commerce and business for rural West Tennessee. Every Pringles potato chip in the world is made in Jackson, which also hosts a number of events, including a Division One women's basketball tournament, the Miss Tennessee pageant, and the West Tennessee State Fair.

Jackson owes its existence to the railroads, and the city has preserved this history at a top-notch museum set right next to the railroad tracks. Jackson is also home to a museum dedicated to the life and death of famous railroad engineer Casey Jones, and another that zeroes in on that endearing art form, rockabilly.

SIGHTS

Jackson's city center is about five miles south of I-40, and the roadways between the interstate and downtown are cluttered with strip malls, motels, and traffic. Most of the attractions, with the exception of Casey Jones Village, are downtown on the blocks surrounding the stately courthouse square.

Casey Jones Historic Home and Railroad Museum

In 1980, the home of the legendary railroad engineer was moved from the city of Jackson to Casey Jones Village, a plaza of shops and restaurants just off the interstate north of Jackson.

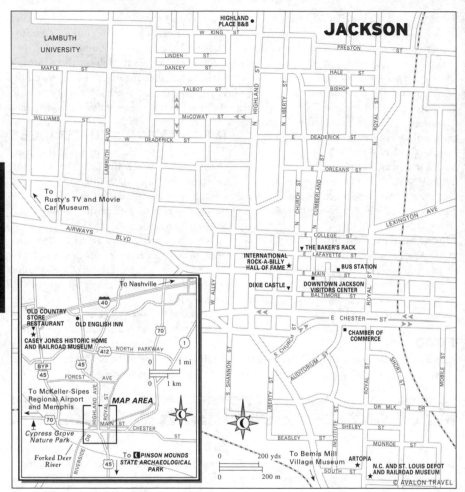

The museum includes Jones's white clapboard home and a replica of the engine that he rode to his death in 1900. The home and engine form the centerpiece of the Casey Jones Historic Home and Railroad Museum (56 Casey Jones Ln., 731/668-1222, www.caseyjones.com, Mon.–Sun. 9 A.M.–5 P.M., adults $6.50, children 6–12 $4.50, children under 6 free), which tells the story of Casey Jones's life and the legend that surrounds him to this day. Exhibits document every detail of the deadly 1900 crash that took his life, but some of the most fascinating parts of the museum deal with the legend of Casey Jones that evolved after his death. There are also elaborate model train sets that you can run for just a few quarters.

N. C. & St. Louis Depot and Railroad Museum

Jackson owes it existence to the railroads that passed through the town, and the N. C. & St. Louis Depot and Railroad Museum

© GARRY THOMPSON

WESTERN PLAINS

The legend of Casey Jones lives on in Jackson.

(582 S. Royal St., 731/425-8223, Mon.–Sat. 10 A.M.–3 P.M., free) documents much of the city's railroad history. Located inside Jackson's oldest railroad station a few blocks south of downtown, the museum walls are covered with photographs and memorabilia of the railroads. There is a large model train in the rear of the station, and outside visitors can explore a dining car and engine.

Over the railroad tracks from the museum is a covered well whose waters once drew thousands of people to Jackson. The **Electro Chalybeate Well** (604 S. Royal St.) was discovered in the late 1800s, and its waters were reputed to cure a host of ailments. In recent years the city of Jackson built the fountain, gazebo, and benches around the well. You can drink the water from a circle of water fountains if you like.

International Rock-a-Billy Hall of Fame

As the city that lays claim to Carl Perkins,

Jackson is home to the International Rock-a-Billy Hall of Fame (105 N. Church St., 731/423-5440, www.rockabilly.org, Mon.–Thurs. 10 A.M.–5 P.M., Fri.–Sat. 10 A.M.–2 P.M., $10). This storefront museum features exhibits about a number of the genre's famous performers. There is also a room of Elvis memorabilia and a performance space for concerts and dancing. A tour with enthusiastic guide Linda McGee costs $10 and is best suited for hardcore rockabilly fans. There are line-dancing lessons Monday and Tuesday beginning at 6 P.M. and live music on Friday night starting at 7 P.M.

Bemis Mill Village Museum

The history of Bemis, a cotton mill town established in 1900, is recorded for the ages at the Bemis Mill Village Museum (2 N. Missouri St., 731/424-0739, www.bemishistory.org, by appointment only, donations encouraged). The museum is housed in the Bemis Auditorium, a large, imposing building constructed in 1922

THE LEGEND OF CASEY JONES

Casey Jones was born John Luther Jones, but he was better known as Casey after his hometown, Cayce, in Kentucky. He started as a telegrapher for the Mobile and Ohio Railroad in Kentucky and worked his way up to be brakeman, fireman, and eventually engineer. Casey had a reputation for running the trains on time, no matter what.

In the early morning hours of April 30, 1900, Jones was running a passenger train from Memphis to Canton, Mississippi, when he crashed into the tail end of a freight train that was blocking a portion of the track near Vaughn, Mississippi. Jones died when his engine, No. 382, collided with the freight train and veered off the tracks. Jones was the only person killed in the accident.

The story of Casey Jones did not end with his death, however. An African American engine wiper, Wallace Saunders, started to sing a song that he composed about the dead engineer, and soon "The Ballad of Casey Jones" was a well-known folk song. The professional songwriting team Sibert and Newton copyrighted the song in 1909, and it became one of the most famous songs in America. Neither the Jones family or Wallace Saunders ever received a penny from its success. The engineer's story also became the inspiration for an eponymous song by the Grateful Dead in 1970.

The story of Casey Jones's life and death was immortalized on television, film, and stage. His widow, Janie Jones, and accident survivor Simeon Webb remained minor celebrities for the rest of their lives.

The story of Casey Jones is told at the Casey Jones Home and Railroad Museum in Jackson.

to be the focal point of community life for the townspeople. The building is an elegant, sophisticated example of Beaux Arts design. It houses exhibits about the Bemis Brothers Bag Company, as well as life in an early-20th-century company town. Additional exhibits, with recently acquired artifacts, are in the works.

Rusty's TV and Movie Car Museum

If you care more about the car than the star, head to Rusty's TV and Movie Car Museum (323 Hollywood Dr., 731/267-5881, www.rustystvandmoviecars.com, Fri.–Sun. 9 A.M.–5 P.M., other days by appointment, $5, kids under five free). This offbeat museum just off I-40 has more than 25 cars that have been used on the big and small screens, as well as other memorabilia. In many cases, these are the real deal—cars from *The Fast and the Furious* and one of many General Lees, not just reproductions.

FESTIVALS AND EVENTS

Jackson hosts three major annual events. The Shannon Street Blues and Heritage Festival

(731/427-7573, www.jacksondowntown.com) brings blues, jazz, and other music to the West Tennessee Farmer's Market in June. The Rock-a-Billy Hall of Fame organizes an **International Rock-a-Billy Festival** (731/427-6262, www.rockabillyhall.org) every August, and the Casey Jones Village puts on an **Old Time Music Fest** (731/668-1223, www.caseyjonesvillage.com) in September.

In addition, every September sees the **West Tennessee State Fair** (731/424-0151), a week of competitions, amusements, performances, and rides at the Jackson Fairgrounds Park.

SHOPPING

Across Royal Street from the N.C. & St. Louis Depot and Railroad Museum is **Artopia** (575 S. Royal St., 731/554-2929, open daily, until 9 P.M. Thurs.–Sat.), a gallery housed in an old hotel. Each old guest room is filled with the work of different artists, and items include paintings, sculpture, fabric, and much more. There is also a salon, coffee shop, and restaurant.

The **Old Medina Winery** (2894 Old Medina Rd., 731/256-1400, www.oldmedinawineclub.

com, Mon.–Sat. 9 A.M.–6 P.M., Sun. noon–5 P.M.) has two rooms and a pleasant outdoor patio where you can taste Tennessee-made wine and other food products. Old Medina Winery is the home of Lauderdale Cellars, a winery once located in Ripley.

SPORTS AND RECREATION
Parks
A few miles southwest of downtown Jackson is **Cypress Grove Nature Park** (Hwy. 70 W., 731/425-8316), a pleasant park with boardwalks, picnic facilities, walking paths, and an observation tower.

Spectator Sports
The **Jackson Generals** (4 Fun Pl., 731/988-5299, www.jacksongeneralsbaseball.com, $6–10) play in Pringles Field just off I-40 in Jackson. A farm team for the Seattle Mariners, the Generals put on a good show for fans during their season April–October.

ACCOMMODATIONS
For the most luxurious accommodations in Jackson, if not the region, choose ◖**Highland Place Bed & Breakfast** (519 N. Highland Ave., 731/427-1472, www.highlandplace.com, $119.50–175). Set in a stately redbrick historic home along central Highland Avenue, a five-minute drive from downtown, the inn has four rooms ranging from a three-room suite to single rooms. Each room has a private bath, cable television, and wireless Internet access. The rooms are decorated with antique and modern handmade furniture. All guests have the run of the numerous public rooms, including a living room, library, and breakfast room. It sure beats a standard hotel room. Pets are not permitted.

The **Old English Inn** (2267 N. Highland Ave., 731/668-1571, www.oldenglishinn.com, $60–75) is a mile or so south of the interstate. Its 103 rooms include suites and wheelchair-accessible rooms and wireless Internet access.

The lobby and common areas enjoy distinctive flair, including stained glass and a fireplace, and all the rooms are nicely furnished with dark wood. The Old English Inn calls itself a Christian hotel, although guests of all religious affiliations are welcome.

FOOD
◖**Dixie Castle** (215 E. Baltimore, 731/423-3359, Mon.–Fri. 10:30 A.M.–2 P.M., Mon.–Sat. 5–9 P.M., $6–14) attracts a large local crowd for lunch and dinner. This diner-style restaurant serves plate-lunch specials, burgers, and sandwiches. The food is home-style, with large portions. You'll be hard-pressed to find a table at the peak of the lunch rush. At dinner, they offer steaks, pork chops, and chicken dinners. They do a brisk takeout trade as well, and the servers are some of the friendliest in town.

Also downtown, **The Baker's Rack** (203 E. Lafayette, 731/424-6163, Mon.–Thurs. 7 A.M.–5 P.M., Fri. 7 A.M.–3 P.M., $3–10) serves a diverse menu of hot and cold sandwiches, baked potatoes, plate lunches, and a famous strawberry salads. They also make decadent desserts: Try the red velvet cake or "better than sex" cake. For breakfast, choose from biscuits, eggs on toast, oatmeal, French toast, or a generous breakfast platter with all the fixings.

In Casey Jones Village off I-40, the **Old Country Store Restaurant** (56 Casey Jones Ln., 731/668-1223, www.caseyjones.com, daily 6:30 A.M.–9 P.M., $7–12) serves specials such as country ham, smothered chicken, and fried catfish, plus burgers and barbecue. The breakfast bar is a popular choice for those with a big appetite. They also have a fruit bar and the usual breakfast choices of eggs, biscuits, pancakes, and omelets.

One of the better restaurants in town is **Candela** (575 S. Royal St., 731/554-3663, Tues.–Sat. 11 A.M.–2 P.M., Thurs.–Sat. 5–9 P.M., $7–17). Located in Artopia, Candela takes a creative approach to dining, and the results are usually excellent. Lunch features tortellini pasta, seared salmon, shrimp salad, and a variety of sandwiches. For dinner try the stuffed mushrooms, lobster ravioli, or fish of the day.

The **West Tennessee Farmer's Market** (91 New Market St., 731/425-8310) takes place under shelters in downtown Jackson Tuesday–Saturday 6 A.M.–5 P.M.

INFORMATION AND SERVICES

Maps and general information on Jackson can be found at the **Jackson Downtown Development Corporation** (314 E. Main St., 731/427-7573, www.downtownjackson.com) or the **Jackson Area Chamber of Commerce** (197 Auditorium St., 731/423-2200, www.jacksontn.com).

The **Jackson-Madison County Library** (433 E. Lafayette St., 731/425-8600, www.jmcl.tn.org) is one of the nicest public libraries in West Tennessee.

GETTING THERE AND AROUND

Jackson is located about midway between Nashville and Memphis along I-40, and most people drive here. The regional **McKellar-Sipes Airport** (MKL, www.mckellarsipes.com) has on-and-off commercial air service, subject to the ups and downs of the airline industry. Check with airport officials to find out if commercial service is available.

Photographers have been known to make a detour to photograph the iconic **Jackson Main Street Greyhound bus terminal** (407 E. Main St., 731/427-1573), with its retro art deco style. The station is convenient to several attractions and restaurants but not close to any hotels. There is daily service to Memphis and Nashville; Paducah, Kentucky; and Jackson, Mississippi.

While trains still travel on Jackson's famous tracks, there is no passenger service to or from the city.

◖ PINSON MOUNDS STATE ARCHAEOLOGICAL PARK

One of the largest complexes of mounds ever built by Woodland Indians is found 10 miles south of Jackson. Pinson Mounds (460 Ozier Rd., 731/988-5614, museum open Mon.–Sat. 8 A.M.–4:30 P.M. and Sun. 1–5 P.M., remainder of park open until dusk, free), now a state park, is a group of at least 17 mounds believed to have been built beginning around 50 B.C. The mounds were discovered in 1820 by Joel Pinson, part of a surveying team that was mapping new territory bought from the Chickasaw Indians in 1818. Early archaeological digs were carried out in the late 1800s, but it was not until 1961 that the first major investigation of the site was completed (by scientists from the University of Tennessee).

Despite continuing archaeological study on the site, many mysteries remain. Among them is the significance of the design and arrangement of the mounds and why the mound builders abandoned the site around A.D. 500. Some scientists believe that the mounds were arranged as markers for the summer and winter solstices.

Visitors to Pinson Mounds begin within a 4,500-square-foot mound replica, which houses a museum and bookstore. The museum is dedicated to telling the story of what is known about the mysterious mounds and the people who built them. The mounds themselves are spread out along six miles of hiking trails that meander through the archaeological park. Many of the trails are across open fields, and walking can be hot during the summer months. A bike is an ideal way to get around, but you need to bring your own since there is no rental facility.

Festivals and Events

Archaeofest is a family-friendly festival celebrating Native American culture. It takes place every September and includes artistic demonstrations, food and craft vendors, storytelling, flintknapping, and more. Contact the park office for more information.

Camping

Pinson Mounds has a **group camp facility** that

© JAKE WARREN

WESTERN PLAINS

Pinson Mounds State Archaeological Park

can accommodate up to 32 people. There is also a day-use picnic area.

BETHEL SPRINGS

About 30 miles south of Jackson on Highway 45, near the community of Bethel Springs, is **Ada's Unusual Country Store** (9653 Hwy. 45, 731/934-9310, www.adascountrystore.com, Mon.–Sat. 8 A.M.–5 P.M.), which is unusual indeed. The shelves are packed with organic and natural food items, including grains, flour, pastas, and snacks. You can buy fresh local eggs, honey, and milk; Amish cheese and cookbooks; and homemade breads and sweets. For a meal on the go, you can get cold drinks, fresh-made sandwiches, and ice cream.

South Along the Tennessee

The Tennessee River flows by Clifton and southward to the state line. It passes Tennessee's most lovely river town, Savannah, and the site of the state's bloodiest Civil War battle, Shiloh.

CLIFTON

Pulitzer Prize–winning author T. S. Stribling was born in the river town of Clifton in 1881. His works include the 1,479-page trilogy *The Forge, The Store,* and *Unfinished Cathedral,* which portray the history of a Florence, Alabama, family from the Civil War to the 1920s. He won the Pulitzer Prize for fiction in 1933 for *The Store.* Stribling was one of the first Southern writers to speak out about issues of social conscience. He also wrote formulaic adventure novels and detective stories. His autobiography, *Laughing Stock,* was published posthumously in 1969.

A museum dedicated to Stribling and his

THE DEATH OF GENERAL JOHNSON

Gen. Albert Sidney Johnston, the Confederate commander of the western department of the army, was concentrating all available forces at Corinth, Mississippi, in early April 1862. His objective was to launch an offensive against the Union army under the command of Gen. Ulysses S. Grant at Pittsburg Landing, Tennessee, before Union reinforcements arrived.

On April 3, Johnston ordered his troops to march north, toward the engagement. Heavy rains and bad roads slowed their progress, and the Southern troops lost a day on their journey, a delay that would prove significant in the coming days.

The Confederates arrived at their camp south of Pittsburg Landing on the late afternoon of April 5, and Johnston decided to delay the attack until morning. During the evening, he and his second-in-command, P.G.T. Beauregard, disagreed about the coming fight; Beauregard argued against attack, saying that the Union army would not be surprised. But Johnston would not be deterred. He wanted to attack the Union forces before reinforcements from Nashville arrived.

As it turned out, the Union army was surprised by the Confederate attack in the early morning hours of April 6. Soldiers described the disorder and chaos of the Union camps as word was quickly spread about the advancing fighters. General Grant, who was breakfasting at the **Cherry Mansion** in Savannah, a few miles north of Shiloh, was surprised by the sound of gunfire and rushed to the scene.

General Johnston would not live to see the outcome of the battle that he orchestrated. Midafternoon on the first day of fighting, just before the Confederates reached the high-water mark of their efforts, Johnston was struck by a minié ball in the leg. His companions did not realize at first the seriousness of his injury, and neither did Johnston. But at 2:45 P.M. on April 6, the Confederate general died, passing command to Beauregard.

Johnston was the highest-ranking officer on either side of the Civil War to be killed in active duty.

---

life's work is located in a building that shares space with the Clifton Public Library. This 1924 Craftsman bungalow is where Stribling and his wife, Lou Ella, lived in their retirement. The museum includes Stribling's typewriter, Bible, papers, and other personal articles. The **T. S. Stribling Museum** (300 E. Water St., 931/676-3678, Tues.–Fri. 11:30 A.M.–6:30 P.M., free) is operated by the City of Clifton. The museum/library has an ongoing book sale to raise funds for its work.

SAVANNAH

A quaint town on the eastern bank of the Tennessee River, Savannah has historic homes, a good museum, and the greatest selection of restaurants and accommodations in this part of the state. You can guess what is on the menu as it is known as the Catfish Capital of the World.

In its early life, the town was Rudd's Ferry,

named for James Rudd, who operated a ferry across the river. The ferry was taken over by David Robinson, whose wife is said to have renamed the town Savannah after her hometown in Georgia. In 1830, Savannah became the seat of Hardin County and soon developed a reputation as a wealthy, cultured town.

Tennessee River Museum

Savannah is a river town, and the mighty Tennessee River is one of its main attractions. The Tennessee River Museum (507 Main St., 731/925-2364, Mon.–Sat. 9 A.M.–5 P.M., Sun. 1–5 P.M., adults $3, kids free) documents the history of the region and the river. Exhibits detail the prehistoric peoples of the region and include an original red stone effigy pipe found inside one of the Shiloh Indian Mounds a few miles south. There are also exhibits on Shiloh and the river during the Civil War, riverboats, and the economic uses of the river, including pearl farming and mussels. One of the most interesting exhibits features receipts issued by Savannah merchants to the U.S. Army party that was escorting 2,500 Cherokee Indians down the river on the Trail of Tears in 1838.

The museum is an informative first stop for visitors to the area, and staff can provide information about other area attractions. Through a partnership with Shiloh National Military Park, guests who show their Shiloh parking pass receive free entry to the museum.

Historic Homes

David Robinson built the **Cherry Mansion** (265 W. Main St.) on the riverbank, on top of what historians believe was an Indian mound. Robinson gave the mansion to his daughter when she married William H. Cherry, for whom it was named. The house, which is closed to the public, is where U.S. general Ulysses S. Grant stayed during the days leading up to the Battle of Shiloh. Cherry was a noted Union sympathizer, and the mansion remained a Union headquarters and field hospital during the war. Although the house is privately owned, visitors are welcome to stop and look. There is a river overlook next door.

Savannah was settled between 1830 and 1850, but many of the old houses were damaged or destroyed during the Civil War. However, beautiful homes were rebuilt, and many of these remain in the leafy residential area just north of Savannah's Main Street. The homes are elegant examples of fine homes of the late 19th century.

Pick up a guide to the **Savannah Walking Tour** at the Tennessee River Museum (507 Main St., 731/925-2364).

Haley Memorial

Savannah is where the paternal grandparents of Pulitzer Prize–winning author Alex Haley are buried. Alex Haley Sr. operated Rudd's Ferry, and his wife, Queen Haley, worked in the Cherry Mansion for the Cherry family. Haley's novel *Queen* was inspired by his grandmother's life. The couple's shared tombstone is located in the Savannah Cemetery. To find the Haley Memorial, take Cherry Street from downtown Savannah and over a small bridge and enter the cemetery. Take the first gravel road to your right, and then walk over the hill, taking a right at the Y. The Haleys, as well as Alex Haley Sr.'s first wife, Tennie, share a gravestone.

Accommodations

You can get a clean, comfortable bed at the **Savannah Lodge** (585 Pickwick St., 731/925-8586, www.savannahlodge.net, $35–55), a motel that boasts the basics for its guests, as well as amenities like a swimming pool. Pets are allowed. Several national chains also have locations in Savannah.

Food

Worleybird Café (990 Pickwick St., 731/926-4882, Mon.–Sat. 5 A.M.–9 P.M., Sun. 5 A.M.–2 P.M., $5–12) is a popular choice for Savannah's locals. Named for beloved son of the soil, country musician Daron Worley, the café serves sandwiches, Cajun catfish, steaks, chicken cordon bleu, and salads, plus eggs, biscuits, and pancakes in the morning.

Another good choice for home-style cooking in Savannah is **Toll House Restaurant** (610 Wayne Rd., 731/925-5128, Mon.–Sat. 5 A.M.–8 P.M., Sun. 6 A.M.–2 P.M., $4–9), whose home fries and eggs draw a crowd in the morning. At lunch and dinner, there is an ample buffet with traditional favorites like macaroni and cheese, fried catfish, and beef tips.

For a more refined dining experience, go to the **Uptown Bistro** (390 Main St., 731/926-1911, Mon.–Sat. 11 A.M.–8 P.M., $12–19), a wine bar and bistro with seafood, pasta, and steak, as well as superb desserts, such as the Oreo cake,

WESTERN PLAINS

Information

Stop at the **Tennessee River Museum** (507 Main St., 731/925-2364, Mon.–Sat. 9 A.M.–5 P.M., Sun. 1–5 P.M.) to pick up maps and other information about Savannah.

You can also contact the **Hardin County Convention and Visitors Bureau** (731/925-8181, www.tourhardincounty.org) for information. For information on the Savannah Historic District, visit www.savannahmainstreet.org.

◖ SHILOH NATIONAL MILITARY PARK

The Shiloh National Military Park (1055 Pittsburg Landing Rd., 731/689-5696, daily 8 A.M.–5 P.M., closed Christmas Day, free) is set along the western shore of the Tennessee River about eight miles south of Crump. The Battle of Shiloh is one of the most remembered of the Civil War; it was the battle that demonstrated to both North and South that the war would be a longer and harder fight than either had imagined. Shiloh today is a landscape of alternating open fields and wooded forest, populated by hundreds of monuments to soldiers who fought and died at Shiloh on April 6–7, 1862. The peacefulness of the present brings into even greater focus the violence of the battle that took place here almost 150 years ago and claimed nearly 24,000 casualties.

You can drive around the battlefield, but some of the most important sites are a short walk from the road. At the visitors center there is a small museum where you can watch a film, *Shiloh-Fiery Trial,* about the battle.

Sights within the park include the peach orchard, now being regrown, where soldiers described the peach blossoms falling like snow on the dead and injured; the "bloody pond," where injured men crawled for water and, in some cases, to die; and the Hornet's Nest, the site of some of the most furious fighting.

The 10-acre **Shiloh National Cemetery** is located next to the visitors center. Two-thirds of the 3,695 bodies interred here are unidentified. Most are Union soldiers killed at Shiloh, but there are others from nearby battles, the Spanish-American War, both World Wars, and the Revolutionary War. The Confederate dead were buried in five trenches around the battlefield and remain there today.

Nearly 800 years before the Civil War, the riverbank near present-day Shiloh was home to a mound-building Mississippian Indian community. The **Shiloh Indian Mounds** that they left behind sit along the west bluff of the riverbank and are one of the largest mound groups in the country. A remarkable effigy pipe was discovered here in the 1890s and is on display at the Tennessee River Museum in Savannah. The mounds are accessible on foot from two points in the park.

Practicalities

A printed guide and map to the battlefield is available at the visitors center, and it takes about an hour to follow its path. For a more detailed examination, you can buy an audio tour from the park bookstore for $12. This tour takes about two hours to complete and includes narratives by soldiers, historians, and civilians.

The bookstore is one of the best in the area and has an extensive collection of books on the Civil War, Tennessee, Native Americans, and African American history.

There are snack and drink vending machines at the visitors center and a picnic area in the park. The closest restaurants are in Shiloh, Savannah, and Counce. For accommodations, look in Savannah.

With its miles of flat roads and restrained traffic, Shiloh is a good place to bicycle. There are no rental facilities nearby, however, so bring your own wheels.

SHILOH

There is not much to the modern town of Shiloh, except a few souvenir shops and one excellent catfish restaurant that has been serving visitors since 1938. **C World Famous Hagy's Catfish Restaurant** (off Hwy. 22, 731/689-3327, Tues.–Sat. 11 A.M.–10 P.M., Sun. noon–9 P.M., $9–15) is set off by itself in a beautiful clearing overlooking the Tennessee River. You can stretch your legs with a walk down to the water's edge. Hagy's menu has fried and grilled catfish, plus other favorites like chicken and steak. But choose the catfish, which is nicely seasoned and expertly fried. It comes with hush puppies and coleslaw. This will be a meal to remember.

Find Hagy's by looking for the large sign for the turnoff along Highway 22 on the northern side of Shiloh National Military Park.

PICKWICK LANDING STATE PARK

Pickwick Landing was a riverboat stop from the 1840s until the 1930s, when Pickwick Dam was built and the lake formed. Pickwick Lake was created in December 1937 when the Tennessee Valley Authority dammed the Tennessee and flooded farmland in the valley. The lake was dedicated in 1940, and a crowd of 30,000 people attended the services on the southern earth dam. Today it attracts vacationers from around the region who enjoy the laid-back atmosphere and top-flight bass fishing.

The lake lies in Tennessee, Alabama, and Mississippi and is one of the premier spots for recreation in the area. Boating, fishing, and swimming are especially popular. There are several nearby golf courses and opportunities to camp, hunt, and hike.

Pickwick Landing State Park (Hwy. 57, 731/689-3129) is one of Tennessee's resort parks, with a modern hotel, conference center, golf course, and marina.

Hiking

There is an easy three-mile hiking trail that meanders along the lakeshore.

Golf

The Pickwick Landing State Park golf course is a par 72 champion's 18-hole course. The pro shop rents clubs and carts, and sells golf accessories. Call 731/689-3149 to reserve a tee time. Greens fees range $13–22, depending on the season and day of the week.

Boating

Pleasure riding, sailing, waterskiing, paddling, and fishing are all popular activities on Pickwick Lake. There are three public boat-launch ramps at Pickwick Landing State Park, and marine fuel and other boating items are available from the park marina.

You can rent a pontoon boat from **Pickwick Boat Rentals** (731/689-5359, www.pickwickboatrentalsinc.com) starting at $225.

Fishing

Fishing on Pickwick Lake is best in the spring and fall. Conditions here include shallow stump flats, well-defined channels, active feeder creeks, steeply falling bluffs, rocky ledges, and long grass beds.

Pickwick Outdoors, Inc. (877/214-4924, www.pickwickoutdoors.com) organizes fishing vacations for groups. For a fishing guide, contact **Big Orange Guide Service** (731/689-3074) or **Rick Matlock's Guide Service** (731/689-5382).

Swimming

Pickwick Landing State Park has three swimming beaches. Circle Beach and Sandy Beach are in the day-use area; Bruton Beach is in the primitive area, which is located across the lake from the main park.

Accommodations

C Pickwick Landing State Resort Park (Hwy. 57, 731/689-3135, rooms $70–80, cabins $100–125, campsites under $20) is the home of one of Tennessee's newest state park inns and conference centers. The modern hotel has 119 rooms, each with a balcony looking out over the lake and the dam. Cabins and campsites are also available. There is a pool and a 135-seat restaurant at the inn, which serves three meals a day, with an emphasis on Southern cuisine.

COUNCE

This humble town is the western gateway to Pickwick Lake. It is also a hub in the region's hardwood timber industry, and you will smell the distinctive scent of the local paper plant at certain times of the day.

Accommodations

If you're planning to stay more than a few days at Pickwick Lake, consider renting a cabin. **Pickwick Lake Cabin Rentals** (11268 Hwy. 57, 731/689-0400, www.pickwick-lakecabins.com) represents the owners of two dozen one-, two-, and three-bedroom cabins on and around the lake. Lakefront cabins will cost $300–400 per night, water-view cabins will cost $175–300, and cabins off the water cost $100–200. Many lakefront cabins come with a private dock and can accommodate large groups.

Food

Don't be mistaken by the rustic appearance of the ☾**Broken Spoke** (7405 Hwy. 57, 731/689-3800, www.brokenspokerestaurant.com, Wed.–Sat. 11 A.M.–10 P.M., $12–27). This is the most upscale and creative dining around Pickwick Lake. The decor is comfortably eclectic but not trashy, and there is tasteful live music several nights a week. The menu is remarkably diverse: You can choose from catfish, po'boys, and burgers, or steaks, pork chops, and chicken cooked expertly on the grill. There are also salads, pasta, and daily specials. Come with an appetite—there are no small portions. The adjacent bar is a popular hangout spot any night of the week, and **Mombie's Pizza** (731/689-8646, Tues.–Sat. 11 A.M.–10 P.M., $9–15), right next door, serves the best pizza, burgers, and wings in Pickwick. You will find the Broken Spoke and Mombie's one mile west of the dam on Highway 57.

Southwestern Tennessee

The southernmost stretch of West Tennessee spans Adamsville in the east to La Grange in the west. Here you'll find a museum dedicated to sheriff Buford Pusser, another dedicated to bird dogs, and one of the loveliest small towns in all of Tennessee.

Information

Seven Tennessee counties have come together to form the **Tourism Association of Southwest Tennessee** (866/261-7534, www.tast.tn.org), which produces brochures and stocks information stands at interstate rest stops and other crossroads. Their guide to the region has helpful listings and a map.

ADAMSVILLE

Famed McNairy County sheriff Buford Pusser worked in Selmer, the McNairy County seat, but he lived in Adamsville, a small town a few miles down Highway 45. Fans of Pusser and the movies that his legacy inspired, starting with the 1973 film *Walking Tall*, can learn more about his life at the **Sheriff Buford Pusser Home and Museum** (342 Pusser St., 731/632-4080, www.bufordpussermuseum.com, Mon.–Fri. 11 A.M.–5 P.M., Sat. 9 A.M.–5 P.M., Sun. 1–5 P.M., $5). Pusser earned a reputation as a no-nonsense lawman during his eight-year career as sheriff. He was famous for raiding moonshine stills and for fighting criminals with little regard for his own personal safety. In 1967 his wife, Pauline, was killed in an ambush when she was riding along with him in his patrol car. Seven years later, Pusser was killed in a single-car accident while he was driving home from the McNairy County Fair in Selmer. When Pusser died, hundreds of people came to his funeral. Elvis Presley visited the family privately to offer his condolences.

The home and museum features a video about Pusser's life, family memorabilia, and two cars that Pusser used.

Shiloh Golf Course and Restaurant (2915 Caney Branch Rd., 731/632-0678) in Adamsville is a par 71 course and driving range.

SELMER

In Selmer, the McNairy County seat, you can see the courthouse where Buford Pusser worked, and where Mary Winkler was put on trial in 2007 for the murder of her preacher husband, Matthew Winkler.

This quiet town is also home to the **McNairy County Historical Museum** (114 N. 3rd St., 731/646-0018, Sat. 10 A.M.–4 P.M., Sun. 1–4 P.M., free), nestled in the old Ritz theater. Exhibits are dedicated to schools, the Civil War, churches, the healing arts, business, and agriculture.

Selmer is also famous for its slugburgers, deep-fried grain burgers that are sold at lunch counters around town.

LA GRANGE

La Grange, a mere speck of civilization 50 miles east of Memphis, feels like the town that time forgot. Old homes—some elegant, some ramshackle—line narrow drives. The post office, town office, and an old-fashioned country store constitute the business district.

La Grange, named in honor of the Marquis de Lafayette's ancestral home in France, seemed destined for great things when it was chartered in 1829. Its population quickly swelled to more than 3,000. The first Episcopal church

in West Tennessee was founded here, and in 1835 stockholders chartered the La Grange & Memphis Railway. The plans for a railroad faltered, however, and La Grange suffered from Union occupation during most of the Civil War. A tornado destroyed part of the town in 1900, and La Grange lost its telegraph station and express mail delivery to nearby Grand Junction. Hopes for La Grange to grow into a city dwindled.

Despite its size, La Grange was and is known for a special refinement and pursuit of the arts and education. In 1855, the La Grange Female College and the La Grange Synodical College for Men were chartered. The town's local newspapers, *The Monitor* and, later, the *Spirit of the Age*, were respected in the region. During the Civil War, La Grange native Lucy Pickens was depicted on the face of the Confederate $1 note and three different $100 notes. Pickens, whose childhood home at 290 Pine Street is still standing, was known as the Queen of the Confederacy.

Sights

In 1998, La Grange dedicated a 2.5-ton bronze and limestone monument to the nearby Wolf River. The **Wolf River Monument,** located near the post office and fire department, was rendered in the shape of a wolf's head and was created by Memphis sculptor Roy Tamboli.

Unfortunately, since the closure in 2007 of Cogbill's Store and Museum, there is not much to do here except look. If you come by on Saturday morning, stop at the La Grange General Store, which is part of the **La Grange Inn** (240 Pine St., 901/878-1000). Both are open by appointment. The town office is open weekday mornings.

Despite the dearth of outright attractions, La Grange, also called La Belle Village, delivers an experience unlike any other town in this part of Tennessee. Its lovingly preserved antebellum homes, rural landscape, and charming people are unique and worth seeing.

WESTERN PLAINS

Ghost River State Natural Area

The Ghost River is a 14-mile section of the Wolf River that meanders through bottom-land forest, cypress-tupelo swamps, and open marshes. The river got its name from the loss of river current as the water flows through marshes and swamps.

About a three-mile drive south of La Grange you can hike or canoe in the Ghost River State Natural Area. To find the 600-foot boardwalk and hiking trail, drive south from La Grange on Yager Road, and then turn west on Beasley Road. The parking area is about 1.5 miles down the road. There is another parking area and a place to put in a canoe along Yager Road, and a marked canoe path so you don't get lost in the swamp. There is another parking area at the canoe take-out on Bateman Road. Grab a map from the La Grange town office or from the State of Tennessee website (www.state.tn.us).

Information

La Grange City Hall (20 Main St., 901/878-1246, Mon.–Fri. 8 A.M.–noon) is the best source of information about the town. They can provide you with a large fold-out map of the town's historic homes.

GRAND JUNCTION

A few miles east of La Grange on Highway 57 is the **National Bird Dog Museum** (5050 Hwy. 57 W., 731/764-2058, Tues.–Fri. 10 A.M.–2 P.M., Sat. 10 A.M.–4 P.M., Sun. 1–4 P.M., free). The collection includes paintings and photographs of champion sporting dogs, plus lots of taxidermy. There's a gift shop for souvenirs for the dog lover in your life. The National Field Trials take place just down the road at the Ames Plantation.

CHICKASAW STATE PARK

Named for the Indians who once lived and hunted in this part of Tennessee, Chickasaw State Park (20 Cabin Ln., Henderson, 731/989-5141, www.tn.gov/environment/parks/Chickasaw, daily 6 A.M.–10 P.M.) encompasses Lake Placid and a golf course. The 14,400-acre park lies midway between Jackson and Bolivar. There are more than four miles of roads for hiking or biking, plus tennis courts, an archery range, horseback riding, campsites, and a 40-room inn. Rowboats and pedal boats are available for rental here, or you can bring your own kayak or paddleboard. A 100-seat restaurant serves Southern specialties.

Bear Trace at Chickasaw (9555 State Rte. 100, 731/989-4700, www.beartrace.com) is par 72 Jack Nicklaus golf course with natural beauty and challenging holes.

BIG HILL POND STATE PARK

Big Hill Pond was created in 1853 when dirt was removed from a borrow pit to build a levee across the Tuscumbia and Cypress Creek bottoms for the Memphis to Charleston Railroad. Over the years, a grove of cypress trees have grown in and around the 35-acre pond.

The centerpiece of the state park (11701 Hwy. 57, 731/645-7967) is the boardwalk through the scenic swamp and the observation tower, which provides views of the swamp and lake. There are 30 miles of hiking trails, 14 miles of horseback riding and mountain bike trails, a campground with 30 sites, a picnic area, and opportunities to fish and hunt.

There's no backcountry camping allowed here, but there are four camp shelters.

NASHVILLE

Nashville is the home of America's music. This city of more than 630,000 on the banks of the Cumberland River is where tomorrow's hits are written, performed, and recorded, and where you can hear them performed on the stage of the longest-running live radio variety show, the Grand Ole Opry.

There is a song in the air all around the city—in the honky-tonks along lower Broadway, on the streets of downtown Nashville, in the studio along Music Row, and in Music Valley, modern home of the Opry. During the annual Country Music Association (CMA) Festival in June, the whole city is alive with the foot-tapping rhythm of country music. But locals like Jack White, Robert Plant, and the Kings of Leon have done their part to make Music City's sound more than just twang.

Nashville is also the city where performers and songwriters come to make it in the music business. Listening rooms and nightclubs all over the city are the beneficiaries of this abundance of hopeful talent, and their creativity and energy seeps into almost everything in this city.

It is wrong to think that music, country or otherwise, is all there is to Nashville. After the Civil War and Reconstruction, Nashville became known as the Athens of the South because it was a center for education and the arts. Still today, Nashville offers visitors much more than a night at the Opry. Art buffs love the Frist Center for Visual Arts and Cheekwood

HIGHLIGHTS

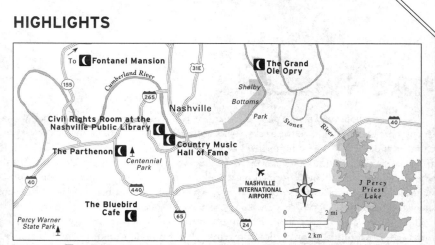

LOOK FOR ◖ TO FIND RECOMMENDED SIGHTS, ACTIVITIES, DINING, AND LODGING.

◖ Country Music Hall of Fame: Pay homage to the kings and queens of country music while you trace its evolution from old-time mountain music to today's megahits (page 125).

◖ Civil Rights Room at the Nashville Public Library: The public library houses the best exhibit about the historic Nashville sit-ins of 1960 and their role in the U.S. civil rights movement (page 131).

◖ The Parthenon: First built in 1897 to mark the 100th anniversary of the state of Tennessee, this life-size replica of the Greek Parthenon, complete with a statue of Athena, is as beautiful as it is unusual (page 134).

◖ Fontanel Mansion: Music and nature come together at the former home of Barbara Mandrell, now a museum and music venue with acres of hiking trails (page 149).

◖ The Grand Ole Opry: The live radio variety show that's been on the air for more than 80 years is still the best place to be entertained in Music City. Neighboring Gaylord Opryland Resort offers a vacation unto its own (page 151).

◖ The Bluebird Cafe: The quintessential Nashville listening room hosts intimate music sessions with songwriters every night of the week (page 154).

Botanic Garden and Museum of Art. The Nashville Symphony Orchestra plays in the elegant, acclaimed, and renovated Schermerhorn Center downtown.

Come to watch the NFL's Tennessee Titans play football, or to play golf at one of the award-winning courses nearby. Admire the Parthenon in Centennial Park, or drive to the southern outskirts of the city for a hike at Radnor Lake State Natural Area.

For a city that is populated by so many

transplants (there's often a double take when one meets an actual native Nashvillian, with all the relocated musicians, university students, and health care executives in town), Nashville has a strong sense of community. This was never as evident as it was in May 2010 after the Cumberland River crested more than 12 feet above its flood stage. Downtown, Music Valley, and other parts of the city were underwater, causing an eventual $2 billion in damage. Major sights, including the Gaylord

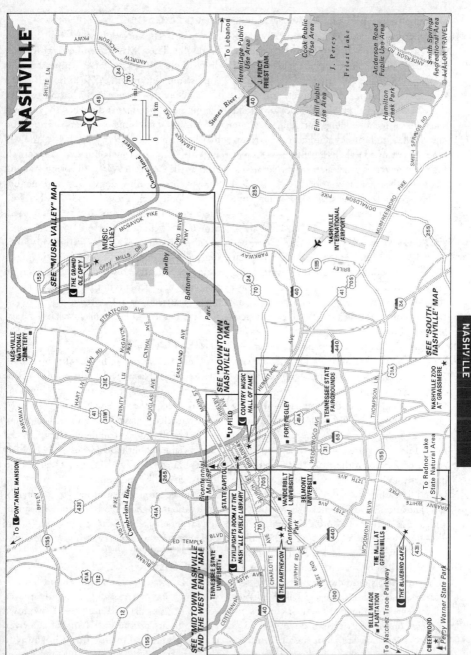

NASHVILLE

SEE "MUSIC VALLEY" MAP

THE GRAND OLE OPRY

SEE "DOWNTOWN NASHVILLE" MAP

COUNTRY MUSIC HALL OF FAME

SEE "MIDTOWN NASHVILLE AND THE WEST END" MAP

SEE "SOUTH NASHVILLE" MAP

To CBELLE MEADE MANSION

NASHVILLE NATIONAL CEMETERY

Bicentennial Mall SP

STATE CAPITOL

CIVIL RIGHTS ROOM AT THE NASHVILLE PUBLIC LIBRARY

THE PARTHENON

LP FIELD

Tennessee State University

FORT NEGLEY

Vanderbilt University

BELMONT UNIVERSITY

Centennial Park

BELLE MEADE PLANTATION

THE MALL AT GREEN HILLS

THE BLUEBIRD CAFE

NASHVILLE ZOO AT GRASSMERE

Tennessee State Fairgrounds

CREEKWOOD

Percy Warner State Park

To Radnor Lake State Natural Area

To Natchez Trace Parkway

NASHVILLE INTERNATIONAL AIRPORT

To Lebanon

Hermitage Public Use Area

J PERCY PRIEST DAM

Cook Public Use Area

J. Percy Priest Lake

Elm Hill Public Use Area

Anderson Road Public Use Area

Smith Springs Recreational Area

Hamilton Creek Park

To AVALON TRAVEL

Cumberland River

Stones River

MUSIC VALLEY

Shelby Bottoms

Shelby Park

N

0   1 mi
0   1 km

Opryland Resort, the Grand Ole Opry, and the Schermerhorn Center were temporarily shuttered. But folks pitched in, as is fitting in a place called the Volunteer State, and most of the public damage was repaired. Some sights are even better than they were preflood.

Downtown is dominated by tall office towers and stately government buildings, including the state capitol. Meat-and-three restaurants serve irresistible Southern-style meals, East Nashville welcomes award-winning chefs, while eateries along Nolensville Pike reflect the ethnic diversity of the city.

Nashville is a city that strikes many notes but sings in perfect harmony.

PLANNING YOUR TIME

Nashville is within a one day's drive for much of the U.S. population, and as a result it is a draw for weekend getaways. In just two days you can see a few of the city's attractions and catch a show at the Grand Ole Opry. Musical pilgrims, history enthusiasts, and outdoors enthusiasts should plan to spend more time in Music City. Even the most disciplined explorers will find themselves happily occupied if they choose to stay a full week.

Downtown is a good home base for many visitors. Hotels here are within walking distance of many attractions, restaurants, and nightclubs. They are also the most expensive accommodations in the city. Visitors who are primarily interested in seeing a show at the Grand Ole Opry or shopping at Opry Mills can shack up in Music Valley, where there is a wide cross-section of affordable hotel rooms, as well as the luxury of the Opryland Resort.

Visitors with a car can opt for accommodation outside of the city center. There are affordable hotels in midtown and smaller bed-and-breakfasts in Hillsboro and East Nashville. All these neighborhoods have their charms but are less tourist centric than downtown and Music Valley. The city's lone hostel is in midtown and is a good choice for budget travelers.

When to Go

Summer is the most popular time to visit Nashville. The CMA Music Festival in June draws thousands to the city. Temperatures in August top out around 90°F, although it can feel much hotter, thanks to the humidity and a thermometer that doesn't dip when the sun sets.

Spring and fall bring mild temperatures and may be the best time to visit Nashville. You will avoid the largest crowds but can still sample all that the city has to offer. In spring you will enjoy sights of tulips, dogwoods, and magnolias in bloom. Beginning in mid-October, foliage around the city starts to turn blazing red, brown, and yellow.

In winter, temperatures range 30–50°F. During November and December, holiday concerts and decorations liven up the city. Many attractions cut back hours during winter, and some outdoor attractions are closed altogether, particularly in the post-Christmas slack of January.

ORIENTATION

For a city of its size, Nashville takes up a lot of space. In fact, Nashville has the second-largest footprint of any major American city. But don't picture a scene of concrete: Nashville is a leafy, suburban city. Outside downtown is a patchwork of traffic lights, strip malls, and tree-lined residential neighborhoods, several of which are incorporated towns with their own elected officials, city halls, and police.

Nashville's attractions are spread out among the city's various neighborhoods. Learn the locations and identities of a few parts of town, and you are well on your way to understanding Music City.

City Center

Nashville straddles the Cumberland River, a waterway that meanders a particularly uneven course in this part of Tennessee. Downtown Nashville sits on the west bank of the river, climbing a gradual incline from Broadway to the Tennessee State Capitol. It is defined by

© HENRYK SADURA/123RF

The "Batman Building" towers over the downtown skyline.

landmarks including the AT&T Building, the tallest building in Tennessee, better known by many as the "Batman Building" for the two tall antennae that spring from the top. (The building was designed to be evocative of the shape of the top of a desk phone, where you place the receiver...in the days before iPhones.)

Downtown is where you will find major attractions like the Country Music Hall of Fame, the Ryman Auditorium, and Printer's Alley, a hotbed of clubs and bars. It includes the traditional business zone, where you'll find office buildings, the Tennessee State Museum, and city parks.

Grab the good walking shoes and leave the car in the garage in central Nashville. Traffic and parking are what'd you expect in a downtown area of a city of this size. But remember: Nashville is built on a hill. Walking between Broadway and the state capitol is perfectly doable, but on a hot summer day, or with small children in tow, you may need to take plenty of breaks (or hop on one of the free Music City Circuit buses).

East Nashville

Shelby Street Pedestrian Bridge spans the Cumberland River, taking you from Riverfront Park to the heart of East Nashville. Now dominated by LP Field, home of the NFL's Tennessee Titans, the eastern reaches of Nashville are also home to some of the most charming residential neighborhoods. **Edgefield,** Nashville's oldest suburb, was a separate city when it first sprang up in the 19th century. Many of its most elegant homes were destroyed in the great East Nashville fire of 1916, but it still boasts a lovely mix of Victorian, Princess Anne, and Colonial Revival homes. Farther east is **Lockeland Springs,** and farther north is **Inglewood.**

While East Nashville is short on tourist-magnet attractions, visitors should consider the growing number of bed-and-breakfast accommodations here. The neighborhoods are close to downtown but also boast their own unique nightlife, restaurants, and character.

North Nashville

North of the state capitol and Bicentennial Mall is **Germantown,** a compact historic neighborhood now home to a few shops, galleries, restaurants, and studios, once the home of European immigrants. Heading west from Germantown, **Jefferson Street** takes you past several of Nashville's African American landmarks, including Fisk University and Meharry Medical College.

A neighborhood created entirely for the tourist trade, **Music Valley** is the zone of hotels, restaurants, and retail that has popped up around the Opryland Hotel and the Grand Ole Opry House. Located inside a narrow loop of the Cumberland River, Music Valley lies northeast of downtown Nashville. It is a quick drive from the airport along Briley Parkway.

If Music Valley is actually a valley, you wouldn't know it. The strip of hotels, restaurants, souvenir shops, and malls is just about as far removed from the natural environment as you can get. But you overlook the neighborhood (and the construction of Dolly Parton's snow and water park) to get to the Grand Ole Opry, the Gaylord Opryland Resort, and the discount shopper's paradise that is Opry Mills. Music Valley is also home to a wide variety of hotel accommodations, including some budget-friendly choices, plus family-friendly restaurants.

West Nashville

Perhaps the most famous neighborhood in all of Nashville, **Music Row** is where country music deals are done. The tree-lined streets of 16th and 17th Avenues, a few blocks southwest of downtown, shade dozens of different recording studios, record labels, and producers.

Lying just west of downtown, **Elliston Place** is a block of nightclubs, restaurants, and two famous Nashville eateries: Elliston Place Soda Shop and Rotier's.

The neighborhood is surrounded by medical complexes and is a few blocks from the city's only

downtown hostel. Centennial Park, Nashville's best urban park, is a few blocks farther west.

The youthful energy of nearby Vanderbilt and Belmont Universities keep **Hillsboro Village** one of the most consistently hip neighborhoods in Nashville. Hillsboro is home to one of Nashville's finest used-book stores, stylish and pricey boutiques, and notable restaurants, including the upscale Sunset Grill, the down-home Pancake Pantry, and Fido, a restaurant/coffeehouse where record contracts are signed and hit songs are written. Hillsboro is also where you will find the alternative movie house the Belcourt, which screens independent and arts movies, plus hosts live music concerts.

Together, Hillsboro and Elliston Place are Nashville's **Midtown.**

Sylvan Park, once a suburb of the city, is located between Charlotte Avenue and Murphy Road, just west of the city center. Noted for neat homes and state-named roads, the neighborhood is quiet and residential, with a growing number of shops and restaurants. Along Charlotte Avenue, facing Sylvan Park, you will find antiques and thrift stores, the Darkhorse Theater, and Rhino Books, specializing in used and rare books. Farther out along Charlotte is a burgeoning number of international eateries.

West End refers to the neighborhoods along West End Avenue. It includes Belle Meade, an incorporated city and one of the wealthiest in the whole state. Head in this direction to find good restaurants, the Belle Meade Plantation, and Cheekwood.

South Nashville

South of the city center are several distinct neighborhoods. **8th Avenue South,** close to downtown, is the antiques district. Restaurants like Arnold's Country Kitchen and the Jackalope Brewery, and clubs including the Mercy Lounge, draw people to this neighborhood.

Follow 12th Avenue as it heads south from downtown to find **the Gulch.** Rising from what was once a railroad wasteland, the Gulch is now the city's hot spot for high-rise housing and urban condos.

A few miles farther south along 12th Avenue is **12 South,** another of Nashville's most popular gentrified neighborhoods. An influx of young professional property owners has given rise to new restaurants, boutiques, and coffee shops.

You have to leave the main drag to find the greenery left in **Green Hills,** a retail hot spot south of Hillsboro Village. If you can tolerate the inevitable traffic jam (particularly after school gets out on weekdays), follow 21st Avenue south to find the tony Mall at Green Hills, the even more upscale Hill Center, media darling Parnassus Books, and the venerable Bluebird Cafe, tucked away in a strip mall a few blocks farther south.

Sights

BROADWAY

This is the entertainment and retail hub of Nashville. Walk along lower Broad, as the blocks from 5th Avenue to the river are called, and you will pass a dozen different bars (honky-tonks), restaurants, and shops catering to visitors. Second Avenue, near where it crosses Broadway, is a neighborhood where old warehouses have been converted to restaurants, shops, office space, and loft condominiums. A $7 million **Johnny Cash Museum** (119 3rd Ave. S.) is being built near lower Broad. The plan is for an 18,000-square-foot museum that will include a live music venue to seat up to 250 people.

◖ Country Music Hall of Fame

The distinctive design of the Country Music Hall of Fame and Museum (222 5th Ave. S., 615/416-2001, www.countrymusichalloffame. com, daily 9 A.M.–5 P.M., adults $20, seniors $18, children $12) is the first thing you will notice about this monument to country music. Vertical windows at the front and back of the building resemble piano keys, the sweeping arch on the right side of the building portrays a 1950s Cadillac fin, and from above, the building resembles a bass clef. The hall of fame was first established, in 1967, and its first inductees were Jimmie Rodgers, Hank Williams, and Fred Rose. The original hall was located on Music Row, but in 2002 it moved to this signature building two blocks off Broadway in downtown Nashville.

Country music fans are drawn by the carload to the hall of fame, where they can pay homage to country's greatest stars, as well as the lesser-known men and women who influenced the music. Those who aren't fans when they walk in generally leave with an appreciation of the genre's varied roots. The hall's slogan is "Honor Thy Music."

The museum is arranged chronologically, beginning with country's roots in the Scotch Irish ballads sung by the Southern mountains' first settlers, and ending with displays on some of the genre's hottest stars of today. In between, exhibits detail themes including the rise of bluegrass, honky-tonk, and the world-famous Nashville Sound, which introduced country music to the world.

There are a half dozen private listening booths where you can hear studio-quality recordings of seminal performances, as well as a special display of a few of the genre's most famous instruments. Here you can see Bill Monroe's mandolin, Maybelle Carter's Gibson, and Johnny Cash's Martin D-355.

If you are interested in learning something about country music while you're here, splurge on the $5 audio guide, which adds depth to the exhibits, and really immerse yourself in the music.

The hall of fame itself is set in a rotunda. Brass plaques honor the 100 inductees, and

NASHVILLE

© RYMAN AUDITORIUM

Even you can make it on stage at the famous Ryman Auditorium...if you take the tour.

around the room are the words *Will the Circle Be Unbroken,* from the hymn made famous by the Carter Family.

The only way to visit Music Row's famous **Studio B,** where Elvis once recorded, is to buy your ticket at the museum box office and hop on the hall of fame's guided tour bus. The tour takes about an hour, including the 10-minute drive to Music Row and back. The Studio B tour is an additional fee to your admission, but you can buy it as a package all at once. The Platinum Package is adults $33 adults, children $24 total, for the audio tour, museum admission, and Studio B.

The Ryman Auditorium

Thanks to an $8.5 million renovation in the 1990s, the historic Ryman Auditorium (116 5th Ave. N., 615/889-3060, www.ryman.com, daily 9 A.M.–4 P.M., adults $13, children $6.50) remains one of the best places in the United States—let alone Nashville—to hear live music.

Built in 1892 by Capt. Thomas Ryman, the Union Gospel Tabernacle, as the Ryman was then called, was designed as a venue for the charismatic preaching of Rev. Samuel P. Jones, to whom Ryman owed his own conversion to Christianity.

Managed by keen businesswoman Lula C. Naff during the first half of the 20th century, the Ryman began to showcase music and performances. In 1943, Naff agreed to the Ryman hosting a popular barn dance called the Grand Ole Opry. The legacy of this partnership gave the Ryman its place in history as the so-called Mother Church of Country Music.

The Opry remained at the Ryman for the next 31 years. After the Opry left in 1974, the Ryman fell into disrepair and was virtually condemned when Gaylord Entertainment, the same company that owns the Opry, decided to invest in the grand old tabernacle. Today, it is a popular concert venue, booking rock, country, and classical acts, plus comedy and more. Performers still marvel at the fabulous acoustics of the hall.

Performers like to show them off, playing a number or two without a mic. The Opry returns here during the Christmas season, and in the summer there's a weekly bluegrass series.

Seeing a show at the Ryman is by far the best way to experience this historic venue, but if you can't do that, pay the admission fee to see a short video and explore the auditorium on your own, which includes museum-style exhibits about the musicians who have performed here through the ages. You can sit a few minutes on the old wooden pews and even climb on stage to be photographed in front of the classic Opry backdrop. A guided tour that takes you backstage (adults $17, children $10.50) isn't just for diehard fans. It gives lots of insight into how stars behaved when they were behind these famous walls. The guides tend to throw in an extra tall tale or two. Plus, you get to walk on the storied stage yourself. More than one marriage proposal has taken place at this point on the tour.

Shelby Street Pedestrian Bridge

Built in 1909, the Sparkman Street Bridge was slated for demolition in 1998 after inspectors called its condition "poor." But citing the success of the Walnut Street Bridge in revitalizing downtown Chattanooga, Tennessee, advocates succeeded in saving the bridge. The Shelby Street Bridge reopened in 2003 as a pedestrian and bike bridge.

The Shelby Street Bridge connects East Nashville neighborhoods with downtown. It is also convenient on Titan game days since the eastern terminus is a few hundred yards from LP Field. On nongame days LP Field often offers free parking. You can take a shuttle or walk across the bridge to get to downtown events. Don't miss the views of the downtown cityscape from here.

Fort Nashborough

Fort Nashborough (170 1st Ave., 615/862-8400, www.nashville.gov/parks, Mon.–Sat.

10 A.M.–4 P.M., Sun. 1–5 P.M., free) is a one quarter-size replica of the fort erected by James Robertson and John Donelson when they first settled what was then called French Lick on Christmas Day 1779. Visitors here will get the feeling that this site has seen better days. While the replica fort is open, it is mostly left unattended, and there is little to see or learn here. The interiors of the five cabins have been gated with iron bars, perhaps to prevent vagrants from settling in. The site is mostly fascinating simply because it looks so out of place among Nashville's skyscrapers and the Tennessee Titans' stadium nearby. But it has a nice view of the river and gives some context for the city's roots.

Tennessee Sports Hall of Fame

Sports fans will enjoy the Tennessee Sports Hall of Fame (Bridgestone Arena, 501 Broadway, 615/242-4750, www.tshf.net, Tues.–Sat. 10 A.M.–5 P.M., $3). Located in a state-of-the-art 7,500-square-foot exhibit space inside Bridgestone Arena, the hall chronicles the history of sports in Tennessee from the 1800s to today's heroes.

Customs House

Located at 701 Broadway, the old Nashville Customs House is a historic landmark and architectural beauty. Construction on the Customs House began in 1875, and President Rutherford B. Hayes visited Nashville to lay the cornerstone in 1877. The building is an impressive example of the Victorian Gothic style. It was designed by Treasury architect William Appleton Potter and was completed in 1916. Although it is called a customs house, the building served as the center of federal government operations in the city: Federal government offices, courts, and treasury offices were housed in the building.

Hume Fogg

Located across Broadway from the Customs

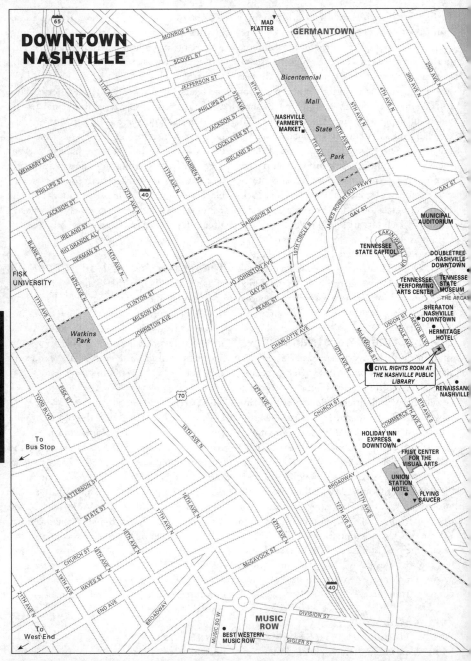

NASHVILLE

DOWNTOWN NASHVILLE

65

MONROE ST

SCOVEL ST

JEFFERSON ST

GERMANTOWN

MAD PLATTER

Bicentennial

Mall

State

Park

NASHVILLE FARMER'S MARKET

MUNICIPAL AUDITORIUM

TENNESSEE STATE CAPITOL

DOUBLETREE NASHVILLE DOWNTOWN

TENNESSEE PERFORMING ARTS CENTER

TENNESSEE STATE MUSEUM

THE ARCA

SHERATON NASHVILLE DOWNTOWN

HERMITAGE HOTEL

CIVIL RIGHTS ROOM AT THE NASHVILLE PUBLIC LIBRARY

RENAISSANC NASHVILLE

FISK UNIVERSITY

Watkins Park

70

HOLIDAY INN EXPRESS DOWNTOWN

FRIST CENTER FOR THE VISUAL ARTS

UNION STATION HOTEL

FLYING SAUCER

To Bus Stop

PATTERSON ST

STATE ST

CHURCH ST

HAYES ST

BROADWAY

To West End

MUSIC ROW

DIVISION ST

BEST WESTERN MUSIC ROW

SIGLER ST

40

PHILLIPS ST

JACKSON ST

LOCKLAYER ST

IRELAND ST

WARREN ST

MEHARRY BLVD

PHILLIPS ST

JACKSON ST

IRELAND ST

RIO GRANDE ALY

HERMAN ST

BLANK ST

CLINTON ST

MILSON AVE

JOHNSTON AVE

JO JOHNSTON AVE

GAY ST

PEARL ST

HARRISON ST

CHARLOTTE AVE

CHURCH ST

COMMERCE ST

BROADWAY

JAMES ROBERTSON PKWY

GAY ST

GAY ST

EAKIN WEAKLON

UNION ST

POLK AVE

CAPITOL BLVD

MALBERRO ST

10TH AVE N

8TH AVE S

9TH AVE S

11TH AVE S

12TH AVE S

McGAVOCK ST

MUSIC SQ W

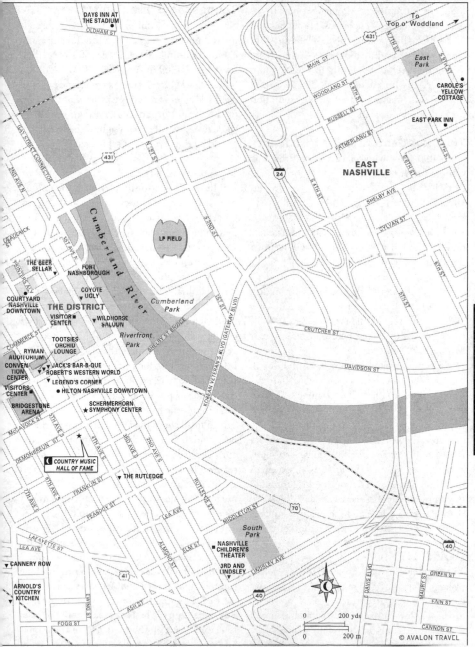

NASHVILLE

House is Hume Fogg Magnet School. It sits on land formerly occupied by Hume School, Nashville's first public school. The four-story stone-clad 1912 building was designed by William Ittner of St. Louis in the Norman Gothic style with Tudor Gothic details. Today, it is a public magnet school with a reputation for high academic standards.

The Frist Center for the Visual Arts

Nashville's foremost visual art space is the Frist Center for the Visual Arts (919 Broadway, 615/744-3247, www.fristcenter.org, Mon.–Sat. 10 A.M.–5:30 P.M., Thurs. and Fri. until 9 P.M., Sun. 1–5:30 P.M., adults $10, seniors, students, and military $7). The Frist is located in a stately building that once housed the 1930s downtown post office (and there's still a working post office in the basement). High ceilings, art deco finishes, and unique hardwood tiles distinguish the museum. Look carefully in the hallways, and you can see the indentations in the walls from folks who leaned here waiting for their turn in line at the post office.

With no permanent collection of its own, the Frist puts on about 12 different major visiting exhibitions annually. At any given time, you will see 3–4 different exhibits, many of which are regional or national premieres. There are typically plenty of ongoing educational activities paired with the exhibitions. ArtQuest, a permanent part of the Frist, is an excellent hands-on arts activity room for children and their parents. The Frist's café serves better-than-expected salads and sandwiches, and has a nice outdoor patio for alfresco dining.

DOWNTOWN

The greater part of downtown is dominated by large office buildings and federal, state, and city government structures. From Commerce Street northward to the state capitol, you will find historic churches, museums, and hordes of office workers.

Tennessee State Capitol

Set on the top of a hill and built with the formality and grace of classic Greek architecture, the capitol building of Tennessee (505 Deaderick St., 615/741-2692, Tues.–Sat. 10 A.M.–5 P.M., Sun. 1–5 P.M., free) strikes a commanding pose overlooking downtown Nashville. Construction of the capitol began in 1845, two years after the state legislature finally agreed that Nashville would be the permanent capital city. Even with the unpaid labor of convicts and slaves, it took 14 years to finish the building.

The capitol is built of limestone, much of it from a quarry located near present-day Charlotte and 13th Avenues. In the 1950s, extensive renovations were carried out, and some of the original limestone was replaced. The interior marble came from Rogersville and Knoxville, and the gasoliers were ordered from Philadelphia. The capitol was designed by architect William Strickland, who considered it his crowning achievement and is buried in a courtyard on the north end of the capitol.

Visitors are welcome at the capitol. Ask at the information desk for a printed guide that identifies each of the rooms and many of the portraits and sculptures both inside and outside the building. If the legislature is not in session, you can go inside both the House and Senate chambers, which look much as they did back in the 19th century. In the 2nd-floor lobby, you can see two bronze reliefs depicting the 19th and 14th amendments to the U.S. Constitution, both of which were ratified by the State of Tennessee in votes held at the capitol.

Guided tours of the capitol depart hourly Monday–Friday 9 A.M.–4 P.M. Ask at the information desk inside for more information.

Other important state buildings surround the capitol. The **Library and Archives** sits directly west of the capitol and next to the **Tennessee Supreme Court.** The **Tennessee War Memorial** is a stone plaza on the south side of the capitol and a nice place to people-watch (and where, in

2000, Al Gore told supporters he would fight on in the election against George Bush) This is where Occupy Nashville protesters gathered in 2011. A number of state office buildings are nearby, and state employees can be seen walking to and fro, particularly at lunchtime.

Tennessee State Museum

If you are used to the flashy multimedia exhibits found in many of today's top museums, the Tennessee State Museum (505 Deaderick St., 615/741-2692, www.tnmuseum.org, Tues.–Sat. 10 A.M.–5 P.M., Sun. 1–5 P.M., free) might seem like a musty throwback to the past. The displays are largely straightforward combinations of text and images, and they require visitors to read and examine on their own. There are but a few video presentations. But for patrons with enough patience to give the displays their due, the museum offers an excellent overview of Tennessee history from the Native Americans to the New South era of the 1880s.

Exhibits detail the state's political development, explore the Revolutionary and Civil Wars, and profile famous Tennesseans including Andrew Jackson and Davy Crocket. They also cast a spotlight on the lifestyles and diversions of Tennesseans of various eras, from the early frontiersmen and frontierswomen to a free African American family before emancipation. Special artifacts include the top hat worn by Andrew Jackson at his presidential inauguration, a musket that belonged to Daniel Boone, and the jawbone of a mastodon.

The **Military Branch Museum** (Legislative Plaza, 615/741-2692, Tues.–Sat. 10 A.M.–5 P.M., free) is associated with the Tennessee State Museum and highlights America's overseas conflicts, beginning with the Spanish-American War in 1989 and ending with World War II. The exhibits examine the beginnings of the wars, major battles, and the outcomes. There is a special exhibit about Alvin C. York, the Tennessee native and World War I hero. The military museum is located in the War Memorial Building on the south side of the capitol.

C Civil Rights Room at the Nashville Public Library

The Nashville Public Library (615 Church St., 615/862-5800, Mon.–Thurs. 9 A.M.–8 P.M., Fri. 9 A.M.–6 P.M., Sat. 9 A.M.–5 P.M., Sun. 2–5 P.M., free) houses a powerful exhibit (615/862-5782, www.library.nashville.org/civilrights/home.html) on the movement for civil rights that took place in Nashville in the 1950s and '60s. Nashville was the first Southern city to desegregate public services, and it did so relatively peacefully, setting an example for activists throughout the South.

The story of the courageous men and women who made this change happen is told through photographs, videos, and displays in the Civil Rights Room at the public library. The library is a fitting location for the exhibit since the block below on Church Street was the epicenter of the Nashville sit-ins during 1960.

Inside the room, large-format photographs show school desegregation, sit-ins, and a silent march to the courthouse. A circular table at the center of the room is symbolic of the lunch counters where young students from Fisk, Meharry, American Baptist, and Tennessee A&I sat silently and peacefully at sit-ins. The table is engraved with the 10 rules of conduct set out for sit-in participants, including to be polite and courteous at all times, regardless of how you are treated. A timeline of the national and Nashville civil rights movements is presented above the table.

Inside a glass enclosed viewing room you can choose from six different documentary videos, including an hour-long 1960 NBC news documentary about the Nashville sit-ins. Many of the videos are 30 minutes or longer, so plan on spending several hours here if you are keenly interested in the topics.

The centerpiece of the Civil Rights Room is

NASHVILLE

The struggles of the 1950s and '60s are examined in the Civil Rights Room at the Nashville Public Library.

NASHVILLE

a glass inscription by Martin Luther King Jr., who visited the city in 1960 and said, during a speech at Fisk University: "I came to Nashville not to bring inspiration, but to gain inspiration from the great movement that has taken place in this community."

Nashville is planning a new and much-needed museum dedicated to its African American history and culture, which will be located at the corner of Jefferson and 8th Avenues, near the farmers market. Until this museum is built, the Nashville Public Library is the best place to learn about the city's racially segregated past and the movement that changed that.

The Civil Rights Room is located on the 2nd floor of the library, adjacent to the room that houses its Nashville collection.

The Arcade

One of Nashville's most distinctive urban features is the covered arcade that runs between 4th and 5th Avenues and parallel to Union Street. The two-story arcade with a gabled glass roof was built in 1903 by developer Daniel Buntin, who was inspired by similar arcades he saw in Italy.

From the moment it opened, the Arcade was a bustling center for commerce. Famous for its peanut shop, the Arcade has also been the location of photo studios, jewelers, and a post office for many years. Today, restaurants (including Manny's House of Pizza) crowd the lower level, while art galleries, artists' studios, and professional offices line the 2nd floor. Don't miss the bustling activities here during the monthly Art Crawl on the first Saturday of the month.

Downtown Presbyterian Church

William Strickland, the architect who designed the Tennessee State Capitol, also designed the Downtown Presbyterian Church (154 5th Ave. N., 615/254-7584, www.dpchurch.com), a place of worship now on the National Register of Historic Places. Built in 1848 to replace an earlier church destroyed by fire, the church is in the Egyptian revival style that was popular at the time. It is, however, one of only three surviving churches in the country to be built in this style.

Downtown Presbyterian, which added the word *Downtown* to its name in 1955, was used as a Union hospital during the Civil War, and it is where James K. Polk was inaugurated as Tennessee governor in 1839. Visitors are welcome to come for a self-guided tour Monday–Friday 9 A.M.–3 P.M.; groups of five or more can call in advance. The church's **Waffle Shop** brunch, held in December, is a local tradition.

MUSIC ROW

Home to the business end of the country music industry, Music Row can be found along 16th and 17th Avenues south of where they cross Broadway. While there are few bona fide attractions here, it is worth a jaunt to see the

THE NASHVILLE SIT-INS

Greensboro, North Carolina, is often named as the site of the first sit-ins of the American civil rights movement. But, in truth, activists in Nashville carried out the first "test" sit-ins in late 1959. In these test cases, protesters left the facilities after being refused service and talking to management about the injustice of segregation. In between these test sit-ins and the moment when Nashville activists would launch a full-scale sit-in campaign, students in Greensboro took that famous first step.

The Nashville sit-ins began on February 13, 1960, when a group of African American students from local colleges and universities sat at a downtown lunch counter and refused to move until they were served. The protesting students endured verbal and physical abuse, and were arrested.

Community members raised money for the students' bail, and black residents of the city began an economic boycott of downtown stores that practiced segregation. On April 19, the home of Z. Alexander Looby, a black lawyer who was representing the students, was bombed. Later the same day, students led a spontaneous, peaceful, and silent march through the streets of downtown Nashville to the courthouse. Diane Nash, a student leader, asked Nashville mayor Ben West if he thought it was morally right for a restaurant to refuse to serve someone based on the color of his or her skin. Mayor West said, "No."

The march was an important turning point for the city. The combined effect of the sit-ins, the boycott, and the march caused, in 1960, Nashville to be the first major Southern city to experience widespread desegregation of its public facilities. The events also demonstrated to activists in other parts of the South that nonviolence was an effective tool of protest.

The story of the young people who led the Nashville sit-ins is told in the book *The Children* by David Halberstam. In 2001, Nashville resident Bill King was so moved by the story of the protests that he established an endowment to fundraise for a permanent civil rights collection at the Nashville Public Library. In 2003, the Civil Rights Room at the Nashville Public Library was opened. It houses books, oral histories, audiovisual records, microfilm, dissertations, and stunning photographs of the events of 1960. The words of one student organizer, John Lewis, who went on to become a congressman from Georgia, are displayed over the entryway: "If not us, then who; if not now, then when?"

NASHVILLE

headquarters of both major and independent music labels all in one place (this might be your best chance for a celebrity sighting).

Music Row's most famous, or infamous, landmark is **Musica,** the sculpture at the Music Row traffic circle. The sculpture, by local artist Alan LeQuire, caused a stir when it was unveiled in 2003 for the larger-than-life anatomically correct men and women it depicts. Regardless of your views on art and obscenity, it is fair to say that *Musica* speaks more to Nashville's identity as the Athens of the South than as Music City USA.

RCA Studio B

As a rule, the music labels in Music Row are open for business, not tours. The lone exception is Historic RCA Studio B (Music Square W., 615/416-2001, www.countrymusichalloffame. com, $22–33). The RCA studio was the second recording studio in Nashville and the place where artists including the Everly Brothers, Roy Orbison, Dolly Parton, Elvis Presley, and Hank Snow recorded hits. Also called the RCA Victor Studio, this nondescript studio operated from 1957 to 1977. Visitors on the one-hour tour, which departs from the Country Music Hall of Fame downtown, hear anecdotes about recording sessions at the studio and see rare footage of a 1960s Dottie West recording session.

Tours can only be purchased in conjunction with admission to the Country Music Hall of Fame. Tours depart hourly Sunday–Thursday 10:30 A.M.–2:30 P.M. On Friday

© MARGARET LITTMAN

The statue of Athena at The Parthenon is of epic proportions.

and Saturday, tours leave every half hour 10:30 A.M.–2:30 P.M.

The Upper Room

Three million Christians around the world know the *Upper Room Daily Devotional Guide,* a page-a-day pocket devotional available in 106 countries and 40 languages. Headquartered in Nashville, the Upper Room Ministry has established a bookstore, museum, and chapel to welcome visitors. **The Upper Room Chapel and Museum** (1908 Grand Ave., 615/340-7207, http://chapel.upperroom.org, Mon.–Fri. 8 A.M.–4:30 P.M., free, $4 suggested donation) features a small museum of Christian-inspired art, including a wonderful collection of Nativity scenes from around the world made from materials ranging from needlepoint to camel bone. Visitors may also tour the chapel, with its 8-foot-by-20-foot stained-glass window and 8-foot-by-17-foot wood carving of Leonardo da

Vinci's *Last Supper.* A 15-minute audio presentation discusses features of the carving and tells the history and mission of the Upper Room.

MIDTOWN

Encompassing the neighborhoods of Elliston Place, Hillsboro Village, and Green Hills, midtown refers to the parts of Nashville between downtown and the West End.

◖ The Parthenon

In 1893, funds began to be raised for a mighty exposition that would celebrate the 1896 centennial of the state of Tennessee. Though the exposition would start a year late—in 1897—it would exceed all expectations. The old West Side Race Track was converted to a little city with exhibit halls dedicated to transportation, agriculture, machinery, minerals, forestry, and African Americans, among other themes. There were Chinese, Cuban, and Egyptian villages; a midway; and an auditorium. The exposition attracted 1.7 million people between May 1 and October 31. While the event turned only a modest profit for its organizers, it no doubt contributed in other ways to the local economy and to the stature of the state.

When the exposition closed in the fall of 1897, all the exhibit halls were torn down except for a life-size replica of the Greek Parthenon, which had housed an art exhibit during the centennial. The exposition grounds were made into a public park, aptly named Centennial Park, and Nashvillians continued to admire their Parthenon.

The Parthenon replica had been built out of wood and plaster, and it was designed only to last through the centennial. Remarkably, it survived well beyond that. But by the 1920s, the Parthenon was crumbling. City officials, responding to public outcry to save the Parthenon, agreed to restore it, and they hired a contractor to rebuild the replica. The contractor did so using tinted concrete.

Today, the Parthenon remains one of Nashville's most iconic landmarks. It is a monument to the creativity and energy of the New South, and also to Nashville's distinction as the Athens of the South.

You can see and walk around the Parthenon simply by visiting Centennial Park. It is, in many respects, most beautiful from the outside, particularly when lit dramatically at night.

As breathtaking as it is from the exterior, it is worth paying to go inside the Parthenon (Centennial Park, 2600 West End Ave., 615/862-8431, www.nashville.gov/parthenon, Tues.–Sat. 9 A.M.–4:30 P.M., June–Aug. Sun. only 12:30–4:30 P.M., adults $6, seniors and children $4). The landmark has three gallery spaces; the largest is used to display works from its permanent collection of 63 pieces of American art. The other two galleries host interesting changing exhibits. But upstairs is the remarkable 42-foot statue of Athena, by local sculptor Alan LeQuire. Athena is designed as a replica of what the statue would have looked like in ancient Greece, in all her golden glory. In ancient Greece the doors of the Parthenon would have been open, and she would have been seen from a distance. In Nashville her scale and gilded loins are front and center.

Vanderbilt University

Named for philanthropist Commo. Cornelius Vanderbilt, who donated $1 million in 1873 to found a university that would "contribute to strengthening the ties which should exist between all sections of our common country," Vanderbilt University (211 Kirkland Hall, 615/322-7311, www.vanderbilt.edu) is now one of the region's most respected institutions of higher education (and the alma mater of this author).

A private research university, Vanderbilt has an enrollment of 6,700 undergraduates and 5,200 graduate students. The university comprises 10 schools, a medical center, public policy center, and The Freedom Forum First Amendment Center. Originally just 75 acres, the university had grown to 250 acres by 1960. When the George Peabody School for Teachers merged with Vanderbilt in 1979, another 53 acres were added.

Vanderbilt's campus life is vibrant, and there is a daily roll call of lectures, recitals, exhibits, and other special events for students, locals, and visitors alike. Check http://calendar.vanderbilt.edu for an up-to-date listing of all campus events.

Prospective students and their parents can sign up for a campus tour. Vanderbilt also offers a self-guided tour of the campus's trees, which form the Vanderbilt Arboretum. Most trees on the tour are native trees common to Nashville and Middle Tennessee. This is a nice activity for people who want to hone tree identification skills. Download a podcast or print a paper copy of the tour from the website or contact the university for more information.

Vanderbilt University also has two excellent art galleries: The **Sarratt Gallery** (Sarratt Student Center, Vanderbilt Place near 24th Ave., 615/322-2471, Mon.–Fri. 9 A.M.–9 P.M., Sat.–Sun. 10 A.M.–10 P.M., free), which has a more contemporary bent, and the **Vanderbilt Fine Arts Gallery** (1220 21st Ave. S., Mon.–Fri. noon–4 P.M., Thurs. until 8 P.M., Sat.–Sun. 1–5 P.M., free), which includes works that demonstrate the development of both Eastern and Western art, plus six different traveling exhibits annually. The Fine Arts Gallery is located near the intersection of West End and 23rd Avenues. Both galleries are closed or limit their hours during university holidays and semester breaks, so it's a good idea to call ahead.

There is designated visitor parking in several lots on the Vanderbilt campus. Look on the eastern edge of the sports facilities parking lot off Natchez Trace, in the Wesley Place parking lot off Scarritt Place, or in the Terrace Place parking lot between 20th and 21st Avenues north of Broadway. Pay attention to these signs, as the university parking monitors do ticket those who park in prohibited areas.

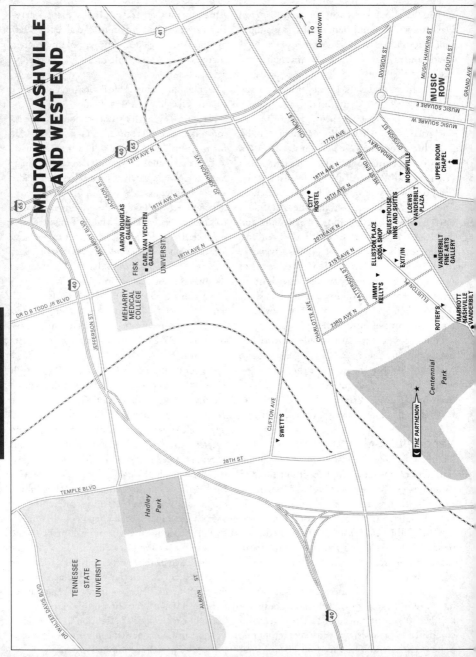

MIDTOWN NASHVILLE AND WEST END

To Downtown

MUSIC ROW

UPPER ROOM CHAPEL

NOSHVILLE

LOEWS VANDERBILT PLAZA

GUESTHOUSE INNS AND SUITES

VANDERBILT FINE ARTS GALLERY

CITY HOSTEL

AARON DOUGLAS GALLERY

CARL VAN VECHTEN GALLERY

FISK UNIVERSITY

MEHARRY MEDICAL COLLEGE

ELLISTON PLACE SODA SHOP

EXIT/IN

JIMMY KELLY'S

ROTIER'S

MARRIOTT NASHVILLE VANDERBILT

THE PARTHENON

Centennial Park

SWETT'S

TENNESSEE STATE UNIVERSITY

Hadley Park

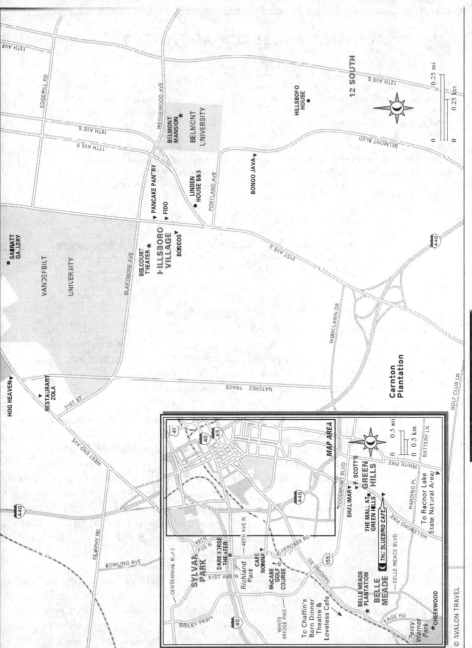

NASHVILLE

© AVALON TRAVEL

McKISSACK AND McKISSACK ARCHITECTS

The oldest African American architectural firm in Tennessee can trace its roots to Moses McKissack (1790-1865), a member of the West African Ashanti tribe. He was sold into slavery to William McKissack of North Carolina. Later, McKissack moved to Middle Tennessee. Moses became a master builder, and he passed his knowledge on to his son, Gabriel Moses McKissack, born in 1840. Gabriel Moses passed his knowledge of the building trade to his own son, Moses McKissack III, born in 1879.

Moses McKissack III was born in Pulaski, where he received a basic education in the town's segregated schools. In 1890 he was hired by a local white architect. Until 1905, McKissack designed and built homes throughout the area, including many in Mount Pleasant in Maury County. He developed a reputation as an excellent architect and tradesman.

In 1905 McKissack moved to Nashville, where he started his own construction company. Within a few years, he was working on major projects. He built a home for the dean of architecture and engineering at Vanderbilt University and the Carnegie Library at Fisk University. In 1922, Moses's brother, Calvin, joined him, and they opened McKissack and McKissack, Tennessee's first black architectural firm.

The McKissacks continued to distinguish themselves in the building industry, and they have also kept the business in the family. Since 1991 the company has been led by Cheryl McKissack, a fifth-generation McKissack. The firm employs more than 100 people and has corporate offices in Philadelphia and New York City.

Belmont University

The school for girls founded in the Belmont Mansion in 1890 evolved in 1913 to the Ward-Belmont School for Women and in 1951 to coed Belmont College. Since 1991, it has been Belmont University (1900 Belmont Blvd., 615/460-6000, www.belmont.edu), a higher-education institution with links to the Tennessee Baptist Convention. Today Belmont is a fast-growing university with highly respected music and music business programs. In 2011 the school opened the first new law school in the state in the last century. Belmont, which hosted one of the 2008 presidential debates, has a student enrollment of 6,400. Campus tours are available twice a day on weekdays.

Several Belmont facilities are of interest to the public, including the student-run **Buzzy's Candy Store** (2006 Belmont Blvd., 615/460-8561, Mon.–Sat. 11 A.M.–8 P.M.) and the **Curb Event Center** (2002 Belmont Blvd., 615/460-8500). The Curb Center hosts sporting events, concerts, and lectures.

Belmont Mansion

The elaborate "summer home" of Adelicia Acklen was constructed in 1853 and was named Belle Monte. Belmont Mansion (1900 Belmont Blvd., 615/460-5459, www.belmontmansion.com, Mon.–Sat. 10 A.M.–4 P.M., Sun. 1–4 P.M., adults $10, seniors $9, children 6–12 $3), as it is known today, is a monument to the excesses of the Victorian age.

Adelicia was born to a wealthy Nashville family in 1817. When she was 22, Adelicia married Isaac Franklin, a wealthy bachelor 28 years her senior. When Franklin died seven years later, Adelicia inherited his substantial wealth. Adelicia remarried to Joseph Acklen, a young lawyer, and together they planned and built Belmont Mansion. The home was built in the Italian style, with touches of Egyptian revival style.

The home boasted 36 rooms and 16,000 square feet of space, including a grand gallery where the Acklens hosted elaborate balls and dinner parties. The property included a private art gallery, aviary, zoo, and conservatory, as well as a lake and acres of manicured gardens. After the Civil War, Adelicia traveled to Europe, where she purchased a number of paintings and sculptures that are now on display in her restored mansion.

Shortly before her death, Adelicia sold Belmont to two female educators who ran a girls school from the property for 61 years. Later, it was purchased by the founders of Belmont College.

Visitors to the mansion are given a 45-minute guided tour of the property, which includes the downstairs sitting and entertaining rooms and three of the upstairs bedrooms.

WEST END

Nashville's most posh neighborhood, Belle Meade, is actually a city with its own government. Named after an antebellum plantation, Belle Meade the city is home to Nashville's elite, and it famously possesses one of the most wealthy zip codes in America. Drive through to spy on mansions that look more like museums and lawns that look like botanical gardens.

Around Belle Meade are other nice neighborhoods where Nashville's professionals and upper class live. West End Avenue, the area's thoroughfare, is home to lots of nice restaurants. As you head westward, you pass Cheekwood, the Warner Parks, and eventually meet up with the Natchez Trace Parkway.

Belle Meade Plantation

The mansion at the former Belle Meade Plantation (5025 Harding Pk., 615/356-0501, www.bellemeadeplantation.com, Mon.–Sat. 9 A.M.–5 P.M., Sun. 11 A.M.–5 P.M., $16) is the centerpiece of present-day Belle Meade Plantation and one of the finest old homes in the city. Its name means beautiful pasture, and indeed it was Belle Meade's pastures that gave rise to the plantation's fame as the home of a superb stock of horses. Purchased as 250 acres in 1807 by Virginia farmer John Harding and his wife, Susannah, the estate grew to 5,400 acres at its peak in the 1880s and 1890s.

Belle Meade was never a cotton plantation, although small amounts of the cash crop were grown here, along with fruits, vegetables, and tobacco. Instead it was the horses, including the racehorse Iroquois, that made Belle Meade famous. The mansion was built in 1820 and expanded in 1853. Its grand rooms are furnished with period antiques, more than 60 percent of which are original to the house. The estate also includes outbuildings, including a smokehouse, dairy, and the original log cabin that Harding built for his family when they moved to Belle Meade in 1807.

The plantation also includes a slave cabin, which houses an exhibit on Belle Meade's enslaved population, which numbered more than 160 at its peak. Two of these slaves are described in detail. Susanna Carter was the mansion's housekeeper for more than 30 years, and she remained with the family even after the end of slavery. On her deathbed, Selena Jackson, the mistress of Belle Meade for many years, called Susanna "one of the most faithful and trusted of my friends." The other African American who features prominently at the museum is Bob Green, whose skill and experience as a hostler earned him one of the highest salaries ever paid to a horse hand of the day.

Visitors to Belle Meade are given a one-hour guided tour of the mansion and then visit the outbuildings and grounds on their own.

Cheekwood

Plan to spend a full morning or afternoon at Cheekwood (1200 Forrest Park Dr., 615/356-8000, www.cheekwood.org, Tues.–Sat. 9:30 A.M.–4:30 P.M., Sun. 11 A.M.–4:30 P.M., adults $12, seniors $10, students and children $5) so you can experience the full scope of this magnificent art museum and botanical garden. Galleries in the Cheekwood mansion house the museum's American and European collections, including an excellent contemporary art collection. Cheekwood has the largest public collection of works by Nashville artist William Edmondson, the sculptor and stoneworker.

Cheekwood usually displays items from its permanent collection as well as traveling exhibitions from other museums. Many exhibits have special ties with Nashville.

But the Cheekwood is far more than just an art museum. The mansion overlooks hundreds of acres of gardens and woods, and it is easy to forget that you are near a major American city when you're at the Cheekwood. Walk the mile-long **Carell Woodland Sculpture Trail** past works by 15 internationally acclaimed artists, or stroll past the water garden to the Japanese garden. There are dogwood gardens, an herb garden, a delightful boxwood garden, and much more. Wear comfortable shoes and pack a bottle of water so you can enjoy the grounds in comfort.

The Cheekwood owes its existence to the success of the coffee brand Maxwell House. During the 1920s, Leslie Cheek and his wife, Mabel Wood, invested in the new coffee brand being developed by their cousin, Joel Cheek. Maxwell House proved to be a success and earned the Cheeks a fortune, which they used to buy 100 acres of land in West Nashville. The family hired New York residential and landscape architect Bryant Fleming to create a 30,000-square-foot mansion and neighboring gardens. Cheekwood was completed in 1933.

Leslie Cheek lived in the mansion just two years before he died, and Mabel lived there for another decade before deeding it to her daughter and son-in-law, who later offered it as a site for a museum and garden. Cheekwood opened to the public in 1960.

Visitors pay admission at a guard gate at the entrance; parking is $3 per car. Once inside, drive to parking lot B so you can explore the art museum and grounds. Parking lot A is for the museum shop and restaurant.

SOUTH NASHVILLE

Head south on 4th Avenue, which becomes Nolensville Pike, toward a diverse array of attractions.

© MARGARET LITTMAN

Along Cheekwood's Carell Woodland Sculpture Trail, some of the art floats above the scenery.

Fort Negley

Early in the Civil War, the Union army determined that taking and holding Nashville was a critical strategic link in their victory. So after Nashville fell in 1862, the Federals wasted no time fortifying the city against attacks. One of the city's forts was Fort Negley, built between August and December 1862 on St. Cloud Hill south of the city center.

Fort Negley owes its existence to the 2,768 men who were enrolled to build it. Most were blacks, some free and some slave who were pressed into service by the Union army. These men felled trees, hauled earth, and cut and laid limestone for the fort. They slept in the open and enjoyed few, if any, comforts while they labored. Between 600 and 800 men died while building the fort, and only 310 received payment.

When it was completed, Fort Negley was the largest inland masonry fortification in

THE SCULPTURE OF WILLIAM EDMONDSON

The first African American artist to have a one-man show at the Museum of Modern Art in New York was Nashville-born sculptor William Edmondson (1874–1951).

Edmondson was born in the Hillsboro area of Nashville. He worked for decades as a laborer on the railroads, a janitor at Women's Hospital, and in other similar jobs before discovering his talent for sculpture in 1929. Edmondson told the Nashville *Tennessean* that his talent and passion were God given: "God appeared at the head of my bed and talked to me, like a natural man, concerning the talent of cutting stone He was about to bestow. He talked so loud He woke me up. He told me He had something for me."

Edmondson was a prolific sculptor. He worked exclusively with limestone, and he created angels, women, doves, turtles, rabbits, and other "varmints." He also made tombstones. Edmondson never learned to read or write, and he called many of his works "mirkels" because they were inspired by God.

In the 1930s, Louise Dahl-Wolfe, a photographer for *Harper's Bazaar* magazine, brought Edmondson and his work to the attention of Alfred Barr, the director of the Museum of Modern Art. Barr and other trustees of the museum admired what they termed as Edmondson's "modern primitive" work, and they invited him to display a one-man show at the museum in 1938. In 1941, the Nashville Art Museum put on an exhibit of Edmondson's work.

Edmondson continued to work until the late 1940s, when he became ill with cancer. After his death in 1951 he was buried in an unmarked grave at Mt. Ararat Cemetery in Nashville. The city park at 17th Avenue North and Charlotte Avenue is named in honor of Edmondson.

There is an exhibit of some of Edmondson's work at the Cheekwood Museum.

North America. It was never challenged. Fort Negley was abandoned by the military after the war, but it remained the cornerstone of one of Nashville's oldest African American communities, now known as Cameron-Trimble. During the New Deal, the Works Progress Administration rebuilt large sections of the crumbling fort, and it became a public park.

In 2007, the city opened a visitors center to tell the story of the fort. **Fort Negley Park** (Fort Negley Dr., 615/862-8470, Tues.–Sat. 9 A.M.–4 P.M., free) includes a museum about the fort and Nashville's role in the Civil War. There is a short paved loop trail around the base of the fort, plus raised boardwalks through the fortifications themselves. Historic markers tell the story of the fort's construction and detail its military features.

City Cemetery

Right next to Fort Negley Park, off Chestnut Street, is the old City Cemetery. Opened in 1822, City Cemetery (1001 4th Ave. S., www.thenashvillecitycemetery.org) was the final resting place of many of Nashville's most prominent early citizens, including founder James Robertson; William Driver, the U.S. Navy captain who named the flag "Old Glory"; Mabel Lewis Imes and Ella Sheppard, members of the original Fisk Jubilee Singers; and 14 Nashville mayors.

During the Civil War, the cemetery was contracted to bury more than 15,000 Union and Confederate dead, although they were later reinterred in different cemeteries.

Visitors are welcome 8 A.M.–5 P.M. daily. Consult the information board in the Keeble Building for help with your self-guided tour. Guided tours and special events, such as living history tours, garden tours, and historical lectures, take place on the second Saturday of each month. The events are aimed at telling the history of Nashvillians who are buried at this historical cemetery.

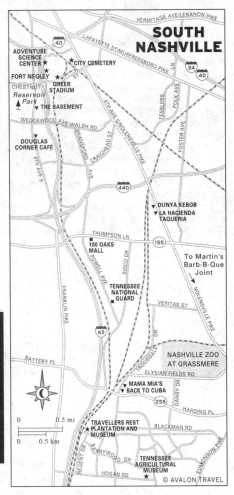

The center's **Sudekum Planetarium** (www. sudekumplanetarium.com) is the largest planetarium in Tennessee. The 164-seat planetarium offers a variety of space-themed shows. There are also star-viewing parties, gravity-suspending rides, and other exhibits about space flight, the moon, the solar system, and other things found in space.

Tennessee Central Railway Museum

Railroad enthusiasts should make a detour to the Tennessee Central Railway Museum (220 Willow St., 615/244-9001, www.tcry.org, Tues., Thurs., and Sat. 9 A.M.–3 P.M., free). This institution is best known for its special railroad excursions, but they also collect railroad equipment and paraphernalia, which are on display at the museum. The museum is located in an otherwise industrial area between the interstate and the railroad tracks, one block north of Hermitage Avenue and east of Fairfield Avenue.

Nashville Zoo at Grassmere

See familiar and exotic animals at the Nashville Zoo at Grassmere (3777 Nolensville Pk., 615/833-1534, www.nashvillezoo.org, Apr. 1–Oct. 15 daily 9 A.M.–6 P.M., Oct. 16–Mar. 31 daily 9 A.M.–4 P.M., closed Thanksgiving, Christmas, and New Year's Days, adults $15, seniors $13, children 3–12 $10, children under 3 free, parking free). Many of the zoo's animals live in beautiful habitats like Lorikeet Landing, Gibbon Islands, and Bamboo Trail. The zoo's meerkat exhibit, featuring the famously quizzical and erect animals, is one of its most popular. The Wild Animal Carousel is an old-time carousel with 39 different brightly painted wooden animals.

The zoo is located at Grassmere, the onetime home and farm of the Croft family. The historic Croft farmhouse has been preserved and is open for guided tours in October and December.

Travellers Rest Plantation and Museum

Travellers Rest (636 Farrell Pkwy., 615/832-8197, www.travellersrestplantation.org,

Adventure Science Center

Children and their caretakers will enjoy the hands-on science education available at the Adventure Science Center (800 Fort Negley Blvd., 615/862-5160, www.adventuresci.com, Mon.–Sat. 10 A.M.–5 P.M., Sun. 12:30–5:30 P.M., adults $12, children $10). Interactive exhibits explore how the body works, the solar system, and other scientific areas. There's a multistory climbing tower in the building's center, which features a giant guitar and other instruments.

© AMIEE STUBB

A cougar plays with a toy egg at the Nashville Zoo.

Tues.–Sat. 10 A.M.–4 P.M., Sun. 1–4 P.M., ages 12 and older $10, seniors $9, children 7–11 $5, children 6 and under free, grounds only $5) was the home of John Overton, a Nashville lawyer who helped found Memphis, served on the first Tennessee Supreme Court, and was a trusted advisor to Andrew Jackson, the seventh U.S. president and the first from Tennessee.

Overton was born in Virginia and studied law in Kentucky before he decided to move to Middle Tennessee, what was then the western frontier of the United States. When workmen were digging the cellar for the original home in 1799, they uncovered Native American skeletons and artifacts—Overton had chosen a Mississippian-era Indian mound for the site of his home. But the archaeological finds did not stop Overton, who initially named his home Golgotha, or hill of skulls. The name did not stick, however; tradition has it that Overton later named the home Travellers Rest because it was his place of rest between long trips as a circuit judge in Middle and East Tennessee.

Travellers Rest underwent two major expansions in its lifetime: one in 1808 and another 20 years later. The additions allowed Overton first to accommodate a growing number of young law students who wished to study law with him; later his wife, Mary, and their children; and, finally, the elaborate parties that Overton hosted to further the political career of Andrew Jackson.

John Overton was many different things in his lifetime. Among them was slave owner. Records show that 30–80 slaves lived at Travellers Rest before emancipation. While Overton's plantation was not the primary source of his wealth, it no doubt contributed to his status and prominence. Sadly, when the L&N Railroad purchased the Overton property in the 1940s, the company destroyed not only the Overton family burial ground and peach orchard, but also the slave cabins that remained at the rear of the house.

Visitors to Travellers Rest may choose to skip the mansion tour; admission to the grounds alone

THE BATTLE OF NASHVILLE

During most of the Civil War, Nashville was occupied by Federal forces. After Fort Donelson, 90 miles northeast of Nashville, fell in mid-February 1862, Nashville was in Union hands. The Federals turned Nashville into an important goods depot for the Northern cause and set strict rules for city residents during occupation.

As the war drew to a close in late 1864, Nashville was the site of what war historians now say was the last major battle of the Western Theater.

The Battle of Nashville came after a string of defeats for the Confederate army of Tennessee, commanded by John Bell Hood. After his bloody and humiliating losses at Spring Hill and Franklin a few miles south, Hood moved north and set up headquarters at Travellers Rest, the home of John Overton. His plan was to set up his troops in an arc around the southern side of the city. Union major general George H. Thomas did not plan to wait for Hood's attack, however. He devised to attack first and drive the Confederates away from Nashville.

A winter storm and frigid temperatures delayed the battle. For two weeks, from December 2 to 14, 1864, the two armies peered at one another across the no-man's-land between the two lines. Then, at dawn on December 15, 1864, the Union attack began. Union troops on foot and horse, including at least four U.S. Colored Infantry brigades, attacked various Confederate posts around the city. By the close of the first day of fighting, Hood withdrew his troops two miles farther south from the city.

The dawn of the second day of battle augured more losses for the Confederates. Unable to hold their line against the Union assault, they fell back again. As darkness fell, Union major general Thomas wired Washington to announce his victory. Pursued by a Union cavalry commanded by Maj. Gen. James Wilson, what remained of the Confederate army of Tennessee marched south, and on the day after Christmas they crossed the Tennessee River into Alabama. Four months later, the war was over.

The **Battle of Nashville Preservation Society, Inc.** (www.bonps.org) offers tours of the battlefield sites.

---

is just $5. But to get the full story and flavor of the property, choose the 45-minute guided tour.

Tennessee Agricultural Museum

The Tennessee Agricultural Museum (Ellington Agricultural Center, 615/837-5197, www.tnagmuseum.org, Mon.–Fri. 9 A.M.–4 P.M., free) celebrates the ingenuity and dedicated labors of farm life from the 17th to the 20th century. Operated by the Tennessee Department of Agriculture and set on the department's pleasant south Nashville campus, the museum depicts various facets of Tennessee farm life. There are exhibits about clothes washing, blacksmithing, coopering, plowing, weaving, and more. Outside, there is a small kitchen garden with heirloom vegetables, and replicas of a log cabin, one-room schoolhouse, and outdoor kitchen. There is also a short self-guided nature trail illustrating the ways that settlers used various types of native Tennessee trees.

Admission to this family-friendly museum is free, but you can prearrange demonstrations for a fee. Staff are available to answer any questions.

JEFFERSON STREET

Jefferson Street runs from downtown through northwestern Nashville, past several of the city's African American landmarks.

Bicentennial Mall

Tennessee celebrated its 100th anniversary in 1896 with the construction of the beloved Centennial Park, so it must have seemed like a good idea to celebrate its 200th anniversary in much the same way. The **Bicentennial Capitol Mall State Park** occupies 19 acres on the north side of the capitol building. It offers excellent views of the capitol, which towers over the mall. The mall and the capitol are separated by a steep hill and more than 200 steps, which may look daunting but are worth the climb for the views and access to downtown.

The mall has dozens of features that celebrate Tennessee and Tennesseans, including a 200-foot granite map of Tennessee embedded in concrete; a River Wall with 31 fountains, each representing one of Tennessee's rivers; and a timeline with Tennessee events, inscriptions, and notable quotes from 1796 to 1996. A one-mile path that circles the mall's perimeter is popular with walkers and joggers, and a 2,000-seat amphitheater is used for special events. The park may be a civics lesson incarnate, but it is also a pleasant place to pass the time. Ninety-five carillon bells (for the state's 95 counties) play "The Tennessee Waltz" every hour on the hour.

To the west of the mall is the amazing **Nashville Farmers' Market,** where you can buy fresh produce, flowers, gourmet breakfasts and lunches, and locally made crafts. Locals often picnic in the mall with goodies from the market. There's plenty of free parking here, but don't speed. Because this is a state park, tickets come from the state police, and they're pricier than metro Nashville tickets.

Fisk University

Founded in 1866 to educate newly freed slaves, Fisk University (1000 17th Ave. N., 615/329-8500, www.fisk.edu) has a long and proud history as one of the United States' foremost black colleges. W. E. B. Du Bois attended Fisk, graduating in 1888, and Booker T. Washington married a Fisk alumna and sent his own children to Fisk. In more modern times, Knoxville native and poet Nikki Giovanni attended Fisk.

Fisk sits at the corner of Jefferson Street and Dr. D. B. Todd Jr. Boulevard, about 10 blocks west of downtown Nashville. The campus is a smattering of elegant redbrick buildings set on open green lawns, although a few more modern buildings, including the library, detract from the classical feel. One of the oldest Fisk buildings is **Jubilee Hall,** on the north end of the campus, which is said to be the first permanent building constructed for the education of African Americans in the country. It was built with money raised by the Fisk Jubilee Singers, who popularized black spirituals during a world tour 1871–1874. Another notable building is the **Fisk Little Theatre,** a white clapboard building that once served as a Union hospital during the Civil War.

At the corner of Jackson Street and Todd Boulevard is the **Carl Van Vechten Gallery** (615/329-8720, Tues.–Sat. 10 a.m.–5 p.m., adults $10, seniors $6, children free), named for the art collector who convinced artist Georgia O'Keeffe to donate to Fisk a large portion of the work and personal collection of her late husband, Alfred Stieglitz. The college still retains much of this collection, although they have sought to sell parts of it to raise funds for the cash-strapped private school, and the legal battle has waged in courts for years. The collection includes works by Stieglitz and O'Keeffe, as well as acclaimed European and American artists including Pablo Picasso, Paul Cézanne, Pierre-Auguste Renoir, Diego Rivera, Arthur Dove, Gino Severini, and Charles Demuth. It is truly a remarkable collection and one worth seeing, but call ahead to confirm hours, particularly when school is not in session. Ring the bell to the right of the door to be let in.

The **Aaron Douglas Gallery** (Jackson St. and 17th Ave. N., Tues.–Fri. 11 a.m.–4 p.m., Sat. 1–4 p.m., Sun. 2–4 p.m., free) houses Fisk's collection of African, African American, and folk art works. It also hosts visiting exhibits and others by Fisk students and faculty. It is named after painter and illustrator Aaron Douglas, who also established Fisk's

FISK'S STIEGLITZ COLLECTION

When photographer Alfred Stieglitz died in 1946, his wife, Georgia O'Keeffe, herself one of the most important artists of her generation, was left with the responsibility of giving away his massive art collection. Stieglitz had collected more than 1,000 works by artists including Arthur Dove, Marsden Hartley, O'Keeffe, Charles Demuth, and John Marin. He also owned several African sculptures.

Stieglitz's instructions regarding this art collection were vague. In his will he asked O'Keeffe to select the recipients "under such arrangements as will assure to the public, under reasonable regulations, access thereto to promote the study of art."

O'Keeffe selected several obvious recipients for parts of the collection: the Library of Congress, the National Gallery of Art in Washington, the Metropolitan Museum of Art, the Art Institute of Chicago, and the Philadelphia Museum of Art. Nashville's Fisk University was a surprise, and Carl Van Vechten, a writer, photographer, and friend of Stieglitz and O'Keeffe, is credited with making the suggestion. Van Vechten was keenly interested in African American art and was close friends with Fisk president Charles Johnson.

O'Keeffe and Fisk were not an easy partnership. According to an account by C. Michael Norton, when she first visited the university a few days before the Carl Van Vechten Gallery would open on campus, O'Keeffe ordered major changes to the gallery space, eventually flying in a lighting designer from New York on the day before the opening. At the opening ceremony on November 4, 1949, held at the Memorial Chapel at Fisk, O'Keeffe declined President Johnson's invitation to the lectern and spoke from her chair, saying curtly: "Dr. Johnson wrote and asked me to speak, and I did not answer. I had and have no intention of speaking. These paintings and sculptures are a gift from Stieglitz. They are for the students. I hope you go back and look at them more than once."

The Stieglitz Collection at Fisk consists of 101 remarkable works of art, including 2 by O'Keeffe, 19 Stieglitz photographs, prints by Cézanne and Renoir, and 5 pieces of African tribal art.

Cash-strapped Fisk has sought to sell parts of the collection to raise funds. A proposal to sell a 50 percent share in the collection for $30 million to Walmart heiress Alice Walton's Crystal Bridges Museum in Bentonville, Arkansas, has been rejected by a court, but Fisk continues to press its case. Several alternative proposals have been made, including one to house the collection in the planned museum of African American culture, art, and history, to be located near the Bicentennial Mall. But that idea offered no immediate financial relief for Fisk and raised many unanswered questions. Meanwhile, Fisk reopened the Van Vechten Gallery in October 2008 so that the legendary collection is once again accessible to the public, as the will directed.

first formal art department. The gallery is located on the top floor of the Fisk library. **Cravath Hall** houses several Aaron Douglas murals that are worth seeing.

Fisk welcomes visitors, but there is no central information desk or printed guide. A map is posted just inside the library, and this is the best place to go to start your visit. Historical markers provide details of each of the main campus buildings. To see the famous painting of the Jubilee Singers, enter Jubilee Hall and bear right to the Appleton Room, where it hangs at the rear.

Meharry Medical College

Just across Dr. D. B. Todd Jr. Boulevard from Fisk is Meharry Medical College (1005 Dr. D. B. Todd Jr. Blvd., 615/327-6000, www.mmc.edu), the largest private, comprehensive, historically black institution educating medical professionals. It was founded in 1876 as the Medical Department of the Central Tennessee

THE JUBLIEE SINGERS

© SUSANNA HENIGHAN POTTER

Jubilee Hall on the Fisk University campus was paid for by the proceeds of the Fisk Jubilee Singers.

In 1871, Fisk University needed money. Buildings at the school established in old Union army barracks in 1866 were decaying while more and more African Americans came to seek education.

So, in what might later be considered a very Nashville-style idea, the school choir withdrew all the money from the university's treasury and left on a world tour. The nine singers were Isaac Dickerson, Maggie Porter, Minnie Tate, Jennie Jackson, Benjamin Holmes, Thomas Rutling, Eliza Walker, Green Evans, and Ella Sheppard. Remembering a biblical reference to the Hebrew "year of the jubilee," Fisk treasurer and choir manager George White gave them their name, the Fisk Jubilee Singers.

The choir struggled at first, but before long audiences were singing their praises. They toured first the American South, then the North, and in 1873 sailed to England for a successful British tour. Their audiences included William Lloyd Garrison, Wendell Phillips, Ulysses S. Grant, William Gladstone, Mark Twain, Johann Strauss, and Queen Victoria. Songs like "Swing Low, Sweet Chariot" and "Nobody Knows the Trouble I've Seen" moved audiences to tears. The singers introduced the spiritual to mainstream white audiences and erased negative misconceptions about African Americans and African American education.

In 1874 the singers returned to Nashville. They had raised enough money to pay off Fisk's debts and build the university's first permanent structure, an imposing Victorian Gothic six-story building now called Jubilee Hall. It was the first permanent structure built solely for the education of African Americans in the United States.

Every October 6, the day in 1871 that the singers departed Fisk, the University recalls their struggle and their triumph with a convocation featuring the modern-day Jubilee Singers.

College of Nashville, under the auspices of the Freeman's Aid Society of the Methodist Episcopal Church.

Meharry was at one time responsible for graduating more than half of all African American doctors and nurses in the United States. Today it has an enrollment of almost 800 students.

Marathon Village

This "new" neighborhood is actually one that dates back to 1881. A former auto factory, Marathon Village (www.marathonvillage.com) now houses sleek urban condos, restaurants, the Corsair Artisan Distillery, Bang Candy Company, and shops, including Antique Archaeology Nashville, owned by Mike Wolfe of *American Pickers* TV fame. Marathon Village's gentrification has been slow, and it still has a ways to go to be a bustling destination. But the 2011 addition of live music venue Marathon Music Works is bringing out the locals, and architecture and history buffs love the buildings' bones.

Hadley Park

Founded in 1912, Hadley Park (1037 28th Ave. N., 615/862-8451) is believed to be the oldest public park developed for African Americans in the South and, most likely, the United States. The park got its start when Fisk University president George Gates requested that the city buy land and create a park for its black citizens. This was in the era of segregation, so other city parks were not open to blacks. The request was granted, and the park opened in July 1912. An old farmhouse was converted into a community center, and benches and a playground were installed. It is now home to a state-of-the-art gym and fitness center, computer labs, meeting rooms, and tennis courts.

Tennessee State University

Founded in 1912 as a normal school for blacks, Tennessee State University (3500 John A. Merritt Blvd., 615/963-5000, www.tnstate.edu) is now a comprehensive university with more than 9,000 students. In 1979, as a result of a court order to desegregate the state's universities, TSU merged with the Nashville campus of the University of Tennessee. Today, TSU's student body is 75 percent African American.

MUSIC VALLEY

A collection of tourist attractions separated from the rest of Nashville by the Cumberland River, Music Valley is most known for being the new home of the Grand Ole Opry. The area was one of those hit hardest by the 2010 flood, leading to some significant improvements and upgrades, and some closures. This strip of motels, restaurants, and country music "museums" is tourist-centric. It is more campy than authentic, although it does offer some fun, affordable ways to explore Music City's kitsch.

If you're game, however, head straight for **Cooter's** (2613 McGavock Pk., 615/872-8358, www.cootersplace.com, Mon.–Thurs. 9 A.M.–7 P.M., Fri.–Sat. 9 A.M.–8 P.M., Sun. 9 A.M.–6 P.M., free), a gift shop and museum dedicated to the *Dukes of Hazzard* television show. The museum features a mind-boggling array of toys, ornaments, and model cars manufactured in the 1970s and '80s to profit off the Dukes' wild popularity. You can also see one of the bright-orange Dodge Chargers that became the Dukes' icon. In the gift shop, buy a pair of "official" Daisy Dukes or any number of General Lee souvenirs. Cooter's is operated by Ben Jones, who played Cooter, the affable sidekick mechanic, in the original television series. In recent years, Jones has been one of the forces behind DukeFest, a wildly popular annual celebration of fast cars and the General Lee held at the Nashville Motor Speedway.

A few doors down from Cooter's, you will find **Willie Nelson and Friends Museum** (2613 McGavock Pk., 615/885-1515, Mon.–Sat. 8:30 A.M.–9 P.M., Sun. 8:30 A.M.–8 P.M., $10), which showcases a number of things that once

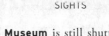

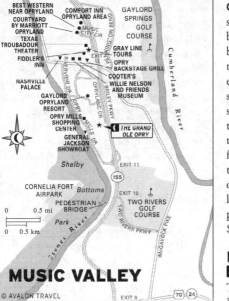

MUSIC VALLEY

© AVALON TRAVEL

belonged to Willie Nelson, including his golf bag, a replica of his tour bus, and the guitar he played during his first performance on the Grand Ole Opry. Many of the Willie Nelson items were purchased by museum operators Jeannie and Frank Oakley at an IRS auction.

The Grand Ole Opry

Since 1974, the Grand Ole Opry (2802 Opryland Dr., 615/871-6779, www.opry.com) has been most often staged at the specially built Grand Ole Opry House in Music Valley. This is the Opry's sixth regular home, and it was completely renovated after it was shuttered due to the 2010 flood. The Opry House may have been closed, but the Opry went on. The show still made the airwaves for every scheduled performance, playing at different venues around town while construction went on around the clock.

The Opry performs at least two times a week, Friday and Saturday, with additional shows on Tuesday night most weeks. The

Grand Ole Opry Museum is still shuttered since the flood (it is unclear if it will reopen), but with the renovated Opry came a renovated backstage tour. Daytime tour tickets go on sale two weeks in advance and are generally offered every 15 minutes; if you are buying tickets to a show, you can also purchase postconcert backstage tours. On this docent-led tour you'll get to see dressing rooms, learn lots of Opry history, and hear plenty of juicy stories about performers and their backstage behavior. One of the highlights of the guided tour is to get to go on stage and have your photo taken under the lights. If you book a postshow tour, you'll see a performer or two. Tickets are $17.50 for adults, $12.50 for children.

NORTH NASHVILLE
◖ Fontanel Mansion

The former estate of country music icon Barbara Mandrell, Fontanel Mansion (4225 Whites Creek Pk., 615/727-0304, www.fon tanelmansion.com, adults $22, seniors $20, children $12) has become a surprising draw for locals and tourists alike since it opened in 2010. These 136 acres include walking trails, a music venue, a restaurant with its own live music, an art gallery, and a gift shop. But the main attraction is the mansion, a 27,000-square-foot log cabin, which is the city's only country music mansion tour. Fans get to see how the most famous of the Mandrell sisters once lived. Tours are sometimes given by Mandrell's daughter, who throws in lots of personal tidbits. Even those who don't love "I Was Country When Country Wasn't Cool" will appreciate the music history, artifacts such as Gretchen Wilson's "Redneck Woman" Jeep, the indoor shooting range, and the bucolic scenery.

TOURS
Nash Trash Tour

Nashville's most notorious tour guides are Sheri Lynn and Brenda Kay Jugg, sisters who ferry good-humored tourists around town in a big pink school bus. The Nash Trash Tour (615/226-7300 or 800/342-2123, www.nashtrash.com, $32) is a raunchy, rollicking, rib-tickling tour of city attractions, some of which you won't even find in this guidebook. Be prepared to be the butt of some of the jokes yourself; their "I Got Trashed" T-shirts have a double meaning. You'll snack on canned cheese, and there's a pit stop to buy beer. Not appropriate for children or adults who aren't comfortable laughing at themselves and others. As Sheri Lynn says: "If we haven't offended you, just give us some time." Nash Trash tours sell out early and often. If you think you want this perspective on the city, make your reservation now. Tours depart from the Nashville Farmers' Market.

Gray Line Tours

Nashville's largest tour company, Gray Line (2416 Music Valley Dr., 615/883-5555 or 800/251-1864) offers more than 12 different sightseeing tours of the city. The three-hour Discover Nashville tour costs $47 per adult and includes entrance to the Ryman Auditorium and the Country Music Hall of Fame, and stops at other city landmarks.

The three-hour Homes of the Stars tour takes you past the homes of stars including Alan Jackson, Vince Gill, Dolly Parton, and the late Tammy Wynette for $35. There is also a one-hour downtown trolley tour for $15 and a 90-minute downtown walking tour for $20.

General Jackson Showboat

Gaylord Opryland's General Jackson Showboat (2812 Opryland Dr., 615/458-3900, www.

generaljackson.com, tickets $57–91, depending on time of day and year) offers campy, big-budget-style musical shows on the stage of a giant riverboat as it lumbers down the Cumberland River. Show dates and ties vary by season, but typically there are midday lunch and evening dinner cruises. A smaller boat, the *Music City Queen,* offers tailgating cruises before Titans football games. Because of the meal and the live entertainment, these cruises aren't necessarily the best way to see the river, as you're focused on the stage rather than the scenery.

Tennessee Central Railway

The Tennessee Central Railway Museum (220 Willow St., 615/244-9001, www.tcry.org) offers an annual calendar of sightseeing and themed railway rides in central Tennessee, including kids' trips, Old West shoot-outs, and murder mysteries. Excursions include fall foliage tours, Christmas shopping expeditions, and trips to scenic small towns. All trips run on the Nashville and Eastern Railroad, which runs east, stopping in Lebanon, Watertown, Cookville, or Monterrey. Prices vary based on the trip but are generally around $32 for adults.

These tours are not just train rides, but well-organized volunteer-led events. You might get "robbed" by a Wild West bandit (the cash goes to charity) or taken to a scenic winery. The volunteers know their railroad trivia, so feel free to ask questions. The cars vary depending on what is available, but there is a car that doubles as a gift shop and another that is a concession stand, although you are welcome to bring your own food on the train. Trips sell out early, so book your tickets well in advance.

Entertainment and Events

From live music to theater, Nashville offers visitors plenty of diversions. Even if you are not a fan of country music, you will find plenty to do in Music City.

LIVE MUSIC VENUES

No trip to Nashville is complete without listening to some live music. Music City overflows with musicians and opportunities to hear them. So whether you catch a show at the Opry, stake out a seat at The Bluebird Cafe, or enjoy a night at the symphony, be sure to make time for music during your visit.

Even before you arrive in the city, you can plan out your nights thanks to the Nashville Convention and Visitors Bureau (www.nashvillecvb.com). Through a handy feature on the bureau's website you can check out upcoming concerts a month or more in advance. Many venues will let you buy tickets in advance over the phone or online. But don't panic if you can't plan ahead. One of the benefits of being in Music City is that there is always a show worth seeing somewhere. And because there are so many shows, there is always something that hasn't sold out.

Published on Wednesday, the *Nashville Scene* always includes detailed entertainment listings and recommendations. The *Tennessean*, the city's daily paper, publishes its entertainment insert on Friday. Now Playing Nashville (www.nowplayingnashville.com), an initiative with the Community Foundation of Middle Tennessee, is a great resource for both entertainment listings and discounted tickets. Now Playing Nashville has a kiosk in the Nashville airport.

◖ The Grand Ole Opry

If there's any one thing you really must do while in Nashville, it's go to see the Grand Ole Opry (2802 Opryland Dr., 615/871-6779 or 800/733-6779, www.opry.com, $35–50). Really. Even if you think you don't like country music. For more than 80 years this weekly radio showcase of country music has drawn crowds to Nashville. Every show at the Opry is still broadcast live on WSM, a Nashville AM radio station. Shows are also streamed online, and some are televised on cable. But nothing beats the experience of being there.

The Opry runs on Friday and Saturday night, with two 2.5-hour shows each night. The early show starts at 6:30 P.M., and the late show starts at 9:30 P.M. Often there is an additional Tuesday evening show. Since this is a radio broadcast, shows start and end right on time.

Every Opry show is divided into 30-minute segments, each of which is hosted by a different member of the Opry. This elite country music fraternity includes dozens of stars that you've heard of and others you haven't. The host performs two songs; one at the beginning of their half-hour segment and one at the end. In between they will introduce two or three other performers, each of whom will sing about two songs. In between segments, the announcers read radio commercials and stagehands change around the stage set.

All in all, it is a fast-paced show that keeps your toes tapping. Even if there's an act that you don't like, they won't be on the stage for too long. Of course, the flip side is that if it's an act you love, well, they're only on the stage for two songs, too. Even when the biggest stars appear on the Opry stage, they rarely sing more than a few numbers. Fans are welcomed, and even encouraged, to walk to the front of the seating area to take photographs during the performances.

The Opry usually releases the full lineup for each show about a week in advance. Some fans wait until then to buy their tickets so they're sure to catch a big-name artist. My advice is

NASHVILLE

The Grand Ole Opry

to forget about bragging to your friends back home about who you saw at the Opry and buy tickets to any show at all. Each show is carefully balanced to include bluegrass, classic country, popular country, and, sometimes, gospel or rock. It is a true showcase that music and Americana fans will enjoy.

Most Opry shows take place in the Grand Ole Opry House, a 4,400-seat auditorium in Music Valley that was renovated after the 2010 flood. A circle of the original stage from the Ryman Auditorium was cut out and placed in the center of the Opry House stage, and it is here that artists stand when they perform. During the Christmas season the Opry returns to its Ryman roots (and the Radio City Rockettes take the Opry House stage).

One advantage of shows at the Opry House is that you can buy tickets for a guided backstage tour. Tickets go on sale two weeks in advance; times vary based on the time of year and time of day. The tours include a peek at the Green Room, Opry stars' mailbox, and other behind-the-scenes treasures. If you book one of the evening tours, you're likely to see performers jamming in folding chairs after a show. Glitzy costumes, juicy stories, and a chance to walk on that stage are all part of the tour offerings.

Tours are $17.50 for adults and $12.50 for children. You can also book combination packages that include the backstage tours, an Opry performance, and hotel rooms and meals at the Gaylord Opryland Resort.

Texas Troubadour Theatre

Known as the Texas Troubadour, Ernest Tubb started a tradition when he set up a live radio show at the back of his Broadway record shop. The **Ernest Tubb Midnite Jamboree** was broadcast after the Opry shut down across the street, and it lived up to its name. The Jamboree continues, now broadcast from the Texas Troubadour Theatre (Music Valley Village, 2416 Music Valley Dr., 615/889-2472,

PRESENTING THE GRAND OLE OPRY

Nashville's most famous broadcast can trace its roots to October 1925, when Nashville-based National Life and Accident Insurance Company opened a radio station in town. Its call letters (then and now), WSM, stood for "We Shield Millions," the company's motto.

WSM hired George D. Hay, a radio announcer who had worked in Memphis and Chicago, to manage the station. Hay—who, while in Chicago, had announced one of the nation's first live country radio shows—planned to create a similar such program in Nashville.

On November 25, 1925, Hay invited a 78-year-old fiddler, Uncle Jimmy Thompson, to perform live on Saturday night over the radio waves. The response was electric, and WSM continued to broadcast live old-time music every Saturday night. In May 1927, the program developed the name the Grand Ole Opry, practically by chance. An announcer named Judge Hay was segueing from the previous program of classical opera to the barn dance. "For the past hour, we have been listening to music taken largely from Grand Opera. From now on, we will present the Grand Ole Opry," he said. The name stuck.

During the first few years, most Opry performers were unknowns who worked day jobs in and around Nashville. But as the show gained popularity, some acts were able to make it professionally, including Uncle Dave Macon, the Vagabonds, and the Delmore Brothers. By 1939,

the Opry gained a slot on the nationwide NBC radio network, allowing it to reach a national audience every week.

Always a live audience show, the Opry was performed in several different venues over the years. It started in the WSM studio, then moved to the Hillsboro Theater (now the Belcourt), the Dixie Tabernacle on Fatherland Street, and the War Memorial Auditorium downtown. In 1943 it moved to the Ryman Auditorium, where it remained until 1974, when National Life built a new 5,000-seat auditorium in a rural area north of Nashville. The first show from the new Opry House in Music Valley was broadcast on March 16, 1974. President Richard Nixon attended. In 1983, the Opry was acquired by Oklahoma-based Gaylord Broadcasting Company. After the 2010 Nashville flood, the Opry House was gutted and renovated by Gaylord Entertainment, who still owns all the Opry properties.

The music that flows from the Opry's stage on a Saturday night (and now, Tuesday and Friday, too) has changed since the first fiddler took the airwaves. Just as country music broadened its appeal by softening its hard edges, the Opry has evolved with its audience. Today it is a showcase for all types of country and country-inspired music, including bluegrass, gospel, honky-tonk, and zydeco. It remains, however, one of the most esteemed and celebrated institutions in American music.

www.ernesttubb.com, no cover). Located across the street from the Gaylord Opryland Resort, the Jamboree gets started early in the evening, while the Opry is still on, but things really get swinging after midnight.

The Texas Troubadour Theatre is also home to the **Cowboy Church** (2416 Music Valley Dr., 615/859-1001, www.nashvillecowboychurch.org). Every Sunday at 10 A.M., locals and tourists dressed in anything from shorts to Stetsons gather here for a lively praise-and-worship country gospel church service led by Dr. Harry Yates and Dr. Joanne Cash Yates.

The church was founded in 1990 with just six souls; today it attracts hundreds to its weekly services. Country and gospel music legends make cameo performances now and again, but the real star is Jesus.

The Ryman Auditorium

The most famous music venue in Nashville, the Ryman Auditorium (116 5th Ave. N., 615/889-1060, www.ryman.com, cover varies) continues to book some of the best acts in town, of just about every genre you can imagine. On the good side, the hall still boasts some of the best acoustics around. On the bad, the pew-style bench seats are just as uncomfortable as ever. But seeing the reverence performers have for this venue makes it hard to notice anything else. Musicians love to show off the acoustics here, often playing a song or two without a mic.

Country Music Hall of Fame

The Country Music Hall of Fame (222 5th Ave. S., 615/416-2100, www.countrymusichalloffame.com) hosts concerts, readings, and musical discussions regularly in an auditorium located inside the hall. These daytime events are often aimed at highlighting one type of country music or another, but sometimes you'll find big names playing. Admission is free with your paid admission to the hall, so it is a good idea to plan your trip to the hall on a day when there's a concert scheduled (separate admission to concerts is not available). Check the website for a listing of upcoming events.

Woods Amphitheater

Opened in 2010, this 4,500-seat outdoor concert venue is nestled, as its name suggests, in the woods at Fontanel, a spot that used to be the home of country star Barbara Mandrell. The Woods Amphitheater (4225 Whites Creek Pk., 615/727-0304, www.woodsamphitheater.com) has space for picnicking on the lawn during a concert and VIP boxes, as well as folding chairs for a more traditional concert experience. Fontanel often operates free shuttles to and from downtown, for those who don't want to drive to Whites Creek for a concert. This can be a bonus, as the driveway to the parking lot can get congested.

Marathon Music Works

The 14,500 square feet at Marathon Music Works (1402 Clinton St., 615/891-1781, www.marathonmusicworks.com, ticket prices vary depending on the performing artist) are some of Nashville's most progressive when it comes to

concertgoing. Located in the historic Marathon Village, this venue has exposed brick, a swanky VIP loft area, multiple bars, and plenty of space for cutting the rug. Musical acts booked run the gamut from The Black Belles to the Younder Mountain String Band.

◖ The Bluebird Cafe

In some ways no other music venue is as quintessentially Nashville as The Bluebird Cafe (4104 Hillsboro Pk., 615/383-1461, www.bluebirdcafe.com, cover varies). It is intimate and homey. It books some of the best up-and-coming country and acoustic acts in the business, as well as the songwriters who penned the lyrics you are used to hearing other people sing. Its shows start as early as 6:30 P.M. There is no talking during the acts and virtually none of the usual bar pickup scene. In short, The Bluebird is a place where music comes first and everything else is a far second.

Opened in 1982 by Amy Kurland, The Bluebird is located next to a dry cleaners in a nondescript shopping mall a few miles south of Hillsboro Village. While it started out as a casual restaurant with live music, over the years it evolved into a destination for music lovers who appreciate its no-nonsense take on live music, and who hope that they just might stumble in on the next big thing. The Bluebird is famous as an early venue for the then-unknown Garth Brooks, but its stage has also hosted the likes of Emmylou Harris, Kathy Mattea, Gillian Welch, Trisha Yearwood, and Steve Earle, among many more. In 2008 it was sold to the Nashville Songwriters Association International, a deal that has improved the venue by streamlining some of the booking and ticket-buying processes.

The Bluebird is open every night of the week, and most evenings the entertainment starts at 6:30 P.M. Cover is usually under $15. There are just 20 tables and a few additional seats at the bar, so, depending on the show, you have to be on your toes to get a spot in the house. Reservations are only taken online (not by email or by phone), and some shows are first come, first seated only.

Once you've successfully nabbed a seat at The Bluebird, sit back and enjoy some fine live music (but really, no talking—you will be shushed). Nashville is the city where anybody can become a somebody, and it's places like The Bluebird that make that happen.

CONCERT SERIES

Dyer Observatory (1000 Oman Dr., 615/373-4897, www.dyer.vanderbilt.edu), a working space observatory operated by Vanderbilt University, has emerged as a popular venue for music, thanks to two ongoing concert series. **Music on the Mountain,** with Blair School of Music, and **Bluebird on the Mountain** ($105 per carload) with The Bluebird Cafe, bring live music to this dramatic and one-of-a-kind spot. Imagine a night of fine music enjoyed under the stars, with the fresh air and the atmosphere of the forest all around you.

Thursday nights in September and October transform downtown's Public Square Park for **Live on the Green** (www.liveonthegreen.net, free). The outdoor concert series tends to attract a lot of indie rock acts, and the crowd is young, hip, and socially aware. Food and arts and crafts vendors line the sidewalks under tents.

Also taking place on Thursday nights in the summer, **Bluegrass Nights at the Ryman** (www.ryman.com/bluegrass, free) is a concert series that features some of the best pickers in the country. Starting in June and ending in July, this Ryman Auditorium series is always popular.

For a laid-back evening in a one-of-a-kind setting, check out the Tennessee Jazz and Blues Society's concert series **Jazz on the Lawn** (www.jazzblues.org). On Sunday evenings May–October, jazz and blues artists take the stage on the lawns of some of Nashville's most historic homes, including Belle Meade and Cheekwood. Bring your own picnic and blanket.

As great as the Opry is (and it *is great*), sometimes the music seems a little, well, dated. On Wednesday nights you can experience an Opry-style live radio show, but with more cutting-edge country, Americana, and bluegrass acts, during **Music City Roots** (www.musiccityroots.com). This two-plus-hour multiple-act show includes live interview segments with the artists, on-the-air commercials, and an audience that often gets up and dances. Stay till the very end for the Loveless Jam, when all the night's performers cram on stage for one last song. The show takes place at the Loveless Barn; tickets are just $10.

CLUBS

Venues here are categorized by their predominant music type, but keep in mind that variety is the name of the game. Most bars and clubs (except for honky-tonks) charge a cover when there is a band or performer, while songwriter nights and open mics are usually free.

Country

Nashville's most colorful country music establishments are the honky-tonks that line Broadway. Once places where country boys and girls would come to shake a leg or meet a sweetheart, these all-day, all-night bars and music clubs now cater to visitors. After the Opry moved to Music Valley in the late 1970s, taking with it the customers who kept Broadway businesses afloat, the street's honky-tonks subsisted first on local barflies and later on the tourist trade. But now they've bounced back, and locals and visitors alike take advantage of the high energy, cheap beer, and talented musicians found here. Whether you're looking for a place to drown your sorrows or kick off a night on the town, Broadway's honky-tonks are a good place to go. They are always open and typically free, although you are encouraged to participate when the hat is passed for the band.

Tootsie's Orchid Lounge (422 Broadway,

615/726-0463, no cover) is painted purple and exudes classic country every day of the week beginning as early as 10 A.M. Three doors down from Tootsie's is **Robert's Western World** (416 Broadway, 615/244-9552, www.robertswesternworld.com, no cover), voted the city's best honky-tonk. Originally a store selling boots, cowboy hats, and other country music regalia, Robert's morphed into a bar and nightclub with a good gift shop. Another choice is **The Stage** (412 Broadway, 615/726-0504, no cover), with a large dance floor and music seven nights a week.

The **Wildhorse Saloon** (120 2nd Ave. N., 615/902-8200, www.wildhorsesaloon.com, cover varies) is a boot-scootin', beer-drinkin' place to see and be seen, although almost exclusively by tourists. When the Wildhorse opened in 1994, promoters drove a herd of cattle through the streets of downtown Nashville. The huge dance floor is often packed with cowboys and cowgirls line dancing to the greatest country hits. Free dance lessons are offered every day (Mon.–Thurs. 6:30–8:30 P.M., Fri. 6–9:30 P.M., Sat. noon–9:30 P.M., Sun. 2–7:30 P.M.). The Wildhorse books big-name acts many nights of the week, including country music, roots rock, and classic rock stars. The Wildhorse opens Thursday–Sunday at 11 A.M. and on Monday at 5 P.M. When there is a show on, doors normally close at 6 P.M. and reopen at 7 P.M. for people with tickets. On other nights the cover charge is $4–6. From 10 P.M. on, the Wildhorse is a 21-and-up club. The Wildhorse is owned by Gaylord, the same folks who own the Ryman, Opryland, and the Opry, and often offers deals for hotel guests. There is a shuttle back to the Opryland Hotel for folks staying there.

It doesn't look like much (or anything) from the outside, but inside this cinder block box is the city's most popular venue for bluegrass and roots music. **The Station Inn** (402 12th Ave. S., 615/255-3307, www.stationinn.com, cover varies) is perhaps the country's best bluegrass club, and it showcases fine artists every night of the week. This homey and casual club opens nightly at 7 P.M., with music starting about 9 P.M. This is a 21-and-over club, unless you come with a parent or guardian. There is no cover for the Sunday-night bluegrass jam. Monday nights feature The Time Jumpers, a world-class Western swing jam band. Most Tuesday nights the hilarious parody **The Doyle and Debbie Show** (www.doyleanddebbie.com, $20) takes the stage.

The **Nashville Palace** (2400 Music Valley Dr., 615/889-1540, no cover) is a restaurant, nightclub, and dance floor across from the Opryland Hotel. Live music is on tap daily starting at 5 P.M., and talent nights on Tuesday and Wednesday always draw a crowd.

Jazz and Blues

If you need to get that country twang out of your head, a good dose of the Memphis blues will do it. **B.B. King Blues Club** (152 2nd Ave. N., 615/256-2727, www.bbkingclubs.com, cover varies) is a good place to start for a night of the blues. The club is a satellite of King's original Beale Street club, and it books live blues every night. The cover charge is usually under $10, unless B. B. King himself is making one of his rare appearances.

In Printer's Alley, the **Bourbon Street Blues and Boogie Bar** (220 Printer's Alley, 615/242-5867, cover varies) is a hole-in-the-wall nightclub that specializes in New Orleans–style jazz and blues.

A fine-dining restaurant next door to the Mall at Green Hills, **F. Scott's** (2210 Crestmore Rd., 615/269-5861, www.fscotts.com, no cover) is also one of the city's premier venues for live jazz. The music goes well with the restaurant's art deco appeal. Come for dinner or for a few drinks at the bar while you listen in. Although there's no cover at the door, there is a two-drink minimum if you're not dining.

While not a club per se, the **Nashville Jazz Workshop** (1319 Adams St., 615/242-5299, www.

nashvillejazz.org, cover varies) has live performances in its Jazz Cave as well as at special events around town. Ticket prices are typically modest.

Eclectic

Clubs listed here may book a rock band one night and folk the next. Always check the free weekly *Nashville Scene* for the latest entertainment listings.

The **Exit/In** (2208 Elliston Pl., 615/321-3340, www.exitin.com, cover varies) has been a favorite rock music venue for years, although it also books alternative country, blues, and reggae. Located on Elliston Place, the club is convenient to Vanderbilt and downtown.

Coffee shop by day, bar and live music venue by night, **Café Coco** (210 Louise Ave., 615/321-2626, www.cafecoco.com, cover varies) in Elliston Place is the best of both worlds. Monday is songwriter's night, Tuesday is open-mic poetry, and Thursday is open mic music. Jazz and rock bands play other nights, when the cover is $2–5.

The Basement (1604 8th Ave. S., 615/254-8006, www.thebasementnashville.com, cover varies) calls itself a cellar full of noise, but it's a good kind of noise. Indie rock is the most common art form here, but they book other types of acts, too. The Basement's New Faces Night on Tuesday is a popular place to hear singer-songwriters. Admission is 21 and over, unless accompanied by a parent or guardian. The brick walls and subterranean feel give the Basement its cool atmosphere. It is nestled under **Grimey's New and Pre-Loved Music,** one of the city's best record stores. Park behind the club and on side streets.

Located in an old warehouse that has housed a flour mill, jam factory, and country music concert hall, **Cannery Row** (One Cannery Row, 615/251-3020, www.mercylounge.com, cover varies) and its derivative **Mercy Lounge** are two cool venues for live music. Cannery Row is a large, somewhat cavernous space with lots of nice cherry-red touches, hardwood floors, and a shiny red bar. It can hold up to 1,000 people. The Mercy Lounge upstairs is a bit more intimate, with a capacity of up to 500 people. The Mercy Lounge hosts 8 off 8th on Monday nights, an open mic where eight different bands get to perform three songs. Both venues book rock, country, soul, and all sorts of other acts. It is located off 8th Avenue South.

A music venue designed by performers, **The Rutledge** (410 4th Ave. S., 615/782-6858, www.therutledgelmv.com, cover varies) has some of the most ear-pleasing acoustics in the city. An intimate venue—it seats only 250—the Rutledge books a wide variety of acts, hosts industry events, and even puts on tribute shows now and then.

3rd and Lindsley (818 3rd Ave. S., 615/259-9891, www.3rdandlindsley.com, cover varies) is a neighborhood bar and grill that showcases rock, alternative, progressive, Americana, soul, and R&B music. Over the years they have developed a reputation for booking good blues acts. They serve a full lunch and dinner menu, the bar is well stocked, and the club offers a great atmosphere and sound quality.

Over In East Nashville, the **French Quarter Cafe** (823 Woodland St., 615/227-3100, cover varies) offers a Thursday night in-the-round songwriter's night. Weekends will find blues, rock, and soul musicians on the stage at this New Orleans–style nightclub. Dine on spicy po'boys, muffuletta, or other Cajun specialties while you enjoy a night out.

The **Douglas Corner Cafe** (2106-A 8th Ave. S., 615/298-1688, www.douglascorner.com, cover varies) offers a Tuesday-night open mic and country and other acts the rest of the week. It is known as a place where singer-songwriters are discovered, and it is laid-back in both attitude and ambience. An intimate setting, full menu, and good acoustics make this a popular choice for music listening. Several live albums have been recorded here.

BARS

Barhopping is best enjoyed downtown, where there is the greatest concentration of

Printer's Alley is home to several nightclubs and bars, including the Bourbon Street Blues and Boogie Bar.

NASHVILLE

nightclubs, restaurants, and bars. Even on weeknights lower Broadway and its side streets are crowded with people, some dressed in designer cowboy boots and fringed shirts, others in Preds jerseys, others in business suits. This is the official entertainment district of Nashville, and it is well patrolled by police and cruisers alike. Outside of downtown, there are several other enclaves of nightlife that cater more to residents than visitors.

Nashville won't issue a liquor license unless the establishment also serves food, so all of the following bars double as restaurants.

Downtown

The honky-tonks along Broadway, Wildhorse Saloon, and B. B. King Blues Club are several of the most popular nightclubs downtown. Right next to the Wildhorse Saloon, **Coyote Ugly** (154 2nd Ave. N., 615/254-8459, www.

coyoteugly.com) draws a youthful, raucous crowd. Drinking beer and making friends are the two primary pursuits here, and for many visitors, there's no better place to do either.

Memorabilia of Nashville's past adorns the walls at **Legends Corner** (428 Broadway, 615/248-6334), a popular and more authentic club for live music and rollicking crowds. There is never a cover, but, as always, be sure to put in a few bucks when they pass the hat for the performer.

A few blocks from downtown, near the Frist Center for the Visual Arts, you'll find one of the city's best beer bars. Behind the Union Station Hotel on the west side of downtown, the **Flying Saucer** (1001 Broadway, 615/259-7468, www.beerknurd.com) has one of the best selections of beer in town. Monday is pint night, when you can get $2.50 pints of just about any of the beers on the wall.

Duck into **The Beer Sellar** (107 Church St., 615/254-9464, www.beersellar.net) to experience its "50 draughts, 150 bottles, and 1 bitching jukebox." Located within walking distance of downtown, this is a cozy bar for conversation and fun.

Another popular brewpub is **Big River Grille and Brewing Works** (111 Broadway, 615/251-4677), an imposing bar and restaurant right near Riverfront Park. They serve food as well as boutique beers from around the world.

Printer's Alley

This narrow strip of downtown, located in between 3rd and 4th Avenues off Church Street, is home to a half dozen nightclubs and bars, some of which cultivate a seedy reputation. While reality is a bit more tame, it is still a popular place to let loose. Elaborate wrought-iron balconies and the historic cobblestone underfoot evoke Bourbon Street, a parallel that seems to suit the place. Bars here include **Bourbon Street Blues and Boogie Bar** (220 Printer's Alley, 615/242-5867) and **Fiddle and Steel** (201 Printer's Alley, 615/251-9002). Printer's Alley also has two terrific karaoke bars and one of the city's most storied adult-entertainment bars. If you think your karaoke skills can keep up with all the Music City pros, head to **Lonnie's Western Room** (208 Printer's Alley, 615/828-7971, www.lonnieswesternroom.com).

Midtown

Elliston Place is home to several live music clubs, plus a few neighborhood bars and college hangouts (Elliston is just blocks from the Vanderbilt University campus). The Exit/In and The End have live bands most nights of the week. You can play a game of pool at **George Elliston's Pool Place Hall** (2200 Elliston Pl., 615/320-9441). This is a back-to-the-basics hangout where good drinks, good pool, and good people make for a good night out. **The Gold Rush** (2205 Elliston Pl., 615/321-1160, www.goldrushnashville.com) is a time-worn but beloved late-night mellow hangout.

Boscos (1805 21st Ave. S., 615/385-0050, www.boscosbeer.com/nashville/story) calls itself a beer-lover's restaurant. While food is important here, it is Boscos' reputation for good beer that keeps patrons coming back. Stake out a front window seat to people-watch in always-hopping Hillsboro Village while you drink your beer.

Also in Hillsboro Village, **Cabana** (1910 Belcourt Ave., 615/577-2262, www.cabananashville.com) is a popular, if trendy, place to people-watch and unwind. It is a bar/restaurant/late-night hangout that attracts a youthful and well-dressed crowd. Lounge at the bar or in the expansive backyard. Choose from dozens of beers, wines, and some excellent martinis.

Blackstone Restaurant and Brewery (1918 West End Ave., 615/327-9969, www.blackstonebrewery.com) is a local favorite, with its own brand of craft beers, a cozy fireplace, and a laid-back vibe. The menu features better-than-bar food.

There's no sign on the exterior, but that hasn't kept people across the country from discovering **Patterson House** (1711 Division St., 615/636-7724, www.thepattersonnashville.

com). Cocktails here are mixed with care, and there's no standing room. You must have a seat in order to be served, both of which contribute to a civilized cocktail hour.

Near the Mall at Green Hills, **The Greenhouse** (2211 Bandywood Dr., 615/385-3357) offers specialty drinks, beers, and lots of hanging plants. To find it, look for the Green Hills Kroger and take a left. Its location means you'll find more locals than tourists. A few doors down, **The Box Seat** (2221 Bandywood Dr., 615/383-8018) is a bona fide sports bar with televisions in every direction.

East Nashville

Edgefield Sports Bar and Grille (921 Woodland St., 615/228-6422) is a no-frills watering hole that caters to East Nashville residents.

No. 308 (407 Gallatin Ave., 615/650-7344, www.bar308.com) is a sleek, mod, hipster hangout with hand-crafted drinks. Come during happy hour, when these custom cocktails are more budget friendly.

Another Nashville mixology house that has received national attention, **Holland House Bar and Refuge** (935 W. Eastland Ave., 615/262-4190, www.hollandhousebarandrefuge.com) specializes in handmade, old-fashioned cocktails. The bar stocks an impressive selection of whiskey and bourbon, and hires bartenders who know how to use them.

You might think you're south of the border at the **Rosepepper Cantina** (1907 Eastland Ave., 615/227-4777, www.rosepepper.com), a Mexican restaurant and bar. Choose from 30 different variations of the margarita, and enjoy the house band on weekend nights.

12 South

The gentrified neighborhood on 12th Avenue South has attracted new residents, and they like to hang out at a number of neighborhood bars.

Snag a seat on the crowded patio outside **Mafiaoza's Pizzeria and Neighborhood Pub**

NASHVILLE

(2400 12th Ave. S., 615/269-4646, www.mafiaozas.com), a popular neighborhood hangout known for its pizza, which you watch be slid into the giant ovens.

The extensive list of brews on tap has earned **12 South Taproom and Grill** (2318 12th Ave. S., 615/463-7552, www.12southtaproom.com) a loyal following. The above-average bar food includes several vegetarian-friendly options.

GAY AND LESBIAN NIGHTLIFE

You don't have to be gay to enjoy **Tribe** (1517-A Church St., 615/329-2912), but it helps to be beautiful, or at least well dressed. The dance floor here is one of the best in the city, and the atmosphere is hip. Martinis and other specialty drinks are the poison of choice at this standard-setting club, which stays open until the wee hours.

Right next door to Tribe is **Play** (1519 Church St., 615/322-9627), the city's highest-energy gay club, with drag shows and performances by adult-film stars.

The Chute Complex (2535 Franklin Rd., 615/297-4571) has karaoke, drag shows, and a dance floor. It caters to gay men.

Women outnumber men at the **Lipstick Lounge** (1400 Woodland St., 615/226-6343, www.thelipsticklounge.com), a cool yet homey club in East Nashville. Live music, pool, and great food attract a crowd nearly every night. Across the street is **Mad Donna's** (1313 Woodland St., 615/226-1617, www.maddonnas.com), where the second floor is home to drag queen bingo, karaoke, and other festivities.

For a low-key evening of pool or a happy-hour stop before dinner, **TRAX** (1501 2nd Ave. S., 615/742-8856) is the place to go. The patio is a nice place to sit in warm weather. There is wireless Internet and big-screen televisions, but little in the way of ambience.

COMEDY

Nashville's only dedicated comedy club is **Zanies** (2025 8th Ave. S., 615/269-0221), where you can hear stand-up comics every weekend and some weeknights. But there's much to amuse you all over town, including **The Doyle and Debbie Show** at **The Station Inn** (402 12th Ave. S., 615/255-3307, www.stationinn.com) and the **Nash Trash Tour** (615/226-7300 or 800/342-2123, www.nashtrash.com, $32). Check out comedy listings at **Nash Comedy** (www.nashcomedy.com).

THE ARTS

Before Nashville was Music City, it was the Athens of the South, a city renowned for its cultural, academic, and artistic life. Universities, museums, and public arts facilities created an environment for artistic expression unparalleled by any other Southern city. It has an opera company of its own, not to mention an award-winning symphony (and symphony center), an innovative arts scene, and ample opportunities

Doyle & Debbie parody (and praise) Nashville at the Station Inn.

FAMOUS NASHVILLIANS

Nashville is used to celebrity, what with all the music stars around. But it's not just musicians who call, or called, Nashville home:

- **"Jefferson Street Joe" Gilliam,** one of the first African American quarterbacks in the National Football League, played college ball at Tennessee State University. The former quarterback for the Pittsburgh Steelers died in 2000 in his hometown of Nashville, five days before his 50th birthday.

- **Madison Smartt Bell** was born and raised in Nashville. The novelist's works include *All Souls Rising, Ten Indians,* and *The Year of Silence.*

- **Oprah Winfrey** was raised in Nashville by her father, Vernon. In her second year at Tennessee State University she was hired as Nashville's first female and first African American TV news anchor on WTVF-TV.

- **Julian Bond,** civil rights activist, political activist, and the chairman of the NAACP, was born in Nashville and lived here until he was five years old.

- **Bobby Jones,** host of BET's *Bobby Jones Gospel,* was once a professor at Tennessee State University. The program is the longest-running show on cable television and is taped in Nashville.

- **Red Grooms** was born and raised in Nashville. Grooms is a prominent modern American artist whose pop art depicts frenetic scenes of urban life.

- **Al Gore Jr.,** though born in Washington DC and raised in Carthage, Tennessee, is closely associated with Nashville. After the Vietnam War he attended Vanderbilt University for one year and then spent five years as a reporter for the *Tennessean.* The former U.S. vice president has had a home in Nashville for many decades.

- Aussie actress **Nicole Kidman** may have moved to Nashville for the career of her country-singing hubby, **Keith Urban,** but she has made it her own. She is frequently seen around town with her family.

to sample contemporary and classic music, film, and theater.

Theater

The **Tennessee Repertory Theatre** (505 Deaderick St., 615/782-4000, www.tennesseerep. org) is Tennessee's largest professional theater company. It stages five big-name shows and three off-Broadway productions annually. The Rep performs in the Tennessee Performing Arts Center, located in the James K. Polk Cultural Center in downtown Nashville. This is the same building that houses the Tennessee State Museum, plus some Nashville Opera performances, and the Nashville Ballet. Some of their productions have included *The Crucible, I Hate Hamlet,* and *Doubt.* The season runs October–May.

Artists' Cooperative Theatre (ACT 1, 615/726-2281, www.act1online.com) is an organization dedicated to bringing theatrical gems, both classic and modern, to Nashville audiences. Founded in 1989, ACT 1 has presented productions of more than 90 of the world's greatest plays. Each year the theater puts on four or five productions. ACT 1 performs at the Darkhorse Theater at 4610 Charlotte Avenue.

New theatrical works are given the spotlight by the **Actors Bridge Ensemble** (1312 Adams St., 615/341-0300, www.actorsbridge. org), a theater company for new and seasoned actors. The Ensemble brings provocative and new plays to Nashville, often performing at the Belmont Black Box Theater in midtown.

Circle Players (www.circleplayers.net) is the oldest nonprofit, all-volunteer arts association in Nashville. As a community theater, all actors, stagehands, directors, and other helpers are volunteers. The company stages four or five performances every year at a variety of theater locations around the city. Performances include classic theater, plus stage adaptations of popular cinema and literature.

Nashville's leading experimental theater group is the **People's Branch Theatre** (615/254-0008, www.peoplesbranch.org). Founded in 2000, the group brings together local actors to produce bold and innovative professional theater. They perform at the Belcourt Theatre in Hillsboro Village.

Children's Theater

Nashville Children's Theatre (724 2nd Ave. S., 615/254-9103, www.nashvillechildrenstheatre. org) is the oldest children's theater company in the United States. During the school year, the company puts on plays for children from preschool to elementary-school age in its colorful theater. In the summer there are drama classes for youngsters, plus lots of activities that include Mom and Dad.

Teenagers own and operate the **Real Life Players** (615/297-7113), a stalwart theater company that produces original plays written by Nashville teens. Profits are donated to teen-related community organizations. Plays are performed at the Darkhorse Theater at 4610 Charlotte Avenue.

Don't miss the **Marionette Shows at the Nashville Public Library** (615 Church St., 615/862-5800). Using marionettes from the collection of former library puppeteer Tom Tichenor, plus others acquired from Chicago's Peekabo Puppet Productions, the library's children's room staff put on excellent one-of-a-kind family entertainment.

Dinner Theater

Chaffin's Barn Dinner Theatre (8204 Hwy. 100, 615/646-9977, www.dinnertheatre. com, adults $60, students 13–18 $40, children 12 and under $30) was Nashville's first professional theater and continues to put on Broadway-style plays for dinner patrons. There's nothing cutting-edge about the shows or the meal, but they are family-friendly fun. If mystery is more your style, have dinner at **Miss Jeanne's Mystery Dinner Theatre** (600 9th Ave. S., 615/902-9566, www.missjeannes. com, $50), where you and your friends try to guess who done it while eating a Southern feast.

Music

The **Nashville Symphony Orchestra** (One Symphony Pl., 615/687-6400, www.nashvillesymphony.org) is housed in the remarkable Schermerhorn Symphony Center next to the Country Music Hall of Fame, one of the downtown buildings that was renovated as a result of 2010 flood damage. Nominated for four Grammies and selling more recordings than any other American orchestra, the symphony is a source of pride for Music City. Costa Rican conductor Giancarlo Guerrero is the symphony's seventh music director.

The symphony puts on more than 200 performances each year, including classical, pops, and children's concerts. Its season spans September–May. Buying tickets online is a breeze, especially since you can easily choose where you want to sit. There is discounted parking for symphony-goers in the Pinnacle at Symphony Place, across the street from the Schermerhorn.

During the summer, the symphony plays its **Centennial Park Concert Series.** Head to the Centennial Park band shell to hear free big-band, ballroom, and classical concerts with other parkgoers. It is a classic Nashville experience.

The **Blair School of Music** (2400 Blakemore Ave., 615/322-7651) presents student, faculty, and visiting artist recitals frequently during the school year. Vanderbilt University's music school, Blair addresses music through academic, pedagogical, and performing activities.

Listen to new works by American composers performed by the **Nashville Chamber Orchestra** (615/322-1226, www.nco.org). The orchestra's concerts include masterpieces and new works commissioned by the chamber orchestra, many of which fuse tradition with new genres, including jazz, Celtic, Latin, and world music.

Opera

Middle Tennessee's only opera association, the **Nashville Opera Association** (www.nashvilleopera.org) puts on an average of four main-stage performances per season (October–April) and does a six-week tour to area schools. They perform at the Tennessee Performing Arts Center at 505 Deaderick Street.

Ballet

Founded in 1981 as a civic dance company, the **Nashville Ballet** (505 Deaderick St., www.nashvilleballet.com) became a professional dance company in 1986. Entertaining more than 40,000 patrons each year, the ballet performs both classical and contemporary pieces at the Tennessee Performing Arts Center.

Cinemas

Once the home of the Grand Ole Opry (as is true of so many buildings in Nashville), the **Belcourt Theatre** (2102 Belcourt Ave., 615/383-9140, www.belcourt.org) is the city's best venue for independent films. Built in 1925 as a silent movie house, the Belcourt now screens a refreshing variety of independent and unusual films, plus hosts live music concerts. In the summer the Belcourt screens some films outdoors. Parking in the theater's Hillsboro Village lot is free for moviegoers. Ask for a code when you buy your ticket.

More mainstream arty flicks are shown at the **Regal Cinemas Green Hills** (3815 Green Hills Village, 615/269-5910). Mainstream multiplex cinemas can be found near Opryland, 100 Oaks, Rivergate, and other neighborhoods.

FESTIVALS AND EVENTS
January

There's only one day all year that **The

Hermitage, the Home of Andrew Jackson** (4580 Rachel's Ln., 615/889-2941, www.thehermitage.com) is free to the public, and that's to celebrate the former president's victory at the Battle of New Orleans. The free day is typically on a weekend closest to January 8.

February

The second week of February is **Antiques Week** (www.nashvilleantiquesweek.com) in Nashville. During this period, four separate antiques events top the bill. At the Tailgate Antique Show at the Fiddler's Inn Hotel in Music Valley, antiques dealers set up their shops in hotel rooms and parking spaces. A similar setup exists at the Radisson Hotel Opryland for the Music Valley Antiques Market. The biggest sale is at the Gaylord Opryland Resort and Convention Center. The final event for Antiques Week is the upscale Antiques and Garden Show of Nashville, which features antiques dealers, exhibition gardens, and lectures at the Nashville Convention Center.

March

Many Nashville music events celebrate the performers. But the **Tin Pan South Songwriters Festival** (www.tinpansouth.com) honors the people who come up with the lyrics for all those great tunes. Typically held the last week of March, Tin Pan South, organized by the Nashville Songwriters Association International, schedules performances at venues across the city.

April

Nashville celebrates the coming of spring in a big way. **Awesome April** (www.visitmusiccity.com) is the name that encompasses the half dozen or more big events that take place during this month, one of the most pleasant on the city's weather calendar.

The **Country Music Television Music Awards** (www.cmt.com) was country music's first fan-voted awards show. Founded in 2002, the show lets fans participate in both the first and final rounds of voting. The show is broadcast live on television from Nashville, usually from the Curb Event Center at Belmont University.

Gospel music hosts its annual awards night in April, too. The **Gospel Music Association Dove Awards** (www.gospelmusic.org) is billed as gospel music's biggest night. The celebration takes place at the Grand Ole Opry House in Music Valley and is preceded by Gospel Music Week at the Nashville Convention Center, part trade show and part fan fair.

Film lovers throughout country look forward to the **Nashville Film Festival** (www.nashvillefilmfestival.org), held every April at the Green Hills Cinema 16. The film festival was founded in 1969 as the Sinking Creek Film Celebration. These days, upwards of 20,000 people attend the weeklong event, which includes film screenings, industry panels, and lots of parties.

The **Country Music Marathon** (www.cmmarathon.com) takes place every April. More than 15,000 professional and amateur runners take part, and tens of thousands more come out for the live music and cheer squads that line the racecourse. The postrace concert usually boasts nationally known country music artists.

May
Held in Centennial Park, the **Tennessee Crafts Fair** (www.tennesseecrafts.org) showcases the work of more than 180 different fine craftspeople. More than 45,000 people come to the three-day event every year, which also includes craft demonstrations, a food fair, and entertainment. The fair repeats in September.

For something a little different, plan to attend the **Running of the Iroquois Steeplechase** (www.iroquoissteeplechase.org) at Percy Warner Park. Taking place on the second Saturday of May, the race is the nation's oldest continuously run weight-for-age steeplechase in the country. Fans in sundresses or suspenders and hats enjoy watching some of the top horses in the country navigate the race course. You can pay for general admission to sit on the hillside overlooking the stadium. Pack a blanket, food, and drinks (and mud boots if it has rained recently), and you'll have an excellent day. Various tailgating tickets are available and are priced according to how good the view is from the parking spot. If you want to tailgate, you need to buy tickets well in advance.

Taking place every weekend in May, the **Tennessee Renaissance Festival** (www.tnrenfest.com) celebrates all things medieval. Come to watch jousting matches, hear 16th-century comedy, or buy capes and swords. The festival takes place off Highway 96 between Franklin and Murfreesboro, about 25 minutes' drive south from Nashville.

June
What was once called Fan Fair, and is now called the **Country Music Association Music Festival** (www.cmafest.com), is a four-day megamusic show in downtown Nashville. The stage at Riverfront Park along the Cumberland River is occupied by day with some of the top names in country music. At night the hordes move to LP Field across the river to hear a different show every night. Four-day passes, which cost $135–355 per person, also give you access to the exhibit hall, where you can get autographs and meet up-and-coming country music artists. This is one of Nashville's biggest events of the year, and you are wise to buy your tickets and book your hotel early. Get a room downtown so you don't need a car; parking and traffic can be a nightmare during the festival. Locals tend to steer clear of downtown during CMA Fest.

Early June sees Nashville's gay, lesbian, bisexual, and transgender community show its colors at the **Nashville Pride Festival** (www.nashvillepride.org), a three-day event at Riverfront Park.

FANS MEET THE STARS AT CMA FEST

Like country music itself, the annual event once known as Fan Fair has evolved from a down-home meet and greet to large-scale musical theater.

The CMA Music Festival, called CMA Fest for short, began in 1972 as a convention for music fans. Each year, the event grew as more and more people wanted to meet their country idols in person. Fans bought tickets months in advance, camped out at the state fairgrounds, and yearned to see, touch, and speak with the stars. It delivered on the name it had back then: Fan Fair. Stars endured marathon autograph sessions—Garth Brooks famously spent 23 hours signing autographs without a bathroom break—and they performed to crowds of their most dedicated fans.

But country music's remarkable boom of the 1990s was the end of that kind of Fan Fair—the music simply outgrew the event. Country music was no longer the stepchild of the recording industry; it was corporate, and it was big business. Fans, politicians, and industry representatives tangled over the future of Fan Fair. One plan to move Fan Fair to the Nashville Superspeedway in Lebanon was nixed because it would take the event out of Nashville.

In the end, CMA Fest replaced Fan Fair in 2000. With venues at Riverfront Park and LP Field, it still has plenty of music. Stars perform day and night. The autograph sessions continue in the Nashville Convention Center, but the artists you'll find here are the unknowns and up-and-comings. You need an invitation to meet and greet the big stars.

The rebirth of Fan Fair as the CMA Fest still attracts criticism, especially from those who remember the glory days of the old Fan Fair. But today's fans delight in the modern event, and even some of the critics are coming around, as it continues to bring tourists to Music City and fans to the genre.

July

Independence Day (www.visitmusiccity.com) is celebrated in a big way with fireworks and a riverfront concert that's broadcast live on television. The event is free and attracts upwards of 100,000 people every year.

The **Music City Brewer's Festival** (www.musiccitybrewersfest.com) is a one-day event at the Music City Walk of Fame downtown. Come to taste local brews, learn about making your own beer, and enjoy good food and live music. Tickets are required, and the event almost always sells out.

The temperature is almost always hot at the **Music City Hot Chicken Festival,** but so is the chicken. This east side event (www.mchcf.blogspot.com) is a feast of Nashville's signature spicy pan-fried dish.

August

The **East Nashville Tomato Art Festival** (www.tomatoartfest.com) is a tongue-in-cheek celebration of tomatoes and the hip, artsy vibe of East Nashville. Events include a parade of tomatoes, the "Most Beautiful Tomato Pageant," biggest and smallest tomato contests, tomato toss, and Bloody Mary taste-off. The festival usually takes place on the second Saturday of August.

September

The Belle Meade Plantation (www.bellemeadeplantation.org) hosts its biggest fundraising event of the year, **Fall Fest,** every September. The two-day festival features antiques, arts and crafts, live music, and children's activities.

Nashville's annual **Greek Festival** (615/333-1047) is hosted by the Holy Trinity Greek Orthodox Church. Nashville residents flock here for homemade Greek food and entertainment, which includes dancing and tours of the historic cathedral.

The **John Merritt Classic** (www.merrittclassic.com), held over Labor Day, starts with fashion shows and concerts, and culminates with

NASHVILLE

a football contest between the Tennessee State University Tigers and another historically black collegiate football team. The annual showdown is named for legendary former TSU football coach John Ayers Merritt.

The **Cumberland River Compact Dragon Boat Festival** (www.nashvilledragonboat.com) is a one-day race that takes place at Riverfront Park. More than 40 boats with big dragon heads and 20 costumed paddlers each race each other on the water near LP Field. There are river-themed activities for spectators.

October

The **Southern Festival of Books** is held during the second full weekend of October on Legislative Plaza in downtown Nashville. Featuring book readings, autograph sessions, and discussions, the festival is a must for book lovers. It has activities for children, too. The festival is organized by Humanities Tennessee (www.humanitiestennessee.org).

Oktoberfest (www.nashvilleoktoberfest. com) is a Nashville tradition. Held in historic Germantown north of the Bicentennial Mall, this weekend festival is enhanced by its setting in what was once Nashville's German enclave.

The events include a walk-run, church services, and a street fair with German music, food, and other entertainment. Oktoberfest usually takes place in mid-October.

The Metro Parks department took over the **Celebrate Nashville Cultural Festival** (www. celebrationofcultures.org) from the Scarritt-Bennett Center. But this international festival in Centennial Park still features food and music from around the world.

November

Beginning in November and continuing through the new year, several Nashville institutions put up special holiday decorations. Belmont University, Travellers Rest Plantation, and Belle Meade all celebrate the holiday season with special decorative flair.

December

The **Music City Bowl** (www.musiccitybowl. com) pits a Southeastern Conference team against a Big Ten rival. This nationally televised football game is held at LP Field and typically includes a night-before free concert downtown.

New Year's Eve in downtown Nashville includes—what else?—a giant guitar drop.

Shopping

You'll find many good reasons to shop in Nashville. Who can pass up Western wear in Music City? Fine boutiques cater to the well-heeled in tony West End. Malls in the suburbs offer upscale department stores or outlet bargains. And downtown you'll find unique art and gifts.

One of the best all-around shopping districts is **Hillsboro Village,** the commercial district that borders Vanderbilt University in midtown. Upscale clothing stores, used books, and trendy housewares are just a few of the things you'll find in this neighborhood, best explored on foot.

MUSIC

The Texas Troubadour, Ernest Tubb, founded his famous record store on Broadway in 1947. The **Ernest Tubb Record Shop** (417 Broadway, 615/255-7503, www.etrecordshop.com) remains an excellent source of classic and modern country music recordings, as well as DVDs, books, clothing, and souvenirs. At the back of the shop you can see the stage where Ernest Tubb's Midnite Jamboree was recorded and aired after the Grand Ole Opry on Saturday nights. The Jamboree still airs, but it's recorded at the Texas Troubadour Theatre in Music Valley.

The Ernest Tubb Record Shop is a Lower Broad mainstay.

For new and used CDs, DVDs, and vinyl, go to **Grimey's New and Preloved Music** (1604 8th Ave. S., 615/254-4801, www.grimeys.com). Here you'll find a wide selection of not just country, but rock, folk, blues, R&B, and other genres. The staff are knowledgeable and friendly.

If you want to make your own music, head to **Gruhn Guitars** (400 Broadway, 615/256-2033), a guitar shop with one of the best reputations in the music world. Founded by guitar expert George Gruhn, the shop is considered by some to be the best vintage guitar shop in the world. Shiny guitars, banjos, mandolins, and fiddles look like candy hung up on the walls of the Broadway storefront, which serves both up-and-coming and established Nashville musicians.

WESTERN WEAR

No city is better endowed with places to buy Western-style wear. The best selection is in shops along Broadway in downtown Nashville, where you'll find hats, boots, shirts, belts, jeans, and everything else you'll need to look the part. Opry Mills, the mall next to the Grand Ole Opry, also has a good selection of Western wear.

Trail West (312 Broadway, 615/251-1711) is a one-stop shop for country clothes. **Boot Country** (304 Broadway, 615/259-1691) specializes in all styles and sizes of cowboy boots and often has a buy two pair, get the third free deal.

Music industry men and women get dressed at **Flavour Clothing** (1522-B Demonbreun, 615/254-2064), a hip clothing store on Music Row. Come here for stylish denim and cowboy boots, plus casual and dressy wear for ladies and gents. This is not your daddy's boot store; this is country music chic.

The name says it all at **Manuel Exclusive Clothier** (1922 Broadway, 615/321-5444), a clothing shop where the cowboy shirts start at $750 and jackets at more than $2,000. This is where to go when you want a custom outfit for your big stage debut.

Even without a ton of cash, you can outfit yourself in some of the best Western designs at **Katy K Designs Ranch Dressing** (2407 12th Ave. S., 615/297-4242, www.katyk.com). This is the showplace of designer Katy K's unique clothing line, which has been worn by the likes of Loretta Lynn and BR549. Ranch Dressing has a well-curated selection of vintage goods, plus clothing from other designers' lines. To find the shop, look for the giant cowgirl on the facade.

CLOTHING

Jamie (4317 Harding Pk., 615/292-4188) has long been the height of couture for Nashville women who want something without rhinestones. Come here for attentive service and killer shoes, but be prepared to pay for it.

Celebrities like Gwyneth Paltrow love 12 South's **Imogene + Willie** (2601 12th Ave. S., 615/292-5005, www.imogeneandwillie.com). The shop carries clothes for men and women, but their specialty is custom-fit blue jeans at a price tag of $200 and up.

With two locations, one in Hillsboro Village and one downtown at 305 Church Street, **Fire Finch** (615/942-5271) is known for trendy jewelry and accessories. Its downtown location has a few home decor items as well.

A relative newcomer on the Nashville clothing scene, **Nashville Clothing Company** (2922 West End Blvd., 615/577-5346) sells stylish men's and women's clothes and shoes. This includes a wide selection of funny T-shirts, purses, and bags.

Bargain-hunting fashionistas cannot skip **UAL** (2918 West End Ave., 615/340-9999, www.shopual.com). Designer samples of clothes, handbags, shoes, and jewelry are shoved onto crowded racks in this shop near the Vanderbilt campus. UAL stocks both men's and women's frocks, but the women's selection is significantly larger.

ART

While not exactly a gallery, **Hatch Show Print** (316 Broadway, 615/256-2805, www.countrymusichalloffame.org/our-work) is one of Nashville's best-known places to buy and see art. Hatch has been making colorful posters for more than a century, and their iconic letterpress style is now one of the trendiest looks in modern design. They continue to design and print handouts, posters, and T-shirts for local and national customers. Visitors to the shop can gaze at the cavernous warehouse operation and buy small or large samples of their work, including reproductions of classic country music concert posters. This is a great place to find a special souvenir of your trip to Nashville or just see another part of Music City's history. Hatch posters are up all over town, including in the airport.

Transplanted New Yorkers Theo Antoniadis and Veta Cicolello opened **Ovvio Arte** (425 S. Chestnut St., 615/838-5699, www.ovvioarte. com) in 2008. This art gallery and performance space is a venue for the unexpected. It offers regular theater, dramatic readings, and art shows.

One of downtown's most accessible and eclectic galleries, **The Arts Company** (215 5th Ave. of the Arts, 615/254-2040, www.theartscompany.com) offers outsider art, the works of local artists, and other contemporary works ranging from the avant-garde to the everyday.

Perhaps the most cosmopolitan of all Nashville's galleries, **The Rymer Gallery** (233 5th Ave. of the Arts, 615/752-6030, www.therymergallery.com) installs thought-provoking exhibits with works from artists of national renown. The Rymer is also home to Nashville's Herb Williams (www.herbwilliamsart.com), a gifted artist who creates sculpture from crayons. Williams's work has been on display in the White House and other prestigious addresses.

The upper level of **The Arcade,** between 4th and 5th Avenues, houses several artist studios that open as galleries during downtown's monthly Art Crawl, which takes place the first Saturday of each month. One favorite is the innovative **Twist Art Gallery** (www.twistartgallery.com).

The **Art + Invention Gallery** (1106 Woodland St., 615/226-2070, www.artandinvention.com) is an East Nashville institution. Proprietors Meg and Bret MacFayden put on 5–6 shows each year, including their signature Tomato Art Show, part of the annual Tomato Art Festival, and are well loved for their support of other Music City creative types.

HOME DECOR

Find fine crystal, tableware, jewelry, and other upscale housewares at **AshBlue** (2170 Bandywood Dr., 615/383-4882). This sophisticated shop is perfect for bridal registries, housewarming gifts, or that special touch for your home or office.

Natural soaps, hand-crafted fragrances, and soy candles are just a few of the things you will find at **Green Pergola Aromatherapy and Soap Company** (223 Donelson Pk., 615/872-0333). One of the best things about the store, however, is its unique partnership with two other businesses. **Teas for Two** sells loose tea, and **One 2 Yoga Studio** offers one-on-one and group yoga instruction. You can also buy a hot or cold cup of tea to drink while you enjoy the relaxing atmosphere of the store.

Edgehill Village's **Nest Interiors** (1200 Villa Pl., 615/383-1511, www.nestnashville.com) stocks vintage and new home goods, with an emphasis on Parisian style finds.

BOOKS

Like many cities, Nashville has lost several of its chain bookstores, but it still has several options for the book lover. **Bookman Bookwoman Used Books** (1713 21st Ave. S., 615/383-6555), in the trendy Hillsboro neighborhood, is chockablock with used books, including cheap paperbacks and rare must-haves.

A famous owner (novelist Ann Patchett) and the willingness to open a new independent bookstore in the "books-are-dead" year of 2011 allowed **Parnassus Books** (3900 Hillsboro Pk., 615/953-2243, www.parnassusbooks.net) to make national headlines. Located in a strip mall across from the Mall at Green Hills, Parnassus specializes in a well-edited selection, personal service, and literary events for both kids and adults.

McKays (5708 Charlotte Pk., 615/353-2595) both buys and sells used books, CDs, and DVDs, which contributes to its always bustling energy. A Knoxville institution for years, the Nashville location of McKays encourages readers to return books for store credit after they've read them.

ANTIQUES

Near the old 100 Oaks Mall in South Nashville you'll find Nashville's largest and most popular antiques mall. **Gaslamp Antique and Decorating Mall** (100 Powell Ave., 615/297-2224, www.gaslampantiques.com) is squeezed behind a Staples and next to a Home Depot. It

has more than 150 vendors and a great selection of all types of antiques.

For something closer to town, head to **Eighth Avenue Antiques Mall** (2015 8th Ave. S., 615/279-9922) or **Wonders on Woodland** (1110 Woodland St., 615/226-5300) in East Nashville, which has a particularly strong collection of midcentury modern finds.

SHOPPING MALLS

The finest shopping mall in Nashville is the **Mall at Green Hills,** an indoor mall located about 15 minutes' drive south from downtown Nashville along Hillsboro Road. Stores include Macy's, Brooks Brothers, Tiffany & Co., and Nordstrom. The mall has spawned additional shopping opportunities nearby, including the upscale Hill Center (www.hillcentergreenhills.com), so this is a good place to head if you're in need of just about anything. Call the mall concierge (615/298-5478, ext. 22) to find out if your favorite store is there. The parking lot can get packed on weekends, but the mall offers free valet service, which makes it tolerable.

Farther south of Nashville, at the Moore's Lane exit off I-65, is the large **Cool Springs Galleria** (1800 Galleria Blvd., 615/731-6255, www.coolspringsgalleria.com). Four major department stores anchor the mall, which includes 100 specialty shops. The mall is surrounded by acres more of drive-up shopping centers and restaurants.

OUTLET SHOPPING

Shuttered for almost two years after the 2010 flood, the **Opry Mills** (433 Opry Mills Dr., 615/514-1000) discount mall in Music Valley is the city's most-maligned favorite destination. Indeed, if upscale shopping is your thing, don't come here. But if good deals on name-brand merchandise appeal to you, or you are looking to kill time before a show at the Opry, Opry Mills is the mall for you. Brands include Old Navy, Disney, LEGO, Coach, Ann Taylor, and Off Fifth. There is also a 20-screen movie theater, IMAX, and Bass Pro Shop with all sorts of outdoor equipment.

A bit farther down the highway in Lebanon, about 30 miles east of Nashville on I-40, **Lebanon Prime Outlets** (800/617-2588) features name-brand outlet stores. Brands include Polo Ralph Lauren, Coach, Tommy Hilfiger, and Ann Taylor. To get to Prime Outlets, take I-40 east from Nashville and get off at exit 238.

FLEA MARKETS

Nashville's largest flea market takes place on the fourth weekend of every month at the Tennessee State Fairgrounds. The **Tennessee State Fairgrounds Flea Market** (615/862-5016, www.tennesseestatefair.org) is a bargain lover's dream, with thousands of sellers peddling clothes, crafts, and all sorts of vintage and used housewares, often at lower prices than you'd find in bigger cities. The fairgrounds are located on 4th Avenue, south of downtown. Admission is free, but parking is $5.

The **Nashville Farmers' Market** (nashville-farmersmarket.org) next to the Bicentennial Mall downtown, has a daily flea market, but it tends to be of the tube sock and T-shirt variety, not furniture and collectibles.

Sports and Recreation

Nashville has good parks, numerous sports teams, and nice weather to enjoy both.

PARKS
Centennial Park
Nashville's best city park, Centennial is best known as home of the Parthenon. It is also a pleasant place to relax. A small lake provides a habitat for ducks and other water creatures; paved walking trails are popular for walking during nice weather. The park hosts numerous events during the year, including Shakespeare in the Park each August and September.

Greenways
Nashville has a remarkable network of connected green spaces thanks to its Greenways (www.nashville.gov/greenways). The master plan is for this system to eventually connect the entire city. Today there are more than 46 miles of paved pathways and 20 miles of primitive trails used by bicyclists, runners, dog walkers, and more. The Greenways run through the city's prettiest natural areas and, in places, along the Cumberland River. Some Greenways include nature centers and other educational facilities. For the most part, the routes are clean and safe. Good maps are available for download from Greenways for Nashville (www.greenwaysfornashville.org).

Radnor Lake State Natural Area
Just seven miles southwest of downtown Nashville, Radnor Lake State Natural Area (Otter Creek Rd., 615/373-3467) provides a natural escape for visitors and residents of the city. Eighty-five-acre Radnor Lake was created in 1914 by the Louisville and Nashville Railroad Company, which impounded Otter Creek to do so. The lake was to provide water for the railroad's steam engines. By the 1940s, the railroad's use of the lake ended, and 20 years later the area was threatened by development. Local residents, including the Tennessee Ornithological Society, successfully rallied against development, and Radnor Lake State Natural Area was established in 1973.

There are six miles of hiking trails around the lake, and Otter Creek Road, which is closed to vehicular traffic, is open to bicycles and walkers. A nature museum at the visitors

COURTESY OF ALTAIRISFAR/WIKIMEDIA COMMONS

Centennial Park

NASHVILLE

center describes some of the 240 species of birds and hundreds of species of plants and animals that live at Radnor. The visitors center is open Sunday–Thursday 9 A.M.–4 P.M. and Friday–Saturday 8 A.M.–4 P.M.

Radnor is well used and well loved by Nashvillians, and for good reason. Very few American cities have such a large and pristine natural area so close to the urban center.

Edwin and Percy Warner Parks

The largest city parks in Tennessee, Edwin and Percy Warner Parks (7311 Hwy. 100, 615/352-6299, www.nashville.gov/parks/locations/warner, open year round) are a 2,600-acre oasis of forest, fields, and quiet pathways located just nine miles southwest from downtown Nashville. Nashvillians come here to walk, jog, ride bikes and horses, and much more. The parks have scenic drives, picnic facilities, playgrounds, cross-country running trails, an equestrian center, bridle trails, a model airplane

field, and athletic fields. Percy Warner Park is also home to the Harpeth Hills Golf Course, and Edwin Warner Park has a nature center that provides year-round environmental education. The nature center also hands out maps and other information about the park.

Warner Parks hosts the annual Iroquois Steeplechase Horse Race in May. A 10-mile bridle path is open to horseback riding year-round. Visit the park's Equestrian Center (2500 Old Hickory Blvd.) for more information.

J. Percy Priest Lake

J. Percy Priest Lake was created in the mid-1960s when the Army Corps of Engineers dammed Stones River east of Nashville. The lake is a favorite destination for fishing, boating, swimming, paddling, and picnicking.

J. Percy Priest Lake sprawls over 14,200 acres. Access is provided through more than a dozen different parks and access areas on all sides of the lake. Many of these areas bear the names of communities that were inundated when the lake was created.

The lake's main visitors center, operated by the Army Corps of Engineers, is located at the site of the dam that created the lake. The visitors center is located on Bell Road at exit 219 off I-40 heading east from downtown Nashville. There you will find a lake overlook and one of four marinas on the lake.

In addition to access areas managed by the Corps of Engineers, Nashville operates **Hamilton Creek Park** (www.hamcreek.com) on the western shore of the lake. The State of Tennessee operates **Long Hunter State Park** on the eastern shore.

There are several hiking trails around the lake. The **Three Hickories Nature Trail** is an easy 1.6-mile trail found in the Cook Recreational Area. **Anderson Road Fitness Trail** is a paved one-mile trail that travels through woodlands and along the lake.

For a long hike, or for horseback riding, go to the **Twin Forks Horse Trail,** an 18-mile trail located in the East Fork Recreation Area on the southwestern shore of the lake. Within Long Hunter State Park there are three hiking trails, including a nature loop trail and the mile-long Deer Trail leaving from the visitors center.

Boating, fishing, and water sports are among the most popular activities on J. Percy Priest Lake. Launch ramps are found in Long Hunter State Park and at several marinas around the lake. **Elm Hill Marina** (3361 Bell Rd., 615/889-5363, www.elmhillmarina.com) is the marina closest to downtown Nashville.

The Corps of Engineers operates three day-use **swim areas** that have sand beaches, bathrooms, and other amenities for a day in the water. These swim areas are located at Anderson Road, Cook Campground, and Seven Points Campground. There is a $4 per-vehicle fee at Anderson and Cook. There is swimming at Long Hunter State Park's Bryant Grove as well.

GOLF

Nashville operates seven public golf courses in the city. Many of these are in parks and offer excellent golf in beautiful settings. You can find details about all city courses at www.nashville.gov/parks/golf. Most courses are open year-round; call ahead for operating hours and to reserve a tee time. Nine-hole greens fees are $18 on weekdays and $17 on weekends, with additional fees for carts and senior and member discounts.

Harpeth Hills Golf Course (2424 Old Hickory Blvd., 615/862-8493) is a par 72 course built in 1965 and renovated in 1991. It is located in Percy Warner Park and is considered one of Tennessee's best public golf courses.

Percy Warner Park is also home of **Percy Warner Golf Course,** a nine-hole course good for beginner golfers, available on a walk-in basis only.

Probably the most-used public golf course in Nashville, **McCabe Golf Course** (615/862-8491) is located in West Nashville near Sylvan Park. McCabe consists of a par 70 18-hole course and 9-hole course. Upgrades have introduced new green complexes and tee complexes.

The oldest city golf course in Nashville is **Shelby Golf Course** (615/862-8474), located in Shelby Park in East Nashville. Shelby is a short course with small mounded greens that places a premium on accuracy.

Situated on the Cumberland River in North Nashville, **Ted Rhodes Golf Course** (615/862-8463) is scenic and pleasant to walk. Built in 1953 as a nine-hole course, Ted Rhodes was expanded to 18 holes in 1992. It is par 72.

Located near Music Valley in Donelson, **Two Rivers Golf Course** (615/889-2675) offers a challenging course for golfers of all skill levels. A bonus is the view of the Nashville skyline at the eighth hole.

There are many privately owned golf courses in Nashville, some of which are open to the public. **Gaylord Springs** (18 Springhouse Ln., 615/458-1730), located next to the Gaylord Opryland Resort in Music Valley, is a par 72 18-hole course built in 1990. Greens fees are

$50–90. **Nashboro Golf Club** (1101 Nashboro Blvd., 615/367-2311) offers a par 72 18-hole course with fees $27–41.

BIKING

The first destination for bikers around Nashville is the **Natchez Trace Parkway** (www.nps.gov/natr), a historic two-lane 444-mile blacktop scenic drive that originates in Nashville and journeys south through Tennessee and Mississippi countryside, eventually terminating in Natchez, Mississippi. The parkway is closed to commercial traffic, and the speed limit is strictly enforced, making it popular for biking.

Biking the Trace can be an afternoon outing or a weeklong adventure. The National Park Service maintains three campgrounds along the Trace, plus five bicyclist-only campsites with more modest amenities. The northernmost bike campsite is located at the intersection of the Trace and Highway 50, about 36 miles south of Nashville.

When biking on the Trace, ride in a single-file line and always wear reflective clothing and a helmet. Pack food and water, and carry a cell phone, ID, and emergency information.

Short paved trails good for biking can be found at Radnor Lake State Natural Area, Warner Parks, and in any of Nashville's greenways, including those at Shelby Bottoms along the Cumberland River.

Nashville's only dedicated mountain bike trail is at **Hamilton Creek Park** (www.hamcreek.com) on J. Percy Priest Lake, on the east side of the Nashville airport. This 10-mile bike trail consists of an eastern trail better for beginning bikers and a western trail for advanced bikers. The two trails meet at a tunnel that crosses Bell Road.

The **Harpeth Bike Club** (www.harpethbikeclub.com) is Nashville's largest bike club. It organizes weekend and weekday group rides April–October, plus races and social events where you can meet other bike enthusiasts.

If you're looking for the inside scoop on biking around Nashville and recommended routes in the surrounding countryside, check out www.nashvillecyclist.com, an online community of bikers.

Bike Shops

There are several good bike shops in Nashville. If you need bike gear, repairs, or advice, check out **Cumberland Transport** (2807 West End Ave., 615/321-4069), **Nashville Bicycle Company** (2817 West End Ave., 615/321-5510), or **Trace Bikes** (8400 Hwy. 100, 615/646-2485), located next to the Loveless Cafe near the Natchez Trace Parkway. East Nashville's **East Side Cycles** (103 S. 11th St., 615/469-1079) has bike tools around back if you need DIY repair during off hours.

TENNIS

The **Centennial Sportsplex** (222 25th Ave. N., 615/862-8480, www.sportsplextennis.com) has 15 lighted outdoor tennis courts and 4 indoor courts, as well as a ball machine, pro shop, and concession stand. The center is open seven days a week; specific hours vary by season. Indoor court rental fees are $18 per hour; courts may be booked up to three days in advance. Outdoor courts are available for $3 per hour per person, and they can be reserved up to six days in advance.

The Sportsplex organizes numerous tennis tournaments, leagues, and classes during the year. Call or stop by for details.

SWIMMING

The city's biggest pool is found at the **Centennial Sportsplex Aquatic Center** (222 25th Ave. N., 615/862-8480, www.centennialsportsplex.com, Mon.–Thurs. 5:30 A.M.–7:50 P.M., Fri. 5:30 A.M.–5:50 P.M., Sat. 9 A.M.–4:50 P.M., adults $6, children 5–12, military, disabled, seniors, and students $5, children 4 and under free). The center, located near Centennial Park in midtown, has both a large lap pool and a small play pool. Various swim classes are offered; call for a schedule.

Take the kids to **Wave Country** (2320 Two Rivers Pkwy., 615/885-1052, Memorial Day–Labor Day daily 10 A.M.–6 P.M., adults $12, children 2–11 $10, children under 2 free; prices tend to increase annually). This water park has exciting slides, wave pool, and sand volleyball courts. Wave Country is managed by the city parks commission.

A great destination for a hot summer day is **Nashville Shores** (4001 Bell Rd., Hermitage, 615/889-7050, www.nashvilleshores.com, Memorial Day–Labor Day Mon–Sat. 10 A.M.–6 P.M., Sun. 11 A.M.–6 P.M., 48 inches and taller $22, under 48 inches $17, children two and under free). Here you'll find miles of sandy beaches along the shore of J. Percy Priest Lake, pools, waterslides, and water sports. Admission includes the opportunity to take a 45-minute lake cruise.

PADDLING

Nashville's easy access to multiple rivers and lakes makes it a natural gateway for kayaking, canoeing, and stand-up paddling. **Nashville Paddle Co.** (www.nashvillepaddle.com) offers lessons and rentals for this fast-growing sport, which is like a hybrid of kayaking and surfing, and is well suited for Middle Tennessee's flat water. **Tip-a-Canoe** (800/550-5810, www.tip-a-canoe.com) is the summer go-to spot for canoe and kayak rental on the Harpeth River.

GYMS

The City of Nashville operates a fitness center in the **Centennial Sportsplex** (222 25th Ave. N., 615/862-8480, www.centennialsportsplex. com, Mon.–Thurs. 5:30 A.M.–8 P.M., Fri. 5:30 A.M.–6 P.M., Sat. 9 A.M.–5 P.M., adults $6, children 5–12, military, disabled, seniors, and students $5, children 4 and under free). The fitness center has modern cardiovascular and weightlifting machines. Fitness classes are also offered.

The Sportsplex also has two pools, tennis courts, and an ice rink. The ice rink offers public skate periods every week, with more during the winter months and holiday season.

SPECTATOR SPORTS
Football

You simply cannot miss 68,000-seat **LP Field,** home of the **Tennessee Titans** (460 Great Circle Rd., 615/565-4000, www.titans-online.com). The stadium, which was finished in 1999 and renovated after the 2010 flood, towers on the east bank of the Cumberland River, directly opposite downtown. Since their move to the stadium in 1999, the Titans have sold out almost every home game. They play September–December.

Tickets sell out early—often months in advance. If you want to see a game on short notice, your best bet is the online NFL ticket exchange, where season ticket holders can sell their seats to games they don't want to attend.

For a different football experience, catch a home game of the minor-league **Nashville Storm** (www.nashvillestorm.com) at Stratford High School. The season starts in April.

Finally, the most distinctive brand of football played in Nashville is Australian rules. The **Nashville Kangaroos** (www.nashvillekangaroos.org) were founded in 1997 and were one of the first Australian football teams in the United States. The "Roos" play at Elmington Park (3500 West End Ave.) and sometimes practice with Vanderbilt's own Aussie rules squad. One of the missions of the club is to promote cultural understanding and exchange, so the social calendar can be just as grueling as the sports one. The Roos also sponsor a women's netball team.

Baseball

What an appropriate name for a minor-league baseball team. The **Nashville Sounds** (534 Chestnut St., 615/242-4371, www.nashvillesounds.com) are a AAA affiliate of the Milwaukee Brewers, and they play about 30 home games a year June–October. Before the

LP Field, home of the Tennessee Titans, is visible from the Shelby Street Pedestrian Bridge.

2008 season opener, the team invested $1 million in stopgap improvements to the aging Greer Stadium, their home in south Nashville. Finding a new home for the Sounds is an ongoing topic of conversation around town. Wherever they go, the guitar-shaped scoreboard better go with them.

Tickets are $12 in advance, $14 at the gate. There's an alcohol-free section of the stadium, which often appeals to families with small kids.

Ice Hockey

Nashville celebrated the 10th anniversary of its National Hockey League franchise, the **Predators** (501 Broadway, http://predators.nhl.com), in 2008. It was a sweet victory for fans, who fought to keep the team in the city in the face of lackluster support from the community with a "Save the Predators" campaign. The Predators play in the 20,000-seat Bridgestone Arena, located on Broadway in the heart of downtown. Home games include live country music performances and other activities for the fans. The regular season begins in October and ends in early April. Single-game tickets start at $20 and can cost as much as $195, although there are often special discounts.

College Sports

In addition to Nashville's smorgasbord of professional and semiprofessional sports teams, the city's colleges provide lots of good spectator sports. Vanderbilt plays football, men's and women's basketball, and baseball in the Southeastern Conference. Tennessee State University and Belmont University play Division 1-A basketball, and Lipscomb University is a member of the Atlantic Sun Division. Vanderbilt football games are an unusual sporting event, as students traditionally dress in coat and tie or dresses and high heels.

Accommodations

Nashville has more than 33,000 hotel rooms. Accommodations range from historic downtown hotels to standard motels, many of which have Music City touches, from recorded wake-up calls from country stars to guitar-shaped swimming pools.

Downtown has the most appealing and convenient hotels. More budget-friendly options are found in midtown and Music Valley.

DOWNTOWN

Hotels in this neighborhood are as close as you can get to attractions including the Country Music Hall of Fame and Broadway honky-tonks.

$150-200

Located across Broadway from the Frist Center for the Visual Arts, **Holiday Inn Express Nashville-Downtown** (902 Broadway, 615/244-0150, $170) offers a comfortable compromise between value and location. There is an on-site fitness room, free wireless Internet, a business center, and a guest laundry. Guest rooms have desks, coffeemakers, and two telephones. Suites ($270) have refrigerators and microwave ovens. All guests enjoy free continental breakfast. On-site parking is available for $19 a day. The Holiday Inn is located about five blocks away from lower Broadway.

Over $200

One of Nashville's most notable downtown hotels is ◖ **Union Station** (1001 Broadway, 615/726-1001, www.unionstationhotelnashville.com, $160–270), a 125-room hotel located in what was once the city's main train station. Distinctions include magnificent iron work and molding, and an impressive marble-floored great hall that greets guests, contributing to what makes this one of the National Trust's Historic Hotels of America. High ceilings and lofty interior balconies make this

one of Nashville's great old buildings, and hotel guests get to make it their home away from home. Union Station is a fine hotel, with amenities like free turndown service, a fitness center, wireless Internet, plasma televisions, complimentary morning newspapers, and room service. Rooms have cathedral ceilings, stylish furnishings, and a subtle art deco touch. The bathrooms have soaking tubs, walk-in showers, and expansive marble vanities. You can choose from a standard room with one double bed or a premium room with a king-size bed or two double beds. Four suites are also available.

The all-suite **Hilton Nashville Downtown** (121 4th Ave. S., 615/620-1000, www.nashvillehilton.com, $180–320) is next door to the Country Music Hall of Fame, Broadway's honky-tonks, and the home of the Nashville Symphony. All of the hotel's 330 suites have two distinct rooms—a living room with sofa, cable television, microwave oven, refrigerator, and coffeemaker, and a bedroom with one or two beds. The rooms are appointed with modern, stylish furniture and amenities. An indoor pool, workout room, valet parking, and two restaurants round out the hotel's amenities.

The **Renaissance Hotel** (611 Commerce St., 615/255-8400, $290–310) is connected to the Nashville Convention Center by a raised and covered walkway. Located one block north of Broadway, it stands 25 stories, providing impressive views of the city below. The Renaissance's 646 rooms offer web TV, hair dryers, ironing boards, crisp linens, coffeemakers, and business services. For an additional $12 daily, guests can enjoy high-speed wired Internet access and unlimited local and U.S. long-distance calls. The fitness center is next door to an indoor heated swimming pool, whirlpool, and sauna.

The last of a dying breed of hotels, the

For more than a century, the Hermitage Hotel has been the place to stay in Nashville.

Hermitage Hotel (231 6th Ave., 615/244-3121, www.thehermitagehotel.com, $300–800) has been the first choice for travelers to downtown Nashville for more than 100 years. The 123-room hotel was commissioned by prominent Nashville citizens and opened for business in 1910, quickly becoming the favorite gathering place for the city's elite. Prominent figures including Al Capone, Gene Autry, and seven U.S. presidents have stayed at the Hermitage. In modern times, its roll call includes some of country music's biggest names. You don't have to be famous to stay at the Hermitage, but having plenty of cash will help your cause. Rooms start at $300 a night, but check for last-minute specials on its website, when rates will dip to $200. You can chose to have $2 from your room rate contributed to the Land Trust for Tennessee. Guests enjoy top-of-the-line amenities, including 24-hour room service, pet walking, valet parking, and laundry services. Rooms are furnished in an opulent style befitting a

luxury urban hotel and have CD/DVD players, refreshment centers, marble baths, and high-speed wireless Internet access. Many rooms have lovely views of the capitol and city.

Courtyard by Marriot (179 4th Ave. N., 615/256-0900, $200–250) is a 181-room renovated hotel set in a century-old downtown high-rise. It is located right next to Printer's Alley and is set midway between the downtown business district and Broadway's entertainment attractions. Guest rooms are tastefully decorated, with web TV, wired Internet access, coffeemakers, ironing boards, cable TV, voice mail, and supercomfortable beds. There are two restaurants on-site, and guests can take advantage of valet parking for $22 a day.

Located just steps from the Tennessee State Capitol and near dozens of downtown office buildings, the **Doubletree Hotel Nashville** (315 4th Ave. N., 615/244-8200, $190–250) is a popular choice for business travelers. Rooms are spacious and bright, and even basic rooms have a comfortable desk and chair, coffeemaker, free Internet access, voice mail, and ironing boards. The hotel boasts a beautiful indoor swimming pool, business center, above-average fitness center, and on-site restaurant and coffee shop. Parking at the Doubletree is valet only and costs $24 per day.

The **Sheraton Downtown Nashville** (623 Union St., 615/259-2000, $200–270) is a city landmark. The 472-room hotel stands tall above neighboring buildings, providing most guest rooms with views of the city below. Located in the middle of Nashville's bustling downtown business district, it is another good option for business travelers. The hotel is 100 percent smoke-free and has a fitness room, business center, indoor pool, and laundry and concierge services. Internet access and on-site parking are available for an additional fee.

MIDTOWN

Midtown hotels are near Music Row, Vanderbilt and Belmont Universities, and the entertainment, dining, and shopping attractions of Hillsboro Village.

Under $100

The **Music City Hostel** (1809 Patterson St., 615/692-1277, www.musiccityhostel.com, $25–79) is located among doctors' offices and commercial buildings in between downtown Nashville and Elliston Place. The low-slung '70s-style building looks like nothing much on the outside, but inside it is cheerful, welcoming, and a comfortable home base for budget travelers. Music City Hostel offers the usual dorm-style bunk-bed accommodations, as well as a handful of private apartments, which rent for $79 a night. You can also have a private bedroom with private bath plus shared kitchen and common room for $49 a night. Common areas include a large kitchen, dining room, reading room, cable TV room, computer with Internet access, and a coin laundry. The entire facility

is smoke-free. Parking is free, and the hostel is within walking distance of restaurants, a bus stop, car rental agency, post office, and hospitals. It is a hike to get downtown on foot from here.

$100-150

Best Western Music Row (1407 Division St., 615/242-1631, $110–150) is a no-nonsense motel with an outdoor pool, free continental breakfast, Internet access, and indoor corridors. Rooms have cable TV, AM/FM alarm clocks, and coffeemakers. Pets are allowed for $10 a day, and parking is free. The 75-room hotel is located a few steps away from the Music Row traffic circle and nearby restaurants.

Located near Elliston Place and Vanderbilt University, **Guesthouse Inn and Suites** (1909 Hayes St., 615/329-1000, $109) offers a free shuttle to nearby hospitals, including Baptist Hospital, Vanderbilt Medical Center, and the Veterans Administration Hospital. All rooms have microwave ovens, refrigerators, and coffeemakers, and guests enjoy free breakfast including made-to-order waffles. Suites ($140) include a sleeper couch. Rooms are typical motel style, with two double beds or a single king-size bed. The property is convenient to Hillsboro Village, Music Row, and Centennial Park.

$150-200

A bed-and-breakfast choice in this part of the city is **1501 Linden House Bed and Breakfast** (1501 Linden Ave., 615/298-2701, www.nashville-bed-breakfast.com, $125–195). This cheerful yellow-brick home on a corner lot has three guest rooms, each with stylish furniture and hardwood floors; one room has a private whirlpool, and another has a fireplace.

Over $200

For luxurious accommodations near Vanderbilt, consider **Loews Vanderbilt Plaza** (2100 West End Ave., 615/320-1700, $260–310), a 340-room hotel on West End Avenue close to Centennial Park and Hillsboro Village. Loews boasts 24-hour room service; luxurious sheets, towels, and robes; natural soaps; and spacious bathrooms. Guests enjoy in-room tea kettles and top-of-the-line coffee, evening turn-down service, and free high-speed Internet access. Many rooms have views of the Nashville skyline; premium rooms provide guests with access to the concierge lounge, with continental breakfast, and evening hors d'oeuvres and a cash bar. All guests can enjoy a fine fitness room, spa, art gallery, and gift shop.

You can't get closer to Vanderbilt University than the **Marriott Nashville Vanderbilt** (2555 West End Ave., 615/321-1300, $180–300). Set on the northern end of the university campus, the Marriott has 301 guest rooms, six suites, and meeting space. It is located across West End Avenue from Centennial Park, home of the Parthenon, and a few steps from Vanderbilt's football stadium. There is an indoor pool, full-service restaurant, concierge lounge, ATM, and business center.

Since its opening in 2009, the **C Hutton Hotel** (1808 West End Ave., 615/340-9333, www.huttonhotel.com, $194–512) has become Nashville's ecofriendly darling. This swanky hotel near the Vanderbilt campus also offers an easy commute to Music Row and downtown, but regular visitors stay here less for the great location and more for the ambience. The lobby and guest rooms are stocked with well-edited art collections, the bathrooms include sleek granite showers, and the entire hotel has an emphasis on sustainability, with biodegradable cleaning products and bamboo flooring. The pet-friendly property has all the expected amenities, such as flat-screen TVs and wireless Internet access. An added bonus is the likelihood of a celebrity sighting.

EAST NASHVILLE

While it has more appeal for locals than it does for visitors, there are a few good reasons to stay in East Nashville. For football fans, this part of the city is close to the Tennessee Titans' stadium. Others will enjoy bed-and-breakfasts in Edgefield, the intimate live music venues, and a cool, laid-back, and diverse residential neighborhood. Good dining and funky shopping abounds, and downtown is a short drive or walk across the Cumberland River.

Under $100

Located on the east bank of the Cumberland River, **Days Inn at the Stadium** (211 N. 1st St., 615/254-1551, $75–100) is near LP Field, where the Tennessee Titans play. The hotel's 180 rooms have clock radios, cable TV, and wireless Internet. Some have nice views of the Nashville skyline. Guests enjoy access to a fitness room, indoor pool, and laundry facilities, plus free breakfast. There is a bar and restaurant inside the hotel. While not within easy walking distance of downtown Nashville, the Days Inn is just across the river from the city's premier attractions. Free parking is a plus.

$100-150

Carole's Yellow Cottage (801 Fatherland St., 615/226-2952, $100–125) is a bed-and-breakfast offering two comfortable guest rooms. The decor is not as fussy as many bed-and-breakfasts, and the atmosphere is homey and low-key. Rooms have a private bathroom, and guests can relax in a library with a TV/VCR. Breakfasts are homemade and feature organic foods when available.

The Big Bungalow (618 Fatherland St., 615/256-8375, www.thebigbungalow.com, $130–185) a Craftsman style early-1900s town house, offers three guest rooms, each with its own private bath and television. Guests have shared access to a computer, microwave, and refrigerator. Common areas are comfortable and stylish, with tasteful decor and hardwood floors. Hostess Ellen Warshaw prepares breakfast for her guests and sometimes hosts in-the-round concerts in her living room. She is also a licensed masseuse and sometimes offers discounted massage rates with room. This is a pet-free, non-smoking facility; children over 10 are welcome. The bed-and-breakfast is located about seven blocks from the Shelby Street Pedestrian Bridge that takes you to the heart of downtown.

The East Park Inn (822 Boscoble St., 615/226-8691, $100–135) is a brightly painted Queen Anne–style bed-and-breakfast in Edgefield, on the east bank of the Cumberland River. Two guest suites offer private bathrooms and elegant furnishings. Guests also enjoy a relaxing terrace and garden, comfortable common rooms, and delicious breakfasts of fresh fruit, breads, quiche, waffles, and fresh-squeezed orange juice. Afternoon tea or wine is served on the front porch, which enjoys a pleasant view of the city skyline. The inn is located 10 blocks from downtown Nashville and 3 blocks from coffee shops and restaurants.

You'll be happy to call **Top O'Woodland** (1603 Woodland St., 888/288-368, www.topofwoodland.com, $145) home during your stay in Nashville. This redbrick home on a corner lot is distinctive and beautiful. Features include a spacious wraparound front porch, original stained-glass windows, a turret, a Steinway baby grand piano, and lots of period and original antiques. The bed-and-breakfast is within five blocks of restaurants and pubs, and a short drive over the Cumberland to downtown Nashville. Guests can choose to stay in the master suite, with a king-size four-poster bed, working fireplace, private bath, and private entrance, or in Mr. Green's Cottage, a detached cottage with kitchenette that can sleep up to six people. The home has wireless high-speed Internet access, and a generous continental breakfast is served at your convenience. Hostess Belinda Leslie is a chaplain and a certified wedding and event planner, and Top O'Woodland is a beautiful place for an old-fashioned wedding or quiet elopement.

MUSIC VALLEY

There are a dozen or more chain hotels in Music Valley, all close to restaurants and a short drive from the Grand Ole Opry and Opry Mills mall. Nashville's most famous hotel, Gaylord Opryland Resort, is luxurious and a destination on its own.

These hotels tend to provide more for your money than downtown digs, but they are a 10- to 15-minute drive to the city center.

Under $100

If you're looking for a clean, comfortable room, look no further than the **Fiddler's Inn** (2410 Music Valley Dr., 615/885-1440, www.fiddlers-inn.com, $60–75). This 202-room no-frills hotel offers a solid Tennessee welcome to its guests, who come in droves to see the Opry and enjoy other Music Valley attractions. It's right next to a Cracker Barrel restaurant, and there's plenty of parking for cars and tour buses. Guests enjoy cable TV, free coffee and pastries in the morning, an outdoor pool, and a gift shop stocked with kitschy Nashville souvenirs.

The all-suite **Best Western Suites near Opryland** (201 Music City Cir., 615/902-9940, $70–80) is a comfortable compromise between the luxury of the Opryland Hotel and the affordability of a motel. Each of the hotel's 100 suites has a couch, desk, high-speed Internet access, coffee- and tea maker, microwave, ironing board, and refrigerator. Rooms with whirlpool tubs are available for about $80 more per night. Guests enjoy an on-site fitness room, 24-hour business center, outdoor pool, free continental breakfast, and weekday newspaper. The Best Western is located along a strip of motels and restaurants about one mile from the Grand Ole Opry and other Opryland attractions.

Located about two miles from the Opryland, **Comfort Inn Opryland Area** (2516 Music Valley Dr., 615/889-0086, $70–75) offers 121 clean, comfortable guest rooms with cable TV, free HBO, wireless Internet, ironing board, hair dryer, and free daily newspaper. There is free outdoor parking, interior corridors, and an outdoor pool. Pets are permitted with an additional fee.

$100-150

Guests at the **Courtyard by Marriott Opryland** (125 Music City Cir., 615/882-9133, $129–150) enjoy refurbished rooms with soft beds, wireless Internet, coffeemakers, ironing boards, and refrigerators. The on-site restaurant serves breakfast, and business rooms come with a desk, dataport, voice mail, and speakerphone.

Over $200

Said to be the largest hotel without a casino in the United States, the **Gaylord Opryland Resort** (2800 Opryland Dr., 615/889-1000, $199 350) is more than just a hotel. Completely renovated after the 2010 flood shuttered it for six months, the 2,881-room luxury resort and convention center is built around a nine-acre indoor garden. Glass atriums invite sunlight, and miles of footpaths invite you to explore the climate-controlled gardens. Highlights include a 40-foot waterfall and flatboats that float along a river.

Set among the gardens are dozens of different restaurants and cafés, ranging from casual buffets to elegant steak houses. Hundreds of room balconies overlook the gardens, providing some guests with views of the well-kept greenery, even in winter. If you stay, choose between a traditional view looking outside the hotel, or an atrium view.

The property has a full-service salon, spa, and fitness center; multiple swimming pools (indoor and outdoor); on-site child care and "kid's resort"; and a car rental agency. You can walk to Opry Mills mall and the Grand Ole Opry from the hotel or take the free shuttle. Guest rooms are luxurious and feature coffee- and tea makers; two telephones; wireless Internet access; pay-per-view movies, games, and music; daily national newspapers; and other usual amenities. Service is impeccable.

Press the "consider it done" button on the phone in your room, and any of your needs will be met. Guests can buy onetime or daily passes on the downtown shuttle for about $15 a day, and the airport shuttle costs $35 round-trip. Parking is $24 a day.

While room rates at Opryland are steep, the hotel offers attractive packages that add on other Gaylord-owned attractions and properties. These often include tickets to the Grand Ole Opry, a ride on the General Jackson Showboat, trips into Nashville to visit the Ryman Auditorium or the Wildhorse Saloon, and extras like spa visits and golf games at the hotel. Many of these packages are a good deal for travelers who want to pay one price for their whole vacation. Christmastime always brings interesting kid-friendly packages.

Together with Opryland, country megastar Dolly Parton is opening a 50-acre water and snow park on the other side of Briley Parkway, due to open in 2014.

AIRPORT
Under $100

The **Alexis Inn and Suites Nashville Airport** (600 Ermac Dr., 615/889-4466, www.nashvillealexishotel.com, rooms $60–70, suites $80–100) is a comfortable and convenient place to stay near the airport. Rooms have all the usual amenities, plus guests get free popcorn in the lobby, a free airport shuttle daily 7 A.M.–9 P.M., and free continental breakfast. All rooms have refrigerators, and most have microwaves. There is a business center on-site.

$100-150

Drury Inns and Suites (555 Donelson Pk., 615/902-0400, $60–130) offers guests an appealing array of extras, including a free hot breakfast, free evening beverages and snacks, a free airport shuttle, 60 minutes of free long-distance calls, and $7 daily park-and-fly parking. There is both an indoor and outdoor pool and a fitness center. Drury Inn is about two miles north of the airport and five miles south of Music Valley.

Hotel Preston (733 Briley Pkwy., 615/361-5900, www.hotelpreston.com, $125–160) is a boutique hotel near the airport. Youthful energy, modern decor, and up-to-date rooms set this property apart from the crowd. Rooms are stocked with Tazo tea and Starbucks coffee, and there's a 24-hour fitness center. The "You-Want-It-You-Got-It" button in each room beckons the 24-hour room service, and whimsical extras including a lava lamp, pet fish, and art kit are available by request when you check in. High-speed Internet is an add-on extra. Naughty packages—like the "Ooey Gooey Night Out" couple's getaway with late check-out, wine, and whipped cream on request—prove that this isn't your parents' motel, though the hotel caters equally to business travelers with meeting rooms and a business center. Two restaurants, including the Pink Skip bar and nightclub, which features a sculpture by local artist Herb Williams, provide food and entertainment. In 2011 the hotel revamped its entire food and beverage program.

Food

You can eat in a different restaurant each day in Nashville and never get bored. Southern cooking stars at meat-and-three diners and barbecue joints, fine-dining restaurants cater to the well-heeled, and international eateries reflect the city's surprising diversity.

The Arcade

One of two downtown food destinations, the Arcade is an old outdoor shopping mall that lies between 4th and 5th Avenues. The ground floor of the Arcade is full of small, casual restaurants that cater to the downtown lunchtime crowd with quick, cheap eats. Upstairs are professional offices and a few art galleries and artists' studios.

Katie's Meat & Three (10 Arcade, 615/256-1055) has four different meat specials daily, which you can get with sides like turnip greens, mashed potatoes, and white beans. A meat-and-three plate costs $7; order your choice of four sides for $5. **The Greek Touch** (13 Arcade, 615/259-9493) has gyro, sausage, veggie, and divine chicken sandwiches, platters, and salads, all for under $6. There are also several sandwich shops, a Chinese restaurant, and **Manny's House of Pizza** (15 Arcade, 615/242-7144, www.mannyshouseofpizza.com), which many consider the city's best slice.

Most restaurants at the Arcade have some seating inside, or you can sit outside and watch the world go by.

Nashville Farmers' Market

The Nashville Farmers' Market (900 8th Ave. N., 615/880-2001, www.nashvillefarmersmarket.org) has undergone a resurgence in recent years and, as a result, is one of the best places to grab an interesting meal in the city. The outdoor components of the market include a farm shed with fresh produce year-round. But when you're hungry, head to the interior for the Market House food court, with choices ranging from Southern specialties to Caribbean cuisine. **Jamaicaway** (615/255-5920, Mon.–Fri. 10:30 A.M.–8 P.M., Sat.–Sun. 10:30 A.M.–5 P.M., $9) serves oxtail, steamed fish, and Jamaican patties Sunday–Friday. *Top Chef* contender Arnold Myint's **AM@FM** (615/291-4585, daily 11 A.M.–6 P.M., $10) offers quick, fresh Asian dishes and even a glass of wine. There are also Mexican, Chinese, barbecue, and Greek choices, as well as enough baked goods to give you a toothache. Hours vary by merchant.

The monthly night market brings specialty

Fresh produce makes life peachy at the daily Nashville Farmers' Market.

food and drink, plus live music, dancing, and a magical ambience to the market.

DINERS AND COFFEE SHOPS
Downtown
Provence (601 Church St., 615/664-1150, Mon.–Fri. 7 A.M.–6 P.M., Sat. 8 A.M.–5 P.M., $5–12), located inside the Nashville Public Library, serves excellent European-style pastries, breads, and salads, as well as coffee. Provence's signature sandwiches include creamy chicken salad and turkey and brie. Or you can try a sampler of the café's salads, including roasted-vegetable salad, parmesan potato salad, or creamy penne pasta. Save room for a decadent pastry, or at least a cookie, which come in varieties like raspberry hazelnut, chocolate espresso, and ginger molasses. For breakfast, nothing beats a buttery croissant spread with jam. Provence also has locations at 1600 Division Street at Roundabout Plaza; at 315 Deaderick Street, in the AmSouth

Building downtown; and in Hillsboro at 1705 21st Avenue South.

For homemade salads, wraps, and sandwiches, follow the crowds of downtown office workers to the **Frist Center Cafe** (919 Broadway, 616/244-3340, Mon.–Wed. and Sat. 10 A.M.–5:30 P.M., Thurs.–Fri. 10 A.M.–9 P.M., Sun. noon–5 P.M., $5–8), located at the rear of the Frist Center for the Arts. Sandwiches are available whole or half, and you can add a soup, salad, or fries for a well-rounded lunch. The café has daily hot lunch entrées, plus a case of tempting desserts.

Midtown
When Nashvillians are in the mood for a hearty deli sandwich, they head to **Noshville** (1918 Broadway, 615/329-6674, Mon. 6:30 A.M.–2:30 P.M., Tues.–Thurs. 6:30 A.M.–9 P.M., Fri. 6:30 A.M.–10:30 P.M., Sat. 7:30 A.M.–10:30 P.M., Sun. 7:30 A.M.–9 P.M., $7–12), which is as close to a genuine New York delicatessen as you'll

FOOD TRUCKS

© MARGARET LITTMAN

Food truck fever has infected Nashville! Some of the city's best eats are on four wheels.

Like every big city with a hipster population worth its salt, Nashville has scores of food trucks driving to and fro, selling gourmet delicacies from their wheel-based restaurants. These snack masters tend to show up places with big lunch crowds, late night after concerts, and at large public events, so you may just run into them.

The **Nashville Food Trucks** website, www.nashfoodtrucks.com, lists menus and upcoming planned stops for more than 25 trucks. If you prefer your meals alfresco, check out this list.

- One of Nashville's first food trucks, **The Grilled Cheeserie** (www.thegrilledcheeserietruck.com) serves delicious grilled cheese sandwiches and tomato soup. It travels all over the city, particularly at farmers markets in the summer. Track it via Twitter (@GrlldCheeserie) or text CHEESE to 88000.

- It is hard to miss the bright pink presence that is **Barbie Burgers.** To find their tasty burgers and sweet potato fries, follow them on Twitter (@BarbieBurgers).

- Ice cream sandwiches, strawberry shortcake, and other classic desserts are the fuel that keeps **Tin Can Treats** going. Their Twitter handle is @tincantreats.

- Locals loved the Mexican cuisine served out of the **Mas Tacos** truck so much that they were forced to open an East Nashville shop, too (732 McFerrin Ave.). The mobile option can be tracked down via Twitter (@mastacos).

- **Riff's Fine Street Food** serves a changing menu of sandwiches, salads, and treats like brisket tacos. A handy calendar (www.riffstruck.com) makes this brightly colored truck easy to find.

find in this southern town. Lox and bagels, oatmeal, and a variety of egg dishes are popular at breakfast. At lunch and supper choose from a variety of sandwiches, all served double-stacked, which means it's really more than any one person should eat. To find Noshville, look for the miniature statue of Lady Liberty on the roof. There is another location in Green Hills (4014 Hillsboro Cir., 615/269-3535), and yet another at the airport.

There's a lot of hype surrounding Nashville's favorite breakfast restaurant, the **Pancake Pantry** (1796 21st Ave. S., 615/383-9333, Mon.–Fri. 6 A.M.–3 P.M., Sat.–Sun. 6 A.M.–4 P.M., $6–14). Founded in 1961 and still family owned, the Pantry serves some of the best pancakes in the city. Owner David Baldwin says that the secret is in the ingredients, which are fresh and homemade. Many of the flours come from Tennessee, and the syrup is made right at the restaurant. The Pantry proves that a pancake can be much more than plain. The menu offers no fewer than 21 varieties, and that doesn't include the waffles. Try the fluffy buckwheat cakes, savory cornmeal cakes, sweet blintzes, or the old standby buttermilk pancakes. And if you decide to order eggs instead, the good news is that most of the other breakfast platters on offer come with a short stack of pancakes, too. To its credit, the Pantry offers no-yolk omelets for the health conscious, and it's very kid friendly as well.

The Pantry also serves lunch, which is limited to sandwiches, salads, and soups. Beware that on weekend mornings, and many weekdays, the line for a seat at the Pantry goes out the door.

In today's retro-happy world, it isn't too hard to find an old-fashioned soda shop. But how many of them are the real thing? **Elliston Place Soda Shop** (2111 Elliston Pl., 615/327-1090, Mon.–Fri. 7 A.M.–7 P.M., Sat. 7 A.M.–5 P.M., $5–9), near Centennial Park and Vanderbilt, is one of these rare holdovers from the past, and it's proud of it. The black-and-white tile floors,

lunch counter, and Purity Milk advertisements may have been here for decades, but the food is consistently fresh and good. Choose between a sandwich or a plate lunch, but be sure to save room for a classic milk shake or slice of hot pie with ice cream on top. In 2011 the shop threatened to close, citing sluggish sales and increasing rent, but public outcry convinced the owners to renew the lease for five more years.

Nashville's original coffee shop, **Bongo Java** (2007 Belmont Blvd., 615/385-5282, Mon.–Fri. 7 A.M.–11 P.M., Sat.–Sun. 8 A.M.–11 P.M.) is just as popular as ever. Located near Belmont University, Bongo, as its frequent patrons call it, is regularly full of students chatting, texting, and surfing the Internet thanks to free wireless Internet. Set in an old house with a huge front porch, Bongo feels homey and welcoming, and a bit more on the hippie side than other Nashville coffee shops. Nonetheless, expect the latest in coffee drinks, premium salads, and sandwiches. Breakfast, including Bongo French toast, is served all day. There is a bulletin board, a good place to find and seek roommates or apartments.

Bongo Java's big brother, **Fido** (1812 21st Ave. S., 615/777-3436, Mon.–Fri. 7 A.M.–11 P.M., Sat. 8 A.M.–midnight, Sun. 8 A.M.–11 P.M.) is more than a coffee shop. It is a place to get work done, see deals made, and see and be seen. Take a seat along the front plate-glass windows to watch the pretty people as they stroll between the Sunset Grill and Posh, one of Nashville's most upscale clothing boutiques. In addition to coffee, sandwiches, and salads, baked goods are on the menu.

Said to have the best burger in Nashville, **Rotier's** (2413 Elliston Pl., 615/327-9892, Mon.–Fri. 10:30 A.M.–10 P.M., Sat. 9 A.M.–10 P.M., $5–12) is also a respected meat-and-three diner. Choose from classic sandwiches or comfort-food dinners. The Saturday breakfast will fuel you all day long. Ask about the milk shake, a city favorite that appears nowhere on the menu. Don't miss the hash brown casserole.

Dessert takes center stage at **Bobbie's Dairy Dip** (5301 Charlotte Ave., 615/292-2112, Mon.–Thurs. 11 A.M.–9 P.M., Fri.–Sat. 11 A.M.–10 P.M., Sun. noon–9 P.M., $4–7), a walk-up ice cream joint. The cheeseburgers and chili dogs are the comfort food you've dreamed of, and you can finish off with soft-serve ice cream, dipped cones, sundaes, and banana splits. Bobbie's closes during the winter months; call ahead to confirm they're open.

East Nashville

Not a deli in the traditional sense, **Mitchell's Delicatessen** (1402 McGavock Pk., 615/262-9862, Tues.–Sat. 7 A.M.–7 P.M., Sun. 7 A.M.–4 P.M., $6–10) is the most creative sandwich shop in town. Order the roasted lamb and raita; a Vietnamese-style creation with pork, liver pate, and veggies; or a BLT fit for a king. Breakfast is served until 11 A.M., and there is also a daily menu of soups and hot plate

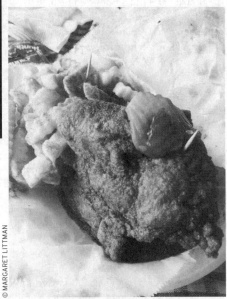

© MARGARET LITTMAN

Hot chicken is a Nashville specialty. It is not for those with meek taste buds.

specials. Stop here for top-notch bread, cheese, and meats for your own sandwiches, too.

SOUTHERN
Downtown

Run, don't walk, to **⟨ Arnold's Country Kitchen** (605 8th Ave. S., 615/256-4455, Mon.–Fri. 10:30 A.M.–2:45 P.M., $7–10) for some of the best Southern cooking in town. Set in a red cinder-block building on the southern edge of downtown, Arnold's is a food-lover's dream. No haute or fusion cuisine here—this is real food. It's set up cafeteria-style, so start out by grabbing a tray while you peer at the wonders before you: chocolate pie, congealed salad (that's Jell-O to those who don't know), juicy sliced tomatoes, turnip greens, mashed potatoes, squash casserole, macaroni and cheese—and that's just the "vegetables." Choose a vegetable plate, with either three or four vegetables, or a meat-and-three for just about a buck more. Common meat dishes include ham, baked chicken, fried fish, and beef tips. All meals come with your choice of pillowy yeast rolls or corn bread. The full lunch, plus a drink, will run you under $10. As you leave, full and happy, the only question on your mind will be, When can I come back?

Midtown

One of Nashville's most beloved meat-and-threes is **Swett's** (2725 Clifton Ave., 615/329-4418, daily 11 A.M.–8 P.M., $8–12), family owned and operated since 1954. People come from all over the city to eat at this Nashville institution, which combines soul food and Southern cooking with great results (and, in 2012, they added barbecue to their offerings). The food here is homemade and authentic, down to the real mashed potatoes, the vinegary greens, and the yeast rolls. Swett's is set up cafeteria-style. Start by grabbing dessert—the pies are excellent—and then you move on to the good stuff: Country-fried steak, pork

NASHVILLE

chops, meat loaf, fried catfish, and ham are a few of the usual suspects. A standard plate comes with one meat, two sides, and a serving of either yeast roll or corn bread, but you can add more sides if you like. Draw your own iced tea—sweet or unsweet—at the end, and then find a seat if you can.

North Nashville

Nashville's most sublime food experience is not to be found in a fine restaurant or even at a standard meat-and-three cafeteria. The food that you'll still be dreaming about when you get home is found at **⟨ Prince's Hot Chicken Shack** (123 Ewing Dr., 615/226-9442, Tues.–Thurs. noon–10 P.M., Fri.–Sat. 2 P.M.–1 A.M., $4–6) in North Nashville. Hot chicken is pan-fried chicken that is also spicy, and you can find hot chicken outlets in Nashville, Memphis, and a few other Southern cities. But no hot chicken shop does it quite as well as Prince's, where the hot chicken comes in three varieties: mild, hot, and extrahot. Most uninitiated will find the mild variety plenty spicy, so beware. It is served with slices of white bread—perfect for soaking up that spicy chicken juice—and a pickle slice. You can add a cup of creamy potato salad, coleslaw, or baked beans if you like. When you walk into Prince's, head to the back, where you'll place your order at the window, pay, and be given a number. Then take a seat—if you can find one—while you wait for your food. You can order to go or eat in. Your food is made to order, and Prince's is very popular, so the wait often exceeds 30 minutes. Take heart, though—Prince's chicken is worth the wait.

Music Valley

Outside of the cuisine at the Gaylord Opryland Resort hotel, Music Valley isn't much known for its food. But the **Opry Backstage Grill** (2401 Music Valley Dr., 615/231-8854, Sun.–Thurs. 11 A.M.–3 P.M. and 4 P.M.–10:30 P.M., Fri.–Sat. 11 A.M.–3 P.M. and 4 P.M.–11:30 P.M., $8–18) tries to offer something that is at least unique to Nashville, albeit with the flair of a chain. This themed restaurant serves classic Southern dishes amid photos and art of classic Opry performers and occasionally hosts live concerts for ambience.

West of Nashville

The **Loveless Cafe** (8400 Hwy. 100, 615/646-9700, daily 7 A.M.–9 P.M., $7–13) is an institution, and some may argue it's a state of mind. But this little café-that-could is increasingly a destination, too, for visitors not just to Nashville but the entire heartland of Tennessee. The Loveless got its start in 1951 when Lon and Annie Loveless started to serve good country cooking to travelers on Highway 100. Over the years the restaurant changed hands, but Annie's biscuit recipe remained the same, and it was the biscuits that kept Nashvillians, including many famous ones, coming back for more. In 1982 then owner George McCabe started the Hams & Jams mail-order business, and in 2003 the Loveless underwent a major renovation that expanded the kitchen and dining rooms, and added additional shops in the rear. The food at the Loveless is good, no doubt about it. The biscuits are fluffy and buttery, the ham salty, and the eggs, bacon, and sausage will hit the spot. The supper and lunch menu has expanded to include Southern standards like fried catfish and chicken, pit-cooked pork barbecue, pork chops, and meat loaf, as well as a few salads. Loveless is located about 20 miles from downtown Nashville; plan on a 30-minute drive out Highway 100. Once you get out of the congestion of West End, it's a pretty trip.

If you are headed to adjacent Loveless Barn for the Wednesday night **Music City Roots** (www.musiccityroots.com) show, don't eat first. You can order from a limited Loveless menu and eat while you listen to the show.

NASHVILLE

BARBECUE
Downtown

If you are downtown and craving barbecue, **Jack's Bar-b-que** (416 Broadway, 615/254-5715, Mon.–Wed. 10:30 A.M.–8 P.M., Thurs. 10:30 A.M.–9 P.M., Fri.–Sat. 10:30 A.M.–10 P.M., $6–15, hours may be extended during the summer) is your best option for a bite on Broadway. It isn't the best in the city, but the location can't be beat. Choose from barbecue pork shoulder, brisket, turkey, ribs, or sausage, and pair it with classic Southern sides like green beans, macaroni and cheese, and fried apples. Jack's serves five types of barbecue sauce, including classic Tennessee, Texas, and Kansas City. Most diners opt for a plate of one meat, two vegetables, and bread for $8–9, but if you're really hungry, go for the three-meat platter for $13. Adding to the appeal of the decent, affordable food is the fact that Jack's service is fast and friendly.

Midtown

Near Centennial Park and Vanderbilt, **Hog Heaven** (115 27th Ave. N., 615/329-1234, www.hogheavenbbq.com, Mon.–Sat. 10 A.M.–7 P.M., $5–10) is a nondescript yet well-known landmark for barbecue. Pulled-pork sandwiches and beef brisket are among the most popular at this mostly takeout eatery; locals like the white barbecue sauce.

South Nashville

Tucked on Nolensville Pike, the land of international eateries, is one of the city's favorite barbecue houses. **Martin's Bar-B-Que Joint** (7215 Nolensville Pk., 615/776-1856, www.martinsbbqjoint.com, Sun.–Thurs. 11 A.M.–8 P.M., Fri.–Sat. 11 A.M.–9 P.M., $4–15) has pulled pork, barbecue spareribs, smoked wings, and beef brisket, plus all the side dishes you could want: coleslaw, green beans, potato salad, and the best corn cakes this side of town. You can also order burgers and a mean catfish po'boy. Martin's is located inside the Nolensville city limits, about 30 minutes' drive south from downtown Nashville.

STEAK HOUSES
Midtown

Jimmy Kelly's (217 Louise Ave., 615/329-4349, www.jimmykellys.com, Mon.–Sat. 5 P.M.–midnight, $18–42) is a family-run old-school steak house. Set in an old Victorian mansion a few blocks from Centennial Park and Vanderbilt, Jimmy Kelly's has been operated by the Kelly family since 1934. During its lifetime, food fads have come and gone, but Jimmy Kelly's has continued to serve excellent steaks and other grill foods. Dinner begins with irresistible corn cakes and continues with classic appetizers like crab cakes or fried calamari. Entrée choices include a half dozen different steaks, lamb, grilled chicken, and seafood, including the best blackened catfish in the city. Jimmy Kelly's offers low lighting, wood paneling, and attentive, but not fussy, service. Tables are set throughout what were once parlors, bedrooms, and porches in the old home, giving diners a feeling of homey intimacy.

CONTEMPORARY
Downtown

The thoughtful menu, careful preparations, and green restaurant credentials at the **Mad Platter** (1239 6th Ave. N., 615/242-2563, www.themadplatterrestaurant.com, Mon.–Fri. 11 A.M.–2 P.M., Wed.–Thurs. 5:30–10 P.M., Fri.–Sat. 5:30–11 P.M., Sun. 5–9 P.M., $18–35) have made it one of Nashville's favorite "nice" restaurants for years. Located among restored town houses in the tiny Germantown neighborhood, just north of the Bicentennial Mall, the Mad Platter is the work of Craig and Marcia Jervis, two chefs who met while catering the mid-1980s Michael Jackson's Victory tour. The Jervises married and opened the Mad Hatter, where they demonstrate their love for food, and each other, every day. Signature entrées include the Mad Platter rack of lamb, which is tender and juicy, and the porcini-dusted shrimp. For a special occasion, or just to enjoy one of the city's best dining deals, choose the five-course special. The chicken salad is sweet and tangy, and comes with fresh banana bread. Reservations are advisable at dinner; for lunch, come early to head off the business crowd.

Rub elbows with legislators, lobbyists, and other members of the jet set at the **C Capitol Grill** (23 6th Ave. N., 615/345-7116, daily 6:30 A.M.–11 A.M., 11:30 A.M.–2 P.M., and 5:30–10 P.M., $18–52). Located in the ground floor of the elegant Hermitage Hotel and set a stone's throw from the Tennessee State Capitol, this is the sort of restaurant where marriages are proposed and deals are done. The menu is fine dining at its best: choice cuts of meat prepared with exacting care and local ingredients. In fact, the ingredients are grown at the nearby Farm at Glen Leven, and this connection to the land has made the restaurant one of the leaders in the farm-to-fork movement. Dinner features rack of elk, sea bass, and pork chops; the provenience of each is noted on the menu. The lunch menu is more modest, including the Capitol Grill burger, a grilled pimento cheese sandwich, and meat entrées for $11–18. The business lunch offers a lunch entrée and your choice of soup or salad for $20. Breakfast ($4–16) may be the most decadent of all, with cinnamon-swirl French toast, eggs Benedict, lobster and shirred eggs, and an array of fresh pastries and fruit. The Sunday Brunch features the best of the grill's lunch and breakfast menus, and is consistently popular.

Adjacent to the Capitol Grill is the old-school Oak Bar, a wood-paneled and intimate bar for pre- or postdinner drinks and conversation.

Midtown

C F. Scott's (2210 Crestmore Rd., 615/269-5861, Mon.–Thurs. 5:30–10 P.M., Fri.–Sat. 5:30–11 P.M., $28–45) is an upscale restaurant and jazz bar with one of the best wine lists in Nashville. Diners are ushered into a black-and-white-tiled dining room, where the sounds of live jazz from the adjacent listening room follow them. Enjoy a relaxed meal with wine pairings and great conversation. Food at F. Scott's is meant to be savored. Appetizers include rabbit tart, or pancetta and scallops with caviar, and entrées might be pan-seared seafood, dressed-up shepherd's pie, and grilled beef tenderloin. Save room for dessert: homemade ice cream, coconut cake, or a cheese plate paired with the perfect dessert wine.

A favorite for Music Row power lunches, special occasions, and late-night bar food is **Sunset Grill** (2001 Belcourt Ave., 615/386-3663, www.sunsetgrill.com, Tues.–Fri. 11 A.M.–3 P.M., nightly 5–10 P.M., Mon.–Sat. until 1:30 A.M., $15–35). Dinner favorites include Voodoo Pasta, a spicy pasta dish with shrimp and andouille sausage, and the grilled beef tenderloin. At lunch, when most choices are less than $12, you can order salads, sandwiches, and pasta. The Cobb salad and chicken-salad sandwiches are always popular. Food here is prepared with care, often using organic and locally produced ingredients. The outdoor patio is popular during warm weather, and it is a great place to people-watch.

East Nashville

Housed in a former Laundromat, the **The Family Wash** (2038 Greenwood Ave., 615/226-6070, www.familywash.com, Tues.–Sat. 6 P.M.–midnight, $9–15) is classic Nashville. Part live music listening room, part bar, part restaurant, part neighborhood gathering place, the Family Wash captures the offbeat energy that so well defines Nashville. Come here to hear local musicians of all stripes (definitely not just country) and eat supper that is better than average bar food. Locals love the shepherd's pie. Reservations are accepted, and they're recommended as the space isn't large and friends of the band may pack the place when favorites take the small stage.

There's something about a place that pays attention to the details, and **Holland House Bar and Refuge** (935 W. Eastland Ave., 615/262-4190, www.hollandhousebarandrefuge.com, Mon.–Thurs. 5 P.M.–midnight, Fri.–Sat. 5 P.M.–2 A.M., Sun. 11 A.M.–2 P.M., $15–40) is one of those spots. This East Nashville hideaway is exactly as its name suggests: a refuge from louder restaurants and more frantically paced bars. The impressive cocktail and food menus change seasonally, and the bartender will craft your drink with precision, so expect to wait for that perfectly sized ginger ice cube or muddle mint (try the truffled popcorn while you wait). The food menu isn't as extensive as the cocktail menu, but everything is made with local and seasonal ingredients, ranging from duck to catfish. Locals like Monday night's happy hour and its burger special. This is not a place to bring little ones—it is a bar as much as a restaurant. Kids are welcome for Sunday brunch, however. The folks at Holland House are the minds behind **The Pharmacy Burger Parlor & Beer Garden** (731 McFerrin, 615/712-9527, www.pharmacynashville.com) right next door. The Pharmacy makes sodas by hand and has a killer grassy backyard beer garden.

INTERNATIONAL
Downtown

There are several Greek restaurants amid Nashville's office towers and state buildings. One of the best is **Santorini** (210 4th Ave., 615/254-4524, Mon.–Fri. 10:30 A.M.–3 P.M., $3.50–5.75). Choose from falafel, gyro, chicken, or spinach pie, served as a plate (with rice, salad, and pita), salad (with pita, tabbouleh, and salad), or meal (with fries). The food is fresh and well prepared, and the premises are neat and clean.

Located in the downtown Arcade, **Manny's House of Pizza** (15 Arcade, 615/242-7144, www.mannyshouseofpizza.com, Mon.–Fri. 10 A.M.–6 P.M., Sat. 11 A.M.–4:30 P.M., $10–30) serves up thick- and thin-crust varieties, massive stromboli, mighty lasagna, and huge meatball subs. The restaurant is small; eating in can be a challenge, particularly because Nashvillians flock here for the best slice in town. Manny's stays open later on the first Saturday of the month thanks to the downtown Art Crawl.

Midtown

The venerable **International Market and Restaurant** (2010 Belmont Blvd., 615/297-4453, daily 10:30 A.M.–9 P.M., $5–10) near Belmont University and Hillsboro Village is a time-honored choice for a cheap lunch in Nashville. The cafeteria serves lots of vegetable, noodle, and rice dishes, many of them Thai in origin, at prices that seem not to have risen much since the restaurant was established in 1975. If you want to splurge, order a "from the kitchen" special of pad thai or another dish, which will be made from scratch just for you. Owner Patti Myint is the mother of *Top Chef* contestant and local restaurateur Arnold Myint.

For the best Italian food in Nashville, head west to the neighborhood of Sylvan Park, where you'll find **Caffe Nonna** (4427 Murphy Rd., 615/463-0133, www.caffenonna.com, Tues.–Fri. 11 A.M.–2 P.M., Mon.–Thurs. 5–9 P.M., Fri.–Sat. 5–10 P.M., $12–21). Inspired by Chef Daniel Maggipinto's own *nonna* (grandmother), the café serves rustic Italian fare. Appetizers include salads and bruschetta, and entrées include the divine Lasagne Nonna, made with butternut squash, ricotta cheese, spinach, and sage. The service at Caffe Nonna is friendly and attentive, and the atmosphere is cozy, but the space is small. Call ahead for a table.

Located just west of the Kroger food store, K&S World Market on Charlotte Avenue, the second in a chain whose original location is on Nolensville Pike, will keep any foodie happy for hours with its obscure and unusual food items. In the same shopping center you'll find Nashvillians' favorite Vietnamese restaurants, **Kien Giang** (5825 Charlotte Ave., 615/353-1250, Tues.–Fri. 11 A.M.–9 P.M., Sat.–Sun. 10 A.M.–9 P.M., $6–12) and **Miss Saigon** (5849 Charlotte Ave., 615/354-1351, Wed.–Sat. 10 A.M.–9 P.M., Sun.–Mon. 10 A.M.–8 P.M., $7–12).

Drive a bit farther out to find **La Hispana Panaderia** (6208 Charlotte Pk., 615/352-3798, daily 6 A.M.–9 P.M.), whose bread and pastries are as good as the finest European bakery but at a fraction of the cost.

One of Nashville's oldest Indian restaurants, **Shalimar** (3711 Hillsboro Rd., 615/269-8577, www.shalimarfinedining.com, Mon.–Sat. 11 A.M.–2:30 P.M. and 5–10 P.M., Sun. noon–8 P.M., $15–17) offers fine food and efficient service. The Saturday lunch buffet brings in mall shoppers and ladies who lunch. At dinner, Shalimar takes on a slightly more elegant cast with vegetarian, chicken, lamb, and seafood entrées in popular preparations including masala, biryani, tikka, saag, or korma. Shalimar is just a few blocks from the Mall at Green Hills.

South Nashville

Chosen by Nashvillians as the best Mexican restaurant in a very crowded field, **La Hacienda Taqueria** (2615 Nolensville Pk., 615/256-6142, www.lahaciendainc.com, Mon.–Thurs. 10 A.M.–9 P.M., Fri. 10 A.M.–10 P.M., Sat. 9 A.M.–10 P.M., Sun. 9 A.M.–9 P.M., $2–14) is located within a colorful storefront on Nolensville Pike, Nashville's most ethnically diverse thoroughfare. The menu offers a dizzying array of choices—tacos, enchiladas, tamales, burritos, quesadillas, and *tortas*, just to name a few. Most come with your choice of chicken, chorizo, tripe, pork, or steak filling, and many have an authenticity often missing from Mexican restaurant fare. Combination platters, which offer three items plus rice and beans, are a good way to sample the options if you aren't sure what to order.

If you aren't in the mood for Mexican, just drive a bit farther along Nolensville Pike for other choices. Among them is **Dunya Kebob** (2521 Nolensville Pk., 615/242-6664, Mon.–Thurs. 11 A.M.–9:30 P.M., Fri.–Sat. 11 A.M.–10:30 P.M., Sun. noon–9:30 P.M., $5–10), which offers Kurdish specialties of chicken, lamb, beef, and seafood kebobs and gyro sandwiches (Nashville has a large Kurdish immigrant population; this is the place to try the cuisine).

Not far from Nolensville, you'll find two more international favorites in the same shopping center on Trousdale Drive. **Back to Cuba** (4683 Trousdale Dr., 615/837-6711, Tues.–Sat. 11 A.M.–9 P.M., $8–12) serves traditional Cuban favorites: Grilled sandwiches of pork, ham, cheese, and pickle are a popular choice at lunchtime. For dinner, try the roast pork or grilled shrimp, and don't skip the lacy fried plantains and spicy black beans.

For homemade, old-school Italian fare (think: red sauce), go to **Mama Mia's** (4501 Trousdale Dr., 615/331-7207, Mon.–Fri. 11 A.M.–2 P.M., Mon.–Sat. 5–10 P.M., $7–16), which offers lasagna, ravioli, chicken, veal, and seafood dishes. Bring your own wine.

MARKETS

For fresh fruits, vegetables, preserves, and honey, go to the **Nashville Farmers' Market** held daily in the large covered building between 8th Avenue and the Bicentennial Mall. Many of the goods for sale here are grown at farms near Nashville; to be sure, ask whether you're getting Tennessee products. During the summer there are many smaller farmers markets around town, including on the Vanderbilt campus, in Franklin, and in East Nashville.

There is an abundance of traditional grocery stores around Nashville. Common chains are Kroger, Harris Teeter, and Publix. There is a Trader Joe's, which specializes in organic and specialty items, in Green Hills, just south of the Mall at Green Hills, as well as a Whole Foods.

Information and Services

VISITORS CENTERS

The main visitors center (615/259-4747, www.visitmusiccity.com/visitors, Mon.–Sat. 8 A.M.–5 P.M., Sun. 10 A.M.–5 P.M.) is located at the corner of 5th Avenue and Broadway, inside the Bridgestone Arena. Here you can pick up brochures, get a free map, and find answers to just about any question. It is open late when there is an event at Bridgestone.

There is another visitors center a few blocks uptown at 1 Nashville Place (615/259-4730, Mon.–Fri. 8 A.M.–5 P.M.).

MAPS

Visitors centers offer a free hand-out map of downtown and an area map that shows major thoroughfares. This will be sufficient for many travelers. However, if you plan to do a lot of driving or off-the-beaten-track exploring, pick up a city map such as those published by Rand McNally or AAA. Detailed maps may be purchased from local drugstores and bookstores. Save time by buying a map before you arrive or downloading a GPS app to your iPhone.

MEDIA
Newspapers

Nashville's daily morning broadsheet is the *Tennessean* (www.tennessean.com). Published under various names since 1812, the *Tennessean* offers what every big-city newspaper does: local, regional, and national news, plus lots more. The paper's entertainment insert is published with the Friday newspaper.

The *City Paper* (www.nashvillecitypaper.com) is a free twice-weekly tabloid with a strong website that specializes in local news, sports, and events. It offers an alternative viewpoint to that of the *Tennessean* and makes a good, compact read for locals and visitors. You can pick up *City Paper* in dozens of downtown locations.

The *Nashville Scene* (www.nashvillescene.com) is a fat tabloid-size alternative weekly that balances its coverage of the local arts, music, and social scene with some political and local news coverage. This is a good go-to choice to understand what's going on in the city.

Nashville Music Guide (www.nashvillemusicguide.com) is a free tabloid published twice a month. It covers the local music scene and music-industry news.

In addition, the *Nashville Business Journal* (615/248-2222, www.bizjournals.com/nashville) is a weekly business publication covering industry, commerce, and finance. It is distributed on Monday. *Nashville Pride* (615/292-9150) covers African American news and is distributed on Friday.

Also published by the *Tennessean, Nashville Lifestyles* is a monthly glossy magazine with local celebrity profiles, home and garden tips, event information, and advertising. You can pick it up at newsstands throughout the city.

American Songwriter Magazine (1303 16th Ave. S., 615/321-6069, www.americansongwriter.com) is a bimonthly magazine devoted to the art of songwriting. It has been published in Nashville since 1984.

Radio

The Nashville dial is chockablock with the usual commercial radio prospects (what else would you expect in Music City?). There are a few radio stations worth mentioning, however. **WSM 650 AM** is the legendary radio station that started it all when it put a fiddler on the air in 1925. Still airing the Grand Ole Opry after all these years, WSM plays country music at other times.

Nashville Public Radio has two stations, **WPLN 90.3 FM** and **91.1 FM.** The first plays National Public Radio news and talk, the second is all classical music. **WPLN 1430 AM** is a companion station with all-day news and talk, including BBC broadcasts. Nashville's only community radio station is **Radio Free Nashville** (107.1 FM, www.radiofreenashville. org). While its signal only reaches a small part of the city now, Radio Free Nashville is looking to expand its reach as soon as it raises the necessary funds.

WKDA 900 AM is Nashville's Spanish-language radio station. **WAMB 1160 AM** plays big-band music, and **WNAH 1360 AM** plays old-fashioned Southern gospel.

Several Nashville universities liven up the radio dial. Fisk's **WFSK 88.1 FM** plays jazz. Middle Tennessee State University has **WMTS 88.3 FM**, the student-run station, and **WMOT 89.5 FM**, a jazz station.

Television

Nashville's network affiliates offer local news morning and night. These include **WKRN** (Channel 2 ABC), **WSMV** (Channel 4 NBC), **WTVF** (Channel 5 CBS), and **WZTV** (Channel 17 FOX).

The local public-television station is **WNPT** (Channel 8 PBS).

Remember that since Nashville is in the Central time zone, most nationally televised programs air one hour earlier than they do on the East Coast.

INTERNET ACCESS

You can go online free at the **Nashville Public Library** (615 Church St., 615/862-5800). There is free wireless access at the visitors center located at 5th and Broadway.

POSTAL SERVICE

Mail a letter or buy stamps from the downtown post offices at 901 Broadway and 1718 Church Street. Both are open Monday–Friday 8:30 A.M.–5 P.M. There is also a post office in the downtown Arcade.

EMERGENCY SERVICES

Dial 911 for police, fire, or ambulance in an emergency. For help with a traffic accident, call the **Tennessee Highway Patrol** (615/741-3181).

Because health care is such a big industry in Nashville, there are a lot of hospitals. The **Monroe Carell Jr. Children's Hospital at Vanderbilt** (2200 Children's Way, 615/936-1000, www.childrenshospital.vanderbilt.org) is among the best in the country. **Baptist Hospital** (2000 Church St., 615/284-5555, www.baptist-hospital.com) is another major player.

Rite Aid, CVS, Walgreens, and the major grocery store chains have drugstores all over Nashville. Try the **CVS** at 426 21st Avenue South (615/321-2590, www.cvs.com).

LIBRARIES

Nashville's downtown library is the crown jewel of its library system. The **Nashville Public Library** (615 Church St., 615/862-5800, www. library.nashville.org, Mon.–Fri. 9 A.M.–6 P.M., Sat. 9 A.M.–5 P.M., Sun. 2–5 P.M.) opened in 2001, replacing an older library that had served the city since 1965. The library is dynamic and busy serving its community. There are story hours, children's programs, art exhibits, a local history collection, and meeting rooms. Visitors to the city will find the public Internet access and wireless Internet network most useful. There is a nice courtyard inside the library where people eat lunch, relax, and enjoy occasional concerts. One Saturday a month the Nashville Shakespeare Festival gathers here for the free **Shakespeare Allowed,** an afternoon where attendees read, not perform, one of the Bard's plays aloud.

If you are visiting the library, you can park in the Nashville Public Library Parking Garage. Enter on 6th or 7th Avenue between Church and Commerce Streets. The first 90 minutes of library parking is free, and the daily maximum is $8. Be sure to validate your ticket at the security desk as you enter the library.

NASHVILLE

Getting There and Around

GETTING THERE
By Air
Nashville International Airport (BNA; 615/275-1675, www.nashintl.com) is located eight miles east of the city center. To get downtown from the airport, head west on I-40; it's a short 15-minute drive. The flat one-way taxi fare from the airport to downtown or Music Valley is $25. The airport has been renovated Music City style. It has outposts of local restaurants and musicians playing live music (and selling CDs).

AIRPORT SHUTTLE
Many of the major hotels offer shuttles from the airport; there's a kiosk on the lower level of the terminal to help you find the right one. **Gray Line Transportation** (615/883-5555, www.graylinenashville.com) offers regular shuttle service from the airport to downtown, West End, and Music Valley hotels. The shuttle departs from the airport every 15–20 minutes 4 A.M.–11 P.M.; reservations are not required. Call ahead to book your hotel pickup. Fare is $14 one-way and $25 round-trip.

By Car
Driving is the most popular way to get to Nashville. The city is 250 miles from Atlanta, 330 miles from St. Louis, 400 miles from Charlotte, 550 miles from New Orleans, and 670 miles from Washington DC.

No fewer than three major interstate highways converge in Nashville. I-40 runs east–west, connecting Nashville with Knoxville and Memphis. I-65 runs north–south, connecting the city with Louisville, Kentucky, and Birmingham, Alabama. I-24 travels at a southeastern angle down to the city, connecting it with the cities of Clarkesville and St. Louis in the north, and Chattanooga and Atlanta in the south.

By Bus
Greyhound (800/231-2222, www.greyhound.com) serves Nashville, with bus service to the city from Memphis, Jackson, Chattanooga, and Knoxville, Tennessee, as well as Paducah and Bowling Green, Kentucky. The **Greyhound station** (1022 Charlotte Ave., 615/255-3556) is well marked and well staffed, with ample parking, and is several blocks west of downtown. Expect to pay about $50 for a one-way ticket from Memphis to Nashville.

GETTING AROUND
Driving
The easiest way to get around Nashville is by car. Although visitors staying downtown will be able to find plenty to do and places to eat within walking distance, many of the best attractions are located outside of the city center. So unless your stay is but a few days, it is best to bring or rent a car to get around.

If you don't bring your own, a dozen different major rental agencies have a fleet of cars, trucks, and SUVs at the airport. Agencies include **Alamo** (615/361-7467, www.alamo.com), **Avis** (615/361-1212, www.avis.com), and **Hertz** (615/361-3131, www.hertz.com). For the best rates, use an online travel search tool, such as Expedia (www.expedia.com) or Travelocity (www.travelocity.com), and book the car early, along with your airline tickets.

NAVIGATING NASHVILLE
Even locals are perplexed by Nashville's city planning, with street names that repeat and change, and few straight roads. The interstates are a little easier to navigate than side streets. I-65 and I-24 create a tight inner beltway that encircles the heart of the city. I-440 is an outer beltway that circles the southern half of the city, while I-40 runs horizontally from east to

west. Briley Parkway, shown on some maps as Highway TN-155, is a highway that circles the north and east perimeters of the city.

City residents use the interstates not just for long journeys, but also for short crosstown jaunts. Most businesses give directions according to the closest interstate exit.

Noninterstate thoroughfares emanate out from Nashville like spokes of a wheel. Many are named for the communities that they eventually run into. Murfreesboro Pike runs southeast from the city; Hillsboro Pike (Route 431) starts out as 21st Avenue South and takes you to Hillsboro Village and Green Hills. Broadway becomes West End Avenue and takes you directly to Belle Meade and, eventually, the Loveless Cafe. It does not take long to realize that roads in Nashville have a bad habit of changing names all of a sudden, so be prepared and check the map to avoid getting too confused.

For real-time traffic advisories and road construction closures, dial 511 from any touch-tone phone, or go to www.tn511.com.

PARKING

There is metered parking on most downtown streets, but some have prohibited-parking signs effective during morning and afternoon rush hours. Always read the fine print carefully.

There is plenty of off-street parking in lots and garages. Expect to pay about $10 a day for garage parking. **Park It! Downtown** (www.parkitdowntown.com) is a great resource for finding downtown parking deals, plus information about the shuttle that transports parkers to LP Field during downtown events.

Public Transportation

Nashville's **Metropolitan Transit Authority** operates city buses. Pick up a map and schedule from either of the two downtown visitors centers, or online at www.nashvillemta.org.

Improvements to the city's public transport system have made it easier to use, but few tourists ride the buses because they can be difficult to understand if you're new to the city. One favorite is the Music City Circuit, a free bus that runs between downtown and the Gulch. These Blue and Green Circuit buses stop at 75 different spots on three different routes. One route that is helpful, however, is the Opry Mills Express that travels from downtown Nashville to Music Valley, home of the Grand Ole Opry, Opryland Hotel, and Opry Mills, the shopping mall. The Opry Mills Express departs the Bridgestone Arena 13 times a day on weekdays. Fare is $1.70 one-way; $0.85 for senior citizens. You can pick up a detailed route timetable from either of the two downtown visitors centers or online.

On Tennessee Titans' game days, the MTA offers its **End Zone Express.** Park at either Greer Stadium (where the Nashville Sounds play) or the state employee lot at 4th Avenue North and Harrison, and for just $6 you get shuttled straight to LP Field.

COMMUTER RAIL

In 2006 Nashville debuted the **Music City Star Rail** (501 Union St., 615/862-8833, www.musiccitystar.org), a commuter rail system designed to ease congestion around the city. With service Monday–Friday, several times a day, trains connect Donelson, Hermitage, Mount Juliet, and Lebanon to downtown Nashville. There is often additional service during special events, such as the Fourth of July celebration downtown. More routes are planned for the future.

One-way tickets can be purchased for $5 each from vending machines at any of the stations. You can prepurchase single-trip tickets, 10-trip packs, and monthly passes at a discount online. For a complete list of ticket outlets, contact the railway.

Taxis

Licensed taxicabs will have an orange driver permit, usually displayed on the visor or dashboard.

Several reliable cab companies are **Allied Cab Company** (615/244-7433 or 625/320-9083, www.nashvillecab.com), **Checker Cab** (615/256-7000), **Music City Taxi Inc.** (615/865-4100, www.musiccitytaxi.com), and **United Cab** (615/228-6969). Taxi rates are $2.10 per mile.

If cruising around in a stretch limo is more your style, call **Basic Black Limo** (615/430-8157, www.basicblacklimo.net). The rate is $125 per hour on Saturday nights; the limo seats up to 14 passengers.

MIDDLE TENNESSEE

Perhaps no region of Tennessee is as diverse geographically and demographically—as Middle Tennessee, which in many ways is the state's heartland. From Clarksville on the Cumberland River to Cowan at the foot of the Cumberland Plateau, Middle Tennessee satisfies visitors with its surprising collection of campuses, kitsch, and countryside.

Much of the this region is familiar. Its scenes are winding country roads cutting through horse pasture; perfectly fried chicken; and charming old railroad towns where the trains still run.

But there are other attractions that just might surprise you: Amish buggies traveling the back roads, a celebration dedicated to the lowly mule, and some of the best shopping in all of the Volunteer State. Middle Tennessee is a landscape of quiet beauty and some outstanding stories that will captivate its visitors.

There's the tale of Sam Davis, boy hero of the Confederacy, who went to his grave without divulging the name of his Union informant. There's the story of the sanctuary for retired circus and zoo elephants, tucked in the lush Tennessee countryside near Hohenwald. And there's the legend of the Natchez Trace, the old Indian road that cuts from Nashville through the countryside bound for the Mississippi port town of Natchez.

In the end, there are dozens of good reasons to travel through Middle Tennessee. But the best one is a wish to slow things down a bit and enjoy

© SUSANNA HENIGHAN POTTER

HIGHLIGHTS

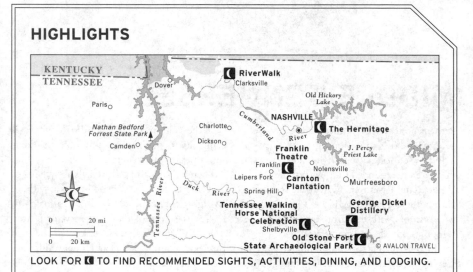

LOOK FOR ◖ TO FIND RECOMMENDED SIGHTS, ACTIVITIES, DINING, AND LODGING.

◖ **RiverWalk:** There's no better way to see Clarksville's gems than to stroll around this 15-acre park along the banks of the Cumberland (page 201).

◖ **The Hermitage:** The home of America's seventh president is also one of Tennessee's finest historic homes and gardens, preserving not only the story of Andrew Jackson, but also that of his family, paid staff, and slaves (page 207).

◖ **Franklin Theatre:** This 1937 movie theater underwent an extensive restoration that brought it back to its original glory (page 218).

◖ **Carnton Plantation:** Let your imagination run free at this mansion, which served as a Confederate field hospital during the Battle of Franklin. It is the fictional setting of the novel *The Widow of the South* (page 219).

◖ **Tennessee Walking Horse National Celebration:** Watch the world's greatest show horses compete in the heart of horse country (page 244).

◖ **George Dickel Distillery:** Tennessee whiskey is world famous, but you can beat the crowds at this lesser-known distillery in beautiful Cascade Hollow (page 260).

◖ **Old Stone Fort State Archaeological Park:** The ancient earthen structure has confounded scientists for decades. Come here to ponder the lives of the earliest Tennesseans (page 262).

the simple pleasure of natural beauty, notable history, and the company of friendly people.

PLANNING YOUR TIME

The rural byways of Middle Tennessee are best explored at a slow pace. The beauty of the region is best enjoyed on small back roads, where the friendliness of its people can be appreciated over a leisurely conversation.

Explore Middle Tennessee gradually if you can. The region can be dipped into over a series of weekend drives or weeklong expeditions. If you have only a few days, choose one of the subregions to explore. If shopping and dining are your preferences, Franklin is a natural choice. For a quaint small-town feel, go to Bell Buckle and Wartrace, crown jewels in Tennessee Walking Horse Country. For

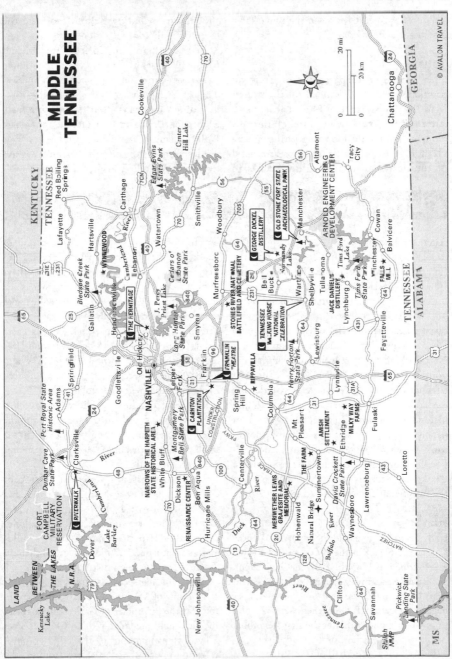

a natural escape, drive down the remarkable Natchez Trace Parkway.

Tours

The Tennessee Department of Tourism promotes several self-guided tours through Middle Tennessee. The **Tennessee Antebellum Trail** (www.antebellumtrail. com) is a 90-mile loop beginning at the Hermitage in Nashville. It stops at several of the best-known antebellum homes in the region, including Belle Meade and the Carnton Plantation.

Bedford, Franklin, Coffee, Lincoln, and Moore Counties have joined forces to promote back-roads tourism in south-central Tennessee. They publish guides to several themed "trails," including a **Tennessee Spirits and Wine Trail,** a **You Pick 'Em Farm Trail,** and the **Tennessee Walking Horse Trail.** You can request free guides from Tennessee's Trails and Byways (www.tntrailsandbyways.com).

Clarksville

Alternately known as the town of spires (for its beautiful historic church spires) and the Queen City (for the Cumberland River that flows by), Clarksville is an old city with a new lease on life. By some accounts the oldest incorporated city in Tennessee (in 1785), Clarksville owed its early prosperity to the Cumberland River and the tobacco industry. Today, the Fort Campbell military base is the city's biggest economic engine, and Clarksville is Tennessee's fifth-largest city. In recent years, Clarksville has done a lot to preserve its waterfront and historic downtown. Its centerpiece waterfront park is a major draw, and so is its historic downtown, which was largely rebuilt after a destructive 1999 tornado. Many riverside properties in Clarksville were also severely damaged when the Cumberland River flooded in May 2010.

History

Early attempts to settle the area that is now Clarksville began in the 1760s, and the town was founded in 1785. In 1806 the first school, the Rural Academy, was established, and two years later the *Clarksville Chronicle* newspaper began publication. By 1819 there were 22 stores in town, and one year later the first steamboat began to navigate the Cumberland River.

During the second half of the 19th century,

no crop or industry was more important to Clarksville than tobacco. In 1855, a special variety of tobacco grown in the fields and valleys of north-central Tennessee was known as the strongest in the world. This "Clarksville dark" tobacco was used primarily to make cigar wrappers and snuff—not cigarettes. During these years, Clarksville grew to be the second-largest tobacco market in the United States, and in 1880 sales moved to a brand-new Tobacco Exchange built near the public square.

The tobacco industry declined by the 1930s, due to changing agricultural practices and the Great Depression, although you can still see small tobacco farms in the valleys and pastures around Clarksville.

The most disruptive event of recent Clarksville history was an F3 tornado that struck downtown at 4:15 A.M. on January 22, 1999. The twister left a 4.3-mile-long, 880-yard-wide path. It destroyed 124 buildings and damaged 562 more, many of them in the historic downtown district.

Clarksville has seen its share of celebrities. It is the home of Miss USA 2007, Rachel Smith, and was the birthplace of U.S. Olympic track-and-field gold medalist Wilma Rudolph. Poet Allen Tate, a member of the Fugitive poets at Vanderbilt in the 1920s, was from nearby

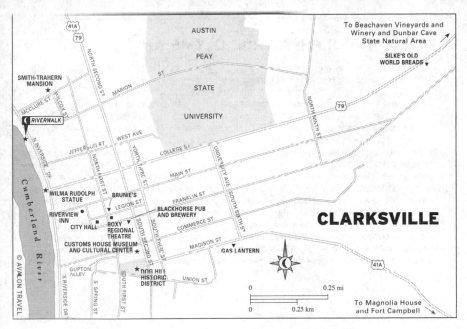

Benfolly, and Robert Penn Warren attended Clarksville High School. Jimi Hendrix lived in Clarksville while he was stationed with the 101st Airborne Division at Fort Campbell in 1962.

SIGHTS

◖ RiverWalk

Opened in 1987, RiverWalk (602 N. Riverside Dr., 931/645-7476, daily 7 A.M.–midnight, free) is Clarksville's crown jewel. The 15-acre park stretches along the Cumberland River, and paved walkways make it easy to enjoy a stroll along the banks of the river. There are also playgrounds, a boat ramp, picnic tables, and an amphitheater where the city hosts events like summer's RiverFest and Christmas on the Cumberland. The Rotary Clubs of Clarksville have also built an avenue of flags designed to reflect the diversity of the city.

If you want to learn more about the river, visit the **Cumberland River Center** (931/645-7476) near the center of the park, where a permanent exhibit chronicles the history of the river and of Clarksville. Among other things, the exhibit describes the river's significance in the Civil War and also its role in the city's lucrative tobacco industry. The center is located near the main parking lot for RiverWalk and is open daily.

At the southern end of RiverWalk you will find a bronze statue of Clarksville native and U.S. Olympic gold medalist **Wilma Rudolph.** The statue sits at the base of the pedestrian overpass at College Street and Riverside Drive.

Historic Clarksville

Pick up a copy of "Walk Clarksville" from the visitors center, RiverWalk, or at the Customs House (or download it from www.clarksvillepartnership.com). This 2.2-mile walking tour allows you to slow down and appreciate the city's fine architecture and its interesting history. The tour begins at the Customs House Museum on South 2nd Street and includes the downtown historic district, the public square,

WILMA RUDOLPH: A TRUE OLYMPIAN

Wilma Glodean Rudolph was born on June 20, 1940, the 20th of 22 children born to her parents, Ed and Blanche Rudolph, in Clarksville. Wilma was diagnosed with polio as a young child and as a result used leg braces to walk. Blanche Rudolph took her daughter to Meharry Medical College in Nashville, a hospital for African Americans, as frequently as she could. When they could not travel, Blanche treated her daughter with homemade remedies, and she spent many evenings massaging her daughter's stricken legs.

When Wilma was 12 she overcame her polio and quickly became a standout athlete. She was a high school basketball star and earned a spot on the U.S. Olympic track-and-field team when she was just 16 years old. At the 1956 Summer Olympics Wilma brought home a bronze medal in the 4 by 100 meter relay.

Four years later, Wilma Rudolph made Olympic history when she became the first American woman to win three gold medals in a single Olympic games. Her medals came in the 100 meters, 200 meters, and the 4 by 100 meter relay. Rudolph was heralded as the "fastest woman in history."

Wilma returned home to Tennessee and retired from athletics in 1962. A year later she enrolled at Tennessee State University, where she earned a degree in education. She later married and had four children. Rudolph wrote her autobiography, *Wilma: The Story of Wilma Rudolph,* in 1977. She died at her home in Brentwood in 1994 of brain and throat cancer; she was just 54 years old.

A bronze statue depicting the young Wilma Rudolph stands on the waterfront in her hometown of Clarksville.

---

the Smith-Trahern Mansion, and Austin Peay State University. Along Franklin Street you will see a large outdoor mural, *Bursting with Pride,* that depicts several of the city's most historic buildings. The walking tour includes a number of historic downtown churches, including Mount Olive Baptist Church, where Wilma Rudolph worshipped as a child, and the First Presbyterian Church, founded in 1822. Don't skip the walk through the Dog Hill Historic District, a clutch of 1890s wood-frame cottages, named Dog Hill because neighborhood dogs would howl at the whistles of passing trains and steamboats. Plan on 2–2.5 hours for the walking tour.

Customs House Museum and Cultural Center

Clarksville's old post office houses its largest museum, which has a wide-ranging collection including regional art and historical artifacts. The Customs House Museum and Cultural Center (200 S. 2nd St., 931/648-5780, www.customshousemuseum.org, Tues.–Sat. 10 A.M.–5 P.M.,

Sun. 1–5 P.M., adults $7, seniors $5, students $3–5) gets points for variety, if nothing else. Its permanent exhibits include Dunwody Boehm porcelains and a "memory lane" exhibit with clothes, forms of transportation, and firearms from the 18th and 19th centuries. The "explorers' floor" has exhibits and activities for children, including bubbles, a grocery store, and optical illusions. A wonderfully intricate model train set is on display, and volunteer engineers run trains on Sunday afternoons.

There is also a small exhibit about the remarkable building itself, which was built in 1898 as a post office and customs house for the collection of tobacco taxes. The unique architecture consists of Italianate ornamentation, a Far East–inspired slate roof, Romanesque arches, and Gothic copper eagles perched at four corners. In addition to the permanent exhibit, the Customs House hosts traveling exhibits year-round.

The Customs House Museum has free admission on the second Saturday of the month.

Smith-Trahern Mansion

Built around 1858 by tobacconist Christopher Smith, this Greek Revival–Italianate mansion sits high above the bank of the Cumberland River. The Smith-Trahern Mansion (311 N. Spring St., 931/648-9998, Mon.–Fri. 9:30 A.M.–2:30 P.M., evenings and weekends by appointment, $2) contains a unique curved staircase and a widow's walk looking out at the Cumberland River. It is now the setting for an education outreach program provided by the University of Tennessee's extension office. Tours are also available to visitors, and the home is used frequently for weddings and other private functions.

Dunbar Cave

The Dunbar Cave has been a site of importance to successive waves of people living around present-day Clarksville. Prehistoric Native Americans took shelter inside the cave as early as 10,000 years ago. Mississippian Indians also used the cave, leaving as evidence cave art on the cavern's walls.

In the 1930s it became a mineral bath resort, and people traveled for miles to take the baths and enjoy big-band and swing music played on the stage at the mouth of the cave. Artie Shaw and Benny Goodman were among the artists who performed at Dunbar Cave, and there are still jazz concerts here in the summer. In 1948, country music star Roy Acuff bought the property and broadcast a live country music show from the location.

Dunbar Cave was purchased by the state in 1973. It is located just four miles from downtown Clarksville, making it a popular retreat for the city's residents. There are three miles of hiking trails, including one-mile and two-mile loops and a short 0.7-mile paved walk to the mouth of the cave. Guided hikes inside the cave were offered on weekends year-round and on certain weekdays in summer, but, as is the case with many publicly owned caves all across the eastern United States, Dunbar Cave's underground tours are closed indefinitely in an effort to curb White Nose Syndrome in bats. This fungus (which looks white on their noses, hence the name) causes low body fat and death. It is transmitted from one bat to another, and by closing caves, the hope is that it will not spread from one cave to another. However, you can still enjoy the aboveground hikes and visit the **nature museum** (401 Old Dunbar Cave Rd., 931/648-5526, daily 8 A.M.–4:30 P.M., staff permitting) at the park office.

There are plans for an interpretive center to be added to the park, which would describe how the cave was used by Native Americans, early European settlers, and the early 20th-century vacationers who came to Dunbar to get well.

Beachaven Vineyards and Winery

You can take a free vineyard tour and sample local wines at Beachaven Vineyards and Winery (1100 Dunlop Ln., 931/645-8867, www.beachavenwinery.com, Mon.–Sat. 9 A.M.–5 P.M., Sun. noon–5 P.M.).

ENTERTAINMENT AND EVENTS
Theater

You can see professional company shows and black-box theater at the **Roxy Regional Theatre** (100 Franklin St., 931/645-7699, www.roxyregionaltheatre.org) in downtown Clarksville. First opened as a movie house in 1912, the Roxy (then called the Lillian Theater) was a first-run movie house until 1980. In 1983 it reopened as a regional theater. The Roxy puts on 10 shows per year, including musicals and classic American and European drama. The Other Space is a black-box theater also located at the Roxy that puts on innovative and cutting-edge productions.

Festivals and Events

Clarksville's biggest party is **Riverfest** (www.clarksvilleriverfest.com, free), a September extravaganza held at the Cumberland RiverWalk. It includes live music, food vendors, children's activities, and fireworks.

Other annual events include **Oktoberfest** (931/647-0243, www.edelweissclarksville. org), held at the Fairgrounds Park in October, and **Jazz on the Lawn** (1100 Dunlop Ln., 931/645-8867, www.beachavenwinery.com), monthly free concerts held during the summer at Beachaven Vineyards and Winery.

SPORTS AND RECREATION

There are three golf courses around Clarksville: **Mason Rudolph Golf Course** (1514 Golf Club Ln., 931/645-7479), which offers inexpensive rates for 9- and 18-hole play; **Swan Lake** (581 Dunbar Cave Rd., 931/648-0479), right next to Dunbar Lake State Natural Area; and **Eastland Green** (550 Clubhouse Ln., 931/358-9051).

There are eight outdoor lighted tennis courts at **Swan Lake Tennis Complex** (2002 Sanders Rd.), which you can use for $4 per hour during warm-weather months. Call the city's parks department at 931/647-6511 for details.

ACCOMMODATIONS

The best hotel in Clarksville has the best location. The **Riverview Inn** (50 College St., 931/552-3331, www.theriverviewinn.com, $98–106) is located just steps from the Cumberland River and Clarksville's historic downtown. Probably even more in its favor, it is located miles from the noisy, congested, and unappealing strip of highway that is home to a seemingly endless array of chain hotel choices. The Riverview offers suites, king-size rooms with a desk and couch, and traditional double rooms. All guests can enjoy breakfast, a fitness room, business center, free wireless Internet, free daily newspaper, and laundry. You can even get your hair done at the on-site salon. And while the exterior of the hotel is about as charming as a concrete box, the inside is cheery and the staff pleasant. A real winner for road warriors.

If you prefer more homey accommodations, call Russ and Almeida Welker at **Magnolia House** (1231 Madison St., 931/552-4545, www. magnoliabb.com, $119–129), a well-run and welcoming bed-and-breakfast in Clarksville's historic district. Margaret has two guest suites, each with a private bathroom, desk, wireless Internet access, fine linens, and a refrigerator. One of the rooms also has a kitchenette and can sleep up to three people.

FOOD

Every town deserves a restaurant like **Silke's Old World Breads** (1214A College St., 931/552-4422, www.silkesoldworldbreads.com, Mon.–Sat. 7:30 A.M.–6 P.M., $6–9). Silke's is a bakery that makes European pastries and breads in a stone hearth oven. There is sourdough, whole wheat, rye, and lots more. On the sweet side, they offer traditional coffee-shop favorites like cheesecake and tiramisu, plus European-style fruit cobblers, turnovers, and genuine pretzels. If you're dining in, you can get sandwiches, salads, or pizzas. The salmon burger is a delicious alternative to another beef burger, and the pizzas are crisp and chewy. Or try one of the German sausage sandwiches, which feature long skinny sausages served on a little round bun. The menu offers a variety of choices for vegetarians and decidedly different breakfast specialties: Try the cheese plate of fresh-baked bread, sliced cheese, herb/cheese spread, and fruit. And don't forget your coffee; you can choose from varieties that include Silke's Old World Blend, designed to taste German! To ease the conscience while you eat, know that Silke goes out of her way to use organic and local ingredients and that she donates leftovers to charity. Silke's is located just north of town inside an old tobacco warehouse.

Keeping with the German theme, Clarksville is home to an old-school German restaurant, **Brunie's** (101 Legion St., 931/645-8414, Mon. 11 A.M.–2 P.M., Tues.–Wed. 11 A.M.–8 P.M.,

Thurs.–Sat. 11 A.M.–midnight, $6–16), a block off the public square. Brunie's is dark and smoky, with a pool table in the back and live music on the weekends. There are at least eight beers on tap. The menu features such German favorites as schnitzel, bratwurst, and sauerkraut, plus American standbys like burgers and steak. Most of the German dishes are available for dinner only, but there is usually one German lunch special, served with a hot toasted roll, potato salad, and cucumber salad. There are few vegetarian-friendly options here.

Clarksville's favorite brewpub, the **Blackhorse Pub and Brewery** (132 Franklin St., 931/552-3726, www.theblackhorsepub.net, daily 11 A.M.–midnight, $7–19) has good beer, of course. But locals swear by the pizza, steak sandwiches, and other pub fare. The restaurant is nestled in the historic downtown area.

INFORMATION AND SERVICES

Clarksville and Montgomery County operate a tourist information center near exit 4 off I-24 north of Clarksville. The center is open daily 8 A.M.–5 P.M. during the summer and 8 A.M.–4 P.M. in winter. Call them at 931/553-8467. You can also pick up brochures and maps of Clarksville at the Customs House Museum and at RiverWalk.

The **Clarksville-Montgomery County Public Library** (Montgomery County Veterans Plaza, 350 Pageant Ln., 931/648-8826) has free public Internet access.

Clarksville's **Leaf-Chronicle,** one of the oldest newspapers in Tennessee, is published daily. Its name reflects the prominence of tobacco during Clarksville's earlier years.

AROUND CLARKSVILLE
Port Royal State Historic Area

One of the earliest settlements in West Tennessee was at Port Royal (3300 Old Clarksville Hwy., Adams, 931/358-9696, www.tn.gov/environment/parks/PortRoyal, daily

8 A.M.–sunset), along the Red River, about 15 miles west of Clarksville. The town was settled in 1782 and incorporated in 1797. Set along an old Native American trail that later became a major stagecoach route, Port Royal was a way-point for travelers of all kinds.

In the 1830s, hundreds of Cherokee Indians who were forcibly removed from their lands in Tennessee, North Carolina, and Georgia traveled through Port Royal on their way to Oklahoma. Diaries of soldiers who traveled with the displaced Cherokee say that some groups remained camped at Port Royal for a day or two to grind corn and rest before they left Tennessee.

Port Royal became a state historic area in 1977 and was later designated one of five sites in Tennessee along the National Trail of Tears Historic Trail.

Sadly, visitors to the park will see little evidence of Port Royal's interesting past, except what they can conjure up in their imaginations while strolling along the bank of the Red River. There are a few picnic tables and a parking area. The park closes at sundown.

Adams

A picturesque rural town, Adams is located about 30 miles west of Clarksville along the Red River. The town isn't famous for much, but it is known as the home of the Bell Witch, a spooky specter that captivated the imaginations of Tennesseans in this neck of the woods around the turn of the 19th century. According to lore, the witch haunted the Bell family after they moved to Adams from North Carolina. The Bell Witch was never visible, but it threw objects, spoke, pulled hair, yelled, and generally behaved very badly. Hearing stories of the witch, Andrew Jackson and some friends came up from Nashville to combat the terror, only to give up after suffering a night of the witch's inhospitable treatment.

You can revel in tales of the Bell Witch at the **Bell Witch Cave** (430 Keysburg Rd., 615/696-3055, www.bellwitchcave.com, June–Aug.

Wed.–Mon. 10 A.M.–5 P.M., weekends only May, Sept., and Oct., $12, with a minimum of $24 per tour). Here you can tour a cave that was on the Bell property, as well as tour a replica of the Bell log home. The cave is closed November–April.

Historic Collinsville

Proprietors JoAnn and Glen Weakley have re-created the old settlement of Collinsville about 15 miles south of Clarksville in lovely rural countryside. Historic Collinsville (4711 Weakley Rd., 931/648-9141, www.historiccollinsville.com, May 15–Nov. 15 Thurs.–Sun. 1–5 P.M., $5, children under five free) includes a restored schoolhouse, log cabin, dogtrot house, and other buildings that would have been seen in the period 1830–1870. There is also a "wildlife center" with a number of stuffed wild animals, including wildcats, owls, and deer.

Fort Campbell

In February 1942, during World War II, construction began on Camp Campbell, which came to be a training ground for the 12th, 14th, and 20th Armored Divisions, and headquarters of the IV Armored Corps and the 26th Infantry Division. In 1950, the camp was redesignated Fort Campbell and became a permanent base.

Over the years, Fort Campbell soldiers have been deployed to many parts of the world and in every war since World War II. The fort is home to more than 30,000 soldiers and 10,500 military family members; 4,300 civilian employees work there. An additional 46,000 military family members live off the base in the Clarksville area. The presence of the military base has a major economic and social impact on Clarksville and the surrounding area. For example, the median age of Clarksville is 32 to the statewide average of 36.

Visit the **Don F. Pratt Memorial Museum** (Bldg. 5702, Tennessee Ave., 270/798-3215, Mon.–Sat. 9:30 A.M.–4:30 P.M., free), which traces the history of the Screaming Eagles from World War II to Operation Iraqi Freedom. The museum also includes the history of Fort Campbell, from its initial survey as Camp Campbell in 1941 to the present day. The museum displays more than 50 uniformed figures and nine historical aircrafts, plus military vehicles and artillery pieces.

Along the Cumberland

Northeast of Nashville, the Cumberland River winds emphatically like holiday wrapping ribbon. It is a calm river, though, and in places impoundment has created "lakes": Old Hickory Lake close to Nashville, Cordell Hull Lake in Jackson County, and Dale Hollow Lake along the Kentucky border.

The Nashville suburbs absorb a little more of this quiet countryside every year. Towns like Hendersonville and Gallatin are within the city commuters' range. Out in the countryside, historic homes and the charm of an almost-forgotten resort town are the main attractions.

This part of Tennessee was hit by powerful tornadoes in February 2008. Macon and Sumner Counties were the most badly affected, with more than two dozen fatalities and widespread damage.

OLD HICKORY

Old Hickory was once a village distinct from Nashville, but now this enclave east of the city is part of the city. Old Hickory is named for Andrew Jackson, whose home, the Hermitage, is located nearby. The town has an interesting history. It was founded in 1918 by DuPont as a company town for a new smokeless gunpowder plant being built nearby. Hundreds of "temporary homes" were built for workers using materials made with

NASHVILLE CONVENTION AND VISITORS BUREAU

Slavery is part of the complicated history of Andrew Jackson, which is examined at The Hermitage.

asbestos. The "permanent village" consisted of more substantial buildings for managers.

The gunpowder plant was short-lived. By 1919 it had closed, and workers moved away. In 1923, however, DuPont returned and retooled the factory into one that would make rayon. The asbestos-riddled houses were torn down, but the permanent village, called Rayon City, was restored and once again became homes for people employed at the factory. In 1946 DuPont sold the village, and Rayon City ceased operating as a company town. Many of the old-style company homes are still standing, however. There are a few small restaurants and bars, including biker bar **Dilligaf's** (333 Swinging Bridge Rd.).

◀ The Hermitage

Andrew Jackson's plantation and home, 16 miles east of Nashville, is the area's best historical tourist attraction. The Hermitage (4580 Rachel's Ln., 615/889-2941, www.thehermitage.com, daily 9 A.M.–5 P.M., adults $19, seniors $16, students 13–18 $14, children 9–12 $9, active military and children 5 and under free) is where Jackson retired following his two terms as president of the United States, and it is where he and his beloved wife, Rachel, are buried. The two have perhaps the most bittersweet love story in American history.

Jackson bought the property in 1809; he and Rachel initially lived in a rustic log cabin, which has since been restored. Jackson first named the home and property Rural Retreat, and later he chose the more poetic name the Hermitage. Jackson ran a successful cotton plantation on the property, owning as many as 150 slaves. In 1819 he and Rachel started construction of what is now the mansion. They moved in in 1821.

In 1831, two years after he became the nation's seventh president, Jackson expanded the mansion so it was more suitable for presidential entertaining. While Jackson was in Washington, his adopted son, Andrew Jackson Jr., managed the property, and when a chimney fire damaged the house in 1834, Jackson Jr. and his wife, Sarah, saw to its restoration. At the end of Jackson's second term in office in 1837, he retired to the Hermitage and lived here happily until his death in 1845.

Following President Jackson's death, the Hermitage remained in family hands until 1853, when it was sold to the State of Tennessee to pay off the family's debts. It opened as a museum in 1889 and was restored largely due to the persistence of the Ladies Hermitage Association. Because the property never left family hands before it was sold to the state, many of the furnishings are original, and even the wallpaper in several rooms dates back to the years when Andrew Jackson called it home.

One major strength of the present-day

MIDDLE TENNESSEE

Hermitage tour and museum is that it focuses not only on Jackson and the construction and decoration of the mansion, but also the African American slaves who worked at the Hermitage plantation, and makes no effort to gloss over some of Jackson's less-favorable legacies. Curators and archaeologists have studied the Hermitage to learn about the hundreds of men and women who made the Hermitage profitable and successful for so many years. The tour of the grounds takes visitors to Alfred's Cabin, a slave cabin occupied until 1901 by former Hermitage slave Alfred Jackson. You also learn about the agriculture that took place on the Hermitage and can see cotton being cultivated during the summer months. To learn even more about the Hermitage's slaves, take an add-on wagon tour, offered April–October ($10).

Visitors to the Hermitage begin with a video about Andrew Jackson and the Hermitage, and can continue on to a museum. Even if you are not typically an audio-tour-type person, consider the one of the grounds, which includes a kids' version narrated by Jackson's pet parrot. Guided tours are offered of the mansion. You wind up in the gift shop and café. Plan on spending at least three hours here to make the most of your visit. Try to come when the weather is good.

Old Hickory Lake

The Old Hickory Dam was built in 1952 and became operational in 1957. At normal water levels, the lake is 22,500 acres.

Old Hickory is well within Nashville's sprawl zone, and private development along the lakeshore is extensive. The Army Corps of Engineers manages the lake, including its public recreation areas.

There are nearly a dozen different day-use facilities along Old Hickory Lake. The following have covered picnic facilities, swimming beaches, and restrooms: Rockland and Lock 3 in Hendersonville, Cedar Creek in Mount Juliet, Old Hickory Beach in Old Hickory, and

Laguardo in Laguardo. Old Hickory is popular with kayakers, stand-up paddlers, boaters, and other water lovers.

Located on the shore of Old Hickory Lake, **Bledsoe Creek State Park** (400 Zieglers Fort Rd., Gallatin, 615/452-3706, www.tn.gov/environment/parks/BledsoeCreek) has six miles of hiking trails, a 26-site campground, boat ramp, and day-use facilities. Bledsoe Creek is located just east of the city of Gallatin.

HENDERSONVILLE

A speck of a town that has become an upscale suburb of Nashville, Hendersonville has a few things going for it: It is home to some of country music's most famous names, it is near Old Hickory Lake, and it is the locale of Trinity Music City U.S.A., a major religious broadcasting attraction.

Trinity Music City U.S.A. (1 Music Village Blvd., 615/822-0093, www.tbn.org, Tues.–Sat. 11 A.M. and 3 P.M., Sun. 3 P.M., free) owes its existence to Conway Twitty, a rock and country musician who opened his house in Hendersonville to fans and called it Twitty City. After Twitty died in 1993, the property sold to Trinity Broadcasting Network (TBN), which retooled the idea and came out with its own "City" destination.

Nationally televised programs are produced at the Hendersonville TBN campus, and visitors can sit in on weekly church services on Friday nights and Sunday afternoons, or a live taping on Tuesday 7–9 P.M. Special religious films are screened throughout the day, and there are exhibits about TBN and Trinity City. Special events are held year-round, and visitors are welcome at other times to tour the grounds and browse the gift shop.

Another star long associated with Hendersonville is Johnny Cash, and his second wife, June Carter Cash. The couple's home on Old Hickory Lake in Hendersonville was where they lived for 35 years. The Cashes died in 2003, and in 2006, former Bee Gee Barry

OLD HICKORY

Andrew Jackson, the seventh president of the United States, was one of the most important American political figures of the first half of the 19th century. His impact was so great that we now refer to his era as the Age of Jackson and his ideology as Jacksonian Democracy.

Jackson was born in 1767 on the American frontier in South Carolina. His father, an immigrant from Northern Ireland, died before Jackson was born. Jackson's two brothers, Hugh and Robert, died during the Revolutionary War. His mother, Elizabeth, died of smallpox in 1781. Jackson was 14 years old and alone in the world.

Remarkably, Jackson not only survived; he flourished. In 1784 he moved to Salisbury, North Carolina, where he studied law. In 1787 he became a licensed lawyer and moved west to Tennessee. In 1790 he was appointed the district attorney for the Mero District, now Middle Tennessee.

In Nashville, Jackson met Rachel Donelson, the daughter of John Donelson, one of the founding fathers of Nashville. Jackson fell in love with Rachel, and in 1791 they were married. The Jacksons set about to establish a home and livelihood. Jackson practiced law, speculated in land, and dabbled in politics. They bought farmland in Davidson County, where they built the Hermitage, which would be the Jacksons' home for the rest of their lives. The couple adopted a nephew, who was known as Andrew Jackson Jr., and reared several Indian orphans.

By 1798 Jackson was a circuit-riding judge on the Tennessee Superior Court, but he also developed a reputation for resolving his own conflicts through violence. He brawled with a set of brothers, killed a man in a duel, caned another, and ran a sword through a third. In 1803 he quarreled publicly with governor John Sevier and nearly dueled him as well.

In 1802 Jackson was elected major general of the Tennessee militia, and with the outbreak of war in 1812, his leadership was required. Jackson earned the nickname "Old Hickory" in 1812 when he disobeyed orders and refused to dismiss his Tennessee soldiers in Natchez, Mississippi, marching them back to Tennessee under great hardship instead. He earned na-

tional fame three years later when he marched his men from Florida to New Orleans, where he resoundingly defeated the British. The American public was so pleased with their new war hero that they did not mind when they learned the British had actually surrendered two weeks earlier. Neither did they mind some of his tactics: military executions, imposition of martial law, suspension of habeas corpus, and defiance of a federal court order.

In the succeeding years, Jackson fought battles with Native American tribes and negotiated land treaties with them. By 1821, he quit his post as major general and came home to the Hermitage for a short retirement.

In 1822 the Tennessee state legislature nominated Jackson for U.S. president, and his nomination was seconded by other states. In the 1824 contest, Jackson received more votes than any other contender in the crowded field. But when the U.S. House of Representatives gave the presidency to John Quincy Adams, Jackson called the decision a "corrupt bargain" that violated the will of the voters. His 1828 presidential campaign had begun.

The 1828 campaign was spirited and dirty, and later historians would point to this as a turning point in American elections. Opponents found seemingly countless stories of Jackson's indiscretions.

During his two terms as president, Jackson enraged his opponents and delighted supporters. He took unprecedented actions in the name of reform, including several controversial banking decisions. He believed in a strong federal government and stood in the way of state nullification of federal laws. By the end of his eight years in the White House, Jackson was known by his opponents as "King Andrew," while his supporters still saw him as a spokesman of the common man.

Jackson, who never remarried, spent the remaining years of his life at the Hermitage, where he entertained guests, helped to manage the farm, and dispensed advice to politicians. His health declined, though, and in 1845, at age 78, he died and was buried in the Hermitage garden next to his beloved Rachel.

Gibb bought the property for $2.3 million. The home was destroyed by fire in 2007. A small cabin used by June and Johnny, and later restored by their son, John Carter Cash, survived, but it is not open to the public. A new Johnny Cash museum, with some of their artifacts, is in the works for Nashville.

CASTALIAN SPRINGS

This small town a few miles east of Gallatin was one of the towns devastated by tornadoes in 2008. Twisters destroyed whole houses and tossed mobile homes around like they were toys. The town made headlines when rescuers found alive an 11-month-old boy who had been tossed some 150 yards.

Previously, what put Castalian Springs on the map were its mineral springs and two nearby historic homes. The Castalian Springs Archaeological Project is researching the extent of a prehistoric Native American town on this location dating to A.D. 1000–1400.

Wynneworld State Historic Area

The largest existing log structure in Tennessee, this imposing home was built in 1828 by A. R. Wynne, William Cage, and Stephen Roberts as a stagecoach inn on the Nashville–Knoxville Road. Six years after it was built, Wynne purchased his partners' shares and moved his family to the inn, where he lived until his death in 1893. Over the years, the inn saw many guests who came to drink and soak in the mineral springs. In the 1940s the present name, Wynneworld, was given to the property, and in 1971 the Tennessee Historical Commission acquired the building as a historic site.

Wynneworld (210 Old Hwy. 25, 615/452-5463) has been closed to the public since the 2008 tornado, pending the completion of a $6 million renovation effort.

Cragfont

Gen. James Winchester was one of those men who seems to have been just about everywhere.

He fought in the American Revolution and the War of 1812, was a Middle Tennessee pioneer, and was one of the founders of Memphis. Winchester's home, Historic Cragfont Mansion (200 Cragfont Rd., 615/542-7070, www.cragfont.org, Apr. 15–Nov. 1 Tues.–Sat. 10 A.M.–5 P.M., Sun. 1–5 P.M., and by appointment, adults $5, seniors $4, children 6–12 $3) is now a Tennessee Historic Site.

Construction on Cragfont started in 1798 and finished four years later. It was the finest mansion of the Tennessee frontier—appropriate for a man of Winchester's stature. Cragfont was so named because it stood on a rocky bluff with a spring at its base. The home was built in the late Georgian style. Today it is furnished with Federal-period antiques.

Following his involvement in the War of 1812, Winchester moved to Cragfont full-time, where he farmed and speculated in land. Winchester died in 1826, but his wife, Susan Black Winchester, lived here until 1862. The property was purchased by the Tennessee Historical Commission in 1958.

CARTHAGE

Carthage, the seat of Smith County, is a river town. The first steamship traveled here from Nashville in 1829, and the trade persisted even into the 20th century, when the first good paved roads were constructed through the rugged countryside.

Landmarks in this quiet town include the **Cordell Hull Bridge,** built in 1936 and noteworthy for its intricate steel grid work, and the **Smith County Courthouse,** a Second Empire–style structure built in 1875. About five miles outside of town is the **Cordell Hull Lock and Dam.**

The **Smith County Heritage Museum** (3rd Ave. N., 615/735-1104, Wed., Fri.–Sat. 10 A.M.–2 P.M., free) houses historical exhibits, including Civil War, steamboat, and farm memorabilia.

Carthage is best known in some circles as the hometown of former U.S. vice president

Al Gore. **Markham's Department Store** (222 Main St. N., 615/735-0184) has a special "Gore-Lieberman Store" where campaign memorabilia from the historic 2000 presidential election is on sale. You can even buy a coffee cup that celebrates a Gore victory in 2000. The Gore family farm is located a few miles outside Carthage along U.S. 70. It's closed to the public.

CORDELL HULL LAKE

The 72 miles of the Cumberland River impounded by the Cordell Hull Dam are popular areas for recreation. Operated by the U.S. Army Corps of Engineers, Cordell Hull Lake's recreation areas consist of two large campgrounds and numerous day-use areas with swimming beaches, picnic facilities, and boat ramps.

Cordell Hull Lock and Dam

The lock and dam that impounds the river was built between 1963 to 1973. You can see the dam from the Tater Knob overlook, located about four miles outside of Carthage off State Route 263. It is an impressive vista.

You can learn more about the science of hydroelectric power and the natural history of the Cumberland River at the **Cordell Hull Lake Visitor Center** (71 Corps Ln., 615/735-1034, www.lrn.usace.army.mil/op/COR/rec, Mon.–Fri. 9 A.M.–3 P.M. in warm-weather months, free), located adjacent to the dam off State Route 263 east of Carthage.

The half-mile **Turkey Creek Nature Trail** departs from the visitors center.

There is a lovely six-mile hiking trail from the Tater Knob overlook to the Defeated Creek Campground and recreation area. The **Bearwaller Gap Trail** follows the lakeshore and is named after bear "wallers," cool depressions where black bears once came to wallow. Today, there are no black bears in these hills. There is a backcountry campsite for hikers about halfway, at the Two Prong camping area.

A campground, marina, and day-use facility,

Defeated Creek was named by early settler John Peyton after his party defeated an Indian attack where they had camped along the creek. (The nearby town, Difficult, was named by the same party after they made the difficult trek back home after the attack.)

Day-trippers will enjoy the sandy beach and marina facilities. The **Bear Wheels Mountain Bike Trail** trailhead is also located at Defeated Creek. The 155-site campground can accommodate tents and RVs; it has showers, bathhouses, a playground, and laundry.

The marina at Defeated Creek offers powerboat rentals for $175–225 per day, with a $100 deposit. Paddleboats are also available for $15 for two hours.

Cordell Hull's second campground, **Salt Lick,** is a 150-site campground. It also has a swim beach, playground, water and electric hookups, dump stations, laundry, and a shower house.

Two more day-use areas have picnic facilities and public swimming beaches. **Wartrace Creek** is located near the town of Gladdice, and **Roaring River** is located near Gainesboro.

RED BOILING SPRINGS

This onetime resort town is still welcoming visitors. Red Boiling Springs had as many as eight different hotels during its heyday from 1890 to 1930, when thousands of people traveled by train and horse-drawn wagon to "take the waters" at the town's mineral springs.

The atmosphere in the holiday town was relaxed but also a tad refined. Tourists spent their days enjoying the cool air, playing croquet on the lawn, taking walks, and soaking in mineral baths. There was live music and good conversation, and mealtimes were a celebration.

Times have changed in Red Boiling Springs, but not as much as in some Tennessee towns. The Salt Lick Creek flows through the city park and is a lovely place to stroll or even wade. Three hotels keep up the town's tradition, and each offers a bona fide welcome to its guests.

If old-time atmosphere is not your thing, perhaps **Cyclemo's Motorcycle Museum** (319 E. Main St., 615/699-5049, www.cyclemos. com, Sat.–Sun. 10 A.M.–5 P.M., adults $8, seniors $6, children $4) is. Here you can see restored antique motorcycles and bike memorabilia, and buy biker clothing and other goods. There are plans in the works for a full restoration center that would specialize in fixing up old bikes. The business hopes to attract bikers who come to the area for the winding country roads so good for motorcycles. The museum has extended hours in the summertime.

About two miles west of Red Boiling Springs along Highway 52 is the turnoff for **Long Hungry Creek Farm** (Long Hungry Rd., 615/699-2493, www.barefootfarmer.com), one of Tennessee's largest and most established organic and biodynamic farms. Farmer Jeff Poppen has also written and taught extensively on the subject of farming. Visitors are welcome but ought to call in advance. The farm hosts special events and workshops during the year.

Shopping

You can order custom-made wooden chairs from **Newberry and Sons Chairs** (1593 Jennings Creek Rd., 615/699-3755, www. newberryandsonschairs.com). Located in the countryside along State Route 56 south of Red Boiling Springs, the Newberry workshop is a testament to doing things the old-fashioned way. Footstools, rocking chairs, corner chairs, and traditional ladder-back dining chairs are among the iconic styles available. Call in advance if you would like to visit the workshop.

Accommodations

The **Donoho Hotel** (500 Main St., 615/699-3141, www.thedonohohotel.com, $32–95, with meals) first opened in 1914 and was renovated in 2001. Guest rooms open onto a generous wraparound porch where rocking chairs invite you to sit a spell and relax. Rooms have an antique feel but modern amenities, including central air and heating, and new bathrooms. Guests can relax in the parlor or lobby, where there are board games and memorabilia from the hotel's early days. Or walk to the nearby Salt Lick Creek. As part of the 2001 renovations, the owners built an entertainment hall that can be used for meetings, performances, or conferences. Family-style meals are served in the 128-seat dining room and feature home-style Southern cooking.

Located on the outskirts of town atop a quiet hill, **The Thomas House** (520 E. Main St., 615/699-3006, www.thomashousehotel.com, $60) is a brick-and-lumber structure dating to the 1890s. Its guest rooms are furnished with antiques, and each is decorated with its own individual flair. There is also a swimming pool. The Thomas House stages frequent dinner theater. Meal plans are available for about $13.50 per person per meal.

Armour's Red Boiling Springs Hotel (321 E. Main St., 615/699-2180, www.armourshotel.com, $85–129) is the only hotel with a working mineral bath on the property. Guests (and nonguests) can enjoy a massage, a stint in the steam room, and a soak in the town's long-revered mineral waters. Built in 1924, Armour's has 16 rooms, including two suites. It was the first brick hotel in Red Boiling Springs, and so it was known for several years as Smith's Brick Hotel, after John Smith, the first owner. Later the hotel was called the Counts Hotel. All rooms have private baths, and each is decorated just a little bit differently. Breakfast is included in the room rate; dinner is available family-style for $14 per person, with reservations. Perhaps the greatest attraction is the wide, open porch that looks out on the hotel's lush green lawn. It is a scene that beckons you to stop and relax.

Food

Red Boiling Springs' three hotels serve

breakfast and dinner daily; reservations are recommended. You can also drive about seven miles east along Highway 52 to the **Hermitage Hill Restaurant** (16150 Hwy. 52, 615/699-3919, daily 6 A.M.–8 P.M., $5–15). This is a traditional country-cooking restaurant with full breakfast offerings, steak, burgers, grilled sandwiches, and country ham. The lunch buffet is served daily, plus a dinner buffet on Friday and Saturday nights.

Big Ed's BBQ (111 Whitley Hollow Rd., 615/699-3288, Wed.–Sat. 8 A.M.–8 P.M., $3–6) serves plates of pork and beef barbecue, as well as sandwiches, burgers, and classic sides such as coleslaw and baked beans.

Information

You can get information about Red Boiling Springs and other towns in Macon County from the **Macon County Chamber of Commerce** (208 Church St., Lafayette, 615/666-5885, www.maconcountytn.com).

West of Nashville

The countryside that lies south of Clarksville, west of Nashville, and north of Columbia is the most rural and sparsely populated in Middle Tennessee. It is ideal for back-roads driving. There are excellent state parks and a few notable pit stops, such as Montgomery Bell State Park and an old-fashioned tearoom at Bon Aqua.

The Duck River, the longest river totally contained in Tennessee, flows from the east toward Hickman and Perry Counties, eventually emptying into the Tennessee River near Johnsonville. The Buffalo River, a tributary of the Duck and the largest unimpounded river in Middle Tennessee, flows westward through Wayne and Lawrence Counties before turning northward through Perry County. Both rivers contribute natural beauty and recreational opportunities to the area.

HARPETH RIVER STATE PARK

Harpeth River State Park (615/952-2009) follows the Harpeth River as it winds through parts of Dickson County near the towns of Bell Town, Kingston Springs, and Pegram. This is a do-it-yourself state park. Bring a map (available at www.tennessee.gov) with you, since there are few signs and even fewer people to assist you should you need it.

The **Narrows of the Harpeth,** located north of Highway 70, is where the river nearly bends back onto itself. Here iron magnate Montgomery Bell built the Pattison Forge, which harnessed the power of the river to manufacture a wide range of iron implements. Slaves built the forge between 1818 and 1820, and it remains a marvel of engineering and labor. The tunnel that brought water power to the forge was 300 feet long, 15 feet wide, and 6 feet high. When the river is low, visitors can wade into the tunnel and look at it.

Recreation

Canoeing, kayaking, stand-up paddling, and fishing are popular along the river. Canoe accesses are found at the U.S. 100 bridge southwest of Nashville, the 1862 Newsom's Mill ruins, and at the McCrory Lane Bridge at Hidden Lake. Downstream, the Narrows of the Harpeth provides an upstream and downstream access, the Bell's Bend five-mile float, and a unique quarter-mile portage. Swimming is also permitted, but there are no lifeguards.

Three different trails originate at a common trailhead at the Narrows. The trails include a two-mile bluff overlook trail, a half-mile trail leading to the site of Pattison Forge, and a half-mile spur that connects the canoe launch to the canoe take-out.

MIDDLE TENNESSEE

MINNIE PEARL'S HOMETOWN

Centerville, in Hickman County, is best known as the hometown of Minnie Pearl. What's less well known is that the first lady of country comedy was not a real person, but rather a character created and portrayed by actress and comedian Sarah Ophelia Colley (1912-1996).

Colley, born in 1912 and raised in Centerville, attended Nashville's prestigious Ward-Belmont College, then a finishing school for women, where she majored in expression. In 1934, Colley joined a theater group for women that traveled throughout the South to organize local dramatic productions. It was in the course of those journeys that Colley experienced the Southern culture that she would later portray through her alter ego, Minnie Pearl. Minnie Pearl, to the extent that she was real at all, was a kind country woman from Sand Mountain, Alabama, who housed Colley when she was stuck in town with no lodging. This lady's comic stories, impeccable timing, and outlook on life left an impression on young Colley, who began performing as Minnie Pearl soon after.

Colley's big break came in 1939 when a Centerville banker invited Colley to perform at a Lions Club event. WSM radio program director Harry Stone spotted her, and the rest is history. "Minnie Pearl" performed on the Grand Ole Opry for more than 50 years. Generations of Americans have heard her greeting, "Howdee! I'm just so proud to be here," and witnessed her frilly dresses and outlandish hats (with the price tag hanging over the brim).

Offstage, Colley married Air Army Corps pilot Capt. Henry Cannon and worked for a number of charities. Colley had a foot in both of Nashville's worlds: its hillbilly opry and the Athens of the South. She was uniquely able to shuttle between these two very different universes.

Minnie Pearl's legacy is on display at the **Grinder's Switch Center** (405 W. Public Sq., Centerville, 931/729-5774). Operated by the local chamber of commerce, the center houses Minnie Pearl memorabilia and recordings of the famous lady of country comedy.

At Gossett Tract, a few miles downriver from the narrows, there are two hiking trails. A one-mile trail circles a meadow, and another one-mile trail winds along the river, providing a glimpse of Mound Bottom Archaeological Site. There are also picnic tables and grills here.

At Hidden Lake, near the town of Pegram, a one-mile trail meanders around and through a wildflower meadow. Another trail offers a half-mile hike through the forest and along majestic bluffs to a small lake with a one-mile spur trail ascending to the top of a ridge where the remains of an old marble dance floor are all that are left of a 1940s resort.

MONTGOMERY BELL STATE PARK

One of Tennessee's resort parks, Montgomery Bell State Park (615/797-9052) has a great deal to offer visitors. Named for iron magnate

Montgomery Bell, who established the iron ore industry in this part of Tennessee, the 3,842-acre park is set amid rolling hills. It was one of three parks built in Tennessee by the federal government in the 1930s. Young men in the Civilian Conservation Corps built the original structures at Montgomery Bell, including the stone dams that impound Lakes Woodhaven and Acorn. In more recent years, the park inn and golf course were built as Montgomery Bell became one of the state's resort parks.

The hardwood forest that was cut to clear farmland and to produce charcoal for the iron furnaces has given way to second-growth forest and a habitat for fox, squirrel, raccoon, opossum, deer, and a wide variety of birds and wildflowers.

The park's proximity to Nashville makes it quite popular for weekend retreats, conferences, and family getaways.

Golf

Montgomery Bell's **Frank G. Clement Golf Course** (615/797-2578) is a par 72 18-hole course. Built in 1973 and redesigned by Gary Roger Baird in 1988, the course is considered one of the top public courses in the state. The entire course is heavily wooded, and you will often see wildlife, including deer and wild turkey.

Tee times are required; greens fees are $13–26. There is a pro shop with club and cart rentals.

Other Recreation

There are some 20 miles of dirt **mountain bike trails,** ranging from easy to difficult. No motorized vehicles are allowed, and bikers must not use hiking trails (and vice versa).

There are 19 miles of **hiking trails** in the park. The longest is 12 miles, and the shortest is less than a mile. There are three overnight shelters for backpackers. You can pick up detailed maps from the park office or at the inn. A short nature trail that departs from the park office is ideal for those with less grand ambitions.

You can rent paddle- and johnboats Memorial Day–Labor Day Monday–Saturday at **Lake Acorn,** a 17-acre lake in the park. Private boats are allowed on Lake Acorn September–April, or on Lake Woodhaven year-round. Outboard attached motors are not allowed; trolling motors are permitted. There is no boating permitted on Creech Hollow Lake, the third lake at Montgomery Bell.

Fishing is allowed in all three lakes. Bluegill, catfish, bass, and creel are some of the species that you will find. A valid Tennessee fishing permit is required; you must also adhere to seasonal limits.

There is a **swimming** beach on Lake Acorn, open Memorial Day–Labor Day. No lifeguards are on duty. There is also a swimming pool for inn and cabin guests.

Other recreational facilities include horseshoe pits, softball fields, basketball courts, playgrounds, and tennis courts.

Accommodations

Montgomery Bell has a 120-room, five-suite park inn (120 Jackson Hill Rd., Burns, 615/797-3101 or 800/250-8613, rooms $68–98, suites $145–195). Rooms are equipped with two beds, telephones, television, and views of Acorn Lake. There are also conference and meeting facilities.

Camping

There are eight two-bedroom vacation cabins with kitchens, bathrooms, and modern amenities. They rent for $75 per night.

There are 40 tent sites ($11) and 75 RV campsites ($17.50) at the Montgomery Bell campground, which is set in a woodland along a creek. Like all Tennessee State Park camping facilities, they are available first come, first served. Reservations are not accepted.

One of the most distinctive features of Montgomery Bell State Park are the 47 1930s-era stone rustic cabins built by the Civilian Conservation Corps during the Depression. These cabins are available for group rental only. The beautiful buildings overlook Lake Woodhaven and are considered a historic site. Central bathroom and cooking facilities are provided.

Food

The restaurant at the **Park Inn and Conference Center** (1000 Hotel Ave., Burns, 615/797-3101, daily 7–10 a.m., 11 a.m.–2 p.m., and 5–8 p.m., $8) serves all three meals, with a seafood buffet Friday night and a steak buffet Saturday night.

DICKSON

Tennessee governor Frank Clemet was born in the old Halbrook Hotel in Dickson, the largest city, but not the county seat, of Dickson County. This old railroad town has a pleasant downtown district.

The **Renaissance Center** (855 Hwy. 46 S., 615/740-5600, www.rcenter.org, Mon.–Fri. 8 a.m.–9 p.m., Sat. 9 a.m.–9 p.m.) is a unique multimedia, technological, and arts center. Designed to encourage interest in all types of artistic expression, the center has visual art exhibits, theater, a planetarium, computer courses, and dance classes. The center is located a few miles south of downtown Dickson, heading toward the interstate.

House Blend (124 N. Main St., 615/446-3311, Mon.–Thurs. 6 A.M.–9 P.M., Fri. 6 A.M.–10 P.M., Sat. 9 A.M.–6 P.M., www.house-blendonline.com, $4–6) has above-average sandwiches, salads, and a whole array of coffee drinks and fruit smoothies. The grown-up grilled cheese is perked up with some parmesan and feta cheeses, and the Mighty Mississippi is a delicate barbecue delight. You get to choose between tortilla chips and orange minimuffins to accompany your sandwich. The chefs will gladly prepare a half-salad, half-sandwich plate; just ask.

WHITE BLUFF

This small hamlet along Highway 70 is home to one of the region's most celebrated barbecue joints. **Carl's Perfect Pig** (4991 Hwy. 70 E., 615/797-4020, Wed.–Thurs. 10:30 A.M.–6 P.M., Fri.–Sat. 10:30 A.M.–7 P.M., Sun. 10:30 A.M.–2:30 P.M., $9) lives up to its name with tender and tangy pulled-pork shoulder and ribs. Chef Carl Teitloff also serves popular lunch specials and grill foods, including fried catfish and burgers.

BON AQUA

Named for the healing waters that once drew people to this area, Bon Aqua is now little more than a huddle of homes and a small business district with some lovely hiking trails. Today, its chief attraction is the **Beacon Light Tea Room** (6343 Hwy. 100, 931/670-3880, www.beaconlighttearoom.com, Tues.–Fri. 4–9 P.M., Sat. 8 A.M.–10 P.M., Sun. 8 A.M.–9 P.M., $7–12), a glorious stop for country ham, skillet-fried chicken, and Biblical wisdom reproduced on the walls, tables, and decor of this unique country eatery. The menu encourages you to "please give your order by number," and you'll be good enough to comply. The No. 4, half a skillet of fried chicken, two vegetables, biscuits, preserves, and gravy, will have you whistling all day long. Breakfast is available on weekends.

The 35-acre **John Noel Natural Area** (www.tn.gov/environment/na/natareas/johnnoel) includes the site of the old Bon Aqua Springs Hotel and Resort. There's room for three cars to park off Old Highway 46, where you can access a pretty, easy one-mile loop hiking trail. From here you can see the remains of the old springs pool, as well as some of Middle Tennessee's picturesque landscape.

Franklin

For much of its life, Franklin was just another small town in Tennessee. The bloody Battle of Franklin that took place in the fields surrounding the town on November 30, 1864, was probably the single most important event to take place in the town. Like other towns in the region, it took many years for Franklin to fully recover from the impact of the Civil War.

Starting in the 1960s, Franklin underwent a metamorphosis. Construction of I-65 near the town spurred economic development. Today, Franklin is a well-heeled bedroom community for Nashville professionals and music industry bigwigs. The city, whose population runs around 62,000, is the 10th largest in Tennessee and one of the wealthiest in the state. What sets Franklin apart from other small towns in the state is the efforts it has made to preserve and protect the historic downtown. Its location only 20 miles from Nashville is also a major plus.

Franklin's attractions are all within a few miles of the city center, except for Cool Springs Galleria, a megamall located several miles out of town along the interstate.

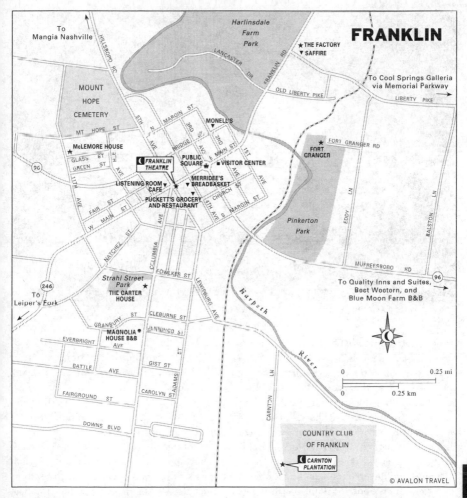

SIGHTS
Historic Downtown

Franklin is one of the most picturesque small towns in Tennessee. Contained within four square blocks, downtown Franklin consists of leafy residential streets with old and carefully restored homes. The center of town is a traffic circle crowned by a simple white Confederate monument. The circle is fronted by banks, more offices, and the 1859 Williamson County courthouse.

The best way to explore downtown Franklin is on foot. Free parking is available along the streets or in two public garages, one on 2nd Avenue and one on 4th Avenue. Pick up a printed walking-tour guide from the visitors center on East Main Street, or download the free iPhone app.

The walking tour takes you past 39 different buildings, including the **Hiram Masonic Lodge,** the oldest Masonic lodge in Tennessee and also the building where Andrew Jackson in 1830 signed the treaty that led to the forced

© 2011 JIM ROOF CREATIVE, INC.

The renovated art deco Franklin Theatre lights up Main Street.

removal of thousands of Native Americans from Tennessee, Georgia, and other Southern states. You will also see the old city cemetery and the old **Franklin Post Office,** as well as lots of beautiful old houses and churches, all of which remain in use today. The walking tour is a good way to become familiar with the town and to appreciate the different types of architecture. It takes 1–2 hours to complete.

Guided walking tours of Franklin are offered by **Franklin on Foot** (615/400-3808, www.franklinonfoot.com). The Classic Franklin tour provides an overview of the history of the town and its buildings. The *Widow of the South* tour is combined with admission to the Carnton Plantation and is a must for lovers of that popular novel. Other tours include a children's tour and Haunted Franklin tour. Tours cost $5–18 per person.

C Franklin Theatre

The newest gem in historic downtown Franklin

is the Franklin Theatre (419 Main St., 615/538-2076, www.franklintheatre.com, box office Wed.–Fri. and Sun. at noon, Sat. at 9:30 A.M.), a 1937 movie theater that had seen better days until it finally closed in 2007. In 2011 it reopened after an $8 million restoration funded primarily by donations from locals through the efforts of the Heritage Foundation. The renovation is spot on, bringing the theater, including its striking outdoor marquee, back to its former glory. Lush carpeting, detailed wallpaper, comfortable seats—everything about the theater evokes moviegoing in a different era.

But the Franklin Theatre isn't stuck in the past. It has many modern amenities that make it a great place to have a night out, complete with a concession stand that serves beer, wine, and spirits, with a menu that delineates Jack Daniel's from bourbon and whiskey (you've gotta love a place that knows its audience). The Franklin Theatre hosts live concerts as well as films.

McLemore House

Five generations of the McLemore family lived in the white clapboard home at the corner of Glass Street and 11th Avenue in downtown Franklin. McLemore House was built in 1880 by Harvey McLemore, a former slave and farmer. Inside, a small museum has been created that documents the story of African Americans in Williamson County.

McLemore House is open by appointment only. Contact Mary Mills at 615/794-2270 or the convention and visitors bureau to arrange a tour; cost is $5.

▌ Carnton Plantation

When Robert Hicks's novel *The Widow of the South* became a best seller in 2005, the staff at the Carnton Plantation (1345 Carnton Ln., 615/794-0903, www.carnton.org, Mon.–Sat. 9 A.M.–5 P.M., Sun. noon–5 P.M., adults $15,

The McGavock Confederate Cemetery at Carnton Plantation is the final resting place to more than 1,500 soldiers.

seniors $12, children 6–12 $8, children under 5 free) noticed an uptick in the number of visitors. The novel is a fictionalized account of Carrie McGavock and how her home, the Carnton Plantation, became a Confederate hospital during the Battle of Franklin in the Civil War (how fictionalized is subject for discussion on the tours here).

The Carnton mansion was built in 1826 by Randal McGavock, a former Nashville mayor and prominent lawyer and businessman. Randal had died by the time of the Civil War, and it was his son, John, and John's wife, Carrie, who witnessed the bloody Battle of Franklin on November 30, 1864. Located behind the Confederate line, the Carnton Plantation became a hospital for hundreds of injured and dying Confederate soldiers. As late as six months after the battle, the McGavock home remained a refuge for recovering veterans.

In the years that followed the battle, the McGavocks raised money, donating much of it themselves, to construct a cemetery for the Confederate dead and donated two acres of land to the cause.

A new visitors center opened at Carnton in 2008, providing much-needed space for the museum and gift shop. Visitors to the Carnton Plantation can pay full price for a guided tour of the mansion and self-guided tour of the grounds, which include a smokehouse, slave house, and garden. You can also pay $5 for the self-guided tour of the grounds. There is no admission charged to visit the cemetery.

Packages include discounts if you want admission to nearby **Lotz House** (www.lotzhouse. com), The Carter House, and Carnton Plantation. It's a good choice for hard-core history buffs but perhaps too much Civil War lore for one day for the average visitor.

Fort Granger

An unsung attraction, Fort Granger is a lovely and interesting place to spend an hour or so.

Built between 1862 and 1863 by Union forces, the earthen fort is set on a bluff overlooking the Harpeth River just south of downtown Franklin. The fort was the largest fortification in the area built by Capt. W. E. Merrill during the Federal occupation of Franklin. It saw action twice in 1863 and also in 1864 during the Battle of Franklin.

Many features of the fort remain intact for today's visitors. You can walk around portions of the breastworks. The interior of the fort is now a grassy field, perfect for a summer picnic or game of catch. An overlook at one end of the fort provides an unmatched view of the surrounding countryside.

You can reach Fort Granger two ways. One is along a short but steep trail departing Pinkerton Park on Murfreesboro Road east of town. Or you can drive straight to the fort by heading out of town on East Main Street. Turn right onto Liberty Pike, right onto Eddy Lane, and, finally, right again onto Fort Granger Drive.

The fort, which is maintained by the City of Franklin, is open during daylight hours only. While there is no office or visitors center at the fort, you may contact Franklin's parks department (615/794-2103) for more information.

The Carter House

Some of the fiercest fighting in the Battle of Franklin took place around the farm and house belonging to the Carter family, on the outskirts of town. The family took refuge in the basement while Union and Confederate soldiers fought hand to hand right above them. Today, the Carter House (1140 Columbia Ave., 615/791-1861, www.battleoffranklintrust.org, Mon.–Sat. 9 A.M.–5 P.M., Sun. noon–5 P.M., $15) is the best place to come for a detailed examination of the battle and the profound human toll that it exacted on both sides.

You will see hundreds of bullet holes, which help to illustrate the ferocity of the fight. Guides describe some of the worst moments of

the battle and bring to life a few of the people who fought it. The house also holds a museum of Civil War uniforms and memorabilia, including photographs and short biographies of many of the men who were killed in Franklin. There is also a video about the battle, which shows scenes from a reenactment.

If you can't get enough Civil War history, consider one of the packages that offer discounts on joint admission to nearby **Lotz House** (www.lotzhouse. com), The Carter House, and Carnton Plantation.

ENTERTAINMENT AND EVENTS
Live Music

Venues that sometimes offer live music include restaurants **Saffire** (The Factory, 230 Franklin Rd., Bldg. 11, 615/599-4995), **Puckett's Grocery and Restaurant** (120 4th Ave. S., 625/794-5527), and **The Bunganut Pig** (1143 Columbia Ave., 615/794-4777). The **Franklin Theatre** (419 Main St., 615/538-2076, www. franklintheatre.com) has an impressive concert schedule, typically with affordable ticket prices.

Theater

The **Boiler Room Theatre** (The Factory, 230 Franklin Rd., Bldg. 6, 615/794-7744, www. boilerroomtheatre.com) is a professional theater company that performs seven or eight productions each year. Shows take place in a 120-seat theater at The Factory and range from light-hearted musical theater to dramas. The theater's season runs year-round.

Franklin's community theater is **Pull-Tight Players** (112 2nd Ave. S., 615/791-5007 or 615/790-6782, www.pull-tight.com). Performing in an intimate theater in downtown Franklin, Pull-Tight Players put on about six productions each season, which runs September–June. Productions include many classic stage favorites.

Cinemas

The restored **Franklin Theatre** (419 Main St.,

615/538-2076, www.franklintheatre.com) shows classic black-and-white films as well as recent releases (although not first-run movies). Movie ticket prices are typically $5, and there are many kid-friendly flicks shown on the weekends.

Head to Cool Springs to find **Carmike Thoroughbred 20** (633 Frazier Dr., 615/778-0775), a 20-screen multiplex showing first-run movies.

Festivals and Events

SPRING

The city's biggest festival of the year is the **Main Street Festival** (615/591-8500, www.historic-franklin.com) during the last full weekend of April. Local arts and crafts are the major draw of this showcase, which also includes food, music, theater, and children's activities.

The town's Rotary Club organizes the annual **Franklin Rodeo** (www.franklinrodeo.com), a weeklong event in May that includes a Rodeo Parade, Miss Tennessee Rodeo pageant, and a PRCA-sanctioned rodeo with steer wrestling and bronco and bull riding. It takes place at the Williamson County Ag Expo Park, and proceeds go to local service projects.

SUMMER

During the first full weekend of June you can join the Heritage Foundation on a **Town and Country Tour of Homes** (www.historic-franklin.com). Tours go to private and historic homes that are closed to the public during the rest of the year.

Franklin celebrates Independence Day with **Franklin on the Fourth** (www.tneventinfo.com/fr_4thofjuly.cfm), a patriotic family concert on the public square. The fireworks finale takes place near Mack Hatcher/Hillsboro Road.

During the last weekend in July the city celebrates **Bluegrass Along the Harpeth** (www.bluegrassalongtheharpeth.com, 615/390-3588, free), a music festival featuring bluegrass, old-time string bands, and buck dancing.

The **Williamson County Fair** (www.williamsoncountyfair.org) starts on the first Friday in August and features agricultural exhibits, a midway, live entertainment, and competitions.

FALL

The **Franklin Jazz Festival** (www.franklinjazzfestival.com) is a two-day music festival that features jazz, Dixieland, and big-band acts in downtown Franklin. Admission is free; the festival takes place on the Sunday and Monday of Labor Day weekend.

WINTER

The Carter House organizes a **holiday tour of homes** during the first full weekend of December. During the second full weekend of the month, the city of Franklin is transformed into a bustling English Victorian town at **Dickens of a Christmas.** There are costumed characters, carolers, artisans, strolling minstrels, and unique foods.

The **Middle Tennessee Civil War Show** has become a favorite destination of history buffs each December.

SHOPPING

In many respects, shopping is Franklin's greatest attraction. Trendy downtown shops, the unique environment of The Factory, and proximity to a major mall make this a destination for shoppers. It is also one of Tennessee's most popular antiques shopping destinations.

Antiques

Franklin declares itself "the new antiques capital of Tennessee." Indeed, antiquing is one of the most popular pursuits of Franklin's visitors, and at least two dozen antiques shops serve to quench the thirst for something old. The town's antiques district is huddled around the corner of Margin Street and 2nd Avenue. Here you'll find no fewer than six major antiques stores. Other shops are found along Main Street in the downtown shopping district.

The best place to start antiquing is the **Franklin Antique Mall** (251 2nd Ave. S., 615/790-8593, www.franklinantiquemall. com), located in the town's old icehouse. The mall is a maze of rooms, each with different goods on offer. Possibilities include books, dishware, quilts, furniture, knickknacks, and housewares. You can also follow 5th Avenue about two blocks south of downtown to find **Country Charm Antique Mall** (301 Lewisburg Ave., 615/790-8998), whose three buildings house a vast array of furniture, quilts, glassware, china, and home decor.

Just outside the Franklin Antique Mall are at least five other antiques shops to roam through, including **J. J. Ashley's** (125 S. Margin St., 615/791-0011), which specializes in French and English country accessories, as well as European furniture. **Scarlett Scales Antiques** (212 S. Margin St., 615/791-4097), located in a 1900s shotgun house, has American country furnishings, accessories, and architectural elements arriving daily.

Downtown

Retail is alive and well in Franklin's downtown. West Main Street is the epicenter of the shopping district, although you will find stores scattered around other parts of downtown as well. Home decor, classy antiques, trendy clothes, and specialty items like candles, tea, and gardening supplies are just a few of the things you'll find in downtown Franklin.

Most shops in downtown Franklin are open by 10 A.M., and many stay open until the evening to catch late-afternoon visitors. You can easily navigate the downtown shopping district on foot, although you may need to stow your parcels in the car now and then.

Bink's Outfitters (421 Main St., 615/599-8777, www.binksoutfitters.com) sells outdoor clothing and equipment. Go to **ENJOUE** (400 Main St., 615/599-8177) for funky fashions and trendy styles.

The city's best bookstore is **Landmark Booksellers** (114 E. Main St., 615/791-6400), found on the other side of the town square. They have a wide selection of used and new books, including many regional titles. It is friendly and welcoming, with fresh coffee for sale in the mornings.

Franklin Tea Merchant (430 Main St., 615/794-6311, www.franklintea.com) has a wide selection of loose tea and various tea accessories. Toys old and new are on sale at **Main Street Toy Co.** (412 Main St., 615/790-4869). For the best in paper, gift wrap, and stationery, go to **Rock Paper Scissors** (317 Main St., 615/791-0150, www.rockpaperscissor.com). **Heart and Hands** (418 Main St., 615/794-2537, www.heartandhandsonline.com) is one of several area shops specializing in crafts and home decor.

The Factory

Franklin's most distinctive retail center is The Factory (230 Franklin Rd., 615/791-1777, www.factoryatfranklin.com). A 250,000-square-foot complex of 11 different old industrial buildings, The Factory once housed stove factories and a textile mill. In the mid-1990s, Calvin Lehew bought the dilapidated eyesore and began the lengthy process of restoring the buildings and converting them to a space for galleries, retail shops, restaurants, and other businesses.

Today, The Factory is a vibrant commercial center for the city of Franklin. It houses a refreshing array of local independent retailers, including galleries, salons, candy shops, and a pet boutique. **The Little Cottage** (615/794-1405) sells children's fashions.

There are also 11 different studios and learning centers, including the **Viking Store** (615/599-9617), which offers cooking demonstrations and classes; **Creation Station** (615/791-9192), where you can practice scrapbooking; and **Arts for Life** (615/995-2778), which offers art classes and music lessons. There are also talent agencies and a tae kwon do academy.

In addition to retail and learning centers, The Factory has four restaurants, a fish market, and free wireless Internet for your surfing needs.

Cool Springs Galleria

Cool Springs Galleria (1800 Galleria Blvd., Cool Springs, 615/771-2128, www.coolspringsgalleria.com) is a mall with 165 specialty stores, 5 major department stores, 20 restaurants, and a 500-seat food court. It is located a few miles north of Franklin, convenient to I-65. Shops include Zales, Wild Oats, Talbots, Pier 1, Pottery Barn, Macy's, JCPenney, and Eddie Bauer. The mall is found at exits 68B and 69 on I-65.

SPORTS AND RECREATION

Pinkerton Park (405 Murfreesboro Rd.), just southeast of town off Murfreesboro Road, is a pleasant city park. Walking trails, playgrounds, and picnic tables draw dozens of town residents, who come to exercise or simply relax. A short hiking trail takes you to Fort Granger, overlooking the city. You can also take the Sue Douglas Berry Memorial pedestrian bridge over the Harpeth River and walk the six blocks to the town square.

Jim Warren Park (705 Boyd Mill Ave., 615/794-2103) is a large public park with baseball and softball fields, tennis courts, covered picnic areas, and 2.5 miles of walking trails.

Harlinsdale Farm

One of the most famous Tennessee Walking Horse breeding farms became a public park in 2007. Harlinsdale Farm (239 Franklin Rd., 615/794-2103) was a famed Franklin landmark for many years, thanks to a very famous horse. Midnight Sun, a stallion, was a world champion Walking Horse in 1945 and 1946, and all subsequent champions can trace their ancestry to him.

In 2004, Franklin bought the 200-acre farm for $8 million, and three years later the first 60 acres opened as a public park. It is a pleasant place to walk or picnic. There are plans for a visitors center, overlook, and extensive walking trails. For now, you can park, picnic, and look at the horses and the landscape.

Golf

Located a few miles southeast of Franklin, **Forrest Crossing Golf Course** (750 Riverview Dr., 615/794-9400) is an 18-hole par 72 golf course designed by Gary Roger Baird. Just shy of 7,000 yards, the course rating is 77.8, and the slope is 135.

There are more golf courses in Cool Springs, a few miles north of Franklin. **Vanderbilt Legends Club** (1500 Legends Club Ln., 615/791-8100, www.legendsclub.com) is a top-of-the-line golf club. There are two 18-hole courses at the club, as well as a complete array of club services, including a putting green and chipping green. Greens fees are $75–85 and include a cart. Lower rates are available after 3 P.M. No blue jeans, T-shirts, or athletic shorts are allowed.

The **Fairways on Spencer Creek** (285 Spencer Creek Rd., 615/794-8223, www.fairwaysonspencercreek.net) is a nine-hole alternative. The course rating is 64.6, and the slope is 105.

ACCOMMODATIONS

Franklin has two types of accommodations: cozy bed-and-breakfast inns and chain motels. The bed-and-breakfasts are located in downtown Franklin and the surrounding countryside. The chain motels are located around exit 65 off I-65, about two miles from the city center. The bed-and-breakfast accommodations are far more congruous with Franklin's charm than the interstate motels.

Under $100

Several chain motels surround the interstate near Franklin. Closest to town are the 89-room **Quality Inns and Suites** (1307 Murfreesboro Rd., 615/794-7591, $65–110) and the 142-room **Best Western** (1308 Murfreesboro Rd., 615/790-0570, $55–70). Both offer wireless

Internet, free continental breakfast, and an outdoor pool. The Quality Inn is pet friendly with a mere $10 fee.

$100-150

The **Magnolia House Bed and Breakfast** (1317 Columbia Ave., 615/794-8178, www.bbonline. com/tn/magnolia, $140–155) is less than a mile from downtown Franklin, near the Carter House. A large magnolia tree shades the early-20th-century Craftsman home. There are four carpeted guest rooms, each with a private bath. Three house queen-size beds; the fourth has two twin beds. Common areas include a polished sitting room, cozy den, and sunroom that looks out on the quiet residential neighborhood. Hosts Jimmy and Robbie Smithson welcome guests and prepare homemade breakfast according to your preferences.

Over $200

Designed for couples, **Blue Moon Farm Bed and Breakfast** (4441 N. Chapel Rd., 800/493-4518, www.bluemoonfarmbb.com, $350–475) is a three-room cottage complete with kitchen, spa-style bathroom, and master bedroom. The art deco decor is unique among country bed-and-breakfasts, as is the sophistication of the welcome. Touches like spa robes, an ultra-luxurious tub, and a decadently dressed king-size bed make this a real getaway. The kitchen is stocked with drinks, snacks, and the ingredients for light meals. A "Grocery Bag Breakfast" is left in the refrigerator for you and your companion to enjoy when you want, and in privacy. During waking hours, you can stroll the grounds or take advantage of wireless Internet access. Hosts Susan and Bob Eidam will also be happy to recommend and arrange activities for your stay in the Franklin area. Children older than one year are welcome at a cost of $20 extra per night.

FOOD
Downtown

The best choice for baked goods, coffee, and light fare, including soups, salads, and sandwiches, is **Merridee's Breadbasket** (110 4th Ave., 615/790-3755, www.merridees. com, Mon.–Wed. 7 A.M.–5 P.M., Thurs.–Sat. 7 A.M.–9 P.M., $3–11). Merridee grew up in Minnesota and learned baking from her mother, a Swede. When Merridee married Tom McCray and moved to Middle Tennessee in 1973, she kept up the baking traditions she had learned as a child. In 1984, she opened Merridee's Breadbasket in Franklin. Merridee McCray died in 1994, but her restaurant remains one of Franklin's most popular. Come in for omelets, scrambled eggs, or sweet bread and fruit in the morning. At lunch choose from the daily soup, casserole, or quiche, or order a cold or grilled sandwich. Merridee's also bakes fresh bread daily; take home a loaf of the always-popular Viking bread. Merridee's attracts a variety of people—students, businesspeople, and families out on the town. The creaky wood floors and comfortable seating make it a pleasant and relaxing place to refuel.

Puckett's Grocery and Restaurant (120 4th Ave. S., 625/794-5527, Mon. 7 A.M.–3 P.M., Tues.–Sat. 7 A.M.–9 P.M., Sun. 7 A.M.–7 P.M., $7–10), the Leiper's Fork institution, has a second location in Franklin (and a third in Nashville). The Franklin shop offers traditional breakfasts with eggs, bacon, country ham, and biscuits, and plate lunches during the day. In the evening, order up a handmade burger (the locals swear that they're the best in town), a Southern dinner of fried catfish, or a traditional steak, chicken, or fish entrée. For vegetarians, they offer a veggie burger or a vegetable plate, as well as salads. Do not skip the fried green beans. The food is well prepared and the service friendly, and there's almost always a crowd, regardless of whether or not there's live music on tap.

The Cool Cafe coffee shop is transformed into **Mangia Nashville** (1110 Hillsboro Rd., 615/538-7456, Fri. at 8 P.M. and Sat. at 6 P.M., $45), a New York–style Italian bistro, only on

Friday and Saturday nights. You'll get an old-school five-course Italian dinner. There's a $5 corkage fee if you BYOB.

Always popular, award-winning **⭐Saffire** (The Factory, 230 Franklin Rd., Bldg. 11, 615/599-4995, Tues.–Sun. 11 A.M.–3 P.M. and reopens at 5 P.M., $14–35) uses primarily organic and biodynamic ingredients. The menu sparkles with unique dishes such as the tender and flavorful Cuban roasted-pork appetizer plate or a simple salad of heirloom tomatoes. Entrées include upscale dishes like prime rib and ahi tuna. Their fried chicken is dusted with panko, topped with country ham gravy, and served with luscious macaroni and cheese. Saffire has an extensive wine and cocktail list, including organic choices. Take $4 off signature cocktails during happy hour (5–6 P.M.), and on Tuesday night most bottles of wine go for half price. The lunch menu is casual, featuring sandwiches, salads, and lunch-size entrées. Or choose the "green plate" daily special, featuring local and organic ingredients. There is also a midday kid's menu with favorites like grilled cheese and chicken bites. Set within an old warehouse, Saffire's dining room is spacious, with exposed brick and beams. The kitchen opens out onto the dining room, so you can watch the cooks work. With live music many nights, Saffire is a solid choice for excellent food in a pleasant and exciting environment.

Farmers Market

The Franklin Farmers Market (230 Franklin Rd., www.franklinfarmersmarket.com, Sat. 8 A.M.–noon) takes place at the rear of The Factory. This is one of the finest small-town farmers markets in the state, featuring a wide variety of fruit and vegetable growers; cheese, milk, and meat sellers; as well as craftspeople and live music.

INFORMATION AND SERVICES

The **Williamson County Convention and Visitors Bureau** (615/791-7554 or 866/253-9207, www.visitwilliamson.com) publishes guides and maintains a website about Franklin and the surrounding area. They also operate the **Williamson County Visitor Center** (209 E. Main St., 615/591-8514, Mon.–Fri. 9 A.M.–4 P.M., Sat. 10 A.M.–3 P.M., Sun. noon–3 P.M.).

The **Williamson Medical Center** (Hwy. 96 E., 615/435-5000) is a 185-bed full-service medical facility with a 24-hour emergency room.

King Neptune (1533 Columbia Ave., 615/790-7682) is a clean and comfortable laundry open 24 hours a day. A single wash costs $1.50.

GETTING AROUND

Traffic can be heavy in and around Franklin. As a bedroom community for commuters working in Nashville, the morning and afternoon rush hours are to be avoided. The City of Franklin offers a **trolley bus** service around the town and to outlying areas, including Cool Springs Galleria, Williamson Medical Center, Watson Glen Shopping Center, and Independence Square. The trolleys run three different routes 6 A.M.–6 P.M.

You can pick up a full schedule and route map from the visitors center or download it from www.tmagroup.org. Fares for the Cool Springs Galleria bus are $3 for a one-way trip and $5 for a round-trip.

If you need a taxi, call Brentwood Taxi at 615/373-4950.

MIDDLE TENNESSEE

The Natchez Trace

The Natchez Trace Parkway cuts a diagonal path through the Middle Tennessee area south of Nashville. The two-lane limited-access highway passes through mostly undeveloped countryside.

Towns and sites in this region are a short drive off the Trace, and these villages and county seats embody small-town Tennessee.

LEIPER'S FORK

Part bucolic small town, part yuppified enclave, Leiper's Fork is a pleasant place to spend a few hours. It is located about 15 minutes' drive from Franklin and near milepost 420 on the Natchez Trace Parkway. The town runs for several miles along Leiper's Fork, a tributary of the West Harpeth River. Beautiful old farmhouses line Old Hillsboro Road, which serves as the main thoroughfare through town.

One of the earliest settlers of the area was the Benton family, including Thomas Hart Benton, who would go on to become a U.S. senator from Missouri. For many years, Leiper's Fork was called Hillsboro after Hillsborough, North Carolina, where many of its early settlers came from. There is another Hillsboro in Coffee County, Tennessee, however, so when this Hillsboro petitioned for a post office in 1818, the U.S. Postal Service insisted that it change its name. Leiper's Fork was born.

Acclaimed furniture maker Dick Poyner was from the Leiper's Fork area. Poyner, a former slave, was famous for his sturdy ladder-back wooden chairs, one of which is on display at the Tennessee State Museum in Nashville.

Leiper's Fork is a pleasant community, with a die-hard group of locals who are proud of their town. Art galleries and antiques shops line the short main drag. Unusually good food can be found at local restaurants, and a laid-back let's-laugh-at-ourselves attitude prevails. Many music powerhouses live here; if you see a celebrity, don't make a fuss. That's why they choose to live in Leiper's Fork.

Bed-and-breakfast inns in the area make it a viable destination or a pleasant pit stop during a tour of the region.

Entertainment

Friday night is songwriter night at **Puckett's Grocery** (4142 Old Hillsboro Rd., 615/794-1308, www.puckettsgrocery.com). For $30 you enjoy dressed-up dinner—fresh seafood, poultry, and steak are usually among the options—at 7 P.M. and an in-the-round performance from Nashville singer-songwriters starting at 8:30 P.M. If you prefer, pay $15 for the concert only. Reservations are essential for either, so call ahead. Check the website to find out who is performing.

Jailhouse Industries operates the Leiper's Fork **Lawn Chair Theatre** behind Leiper's Creek Gallery from May to September. Bring your lawn chair or blanket and enjoy classic movies and kids' favorites on Friday and Saturday nights, plus concerts. Call 615/477-6799 for more information, or just ask around.

Shopping

Leiper's Fork retailers are open Wednesday–Saturday 10 A.M.–5 P.M. and Sunday 1–5 P.M.

Opening its doors in 2007, **R Place** (4154 Old Hillsboro Rd., 615/794-8592) sells the artwork of Anne Goetz, the handmade furniture of Reed Birnie, and used books curated by Renee Armand. You can also get homemade pie and coffee if you need sustenance while you browse the shop, housed in an old home.

The **Leiper's Creek Gallery** (4144 Old Hillsboro Rd., 615/599-5102, www.leiperscreekgallery.com) is the finest gallery in town. It shows a wide selection of paintings by local and regional artists, and hosts a variety of arts events year-round.

THE NATCHEZ TRACE PARKWAY

The first people to travel what is now considered the Natchez Trace were probably Choctow and Chickasaw Indians, who made the first footpaths through the region. French and Spanish traders used the 500 miles of intertwining Indian trails that linked the Mississippi port of Natchez to the Cumberland River.

Early white settlers quickly identified the importance of a land route from Natchez to Nashville. In 1801, the Natchez Trace opened as an official post road between the two cities. Boatmen who piloted flatboats from Nashville and other northern cities to Natchez and New Orleans returned along the Trace by foot or horse, often carrying large sums of money. One historian characterized the diverse array of people who used the Trace as "robbers, rugged pioneers, fashionable ladies, shysters, politicians, soldiers, scientists, and men of destiny, such as Aaron Burr, Andrew Jackson, and Meriwether Lewis."

The Trace developed a reputation for robberies, and few people traveled its miles alone. Many thieves disguised themselves as Indians, fanning the flames of racial distrust that existed during this period of history. By 1820, more than 20 inns, referred to as "stands," were open. Many were modest—providing food and shelter only.

In 1812, the first steamship arrived at Natchez, Mississippi, marking the beginning of the end of the Trace's prominence. As steamboat travel became more widespread and affordable, more and more people turned away from the long, laborious, and dangerous overland route along the Trace.

The road's historical importance is evident in the fact that it was not easily forgotten. While it faded from use, the Natchez Trace was remembered. In 1909, the Daughters of the American Revolution in Mississippi started a project to mark the route of the Trace in each county through which it passed. The marker project continued for the next 24 years and eventually caught the attention of Rep. Thomas J. Busby of Mississippi, who introduced the first bills in Congress to survey and construct a paved road along the route of the old Natchez Trace.

During the Great Depression, work on the Natchez Trace Parkway began under the Public Works Administration, the Works Project Administration, and the Civilian Conservation Corps. Following the New Deal, construction slowed dramatically, and it was not until 1996 that the final leg of the parkway was completed.

The 445-mile parkway follows the general path of the old Natchez Trace; in a few places, they fall in step with each other. More than 100 miles of the parkway lie within Tennessee. It runs along the Western Highland Rim through Davidson, Williamson, Hickman, Maury, Lewis, and Wayne Counties.

The parkway passes scenic overlooks, historic sites, and quiet pastures. In many places along the route you have the opportunity to walk along the original Trace.

ACCOMMODATIONS AND FOOD

There are no hotels on the parkway. Look for accommodations in nearby cities, including Franklin, Columbia, and Lawrenceburg. The Hampshire-based **Natchez Trace Reservation Service** (800/377-2770, www.bbonline.com/natcheztrace) books bed-and-breakfast inns along the parkway, from Nashville all the way to Natchez. This service is worth considering, especially since many of these inns are located closer to the parkway than motels are.

The closest accommodations to the parkway are three **campgrounds,** one of which lies in Tennessee. The Meriwether Lewis Campground at milepost 385 has 32 sites and a bathhouse. The next campground is Jeff Busby, at milepost 193 in Mississippi.

There are no restaurants or food concessions along the parkway. Picnic facilities abound, however, so wise travelers will pack a few sandwiches and avoid traveling off the parkway to eat.

INFORMATION AND SERVICES

The **National Park Service** (800/305-7417, www.nps.gov/natr) publishes a fold-out map and guide to the parkway. The official visitors center for the parkway is in Tupelo, Mississippi. For detailed hiking information, visit the website about the Natchez Trace National Scenic Trail at www.nps.gov/natt.

The only gas station along the parkway is at Jeff Busby, milepost 193 in Mississippi. Fill up your tank before you take off to explore.

Neena's Primitive Antiques (4158 Old Hillsboro Rd., 615/790-0345) specializes in primitive antiques, linens, home decor items, and leather goods.

The 3,000-square-foot **Serenite Maison** (4149 Old Hillsboro Pk., 615/599-2071, www.serenitemaison.com) houses a well-edited inventory thanks to the smart design sense of Alexandra Cirimelli. A California transplant, Cirimelli has appeared on an episode of *American Pickers* and is known for finding her well-heeled clients the perfect farm table or pie safe for their kitchen. Don't overlook the pickin' corner, where locals stop in to play the antique guitars, banjos, and mandolins that hang on the walls.

Recreation

The Leiper's Fork District of the Natchez Trace National Scenic Trail runs for 24 miles, starting near milepost 427 and ending at milepost 408, where State Highway 50 crosses the parkway. The trail follows the old Natchez Trace through rural countryside. The best access point is from Garrison Creek Road, where there is parking, restrooms, and picnic facilities. You can also access the trail from Davis Hollow Road.

Food

⟨ Puckett's Grocery (4142 Old Hillsboro Rd., 615/794-1308, www.puckettsgrocery.com, summer Mon.–Thurs. 6 A.M.–7 P.M., Fri.–Sat. 6 A.M.–10:30 P.M., Sun. 6 A.M.–6 P.M., Dec.–Feb. reduced hours, $6–25) is the heartbeat of Leiper's Fork. An old-time grocery with a small dining room attached, Puckett's serves breakfast, lunch, and dinner to the town faithful and visitors alike. The original country store opened about 1950. In 1998, Andy Marshall bought the store and expanded the restaurant offerings. Solid country breakfasts are the order of the day in the mornings, followed by plate lunches. The pulled pork is a favorite, as is the Puckett Burger. Dinner specials include catfish nights,

family nights, and a Saturday-night seafood buffet. Friday night the grocery turns upscale with a supper club and live music. Reservations are essential for Friday night. Puckett's hours vary by the season, so it is best to call ahead, especially for dinner arrangements. A second Puckett's Grocery location in Franklin offers a more varied menu.

For a casual sandwich, decadent pastry, or cup of coffee, head to the **Backyard Cafe** (4150 Old Hillsboro Rd., 615/790-4003, Mon.–Sat. 11 A.M.–3 P.M., Sun. noon–3 P.M.).

Information

The **Leiper's Fork Merchant's Association** (615/972-2708, www.leipersforkvillage.com) promotes the town, maintains a listing of local businesses, and publishes an annual calendar of events.

ARRINGTON

The sleepy town of Arrington wasn't much more than a dot on a map for tourists (or locals, for that matter) until 2005. That's when country megastar Kix Brooks and his business partners picked these rolling hills as the place they were going to start a winery and set out to change the perception of Tennessee wines.

While no one (yet) is confusing these vintages for those grown in Napa, and, in fact, some of the grapes used are brought into the state at this point, **Arrington Vineyards** (6211 Patton Rd., 615/395-0102, www.arringtonvineyards.com, Mon.–Sat. 11 A.M.–8 P.M., Sun. noon–6 P.M.) has impressed even the skeptics.

You don't have to be an oenophile to appreciate a day at Arrington, however. There's a popular free Music in the Vines concert series in the summer, and almost any pleasant day of the year you'll see others with picnics who came enjoy the scenery and the great outdoors. There's not a restaurant on the premises, but you can buy boxed meals, cheeses, and chocolates. The place is kid friendly, and there are board games to borrow while you stretch out

© PAUL T-OMASSON

Port, cabernet, and more are ready for the sipping at Arrington Vineyards.

on the lawn. Because of Tennessee's quirky liquor laws, you can't buy a glass of wine here, but you can buy a bottle that you can then go open on your picnic blanket.

New initiatives have converted some of Arrington's building to solar power, and the vineyard is becoming a green leader in the area.

SPRING HILL

A small town midway between Franklin and Columbia, Spring Hill is best known by many as the site of a large General Motors automobile factory. To students of the Civil War, the town is the site of one of the South's greatest missed opportunities of the war. While it is doubtful that a different outcome at Spring Hill would have changed the course of war, it would very likely have saved the many thousands of lives lost at the Battle of Franklin.

Spring Hill is located along U.S. 31. Downtown consists of a few blocks between Beechcroft and Kendron Roads. The town's

main street was destroyed by fire and tornado in 1963, leaving only a few remnants of Spring Hill's former charm. To see these remainders, drive up and down the town's side streets, including Murray Hill, Depot, and McLemore Streets. Spring Hill's main attractions are along Highway 31, less than a mile outside of town.

The **Spring Hill Battlefield** (931/486-9037) is a 118-acre park with a one-mile trail that climbs to the top of a hill overlooking the battlefield. Interpretive markers tell the story of Spring Hill. The park is open during daylight hours. To find it, turn east onto Kendron Road and look for the park on the right-hand side of the road, just before the road passes I-65.

Rippavilla

You can tour an 1850s-era mansion at Rippavilla Plantation (5700 Main St./Hwy. 31, 931/486-9037, www.rippavilla.org, Tues.–Sat. 10 A.M.–4 P.M., adults $10, seniors $8, children 6–12 $5, children under 6 free), just

MIDDLE TENNESSEE

THE SOUTH'S LAST STAND

In the waning days of the Confederacy, Confederate president Jefferson Davis met with his commanders to plan strategy. It was September 1864, and the Federals were pushing southward in Virginia and Georgia.

The plan that Davis and his commanders agreed upon was a daring march northward through Middle Tennessee. It was hoped that General Hood's Army of the Tennessee would draw Federal forces away from the battles elsewhere and that they would eventually be repelled from the South entirely.

The last-ditch plan failed and cost the Confederacy some 13,500 lives. The battles of Spring Hill, Franklin, and Nashville were major blows to the Southern cause and its last losing stratagem.

SPRING HILL

On November 29, 1864, Gen. John M. Schofield and his Federal troops were stationed in Columbia. Moving northward, Hood went around Columbia and headed toward Spring Hill. From here, Hood could either have marched to Nashville ahead of the Federals or returned to Columbia and attacked them from the rear. It was a promising position.

But the opportunity was squandered when the Confederates camped just short of a critical road northward. Schofield, who suspected Hood's strategy, moved his men in the dead of night and marched them safely northward.

Explanations for Hood's mistake suggest that he was not himself on that day. He was probably in tremendous physical pain from earlier war injuries (Hood had already lost the use of his left arm and had his right leg amputated below the hip) and was probably taking opium. He may also have been drunk.

Whatever the cause, on the morning of November 30, when Hood realized what had happened, he resolved to battle the Federals in Franklin. Fueled by shame and desperation, Hood ordered the charge at the Battle of Franklin, one of the South's bloodiest defeats of the war.

FRANKLIN

By the time Hood and his army reached Franklin on November 30, 1864, the general was frustrated and the men exhausted. The missed opportunity at Spring Hill stung, but worse was yet to come.

Ignoring the advice of his commanders, Hood ordered a full frontal attack on the Federal line around Franklin. Unlike many other battles of the Civil War, the troops at Franklin had a full view of each other. There were some 23,000 Federal soldiers on one side and 20,000 Confederates on the other. That evening, 18 brigades of Confederate soldiers, many of them from Tennessee, marched toward the Federal line. With the rebel yell that made them famous, the attack had begun.

It was a bloody and fierce battle. Even those commanders and soldiers on the Confederate side who had doubts about the battle strategy fought bravely and often to the death. The hand-to-hand combat around the Carter House near downtown Franklin was some of the fiercest of the battle. One Federal soldier said that the fighting was in such close quarters that "even the poorest marksman could not fail to hit a human target."

The Confederate assault failed. The fighting ended around 9 P.M., and overnight Federal general John M. Schofield and all his soldiers who could walk marched to Nashville. They left their dead on the battlefield. Two weeks later, they defeated Hood's army again during the Battle of Nashville.

The death toll at Franklin was staggering. Some 7,000 Confederates were killed, wounded, or captured in just five hours of battle. The Federals lost 2,500 men. Many injured warriors died on the battlefield overnight, when temperatures dropped below freezing.

The townspeople of Franklin were left to tend to the wounded on both sides of the battle. Nearly every home in the city became a makeshift hospital. The most famous of these was the Carnton Plantation, where visitors today can still see bloodstains on the floor left by injured and dying soldiers.

In 1866, John and Carrie McGavock established a Confederate cemetery on the grounds of Carnton. It holds 1,500 graves, making it the largest private military cemetery in the nation, and it's still a solemn place. Carrie kept a careful record of the men who were buried there, and her cemetery book was used by thousands of people who came to Franklin to mourn loved ones who died there.

south of downtown Spring Hill on Highway 31. Rippavilla, originally called Rip-o-villa, was built in 1851 by wealthy plantation owner Nathaniel Cheairs and his wife, Susan. The story is told that there was a tradition in the Cheairs family for the men to marry women named Sarah, so when Nathaniel told his father that he intended to ask Susan McKissak to marry him, his father offered to pay the young man $5,000 in gold not to. Susan McKissak's father, one of the richest men in the area, heard of this, and in reply he offered Cheairs all the bricks and slave labor he needed to build his home.

In the end, Cheairs married Susan and received both the gifts from his father-in-law and the $5,000 from his father—not a bad way to start out in life.

Rippavilla was sold out of the family in the 1920s, and the new owner modernized many of the finishes and also connected what was once a detached smokehouse and kitchen to the main building. Guided tours of the mansion last about 45 minutes, and guests may also walk around the property, which includes an 1870s freedman's school that was moved from another part of the county when it was threatened to be destroyed.

Tennessee Museum of Early Farm Life

For an educational trip back in time, stop at the Tennessee Museum of Early Farm Life (5700 Main St./Hwy. 31, 931/381-3686, Apr.–Oct. Fri.–Sat. 9 A.M.–3:30 P.M. and by appointment, adults $3, children and seniors $2), which displays farm, kitchen, and other useful implements used at Tennessee farms and homes in days gone by. Operated by a group of enthusiastic and knowledgeable retired farmers, the museum lovingly preserves plows, cultivators, seeders, wagons, and many other pieces of machinery that helped make a hard life just a bit easier for farmers and their families. You can see machinery and equipment used to make brooms, to make molasses, to sow seeds, to bale hay, and to cure pork. Through the descriptions provided by your tour guide, you begin to understand the ingenuity and inventiveness of these pioneers, as well as the hard work that went into fulfilling their basic needs.

The museum is located a few hundred yards behind the Rippavilla Plantation and was once called the Mule Museum, the name that is still reflected on the road sign at Rippavilla.

Accommodations

There is a **Best Western** (102 Kedron Pkwy., 931/486-1234, $95–130) in town with an outdoor pool, laundry facility, free full breakfast, fitness room, and business services.

COLUMBIA

Columbia is the seat of Maury County. Founded in 1809 and named for Christopher Columbus, Columbia was the commercial hub for Middle Tennessee's rich plantations. In 1850 it became the third largest city in Tennessee, behind Nashville and Memphis. A decade later Maury County was the wealthiest county in the whole state. The city's prominence did not survive, however. The economic trauma of the Civil War was largely to blame.

No city in all of Tennessee is more closely associated with mules than Columbia. During the 19th and early 20th centuries, Columbia's mule market opened on the first Monday of April, and people flocked here to buy and sell mules. Other towns, including Lynchburg and Paris, were known for large "First Monday" sales, but Columbia's was the largest.

Younger travelers may be interested to know that the Hannah Montana movie was filmed here in 2008.

Ancestral Home of James Knox Polk

The United States' 11th president, James Knox Polk, was born in North Carolina but moved to Middle Tennessee with his family when he was 11 years old. Before moving to town, Polk's

© SUSANNA HENIGHAN POTTER

President James K. Polk's family home in Columbia is now a museum.

Polk died of cholera just five months after leaving office and so had little opportunity to enjoy the home; Sarah Polk lived for another 42 years following her husband's death, and she spent them all at Polk Place.

The Polk home in Columbia was comfortable, but not luxurious, for its time. It was while living here that Polk began his career as a Tennessee lawyer and eventually won his first seat in the U.S. House of Representatives. He would go on to serve 14 years in the House, four of them as Speaker. He was governor of Tennessee from 1839 to 1841 and defeated Henry Clay, a Whig, to become president in 1845. Polk's presidency was defined by his drive to expand the Union westward, and it was during his term in office that the United States added California, Texas, and Oregon to the territory of the United States.

The Polk home provides a good introduction to this little-known, but nonetheless important, U.S. president.

The Athenaeum Rectory

Once part of a famous finishing school for girls, The Athenaeum Rectory (808 Anthenaeum St., 931/381-4822, Tues.–Sat. 10 A.M.–4 P.M., closed in Jan., adults $6, seniors $5, children $1–4) is also an unusual architectural gem. Designed and built by Maury County master builder Nathan Vaught, the Rectory was the home of Rev. Franklin Gillette Smith and his family. Smith came to Columbia from Vermont in 1837 to run the Columbia Female Institute, an Episcopal girls' finishing school.

In 1851, Smith decided to open his own school for girls. He built the Columbia Athenaeum School next to the Rectory, which remained his family home. Its name refers to Athena, the goddess of wisdom, and has come to mean "seat of learning."

For 52 years the Athenaeum educated young women in art, music, history, science, and business. The library houses more than 16,000

family lived for several years on a farm north of Columbia, from where Polk's father ran successful plantations, speculated in land, and was involved in local politics.

The home where James Polk lived as a teenager and young man in Columbia is the only house remaining, besides the White House, where Polk ever lived. It is now the Ancestral Home of James Knox Polk (301–305 W. 7th St., 931/388-2354, www.jameskpolk.com, Apr.–Oct. Mon.–Sat. 9 A.M.–5 P.M., Sun. 1–5 P.M., Nov.–Mar. Mon.–Sat. 9 A.M.–4 P.M., Sun. 1–5 P.M., adults $7, seniors $6, youths 6–18 $5, children under 6 free) and home to a museum about Polk's life and presidency.

The home has a number of furnishings that belonged to President Polk and his wife, Sarah, while they lived at the White House. Other pieces come from Polk Place, the home that the couple planned and built in Nashville following the end of Polk's presidency in 1849. Sadly, volumes, and the school sat on 22 wooded acres of land. Ladies took part in gymnastics, bowling, croquet, and tennis. At its peak, the Athenaeum housed 125 boarding students, plus day students from the surrounding area.

The Athenaeum remained open until 1904; after the deaths of Rev. Smith and his wife, it was operated by their son. From 1904 to 1914, the Athenaeum served as the community's high school, and in 1915 the school was torn down and the Columbia High School built in its place. The Athenaeum Rectory was preserved, however, and visitors can tour the Moorish-Gothic structure that housed the parlor and reception area for the school.

The rectory is operated by the Association for the Preservation of Tennessee Antiquities (www.theapta.org). For a week every summer they offer the 1861 Athenaeum Girls' School, when girls 14–18 years old dress up in period clothing and study topics like etiquette, penmanship, and archery. Every May, they offer a weekend course for women 19 and older.

Mule Day

Columbia's Mule Day (931/381-9557, www.muleday.com) takes place over four days in mid-April and is perhaps the thing for which Columbia is best known. The festival's roots are in the First Monday mule market that took place in Columbia during the period when work animals were indispensable to Tennessee farmers. In many cases, mules were a farmer's most valuable asset—a good pair of mules could make a poor farmer rich.

Mules were more expensive than horses or oxen because they were more highly prized. They were said to be stronger, smarter, and more surefooted than other work animals. Their temperament can be stubborn, but some mules are easy and willing to work. For this reason, mule breeders were important, influential, and, often, quite wealthy.

Today's Mule Day is more festival than mule market, although the event still does includes mule sales, mule and donkey seminars, and mule shows and competitions. The highlight is Saturday morning's Mule Day Parade, when thousands of people crowd to see school bands, mules, and colorful troops parade down the road. There is also live music, storytelling, dancing, gospel singing, and the crowning of the Mule Day Queen. Activities take place at various locations in Columbia, but the heart of Mule Day is the Maury County Park on Lion Parkway.

Accommodations

Columbia has more choices of chain hotels than any other city in Maury County. **Jameson Inn** (715 S. James M. Campbell Blvd., 931/388-3326, $85–105) is a 55-room hotel with all the amenities: complimentary breakfast, fitness center, free wireless Internet, pool, big televisions, movie channels, and ironing boards. Premium rooms add microwaves, refrigerators, and coffeemakers. The inn is located across the street from the Columbia Mall and downtown.

Locally owned, the **Richland Inn** (2405 Pulaski Hwy., 931/381-4500, www.richlandinn-columbia.com, $65–135) is a 107-room inn with singles, doubles, and suites. There is a continental breakfast and a family restaurant next door.

A host of motels are found around exit 46 on I-65, about 10 miles east of Columbia. They include **Comfort Inn** (1544 Bear Creek Pk., 931/388-2500, $75–100) and **Holiday Inn Express** (1558 Bear Creek Pk., 931/380-1227, $75–120).

Food

Located on the courthouse square, **Square Market and Cafe** (35 Public Sq., 931/840-3636, www.squaremarketcafe.com, Mon.–Thurs. 9 A.M.–4 P.M., Fri. 9 A.M.–9 P.M., Sat. 10:30 A.M.–9 P.M., $6–19) serves breakfast and lunch throughout the week, and dinner on Friday and Saturday nights. The weekday menu features salads, sandwiches, and soups. The signature Polk's Roasted Pear Salad of greens, blue cheese, walnuts, and roasted-pear vinaigrette is a favorite for lunch. Heartier appetites can choose hot steamed sandwiches or the Tennessee Hot Brown, a hot open-faced turkey sandwich topped with white sauce, cheddar cheese, and bacon. The café brews good coffee, and the desserts are homemade. Weekend dinner includes entrées like baked salmon with dill caper sauce, spinach-and-garlic ravioli, and Eastern Shore crab cakes. There is live music, too.

For country cooking, hearty breakfasts, and plate-lunch specials, head to **Bucky's Family Restaurant** (1102 Carmack Blvd., 931/381-2834, daily 5 A.M.–2 P.M., $4–12).

Considered one of the best steak houses in the area, **The Ole Lamplighter Inn** (1000 Riverside Dr., 931/381-3837, Mon.–Sat. 4:30–9 P.M., $10–26) will satisfy the biggest appetite with charbroiled steak, all-you-can-eat soup and salad buffet, bottomless soft drinks, plus seafood and shrimp options. The Lamplighter looks a bit like a log cabin from the outside, and inside it has a low-light tavern feel that hastens relaxation. Come here to enjoy good food at good prices.

Information

The **Maury County Visitors Bureau** (8 Public Sq., 888/852-1860, www.antebellum.com) operates a **visitors center** (931/840-8324, Mon.–Sat. 9 A.M.–4 P.M.) across the street from the James K. Polk house. There's also a free iPhone app with more details on what to see in Columbia.

MOUNT PLEASANT

A few miles down Highway 43 from Columbia is the small town of Mount Pleasant. Once known as the Phosphate Capital of the World, Mount Pleasant is now a quiet town with an unusually large number of beautiful antebellum homes. Many of them were built with money earned from the phosphate industry. During the early boom years of the 1890s, the promise of quick money attracted hundreds of men to work in the mines. Law and order was haphazard until a Texas Ranger named Captain Russell arrived.

Sights
HISTORIC BUILDINGS IN TOWN

You can learn about the phosphate industry at the **Mount Pleasant/Maury County Phosphate Museum** (Public Sq., 931/379-9511, Mon.–Sat. 9:30 A.M.–4:30 P.M., free, donations accepted). In addition to information about phosphate, the museum houses artifacts of local history, Civil War memorabilia, and local crafts.

Mount Pleasant has a nice variety of historic homes, but most are closed to the public. The **Breckenridge Hatter's Shop** (205 N. Main St.), believed to be the oldest building still standing in town, is an original log cabin covered with weatherboarding in the 1920s. It is on the National Register of Historic Places. The **Price-Jackson House** (209 N. Main St.) was built in 1849 and served as an insurance office for many years.

A few blocks away from the town square, Pleasant Street is home to at least three elegant old homes. **Manor Hall** (300 Pleasant St.) once sat on a property of more than 1,200 acres. Martin Luther Stockard had it built in 1859 for his second wife, using money he inherited from his first wife and her brother. The **John Ruhm-Graham Home** (106 Pleasant St.) was built in 1910 for Mr. John Ruhm, one of the "captains of the phosphate industry." It has the only elevator in Mount Pleasant. The **Jenkins-Bradburn House** (104 Pleasant St.) is a three-story log house built in 1917.

Drive northward on Main Street (Highway 243) to find more stately homes. **Walnut Grove** (510 N. Main St.) was built in 1858 and includes a detached kitchen believed to be the oldest brick building in Mount Pleasant. Inside, ash floors are laid at random widths.

RATTLE AND SNAP

Considered by some to be the finest antebellum home in Tennessee, Rattle and Snap (1522 N. Main St./Hwy. 243, 931/379-1700, www.rattleandsnapplantation.com, adults $20, children 7-12 $8 for groups of 2-3, adults $15, children 7-12 $8 for groups of 4-14, adults $13, children 7-12 $8 for groups of 15 or more, children under 7 free) was built by George Washington Polk in 1845. Its extravagance was unmatched by any other home of the period: The 10 Corinthian columns that stand at the front of the mansion were made in Cincinnati, shipped by steamboat to Nashville, and brought overland by oxcart to Maury County. The marble mantels came from Italy, the gardens were designed by a German landscape architect, and a glorious Waterford chandelier hangs over the dining room table. The fine craftsmanship throughout the home is attributed to slaves who labored on the construction.

The story goes that Rattle and Snap was named after an eponymous popular game of the period involving dried beans that were rattled and rolled with a snap of the fingers. Polk claimed that he won the land on which the mansion sits in a rattle and snap game with the governor of North Carolina.

The house was spared during the Civil War, reportedly after the Union commander and field captain noticed that Polk was wearing a Masonic ring in his portrait. Polk's wealth did not survive the war, however, and in 1867 he sold the property to J. J. Granberry, who occupied the home for 50 years and renamed it Oakwood Hall. In 1919 it changed hands again, and for many years tenant farmers lived in the deteriorating mansion. Rattle and Snap owes its restoration to Amon Carter Evans, former publisher of the *Tennessean*.

Today, Rattle and Snap is open year-round for group tours of two people or more. Tours must be booked and paid for in advance. Overnight guests are also welcome at its Carriage House, and special events are hosted here. Even without a tour, you can admire the property from the highway.

Accommodations

Sleep in the Carriage House at **Rattle and Snap Plantation** (1522 N. Main St./Hwy. 243, 931/379-1700, www.rattleandsnapplantation.com, $250 for up to two guests, $25 for each additional person), and you will enjoy your own private tour of one of the state's most famous antebellum homes. The Carriage House is a three-bedroom guesthouse located at the rear of the mansion. It includes two queen-size bedrooms and a sleeping loft with two twin beds. There is also a kitchen, sitting room, and patio where guests can relax and prepare meals. No children are allowed, and smoking is not permitted. There is a two-night minimum stay.

HOHENWALD

The unassuming county seat of Lewis County, Hohenwald developed in the 1890s when a railroad was built through rural Lewis County. Starting in 1895, immigrants from Switzerland moved to the area as part of a settlement scheme advanced by a Swiss American developer, J. G. Probst. The immigrants laid out and built New Switzerland immediately adjacent to the older town of Hohenwald. The two communities are now united.

For many years, the Alpine character of Hohenwald was evident. A Swiss Singing Society was formed, and Swiss and German Reformed Churches held services in German. The European heritage survived until World War II, when anti-German sentiment caused many to abandon their cultural heritage. Today, traces of Hohenwald's Alpine heritage are faint, having been supplanted by those of Middle Tennessee.

Meriwether Lewis Gravesite and Memorial

Lewis County is named for Meriwether Lewis,

THE ELEPHANT SANCTUARY

Tucked into the rural landscape of central Tennessee near the small town of Hohenwald, more than 20 African and Asian elephants retired from circuses and zoos have found refuge.

The Elephant Sanctuary at Hohenwald is a licensed and enlightened nonprofit program that provides a place where retired elephants can live peacefully and as naturally as possible.

The sanctuary was established in 1995 and has grown with support from donors and grants. Today it is a 2,700-acre park with a heated barn (this is the South, but it can get cold in January) and a spring-fed lake. There are presently more than 20 elephants living at the sanctuary. They spend their days walking around, interacting with each other, eating, and being bathed or cared for in other ways.

In 2006, elephant caregiver Joanna Burke was killed in a tragic accident when Winkie, one of the sanctuary elephants, knocked her over and stepped on her. The elephant was apparently afraid that Joanna would touch her right eye, which had been stung and was swollen and painful. Elephant experts say that Winkie's behavior was consistent with posttraumatic stress disorder, which has been diagnosed in other retired zoo and circus elephants.

Burke's death was a sad event for the sanctuary, but in keeping with the wishes of Burke and her family, Winkie was not put to sleep, although new protocols were established for animals with a history of aggression. Burke is buried at the elephant sanctuary.

Visitors are not allowed at the elephant sanctuary (unless you are a major donor), but you can watch live elephant cams on their website at www.elephants.com. The sanctuary is planning to build a visitors center once it raises the necessary funds.

the U.S. army captain and private secretary to President Thomas Jefferson, who is best known as the leader, along with William Clark, of the Lewis and Clark expedition to the Pacific Ocean from 1805 to 1806. His gravesite and a memorial sit along the Natchez Trace Parkway about seven miles east of Hohenwald. This is where Lewis died, under mysterious circumstances, while traveling the Trace bound for Washington DC in 1809.

According to accounts, Lewis, who was appointed governor of the Louisiana Territory following his successful expedition, was upset by accusation of financial mismanagement. He was traveling to Washington to clear his name, and on the night of October 11, 1809, he stayed at Grinder's Stand, a homestead whose owners boarded travelers along the Trace. In the morning, Lewis was found shot to death in his bed. His death was called a suicide, although a few months later a friend came to investigate the circumstances and pronounced that Lewis was murdered. Lewis was just 35 years old when he died.

While the circumstances of Lewis's death remain a mystery, his legacy remains alive. Several monuments to him have been erected at and around his gravesite, and a modest museum tells the story of his life.

The Meriwether Lewis site is located at the intersection of the Natchez Trace Parkway and U.S. 20. There is a campground, picnic area, and restroom nearby.

Natural Bridge

Hidden away at the privately owned and operated **Tennessee Fitness Spa and Retreat** (299 Natural Bridge Rd., 931/722-5589, www.tfspa.com) is one of this area's most remarkable natural attractions, a double-span natural bridge.

Here a tributary of the Buffalo River has etched away at the bedrock for thousands of years, eventually creating a natural bridge formation that is marvelous to look at.

The bridge invites exploration. You can walk along the side of the trickling stream and climb up to view the bridge from above. The sight of layer upon layer of rock, which has been carved out over many thousands of years, is remarkable.

A few hundred yards from the natural bridge is a small cave, also open to visitors. Lights have been placed inside to make it easy to explore.

Natural Bridge is located along State Route 99, between Hohenwald and Waynesboro. Tennessee Fitness allows the public to visit Natural Bridge and the cave on Sunday only. Come between 9 A.M. and 5 P.M. and check in at the office first. Admission is free.

Buffalo River
The Buffalo River, a tributary of the Duck River, flows through northern Wayne County. It is a picturesque and placid river, ideal for canoeing.

Located on Highway 13 where it crosses the Buffalo, **Clearwater Canoe Rental** (931/722-3081, www.clearwatercanoes.com) offers canoe rentals, an RV park, and rustic cabins. A four-hour float costs $35 per canoe; discounts are available for large groups.

Accommodations
Located about 15 minutes from Mount Pleasant in Hampshire, **Ridgetop Bed and Breakfast** (Hwy. 412, 931/285-2777, $85–105) is a rural getaway with a standard guest room and two private cottages. The cottages are unique: The Swiss Cottage is a postage-stamp-size Swiss chalet with a queen-size bed downstairs and sleeping loft with two additional beds upstairs. The log cabin evokes frontier life, but with modern amenities including air-conditioning and a private bathroom. All meals are served in the main dining room.

Food
The **General Cafe** (101 Park Ave. N., 931/796-3990, Mon.–Thurs. 5 A.M.–8 P.M., Fri.–Sat. 5 A.M.–9 P.M., Sun. 5 A.M.–2 P.M., $3–7) is the best place to eat in Hohenwald and a good place to meet lots of people. The menu has burgers and sandwiches, catfish, and daily plate-lunch specials, like meat loaf, chicken and dressing, and baked chicken. For breakfast, have the ham and eggs with biscuits.

THE FARM
In 1970, hippie spiritual leader Stephen Gaskin and 320 others established a commune in the rural countryside near Summertown, Tennessee. Initially governed by beliefs that forbade alcohol and birth control and promoted nonviolence and respect for the environment, the Farm has evolved over the years. While it has loosened some rules, it remains committed to peace, justice, and environmental sustainability.

The Farm (Summertown, 931/964-3574, www.thefarmcommunity.com) has established a number of successful businesses, and it has contributed to its mission for a more peaceful and healthy world. Its businesses include a book publishing company, a soy dairy that manufactures tofu and soy milk, and a yoga studio. Farm books include *The Farm Vegetarian Cookbook* and Ina May Gaskin's works on natural childbirth. Nonprofits on the Farm include Plenty International, an international aid organization, and the Farm School, which provides alternative education for primary through secondary grades.

The Farm is glad to receive visitors. The Ecovillage Training Center puts on workshops and conferences throughout the year, many of them dealing with organic gardening, permaculture, construction, and other sustainable technologies. The Farm also operates a midwifery training center and birthing houses where women can come to give birth.

About 200 people live at the Farm today. A few have been there since the beginning, but there are also recent transplants. Some work at Farm enterprises, but others have jobs "off the Farm." Farm members become shareholders in the company that owns the Farm land and other assets.

Visiting the Farm

The Farm is a welcoming and friendly place where people wave at each other and you can strike up a conversation with just about anybody. The **Welcome Center** (100 Farm Rd., Mon.–Fri. 1–4 P.M., reduced hours Nov.–Mar.) has a museum about the community and sells Farm books, T-shirts, and other products. It is a good idea to call ahead to confirm hours. You can arrange for a tour with a member of the Farm by calling the welcome center. There are also twice-yearly Farm Experience weekends for people who want to see what Farm living is about.

The **Farm Store** (931/964-4356, daily 9 A.M.–7 P.M.) sells organic and natural groceries, household items, vegetarian sandwiches, and drinks.

Accommodations

You can sleep the night at the Farm. The **Inn at the Farm** (184 Schoolhouse Rd., Summertown, www.thefarm.org, 931/964-4474, $12) is part of the Ecovillage Training Center, and it offers dormitory-style accommodations. Reservations are required, and the inn is sometimes full when there are workshops or conferences under way.

A half dozen Farm residents rent out rooms to visitors, usually for about $40–80 a night. Meals may be available for an additional fee. There is also a campground, where you can pitch your own tent for about $16. For more information about staying at the Farm, call the welcome center or go online.

Getting There

The Farm is located off Drake's Lane Road, a few miles west of Summertown along Route 20. Detailed directions and a map are available on the Farm website.

ETHRIDGE

In 1944, three Amish families moved to the countryside near Ethridge, in rural Lawrence County. According to some accounts, they came

seeking a place where they would not be required to send their children to large, consolidated secondary schools. They also were in search of land where they could farm and make a home.

Over the years the Amish population in Lawrence County has waxed and waned, with estimates of 100–200 families now. The Amish are known for their conservative dress; rejection of modern technology, including electricity; and their preference to keep to themselves. They are also excellent farmers, craftsmen, and cooks; devout Christians; and peace lovers. Most of the Amish in this part of Tennessee speak English and Pennsylvania Dutch, and some also know German.

As you drive through the back roads that crisscross the Amish area, you will be able to identify the Amish homes because they are old-fashioned farmhouses without electricity wires, cars, or mechanized farm equipment. You will also notice their fields of corn, peanuts, wheat, tobacco, hay, and oats, and you may see a black horse-drawn buggy—their primary form of transportation.

Many Amish sell goods, ranging from handmade furniture to molasses. As you drive, you will see signs advertising various products for sale. You are welcome to stop by and buy something. Remember that due to their religious beliefs, the Amish do not allow their pictures to be taken. Please respect this fact when you visit them.

If you prefer, you can explore Amish country with a guide on a wagon tour. Such tours are offered by local Lawrence County residents who are not Amish. Each tour lasts about 90 minutes and will take you to several farms where you can meet the Amish and buy products from them. Tours are provided twice daily Monday–Saturday at 10 A.M. and 3:30 P.M. by the **Amish Country Store** (4011 Hwy. 43 N., 931/829-1621). The rate is $10 for adults. You can also call **Jerry's Amish Buggy and Wagon Tours** (931/629-5055).

If you want to drive through on your own, start in Ethridge and explore the narrow back roads bounded by Highway 43 on the east, State Route 242 on the west, Highway 20 on the north, and U.S. 64 on the south. You can pick up a free detailed map of Amish country, with specific farms identified, from the **Lawrence Chamber of Commerce** (1609 Locust Ave./Hwy. 43, 931/762-4911, www. selectlawrence.com). You can also buy a map from the **Amish Country Mall** (4011 Hwy 43 N., 931/829-1621) for $3.

A half dozen stores along Highway 43 just north of Ethridge sell Amish-made goods for those who don't have time to venture into Amish territory themselves. One of the best is **Dutch Country Bakery** (3939 Hwy. 43 N., 931/829-2147, Mon.–Sat. 7 A.M.–5 P.M.), which sells Amish baked goods, cheeses, and bulk goods. It also serves breakfast and lunch daily.

The Amish work Monday–Saturday. Sunday is their Sabbath, the day that they worship and spend time with family. You won't find Amish farm stands or homes open for business on Sunday.

LAWRENCEBURG

Lawrenceburg is the seat of Lawrence County, named for a U.S. naval hero of the War of 1812. Built along the Jackson Military Road, Lawrenceburg has long been a center of trade and commerce for the surrounding countryside. It is the hometown of former Tennessee senator, actor, and unsuccessful presidential aspirant Fred Thompson.

Sights

Founded in 2003 by local Cherokee, the **Cherokee and Davy Crockett Museum** (1 Public Sq., 931/762 3733, Mon.–Sat. 9:30 A.M.–4 P.M., free) seeks to preserve the heritage of Lawrence County's Native Americans. It also pays tribute to Davy Crockett, who lived in Lawrence County for about four years and won his first elective office, as justice of the peace, while there.

You can see a replica of Davy Crockett's

office at the **Davy Crockett Museum,** located one block south of the public square. It is free and open daily during daylight hours.

The man who popularized Southern gospel music called Lawrenceburg home, and the town has remembered him with a museum. The **James D. Vaughan Museum** (SunTrust Bank Bldg., Public Sq., 931/762-8991, http://vaughanmuseum.tripod.com, Mon.–Fri. 9:30–11:30 A.M. and 1–2:30 P.M., weekends by appointment, free) tells the story of its namesake, who sponsored and recorded the first professional gospel quartets and established the first Southern gospel magazine and radio station. He also established the Vaughn School of Music, where he taught students to sing, and published millions of shape-note songbooks. Vaughn has been called the father of Southern gospel music, and Lawrenceburg has been declared its birthplace.

Festivals and Events

Taking place in early June and again over Labor Day weekend, the **Summertown Bluegrass Reunion** (64 Monument Rd., Summertown, 931/964-2100, www.summertownbluegrassreunion.com, Fri. $8, Sat. $10) is an authentic showcase of homegrown bluegrass music. Bring your lawn chair and take a seat under the canopy of trees to enjoy a seemingly limitless smorgasbord of bluegrass music. During the late afternoons, the main stage closes for an hour for a shade-tree band contest, a real case of dueling banjos. The audience picks the winner. Dance for fun, or in one of the afternoon buck dancing contests.

The bluegrass reunions take place at a private campground in Summertown, located about 13 miles north of Lawrenceburg. Most festival attendees camp in RVs on the grounds; tents are also allowed.

Accommodations

Choose from a handful of standard-issue motels

in Lawrenceburg. The **Best Western/Villa Inn** (2126 N. Locust Ave./Hwy. 43, 931/762-4448, $65–80) has been refurbished, is pet friendly, and has free wireless Internet. The **Richland Inn** (2125 N. Locust Ave./Hwy. 43, 931/762-0061, $60–75) has double and king-size rooms, plus executive suites. Rooms have cable TV, in-room dataports, and irons. There is a free continental breakfast, a business center, and plenty of RV and truck parking.

Food

Square Forty Restaurant (40 Public Sq., 931/762-2868, Sun.–Fri. 7 A.M.–2 P.M., Sat. noon–2 P.M., $5–15) serves traditional Southern food and a popular Sunday-morning buffet, and a view of a statue of Davy Crockett.

Information

Visitor information for Lawrenceburg and Lawrence County is available from the **Cherokee and Davy Crockett Museum** (1 Public Sq., 931/762-3733). The **Lawrence County Chamber of Commerce** (1609 Locust Ave./Hwy 43, 931/762-4911, www.selectlawrence.com) publishes brochures and has information about local businesses and attractions.

DAVID CROCKETT STATE PARK

One of Lawrenceburg's earliest residents was also one of its most famous. David Crockett, the larger-than-life frontiersman who seems to have been everywhere in Tennessee, was one of Lawrenceburg's first commissioners and justices of the peace. He and his family operated a gristmill, powder mill, and distillery on the Shoal River a few miles west of town starting in 1817. In 1821, after a flood swept away their home and businesses, the Crocketts moved to northwest Tennessee, where Crockett was elected to Congress. Crockett died in 1836 at the Alamo Mission. The place where he lived in Lawrence County is now the David Crockett State Park (1400 W. Gaines, Lawrenceburg, www.

tn.gov/environment/parks/DavidCrockettSP, 931/762-9408, daily 7 A.M.–dark).

Recreation

David Crockett is a pleasant park with a lot of amenities, including picnic tables, tennis courts, a restaurant, and an Olympic-size swimming pool. Crockett Falls is a pleasant place for a picnic.

You can rent paddleboats or fishing boats to explore 40-acre Lindsey Lake (no private boats are allowed). Fishing is permitted from the lake banks or from a boat; people older than 13 need a valid Tennessee fishing license, and everyone must follow state regulations. There is a paved 2.3-mile bike trail and three different hiking trails.

Festivals and Events

Davy Crockett and the pioneer spirit that he symbolizes is celebrated during **Davy Crockett Days** (931/762-9408), a two-day festival that takes place in early October at David Crockett State Park. Festival enthusiasts spend the weekend dressed in period costumes and do things that Crockett and his contemporaries would have. Activities include shooting, games, music, food, and old-time traders.

Camping

There are 107 campsites, each with a picnic table, fire pit, and electrical and water hookups for RVs. Bathhouses have hot showers and commodes. As is the case with all Tennessee State campgrounds, sites are allocated on a first-come, first-served basis only.

WATERTOWN

Quaint Watertown (615/237-0270, www.watertowntn.com) has a charming downtown filled with shops and restaurants, fueled by **Historic Watertown, Inc.** (615/237-9999), an organization that works hard to keep it that way. Some days Watertown can come off as sleepy, but not

Watertown is a sweet town for an afternoon stroll.

when the **Tennessee Central Railway** (www. tcry.org) drops off a trainload of passengers for lunch, shopping, and a good old-fashioned shoot-out. The Fourth of July festivities include a squirt gun parade. Nashvillians make this 40-minute drive to go to a real drive-in movie.

Entertainment

The **Stardust Drive-In Theatre** (310 Purple Tiger Dr., 615/237-0077, www.stardustdrivein. com, adults $7.50, children $5) is just like you remember. Or, just like you remember hearing about drive-ins. The Stardust plays first-run flicks after dark; prices include a double feature. There's no sneaking in folks in the trunk; price is per person, not carload. And no sneaking outside food, either. You must buy from the concession stand or pay a $6 outside food permit. Fortunately, the concession stand has decent choices, including Philly cheesesteak and pizza. Once you get past the rules, this is good, clean old-fashioned fun. If you are using

a GPS, enter "201 Tennessee Boulevard"; the Purple Tiger address often does not come up.

Shopping

Watertown's Public Square, at the intersection of Main and Depot Streets, is surrounded by antiques stores, jewelers, artisans, and others who set up in storefronts. These vendors change often, and many don't have predictable hours, but they are certain to be open during Watertown events, such as when the train rolls in. Standouts include Susan Thornton's **Thornton Metals Studio** (100 Public Sq., www. thorntonmetals.com) and **Jim's Antiques** (312 Public Sq., 615/237-1777).

Accommodations

On a street between the train tracks and Main Street sits the beautiful **Watertown B&B** (116 Depot Ave., 615/478-1678, www.watertown-bandb.com, $70–125). The building used to be the railroad hotel and oozes history in every

MIDDLE TENNESSEE

corner. Each of the bed-and-breakfast's four rooms are named after a place that the owners, Sharon and Bob McComb, have lived. This bed-and-breakfast offers the unusual combo of both a bicycle built for two for use by guests and access to RV parking.

Food

The oft-crowded **Depot Junction Café** (108 Depot Ave., 615/237-3976, Mon.–Sat. 5 A.M.–8 P.M., $3–12) is known for its cheese sticks, burgers, and milk shakes. When there is a special event in Watertown, expect a wait, as this is one of the places visitors stop first.

Nona Lisa Pizzeria (208 E. Main St., 615/237-0102, Wed.–Thurs. 4–9 P.M., Fri.–Sun. 11 A.M.–9 P.M., $10–22) caters to families, vegetarians, and others looking for something other than Southern classics. Locals love the plum chicken, made with locally grown plums.

Walking Horse Country

The countryside surrounding Shelbyville is the capital of the Tennessee Walking Horse. The beloved high-stepping creatures known for their smooth gait are bred and shown at farms that dot the rolling hills of south-central Tennessee. The annual Walking Horse National Celebration is one of the largest horse shows in the world. Small towns Wartrace and Bell Buckle are two of the most charming in the whole of Middle Tennessee.

The Tennessee Walking Horse Parkway

Highway 31A from Pulaski to Lewisburg, and Highway 64 from Lewisburg to Wartrace, via Shelbyville, has been designated the Tennessee Walking Horse Parkway, and it is the best scenic route through this beautiful terrain. You will pass dozens of horse farms—some large and some small—and you will see some of the handsome horses out grazing in the field.

LEWISBURG

Lewisburg is best known for two very different animals: the Tennessee Walking Horse and the fainting goats of Marshall County. Lewisburg is the home of the business end of the famous horse breed: It is here that the Tennessee Walking Horse Breeders' and Exhibitors' Association is located. As for the goats, the story goes that in the 1880s, a mysterious man named Tinsley moved to Marshall County with four goats and a cow. He stayed for only one growing season, and when he left, he sold his "bulgy-eyed" goats to a local doctor. The goats displayed a strange habit of becoming rigid to the point of losing their balance when startled. Over the years, the fainting goats reproduced. It is now known that their condition is a neurological abnormality called mytonia, which doesn't harm the animals.

Downtown Lewisburg is set around the 1920s-era courthouse. On the north side of the square you'll find one of the most unusual buildings in all of Tennessee. The **Ladies' Rest Room** on 3rd Avenue was built in 1924 to accommodate rural women who traveled to town to shop or sell goods. The building included a reception room, toilets, a bedroom, and a kitchen. In his excellent guide to the area, Judge Robert Brant quotes an unsigned letter received at the county court not long after the restroom was built:

> In behalf of the ladies of the county, I desire to thank the gentlemen of the County Court for the beautiful restroom they have given us.... We praise this beautiful gift, not merely for its beauty and many conveniences but because it shows

VANNOY STREETER'S WIRE HORSES

Self-taught folk artist Vannoy "Wireman" Streeter (1919-1998) drew inspiration for his life's work from the elegant stride and unique step of the Tennessee Walking Horse. Born in Wartrace in 1919 and raised on a horse farm, Streeter first displayed his remarkable talent as a child. His family could not afford to buy toy airplanes and cars, so he made them—bending them out of bailing wire.

Streeter was in Wartrace for the first Walking Horse Celebration, and in later years he returned to the event after it moved to Shelbyville. Streeter was proud of the fact that African Americans trained Strolling Jim and many other world-champion Walking Horses. He created hundreds, if not thousands, of sculpted horses, each with the distinctive high-stepping front leg and each with an African American rider on the back. Other favorite subjects were performers—he sculpted Tina Turner and Elvis Presley in particular—and vehicles, including big-rig trucks, locomotives, and airplanes.

Streeter made most of his sculptures out of coat-hanger wire; he bought hangers by the hundreds. He did detail work with fine-gauge wire and large scale work with bracing wire. He worked with regular pliers, wire cutters, and needle-nose pliers.

Streeter worked on the railroads and as a lumberyard hand, janitor, and hospital orderly. In 1960 he met and married his wife, Marie, and became father to her six children. He continued to make his wire sculptures, eventually gaining national attention. In 1990 he was a demonstrating artist at the National Black Arts Festival in Atlanta. Shelbyville proclaimed April 25, 1992 Vannoy Streeter Day. His work has been displayed in the White House and at the Tennessee State Museum in Nashville.

Streeter continued to work until his death in 1998, although his productivity declined after his wife's death. His work is sold in folk art galleries in Nashville and other cities, and has been included in African American and folk art exhibits in Tennessee and elsewhere.

---

that the women of the county are held in love and honored by our men.

Today, the restroom is no longer open to the public and is in disrepair, although efforts are being made to preserve it.

Entertainment and Events

The **Marshall County Community Theater** operates in the historic Dixie Theater (www.dixietheatre.org) on the east side of the town square. Check local listings or contact the chamber of commerce to find out about upcoming performances.

There is an authentic 1940s-era drive-in movie theater less than two miles out of town. The **Hi-way 50 Drive In** (1584 Fayetteville Hwy., 931/270-1591) screens first-run movies Friday, Saturday, and Sunday evenings. For just $5 for adults and $2 for children, guests get to see back-to-back movies at this vintage drive-in

theater. The sound system is modern, however (it's tuned to your car radio). There is a concession stand that sells burgers, fries, pizza, and popcorn, but patrons are also welcome to bring their own food. This is a popular weekend treat for local residents.

To celebrate Marshall County's fainting goats, the city of Lewisburg hosts the **Goats, Music, and More Festival** (931/359-1544, www.goatsmusicandmore.com) in October. The free two-day fair features goat shows, arts and crafts displays, live music, and a barbecue cook-off. In the evening major country music and rock acts perform at the town's Rock Creek Park.

Information

For information about Lewisburg, contact the **Marshall County Chamber of Commerce** (227 2nd Ave. N., 931/359-3863, www.marshallchamber.org),

MIDDLE TENNESSEE

HENRY HORTON STATE PARK

A few miles north of Lewisburg, near the small town of Chapel Hill, is Henry Horton State Park (4358 Nashville Hwy., 931/364-2222). The park is known for its 18-hole championship golf course, skeet range, and inn and conference facilities.

Park amenities include an on-site restaurant that serves country-style meals and buffets, an Olympic-size swimming pool (inn and cabin guests swim free), hiking trails, and a gift shop.

The park's 18-hole **Buford Ellington golf course** (931/364-2319) is a popular destination for golfers in the region. It has a pro shop, dressing rooms, rental clubs, gasoline and pull carts, a driving range, and a practice green. Greens fees are $14–24, depending on the season and day of the week.

Day-trippers can also enjoy the skeet range, fishing on the Duck River, picnics, horseshoes, tennis courts, volleyball, basketball, and table tennis.

Accommodations

Accommodations include the park inn, with motel-style rooms; a campground with both tent and RV sites; and seven cabins ideal for families or small groups. Rooms at the park inn rent for $65–80, depending on the season and day of the week. Rooms are air-conditioned and come with a television and telephone. Cabins, which are fully equipped for cooking and housekeeping, rent for $110 a night. Campsites are available for $14.50 or $17.50, depending on the season, but cannot be reserved in advance.

SHELBYVILLE

If any one Tennessee city is home to the Tennessee Walking Horse, it is Shelbyville. Considered the world's greatest pleasure, trail, and show horse, the Tennessee Walking Horse is the first breed of horse to bear the name of a state. Tennessee Walkers existed for many years before the breed was identified and named; early settlers needed horses that could travel easily and comfortably over rocky and uneven terrain. These early Walkers were not trained to show—they were purely utilitarian.

Tennessee Walkers are known for their docile temperament and kind manner. They are also known for their unique running walk—in which each of the horse's hooves hit the ground separately at regular intervals. In this gait, the animal's front legs rise in an exaggerated step, and the horse's head nods in time with the rhythm of its legs.

Sights

A few miles east of Shelbyville on Highway 64 is **Waterfall Farms** (2395 Hwy. 64 E., 931/684-7894, www.waterfallfarms.com), one of the few horse farms in this area with an open-door policy on visitors. Just drive on in and check in at the office, where you can ask questions and see photographs of some of the farm's award-winning stallions. You are welcome to walk around the farm and see the magnificent horses, who may be out in the field, in their stables, or otherwise occupied.

For information on other farms that welcome visitors, or opportunities to ride a Tennessee Walking Horse, contact the **Walking Horse Owners' Association** in Murfreesboro at 615/494-8822.

One of only two wineries in the region, **Tri-Star Vineyards and Winery** (168 Scales Rd., 931/294-3062, www.tristarwinery.com, Fri.–Sat. 10 A.M.–5 P.M., Sun. noon–5 P.M., closed Jan., major holidays, and some postholiday weekends) is located about seven miles north of Shelbyville, off Highway 41A. In operation for more than 40 years, Tri-Star makes wines from grapes, muscadines, berries, and fruit.

◖ Tennessee Walking Horse National Celebration

The premier event in Shelbyville is the annual Tennessee Walking Horse National Celebration (931/684-5915, www.twhnc.com), which takes

© JOHN I. CARNEY/SHELBYVILLE GAZETTE

More than 2,000 horses (and riders) compete in the Tennessee Walking Horse National Celebration.

place in late summer for 11 days, ending on the Saturday before Labor Day. This is the event that determines the best of the high-stepping Walking Horses, and it is an exciting time to be a horse fan.

The national celebration routinely attracts 30,000 people per night and more than 5,000 entries. The event takes place at the Celebration Grounds, a few blocks from the courthouse square in Shelbyville.

The Celebration was founded in 1939 as a way to promote Tennessee Walkers. It is an economic experiment that worked. Prize money now tops the half-million-dollar mark, and organizers boast that more than a quarter million tickets are sold over the 11-day event. Winning a show at the Celebration makes a horse more valuable and cements its reputation in the industry.

For horse lovers, the Celebration is exciting and beautiful. For breeders and horse farmers, it is their chance to make it in this competitive and high-stakes business. For the city of Shelbyville and the whole region, it is an economic powerhouse, pumping more than $20 million into the local economy every year.

The Celebration Grounds are used for other horse shows, plus sporting and musical events, year-round. The Nashville Symphony has played here, and shows featuring alpaca, miniature horses, and ponies take place.

Tickets for reserved seats at the Celebration range $7–20 per night, and a pass for the whole event is $100. Box seats are more expensive, while general admission tickets to the South Grandstand are cheaper. While tickets for the best seats must be reserved in advance, you can almost always get a seat at the Celebration, even if you show up on the day of the event.

Accommodations

Located within walking distance of the Celebration Grounds in Shelbyville, **Cinnamon Ridge Bed and Breakfast** (799 Whithorne St., 931/685-9200, $65–75) is a five-bedroom guesthouse. Each room has a private bath and television; provisions may be made for a private telephone, daily newspaper, and other services that appeal to business travelers. Full breakfast is served in your choice of the formal dining room or the sunny garden room. There is also a family room, patio, and backyard deck where you can unwind.

Also within walking distance of the Celebration Grounds, the **Bedford Inn** (727 Madison St., 931/684-7858, $40) is a stalwart motel with clean and comfortable rooms. Amenities include televisions, telephones, microwaves and refrigerators, and plenty of parking.

You will enjoy privacy in a rural setting at the **Tennessee Horse Country Bed and Breakfast** (311 Robinson Rd., 931/684-1863, www.tennesseehorsecountry.com, $55–145), located on a horse farm about eight miles south

MIDDLE TENNESSEE

of Shelbyville along Highway 231. The property has a guesthouse that sleeps up to four people, with a whirlpool tub, full kitchen, living room, and porch, as well as a smaller cottage with a queen-size bed, full bath, and kitchenette. Both accommodations are entirely private. Your kitchen will be stocked with breakfast foods if you request.

Immerse yourself in the world of the Tennessee Walking Horse at the **☾ Clearview Horse Farm** (2291 Hwy. 231 S., 931/684-8822, www.clearviewhorsefarm.com, $65–125). This working horse farm has an indoor area for horse shows, a comfortable and modern barn, and horse trainers. There are three guest rooms at the farm, each with a private bath. The rooms are modern and neat, with ranch-like touches. The Tennessee Walking Horse Room can sleep up to four and would be ideal for families. Guests can enjoy a pool on the property, as well as a fishing lake. There is a continental breakfast. Many guests here are horse owners themselves, although "nonhorseys" are welcome, too.

Located in the countryside between Lewisburg and Shelbyville, **Haha Farm** (482 Cortner Hollow Rd., Petersburg, 931/680-0423, www.hahafarm.com, $80–90) is a working alpaca and llama farm. The guest room is modest, but the experience here is one of a kind. Breakfast is served family-style, and you are invited to explore the farm and meet its unusual residents. The farmhand special offers accommodation at a reduced rate ($60 per night) in exchange for three hours of work on the farm. On the other side of the spectrum is the farm spa pampering special, which includes a daily massage, for about $145 a night. Owners Steve and Kathie Haber warn that alpacas and llamas are addictive, and that your first llama kiss might well change your life.

Food

For coffee and other pick-me-ups, try **The Coffee Break** (121 South Side Sq., 931/680-2552, Mon.–Fri. 7 A.M.–3 P.M., Sat. 8 A.M.–3 P.M., $4–7).

WARTRACE

This tiny railroad town about 10 miles east of Shelbyville is the birthplace of the Tennessee Walking Horse. It was on the grounds of the town's Walking Horse Hotel, across the railroad tracks from the town square, that Albert Dement trained a $350 plow horse into **Strolling Jim,** the first world grand champion Walking Horse. Strolling Jim died in 1957 and is buried in the pasture behind the hotel.

The annual Walking Horse celebration that now draws a quarter million people to Shelbyville every year started in Wartrace, but it got too big for the small town and moved to Shelbyville in 1935.

Today, Wartrace is a sleepy yet pleasing town. The old residential district lies along a few quiet side streets that climb gently along a hillside. The howl of frequent freight trains—20–25 pass through daily—harkens to an earlier era.

Shopping

In certain circles, the name J. W. Gallagher is well known. Gallagher was born near Wartrace in 1915 and opened a woodworking shop in 1939. Skilled at furniture and cabinet making, Gallagher's guitars are what made him famous. From 1969 onwards Gallagher only made guitars. In 1976, Gallagher's son, Don, took over the business. There are not many Gallagher guitars out there—between 1965 and 1990 just over 2,000 were made—because each heirloom instrument is handcrafted from beginning to end. **Gallagher's Guitar Shop** (5 Main St., 931/389-6455, www.gallagherguitar.com) is an otherwise nondescript storefront with the word *Gallagher's* on the front.

Accommodations

The **☾ Walking Horse Hotel** (101 Spring St., 931/389-7030, www.walkinghorsehotel.

com, $100) is the best place to stay not only in Wartrace, but for a good distance in any direction. When Joe Peters bought the hotel in 2007, he was intent on paying tribute to his late wife, Chais, who loved the old 1917 hotel. Peters and his family have brought new life to the old hotel by refurbishing the rooms, recruiting beloved chef Bill Hall to run the Strolling Jim Restaurant, and opening the Chais Music Hall, a state-of-the-art venue for all types of music. Rooms are a fusion of old and new. Classic touches from the hotel's early days have been preserved, but guests can expect the best modern amenities, including flat-screen televisions, free wireless Internet, supercomfortable beds, and good linens. The hotel, which may or may not be haunted, is not pet friendly, but they do offer pet boarding.

Food

The **Iron Gait** (106 Fairfield Rd., 931/389-6001, Mon.–Fri. 7 A.M.–2 P.M., Sat. 7 A.M.–7 P.M., Sun. 1–4 P.M., $3–8) serves breakfast, burgers, and meat and three dinners. The monster burger is a favorite, as are the plate lunches. Find the Iron Gait just around the corner from Main Street, on the road to Bell Buckle.

In spring and summer head to **Valley Home Farm** (310 Potts Rd., 931/389-6470, www.valleyhomefarm.com) to pick your own tasty strawberries.

For other dining choices, look in Bell Buckle, Normandy, and Shelbyville.

Information

The **Wartrace Chamber of Commerce** (931/389-9999, www.wartracechamber.org) promotes the town.

BELL BUCKLE

A tiny town nestled in the northern reaches of the Walking Horse region, Bell Buckle is a charming place to visit. Founded in 1852 and once a railroad town, Bell Buckle has successfully become a destination for antiques shopping, arts and crafts, small-town hospitality, and country cooking. The town's single commercial street faces the old railroad tracks; handsome old homes—some of them bed-and-breakfast inns—spread out along quiet residential streets.

What makes Bell Buckle so appealing is the sense of humor that permeates just about everything that happens here. T-shirts for sale on the main street proclaim "Tokyo, Paris, New York, Bell Buckle," and the town's quirky residents feel free to be themselves. Tennessee's poet laureate, Margaret "Maggi" Britton Vaughn, who operates the Bell Buckle Press and had an office on Main Street for many years, once told an interviewer that William Faulkner "would have killed" for a community with the ambience, and characters, of Bell Buckle.

Bell Buckle's name is derived from the Bell Buckle Creek, named thus because a cow's bell was found hanging in a tree by the creek, attached by a buckle.

The town's annual RC and Moon Pie Festival in June attracts thousands to the small town, and the well-respected Webb School Arts and Crafts Festival in October is one of the finest regional arts shows in the state. This is also home to the annual Tennessee Shakespeare Festival each summer.

Sights

Bell Buckle is noted as the home of the elite and well-regarded **Webb School** (319 Webb Rd. E., www.thewebbschool.com, 888/733-9322). Founded in 1870 and led by William Robert Webb until his death in 1926, Webb School has graduated 10 Rhodes scholars, several governors, attorneys general, and numerous successful academics. The school now has about 300 students in grades 8–12 from around the country and the world. While it was all male for many years of its life, Webb School now admits both male and female students. Its athletic mascot is the "Webb Feet."

© HANNAH L. COFFEY

The Bell Buckle Cafe is local institution.

The Webb campus is about three blocks north of downtown Bell Buckle. You can visit the main administrative office during regular business hours, where there are photographs and school memorabilia on display. Pay attention as you drive by; the speed limit in this school zone is considerably lower than that on all the nearby country roads.

Festivals and Events

Bell Buckle's biggest annual event is the **RC and Moon Pie Festival** (931/389-9663) in mid-June, a nod to one of the South's favorite culinary combos. This hilarious weekend event includes country and bluegrass music, Moon Pie games (such as the Moon Pie toss), arts and crafts booths, the crowning of a Moon Pie King and Queen, and a 10-mile run. You can also witness the cutting of the world's largest Moon Pie (and if you are willing to join the mob, you can taste it, too). In case you're wondering why Bell Buckle has rights to the Moon Pie festival, it's because they asked for it.

It is June in Tennessee, so it is almost always oppressively hot at the Moon Pie Festival, which is a good excuse to drink another RC.

The **Webb School Arts and Crafts Festival** (931/389-9663, www.bellbucklechamber.com) in October brings hundreds of artisans to town. It is one of the finest arts and crafts shows in the region, attracting fine and folk artists from Tennessee and beyond.

Since 2008 the Webb School also has hosted the **Tennessee Shakespeare Festival** (www.tennesseeshakespearefestival.com) each summer. This open-air performance brings in actors from across the country to perform one of the Bard's works each season, led by Artistic Director Lane Davies (of NBC's *Santa Barbara* fame). Tickets are typically a reasonable $5–15.

Shopping

The single most popular pursuit in Bell Buckle is shopping. Antiques are the main attraction, but arts and crafts are a close second. Several Nashville interior designers and antiques dealers have booths in shops in Bell Buckle because of the goods found here. You can spend an entire day rummaging through these shelves, although it is generally too crowded to do so the day of the Moon Pie Festival.

The **Bell Buckle Art Gallery** (26 Railroad Sq., 931/389-0004) sells a wide selection of artwork, from pottery and sculpture to paintings. Most pieces here have a fresh, modern appeal.

The Cat's Meow (25 Railroad Sq., 931/389-0064) has purses, totes, linens, throws, and jewelry, plus lots of gifts for babies and new parents. The **Doodle Bug** and **Doodle Bug Too** (Railroad Sq., 931/389-9009) are sister shops that sell jewelry, housewares, gifts, and folk art.

For antiques try the **Bell Buckle Antique Mall** (112 Main St., 931/389-6174) or **Blue Ribbon Antiques** (Railroad Sq., 931/684-2588).

Accommodations

Host and hostess James and Ina Mingle run the **Mingle House Bed and Breakfast** (116 Main St., 931/389-9453, www.theminglehouse.blogspot.com, $80–85) in a restored 1898 Victorian home. Rooms are furnished with antiques, and guests can fuel up with a country-style breakfast of eggs, sausage, bacon, and more in the morning.

Food

There's no debate about where to eat in Bell Buckle. The ◖ **Bell Buckle Cafe** (Railroad Sq., 931/389-9693, Mon. 10:30 A.M.–2 P.M., Tues.–Thurs. 10:30 A.M.–8 P.M., Fri.–Sat. 10:30 A.M.–9 P.M., Sun. 11 A.M.–5 P.M., $5–15) is not only a Bell Buckle institution, but it is also one of the only games in town. The menu is Southern, with a few refined touches (like ostrich burgers and spinach-strawberry salad) you won't find at most small-town cafés. The menu is also mighty diverse, with

seafood, pasta, and sandwiches in addition to the usual plate lunches and dinner entrées. The large dining room fills up quick, especially for lunch, so there's no shame in coming a bit early. The Bell Buckle Cafe takes care of your entertainment needs, too. There's always live music on Thursday, Friday, and Saturday nights, usually bluegrass or country. Local radio station WLIJ broadcasts a musical variety show from the café on Saturday 1–3 P.M., which is a great reason to come to the café for lunch.

If you managed to pass up homemade dessert at the Bell Buckle Cafe, then head to **Bluebird Antiques and Ice Cream Parlor** (15 Webb Rd., 931/389-6549). Here you'll find a turn-of-the-20th-century soda fountain with hand-dipped ice cream and homemade waffle cones. Come in the morning to see (and smell) them making the cones. Not to be missed.

Information

The **Bell Buckle Chamber of Commerce** (931/389-9663, www.bellbucklechamber.com) publishes brochures, promotes the town, and operates as a clearinghouse for information.

The Southern Heartland

The region of Tennessee south of Walking Horse Country and east of the Natchez Trace is a fertile area known for farming, the railroad, and a very famous brand of sipping whiskey. The Jack Daniel's Distillery in Lynchburg is the greatest single draw in this region, but there are many other reasons to come.

Tims Ford Lake near Winchester and Tullahoma is ideal for boating and fishing. The Elk River that runs near Fayetteville is perfect for canoeing, and the tiny railroad town of Cowan is a down-home gem waiting to be discovered. The biggest music festival in all of Tennessee, Bonnaroo, takes place every

June near Manchester. Perhaps the best-kept secret in the whole area is the George Dickel Distillery in lovely Normandy.

PULASKI

The city of Pulaski has two significant claims to fame. The first is that it was here that a 21-year-old Confederate soldier, Sam Davis, was executed by the Union army for spying. Davis was captured in Giles County on November 20, 1863, carrying sensitive Union papers. When he refused to say where he got them, Davis was sentenced to death. The young soldier's final words, written in a letter to his mother, immortalized his sacrifice: "If I had a thousand lives,

© SUSANNA HENIGHAN POTTER

A statue of Confederate hero Sam Davis stands outside the Giles County Courthouse in Pulaski.

I would give them all before I would betray a friend or the confidence of my informer."

Pulaski's second, and better-known, claim to fame (or claim to infamy, rather) is that it was here that the Ku Klux Klan was established, in the spring of 1866.

Sights

If you see only one county courthouse in this part of Tennessee, let it be the **Giles County Courthouse** (1 Square, Pulaski, 931/424-4044), an elegant neoclassical courthouse that has been called the most beautiful in Tennessee. Built of brick and marble, its finest feature is a three-story rotunda capped by a dome and skylight. In the cupola, the 1858 bell strikes the hours. A ladies' restroom in the basement was a place where women and children who had come to town to shop could rest a spell before making the long journey back into the countryside. The restroom was furnished with several beds and a cradle.

The courthouse is the county's fifth. The first was a rough log cabin, and it was abandoned as the county grew. The second and third courthouses were destroyed by fire, and the fourth courthouse, completed in 1859, survived the Civil War only because Thomas Martin, a prominent citizen and the founder of Martin College, paid a $3,000 bribe to the Federals. The fourth courthouse did not survive to the present, however; it too was destroyed by fire, this time in 1907. The current courthouse was completed in 1909 at a cost of $132,000 and was made fireproof.

The courthouse is surrounded by a bustling courthouse square, fronted by businesses including antiques shops and restaurants.

Pulaski has two monuments to the boy hero of the Confederacy. A statue of Sam Davis stands at the south side of the courthouse. The statue was erected in 1909 by the United Daughters of the Confederacy.

The second monument is on Sam Davis

THE ORIGINS OF THE KU KLUX KLAN

The Ku Klux Klan was established in the spring of 1866 in Pulaski by six ex-Confederate soldiers who saw it as a secret society for fun and entertainment. They adopted some of the trappings of a college fraternity and performed initiation rituals and pranks. During the second half of 1866, new "dens" of the Ku Klux Klan were formed in nearby counties, but there was no evidence of the vigilantism and violence that has come to be associated with the KKK.

Between 1867 and 1868, the political nature of the KKK emerged. Ex-Confederate soldiers home from the war were unhappy with Reconstruction policies that promoted voting rights for African Americans and gave preferences to former Union soldiers and sympathizers. The KKK was seen as a way to resist these policies. Members met for a convention in Nashville in 1867, and a year later Nathan Bedford Forrest was elected to be the grand wizard of the Klan.

During this period, the Klan was strongest in Giles, Humphreys, Lincoln, Marshall, and Maury Counties in Middle Tennessee and Dyer, Fayette, Gibson, Hardeman, and Obion Counties in West Tennessee. Klansmen intimidated African Americans with attacks, whippings, and murder. They were particularly active during the 1868 election, when many African Americans voted for the first time.

Tennessee governor William Brownlow was a staunch Unionist and was resolved to put an end to the Klan's activities. In 1868 he announced new, harsh penalties for being associated with the Klan. He hired a private detective from Cincinnati to infiltrate the Klan and give names of people who were involved. After the detective turned up dead in February 1869, Brownlow declared martial law in six Middle Tennessee counties.

Brownlow's tenure as governor was just about up, however. A week later he resigned to take a seat in the U.S. Senate. His successor, Dewitt Senter, was less strident in his views and less controversial in his actions. Later that year, Forrest called for the end of the Klan, saying that it had served its purpose.

For about 50 years, the KKK was dormant. But in Georgia in 1915 it was resurrected, and it remained active in the Deep South, including Tennessee, for the next three decades. Members intimidated and terrorized blacks, Jews, and other minorities; they murdered and maimed men and women; and they attacked whites who were seen to sympathize with minorities. The Klan's political influence helped to elect Tennessee governor Austin Peay in 1923 and U.S. senator Lawrence D. Tyson in 1924, among others.

Since the Klan was officially disbanded in 1944, its name has been adopted by various extremist organizations, some of which have tried to stage events in Pulaski, the birthplace of the KKK. Town residents have fought these events, wishing to leave behind their historic association with the Ku Klux Klan.

Avenue, where Davis was executed. A small museum is located here, but it does not have regular hours. Call the Giles County Tourism Foundation at 931/363-3789 during business hours to arrange for someone to open it for you.

Pulaski is a lovely town, with a number of beautiful old homes. Two of the most noteworthy are the **Brown-Daly-Horne Home** (307 W. Madison St.), which was the home of onetime Tennessee governor John C. Brown. Brown served as the chairman of the convention that rewrote the Tennessee constitution in 1870. He did so well that Tennesseans elected him their 19th governor in 1870. The home is an excellent example of the Queen Anne style and is on the National Register of Historic Places.

The second prominent home is the **Thomas Martin House** (302 S. 2nd St.), built in 1842 by Thomas Martin, who founded Martin College. It was a hotel in the early 20th century and is now a bank.

Two different groups of Cherokee Indians passed through Pulaski during the 1838–1839 removal, now called the Trail of Tears. The city is developing a park and interpretive center about the Trail of Tears on Stadium Street (www.trailoftearspulaski.com). The center is still in the process of raising funds, but until then there are sculptures and other educational monuments to this dark portion of America's past.

Entertainment

The **Martin Movie Theater** (S. 5th St., 931/424-7373, www.moviesatmartin.com) shows movies on Friday and Saturday nights and Saturday and Sunday afternoons.

Accommodations

Located on a quiet residential street in town, **Miss Butler's Bed and Breakfast** (429 W. Jefferson St., 931/424-0014, www.missbutlers.com, $95–125) is an 1888 Georgian-style town house that has five separate guest rooms. Each room is named for a historical figure with ties to Giles County: Among them are Sam Davis, Frank Mars, and Tennessee governor John C. Brown. The house is named after Miss Margaret Butler, an educator and historian of the area. Each room has a private bath and telephone. Guests have access to a fax machine, and there is wireless Internet throughout the home. Guests also enjoy privileges at the local Hillcrest Country Club, where you can play golf or tennis or swim.

For standard hotel accommodations, choose from the **Richland Inn** (1020 W. College St., 931/363-0006, $80–85) and the **Comfort Inn of Pulaski** (1140 W. College St., 931/424-1600, $130).

Food

There are several casual restaurants downtown, perfect for lunch. **Reeves Drugs** (125 N. 1st St., 931/363-2561, Mon.–Sat. 8 A.M.–5:45 P.M., $3–5) is an old-fashioned drugstore lunch counter and soda fountain serving sandwiches and ice cream. Skip the postschool rush if you are in a hurry. **The Coffee Corner** (102 S. 2nd St., 931/363-1911, Mon.–Fri. 7 A.M.–6 A.M., Sat. 10 A.M.–4 P.M., $2–5) serves sandwiches, wraps, salads, pastries, and coffee.

The Pulaski **farmers market** takes place on Saturday mornings during the growing season on the south side of the courthouse.

Information

The **Giles County Tourism Foundation** (110 N. 2nd St., 931/363-3789, ext. 22, www.gilescountytourism.com) publishes brochures and keeps information about attractions, events, and accommodations. Stop in at their office in Pulaski to ask questions or pick up brochures.

CORNERSVILLE

If you've ever fantasized about staying in a log cabin, here's your chance. **Lairdland Farm Bed and Breakfast** (3174 Blackburn Hollow Rd., 931/363-9090, www.bbonline.com/tn/lairdland, $145) consists of two genuine log cabins set on a large 19th-century horse farm. Both the Clock Creek Cabin and the Springhouse Cabin can sleep up to six people. And while they are log cabins, modern amenities abound. Each has a kitchen, bathroom, television, and heating and air-conditioning. The downstairs living rooms are centered on a working fireplace.

The kitchens come stocked with the makings for a country breakfast—ham, coffee, biscuits, pastries, and more—and you can prepare other meals in the kitchen or on the grill. Since Lairdland is a working horse farm, there are also opportunities for recreation. Horse owners can bring their own animals and board them for $15 per night. Miles of wooded trails on the farm are ideal for horseback riding, hiking, or mountain biking.

Lairdland Farm is located about 15 minutes' drive northeast of Pulaski, off Highway 31A.

LYNNVILLE

About 15 miles north of Pulaski is the quaint town of Lynnville. Almost 60 different buildings in this small town of just about 400 people are listed on the National Register of Historic Places.

Sights

The **Lynnville Depot Museum and Train**

Station (162 Mill St., 931/527-3158, www. lynnvillerailroadmuseum.com, Mon.–Sat. 10 A.M.–4 P.M., Sun. noon–4 P.M., free) is the town's main attraction. Built around a 1928 locomotive, the museum invites you to climb aboard an old passenger train.

The museum also includes an exhibit about the nearby Milky Way farm, where candy bar giant Frank Mars lived. The farm was built between 1930 and 1934 with money Mars earned from the sale of Milky Way candy bars. He had invented the Milky Way in 1923, and by 1930 it was the number-one selling candy bar in the world. The Milky Way farm included several dozen buildings, cottages, and miles of fences. The crown jewel was a 25,000-square-foot 21-bedroom English Tudor–style manor house. Frank Mars died in 1934, and the property continued to operate as a horse farm for many years. More recently, it fell into disrepair, and parts of the 2,000-plus-acre estate were sold. In 2005, the property was purchased by a real estate development company that plans to preserve the manor house and turn it into a clubhouse and inn. On the surrounding farmland, they will build an upscale gated community with amenities including a polo field, golf course, equestrian center, spa, and shopping complex.

Food

In Lynnville, you must stop at **Soda Pop Junction** (111 Mill St., 931/527-0001, Mon.–Thurs. 7 A.M.–2 P.M., Fri.–Sat. 7 A.M.–9 P.M., Sun. 7 A.M.–5 P.M., $3–13), a classic old soda fountain. Besides the fountain drinks, malts, and other treats, Soda Pop Junction serves breakfast, grilled sandwiches, and dinner plates. The burger is a third of a pound, juicy, and costs less than $3. The grilled bologna sandwich is a favorite, and dinners include steak, pork chops, and fried catfish. Friday night is the fish fry, and on Sunday a country buffet is on offer for just $7 per person. The Soda Pop Junction is a great place to fuel up. There's live music on weekend nights.

Information

The **Giles County Tourism Foundation** (110 N. 2nd St., 931/363-3789, ext. 22, www.gilescountytourism.com) publishes brochures and keeps information about attractions, events, and accommodations. Stop in at the office in Pulaski to ask questions or pick up brochures.

FAYETTEVILLE

The county seat of Lincoln County, Fayetteville is a bustling little city. Its proximity to Huntsville, Alabama, helps keep it lively, and its old homes and classic courtyard square make it attractive.

Sights

From 1861 until 1969, Fayetteville's most famous structure was a stone bridge that spanned the Elk River. It included six elliptical arches spanning 450 feet and was very rare. Legend has it that after marching his troops over it in 1863, Union general William Tecumseh Sherman ordered it destroyed, but the man chosen to carry out the mission could not bear to destroy such a beautiful bridge.

In 1969 the bridge collapsed into the Elk River, but the town has built a replica at **Stone Bridge Memorial Park,** located at the corner of Highway 431/231 and Thornton Taylor Parkway.

Located in the old Borden Milk factory, the **Fayetteville Lincoln County Museum and Civic Center** (521 Main Ave. S., 931/438-0339, www.flcmuseum.com, May–Nov. Thurs. and Sat. 12:30–4:30 P.M., free) preserves the history and heritage of Fayetteville and Lincoln County. The museum houses military, medical, and agricultural exhibits, including an outstanding arrowhead collection. The building also houses a community center. To visit at times other than the listed hours, call the chamber of commerce at 931/433-1234 in advance to make arrangements.

Fayetteville's town square and the adjoining residential streets are dotted with beautiful and historic buildings. Ask at the Chamber of Commerce Welcome Center for a printed guide to historic structures, and spend an hour or so strolling the streets of this lovely town.

Festivals and Events

The second week of September is the **Lincoln County Fair** (931/433-6387, www.lincolncountyfairinfo.com), considered by many to be the best county fair in the entire state. Come for demolition derbies, harness races, farming exhibits, carnival rides, a 4H contest, pageants, and other entertainment.

The **Lincoln County Bluegrass and Crafts Festival** (931/433-1234) in September attracts regional musicians who compete in bluegrass, band, and dance contests. It takes place at the Lincoln County Fairgrounds.

Fayetteville gets a head start on the holiday season with **Host of Christmas Past** (931/433-1234) over the second weekend of November. The festival includes high tea, trolley rides, strolling musicians, and a candlelight walking tour of the city.

Shopping

Fayetteville may be the only city in Tennessee whose most celebrated retail establishment is a fabric store. **Sir's Fabric Store** (110 N. Elk Ave., 931/433-2487, www.sirsfabric.com, Mon.–Sat. 9 A.M.–5 P.M.) has been in business since the 1940s and is still operated by the Sir family. It receives new fabric shipments every week and sells them at outlet prices.

Accommodations

Little Young House Bed and Breakfast (210 Bright Ave., 931/433-5873, $80) is an 1869 town house that is listed on the National Register of Historic Places. Located four blocks from the town square, Little Young has three guest rooms, each furnished with elegant antiques and wall-to-wall carpeting. Afternoon tea is served in the parlor and breakfast in the dining room. A modern entertainment room is decorated to resemble an old-fashioned gentleman's smoking room; it houses a television, DVD player, and DVD library.

The **Green Haven Creek** (269 Hughey Rd., 931/532-0399, $85–179) is a farmhouse on 18 acres with modern amenities, including wireless Internet and a Jacuzzi tub.

Two miles outside of town in an 1880s colonial mansion, the **Old Cowan Plantation** (126 Old Boonshill Rd., 931/433-0225, $65) is a peaceful country getaway. Two guest rooms with private baths are comfortable and well appointed. A continental breakfast is served downstairs; sip your morning coffee out on the verandah overlooking the rural landscape.

Food

The old Fayetteville jail is now **Cahoots Restaurant** (114 W. Market St., 931/433-1173, Mon.–Thurs. 10:30 A.M.–8 P.M., Fri.–Sat. 10:30 A.M.–9:30 P.M., $13–20). This is a popular choice for just about any meal; the menu is diverse, with burgers, chicken, and Mexican cuisine on offer. Locals like the homemade chips and salsa.

For steak and barbecue, choose the top-rated **Cattleman's Steakhouse** (520 Main Ave. S., 931/433-8834, Sun.–Thurs. 5–9 P.M., Fri.–Sat. 5–10 P.M., $13–40), which scores a 10 for its hand-carved steaks and satisfying sides (or you can choose from seafood or chicken). The service is sometimes slow.

Information

The **Fayetteville-Lincoln County Chamber of Commerce** (208 S. Elk Ave., 931/433-1234, www.fayettevillelincolncountychamber.com) operates a welcome center and publishes visitor information, including a guide to historic homes and buildings in the city.

KELSO

Located about 10 miles east of Fayetteville along the Elk River is Kelso. Here you will find the award-winning **Prichard's Distillery** (11 Kelso Smithland Rd., 931/433-5454, www. prichardsdistillery.com, Mon.–Sat. 9 A.M.– 4:30 P.M., free), which uses water and premium molasses to create rum, which they then age in handmade charred white-oak barrels. Visitors can see the copper pot stills and the barrel warehouse. The distillery, which also makes bourbon and country lightning, is open for tours, but they ask that you call before visiting to arrange a tour time.

Recreation

The Elk River winds up from Alabama and empties into Tims Ford Lake. The river, tamed by damming, is an ideal river to float in a canoe. Its current is strong yet calm, and it winds through beautiful countryside. **Elk River Canoe Rental** (190 Smithland Rd., 931/937-6886, www.elkrivercanoes.com) is a rental outfit located nine miles east of Fayetteville along Highway 64. They rent top-quality canoes ($15–27 per person), along with lifejackets and paddles. They also provide transportation to and from put-in and take-out points, and will arrange for multiple-day journeys if you like. They are open April–October. Call ahead to reserve your canoe.

LYNCHBURG

Lynchburg, no longer population 361, has been transformed by the popularity of Jack Daniel's Tennessee Whiskey, which is made a few blocks from the town square. No other small town in Tennessee sees as many visitors, from as many different places, as this one.

Critics may object to the tour buses and crowds, but for now, the town has managed to survive its success with relative grace. It has maintained its small-town feel, and it offers its guests a hospitable and heartfelt welcome.

Lynchburg is centered around the Moore County courthouse, a modest redbrick building. Souvenir shops, restaurants, and a few local businesses line the square. Outside of this, Lynchburg is quiet and residential. The Jack Daniel's Distillery is about three blocks away from the town square; a pleasant footpath connects the two.

Jack Daniel's Distillery

As you drive into Lynchburg, or walk around the town, you might notice some odd-looking gray warehouses peeking out above the treetops. These are barrel houses, where Jack Daniel's Distillery ages its whiskey. Around Moore County there are 74 of these warehouses, and each one holds about one million barrels of whiskey.

Thousands of whiskey drinkers make the pilgrimage every year to Jack Daniel's Distillery (280 Lynchburg Hwy./Hwy. 55, 931/759-4221, www.jackdaniels.com, daily 9 A.M.–4:30 P.M., free) to see how Jack Daniel's is made. And what they find is that, aside from the use of electricity, computers, and the sheer scale of the operation, things have not changed too much since 1866, when Jack Daniel registered his whiskey still at the mouth of Cave Spring near Lynchburg.

Jack Daniel was an interesting man. He stood just five feet, two inches tall and liked to wear three piece suits. He was introduced to the whiskey business by a Lutheran lay preacher named Dan Call, who sold the distillery to Daniel shortly after the Civil War. In 1866, Daniel had the foresight to register his distillery with the federal government, making his the oldest registered distillery in the United States. He never married and had no known children.

Daniel died of gangrene in 1911. He got it from kicking a metal safe in frustration after he couldn't get it open and breaking his toe. After Daniel died, the distillery passed to his nephew, Lem Motlow. The distillery remained in the Motlow family until it was sold in 1957 to the Brown-Forman Corporation of Louisville, Kentucky.

The one-hour tour of the distillery begins with a video about the master distillers—Jack

MIDDLE TENNESSEE

You can see the Tennessee whiskey process in action at Jack Daniel's Distillery.

Daniel's has had seven in its lifetime—who are the final authority on all facets of the product. You then board a bus that takes you up to the far side of the distillery, and from here you'll walk back to the visitors center, stopping frequently to be told about the key steps in the process. The highlight of the tour for some is seeing Cave Spring, where the distillery gets its iron-free spring water. Others enjoy taking a potent whiff of the sour mash and the mellowing whiskey.

The tour ends back at the visitors center, where you are served free lemonade and coffee. Moore County, where Lynchburg is located, is a dry county, and for 86 years the irony was that Jack Daniel's could not sell any of its whiskey at the distillery. In 1995, however, the county approved a special exemption that allows the distillery to sell souvenir bottles of whiskey at its visitors center. That is all they sell, however; you have to buy other Jack Daniel's merchandise at one of the other gift shops in town.

Other Sights

A stately two-story brick building on the southwest corner of the square is the **Moore County Jail** (231 Main St., 931/993-1791, www.lynchburgtn.com/JailFlyer, mid-Mar.–Dec. Tues.–Sat. 11 A.M.–3 P.M., adults $1 donation), which served as the sheriff's residence and the county jail until 1990. The building is now a museum and is operated by the local historical society. You can see law-enforcement memorabilia, old newspaper clippings, and vintage clothes. Go upstairs to see the prisoners' cells.

Just down Main Street is the **Tennessee Walking Horse Museum** (Public Sq., 931/759-5747, www.twhbea.com/TWHMuseum.htm, Tues.–Sat. 9 A.M.–5 P.M., free). The museum was originally located in Shelbyville, heart of Walking Horse country, but moved to Lynchburg in the early 2000s to take advantage of the bustling tourist trade here.

The Walking Horse Museum displays photographs, trophies, and other memorabilia from walking horse champions. You can admire both show and posed photographs of top horses and watch a video that explains what makes the Walking Horse so special. The films include show footage of the breed's distinctive flat walk, fast walk, and canter.

Festivals and Events

Spring in the Hollow is an arts, crafts, and music festival that takes place in early May. At the end of May, the **Spotted Saddle Horse Show,** an annual horse show, takes place.

Frontier Days in mid- to late June is a weekend celebration of early settlers. Costumed performers and traders evoke bygone days. July sees the **Tennessee Walking Horse Show** and August the second Spotted Saddle Horse Show.

The biggest event of the year in Lynchburg is the **Jack Daniel's World Champion Invitational Barbecue,** which takes place the last weekend of October. Teams must qualify to take part—they must have won another large barbecue tournament—and even then teams must be invited. Despite serious competition, the event is a whole lot of fun. Spectators compete in bung tossing and butt bowling. There is clogging and bluegrass music, and lots of county-fair-type food is sold. The barbecue competition takes place at Wiseman Park on the outskirts of the town square. An arts and crafts festival takes place at the town square.

Christmas in Lynchburg livens up an otherwise quiet time in town with seasonal performances and decorations.

For information about any events, contact the Metropolitan Lynchburg Moore County Chamber of Commerce (931/759-4111, www.lynchburgtn.com).

Accommodations

The **Tolley House** (1253 Main St., 931/759-7263, www.tolleyhouse.com, $100–150) is located about a mile from the town square and is a pleasant country retreat. A handsome antebellum farmhouse once owned by Jack Daniel's master distiller Lem Motlow, the Tolley House provides touches of luxury. Rooms have private baths, television, and wireless Internet access, and are furnished tastefully with antiques. Hosts Frank and Karen Fletcher provide your choice of a full country or light continental breakfast. Discounts are available for stays of two or more nights.

The closest thing to a motel in Lynchburg is the **Lynchburg Country Inn** (423 Majors Blvd., 931/759-5995, www.lynchburgcountryinn.com, $55–65). Its 25 rooms are each furnished with a microwave, refrigerator, and cable TV. There's a pool out back and rocking chairs on the front and back porches. The building is modern, built in 2003, but the decor is pure country.

Food

The most popular place to eat in Lynchburg is **Miss Mary Bobo's Boarding House** (295 Main St., 931/759-7394, Mon.–Sat. 11 A.M. and 1 P.M., with a 3 P.M. service in high season, $19). Miss Mary's started life as the home of Thomas Roundtree, the founder of Lynchburg. It later became the home of Dr. E. Y. Salmon, a Confederate captain who maintained an office there and rented out rooms to boarders. In 1908, Lacy Jackson Bobo and his wife, Mary Evans Bobo, bought the house and continued to operate it as a boardinghouse until the 1980s. Over the years, word of Mary Bobo's legendary home-cooked meals spread, and this boardinghouse became one of the region's best-known eating houses. Today, Miss Mary's is no longer a boardinghouse, and the restaurant is operated by Miss Lynne Tolley, who has worked hard to keep up the traditions established by Miss Mary. The restaurant is owned by the Jack Daniel's Distillery, and servers are hired from the local community college. A meal at Miss Mary's will easily be the most distinctive of your trip. Guests should arrive at least 15 minutes early to check in, pay, and be assigned to a dining room. When the dinner bell rings, you will be taken to your dining room by a hostess who stays with you throughout the meal. Everyone sits family-style around a big table. The meal served at Miss Mary's is a traditional Southern dinner with no fewer than six side dishes and two meats, plus iced tea (unsweetened), dessert, coffee, and bread. Almost every meal features fried chicken. Side dishes may include green beans, mashed potatoes, fried okra, carrot slaw, and corn bread. Your hostess will make sure that everyone has enough to eat, answer questions about the food, and tell you some stories about the restaurant—if you ask. Be sure to call well ahead to make your reservations. Meals are fully booked weeks and even months in advance, especially during the busy summer months and on Saturdays.

For a more low-key meal, go to the **Bar-B-Que Caboose Cafe** (217 Main St., 931/759-5180, www.bbqcaboose.com, year-round daily 11 A.M.–5 P.M., Apr.–Oct. Fri. 6:30–8 P.M., $7–12). The menu offers pulled-pork barbecue sandwiches, jambalaya, red beans and rice, and hot dogs. You can also get pizzas. On Friday night you can enjoy a barbecue plate dinner ($9) while you listen to live music. On Saturday 10–11 A.M. a live country music radio show is broadcast from the Caboose Cafe.

There are a handful of other restaurants in Lynchburg, all on the town square. **Elk River Coffee** (12 Short St., 931/759-5552, Mon.–Sat. 8 A.M.–5:30 P.M., Sun. noon–5 P.M., $6–12) sells lighter fare, including wraps and salads.

Be prepared that it is next to impossible to get an evening meal in Lynchburg. By 6 P.M. the place is a ghost town.

Information

The **Lynchburg Welcome Center** (182 Lynchburg Hwy./Hwy. 55, 931/759-6357, www.lynchburgtenn.com, open daily), at the intersection of Majors Boulevard and Mechanic Street, has public restrooms and information about local businesses and attractions.

TULLAHOMA

A quintessential railroad town, Tullahoma straddles what was once the Nashville and Chattanooga Railroad. Atlantic Street, actually two streets, runs on both sides of the tracks. The Depot Historic District on the east side of the railroad has a fine collection of old Victorian-era homes.

Sights

Arnold Engineering Development Center

(Arnold Air Force Base, 931/454-5655, www.arnold.af.mil) is the nation's premier aerospace ground flight testing facility. Founded in 1951 by President Truman and named for Gen. Henry H. Arnold, a World War II commander, the center is also a major economic engine for the Tullahoma and Manchester area. The base has more than 50 different test facilities, ranging from large wind tunnels to space chambers. It has played a key role in developing all of the military's high-performance jet aircraft, missiles, and space systems.

Free tours for groups of 12 or more are available by prior reservation only. They last about three hours and require a good deal of walking; wear comfortable shoes. While individual tours are not provided, you can ask to be scheduled with a larger group, usually on Fridays.

Immediately adjacent to the Tullahoma Regional Airport is the **Beechcraft Heritage Museum** (570 Old Shelbyville Hwy., 931/455-1974, www.beechcraftheritagemuseum.org, Mon.–Sat. 8:30 A.M.–4:30 P.M., adults $10, students $5, children under 12 free). The museum tells the story of Beech Aircraft Company, founded by aviation pioneer and Pulaski native Walter H. Beech. The museum features dozens of antique airplanes, including the very first Beechcraft ever made. Built out of love of aviation and Beechcraft planes, the museum is a must if you share either of those passions. Children will also enjoy seeing old-fashioned planes that look like modern-day cartoon characters.

The **Tullahoma Fine Arts Center** (401

S. Jackson St., 931/455-1231, Tues.–Fri. noon–6 P.M., Sat. 11 A.M.–4 P.M., free) offers art classes, hosts the annual Tullahoma Fine Arts and Crafts Festival every May, and operates an art museum with regional art exhibits displayed on a changing basis. The center is usually open during its listed hours, but it is a good idea to call ahead. Look for the bronze sculpture of a female dancer, called *Summer Song*, in the front yard of the center.

The arts center is located in a historic Italianate home built by the Baillet family after they migrated from New York to rural Tennessee in 1868. The three Baillet sisters, Jane, Emma, and Affa, were noted milliners, poets, and artists, and it was their memory and legacy that inspired local residents to restore the home and open the arts center in the 1960s and '70s.

Located in the South Jackson Civic Center, the **Mitchell Museum** (404 S. Jackson St., 931/455-5321, www.southjackson.org, first Sun. of each month 2–4 P.M. and by appointment, free) displays items collected over a lifetime by former Tullahoma postmaster Floyd Mitchell and his wife, Margaret Noland Mitchell. Other citizens have donated artifacts to the collection over the years.

Accommodations

Designed for business travelers, small-scale conferences, and those seeking upscale accommodations, ◖ **The Grand Lux Inn** (212 E. Lincoln St., 931/461-9995, www.thegrandluxinn.com, $115–125) is a stunning old Victorian home now converted into a thoroughly modern inn. Six guest rooms are available, each with a private entrance, bath, and amenities including cable television, writing desks, hair dryers, and wireless Internet. The styling is modern. A continental breakfast of hot and cold cereals, fruit, pastries, coffee, and juice is served in the Breakfast Room, but this is not a traditional bed-and-breakfast. An added bonus is that Tullahoma's best restaurant, Emil's, is right next door.

Jameson Inn (2113 N. Jackson St., 931/455-7891, $75–85) is a 60-room motel with the usual amenities: continental breakfast, fitness room, outdoor pool, cable TV, wireless Internet, and free weekday newspapers.

The **Lodge at Gunter Hollow** (149 Gunter Hollow Rd., 931/433-5214 or 931/438-1665, www.lodgeatgunterhollow.com, $95) is a Christian conference center and bed-and-breakfast inn. Its seven guest rooms are new, neat, and comfortable. Each has its own private entrance, a spacious private bath, and a covered deck outside. Breakfast is served in the conference center dining room. There is also a parlor where you can watch television or relax with a book.

Food

The best place to eat in Tullahoma is **Emil's** (210 E. Lincoln St., 931/461-7070, www.emilsfinedining.com, Tues.–Fri. 10 A.M.–2 P.M., Thurs.–Sat. 5–8:30 P.M., lunch $7.50–14, dinner $16–30). Chef Georges Martin is the brain behind the menu, which combines genteel Southern fare and fine French cuisine. Lunch is casual, with an array of salads (the crab cake salad is a favorite) and sandwiches, as well as entrées like penne pasta with ham and peas. Many diners opt for the daily lunch special ($7.50) or the platter of soup, chicken salad, crackers, dessert, and a drink ($9). Three nights a week Emil's serves dinner. Entrées include roast duck, braised lamb shank, and barbecue salmon. In deference to the region, you'll also find fried chicken. Emil's is located in a restored 1905 home, and it is almost always full. It is a good idea to reserve your table in advance and to call ahead to check the hours, which vary by season.

For something a bit more casual, head to **Fast Jack's** (122 W. Lincoln St., 931/455-2194, www.fastjacks.net, Mon.–Thurs. 11 A.M.–11 P.M., Fri.–Sat. 2–10 P.M., $5–12). At this popular spot you can choose from the daily plate-lunch special, burgers, or a nine-inch lunch pizza. The plate lunches are the real draw: hamburger steak, fried shrimp, meat loaf, chicken and dressing, and a host of tempting side dishes are usually on offer. There's extra parking at the rear of the restaurant.

On the outskirts of town, as you drive toward Lynchburg, you'll find **Sweet Aroma Cafe** (401 Wilson Ave., 931/461-5535, www.sweetaromacafe.net, Mon.–Fri. 7 A.M.–4 P.M., Sat. 7 A.M.–2 P.M., $6–9). Stop here for breakfast or lunch; breakfast runs the gamut from hearty omelets and biscuits and gravy to pastries and peanut butter and banana sandwiches. At lunch they serve wraps, salads, and specialty sandwiches, including an appetizing chicken peach salad adorned with tomato slices and crackers. They serve hot and cold coffee all day long.

Information

The **Tullahoma Chamber of Commerce** (135 W. Lincoln St., 931/455-5497, www.tullahoma.org) publishes a directory of local businesses and hands out brochures and other information to stoppers-by.

NORMANDY

Normandy is a tiny one-street town notable for its position on the railroad and its location amid some of the most beautiful countryside in this part of Tennessee. The rural routes surrounding Normandy are well worth exploring.

◖ George Dickel Distillery

About seven miles south of Wartrace, just outside of the old railroad town of Normandy, is one of the best-kept secrets in this part of Tennessee. The George Dickel Distillery (Cascade Hollow, 931/857-3124, Tues.–Sat. 9 A.M.–4 P.M., free) makes thousands of gallons of Tennessee sipping whisky every year, and all of it comes from the Dickel distillery up Cascade Hollow on the Highland Rim of the Cumberland Plateau. (In deference to its

Take a tour of that other Tennessee whiskey-maker: George Dickel Distillery.

connection to scotch, Dickel uses the Scottish spelling for whisky, without the *e*.)

It's no secret that the best-known name in whiskey is distilled a few miles down the road in Lynchburg, but the folks at George Dickel don't seem to mind. The Dickel distillery is a smaller operation, and visitors are given a more personalized and detailed look at the operations of the plant. And the setting in the Cascade Hollow is one of the most charming in this part of the state.

George Dickel, a German immigrant, distilled his first bottle of whisky at Cascade Hollow in 1870. Dickel created a unique cold mellowing process, which made his product smoother than others. The distillery still uses Dickel's cold mellowing process, as well as his signature proportions of corn, malt, and rye. The Dickel distillery closed down during Prohibition, only to reopen in the 1950s. The distillery has changed hands several times over the past 50 years, and it is now owned by Diageo, one of the largest beer, wine, and spirits manufacturers in the world.

Visitors are welcome to take a free one-hour tour of the distillery, which takes you through every step in the process. The last tour departs at 3:30 P.M.

To find George Dickel, take Route 269 to Normandy, where you will see signs pointing you to Cascade Hollow Road.

Accommodations

For a high-class country escape, head to the **Parish Patch Farm and Inn** (1100 Cortner Rd., 931/857-3017, www.parishpatch.com, $93–243), an inn, conference center, and restaurant set in the rural countryside near Normandy. The more than 30 guest rooms are scattered in various buildings on this working farm. They include spacious suites, private cottages, standard-size bedrooms, and rustic rooms in an old gristmill. The two least-expensive rooms share a bath; all other rooms have private bathrooms, televisions, and telephones. Rollaway beds are available. All guests can enjoy the full country breakfast served daily in the inn dining room. Other amenities include a swimming pool, walking trails, a book and video library, hammocks, and lots of countryside to explore. Parish Patch is a working farm, so you can also watch (or join in on) farm chores, pick your own blackberries (in season, of course), or just watch the animals. The Duck River flows through the property, providing opportunities for fishing and canoeing.

Food

The **Cortner Mill Restaurant** (1100 Cortner Rd., 931/857-3018, www.parishpatch.com, Tues.–Sat. 5:30–9 P.M., Sun. 11:30 A.M.–1:30 P.M., $16–44) is an upscale country restaurant that serves dinner five nights a week and is often booked for special events. Specialties include Memphis-style dry-rub barbecue ribs, grilled rack of lamb, baked rainbow trout, and frog legs. There is an extensive wine list, and desserts include a flaming bananas Foster made tableside. The restaurant hosts special buffets on Easter, Thanksgiving, Christmas, and New Year's Day, and the Champagne Sunday Brunch is a popular treat for locals and visitors.

The restaurant is located in a restored 1825 gristmill, and the dining room overlooks the river. It is an elegant choice for a special dinner.

NORMANDY LAKE

The largest non-power-generating lake created by the Tennessee Valley Authority, Normandy Lake is a 3,200-acre reservoir located between Tullahoma, Shelbyville, and Manchester. It is named for the tiny railroad town of Normandy nearby.

The lake was created in 1976 by a 2,800-foot-long dam across the Duck River. The river was dammed to control flooding and create recreational opportunities.

On the southern shore of the lake is the **Barton Creek Recreation Area** (158 Barton Springs Rd., 931/857-9222). Here you will find

MIDDLE TENNESSEE

a campground with 67 sites, including 40 with electricity and water; a swimming beach; boat dock; picnic tables; and playground. Campsites cost $16–20 per night. The facility is managed by the Tennessee Valley Authority.

A 420-acre protected area near Normandy Lake north of Tullahoma, **Short Springs Natural Area** is a delightful corner of the world. Gorges and slopes carved by water, waterfalls, and abundant wildflowers characterize the area. It also captures two of Tennessee's defining geologic regions, the Highland Rim and the Central Basin. Because of the difficult terrain, parts of the natural area were never farmed and remain undisturbed to this day.

Access to the area is provided across from a parking area and water tower on Short Springs Road. To find the access point from Tullahoma, drive northward on Jackson Street (Highway 41A). Turn right onto Hogan Street after four blocks, and then left onto Country Club Drive after five blocks. Country Club Drive becomes Short Springs Road.

From the parking area, hiking trails head to Upper and Lower Busby Falls as well as the 60-foot Machine Falls. The Machine Falls loop is 1.4 miles, and the Busby Falls Loop is just under one mile. The 1.4-mile Laurel Bluff Loop circles the top of Laurel Bluff, providing lovely views of the area.

Short Springs is managed by the Tennessee State Natural Area Program and the City of Tullahoma. Camping, biking, horseback riding, rock climbing, motorized vehicles, and collecting plants are all prohibited.

You can download a color map from the State of Tennessee website (www.state.tn.us/environment) or call 615/532-0431 for more information.

Long a favorite destination for area residents, **Rutledge Falls** is a natural beauty. Located near Short Springs Natural Area and sharing many of its characteristics, Rutledge Falls is on private property (the property owners allow visitors). Look for the Rutledge Falls Baptist Church on Short Spring Road. There is a parking lot just beyond the church, in front of an old brick farmhouse. Follow the short path to the falls.

MANCHESTER

Opened in 2003, **Beans Creek Winery** (426 Ragsdale Rd., 931/723-2294, www.beanscreek.com, Mon.–Thurs. 10 A.M.–6 P.M., Fri.–Sat. 10 A.M.–7 P.M., Sun. 1–5 P.M.) is a pleasant diversion. Using grapes and fruits grown themselves or on farms in the region, Beans Creek makes a wide variety of wines, ranging from dry to sweet to sparkling. Their tasting bar and store is welcoming and spacious, and they sell other Tennessee wines as well. "Walk-throughs" around the property and plant are also offered.

People come from around the world to visit **Northside Clocks** (2032 McArthur Dr., 931/728-4307, www.northsideclock.com) in Manchester. This family-owned shop sells and repairs clocks. Its inventory includes new and antique pieces, including beautiful grandfather clocks, mantel clocks, and cuckoo clocks. They also sell exquisite Lefton lighthouses and Fenton Glass porcelain.

◖ OLD STONE FORT STATE ARCHAEOLOGICAL PARK

Located a few miles' drive north of Manchester, on Highway 41, is one of the most mysterious historic sites in Tennessee. The Old Stone Fort State Archaeological Park (732 Stone Fort Dr., 931/723-5073) is home to a Native American construction some 2,000 years old.

Sometime around the birth of Christ, early Woodland Indians started to build a massive stone and dirt embankment encompassing 52 acres of woodland between two branches of the Duck River. The embankment was not constructed for military purposes, and there is no evidence that it was the site of a settlement. Archaeologists don't know why the Native Americans undertook such a mammoth job—without pack animals or wheels—but they

© PAUL THOMASSON

Old Stone Fort State Archaeological Park

suspect that the site was of spiritual, political, or community significance for a great number of Woodland Indians. Studies have shown that the site was built and used for 13 generations.

After Indians left the area, white settlers used the site for industry. They built mills on the river and called the enclosure a "stone fort" since that is what it looked like to them.

Sights

Since the 1970s, the site has been owned by the State of Tennessee, and it is now a state park. The **museum** (8:30 A.M.–4:30 P.M., free) explains what is known about the so-called fort, including the people who built it. You can watch a 15-minute video about the site and learn about the paper and gristmills that 19th-century settlers built on the site.

The museum's gift shop carries a wide selection of works about Native Americans.

Festivals and Events

Flintknapping is the art of creating spears and arrowheads from stone, and twice a year the Old Stone Fort plays host to an eponymous event celebrating the ancient art form. Held over the first weekend of May and the last weekend of September, **Flintknapping** includes demonstrations, competitions, and material sales.

Recreation

About two miles of trails circle the fort and are a delightful and easy hike. The paths take you along the Duck River, past three waterfalls, and along the interior of the site, now a serene and beautiful prairie. The sound of rushing water mingles with the symphony of prairie insects and birds.

Parts of the trail take you along and over the embankments constructed so painstakingly by Native Americans more than 2,000 years ago.

The Old Stone Fort park also has a picnic area with grills, a restroom, and picnic shelters.

About two miles down the highway from the park is the **Old Stone Fort Golf Course** (931/723-5075), a nine-hole golf course built

MIDDLE TENNESSEE

BONNAROO MUSIC AND ARTS FESTIVAL

Bonnaroo Music and Arts Festival (www.bonna-roo.com) started out in 2002 as a jam band music festival, but diversification has made this summertime megaevent a destination for all types of music fans. The Bonnaroo takes place over four days in June on a rural farm in Manchester. Between 75,000 and 90,000 people come each year.

Bonnaroo has a hippie heart with a slightly hard edge. Place-names are Suessian–the music tents are called, from largest to smallest, What Stage, Which Stage, This Tent, That Tent, and The Other Tent. Activities run the gamut from a Mardi Gras parade to children's art activities. Of course, it's the music that really draws the crowds: reggae, rock, Americana, jam bands, world, hip-hop, jazz, electronic, folk, gospel, and country. The event is truly a feast for the ears.

In 2007, the Police were reunited at Bonnaroo. In 2008, headliners included Kanye West, Willie Nelson, and Pearl Jam. But quality permeates every echelon of the stage. Unknowns and barely knowns routinely wow audiences, including names like The Civil Wars, Moon Taxi, and Feist. There is an emphasis on world artists and folk music. A jazz tent provides nightclub ambience, and there's even a comedy tent.

A few things to know about Bonnaroo: First, it's huge. The event takes place on a 700-acre farm, and the list of offerings is seemingly endless: four stages of music, whole villages dedicated to the arts, a 24-hour movie tent, yoga studio, salon, music-industry showcase, food vendors, and a whole lot more.

Second, Bonnaroo has above-average logistics. Organizers seem to consider everything, including the basics: drinking water, medical care, parking, traffic control, and a general store where you can buy necessities. Food vendors sell Tennessee barbecue, veggie burgers, and just about everything in between. A shuttle service between the Nashville airport and the Bonnaroo helps minimize traffic. Rules about camping, RVs, reentry, and security are commonsense and easy to follow.

All that said, you can't turn up with the clothes on your back and expect to have much fun. It's important to pack well: A good camping tent, folding chairs, and water bottles are necessities. It is June in the South, so it will be unspeakably hot. If it rains, it will be muddy. If it doesn't, it will be dusty. Even if you plan to buy most of your food at the festival, at least pack some snacks. There are ATMs at the Bonnaroo, but lines can be very long, so bringing plenty of cash is also a good idea (but not so much that you attract trouble). Also bring garbage bags, sunscreen, and hot-weather, comfortable clothes.

Plenty of Bonnaroo fans take the opportunity to do a lot of drinking and drugs, partly because they're somewhere they don't have to drive for four days. There are police at the festival, but they don't seem to crack down on every recreational drug user at the fest (although they do comb the streets on the way in). Beer–including good microbrews–are sold and consumed generously.

Most people buy a four-day pass to the festival, but day-pass tickets are available, too. Four-day passes cost $200 and up; a limited number of reduced-price early-bird tickets go on sale in January each year. Regular tickets go on sale in the spring after the lineup has been announced, typically in February. VIP packages are pricier but offer amenities that are priceless, such as VIP restroom and shower facilities.

along the Duck River. It is open year-round; carts and clubs are available for rent from the pro shop.

Camping

There are 51 campsites with water and electrical hookups, grills, picnic tables, and hard-surface pads. A dump station is available during the summer. One of two restroom facilities includes showers. Campsites are available on a first-come basis; the maximum stay is two weeks.

WINCHESTER

The seat of Franklin County is named for Gen. James Winchester, whose influence during the first 50 years of Tennessee state history went far beyond the military (www.winchester-tn.

© ADAM MᴀᴄCCHIᴀ

Bonnaroo Music and Arts Festival lights up sleepy Manchester each June.

com). Among other things, Winchester was Tennessee's first speaker of the Senate and voted in the North Carolina convention that ratified the U.S. Constitution in 1788. He fought in both the Revolutionary War and the War of 1812. When Franklin County was created in 1807, it was decided to name its main city in honor of Winchester.

The town's most famous daughter is Dinah Shore, born Francis "Fannie" Rose Shore. Although she moved away at age seven, Dinah Shore is remembered fondly in her hometown. So fondly, in fact, that the main drag is named Dinah Shore Drive. Shore became famous singing for World War II troops and is best known for her television shows, including *The Dinah Shore Chevy Show.* She wrote cookbooks, was an avid golfer, and won nine Emmy awards. Shore died of cancer in 1994. There is a Dinah Shore exhibit at Winchester's Jail House Museum.

Sights

Franklin County's old jail was retired from use as a detention center in 1972, but instead of tearing it down, city officials decided to turn it into a museum. **The Jail House Museum** (400 Dinah Shore Dr., 931/967-0524, mid-Mar.–mid-Nov. Tues.–Sat. 10 A.M.–4 P.M., adults $1, children $0.50) now houses exhibits on local history, the Civil War, and Dinah Shore, among other things. The highlight for many is seeing an old jail cell, leg irons, and handcuffs.

One of Winchester's most notable structures is the **Hundred Oaks Castle** (Hundred Oaks Dr., 931/967-8583, open for guided tours by appointment). Originally built as a two-story plantation home in the 1830s, the property was purchased in the 1860s by Albert Marks, the 21st governor of Tennessee. Marks's son, Arthur Handley Marks, was inspired by the castles and estate homes of Europe. Starting around 1880, Arthur Marks and his wife, Mary Hunt, a wealthy native of Nashville,

MIDDLE TENNESSEE

turned Hundred Oaks into a castle. When the work was completed, Hundred Oaks was a 12-bedroom building with a 40-foot-high great hall, a wine cellar, and many features of medieval architecture. The stones were quarried at Sewanee and the bricks baked locally. Unfortunately for Arthur Marks, he did not get to enjoy the fruits of his investment. Marks died in 1882 at age 28 of typhoid fever. Mary Hunt remarried, and the estate was the subject of a long-running legal battle. From 1900 until 1990, the property went through a number of different incarnations, from a Roman Catholic church and school to a dairy creamery and a private restaurant and club. In 1981 it was leased to the Franklin County Adult Activity Center, which used it as an adult training center for many years. The castle was badly damaged by fire in 1990. In 1997 it was purchased by the Kent Bramlett Foundation, a charitable organization. Special events take place here. Guided tours are available only to groups of at least 20 at a cost of $15 per person.

Entertainment
Winchester's downtown movie theater is **The Oldham** (115 1st Ave. NE, 931/967-2516).

Estill Springs
North of Winchester on the road to Tullahoma, Estill Springs is home to the **Montana Drive-In** (10251 Tullahoma Hwy., 931/694-3454, www. montanadrivein.com), one of only a few drive-in movie theaters left in the state. The double feature begins at 7 P.M. nightly. Admission is per person, not per car, so no hiding in the trunk.

Franklin State Forest
A 7,291-acre forest managed by Tennessee's Forestry Division, Franklin State Forest (310 Firetower Rd., Sewanee, 931/598-0830) was acquired in 1936 from the Cross Creek Coal Company. Trails were built by the Civilian Conservation Corps during the Great

Depression. Many of these trails remain today. Hunting and hiking are the two most popular activities here.

Belvidere
Named for Belvidere, Illinois, this community set amid beautiful and productive countryside west of Winchester was settled by Midwesterners after the Civil War.

A few miles west of Belvidere on Highway 64 there is a historical marker for Polly Finlay, Davy Crockett's first wife. The Crocketts settled on the banks of Beans Creek in Franklin County in 1812. The couple had two sons, and they named their Franklin County home "Kentuck." In 1815 Polly died. A year later, Davy Crockett married Elizabeth Patton, a widow with several small children of her own. The new family moved to Lawrence County in 1817.

The pretty **Falls Mill** (134 Falls Mill Rd., 931/469-7161, www.fallsmill.com, Mon.–Tues. and Thurs.–Sat. 9 A.M.–4 P.M., Sun. 12:30–4 P.M., adults $4, seniors $3, children $2) makes a perfect pit stop. The large three-story mill is a lovingly restored 1873 cotton factory. The water-powered mill now grinds flour and cornmeal, and the Falls Mill country store sells whole wheat flour, grits, cornmeal, and pancake mix. Visitors can also pay the modest admission fee to hear a presentation about the old mill and take a self-guided tour of the picturesque grounds.

In addition to a grain mill and country store, Falls Mill also has a two-story log cabin **bed-and-breakfast cottage** (134 Falls Mill Rd., 931/469-7161, www.fallsmill.com, $110). The cozy cabin includes a full kitchen, sitting room, and bedroom with queen-size bed. There is a television, heat and air-conditioning, and a working fireplace. The kitchen is stocked with the makings for breakfast, and guests can sample the home-milled pancake mix and grits. The cabin can sleep up to five people.

To find Falls Mill, travel to the Old Salem

© B. KIM HAGAR

Stop and see the restored cotton mill at Falls Mill.

community along Highway 64. Turn north off the highway onto Salem-Lexie Road. Drive 1.3 miles, and turn left onto Falls Mill Road.

TIMS FORD STATE PARK

Tims Ford State Park (931/962-1183) is a 431-acre park built on the shores of Tims Ford Lake, between Winchester and Tullahoma. Tims Ford Lake was created in 1970 when the Tennessee Valley Authority dammed the Elk River; eight years later the park opened. The park is named for an early river crossing.

Recreation

Fishing and boating on the lake are the two most popular activities at the park. There are seven public boat ramps in the park and two marinas: **Lakeview Marina** (931/967-6711) has pontoon and johnboat rentals, fishing

bait, camp supplies, and marine gas; **Holiday Landing Resort and Marina** (931/455-3151) is a full-service marina with slip rentals, gas, and pontoon boat rentals.

The lake is known for smallmouth and striped bass, but you may also catch largemouth bass, crappie, catfish, and bluegill. Bait and cleaning stations are available at the Lakeview Marina.

There are eight miles of trails. They include the **Marble Plains Trail,** a 1.1-mile handicapped-accessible paved path that winds through trees and fields past the Old Marble Plains Church and ends at an overlook of the Tims Ford Lake. From the overlook you can press on along the **Shoreline Trail,** a 3.1-mile path that follows the shoreline of the lake. The **Bicycle Trail** is a 4.4-mile paved bike path that winds through wooded coves on the Weaver's Point peninsula. Walking is also allowed.

MIDDLE TENNESSEE

There is an Olympic-size swimming pool, open Memorial Day–mid-August.

Bear Chase at Tims Ford is an award-winning 18-hole Jack Nicklaus signature golf course. It is located on a peninsula and offers beautiful views of the lake. Call 931/968-0995 for tee times. Greens fees are $40–50, but there are reduced rates for senior citizens and juniors.

Camping

There are two campgrounds associated with the park. The **Tims Ford Campground** has 52 RV and tent sites set in a wooded area in the main park. It is open year-round and has bathhouses with hot and cold showers. The **Fairview Campground** is located eight miles away on Highway 50, toward Winchester. Its 88 RV and tent sites are located on the lake. Fairview Campground is open April–October. Campsites at both campgrounds are $17.50 per night, or $20.50 with a sewer connection. No reservations are accepted for campsites.

Cabins

The park has 20 large cabins overlooking the lake. Each cabin can sleep up to eight people in two bedrooms. There is a full kitchen with modern appliances, a full bath with shower, a living area with a gas log fireplace, and a deck off each room overlooking the lake. Cabins rent for $90–125 a night, depending on the season and day of the week. There is a two-night minimum stay, and the cabins are open year-round. For reservations, call 800/471-5295.

Food

There is a full-service restaurant, **The Blue Gill Grill** (912 Old Awalt Rd., Tullahoma, 931/455-3151, Sun.–Thurs. 7 A.M.–8 P.M., Fri.–Sat. 7 A.M.–9 P.M., $5–13) at the Holiday Landing Resort and Marina inside the park.

COWAN

The town of Cowan, a few miles east of Winchester, is proving itself to be the little engine that could. A town of and for the railroad, Cowan is reinventing itself as a lovely tourist destination. Located just off the Cumberland Plateau, its attractions include historical railroad-inspired landmarks and the lovely scenery of the surrounding countryside.

The railroad was important in Cowan's history and development. The Nashville & Chattanooga line, chartered in 1848, made its first complete journey between the two cities in 1854. Engines based in Cowan helped trains make it up the steep, winding track to Tracy City. This portion of the rail rose 1,200 feet in seven miles and was referred to as the "Mountain Goat" because of the steepness of the climb. The Cowan station that still exists was built in 1904.

The last passenger train stopped in Cowan in 1965. Eleven years later a group of citizens with foresight purchased the old railroad depot with the hopes of turning it into a museum. They succeeded, and it is now the most charming railroad museum in the state. And while passenger trains no longer pass through Cowan, it remains a stop on the CSX freight train system.

Sights

Cowan's old railroad station is now the **Cowan Railroad Museum** (108 Front St., 931/967-7365, www.cowanrailroadmuseum.org, May–Oct. Thurs.–Sat. 10 A.M.–4 P.M., Sun. 1–4 P.M., free). The museum displays an antique locomotive and train memorabilia and equipment. Photographs, period costumes, old railroad timetables, and machinery combine to evoke the heyday of railroad travel and transportation. There are also model trains and a pleasant park with picnic tables and other facilities outside. Call in advance if you would like to see the museum outside its usual open hours.

Accommodations

Cowan's heyday as a railroad depot is

remembered at the **Franklin Pearson House Bed and Breakfast** (108 E. Cumberland St., 931/962-3223, www.franklinpearson.com, $75–99). Originally a modest railroad boardinghouse, it enjoyed a period of success from 1906 until World War II as the elegant and sophisticated Franklin House, and, later, the Parker House. Today this historic downtown property is a nine-room bed-and-breakfast.

The end of passenger rail service and a major fire in 1965 threatened to destroy Cowan's downtown hotel. After almost 40 years of various uses, the property was restored and reopened in 2003 as a bed-and-breakfast. The handsome white brick facade and elegant reception era evoke a bygone era, but one that is alive in spirit.

Each of the nine rooms has its own look and feel. Antique furniture, some of it original to the property, adds to the ambience. Rooms include several with a king- or queen-size bed, one room with twin bed accommodations, and two suites. All rooms have a private bathroom, cable television, and a telephone. Breakfast is served in the lobby each morning and includes cereal, fruit, and hot specialties including eggs. In addition to the lobby, guests can relax in an upstairs library and sitting room.

Food

For a town of its size, Cowan offers a pleasant variety of dining. The **Corner House** (401 E. Cumberland St., 931/967-3910, Mon.–Sat. 11 A.M.–2 P.M., $7–9) is a traditional Southern teahouse located in a Victorian-style home. Dine in homey sophistication on seasonal sandwiches, salads, and casserole entrées. The luncheon plate includes a muffin, entrée, and salad. Be sure to save room for dessert.

If Italian cooking is more your style, then head to **Sernicola's** (108 S. Tennessee Ave., 931/962-3380, www.sernicolas.com, Tues.–Sat. 11 A.M.–2 P.M. and 5–8:30 P.M., $9–15). Sernicola's has taken the unusual path of combining Italian specialties with good Southern cooking. The result is bound to please just about anyone. The weekday lunch buffet ($6–8) is always popular, as are the pizzas and the Pusher Burger, named for Cowan's pusher railroad engines.

Information

Cowan welcomes its visitors at the **Monterey Café and Welcome Center** (101 E. Cumberland, 931/968-9877, www.visitcowan. com, daily 9:30 A.M.–5 P.M.), in the Texaco Station. Stop here for a refreshment and to pick up brochures and maps.

Murfreesboro

A city of more than 80,000 people, Murfreesboro is, quite literally, the heart of Tennessee. The geographic middle of the state lies just northeast of the city's courthouse square and is commemorated with a stone marker.

The presence of **Middle Tennessee State University** enlivens Murfreesboro. The public university with more than 26,000 students was founded in 1911 as a teacher's college and became a university in 1965. Student life revolves around the campus, located just east of downtown.

SIGHTS

Murfreesboro's downtown is centered on its 1857 **courthouse,** the oldest in the state. It is one of only six pre–Civil War courthouses remaining in Tennessee.

Stones River National Battlefield

The second most deadly Civil War battle in Tennessee is remembered at the Stones River National Battlefield (3501 Old Nashville Hwy., 615/893-9501, www.nps.gov/stri). Only a fraction of the actual battlefield is included in the

MIDDLE TENNESSEE

national park, but enough remains to give you a sense of the battle that took place here from December 31, 1862, to January 2, 1863.

Start your visit to Stones River at the **Visitor Center** (daily 8 A.M.–5 P.M., free). Here is one of the best interpretive Civil War museums in all of Tennessee. It is modern and dynamic, and portrays much more than the tactical events of the battle. It depicts the lives and privations experienced by Civil War soldiers, the effect of the battle on Murfreesboro, and the propaganda war that took place after the battle to determine which side was considered "winner." Plan on spending at least one hour at the museum; the visitors center also has a gift shop and bookstore, restrooms, and staff who can answer your questions.

There are self-guided walking and driving tours to other Stones River landmarks. These include the **Stones River National Cemetery,** where some 6,100 Union dead were buried. Confederates killed at Stones River were taken to their hometowns or buried in a mass grave south of town. Later, these soldiers were reinterred in a mass grave at Evergreen Cemetery in Murfreesboro.

Following the Battle of Stones River, General Rosencrans ordered the construction of the depot and fortification at Murfreesboro. He wanted to press on along the railroad to Chattanooga, but he needed a place from which to launch the attack. From January to June 1863, soldiers and African American laborers built **Fortress Rosencrans,** the largest enclosed earthen fortification built during the Civil War. Part of the fort remains standing today.

Historic Sites

The elegant Italianate mansion at **Oaklands** (900 N. Maney Ave., 615/893-0022, www.oaklandsmuseum.org, Tues.–Sat. 10 A.M.–4 P.M., Sun. 1–4 P.M., adults $10, students and children $5) was one of Murfreesboro's finest. It started as a modest two-room brick house in 1818 on the property of Dr. James Maney and his wife,

Sallie Hardy Murfree. Additions in 1820, 1830, and 1857 left an elaborate and elegant mansion, now restored to its former glory. The tour of the home lasts about 45 minutes. You will see evidence of the various additions and hear stories about some of the notable people who visited at Oaklands, including Confederate president Jefferson Davis. Oaklands was badly deteriorated, vandalized, and quite nearly razed during the 1950s. Local residents fought for its preservation, and in 1958 it was purchased by the City of Murfreesboro. It was later deeded to Oaklands Association, which restored the home and opened it as a museum in the early 1960s. Today, Oaklands offers a range of special events and educational programs for local schools.

The **Bradley Academy Museum and Cultural Center** (415 S. Academy St., 615/867-2633, www.bradleymuseum.com, Tues.–Sat. 10 A.M.–4 P.M., adults $5, students and seniors $3, children under 13 $1) is located in an old schoolhouse. Bradley Academy was established in 1806 as the only school for Rutherford County. Students paid $24 a session and were required to bring firewood. Courses included Latin, Greek, mathematics, logic, writing, and literature. James K. Polk, who would go on to become president of the United States, was one of the school's early students.

Bradley Academy closed in the 1850s after it was absorbed into the newer Union University. During the Civil War the building served as a hospital for the wounded. In 1884, it was repaired and opened as a school for African Americans. In 1918, the old building was torn down and a new one built in its place.

Bradley Academy remained a school, cultural center, and gathering place for the African American community until it closed in 1955. Today, it houses a museum about Rutherford County, a restored 1917 classroom, and changing local art exhibits. It also serves as a community center.

The museum is sometimes closed, even during its published opening hours. It is a good idea to call ahead.

THE BATTLE OF STONES RIVER

After Union forces took Nashville in early 1862, the Federals looked southward toward Chattanooga and Atlanta. It was their objective to drive a wedge through the southland, using the railroad as their path.

Following the Battle of Perryville in October 1862, two large armies were gathering for a battle. Maj. Gen. William S. Rosencrans's 43,000-strong Army of the Cumberland was camped in Nashville, and Gen. Braxton Bragg's 38,000 Confederates were camped 33 miles southeast in Murfreesboro. On the day after Christmas 1862, Rosencrans marched his men to Murfreesboro to prepare for the fight that was to come.

In a strange prelude to battle, on the still night of December 30, 1862, military bands from both sides played long into the night. It began as a musical duel between armies, with songs like "The Bonnie Blue Flag" and "Hail Columbia." But after one army began playing "Home Sweet Home," the other joined in. It was a poignant and unusual moment before one of the war's bloodiest battles.

The Battle of Stones River took place on December 31, 1862, and January 2, 1863. The first day's fighting was fierce and deadly. When dawn broke on New Year's Day, both sides tended to wounded men and gathered the dead from the battlefield. Fighting resumed on January 2 in a cold and driving rain. In what would eventually become the definitive moment of the battle, a brutal Confederate drive to push the Federals back failed in the late afternoon on January 2. Overnight, after he heard that Rosencrans was getting reinforcements, Bragg ordered retreat. The low-spirited Southerners, who up until the retreat felt they had won the battle, marched 30 miles south toward Tullahoma in cold, wet weather. They were forced to leave their fallen brothers on the battlefield.

Tactically speaking, the battle was a draw, but Bragg's withdrawal allowed Rosencrans to declare it a Union victory. His claim was quickly accepted by the North, which was in bad need of a win. President Abraham Lincoln wrote to General Rosencrans these words: "I can never forget, whilst I remember anything, that about the end of last year and at the beginning of this, you gave us a hard-earned victory, which, had there been defeat instead, the nation could scarcely have lived over."

Stones River was the second-bloodiest Civil War battle in Tennessee, behind Shiloh. Nearly 24,000 men were killed or injured at the battle—13,249 Federal and 10,266 Confederate.

Murfreesboro pays tribute to its pioneer past at **Cannonsburgh Village** (312 S. Front St., 615/890-0355, May–Dec. Tues.–Sat. 10 A.M.–5 P.M., Sun. 1–5 P.M., adults $2.50, children $1.50). Reconstructed log cabins, a one-room schoolhouse, general store, and working blacksmith's shop evoke the town's early settlement. Cannonsburgh was the original name for Murfreesboro. The village grounds are open year round, and admission is free if you simply want to look around. Fees are charged for a guided tour.

ENTERTAINMENT AND EVENTS
Nightlife
Liquid Smoke (Public Sq., 615/217-7822, Mon.–Sat. 2 P.M.–late night) is a pub that sells cigars and specialty and imported beer.

For live music, head to **Wall Street Restaurant and Bar** (121 N. Maple St., 615/867-9090, www.wallstreetintheboro.com). In addition to serving breakfast and lunch daily, they have happy hour 5–10 P.M. and live music on the weekends.

The Arts
Local and regional artists are shown at the **Murfreesboro/Rutherford County Center for the Arts** (110 W. College St., 615/904-2787, www.boroarts.org, Tues.–Sat. 10 A.M.–4 P.M., free). The center is located in a restored 1909 Italian Renaissance building that served as

the customs house and later a post office. Since 1995 it has been an arts center with gallery space. Theater performances take place on weekends in a charming 168-seat theater. Tickets are usually $12 for adults, with discounts for students and seniors.

Horse and Livestock Shows

Check the calendar at the **Tennessee Miller Coliseum** (340-B W. Thompson Ln., 615/494-8961, www.mtsu.edu), a 220,000-square-foot air-conditioned coliseum specially designed for horse and other livestock shows.

Festivals and Events

In May, the Main Street Association and MTSU's McLean School of Music present the two-day **Main Street JazzFest** (www.jazzfestmainstreet.com) in downtown Murfreesboro.

Oaklands presents **Oaklands Victorian Fair** (www.oaklandsmuseum.org) in early June. This daylong event features tours, craft and game demonstrations, storytelling, Victorian music, and an old-fashioned cake walk.

In mid-July, Murfreesboro celebrates **Uncle Dave Macon Days Festival** (615/890-0355) in Cannonsburgh Village. Old-time music is the main draw at this free festival, which features banjo music, buck dancing, and clogging. There is also a gospel showcase.

RECREATION

Murfreesboro has 4.5 miles of paved **greenways** for walking, biking, and in-line skating. There are two **canoe access points** and four **fishing piers.** Trailheads are located at Thompson Lane, Broad Street, Redoubt Brannan, Manson Pike, and Cannonsburgh Village.

ACCOMMODATIONS

The **Carriage Lane Inn** (337 E. Burton St., 615/890-3630, www.carriagelaneinn.com, $125–195) is unique among bed-and-breakfasts, quite simply for its size. The property comprises three individual buildings located next to each other in a quiet residential neighborhood. All three are historic homes, and each has been carefully restored to preserve the antique feel of the homes but to also provide guests with modern comforts and amenities. The Main Inn, the Cottage, and the Yellow House can each be rented as a whole or by the room. Individual rooms rentals include a hearty breakfast. The property hosts frequent family reunions, weddings, and special events.

The interstate exits surrounding Murfreesboro are host to dozens of different chain motels, including **Fairfield Inn and Suites** (175 Chaffin Pl., 615/849-1150, $90–120), **Wingate Inn** (165 Chaffin Pl., 615/849-9000, $80–100), and **Super 8** (127 Chaffin Pl., 615/867-5000, $60–90).

FOOD

For something a bit more elegant, go to **B. McNeel's** (215 N. Church St., 615/896-1002, Mon–Fri. 11 A.M.–2 P.M., $10–30). Exposed brick walls, high ceilings, and a charming outdoor patio put this downtown lunch spot high on the ambience list. Choose from designer salads and sandwiches or midday versions of entrées usually seen only on dinner menus, including steak, chicken, and seafood. The fried oysters are a favorite.

Another favorite downtown eatery is **Marina's Italian Restaurant** (125 N. Maple St., 615/849-8881, Tues.–Sat. 11 A.M.–9 P.M., $5–18). Choices include pizzas, calzones, pasta, and the gargantuan stuffed pizza, a real crowd pleaser. The lunchtime menu features full- and half-size plates, all under $8. For dinner you can choose from the standards, as well as upscale dishes like shrimp pasta and baked salmon.

INFORMATION

The **Rutherford County Chamber of Commerce and Visitors Center** (501 Memorial Blvd., 615/893-6565, www.

rutherfordchamber.org, Mon.–Fri. 8 A.M.–4:30 P.M.) publishes visitor information and operates a visitors center. If you arrive on the weekend or after hours, there is an outdoor information kiosk available.

AROUND MURFREESBORO
Smyrna

Boy hero of the Confederacy Sam Davis grew up in Smyrna, once a hamlet, now a stop on the interstate highway. Davis's legacy brings travelers here today to see his boyhood home. The city of more than 33,000 people is also home to Nissan's North American headquarters, which attracts workers and a few visitors interested in seeing how cars are made.

Sam Davis Home and Museum (1399 Sam Davis Rd., 615/495-2341, www.samdavishome. org, Mon.–Sat. 10 A.M.–4 P.M., Sun. 1–4 P.M., closed in Jan., adults $8.50, seniors $6.50, children $3) is the childhood home of Confederate hero Sam Davis. Born in Smyrna and raised in an upper-middle-class family, Davis was enrolled at the Western Military Academy in Nashville when the Civil War broke out.

Davis volunteered for the Confederate cause, and in 1863 he was a member of Coleman's Scouts, soldiers who worked behind enemy lines to disrupt communications. He was detained by Union troops in November 1863 on his way to Chattanooga. Davis had in his possession papers that could only have been given to him by a high-level Union official.

Thinking that Davis would betray the name of his informant, Gen. Grenville Dodge arrested Davis and charged him with spying. Sentenced to hang, Davis still refused to say the name of his source, and he went to the gallows with the secret. His sacrifice made him a legend and a hero among Confederates.

His childhood home and museum keep this legend alive. Visitors see a short video about Davis and his sacrifice, and are then taken on a guided tour of the boyhood home. The house,

which has been a museum since the 1930s, includes hundreds of original Davis family items.

Nissan North America (983 Nissan Dr., 615/459-1444, tours Tues. and Thurs. at 10 A.M., free) is Rutherford County's largest single employer, with some 6,700 workers. The plant sprawls over 884 acres and cost $2.1 billion to build. Some half million vehicles roll off the assembly line yearly, including Maxima and Altima sedans, and the new all-electric LEAF. Advance reservations for the tours are required; no children under 10 are allowed, and cameras, including camera phones, are not permitted.

LONG HUNTER STATE PARK

Long hunters were traders and hunters who ventured into the yet-unsettled western frontier to trap wild animals and trade with Native Americans. They existed in Middle Tennessee during the 18th century, sometimes establishing rough farmsteads, called stations. One such long hunter was Uriah Stone, and the river that runs southeast of Nashville still bears his name.

Stones River was impounded in the mid 1960s to form J. Percy Priest Lake. Located on the lake's eastern shore is **Long Hunter State Park** (2910 Hobson Pk., 615/885-2422). Consisting of some 2,600 acres, the park comprises four units: Couchville, Baker's Grove, Sellar's Farm, and Bryant Grove, each named for farming communities that were inundated when the lake was made. Notably, Bryant Grove was named for Sherrod Bryant, who in the 1850s was one of the state's wealthiest African American landowners. In addition to the park's natural attractions, hikers may see stone remnants of early homesteads, standing witness to the area's past.

Recreation

J. Percy Priest Lake is the main attraction at Long Hunter State Park. There are two boat ramps that provide access to the 14,000-acre lake. Pleasure boating, fishing, and waterskiing are popular pursuits. Catches include large- and smallmouth bass, rockfish, striper, crappie, bream, and catfish. Rental boats are available at the Couchville unit.

For hiking, choose from the short Lake Trail, Nature Loop Trail, or Inland Trail. Deer Trail is a mile-long path through woodland beginning at the park office. The Bryant Grove Trail connects Bryant Grove and Couchville.

Longer hikes include the Day Loop and Volunteer Trail. Overnight camping shelters are available on these longer hikes.

In addition, there is a small swimming beach, volleyball courts, playground, and picnic facilities.

Camping

There is no campground at Long Hunter State Park. A group camp facility can be reserved by youth groups and other organized groups with advance reservations.

CUMBERLAND PLATEAU

The Cumberland Plateau stretches across the entire state of Tennessee from north to south. A flat-topped ridge that stands 1,000 feet higher than its surroundings, the plateau covers 4,300 acres, or about 10 percent of the state.

In the northeastern corner of the plateau are the Cumberland Mountains, a rugged and rural region with Tennessee's largest deposits of coal. At the southern end of the plateau is the Sequatchie Valley, a pleasant, agriculturally rich valley that lies in the middle of the plateau.

The Cumberland Plateau takes in swaths of wilderness including Fall Creek Falls, one of the state's best (and most popular) parks and home of the eponymous Fall Creek Falls, the highest waterfall east of the Rockies. In the northern plateau is the Big South Fork National River and Recreation Area, where the Big South Fork River cuts a dramatic gorge into the plateau. Hiking, horseback riding, and rafting are at their best here. In the southern plateau, Savage Gulf is a natural area with dramatic rock formations and steep gorges.

Cookville and Crossville are the largest cities of the plateau—mostly it is a rural, sparsely populated area. The New Deal–era project at Cumberland Homesteads is a remarkable story of idealism and perseverance. Historic Rugby, an English-style village founded by British author Thomas Hughes, is enchanting even today. The story of the Children's Holocaust Memorial at Whitwell Middle School on the

HIGHLIGHTS

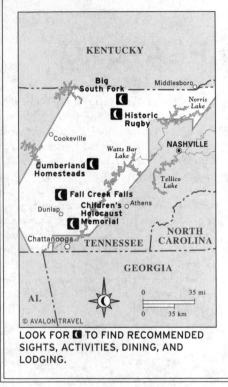

⟨ Historic Rugby: In the 1880s, English settlers founded a utopian colony on the Cumberland Plateau. This site remains a beautiful, spellbinding, and now educational place (page 280).

⟨ Big South Fork: The river gorge carved by the Big South Fork over millions of years is untamed wilderness and a lush playground for hikers, bikers, riders, and paddlers (page 282).

⟨ Cumberland Homesteads: Remnants of a New Deal project to bring homesteaders to the plateau are still apparent in this town near Crossville (page 295).

⟨ Fall Creek Falls: The tallest falls east of the Rocky Mountains are dramatic, but they are not the only waterfalls at Fall Creek Falls State Park; three others dot this expansive and popular outdoor destination (page 305).

⟨ Children's Holocaust Memorial: What started as a project to teach middle school students about tolerance is now a public monument to peace and activism (page 315).

LOOK FOR ⟨ TO FIND RECOMMENDED SIGHTS, ACTIVITIES, DINING, AND LODGING.

lower plateau is a modern-day miracle, which inspired a major studio film in 2004.

PLANNING YOUR TIME

The Cumberland Plateau is a region best explored leisurely. You should get off the interstate and take secondary routes to small towns like Jamestown, Oneida, Grassy Cove, Dayton, and Sewanee. Many of the parks and recreation areas are relatively rugged and undeveloped, so you will want to get out of the car and hike a little.

It is usually a few degrees cooler on the plateau than it is in the surrounding countryside, a plus during the hot, humid Tennessee summer. Also remember that the boundary between **Eastern time** and **Central time** cuts right through the plateau, so you need to be mindful when making plans in this part of Tennessee.

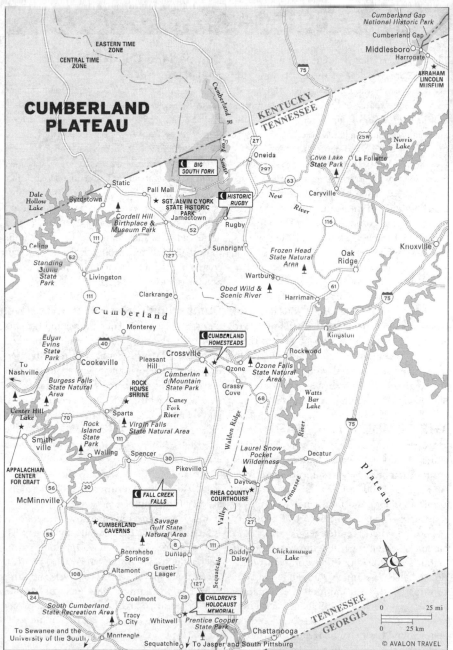

CUMBERLAND PLATEAU

Cumberland Gap
National Historic Park

Cumberland Gap

Middlesboro

Harrogate

★ ABRAHAM
LINCOLN
MUSEUM

EASTERN TIME
ZONE

CENTRAL TIME
ZONE

KENTUCKY

TENNESSEE

75

25W

Norris
Lake

27

Oneida

Cove Lake
State Park

La Follette

☾ BIG
SOUTH FORK

297

63

New

River

Caryville

Static

Pall Mall

Dale
Hollow
Lake

Byrdstown

★ SGT. ALVIN C YORK
STATE HISTORIC
PARK
Jamestown

☾ HISTORIC
RUGBY

116

Cordell Hill
Birthplace &
Museum Park

111

52

Rugby

Knoxville

Celina

Standing
Stone
State
Park

52

Livingston

127

Sunbright

Frozen Head
State Natural
Area

Oak
Ridge

111

Clarkrange

Wartburg

61

75

Obed Wild &
Scenic River

Harriman

Cumberland

Monterey

Kingston

Edgar
Evins
State
Park

40

☾ CUMBERLAND
HOMESTEADS

To
Nashville

Cookeville

Pleasant
Hill

Crossville

Rockwood

Burgess Falls
State Natural
Area

ROCK
HOUSE
SHRINE

Cumberlan
d Mountain
State Park

Ozone

Ozone Falls
State Natural
Area

Center Hill
Lake

70

Sparta

Caney
Fork
River

Grassy
Cove

68

Watts
Bar
Lake

Smith-
ville

Rock
Island
State
Park

111

Virgin Falls
State Natural Area

Walden Ridge

75

Walling

Spencer

30

Laurel Snow
Pocket
Wilderness

Decatur

APPALACHIAN
CENTER
FOR CRAFT

Pikeville

Dayton

Tennessee

56

30

☾ FALL CREEK
FALLS

Savage
Gulf State
Natural Area

RHEA COUNTY
COURTHOUSE ★

Plateau

McMinnville

55

★ CUMBERLAND
CAVERNS

27

Valley

Beersheba
Springs

Dunlap

111

Soddy-
Daisy

Chickamauga
Lake

108

Altamont

Gruetti-
Laager

127

Sequatchie

Coalmont

28

☾ CHILDREN'S
HOLOCAUST
MEMORIAL

24

South Cumberland
State Recreation Area

Tracy
City

Whitwell

Prentice Cooper
State Park

TENNESSEE

GEORGIA

To Sewanee and the
University of the South

Monteagle

Chattanooga

0   25 mi

0   25 km

Sequatchie ↓ To Jasper and South Pittsburg

© AVALON TRAVEL

The Upper Plateau

The northern reaches of the Cumberland Plateau contain some of the most rural and isolated countryside in the state of Tennessee. Here the flat expanse of the plateau gives way to the rugged terrain of the ancient Cumberland Mountains, creating a landscape that is as beautiful as it is difficult to penetrate.

Case in point: When Tennessee officials were looking for a remote and desolate place to put a state prison back in 1893, they chose Brushy Mountain in Morgan County, where the prisoners could conveniently work in nearby coal mines, too. The isolation of this region makes it a lovely place to visit, as long as you are happy to slow down to the pace of winding two-lane roads.

Today, visitors who make the journey to the northern plateau are rewarded with beautiful landscape—mostly rural with small towns here and there. Prosperity is only modest in these parts; these counties are among the poorest in the state of Tennessee. Coal mining has been and continues to be a mainstay of the economy here, along with logging and manufacturing.

THE CUMBERLAND GAP

Once the gateway to the western frontier, Cumberland Gap is now a national park with great natural beauty and historical significance. An estimated 30,000 people walked, rode, or were carried through the Cumberland Gap over the Appalachian Mountains between 1760 and 1850.

Located where Tennessee, Virginia, and Kentucky come together, the Cumberland Gap has remained an important transportation link. The first tunnel through the gap was constructed in 1888, and soon after a macadamized road was built. In 1996, new twin tunnels were built through the mountain and the aboveground highway removed in an effort to return the gap to its 1750 appearance.

Cumberland Gap National Historical Park

Most of Cumberland Gap National Historical Park lies in Kentucky and Virginia; only the southernmost reaches are in Tennessee. The **Cumberland Gap Visitor Center** (U.S. 25E, Middlesboro, Kentucky, 606/248-2817, daily 8 A.M.–5 P.M., free) is located just over the Tennessee-Kentucky state line; it offers exhibits about the Cumberland Gap, information about recreation opportunities, and tours of Gap Cave and the historic Hensley Settlement.

Take a drive to the **Pinnacle Overlook,** located at the end of a windy four-mile road that climbs more than 1,000 feet. From the pinnacle you can see the Great Smoky Mountains 80 miles away, and the gap itself, some 900 feet below.

Cumberland Gap

The small, quiet town of Cumberland Gap sits on the southern side of the gap, surrounded on all sides by hills. Set as it is in the bottom of a geological bowl, the town of Cumberland Gap has been protected from the ravage of development. Historic homes line the streets, and there is a circa-1899 railroad depot and a railroad tunnel that was carved by hand in the late 1890s. Modern-day improvements include a network of greenways and hike-bike trails, which connect the town with the Wilderness Road Trail, which in turn makes its way to the saddle of the Cumberland Gap.

One of the most unusual attractions in town is **Little Congress Bicycle Museum** (Llewellyn St., 423/869-9993, www.bicyclemuseum. net, daily 8 A.M.–8 P.M., free). Here you can see antique bicycles from the 19th and 20th centuries, including a 1934 quadrocycle and an 1895 Penny Farthing. Curator and owner Ralph McClanahan II, a district judge in Kentucky, is a bicycle enthusiast who grew up in Cumberland Gap.

Accommodations

Located in a charming historic mill, the **Olde Mill Bed and Breakfast Inn** (603 Pennlyn Ave., 423/869-9839, www.oldemillinnbnb.com, $115–140) offers unique accommodations in a lovely setting. The six rooms and one suite range from rustic comfort to modern luxury. There is a private log cabin, cozy upstairs "pinnacle" room, and a honeymoon suite with whirlpool tub and a beautiful four-poster bed. All rooms have private bathrooms and comforts like air-conditioning, microwave, refrigerator, and wireless access. A hearty home-style breakfast is served buffet-style in the morning.

HARROGATE

This small town a few miles south of the Cumberland Gap is home to Lincoln Memorial University, an independent four-year university with more than 3,200 students. The LMU mascot is the Railsplitters. To the visitor, LMU offers the **Abraham Lincoln Museum** (U.S. 25E, 423/869-6235, www.lmunet.edu/museum, Mon.–Fri. 10 A.M.–5 P.M., Sat. noon–5 P.M., Sun. 1–5 P.M., adults $5, seniors $3.50, children 6–12 $2.50, children under 6 free), dedicated to the life of this celebrated president. This somewhat dated museum follows Lincoln from his boyhood in Kentucky to his leadership during the Civil War. A highlight is a wall that contains more than 100 different photographs of Lincoln, from the iconic to lesser-known images, which gives the viewer a greater sense of what Lincoln actually looked like. Among the museum's collection are the bed in which Lincoln slept on the night of his 52nd birthday and a rare photograph of his father, Thomas Lincoln.

Food

For a bite to eat, stop at **Webb's Country Kitchen** (602 Colwyn Ave., 423/869-5877, Mon.–Thurs. 11 A.M.–8 P.M., Fri.–Sat. 8 A.M.–9 P.M., Sun. 8 A.M.–4 P.M., $5–15), where biscuits and gravy, country ham, and delicacies like chicken-fried steak are the specialties. At lunch you can order a bowl of pinto beans or a four-vegetable plate, or any number of filling sandwiches; there are even a few gluten-free options. On Friday nights there is an open mic with bluegrass, country, and gospel music; on Saturday nights enjoy live bluegrass.

ONEIDA

Oneida is the largest town in Scott County and one of the principal gateways to the Big South Fork National River and Recreation Area. Incorporated in 1913, it was a way station for the Cincinnati Southern Railroad. After Highway 27 opened in the late 1920s, Oneida continued to serve as a transportation hub for the logging and mining industries of this remote and largely rural county.

Today, Oneida is a workingman's town. The railroad still passes through town, and local industries include manufacturing, health care, and education.

Accommodations and Food

For accommodations, check into the **Grand Vista Hotel** (11597 Scott Hwy., 423/663-2555, www.grandvistahotels.com, $80), located at the intersection of Highways 27 and 63, near Huntsville. This full-service hotel offers free hot (biscuits and gravy) breakfast, refrigerators and microwaves, a heated pool, a business center, Internet access, and a fitness room. There are picnic areas if you want to enjoy the great outdoors before hitting the road.

Phillip's Drive In (18499 Alberta St., 423/569-4002, Mon.–Thurs. 8 A.M.–10 P.M., Fri.–Sat. 8 A.M.–10:30 P.M., $5–14) is home to the juicy Jerryburger, plus milk shakes, hot dogs, chicken tenders, taco salad, BLTs, and other diner food. Phillip's is a longtime fixture in Oneida, and locals say the food is as good as it has always been.

RUGBY

North of Wartburg, the terrain of the plateau becomes more rugged and the towns

© JOEL KRAMER

Christ Church Episcopal is a fixture in Historic Rugby.

of community, hard work, education, and the arts. Rugby opened in 1880, and "colonists" from America and Europe settled here. The experiment attracted considerable attention from the media, which both praised and ridiculed Rugby's unusual ambitions.

There were triumphs and tragedies: Typhoid outbreaks felled dozens of settlers, and economic pursuits failed due to harsh weather, poor soil, and the seeming lack of interest in hard manual labor among many colonists. For a time, tourism was a mainstay of the enterprise, since people were attracted to this odd English village in the Cumberland Mountains where residents stopped to drink tea in the afternoon. One of the oldest libraries in the state of Tennessee was founded in Rugby in 1882, and other pursuits such as a letterpress and restaurant were successful.

But Rugby could not overcome its challenges. A bad drought in 1887 was the final blow. When Thomas Hughes died in 1896, after investing a considerable portion of his own personal fortune in the colony, Rugby was considered to be a failure and an embarrassment. While most settlers moved away by the turn of the 20th century, a handful stayed on and passed the old Victorian-era homes built by colonists down to their children and grandchildren.

In the 1960s, a young man from Deer Lodge name Brian Stagg became fascinated by the enchanting ghost town of Rugby, and he organized Historic Rugby, the private nonprofit corporation that now runs the town.

Begin your visit to Historic Rugby at the **visitors center** (5517 Hwy. 52, no phone, Mon.–Sat. 10 A.M.–5 P.M., Sun. noon–6 P.M., tours $7), where, after paying your tour fee, you'll watch a video about Rugby and view a small museum. A guided walking tour of the grounds covers just about one city block but much information, including **Christ Church Episcopal,** a one-room wooden chapel with original hanging lamps, stained glass, and an

less frequent. Settlements like Deer Lodge, Sunbright, and Burrville appear to be past their prime. If the countryside seems remote now, imagine how it must have felt to hundreds of young English gentry and American settlers who came to the Tennessee wilderness in the 1880s to develop a new type of colony.

◖ Historic Rugby

The story of these unlikely settlers, and what remains of their community, is well preserved in Historic Rugby (5517 Rugby Hwy./Hwy. 52, 888/214-3400, www.historicrugby.org), located in the northernmost corner of Morgan County (and, also, the westernmost edge of Eastern time).

Rugby was the creation of British author and social reformer Thomas Hughes, who imagined a place where the second sons of English gentlemen, who would not inherit their fathers' wealth, could come to make their way in the world. Rugby was founded on principles

1849 rosewood organ. The church was built in 1887 and remains in use today. The public is welcome at Sunday service at 11 A.M. The **Hughes Public Library** looks almost exactly as it did when it opened in 1882, down to the original paint colors. Its simple unadorned walls are covered floor to ceiling with one of the best collections of Victorian literature in the country (about 7,000 volumes donated by American publishers). The tour also stops at **Kingstone Lisle,** the modest home that Hughes built for his mother, who lived out the end of her years, happily by all accounts, at Rugby.

Rugby's old commissary has been restored and converted into a **gift shop** (5569 Rugby Hwy., 423/628-5166, Mon.–Sat. 10 A.M.–6 P.M., Sun. noon–6 P.M.), which stocks an above-average selection of handicrafts, plus English- and Victorian-inspired specialty items. You can also pick up a copy of *Tom Brown's School Days,* the novel that made Thomas Hughes famous and rich enough to bankroll Rugby in the first place.

Rugby today is a marriage of old and new. The new visitors center was opened in 2006, and house lots are being sold according to the original Rugby development plan. But the presence of original Rugby buildings like the Hughes Public Library anchors the newness to its past.

In Rugby you cannot help but be enchanted by the atmosphere of natural beauty, unhurried life, and Victorian-era buildings. Coming here is a journey, not necessarily back in time, but certainly away from it.

Festivals and Events

Rugby puts on dozens of workshops and special events year-round, from heirloom plant sales to yarn spinning to other craft workshops, so you can pick the time of year that fits with your interests. Naturalists, artists, craftspeople, and historians lead these courses, which take place many, if not most, weekends during the year. Download a calendar from the Historic Rugby website.

Rugby's premier event is the **Festival of British and Appalachian Culture** (www.historicrugby.org) in mid-May. Entertainers usually include well-known bluegrass and folk musicians, and there are traditional arts-and-crafts demonstrations. The British bit comes in with a maypole, bagpipe players, and food of the British Isles.

Accommodations

Fall completely under Rugby's spell by staying the night at **C Historic Rugby Lodging** (423/628-2441, $70–135). Historic Rugby offers overnight accommodations in the Newbury House, Pioneer Cottage, Percy Cottage, and Linden Carriage House, all of which are on the National Register of Historic Places. In Newbury House, restored in 1985, there are five guest rooms and one suite. Two of the guest rooms share a bath; others have private facilities. All guests can relax in the downstairs parlor or on the sunporch, and there are coffee, tea, and cookies in the kitchen. Percy Cottage offers free wireless Internet. Rates at Newbury include breakfast. The three- and five-bedroom cottages rent for $80–135 per room, and guests have the use of a kitchen.

All Rugby accommodations are comfortable and unique among Tennessee lodging. Not quite your typical bed-and-breakfast and certainly not your average hotel, these accommodations are rustic yet entirely comfortable, with DVD players, wireless, and other modern amenities, depending on the property. They are a favorite escape for many travelers in the region.

Grey Gables (Hwy. 52, 423/628-5252, www.rugbytn.com, $135) is a bed-and-breakfast unaffiliated with Historic Rugby but influenced by it nonetheless. The farmhouse-style inn has eight bedrooms, each furnished with antique furniture and colorful draperies and linens. The overnight rate includes breakfast and dinner prepared by hostess Linda Brooks Jones, a celebrated local chef. She also hosts a number of themed special events during the year.

Food

The **C Harrow Road Cafe** (5517 Hwy. 52, 423/628-2350, Sun.–Thurs. 8:30 A.M.–3 P.M., Fri.–Sat. 8:30 A.M.–8:30 P.M., $5–12) rounds out Rugby's attractions. Serving breakfast and lunch, and offering dinner by lamplight on weekends, the café is the heartbeat of Rugby. Tourists, residents, and the legions who drive Highway 52 daily meet here in the name of good eats. The menu reflects the hybrid nature of Rugby's appeal: There is Welsh rarebit and shepherd's pie next to fried catfish and turnip greens. All the food is good, though, and there is an effort to stay true to some of the English traditions. You can order hot tea without fear of being laughed out of the room. They may even offer milk. If you get hooked on a particular dish, check the website; recipes are often posted.

The Harrow Road Cafe closes at 3 P.M. on weeknights in winter.

C BIG SOUTH FORK

Big South Fork National River and Recreation Area (4564 Leatherwood Rd., Oneida, 423/286-7275, www.nps.gov/biso) was established in 1974 to preserve this northern-flowing large tributary of the Cumberland River and approximately 119,000 surrounding acres. Threatened with coal-mine damage and what would have been the highest dam in the eastern United States, local conservationists, with the help of then U.S. senator Howard Baker from nearby Huntsville, Tennessee, succeeded in saving this outstanding gorge and rim terrain in one of the most remote areas of Tennessee and Kentucky. About three-fourths of the park is in Tennessee. It is a land bejeweled with a wild river surrounded by natural forms such as steep sandstone bluffs and high arches, including famous side-by-side arches, arguably the largest in the eastern United States. It isn't as well known as the nearby Smokies, but it is some of the loveliest scenery in the state.

Orientation

State Highway 297 cuts through the Tennessee portion of the Big South Fork. It is a pleasant, scenic drive that takes you down to the bottom of the river gorge and back up again. The closest towns are Oneida to the east and Jamestown to the west.

Sights

Soon after you enter the park from the east, you pass the park headquarters and a turnoff to the East Rim Overlook, a picturesque spot where you can peer out over the gorge. From the overlook it is a quick, steep descent to the bottom of the gorge at Leatherwood Ford, where you'll find picnic tables, an information kiosk, and trailheads.

Past the gorge is Bandy Creek, a focus of activity and recreation on the Tennessee side of the park. The complex, which sits on the site of an abandoned homestead of earlier days, includes a campground, horse stables, visitors center, and trails. The visitors center (423/286-7275, daily 8 A.M.–4 P.M.) offers free information and detailed maps, guidebooks, and ice for sale. For those preferring a pool to the many swimming holes along the river, there is Bandy Creek Pool.

Hikers in the Big South Fork love the Twin Arches, a remarkable double natural bridge formation. This is one of their favorite destinations.

In the Kentucky portion of the park there are attractions that commemorate the historic coal-mining communities and railroads of the region. From 1937 to 1962, people lived in Blue Heron, a remote coal-mining town operated by the Stearns Coal and Lumber Company. Today, **Blue Heron Mining Community** (Kentucky Hwy. 742, 606/376-3787, year-round during daylight hours, free) is an outdoor museum where visitors can hear the stories of onetime residents, told through audio recordings and displays about daily life in this remote and beautiful place. From April to October, rangers are on hand to answer questions. At other times, you may explore on your own. From mid-April through November you can ride the **Big South Fork Scenic Railroad** (800/462-5664, www.bsfsry.com, adults $18, seniors $16.50, children 3–12 $9) from Stearns, Kentucky, to Blue Heron.

In addition, the park hosts two festivals each year, usually in late April and late September, which celebrate the cultural heritage of the area. While Blue Heron is the largest cultural heritage site in the park, the Big South Fork is sprinkled with the remains of many more old settlers' cabins and farmsteads. Hikers, bikers, and horseback riders are asked not to disturb or dig around ruins that may be encountered.

River Recreation

The Big South Fork is a center for white-water sports, including canoeing, kayaking, stand-up paddling, and rafting. Floating through the Big South Fork gives you entry to a remote and beautiful countryside where you can still see evidence of previous agricultural, mining, and

© CHARLES SUTHERLAND

Beautiful Big South Fork is one of the state's lesser-known outdoor gems.

logging use. The rivers and streams in the park offer placid floats and dangerous white water. The character of the rivers can change with heavy rains; check conditions before setting out.

For those without their own craft, there is only one permitted outfitter. **Sheltowee Trace Outfitter** (Whitley City, Kentucky, 800/541-7238, www.ky-rafting.com) leads beginner and intermediate white-water rafting trips down the Big South Fork mid-May–mid-September. Participants in these trips meet near Oneida. Sheltowee also rents canoes, kayaks, and tubes. They offer shuttle service to put-in points and provide maps and itineraries to help plan your river outing.

For those needing only a guide, **Against the Flow** (Byrdstown, 931/510-6939) offers professional guide services for the park's waters and others in the area. The river can be hazardous, and floaters need to be sure of their skills and equipment and know the area they are floating.

Horseback Riding

On land, there are 300-plus miles of trails marked by self-evident icons for specific uses. The remoteness of this park calls for horseback travel, and there are 130 miles of backcountry horse trails. The *Trails Illustrated* map of the Big South Fork is the best resource for trail navigation in the park.

Southeast Pack Trips (276 Dewey Burke Rd., Jamestown, 931/879-2260, www.southeastpacktrips.com) and **Saddle Valley Campground** (350 Dewey Burke Rd., Jamestown, 931/879-6262, www.saddlev-alleycampground.com) are permitted horse outfitters for the Big South Fork. They offer overnight horseback excursions or half day journeys. Expect to pay about $20 per hour to rent a horse or $100 per day for a guide if you have your own horses. Short as well as longer rides may be arranged directly at the **Bandy Creek Stable** (1845 Old Sunbright Rd., Jamestown, 423/286-7433, www.bandycreek-stables.net) in the park, which is also a place to board horses while you camp in the nearby Bandy Creek Campground.

Other Recreation

Big South Fork allocates trails for all manner of uses. Hikers may use all of the trails in the park. Mountain bikers may use specified bike trails or any horse trail. Wagon trails are open for all nonmotorized traffic, and multiuse trails include motor vehicles, such as ATVs. Users should check for specific ATV regulations before setting out.

Fishing and hunting in season and with appropriate licenses are allowed and popular. Big South Fork also has many locations open for rock climbing and rappelling, though arches and other fragile landforms are closed to these activities. There are no outfitters for these activities.

Accommodations

For an experience unique in the Big South Fork, reserve a bed at the **C** **Charit Creek Lodge** (865/429-5704, www.charitcreek.com). This is a privately operated concession offering rustic overnight stays at an old farmstead, plus supper and breakfast. It is especially good for groups since each cabin or lodge room can sleep up to 12 people.

The complex consists of three cabins (two for visitors), a barn, and a communal dining/gathering hall. There is no electricity or telephones, and pack light; the lodge is accessible only on horseback, foot, or bike. Full accommodations cost $65 per night per adult ($53 for children under 10) and includes dinner and breakfast. Hostel accommodations cost $20 per night and include access to showers, restrooms, and modest kitchen privileges. All guests enjoy wood-burning fireplaces, heated (in season) showers, and access to outdoor games, including volleyball and horseshoes. Meals are hearty and served family-style.

Charit Creek Lodge is situated about a mile down the trail from the Fork Ridge Road, at the confluence of the Charit Creek and the Stations Camp Creek. You can also reach it via the Twin Arches Trail.

Charit Creek is operated by the same company that operates LeConte Lodge in the Great Smoky Mountains National Park, and the reservation office is at 250 Apple Valley Road, Sevierville.

Camping

Bandy Creek Campground ($19–22) is the only campground in the Tennessee section of the Big South Fork, and it is easily accessible from Leatherwood Road (Highway 297), the only paved road through the heart of the park. There are 181 sites, 96 with water and electricity hookups, and 49 for tents only, and two group camping loops with 19 sites in one and 17 sites in the other. The facility is open year-round, with reservations (877/444-6777, www.nps.gov/biso) accepted April–October. Bandy Creek is popular with families in part because it is that rare campground with a swimming pool ($3). Campgrounds located in Kentucky include Blue Heron ($17) and Alum Ford ($5).

Backcountry camping is allowed in some areas with a permit, available at the park and from many area businesses.

PICKETT STATE PARK

Pickett CCC Memorial State Park (4605 Pickett Park Hwy., 931/879-5821) and the surrounding Pickett State Forest comprise 11,000 acres of land obtained by the state from the Sterns Coal & Lumber Company in the midst of the Great Depression of the 1930s. The park is named after the small and isolated county in which it is located, which in turn was named after Howell L. Pickett, an otherwise unnoted Tennessee state representative involved in the county's formation in 1879. The Civilian Conservation Corps (CCC), a New Deal program to assist the unemployed, built the basic infrastructure of the park in its early days. The original administrative buildings, various roadside and trailside improvements, several rustic stone cabins (still comfortably in use), and the Thompson Creek Dam that creates the park's 15-acre recreation lake were constructed by the local workers who joined the CCC.

Recreation

Seasonal uses of the lake include a free swimming area with a fine sand beach, changing facilities, and rental canoes and fishing boats. No private boats are allowed, but limited recreation equipment such as horseshoes and tennis rackets can be borrowed.

The jewels of Pickett, however, are the natural features and forms that the slow forces of deep geological time have wrought. The soft sandstone under harder caprock and above less permeable layers eroded to form numerous rock overhangs called variously caves or rock houses, or more spectacularly, the famous natural bridges of the park. In the case of natural bridges, the forces of erosion have worked on both sides of a narrow ridge to form a passage all the way through the sandstone. Several of these forms, such as **Hazard Cave, Indian Rock House,** and a natural bridge, can be reached by short and clearly marked walks from State Highway 154, the road to and through the park.

There are 58 miles of hiking trails in Pickett. A network of one- to two-mile loops highlights the park's features. Those seeking backcountry hiking can set out on either the **Hidden Passage Trail** or the **Rock Creek Trail.** The former follows Thompson Creek into the adjacent Big South Fork National River and Recreation Area, where it becomes the Shiltowee Trace Trail and can take the hiker some 40 miles into the Daniel Boone National Forest in Kentucky. The Rock Creek Trail follows this creek into the Big South Fork, where it becomes the John Muir Trail and extends a further 40 miles. The two Pickett trails intersect and form a pair of double loops each about 8–10 miles long, just right for a pleasant day of hiking.

Backcountry camping in Pickett can be arranged at the park office (931/879-5821), and Big South Fork allows it with a permit as well. Pets are allowed on a leash on trails. Hunting is allowed in backcountry areas during specific fall and winter hunting seasons.

Accommodations and Camping

Pickett's overnight facilities include 34 tent and trailer camping sites available year-round on a first-come, first-served basis ($13 per night); a large group facility with dorm space for 144 people and an indoor dining and cooking facility ($3 per person per night, minimum charge $200 per night); and four types of cabins: rustic (sleeps four), chalet (sleeps two), deluxe (sleeps six), and villa (sleeps eight). Only one cabin (the deluxe unit) is pet friendly, and there is a $15 pet fee. Cabins cost $80–120 per night, with a $20-per-night discount during the off-season, November–March. Reservations can be made up to a year in advance. There is no restaurant, but there is a large picnic area with a few rentable covered sites.

For more information, call the park office at 931/879-5821. Cabin reservations can be made by calling 877/260-0010.

JAMESTOWN

Jamestown is the second gateway city to the Big South Fork. Located on the western side of the wilderness, Jamestown is the seat of Fentress County and features a lovely stone courthouse. The town's claim to fame is that Samuel Clemens, better known as Mark Twain, was conceived here. Twain was born in Missouri seven months after his family left Jamestown. It is said that Obedstown in Twain's book *The Gilded Age* approximates Jamestown. The folk of Jamestown created **Mark Twain Spring Park,** across from the post office, to celebrate their connection with this literary genius. (For those who want to take the story even further, note that you may see the Tennessee home where the

Clemenses lived on display at the Museum of Appalachia, in Norris.)

Jamestown's main attraction is the **Ye Olde Jail Museum** (114 Central Ave. W., 931/879-9948, Mon.–Fri. 8 A.M.–4:30 P.M., free). The old jail housed prisoners from 1900 to 1979 and now houses the Fentress County Chamber of Commerce. You may tour the old cells, which now include exhibits about local history.

Tennessee's oldest licensed winery is the **Highland Manor Winery** (2965 S. York Hwy., 931/879-9519, www.highlandmanorwinery.net, Mon.–Sat. 9 A.M.–5 P.M., Sun. 11 A.M.–5 P.M., free), located about four miles south of Jamestown. This Tudor-style winery makes grape, muscadine, and other fruit wines for sale and tasting. The winery hosts two large annual events, Wine and Swine Day in May and Upper Cumberland Cajun Day in July.

Practicalities

Visitors to Jamestown will find plenty of grocery stores, gas stations, and camp supplies with which to stock a trip to the Big South Fork or Pickett State Park, or for thrifting on the World's Longest Yardsale. Highways 154 and 297 leading out of town toward the parks are littered with enterprises geared to outfitting hunters and hostlers.

For a casual meal near Jamestown, try **Cherokee Trails Market and Cafe** (2880 Pickett Park Hwy., 931/879-0895, Mon.–Fri. 6:30 A.M.–9 P.M., Sat. 7 A.M.–9 P.M., Sun. 7 A.M.–4 P.M., $2–5) for burgers, sandwiches, and hearty breakfasts.

ALVIN C. YORK STATE HISTORIC AREA

Alvin C. York State Historic Area, established in 1968, is located approximately 8.5 miles north of Jamestown on U.S. 127. Situated on the edge of the beautiful valley of the Wolf River, not far from Kentucky, it is a remembrance of the most decorated American military hero of World War I. The small town of Pall Mall includes the York home and farm, which he received as a gift from grateful Tennesseans when he returned here. There is also his store and gristmill. Nearby are York's grave and the church where he served as Sunday school teacher, elder, and occasional preacher.

Alvin York was a poor, ill-educated farm boy when he left America to fight in World War I. He returned an international hero, after his courage and marksmanship led him and seven surviving members of his squad to kill 25 German soldiers and capture 132 prisoners in a single engagement on October 18, 1918. York was feted by the Allied countries and their leaders, and offered wealth and fame when he returned to the United States. He chose instead to return to rural Tennessee, marry his childhood sweetheart, and live his life there, while seeking to improve the future for his remote community. York used his celebrity to obtain better roads and educational improvements for the Upper Cumberland Plateau. The Alvin York Institute was founded in 1929 and provided generations of mountain children with education and vocational opportunities. When York died in 1964, 7,000 people attended his funeral.

The bucolic Alvin York State Historic Area (Pall Mall, 931/879-6456, free) is a fitting tribute to this most remarkable American war hero. The park includes the old York home, which is full of photographs and memorabilia reflecting on the famous soldier and his community. The old York gristmill is picturesque, and a picnic ground provides an excuse to linger.

DALE HOLLOW LAKE

Dale Hollow Lake is a 27,700-acre man-made lake located in parts of Pickett, Clay, Fentress, and Overton Counties, plus Clinton and Cumberland Counties in Kentucky. Created in 1943, the Dale Hollow Dam impounds the Obey River about seven miles above its junction with the Cumberland. Byrdstown on the

THE WORLD'S LONGEST YARD SALE

©FAITH LIM

You never know what you'll find on the Highway 127 World's Longest Yard Sale.

In a place where "yard saleing" is a bona fide pastime as well as a spectator sport, it should be no surprise that the world's biggest, baddest, and longest yard sale makes its way through the Cumberland Plateau. Officially headquartered in Jamestown, the Highway 127 World's Longest Yard-sale (800/327-3945, www.127sale.com) wends its way through 690 miles from Michigan to Alabama, although the Tennessee and Kentucky sections are generally the busiest and best for bargain hunters.

It works like this: On the first weekend of August, thousands of people set up booths and tents to sell their unwanted goods along Highway 127. Some of these folks are antiques dealers who come from all over to get in front of a high concentration of shoppers. Others are folks who happen to live on Highway 127, which the other 51 weeks of the year may be a sleepy stretch of road, and drag the stuff from the attic to their front yard. Along with goods for sale there's plenty of food and drink and home-spun entertainment. Many people make driving this sale an annual trip with friends.

There is no telling what you'll find for sale, but expect things like quilts, antiques, household items, books, clothing, crafts, and toys. There are a few things, however, that are certain:

· It will be hot. It is summer in the South. Pack water bottles and stop often to hydrate.

· It will be crowded. People drive along the road and pull over when something catches their eye, so drive slowly and pay attention.

· It will be booked up. In some areas, like Jamestown and Crossville, hotel rooms are booked well in advance. If you can't get enough of *American Pickers*-style adventures, make your reservations now.

east and Celina on the west are the main gateways to the lake and its recreational opportunities. You're likely to see bald eagles flying above in the fall and winter.

The **Dale Hollow National Fish Hatchery** (50 Fish Hatchery Rd., Celina, 931/243-2443, www.fws.gov/dalehollow, daily 7 A.M.–3:30 P.M., free) produces rainbow, brown, and lake trout for restocking rivers and lakes in Tennessee and neighboring states. The hatchery yields more than 300,000 pounds of trout each year for stocking programs. There is a visitors center where you can learn about trout and the hatchery process. You can also tour the facility.

Recreation

Fishing, paddling, and boating are popular pastimes on Dale Hollow Lake. There are 14 commercial marinas on the lake, including **East Port** (5652 East Port Rd., 931/879-7511), near Alpine, and **Star Point** (4490 Star Point Rd., 931/864-3335) and **Sunset Marina** (Hwy. 111, 931/864-3115), both near Byrdstown. Because of its above-average water quality, the lake is sometimes used by freshwater scuba divers. The only commercial dive shop is located at **Willow Grove Resort and Marina** (9990 Willow Grove Hwy., 931/823-6616, www.willowgrove.com), near Allons.

Camping

The U.S. Army Corps of Engineers provides six campgrounds around the lake. They include the **Obey River Campground** (931/864-6388, $12–24), which has 131 RV and tent sites, dump stations, electrical hookups, bathhouses, and a developed swimming area on the lake. Obey River Campground is located near Byrdstown, sitting picturesquely on the lakeshore. Reserve campsites by calling 877/444-6777 or by visiting www.reservation.gov.

CORDELL HULL BIRTHPLACE STATE HISTORIC AREA

Congressman, U.S. secretary of state, and Nobel Laureate, Cordell Hull was born in 1871 and raised in upper Pickett County. Hull's family was poor; he was educated in part at home and then in free schools until his parents were able to afford a private education.

Education was not wasted on Cordell Hull, who possessed a quick and astute mind. In 1891 he received a law degree after just one year of course work at Cumberland University in Lebanon. Hull went on to work as a lawyer and judge before entering into a political career that would eventually take him to the highest reaches of the U.S. government.

Hull was a member of the U.S. House of Representatives from 1906 to 1931, when he was elected to the U.S. Senate. In 1933, Hull was chosen as secretary of state under President Franklin D. Roosevelt, a position he would hold for 11 years. Hull received the Nobel Peace Prize in 1945 for his role in helping to establish the United Nations. He was also an ardent supporter of free trade, believing that world peace and progress depended on nations having free access to the raw materials and markets of the world.

Hull left public service in 1944 and lived out the remainder of his years in Washington DC. He did not return to the rural Tennessee countryside from whence he came.

The Cordell Hull Birthplace State Historic Area (Hwy. 325, Byrdstown, 931/864-3247) consists of a visitors center, a replica of Hull's childhood home, a one-mile nature trail, and a day-use picnic area. Special events are scheduled all year long. A **museum** (daily 9 A.M.–5 P.M., closes at 4 P.M. Nov.–Mar., free) contains artifacts belonging to Hull, including his Nobel Peace Prize, plus original papers and photographs. The cabin portrays the lifestyle that Hull would have experienced while he lived here from 1871 to 1874.

T. B. Sutton General Store, on the lake in nearby Granville, has antiques, ice cream, and live bluegrass every Saturday.

STANDING STONE STATE PARK

Covering almost 11,000 acres of hills and valleys on the Upper Cumberland Plateau, Standing Stone State Park (1674 Standing Stone Hwy., Hilham, 931/823-6347) is a place for relaxing recreation. The 12-foot-tall "standing stone" for which it was named once stood along the Avery Trace, an early road that is now Highway 70. The stone is no longer in its original site; a portion of it is on display in Monterey.

Recreation

The 70-acre **Standing Stone Lake** offers fishing and boating. **Paddleboats** may be rented from the park office year-round, and you can bring your own electric trolling motor and battery if you wish. No private boats are allowed. Fishers often catch largemouth bass, bluegill, crappie, lake trout, and catfish.

There are eight miles of day-use **hiking trails,** including several that climb to points where you can enjoy views of the surrounding area.

The park **swimming pool** is open Memorial Day–Labor Day.

Camping

A pleasant campground has 36 trailer and tent sites ($20), each equipped with a table, charcoal grill, and water and electrical hookups. The campground is open year-round, but the bathhouses close December–March. Sites are available on a first-come, first-served basis.

Cabins

Standing Stone has 14 rustic cabins ($60–65) that can accommodate 2–8 people and are open April–October. Eight timber lodges ($90–150) have central heat and air-conditioning and are open year-round. They sleep up to 10 people. Four modern cabins ($80–90) are also open year-round and can accommodate

boathouse at Standing Stone Lake

up to eight people. There are also a group lodge and a meeting room.

All cabins are equipped for housekeeping; however, there are no televisions, microwaves, or telephones.

CLARKRANGE

Located on Highway 127 south of Jamestown is Clarkrange and the **Cumberland Mountain General Store** (Hwy. 127, 931/863-3880, www.cumberlandmountaingeneralstore.com, May–Nov. Tues.–Sat. 10 A.M.–5 P.M., Sun. noon–5 P.M.), an old-time general store that dates back to 1923. Inside, it is stocked with old-fashioned household items, antiques, and local crafts. A 1950s-style diner serves burgers, fries, and milk shakes. Hours are erratic, particularly in the off-season. Call before you make a special trip.

COOKEVILLE

Cookeville is the seat of Putnam County and the largest city on the Upper Cumberland Plateau. Cookeville is closely associated with I-40, which passes just south of town. For road-weary travelers, Cookeville is a pit stop or a mile mark to show one's progress.

Off the interstate, Cookeville's greatest source of energy and vitality is **Tennessee Tech University** (1000 N. Dixie Ave., 931/372-3888, www.tntech.edu), a public university with an enrollment of more than 10,000. Tennessee Tech was founded in 1909 as Dixie College and was affiliated with the Church of Christ. Since 1965 it has been part of the state's higher-education system. The campus is located on the northwest side of town, near 12th Street and Peachtree Avenue, and includes historic Henderson and Derryberry Halls. The Bryan Fine Arts Building hosts concerts and the campus **art gallery.**

Sights

Visitors to Cookeville should find their way to the **West Side District,** located along West Broad Street, North Cedar and Church Avenues, and 1st Street. This is the best area for shopping and dining. It is also where you will find the **Cookeville Depot Museum** (116 W. Broad St., 931/528-8570, Tues.–Sat. 10 A.M.–4 P.M., free). Located in the town's old train depot, the museum houses railway artifacts, memorabilia, and photographs of the railroad in Putnam County over the years. The depot was built in 1909.

The **Cookeville History Museum** (40 E. Broad St., 931/520-5455, www.cookevillehistorymuseum.com, Wed.–Sat. 10 A.M.–4 P.M., free) houses an extensive collection of artifacts, photographs, and other items of interest from Cookeville's history.

Families love the **Kiwanis Cookeville Children's Museum** (36 W. 2nd St., 931/979-7529, www.kiwaniscookevillechildrensmuseum.org, Mon.–Wed. and Fri.–Sat. 10 A.M.–4 P.M., Thurs. noon–5:30 P.M., adults $4, children two years and up $3). Opened in 2007, the children's museum houses interactive and educational exhibits for children 2–12. They include music making, arts exploration, and outdoor games.

Entertainment

Tennessee Tech University lends sophistication to Cookeville's arts scene. The university's Bryan Fine Arts Building is home of the Bryan Symphony Orchestra, which performs six times per year. The **Jean Derryberry Gallery** (Roaden University Center, 931/372-3123, Mon.–Fri. 10 A.M.–4:30 P.M., free) exhibits student and faculty work, plus special exhibits from the university's collection.

The **Cookeville Drama Center** (10 E. Broad St., 931/528-1313, www.cookeville-tn.org/cpac) is a performing-arts venue where local and touring productions are staged. The Cookeville Mastersingers also perform here.

CUMBERLAND TRAIL STATE PARK

In 1998, Tennessee established its 53rd state park, the **Justin P. Wilson Cumberland Trail State Park** (423/566-2229). When it is completed, the park will be a 300-mile linear trail that runs from Cumberland Gap National Park, on Tennessee's northern border, all the way to Chickamauga and Chattanooga National Military Park and Prentice Cooper Wildlife Management Area in the south.

More than 175 miles of the Cumberland Trail are open, and others are being developed. The nonprofit **Cumberland Trail Conference** (www.cumberlandtrail.org) is spearheading trail projects and is the best source of information on current conditions, campsites, and other useful hiking information.

The trail traverses the ancient Cumberland Mountains. Passing through 11 counties, the trail and associated parklands encompass gorges, valleys, mountain peaks, waterfalls, and geological formations.

Portions of the trail include:

- **Cumberland Mountain,** which begins in Cumberland Gap National Park and travels to Cove Lake State Park;

- **Smoky Mountain,** a 25-mile segment beginning at Cove Lake and crossing through the heart of the Cumberland Mountains to Frozen Head State Park;

- **Frozen Head,** which begins at Frozen Head State Park and ends at the Obed Wild and Scenic River, traversing from the ridgeline to a watershed gorge;

- **Obed River,** a 17-mile pass through the Obed Wild and Scenic River and the Catoosa Wildlife Management Area;

- **Grassy Cove,** which traverses Brady and Black Mountains surrounding Grassy Cove;

- **Stinging Fork,** a 15-mile segment using an already-established trail system through the Bowater Pocket Wilderness;

- **Piney River,** a 22-mile segment that includes 10 miles of the Piney River Pocket Wilderness Trailhead, and then leaving the escarpment above Spring City;

- **Laurel-Snow,** a 32-mile segment passing through the existing Laurel-Snow Bowater Pocket Wilderness Trail;

- **North Chickamauga,** a 20-mile segment located almost exclusively within the North Chickamauga Creek Gorge; and

- **Tennessee River Gorge,** the final leg of the trail, located in Prentice Cooper State Forest.

The trail terminates at Signal Mountain.

The Drama Center also organizes summer shows at the **Dogwood Park and Performance Pavilion,** including Shakespeare in the Park and Symphony in the Park.

For visual arts, visit the **Upper Cumberland Arts Alliance Gallery** (Cookeville Mall, 931/265-0338), which displays and sells works from artists in 14 Upper Cumberland counties. The **Cumberland Art Society Backdoor Gallery** (186 S. Walnut St., 931/526-2424) showcases fine art and photography, plus an annual juried membership show. Visitors may see an artist at work in the open studio space. The gallery offers special workshops and demonstrations throughout the year.

Accommodations

There is no shortage of chain hotels and motels in Cookeville, with the majority clustered around exit 287 off I-40. The town's most distinctive accommodations are found at **Cookeville Manor Bed and Breakfast** (7241 Hilham Hwy., 931/372-8236, $80–110), a red-brick colonial house on six acres near downtown. Guest accommodations include one suite and two rooms. A full breakfast is served, and guests may use several downstairs sitting rooms, plus a conference room facility.

Food

For a fine Italian meal, make reservations

at **Mauricio's Ristorante Italiano** (232 N. Peachtree Ave., 931/528-2456, www.mauricioscookeville.com, Thurs.–Fri. and Sun. 11 A.M.–2 P.M., Tues.–Sat. 4–9 P.M., $15–32), a perfect place for a special night out or a business meal. The richly painted walls and rustic decor are easy yet elegant, and the service is careful but not fussy. The menu offers authentic and well-executed Italian dishes.

For a casual lunch in the West Side district, head to **The Soup Kitchen** (20 W. Broad St., 931/528-7687, Mon.–Fri. 8 A.M.–8 P.M., $5–12) for deli-style sandwiches, fresh soups, and salads. **Dipsy Doodle Drive Inn** (2331 W. Broad St., 931/372-2663, Mon.–Thurs. 5:30 A.M.–8 P.M., Fri.–Sat. 5:30 A.M.–8:30 P.M., $5–12) offers Southern-style cooking in a classic diner setting, and **Bobby Q's BBQ** (1070 N. Washington Ave., 931/526-1024, www.bobbyqsrestaurant.org, Tues.–Thurs. 11 A.M.–8:45 P.M., Fri.–Sat. 11 A.M.–9:45 P.M., $5–12) is one of Cookeville's oldest, and most favorite, barbecue restaurants.

MONTEREY

The city park in downtown Monterey is home to part of the stone that once stood in Standing Stone State Park, north of town.

The countryside north of Monterey is home to the Muddy Pond Mennonite Community. This is good countryside to explore if you are looking for handicrafts or home-baked bread and other specialty items. It is also a beautiful area to drive through.

To find Muddy Pond, drive north from Monterey on Highway 164 until you reach Muddy Pond Road. Turn right onto Muddy Pond, and travel a couple miles. You have arrived. The **Muddy Pond General Store** (3608 Muddy Pond Rd., 931/445-7829) sells handicrafts, quilts, pottery, bulk foods, and clothing. The **Country Porch** (3130 Muddy Pond Rd., 931/445-7370) also has gift items, as well as light lunch fare, including soups and sandwiches.

One of the community's best attractions is the **Guenther's Sorghum Mill** (4064 Muddy Pond Rd., 931/445-3357, www.muddypondsorghum.com). On Tuesday, Thursday, and Saturday in September and October you can watch as the sorghum mill makes its molasses. If you come at this time, you may see a horse-powered mill squeezing cane juice from the sorghum stalks. The juice is boiled in the evaporator pan until it turns into the thick, golden-hued syrup.

At other times of the year, come by the mill to purchase sorghum and other specialty items in their variety store.

Accommodations

For lodging, check out the chain hotels along the interstate, or call for a room at **The Garden Inn Bed and Breakfast** (1400 Bee Rock Rd., 931/839-1400 or 888/293-1444, www.thegardeninnbb.com, $145–155). This 11-room inn offers private bathrooms, full breakfast, and a lovely, rural location on the plateau. The grounds include the Bee Rock overlook, from which you can see Calfkiller Valley and Stamps Hollow below.

OBED WILD AND SCENIC RIVER

The Obed Wild and Scenic River, added to the National Park system in 1976, is—like its nearby and better-known neighbor, the Big South Fork National River and Recreation Area—based around a prized white-water recreation stream. The Obed park, managed jointed by the U.S. Department of the Interior and the Tennessee State Wildlife Management Agency, encompasses 56 miles of the rugged Obed and Emory River system, with adjacent riparian areas. The park offers Class II–IV white water and excellent rock-climbing opportunities. For hikers there is a 14.2-mile section of the Cumberland Trail State Park along the Obed and its Daddy's Creek tributary, though portions of this trail are closed during certain hunting seasons.

Camping

The **Rock Creek Campground,** a no-reservation, 12-site facility with pit toilets and no water or electric hookups, provides a place to sleep. Backcountry camping is also allowed. There is a $7 fee per campsite.

Information

The park's **visitors center** (208 N. Maiden St., Wartburg, 423/346-6294, www.nps.gov/obed, daily 8 A.M.–4:30 P.M., free) has a small museum and information about recreation in the park.

FROZEN HEAD STATE NATURAL AREA

Frozen Head State Natural Area (964 Flat Fork Rd., Wartburg, 423/346-3318) is famous for its beautiful spring wildflowers. The park takes its name from Frozen Head Mountain, a 3,324-foot peak often covered by ice and snow in winter.

On a clear day, the views from the top of Frozen Head extend to the Smoky Mountains in the east, the Cumberland Mountains to the north, and the Cumberland Plateau to the west. Cross Mountain (3,534 feet), the tallest peak in the Tennessee portion of the plateau, is within view.

You can reach the summit of Frozen Head Mountain on the South Old Mac Trail (2.4 miles) or the North Old Mac Trail (3.3 miles).

The land here was not always a park. Much of Frozen Head State Natural Area was part of Brushy Mountain State Prison, and convict labor was used to mine coal from the hills. During the early 20th century, the forest was heavily logged, and in 1952 it was burnt by forest fire. Over the past decades, a new forest has grown up, including an exceptional array of spring wildflowers.

To see the blooms, hike along any of the lower trails, especially those that hug the Flat Fork Creek that flows through the park. Panthers

© DOUG SCHWEIGER

The waterfalls of Frozen Head State Natural Area are an attraction for hikers.

Branch Trail (2.1 miles) is a favorite walk for flowers. It also passes the DeBord Falls.

There are 20 primitive campsites for backpackers in Frozen Head. As many as 75 people can be accommodated at the group camp. There are picnic tables, pavilions, an amphitheater, and a visitors center, plus a 6.9-mile bike-horse trail. All the rest of the 50 miles of trail are for hiking only.

The Flat Fork Creek is stocked with rainbow trout in the spring, and it is a favorite place for fishing.

The Middle Plateau

The center swath of the plateau is the most populated—it is close to I-40 and the population centers of Crossville and Cookeville. Universities in the area lend greater sophistication and wealth to some parts of the middle plateau. Highway 70, once called the Broadway of America, runs east–west through this part of the plateau, providing a much more pleasant experience than the nearby interstate.

KINGSTON

This town, the seat of Roane County, sits on the banks of Watts Bar Lake. The lake was formed in 1942 when the Clinch, Emory, and Tennessee Rivers were dammed by the Tennessee Valley Authority's Watts Bar Dam.

Kingston is an old city. It was founded in 1799 around an army garrison on the Clinch River. You can see a replica of this installation at **Fort Southwest Point** (1226 Hwy. 58, 865/376-3641, www.southwestpoint.com, Apr.–mid-Dec. Tues.–Sat. 10 A.M.–4 P.M., $1). The fort was built in 1797 as settlers moved westward and came into conflict with Native Americans whose lands were being encroached upon. The fort and its soldiers were supposed to protect the Cherokee land from white settlement. At its peak, Fort Southwest Point housed 600 soldiers.

Fort Southwest Point was abandoned by the army in 1811. Beginning in 1974, archaeologists began to study the ruins. Today, parts of the original fort have been re-created, including a barracks, blockhouse, and more than 250 feet of palisade walls. The museum also has artifacts found on the site.

In the heart of downtown Kingston is the **Roane County Courthouse,** one of only seven remaining pre–Civil War courthouses in Tennessee. Inside is the **Roane County Museum of History** (119 Court St., 865/376-4201, www.roanetnheritage.com, Mon. 8:30 A.M.–6:30 P.M., Tues.–Fri. 8:30 A.M.–4:30 P.M., closed noon–1 P.M. for lunch, free), which is part of the Roane County Archives.

Recreation

Watts Bar Lake is located just a few blocks from downtown Kingston. There is a walking trail along the riverbank. Popular activities include fishing and boating.

Accommodations

Nestled on Watts Bar Lake is **Whitestone** (1200 Paint Rock Rd., 865/376-0113, www.whitestoneinn.com, $165–325). Just 15 minutes' drive south of Kingston, this B&B offers 21 rooms in serious luxury. You'll find spa showers and fireplaces in the rooms, and kayaks, canoes, and hiking trails outside. Whitestone is popular for weddings in this bucolic setting.

HARRIMAN

Harriman, a town of fewer than 10,000, has an interesting history. It was founded in 1890 by a Methodist minister who wanted to form a town on the foundation of social temperance and industry, where no alcohol would be permitted. His idea struck a chord with people from all over the country, and when he held a one-day land sale in 1890, more than 570 lots were sold and more than $600,000 made.

The town's **Cornstalk Heights** historic district between Roane and Cumberland Streets comprises 135 historic Victorian houses, many built by these early investors. The **Harriman Heritage Museum** (330 Roane St., 865/882-3122, free) is open by appointment and tells the story of the city's founding. A guide to the town's historic homes has been published by the Cornstalk Heights Community Organization and is available from the **Roan County Visitors Bureau** (119 Court St., 423/376-4201), located in the courthouse.

The **Midtown Drive-In Theatre** (2734 Roane Hwy./Hwy. 70, 865/882-6119), located just south of town, shows movies during the summer.

OZONE FALLS STATE NATURAL AREA

Ozone Falls is located a few steps from Highway 70, near the town of Ozone, located between Harriman and Crossville. This dramatic waterfall is also a short drive from I-40 (you can get there from either exit 329 or 338), so it's a popular stop for road-weary travelers who want to breathe some fresh air and stretch their legs. Be wary, however, because the path that goes to the top of the falls dead-ends at a 110-foot drop. There is no guardrail or fence to keep you from falling, so exercise caution. Families with small children may want to skip this trail altogether.

For a safer and better look at the falls, take the half-mile path to the bottom of the falls. It passes through a lovely gorge with interesting rock formations and old-growth forest.

Ozone Falls is a unit of the Cumberland Mountain State Park (931/484-6138). There is an information board at the parking area, but no rangers are on duty.

GRASSY COVE

On Highway 68, just a few miles outside the town of Homestead, is the lovely rural community of Grassy Cove. Surrounded by Brady and Black Mountains, the cove is more than 10,000 acres. In 1974 it was declared a National Natural Landmark because it is one of the largest limestone sinkholes in North America. Remarkably, the cove is drained by a cave, and after the water flows into the cave, it emerges some 6–7 later at the mouth of the Sequatchie River, on the other side of the mountain.

For casual visitors, however, Grassy Cove's appeal is not geologic; it is the countryside. Drive along any of the secondary roads and soak in the landscape of lightly rolling hills, largely used for livestock farming, surrounded by steep wooded hillsides. Take Kemmer Road off Highway 70 to find the **Grassy Cove Methodist Church and Cemetery,** built in 1803, and the picturesque **Grassy Cove Community House,** built in 1894 and used as part of the Presbyterian Grassy Cove Academy from 1880 to 1906.

On Highway 68 check out the classic mercantile **J. C. Kemmer & Sons General Store** (931/484-4075). It offers old-fashioned cookware, overalls and other workingman's attire, and an array of other odds and ends, some of which you may actually need.

◀ CUMBERLAND HOMESTEADS

The town of Homestead, southeast of Crossville, is named for Cumberland Homesteads, the New Deal project that saw the construction of more than 250 homesteads for poor families during the Great Depression. Organized by the government's Division of Subsistence Housing (later called the Resettlement Administration), the project was designed to give poor Tennessee families an opportunity to work for the basics of life, plus learn new skills and acquire a permanent home.

The countryside around Homestead—U.S.

CUMBERLAND PLATEAU

The Cumberland Homesteads Tower was a project of FDR's New Deal.

© BRIAN STANSBERRY/CREATIVE COMMONS

127 and 70, and Highway 68—is dotted with old Homestead houses, distinctive for their cottage features and the use of golden-hued Crab Orchard stone.

To learn more about the Homestead experiment, visit the **Homesteads House Museum** (2611 Pigeon Ridge Rd./U.S. 127, 931/456-9663, www.cumberlandhomesteads.org, Apr.–Oct. Mon.–Sat. 10 A.M.–5 P.M., Sun. 1–5 P.M., adults $2, youths $1, children under six free). Located in the distinctive Homestead tower and administration building, the museum tells the story of the project, depicts what life was like for Homesteaders, and includes a gallery about the original Homestead families. The building itself is remarkable; the ground floor consists of four "wings," each of which now houses exhibits. The tower, which housed a water tank for the Homesteaders, reaches up above the trees and offers views of

the surrounding countryside. No one can really explain why the planners chose to build such an unusual building, but one theory is that it was to expose the workmen to advanced building techniques.

The folks at the Homesteads museum are remarkably friendly, and the gift shop has local-made crafts, books and pamphlets about the project, and a hefty cookbook of recipes collected from Homesteaders.

CUMBERLAND MOUNTAIN STATE PARK

Cumberland Mountain State Park (U.S. 127 S., 931/484-6138) was developed as a recreation area for the Cumberland homesteaders and built between 1938 and 1940 by the Civilian Conservation Corps (CCC). Its focal point is a seven-arch dam and bridge made from Crab

A NEW START AT THE CUMBERLAND HOMESTEADS

President Franklin Roosevelt's New Deal made anything seem possible. On several thousand remote acres of land atop the Cumberland Plateau, that thing was Cumberland Homesteads, a radical project to give hundreds of out-of-work laborers a second chance.

Under the plan, poor families would agree to work and contribute to collective projects, including the construction of their own homes. In return, workers were paid for a portion of their labor. The rest was turned into credits in order to pay off their own homestead, which consisted of a family home, chicken pen, smokehouse, privy, two-story barn, and lands where families were expected to raise their own food.

Between 1934 and 1938, 262 homesteads were built, and thousands of people, many of them from other parts of Tennessee, moved to the Cumberland Plateau to make a new life. It was, by all accounts, a hard life, but also a happier and more promising one than many people left behind. In addition to the homesteads themselves, the community built a school where children could be educated. There were also opportunities to learn new skills—from canning to masonry—which would help families after the Depression, and the New Deal, ended.

There were a handful of similar homestead projects around the country, including one for African Americans in Virginia. To reformers and planners, the project meant an opportunity to demonstrate that a planned, cooperative community could work.

Cumberland Homesteads did work for several years. A labor dispute in which Homesteaders complained they were being shortchanged on work credits created animosity between the project architects and those who lived there. But despite the difficulties, many Homestead families remained, even after the formal project wrapped up around 1940.

The legacy of Cumberland Homesteads is strong. A handful of Homestead family members are still alive, and their descendants live all over the plateau. Some still live in the Homestead houses, distinctive for their common Tudor-style cottage design and the Crab Orchard stone with which they were built. An association of Homestead descendants and other supporters runs the Cumberland Homesteads Museum (www.cumberlandhomesteads.org) in the old administration building and water tower, at the intersection of Highway 68 and U.S. 70 southeast of Crossville.

Orchard stone, which impounds Byrd Creek to make pleasant 50-acre Byrd Lake. The 70-year-old dam, which got a face-lift in 2008, is a monument to the labors of the young men of the CCC. World War I hero Sgt. Alvin York briefly served as a foreman on the project until he was called away in 1940 for the filming of his life story.

Recreation

There are six **hiking** trails, ranging from easy paths around the lake to an overnight loop. During the summer months, you can rent boats for use on Byrd Lake, and fishing is popular. There is a swimming pool and tennis courts.

Accommodations

There are 37 cabins, which range from modern to rustic, and a group lodge. The campground has 147 sites with electric and water hookups.

Food

The **park restaurant** (931/484-6138, summer daily 11 A.M.–2:30 P.M. and 4–8 P.M., Jan.–Apr. Tues.–Sat. 11 A.M.–2:30 P.M., Fri.–Sat. 4–8 P.M., $6–16) overlooks the lake and serves three meals daily. Friday evening is catfish night.

CROSSVILLE

Named because it was here that the old Nashville–Knoxville road crossed the Chattanooga–Kentucky road, Crossville is now a pleasant town and the unofficial capital of the Cumberland Plateau. Smaller than nearby Cookeville and more appealing, Crossville is a

© SUSANNA HENIGHAN POTTER

The Palace Theatre is one of many buildings created out of Crab Orchard stone.

pleasant place to spend a few hours. This is one of the most popular places to jump on the Highway 127 World's Longest Yardsale, which takes place the first weekend in August. Crossville is also one of the state's premier golfing destinations.

One of the first things you should look for in Crossville is Crab Orchard stone, a distinctive tan-colored sandstone that is quarried in the area and derived its name from the community of Crab Orchard just down the road. Crab Orchard stone was used by local builders for years, but in 1925 it grew in popularity after a Nashville architect used it at Scarritt College. It has been used all over the country.

Crab Orchard stone was used to build Crossville's first courthouse and the Palace Theatre on Main Street, among many other buildings around town.

Sights

The **Cumberland County Courthouse,** designed by W. Chamberlin and Company and built in 1905, sits in the center of town. Its yard has been used over the years for public art displays and memorials, the most recent being a memorial to U.S. soldiers killed in Iraq and Afghanistan. Across Main Street from the present-day courthouse is the older one, built in 1886. It houses the homegrown **Upper Cumberland Military Museum** (20 S. Main St., 931/456-5520, Mon.–Fri. 9 A.M.–4 P.M., free), with memorabilia from the Civil War through to the war in Iraq. There is an interesting display about the prisoner of war camp built in Crossville during World War II.

About a block away from the courthouse is the **Palace Theatre** (72 S. Main St., 931/484-6133, www.palacetheatre-crossville.com). Built in 1938 out of Crab Orchard stone with art deco flourishes, the Palace was a first-run movie theater for 40 years. In 1993 it was listed on the National Register of Historic Places, and after being abandoned and derelict for many years, the community decided to preserve the Palace.

A restored and expanded Palace Theatre opened in 2001.

The 302-seat facility hosts events ranging from high school band concerts to regional musical events. They also show movies. Pop in while you're in town, and someone is bound to offer to show you around, as long as it is not in use.

At the corner of North and Main Streets is the old **Crossville Depot** (931/456-2586). The depot was built in 1900 and served as the town's train station until 1968, when the trains stopped running through Crossville. In the 1980s the old tracks were removed. In 1996 three local Rotary Clubs spearheaded a project to restore the old depot. Today, it houses a gift shop/art gallery/tearoom. Inside there are a few photographs and displays about the old railroad.

For more than 25 years, flea market types have flocked to the **Highway 127 World's Longest Yardsale** (first weekend of Aug., 800/327-3945, www.127sale.com). It spans 690 miles, and Jamestown is officially considered the epicenter, but the area near Crossville is a great spot for newcomers to try it out. Crossville is near the I-40 intersection and is often filled with antiques dealers who set up booths, rather than just locals who drag the contents of the basement to the yard (not that there's anything wrong with that). Plan ahead if you want to stay here during the sale; small inns and hotels can get all booked up a year in advance.

Entertainment

The Cumberland Plateau's foremost arts facility is the **Cumberland County Playhouse** (221 Tennessee Ave., 931/484-5000, www.ccplayhouse.com), located a few miles west of downtown Crossville, near the Crossville airport. Founded in 1965 and nurtured by successive generations of committed Cumberland residents, the playhouse presents mainstream theatrical works like *Hello Dolly* and *Oklahoma*, plus regional and local works. They also organize acting, dance, and music classes for all ages.

Recreation

Crossville calls itself the Golf Capital of Tennessee because there are 10 different golf courses in the area. **The Bear Chase at Cumberland Mountain** (407 Wild Plum Ln., 931/707-1640, www.tngolftrail.net) is one of the public golf courses operated in partnership with the state park system. It was designed by Jack Nicklaus. The 6,900-yard, par 72 layout features a design that capitalizes on elevation changes as well as nature features, such as flowing brooks and clustered, mature pines. The club also offers a driving range, practice green, pro shop, rental clubs, and golf lessons.

Lake Tanasi Village (2479 Dunbar Rd., 931/788-3301, www.laketansipoa.com) is a top-rated golf course that places a premium on accuracy off the tee. The fairways of this 6,701-yard course are gently rolling, with tiered greens, water hazards, bunkers, and thick rough. There is also a driving range, practice green, pro shop, rental clubs, golf lessons, and on-site lodging.

For a detailed rundown of each golf course in the Crossville area, and special packages and discounts, contact the Crossville Chamber of Commerce's special golf desk (877/465-3861, www.golfcapitaltenn.com).

Accommodations

A number of chain hotels are located near Crossville's three interstate exits. The **Best Western Leisure Inn** (exit 317, 4035 Hwy. 127 N., 931/484-1551, $75–100) is a sprawling hotel with indoor corridors, queen- and king-size rooms, and a hot breakfast. There is also an indoor heated pool, fitness room, and business center. Children 12 and under stay free. Discounts are available for 7-, 14-, and 30-day nonrefundable advance reservations.

The **Cumberland Mountain Lodge** (1130 Clint Lowe Rd., 931/788-5833, www.cumberlandmountainlodge.com, $200) is a rural bed-and-breakfast located on a working livestock farm. The farmhouse was fully restored in 2005, and the three guest rooms are comfortably and elegantly furnished in Mission style. Hardwood paneling and Crab Orchard stone feature prominently in the construction. Amenities include continental breakfast, high-speed Internet, wood-burning fireplaces, stocked fishing pond, and miles of hiking trails. Guests may also relax in the common areas, including the great room and a large, homey dining area.

Rates at Cumberland Mountain Lodge are $250 per night per couple, and $50 for each additional adult in your party. The lodge can sleep up to six adults.

The farm is located on a permanent conservation easement, and it is a relaxing and quiet place. It is located about 15 miles from Crossville, south of Cumberland Mountain State Park.

The **McCoy Place Bed and Breakfast** (525 McCoy Rd., 931/484-1243, $85) has three rooms and traditional B&B ambience.

Food

Folks in Crossville like to eat lunch at **Boston's** (42 North St., 931/456-1925, Sun. 11 A.M.–2 P.M., Mon.–Fri. 10:30 A.M.–3 P.M., closed Sat., $4–12). They offer daily hot lunch specials, plus sandwiches, salads, and soups.

For something a bit more upscale, try **Rembrandt's Cafe** (52 N. Main St., 931/456-3636, Tues.–Wed. 8 A.M.–6 P.M., Thurs. 8 A.M.–8 P.M., Fri. 4:30–8 P.M., Sat. 1:30–8 P.M., $5), which serves pasta dishes, salads, panini, and delectable desserts. You won't find food like this in many small Tennessee towns. There is also a full coffee bar. This friendly shop also has an Internet café and tables for playing cards.

The **Stagecoach Place Cafe** (4355 Hwy. 127, 931/456-9631, Tues.–Sun. 10 A.M.–8 P.M., $12–18) is inside the Stagecoach Place inn and offers Indian, Italian, and French-inspired lunches and dinners.

Information

The **Cumberland County Chamber of Commerce** (34 S. Main St., 931/484-8444, www.crossville-chamber.com, Mon.–Fri. 9 A.M.–5 P.M.) has an information center, or you can order a package of brochures before you arrive. The **Palace Theatre** (72 S. Main St., 931/484-6133, www.palacetheatre-crossville.com) also has an information center with brochures, and the staff there are friendly and helpful.

PLEASANT HILL

About 10 miles west of Crossville on Highway 70 is the small town of Pleasant Hill. The **Pioneer Hall Museum** (Main St., 931/277-3872, May–Oct. Wed. 10 A.M.–4 P.M., Sun. 2–5 P.M., free) is a local history museum. Pioneer Hall was a dormitory for the Pleasant Hill Academy, established in 1884 and closed in 1947.

SPARTA

There is just something special about downtown Sparta, but it's hard to put your finger on the one thing that makes it so. Taken individually, each component seems insignificant, but together they make a pleasant whole and a nice place to stop to stretch your legs or grab a meal.

Storefronts along Liberty Square and Bookman Way are colorful with art deco touches. The old movie theater facade was rebuilt, and there are plans to fix up the inside and make it into a functioning performing-arts center. The town amphitheater is used frequently for concerts and civic events, plus a monthly bluegrass concert. Down by the Calfkiller River, the river park has covered picnic tables, a playground, and walking paths.

Bluegrass star Lester Flatt was raised in Sparta, and he maintained a home here throughout this life. There is a historical marker on the east side of town and a monument in his honor in front of the courthouse.

Sparta, the seat of White County, was founded in 1809. Over the years the town grew along with coal, lumber, and other industries on the plateau. Sparta's newspaper is the *Expositor*, and it has been in print for more than a century.

Shopping

Sparta has several antiques stores. **Brasel's Antiques and Collectibles** (222 W. Bockman Way, 931/837-2805) has furniture, glass, quilts, porcelain, and Barbies, just for starters. **Anderson Antiques** (9 Maple St., 931/837-9044, Fri.–Sat. 10 A.M.–3 P.M. and by appointment) on Liberty Square specializes in imported Scottish period antiques. A few blocks from the town square is **J&J Antiques** (133 S. Young St., 931/836-8123), three buildings of antiques, primitives, and collectibles.

Wheel-thrown pottery, soaps, and candles are the specialties at **The Fragrant Mushroom Pottery Gallery & Studio** (15 Rhea St., 931/836-8190, www.fragrantmushroom.com).

Perhaps Sparta's most distinctive store is **Simply Southern Quilts & Gifts** (12 Liberty Sq., 931/836-3271, www.simplysouthernquilts.com). Opened in 2007, Cheryl Hackett's shop sells all the equipment you need to make a quilt. But what makes her store special are the sewing and quilting classes that she offers upstairs and her open-door policy for area quilters. Anyone is welcome to come in and sew in her spacious third-floor classroom (provided there's not a class in session, of course). There is a "men's lounge" on the mezzanine with a television, comfortable couch, and snacks. Crafters of all kinds will feel as if they have come home when they arrive at Simply Southern.

Food

Brenda Pope serves homemade soups, fresh salads, and light sandwiches at **Miss Marenda's Tea Room** (5 E. Maple, 931/836-2542, Tues.–Fri. 11 A.M.–2 P.M., $5–8). The **Sparta Cafe** (104 E. Bockman Way, 931/837-2233, Mon.–Tues., Thurs.–Fri. 4:30 A.M.–2 P.M., Sat. 5:30–11 A.M., Sun. 5:30 A.M.–2 P.M., $2–8) is the place to come for a hearty breakfast or

lunch. The breakfast menu offers variations on a theme: Hungry Man's Breakfast, Big Breakfast, and Steak Breakfast. Lighter appetites can order a bowl of oatmeal for $0.80. At lunch- and dinnertime, choose from entrées like country ham, popcorn shrimp, and catfish. Sandwiches are also on offer.

Information

Stop at the **Sparta-White County Chamber of Commerce** (16 W. Bockman Way, 931/836-3552, www.sparta-chamber.net) for information, maps, and brochures.

AROUND SPARTA
Rock House Shrine

About four miles east of Sparta off Highway 70 is Rock House Shrine (931/761-2885, Apr.–Oct. Wed., Fri., Sat. 10 A.M.–3 P.M., adults $5, children $3), a 175-year-old sandstone house that once served as a stagecoach stop on the Wilderness Road. The likes of Andrew Jackson and Sam Houston slept here, along with hundreds of less-famous men and women. The Daughters of the American Revolution has maintained and protected the building over the years. It is usually open for tours during the published hours, but call to confirm.

You can get to the Rock House from Sparta two ways. Follow the new Highway 70 if you like, but a more pleasant drive departs Gains Street downtown and becomes Country Club Lane. This is the old Highway 70 and takes you directly there.

Virgin Falls State Natural Area

One of the best all-day hikes in the Sparta area is to the **Virgin Falls**, a mysterious 110-foot waterfall. No surface water leads to the falls or away from it; the falls appear from an underground stream and disappear at the bottom into another cave.

The eight-mile round-trip hike to Virgin Falls is through the state-owned 1,157-acre Virgin Falls State Natural Area. The natural area has at least three additional waterfalls and several caves and sinkholes. From the Caney Fork Overlook you enjoy a dramatic view of Scott's Gulf and the Caney Fork River 900 feet below.

The parking lot for the natural area is located on Scotts Gulf Road southeast of Sparta. To find it, drive 11 miles east of Sparta along Highway 70. Turn onto Eastland Road (also called Mourberry Road) and drive six miles until you reach Scotts Gulf Road. The parking lot and trailheads are two miles up the road, on the right side.

For information contact the State's Division of Natural Areas in Nashville at 615/532-0431.

Mennonite Community

There is a Mennonite community just outside of Sparta. Follow Young Street south out of town about three miles and look for Pleasant Hill Road. Take a right, and in less than 100 yards is the **Country Store and Bakery,** operated by Mennonites. The store carries salvage groceries, a handful of Amish- and Mennonite-made goods, and some practical goods specific to Mennonite people, such as dark-blue cloth. You can also buy bulk cheese and Amish and Mennonite cookbooks. The store is next door to a Mennonite school and church. It is open Monday–Saturday and does not allow patrons wearing shorts, sleeveless shirts, or tank tops inside.

Walling

Real Cajun food is on the menu at the **Foglight Foodhouse** (275 Powerhouse Rd., 931/657-2364, Tues.–Sat. 5–9 P.M., $15–38). The first thing you will notice here is a view of the Caney Fork River. In nice weather, you can eat in the fresh air on a deck overlooking the river. Cajun specialties include pecan fried catfish, smoked rib-eye steak, and grilled entrées.

CENTER HILL LAKE

Formed when the Army Corps of Engineers dammed the Caney Fork River, Center Hill Lake sprawls out between Smithville and Sparta. There are seven recreation areas around the lake, where you can picnic, swim, and enjoy being near the water. Eight commercial marinas cater to boaters. **Edgar Evins State Park** (Silver Point, 931/858-2446) sits on the northern banks of the lake, near I-40. Boating and other forms of water recreation are the focus at this 6,000-acre park. The **Edgar Evins Marina** (931/858-5695) is the center of activity for boating and fishing.

There are also 11 miles of hiking trails, including the nine-mile Jack Clayborn Millennium Trail and a short nature walk departing from the park visitors center.

Rock Island State Park (931/686-2471), at the south end of the lake, is located near the town of Walling, southwest of Sparta. The Tennessee Electric Power Company built a dam and hydroelectric plant here in 1917, creating the Great Falls Reservoir. Later, the Tennessee Valley Authority took over the facility, and in 1971 the state leased the first 350 acres from TVA to form the park.

Rock Island has a sandy beach for swimming, public boat ramps, picnic tables, playgrounds, and facilities for basketball, volleyball, tennis, and more. Fishing is popular on the lake, especially during spring.

You can stay in one of 10 cabins ($100–135) or at the 60-site campground ($20), which is unusual in that it has wooden platforms, some with great views, for the campsites.

BURGESS FALLS STATE NATURAL AREA

The Falling Water River is the focal point of Burgess Falls State Natural Area (931/432-5312), located northwest of Sparta near the town of Bakers Crossroads. A three-quarter-mile hike brings you to the breathtaking 130-foot Burgess Falls, named for the 18th-century Revolutionary War veteran who received this land as payment for his service to the young country. There is also a picnic area and fishing piers.

© MARAGARET LITTMAN

The workout from the steep trail pays off when you get to this majestic view of Burgess Falls.

This stretch of river has long been acknowledged as a source of energy. The Burgess family operated a gristmill here for many years, which used the power of the water to grind flour and cornmeal. During the early 1920s, the City of Cookeville built a dam and power plant along the river to provide electricity for the city. The dam broke during a 1928 flood, but a new one was built in its place. The new dam operated until 1944, when it became obsolete due to the Tennessee Valley Authority's hydroelectric projects.

Get to Burgess Falls along Highway 135 or 136. The park is located between Sparta and Smithville, north of Highway 70.

SMITHVILLE

Smithville, the seat of DeKalb County, is known as the venue for the **Smithville Fiddler's Jamboree** (615/587-8500, www.

smithvilletn.com), held over Fourth of July weekend. Arts and crafts sellers line the street, and a stage is built in front of the courthouse for two days of Appalachian music and dance.

Smithville is also associated with the Evins family, prominent businesspeople and politicians. Joe L. Evins was a U.S. congressman representing Smithville and its neighbors from 1947 to 1977. Joe's father, Edgar, was one of the chief developers of Smithville. The nearby state park is named in his honor.

Quilters, sewers, and other craftspeople might like to stop at **Becky's Fabrics and More** (105 W. Main St., 615/597-8521, Mon.–Tues. and Thurs.–Fri. 9 A.M.–5 P.M., Sat. 9 A.M.–2 P.M.), which has more than 2,000 bolts of fabric in stock, plus fat quarters by the thousands. It also stocks specialty equipment for hand and machine quilting.

Food

Smithville is a good place to stop for lunch. **Ashburn's Alley Cafe** (109 W. Walnut St., 615/597-2559, Tues.–Sat. 10 A.M. 2 P.M., $4–8) serves a daily plate-lunch special, plus salads, soups, and sandwiches. Across the street is **Fiddler's** (108 W. Walnut St., 615/597 8646, Mon., Tues., Thurs. 7 A.M.–2 P.M., Fri.–Sat. 7 A.M.–9 P.M., Sun. 8 A.M.–2 P.M., $8–18), with home-style luncheon fare. Try the shepherd's pie or roasted rib eye. Fiddler's presents live music after 6 P.M. on Friday and Saturday.

On the other side of the courthouse you'll find **C Sundance** (107 E. Main St., 615/597-1910, Tues.–Fri. 10 A.M.–2 P.M., Fri.–Sat. 5–8:30 P.M., $7–20), a popular choice for its daily home-cooked lunch specials, specialty salads, fresh-brewed fruit teas, and hot-from-the-oven desserts. The menu is not extensive, but it changes daily, and you can be assured that everything is made from scratch. Sundance serves dinner on weekends, when diners will also enjoy live acoustic guitar music while they eat.

AROUND SMITHVILLE
Appalachian Center for Craft

A fine-arts education center affiliated with Tennessee Tech University in Cookeville, the Appalachian Center for Craft (615/597-6801, www.tntech.edu/craftcenter, daily 9 A.M.–5 P.M., closed holidays, free) is located on the banks of Center Hill Lake about six miles north of Smithville.

The name is a bit misleading: The center is not located in the Appalachian Mountains (it's on the Cumberland Plateau), and it is not focused on traditional crafts. Instead, the center teaches students the latest techniques in clay, fibers, glass, metal, and woods. The results are pieces that are more a reflection of trends in contemporary art making than of the mountain heritage of the area. But it is remarkable and housed in a breathtaking setting.

Visitors can tour three exhibit areas, which feature the works of artists in residence, students, and others. The gallery has a variety of artwork for sale, ranging from jewelry to candles to sculptures, all of which make great one-of-a-kind gifts. The pieces are serious works of art. The shop also sells some art-making supplies, should you be hit with creative inspiration while here.

The Lower Plateau

As you head south, the Cumberland Plateau narrows, eventually reaching a width of about 38 miles near Chattanooga. The Sequatchie River flows down the southern half of the plateau, creating the Sequatchie Valley, a wide, fertile valley that extends all the way to Chattanooga. West of the Sequatchie Valley is the Cumberland Plateau, and to the east the ridge is called Walden's, or Walling, Ridge.

FALL CREEK FALLS STATE PARK

Tennessee's largest state park, Fall Creek Falls State Park (2009 Village Camp Rd., Pikeville, 800/250-8611) is a prime area for outdoor recreation on the Cumberland Plateau. The 25,000-acre park derives its name from its largest waterfall and chief attraction, but there are three other falls within the bounds of the park. In addition, Fall Creek Lake offers fishing and boating, and the Cane Creek Gorge offers dramatic vistas and bluffs. An oak and hickory forest that covers most of the park gives way to tulip poplar and hemlock in the gorges.

Fall Creek Falls got its start as a public park in the 1930s when the National Park Service established a Recreation Demonstration Area here around the falls. During the New Deal, some park infrastructure was built. In 1944, the park was deeded to the State of Tennessee. Construction of the dam began in 1966, and in 1970 other major park facilities, including the inn, were built. In the 1990s, an 18-hole golf course was added.

PLANNING YOUR TIME

If you have only a few minutes, go to the Fall Creek Falls overlook and then drive to the nature center, where you can see two more waterfalls and walk across a swinging bridge. If you have a few hours, travel to the nature center, view the Cane Creek Falls, and then hike the two-mile loop that takes you along the Cane Creek Gorge and Fall Creek Falls.

Over a few days you could hike to all the falls and add the recreational activity of your choice: swimming, boating, bicycling, fishing, or even shuffleboard.

Fall Creek Falls is located within a few hours' drive of three of Tennessee's biggest cities, but it is far from any real towns. The park is about a 45-minute drive along two-lane blacktop roads to the nearest towns of McMinnville, Sparta, Crossville, and Dayton. On the outside bounds of the park are convenience stores that sell canned goods and a few basic necessities. Pikeville, a small town with a few restaurants and a grocery, is located about 20 minutes' drive away.

Fall Creek Falls is beautiful year-round—there are those who think the falls are even lovelier in winter (and certainly less crowded)—but the summer and fall are the most popular times to visit. The fall foliage show here is spectacular; book your cabin or other accommodations early to avoid being disappointed.

◖ Fall Creek Falls

At 256 feet, Fall Creek Falls is the tallest waterfall east of the Rocky Mountains. Here water plunges past millennia of rock layers and into a pool of water that is deep and mysterious. Talking is difficult at the overlook, because you have to shout to speak over the sound of falling water.

Visitors to Fall Creek Falls can take an easy stroll from the parking lot to the overlook. The

© SUSANNA HENIGHAN POTTER

Fall Creek Falls is the highest waterfall in the eastern part of the United States.

hike down to the bottom of the falls is a strenuous half-mile trip, but it's worth the effort for the sure-footed. You can also hike a two-mile loop from the nature center to Fall Creek Falls.

There are other waterfalls at the state park. **Cane Creek Falls** and **Cane Creek Cascade** are immediately behind the park's nature center. In the summer you'll see families playing in the water at the bottom of these falls. Though not as tall as Fall Creek Falls, these are just as splendid. **Piney Falls,** accessible from an overlook on the western side of the park, is considered by some to be the park's most beautiful falls.

For impressive views of the Cane Creek Gorge, go to **Millikan's Overlook** and **Buzzard's Roost.** At Millikan's you are looking out at the point where the Cane Creek Gorge joins the Piney Creek Gorge. A five-minute walk from the parking lot brings you to Buzzard's Roost, where you are eye level with the hawks and turkey vultures that soar along the bluffs.

For information about the flora, fauna, and geologic history of the Cumberland Plateau, visit the **nature center** (423/881-5708, daily 9 A.M.–4 P.M., free). Here you can see a three-dimensional map of the park and learn about the plants and animals that make it home. There is also a movie about the park.

Recreation

Fall Creek Lake is fun to explore by **boat.** Paddleboats, canoes, and fishing boats without motors are available for rent for $6–9 a day; hourly rates are available. A fishing permit costs an extra $2, and you'll need to make sure you have a Tennessee fishing license, too. You can also fish from the lakeshore.

There is an 18-hole **golf** course at the park. Greens fees are $22–25 depending on the day. You can rent carts and clubs, and there is a driving range and practice green. Call the pro shop at 423/881-5706 for details.

There is a **swimming** pool at the inn, which

nonguests can use for $3. Swimming is not permitted in the lake.

There are three paved **bicycle** paths, for a total distance of just over three miles. Bikes are also permitted on the park roads. Chinquapin Ridge and Piney Creek are mountain bike trails. Both are about seven miles long and are appropriate for intermediate or advanced mountain bikers. For details on the trails, including current conditions, call the nature center (423/881-5708).

During the summer, the Fall Creek Falls Stables, a private concession, offers guided **horseback riding** tours of the park for $20 per person. Contact them directly at 423/881-5952 for reservations.

There are a half dozen **hiking** trails in the park, many of which leave from the nature center. The **Woodland Trail** is a 0.8-mile path that passes through forest to Fall Creek Falls. The **Gorge Overlook Trail** is 1.1 miles and passes three overlooks on its way to Fall Creek Falls. The three-mile **Paw Paw Trail** is the longest hike at the park and crosses Rockhouse Creek. Experienced hikers may want to try the **Cable Trail,** a steep path that runs from the Paw Paw Trail to the base of the Cane Creek Falls. It's so steep that the park has erected a cable to help you, and you should consult with park staff about the trail's condition before setting out.

Leaving from the rear of the inn parking lot is a paved 1.35-mile trail that follows the lakeshore.

Several of the trails can be combined to make for longer hikes, and there is one overnight campsite for backpackers.

Accommodations

Fall Creek Falls has an inn, campground, and cabins for its visitors. The lovely blue ◖ **fisherman's cabins** sit picturesquely on the lakefront. The landside cabins are tucked into the woods, with partial views of the water. All cabins sleep up to eight people and rent for

$135 per night; between Memorial Day and Labor Day you must rent them by the week.

The inn is a concrete fortress on the lake, with about as much charm as a worn-out college dormitory. The view of the lake out your window is not enough consolation for the spiritless decor and institutional feel. Nonetheless, the beds are comfortable, and it does beat an interstate motel—but just barely. Rooms rent for $93–103.

Campsites are set in a pleasant forest near the nature center. Rates are $20, but you'll pay $5 extra for a site with sewer hookup.

For inn and cabin reservations, call 423/881-5241 or 800/250-8610. For camping information, call 800/250-8611.

Food

The **Fall Creek Falls Restaurant** (daily 7 A.M.–8 P.M., $4–12) is located at the inn and serves breakfast, lunch, and dinner. Billing itself as country cooking at affordable rates, the menu features burgers, sandwiches, fried fish, and a buffet. The buffet ($10 at supper, less at other times) includes a salad bar, about five side dishes, and three main-dish meats, plus dessert and soup. The quality of the food is mediocre, however, and the health-conscious will struggle to cobble together a satisfying meal.

Around the Park

A few commercial enterprises have popped up around Fall Creek Falls. Four miles from the south gate of the park is **The Way Inn Grill** (Hwy. 284, 931/946-2800, Mon.–Sat. 7 A.M.–5 P.M., Sun. 10 A.M.–5 P.M., $2–4), which serves food off the grill. Their lunch special is popular and home cooked. They also stock groceries and select camping supplies.

On the north side of the park, **The Fire House Grill** (12959 Park Rd., 423/881-5118, Fri. 4–8 P.M., Sat. noon–8 P.M., Sun. noon–6 P.M., $9) sells pizza, barbecue, and groceries.

For more luxurious accommodations near the park, go to the **Fall Creek Falls Bed and**

Breakfast (184 Deweese Rd., 423/881-5494, www.fallcreekfalls.com, $86–150). Located near the north entrance of the park, the bed-and-breakfast has six guest rooms, a two-room suite, and a private cabin that overlooks the rural countryside. Rates include breakfast and tax.

Also near the north entrance to the park, **Dogwood Manor** (34 Rozzell Rd., 423/881-5898, www.dogwoodmanorbb.com, $125–130) is a four-suite inn. Built in 2006, the inn's suites have living rooms and kitchenettes. Breakfast is served on the upstairs balcony.

DAYTON

This town of 7,000 is the seat of Rhea County and the site of one of Tennessee's (if not the country's) most famous legal events: the trial in July 1925 of teacher John Scopes on the charge that he taught evolution at the local high school.

Sights

Visitors should head directly to the **Rhea County Courthouse,** where the trial took place. In the basement there is a **museum** (Mon.–Fri. 8 A.M.–4:30 P.M., free) that gives an overview of the trial, including panels about its two principal characters: defense attorney Clarence Darrow and lawyer for the prosecution Williams Jennings Bryan. Thanks to the widespread media coverage of the trial, there are photographs and contemporary accounts of the events.

If court is not in session, you can head upstairs and see the courtroom, a broad, high-ceilinged, and elegant room. The original hard-backed chairs fill the gallery, and it is easy to imagine the heat and emotions that were stirred up here in 1925. It was so hot, in fact, that on at least one occasion court adjourned to a stage set up on the lawn outside.

Bryan, who won the case for the prosecution, died during an afternoon nap five days after the trial, while he was still in Dayton. A college was founded in his honor five years later, and today **Bryan College,** on the outskirts of town, is a Christian college with an extensive collection

relating to Bryan and the Scopes trial. The college celebrates Bryan's position that the Bible is the literal truth.

Festivals and Events

Every July since 1988, the Dayton Chamber of Commerce and Bryan College have organized a four-day performance of **The Scopes Trial,** a documentary drama of the court case, based closely on the actual transcripts. Tickets are about $15 per person, and onlookers are expected to dress as their counterparts in the mid-1920s would have. That means no blue jeans or T-shirts, and no pants for the ladies.

During the Scopes festival, there are arts and crafts booths open on the courthouse lawn, while the reenactment takes place upstairs in the courthouse. For information and tickets, call the chamber of commerce at 423/775-0361.

Accommodations

Rooms at the **Holiday Inn Express** (2650 Rhea County Hwy., 423/570-0080, $80–105) come with cable TV, microwaves, refrigerators, coffeemakers, hair dryers, and speakerphones, among other things. There is a free hot breakfast in the morning, a business center, and a fitness room.

Food

Dayton's most distinctive restaurant is the **Fehn's 1891 House** (449 Delaware Ave., 423/775-1892, www.fehns1891house.com, Thurs. 5–8:30 P.M., Fri. 5–9 P.M., Sat. 4–8:30 P.M., 2nd and 4th Sun. 11:30 A.M.–2:30 P.M., $12–20), located in an old boarding school. The setting is elegant, yet relaxing, and the menu features standby favorites such as prime rib, fried chicken, salmon, and filet mignon. Try the homemade fruit tea and the daily special dessert.

Travel by boat or car for dinner at **Jacob Myers** (185 Chickamauga Dr., 423/570-0023, www.jacobmyersrestaurant.com, Tues.–Thurs. 11 A.M.–9 P.M., Fri.–Sat. 11 A.M.–10 P.M., Sun. 11 A.M.–6 P.M., $6). Coffee and pastries are available at **Harmony House**

THE SCOPES MONKEY TRIAL

© SUSANNA HENIGHAN POTTER

The Rhea County Courthouse was the site of the Scopes Monkey Trial.

For a few weeks in the heat of July 1925, Dayton, Tennessee, was the site of much national attention. If it had been 2012, it would have been flooded with 24-hour news crews. High school football coach and biology teacher John Scopes was on trial for violating a new and controversial Tennessee law, passed just four months earlier, which made it illegal to teach "any theory that denies the story of Divine Creation of man as taught in the Bible, and to teach instead that man has descended from a lower order of animal."

F.E. Robinson, owner of a local drugstore, is often credited with proposing and championing the cause that Dayton be the first city to test Tennessee's new antievolution law. He recruited Scopes, who agreed to be the test case. Scopes's alleged crime took place the previous April when he taught biology out of a state-sanctioned textbook.

Dayton's interest in testing the law had little to do with the issue of evolution (although most town residents took the Fundamentalist view of Divine Creation). Instead, it was an economic decision, since many in town knew that a trial like this would fill up all the hotels and put Dayton on the map in a way it had never been before. But Robinson and other organizers probably never imagined that more than 80 years after the fact, people would still be coming to Dayton on account of the trial.

One reason for the continued interest in the Scopes trial is the charismatic cast of characters who took part. Clarence Darrow was one of three volunteer lawyers who took up for Scopes's defense. "Great Commoner" William Jennings Bryan was a special prosecutor. The climax of the trial took place on July 20, when Darrow called Bryan to the stand as an expert witness on the Bible.

The courtroom duel between these two lawyers was captured in the 1955 play *Inherit the Wind*, which was performed on Broadway and was made into a Hollywood film in 1960 starring Gene Kelly, Spencer Tracy, and Fredric March. The story has been the subject of at least three subsequent television remakes.

The narrow legal question of whether Scopes taught evolution to Dayton high school students was not at issue during the trial, and on July 21 the jury took 10 minutes to return a guilty verdict. The judge fined Scopes $100. Later, the Tennessee Supreme Court overturned the conviction on a technicality. Dayton prosecutors decided not to retry John Scopes, who by then was at the University of Chicago studying geology.

The legacy of the Scopes trial, and the publicity it stirred, was a wave of similar state laws banning the teaching of evolution. Tennessee's own antievolution statute remained on the books until 1967, although there were no other prosecutions.

Savage Gulf State Natural Area

Coffee (447 Haywood Ln., 423/570-7656, Mon.–Fri. 7 A.M.–6 P.M., Sat. 8 A.M.–8 P.M.).

McMINNVILLE

The roads leading to McMinnville are scattered with dozens of tree and plant nurseries. Several are retail operations, but most are wholesale, selling only to garden and home stores around Tennessee and the southeast. As a result, McMinnville and Warren County are known as the Nursery Capital. The nurseries are attracted by the good soil, temperate climate, and availability of supplies and specialist services.

The greatest tourist attraction in this part of the plateau is Cumberland Caverns (1437 Cumberland Caverns Rd., 931/668-4396, www.cumberlandcaverns.com, May–Aug. daily 9 A.M.–5 P.M., Sept.–Apr. daily 10 A.M.–4 P.M., adults $18, children $10). Best known for its underground ballroom, equipped with seating and a quarter-ton crystal chandelier, Cumberland Caverns also has cave formations, underground waterfalls and pools, and a

historic 1812 saltpeter mine. The underground tour is 1.5 miles long and includes the sound and light show *God of the Mountain*. Kids will also enjoy the Cumberland Caverns gem mine, where they can search for semiprecious stones. It is a constant 56 degrees down in the cave.

Cumberland Caverns is located six miles southeast of McMinnville, off Highway 8.

SAVAGE GULF STATE NATURAL AREA

Carved over millions of years by Big Creek, Collins River, and Savage Creek, Savage Gulf is a network of gorges resembling a giant chicken's foot. It is also one of the Cumberland's most lovely natural areas, but you have to get out of your car to enjoy it. Fast-moving streams, steep bluffs, and the divergent habitats of the gorge and the plateau make it a fascinating place to explore.

Savage Gulf comprises 14,500 acres, 500 of which are virgin forest. There are 55 miles of trails. We owe its existence to several local residents who raised money and support for the area to be preserved. Several of the most prominent champions of the park were descended from the Swiss immigrants who settled this area in the 19th century.

ORIENTATION

There are two ways to access Savage Gulf. The Stone Door Ranger Station (931/692-3887) is located off Highway 56 near Beersheba Springs. The Savage Ranger Station (931/779-3532) is located off Route 399 between Palmer and Cagle. It is a half-hour drive from one ranger station to the other.

The park offers programs and guided hikes year-round. Contact South Cumberland State Park (931/924-2956) for an upcoming calendar.

Recreation

There are 16 hiking trails through the natural area. Some are easy and flat; others are strenuous, taking you up, down, and around the deep gorges. Some 10 primitive campsites scattered throughout the park make it easy to plan an overnight hiking trip. A camping permit is required; contact the ranger stations for details.

The single greatest sight at Savage Gulf is the **Stone Door,** a rock formation that looks like a giant door that has been left ajar. Native Americans used it to travel from the plateau to the gorges. It is an 0.8-mile hike from the Stone Door Ranger Station along the plateau to the Stone Door. Also leaving from the Stone Door Ranger Station is the **Laurel Falls Loop,** a short 0.3-mile walk to a waterfall.

The **Savage Day Loop** is a 4.2-mile hike that begins and ends at the Savage Ranger Station. Along the way you walk across a suspension bridge, stop at Rattlesnake Point Overlook, and follow an old logging road.

For a detailed map of the hiking trails and campsites at Savage Gulf, stop by or call one of the ranger stations and ask for the trails map.

DUNLAP

Dunlap, Tracy City, Coalmont, and other small towns in this part of the plateau owe their existence to coal. From the 1860s until the 1920s, coal was mined in this area. During the 20th century, much of the coal was turned to coke—a refined coal product used in iron and steel foundries. Coke ovens were built all over the countryside.

Dunlap has preserved the history of these coke ovens at the **Dunlap Coke Oven Park** (423/949-3493, www.cokeovens.com, free), a 62-acre park where some 268 old coke ovens have been preserved. The Coke Oven Museum at the park is open by appointment. To find the park, drive south on Highway 127 through Dunlap and turn right on Cherry Street at the stoplight. Cross the railroad tracks and follow the signs to the park.

For more information about the park and the coke ovens, contact the Sequatchie Valley Historical Association at 423/949-2156.

TRACY CITY

Tracy City is a quiet town today. From 1858 until the 1920s, it was a busy coal mining town and the site of bitter labor disputes between miners and the owners of the mines.

Sights

Several historic buildings have links to the city's mining history. **Miner's Hall** on Jasper Road was the headquarters of the local United Mine Workers Union. You can see homes built by coal capitalists next door to each other along Depot Street.

Grundy Lakes State Park (Hwy. 41, 931/924-2980) is a lovely little park and the best place in the area to see old coke ovens. A one-way road skirts a small lake, built by the Civilian Conservation Corps during the New Deal of the 1930s. You can see old ovens across the lake from the swimming beach, and also along the road just past the beach entrance. As you become better at spotting the ovens, you will notice that they are scattered all over the forest through the park.

In addition to the coke ovens, Grundy Lakes has a playground, picnic tables, and walking trails. The 1.3-mile **Lone Rock Trail** skirts the lake. The 12.5-mile **Fiery Gizzard Trail** starts at Grundy Lakes and traces the Fiery Gizzard Gorge. It is a beautiful and challenging hike through a diverse and rugged landscape. This hike includes incredible views from Raven's Point and several waterfalls along the way. But there are boulders to climb along the way and no way other than to walk back out if you slip. Wear hiking boots and be prepared before you do this lovely hike. There are two backcountry campsites along the way, and the trail ends up at the parking area for **Foster Falls,** a 60-foot waterfall. You can also drive to Foster Falls by heading east along Highway 41 from Tracy City. The access point is located shortly after you pass into Marion County.

Shopping
Stop at **The Marugg Company** (88 Depot, 931/592-5042), manufacturers of hand-hewn rakes and other implements. They also operate an antiques shop next door. Hours are limited in the winter.

Food
The Swiss heritage of this part of Tennessee is evident at **◖ Dutch Maid Bakery** (109 Main St., 931/592-3171, www.thedutchmaid.com, Mon.–Sat. 7 A.M.–5 P.M., Sun. 10 A.M.–2 P.M.). The bakery was founded in 1902 by six brothers of the Baggenstoss family, and it remained in the family until 1992. In 2005, it was purchased by Cynthia Day, who continues to use the old Baggenstoss recipes, plus some of her own. You will find loaves of breakfast bread and whole wheat, potato, and salt-rising bread, along with pastries and fruitcakes.

A café (Mon.–Sat. 7 A.M.–2:30 P.M., Sun. 11 A.M.–2:30 P.M., $4–8) next door serves breakfast and lunch Monday–Saturday and a buffet lunch on Sunday. There are traditional breakfast options, all served with toasted bread made at the bakery. At lunch you can get sandwiches or choose the daily lunch special, such as pork chops, chicken and dumplings, or meat loaf. The café closes at 2:30 P.M. throughout the week.

SOUTH CUMBERLAND STATE PARK
To newcomers, South Cumberland State Park (Hwy. 41, 931/924-2980) is confusing because it seems to be in so many places at the same time. The reality is that South Cumberland is an umbrella park for 10 different "units" that are scattered around the southern plateau. Units will be presented in this book where they fit in geographically.

The headquarters of the park is located along Highway 41 about halfway between Monteagle and Tracy City. There is a visitors center, museum, and gift shop, and recreation facilities including a ball field and picnic tables. The museum eloquently describes the natural and human history of the area through hand-stitched narrative panels. It is a good starting place for an overview of the area.

MONTEAGLE
Few communities in Tennessee are as surprising as Monteagle. A speck on the map and a rest stop on the interstate, Monteagle is also home to a 125-plus-year-old summer retreat that continues to this day. The **Monteagle Assembly** (76 Assembly St., 931/924-2286, www.monteaglesundayschoolassembly.org) was founded in 1882 as the Chautauqua of the South. Created out of enthusiasm for Christian living, temperance, and intellectual and artistic development, the Monteagle Sunday School Assembly was initially meant as an ecumenical training center for Sunday school teachers. Over the years, the assembly became more secular in its focus; the annual summer program taught literature,

The Monteagle Assembly provides plenty of opportunity for reflection.

physics, drawing, music, and education. For a time, Nashville's Peabody College held its summer school here.

What is most remarkable about the Monteagle Assembly is that it persists. Of the hundreds of similar assemblies patterned after the Chautauqua Institution in New York, fewer than 10 remain active. Monteagle is one of them. After a period of decline in the mid-20th century, Monteagle came back, and the 100th-anniversary celebrations in 1982 were a major success.

Every summer, from early June until August, families return to Monteagle to live and take part in workshops, church activities, lectures, and community events. If you are having a hard time understanding what happens, imagine it as a wholesome summer camp for the whole family.

Even if you're not a member of the Assembly, you can attend workshops and other events by buying a daily gate ticket ($16). Temporary passes are also available if the workshop lasts only a few hours. Workshops range from art classes to bridge instruction. Lecture topics are equally diverse. Many have a religious perspective, but others focus on local history, health and fitness, or nature and the environment. There are also musical performances.

Part of Monteagle's appeal comes from its physical setting. The Assembly is located in a wooded, hilly area, and the 161 cottages are charming examples of 19th- and early-20th-century architecture, including Carpenter Gothic, Queen Anne, and Craftsman. All are well maintained, and walking or driving through the community makes you feel as if you have stepped back in time.

If you visit during the summer, you will have to pay the gate fee, which is $16 for adults per day. Outside of the summer season, visitors may drive or walk through the Assembly on their own. Stop in at the office, located to the right of the gate, for a map and other information. If you come during the summer, respect the quiet hours, which are 1–2:30 P.M. daily.

Accommodations

The 🌙 **Edgeworth Inn** (No. 23 Monteagle Assembly, 931/924-4000, www.edgeworthinn. com, $110–225) is a seven-room bed-and-breakfast located inside Monteagle Assembly. Built in 1896, this handsome Victorian offers atmosphere unmatched by other area bed-and-breakfasts. Each room has a private bath, and several suites are available. The generously proportioned porch is a focal point for visitors, as is the lovely garden. The same owners also have two suites available on the University of the South campus in beautiful Sewanee.

Just outside the gates of the Assembly is the 🌙 **Monteagle Inn** (204 W. Main St., 931/924-3869, www.monteagleinn.com, $165–245), a 13-suite boutique bed-and-breakfast. Guest rooms are neatly appointed with plush linens, four-poster beds, newly refurnished bath rooms, and color schemes reminiscent of Italy. Common rooms include a comfortable sitting room, gardens, and a front porch.

You can also rent a room inside the Assembly from one of the more than 150 Assembly members. Ask at the office for a listing of properties and contact information. Rates, policies, availability, and amenities vary considerably among properties, and many book up for the season well in advance.

Food

Thanks to the presence of the Assembly, Monteagle supports more than the average number of upscale restaurants. **The High Point** (224 E. Main St., 931/924-4600, daily

5–10 P.M., www.highpointrestaurant.net, $24–46) is Monteagle's original fine-dining restaurant. Built in 1929 by Al Capone, the High Point is famous for its hidden escape hatches and secret storage areas where Capone hid liquor and other contraband. Today, the High Point is hardly criminal. Its upscale ambience emanates from a sturdy stone facade, hardwood floors, and beautiful dark wood window casings. During the summer, you may dine on the stone terrace. The menu features an array of fresh seafood—grouper, mahimahi, lobster, and shrimp—plus prime steaks, pork chops, and lamb. The wine and spirits bar is superb.

Located on the road to Sewanee, 🌙 **Pearl's Foggy Mountain Cafe** (15344 Sewanee Hwy., 615/598-9568, daily at 5 P.M., Sun. 11 A.M.–2 P.M., $18–32) is your best choice for an innovative yet comforting meal in these parts. Proprietors Jim and Susan Wofford escaped the rat race of Atlanta to open a high-quality restaurant in the wilds of the Cumberland Plateau. A favorite among Sewanee and Monteagle residents and visitors, the Foggy Mountain serves a modern version of Southern-style cuisine for dinner and Sunday brunch. Home smoked trout, stuffed pork chops, and lots of fresh salads are just some of the dishes you can expect.

For something more everyday, go to **Papa Ron's Pizza and Pasta Grill** (402 W. Main St., 931/924-3355, www.paparons.net, Mon.–Thurs. and Sun. 11 A.M.–9 P.M., Fri.–Sat. 11 A.M.–10 P.M., $6–18), which serves lunch and dinner daily. The menu offers a variety of creamy and tomato-based pasta dishes, personal and large pizzas, soup, and sandwiches. The service is efficient.

The **Monteagle Diner** (740 W. Main St., 931/924-4177, Sun.–Mon. 6:30 A.M.–3 P.M., Wed.–Sat. 6:30 A.M.–9 P.M., $4–12) serves comfort food for breakfast, lunch, and dinner. The breakfast buffet and lunch specials are popular.

SEWANEE

The town of Sewanee is synonymous with the **University of the South** (735 University Ave., 931/598-1000, www.sewanee.edu), the private liberal arts college that has educated 24 Rhodes scholars and earned a reputation as one of the South's finest universities.

It was 1857 when the Episcopal Church announced it was planning to establish an educational center in the region. The plans were grand: The center would include 30 schools and colleges offering classical education as well as practical subjects like agriculture and forestry. The citizens of Franklin County and the Sewanee Mining Company offered 10,000 acres of land on the Cumberland Plateau for the school, and in 1860 the cornerstone was laid.

The Civil War nearly dashed all hopes for this educational paradise. By the end of the war all the original leaders were dead, and the cornerstone had been blown apart. Promised funds for the school had evaporated.

Despite the challenges, bishops Charles T. Quintard and William M. Green persisted with the dream. They raised 2,500 British pounds, built a clapboard chapel, donned ecclesiastical robes, and led a procession to establish the University of the South on September 18, 1868. During its first year, nine students were enrolled.

Over the years, Sewanee's fortunes have improved. Today, it has one of the largest per-student endowments in the country. Its academic reputation is strong, and the *Sewanee Review* is the oldest literary quarterly in the United States. The university is still owned by the Episcopal Church, and in addition to its undergraduate liberal arts college, it is home to the Episcopal School of Theology.

Sewanee enrolls about 1,500 students. The original "domain" of 10,000 acres that was donated to establish the school remains, making it the largest college campus in America. The campus, with its Gothic-style architecture and classical feel, is a pleasant place for a walk. Stop at the admissions office for a campus map.

Sewanee's architecture is grand. Even the newer buildings are carefully constructed to fit in on the campus, which feels like it would be just as at home in old England as on the Cumberland Plateau of Tennessee.

For a dramatic view over the western edge of the plateau, drive to an overlook located at the end of Tennessee Street, past the School of Theology.

Of note is the **University Bookstore** (735 University Ave., 931/598-1153), which is the best bookstore between Chattanooga and Nashville. The shelves include an extensive selection of religious works, Sewanee merchandise, and a wide selection of modern and classic works. The *Sewanee Review* is on sale for $8 a copy.

Accommodations

Accommodations in Sewanee itself are limited. **Cabin 111** (289 University Ave., 931/598-5311, www.cabin111.com, $95) is a cozy one-bedroom cottage located half a mile from the university campus. The simple yet comfortable accommodations include a queen-size bed and kitchenette. The cabin is nonsmoking, and pets are not permitted.

The owners of the **Edgeworth Inn** in Monteagle have two **Sewanee Suites** (931/924-4000, www.edgeworthinn.com, $200) available for rent on campus.

If you are in some way affiliated with the university, you may reserve a room at **The Sewanee Inn** (University Ave., 931/598-1686). For other choices, look in nearby Monteagle.

Food

On campus, the **Global Cafe** (735 University Ave., 931/598-1120, Mon.–Sat. 8 A.M.–10 P.M., $5–13) serves breakfast, lunch, and dinner six days a week. The menu includes sandwiches, salads, and homemade potato chips. You can also get coffee and snacks. The café is next door to the campus bookstore.

© KIM HEADRICK

Children's Holocaust Memorial is a moving tribute to events that took place across the globe.

Sewanee's commercial district is located along Highway 41, a few blocks south of the university. **The Blue Chair** (41 University Ave., 931/598-5434, www.thebluechair.com, opens Mon.–Fri. at 7 A.M., Sat. at 7:30 A.M., $7–14) should be your first stop for coffee, sandwiches, breakfast, and take-away dinners and boxed lunches. Call ahead for hours; closing time varies with the season and the university's schedule.

Around Sewanee

The **Sewanee Natural Bridge** is about four miles outside of town. Part of South Cumberland State Park, the rock formation is 25 feet tall with a 50-foot span. Visitors reach it at the end of a short footpath from a parking area. Take care as you walk over and around the natural wonder.

To find the natural bridge, drive west out of town along Highway 41. Turn left onto Highway 56 and follow the signs.

WHITWELL

A small town on the southern end of the Sequatchie Valley, Whitwell is the type of place you might just pass right through. Don't. This rural community that huddles along Highway 28 northeast of Chattanooga is home to one of the most moving sights in this part of Tennessee, the Children's Holocaust Memorial.

◖ Children's Holocaust Memorial

The story started in 1998, when the principal of Whitwell Middle School wanted to start a project about tolerance. She sent an eighth-grade teacher, David Smith, to a workshop on the subject. Mr. Smith returned with an idea to offer an after-school class about the Holocaust. Another teacher, Sandra Roberts, led the first session in the fall of 1998. As Roberts told the students about the six million Jews killed by the Nazis, she realized that six million was a number that her students just could not grasp.

It was a student who first suggested the

NATIONAL CORNBREAD FESTIVAL

If there is one thing Southerners know, it is corn bread. They have strong opinions on what makes for a good corn bread and how to prepare it, and they descend on South Pittsburg at the end of April each year to share these thoughts at the National Cornbread Festival (www.nationalcornbread.com).

A $5 admission gets you inside the festival, which features Cornbread Alley (locals showing off their favorite recipes), corn bread cook-offs, buttermilk-chugging and ice-cream-eating contests, arts and crafts shows, a quilt exhibit, and tours of the local Lodge Foundry Plant, where cast-iron skillets (essential for corn bread making) are manufactured. Winning recipes tend to shy away from straight-up corn bread—one of 2012 finalists was a sweet corn bread shrimp cakes with mango salsa—but there is plenty of unadulterated corn bread around, too.

paper clips. The idea was for students to collect 6 million paper clips as a way of demonstrating the horrific scale of the Holocaust. The idea caught on. Over the years that followed, Whitwell Middle School received paper clips from all 50 states and more than 50 countries. Along with them have come letters and documents, over 30,000 of them. The school still receives paper clips.

The tale of the Children's Holocaust Memorial goes even further. After the paper clips began to pour in and interest in the project grew, the school recognized the need for a memorial. Things came together when two correspondents for a German newspaper bought a 1917 German rail car that had been used to transport Jews during the Holocaust and donated it to the school. Local businesses pitched in to build the memorial, where visitors can come to see the millions of paper clips that the students collected. The message of the memorial is one of rebirth and call to action: The students ask you as you leave to reflect on what you can do to eliminate hatred and bigotry from the world.

Visitors can see the Children's Holocaust Memorial (1130 Main St., 423/658-5631, www.whitwellmiddleschool.org) at any time. During school hours, stop at the front door of the school, where you can pick up an audio tour. On Friday when school is in session there are student-led tours at 10:40 A.M. Reservations are required. After hours you can pick up an audio tour from the police station or simply look at the memorial on your own.

In 2004, Miramax Pictures released a documentary by Joe Fab about the project, titled *Paper Clips.*

SOUTH PITTSBURG

Established in the 1870s and named in the hope it would become an industrial center of the New South, South Pittsburg is a small town that has seen better days. It is located just a few miles north of the Alabama state line.

Thousands of people head to South Pittsburg for the **National Cornbread Festival** (www.nationalcornbread.com), which takes place during the last weekend of April and includes cook-offs, live music, church services, and lots of corn bread.

It is almost impossible to fight the lines at the **Lodge Factory Store** (503 S. Cedar Ave., 423/837-5919) during the corn bread festival. (Everyone needs cast iron for their new corn bread recipes.) But the rest of the year it is a less hectic place to stock up on this beloved brand.

South Pittsburg is near I-24, and so there are several mainstream hotels nearby. **Comfort Inn** (exit 152, 205 Kimball Crossing Dr., 423/837-2479, $75–85) and **Holiday Inn Express** (exit 152, 300 Battlecreek Rd., 423/837-1500, $76–115) are two choices.

CHATTANOOGA AND THE OVERHILL COUNTRY

Nicknamed the Scenic City, Chattanooga, the smallest of Tennessee's four main cities, is also regarded as its most livable. In 2011 *Outside* magazine's readers named it their "ultimate dream city." Perched on the bank of the Tennessee River, surrounded by mountains, Chattanooga was once an industrial powerhouse. After some hardscrabble years, now it is a model for urban ecofriendly redevelopment. City parks, a pedestrian bridge, free downtown (electric, zero-emission) buses, and an abundance of nearby recreation have brought people back downtown. Its arts district is anchored by a museum with one of the best collections of American art in the South. The University of Tennessee has a downtown Chattanooga campus, which lends an additional youthful energy to the city.

In addition, Chattanooga is one of the best destinations for families in Tennessee. Perhaps with the exception of the Great Smoky Mountains, no other part of Tennessee has as much to offer its pint-size visitors. The Tennessee Aquarium is its flagship attraction, but there is also a downtown IMAX theater, the Chattanooga Zoo, and railroad excursions. On Lookout Mountain, families will enjoy riding the Incline Railroad, going beneath the earth to see the hard-to-describe Ruby Falls, and exploring the fairyland style rock gardens at Rock City. On top of this are downtown parks, the local AA baseball team, nearby Lake

© MELINDA FAWVER/123RF

HIGHLIGHTS

◖ **Tennessee Aquarium:** See freshwater and ocean creatures up close at one of the best aquariums in the country (page 323).

◖ **Lookout Mountain:** This narrow finger of the Cumberland Plateau offers great views as well as Rock City, Ruby Falls, and the setting of a Civil War battle (page 326).

◖ **Rafting the Ocoee:** High-velocity rapids keep even the most experienced paddlers at the edge of their rafts on a journey down the Ocoee River (page 346).

◖ **Ducktown Basin Museum:** Learn about the legacy of copper mining at this top-notch, yet down-home, museum (page 349).

◖ **Tennessee Valley Railroad Excursions:** All aboard! See old mining towns and beautiful mountain passes on a scenic railroad ride (page 354).

◖ **Fort Loudoun State Historic Area:** The complex dynamics of the Tennessee frontier come to life at this re-created 18th-century British fort (page 359).

LOOK FOR ◖ TO FIND RECOMMENDED SIGHTS, ACTIVITIES, DINING, AND LODGING.

Winnepesauka, and an amusement park, not to mention lots of hiking, paddling, and other outdoor activities.

The nearby Overhill region in southeastern Tennessee is a region of natural beauty and rich heritage. Five rivers wind down the mountains and through the valleys here, with names—Hiwassee, Ocoee, Tellico, Conasauga, and Tennessee—that trace back to the Overhill Cherokee people. The Ocoee's white-water rapids attract rafters and kayakers; the calms of the Hiwassee are a refuge for Sandhill crane and other waterfowl.

The foothill country here is dotted with towns and landmarks named in the Cherokee language, and others—like Reliance, Copperhill, and Cleveland—that are linked to lives and industries of more modern settlers. Museums in Ducktown, Etowah, and Englewood preserve the stories of Tennesseans who earned their livelihoods in the mines, on the railroads, and in the textile factories of East Tennessee.

It is the natural beauty of the region that is its greatest calling card, however. The Cherokee National Forest contains hiking trails, bike paths, lakes, and rivers. The landscape invites you to slow down and enjoy the seasons and the gentle passage of time. For more to do near Chattanooga, Monteagle and Sewanee are good places to visit.

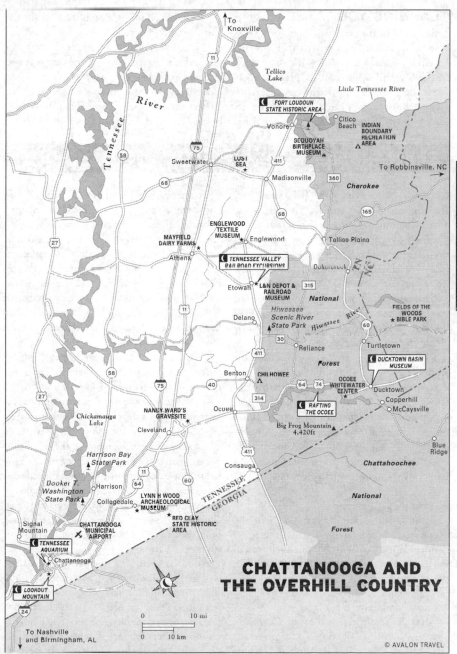

CHATTANOOGA AND THE OVERHILL COUNTRY

To Knoxville

Tellico Lake

Little Tennessee River

Tennessee River

FORT LOUDOUN STATE HISTORIC AREA

Citico Beach

Vonore

INDIAN BOUNDARY RECREATION AREA

SEQUOYAH BIRTHPLACE MUSEUM

To Robbinsville, NC

Sweetwater

LOST SEA

Cherokee

Madisonville

ENGLEWOOD TEXTILE MUSEUM

Englewood

Tellico Plains

MAYFIELD DAIRY FARMS

Athens

TENNESSEE VALLEY RAILROAD EXCURSIONS

Ocoeroeck

TN NC

FIELDS OF THE WOODS BIBLE PARK

Etowah

L&N DEPOT & RAILROAD MUSEUM

National

Delano

Hiwassee Scenic River State Park

Hiwassee River

Reliance

Turtletown

DUCKTOWN BASIN MUSEUM

Benton

CHILHOWEE

Forest

OCOEE WHITEWATER CENTER

Ducktown

Copperhill

Chickamauga Lake

NANCY WARD'S GRAVESITE

Ocoee

RAFTING THE OCOEE

McCaysville

Cleveland

Big Frog Mountain 4,420ft

Chattahoochee

Blue Ridge

Harrison Bay State Park

Consauga

Booker T. Washington State Park

Harrison

National

Collegedale

LYNN H WOOD ARCHAEOLOGICAL MUSEUM

TENNESSEE GEORGIA

Signal Mountain

CHATTANOOGA MUNICIPAL AIRPORT

RED CLAY STATE HISTORIC AREA

Forest

TENNESSEE AQUARIUM

Chattanooga

LOOKOUT MOUNTAIN

To Nashville and Birmingham, AL

0   10 mi

0   10 km

© AVALON TRAVEL

PLANNING YOUR TIME

This region of the state is perfect for a two-in-one vacation: Start with three days in Chattanooga and follow it with three days in the Overhill region. It's a plan that offers a nice balance of urban sophistication and outdoor exploration, and can be an ideal family vacation. If you have more time,

add a day in Monteagle and Sewanee (in the Cumberland Plateau).

If you have only a long weekend and pine for the outdoors, cut your time in Chattanooga to two days and spend your third day at the Ocoee River.

Remember that many attractions in Chattanooga—such as the aquarium—may be very crowded during summer weekends.

Chattanooga

Cradled in a tight bend of the Tennessee River, Chattanooga is a city that has risen from the ashes. Chattanooga's first boom was after the Civil War, when industry and transportation flourished. Expansive warehouses and railway yards bustled with activity, and the city that grew up around them was lively and sophisticated.

Chattanooga's prosperity was not to last, however. By the 1970s and '80s, the Scenic City was dirty, dilapidated, and nearly deserted by all but the most loyal residents.

Chattanooga's turnaround is one of the great stories of the success of urban planning and downtown development. Starting with the flagship Tennessee Aquarium in the early 1990s, Chattanooga has flourished with the addition of new attractions. Planners have also emphasized quality of life for residents; Chattanooga is pedestrian friendly, easy to navigate, and boasts several lovely downtown parks.

History

Chattanooga's location in the bend of the Tennessee River made it secure, temperate, and fertile. Native Americans are believed to have settled here more than 8,000 years ago. The Cherokee called the area *Chado-na-ugsa* (rock that comes to a point), referring to nearby Lookout Mountain.

After the forced removal of the Cherokee, settlers established Ross's Landing, a trading post on the river. In 1839, the town of

Chattanooga was incorporated. Eleven years later, the first rail line, the Western and Atlantic, arrived in the city.

Chattanooga was called the city where cotton meets corn. It was the gateway to the Deep South. Goods passed through Chattanooga whether by rail or river, giving rise to a massive warehouse and transportation industry. Residents here were sympathetic with the Confederate view, even before the State of Tennessee voted to secede from the Union in 1861.

Chattanooga was of great strategic importance during the Civil War. Confederates moved in to defend her in 1861, and for the first two years of the war Chattanooga was an important supply depot for the Southern states. In the fall of 1863, after the bloody battles of Chickamauga and Chattanooga, the city was in Federal hands. Once again, Chattanooga's infrastructure and strategic position proved useful to its occupiers. Sherman used Chattanooga as a staging point for his march through Georgia and South Carolina, and Union troops built warehouses, stockyards, and hospitals to support the army.

After the Civil War, northern industrialists sought to capitalize on Chattanooga's location, infrastructure, and proximity to natural resources. These industrialists were also the political leaders of the city, and they relied heavily on the political support of newly enfranchised African Americans. During this period,

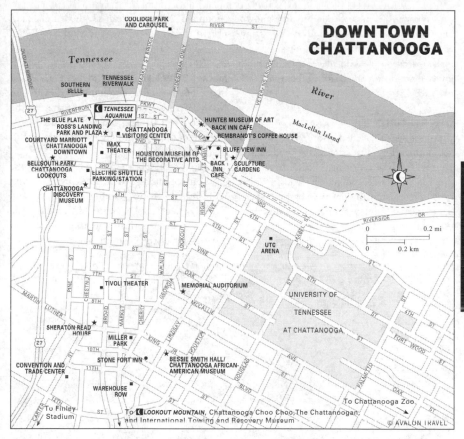

DOWNTOWN CHATTANOOGA

African Americans were elected to local office, established businesses, and pursued education.

Economic woes of the 1890s, combined with the social and political backlash against postwar policies that empowered African Americans, led to hard times for the city's blacks. Jim Crow arrived in Chattanooga and would remain until the civil rights movement of the 1950s and '60s.

Chattanooga remained a city based on industry and manufacturing. In 1899 the city secured exclusive bottling rights to Coca-Cola, and the Chattanooga Coca-Cola bottling plant grew into one of the city's largest and most successful businesses. (Coke still rules the beverage

counters in town today. You might also find an RC, but likely not a Pepsi.) After the Tennessee Valley Authority built dams, increased electricity supply, and eased flooding during the 1930s and '40s, Chattanooga experienced another boom, further bolstered by World War II. The economic success was not without problems, however. By the late 1960s Chattanooga was one of the most polluted cities in America.

Over the past two decades, Chattanooga has experienced an exciting period of rebirth. In 2008 Volkswagen Group of America announced that it was putting its U.S. headquarters in the city, a move that lead to building a $1 billion green assembly plant. Spurred by the success of the Tennessee Aquarium, downtown Chattanooga is once again alive. Pedestrian walkways and good public transportation help make the city a pleasant place to be, while its lovely location on the bank of the Tennessee makes it distinctive.

Orientation

Chattanooga is defined and confined by its geography. The city sits in the bend of the Tennessee River and is hemmed in by mountains on three sides. Missionary Ridge, which runs along the fourth side, was a barrier for earlier residents, but now tunnels pass through it.

The best place to get an understanding of Chattanooga's setting is from atop Lookout Mountain, where you can see the Cumberland Plateau, the Tennessee River, and Missionary Ridge.

DOWNTOWN

Market Street and **Broad Street** are the two major north–south thoroughfares downtown. Market Street continues across the river via the Market Street Bridge; Broad Street dead-ends in front of the aquarium. Cross streets 1st–9th make navigation simple.

South and east of the aquarium district is the city's business and government center. Here you will find large office buildings; city, state, and federal offices; the University of Tennessee; the city's African American museum; and Warner Park, home of the Chattanooga Zoo.

Market Street Bridge

© MELINDA FAWVER/123RF

Farther south is the world-famous Choo Choo and Chattanooga's old commercial district, centered along **Main Street.** Explore around the Choo Choo, and you will see lots of old brick buildings that once housed warehouses, hotels, and manufacturers that needed to be near the railroad. Many of these buildings have been restored and now house new businesses; some still sit empty.

Bluff View is a smattering of elegant old homes located about three blocks east of the aquarium, along the river, with, as its name suggests, a view from the bluff over the river. The city's art museum is here, along with a collection of outstanding restaurants. You can get to Bluff View on foot either by walking about four blocks along 3rd Street from downtown, along the Riverwalk boardwalk that follows the river, or across the remarkable Holmberg pedestrian bridge, a 250-foot lighted glass bridge that connects the south end of Walnut Street to Bluff View.

Across the river from downtown is the **Northside.** Accessible by car via the Market Street Bridge or by foot along the Walnut Street pedestrian bridge, Northside is a dining, shopping, and entertainment center with a fresher, more youthful feel than downtown. Coolidge Park along the waterfront is another attraction on this side of the river.

LOOKOUT MOUNTAIN

Many of Chattanooga's most famous attractions are on Lookout Mountain, located south of downtown. The best way to get to Lookout Mountain from the city is by driving south on Broad Street. After about two miles, Broad splits into the Ochs Highway (Route 58) and the Cummings Highway (Highways 42, 72, 11, and 64). Follow Ochs to get to the base of the Incline Railroad or Rock City; follow Cummings to get to Point Park and Ruby Falls. Both roads take you to Lookout Mountain.

You can also get to Lookout Mountain by parking at the bottom and riding the Incline

Railroad. When you reach the top, you can walk to Point Park. Other attractions are beyond walking distance, however.

Whenever you are driving on Lookout Mountain, do it with caution. The roads are narrow, windy, heavily trafficked, and—in some places—precarious. Drive slowly and carefully (seriously, no texting!).

SIGHTS
◖ Tennessee Aquarium

The Tennessee Aquarium (1 Broad St., 800/262-0695, www.tnaqua.org, daily 10 A.M.–6 P.M., adults $24.95, children 3–12 $14.95) is Chattanooga's landmark attraction. Two huge buildings with angular glass roofs house Ocean Journey and River Journey, salt- and freshwater aquariums with more than 12,000 animals in all. It has a more educational bent than facilities like Atlanta's Georgia Aquarium, which is more entertainment focused. Built in 1992, the aquarium was the first act in Chattanooga's remarkable comeback as a city.

Ocean Journey showcases saltwater creatures, including sharks, rays, and colorful coral reef fish. River Journey follows the watershed from an Appalachian cove forest to a humid delta swamp and includes exhibits on the major rivers of the world, including the Tennessee, which is literally right out front. Standout exhibits include the playful river otters, the boneless beauties—jellyfish, octopus, and cuttlefish—and the American alligator. In between these, there are literally hundreds of captivating and high-quality exhibits of all types of water creatures. The music you hear is designed to reflect the music you'd hear in the region of the world where you'd find the fish you see. On some days you may even experience live music, such as a bluegrass fiddler in the delta exhibit.

Outside the aquarium there are fountains and a wading pool. Or you can walk over the riverfront and look out at the mighty Tennessee. In addition to the aquarium itself, there is an

sandbar shark at the Tennessee Aquarium

IMAX 3-D Theater, which shows nature-related films daily. Tickets may be purchased separately (adults $9.95, children $8.50) or as part of a discounted admission package with the aquarium.

The aquarium can get crowded on weekends, as well as on weekdays in summer. Start out early to avoid the worst crowds, and remember that your admission ticket is good all day, so you can take a midday break for lunch and return.

Other Downtown Sights

Chattanooga's African American history is preserved at the **Bessie Smith Hall and Chattanooga African American Museum** (200 E. Martin Luther King Blvd., 423/266-8658, www.bessiesmithcc.org, Mon.–Fri. 10 A.M.–5 P.M., Sat. noon–4 P.M., adults $7, seniors and students $5, children 6–12 $3). The museum is located at the site of the Martin Hotel, once a popular African American hotel and restaurant. There are hundreds of photographs of black Chattanoogans, with panels that describe the African American community's contributions in sports, the arts, business, government, and culture. There are pictures of famous black Chattanoogans including Bessie Smith, Samuel L. Jackson, Valaida Smith, and Roland Hayes. The exhibits include information about African culture, accomplishments, and art.

Just down the hall, in the lobby of the Bessie Smith Hall, is an exhibit dedicated to the legendary blues singer. Smith grew up poor in Chattanooga, having been orphaned at age nine. She developed her singing talent performing for pennies on the streets of Chattanooga. Smith was discovered by Ma Rainey and, later, Columbia Records, and for a period in the 1920s she was the highest-paid American black woman in the entertainment world.

Smith's success did not last. After a bad marriage and personal problems including alcohol abuse, Smith was in the early stages of a comeback when she died in a car accident in north Mississippi in 1937. She was buried in an unmarked grave in Philadelphia. In 1970, rock singer Janis Joplin found out about the grave and bought a headstone, which reads "The greatest blues singer in the world will never stop singing."

Inside the hall you will see photographs of Smith, old concert posters, and a dress she wore in the early days of her singing career.

The **International Towing and Recovery Hall of Fame and Museum** (3315 Broad St., 423/267-3132, www.internationaltowingmuseum.org, Mar.–Oct. Mon.–Sat. 9 A.M.–5 P.M., Nov.–Feb. Mon.–Sat. 10 A.M.–4:30 P.M., year-round Sun. 11 A.M.–5 P.M., adults $8, seniors $7, children 6–18 $4) showcases antique and modern tow trucks and other recovery vehicles. The museum is located in Chattanooga because the first tow truck was fabricated nearby at the Ernest Holmes Company. The museum's hall of fame memorializes people who have made significant contributions to the towing and recovery industry. The Wall of the Fallen remembers operators who lost their lives on the job.

The **Chattanooga Discovery Museum** (321 Chestnut St., 423/756-2738, www.cdmfun.org, Mon.–Sat. 10 A.M.–5 P.M., extended summer hours 9:30 A.M.–5:30 P.M., Sun. noon–5 P.M., closed on Wed. Sept.–Feb., $11.95, discounts with your aquarium ticket stub) is a hands-on museum specifically designed for children under 12. Activities include RiverPlay, where kids can pilot a riverboat, and an archaeological dig area, plus a regularly rotating collection of temporary exhibitions. There is a special play area for toddlers, too.

The **Chattanooga History Center** (2 Broad St., 423/265-3247, www.chattanoogahistory.com, Mon.–Fri. 9 A.M.–5 P.M.) closed its location at 400 Chestnut Street in 2007. The museum is developing its new facility, and the exhibits are still in the works. Even so, the center is worth a visit. The center also leads themed tours around the city, including several Civil War tours. Fees vary based on tour. Custom tours can also be arranged.

The **Chattanooga Zoo** (Warner Park, 1254 E. 3rd St., 423/697-1322, www.chattzoo.org, daily 9 A.M.–5 P.M., adults $8.95, seniors $6.95, children 3–12 $5.95, children 2 and under free) is a modest yet fun animal park. The six-acre facility located inside Warner Park houses chimpanzees, red pandas, snow leopards, spider moneys, and jaguars, among others. There is also a petting zoo. A $4.2 million front entrance to the zoo from Holtzclaw Avenue (Warner Park) was constructed in 2008; this makes it easier to see and find the zoo. The zoo celebrated its 75th anniversary in 2012. The zoo is not in walking distance of the main downtown attractions.

Bluff View

The bluff overlooking the Tennessee River and downtown Chattanooga is the city's arts center. The foremost attraction here is the **Hunter Museum of American Art** (10 Bluff View, 423/267-0968, www.huntermuseum.org, Mon.–Tues., Fri.–Sat. 10 A.M.–5 P.M., Wed. and Sun. noon–5 P.M., Thurs. 8 A.M.–8 P.M., adults $9.95, children 3–17 $4.95, children under 13 free holidays and weekends). Housed in the former home of Coca-Cola magnate and philanthropist George Thomas Hunter, the Hunter Museum has one of the most important collections of American art in the Southeast. The permanent collection includes works from the Hudson River School, American Impressionism, Ashcan School, Regionalist, Early Modern, and Contemporary movements. Major touring exhibits are also on display, and visitors enjoy dramatic views of the river below.

On a pleasant day, stroll through the **Bluff View Art District Sculpture Garden,** affiliated with the Hunter Museum but open to the public at no charge.

The **Houston Museum of the Decorative Arts** (201 High St., 423/267-7176, Mon.–Fri. 9:30 A.M.–4 P.M., Sat. noon 4 P.M., adults $8, children 4–17 $3.50) houses the decorative arts collection of Anna Safley Houston. Houston was a colorful character who died in relative poverty in 1951, having refused to sell any part of her valuable collection of porcelain and glassware.

Inside the museum you will find parts of Houston's remarkable collection, including antique money banks, steins, face mugs, miniature lamps, and glass baskets, as well as early American furniture and coverlets.

Main Street

South of downtown, at the corner of Main and Market Streets, is the legendary **Chattanooga Choo Choo** (1400 Market St., 423/266-5000, www.choochoo.com), a railroad car. The Choo Choo is located inside the city's old Terminal Station, which is now a hotel. The terminal was built in 1909 to accommodate the increasing number of passengers who arrived in the city aboard trains including the Chattanooga Choo Choo, which ran from Cincinnati, Ohio, to Chattanooga starting in 1880. The train was made famous in a song by Harry Warren and Mack Gordon, performed in the late 1940s by the Glenn Miller Orchestra. The tune starts with the lines: "Pardon me, boy, Is that that Chattanooga Choo Choo?" It is impossible to stand here and not have that refrain pass through your head.

The main sight here is an old wood-burning engine, which is similar to what would have powered the famous Choo Choo. The engine you see actually came from the Smoky Mountain Railroad, which ran between Knoxville and the Smokies in the 1940s.

There are shops, restaurants, and a small garden around the old railroad engine. Children will enjoy the **Model Railroad Museum** (1400 Market St., 423/266-5000, Mon.–Thurs. 3–7 P.M., Fri.–Sun. 10 A.M.–7 P.M., adults $4, children 3–17 $2), a miniature world with 3,000 feet of model railroad track, 120 locomotives, and 80 passenger cars.

Better than the Choo Choo, however, is Chattanooga's real, working railroad. The **Tennessee Valley Railroad** (4119 Cromwell Rd., 423/894-8028, www.tvrail.com, adults $16, children $10) offers railroad excursions departing from Grand Junction Station on the other side of Chickamauga Creek and Missionary Ridge. The hour-long ride covers six miles, travels through the Missionary Ridge railroad tunnel, and includes a stop at the East Chattanooga repair shop and turntable. The Missionary Ridge Local, as the excursion is named, leaves several times per day, depending on the time of year.

The railroad also offers occasional trips to other destinations in Tennessee and north Georgia.

◖ Lookout Mountain

Lookout Mountain is part of the Cumberland Plateau. It extends 83 miles through Tennessee, Alabama, and Georgia, but the northernmost tip, which overlooks Chattanooga, is its most famous part. No journey to the city is complete without taking a drive up the mountain to enjoy exceptional views and some of the most iconic of Tennessee attractions.

Point Park (1110 E. Brow Rd., adults $3, children 15 and under free) offers the best views off Lookout Mountain. This park is maintained by the National Park Service as part of the Chickamauga and Chattanooga National Military Park, and there is a **visitors center** (423/821-7786, daily 8:30 A.M.–5 P.M.) at the gates of the park. The best thing about the park, however, are the views of the Cumberland Plateau, Chattanooga, and the Cherokee National Forest in the eastward distance. The Tennessee River winds languidly through the landscape. On a clear day, it is stunning.

Students of the Civil War should visit the **Battles for Chattanooga Electric Map and Museum** (1110 E. Brow Rd., 423/821-2812, www.battlesforchattanooga.com, daily 10 A.M.–5 P.M., summer 9 A.M.–6 P.M., adults $8, children 3–12 $6), a private museum that

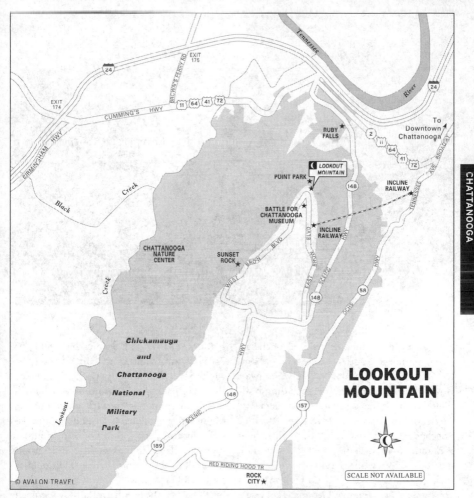

chronicles several Civil War battles, including the Battle Above the Clouds on Lookout Mountain, that took place in the area. An electric map, which shows 5,000 miniature soldiers and hundreds of lights, is a showpiece of the museum. Don't miss the gift shop if you are a collector of things relating to Civil War history. The museum is located next door to Point Park.

Chattanooga's most famous attraction may well be **Rock City** (1400 Patten Rd., 800/854-0675, www.seerockcity.com, Jan.–Mar. 10 and Nov. 4–15 daily 8:30 A.M.–5 P.M., Mar. 11–May 25 and Sept. 4–Nov. 3 daily 8:30 A.M.–6 P.M., May 26–Sept. 3 daily 8:30 A.M.–8 P.M., Nov. 16–Jan. 5 daily 8:30 A.M.–4 P.M., adults $18.95, children 3–12 $10.95, package discounts available if you buy the tickets in combination with Lookout Mountain attractions). A remarkable, yet hokey, rock garden with exceptional views, including one that encompasses seven states, Rock City was one of the first tourist attractions in the area, opening in 1932. The

From Rock City you can see seven states.

See Rock City billboards painted on barns throughout the South were legendary and iconic; today the gift shop at Rock City overflows with related mementos, including birdhouses with the message painted on them.

Visitors to Rock City travel a 4,100-foot "Enchanted Trail" that winds through ancient rock formations, including a 90-foot waterfall, narrow walkways, and a 1,000-ton balancing rock. Lover's Leap is the viewpoint from which you can see, on a clear day, Georgia, Tennessee, Alabama, North Carolina, South Carolina, Virginia, and Kentucky. Fairyland Caverns and Mother Goose Village are underground collections of quirky folk art (illuminated by black light). The 180-foot swinging bridge over the open air is memorable, as are the gardens of perennials and native plants. Unlike most botanic gardens, Rock City welcomes dogs. More than half a million people check out Rock City every year, but the parking lots and trails are well designed to handle crowds.

Ruby Falls (1720 S. Scenic Hwy., 800/755-7105, www.rubyfalls.com, daily 8 A.M.–8 P.M., adults $17.95, children 3–12 $9.95, although there are package discounts if you buy the tickets in combination with other Lookout Mountain attractions) is an underground waterfall located deep within Lookout Mountain (in fact, it claims to the be tallest underground waterfall in the country). The traditional entrance to Lookout Mountain Cave was closed in 1905 when the Southern Railway Company sealed it during the construction of a railroad along the side of the mountain. Chemist and entrepreneur Leo Lambert had explored the cave before and believed it would be a lucrative tourist attraction. So in 1928 he started to bore an elevator shaft down into the mountain to the cave. Lambert's unusual plan worked, and by 1930 visitors were touring the cave and the 145-foot waterfall, which Lambert named not for a color, but for his wife, Ruby.

The entrance to Ruby Falls is in a massive

© R&R MARKETING

Take in the view from Lookout Mountain Incline Railway.

limestone building modeled after an Irish castle. It was built out of stone brought up while Lambert was drilling the elevator shaft through the mountain; the top floor was added in 1976.

The tour of Ruby Falls takes about 1.5 hours in total and involves walking a bit less than a mile on paved underground paths. Your tour guide will tell the standard kitschy jokes, and the lighting on many of the rock formations feel forced. But when you get to the spot where Ruby Falls' waters thunder 145 feet to the pool beneath, it is hard not to be impressed. The tour guide will turn off the lights and then turn on the ruby-tinted bulbs, and you'll get the chance to hear and see the falls close up, if you choose.

Much of the power that now illuminates the Ruby Falls complex is generated by green energy options.

The steepest passenger train in the world is the **Incline Railway** (3917 St. Elmo Ave. and 827 E. Brow Rd., 423/821-4224, www.ride theincline.com, Apr.–May and Sept.–Oct.

daily 9 A.M.–6 P.M., June–Aug. daily 8:30 A.M.–9:30 P.M., Nov.–Mar. daily 10 A.M.–6 P.M., adults $14, children 3–12 $7, although there are package discounts if you buy the tickets in combination with other Lookout Mountain attractions), which climbs from Chattanooga to the top of Lookout Mountain. The railway was built in 1895 and has been ferrying visitors up the mountain ever since.

It takes about 10 minutes to make the journey from the bottom of the mountain to the top, where there are gift shops and restaurants. Point Park is a short walk away, but other Lookout Mountain attractions require a car. Parking is free at the bottom of the mountain, but a fee is charged to park at the top.

On the western edge of Lookout Mountain, in the midst of the upscale residential neighborhood, is **Sunset Rock.** A natural landmark admired for generations, this sheer bluff looks westward, and the view at sunset is indeed spectacular. It draws rock climbers who rappel down the sheer face of the bluff. The short hike (0.2 mile) down to the rock is steep and rough; wear comfortable shoes and take your time. There is no wall or fence blocking the sheer drop down the face of the rock (which makes for much better pictures).

Nestled on Lookout Mountain are 317 acres of the **Chattanooga Arboretum and Nature Center** (400 Garden Rd., 423/821-1160, www.chattanooganaturecenter.org, Mon.–Sat. 9 A.M.–5 P.M., Sun. (summer only) 1–5 P.M., adults $8, seniors and children 4–11 $5). This is a park, nature preserve, and environmental education facility. Visitors have the opportunity to see 30 different native animal species, including red wolves, bald eagles, bobcats, and raccoons, in the Wildlife Wanderland. There is also a 1,400-foot boardwalk that meanders through a seasonal wetland and lowland forest, and takes you to the George S. Bryan Tree House. Gardens include a fragrance garden and organic community garden, and there is a bird and butterfly café. In addition, there are miles of trails for hiking or biking in the adjoining Reflection Riding Arboretum and Botanical Garden. Come on a pleasant day and plan on spending several hours exploring the nature center. As is the case at many nature centers, dogs are not permitted.

Signal Mountain

Signal Mountain perches on the top of Walden's Ridge about 15 minutes' drive north of Chattanooga. Named because it is believed the Cherokee used it for signal fires, Signal Mountain later evolved into an upscale residential community. The Signal Mountain Inn once was a popular tourist destination; today it is a retirement home.

Visitors should make the challenging uphill drive to visit **Signal Point** (Signal Point Rd., 423/821-7786), a park that offers a dramatic view of the Tennessee River below. The site, managed by the National Park Service, is part of the Chickamauga and Chattanooga National Military Park and was an important vantage point during the Civil War. It is the southern terminus of the 300-plus-mile Cumberland Trail.

To get to Signal Mountain, take Highway 127 to Mountain Creek Road.

ENTERTAINMENT AND EVENTS
The Arts

Chattanooga has made significant investment in its arts offerings during the last decade, and it shows. Programs like CreateHere (www.createhere.org) helped develop loans for individual artists to encourage them to buy property in the Main Street/Southside District, and that had the intended effect of attracting more artists of all stripes to the city.

The **Allied Arts Alliance of Greater Chattanooga** (406 Frazier Ave., 423/756-2787, www.alliedartschattanooga.org, Mon.–Fri. 8:30 A.M.–5 P.M.) is an umbrella organization

that promotes the arts. Contact them for an arts guide to the city or for information about upcoming events.

Chattanooga's **Arts and Education Council** (3069 Broad St., 423/267-1218, www.artsedcouncil.org) organizes a variety of programs, including film festivals and literary conferences.

VENUES

The jewel of Chattanooga's arts venues is the **Tivoli Theater** (709 Broad St., 423/757-5050), a beaux arts–style performance hall that has been restored and equipped with modern amenities. Built in 1921, the Tivoli played films and live dramas to sold-out Chattanooga audiences through the 1950s. But with the advent of television, shopping malls, and the automobile, the downtown theater declined and narrowly escaped demolition in 1961.

After years of consideration and fundraising, the Tivoli was totally restored in the late 1980s and reopened to adoring crowds in 1989. Its domed ceiling, crystal chandeliers, and ornate finishes make this a lovely venue. There's typically free parking for ticketholders at the BlueCross/BlueShield of Tennessee garage.

Chattanooga's **Memorial Auditorium** (399 McCallie Ave., 423/642-8497) is another popular venue for concerts, performances, and special events. Built in 1924 as a memorial to the soldiers and sailors of World War I, Memorial Auditorium was then the largest space in Chattanooga for concerts other events. It housed boxing matches, roller derbies, tennis matches, banquets, and religious revivals.

VISUAL ARTS

Once a forgotten part of the city, the **Southside** neighborhood (http://southsidechattanooga.org), which largely is made up of Main Street, is a collection of former industrial buildings that have been repurposed as artist studios, galleries, boutiques, and more. On the last Friday of every month 5–8 P.M. is the art stroll here,

© HANNAH L. COFFEY

The Tivoli Theater has been a sign of entertainment in Chattanooga for more than 85 years.

when galleries are open late and artists are on hand to talk about their new works, but any day is a good day to walk by and gaze at the creativity on display in these windows.

The work of local and regional artists is featured at the **Association for Visual Artists Gallery** (30 Frazier Ave., 423/265-4282, www.avartists.org, Tues.–Sat. 11 A.M.–5 P.M.), located on Chattanooga's North Shore.

The **River Gallery** (400 E. 2nd St., 423/265-5033, www.river-gallery.com, Mon.–Sat. 10 A.M.–5 P.M., Sun. 1–5 P.M.) is located in a turn-of-the-20th-century home in the Bluff View Arts District. It exhibits fine arts and crafts from local, regional, and international artists.

MUSIC AND DANCE
The **Chattanooga Symphony & Opera** (701 Broad St., 423/267-8583, www.chattanoogasymphony.

org) performs classical, opera, pops, and family concerts every year at the Tivoli Theater.

Ballet Tennessee (3202 Kelly's Ferry Rd., 423/821-2055, www.ballettennessee.org) is Chattanooga's foremost ballet company and school. They perform at the Tivoli Theater and Memorial Auditorium.

Track29 (1400 Market St., 423/521-2929), named for its location at the historic Chattanooga Choo Choo, is the city's hippest concert venue. Shows are booked by the same folks who pull together Bonnaroo, so they get access to a diverse cross section of acts.

THEATER
The **Chattanooga Theatre Centre** (400 River Rd., 423/267-8534, www.theatrecentre.com) is a community theater that produces musicals, comedies, and dramas.

CINEMAS
The **Independent Film Series** (www.artsedcouncil.org) brings award-winning independent films to Chattanooga's downtown Bijou Theatre two times per year. The **Back Row Film Series** (www.backrowfilms.com) takes place at the Hunter Museum and features film screenings followed by a related guest speaker.

Festivals and Events
SPRING
Billed as a writer's conference for readers, the biennial **Conference on Southern Literature** (www.southernlitconference.org) brings heavyweights in Southern literature to Chattanooga for three days of lectures, discussions, and readings in March. On off years, the Arts and Education Council hosts the **Chattanooga Festival of Writers,** a celebration of the craft of writing.

In April the **4 Bridges Arts Festival** (www.4bridgesartsfestival.org) brings 150 artists (chosen from more than 700 applicants) to the First Tennessee Pavilion downtown for two days of exhibits, children's activities, and acoustic music. It is a good opportunity to purchase original artwork in a wide variety of formats or just people-watch (in 2011, more than 18,000 people attended). There is typically a modest admission fee.

In May, the Chattanooga Bicycle Club and Outdoor Chattanooga host **3 States, 3 Mountains** (www.chattbike.com), a 100-mile bicycle race that originates and ends at Finley Stadium in downtown Chattanooga. There are also options for 88-, 62- and 25-mile courses.

SUMMER
One of Chattanooga's largest annual events is the **Riverbend Festival** (www.riverbendfestival.com). Taking place in mid-June, the festival stretches for one mile along the city's waterfront and features multiple stages with jazz, blues, rock, pop, country, folk, and classical performers. The festival also includes the Bessie Smith Strut, a street festival along Martin Luther King Boulevard.

On Fridays May–August, **Rhythm and Noon** provides free midday concerts at Miller Plaza downtown. Performers play classical, folk, rock, jazz, swing, choral music, and blues. The concerts are a warm-up for **Nightfall** (http://nightfallchattanooga.com), free Friday-evening concerts held at Miller Plaza Memorial Day–the last weekend in September. Each concert starts out with a local act and concludes with a headliner. The schedule includes a wide range of genres, from world music to bluegrass.

FALL
On the Friday night of Labor Day weekend, kick off your shoes at **SwingFest** (www.downtownchattanooga.org), an open-air concert featuring local and regional big-band performers.

Every September, Chattanooga's **Culture Fest** (www.artsedcouncil.org) turns Coolidge Park into a festival of diverse cultures. International performers, foods from around the world, a merchandise bazaar, and unique arts and crafts are a few of the attractions.

Bluegrass music comes to the waterfront with the **Three Sisters Festival** (www.3sistersbluegrass.com), a three-day festival held in early October at Ross's Landing. Three Sisters is held in conjunction with **RiverRocks Chattanooga** (www.riverrockschattanooga.com), a nine-day celebration of all things outdoor. There are more than 90 events at RiverRocks, including stand-up paddling races, hot-air balloon rides, cycling, biking, and running events, plus live music, kids' activities, and funky demonstrations.

WINTER
Each November brings the **Head of the Hooch Regatta** (www.headofthehooch.org), the second-largest regatta in the country, to Chattanooga.

SHOPPING
Malls
Hamilton Place (2100 Hamilton Place Blvd., 423/894-7177, www.hamiltonplace.com) is Chattanooga's foremost place for shopping. Located at exit 4A off I-75 northeast of downtown, Hamilton Place has more than 150 stores, including JCPenney, Sears, Dillard's, and Belk.

Books
Chattanooga's best downtown bookstore is **Winder Binder** (40 Frazier Ave., 423/413-8999, www.winderbinder.com), which is also an art gallery and hipster hangout.

RECREATION
Parks
In many ways, Chattanooga, with countless ways to get out and enjoy nature, is like one big park. It seems like there are as many boat access spots along the banks of the river as there are parking lots.

Two of the best city parks are located on the banks of the Tennessee River. **Ross's Landing Park and Plaza,** adjacent to the Tennessee Aquarium at the end of Broad

Street, is a sculpted park that uses concrete, glass, stone, and grass to depict the timeline of Chattanooga's history. It is a nice place to stroll, people-watch, or enjoy a picnic.

On the other side of the river, **Coolidge Park** is even nicer. This grassy park has paths for walking, benches for sitting, and a glass-enclosed carousel to entertain children and adults. A ride on the old-style merry-go-round is just $0.50. Come here for lovely views of Chattanooga's downtown.

Outside of town, **Booker T. Washington State Park** (5801 Champion Rd., 423/894-4955) is a day-use park located off Highway 58, on the northeast side of town, whose primary attraction is Lake Chickamauga. There are several boat launching ramps. Waterskiing, fishing, stand-up paddling, kayaking, and pleasure cruising are popular activities. There are also picnic facilities and an Olympic-size swimming pool.

Farther outside of town, **Harrison Bay State Park** (8411 Harrison Bay Rd., Harrison, 423/344-6214) is also located on Lake Chickamauga. It is named for part of the lake, Harrison Bay, that covers what was once the last Cherokee Indian settlement in this area. The land was inundated in 1940 with the construction and closure of the Chickamauga Dam by the Tennessee Valley Authority.

There are public boat ramps, and all types of boats are allowed. In addition, there are picnic facilities, an Olympic-size pool, and a campground with RV and tent sites. There are also six miles of hiking trails and a bike path.

Biking

Bicycling is a required mode of transport for Chattanoogans. With bike-to-work programs and an innovative 300-bike fleet initiative, Chattanooga is well ahead of the curve when it comes to promoting alternative ways of getting around town.

There are bike lanes on many downtown streets, as well as bike-friendly trails along the Chattanooga waterfront, at the Chickamauga Dam, and at the TVA's Raccoon Mountain Reservoir, making the area accessible on two wheels for both visitors and locals.

Bike Chattanooga (www.bikechattanooga.org) provides safety courses for bikers, promotes bike riding, and publishes information about recreational bike riding in the area, as well as details on the new public bike sharing program. The **Chattanooga Bicycle Club** (www.chattbike.com) is another good option for local biking info.

For rentals and other bike-gear needs, try **Trek Bicycle Store of Chattanooga** (307 Manufacturers Rd., 423/648-2100, http://trekstorechattanooga.com), **River City Bicycles** (122 Tremont St., 423/265-7176, http://rivercity-bikes.com), or **Suck Creek Cycle** (501 Cherokee Blvd., 423/266-8883, http://suckcreek.com).

River Cruises

When visiting a city built on the river, you might as well take advantage and get *on* the river. **Blue Moon Cruises** (888/993-2583, www.bluemooncruises.org, $40) offers seasonal cruises down the Tennessee River aboard a 70-foot Skipperliner cruise boat. Blue Moon's cruise down the Tennessee River Gorge lasts about 3.5 hours and departs morning and afternoon from the Chattanooga Pier, off Ross's Landing waterfront park. The naturalist-led ecocruise emphasizes the animals and plants you see on the riverbanks, as well as the cultural and historical significance of the river over the years. There are also seasonal fall color cruises and other specialty tours.

Spectator Sports

The **Chattanooga Lookouts** (201 Power Alley, 423/267-2208, box office 423/267-4849, www.lookouts.com, general admission adults $4, children $2, box seats $6–8), a farm team for the Cincinnati Reds, play at AT&T Field downtown. The baseball season runs April–September.

Amusement Parks

Just over the state line in Georgia is **Lake Winnepesaukah** (1730 Lakeview Dr., Rossville GA, 706/866-5681, www.lakewinnie.com, Apr.–Sept. Wed.–Thurs. 10 A.M.–8 P.M., Fri.–Sat. 10 A.M.–10 P.M., Sun. noon–10 P.M., unlimited rides pass adults $26, seniors and children $10), a family-oriented amusement park operating since 1925. The Cannon Ball is a wooden roller coaster, and the Boat Chute is the oldest mill chute ride in the United States. There are also modern rides, including the Oh-Zone and Wild Lightning. In addition to rides, Lake Winnepesaukah has a midway and food vendors. In addition to the unlimited pass, tickets to rides can be purchased individually.

To find Lake Winnepesaukah, drive south on I-75 to the Route 41 exit. Drive on Ringold Road for two miles to McBrien Road. Turn left, and the park is two miles ahead on Lakeview Drive.

Hang Gliding

The mountains around Chattanooga are ideal for hang gliding. The **Lookout Mountain Flight Park** (7201 Scenic Hwy., Rising Fawn GA, 706/398-3541, www.hanglide.com, daily 9 A.M.–6 P.M., closed Wed.) offers tandem glides with a certified instructor and lessons appropriate for all levels. The flight school is the largest hang gliding school in America. A single tandem flight, which lasts about 15 minutes, is $149. A daylong package that includes a tandem flight plus five "bunny hill" low-altitude flights is $199.

Paddling

Whether it is in a kayak, canoe, or on a stand-up paddleboard, Chattanoogans love to get on the local waters, both flat water and white water. Rent boards from **SUP Paddleboard** (900 Dallas Rd., 423/421-1403, www.suppaddleboard.com) or **L2 Boards** (First and Market Sts., 423/531-7873, www.l2boards.com). For canoes, try **Chattanooga Nature Center** (400 Garden Rd., 423/821-1160, www.chattanooganaturecenter.org). **OutVenture Kayak** (5051 Gann Store Rd., 423/842-6629) offers guided kayak trips all over the area, including a downtown kayak trip.

ACCOMMODATIONS
Under $100

Interstate motels offer good value in the Chattanooga area. In this category, the **Econo Lodge Lookout Mountain** (150 Browns Ferry Rd., 423/821-9000, $65–85) is a good choice for its location convenient to downtown and Lookout Mountain, and for its clean rooms and amenities, including in-room microwaves, refrigerators, free wireless, and coffeemakers. Guests also enjoy a free continental breakfast. There's an outdoor pool open in the summer.

$100-150

⟨ **Bluff View Inn** (Bluff View Art District, 423/265-5033, ext. 2, www.bluffviewartdistrict.com, $105–240) consists of 16 rooms in three different historic properties located in the peaceful Bluff View Art District. Guest rooms in the Maclellen House, Martin House, and Thompson House range from modest-size quarters with a shower-tub combination to luxurious suites with river views, private balconies, and sitting rooms. A full sit-down breakfast is included in room rates and is served at the Back Inn Café.

If you thought it was a new idea to turn an outmoded train station into a hotel, think again. The Chattanooga Station stopped operating as a train station in 1970, and just three years later it reopened as a tourist attraction. Nineteen years later it was retooled again, this time into the hotel that you see today. The **Chattanooga Choo Choo Holiday Inn** (1400 Market St., 800/872-2529, www.choochoo.com, $120–190) consists of three buildings of hotel rooms, plus distinctive train-car accommodations. The hotel rooms are clean and generous in size, although not particularly modern or charming;

Today, the old Chattanooga Choo Choo train station is a magnificent hotel lobby.

they feature amenities such as wireless Internet, in-room coffeemakers, and king-size beds.

But what makes the Choo Choo special is its railcar accommodations. These old sleeper cars have been converted into hotel-style rooms with four-poster beds, desks, and private bathrooms. Each room has a queen-size bed, and some feature pull-out trundle beds ideal for family accommodations, although all are very small (because they used to be sleeper cars). The lobby is the most interesting feature of the hotel.

In addition to hotel rooms, the Choo Choo has three different restaurants, an ice cream shop, retail shops, and a railway museum. The lobby and upscale restaurant located in the atrium of the old train station lobby are dramatic and beautiful.

The **Stone Fort Inn** (120 E. 10th St., 423/267-7866, www.stonefortinn.com, $120–190) is an old-fashioned city hotel with a modern, chic feel. Located about 10 blocks from the aquarium and close to federal and state office buildings, the Stone Fort Inn has 20 guest rooms of varying sizes. All rooms have high-speed Internet connections, oversized whirlpool tubs, luxury bath soaps, claw-foot soaking tubs, TV/VCRs, and cheerful decor. Polished terrazzo floors, marble fireplaces, well-stocked bookshelves, an 1885 grand piano, and a 1920s slate pool table all conjure an atmosphere of cozy elegance in this circa-1909 hotel building. On weekdays there is a continental breakfast and on weekends a gourmet sit-down morning meal. The dining area becomes a public café and restaurant on Wednesday and Thursday evenings, with inviting selections from the bar, live acoustic music, and a menu of inventive small plates. Children under 12 are not permitted at the Old Stone Fort, unless you rent the whole hotel for a special event.

The **Chattanoogan** (1201 S. Broad St., 423/756-3400, www.chattanooganhotel.com, $119–159) is an upscale hotel and conference center located just south of downtown. The hotel offers 199 guest rooms and suites, many of them with views of Lookout Mountain, and all appointed with modern furnishings, fabrics, and amenities. A dramatic see-through glass fireplace in the lobby is a talking point and attraction in its own right. An on-site spa, conference center, and three restaurants round out the resort's amenities. The Chattanoogan opened in 2001 and underwent extensive renovation in 2007 to keep the decor current and comfortable.

$150-200

Mayor's Mansion Inn (801 Vine St., 423/265-5000, www.mayorsmansioninn.com, $160–295) is a luxury bed-and-breakfast located in an 1889 Victorian mansion built for the mayor of Chattanooga. Mayor's Mansion has 11 guest rooms and is located in the Fort Wood District near the University of Tennessee, less than one mile from downtown Chattanooga. Each guest room is unique, with distinctive fabrics, wallpaper, and antique furniture. Guests may feel like they are bedding down in a home that could just as easily be open for tours. Common areas include a stone terrace, verandahs, and a library. Elegant indulgences include nightly turn-down service, a three-course breakfast, and soft cotton robes. Guests may also take advantage of concierge service, Internet access, and other amenities like ironing boards and a video library.

Another longtime favorite downtown hotel is the **Sheraton Read House Hotel** (827 Broad St., 800/691-1255, $115–290). Located in a historic redbrick Georgian-style building near the theater district, and about 10 blocks from the aquarium, the Sheraton offers its guests luxury and comfort. Its 219 guest rooms and suites include high-speed Internet, Drexel Heritage furniture, and luxurious beds. There is an indoor zero-edge pool with a waterfall, top-notch workout room, on-site steak house, and

The historic Sheraton Read House Hotel has a great location in downtown Chattanooga.

Starbucks coffee shop. It is a short walk to the riverfront attractions.

Camping

Harrison Bay State Park (8411 Harrison Bay Rd., Harrison, 423/344-7966), located about 20 minutes drive from downtown, has 134 RV sites and 28 tent-only sites in its lakefront campground. Rates are $12–18.50. No reservations are accepted; Tennessee State Parks are first come, first served.

FOOD

Downtown

For good food, casual-yet-polished service, and a convivial atmosphere, go where many Chattanoogans go for a meal out. **212 Market** (212 Market St., 423/265-1212, daily 11 A.M.–3 P.M., Mon.–Thurs. 5–9:30 P.M., Fri.–Sat. 5–10 P.M., Sun. 5–9 P.M., lunch $7–14, dinner $15–30) serves upscale daily lunch and dinner specials like ginger-glazed salmon, wild mushroom ravioli, and Carolina mountain trout. The 212 Pecan Chicken Club is a delectable lunchtime favorite. This was one of the first downtown restaurants to open following the area's rebirth in the early 1990s, and it is still a first choice for dining in the city.

When you give an old-fashioned diner a makeover, the result is **The Blue Plate** (191 Chestnut St., Unit B, 423/648-6767, Mon.–Thurs. 11 A.M.–9 P.M., Fri. 11 A.M.–10 P.M., Sat. 9 A.M.–10 P.M., Sun. 9 A.M.–9 P.M., $6–18), a downtown eatery with sleek lines, fresh food, and a home-style heart. You can order breakfast eggs and pancakes all day, or choose a plump, juicy burger. The chef salad is piled high with pulled chicken, diced eggs, and mixed cheeses, and the entrées include fried to order chicken and not your mother's baked meat loaf. Don't skip the green beans. Or the Moon Pie cheesecake. To prove that this is not your everyday lunch counter, you can also order from a full bar, although the spot is perfectly kid friendly.

Tucked away in the downtown business district is Chattanooga's favorite vegetarian eatery, albeit only open for lunch. The **Country Life Vegetarian Restaurant** (809 Market St., 423/634-9925, Mon.–Thurs. 11:30 A.M.–2:30 P.M., $5–10) serves whole-grain, home-grown, all-vegetarian food. The specials change daily and include things like tofu and brown rice, butternut squash quiche, and veggie fajitas. There is also a well-stocked salad bar.

You might be surprised how good England tastes in Chattanooga. The **English Rose Tearoom** (1401 Market St., 423/265-5900, Tues.–Sun. 11 A.M.–5 P.M., $5–15) serves authentic British Isles fare, including finger sandwiches, ploughman's lunch, and cottage pie. Come into this welcoming spot for an afternoon tea with scones and sandwiches, or for a meal of steak pies, Dover sole, flounder, or Cornish pasties. The atmosphere is on the refined side, but it's not uptight. The English Rose offers a nice change of pace.

Upscale Southern comfort food is the draw at **Mt. Vernon Restaurant** (3535 Broad St., 423/266-6591, www.mymtvernon.com, Mon.–Thurs. 11 A.M.–9 P.M., Fri. 11 A.M.–9:30 P.M., Sat. 4–9:30 P.M., $9–16). Located near the base of Lookout Mountain, Mt. Vernon is a favorite among Chattanoogans, who come for its familiar food, generous portions, and hometown feel. Specialties include Southern fried chicken ($13) and Maryland crab cakes ($17). The fried green tomatoes appetizer is always a favorite. At lunchtime you can also order from the under-$10 sandwich menu, with choices like BLT, grouper sandwich, and the Mt. Vernon Club.

Chattanooga's best meat and three diner is **Zarzour's Café** (1627 Rossville Ave., 423/266-0424, Mon.–Fri. 11 A.M.–2 P.M., $5–8), a hole-in-the-wall tucked away in the wrong part of town. Zarzour's was founded by Lebanese immigrant Charles Zarzour in 1913, and the eatery has persisted through good times and bad for the past nine-plus decades under the family's ownership. But it is not Middle Eastern specialties that bring in the regulars; it is some of the best home-cooked Southern food in the city. Flavorful turnip greens, creamy potatoes, comforting baked spaghetti, and hot-from-the-skillet corn bread are among the dishes on the menu. Each day you can choose from one of three main-dish entrées, accompanied by your choice of two side dishes. Or order a hand-patted burger from the grill. This is a cash-only joint.

Bluff View

As ubiquitous as the coffee-sandwich-dessert bar is these days, it is still refreshing when someone does it well. **Rembrandt's Coffee House** (204 High St., 423/265-5003, Mon.–Thurs. 7 A.M.–10 P.M., Fri. 7 A.M.–11:30 P.M., Sat. 8 A.M.–11:30 P.M., Sun. 8 A.M.–10 P.M.,

The Bluff View Art District is one of Chattanooga's best places to stroll.

$5–7) is one such place. Located catty-corner from the Hunter Museum of American Art, Rembrandt's serves excellent hot and cold sandwiches on superb locally baked bread. The menu also offers salads, including a delicious spinach salad with bacon, hard-boiled eggs, and walnuts. The ingredients are fresh and flavorful. For breakfast choose from French toast panini filled with fruit compote and mascarpone cheese, hot breakfast sandwiches, or lighter options such as bagels, yogurt and fruit, or banana bread. The coffee here is excellent, and you can finish off your meal with a wide array of sweets. Rembrandt's is not without a sense of humor. Step outside, and you will see a plate-glass window with a sign reading Working Artist. He or she will be making hand-dipped chocolate treats you can buy inside. There's a second location inside Memorial Hospital.

The setting at ◖**Back Inn Café** (412 E. 2nd St., 423/265-5033, Mon.–Fri. 7 A.M.–9 P.M., Sat. 8 A.M.–10 P.M., Sun. 8 A.M.–9 P.M., $14–28) is romantic and relaxing. Located in a stately old home, the Back Inn offers diners the choice of dining in the library, sunroom, or on the terrace overlooking the river. Polished wood floors, elegant old-world finishes, and a lovely view make you feel distinctly at home in this restaurant. The menu features global cuisine with a good wine list.

Lunchtime entrées include Japanese bento boxes, penne carbonara, and shrimp and grits. There are also salads and sandwiches, and gluten-free options. At dinner, choose from entrées such as Thai curry chicken, seafood gratin, and the house specialty Martin House steak tenderloin. Reservations are recommended.

Southside

Main Street, near the famous Choo Choo, has become one of the city's favorite dining districts. The sleek, modern **Alleia** (25 E. Main St., 423/305-6990, http://alleiarestaurant.com, Mon.–Thurs. 5–9:30 P.M., Fri.–Sat. 5–10 P.M.,

The Bluegrass Grill on artsy Main Street is a favorite for breakfast.

$6–27) is cozy enough for date night, but not so romantic that it doesn't work for a business dinner. The wine list is impressive.

For morning meals, join the locals at C **Bluegrass Grill** (55 E. Main St., 423/752-4020, http://bluegrassgrillchattanooga.com, Tues.–Fri. 6:30 A.M.–2 P.M., Sat. 6:30 A.M.–1 P.M., $2–9). Breakfast is served whenever this homey joint is open; don't miss the homemade breads and potatoes. Look for the sign with the banjo on it.

North Shore

In recent years, the streets across the river from downtown Chattanooga have become popular locations for restaurants.

Terra Nostra Restaurant and Wine Bar (105 Frazier Ave., 423/634-0238, www.terranostratapas.com, Mon.–Thurs. 4:30–10 P.M., Fri. Sat. 4:30 11 P.M., Sun. 4:30–9 P.M., $7–15) is a tapas restaurant with vegetarian,

seafood, and meat plates. Come for an afternoon glass of wine to be enjoyed with a plate of cheese and bread. Or come for a more filling dinner; try the handcrafted spinach ravioli, fresh seafood plates, or osso buco. The restaurant's bold colors and metal sculptures give it a rustic-hip feel. In the tapas tradition, each plate is a small portion, about appetizer size, and you should order several as part of your multicourse meal. In addition to tapas, Terra Nostra has 80 different wines available by the glass and 90 available by the bottle.

For sushi, many Chattanoogans head to **Sushi Nabe** (110 River St., 423/634-0171, www.sushinabechattanooga.com, Mon. 4–9 P.M., Tues. Thurs. and Sun. 11:30 A.M.–2:30 P.M. and 5–9:30 P.M., Fri.–Sat. 11:30 A.M.–2:30 P.M. and 5–10:30 P.M., sushi $4–7 per roll, combination plates $15–18). Located adjacent to Coolidge Park, this chic eatery offers seating at the sushi bar or at tables. In addition to sushi, you can order stir-fries and other Japanese specialties. There are also convenient dinner combination plates.

INFORMATION AND SERVICES
Visitor Information

The **Chattanooga Area Convention and Visitors Bureau** (2 Broad St., 423/756-8687 or 800/322-3344, www.chattanoogafun.com) provides information online, over the telephone, and in person at its visitors center, located right next door to the Tennessee Aquarium.

Media

The *Chattanooga Times Free Press* (www.timesfreepress.com) is the city's daily newspaper. *The Pulse* (www.chattanoogapulse.com) is a free alternative weekly paper with a focus on arts, entertainment, and culture.

Libraries

The **Chattanooga-Hamilton County Bicentennial Library** (1001 Broad St.,

423/757-5310, Mon.–Thurs. 9 A.M.–9 P.M., Fri.–Sat. 9 A.M.–6 P.M.) is the city's main downtown library. The entire library is a wireless Internet hot spot, and there is also free Internet access on library terminals.

Laundry

Gordon's Cleaners (315 N. Market St. and 3546 Broad St., 423/265-5877) has dry cleaning and laundry service downtown.

GETTING THERE

Chattanooga is located along three major interstate highways. I-75 travels north–south from Knoxville in the north to Atlanta in the south. I-24 runs from Nashville to Chattanooga, and I-59 runs from Birmingham to Chattanooga.

Chattanooga is about 115 miles from Knoxville, 130 miles from Nashville, 120 miles from Atlanta, and 150 miles from Birmingham.

The **Chattanooga Metropolitan Airport** (CHA, 423/855-2202, www.chattairport. com) is served by a half dozen airlines providing nonstop service to nine different U.S. cities, although many people fly to either Atlanta or Nashville and take shuttles to Chattanooga.

The Chattanooga airport is located about 14 miles east of the city center. To get downtown from the airport, take Highway 153 south to I-75 and follow the signs to downtown Chattanooga.

GETTING AROUND

Chattanooga is an exceedingly pedestrian-friendly city. There is plenty of downtown parking, and it is easy to get around on foot or by the free public trolleys. You can walk from downtown to Bluff View and even to the North Shore via the Walnut Street pedestrian bridge.

You'll need a car to get to Lookout Mountain attractions.

Public Transportation

Chattanooga's public transit service operates an electric (zero-emissions) shuttle bus service around downtown. The **CARTA Electric Shuttle** (www.carta-bus.org, runs every five minutes Mon.–Fri. 6:30 A.M.–11 P.M., Sat. 9 A.M.–11 P.M., Sun. 9 A.M.–8:30 P.M., adults $1.50, children $0.75, 24-hour unlimited-ride pass $4) runs from the Chattanooga Choo Choo building on the south side of town to the Tennessee Aquarium along the waterfront. There are stops about every block; if you need to get to a specific place, just ask your driver. Maps are posted around the city, and free guides are available at the north parking lot.

The route is convenient to all downtown hotels. There are large parking garages at both ends of the shuttle route. It costs $3 to park by the Choo Choo and $7 to park by the aquarium. Since there is no such thing as free parking anywhere around downtown Chattanooga, parking and riding the shuttle is a very good idea.

Parking

All parking around downtown Chattanooga is paid. If you find a metered space along the road, grab it, because these are the cheapest, at least for short-term parking. There are large lots located across from the Tennessee Aquarium. All-day parking will run you about $7, and evening parking will cost $5. There is a large public lot next to the Choo Choo, where all-day parking is just $3. Rates are higher during special events.

The Ocoee

The lands east of Chattanooga are speckled by towns that still bear names bestowed by some of their first settlers. Citico, Chota, Hiwassee, and Tellico were named by Overhill Cherokee who made the journey over the mountains and into southeastern Tennessee during the 17th century. Red Clay State Historic Park was the site of the last council meeting of the Cherokee before their forced removal in 1838. Today, these lands are part of the southern portion of the Cherokee National Forest, an expanse of 300,000 acres of federal lands that contain rivers, mountains, and rural farmland.

The southern part of the Cherokee National Forest is defined by the powerful Ocoee River, which attracts thrill-seeking rafters and kayakers. Sightseers enjoy scenic drives up Chilhowee Mountain and along the river, past recreation areas and opportunities for hiking and swimming.

Several towns in the southeastern corner of this region have strong mining histories. Ducktown, Copperhill, and Coker Creek are among the quiet towns that now preserve their unique history with museums and historic tours.

The Hiwassee River cuts through the national forest north of the Ocoee, passing the historic town of Reliance and posing opportunities for laid-back canoe and raft outings.

CLEVELAND

Cleveland is one gateway to the Cherokee National Forest. The seat of Bradley County, Cleveland is home to Lee University, a four-year Christian college operated by the Church of God, as well as the Church of God Theological Seminary, a graduate school for Christian ministry.

Sights

Find your way to Johnston Park downtown to see the *Cherokee Chieftain*, a large sculpture carved by Peter "Wolf" Toth. The sculpture was presented to the city of Cleveland in 1974 and represents the close association this region has with the Cherokee people.

The **Museum Center at Five Points** (200 Inman St., 423/339-5745, www.museumcenter.org, Tues.–Fri. 10 A.M.–5 P.M., Sat. 10 A.M.–3 P.M., adults $5, children $4) is a history museum dedicated to telling the story of the different groups of people who have lived along the Ocoee River. The museum is located at the end of the Old Copper Trail, the road by which copper traveled from the Copper Basin, through the mountains, and to the railroad at Cleveland.

Accommodations

The **Whitewater Lodge** (2500 Pointe South Rd., 423/479-7811, $30) is a bit far from the action of the Ocoee River, but the price can't be beat. Rooms have a kitchenette with coffeemaker, sink, and stovetop, adding to the bargain. Weekly rates are also available.

COLLEGEDALE

More than 200 ancient artifacts from the Near East are on exhibit at the **Lynn H. Wood Archaeological Museum** (Industrial Dr., Southern Adventist University, 423/236-2030, http://archaeology.southern.edu, Tues.–Thurs. 9 A.M.–noon and 1–5 P.M., Fri. 9–11 A.M., Sat.–Sun. 2–5 P.M., free). Museum curators strive to depict life in the Biblical world with artifacts from Egypt, Babylonia, Persia, Syria-Palestine, Greece, Cyprus, and Anatolia. Highlights include a complete series of lamps from the Chalcolithic to early Arabic periods and hand written cuneiform tablets from Ur.

RED CLAY STATE HISTORIC PARK

Red Clay State Historic Park (1140 Red Clay Park Rd., 423/478-0339, daily 8 A.M.–sunset,

CHATTANOOGA

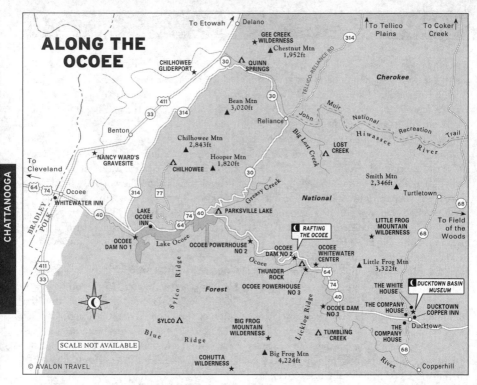

ALONG THE OCOEE

$3 per vehicle) was the site of the Cherokee capital from 1832 to 1838. In the years leading up to 1832, the State of Georgia outlawed Cherokee councils, so in 1832 the Cherokee moved their capital from New Echota, Georgia, to Red Clay, Tennessee, just over the state line. As many as 5,000 people attended the 11 council meetings held here until 1838, the year of the Cherokee's forced removal via the Trail of Tears. It was here at Red Clay that many Cherokee first learned of the planned removal.

The park consists of a **visitors center** (Mon.–Sat. 8 A.M.–4:30 P.M., Sun. 1–4:30 P.M.), re-created Cherokee settlement and council house, and a permanent exhibit on the Cherokee culture. The most prominent natural landmark is the spring, which rises from beneath a limestone ledge to form a deep pool that flows into Mill Creek, a tributary of the Conasauga and Coosa River system. The spring is about 15 feet deep and produces more than 500,000 gallons of water each day.

The park is an official interpretive center on the National Historic Trail of Tears. Cherokee Days of Recognition is held on the first weekend of August each year. It includes authentic Cherokee crafts, food, storytelling, and music.

OCOEE

The town of Ocoee is a smattering of businesses and homes located on Highways 64 and 411.

A few miles north of the intersection, along Highway 411, is the **Gravesite of Nancy Ward,** located atop a small hill. There is a parking area and pathway to the summit. Nancy Ward was born in 1738 at the Cherokee town of Chota, and she was named Nanye-hi. Nanye-hi had a queenly appearance and commanding bearing,

THE CHEROKEE NATIONAL FOREST

The Cherokee National Forest covers 640,000 acres of land on the eastern edge of Tennessee. The southern portion extends from the Georgia state line all the way to the southern boundary of the Great Smoky Mountains National Park, encompassing some 300,000 acres. The northern portion—which covers 327,000 acres—ranges from the northern boundary of the Smokies to the Virginia state line.

The federal government began buying land in East Tennessee around 1912. The government's action was in response to the environmental effects of widespread logging in the southern mountains. Clear-cutting, erosion, and wildfires ravaged the environment, and the federal government stepped in to preserve the headwaters of area rivers. In 1920, President Woodrow Wilson declared the lands to be the Cherokee National Forest, and in 1936 the boundaries were redrawn to put the forest entirely within the state of Tennessee (Pisgah and Natahala National Forests were established in North Carolina). During the New Deal, the Civilian Conservation Corps (CCC) built many of the trails that still exist today in the forest, and the Tennessee Valley Authority built dams and reservoirs.

National forests differ from national parks in several important ways. The motto of the forest service is "Caring for the land and serving the people," a statement that reveals its dual purpose. So while environmental stewardship is one objective of park managers, they are also concerned with encouraging recreation and the use of natural resources. Activities such as off-road mountain biking, hunting, and logging—which are not permitted in the Great Smoky Mountains National Park—are allowed in the Cherokee National Forest. Equally significant, commercial and residential development is allowed in certain parts of the national forest.

Some 66,000 acres of the forest is classified as wilderness, a designation that prohibits logging, motorized vehicles, construction, and development. Some 20,000 acres are classified as scenic, a designation that prohibits logging and allows only limited vehicle use. Meanwhile, 46,000 acres have been classified as primitive, which opens them up to low-impact recreation in a nonmotorized environment. There is a recurring tension between those who want more environmental protection in the forest and those who want to open the lands up to more intensive uses and development.

Despite this, the Cherokee National Forest remains a beautiful, ecologically rich, and—in some parts—wild area. The forest is home to some 120 bird species, including wild turkey, golden eagle, and peregrine falcon; 47 mammal species, including the black bear, red wolf, wild boar, and coyote; and 30 species of reptile, including rattlesnake, copperhead, and salamander. It is home to many endangered species, including the northern flying squirrel and two varieties of river mussels.

Hiking, camping, horseback riding, swimming, boating, white-water sports, and biking are just a few of the activities that draw people to the Cherokee National Forest.

The supervisor's office for the entire forest—north and south—is at 2800 North Ocoee Street in Cleveland. Call them at 423/476-9700. The southern forest has two ranger districts and corresponding ranger stations. The **Ocoee/ Hiwassee District** (3171 Hwy. 64, 423/338-5201) is located along the Ocoee River near Benton. The **Tellico Ranger Station** (250 Ranger Station Rd., 423/253-2520) is located along the Cherohala Skyway near Tellico Plains.

The northern forest has two ranger stations. The **Nolichucky/Unaka District Ranger Station** (4900 Asheville Hwy./State Rte. 70, 423/638-4109) is located near Greeneville. The **Watauga District Ranger Station** (4400 Unicoi Dr., Unicoi, 423/735-1500) is in Unicoi.

Ranger stations are generally open daily 8:30 A.M.-4:30 P.M., and they are the best places to buy maps and get other information about recreation in the national forest. You can also visit the online store maintained by the Cradle of Forestry (www.cradleofforestry.com).

CHATTANOOGA

and she fought alongside her husband and other men in a raid on the Creeks during the 1755 Battle of Taliwa. Ward was chosen as *Agi-gau-u-e* (Beloved Woman) of the Cherokee. As such, she sat on the Council of Chiefs, had complete power over prisoners, and led the Women's Council.

In the late 1750s, an English trader named Bryant Ward moved in to the area and married Nancy, as she was called by the white settlers, although he already had a wife and family in South Carolina. They had a daughter, Betsy, who joined Five Killer and Catherine, children of Ward's first marriage, as her offspring.

Ward was influential in her tribe and with the white settlers. She advocated peace between Indians and settlers, and more than once she warned settlers of an impending Indian attack. She spoke at the negotiations held on the Long Island of the Holston and at the Treaty of Hopewell.

With the Hiwassee Purchase of 1819, Ward along with all Cherokee was forced to abandon Chota, their capital city of Overhill Tennessee. She moved south and settled near where her gravesite lies today. Ward died in 1822.

The oldest monument at Ward's gravesite was erected in 1923 by the Nancy Ward Chapter of the Daughters of the American Revolution. Newer exhibits by the Tennessee Overhill Association detail her life.

Accommodations

The **Whitewater Inn** (120 Whitewater Dr., 423/338-1201, www.ocoeewhitewaterinn.com, $63–103) is a standard-issue motel that still has a good deal of polish left. Designed to feel a bit like a mountain lodge, this inn offers comfortable rooms with two queen-size beds, satellite TV, and telephones. There is free continental breakfast, wireless Internet, and fax and copy service. Rates are higher in season. Apartments with a full kitchen ($150) are also available.

ALONG THE OCOEE

Just past Ocoee on Highway 64, you enter the Cherokee National Forest. The next 26 miles are a winding two-lane blacktop that follows the Ocoee River.

Chilhowee Mountain

For breathtaking views of Parksville Lake, the Ocoee River, and the Great Eastern Valley of Tennessee, take a seven-mile detour up Forest Service Road 77 to the summit of Chilhowee Mountain. There are no fewer than five overlooks on the drive, which terminates at the Cumberland Recreation Area, a day-use facility and campground. There is also a historical marker that recalls the Confederate soldiers who camped in these hills and waged guerilla war on Unionists during the Civil War.

Once at the Cumberland Recreation Area, you can hike 1.5 miles to **Benton Falls** or take any of the seven other trails in the area. There is also a swimming beach, bathhouses, and picnic tables.

Parksville Lake

This nearly 2,000-acre lake formed by the Ocoee River is operated as a Forest Service recreation area. There is a swimming beach, campground, picnic area, and boat launches. The lake is popular for fishing, waterskiing, and riding personal watercraft.

Ocoee River Dams

The Tennessee Valley Authority operates three powerhouses along the Ocoee River, which together produce some 70,000 kilowatts of electricity. Ocoee 1, the westernmost facility, predates TVA and forms the Parksville Lake (also called the Ocoee Lake). There is a marker and overlook next to the dam, which was built in 1910.

Ocoee 2 was built in 1913 and consists of a diversion dam, wooden flume, and powerhouse. When the powerhouse is on, the river water is diverted into the flume, which carries it five miles downstream to the Ocoee 2

HIKING IN THE SOUTHERN CHEROKEE

If you plan to do much hiking in the southern Cherokee National Forest, you should invest in good boots, a water bottle, a GPS, and a good trail map. The best is National Geographic's Trails Illustrated No. 781 *Tellico and Ocoee River Cherokee National Forest.*

There are dozens of hiking trails in the southern Cherokee National Forest. The following are some of the best.

The **Old Copper Trail** begins at the Ocoee Whitewater Center and is a 2.3-mile (one-way) hike along an old mining road. The Old Copper Trail is the last remaining portion of a road that was built around 1851 to connect the copper-mining towns of Ducktown and Copperhill with Cleveland. It took miners two days to haul the copper by mule the 33 miles to Cleveland. When Highway 64 was built in the 1930s, it followed the old Copper Road route, and subsequent upgrades widened and improved the current highway.

The present-day hiking trail follows the edge of the river, passing apple trees and stone foundations left by farm families, some of whom were Cherokee Indians, in the early 19th century. You'll also pass a beaver pond and cross four footbridges, including three timber stringer plank bridges and one heavy timber bridge.

Other hikes that start at the Whitewater Center include **Bear Paw Loop** (1.7 miles) and the **Chestnut Mountain Loop** (6 miles).

One of the most famous trails in the forest is the **Benton MacKaye Trail** (www.bmta.org), a 150-mile trail named for the creator of the Appalachian Trail (AT). When the AT was getting congested, a group of dedicated hikers set out to create a new long-haul hike through the Southern mountains. The Benton MacKaye Trail begins at Spring Mountain, Georgia, as does the AT. It follows a different path, however, and ends at Davenport Gap, North Carolina, in the Great Smoky Mountains National Park. The trail enters the Cherokee National Forest at Big Frog Mountain. Access points are at Forest Service Road 221, Forest Service Road 45, Thunder Rock Campground, and Highway 64 across from Ocoee Powerhouse No. 3.

Benton Falls Trail is an easy 1.5-mile (one-way) trail that leaves from Chilhowee Campground and follows Rock Creek to 65-foot Benton Falls.

The **John Muir Trail** covers 18.8 miles along the Hiwassee River from Childers Creek near Reliance to Highway 60 at Farmer. The trail follows a route described by naturalist and writer John Muir in his book *A Thousand Mile Walk to the Gulf.*

The **Oswald Dome Trail** climbs 3.9 miles up Bean Mountain from the Quinn Springs Campground on Highway 30 near Reliance. The trail ends at an elevation of 3,500 feet near the Oswald Dome fire tower.

Lastly, the **Unicoi Turnpike Trail** is a 2.5-mile portion of the historic Unicoi Turnpike, an old road that settlers, hunters, and Native Americans used to get over the mountains. The trail connects Doc Rogers Fields near Coker Creek with the Unicoi Gap. Along the way you will see a marker for a murdered tollgate keeper and the remnants of Rolling Stone Civilian Conservation Corps (CCC) Camp.

---

powerhouse, where it is dropped from a height of 250 feet, creating far more power than it would otherwise. The flume, which is visible as you drive along the river, is on the National Register of Historic Places. Ocoee 3, built in 1942, follows a similar pattern. It has a diversion dam, a tunnel, and a powerhouse.

When the river water is being used to generate electricity, the Ocoee River is just a trickle down a dry riverbed. But TVA releases water for recreation on certain days of the year, according to a published schedule. A one-mile section below Ocoee 3 is the Olympic whitewater section, and it passes in front of the Ocoee Whitewater Center. A four-mile segment below Ocoee 2 is used by commercial outfitters and water-sports enthusiasts for rafting and kayaking trips.

The Ocoee River was not always recognized as a site for white-water sports. In fact, it was

BIKING IN THE SOUTHERN CHEROKEE

Mountain biking is permitted on dozens of trails within the Cherokee National Forest, making this a popular destination for off-road bicyclists. The **Chilhowee Mountain Bike Trail System** is centered in the Chilhowee Mountain recreation area, near the town of Ocoee. It includes nine different trails ranging from easy to advanced. The two-mile Azalea Trail is a favorite; the 5.4-mile Clear Creek Trail is challenging, with wrenching uphill and screaming downhill segments.

The **Tanasi Mountain Bike Trail System** is located near the Ocoee Whitewater Center and has five trails, including the 11.5-mile advanced Chestnut Mountain–West Fork Loop. The Thunder Rock Express is a 1.5-mile stretch of trail with exciting downhill segments and lots of jumps. The Tanasi system is so revered by mountain bikers that a top-of-the-line titanium-frame mountain bike is named after it.

Elite road bikers head to the **Cherohala Skyway** for endurance rides. The road climbs for 21 miles on the Tennessee side before beginning a 15-mile descent in North Carolina. Steep switchbacks and high elevation make this a challenging ride for even the most experienced bikers. The Skyway is the location of the 100-mile **Cherohala Challenge** every June.

The **Tellico Ranger District Trail System,** north of the Cherohala Skyway, includes the 11-mile Citico Creek and Tellico River Trail, a challenging ride along a gravel road, and the Indian Boundary Loop, a 3.2-mile level track that circles Indian Boundary Lake.

Bike rentals and gear are available from **Trailhead Bicycle Company** (225 1st St. NE, Cleveland, 423/472-9899), which offers superior gear and repair services.

Copperhill's **Ocoee Adventure Center** (4654 Hwy. 64, 423/496-4437, www.ocoee-adventurecenter.com) offers guided mountain bike trips and personalized instruction. Rates are $45 per person for a half-day, and $89 per person for a whole day. **Outdoor Adventure Rafting** (629 Welcome Valley Rd., 423/338-5746, www.raft.com) near Benton rents bikes for $15 per hour or $40 per day and will also create custom bike trips for your group.

only due to the deterioration of the Ocoee 2 water flume that the river's recreational potential was discovered. It was around 1976 that years of weathering caused TVA to shut down the flume for repairs, causing river water to flow unimpeded down the Ocoee for the first time in decades.

It did not take long for the first daredevils to discover the thrill of the rapids; the first river riders rode Navy surplus rafts. The first two outfitters, Ocoee Outdoors and Sunburst Expeditions, opened their doors in 1977.

But meanwhile TVA was repairing the flume, and in 1984 it was ready to again divert the river water away from the riverbed. By this time, however, the rafting industry had blossomed. So in 1984 the Outfitters Association and TVA reached a 35-year agreement where rafting companies would get a minimum of 116 days of rafting water each year and would pay $2 per customer to compensate TVA for the loss of power generation. It is an agreement that has allowed TVA to continue operation and the rafting industry to flourish.

◖ Rafting the Ocoee

White-water rafting is the most popular activity of the southern Cherokee Forest between June and September. The four miles between the Ocoee 2 diversion dam and the Ocoee 2 powerhouse are where the fun happens, over 20 different rapids with names like Grumpy, Broken Nose, Double Suck, Slingshot, and Hell's Hole.

The Ocoee River is for experienced or adventurous outdoorspeople. With Class III–IV rapids, the river can be frightening or dangerous if you're not experienced or confident enough. No one under 12 is permitted to raft anywhere

COURTESY OF CHATTANOOGA VISITOR'S BUREAU

There are few better ways to catch a buzz than rafting the Ocoee River.

Don't carry anything with you, like a camera, that can't be submerged. In summer, wear your bathing suit, shorts, a T-shirt, and tennis shoes. During the cooler months, suit up in a wet suit or wear a windbreaker or wool sweater to keep warm. Wool socks and tennis shoes are also nice. Regardless of the season, avoid cotton clothing and bring a change of clothes to put on after your trip. Most rafting companies offer somewhere to store your belongings until after the trip.

There are more than 20 companies offering rafting trips down the Ocoee. Some of the best are **Ocoee Rafting** (Ducktown, 423/496-3388, www.ocoeerafting.com), **Nantahala Outdoor Center (NOC)** (13077 U.S. 19, Bryson City NC, 423/338-5901, www.noc.com), and **Ocoee Inn Rafting** (2496 Hwy. 64, 423/338-2064, www.ocoeeinn.com).

If you want to make a more significant commitment to the sport of kayaking, sign up for a clinic at **Ocoee Adventure Center** (4651 Hwy. 64, 423/496-4437, www.ocoeeadventurecenter.com) or NOC,

on the Ocoee. Beginners or families with young children should raft down the Hiwassee instead. If you are uncertain, talk to an experienced outfitter about which rafting trip would be best for your group.

Watching as other people make their way down the river is also an enjoyable pastime. Places where you can pull over and parking areas along the rafting portion of the river are often full of onlookers on summer afternoons and other busy periods.

The Ocoee rafting and floating season runs March–September. During the spring and fall, outfitters will offer trips on weekends or holidays only. During the summer, there are trips every day. Rafting on the river is dependent on TVA's schedule of water releases. You can pick up a schedule from the Ocoee Whitewater Center (Hwy. 64 W., 423/496-5197, www.fs.fed.us/r8/ocoee).

When you go rafting, do plan to get wet.

OCOEE WHITEWATER CENTER

Built for the 1996 Atlanta Summer Olympics, the Ocoee Whitewater Center (Hwy. 64 W., 423/496-5197, www.fs.fed.us/r8/ocoee, Apr.–Nov. daily 9 A.M.–5 P.M., Thanksgiving–Mar. Fri.–Sun. 9 A.M.–5 P.M., free) is a central source of information about the Ocoee River, has restrooms and other amenities, and is a starting point for several hikes.

The riverbed in front of the center is pockmarked and rugged; the natural contours of the river were "improved" in preparation for the Olympics. When the water is low, children and adults will enjoy walking around the pools and streams on the riverbed or sunning on the rocks. When the water is high, marvel at the power and sound of fast-running water while you watch rafters and kayakers maneuvering down the rapids.

There are rocking chairs and plenty of benches around for relaxing. The Olympic

Legacy Bridge spans the river, providing nice views of the water below. During spring and summer, plan to walk through the gardens, which showcase native plants. You can find a guide to the gardens at the visitors center, which has great additional information about the area.

Visitors to the center can park for 30 minutes in the lot right next to the center. Long-term users must park below and pay a fee of $3 per vehicle.

Accommodations

The **⟨** **Lake Ocoee Inn** (2496 Hwy. 64, 423/338-2064, www.ocoeeinn.com, $55–65) is located about 15 miles west of the Ocoee Whitewater Center and sits on the shore of placid Lake Ocoee (Parksville Lake). This motel opened in 1936 and has nondescript motel rooms, plus four fully equipped cabins. There is also a marina. Generally speaking, Lake Ocoee attracts an outdoorsy crowd. It is also family friendly.

Practicalities

Gas, food, and lodging are somewhat limited along the Ocoee River. There are **gas stations** at Ocoee, Ducktown, and at Greasy Creek, about five miles up Highway 30. There are restaurants in Ocoee, Ducktown, and Copper Hill, plus one restaurant along the river. The best way to handle food during a trip to the river is to pack a picnic lunch and enjoy it at one of the many picnic areas in the forest. There are modest groceries in Greasy Creek, Reliance, and Ocoee. In Ducktown, there's a **Piggly Wiggly** (125 Five Points Dr.).

DUCKTOWN

Ducktown, and its sister city Copperhill, are the heart of the Copper Basin of Tennessee. Here, copper was mined from the 1850s until the 1980s.

In order to fuel the copper smelters, timber was harvested all around. By 1876, all the trees in the area were gone, and logs had to be floated in from Fannin County, Georgia. Between 1865 and 1878, 24 million pounds of copper were removed from the earth and 50 square miles of the basin had been stripped of its trees.

The area's mines declined between 1878 and 1890, until a new railroad spur arrived in the area. In 1899 the Tennessee Copper Company opened the Burra Burra Mine in Ducktown and built a new smelter. During this period, mining companies used an open roasting process to remove copper from the raw ore. This open roasting required lots of timber for fuel, and it let off sulfuric acid, which killed vegetation and left the landscape eerily empty. Acid rain fell, polluting the Ocoee River and other nearby bodies of water.

The environmental abuse of more than a century left its mark on Tennessee's Copper Basin. For years, this area was distinctive for its barren orange-red hills and craters, the legacy of many years of deforestation and the open release of sulfuric acid. Residents had mixed feelings about the landscape—it was strangely beautiful, but at the same time it was a constant reminder of environmental damage. There were also concerns about health effects. Early efforts to reforest the old mines date back to the early 20th century, but it was not until the 1970s that scientists figured out a way to successfully introduce trees back into the denuded landscape. Since then, pine trees have grown to cover virtually all of the hills that were once barren.

Copper was mined here until 1987, and the plant at Copperhill still processes sulfur, although the raw materials are trucked in—not mined.

Ducktown was a company town, a fact that is evident as you take a short drive around. Main Street is little more than two blocks with a handful of elegant homes built by mine owners and bosses. The main residential neighborhood is a collection of modest homes in a slight hollow. The newer parts of town, including gas stations, motels, and a school, are found near the intersection of Highways 64 and 68.

CAMPING IN THE SOUTHERN CHEROKEE

There are more than a dozen developed camp grounds in the southern region of the Cherokee National Forest. Campgrounds vary from developed areas with electrical hookups for RVs and hot showers to rustic grounds with chemical toilets and no shower facilities at all. Most Forest Service campgrounds are open mid-March–December, although some are available year round, and most are open on a first-come, first-served basis. Where reservations are available, they must be made through the government's centralized reservation service at www.reserveusa.com or by calling 877/444-6777.

Camping rates range $10–20 depending on the type of site you choose and the popularity of the campground. The following are some of the most popular campgrounds; for a complete list, contact the nearest ranger station.

OCOEE/HIWASSEE DISTRICT
The largest campground is **Chilhowee Recreation Area,** located along Forest Service Road 77. There are 86 campsites, warm showers, and flush toilets. You are next door to the McKamy Lake beach and have easy access to 25 miles of hike/bike trails.

Thunder Rock is located near Ocoee Powerhouse No. 3 and is convenient to the Whitewater Center. There are 39 sites, warm showers, and flush toilets. This is a popular campsite for rafters and other water-sports enthusiasts.

Parksville Lake, open April 1–October 31, is located along Rock Creek and has 17 campsites, warm showers, and flush toilets. It is convenient to the white-water section of the Ocoee River and to swimming, boating, and fishing on Parksville Lake.

Lost Creek, located off Highway 30 near Reliance, has 15 sites and is set in a mature hardwood forest next to Big Lost Creek. It is a peaceful and wild area, but the flush toilets and hot showers provide basic creature comforts. RVs are welcome.

TELLICO DISTRICT
Big Oak Cove is an 11-site campground located on the banks of the Tellico River. A retreat for tent campers, the grounds are open mid-March–December. Hiking, fishing, and wading are available nearby. The fee is $10 per night. There are chemical toilets and cold showers.

Located off the Cherohala Skyway at an elevation of 1,800 feet, **Holly Flats** is an 18-site tent-friendly campsite with limited facilities. There are chemical toilets and cold showers, but little in the way of other comforts. The setting is peaceful and typically uncrowded.

One of the most popular campgrounds in this part of the forest is **Indian Boundary,** an 88-site campground located on Indian Boundary Lake along the Cherohala Skyway. Four loops offer various levels of comfort, from full RV hookups to rustic tent sites. Recreation includes hiking or biking around the lake, boating, fishing, and swimming. Reservations are accepted.

CHATTANOOGA

◖ Ducktown Basin Museum
The Ducktown Basin Museum (212 Burra Burra St., 423/496-5778, Mon.–Sat. 10 A.M.–4:30 P.M., hours may be extended 30 minutes in summer, adults $4, seniors $3, children $0.50) captures the unique history and culture of Tennessee's Copper Basin. Located in the offices of the old Burra Burra Mine, the museum has displays about the historical development of the mines, the culture that developed in the company towns, and the mining business itself. Special topics include mine safety, the railroad, and the history of strikes at the mine. The visit includes a 15-minute video that tells the story of the entire region and describes the three periods during which the hills here were mined for copper and other minerals.

At the rear of the museum is one of the only "copper craters" that was not reforested. Although volunteer pine trees are beginning to take root in the red soil, you can still imagine how distinctive the landscape once looked.

Accommodations
Ducktown is close enough to the Ocoee and several outdoor outfitters to make it a popular

CHATTANOOGA

© DUCKTOWN BASIN MUSEUM

Learn about the history of copper mining at the Ducktown Basin Museum.

place for outdoor thrill seekers. But the additional draw of the mining museum is another reason to make this your home base in the Overhill region.

For a bed-and-breakfast option in Ducktown, try **The Company House** (125 Main St., 423/496-5634, www.bbonline.com/tn/companyhouse, $89–99). It has six guest rooms, each named for a mine in the area. All rooms have private baths and in-room telephones.

If motel lodging is more your thing, then there are two options. The **Ducktown Copper Inn** (U.S. 64 and Hwy. 68, 423/496-5541, $55–65) is an aging motel with no-frills accommodations. Rooms have microwaves, refrigerators, and televisions. The **Ocoee River Inn** (5082 Hwy. 64, 877/546-2633, $60–80) is a newer outfit, with many of the same amenities (but less grunge) than its nearby neighbor.

Food

With the exception of a gas-station convenience store, **Brother's Copper Kettle** (5750 Hwy. 64, 423/496-5001, Mon.–Sat. 11 A.M.–9 P.M., $4–12) is the only game in town. The menu includes a buffet, salad bar, and barbecue sandwiches.

COPPERHILL

Copperhill sits on the state line and on the banks of the Ocoee River. On the Georgia side, the town is called McCaysville and the river is called the Toccoa.

There is more going on in Copperhill than Ducktown, due largely to the scenic train excursions that stop here for midday layovers. A pleasant main street district with restaurants and shops makes this a nice place to spend an hour or so. Walk up the hillside that faces Ocoee Street for views of the town and the Ocoee/Toccoa River.

Rail Excursions

In addition to the rail excursions offered by the Tennessee Valley Railroad, the **Blue Ridge**

Scenic Railway (241 Depot St., Blue Ridge, GA, 706/632-9833, www.brscenic.com, adults $28–43, children about half price) offers railroad excursions that come to Copperhill. The trip leaves from Blue Ridge, Georgia, and makes a one-hour journey north through the mountains to Copperhill, where you have two hours to eat and shop.

Food

More than 70 years after its founding, the **New York Restaurant** (121 Ocoee St., 423/496-3855, www.thenewyorkrestaurant.com, daily 7 A.M.–3 P.M., $2–6) was remodeled and came under new management in 2007. You can eat at the classic lunch counter or dine on white tablecloths at a table.

The menu includes plate lunches of hamburger steak, chicken breast and gravy, or chicken salad, and sandwiches including tuna melts and Philly cheesesteaks. There are some modern additions, too: hummus in pita and black-bean veggie burgers. If you prefer omelets and eggs, order from the breakfast menu all day. After a day rafting the river, you'll appreciate that beer is served.

TURTLETOWN

Drive north from Ducktown on Highway 68 to find more quiet towns and rural countryside.

Just beyond the small community of Turtletown, Highway 294 splits off Highway 68, headed toward North Carolina. About four miles down this road, and about two miles past the state line, there is a remarkable monument to the Christian faith. **Fields of the Wood Bible Park** (10000 Hwy. 294, Murphy NC, 828/494-7855, www.fieldsofthewoodbiblepark.com, daily sunrise–sunset, free) is a project of the Church of God of Prophecy that contains, among other things, the world's largest cross and the largest representation of the Ten Commandments. The latter is located just inside the park's gates and is laid out on a hillside. Each letter spelling out the commandments is five feet high and four feet wide. This is just the beginning of what Fields of the Wood has to offer. You will also find replicas of Joseph's tomb, where Christ was buried and rose from the dead, and Golgotha, where Jesus offered himself as a sacrifice. There is also a gift shop and the Burger Mountain Café, which are open Monday–Saturday 9 A.M.–5 P.M.

The Hiwassee

Named from the Cherokee word *ayuwasi* (savannah or meadow), the Hiwassee River drains fertile agricultural lands and passes through the heartland of the southern Cherokee National Forest.

RELIANCE

The Reliance historic district is located along the Hiwassee River, near where Highways 30 and 315 intersect. The **Hiwassee Union Church** is a two-story board structure built jointly by the local Masonic lodge and the Union Church in 1899. On the north side of the river is the **Higdon Hotel,** also built around 1899.

Your pit stop in Reliance should be the **Webb Brothers Texaco** (3708 Hwy. 30, 423/338-2373, www.webbbros.com), a gas station, post office, general store, river outfitter, and community hub. Inside the shop you'll find a placard with historical information about Reliance.

Reliance is located about 10 miles north of the Ocoee River, along Highway 30. The drive south follows Greasy Creek, a pretty, clear stream that defies its name. You will pass old wood-frame houses and farms that have been in this valley for generations.

HIWASSEE SCENIC RIVER STATE PARK

A 23-mile section of the Hiwassee River has been designated a Tennessee Scenic River.

CHATTANOOGA

CHATTANOOGA

From Highway 411 to the North Carolina state line, the Hiwassee River offers prime opportunities for canoeing, rafting, fishing, hiking, and wildlife viewing.

Hiwassee Scenic River State Park (404 Spring Creek Rd., Delano, 423/263-0050, www.tn.gov/environment/parks/Hiwassee) and the neighboring **Gee Creek Campground** (Spring Creek Rd., Delano, 423/263-0050) are good places to come to explore the river. There are picnic grounds, restrooms, and boat-launch areas. The Gee Creek Campground has 47 particularly tent-friendly campsites, some of which are right next to the river. As is the case with Tennessee state parks, campsites are available on a first-come, first-served basis only.

Fishing is popular along the river; anglers frequently catch rainbow and brown trout, largemouth bass, yellow perch, and catfish.

Unlike the Ocoee River, the Hiwassee is a calm river, with Class I–II (rather than III–IV) rapids. Children six and up are allowed on the Hiwassee.

Because the Hiwassee is calmer, many people rent the necessary equipment and make the journey downriver without a guide. Expect to pay $40 and up per day for a six-person raft or $24 per day for a one-person Duckie. Inner tubes and other equipment are also available. Hiwassee outfitters include **Hiwassee Scenic Outfitters, Inc.** (155 Ellis Creek Rd., Reliance, 423/338-8115, www.hiwasseeoutfitters.com) and **Webb Brothers Float Service** (Reliance, 423/338-2373, www.webbbros.com).

SANDHILL CRANES

Located along the Hiwassee River between Dayton and Birchwood, the **Blythe Ferry Unit of the Hiwassee Refuge** (423/614-3018) is a good place for bird-watching. Besides seasonal shorebirds, waders, and common waterfowl such as wintering ducks and geese, the unit has become a winter stopover for migrating sandhill and whooping cranes. The concentration has grown from just a few birds to more than 6,000 at times, making this one of Tennessee's premier wildlife spectacles November–March. The refuge is closed to the public during the winter except for a Sandhill Crane Festival in January, but viewing is possible along the roads and from an observation deck.

To get to the refuge, find the junction between Highways 58 and 60 near Georgetown. Drive 7.8 miles west on Highway 60 and turn right at the wildlife sign.

The best way to get up close to the cranes and other wildlife of the Hiwassee Refuge is aboard **Blue Moon Cruises** (5637 Hwy. 411, Benton, 888/993-2583, www.bluemooncruises.org, Dec.-Mar., $40), which depart from Sale Creek Marina near Soddy-Daisy. For 3.5 hours you will ply the waters of the Hiwassee on a naturalist-led tour that includes viewing of sandhill cranes.

DELANO

Located on the edge of the national forest, between Etowah and Benton, the town of Delano is known for **Delano Daylilies** (153 County Rd. 854, 423/263-9323, www.delanodaylilies.com, late May–early June Tues.–Sat. 10 A.M.–5 P.M., free), a noteworthy seasonal attraction and nursery. This nursery raises some 1,300 varieties of colorful daylilies, and from late May to early June every year their garden is busy with area growers shopping for blooms. Casual visitors are also welcome to come and enjoy a stroll throughout the patches of daylilies, but you'll be hard-pressed not to wind up with at least one plant in your possession by the end of your visit. A covered pavilion is a lovely place to sit and relax while your traveling companion chooses lilies. There are also benches throughout the gardens.

An 1861 barn provides the centerpiece for the 11,000 acres of vineyard at **Savannah Oaks Winery** (1817 Delano Rd., 423/263-2762, www.savannah-oaks-winery.com,

Mon.–Thurs. 10 A.M.–6 P.M., Fri.–Sat. 10 A.M.–7 P.M., Sun. 1–6 P.M., free). Tours and wine and cheese tastings are available by appointment, and in the summer the winery hosts a number of events with live music.

Gliding

Gliding is flying without an engine, and you can experience this sublime form of travel at **Chilhowee Glideport** (Hwy. 411, 423/388-2000, www.chilhowee.com), near Benton. A half-hour ride costs $219 and takes you high above the scenic Cherokee National Forest and the Hiwassee and Ocoee Rivers. Chilhowee Glideport also offers lessons and rentals for gliding enthusiasts.

COKER CREEK

Before copper was mined in the Copper Basin, this area was famous for its gold. The Cherokee Indians had known about the gold for years, but whites discovered it around 1825. It didn't take long for a full-fledged gold rush to begin. Trouble was that the gold was on Cherokee land. When the Indians complained to the federal government in 1826, the U.S. army established a garrison here supposedly to enforce the Cherokee's land rights. Even the presence of soldiers did little to keep settlers from tapping into the Cherokee's resources, and the pressure from people such as these was probably one thing that sealed the Cherokee's later fate.

Sights

For the best views of this part of the Cherokee Forest, drive to **Buck Bald,** the site of an old fire tower. The tower was removed in the 1970s, but the site remains a place to enjoy 360-degree views of the surrounding landscape. To get there, drive seven miles south of Coker Creek along Highway 68, then turn left onto Buck Bald Road. It is 2.5 miles to the top.

A designated scenic area with four waterfalls and several miles of hiking trails, **Coker Creek**

Scenic Area and Falls is a wonderful place for a picnic. The four waterfalls—Upper Coker Creek Falls, Coker Creek Falls, Hiding Place Falls, and Lower Coker Creek Falls—are all located within a quarter mile of the parking area. There are picnic tables, but no toilets or potable water.

To find the falls, drive south of Coker Creek 3.1 miles along Highway 68. Turn right onto County Road 628 (Ironsburg Road) and travel 0.8 mile. Veer left at the Ironsburg Cemetery onto County Road 626 (Duckett Ridge Road) and travel for three miles. The road will become gravel. Turn left onto Forest Service Road 2138 and travel one mile to the parking area.

Festivals and Events

Since 1968 Coker Creek's **Autumn Gold Festival** (www.cokercreek.org) has been the community's largest event of the year. Taking place during the second full weekend of October—while the autumn leaves are on full display—the festival includes a crafts fair, gold panning, and the crowning of the Autumn Gold Queen.

Shopping

Coker Creek is home to several art galleries. **Designs by Baerreis** (12203 Hwy. 68, 423/261-2731, www.climbingbear.com) is a family-owned gallery showcasing the work of Phil and Martha Baerreis as well as their children. Highlights include Phil's hand-turned wooden boxes and custom-made jewelry by Elisabeth Baerreis. The **Coker Creek Gallery** (206 Hot Water Rd., 423/261-2157), located just a few hundred yards from Highway 68, has wind chimes, pottery, glass and metal sculptures, jewelry, and more.

Panning for Gold

Although the gold industry petered out at Coker Creek after the Civil War, hobby mining and panning continues. You can buy panning supplies at the **Coker Creek Welcome Center** (Hwy. 68, 423/261-2286, www.cokercreek.org).

It's unlikely that anyone will tell you the best places to pan for gold, but the most popular are easy to find. You can pan at **Coker Creek** just 0.3 mile from the welcome center, near Doc Rogers Field. **Coker Creek Falls**, eight miles south of the welcome center, is also a nice place to pan, although you may soon grow weary of the work and choose to enjoy the falls and swimming hole instead.

ETOWAH

Etowah didn't much exist until 1902, when the Louisville and Nashville Railroad chose the settlement for its new headquarters and rail center. The railroad was planning a new, more direct route between Cincinnati and Atlanta, and it needed a place for crew changes and engine servicing. The passenger station was built first, in 1906. A veritable railroad complex followed: roundhouse, sand house, cinder pits, coal bins, oil house, machine shop, blacksmith shop, boiler shop, planing mill, cabinet shop, powerhouse, car repair shop, water tanks, a store, offices, freight depot, and nearly 20 tracks.

The L&N also built houses for its workers, and Etowah was truly a company town where everyone lived, breathed, and worked the railroad. At its peak, more than 2,000 men were employed by the L&N here.

Etowah and its railroad industry flourished until 1928, when the L&N started to replace its wooden railroad carts with steel ones. Two hundred shop men were laid off. In the same year, the L&N closed its headquarters in Etowah, moving them to Knoxville. By 1931, the workforce at Etowah had shrunk to just 80.

Over the succeeding decades, Etowah diversified, and people found other work. Passenger trains continued to run until 1968. CSX, the freight train company, still operates a terminal in Etowah.

There isn't much in the way of accommodations in Etowah, so look at nearby Athens for a comfortable bed-and-breakfast.

Sights

Etowah's downtown district faces Highway 411 and the railroad. The historic **Gem Theater** (700 S. Tennessee Ave./U.S. 441, www.gemplayers. com), built in 1927, has been renovated and is the home of the Gem Theater Players. For information about upcoming shows, contact the Etowah Arts Commission at 423/263-7608. They typically produce about five shows annually.

You can relive Etowah's railroad history at the **L&N Depot and Railroad Museum** (Tennessee Ave./Hwy. 411, 423/263-7840, Mon.–Sat. 10 A.M.–4 P.M., free). The old passenger station is elegant, with high ceilings and delicate wood finishes. It comes alive through old photographs and recollections by area residents who talk about the hardships and pleasures of a railroad life. The exhibit, called "Growing Up with the L&N: Life and Times of a Railroad Town," is more about the social history of Etowah than the railroad itself, although the two are interlinked.

Ask to go upstairs, where you can see more general exhibits about Etowah's history. Sometimes there are local art exhibits on display.

After touring the museum, go outside to see a railroad caboose. There is also a picnic area and a walking trail that follows the railroad tracks.

◀ Tennessee Valley Railroad Excursions

The Tennessee Valley Railroad (423/894-8028, www.tvrail.com), based in Chattanooga, organizes sightseeing tours of the Cherokee National Forest during the summer and fall. The **Hiwassee River Rail Adventure** (adults $34, children $24) is a 3.5-hour, 50-mile journey that follows the path of the Hiwassee River and includes the breathtaking corkscrew loop around Bald Mountain. The **Copperhill Special** (adults $52, children $35) follows the same route as the Hiwassee journey but adds an additional 40-mile trip and lunchtime layover in Copperhill.

Passengers on either journey meet at

the L&N Depot and Railroad Museum in Etowah and are bussed to nearby Gee Creek State Park, where they board the train. Train cars are comfortable, with big windows and air-conditioning.

The scenic train excursions are made possible by the combined efforts of the Tennessee Overhill Association and the Tennessee Valley Railroad Museum.

Food

Directly across Tennessee Avenue (otherwise known as Highway 411) from the L&N Depot is **Tony's Italian Restaurant** (718 Tennessee Ave., 423/263-1940, daily 11 A.M.–10 P.M., $5–8), which serves pasta, pizza, calzones, and Italian-style subs. There is a buffet at lunch and dinner that includes lasagna, pizza, salad, and other house specialties.

A short drive north on Tennessee Avenue will take you to **Hah-Hah's Deli and Coffee Shoppee** (235 Hwy. 411 N., 423/263-7914, Mon.–Fri. 9 A.M.–4 P.M., $5–6), which serves coffee, sandwiches, and ice cream.

Information

Contact the **Etowah Area Chamber of Commerce** (727 Tennessee Ave., 423/263-2228, www.etowahcoc.org), located in the L&N building next to the museum, for visitor information. The **Tennessee Overhill Heritage Association** (423/263-7232, www.tennesseeoverhill.com) is a regional tourism agency based in Etowah, with offices in the railroad depot.

CHATTANOOGA

The Tellico

The headwaters of the Tellico River are high atop the peaks of the Cherokee Forest. The stream, noted for fishing, flows down the mountain and along the scenic Cherohala Skyway to Tellico Plains, where it flows northward to its confluence with the Little Tennessee. The Tellico Dam impounds the rivers and forms Tellico Lake. Here, near the town of Vonore, are two of the most significant historic attractions in the region: Fort Loudoun State Historic Area and the Sequoyah Birthplace Museum. Both have important ties to Cherokee history.

Towns including Athens, Englewood, and Madisonville are located in the foothills of the mountains, in the Great Valley of East Tennessee. These centers of industry, education, and commerce are still the heartbeat of the Overhill region.

TELLICO PLAINS

Located where the Tellico River emerges from the national forest, Tellico Plains was once a logging and industrial town. It is now a gateway to the Cherokee National Forest and the official beginning point of the Cherohala Skyway, a scenic parkway that extends into North Carolina.

The **Cherohala Skyway Visitor Center** (225 Cherohala Skyway/Hwy. 165, 423/253-8010, www.cherohala.org/visitorcenter.html, daily 9 A.M.–5 P.M.), near the official start of the skyway, has maps as well as staff to answer questions. There is also a large gift shop and bathrooms. Right next door is the **Charles Hall Museum** (229 Cherohala Skyway, 423/253-6767, www.charleshallmuseum.com, Mon.–Sat. 10 A.M.–5 P.M., Sun. noon–5 P.M., free), a local history museum packed with antiques, 98 percent of which came from the collection of Tellico-area resident Charles Hall. There are more than 200 guns, an extensive telephone collection, and an impressive coin collection, among others. In 2010 more than 30,000 people visited this small museum.

Tellico Plains consists of an older "downtown" located on the south side of Highway 165, and several miles of sprawl along Highway 68. The downtown area is home to several real estate offices, building supply companies, local businesses, restaurants, and shops. **Motorcycle Outfitters** (106 Scott St., 423/253-2088, www.tellicomoto.com) sells clothes and equipment for bikers, and **The Bookshelf** (108 Scott St., 423/253-3183, www.tellicobookshelf.com) is a used-book store with a knowledgeable staff that also repairs books. Galleries including **The Tellico Arts Center** (113 Scott St., 423/253-2253) cater to visitors looking for local arts and crafts.

For food, head first to **Tellico Grains Bakery** (105 Depot St., 423/253-6911, www.tellico-grains-bakery.com, Tues.–Sat. 8 A.M.–4 P.M., $4–8), a bakery and café with its own wood-fired oven. The menu of bread, sandwiches, and pizza are as clever as the bakery's name.

For plate lunches, burgers, and other grilled sandwiches, go to **Town Square Café and Bakery** (Public Sq., 423/253-2200, Mon.–Sat. 6 A.M.–7:30 P.M., Sun. 6 A.M.–3 P.M., $3–8), a cozy eating house where everyone seems to know each other. The daily lunch special comes with your choice of two sides and bread. They also sell pizza, but it is the homemade gravy on the breakfast dishes that brings in the locals.

Cherohala Skyway

Completed in 1996, this is a two-lane highway that passes through the highest peaks of the southern Unaka Mountains. The 54-mile road, which begins in Tellico Plains, climbs to more than 5,300 feet at its highest level and provides stunning scenic views. It follows the Tellico River for several miles at the beginning before starting its serious ascent. The road terminates in Robbinsville, North Carolina; about one-third of the road is in Tennessee.

The Cherohala Skyway was originally called the Cheoah Parkway and the Overhill Skyway; the states of Tennessee and North Carolina eventually agreed on the existing name, which combines the words *Cherokee* and *Nantahala*. The highway, which took

34 years and some $100 million to build, replaced narrow, unpaved Forest Service roads that had for many years been the only means of travel over the peaks in this part of the forest. Despite predictions to the contrary, the skyway remains relatively uncrowded, providing a pleasant alternative to congested highways through the Great Smoky Mountains National Park.

It will take you about 1.5 hours to drive nonstop from one end of the skyway to the other. Although the road is well maintained and easy to drive, plan to take it slow. It is windy, and you will want to stop frequently to admire the view. Beware of snow and ice during winter.

Sights and stops along the way include **Tellico Ranger Station** (250 Ranger Station Rd., 423/253-2520), a source of information about the forest, the area, and the drive. The station is located in a New Deal–era CCC building. **Bald River Falls,** a 100-foot waterfall, is located off the skyway along Forest Service Road 210.

After you pass the ranger station, the road begins to climb. Overlooks on the Tennessee side include **Turkey Creek, Lake View,** and **Brushy Ridge.** There are picnic tables at Turkey Creek and Brushy Ridge. All overlooks are wheelchair accessible.

The skyway is popular with motorcyclists and serious bicyclists who enjoy the scenic curves and fresh mountain air.

Indian Boundary

One of the most popular destinations in the southern Cherokee Forest, Indian Boundary (Forest Service Rd. 345, Apr.–Sept.) is a Forest Service campground and recreation area. Located high atop the mountains off the Cherohala Skyway, Indian Boundary is cool in the summer and an ideal place for a camping vacation. Cool off with a swim at the Indian Boundary beach, hike or bike along the three-mile loop that circles the 100-acre Indian

Boundary Lake, or go for a boat cruise on the lake. No gasoline engines are allowed in the lake.

The **campground** (877/444-6777, www.reserveusa.com, $20) has 91 sites, hot showers, and potable water available from spigots around the campground. Several sites have electricity. There is also a camp store (no phone) and picnic area. Despite Indian Boundary's isolation, it is quite popular, particularly during the summer. For information on recreation, contact the Tellico Ranger Station at 423/253-2520.

ENGLEWOOD

A small town located in the foothills of the Appalachian mountains, Englewood is home to the **Englewood Textile Museum** (17 S. Niota St., 423/887-5455, Tues.–Sat. noon–5 P.M., free). The museum remembers the hundreds of area working-class women who toiled at textile mills in Englewood. A hand-painted mural on the outside of the museum depicts a pastoral company town. Inside, you can see some of the clothing that was manufactured here for nearly 100 years. There is an adjacent antiques store.

Food

The ◖ **Tellico Junction Café** (17 Main St., 423/887-7770, Mon.–Fri. 6 A.M.–8 P.M., Sat. 7 A.M.–4 P.M., Sun. 7 A.M.–noon, $5–12) is a large, open restaurant facing the railroad tracks in downtown Englewood. Dozens of polished wood tables and a wide lunch counter invite you to stop and linger over cups of coffee or plates of grilled sandwiches, plate-lunch specials, or homemade dessert. Locals head here after church on Sunday or for fish fry on Friday. No matter when you come, don't miss the chance to check out the decor in the men's restroom.

ATHENS

The seat of McMinn County, Athens is home to **Tennessee Wesleyan University** (204 E. College St., 423/745-7504, www.twcnet.edu), a Methodist-affiliated four-year university.

Chartered in 1857, it is the home of the Old College Harp Singers, a shape-note singing group.

The **McMinn Living History Museum** (522 W. Madison Ave., 423/745-0329, Mon.–Fri. 10 A.M.–5 P.M., adults $5, students and seniors $3) is home to 30 different exhibit rooms, including an extensive collection of antique quilts.

One of the Southeast's most distinctive food brands is Mayfield, a maker of milk, dairy, and juice products. Mayfield's largest bottling and processing plant is located just outside of Athens, near where Thomas B. Mayfield Sr., a local dairy farmer, first opened his creamery in 1923. Visitors are welcome at **Mayfield Dairy Farms** (4 Mayfield Ln., 800/629-3435, www.mayfielddairy.com, Mon.–Fri. 9 A.M.–5 P.M., Sat. 9 A.M.–2 P.M., free). The 40-minute tour includes a short video and visits to viewing areas where you can see Mayfield's distinctive yellow milk jugs being made, jugs and other containers being filled, and ice cream being packaged. You also walk by giant vats of milk being pasteurized, and others that are being made into buttermilk. Milk is not made on Wednesday, and ice cream is not made on Saturday.

Don't expect to see any cows, though, except for the bronze cow sculpture outside the welcome center. Mayfield buys its raw milk from area dairy farmers; it arrives in giant trucks that enter the dairy gates by the dozens every day.

The tour is free, but be aware that it is awfully hard to pass up the ice cream shop at the end, particularly on a hot summer day. It's almost as if they planned it that way.

Accommodations

The **Majestic Mansion** (202 E. Washington Ave., 423/746-9041, www.themansionbnb.com, $115–145) is a bed-and-breakfast in downtown residential Athens. Four guest rooms offer classic country decor with elegant touches such as claw-foot tubs, feather beds, and polished brass fittings. Each room has a

CHATTANOOGA

CHATTANOOGA

COURTESY OF THE LOST SEA ADVENTURE

Take an easy stroll to an underground lake at The Lost Sea Adventure.

private bath, air-conditioning, and television. For breakfast choose between "fitness fare" and "full power breakfast." Spend a quiet afternoon relaxing on the screened-in front porch or in the sitting room. In-room spa service is available at reasonable prices.

MADISONVILLE

Epicureans should make a beeline to **Benton's Country Hams** (2603 Hwy. 411, 423/442-5003), a family-run ham house where they depend on brown sugar, salt, and a lot of time to cure their hams. Housed in a low-slung inconspicuous cinderblock building on the side of busy Highway 411, Benton's has been a destination for cooks and eaters for generations. Their smoked and unsmoked country hams sell like hotcakes. You can also buy prosciutto, bacon, and luncheon meats that will have you dreaming pig. You know this is the real thing because the scent of hickory smoke clings to your clothes and hair after you depart.

SWEETWATER

The Lost Sea Adventure (140 Lost Sea Rd., 423/337-6616, www.thelostsea.com, Nov.–Feb. daily 9 A.M.–5 P.M., Mar.–Apr. and Sept.–Oct. daily 9 A.M.–6 P.M., May–June and Aug. daily 9 A.M.–7 P.M., July daily 9 A.M.–8 P.M., adults $16, children $8) is a cave noted for its four-acre underground lake. Tours include a 0.75-mile guided tour of the caverns, as well as a ride aboard a glass-bottomed boat on the lake. You can even sign up to camp out down in the cave in one of the Lost Sea's so-called wild tours. This is a memorable experience. The Lost Sea is located at exit 60 off I-75.

While in Sweetwater, satisfy your sweet tooth at **Hunter's Bakery and Café** (101 E. Morris St., 423/351-1098, www.huntersbakeryandcafe.com, Mon.–Thurs. 10 A.M.–4 P.M., Fri.–Sat. 9 A.M.–8 P.M., lunch $2–16, dinner $10–25). This cozy downtown hot spot has a fox-hunting theme and solidly good food that keeps people coming back again and again.

© J BRIAN AND MERRI E LONG

Boating, fishing, and history lessons come together at the Fort Loudoun State Historic Area.

Salads, pasta, and entrées including steak, pork, chicken, and shrimp are offered at lunch and dinner. At the midday meal, you can also pick from signature sandwiches like the tuna melt or the Reuben.

No matter how full you are after your meal, grab one of the café's home-baked big cookies or other confectionaries for the road.

VONORE

Two side-by-side historical attractions located on Tellico Lake focus on the state's Native American history, but from distinctly different eras and perspectives. Fort Loudoun State Historic Area marks the early era of contact between colonists and Cherokee Indians, while the Sequoyah Birthplace Museum looks in greater detail at the tribe's later interactions with white settlers, including its tragic removal via the Trail of Tears in 1838.

◀ Fort Loudoun State Historic Area

The Fort Loudoun State Historic Area (338 Fort Loudoun Rd., 423/884-6217, daily 8 a.m.–4:30 p.m., free) recalls the British fort that was built in this spot in 1756 to woo the Cherokee Indians during the French and Indian War. The war between the British and the French, and their respective Indian allies, was fought to decide which European power would control the new American colonies. The British built Fort Loudoun in an effort to cement its alliance with the Cherokee, and therefore strengthen their position to win the war against the French.

Fort Loudoun was located along the Little Tennessee River, and it was the very edge of the American frontier. At first, the British managed to maintain good relations with their Cherokee neighbors. But the uncertain alliance ultimately failed, and violence broke out, with each side blaming the other for the problems. After a five-month siege of Fort Loudoun in 1760, the British surrendered. The British negotiated the terms of their surrender with the Cherokee, who agreed to let the 180 men together with 60 women and children retreat to Charleston, South Carolina.

When the British party stopped to camp their first night, their Cherokee guides slipped into the forest, and by the next day some 29 of the Fort Loudoun party had been killed, including three women. While the basic facts of the ambush are clear, the motivation of the Cherokee is not. Their actions may have been in retribution for the earlier deaths of some 30 Cherokee at the hands of the British. Or they may have been angry that the British had buried the cannons and destroyed the gunpowder at the fort, contrary to the terms of the surrender.

Whatever the cause, it was a bloody and somber end to the Cherokee-British alliance in the Overhill Tennessee region.

Today, Fort Loudoun sits on the bank of

Tellico Lake. The last and most controversial of TVA's dam projects, Tellico Dam was finally closed in 1979 after nearly a decade of debate over its impact on the environment and the loss of historic Cherokee sites.

The park visitors center houses a good museum about the fort, and the film here is one of the best at a Tennessee state park. About 200 yards behind the visitors center is a replica of Fort Loudoun, built according to the archaeological evidence and contemporary accounts from the fort. The simple wooden buildings and the fort walls have been faithfully reconstructed. It is a pleasant place that conjures up the remoteness that would have existed in the 18th century, when the original fort was built.

Every September the **18th Century Trade Faire** depicts a colonial-era marketplace with merchants, artisans, and entertainers. At Christmas, there are candlelight tours of the fort. In addition, every month there are special programs that include costumed British soldiers and Cherokee Indians.

Fort Loudoun State Historic Area also has a picnic area, five miles of hiking trails, and fishing from a 50-foot pier that projects over Tellico Lake.

Sequoyah Birthplace Museum

Sequoyah was a Cherokee Indian born in about 1776 to Nathaniel Gist, a Virginia fur trader, and Wurteh, the daughter of a Cherokee chief. A silversmith by trade, Sequoyah is most famous for creating a written syllabary for the Cherokee language.

It was 1809 when Sequoyah first started to experiment with a written language for the Cherokee. During this period there was extensive interaction between white settlers and the Cherokee, and Sequoyah saw that a written language would allow his people to record their history, write letters, and communicate news.

Sequoyah developed the language independently, and his first student was his young daughter, Ayoka. Together, in 1821, Ayoka and

Sequoyah introduced the language to Cherokee elders, and within a few months thousands of Cherokee were using the system of 85 symbols. By 1825 much of the Bible and numerous hymns had been translated, and in 1828 the *Cherokee Phoenix* became the first national bilingual newspaper in the country.

The story of Sequoyah's accomplishment and the broader legacy of the Cherokee people is preserved at the **Sequoyah Birthplace Museum** (Hwy. 360, 423/884-6246, www.sequoyahmuseum.org, Mon.–Sat. 9 A.M.–5 P.M., Sun. noon–5 P.M., adults $3, seniors $2.50, children 6–12 $1.50), a museum that is managed by the Eastern Band of the Cherokee.

Though dated, the museum provides a thorough and detailed rendering of the Cherokee way of life, the history of the tribe, and the story of Sequoyah himself. At the rear of the museum, at the end of a 100-yard gravel walkway, there is a mound where the remains of 221 Cherokee people are buried. The graves were moved here during the excavation that took place before Tellico Lake was formed.

Every September, the Sequoyah Birthplace Museum hosts a **Fall Festival,** featuring a Cherokee living-history camp, music, storytelling, Cherokee games, and dance.

Chota and Tanasi Memorials

The towns of Tanasi and Chota were the mother towns of the Overhill Cherokee. It is from the word *Tanasi* that the name Tennessee is derived. The Cherokee were forced to leave Tanasi, Chota, and other settlements as white settlers moved west into Tennessee, taking more and more Cherokee land.

When Tellico Lake was created in 1979, the sites of these historic Cherokee settlements were flooded. Before the inundation, University of Tennessee archaeologists explored the sites and found the remains of a great town house and the grave of the Cherokee warrior and chief Oconostota, who died in 1783.

After the lake was formed, the Tennessee Historical Commission erected a stone memorial that overlooks the actual site of Tanasi. The pavement in front of the marker is an octagonal slab representing a town house, and in the center of this is a granite marker engraved with a seven-pointed star, which represents the seven clans of the Cherokee.

One mile north of the Tanasi monument is the parking area for the Chota memorial. It is a quarter-mile walk from the parking area to the memorial, which consists of a full-scale replica of a Cherokee town house. The memorial, which stands on a raised surface built above the level of the lake, was erected by the Eastern Band of the Cherokee.

The Tanasi and Chota memorials are located off Bacon Ferry Road. To get there, take Highway 360 to Monroe County Road 455. After about six miles on Route 455, you will see the turnoff for Bacon Ferry Road and signs to the memorials. Both sites are also popular places for bird-watching.

CHATTANOOGA

KNOXVILLE

Perhaps Tennessee's most underappreciated city, Knoxville sits on the banks of the Tennessee River, in the foothills of the Appalachian Mountains. Knoxville lacks the immediate identity of other major Tennessee cities—it is not the birthplace of the blues, Music City USA, or the home of the Choo Choo. (Unless, of course, you are a college sports fan.) But that's okay with locals. Knoxville's viewpoint is ultimately an insular one—this is a city that does not strive to be. It just is.

And what is Knoxville? It is the gateway to the Smokies and the home of the orange-clad University of Tennessee Volunteers. It is an old industrial city with a long, rich history.

Whatever name you choose to put on Knoxville, dedicate some time to exploring it. The city skyline is dominated by the iconic gold-plated Sunsphere, built during the 1982 World's Fair. Along Gay Street and in the Old City downtown you will find restaurants, bars, and concert halls that are putting Knoxville on the musical map. The University of Tennessee campus is a hotbed of athletic and cultural events. In old suburbs scattered around the city you will find jewels in the rough, including the Knoxville Zoo, Beck Cultural Center, and Ijam's Nature Center.

Knoxville is a city without pretensions. It is a place that gets better the more you get to know it.

Within a half-hour drive from Knoxville are several must-see communities with their

HIGHLIGHTS

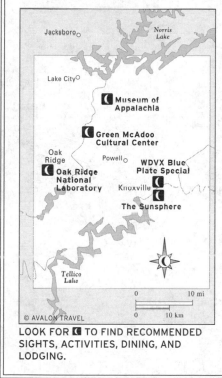

◖ The Sunsphere: Love it or hate it, the gold-plated globe of the Sunsphere defines the Knoxville skyline. Ride to the top for views of Knoxville and the surrounding area (page 370).

◖ WDVX Blue Plate Special: Almost every city in the state has a musical icon. Community radio station WDVX is it in Knoxville. It provides a live lunchtime concert every weekday at the Knoxville Visitor Center (page 379).

◖ Green McAdoo Cultural Center: The story of the desegregation of Clinton's high school is movingly presented at this multimedia museum (page 391).

◖ Museum of Appalachia: This museum pays tribute to the ingenuity, creativity, and tenacity of the mountain folk who settled in the southern Appalachian mountains (page 392).

◖ Oak Ridge National Laboratory: Get the behind-the-scenes look at what makes The Secret City tick when you tour this essential stop in atomic history (page 397).

LOOK FOR ◖ TO FIND RECOMMENDED SIGHTS, ACTIVITIES, DINING, AND LODGING.

own history and attractions. Oak Ridge is one of three places in the United States that built the components of the atomic bombs used at Hiroshima and Nagasaki, and it continues to be home to a nuclear facility. The glimpse of the United States you'll find here is unlike anything anywhere else in the United States. Sleepy Norris houses a remarkable museum about the Appalachian way of life, and Clinton is the site of a significant, but oft-overlooked, scene in the U.S. civil rights movement.

HISTORY

Knoxville's first settler was James White, who in 1786 built a fort where First Creek flows into the Tennessee River and named it after himself. In 1791 governor William Blount chose the fort as capital of the Territory South of the River Ohio and renamed it after secretary of war Henry Knox.

In the same year the first lots of land were sold, and the town of Knoxville was born. Street names were borrowed from Philadelphia and Baltimore, and four lots were reserved for Blount College, to be Knoxville's first school. Shortly after the town was laid out, Governor Blount built a frame house overlooking the river, which became the territorial capitol. Knoxville was incorporated in 1815.

During its first 50 years, Knoxville was primarily a way station for travelers making their

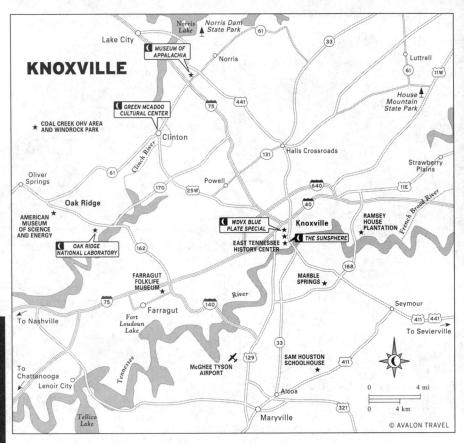

way along the Tennessee River or overland on stage roads. The population grew slowly to about 2,000 in 1850, and during the decade before the Civil War the number of residents more than doubled to about 5,000, thanks to the arrival of the East Tennessee and Georgia Railroad.

A majority of Knoxvillians voted to secede from the Union in the June 1861 referendum. But some city residents, and most East Tennesseans who lived in the rural countryside surrounding Knoxville, supported the Union. Initially Knoxville was occupied by the Confederate Army under Gen. Felix Zollicoffer, whose job was to keep the rail lines open. After East Tennessee Unionists started to

harass the Southern troops and burn up railroad bridges, General Zollicoffer launched a campaign of repression against Union supporters in the city and surrounding areas.

Zollicoffer's troops were called south to fight in the fall of 1863, and Federal troops under the command of Gen. Ambrose Burnside quickly took Knoxville. Burnside built a series of forts around the city, which enabled him to easily repulse an attempted attack by Confederates under command of Gen. James Longstreet in November 1863. Knoxville remained under Union control for the duration of the war. Union supporters returned to the city and retaliated against the Confederate sympathizers who had had the upper hand during the early period of the war.

After the Civil War, Knoxville experienced an industrial expansion. Iron and cloth mills, machine shops, apparel and furniture factories, and marble quarries were built. Thanks to the railroad, the city was a major distribution center; in 1896 Knoxville was the third-largest wholesale center in the South, behind Atlanta and New Orleans.

During this time, the first suburbs developed. West Knoxville, now called Fort Sanders, became the city's premier residential area, with many fine homes and mansions built around the turn of the 20th century. With prosperity came people; by 1900 Knoxville had a population of 32,637.

Like any city, Knoxville was not without problems. Pollution from factories made the city air and water unhealthy. Race relations were strained, and African Americans were stripped of power by political gerrymandering and economic discrimination. As urban problems grew, the city's elite moved into suburbs farther and farther from the city center.

Events in 1919 showed the tensions of the day. In August of that year, a riotous white mob tore down the city jail in search of a mixed-race man who had been charged with murdering a white woman. When the mob did not find the suspect, Maurice Mayes, they headed to the black section of town to cause havoc. When the dust settled, one National Guard officer and one African American had been killed. Thirty-six white men were arrested for their actions, but an all-white jury refused to convict. It was a different story for Maurice Mayes, who was convicted and eventually executed for murder.

During the mid-20th century the trend of outward expansion continued in Knoxville. From the 1950s to the 1980s, Knoxville's downtown deteriorated as retail shops closed and people moved to the suburbs. Central Knoxville became a no-man's-land where only downtown office workers dared to venture.

In the early 1980s, Knoxville was famously dubbed "a scruffy little city."

Some people trace the present downtown renaissance to the 1982 World's Fair, when the Sunsphere and the World's Fair Park were built and 11 million people came to visit the internationally themed festival event. *Time* magazine uncharitably dubbed the event "Barn Burner in a Backwater," and the *Philadelphia Inquirer* said the grounds were built along a wasted gully of Second Creek, a place that was "like a hole in your sock."

Despite the fears that the World's Fair was overly ambitious, it did break even financially and left Knoxville with a park that the city—some 20 years later—finally decided to use to its full advantage. Over the succeeding years, downtown Knoxville has staged a comeback, with the addition of a downtown art museum, the birth of an entertainment district in the Old City, and, most recently, the rebirth of Gay Street and Market Square as centers for business, commerce, and residential living.

PLANNING YOUR TIME

Knoxville is an ideal destination for a long weekend: Spend a day exploring downtown attractions around Gay Street and the World's Fair Park, and then choose two destinations outside of town—such as the Museum of Appalachia, Oak Ridge, or Clinton—for your second and third days. For the best atmosphere, find a hotel within walking distance of Gay Street and the Old City so you can walk to restaurants and music venues.

Whatever you do, don't plan your trip to coincide with a University of Tennessee home football game, unless that's your purpose for coming to town.

ORIENTATION

Knoxville lies on the shore of the Tennessee River, also called Fort Loudoun Lake. The original city and today's downtown center sit atop a bluff overlooking the river. The main thoroughfares through downtown are **Gay**

Street, with its delightful historic storefronts, and **Henley Street,** which becomes Chapman Highway to the south and Broadway to the north. The Henley Street and Gay Street bridges are the primary routes over the Tennessee River.

Immediately west of downtown is the **World's Fair Park,** identifiable by the gold-plated Sunsphere. The **University of Tennessee** and one of the city's first suburbs, **Fort Sanders,** lie just west of the World's Fair park. Cumberland Avenue, also known as "The Strip," is the university's main drag, and it divides UT from Fort Sanders. In recent years, many beautiful old historic homes in Fort Sanders have been torn down for the construction of condominiums.

Cumberland Avenue turns into Kingston Pike, which heads westward from UT, passing suburbs of progressive vintage, beginning with **Sequoyah Hills** and **Bearden.** This land of shopping malls, traffic jams, and sprawl is now called **West Knoxville.**

There are several pleasant historic neighborhoods north and east of the city center. **Fourth and Gill** lies north of town near Emory Place, once a commercial center at the northern end of Gay Street. **Mechanicsville,** north of Western Avenue, developed as housing near Knoxville's old industrial center and is now anchored by Knoxville College. Magnolia Avenue was the primary thoroughfare headed eastward, to neighborhoods including **Park City** and **Holston Hills.**

Sights

DOWNTOWN

Downtown Knoxville lies east of Henley Street and includes the oldest areas of the city, plus its modern-day commercial and government center.

East Tennessee History Center

There is an excellent museum about the history of East Tennessee at the East Tennessee History Center (601 S. Gay St., 865/215-8824, www.easttnhistory.org, Mon.–Fri. 9 A.M.–4 P.M., Sat. 10 A.M.–4 P.M., Sun. 1–5 P.M., free). The permanent exhibit, titled "Voices of the Land: The People of East Tennessee," offers a sweeping survey of East Tennessee history, from its early Native American inhabitants to the beginnings of the modern-day tourist trade in the Great Smoky Mountains. In between, you learn about the region's groundbreaking abolitionists, its writers and musicians, and the everyday lives of residents during tumultuous periods like the Civil War and the civil rights movement. The voices of more than 350 people are used to bring the tale to life, as are artifacts

such as Davy Crockett's rifle, a ring once belonging to Cherokee "Beloved Woman" Nancy Ward, and the painting *Hauling of Marble* by Lloyd Branson. The underlying message is that East Tennessee's story cannot be lumped into that of the entire state; the region is unique.

The exhibit includes several audio and video presentations, and hundreds of panels to read and examine. Plan on spending at least two hours here.

The history center is located in the city's old customs house, a handsome white marble structure built in 1874. For most of its life, the building housed federal offices and a U.S. post office. Later, it was a headquarters for the Tennessee Valley Authority.

James White Fort

The oldest home in Knoxville is found at James White Fort (205 E. Hill Ave., 865/525-6514, www.jameswhitesfort.org, Apr.–Nov. Mon.–Sat. 9:30 A.M.–5 P.M., closed during UT home football games, Dec.–Mar. Mon.–Fri. 10 A.M.–4 P.M., adults $7, children 5–17 $3).

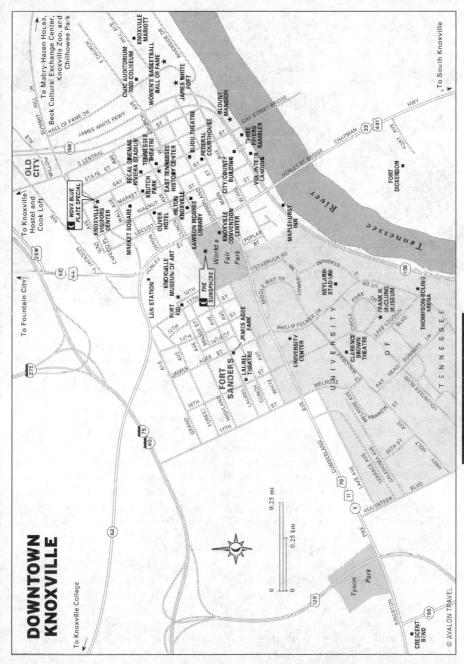

DOWNTOWN KNOXVILLE

© AVALON TRAVEL

East Tennessee History Center

Gen. James White acquired more than 1,000 acres of land in 1783 under the so-called Land Grab Act passed by the North Carolina legislature. White and his wife, Mary Lawson, moved to the frontier in 1785 and constructed a log cabin near the junction of the French Broad and Holston Rivers, to the west of First Creek. Soon, White built additional log structures and protected them with a stockade; he called the place James White's Fort. Later, William Blount chose the location as the first capital of the Southwest Territory and renamed the fort Knoxville.

White hired Charles McClung to survey his 1,000 acres, and in 1791 he sold lots in the new city of Knoxville for $8 each. White donated lots for a town common, church, and cemetery, and he sold lots for Blount College for a nominal amount.

As Knoxville grew, White's rough-hewn log cabin was threatened by development. In 1906 a local citizen, Isaiah Ford, bought the fort and carefully moved the structures to a site on Woodland Avenue. In 1960, the fort was moved again to its present location on Hill Avenue. Visitors will learn about White, the establishment of Knoxville, and the rugged way of life on the Tennessee frontier.

Blount Mansion

The Blount Mansion (200 W. Hill Ave., 865/525-2375, www.blountmansion.org, summer Tues.–Sat. 9:30 A.M.–5 P.M., Oct.–May Tues.–Sat. 10 A.M.–5 P.M., adults $7, seniors $6, children 6–17 and students $5) is Knoxville's best historic attraction. First built between 1792 and 1796 by territorial governor William Blount, the "mansion" underwent no fewer than six periods of construction and alteration during its lifetime. The original structure was the first frame home in Knoxville and one of the first in the whole state. The Cherokee called Blount's home the House with Many Glass Eyes because of its large glass windows.

Significant events in Tennessee history took place at Blount Mansion. It is believed that it

THE CRADLE OF COUNTRY MUSIC

Knoxville's place in country music history is not as well known as that of Memphis or Nashville, but the roots of several seminal country artists are buried deep in Knoxville history. Several Knoxville institutions are also closely linked with the emergence of country music on the national stage.

The **Andrew Johnson Hotel** (912 S. Gay St.) is now a government office building, but for many years it was Knoxville's landmark hotel. WNOX broadcast the live *Midday Merry-Go-Round* from the hotel, and in 1952, Hank Williams checked in on what would be the final day of his life. It is still a matter of discussion whether Williams was alive when his teenage chauffeur put him in the backseat of a Cadillac and drove north for a gig in Canton, Ohio. During a pit stop in Oak Hill, West Virginia, the driver discovered that Williams was dead; he was just 29 years old.

In 1932 the **Tennessee Theatre** (604 S. Gay St.) hosted the first public performance by Union County native Roy Acuff, who performed in a talent contest with his band, Three Rolling Stones.

Knoxville has memorialized its musical history at the **Knoxville Music Monument** (Gay St. and Summit Hill Dr.), which features likenesses of Chet Atkins, an East Tennessee native later known as Mr. Guitar; Archie Campbell, a country music comedian and radio host from nearby Bulls Gap; and Unknown Musicians, representative of jazz, blues, country, and rock 'n' roll artists whose contributions have gone largely unwritten.

It was from a storefront on **Market Square** that Sam Morrison of Bell Sales Company promoted Elvis Presley's "That's All Right (Mama)" by playing it on a loudspeaker outside. Morrison sold hundreds of copies of the single, including two to an RCA talent scout. Several months later, RCA bought Presley's recording contract from Sun Studio in Memphis.

For a detailed tour of Knoxville music history, follow the Cradle of Country Music Walking Tour. A printed guide is available from the Knoxville Visitor Center (301 S. Gay St., 865/523-7263, www.knoxville.org).

was here that governor William Blount wrote the first Tennessee constitution. The mansion also served as the second territorial capitol of the soon-to-be state.

Blount Mansion consists today of restored living quarters, office, kitchen, and gardens, as well as a visitors center that houses exhibits about Blount and his home. Guided tours depart at the top of every hour.

Market Square

Knoxville's old Market Square has been given new life thanks to downtown redevelopment over the past 20 years. Once a dirty and depressing corner of the city, Market Square is alive again with commerce. Restaurants, boutiques, and nightclubs populate the square. It is the venue for the city's farmers market on Saturday and Wednesday during the summer, and it is a popular location for outdoor events and concerts.

Come here to people-watch or to soak up some of Knoxville's youthful downtown vibe.

Find Market Square near the intersection of Market Street and Union Avenue, just a few blocks behind Gay Street. It is within easy walking distance of downtown attractions.

Women's Basketball Hall of Fame

In 1892, one year after James Naismith invented basketball, a woman coach introduced the sport at Smith College. The female sport underwent countless changes during its 100-plus-year history. A few of them: In 1918 bounce passes were legalized, in 1926 the first national women's collegiate championship was held, in 1962 players were permitted to "snatch" the ball from each other, and in 1976 women's basketball made its Olympic debut.

These and many other milestones are remembered at the Women's Basketball Hall of Fame

(700 Hall of Fame Dr., 865/633-9000, www.wbhof.com, summer Mon.–Sat. 10 A.M.–5 P.M., Sept.–Apr. Tues.–Fri. 11 A.M.–5 P.M., Sat. 10 A.M.–5 P.M., adults $7.95, seniors and children 6–15 $5.95), a museum dedicated to celebrating women's achievement on the basketball court and to fostering future talent.

The hall of fame consists of interactive exhibits that recall the history and development of women's basketball. Visitors will hear women's basketball "inventor" Senda Berenson share her thoughts on the early days of the game. They will sit in a modern-day locker room and hear half-time talks by some of the best coaches in the modern sport. This is not just a spectator museum. Downstairs are basketball courts where you can test your skill against the sport's best, shoot into baskets from different eras in history, and try on old and new uniforms. In addition, there are exhibits about international women's basketball, the WNBA, and top women's basketball college programs. Finally, visitors can pay tribute to the sport's best at the 127-member hall of fame.

The Women's Basketball Hall of Fame is located in an eye-catching building near the eastern end of Knoxville's waterfront. It is home to the world's largest basketball—30 feet tall and 10 tons heavy—which protrudes from the roof.

The hall of fame opened in Knoxville in 1999, and there was really no better city for it. The Tennessee Lady Vols are one of the most successful women's basketball teams in the country. Their former coach, Pat Summit, was renowned for style and success. Current coach Holly Warlick worked with the legendary Summitt, first as a player, then as an assistant and associate head coach. Summitt is the all-time winningest coach in men's or women's collegiate basketball, and Warlick was there for 922 of the 1071 wins collected by her mentor.

Volunteer Landing

A one-mile city park sits along the bank of the Tennessee River, providing a nice place to walk or bring the family.

At the eastern end of the park there is a playground and a statue symbolizing the Treaty of the Holston, which took the land on which Knoxville sits away from the Cherokee. This is where Tennessee riverboats depart.

Farther west is another playground and a series of fountains, perfect for romping around in on a hot summer day.

There are several commercial marinas and restaurants along the park. The best way to get here is to take the pedestrian bridge over Neyland Drive, which departs from the southwestern corner of the Knoxville City/County Building along Walnut Street.

WORLD'S FAIR PARK

Lying between the University of Tennessee and downtown is the grassy, pleasant grounds of the World's Fair Park. There are several reasons for visitors to head to this area.

◖ The Sunsphere

Knoxville's foremost landmark is the Sunsphere (World's Fair Park, Apr.–Oct. daily 9 A.M.–10 P.M., Nov.–Mar. daily 11 A.M.–6 P.M., free). Built for the 1982 World's Fair, the Sunsphere has been both a source of pride and consternation for Knoxvillians in years since. The Sunsphere, symbolic of the World's Fair theme "Energy Turns the World," is 266 feet tall. It consists of a five-story golden sphere—which the *New York Times* described as similar to a gold golf ball—perched atop a steel shaft. During the World's Fair, it housed two restaurants.

After the World's Fair ended, Knoxville couldn't decide what to do with the odd monument. Ideas came and went—restaurants, advertising billboard, visitors center—but from 1999 until 2007 the sphere was essentially closed all together. Around the 20th anniversary of the World's Fair, the city began to think again about what it could do with this iconic

The Sunsphere was built for the 1982 World's Fair.

Knoxville Museum of Art

Located in a building faced dramatically with white marble and designed by New York architect Edward Larabee Barnes, the Knoxville Museum of Art (1050 World's Fair Park Dr., 865/525-6101, www.knoxart.org, Tues.–Sat. 10 A.M.–5 P.M., Sun. 1–5 P.M., free) is Knoxville's preeminent visual arts institution. Originally called the Dulin Gallery of Art and located in an early-20th-century mansion, the Knoxville Museum of Art moved to the World's Fair Park after the 1982 World's Fair. The current structure opened in 1990.

The museum has five galleries, an outdoor sculpture garden, gift shop, and an interactive exploratory gallery for children. From the rear of the great hall, visitors can step outside on the museum balcony for views of the World's Fair Park and downtown Knoxville. The museum's growing permanent collection is bolstered by numerous visiting exhibitions. On Friday evening the museum hosts Alive After Five, with jazz performances.

UNIVERSITY OF TENNESSEE

The preeminent public university in Tennessee, the University of Tennessee was founded in 1784 as Blount College. Originally centered at "the hill" on the eastern end of Cumberland Avenue, UT has spread out along the entire length of Cumberland. Its colors—orange and white—were inspired by the orange and white daisies that grow outside on the hill. UT has a student enrollment of more than 21,000.

At UT, it is athletics that are truly center stage, or at least so it seems. Take, for example, the fact that in recent years UT has renamed two major roads throughout the campus not after prizewinning scientists or writers, but after Peyton Manning, the UT quarterback who went on to take the Indianapolis Colts to the Super Bowl (and now plays for the Denver Broncos), and Phillip Fulmer, UT football's former head coach.

landmark, and five years and $280,000 later, in time for the 25th anniversary of the fair, the city reopened the observation deck to visitors.

The observation deck is located on the 4th floor of the Sunsphere. After a long and clanky elevator ride up, you are deposited in a narrow circular room with a 360-degree view of Knoxville. It is a pretty neat view, and it puts the city in perspective. The Tennessee River sweeps southward, the University of Tennessee sits on the river bluff, and the interstate highways slice this way and that. You look right down on the World's Fair Park, and it's like seeing the world in miniature.

Panels around the observation deck tell about some of Knoxville's attractions and history, and there is a running video with footage from the 1982 World's Fair.

Other floors in the Sunsphere are rented by local businesses.

Frank H. McClung Museum

The best all-around museum in Knoxville, the Frank H. McClung Museum (1327 Circle Park Dr., 865/974-2144, http://mcclungmuseum.utk.edu, Mon.–Sat. 9 A.M.–5 P.M., Sun. 1–5 P.M., free) houses a wide variety of historical, cultural, and natural-history exhibits. Longstanding exhibits explore ancient Egypt, the native peoples of Tennessee, and the Civil War in Knoxville. Other exhibits look at Tennessee's freshwater mussels and decorative arts in the state. The museum also hosts special temporary exhibits.

Ewing Gallery

UT's art museum is the Ewing Gallery (1715 Volunteer Blvd., 865/974-3200, www.ewing-gallery.utk.edu, Mon.–Fri. 10 A.M.–5 P.M., during the school year also on Sun. 1–4 P.M., free). Located on the first floor of the university's Art and Architecture Building, the Ewing Gallery is named for the founder of UT's art program. Student and faculty art share the 3,000-square-foot exhibition space with visiting shows from other museums.

Fort Sanders

Knoxville's original suburb, Fort Sanders is a quickly disappearing historic neighborhood that lies between the World's Fair Park and UT. The site of an earthen fort named for Gen. William Sanders, who died in the Battle of Knoxville in 1863, Fort Sanders was developed into a residential area beginning in the 1880s. This was home to Knoxville's upper-class merchants, mayors, university professors, and other persons of note. Author James Agee was raised in Fort Sanders.

Because of its vintage and the relative affluence of its residents, Fort Sanders's homes are lovely examples of American Victorian and early-20th-century architecture. Towers, broad porches, colorful shutters, and intricate detail work set Fort Sanders homes apart.

As the university grew, Fort Sanders was encroached. By the 1970s, many owners stopped occupying their homes and instead rented them to students. Homes deteriorated. During the 1990s and early years of this century, development has taken a great toll on Fort Sanders. In 1999 alone, 15 historic homes were razed to make room for condominium developments. The destruction caused an outcry, and some of Fort Sanders's historic homes are now protected from development.

You can see what is left of Fort Sanders along Highland, Laurel, Forest, and Grand Avenues, between 11th and 17th Streets. In 2009, the City of Knoxville and the Metropolitan Planning Commission began work on developing a long-range plan for sustainable development. A historical district was created, so steps are being taken to save this neighborhood and enhance its beauty. **James Agee Park,** at the corner of James Agee Street and Laurel Avenue, is located near the site of Agee's childhood home, where parts of Agee's Pulitzer Prize–winning work *A Death in the Family* are set.

WEST KNOXVILLE

Kingston Pike is the thoroughfare that connects downtown Knoxville with its western suburbs. Immediately past the University of Tennessee, Kingston Pike passes several historic homes. Farther west, you reach the communities of Bearden, West Hills, and Farragut.

Crescent Bend

The Armstrong-Lockett House, also called the romantic-sounding Crescent Bend (2728 Kingston Pk., 865/637-3163, www.crescent-bend.com, Wed.–Fri. 10 A.M.–4 P.M., Sat. 10 A.M.–2 P.M., adults $7, students $5, children 12 and under free), was built in 1834 by Drury Paine Armstrong, a local merchant and public official. The brick farmhouse was once the centerpiece of a 600-acre farm. Now it consists of the elegant home and formal Italian gardens facing the Tennessee River.

Visitors who take the guided tour will see a fine collection of china, silver, and other antiques, including wallpaper originally meant for the Hermitage, President Andrew Jackson's home near Nashville.

During March and April Crescent Bend celebrates spring with Tuliptime. This is a delightful time to visit, when more than 20,000 tulips are in bloom. During Tuliptime, the home schedules candlelight dinners, high teas, and other special events.

Bleak House

Knoxville's Confederate Memorial Hall, better known as Bleak House (3148 Kingston Pk., 865/522-2371, www.knoxvillecmh.org, Wed.–Fri. 1–4 P.M., adults $5, seniors $4, discount for students and children, call first as hours are subject to change) was Gen. James Longstreet's headquarters during the Battle of Fort Sanders and other Civil War battles that took place November–December 1863. Built in 1858 for Robert Houston and Louisa Armstrong, the Italian villa–style home was named after the popular Charles Dickens novel of the day.

Visitors may be given a tour, which includes the tower where, legend has it, Confederate sharpshooters were stationed during the Civil War. There is a museum that includes Confederate artifacts.

Girl Scout Museum

Whether you have a sash of badges in the basement or just like the cookies, you'll want to make a stop here. East Tennessee's Girl Scout Council operates the Girl Scout Museum at Daisy's Place (1567 Downtown West Blvd., 865/688-9440, www.girlscoutcsa.org/about/museums-2, Mon. 8:30 A.M.–7 P.M., Tues.–Fri. 8:30 A.M.–4:30 P.M., free). The museum, one of six such Girl Scout museums in the United States, features exhibits about the history of Girl Scouting, Girl Scout cookies, and scouting in East Tennessee. You can see handbooks, songbooks, vintage uniforms, and scrapbooks dating back to 1912. There are lots of hands-on exhibits to experience. Bring a pin or trinket from your troop to swap for another.

Farragut Folklife Museum

The first U.S. admiral, David Glasgow Farragut, was born west of Knoxville in an area called Stoney Point. The family moved to New Orleans when Farragut was just five years old. When his mother died of yellow fever, Farragut was adopted by David Porter and moved to Chester, Pennsylvania. Farragut, who was born James Glasgow Farragut, changed his name to David in honor of his patron and entered the U.S. navy. His naval career was long and proud; Farragut's military service during the Civil War led to his promotion in 1866 to the rank of admiral. It was during an August 1864 battle aboard the USS *Hartford* when Farragut reportedly said, "Damn the torpedoes, full speed ahead," a phrase that lives on today.

The town that now exists near Admiral Farragut's birthplace took his name, and now the Farragut City Hall houses a museum dedicated to this mostly unknown Tennessean. The Farragut Folklife Museum (11408 Municipal Center Dr., Farragut, 865/966-7057, www.townoffarragut.org, Mon.–Fri. 10 A.M.–4:30 P.M., free) also houses exhibits about the local marble industry, the Battle of Campbell's Station, and arts, crafts, and other memorabilia from the communities of Farragut and Concord.

Farragut is located near the intersection of Kingston Pike and Campbell Station Road, off I-40 exit 373.

EAST KNOXVILLE

Magnolia Avenue (U.S. 25 West) and Martin Luther King Boulevard are two thoroughfares that head east from downtown Knoxville. Originally a series of quiet residential neighborhoods, East Knoxville has gradually evolved into a mixture of low-rise office buildings, modest sprawl, and historic homes.

Mabry-Hazen House Museum

The Mabry-Hazen House Museum (1711 Dandridge Ave., 865/522-8661, www.mabry-hazen.com, Wed.–Fri. 11 A.M.–5 P.M., Sat. 10 A.M.–3 P.M., adults $5, students K–12 $2.50) is located on a pleasant rise in East Knoxville. This handsome home, with green shutters and a wide porch, housed three generations of the same family from 1858 to 1987 and served as headquarters for both Confederate and Union troops during the Civil War. Since 1992 it has been open to the public for tours. The Mabry name comes from Joseph Alexander Mabry Jr., a businessman who donated the land for Market Square and owned the *Knoxville Whig* from 1869 to 1870. The murders of Mabry and his son on Gay Street in 1882 were documented in Mark Twain's *Life on the Mississippi*. Mabry's daughter, Alice Mabry, married Rush Strong Hazen, a wealthy businessman. The third generation to live in the house was Evelyn Montgomery Hazen, who helped author the *Harbrace College Handbook,* a reference guide used by generations of English students.

Because staff at the home is limited, the house sometimes closes for appointments or tours of the nearby **Bethel Civil War Cemetery Museum** (1711 Dandridge Ave., Wed.–Fri. 11 A.M.–5 P.M., Sat. 10 A.M.–3 P.M.). Call the museum director at 865/951-6614 if you arrive and find no tour guide. Your wait until one arrives may be just a few minutes.

Beck Cultural Exchange Center

Knoxville's foremost African American historical and cultural center is the Beck Cultural Exchange Center (1927 Dandridge Ave., 865/524-8461, www.beckcenter.net, Tues.–Sat. 10 A.M.–6 P.M., free). Founded in 1975, Beck is a museum, education center, archive, and community gathering place. In addition to putting on a variety of programs throughout the year, Beck also welcomes visitors who want to learn more about Knoxville's African American history.

Among Beck's permanent exhibits is the William H. Hastie Room, dedicated to preserving the memory of the Knoxville native who became the first black governor of the U.S. Virgin Islands in 1946 and the first African American federal judge in the United States four years later. Beck also features a gallery with photographs and biographies of prominent African Americans from Knoxville.

The center also preserves the history of the struggle to desegregate Knoxville's public schools, the University of Tennessee, and Maryville College. There is also information about the historic desegregation of schools in Clinton, Tennessee, and the legacy of Austin High School, Knoxville's onetime all-black secondary school.

Alex Haley Square

Pulitzer Prize–winning author Alex Haley has roots in both East and West Tennessee. He grew up in Henning, a sawmill town along the Mississippi River, but he spent a great deal of his adult life in East Tennessee, giving both regions a claim to his legacy.

Haley's preeminence—but also his disarming and loving nature—is evident in a larger-than-life statue of the writer at Alex Haley Square (1600 Dandridge Ave.) in East Knoxville. In the figure, Haley is reading a book, seeming to invite the viewer to gather round and listen to a story. The statue, park, and playground opened in 1998, six years after Haley's death.

Knoxville Zoo

Children and adults alike love the Knoxville Zoo (3500 Knoxville Zoo Dr., 865/637-5331, www.knoxville-zoo.org, summer daily 9:30 A.M.–6 P.M., winter daily 10 A.M.–4:30 P.M., adults $19.95, seniors 65-plus and children 2–12 $15.95). More than 800 species of animals live at the zoo, in habitats including Grassland Africa, the Red Panda Village, and penguin pool. Giraffes, elephants, camels, giant tortoise, and gorillas are just a few of the iconic animals you will see at the zoo.

Attractions include a petting zoo, camel rides ($5), a colorful carousel ($2), and a Komodo dragon named Khaleesi.

Surrounding the zoo is Chilhowee Park, with picnic tables, walking paths, and a lake. Parking at the zoo costs $5 per vehicle.

East Tennessee Science Discovery Center

Also located at Chilhowee Park is the East Tennessee Science Discovery Center (Chilhowee Park, 865/594-1494, www.etdiscovery.org, Mon.–Fri. 9 A.M.–5 P.M., Sat. 10 A.M.–5 P.M., adults $4, seniors and children 5–18 $3, children 3–4 $2), an interactive children's museum. Exhibits include aquariums, whisper dishes, a replica space shuttle, and a liquid-crystal wall. There is also a planetarium; shows are offered most days at 2 and 4 P.M.

SOUTH KNOXVILLE

Chapman Highway (U.S. 441) begins south of the Henley Street Bridge and brings you to South Knoxville.

Ijams Nature Center

Knoxville's best outdoor attraction is Ijams Nature Center (2915 Island Home Ave., 865/577-4717, www.ijams.org, visitors center Mon.–Sat. 9 A.M.–5 P.M., grounds daily 8 A.M.– dusk, free). The visitors center is a modern earth-friendly construction that houses exhibits about lost animal species and the Ijams family. There is also an enclosure with a red-tailed hawk and a turkey vulture, plus native plant and animal species.

The real attraction at Ijams is the 160 acres of protected woodlands and meadows. Come here for a walk through the woods or a stroll along the Tennessee River boardwalk. The grounds also include the Ijams family historic homesite and Mead's Quarry. In total, there are seven miles of walking trails.

Ijams offers a regular schedule of special events: workshops, talks, guided walks, and fairs. Check the website for details.

Fort Dickerson

A Civil War–era earthen fort and three replica cannons are the historical attractions at the Knoxville city park on the south side of the Tennessee River. Panels explain the fort's significance during the battles of Knoxville that took place in the fall of 1863.

Visitors will also enjoy the view (particularly during the fall and winter, when the trees have shed their leaves) of the Knoxville skyline and the view of an old quarry.

Fort Dickerson Park is located three-quarters of a mile south of the Henley Street Bridge on Chapman Highway (U.S. 441). Look for the signs on your right.

Ramsey House Plantation

The home called "the most costly and most admired building in Tennessee" by the 1800 census taker is open for public tours in the 21st century. Ramsey House Plantation (2614 Thorngrove Pk., 865/546-0745, www.ramseyhouse.org, Wed.–Sat. 10 A.M.–4 P.M., adults $7, children 6–12 $5) was built between 1795 and 1797 by master carpenter and cabinetmaker Thomas Hope for Col. Francis Alexander Ramsey. Built in the late Georgian style out of pink marble, Ramsey House features intricately carved consoles and other distinctive decorative features. It was said to be the first stone house in Tennessee, as well as the first home in the state with an attached kitchen.

The site of the house is near the fork of the Holston and French Broad Rivers. It was close to a site called Swan Pond, a beaver dam pond well-known by hunters and travelers. Col. Ramsey drained the pond to create pasture and farmland.

Ramsey House was the home of Colonel Ramsey's son, James G. M. Ramsey, a doctor, businessman, and author of an authoritative early history of Tennessee, *The Annals of*

© BRIAN STANSBERRY/CREATIVE COMMONS

Old Gray Cemetery

Tennessee to the End of the Eighteenth Century. James Ramsey and his wife, Margaret Crozier, raised 11 children at the home, then called Mecklenburg. Ramsey supported the Confederate cause during the Civil War, and Mecklenburg was burned by Union troops during the war, destroying a valuable library and collection of early Tennessee antiquities. During the war years and until the early 1870s, Ramsey and his family lived in Atlanta, Savannah, and North Carolina. He returned to East Tennessee in the 1870s and remained here until his death in 1884.

Ramsey House was purchased in 1952 by the Association for the Preservation of Tennessee Antiquities. It has been fully restored and is open for tours, which include all rooms of the house, the kitchen, and the grounds. Ramsey House has a nice garden where heirloom vegetables and other plants are grown.

Ramsey House is located off Gov. John Sevier Highway southeast of downtown. The easiest way to get there from downtown is to take Chapman Highway (U.S. 441) south out of town. Turn left onto John Sevier Highway (Highway 168). After crossing the Tennessee River, look for Thorngrove Pike on your right and signs to Ramsey House.

Marble Springs

The early home of Tennessee's first governor, John Sevier, is preserved at Marble Springs (1220 John Sevier Hwy., 865/573-5508, www.marblesprings.net, Wed.–Sat. 10 A.M.–5 P.M., Sun. noon–5 P.M., tours $4), five miles south of downtown Knoxville. Sevier received 640 acres at the foot of Bays Mountain for his service in the Revolutionary War, and he named the property Marble Springs because there were marble deposits and a large spring. By 1792 Sevier established a farm residence at Marble Springs, although he and his family lived here only periodically. They also had a home in Knoxville.

After Sevier died in 1815, the property changed

hands several times until the State of Tennessee bought it in 1941. It remains state owned and is operated by the Gov. John Sevier Memorial Association. Over the years, the log home has been restored, and several historically accurate outbuildings have been added. Workshops and living-history days are offered year-round.

NORTH KNOXVILLE

Broadway (U.S. 441) travels from downtown Knoxville to Fountain City, an early suburb of the city.

Old Gray Cemetery

Just past Knoxville's scruffy Mission District—past the old 5th Avenue Hotel, a flophouse turned affordable housing project—is the Old Gray Cemetery (543 N. Broadway, 865/522-1424, www.oldgraycemetary.com). This 13-acre cemetery was established in 1850 and is the final resting place of hundreds of prominent and not-so-prominent city residents. It is a pleasant, wooded, parklike place—nice for a quiet stroll.

Among the buried are William "Parson" Brownlow, minister, journalist, governor, and one of Tennessee's most colorful historical characters; feminist Lizzie Crozier French; and C. C. Williams, the father of playwright Tennessee Williams.

Knoxville College

Presbyterian missionaries established a school for freedmen in Knoxville in 1875, and two years later this educational institution was designated as a college. Knoxville College (901 Knoxville College Dr., 865/524-6525) has been educating African Americans since. The campus is an architectural mixed bag—elegant historic structures share space with low-slung modern buildings. Budget challenges have dogged Knoxville College over its modern history, but it has persisted nonetheless in its mission to educate the next generation of black leaders.

Knoxville College is located in Mechanicsville, an old neighborhood found at the intersection of Western Avenue and Middlebrook Pike.

Entertainment and Events

Knoxville boasts a lively local music scene, plus venues that attract big-name artists. The arts scene also includes professional theater, dance, and music companies.

NIGHTLIFE

Downtown Knoxville offers plenty of options for entertainment after the sun sets.

The Old City

Near the intersection of Jackson and Depot Streets, a few blocks northeast of Gay Street, is the Old City. Knoxville's former warehouse district, near the train tracks, is now its chief entertainment district. Here you will find **Patrick Sullivan's** (100 N. Central St., 865/637-4255),

an Irish-inspired restaurant and bar that is a good place to meet for drinks.

Barley's Taproom and Pizzeria (200 E. Jackson St., 865/521-0092, cover varies) is a large taproom with lots of space for mingling and a stage where folk, rock, and country performers can be found just about every night of the week. The 1st-floor bar offers 40 different beers on tap, a full-service restaurant, and a stage. Upstairs are pool tables and dartboards. Outside is a patio where you can witness Knoxville's skyline as you meet and mingle.

Downtown

Downtown nightlife centers on Market Square. Here you can catch up with friends at

Preservation Pub (28 Market Sq., 865/524-2224, cover varies). In the shadow of its exposed-brick walls decorated with funky art, you just can't help but feel cool. Fabulous drink specials; a hip, youthful attitude; and a steady stream of local rock, folk, and country acts make Preservation Pub a popular destination. It is also a restaurant.

Located in the Fourth and Gill neighborhood, a few blocks north of downtown, is the cozy and intimate **Sassy Ann's House of Blues** (820 N. 4th Ave., 865/525-5839, cover varies). As the name suggests, Sassy Ann's specializes in the blues—visiting musicians, homegrown talent, and open-mic-style performers—but they also book rock and folk artists. Housed in a 100-plus-year-old town house with two bars and lots of intimate pockets for seating, Sassy Ann's is a bit like going to a grown-up house party, with live music to boot. Generally speaking, Sassy Ann's has DJ music on Sunday and Thursday nights, with bands on Wednesday, Friday, and Saturday.

The Valarium (1213 Western Ave., 865/522-2820, cover varies) is a 1,000-person standing-only entertainment venue located under the Western Avenue Viaduct, in a seeming wasteland of highway interchanges. Once a venue for cutting-edge bands, then a gay dance hall, this cavernous hall now books performing artists of all types. The bar is outside, allowing the owners to make this an all-ages club.

THE ARTS
Venues

Knoxville's historic theaters are something special. In 1928 the **Tennessee Theatre** (604 S. Gay St., 865/684-1200, www.tennesseetheatre.com) opened its doors on Gay Street. The theater operated nearly uninterrupted for 50 years as a movie house and concert hall. After being shuttered for a few years, the theater operated during the 1980s and 1990s, although the venue was showing its age. Thankfully, in

2001 plans were announced for a full-fledged restoration that would bring the Tennessee back to its former glory.

Since 2005, when the Tennessee Theatre reopened to praise from concertgoers and performers alike, it has become Knoxville's favorite venue for music, theater, and film. Its interior is awash with ornate detail, including plush fabric, intricate woodwork, gold-painted trim, and glistening chandeliers—all reminiscent of the roaring twenties, when the theater was built. The theater's 1928 original Mighty Wurlitzer pipe organ is also a showstopper.

Check the theater's website for upcoming performances for an opportunity to experience entertainment at its finest. You can also call to request a tour of the theater, if no show is in the offing.

Knoxville's best-sounding concert hall is also located on Gay Street. The **Bijou Theater** (803 S. Gay St., 865/522-0832, www.knoxbijou.com) opened in 1909 as part of the Lamar Hotel. Since then, it has been a venue for concerts and other performances. With a capacity of 700, it is more intimate than the Tennessee Theatre; it is also far less ornate and upscale. The Bijou underwent restoration in 2005, which resulted in a brand-new sound and stage system, better seats, and a new heating and air-conditioning system.

Other Knoxville concert and theater venues include the **Knoxville Civic Auditorium and Coliseum** (500 E. Church Ave., 865/215-8999, www.knoxvillecoliseum.com), which seats 2,500, and the **Thompson-Boling Arena** (1600 Phillip Fulmer Way, 865/974-0953, www.tbarena.com), with a capacity of almost 25,000.

Dance and Opera

The **Appalachian Ballet Company** (865/982-8463, www.appalachianballet.com) is a regional dance group chartered in 1972. The company puts on three performances each year, including a holiday production of *The Nutcracker*.

Circle Modern Dance (865/309-5309, www.

circlemoderndance.com) is a grassroots dance group founded in 1990 to provide an alternative to mainstream dance performances. They offer classes as well as the occasional show.

The **Knoxville Opera** (865/524-0795, www.knoxvilleopera.com) offers four performances annually at the Tennessee Theatre in downtown Knoxville. The opera also organizes the Rossini Festival and International Street Fair, an Italian street fair, every April.

Theater

The University of Tennessee's **Clarence Brown Theatre Company** (865/974-5161, www.clarencebrowntheatre.com) presents a wide repertoire of plays featuring nationally and internationally recognized guest artists. The company performs in the 570-seat Clarence Brown Theatre (1714 Andy Holt Blvd.) on the UT campus, named for UT alumnus and distinguished film director Clarence Brown. UT is also home to the 350-seat Ula Love Doughty Carousel Theater and a 100-seat black-box theater, which are used for campus productions.

Knoxville's **Carpetbag Theatre** (865/544-0447, www.carpetbagtheatre.org) is a community-based nonprofit professional theater company founded in 1970. It is one of the few tenured African American professional theater companies in the South. The company produces plays, festivals, youth theater workshops, and other events throughout the year. Their performances often bring to the fore the stories and experiences of people who are otherwise overlooked by history.

The **Tennessee Stage Company** (865/546-4280, www.tennesseestagecompany.com) produces Shakespeare in the Square, a free summertime production of Shakespeare's work at Market Square Mall, and the New Play Festival, which brings to life unpublished theatrical works.

Music
◖ WDVX BLUE PLATE SPECIAL

Back in the 1930s and '40s, Knoxville radio station WNOX hosted a lunchtime musical variety show called the *Midday Merry-Go-Round*. Hosted by Lowell Blanchard, the show attracted hundreds of patrons and thousands more who tuned in to listen to the show live on radio. It was a stepping stone to the Grand Ole Opry, and legendary performers like Roy Acuff, Chet Atkins, Kitty Wells, and Bill and Charlie Monroe were among the entertainers.

So when Knoxville radio station WDVX started its own lunchtime live music program back in the 1990s, it was following in hallowed footsteps. But it also felt like something quite new and exciting for downtown Knoxville.

Today, the WDVX Blue Plate Special takes place Monday–Friday noon–1 P.M. at the Knoxville Visitor Center at 301 South Gay Street (the building also houses the WDVX studios). The performers vary from bluegrass to Americana to rock. It is a wonderful way to pass an hour since you get to listen to live music and watch a radio show being made at the same time. The atmosphere is intimate, casual, and—at times—electric. A coffee bar serves sandwiches and drinks, but you are welcome to bring your own bag lunch as well.

KNOXVILLE SYMPHONY ORCHESTRA
Established in 1935, the Knoxville Symphony Orchestra (865/291-3310, www.knoxvillesymphony.com) is one of the oldest orchestras in the southeast. The KSO, a professional orchestra since 1973, performs its season September–May in Knoxville venues including the Civic Auditorium, the Tennessee Theatre, and the Bijou. Special guest conductors and soloists are frequent additions, and seasonal shows include the annual holiday concert.

UNIVERSITY OF TENNESSEE
The University of Tennessee's music program (www.music.utk.edu) puts on a full schedule of recitals and concerts during the academic year. All events are free and open to the public. They take place in one of three performance halls in the **Alumni Memorial Building** (1408 Middle Dr.).

KNOXVILLE

JUBILEE COMMUNITY ARTS

One of Knoxville's finest musical institutions is Jubilee Community Arts, which promotes traditional Appalachian music and other folk traditions. Jubilee offers a full schedule of concerts and other special events at the **Laurel Theater** (1538 Laurel Ave., 865/522-5851, www.jubileearts.org), a 19th-century church in the Fort Sanders neighborhood that has been converted into a performance hall. The space is intimate, with excellent acoustics and a homey atmosphere. The concert schedule is heavy on regional bluegrass, folk, Americana, and country performers. It also includes Celtic, zydeco, and world music artists. Concerts are scheduled most weeks. The Jubilee Festival in March is a three-day weekend event with a smorgasbord of performances.

When the Laurel Theater is not being used for a concert, various community groups use the space for meetings and other purposes. Several community dance groups have weekly sessions here, as does the Knoxville Writer's Guild. In addition to its live performance schedule, Jubilee Community Arts works with local radio stations to produce programming for the airwaves, including the long-running *Live at Laurel* program, which features recordings of Laurel Theater concerts and is broadcast on WDVX (89.9 FM and 102.9 FM) at 7 P.M. on Sunday.

Cinemas

First-run movies came back to downtown Knoxville with the opening of **Regal Cinemas Riviera Stadium** (510 S. Gay St., 865/522-5160), an eight-screen theater in the heart of downtown.

Knoxville's best art-house movie theater is at **Downtown West** (1640 Downtown West Blvd., 865/693-6327), in the West Hills area near West Town Mall.

FESTIVALS AND EVENTS

Spring

Knoxville's stalwart arts festival celebrated its 50th anniversary in 2010. The **Dogwood Arts Festival** (www.dogwoodarts.com) takes place in April to coincide with the springtime blooming of dogwood trees. The core of the festival is the opening of 70 miles of dogwood trails that pass through historic and architecturally significant neighborhoods and by thousands of blooming dogwood trees.

The Dogwood Arts Festival also includes a variety of art shows and other events—workshops, festivals, and concerts—aimed at promoting the arts in the community and in area schools.

In April, the Knoxville Opera organizes the **Rossini Festival** (www.rossinifestival.org), an Italian street fair that takes place on Gay Street and at Market Square Mall in downtown Knoxville. Special wine tastings, opera performances, and European music combine with a vibrant street fair with a pronounced Mediterranean theme.

Summer

The **Kuumba Festival** is an African-inspired street festival that takes place in late June at Market Square downtown and in Chilhowee Park in East Knoxville. The event features parades, music, arts demonstrations, and vendors, all with an African theme.

The end of summer is marked annually with **Boomsday,** the largest fireworks display in the nation over the Tennessee River, on Labor Day.

Shopping

GAY STREET

Some of Knoxville's most distinctive stores are found on Gay Street. The first **Mast General Store** (402 S. Gay St., 865/546-1336, Mon.–Wed. 10 A.M.–6 P.M., Thurs.–Sat. 10 A.M.–9 P.M.) opened in Valle Crucis, North Carolina, in 1883, and it sold everything that folks needed, "from cradles to caskets," as it is said. Mast is now a chain with locations in several Southern mountain cities, including Asheville, North Carolina, and Greenville, South Carolina. Like the others, Knoxville's Mast General Store sells a satisfying variety of sturdy clothing and footwear, classic cookware like cast-iron skillets, old-fashioned candy, and games.

Also on Gay Street, the **East Tennessee Historical Society Gift Shop** (601 S. Gay St., 865/215-8824, Mon.–Sat. 10 A.M.–4 P.M., Sun. 1–5 P.M.) has a good collection of books about Tennessee, local arts and crafts, and T-shirts from the 1982 World's Fair.

GALLERIES

Gay Street is a major contributor to Knoxville's vibrant gallery scene. Knoxville's Arts & Culture Alliance manages an art gallery in an old furniture store at the **Emporium Center for Arts & Culture** (100 S. Gay St., 865/523-7543, www.theemporiumcenter.com, Mon.–Fri. 9 A.M.–5 P.M., free). Home to two art galleries, the Emporium puts on 12 different shows annually that showcase local and regional arts.

The Emporium also provides studio space for area artists and office space for arts organizations. The galleries are open until 9 P.M. on the first Friday of each month and 11 A.M.–3 P.M. on the first Saturday of each month.

Located next door to the Emporium galleries is a downtown satellite of UT's Ewing Gallery. The **University of Tennessee Downtown Gallery** (106 S. Gay St., 865/673-0802, Wed.–Fri. 11 A.M.–6 P.M., Sat. 10 A.M.–3 P.M., free) has a modern, fresh feel. Student and faculty artwork are exhibited alongside shows of regional and national artists.

The Art Market (422 S. Gay St., 865/525-5265, Mon.–Sat. 11 A.M.–6 P.M., Sun. 1–5 P.M.) is a stalwart artists' cooperative that traces its roots to the 1982 World's Fair. More than 60 area painters, sculptors, jewelers, weavers, and printmakers display their work at this attractive and welcoming space.

BOOKSTORES

Central Street Books (842 N. Central St., 865/573-9959, Mon.–Sat. 11 A.M.–6 P.M., Sun. 1 P.M.–5 P.M., call for winter hours) is an above-average used-book store with a notable collection of local books and collector's editions. As a bonus, it's located next to Magpie Bakery, reportedly the best bakery in Knoxville.

Another option for used books is **McKay's** (230 Papermill Place Way, 865/588-0331, Mon.–Thurs. 9 A.M.–9 P.M., Fri.–Sat. 9 A.M.–10 P.M., Sun. 11 A.M.–7 P.M.), a warehouse-size bookstore that is well organized and well loved by readers of all stripes. McKay's also has a giant location on the west side of Nashville.

The closest new-book store to downtown Knoxville is **Barnes and Noble** (8029 Kingston Pk., 865/670-0773, Mon.–Thurs. 9 A.M.–10 P.M., Fri.–Sat. 9 A.M.–11 P.M., Sun. 11 A.M.–9 P.M.), located next to West Town Mall.

Sports and Recreation

Sports may be Knoxville's single biggest draw. The University of Tennessee Vols play football at Neyland Stadium, on the banks of the Tennessee River. The Lady Vols basketball team is the most successful sports team at UT. There are sporting events and sports museums and, of course, plenty of sports fans.

But Knoxville is more than just UT sports. There are nice parks, too.

PARKS

Knoxville has more than two dozen city parks. For a complete list of parks and facilities, visit the city website (www.cityofknoxville.org).

World's Fair Park

Knoxville's best city park is the 10-acre World's Fair Park, which connects downtown with UT and brings new life to the site of the 1982 World's Fair. The park consists of walking paths, fountains, a man-made lake, grassy spaces, and a statue of Russian musician and composer Sergei Rachmaninoff, whose last public performance was at UT on February 17, 1943. The fountains are a popular attraction on hot summer days, when families come to romp in the water.

North of the fountains and adjacent to the East Tennessee Veteran's Memorial is a 4,150-square-foot playground that features a climbing wall, neutron spinner, several slides, a dual-track ride, and more. Features included were chosen by local elementary school students for their fun factor.

Tyson Park

Located at the western edge of the UT campus along Alcoa Highway, Tyson Park is a venerable city park with playgrounds, picnic tables, walking paths, tennis courts, and a skate park.

Sequoyah Park

Located in West Knoxville on the banks of the Tennessee River, 87-acre Sequoyah Park is a good place for walking, biking, or relaxing outdoors. There are playgrounds, baseball/softball fields, and lots of open space ideal for a picnic or game of Frisbee.

Sequoyah is located at 1400 Cherokee Boulevard. Get there by driving west on Kingston Pike and turning left onto Cherokee Boulevard.

Chilhowee Park

Chilhowee Park (3301 Magnolia Ave.), located off Magnolia Avenue in East Knoxville, was the city's first major park. The first streetcar line in the city connected downtown with Chilhowee, and on weekends, holidays, and hot summer days, throngs would come here to picnic, splash in the lake, or watch baseball games, horse races, or concerts.

Today the reasons to head here are spectator driven rather than recreational, such as tractor pulls and gun expos. The Knoxville Zoo, Knox County Fairgrounds, and East Tennessee Science Discovery Center all abut Chilhowee Park for a nearby recreation bonanza.

Greenways

Knoxville has an expanding array of greenways that connect parks and make it possible to get around the city on foot or by bike. Those of special note include the **James White Greenway** that originates at the South Knoxville bridge and follows the Tennessee River to Volunteer Landing downtown. On the other end of Volunteer Landing, you can follow the **Neyland Greenway** to Tyson Park and onward to the **Third Creek Greenway,** which connects with both the **Bearden Greenway** and the **Sequoyah Greenway.**

On the south side of the river, the **Will Skelton Greenway** begins at Island Home Park, passes through Ijams Nature Center, and follows the shore of the Tennessee to the Forks of the River.

For information about Knoxville greenways, go to www.cityofknoxville.org/greenways or call 865/215-4311 for the Parks and Recreation Department. The Knox Greenways Coalition (865/215-2807, www.knoxgreenwayscoalition.com) supports the use and development of greenways in the city.

Knoxville Botanical Garden and Arboretum

The Knoxville Botanical Garden and Arboretum (2743 Wimpole St., 865/862-8717, www.knoxarboretum.org, daily sunrise–sunset, free) is a dream that is slowly taking shape. Located on grounds once occupied by a plant nursery, the gardens are an effort by volunteers and family members of the former landowners.

The grounds are leafy and pleasant, though not very manicured. It is a pleasant place to come for a walk. Staff members are generally present on weekdays 9 A.M.–5 P.M.; at other times the garden is unattended.

SPECATATOR SPORTS

Watching sports in Knoxville means one thing: the University of Tennessee Volunteers. Knoxville is the epicenter of Big Orange country, and this is a city that is serious about sports. UT is a member of the competitive Southeastern Conference.

Football

UT's biggest spectator sport is football. Neyland Stadium, home of the football team, is awash with bright orange on game days. Named for Gen. Robert Neyland, head coach of the UT football team from 1926 to 1952, Neyland Stadium has a capacity of just over 100,000. Most home games sell out.

The regular college football season runs September–November. Single tickets go on sale in late July or early August for the upcoming fall season and cost $45–90. You can buy tickets from the **UT box office** (1600 Phillip Fulmer Way, 865/656-1200, www.utsports.com). On game days, tickets are sold at Gate 21 at Neyland Stadium beginning four hours before kickoff.

A word to the wise: If you are not coming into town to watch the football game, avoid downtown Knoxville on a game day. The entire city becomes a knot of congestion and Big Orange mania on these days, and if you don't want to be part of it, you'll hate the experience. Longtime residents who don't particularly fancy college football say that game days are good times to go to the mall, visit the Great Smoky Mountains National Park, or just stay home. Whatever you do, plan ahead.

Basketball

In Knoxville, UT's men's basketball team plays second fiddle to the legendary Lady Vols, eight-time national champions who have been leaders of the women's college basketball pack for a generation. The Lady Vols, under the leadership of coach Holly Warlick, play home games at Thompson-Boling Arena November–March.

Single-game tickets go on sale in October and cost $45–80 depending on your seat and the opponent. Buy tickets from the **UT box office** (1600 Phillip Fulmer Way, 865/565-1200, www.utladyvols.com).

Other UT Sports

UT plays a full schedule of sports: track and field, baseball, softball, tennis, soccer, rowing, tennis, swimming, golf, and volleyball. The UT women's softball team has performed well in recent years and is developing a reputation as a Southeastern Conference leader. UT tennis and track have good records, and in 2010 the university built a new golf center to bolster its program in that sport. For a full rundown of UT sports events, contact the athletics box office (1600 Phillip Fulmer Way, 865/656-1200, www.utsports.com).

Ice Hockey

The **Knoxville Ice Bears** (www.knoxvilleicebears.com) play at the Knoxville Civic Coliseum. The Ice

KNOXVILLE

Bears are a member of the Southern Professional Hockey League and play October–April.

TOURS

The **Three Rivers Rambler** (Volunteer Landing, 865/524-9411, www.threeriversrambler.com, adults $26.50, seniors $25.50, children 3–12 $15.50, toddlers 1–2 $7.50) is an 11-mile scenic railroad excursion that departs from downtown Knoxville. The ride travels along the Tennessee River past Island Home airport to the confluence of the Holston and French Broad Rivers. The journey takes 90 minutes and takes you past farmland and old quarries. The open-air car is a real treat in pleasant weather.

Rambles take place on holiday weekends such as Father's Day, Independence Day, and Halloween. Call ahead for a current schedule. You can reserve tickets online or up to 30 minutes before departure at the ticket counter.

To get to the Three Rivers Rambler, take Neyland Drive (Highway 158) along the Tennessee River. Look for parking lot C-18 on the shore side of the road, where Rambler guests may park for free.

The **Tennessee Riverboat Company** (300 Neyland Dr., 865/525-7827, www.tnriverboat.com) offers dinner cruises and daytime sightseeing cruises down the Tennessee River on an old-fashioned paddleboat.

Accommodations

On the up side, Knoxville's downtown hotel rooms run a bit cheaper than those in other major Tennessee cities. On the down side, the city has one of the highest combined sales- and room-tax rates in the state: 17.25 percent. Be sure to figure this in when planning your budget.

DOWNTOWN

There is a pleasant array of boutique and chain hotels in downtown Knoxville, many of which are convenient to Gay Street, Market Square, and the riverfront.

$100-150

Knoxville's most distinctive hotel is a bit hard to find. The renovated and renamed **C Oliver Hotel** (407 Union Ave., 865/521-0050, www.theoliverhotel.com, $135–278) is located just around the corner from Market Square, but the 1876 town house easily blends into its surroundings. Built by German baker Peter Kern in the 19th century, the former St. Oliver was converted into a hotel for the 1982 World's Fair. It is not well advertised, but patrons find

it nonetheless. Far from the cookie-cutter, the Oliver Hotel offers superior location and genuinely friendly service. Its 24 guest rooms have elegant beds, refrigerators, wet bars, and coffee service. Perhaps the best perk is the downstairs library, with soft couches and inviting reading nooks that beg you to come in and sit a spell.

Offering an ideal location and intimate, personalized service, the **C Maplehurst Inn** (800 W. Hill Ave., 865/254-5240, www.maplehurst-inn.com, $79–145) is worth considering. Each of the 11 guest rooms has a private bath and personalized touches to make you feel like you're at home. Breakfast is served in a cozy dining room overlooking the Tennessee River. Maplehurst dates from the early 20th century, when the town house was built for a wealthy merchant. It was converted to a bed-and-breakfast for the 1982 World's Fair and remains one of the only bed-and-breakfasts in downtown Knoxville.

Located at the north end of downtown, near the Old City and Gay Street, is the **Crowne Plaza Knoxville** (401 W. Summit Hill Dr., 865/522-2600, $144–174). This 197-room

The renovated Oliver Hotel is now a landmark and a Market Square must-stay.

The **Hilton Knoxville** (501 W. Church Ave., 865/523-2300, $99–159) is a high-rise hotel located in the midst of downtown office buildings. It is a few blocks from Gay Street and Market Square Mall. The Hilton offers guest rooms, suites, and executive guest rooms with upgraded amenities and the best views of the city. There is a business center, fitness room, pool, cribs and high chairs for children, an on-site ATM, car rental, and café.

Over $200

Feel like part of Knoxville's downtown renaissance at **Cook Loft** (722 S. Gay St., 865/310-2216, www.cookloft.com, $450–500), an urban guesthouse and event venue. Skylights, hardwood floors, high ceilings, exposed-brick walls, large windows, and sleek lines bring the loft concept to life. Two bedrooms and a spacious living room invite you to relax and spread out. The kitchen is well furnished with restaurant-grade appliances, but you probably won't be doing much cooking with all the great restaurants in your backyard. Weekly rates ($2,100) are also available.

UNIVERSITY OF TENNESSEE
$100-150

Located near the World's Fair Park on the edge of Fort Sanders, the **Cumberland House Hotel** (1109 White Ave., 865/971-4663, $145–175) is a Sheraton. The 130 guest rooms have flat-screen televisions, coffeemakers, hair dryers, and CD players. Suites with kitchenettes and couches are available. The hotel, built in 2005, boasts an on-site restaurant as well as a fitness center. Cumberland House is convenient to UT and to Neyland Stadium.

FOURTH AND GILL
Under $100

The historic residential neighborhood of Fourth and Gill, near the Old City and slightly north of downtown, is home to the **Knoxville**

high-rise hotel has full business services, an indoor pool and fitness center, 24-hour lounge, and updated guest rooms.

$150-200

Located in a pyramid-shaped building on the Knoxville waterfront, the **Knoxville Marriott** (500 Hill Ave. SE, 865/637-1234, $119–169) is one of the city's most distinctive landmarks. The unusual design creates a lofty lobby and gives many of the guest rooms impressive river views. In addition to novelty, the Marriott also offers its guests a slew of thoughtful amenities especially designed for business travelers. There is an outdoor swimming pool, fitness center, and full-service salon on-site. There are also two restaurants, a gift shop, and lots of meeting space. The Knoxville Marriott is located next door to the Women's Basketball Hall of Fame and is within walking distance of downtown attractions like Blount Mansion and James White Fort.

KNOXVILLE

Hostel (404 Fourth Ave., 865/546-8090, $17). Located in a homey urban cottage with hardwood floors, a generous porch, and small backyard, the Knoxville Hostel offers its guests bunk-bed dorm-style accommodation in sex-segregated bedrooms. Guests can lounge by the TV, use the kitchen, or surf the Internet for free on the hostel computer. Linens are provided, as is a free continental breakfast. All in all, it's a good deal, even for the budget conscious. The hostel is within walking distance of the Old City, Gay Street, and the trolley line.

WEST KNOXVILLE
$100-150

There's no shortage of chain hotels and chain restaurants in the development near Turkey Creek Medical Center. But that means you get reliably clean, safe, albeit not necessarily interesting, places to sleep. Top among them is the **Homewood Suites** (10935 Turkey Dr., 865/777-0375, $99–139). A friendly staff, easy parking, and free access to a nearby gym make it an easy place to stay.

Food

Knoxville dining is impossible to pigeonhole. Downtown eateries cater to the business lunch crowd, college students, and downtown's new young professional residents. Older neighborhoods outside of the city center are home to hole-in-the-wall eateries that defy expectation.

Whatever you do, don't head straight for the familiar chain restaurant. Explore a bit; you'll be richly rewarded.

DOWNTOWN

Gay Street, the Old City, and Market Square have a large concentration of restaurants that cater to all tastes and budgets.

Casual

For coffee, baked treats, and sandwiches, grab a table at **Old City Java** (109 S. Central St., 865/523-9817, Mon.–Fri. 7 A.M.–10 P.M., Sat.–Sun. 8 A.M.–10 P.M., $4–9). Hardwood floors, plenty of cozy tables, and wireless Internet make this a popular place to while away a few hours.

Market Square's most celebrated restaurant is ◖**The Tomato Head** (12 Market Sq., 865/637-4067, Mon. 11 A.M.–3 P.M., Tues.–Thurs. 11 A.M.–10 P.M., Fri. 11 A.M.–11 P.M., Sat. 10 A.M.–11 P.M., Sun. 10 A.M.–9 P.M., $4–9), which opened its doors downtown long before it was cool. Originally a pizza joint, the Tomato Head now serves soup, sandwiches, salads, burritos, and pizza made with only the best organic and otherwise pure-at-heart ingredients. The results are way above average. Vegetarians and meat eaters can rejoice, for options range from a vegetarian sandwich made with flavorful tofu to a roast beef sandwich heaped with meat. The pizza is still mighty popular, and for good reason. They offer 14 official varieties, but you can build your own pie from a list of 45 different toppings (homemade lamb sausage, anyone?). The Tomato Head is generally crowded and noisy. You step to the counter, order, and pay, and then one of the low-key staff members will bring your order to the table. It's a good meeting place and also a great place for a quick solo lunch. The owners are working on another location in West Knoxville (the one in downtown Maryville closed). They also own Flour Head bakery.

The **Downtown Grill & Brewery** (424 S. Gay St., 865/633-8111, Sun.–Thurs. 11 A.M.–midnight, Fri.–Sat. 11 A.M.–3 A.M., $8–18) is as popular for its selection of handcrafted brews as it is for its easy bar-style menu. Mesquite-grilled steak, jumbo pasta plates, pizza, and fajitas all come with a recommendation from the chef for the right beer accompaniment. With outdoor sidewalk seating and a prime location on Gay Street, this is a popular restaurant to meet and mingle.

Pete's Coffee Shop (540 Union Ave., 865/523-2860, Mon.–Fri. 6:30 A.M.–2:30 P.M., Sat. 7 A.M.–2 P.M., $4–10) is the best downtown destination for diner-style breakfasts and plate lunches. Located in a storefront a few blocks from Market Square, Pete's attracts a loyal following among downtown office workers and new residents. It is the type of place that offers you a bottomless cup of joe and no-nonsense food like club sandwiches, fried chicken, and omelets.

Japanese

Handcrafted sushi along with cuisine that fuses Japanese, Korean, and Spanish ingredients and styles: That is what **Nama** (506 S. Gay St., 865/633-8539, Mon.–Sat. 11 A.M.–midnight, Sun. noon–midnight, $8–25), a trendy sushi house on Gay Street, offers. The enlightened business set dines here at lunchtime; at night it attracts a youthful, well-heeled crowd. The half-price maki happy hour 4–6 P.M. is a good deal for the budget diner.

Fusion

◖ **31 Bistro** (31 Market Sq., 865/566-0275, Mon.–Fri. 11 A.M.–3 P.M. and 4 P.M.–midnight, Sat. 10 A.M.–3 P.M. and 4 P.M.–midnight, Sun. 10 A.M.–3 P.M., $16–23) offers a serious farm-to-table commitment in a cozy Market Square storefront. The seasonally changing menu offers Southern-fusion shrimp and grits, mountain trout with sage butter, and select local cuts of beef. Brunch is served on weekends.

English

Who knew that English cuisine would have its day? ◖ **The Crown & Goose** (123 S. Central St., 865/524-2100, Mon.–Thurs. 11 A.M.– 11 P.M., Fri. 11 A.M. 2 A.M., Sat. noon–2 A.M., Sun. 11 A.M. 4 P.M., $12–28) in the Old City

is proving that Welsh rarebit, fish-and-chips, and bangers and mash are indeed good food. But to be fair, the Crown & Goose is far more than British Isle pub food. They have adopted the best of the Continent, as well, and put it on display in dishes like spring vegetable and wild mushroom risotto, San Marzano tomato and Stilton bisque, and the Frenchman's Lunch, a European cheese board served with bread. Best of all, the Crown & Goose has a stylish but unpretentious atmosphere. This is a nice choice for an unexpectedly good dinner.

Sandwiches

Hefty sandwiches on home-baked bread keep the patrons coming to venerable **Steamboat Sandwiches** (7 Market Sq., 865/546-3333, Mon.– Fri. 10 A.M.–8 P.M., Sat. 11 A.M.–8 P.M., Sun. 11 A.M.–3 P.M., $5–8). The Steamboat is an over-sized sandwich packed with ham, Genoa salami, and swiss cheese, finished with a mild hot sauce, mayonnaise, mustard, and pickle. Thankfully for those with smaller appetites, you can also order a half size.

UNIVERSITY OF TENNESSEE
Fusion

Knoxville's best restaurant for vegetarians is the **Sunspot** (1909 Cumberland Ave., 865/637-4663, Mon.–Sat. 11 A.M.–10 P.M., Sun. 10:30 A.M.– 10 P.M., limited late-night menu, $8–17), an institution on the UT strip that features eclectic cuisine with strong Southwestern and Latin American influences. For vegetarians there is the baked enchilada, the Tofu Tier (a stack of baked tofu and fried eggplant in a savory miso sauce), and an awesome veggie burger. Carnivores have options like pan-seared tilapia served over cheese grits, and Pasta Rustica, chorizo sausage and red peppers served in a spicy tomato sauce. There are dozens of beers on tap and in the bottle.

WEST KNOXVILLE
Fine Dining

For a taste of Knoxville's most elegant food,

KNOXVILLE

make reservations at **The Orangery** (5412 Kingston Pk., 865/588-2964, Mon.–Thurs. 11:30 A.M.–2 P.M. and 5:30–10 P.M., Fri. 11:30 A.M.–2 P.M. and 5:30–11 P.M., Sat. 5:30–11 P.M., lunch $9–14, dinner $23–44). A French-inspired menu, impeccable wine list, and refined atmosphere make for a luxurious dining experience. Come for lunch for salad Niçoise, roasted-vegetable ravioli, and sautéed shrimp. Dinner specialties include veal porterhouse, prime New York strip, buffalo with caramelized shallots, and elk chop with vegetable puree. Bet you can't get that at home. Also consider the $35 prix fixe menu, which begins with an amuse-bouche and ends four courses later with desserts such as raspberry tiramisu or an amaretto brownie served with whipped cream and caramel pecan sauce.

Italian

The best New York–style pizzas, handcrafted calzones, and other authentic Italian favorites are offered at **Savelli's** (3055 Sutherland Ave., 865/521-9085, Mon.–Thurs. 11 A.M.–9 P.M., Fri.–Sat. 11 A.M.–10 P.M., $9–19). This homey restaurant is small and often crowded, for good reason: Savelli's serves made-from-scratch Italian food at good prices. Beer is served, but bring your own wine.

SOUTH KNOXVILLE
Steak

Beef lovers rule at **Ye Olde Steak House** (6838 Chapman Hwy., 865/577-9328, Sun.–Thurs. 4–9 P.M., Fri.–Sat. 4–9:30 P.M., $12–35), where the menu features nearly a dozen different cuts of beef, including a generous hand-patted burger. Seafood and chicken are also served. Ye Olde Steak House is a family-owned steak house set in a Tudor-style home (hence the name). It is a funky, family-friendly destination for diners with big appetites.

Beer is served at Ye Olde Steak House, but liquor and wine are not. You may bring your own.

Middle Eastern

For a dining experience like no other, head directly to **◖ King Tut Grill** (4132 Martin Mill Pk., 865/573-6021, daily 11 A.M.–8 P.M., $6–12), a family-owned restaurant in otherwise unremarkable Vestal, a few miles south of the Henley Street bridge. King Tut's has established a loyal following thanks largely to the charisma of its owner, Mo, who serves drinks in flower vases, tells you what to order, and is famous for sending out extra food to his favored customers. Mo and his family offer traditional diner-style meals—hamburgers, meat loaf, baked chicken, and the like—to appease the locals, but the reason to come here is to eat home-style Egyptian fare. The daily menu offers a handful of such favorites, like falafel sandwiches, an Egyptian platter, and the best Greek salad in Knoxville. But it is on Mo's Middle Eastern night that he and his family go all out with stuffed grape leaves, homemade *basboosa,* and the works. Believe what they tell you: This is a restaurant not to be missed.

EAST KNOXVILLE
Southern

Arguably Knoxville's best meat-and-three Southern-food house, **Chandlers** (3101 E. Magnolia Ave., 865/595-0212, Mon. 11 A.M.–3 P.M., Tues.–Thurs. 11 A.M.–7:30 P.M., Fri. 11 A.M.–8:30 P.M., Sat. noon–8:30 P.M., Sun. noon–6 P.M., $4–10) is a cafeteria-style restaurant where workingmen and businesspeople rub elbows when the dinner bell rings. The fried chicken is always reliable and comes with sides like hot rolls, collard greens, fried okra, and stewed apples.

NORTH KNOXVILLE
Diners

◖ Litton's (2803 Essary Dr., 865/688-0429, Mon.–Thurs. 11 A.M.–8 P.M., Fri.–Sat. 11 A.M.–9:30 P.M., $7–17) is a North Knoxville institution where Knoxvillians go for the city's best burgers, blue-plate lunches, and homemade dessert. Hand-cut fries, jumbo onion rings, red velvet cake, and baked sweet potatoes are some of the things that keep people coming back to Litton's again and again. A family restaurant that began as a humble grocery in 1946, Litton's is worth the drive. To get there, drive north on Broadway (U.S. 441), passing the I-640 overpass. Litton's is located across the street from the Fountain City park.

Information and Services

VISITOR INFORMATION

For information about Knoxville, contact the **Knoxville Tourism & Sports Corporation** (865/523-7263 or 800/727-8045, www.knoxville.org).

Downtown Knoxville (17 Market Sq., 865/637-4550, www.downtownknoxville.org) promotes the city center by publishing maps and guides, and maintaining a website.

The **Knoxville Visitor Center** (301 S. Gay St., 865/523-7263, Mon.–Fri. 8:30 A.M.–5 P.M., Sat. 9 A.M.–5 P.M., Sun. noon–4 P.M.) is at the corner of Gay Street and Summitt Hill Drive. This is the place to pick up information and maps, but it is also a Knoxville gift shop and bookstore, wireless Internet hot spot, and the venue of the weekday WDVX Blue Plate Special, a midday concert and live radio broadcast. The coffee bar serves hot beverages, basic sandwiches, and sweets.

NEWSPAPERS

Knoxville's daily paper is the **Knoxville News Sentinel** (www.knoxnews.com). Its alternative weekly, **Metropulse** (www.metropulse.com), is a far better read. Smart commentary, up-to-date entertainment listings, and columns like "Secret History" make it great. Pick yours up free on Wednesday at local groceries, coffee shops, and restaurants.

RADIO

The Knoxville radio dial is crowded with the usual suspects, but a few frequencies are worth seeking out. Chief among them is **WDVX** (89.9 FM and 102.9 FM), a community-supported grassroots radio station that plays a mix of early country, contemporary Americana, and other roots music.

WUOT (91.9 FM) is the university's public radio station. It airs NPR news programs and classical music.

LIBRARIES

Knoxville's main public library is the **Lawson McGhee Library** (500 W. Church Ave., 865/215 8750, Mon.–Thurs. 9 A.M.–8 P.M., Fri. 9 A.M.–5:30 P.M., Sat. 10 A.M.–5 P.M., Sun. 1–5 P.M.). It has public Internet access.

GAY AND LESBIAN RESOURCES

In 2012, standard-bearer *The Advocate* named Knoxville the eighth most gay-friendly city in the United States, citing the university's LGBT groups, the Tennessee Valley Unitarian Universalist Church (www.tvuuc.org), and the gay softball league as some of the evidence of the welcoming community.

One place to network with LGBT people is at the **Metropolitan Community Church** (7820 Redeemer Ln., 865/531-2539, www.mccknoxville.org) in West Knoxville.

KNOXVILLE

Getting There and Around

GETTING THERE
By Air
The **McGhee Tyson Airport** (TYS, www.tys.org) is the Knoxville area's airport. It is located 12 miles south of the city in Blount County.

A half dozen airlines serve McGhee Tyson with direct flights from 20 U.S. cities, including Orlando, Dallas, Houston, Denver, Memphis, Chicago, Cleveland, St. Paul, New York, Philadelphia, and Washington DC. Airlines with service to Knoxville include US Airways, United, Delta, American, Continental, Northwest, and Allegiant Air.

Taxis and car rentals are available at the airport. To get to downtown Knoxville from McGhee Tyson, take Alcoa Highway (U.S. 129) north to the city.

By Car
Two major interstate highways cross in Knoxville. I-75 is a north–south highway that connects with Lexington, Kentucky, in the north and Chattanooga to the south. I-40 is an east–west thoroughfare. About 35 miles east of Knoxville I-40 peels off and heads into North Carolina, while I-81 heads to the Tri-Cities and points northeast. I-40 west heads to Nashville and Memphis.

By Bus
Greyhound (www.greyhound.com) serves Knoxville with bus service to Nashville, Chattanooga, Asheville, Atlanta, and many other cities. The **Greyhound station** (100 East Magnolia Ave., 865/524-0369) is on Magnolia Avenue.

GETTING AROUND
Driving
Knoxville is a city where everyone drives to get where they're going. Sprawling suburbs, shopping malls, and the interstate are evidence of this.

I-640 is a bypass interstate that makes a circle on the northern fringe of Knoxville and allows I-40 through traffic to avoid downtown. Part of I-640 is also I-275.

While the interstate is efficient, there are good reasons to get off the highway. Thoroughfares like Cumberland/Kingston Pike, Chapman Highway/Henley Street/Broadway, and Central, Magnolia, and Western Avenues will give you a better sense of the character and geography of Knoxville. And with the possible exception of Kingston Pike, there's likely to be less traffic, too.

PARKING
Drive around downtown searching for a meter, or park in one of the many paid parking lots downtown. No matter what you do, all-day parking in Knoxville will rarely cost you more than $5 per day.

Public Transportation
The **Knoxville Trolley Line** (865/637-3000, www.katbus.com) offers free air-conditioned easy transit throughout downtown Knoxville most weekdays. The Vol Line (Mon.–Thurs 7 A.M.–6 P.M., Fri. 7 A.M.–10 P.M., Sat. 9 A.M.–10 P.M.) connects UT and the World's Fair Park with downtown, including Gay Street. The Downtown Loop (Mon.–Fri. 6 A.M.–6 P.M.) connects Hall of Fame Drive and the Civic Coliseum with Henley Street and downtown. The Gay Line runs on Gay Street to Hill (Mon.–Thurs 7 A.M.–6 P.M., Fri. 7 A.M.–10 P.M., Sat. 9 A.M.–10 P.M.).

Most Knoxville Trolleys are red, although sometimes orange Knoxville Transit Authority vans fill in. They stop at locations designated by a trolley sign.

Around Knoxville

CLINTON

◖ Green McAdoo Cultural Center

In 1955, Green McAdoo School was the segregated primary school for Clinton, a mill town of 4,000 people located about 20 miles northwest of Knoxville. Under the "separate but equal" policy of the segregationist South, graduates of the black primary school were bussed to Knoxville's all-black Austin High School for their secondary education.

Fifty years later, the school building became the Green McAdoo Cultural Center (101 School St., 865/463-6500, www.greenmcadoo. org, Tues.–Sat. 10 A.M.–5 P.M., free), which records and celebrates the remarkable story of the integration of Clinton's high school back in 1956. Don't speed, or you'll miss it—and this is definitely something you do not want to miss.

Tales of school desegregation in the South normally begin with Little Rock, Arkansas. But they really ought to begin with Clinton. That's because even before the Little Rock Six entered Little Rock Central High School in the fall of 1958, there were black and white students attending Clinton High School together in rural Tennessee.

In 1951, five black high school students petitioned the Anderson County Board of Education for the right to attend all-white Clinton High School. At this time, black students in Clinton were bussed a long 18 miles into Knoxville to attend the all-black Austin High School.

At first, the students lost their suit. U.S. District Judge Robert Taylor declared that the bussing arrangement met the requirements of separate but equal. However, when the U.S. Supreme Court decided the landmark Brown vs. Board of Education in the spring of 1954, Judge Taylor reversed his earlier ruling and ordered that Clinton High School be integrated at the beginning of the school term in September. What followed is a remarkable story,

recounted at the cultural center through newspaper clippings, video remembrances by the participants, and evocative photographs of the events. Integration went smoothly at first, but as the eyes of the world focused on this trendsetting Tennessee town, tensions began to run high. The National Guard was called in, and the school building was bombed. But the school principal, student body president, local Baptist minister, and other leaders in Clinton took a strong stand in favor of the rule of law—and, therefore, for integration.

One of the most moving displays in the museum is a glass case with letters that were received by Rev. Paul Turner, the white Baptist minister who helped to escort the black students to school and preached against the segregationists. There are anonymous and hateful postcards and letters that decry Rev. Turner, as well as letters of support from unknowns to celebrities, including Rev. Billy Graham and Edward R. Murrow.

Eventually, the world stopped paying a lot of attention to Clinton. New civil rights struggles were taking place all over the South, and the outsider segregationists who fomented the worst of the violence and unrest were gone. Photographers traveled to Clinton to take pictures when Bobby Cain became the first black male to graduate from a desegregated public school in May of 1957, but when Gail Epps followed in his footsteps the following year, no one paid any attention.

The events that took place in Clinton were recounted in an hour-long 1957 *See It Now* television program, and its 1960 sequel from CBS Reports, both of which may be seen at the museum. In 2006, the Green McAdoo Cultural Center produced an award-winning documentary about the events titled *Clinton 12,* which was narrated by James Earl Jones.

GRAINGER COUNTY AGRITOURISM

Grainger County lies northeast of Knoxville. One of the state's most rural counties, Grainger has a rugged landscape, defined by steep ridges and long valleys. The area is perhaps best known for its tomatoes–during the summer it is not uncommon to see farm stands set up around Knoxville with signs touting Grainger County Tomatoes.

You can get to the source of the abundance by visiting farms in Grainger County yourself. **Ritter Farms** (2999 Hwy. 11-W S., 865/767-2575, www.ritterfarms.com) is one of the largest family-owned farms in the area. They have a commercial kitchen where they prepare jams, jellies, salsas, and other farm-fresh provisions for retail sale. The farm market is open Monday–Saturday year-round; in the spring, summer, and fall you can buy seasonal fresh produce, and in winter they specialize in handicrafts, preserves, and baked goods. Call ahead

to confirm hours. The farm is located between Bean Station and Rutledge.

Tennessee Homegrown Tomatoes (865/828-8316), located near Cherokee Lake on Route 375, about 3.5 miles east of Highway 92, grows all sorts of vegetables–not just tomatoes. They offer farm tours and host events throughout the growing season.

If you want some wine with your vegetables, you can get some at **Clinch Mountain Winery** (Thorn Hill, 865/767-3600, www.clinchmountainwinery.com, Mon.-Sat. 10 A.M.-7 P.M., Sun. noon-7 P.M.), located on Bullen Valley Road in the Thorn Hill community. Try their most popular varieties, Scooter Trash and Hound Dog Red, at the tasting room.

The crowning event for Grainger County farmers is the **Grainger County Tomato Festival** (www.graingercountytomatofestival.com), which takes place in Rutledge in late July every year.

Outside the museum is a life-size statue of the Clinton 12, the 12 African American young people who enrolled at Clinton High School in the fall of 1956. When the museum was opened in 2006, 9 of the 12 were on hand to see the statue being unveiled.

The Green McAdoo Cultural Center was funded in part by federal, state, and local funds, as well as through private donations. In 2007, legislation was introduced in Congress that would designate the Green McAdoo Cultural Center as part of the National Park Service.

The old Clinton High School building now houses Clinton Middle School, just a few blocks from the Green McAdoo center.

Get to Clinton by taking Clinton Highway (Highway 25 West) about 15 miles out of Knoxville. Once in Clinton, there are signs directing you to the center.

Appalachian Arts Craft Center

Locals love the Appalachian Arts Craft Center (2716 Andersonville Hwy., Norris, 865/494-9854, www.appalachianarts.net, Mon.–Sat. 10 A.M.–6 P.M., Sun. 1–5 P.M., closed Sun.–Mon. Jan.–Feb.) because they get to meet artists and learn to make works of art in ongoing workshops. But this small nonprofit gallery is a must-see for visitors, too, particularly if you want that one-of-kind souvenir to take home. Specialties include pottery, weaving, and quilting.

◖ Museum of Appalachia

There is one place that every visitor to this region should visit if they are the least bit interested in the lifestyles and folk traditions of Appalachia. The Museum of Appalachia (2819 Andersonville Hwy., 865/494-7680, www.museumofappalachia.org, Jan.–Feb. daily 10 A.M.–5 P.M., Mar. and Nov.–Dec. daily 9 A.M.–5 P.M., Apr. weekdays 9 A.M.–5 P.M., weekends 9 A.M.–6 P.M., May–Oct. daily 9 A.M.–6 P.M. adults $18, seniors $15, teens 13–18 $10, children 5–12 $6) is one of a kind.

blacksmith shop at the Museum of Appalachia

Its 65 acres contain more of the history of this region than any other place in Tennessee. The collection includes more than 250,000 artifacts, and more than 100,000 people visit annually. This is all the more remarkable given that the museum, which is now a Smithsonian Institution affiliate, started as a collection from one man's garage.

The museum is a story told in several chapters. Its indoor exhibits include the Appalachian Hall of Fame, a remarkable collection of things that were made, used, and treasured by the people who came and created a life in the rugged land of the southern Appalachians. There are dolls that were whittled by rugged mountain men, banjos created from food tins, and the remains of a supposed perpetual motion machine. The exhibits are the work of John Rice Irwin, as is the whole museum. Irwin, a mountain man himself, has spent his life motivated by his admiration and love for the people who settled the mountains. He believes that the items of

everyday life are important, and that through them, we can understand the people who made them and made the region what it is. It certainly seems like he's right. Take the time to read the detailed and loving descriptions of each item in the hall of fame (most handwritten), and soon you will feel admiration and marvel for the people who made them, in the midst of what we would now consider hard times.

Music fans should not overlook the museum. Its collection of handmade fiddles, guitars, banjos, and mouth harps is unrivaled, and its displays about musicians tell not only who, what, and when, but also why and how. It's not to be missed.

Outside the hall of fame, the museum has a collection of mountain buildings. There is a log church, schoolhouse, pioneer homestead, and the log home where Mark Twain's parents lived in Possum Trot, Tennessee. As you explore these old buildings—all of which have been carefully moved from original locations throughout the region—look for members of the museum's menagerie: peacocks, horses, fainting goats, and sheep.

The Museum of Appalachia hosts several events during the year, but none is better known and as well loved than its annual **Homecoming** in October. The best musicians, writers, and artists come for the weekend, which offers the most authentic celebration of mountain arts in the region. Perhaps better loved by locals is the Fourth of July Anvil Shoot (yes, an actual anvil is shot into the air), which also includes music and crafts of the region.

In 2008, Irwin announced that he could no longer afford to keep the museum afloat with regular, large personal contributions, and locals, museumgoers, and historians alike were concerned that the museum would have to cut hours or otherwise look for cost-cutting measures. But his daughter, Elaine Irwin Meyer, took the reigns, forged the relationship with the Smithsonian, and took steps to preserve her father's legacy, and that of his forefathers, for the future.

Wear comfortable shoes, charge the camera battery, and prepare to stay for a good part of the day to see everything this site has to offer. Don't skip the gift shop or the on-site restaurant.

NORRIS DAM STATE PARK

TVA's first hydroelectric project was to construct a dam on the Clinch River, in Anderson County north of Knoxville. Construction of the 1,860-foot-long, 265-foot-tall dam started in 1933 and was completed in 1936. It was named for senator George Norris of Nebraska, who conceived of and championed the idea of a public power company in the Tennessee Valley. This was one of a number of projects that displaced mountain families in this region.

Hungarian-born architect Roland Wank designed Norris Dam. Wank cared not only about the function of the dam, but its appearance as well. He considered the placement of overlooks on either side of the dam and designed a visitors center. The dam was proportional; carefully placed window openings and the placement of the formwork boards created texture and pattern.

Today, Norris Dam is part of Norris Dam State Park (125 Village Green Circle, Lake City, 865/426-7461 or 800/543-9335). Visitors may see the picturesque dam from overlooks on both sides of the lake; U.S. 441—the main thoroughfare in the park—tracks along the top of the dam. It is an impressive sight. The visitors center, on the east side of the dam, has public restrooms and displays about construction of the dam.

Norris Dam is also home to the **Lenoir Museum** (865/494-9688, Wed.–Sun. 9 A.M.–5 P.M., free), named for Will G. Lenoir, a local resident who amassed a mind-boggling collection of mountain artifacts during his lifetime. Lenoir traveled the back roads of East Tennessee to purchase housewares, old farm implements, mementos, and other remnants of everyday life of the early 20th century. When Lenoir died, he donated his collection to the State of Tennessee, and eventually the Lenoir Museum was built at Norris Dam State Park.

In addition to Lenoir's collection, the museum houses displays about Native Americans and the construction of Norris Dam.

Next to the Lenoir Museum are two authentic structures that were moved to the park during construction of TVA dams and lakes. The **Caleb Crosby Threshing Barn** once sat on the Holston River where the David A. Green Bridge now spans Cherokee Lake on Highway 25 East. Before the lake flooded the farm site, the barn was carefully dismantled and put in storage, where it was kept for 34 years until 1978, when it was reconstructed at Norris Dam.

Next to the threshing barn is the **18th Century Rice Gristmill,** originally constructed in 1798 by James Rice along Lost Creek in Union County. Four generations of the Rice family operated the mill from 1798 until 1935,

BRIAN STANSBERRY/CREATIVE COMMONS

the 18th Century Rice Gristmill at the Lenoir Museum Cultural Complex

when TVA bought the land on which it sat in preparation for flooding of Norris Lake. The Civilian Conservation Corps labeled all the components of the mill, disassembled it, and reassembled it on its present land. During the summer, park staff still operate the mill and have gift items for sale.

Recreation

Despite its rich history, most people come to Norris Dam State Park to relax and enjoy the outdoors. Boating and fishing are popular on the Clinch River and on Norris Lake, in part because the water is so deep and cool, and the fish so plentiful. There are several licensed commercial marinas (865/494-8138) on the lake, including ones where you can rent houseboats for your stay. There are 15 miles of hiking trails and another 15 miles of multiuse dirt and gravel paths ideal for biking. An Olympic-size swimming pool is open during the summer Wednesday–Sunday 10 A.M.–6 P.M.

Cabins and Camping

Norris has 19 rustic cabins (865/426-7461, $60–85) and 10 three-bedroom deluxe cabins ($70–105). All cabins are located in a wooded setting and have kitchens, bathrooms, fireplaces, linens, and outdoor picnic tables and grills. The Norris campground has 75 sites ($20) with electrical and water hookups. Houseboat rates vary by season, size of boat, and availability.

OLIVER SPRINGS

The town of Oliver Springs is just a blip on the map, but it's worth stopping to see the general store, the library (housed in the old train depot), and the town hall.

The real reason people head to Oliver Springs, though, is to get to the **Coal Creek OHV Area and Windrock Park** (865/435-1251, www. coalcreekohv.com). The park offers more than 72,000 acres of wide-open spaces, including trails, camping, cabins, and fantastic scenery.

COURTESY OF ANDERSON COUNTY TOURISM COUNCIL

There are 72,000 acres of off-road fun at Coal Creek OHV Area and Windrock Park.

OAK RIDGE

America created the atomic bomb—or parts of it, at least—at the Y-12, X-10, and K-25 plants in this city, northwest of Knoxville. Talk about top secret! Even those involved didn't really know what was happening, and The Secret City moniker remains one people use. Today, Oak Ridge and its plants are still an important component in the national defense industry. Oak Ridge's heritage is part of everything in the city. You can sense how smart everyone in town is (the government recruited the best and brightest to work here, and many of their offspring have stayed): This is a little brain trust in the mountains. You can't walk away from here without a different perspective on the country.

History

Oak Ridge did not exist before 1942. When nuclear fission was discovered in the late 1930s, American scientists warned that this technology could be used to create a weapon more powerful than any known to man. As World War II escalated, and the United States joined the conflict in 1941, the U.S. military decided to exploit this technology. Sites in New Mexico, Washington state, and East Tennessee were chosen for the work. The isolated hills in Tennessee were chosen because they were close to roads and rail lines, they had ample supply of electricity, and they would be hard for spies and the curious to discover. Before the land was taken over by the government, about 3,000 people lived in homes that were scattered around the hills and valleys. Each homeowner received a letter stating that their land and home were being taken, and how much money they would receive in exchange.

Oak Ridge was built seemingly overnight. Between the spring of 1943 and the fall of 1944, the 59,000-acre tract of land bought for the project was developed into 10,000 homes and apartments, 13,000 dormitory spaces, 5,000 trailers, and more than 16,000 barracks. One of the facilities, K-25, where they processed uranium, was at the time the largest building in the world under one roof. Workers rode bicycles to get from one side of the massive structure to the other.

Social societies, schools, churches, theaters, barber shops, and much more were developed to entertain and meet the needs of the new residents.

When the United States dropped atomic bombs in Hiroshima and Nagasaki on August 6 and September 2, 1945, many workers at Oak Ridge learned for the first time what they had been doing all this time. Many believed and were proud that they had helped to end World War II.

The end of the war did not mean the end of Oak Ridge. Y-12 continues to research, develop, and produce weapons for the U.S. military. In 1948, X-10 became the Oak Ridge National Laboratory, a center for science and research managed successively by the University of Chicago, Monsanto Chemical, Union Carbide, and Lockheed Martin corporations. It is now managed by the University of Tennessee and Battelle, and remains a center for scientific research in a wide range of fields.

American Museum of Science and Energy

Oak Ridge's premier attraction is the American Museum of Science and Energy (300 S. Tulane Ave., 865/576-3200, www.amse.org, Mon.–Sat. 9 A.M.–5 P.M., Sun. 1–5 P.M., adults $5, seniors $4, children 6–17 $3). The museum serves double duty: It houses an exhibit about the development of Oak Ridge, and it is a science museum for young people. The historical exhibit relies on newspaper clippings, original documents, and audiovisuals to describe Oak Ridge during World War II. The science museum has features dedicated to types of energy, including nuclear.

◖ Oak Ridge National Laboratory

Before September 11, 2001, visitors were allowed walk-in tours of Y-12/Oak Ridge National Laboratory (865/574-7199, www.ornl. gov). But in today's security-anxious world, casual visitors are not allowed on the campus of the nuclear plant without an advance reservation. Call to arrange a tour, or get on one of the public bus and train tours offered in collaboration with the American Museum of Science and Energy (AMSE). These tours run daily June–September. To get on board the bus tour, you must sign up in person at the AMSE before 9 A.M. on the day of the tour. The bus leaves at noon and returns at about 3 P.M. The bus tour is free with paid admission to the museum.

If you're short on time or don't want to get tangled up at the AMSE, then head for the **K-25 overlook** (Highway 58), a minimuseum and viewing station located about 10 miles south of Oak Ridge. You'll drive through the city's industrial park before arriving to the overlook. Inside a small enclosed building is a short version of Oak Ridge's history. Outside you can see the K-25 plant as well as other Oak Ridge infrastructure. It is not scenic, but it's still a view.

Across from the K-25 Technology Park is the **Wheat African Burial Ground,** which houses 90 unmarked graves believed to be those of slaves from the Wheat Plantation. The cemetery dates back to 1850.

Other Sights

While most of "old Oak Ridge" has been razed and rebuilt in the ubiquitous modern American style of strip malls and parking lots, parts of the city date back to the 1940s. **Jackson Square** remains largely unchanged since it was built as Oak Ridge's original town center. The low-slung horseshoe-shaped shopping center is home to professional offices, a few cafés, and the Oak Ridge Playhouse. Across Kentucky Street from the square are the remains of the **Alexander Motor Inn,** Oak Ridge's original and only hotel during the war. Above the inn is the **Chapel on the Hill,** a church that served as the place of worship for numerous denominations during the war.

Other don't-miss attractions in Oak Ridge include the **International Friendship Bell,** located downtown, which is a monument to peace. The **Secret City Commemorative Walk,** also downtown, is a memorial to the 75,000 men and women who built Oak Ridge during the 1940s.

The **Children's Museum of Oak Ridge** (461 W. Outer Dr., 865/482-1074, www. childrensmuseumofoakridge.org, Tues.–Fri. 9 A.M.–5 P.M., Sat. 10 A.M.–4 P.M., Sun. 1–4 P.M., adults $7, seniors $6, children 3–18 $5) building was the Highland View Elementary School during the Manhattan Project era. Founded as a Girl Scout project in 1973, this is probably Tennessee's best children's museum, and it does a remarkable job explaining the area's complex history to even the youngest of visitors. In addition to The Secret City history, there's a child-size dollhouse, a rain forest, a bird room, a water flume, and a spectacular model railroad. Model-train buffs from Knoxville make the trek to keep this exhibit running.

When you've had enough Manhattan Project–era tourism in Oak Park, head to the **University of Tennessee Arboretum** (901 S. Illinois Ave., 865/483-3571, daily 8 A.M.–sunset). Here you can stroll through 250 acres of trees. There are a number of easy, self-guided walking trails, each well marked should you want to learn about the flora of the region. If you just want some time to commune with nature, that works, too.

Tours

The **Secret City Scenic Excursion Train** (865/241-2140, www.techscribes.com/sarm/srm_scs.htm, Apr.–Sept. first and third Sat., Oct.–Nov. selected weekends, Sat. 11 A.M., 1 P.M., and 3 P.M., Sun. 1 P.M. and 3 P.M., adults $17 children 4–18 $13, call ahead) combines pretty scenery with the history of Oak Ridge.

The train departs from Wheat Union Station, near the K-25 overlook on Highway 58. The journey travels a 12-mile route through the Manhattan Project site. The guides cram in a lot of information on these rides; the train will likely be of more interest to little ones than the lecture.

Entertainment and Events

The Oak Ridge Art Center (201 Badger Rd., 865/482-1441, www.oakridgeartcenter.org, Tues.–Fri. 9 A.M.–5 P.M., Sat.–Mon. 1–4 P.M., free) displays local and regional artwork. Exhibits change regularly and are fairly small. Getting a glimpse of the working studio is the appeal of this attraction.

Each June Oak Ridge tells its story during the **Secret City Festival** (www.secretcityfestival.com). There are World War II reenactments, live music, a juried art show, tennis tournaments, and plenty of activities for kids.

Food

For a meal in Oak Ridge, head to Jackson Square, where you can join the crowds at **Big Ed's Pizza** (101 Broadway, 865/482-4885, Mon.–Sat. 11 A.M.–11:30 P.M., $8–15), the city's most famous restaurant and a well-loved pizza parlor. Also on Jackson Square is **The Soup Kitchen** (47 E. Tennessee Ave., 865/482-3525, Mon.–Fri. 11 A.M.–7:30 P.M., Sat. 11 A.M.–2 P.M., $5–12), which serves excellent sandwiches, salads, and soups. Don't skip the Chilios (a combination of Fritos, chili, and cheese). End the meal with ice cream at **Razzleberry's Ice Cream Lab and Kitchen** (223 Jackson Sq., 865/481-0300, Mon.–Thurs. noon–8 P.M., Fri.–Sat. noon–9 P.M.).

With menu items including the Y-12 and K-25 breakfast specials, you know you are in Oak Ridge when you are at the **Jefferson Soda Fountain** (22 N. Jefferson Cir., 865/482-1141, Mon.–Fri. 7 A.M.–3 P.M., Sat. 6:30 A.M.–2 P.M., $6–10). Try the Myrtle Burger and stay long enough to hear longtime Oak Ridgers tell their tales.

Take in the scenery at the **Riverside Grille**

SAM HOUSTON: THE RAVEN

·The word *colorful* does not do justice to Sam Houston, onetime Tennessee governor and one of the state's most complex and controversial citizens during the first half of the 19th century.

Born in Lexington, Virginia, in 1793, Houston was just 13 when his father died. His mother, Elizabeth, brought Sam and his eight siblings to Blount County, where he went to school for the first time and promptly memorized Pope's translation of Homer's *Iliad*. When his teacher refused to teach Houston Greek and Latin, the teenager disappeared from his family home. Houston traveled the rural mountainsides of East Tennessee and spent long periods in a Cherokee village. Oo-Loo-Te-Ka, a Cherokee chief, became a surrogate father to Houston and named him the Raven. Houston learned the language and ways of the Cherokee.

Some years later Houston needed to pay off debts, and in 1811 he opened a school in Blount County where he charged the then-astronomical fee of $8 per student per year. After about a year, when he was 20 years old and had paid his debts, Houston joined the army and quickly rose to an officer rank. Andrew Jackson noticed Houston's bravery and intelligence at the Battle of Horseshoe Bend during the Creek Wars of 1814. The future president stationed Houston to his regional headquarters in Nashville, and the young East Tennessean became part of Jackson's so-called Tennessee Junto, his political machine.

In 1819 Houston quit the army to study law and shortly after was appointed attorney general for Davidson County. Houston ran successfully for a seat in the U.S. House of Representatives, where he served two terms. In 1827 he was elected governor of Tennessee.

Houston's station at the top of Tennessee politics was not to last. He had a tumultuous private life, fueled by bouts of drinking and depression. While campaigning for his second term as Tennessee governor, Houston married Eliza Allen, the daughter of a prominent Middle Tennessee family. She left him after just 80 days of marriage, and Houston resigned the governorship and fled to the Cherokee, now living in Oklahoma.

So began the next chapter for Houston, who went on to marry a Cherokee wife, lead the Texas army against Mexico, and be elected president of the Republic of Texas. Later, in 1840, he married again, this time to Margaret Lea of Alabama, with whom he would have eight children. He worked tirelessly to achieve Texas annexation to the United States, which occurred in 1845. While Houston served as a senator from Texas from 1846 until 1858 he promoted the transcontinental railroad, criticized the army, and supported the Union. In 1859 Houston was elected governor of Texas, where he opposed the state's secession. He died in 1863.

Tennessee historian and writer Wilma Dykeman described Houston this way: "A strange, interesting combination of scout and scholar, woodsman and humanitarian, Sam Houston balanced Homer with humor and represented a sense of the total community of man."

(100 Melton Lake Peninsula, 865/862-8646, www.riversidegrilletn.com, Mon.–Thurs. 11 A.M.–9 P.M., Fri.–Sat. 11 A.M.–10 P.M., Sun. 11 A.M.–4 P.M., $4–18). Here you will enjoy steaks, salads, and a view of Melton Hill Lake.

Information

The **Oak Ridge Welcome Center** (102C Robertsville Rd., 865/482-7821, www.oakridgevisitor.com, year-round Mon.–Fri. 9 A.M.–5 P.M., June–Oct. also open Sat. 9 A.M.–1 P.M.) hands out maps and brochures, and helps travelers plan their visit to the city.

MARYVILLE

One of the oldest cities in East Tennessee, Maryville was named for Mary Grainger Blount, the wife of territorial governor William Blount. It is the home of Maryville College, a four-year college founded in 1819. Maryville College was among the first Southern schools to admit Native Americans, African Americans, and women.

On the northern outskirts of Maryville is Alcoa, established as a company town for the Aluminum Corporation of America in 1914. ALCOA remains an important economic engine for Blount County.

Sights

The **Sam Houston Schoolhouse** (3650 Sam Houston Schoolhouse Rd., 865/983-1550, www.samhoustonhistoricschoolhouse.org, Tues.–Sat. 10 A.M.–5 P.M., Sun. 1–5 P.M., adults 17 and older $5, children 9–16 $3) is the one-room schoolhouse where Sam Houston taught for about a year beginning in 1812. Houston, one of early Tennessee's most remarkable citizens, was mostly self-educated. Raised in part by the Cherokee, who named him Raven, Houston went on to be governor of Tennessee, president of the Republic of Texas, and senator and governor of the state of Texas.

The Sam Houston Schoolhouse was built around 1794 by area settlers who wanted a place for their children to be educated. Several different teachers held class in this little one-room schoolhouse until Houston's arrival in 1812. Houston, who took up teaching in order to pay off his debts, stayed for only a year. But his name has remained tied with the institution up to the present day.

Today, the Sam Houston Schoolhouse re-creates early schools on the Tennessee frontier. Reenactments can be arranged for groups.

Shopping

Southland Books (1519 E. Broadway, 865/984-4847, daily 10 A.M.–1 P.M.) is an excellent used-book store, popular meeting place, art gallery, and coffee shop. Stop in at any time for a pick-me-up pastry and coffee drink. Owner Lisa Misosky serves a special homemade lunch special every weekday.

Accommodations

Located at McGhee Tyson Airport is the **Hilton Knoxville Airport** (2001 Alcoa Hwy., Alcoa, 865/970-4300, www.hiltonknoxvilleairport.com, $150–190). Its 326 guest rooms offer work desks, high-end bedding, coffeemakers, and MP3-player plug-ins.

Food

Local chains include Knoxville-based **Aubrey's** (909 W. Lamar Alexander Pkwy., 865/379-8800, Sun.–Thurs. 11 A.M.–10 P.M., Fri.–Sat. 11 A.M.–11 P.M. $12), which serves pasta and steaks; there's also **Lemon Grass Thai Cuisine and Sushi Bar** (912 W. Lamar Alexander Pkwy., 865/681 8785, www.mylemongrass.com, Mon.–Thurs. 11 A.M.–3 P.M., 5–10 P.M., Fri.–Sat. 11 A.M.–3 P.M., 5–11 P.M., Sun. noon–10 P.M., $11).

GREAT SMOKY MOUNTAINS

The Smokies are the most popular national park in the United States, and it is no wonder why. The park's iconic vistas of blue-green mountains topped by the namesake smoky mists are awesome, yet somehow comforting. These are ancient mountains whose hills and valleys have secrets to keep.

The scenery in the Smokies is unrivaled. Mountaintops such as Clingmans Dome and Mount LeConte offer panoramic vistas of soft edged mountains. Balds—clearings high up in the mountains—are enchanted places where wild blueberries and rhododendron grow, and where the sunshine is pure and warm.

Valleys such as Cades Cove are ideal for wildlife viewing—here you'll see lovely creatures like elk and deer. Mountain streams and rivers offer a kaleidoscope of sights, both under the cold, rushing water and around the water's edge. Within the 800 square miles of parkland, scientists have documented some 10,000 species of plants, animals, and invertebrates, but they believe that as many as 90,000 more live in this remarkably diverse natural wilderness.

No matter what interests you, you won't be bored in the Smokies. There are 800 miles of hiking trails within the park, and traveling them brings you face-to-face with wildlife, waterfalls, and breathtaking viewpoints. Once you start hiking the trails of the Smokies, you might never want to stop. Cool mountain

© BEN ALLEN PHOTO/123RF

HIGHLIGHTS

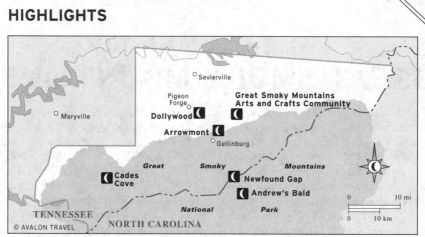

LOOK FOR ◖ TO FIND RECOMMENDED SIGHTS, ACTIVITIES, DINING, AND LODGING.

◖ **Newfound Gap:** The most prominent mountain pass in the Smokies offers breathtaking vistas, cool mountain air, and a chance to hike along the famed Appalachian Trail (page 408).

◖ **Cades Cove:** Historic cabins, churches, and farms dot this popular pastoral mountain cove, ideal for walking, biking, or auto touring (page 410).

◖ **Andrew's Bald:** A high mountain clearing accessible only on foot, Andrew's Bald is one of the Smokies' mysterious bald spots. This landscape of wild grasses, rhododendron, and clear air is the perfect destination for a day hike (page 418).

◖ **Arrowmont:** Established in the early 20th century as a settlement school for mountain folks in Gatlinburg, Arrowmont is an arts school and gallery with a focus on Appalachian decorative arts (page 427).

◖ **Great Smoky Mountains Arts and Crafts Community:** Drive the back roads near Gatlinburg to meet artisans who keep the creativity and ingenuity of mountain crafts alive. This is a must-stop for take-home gifts (page 428).

◖ **Dollywood:** Don't turn up your nose at Dolly Parton's Pigeon Forge theme park. With roller coasters, live music, artisans, and lots more diversions, this place is the definition of good, clean fun (page 433).

streams are ideal for wading and offer some of the best mountain fishing in the country. Visitors also enjoy picnicking and driving along the park's windy, quiet roads. The Smokies are also more car accessible than other national parks, meaning even those who can't or don't want to hike, walk, or bike can enjoy the sights.

More than 9.4 million people visit Great Smoky Mountains every year, and they need places to stay and to eat. The

gateway communities in Tennessee—Cosby, Gatlinburg, Pigeon Forge, and Townsend—offer the necessities of life and so much more. If the Smokies soothe the spirit and revive your mind, then Gatlinburg and Pigeon Forge, with theme parks, minigolf, dinner theaters, and any type of retail store you can imagine, send you crashing right back down to the real world. It's the yin and the yang of East Tennessee. The quieter sides of Cosby and Townsend offer a middle road for those who want it.

HISTORY
Geologic History

The Smoky Mountains are old. They were formed between 200 and 300 million years ago, when the African and North American continental plates collided, causing great peaks to form. Over the succeeding millennia, the Smoky Mountains weathered away, creating the soft, rounded peaks that now define the mountain range. By comparison, the Himalayas are nearly newborn at 50 million years old.

The park's diverse array of ecosystems, plants, and animals can be traced to the last ice age, when glaciers covered large parts of what is now the United States. Animals and plants from northern climes moved southward to escape the ice, and they found refuge in the Smoky Mountains. When the ice receded, many species remained, having adapted to their new home.

Human Settlement

Native Americans lived in the Smokies and their foothills beginning around 7000 B.C. When the first European explorers traveled through what today is Tennessee, they found the Cherokee Indians, a politically and economically sophisticated tribe linked to the Iroquois nation.

The first white settlers established homesteads in the Smoky Mountains near Cherokee, North Carolina, in 1795. In 1814 the first families settled in Cataloochee, and seven years later settlers arrived in Cades Cove. Mountain homesteads began to appear in other lowland areas of the Smokies, and along rivers and streams. By 1850 there were 451 residents in Cades Cove, and other large settlements in Cataloochee and Greenbrier.

Life in the mountains was not easy. Families survived off the land, growing crops and raising livestock. Nearly everything they had—tools, clothing, household goods, and games—came from the forests around them. Corn was the most important crop, and water-powered gristmills were used to grind corn into cornmeal—a staple of life.

The landscape of the Smokies changed dramatically during the first 30 years of the 20th century. Logging companies, which had previously passed by the mountains thanks to their difficult terrain, looked again, inspired by the possibility of expansion and the arrival of railroads in the region. Little River Lumber Company was the first logging company to arrive in the Smokies, in 1903, and the last to leave, in 1939, after the creation of the national park. Loggers felled millions of old-growth trees—by the time the last axe struck, just 20 percent of the virgin forest remained. Logging led to forest fires, which sometimes raged for months, and erosion, which polluted rivers and streams.

Logging changed the lifestyle of mountain residents, too. Logging towns appeared seemingly overnight. Logging jobs paid money, and so began the evolution from subsistence to wage living. Residents were also able to sell goods and services to the loggers and logging executives; the first hotel in Gatlinburg opened to house timber buyers who came to the area.

The environmental toll of such aggressive logging was one of the reasons that folks started to talk about protecting the mountains through a national park.

Establishing the Park

Looking back today, it is remarkable that the Great Smoky Mountains National Park exists at all. It took 17 years, and the combined efforts of Tennessee and North Carolina residents, plus local, state, and federal politicians, to achieve the complicated and daunting job of setting up the park.

The primary challenge was that by the 1920s, when talk of the park began in earnest, the land was in private hands. A portion was owned by about 4,000 mountain residents, but the greatest expanses belonged to lumber companies, which had been harvesting the mountainsides for timber since the turn of the 20th century.

Early park boosters were businesspeople and

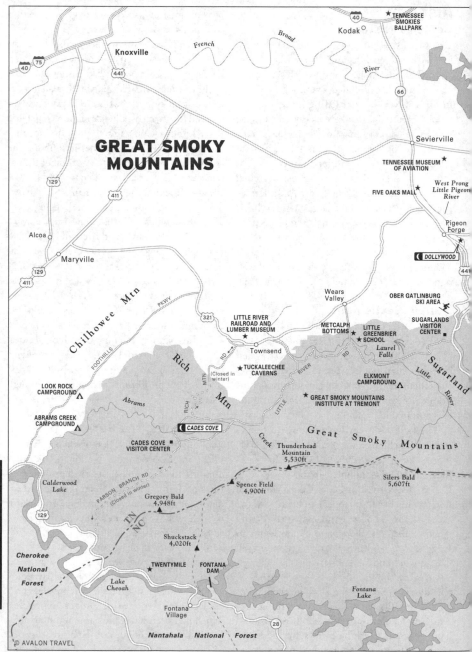

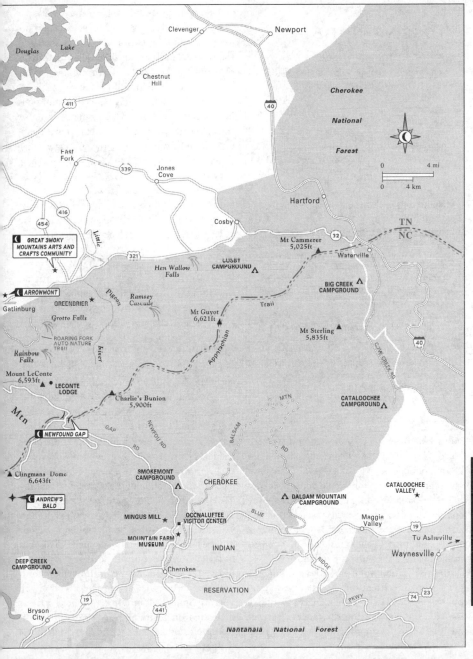

LOGGING IN THE SMOKIES

You wouldn't know it from looking at the lush treetops today, but at the time the Great Smoky Mountains National Park was dedicated in 1940, it had been largely denuded by logging. Beginning around 1903, timber companies logged the mountains, felling trees to satisfy the growing demand for lumber. It is estimated that two billion board feet of lumber came out of the Smokies during this period.

Logging companies built railroads, roads, and towns, the names of which—Elkmont, Tremont, Smokemont, and Proctor—remain as place-names in the park today. The environmental effects of logging were devastating. Fires burnt logged areas, leaving the mountainside bare. Streams and rivers swelled with muddy water, caused by erosion and landslides.

Lumber companies fought against the creation of a park. They took the government to court—one case reached the U.S. Supreme Court. The last timber was extracted from the Smokies in 1939 by Little River Lumber Company in the Tremont area. By 1940, only 20 percent of the park's lands were covered by old-growth forests.

politicians from East Tennessee and western North Carolina who argued that a park would be an economic boon for the region. They foresaw a future when visitors would come in droves to see the park, spending money in the gateway communities on their way. Boosters launched an all-out public relations campaign to promote a park, and in 1926 alone residents pledged $1 million toward the purchase of lands.

The popularity of the park idea among residents drew the attention of state and federal politicians. In 1926 President Calvin Coolidge signed a bill committing the federal government to begin development of a national park in the Great Smokies, as soon as 423,000 acres of land were provided by the states of North Carolina and Tennessee. The states then offered $1 million each for land purchases, and the final $5 million was given by philanthropist John D. Rockefeller Jr. in memory of his mother, Laura Spellman Rockefeller.

Money in hand, states-appointed commissions had the difficult task of purchasing land. The timber companies resisted. First they tried to derail the project itself, and later they sought to get the highest possible price for their land—much of which had now been stripped bare of trees. The states took five of the companies to court, a process that depleted funds meant for land purchase and allowed the timber companies time to continue logging in the Smokies.

In part because of the devastating effects of continued logging, support for a park grew even stronger. In 1933 President Franklin D. Roosevelt reversed a previous federal position and earmarked federal money for the purchase of land. By 1940, when the park was dedicated, the U.S. government had contributed more than $2 million.

Perhaps the biggest losers from the park project were the 4,000 people who lived within park boundaries. Without deep pockets like those of the timber companies, they were often stuck taking very little in financial compensation for their homes and farms. Some older residents chose to stay in the park—they sold their property to the government and leased it back for the duration of their lives. But making a livelihood on a land where they were now forbidden to hunt, fish with bait, or cultivate crops was close to impossible. Some residents, including the five Walker sisters who lived in a cabin in Little Greenbrier until the 1950s, managed to survive. Others, however, moved to communities outside the park and began new lives.

Great Smoky Mountains National Park was dedicated on September 2, 1940. President Roosevelt stood at Newfound Gap to dedicate the park, and among his words were these:

In this park we shall conserve the pine, the redbud, the dogwood, the azalea, the rhododendron, the trout and the thrush for the happiness of the American people. The old frontier that put the hard fiber in the American spirit and the long muscles on the American back, lives and will live in these untamed mountains to give future generations a sense of the land from which their forefathers hewed their homes.

If you watch the short introductory video at park visitors centers, you will see footage of the presidential caravan as it made its way up the mountain to Newfound Gap for the dedication ceremony. The footage of that difficult drive up to the top of the mountain is a powerful symbol of the remarkable efforts and convergence of circumstances that gave rise to this remarkable national park.

ORIENTATION

The crest of the Smokies forms the boundary between Tennessee and North Carolina, bisecting the park from northeast to southwest in an unbroken chain that rises more than 5,000 feet for more than 36 miles. Elevations in the park range from 875 feet to 6,643 feet.

Most people arrive in the park through Gatlinburg, a touristy hamlet (and popular wedding destination) located in the middle of the northern park boundary. To the southwest is Townsend, which has hotels and restaurants but far, far less of both. Cosby, at the eastern side of the Tennessee boundary, is the quietest gateway point of all.

PLANNING YOUR TRIP

As the most-visited national park in the nation, Great Smoky Mountains can feel crowded at peak times of the year. More than nine million people visit the park each year, most of them in their own cars, which clog roadways and fill parking lots. The busiest months are June, July, and August, when more than 3.5

million people will visit. The second most popular time is during the peak of the fall foliage show, which generally happens during the last two weeks of October. More than one million people come to the Smokies each October.

There are some effective strategies for circumventing the crowds. First, avoid peak season. If you must come during the summer, or October, visit during the week instead of on weekends. Next, don't sleep in! Set out early in the day. Most park roads get busy after 10 A.M., and the early mornings can be lovely times to see the sights.

Another good way to avoid the crowds in the Smokies is to get off the beaten track. There is a crowd mentality among most park visitors, which takes them to Sugarlands, Cades Cove, Newfound Gap, and Clingmans Dome, leaving the rest of the park to you. Plan an itinerary that allows you to enter the park through Cosby, Townsend, or another of the secondary gateways and then to explore some of the lesser-known attractions, such as Abrams Creek, Greenbrier, and Cosby.

The final, and single best, way of shedding the crowds is to get out of your car. Among the miles of hiking trails in the Smokies, only a few are highly trafficked. Even the most popular of hiking trails, such as Chimney Tops and Grotto Falls, are downright empty compared to the park's roads. It is well worth a few sore muscles and a little sweat to enjoy some of the park's majesty all alone.

Driving

Distances to various sites within the park are relatively short; it is just 34 miles from Cherokee, North Carolina, to Gatlinburg. But the drives are not quick (nor should they be). National park roads are winding two-lane blacktops. It can take hours to drive from Gatlinburg to Newfound Gap due to traffic congestion and the steep and windy nature of the road. If you are keen on avoiding traffic jams, consider entering the park through either Townsend or Cosby, and start your day early.

Weather

Always check the weather forecast before you come to the Smokies. Temperatures in the park, and particularly at the high elevations, can be as much as 30°F colder than those in the surrounding area. In summer this is welcome, but in the winter it can be deadly. Rainfall in the park ranges from 55 inches per year in the valleys to 85 inches per year on the peaks, more than is received anywhere else in the United States except the Pacific Northwest.

Seasons

Spring in the Smokies is the season of variable weather; it can be sunny and warm one day and snowy the next. Spring rainfall can cause rivers and streams to swell without warning. Summer is generally hot, with lots of haze and humidity. Afternoon thunderstorms are not uncommon.

Autumn is the park's greatest season. The fall foliage draws thousands of people, and for good reason. The weather is generally cool and crisp, with snow beginning at the high elevations in November. Winter snow is deep in the high elevations; Newfound Gap experiences an average of 69 inches of snowfall per year. In lower elevations only a few inches fall. Many secondary roads are closed during the winter due to frequent snow and ice.

Planning Your Time

If you have only one day in the Smokies, choose between a day hike or a drive to Clingmans Dome. Make the choice based on your own capacity for hiking, the weather (Clingmans Dome is often enveloped in haze), and the season (avoid Clingmans Dome during peak visitation periods).

If you have a few days, go camping. Spend one day hiking, one day driving, and one day exploring Cades Cove. Ambitious hikers should make reservations at LeConte Lodge and plan a rest day between the hike in and the hike out to enjoy the peace and quiet at the top of the mountain.

Sights

◖ NEWFOUND GAP

This mountain pass, located at 5,048 feet, is one of the Smokies' greatest attractions. Named because it was not discovered until the 1850s, Newfound Gap is the lowest pass over the mountains. Today's visitors enjoy its refreshing cool air, its views, and the fact that you can straddle the state line between Tennessee and North Carolina. It was here, on September 2, 1940, that President Franklin D. Roosevelt dedicated the Great Smoky Mountains National Park.

There is a large parking lot here, with the best views looking southward into the Oconaluftee River Valley in North Carolina. The Appalachian Trail, which travels the ridge of the mountains through the Smokies, crosses the road here at Newfound Gap. You can hike along the AT in either direction for as long as you like.

Clingmans Dome

Come to Clingmans Dome for the views. Here at the highest point in the park (6,643 feet), you can climb an observation tower that takes you up above the treetops. It is a stunning view and a refreshing experience, and afterward you can say that you were on the top of Ol' Smoky.

Clingmans Dome is the highest peak in the Smokies, and the third-highest peak in the eastern United States. Once called Smoky Dome because it is rounded like a dome, it is now called Clingmans after Thomas Lanier Clingman, a North Carolina attorney and politician who was involved in early attempts to measure and catalog mountain peaks.

The concrete observation tower atop Clingmans Dome dates to the 1960s. Immediately in front of the tower there are two steel-frame towers, a communications tower and a climactic data collection tower. On a clear day, the 360-degree view is truly awesome. Fontana Lake, Mount Mitchell, Knoxville, and Mount LeConte are just a few of the landmarks visible from the tower. Unfortunately, visibility from Clingmans Dome is often limited—often just 20 miles—by air pollution. Park officials blame coal-burning power plants in the southeastern United States for most of the pollution, which can also pose a health risk for people with breathing difficulties.

Another environmental problem evident at Clingmans Dome is the infestation of mature Fraser fir trees by the balsam woolly adelgid. The dry skeletons of these once-majestic evergreens haunt the mountainsides here. Fraser firs were the iconic champions of the unique spruce-fir forest that exists in the high elevations of the Smokies. But beginning in 1963, the adelgid, an aphid-like insect less than one millimeter long, arrived in the Smokies after coming to the United States from Europe, probably on nursery stock. Without any natural predators, the adelgids thrived on the sap of mature Fraser fir trees. Today, park officials estimate that some 70 percent of mature Fraser fir trees have been killed by the adelgids; the rest are infested. You can identify an infested tree by the white woolly mass covering its bark. Sometimes it causes the tree to look whitewashed.

Park rangers treat Fraser fir trees in developed areas and sites accessible by road with a soap solution sprayed from truck-mounted spray units. Other treatments to trees that the trucks can't reach include drenching the soil with the active ingredient in flea and tick medication for dogs. This has been very successful and is effective up to five years. The park rangers have also been releasing predatory beetles that feed exclusively on adelgids, but it will take years for the population of these beetles to have any effect on the adelgids. By 2011, the park had released more than half a million beetles.

Preliminary monitoring has been encouraging. The park has also transplanted some firs to lower elevations in the park, where they can be protected and preserved in the event that scientists discover a way to guard against the microscopic predators.

When planning to visit Clingmans Dome, check the weather first. Remember that it is often much more cold and wet on top of Ol' Smoky than it is in the lowlands. On cloudy or overcast days, there will be no visibility at all.

Clingmans Dome is located at the end of a seven-mile spur road. It is a half-mile walk along a steep, but paved, footpath from the parking area to the base of the observation tower. The road to Clingmans Dome is closed December 1–March 31.

Mount LeConte

It is as if Mount LeConte keeps watch over the Smokies. The 6,593-foot peak stands sentry over the foothills; its size makes it easy to identify, even from a distance. Accessible only by foot, Mount LeConte is a destination for hikers who yearn for a sense of accomplishment. And what an accomplishment it is, with spectacular views and beautiful scenery along the way. The peak is also home to LeConte Lodge, the only indoor accommodations in the park.

ELKMONT

An old logging town that later became a summer resort community, Elkmont is now a campground and the starting point for several day hikes. The park has considered tearing down the deteriorating remains of summer cottages here, but for now they still stand—a reminder of the days before the park existed. Present-day vacationers can lay their heads at the 208-site Elkmont campground.

Elkmont is noted for the appearance here every June of synchronous fireflies. People come in droves to watch the insect show, which normally lasts about two weeks and begins

Deer are among the wildlife residents you'll see in Cades Cove.

around the second week of June. The park service offers trolley transportation to Elkmont during the firefly show.

Metcalph Bottoms

Metcalph Bottoms is a day-use area popular for picnicking and swimming. From here you can walk one mile to **Little Greenbrier School,** a 19th-century split-log schoolhouse with original furniture.

Just west of Metcalph Bottoms along the Little River Road are two water attractions. **The Sinks** is a waterfall with a pool so deep it once swallowed an entire derailed logging train, or so they say. Swimming here is not recommended, but it is nice to sit and watch the water crash over the falls.

Close to the intersection with Highway 73, which goes to Townsend, is the **Townsend Y,** probably the most popular swimming hole in the park. The river here is relatively wide and smooth, and the grassy bank is perfect for sunbathing.

◖ CADES COVE

Historical and natural attractions lie side by side in Cades Cove, a flat mountain valley on the Townsend side of the park. It was a population center before the park was established.

There are indications that Cherokee and other Native Americans used Cades Cove for hunting and as a way to travel through the rough mountain terrain. But it is believed that whites were the first people to settle permanently in this fertile yet remote place. Early homesteaders came in the 1820s, and by 1850 the population was nearly 700. Families—with names such as Jobe, Oliver, Tipton, Shields, Burchfield, Cable, Sparkes, and Gregory—farmed, raised cattle, collected wild chestnuts, and hunted. They built churches, a school, a gristmill, and homes. Theirs was the hard yet happy life of the mountains.

In the 1920s and '30s, the government came to buy up Cades Cove land for the park. Some of the remaining 600 residents agreed to the financial settlement and left the cove. Others took less money but retained the right to live in Cades Cove until they died. One man, John W. Oliver, took Tennessee to court, but he lost and moved out in 1937. During the 1940s, the population of Cades Cove dropped quickly. The school closed in 1944, and the post office was shuttered in 1947. By the end of the decade it was a ghost town, left to the imaginations of visitors yet to come.

Access to Cades Cove is along an 11-mile one-way loop road. Traffic moves slowly through this pastoral landscape, so plan on spending at least two hours on the loop. Two two-way lanes cross the cove and allow you to shorten or lengthen your drive.

The roads in Cades Cove are closed to vehicular traffic on Wednesday and Saturday mornings until 10 A.M. May–September. Exploring on foot or bike is a lovely way to experience the cove.

Historic Buildings

Cades Cove is home to more than 70 historic buildings, which makes it the best place in the park to learn about human inhabitation of the Smokies. Along the 11-mile loop you will have the opportunity to explore various homesteads, including the **John Oliver Place,** the **Henry Whitehead Place,** and the **Carter Shields Cabin.** Historic churches include the 1902 **Methodist Church,** the 1887 **Primitive Baptist Church,** and the 1915 **Missionary Baptist Church.**

At the extreme western end of the loop is the **Cable Mill** area, which you should explore on foot. The gristmill here is original; it was built by John P. Cable in the 1870s. Outbuildings around the mill were moved here from other parts of the park. They include a cantilever barn, blacksmith shop, smokehouse, and the Gregg-Cable House, believed to be the first frame house built in the cove.

There is a parking lot, visitors center, and restrooms at the Cable Mill.

Wildlife

Deer are a common sight in Cades Cove. You may also see bear, river otter, elk, woodchuck, wild turkey, rabbit, and squirrel. Elusive animals of the cove include bobcat, raccoon, and gray and red fox.

Over the years, the park service has debated how to manage the Cades Cove environment. Since it is a "historical district," the objective is not to return the cove to nature but to preserve its open spaces and historic buildings. In the early years, the park service issued grazing permits, built large drainage ditches, and introduced nonnative fescue grass. More recently, they have rethought these policies. They are phasing out grazing and haying, resorting instead to prescribed burns to keep the cove open. Native grasses and wildflowers are being reintroduced, and drainage ditches are being plugged so that low-lying areas will return to being wetlands.

Rich Mountain

You can leave Cades Cove (but not enter it) along the one-way Rich Mountain Road, which climbs up and over Rich Mountain and deposits you in Tuckaleechee Cove, near Townsend. The road is steep and curvy, offering lovely views of the cove below. It is closed mid-November–mid-March.

Parsons Branch

Another exit from Cades Cove is Parsons Branch Road, a one-way seasonal road that departs the cove near the Cable Mill and heads through unspoiled mountains. After joining with Forge Creek Road, this route ends at Highway 129 and Calderwood Lake. It is 10 miles from Cades Cove to Highway 129.

From 129 you can drive east into North Carolina or west to Chilhowee and the Foothills Parkway in Blount County.

ABRAMS CREEK

Abrams Creek is a lovely and relatively uncrowded corner of the Smokies. Accessible by car only from Happy Valley Road, this is one part

BLACK BEARS

Black bears are cute and photoworthy, but they are also wild animals. Attacks by black bears in the Smokies are rare, but they have happened. In May 2000 a 50-year-old schoolteacher from Cosby was attacked and killed by two bears in the Elkmont area of the Great Smoky Mountains National Park. In 2006, a six-year-old girl was killed near Benton Falls in the southern Cherokee National Forest; the girl's mother and two-year-old brother were injured in the same attack.

If you see a bear in the woods, proceed with extreme caution and follow this advice from the National Park Service:

If you see a bear, keep your eyes on it. Do not approach it. If your presence causes the bear to change its behavior (stops feeding, changes its travel direction, watches you, etc.), then you're too close. Being too close may promote aggressive behavior from the bear, such as running toward you, making loud noises, or swatting the ground. The bear is demanding more space. Don't run, but slowly back away, watching the bear. Try to increase the distance between you and the bear. The bear will probably do the same.

If a bear persistently follows or approaches you without vocalizing or paw swatting, try changing your direction. If the bear continues to follow you, stand your ground. If the bear gets closer, talk loudly or shout at it. Act aggressively and try to intimidate the bear. Act together as a group if you have companions. Make yourselves look as large as possible (for example, move to higher ground). Throw nonfood objects such as rocks at the bear. Don't run and don't turn away from the bear. Don't leave food for the bear; this encourages further problems.

Most injuries from black bear attacks are minor and result from a bear attempting to get at people's food. If the bear's behavior indicates that it is after your food and you're physically attacked, separate yourself from the food and slowly back away.

If food isn't the lure and you're physically attacked, fight back aggressively with any available object—the bear may consider you as prey. Help protect others by reporting all bear incidents to a park ranger immediately. But prevention is the best course of action: Keep your distance from bears.

of the park you can enjoy without setting foot (or tire) in any of the traditional entry points.

Abrams Creek is the focal point of this recreation area. The creek is deep and wide enough for swimming along the picnic area and campground. It is a good place for fishing, too. From the campground, you can hike four miles to **Abrams Falls,** a 20-foot waterfall. Continue on past the falls another 2.5 miles, and you reach Cades Cove.

Foothills Parkway

An 18-mile limited-access scenic parkway, the Foothills Parkway's western portion connects Chilhowee Lake with Townsend. While strictly located outside the bounds of the national park, the parkway offers stunning views of the western reaches of the Smokies. It is lightly traveled and a good alternative to other more crowded scenic roads.

The parkway follows the ridge of Chilhowee Mountain. There is a campground, picnic area, and observation tower at **Look Rock.**

Seemingly in an effort to confuse visitors, the parkway actually consists of two separate roadways. The eastern section, also called the Foothills Parkway, is a six-mile stretch that connects Cosby with I-40.

Fontana Dam

The tallest dam east of the Rocky Mountains, Fontana was built in 36 short months starting in 1942. Spurred by World War II, crews worked in three shifts 24 hours a day on the construction. Fontana is some 480 feet tall and required a mind-boggling three million cubic yards of concrete. Completed, it had a power-generating capacity of 293,600 kilowatts.

The Appalachian Trail passes over the top of the dam, and you can, too. It is a mammoth concrete creation—equivalent to a 50-story skyscraper. The **visitors center** (daily 9 A.M.–6 P.M.) is open May–November, but only when the U.S. Homeland Security threat level is below high (orange). There are picnic tables and an overlook around the dam. Of note to hikers are the restrooms with hot-water showers, dubbed the Fontana Hilton by through-hikers on the Appalachian Trail.

Fontana impounds the Little Tennessee River. The resulting **Fontana Lake** is popular for fishing, boating, and swimming. Fontana Village in North Carolina offers shopping, dining, and lodging options.

GREENBRIER

Greenbrier is a pleasant day-use area located on the banks of the Little Pigeon River. Greenbrier Cove, located where the Middle Prong runs into the Pigeon River, was a population center before the park was formed. Swimming and fishing are popular pursuits here today.

Greenbrier is accessible from Highway 321, which runs from Cosby to Gatlinburg. It is possible to get here without driving through Pigeon Forge or Gatlinburg, which is a plus for many visitors. It is a 3.2-mile drive along the Little Pigeon from Highway 321 to Greenbrier Cove. At the cove, the road forks. Turn left along the Middle Prong to find the trailheads for the Old Settlers Trail and the Ramsey Cascades Trail. Turn right for picnic areas and a one-mile trail that leads you to historic homesteads and a cemetery.

COSBY

Here, Cosby refers to the recreation area at the northeast corner of the park, not the town that lies nearby, outside the bounds of the park. This is one of the least-visited areas in the park, offering hiking, waterfalls, camping, and swimming. The Cosby Creek provides opportunities for swimming and wading. It is a 2.1-mile hike along the Gabes Mountain Trail to **Hen Wallow Falls.** Several other hiking trails pass through Cosby, including the Low Gap Trail, which climbs 2.5 miles to the Appalachian Trail.

OCONALUFTEE

This is North Carolina's main gateway to the park. Adjacent to the Oconaluftee Visitor Center is the **Mountain Farm Museum** (828/497-1900, daily sunrise-sunset, free), a village of original log structures collected from throughout the park. A historical highlight is seeing a log home built of American chestnut before the chestnut blight. About a half mile north of the Farm Museum is the **Mingus Mill** (no phone, mid-Mar.–mid-Nov. daily 9 A.M.–5 P.M., plus Thanksgiving weekend, free), a water-powered gristmill that still operates. Watch corn ground into cornmeal.

About three miles north of Oconaluftee is Smokemont. Once a lumber company town, Smokemont is now a recreation area with hiking trails, a picnic area, and a campground.

Located near Bryson City, North Carolina, **Deep Creek** is a recreation area noted for its waterfalls. It is also the location of the Deep Creek and Indian Creek Trails, both of which allow mountain bikes.

A North Carolina attraction of special note is the **Blue Ridge Parkway,** a two-lane scenic blacktop highway that traverses Nantahala and Pisgah National Forests before heading north into Virginia.

CATALOOCHEE

Cataloochee is, in some respects, another Cades Cove. In other respects, it is quite different. A valley surrounded by mountains, Cataloochee was once the most populous community in what is now the national park. Its name is derived from the Cherokee word for the area, *Gadalutsi* (standing up in a row or wave upon wave).

Like Cades Cove, Cataloochee is a cove surrounded by wooded mountains. Historic buildings, including a school, churches, a barn, and several homesteads, provide a sense of human inhabitation. In 2001, the park service introduced a herd of elk in Cataloochee; elk are most likely to be seen in the early morning or evenings.

Unlike Cades Cove, Cataloochee is not crowded. The most obvious reason for this is that getting here is a bit of a challenge. The easiest way to get to Cataloochee is to take I-40

east into North Carolina. At exit 20, it's 11 miles along Cove Creek Road to Cataloochee. The last two miles of your journey are along a gravel road, which is fine for standard passenger vehicles but slow going nonetheless.

Those who make the journey to Cataloochee will be rewarded with scenes of an idyllic mountain valley and notable trout fishing, as well as facilities to camp, hike, and picnic.

Driving Tours

Taking a relaxing drive through the park is a great way to see its most prominent attractions. During weekends in the summer and October expect long lines of traffic on the most popular roads. Try to choose a weekday and strike out early to avoid crowds.

The mountain ascents and descents can strain your vehicle. Watch your engine temperature carefully, particularly in the summer, and use a low gear when coming down the mountain. Slow-moving vehicles should use pullouts.

Several park roads are closed in winter. If you plan to visit between November and April, call the park first to confirm closures.

As you drive through the park, you will see signs for **Quiet Walkways.** These trails are designed to encourage you to get out of your car and stroll for a few minutes through the forest. Some of the walkways are short—about a half mile—while others join up with longer trails. Walk as far as you like, and then turn back and return to your car the way you came.

NEWFOUND GAP ROAD

Journey through the mountain pass that early settlers used to reach the Tennessee side of the mountains. Newfound Gap Road travels 30 miles from Sugarlands Visitor Center to Oconaluftee in North Carolina. The road climbs some 3,000 feet, traveling through

ecosystems including cove hardwood, pine-oak, and northern hardwood forests. At the top of the pass you will see an evergreen spruce-fir forest.

About two miles into your drive, you will find the **Campbell Overlook,** where you can see Mount LeConte and other large peaks. There is also a display that identifies the different types of forest found in the Smokies.

At 4.6 miles is the Chimney Tops Picnic Area, once a common place for bear sightings. If you see a bear, remember to keep your distance. Admire it, take photos with a zoom lens, but do not feed it. Less than a mile past the picnic area is a series of three overlooks giving you views of **Sugarland Mountain** and **Chimney Tops.** From here you can see some of the only virgin spruce forest left in the eastern United States.

After passing along the West Prong of the Little Pigeon River and entering into the harsh northern elevations of the Smokies, you will find **Morton Overlook,** situated at 4,837 feet. Here you can look down on the ribbon of asphalt that you just traveled.

Newfound Gap is located at mile 13.2 on your journey. This mountain pass offers spectacular views. Just two-tenths of a mile beyond Newfound Gap is the entrance to the seven-mile spur road that will take you to Clingmans Dome, the highest point in the park.

From this point, the road descends along

© MELINDA FAWVER/123RF

Newfound Gap vista

the Oconaluftee Valley through the North Carolina side of the park. You will pass several more overlooks and quiet walkways. At mile 29 is the **Mingus Mill,** an old gristmill that operates from early spring through the fall. The drive ends at the **Oconaluftee Visitor Center,** located adjacent to the **Mountain Farm Museum.**

CADES COVE LOOP

Cades Cove is one of the most popular sights in the national park and a favorite place for exploring by car. Traffic along the one-way 11-mile loop road proceeds slowly, and there are frequent opportunities to stop and explore on foot. Beware that during peak visitation, it can take five hours to drive the loop—longer than it would take to walk it. Set out early in the day to have it more to yourself.

The drive begins at the **orientation shelter,** located near the Cades Cove campground and picnic area. If you don't already have one, pick up the detailed guide to Cades Cove here. The first homestead you arrive at is that of John Oliver. If it's crowded, drive on—there are more cabins later in the tour.

You will next pass Cades Cove's three extant churches. These beautiful buildings date from 1887 to 1915. Opposite the Missionary Baptist Church is Rich Mountain Road, a winding, steep road that goes to Townsend. It is closed during the winter.

At the extreme southwestern corner of the cove is the **Cable Mill** area. Here you will find restrooms and Cades Cove's most substantial visitors center. There is also a collection of historic buildings to explore on foot.

As you drive along the southern side of the cove, you will pass a series of homesteads, including the Dan Lawrence Place, Tipton Place, and the Carter Shields Cabin.

There are two north–south "lanes" that cut through the loop. If you have time, and traffic allows it, drive through one of them to see the broad, flat expanse of the cove more closely.

GREAT SMOKY MOUNTAINS

ROARING FORK AUTO NATURE TRAIL

This six-mile paved road departs from Gatlinburg. To find it, turn left at traffic light No. 8 in Gatlinburg and follow the signs to the park. As you enter the park, roll down your windows to feel the cooler and fresher air of the forest. Sights along the way include the **Noah "Bud" Ogle Place,** where you can get out and walk a short nature trail through the forest.

Here you'll see parts of the homestead, including a tub mill and wooden flume.

Just past the Ogle Place, the road becomes one-way and winds for six miles along Roaring Fork, a fast-moving mountain stream. Along the way you will pass more historic structures and the trailhead for Grotto Falls, a popular and relatively easy hike. At the end of the drive is the waterfall **Place of a Thousand Drips,** which runs during wet weather.

Hiking

Hiking is the best way to experience the grandeur of the Smoky Mountains. On the trail you will feel, smell, and breathe the mountain air; see wildflowers and trees; and experience views inaccessible by road. Hiking destinations can be historic structures, crisp waterfalls, or one of the Smokies' seemingly enchanted highland balds. Or you may just wish to walk for walking's sake—to acquire a more intimate understanding of the forest and its inhabitants.

In total the Smokies have a whopping 850 miles of hiking trails! Not bad for a park known for its car-friendly access. Only Yellowstone and Yosemite have more miles of trails.

PLANNING YOUR HIKE

The Great Smoky Mountains Association publishes the best and most reliable guides to hiking in the Smokies. These guides provide detailed descriptions of hikes, elevations, hazards, and features you will see along the way. They are a worthwhile investment if you plan to do a lot of hiking. *Hiking Trails of the Smokies* is the authoritative volume. *Day Hikes in the Smokies* and *History Hikes in the Smokies* offer specialized focus.

You can buy the official NPS trail map for less than a dollar at any visitors center or download it for free (www.nps.gov/grsm/planyourvisit/hiking.htm). This map shows trail locations, distances, and the locations of backcountry campsites. The National Geographic/Trail Illustrated map of the Smokies, available at visitors centers and online, is worth the $12 investment, however. It includes much more detail and will hold up to the elements.

Guides and Gear

The best guide service in the Smokies is offered by **A Walk in the Woods** (4413 Scenic Dr. E., Gatlinburg, 865/436-8283, www.awalkinthewoods.com), run by husband-and-wife team Erik and Vesna Plakanis, naturalists and mountain (and park) enthusiasts. These helpful folks do it all: They lead day hikes and backpacking trips, they offer trip plans for backpackers too busy to do the advance legwork themselves, they shuttle hikers to trailheads or pick them up at their destination, and they offer special classes about birds, wildflowers, and medicinal plants of the Smokies. They also rent backpacking and other mountain gear, so you can try the whole thing out as a hobby before making an investment in expensive gear.

DAY HIKES

There are as many day hikes in the Smokies as there are days. The following are some of the most highly recommended choices.

SAFE HIKING

Getting out of the car and onto your feet is one of the best ways to see the Smokies. When planning a day hike, take time to consider your safety. These commonsense precautions will ensure you have a memorable hike, for the right reasons.

Plan ahead. Using trail maps or guides, determine your route before you set out, and let someone know where you'll be headed and when you expect to be back. Cell phones rarely work on the trail.

Dress the part. Your clothes must protect you from the elements. Layering is a smart choice because temperatures can vary on the trail and weather conditions can change. Wear sturdy shoes with ankle support. Wear wool or fleece clothing (especially socks), not cotton, which holds water and can make you cold.

Wear ID. Whether it is a Road ID bracelet, a medic alert, or just carrying your driver's license, the information about who you are and what ER staff needs to know if you are injured should be easily accessible.

Don't overestimate your ability. Be conservative when planning your walk. Most people average about 1.5 miles per hour. If you have never hiked before, or if it's been a while, start with a day hike no longer than 5 miles. Be sure to give yourself enough time to wrap up before sunset, which can be as early as 5:30 P.M. in winter (and as late as 9 P.M. in summer).

Eat and drink for energy. Bring water and food, even if you don't think you'll need it. Eat before you're hungry and keep hydrated as you walk. Nuts, dried fruit, and chocolate are good energy foods, as are apples and oranges.

Loop Hikes

RICH MOUNTAIN LOOP
(8.5 miles, moderate)

This loop offers lovely views of Cades Cove. In spring you may see mountain laurel, and in the fall the colors are spectacular. Park in the large lot at the start of the Cades Cove Loop Road. You will travel along the Rich Mountain Loop Trail (2.9 miles), Indian Grave Gap Trail (2.5 miles), and the Crooked Arm Ridge Trail (2.2 miles).

CUCUMBER GAP
(5.5 miles, easy)

Cucumber Gap explores the Elkmont area and follows the Little River. Expect beautiful wildflowers in spring. Park near the barricade at the start of Little River Trail above Elkmont campground. You will travel on Little River Trail (2.4 miles) before turning back along the Cucumber Gap Trail (2.4 miles) and Jakes Creek Trail (0.3 mile), which passes Elkmont's abandoned summer cottages. Return to your car along the road.

Waterfall Hikes

LAUREL FALLS
(2.6 miles round-trip, easy)

Laurel Falls may be the most popular hike in the Smokies. The pathway is paved all the way to the falls, and the trailhead is located a short drive east of Sugarlands along the Little River Road. If you walk another 0.75 mile past the falls, you will reach stands of old-growth forest. Parking is limited at the trailhead.

RAMSEY CASCADES
(8 miles round-trip, strenuous)

Ramsey Cascades takes you to a spectacular 100-foot waterfall. The last two miles of the hike are through old-growth forest. The trailhead is located near the Greenbrier day-use area of the park.

HEN WALLOW FALLS
(4.4 miles round-trip, moderate)

Hen Wallow Falls takes you to a 45-foot waterfall. The walk originates near the Cosby picnic area.

Hikes with a View

CHIMNEY TOPS
(4 miles round-trip, strenuous)

This is a difficult, but rewarding, hike that

GREAT SMOKY MOUNTAINS

Try to hike Andrew's Bald when the azaleas are in bloom.

COURTESY OF GATLINBURG CONVENTION AND VISITOR'S BUREAU

takes you to the rock formations known as the Chimneys. The trail has been badly eroded from heavy use, rain, and the steep terrain. It is undergoing reconstruction each Monday–Thursday. Work is expected to be complete by the 2014 season. The trailhead is located almost seven miles south of Sugarlands Visitor Center along the Newfound Gap Road.

ALUM CAVE BLUFF AND MOUNT LECONTE
(10 miles round-trip, strenuous)

Alum Cave Bluff and Mount LeConte are destinations for seasoned hikers. It is 2.3 miles from the trailhead to Alum Cave Bluffs and another 2.7 miles to Mount LeConte. (Don't be misled by the relatively short distances; this is a challenging hike.) Pause for views at Cliff Tops and Myrtle Point. The trailhead for this excursion is located 6.8 miles south of Sugarlands along the Newfound Gap Road.

◖ ANDREW'S BALD
(3.6 miles round-trip, moderate)

Andrew's Bald is one of the Smokies' mysterious highland grassy meadows, called a bald. It is a lovely, magical place, great for relaxing in the sun or even playing a game of Frisbee or catch. The hike departs the Clingmans Dome parking area and travels Forney Ridge Trail.

CHARLIES BUNION
(8 miles round-trip, strenuous)

Charlies Bunion follows the Appalachian Trail along the ridge of the mountains. The trail departs Newfound Gap and provides lovely views along the way. It passes through the spruce-fir forest, where you can see evidence of the Fraser fir's demise.

Strolls
GATLINBURG TRAIL
(3.8 miles round-trip, easy)

This trail connects the city of Gatlinburg with Sugarlands Visitor Center and follows the West Prong of the Little Pigeon River. The path is paved. Leashed dogs and bicycles are allowed.

CADES COVE NATURE TRAIL
(0.75 mile round-trip, easy)
Cades Cove Nature Trail takes you through pine and oak forest. The trail departs from near the Henry Whitehead Place, just past the intersection with Parsons Branch Road. A trail guide ($0.50) available on-site points out notable plants and other sights.

BACKCOUNTRY CAMPING
Backcountry camping allows you to hike longer and reach more remote sights in the park. Backpackers can plan journeys of one, two, three, or more days, with nights spent at backcountry campsites and shelters. For many people, the self-sufficiency of carrying all that you need on your back is a joy. Twenty-four-hour immersion in the wilderness—sometimes without seeing another person—is equally appealing.

Preparation
Multiday hiking expeditions require planning. Consult reference guides and maps carefully. You can also call the volunteers at the **Backcountry Information Office** (865/436-1297, daily 9 A.M.–noon) for help planning your trip. As you plan your route, remember that 5–8 miles is a reasonable distance to cover each day. You'll be carrying a heavy pack and will need time at the beginning and end of each day to set up and break down camp.

Rules and Regulations
Every backcountry hiker is required to have a free permit from the park service. You can obtain these from most visitors centers and campgrounds, including Sugarlands, Cosby Campground Office, Greenbrier Ranger Station, Elkmont Campground, Cades Cove Campground Office, Abrams Creek Ranger Station, and Great Smoky Mountains Institute at Tremont.

All backcountry sites are near sources of water—although depending on the weather, sometimes springs or creeks go dry. They each have a cleared area for your tent and an important cable system for hanging your food out of the reach of bears. Seventeen campsites and all of the Appalachian Trail shelters require advance reservations. These may be made up to a month ahead with the **Backcountry Reservation Office** (865/436-1231, daily 8 A.M.–6 P.M.). Remember, camping is allowed at backcountry sites only.

Several rules apply at backcountry sites: You can stay at any one site for a maximum of three nights, and a maximum of one night at any backcountry shelter. No more than eight people can camp together at one site. Fires are prohibited, except at designated sites. Neither are you allowed to stake your tent at a shelter site. Due to quarantines, you should buy local firewood rather than bring some from outside the park.

Equipment
Certain equipment is essential for backcountry camping. You are advised to bring two flashlights, water, raingear, comfortable ankle-supporting shoes, high-energy food, and extra clothing. Always carry a map and compass, and know how to use them. A camp stove, water-purification tablets, and a spade for burying human waste are also very useful. Of course, you will also need to carry a sleeping bag and tent for the night.

In the higher elevations, you must be prepared for cold, wet weather. Expect snow as early as October and as late as April.

Leave No Trace
As you hike and camp in the backcountry, remember that it is up to you to leave the environment as you found it. Never cut, deface, or take any plant, animal, or historical feature. Don't use soap to wash your dishes or bathe in streams and rivers. Human feces should be buried at least six inches deep at least 100 feet from the nearest water source.

GREAT SMOKY MOUNTAINS

Perhaps the most important rule is that all food should be stored at least 10 feet off the ground and 4 feet from the nearest tree limb. All backcountry sites have special cable systems for this purpose. This keeps food out of the reach of bears, who are regular residents of the park.

Other Recreation

BIKING

There are no dedicated mountain biking trails in this national park. While you can bike on any park road, many are unsuitable because they are narrow, steep, and clogged with cars. The best biking experience is the 11-mile Cades Cove loop, which is closed to vehicular traffic until 10 A.M. on Wednesday and Saturday mornings May–September. You can rent bikes ($4–6 per hour) during the summer and fall from the **Cades Cove store** (865/448-9034), which is open March 5–May 31 and August 16–December 4 daily 9 A.M.–5 P.M., June 1–August 15 daily 9 A.M.–9 P.M., with a 7 A.M. opening time on Wednesday and Saturday during the biking season.

Bikes are not allowed on park trails, with the exception of the Gatlinburg Trail, Oconaluftee River Trail, and the Deep Creek Trail. Less-traveled park roads that are usually good for biking are Greenbrier and Tremont Roads.

In the state of Tennessee, all children 16 years and younger are required to wear a helmet when they ride a bike. Of course, adults are encouraged to do so as well.

HORSEBACK RIDING

Four concessionaires offer horseback riding trips in the park, starting in mid-March and ending in November. These outfitters will rent you a horse for about $30 an hour. Overnight packages are available.

Tennessee outfitters are **Cades Cove Stables** (Cades Cove, 865/448-9009, www.cadescovestables.com), **Sugarlands Stables** (865/436-3535, www.sugarlandridingstables.com), and **Smoky Mountain Stables** (Gatlinburg, 865/436-5634, www.smokymountainridingstables.com). In North Carolina, **Smokemont Stables** (828/497-2373, www.smokemontridingstable.com) is located near Cherokee.

Horses are allowed on certain trails inside the park. The NPS trail map indicates horse trails, as well as backcountry campsites where horses are allowed. In addition, there are five drive-in horse camps that provide access to backcountry horse trails. These camps are located at Cades Cove, Big Creek, Cataloochee, Round Bottom, and Towstring, and are open April–mid-November. Reservations may be made by calling 877/444-6776 or visiting www.recreation.gov.

FISHING

All streams in the Smokies originate as mountain springs, burbling up along the high mountain ridge. At high elevations they flow quickly over steep, rocky beds. As more streams flow into one another, and the elevation drops, the streams widen and flow more slowly. They are no longer sheltered entirely by the forest canopy, and they become warmer. By the time they reach the park boundaries, they are rivers.

The diversity of the Smokies' streams and rivers means a diversity of fish. The fast-moving headwaters at high elevations are the native habitat of brook trout, also called brookies, or speckled trout. As streams reach elevations lower than 3,000 feet, other types of trout begin to appear, such as nonnative rainbow and brown trout. Near the park boundaries, where waters are warmer and move more slowly, you will find these trout as well as bass, shiners, minnows, suckers, and darters.

THE BROOKIES ARE BACK

The Smokies' greatest fish story is that of the native brook trout. These beautiful fish, also called brookies or speckled trout, were once the only type of trout swimming in the Smokies' waters and are the only trout native to the area. They were high-elevation fish, found in fast-moving mountain streams as they dashed down mountainside. But developments in the early 20th century nearly wiped out the brook trout. From 1934 to 1974, officials stocked park streams with other types of trout, including rainbow and brown trout, which quickly took over previous brook trout habitats. In 1976 park officials banned fishing for brook trout to protect the disappearing species. They also made a policy decision that stocking fish was contrary to the mission of the park.

But the story does not end there. In 1986, the National Park Service, working alongside other agencies and nonprofits, started to reintroduce the native brook trout, as well as remove rainbow and brown trout from certain streams. Park fishery managers used a combination of electro-fishing and chemicals to remove nonnative trout from stream segments that lie above waterfalls and other barriers that prevent upstream movement of fish.

The result of the reintroduction effort was that beginning in 2006, anglers were able fish for and keep brook trout in all park streams for the first time in almost 30 years. The population of brook trout is being carefully monitored, and studies have shown that even with fishing, the population remains healthy and self-sustaining. For example, in 2007 officials found that brook trout were the only species of trout in 17 miles of streams, and they were coexisting with other types of trout in 69 additional miles.

Hurdles remain, of course, among them being the acidification of high-elevation mountain streams due to air pollution and climate change, which impact water temperature. But for now, chalk one up for the brookies.

Fishing in the Smokies is a sport, but it is also an opportunity to view wildlife and experience the rich ecosystem of mountain streams. Anglers, particularly those who venture away from roads and into more remote areas of the park, will enjoy the sounds of running water and the sights of salamanders, insects, mammals, and wildflowers.

Guides

Get helpful local knowledge or brush up on your technique with a fishing guide. **Smoky Mountain Anglers** (466 Brookside Village Way, Ste. 8, Gatlinburg, 865/436-8746, www. smokymountainangler.com) offers full- and half-day guided fishing trips starting at $175. They also sell hand-tied and commercial flies, plus all the other gear an angler would need.

Rules and Regulations

Fishing is governed by rules that have been established to protect species and the environment. It is up to individual anglers to takes these rules to heart so that the fishery remains strong and the surrounding environment remains in balance.

Fishing is allowed in almost all streams and rivers in the park. The park service closes one or two each season due to active brook trout restoration activities; call ahead or check the NPS website to find out which streams are closed.

Anglers must be in possession of a valid Tennessee or North Carolina fishing license, depending on where in the park they are fishing. The park service does not sell these licenses, but they are available online and from outfitters in Townsend, Gatlinburg, Cosby, and other gateway communities.

Live bait may not be used, and only single hooks are allowed. Fishing is allowed 30 minutes after official sunrise and must cease 30 minutes before official sunset. The daily limit is five fish, although up to 20 rock bass are allowed. Anglers must stop fishing as soon as they reach their bag limit. Smallmouth bass and brook, rainbow, and brown trout must be at least seven inches long to be kept. There is no size limit for rock bass.

As you fish, be a good park citizen. Pick up any trash you may find and don't move or disrupt rocks, which are where many fish lay their eggs.

SWIMMING

There is nothing as refreshing or enlivening as a dip in the icy-cold waters of a mountain stream. The "Y," near the Townsend entrance to the park, is one of the most popular swimming holes in the park. Other good places to swim are at the Abrams Creek campground, the Greenbrier picnic area, and at Cosby.

Because swimming in rocky, fast-moving rivers can be dangerous, the park service officials frown on swimming. Despite this, many people do it. If you swim, remember that there are no lifeguards in the park, and that hidden rocks and ledges lurk beneath the surface of the water. Never dive into streams or rivers.

FESTIVALS AND EVENTS
Spring Wildflower Pilgrimage

Wildflowers in the Smokies are legendary, and every April they are in the spotlight at the Spring Wildflower Pilgrimage (www.springwildflowerpilgrimage.org). This five-day event organized by the Friends of the Great Smoky Mountains National Park consists of wildflower, fauna, and natural history walks, motorcades, photographic tours, art classes, and indoor seminars.

Pilgrimage events are very popular, and advance registration is almost always a must. Registration is $50 per day, $75 for two or more days for an adult, and $10 per day for high school and college students. Children under 12 are free with a registered adult. A detailed schedule is posted online, and reservations are accepted beginning in October the year before.

Townsend Winter Heritage Festival

In 2007, Townsend and the Great Smoky Mountains National Park established the annual Townsend Winter Heritage Festival (800/525-6834, www.smokiemountains.org). Featuring concerts, lectures, guided hikes, and other special events, the festival focuses on the music, food, history, and culture of people who once lived inside the park. It takes place in early February.

CLASSES
Great Smoky Mountains Institute at Tremont

The Great Smoky Mountains Institute at Tremont (9275 Tremont Rd., 865/448-6709, www.gsmit.org) offers residential environmental education programs year-round. They include naturalist certification and education, photography workshops, hiking weeks, family camping events, and programs for children and teachers.

Accommodations are in large air-conditioned and heated dormitories, and meals are served family-style in a large dining hall. Program fees apply, and reservations are essential.

Smoky Mountain Field School

A partnership between the University of Tennessee and the national park, the Smoky Mountain Field School (865/974-0150, www.smfs.utk.edu) offers workshops, hikes, and hands-on instruction. Programs range from day-long seminars on medicinal plants of the Smokies to a two-day program on fly-fishing. Other topics include orienteering, waterfalls of the Smokies, and salamanders in the park. Fees apply to all programs, and advance registration is required.

Ranger-Led Programs

The park service offers lectures, guided walks, and cultural presentations year-round. Check the park service website (www.nps.gov/grsm) for a schedule, or call a visitors center for more information.

Practicalities

ACCOMMODATIONS

There is one lodge inside the national park. **LeConte Lodge** (Mt. LeConte, 865/429-5704, www.leconte-lodge.com, adults $121, children $85), located at the peak of Mount LeConte, is a rustic inn accessible only by foot. While the amenities are sparse, the lodge is a palace for trail-worn hikers.

Accommodations are in rough-hewn log cabins scattered around the compound. Each guest gets a bunk bed with warm wool blankets. There are flush toilets, but no showers or electricity. Cabins are lighted with kerosene lamps and warmed with kerosene heaters.

The standard cabins sleep four or five people and are suitable for two couples or a family. LeConte Lodge does not put strangers in cabins together. Larger "lodges" that sleep up to 13

people are also available. Rental rates include breakfast and dinner, and LeConte's meals are famously filling—perfect after a day of fresh air and hiking. If you're a vegetarian, say so when you make your reservation so that arrangements can be made.

LeConte Lodge is open from mid-March–November. Even though you won't be there in the dead of winter, be prepared for cold temperatures and inclement weather. The temperatures here are often 20–30°F cooler than the lowlands, and it has never gotten above 80°F. During spring and fall, there is often snow on the ground and temperatures in the teens.

Reservations are available starting on October 1 for the next year. The lodge is almost always fully booked by November, although you might still find a vacancy for midweek dates

© DAN TROYKA

You'll be 6,593 feet above the everyday when you hike to LeConte Lodge.

during the spring or fall. If you can't get a room at the inn, there is a park service shelter nearby.

Guests are advised to pack a flashlight and hand towel. You should also pack an extra sweater or coat for the cold weather, plus snacks and water for the trail. Lunch is provided only to guests who are staying more than one night.

CAMPING

There are 10 developed campgrounds in Great Smokies, 5 on the Tennessee side of the park. None of the campgrounds have showers or hookups, and each campground has different size limits for RVs. You can make reservations up to six months in advance for sites at Elmont, Smokemont, Cosby, Cataloochee, and Cades Cove by calling 877/444-6777 or online at www.recreation.gov. All other sites are on a first-come, first-served basis.

A single campsite may be occupied by no more than six people, in two tents or an RV and one tent.

Townsend Entrance

◖ **Abrams Creek** (Mar.–Oct., $14) has 16 sites located along Abrams Creek and at the trailhead to Abrams Falls. Accessible only from the extreme western end of the park, this is usually one of the quietest campgrounds.

Located along the Foothills Parkway, which travels from Tellico Lake to Walland, **Look Rock** (May–Oct., $14) is the highest-elevation campground on the Tennessee side of the park. **Cades Cove** (year-round, $17–20) has 159 sites and is located at the head of the Cades Cove loop.

Gatlinburg Entrance

Elkmont (Mar.–Nov., $17–23) is the largest campground in the park. Its 220 sites are situated in a pleasant mountain valley along the Little River.

Cosby Entrance

From Cosby you can easily access two pleasant campgrounds. **Cosby** (Apr.–Oct., $14) has 165 sites along the Cosby Creek. **Big Creek** (Apr.–Oct., $14) is a tents-only campground with 12 sites. It is located just over the North Carolina line along Big Creek.

North Carolina

Other North Carolina sites are **Deep Creek** (Apr.–Oct., $17), located near Bryson City, and **Cataloochee** (Mar.–Oct., $20, reservations required), on the eastern end of the park. **Smokemont** (year-round, $17–20) is located about two-thirds of the way from Newfound Gap to Oconaluftee. **Balsam Mountain** (May–Oct., $14), which at more than 5,300 feet is the highest-elevation campground in the Smokies, is located on the remote Balsam Mountain Road and is accessible only from the eastern end of the Blue Ridge Parkway.

FOOD

There are no restaurants or concessions inside the park. The best way to eat is to pack a picnic and enjoy it at one of the many picnic grounds throughout the park. All picnic grounds include tables and fire grates.

HEALTH AND SAFETY

According to the park, motor vehicle accidents and drowning are the leading causes of death in the Smokies. Drive and swim with care. Pay attention to the road even when admiring the scenery. Do not climb on top of waterfalls, and do not go tubing inside the park. If you swim, don't try to show off, and never dive into the water—you cannot see underwater obstructions.

Venomous Snakes

Two species of venomous snakes live inside the park. Northern copperheads and timber rattlesnakes are particularly fond of rocky areas, including stone walls and buildings.

Insects

Look out for yellow jackets, a type of wasp

with a feisty sting. Yellow jackets build their nests in the ground and get mad when you disturb them. People with allergies should bring epinephrine kits. Remove any rings from your fingers right away if you're stung on the hand.

Medical Care
LeConte Medical Center (865/446-7000) is located in Sevierville, 15 miles from Gatlinburg. **Blount Memorial Hospital** (865/983-7211) is in Maryville, 25 miles from Cades Cove.

INFORMATION
The national park publishes a free quarterly newspaper, *Smokies Guide,* which is available from any NPS-affiliated visitors center. The newspaper includes information about seasonal hazards, road closures, and upcoming events.

To request general park information, contact the park headquarters at 865/436-1200. Campground and other reservations may be made at 877/444-6777 or www.recreation.gov. For backcountry campsites call 865/436-1231. You can order maps and guides at 888/898-9102.

A wide selection of brochures, guides, and books are available for purchase at visitors centers or online at www.smokiesinformation.org.

The park website (www.nps.gov/grsm) has a lot of information about attractions, activities, and current conditions. The website offers webcams that show current conditions at Look Rock and Purchase Knob within the park.

Visitors Centers
There are three park visitors centers inside the park and four outside its boundaries. Each visitors center sells maps, guides, and books. There are volunteers at each center who can help you plan your visit to the park. Information about current weather conditions, road closures, and ranger-led events is also available. All visitors centers both in and outside the park are open daily year-round but close on Christmas Day.

Sugarlands Visitor Center (865/436-1291,

Dec.–Feb. daily 8 A.M.–4:30 P.M., Mar. and Nov. daily 8 A.M.–5 P.M., Apr.–May and Sept.–Oct. daily 8 A.M.–6 P.M., June–Aug. daily 8 A.M.–7 P.M.), located two miles south of Gatlinburg on Highway 441, is the busiest visitors center. In addition to the aforementioned services, the visitors center has a museum about the flora and fauna of the park and a free 20-minute video about its history and natural features.

Cades Cove Visitor Center (no phone, Jan. and Dec. daily 9 A.M.–4:30 P.M., Feb. and Nov. daily 9 A.M.–5 P.M., Mar. and Sept.–Oct. daily 9 A.M.–6 P.M., Apr.–Aug. daily 9 A.M.–7 P.M.) is located at the midway point of the 11-mile Cades Cove Loop Road.

On the North Carolina side of the park, the **Oconaluftee Visitor Center** (828/497-1904, Jan.–Feb. and Dec. daily 8 A.M.–4:30 P.M., Mar. and Nov. daily 8 A.M.–5 P.M., Apr.–May and Sept.–Oct. daily 8 A.M.–6 P.M., June–Aug. daily 8 A.M.–7 P.M.) is located two miles north of Cherokee, North Carolina.

In addition to the visitors centers located inside the park, the park service operates centers in gateway communities surrounding the Smokies. All these visitors centers sell maps, guides, and books. They are staffed with people who can answer questions and who have up-to-date information about weather and roads. They cannot help with reservations or backcountry permits, however.

The **Gatlinburg Welcome Center** (520 Parkway, 865/436-0504, Apr.–Oct. daily 8 A.M.–7 P.M., Nov.–Mar. daily 8 A.M.–5:30 P.M.) is located on the spur road between Pigeon Forge and Gatlinburg.

The **Sevierville Visitor Center** (3099 Winfield Dunn Pkwy., 865/932-4458, Mon.–Fri. 8:30 A.M.–5:30 P.M., Sun. 1–6 P.M.) is located on Highway 66 between I-40 and Sevierville.

The **Townsend Visitor Center** (7906 E. Lamar Alexander Pkwy., 865/448-6134, Jan.–May and Nov.–Dec. daily 9 A.M.–5 P.M., June–Oct. daily 9 A.M.–6 P.M.) is located on Highway

321 in Townsend. It is closed on Thanksgiving and Christmas Day.

Pets

You may bring your pet to campgrounds and roadside stops as long as they are restrained at all times. Pets are not allowed on trails, except for the Gatlinburg and Oconaluftee River Trails.

Communications

Do not count on your cell phone working inside the park. While you are likely to get service in the gateway communities surrounding the park, most parts of the Smokies are outside of cell phone range. Campgrounds and visitors centers do have pay phones.

Gateways to the Smokies

The most popular way to get to the Smokies is along the Sevier County corridor, which begins at exit 407 off I-40 and passes through Sevierville, Pigeon Forge, and Gatlinburg. These three communities long ago shed their quiet, rural roots to become pinnacles of hyperactive commercialism. It is hard to imagine a landscape so opposed to the peace and majesty of the national park.

In this land of plenty you will find pancake houses next to outlet malls, monster truck rides next to a Bible museum, and country music dinner theater next to helicopter rides. The "live black bear" attractions seem to have faded into history, but they have been replaced by a rain forest zoo, Christian-themed entertainment complexes, and a theme park owned and operated by Sevier County native Dolly Parton.

The cost of exuberant development is traffic jams, and Sevier County has plenty. It may be a short 15 miles from Sevierville to the park, but it will feel like far more as you stop dozens of times at traffic lights along the way. At least it makes your eventual arrival inside the cool, fresh air of the park that much more welcome.

It may seem incongruous to pass through this corner of the world on the way to a national park. But there is a time in every person's life for minigolf, and back-to-school shopping is achieved quickly and inexpensively at outlet malls. Or celebrate your big day with a hot-air balloon ride over the foothills. The most

open-minded among us might find themselves pleased at the opportunity to "live the nightmare" at Ripley's Haunted Adventure or pause, mesmerized, to watch a taffy machine in action.

If you don't want to join in the fun, then bypass these cities entirely by entering the park through one of the side doors: Townsend or Cosby. It's up to you.

GATLINBURG

Surrounded on three sides by the national park, Gatlinburg is the capital city of the Smokies. Once a quiet mountain hamlet where folks lived off the land, the "Burg" is now a busy tourist trap where anything goes. Anything may include new generations of ever more gargantuan hotels and condominiums, or new attractions that try to giggle, wow, or scare the money out of you. Anything is also the unrelenting commercial machine that peddles pancakes, taffy, T-shirts, and mountain-kitsch goodies to whoever passes by.

Gatlinburg is the Tennessee city closest to the Smokies, but the mountains seem oh so far away. If you came to the Smokies strictly to enjoy nature, this isn't where you want to stop. But if your idea of fun includes a little kitsch, then maybe you'll find it in your heart to spend an afternoon gorging on cotton candy and taking funny pictures with your traveling companions. Gatlinburg's scenery and family-friendly atmosphere have made it a popular wedding

COURTESY OF GATLINBURG CONVENTION AND VISITOR'S BUREAL

The ski town of Gatlinburg is worth visiting in summer, too.

destination. You'll see wedding chapels and honeymoon deals offered around town.

Ripley's Aquarium of the Smokies

Exactly why you need an aquarium at the doorstep of one of the country's most biologically diverse mountain parks is hard to understand, but too much thought will ruin any trip to Gatlinburg. So if you've grown tired of the environment of the Smoky Mountains, trade it in for exotic ocean seascapes at the Ripley's Aquarium of the Smokies (Jan.–Feb. Mon.–Thurs. 9 A.M.–8 P.M., Fri.–Sat. 9 A.M.– 10 P.M., Mar.–Memorial Day Mon.–Thurs. 9 A.M.–9 P.M., Fri.–Sat. 9 A.M.–10 P.M., Memorial Day–Labor Day Mon.–Thurs. 9 A.M.–10 P.M., Fri.–Sat. 9 A.M.–11 P.M., Labor Day–New Year's Day Mon.–Thurs. 9 A.M.–9 P.M., Fri.–Sat. 9 A.M.–10 P.M., 888/240-1358, www.ripleyaquariums.com/gatlinburg/, adults $23, children 6–11 $12, children 2–5 $6). Here you will see sharks,

stingrays, crabs, and lots of colorful tropical fish. There are touch tanks and daily feeding demonstrations. A highlight is walking through an underwater tunnel where you are surrounded on three sides by aquarium tanks. Ripley's latest exhibit is "Perfect Predators: SHARKS!"

◖ Arrowmont

Gatlinburg has bulldozed much of its history, but a few remnants remain. One of the best enduring is Arrowmont School of Arts and Crafts (556 Parkway, 865/436-5860, www.arrowmont.org). Arrowmont began as a settlement school for mountain folks. It opened in 1912 as the Pi Beta Phi Settlement School, named for the Pi Beta Phi fraternity. In addition to providing an education for mountain children, the school promoted local handicrafts. In 1926, Arrowcraft Shop opened in Gatlinburg as a retail outlet for local crafts.

By the mid-1960s Sevier County took over public education, and the settlement school

© KATIE RIES

Visit artists at work at the Arrowmont School of Arts and Crafts in Gatlinburg.

turned its focus to crafts. In 1970 the main studio complex was built. Today, Arrowmont is known for its contemporary arts-and-crafts education. Adults from around the country come here for one- and two-week residential programs in clay, paper, metals, fiber, glass, enamels, weaving, basketry, sculpture, polymer clay, woodturning, and woodworking, among others. **Arrowmont Galleries** (year-round Mon.–Sat. 8:30 A.M.–5 P.M., free) hold more than 10 juried, invitational, themed, and media-oriented exhibitions each year held. The art supply store and bookshop stocks tools, art materials, and other specialty items.

Located next to Arrowmont's retail outlet is the **Ogle Cabin** (556 Parkway). Built of rough-hewn logs around 1807, this cabin was the first homestead in Gatlinburg. The location was chosen by William Ogle, but he died before his family could make the move from South Carolina to the mountains of East

Tennessee. His widow, Martha Jane Huskey Ogle, and her seven children, together with her brother Peter Huskey and his family, moved to Gatlinburg—then called White Oak Flats—in 1807. The Ogle family remained in the cabin until about 1910, and in 1921 it was sold to the Pi Beta Phi fraternity, which converted it into a clinic and later a museum. Ogle and Huskey remain two of the most common names in Gatlinburg.

◖ Great Smoky Mountains Arts and Crafts Community

Craft connoisseurs should head to the Great Smoky Mountains Arts and Crafts Community (light No. 3A, E. Parkway/Hwy. 321 N., www.gatlinburgcrafts.com). The community started during the 1930s when area artisans decided that instead of selling their wares in downtown Gatlinburg, they would invite tourists out to their studios and homes. During the early years, the community featured traditional, local artisans making brooms, furniture, candles, quilts, and more.

Nowadays, authentic country craftsmen share the stage with modern artisans who have adopted new styles and media. The community, strung along eight miles of back roads, is home to more than 100 different studios, gift shops, and restaurants.

Ogle's Broom Shop (670 Glades Rd., 865/430-4402) is a third-generation workshop making brooms, walking sticks, and canes. **The Chair Shop** (830 Cantrell Cir., 865/436-7413) sells custom-designed handmade rocking chairs. One of the most remarkable stories of the community is the **Cliff Dwellers Gallery** (668 Glades Rd., 865/436-6921). This chalet-style gallery was built in downtown Gatlinburg in 1933 and served as a gallery and workshop for many years. In 1995, threatened with destruction, the building was moved to Glades Road to form part of the Great Smoky Mountains Arts and Crafts Community. It is

Broommaker David Ogle is one of the artisans you may meet on the Great Smoky Mountains Arts and Crafts Community Trail.

owned cooperatively by 6 artists and carries the work of some 60 more.

The community is located three miles east of downtown Gatlinburg, along East Parkway (Highway 321 North). The route follows Glades Road and Buckhorn Road before running back into Highway 321. The Gatlinburg Trolley travels the route of the arts community. There are also parking areas and public restrooms along the way.

Because of the sheer number of galleries, think ahead about what you seek. Pick up a copy of the arts community brochure and map, which shows the exact location of each gallery and includes a brief description of what they sell. Or visit the community's website and search for galleries selling the kinds of items you prefer.

Attractions

Attractions are Gatlinburg's special variety of fun, so much so that the Attractions Association

of Gatlinburg (www.attractions-gatlinburg.com) was formed to help keep them all straight. New attractions open each year, offering variations on the theme of mindless, family-friendly, fun activities.

Some attractions that stand out from the rest are the **Amazing Mirror Maze** (919 Parkway, 865/436-4415, daily 9 A.M.–midnight in season, daily 9 A.M.–10 P.M. off season, adults and children 10 and up $9, children 3–9 $7), touted as the world's largest, and **Ripley's Believe It or Not Odditorium** (lights Nos. 7 and 8, Parkway, 865/436-5096, daily 10 A.M.–11 P.M., adults and children 12 and up $15, children 3–11 $8), where you can see some of the strangest and most extreme sights in the world, such as two-headed cows and shrunken heads. **Mysterious Mansion** (424 River Rd., 865/436-7007, May–Oct. daily 10 A.M.–11 P.M., $9) is a classic haunted house, and **Motion Ride Movie Theater** (716 Parkway, Reagan Terrace Mall, 865/430-8985, daily 10 A.M., five and older $11–16, children under eight must be accompanied by an adult) shows eight different movies where the seats move in tandem with the on-screen action, making you feel like you're really in the cab of an 18-wheeler as it descends, without brakes, down the side of a mountain.

Other attractions in Gatlinburg fall in the category of higher-is-better. The **Space Needle** (115 Historic Nature Tr., 865/436-4629, Mon.–Thurs. 9 A.M.–11 P.M., Fri.–Sun. 9 A.M.–midnight, adults $7.95, children 5–12 $4) is more than 400 feet tall and offers 360-degree views of scenic Gatlinburg and the surrounding mountains. As if the view were not enough, there is a high-tech arcade, virtual-reality roller coaster, and minigolf inside at the base of the needle.

The **Gatlinburg Sky Lift** (light No. 7, 765 Parkway, 865/436-4307, www.gatlinburgskylift.com, Apr.–May daily 9 A.M.–9 P.M., June–Aug. daily 9 A.M.–11 P.M., Sept.–Oct. daily 9 A.M.–10 P.M., Nov.–Mar. as posted, weather permitting, adults $13, children 3–11 $9.75) is an old-fashioned attraction dating back to the

GREAT SMOKY MOUNTAINS

1950s. Take a seat in a chairlift and climb gently up 518 feet, enjoying views of Gatlinburg and the mountains along the way. This attraction is as near to a timeless pleasure as you'll find in Gatlinburg.

Festivals and Events

The **Craftsmen's Fair** (865/436-7479, www.craftsmenfair.com) takes place at the Gatlinburg Convention Center in July and October. For $6 admission, you can watch more than 180 craftspeople from around the country make traditional crafts such as baskets, pottery, brooms, and stained glass.

Shopping

The best arts-and-crafts shop in downtown Gatlinburg is **Arrowcraft** (576 Parkway, 865/436-4604), a member of the Southern Highland Craft Guild and affiliate of Arrowmont School of Arts and Crafts. The gallery has a wide selection of crafts, from jewelry to pottery to handwoven clothing, all made by regional craftspeople.

For fishing gear, go to **Smoky Mountain Angler** (466 Brookside Village Way, Ste. 8, 865/436-8746, summer Mon.–Sat. 8 A.M.–6 P.M., Sun. 10 A.M.–5 P.M., fall–spring Mon.–Sat. 8 A.M.–5 P.M., Sun. 10 A.M.–4 P.M.).

For a full-service outfitter to get you ready for day hikes or camping trips, go to **Nantahala Outdoor Center** (1138 Parkway, 865/277-8209, www.noc.com, Mon.–Sat. 10 A.M.–9 P.M., Sun. 10 A.M.–6 P.M.). Beyond the basics, this outfitter has climbing gear and clinics in fly-fishing, hiking, and bird-watching. They can also guide your river rafting or take you on a zip line.

Skiing

Yes. Skiing in the South. It is one of the outdoor pleasures of Gatlinburg. You can drive Ski Mountain Road up to **Ober Gatlinburg** (865/436-5423, www.obergatlinburg.com), but most people prefer to take the aerial tramway

(adults $11, children 7–11 $8.50) that departs from 1001 Parkway.

Ober Gatlinburg's slopes are not spectacular, but they are good for beginners and the best you'll find in this neck of the woods. In addition to skiing (adults $20–51, seniors and children 7–11 $20–41), you can enjoy year-round ice skating ($9), a black bear habitat ($7), and amusements such as an arcade, alpine slide ($7), and minigolf ($3.50).

Accommodations

There are more than 10,000 hotel rooms in and around Gatlinburg. That means even at the top of peak season, you will find a place to lay your head. Prices vary according to season; summertime and fall foliage (October) are peak periods, along with Christmas and New Year's.

While there are some high-end hostelries, Gatlinburg's specialty is affordable family-friendly lodging.

UNDER $100

Gatlinburg is chockablock with motels, particularly along River Road, the road that runs parallel to the Parkway. Some are chain motels, and others are independent. The **Riverhouse Motor Lodge** (610 River Rd., 865/436-7821, www.riverhousegatlinburg.com, $66–174) has the most secluded riverfront rooms in town. Rooms have either two queen-size beds or one king, and many come with fireplaces (gas or wood burning) and balconies overlooking the river. Rates vary based on your choice of amenities and the season. Continental breakfast is included.

Located right on the Parkway, **☾ The Gatlinburg Inn** (755 Parkway, 865/436-5133, www.gatlinburginn.com, $58–150, family suites $94–150) was the third hotel to open in Gatlinburg. Today it holds on to an aura reminiscent of times gone by. The inn was built in 1937 by R. L. Maples Sr. His wife, Wilma Maples, continues to manage the hotel. The inn has 67 rooms and seven suites. There is a swimming pool and tennis courts, and a common sitting area at the front. Lady Bird Johnson, Liberace, Dinah Shore, Tennessee Ernie Ford, and J. C. Penney stayed here, and Boudleaux and Felice Bryant wrote the song "Rocky Top" in room 388. The Gatlinburg Inn is clean and comfortable, with decor (and maids' pink uniforms) frozen in the 1970s. All in all, it is a joyful retreat from the Parkway hustle and bustle, where the hospitality is still genuine. Its motto is "clean, quiet, and comfortable." The Gatlinburg Inn is open April–October. Infant cribs are available by request. No motorcycles or motor homes permitted.

$100-150

Located on River Road, **The Edgewater Inn** (402 River Rd., 865/436-4151, www.edgewater-hotel.com, $87–139) is a full-service hotel and conference center ideal for families or business travelers. Guests enjoy free continental breakfast, indoor and outdoor swimming pools, and in-room fireplaces, plus free parking and wireless Internet.

Situated in a 1930s home, **Laurel Springs Lodge** (204 Hill St., 865/430-9211, www.laurelspringslodge.com, $129–159) is a bed-and-breakfast with five guest rooms. Each room has a private bath, television, and fine linens. Minisuites have a DVD/VCR and bathrobes. Breakfast is served each morning at 8:30 A.M. and features fresh, hearty home-style fare, although light options are also available. The inn is located within walking distance of many Gatlinburg attractions and restaurants.

Located just a few miles from the Greenbrier area of the Great Smoky Mountains National Park and five miles from Gatlinburg, **Buckhorn Inn** (2140 Tudor Mountain Rd., 865/436-4668, www.buckhorninn.com, $115–320) is a peaceful and elegant retreat. Situated in the Great Smoky Mountains Arts and Crafts Community on 25 acres of land, the Buckhorn Inn has four types of accommodations.

Standard rooms ($115–130) have king-size beds, phones, baths, and sitting areas. Premier rooms ($175) add a fireplace, private balcony, whirlpool tub, coffeemaker, and refrigerator. Private cottages ($175) offer the same amenities as a premier room but in a small private cottage. Private guesthouses ($195–320) are two-bedroom accommodations with full kitchens, fireplaces, living rooms, and ample outdoor spaces. All Buckhorn rooms are furnished in an elegant, yet homey, style. Comforts abound. Overnight guests enjoy breakfast in the sunny dining room, with views of Mount LeConte in the park. A four-course dinner is served nightly at an additional charge of $35 per person. The food at Buckhorn Inn is superb. You can pass the time walking the nature trail or strolling in Rachael's Labyrinth. Relax in the library or watch the view from the flagstone terrace. Children under 12 are not permitted at in the lodge but are welcomed in cottages and guesthouses. On weekends and holidays there is a two-night minimum stay. The innkeepers offer special packages for honeymooners, hikers, fly fishers, and others.

$150-200

Located on a mountainside far above Gatlinburg, **The Lodge at Buckberry Creek** (961 Campbell Lead Rd., 865/430-8030, www.buckberrylodge.com, $180–460) is an all-suite luxury lodge. Modeled after the Adirondack-style mountain lodge, with lots of exposed wood and rustic finishes, Buckberry feels a bit like an elite mountain club that you're lucky to be a member of. Guest suites have king-size beds, sitting areas, balconies, and kitchens. Fine dinners are served nightly in the restaurant, which is praised as one of the area's most upscale.

CHALETS AND CABINS

In addition to hotel rooms, Gatlinburg guests can stay in private cabins and "chalets." The term *chalet* traditionally referred to an

A-frame–style vacation home, but now it encompasses just about every type of vacation apartment. Most chalets and cabins offer amenities like fireplaces, whirlpool tubs, full kitchens, and balconies. They are located on the hillsides and valleys surrounding Gatlinburg.

Rates range $500–1,200 weekly for one- and two-bedroom cabins. Large four- and five-bedroom properties can cost as much as $3,000 per week. Daily rates are often available and start around $120.

There are dozens of different chalet and cabin developments, and thousands of individual properties. The best way to make a reservation is to use a reservation service. The friendly folks at **Smoky Mountain Accommodations** (865/436-6943, www.smagatlinburg.com) can recommend a property that fits within your price range and meets your needs(e.g., kid friendly, close to the park, close to Gatlinburg, etc.). On the website you can look at pictures and read a description of each property.

The Chalet Company (865/436-3029, www.thechaletcompany.com) also represents dozens of properties at various prices.

Food

Restaurants in Gatlinburg serve pancakes. Also steaks, barbecue, burgers, and other crowd-pleasing country-style food. But lots of pancakes. Snack shops sell sweets, candy, doughnuts, and other temptations. There's even a Hard Rock Café here.

The Peddler Restaurant (820 River Rd., 865/436-5794, http://peddlergatlinburg.com, Sun.–Fri. 5–10 P.M., Sat. 4:30–10 P.M., $20–40) is Gatlinburg's best steak house, with a super salad bar. In addition to New York strip, prime rib, and filet mignon, you can order fresh trout, shrimp, or blackened chicken. The extralarge salad bar comes with dinners or is available for $13 on its own.

The fine folks who own The Peddler also operate **Park Grill Steakhouse** (1110 Parkway, 865/436-2300, www.parkgrillgatlinburg.com,

opens Sat. 4:30 P.M., Sun.–Fri. 5 P.M., $20–40), giving you another good option for a hearty meal.

For breakfast all day, the **Pancake Pantry** (628 Parkway, 865/436-4724, June–Oct. daily 7 A.M.–4 P.M., Nov.–May daily 7 A.M.–3 P.M., $6–16) cannot be beat. Its 24 different varieties of pancakes share the menu with waffles, eggs, and other traditional hearty breakfast favorites. Beginning at 11:30 A.M. daily, the Pantry offers sandwiches, soups, and salads. There's a Pancake Pantry in Nashville, too, and people across the state are loyal to this restaurant.

Follow Highway 321 north 1.5 miles to Newman Road to find **C Greenbrier Restaurant** (370 Newman Rd., 865/436-6318, Sun.–Thurs. 4:30–9 P.M., Fri.–Sat. 4:30–10 P.M., $15–30), which serves dinner specialties including steak and shrimp, and indulgent desserts. Vegetarian options include sautéed vegetables with provolone cheese and pasta Alfredo. There is a children's menu ($7–8).

Information

Gatlinburg operates two visitor information centers. The first (1011 Banner Rd., 865/436-0519, Memorial Day–Oct. 31 daily 8:30 A.M.–7 P.M., Nov–May daily 8 A.M.–5:30 P.M.) is located along U.S. 441 before you arrive in the city. This is also a national park visitor information center, and it is a park-and-ride facility for the Gatlinburg Trolley.

The second (88 River Rd., 865/436-0535, Jan.–Mar. 31 Sun.–Thurs. 9 A.M.–5:30 P.M., Fri.–Sat. 9 A.M.–9:30 P.M., Apr.–Dec. 31 Sun.–Thurs. 9 A.M.–9 P.M., Fri.–Sat. 9 A.M.–9:30 P.M.) is located at traffic light No. 5, right next to Ripley's Aquarium.

To request information, contact the **Gatlinburg Chamber of Commerce** (800/588-1817, www.gatlinburg.com).

Services

The **Anna Porter Public Library** (158 Profitt Rd., 865/436-5588) has free Internet access and a

Smoky Mountain Collection where you can browse history books, guides, and nature reference books.

Gatlinburg's largest food store is **Food City** (1219 E. Parkway, 865/430-3116), located on Highway 321 opposite the Gatlinburg post office. **Parkway Liquor Store** (286 Parkway, 865/436-9635) sells wine, liquor, and premixed cocktails.

Getting There and Around

Gatlinburg is easy to find, but traffic can be intense. Vehicles creep slowly along the Parkway, and you feel more like you're cruising than driving. Parking, when you find it, costs around $2 per hour or $8 a day.

The **Gatlinburg Trolleys** are the answer. Free parking is available at the Gatlinburg Welcome Center on the Spur, outside of town, and at the municipal garage located on Highway 321. From either stop you'll pay $0.50 for the trip into town, and the trolley will deposit you right in front of the aquarium. From there you can catch rides up River Road ($0.50), out Highway 321 to the Great Smoky Mountains Arts and Crafts Community ($1), or into the national park ($2), or purchase an all-day pass ($2). Exact change is required on all routes. Or you can hoof it—walking distances in Gatlinburg are short.

Trolley route maps are available from visitors centers, by download (www.gatlinburg.com/maps/), or by calling the Mass Transit Center at 865/436-3897.

If you are traveling through Gatlinburg only to get to the national park, skip it all by taking the **Gatlinburg Bypass.** The bypass veers off Highway 441 shortly after the Gatlinburg Welcome Center and climbs the mountainside overlooking Gatlinburg. It deposits you back on Highway 441 inside the national park.

PIGEON FORGE

Nothing can truly prepare you for Pigeon Forge. This long strip of highway that lies between Gatlinburg and Sevierville on the road to the Smokies takes tacky to the 10th degree. You

can see the evolution of lowbrow consumerism here, where roadside pit stops selling concrete lawn ornaments seem quaint next to the fruits of modern-day developers' machinations, some of which have been hit by postrecession foreclosures. Consider this: In 2008 Pigeon Forge welcomed its newest development—Belle Island, a massive $110 million Disney World–esque development with 95 retail shops, 126 hotel rooms, and four major restaurants. Located on an actual island, the development went belly-up and has been demolished. But new plans were in the works for a 200-foot-tall billboard, parking, restaurants, and entertainment on the island. That's Pigeon Forge; love it or hate it, you can't keep it down.

Before you discard Pigeon Forge, consider what it has going for it. The Dollywood theme park is truly something, with its fun rides, mountain craft demonstrations, and musical performances. During the hot summer months, who can resist Dollywood's Splash Country, the crème de la crème of water parks? If shopping is on your list, then try on Pigeon Forge's myriad outlet malls. If you truly let go, then dive right in to all the rest: comedy barns, Elvis museums, indoor skydiving, bungee jumping, car museums, minigolf, and country music dinner theater.

Dollywood

There is no way around it: Dollywood (2700 Dollywood Parks Blvd., 800/365-5996, www.dollywood.com, adults $54, seniors 60 and older $49, children 4–11 $42) is just good clean fun. Owned and operated by Sevier County native Dolly Parton, the Dollywood theme park combines excellent rides with family-friendly entertainment. Mountain craft demonstrations keep Dolly's childhood alive. The park's wooden roller coaster, the Thunderhead, is thrilling and fun; at River Battle you get to aim and shoot water cannons at fellow riders; and the Blazing Fury takes you through an 1880s frontier town engulfed in flames. Dollywood

© JOHN ROOST – PARKADVISOR.COM

Thunderhead, the wooden roller coaster at Dollywood

also has plenty of less-thrilling attractions. The county fair has Ferris wheels and other classic amusements. Calico Falls Schoolhouse is a replica of a one-room mountain school, and the Dollywood Express takes you on a five-mile railroad journey through the foothills of the Smokies. There is also a bald eagle sanctuary and the Southern Gospel Music Hall of Fame.

Dollywood also offers live music. Performers on various stages play bluegrass, country, gospel, and oldies. All shows are free with your admission to Dollywood.

Arts-and-crafts demonstrations are also a big part of Dollywood. You can watch glassblowers at work, see lye soap being made, and observe candles being dipped. A blacksmith shop produces metalwork, and a woodcarver makes one-of-a-kind pieces of artwork.

As if this weren't enough, Dollywood puts on several major events each year, when special entertainment is offered. The Festival of Nations, held March–May, includes singers, dancers, and performers from around the world. Barbeque and Bluegrass, held during September, offers special concerts by bluegrass favorites, and Smoky Mountain Christmas in December is a remarkable display of lights. Other events are KidsFest (June–August) and Harvest Celebration (October–November).

For less than the price of two general admission tickets, you can buy a season pass to Dollywood. Many area residents choose this option so they can come back again and again, and so they won't feel compelled to cram everything Dollywood into a single visit.

Dollywood's doors open at 9 or 10 A.M. and close between 6 and 9 P.M., depending on the season. Call ahead or check the website to find out what time the gates open on any particular day. Dollywood is closed January–March.

Dollywood's Splash Country (light No. 8, 1198 McCarter Hollow Rd., 865/429-9910, mid-May–mid-Sept. daily 10 A.M.–6 P.M., late June–July closes at 7 P.M., adults $44, seniors

60 and older and children 4–11 $39) is a super-duper water park with 23 different rides and slides. Some are thrilling white-water adventures, and others are placid kid-friendly games. Swiftwater Run takes you round and round a tightening corkscrew until you're sent down the chute. The Cascades is an 8,000-square-foot lagoon-style pool with interactive elements ideal for younger children.

Plan to stay all day to get your money's worth. On top of the admission fee, you'll pay $8 for parking unless you have a gold season pass or gold super season pass. Guests are not permitted to bring coolers, food, or other picnic goods inside the park, although you can leave the park and return later in the day. Food is available for purchase.

Children under 13 are not allowed in Splash Country without an adult.

Other Sights

Pigeon Forge's city park is **Patriot Park,** located behind the Old Mill. Named for the Patriot Bomber that is on permanent display, the park is the site of festivals, fairs, and other events.

You can't help but notice **WonderWorks** (Parkway, 865/868-1800, www.wonderworks-tn.com, daily 9 A.M.–midnight, adults 13 and up $23, children 4–12 and seniors 55 and up $15), whose facade is turned completely upside down. The illusion is merely cosmetic, but it sets the stage for the over-the-top kid-friendly activities inside. WonderWorks includes a disaster zone where you can feel what it would be like to experience a major earthquake or hurricane. There is a gallery of optical illusions, and laser tag ($7 extra). WonderWorks is also home to *Terry Evanswood: The Wonders of Magic,* a family-friendly magic show that is staged several times a day.

The **Hollywood Wax Museum** (106 Showplace Blvd., 865/428-5228, www.hollywoodwaxmuseum.com/pigeonforge, daily 9 A.M.–10 P.M., closes at midnight many weekends and during summer, adults $17.95, children $8.95) was moved from Gatlinburg to Pigeon Forge. Look for the giant King Kong replica hanging from the building. Inside you'll see wax creations of other celebrities, both real and imagined. The museum is pure camp, but it's fun. Check the website for online discounts on tickets before you head over.

Entertainment

Gaudy stage entertainment is another Pigeon Forge hallmark. Massive theater complexes line the Parkway, surrounded by even more massive parking lots. **Country Tonite** (129 Showplace Blvd., 865/453-2003, www.countrytonitepf.com, adults $29, children 12 and up $19.75) is a country music show with patriotic and gospel thrown in. **The Comedy Barn** (2775 Parkway, 865/428-5222, www.comedybarn.com, adults $34, one free ticket for a child 11 and under per adult ticket, otherwise $12) offers terribly hokey country-style comedy.

Memories Theatre (140 Showplace Blvd., 865/428-7852, www.memoriestheatre.com, adults $27, seniors $25, teens $20, children 6–11 $5, children 5 and under free) is one of the longest-running shows in town, with perennial Elvis tribute shows plus tributes to other stars such as Dolly Parton and Garth Brooks.

The most famous of dinner theaters is the **Dixie Stampede** (3849 Parkway, 865/453-4400, www.dixiestampede.com, adults $48–55, children 4–11 $24–30). Here guests are seated around a circular arena where actors and animals put on a rodeo-inspired dinner show. A four-course barbecue meal is served while you watch.

Shopping

Pigeon Forge is a destination for outlet shopping. **Pigeon River Crossings** (2655 Teaster Ln., 865/453-7316, www.pigeonrivercrossings.com/) houses dozens of name-brand discount stores, such as Bass, Dress Barn, Izod, and Rue 21. Right next door, at the **Shoppes of Pigeon Forge** (161 E. Wears Valley Rd.), you'll find Eddie Bauer, Burlington Brands, and Reebok Outlet Stores.

The **Factory Outlet Mall of Pigeon Forge** (2850 Parkway) is easily identified by its red roof. It isn't the destination it once was (at press time more than half the space was available for lease), but here you'll find Corningware, Osh Kosh, and New York New York, plus clothing and shoe outlets.

Though it is technically located inside Sevierville's city limits, the **Tanger Five Oaks Mall** (1645 Parkway, Sevierville, 865/453-1053) is Pigeon Forge at heart. Five Oaks is the area's newest and largest outlet mall, with Old Navy, Gap, Van Heusen, Brooks Brothers, and Reebok, among many others. Many retailers relocated here from other outlet malls.

Most outlet malls open at 10 A.M. during the winter and 9 A.M. during summer. They usually stay open until sunset.

Pigeon Forge Pottery was a Pigeon Forge institution. In 1946, Douglas Ferguson established the business, and over the years he formed a reputation for excellent pottery. Visitors enjoyed watching craftspeople work when they visited the shop, and the pottery's famous black bears were collector's items. Ferguson died in 2000, and the pottery was sold to the Old Mill. Today, **Pigeon River Pottery** (Old Mill Sq., 865/428-0771) sells beautiful handmade pottery in a variety of styles, but you won't find many of the designs that made the pottery famous in the first place. Check the seconds corner for discounted pieces.

Recreation

Pigeon Forge leads the United States in far-fetched extreme activities—the type of thing you'll be talking about after you get home.

Case in point: Pigeon Forge was the first U.S. location of Zorb, the New Zealand–invented sport of rolling downhill in an 11-foot inflatable ball. In Zorbit, you are harnessed in

and watch as the world spins around as you roll 600 feet downhill. In Zydro, they throw in a bucket of water, and you cascade downhill in a cross between a waterslide and a roller coaster. A ride costs $35–70, but prices decrease if you have a larger group. **Smoky Mountain Zorb** (203 Sugar Hollow Rd., 865/428-2422, www.zorb.com/smoky, Sept.–Feb. Mon. and Wed.–Thurs. 10 A.M.–5 P.M., Fri.–Sun. 9 A.M.–5 P.M., Mar.–May daily 9 A.M.–5 P.M., June Mon.–Thurs. 10 A.M.–6 P.M., Fri.–Sat. 9 A.M.–7 P.M., Sun. 9 A.M.–6 P.M., July Mon.–Thurs. 10 A.M.–7 P.M., Fri.–Sun. 9 A.M.–7 P.M., Aug. Mon.–Thurs. 10 A.M.–6 P.M., Fri.–Sun. 9 A.M.–6 P.M.) is located near traffic light No. 1 in Pigeon Forge.

Indoor skydiving is a Pigeon Forge tradition. At **Flyaway** (3106 Parkway, 877/293-0639, www.flyawayindoorskydiving.com, daily 10 A.M.–7 P.M., $34) you can "body fly" in a vertical wind tunnel. You'll get about 20 minutes of instruction, plus the use of a suit, helmet, and other safety gear. Then you'll get about three minutes of flying time inside the tunnel. What fun!

Finally, there is bungee jumping at **The Track** (2575 Parkway, 865/453-4777, www.pigeonforgetrack.com, $16). Jump from a 65-foot platform attached by a harness and elastic bungee cord. The Track also has bumper cars, go-karts, and an arcade.

Food

Like Gatlinburg, Pigeon Forge has a lot of family-friendly eateries, chain restaurants, and a lot of places to grab pancakes.

The **Old Mill** (175 Old Mill Ave. at light No. 7, 865/428-0771, www.old-mill.com, daily 8 A.M.–9 P.M., $5–25) is a favorite for Southern-style dining. Come here for hearty meals all day—the dinner menu offers no fewer than five different Southern fried specialties: chicken, steak, pork chop, beef liver, and country ham.

Mel's Diner (119 Wears Valley Rd.,

865/429-2184, www.melsdinerpf.com, daily 7 a.m.–midnight, $6–9) is a classic diner in the traditional sense, with affordable breakfasts (pancakes, of course), burgers, and other items from the grill, plus the iconic facade.

Getting Around

Pigeon Forge and Sevierville have joined forces to offer the **Fun Time Trolley** (865/453-6444, www.pigeonforgetrolley.org). All trolleys originate at Patriot Park. The **North Parkway Trolley** ($0.50) travels north through Pigeon Forge and continues on into the city of Sevierville. After traveling north to the Governor's Crossing and Walmart areas, it turns south again and returns to Patriot Park. The **South Parkway Trolley** ($0.50) travels north to traffic light No. 6, then turns west bound onto Pine Mountain Road. It then travels to the south city limits, serving campgrounds in the area and the Dixie Stampede before returning to Patriot Park. The **Gatlinburg Welcome Center Trolley** ($0.75) travels nonstop to the Gatlinburg Welcome Center on the spur just outside the city. The **Dollywood Trolley** ($0.50) travels to and from Dollywood. The **Splash Country Trolley** ($0.50) goes to and from Splash Country. The **Wears Valley Trolley** ($0.50) travels north on Teaster Lane through the Pigeon River Crossing/Riverview Mall area to traffic light No. 2 on the Parkway. From light No. 2 it goes to Community Center Drive, McGill Street, and then on to Wears Valley Road, continuing past campgrounds and other businesses to the city limits before returning to Patriot Park by the same route. The **Courthouse Trolley** ($0.50) travels north on Teaster Lane, passing through mall areas and entering the Parkway northbound at traffic light No. 2. It continues north into downtown Sevierville before turning around at the Sevier County Courthouse. Stops include Tanger Five Oaks Mall, Walmart, Kmart, and the River Place Shops.

Trolleys run early March–October daily 8:30 a.m.–midnight and November–December daily 10 a.m.–10 p.m. Exact fare is required, and fare applies each time you get on the trolley. Parkway trolleys run every 20–25 minutes, Dollywood trolleys every 15–20 minutes, Wears Valley trolleys every 40–45 minutes, the Gatlinburg Welcome Center trolley every 20–25 minutes, and the Courthouse trolley runs every 25 minutes.

SEVIERVILLE

It used to be that the sprawl of malls, oversized theaters, restaurants, and tourist attractions was pretty much contained to Pigeon Forge. Sevierville (se-VEER-ville), the Sevier County seat and first city on the journey from interstate to national park, was a laid-back place. But the lure of tapping into tourist dollars was too much, and Sevierville is beginning to look like a young Pigeon Forge. Shopping malls, giant flea markets, minigolf, and hotels now line the entire route along Highways 66 and 441. The old city center of Sevierville is just a dot on the map.

Sights

Sevier County's elegant Victorian courthouse dominates the Sevierville skyline. Stop here to see a life-size statue of a willowy young Dolly Parton, Sevier County's hometown girl.

Located at the Sevierville municipal airport, the **Tennessee Museum of Aviation** (135 Air Museum Way, 865/908-0171 or 866/286-8738, www.tnairmuseum.org, Mon.–Sat. 10 a.m.–6 p.m., Sun. 1–6 p.m., adults $12.75, seniors $9.75, children 6–12 $6.75, children under 6 free) is an enthusiast's dream. Glass-enclosed cases display memorabilia associated with Tennessee aviation, and the heated exhibit hangar houses airworthy planes, including two P-47D Thunderbolts and a Navy TBM Avenger. The aviation museum is located two miles outside of downtown Sevierville along Highway 411. Look for the signs to the airport and aviation museum.

Entertainment

Sevier County's only movie theater is **Reel Theatres** (Hwy. 66, 865/453-9055, www.reel-theatres-sevier.com), located one mile north of downtown Sevierville along Highway 66. Its screens show first-run movies daily.

Recreation

The Knoxville K-Jays moved east to Sevier County in 2000 and became the **Tennessee Smokies** (Hwy. 66, 865/286-2300, www.smokiesbaseball.com, field-level seats: adults $9, seniors and children $8, bleacher seats: adults $7, seniors and children $6, grass berm seating $6). The Smokies, a AA Cubs affiliate, play in a stadium located right next to I-40 at exit 407. The regular season runs April–August. Smokies games are heavy on between-inning entertainment and promotions. Special no-alcohol seating areas are available. Reserved-seat tickets are $1 more if you buy them at the gate. Advance tickets are available online and in person at the Smokies box office.

For something totally different, sign up for a hot-air balloon ride with **Smoky Mountain Balloon Adventures** (865/622-1394, www.smokymtnballoons.com). For $249 per adult (less if you agree to join up with another group), you'll get 1–1.5 hours in a hot-air balloon, floating over the foothills of the Smokies. These are private balloon trips; you'll be with members of your own party and will only be put in with another group if you arrange it that way at the time of your reservation. Typically you'll meet at the Starbucks (646 Winfield Dunn Pkwy./Hwy. 66) in Sevierville and be shuttled to the launch site, but you'll get directions when you book. Launch sites vary based on wind and weather conditions. After your flight, you'll enjoy a toast with the captain, and you'll get a special certificate as a keepsake. Balloon flights are offered April–November. Most flights depart early in the morning or late in the afternoon and reach 1,500–2,000 feet above the ground.

The **Wilderness at the Smokies Resort** (1424 Old Knoxville Hwy., 877/325-9453, www.wildernessatthesmokies.com) is for families who want a little adrenaline on their vacation and didn't get it in Pigeon Forge. After all, one of its water park rides features a trap door launching pad and a gravity-powered loop-the-loop experience at 2.5 g (g-force). The resort has both "dry" amusement-park-type rides and both indoor and outdoor water parks, plus a conference center, hotel, and other resort amenities.

Food

One of Sevierville's most beloved restaurants is the ◖ **Applewood Farmhouse Restaurant** (240 Apple Valley Rd., 865/428-1222, daily 8 A.M.–9 P.M., $7–20), a country-cooking institution. Applewood is located next to the Apple Barn, a general store and cider press where you can watch as apple cider and other goodies (from apples) are being made.

Getting Around

Traffic congestion is a problem in Sevierville. In 2006, officials opened State Route 448, which is supposed to speed up your journey through town. Traffic headed toward Pigeon Forge and the national park should remain on Highway 441 (the Parkway), but traffic headed in the other direction, toward the interstate, should follow the signs to the new Route 448 through town.

An even newer alternate route worth noting is Veteran's Drive, or Highway 449. This four-lane divided highway runs from Highway 411 to Pigeon Forge, bypassing the sprawl and traffic lights. You enter Pigeon Forge near Dollywood.

COSBY

Located on the northeastern side of the Great Smoky Mountains, Cosby is a rural town with services and accommodations for visitors. From the Cosby entrance to the park, you can explore Cosby campground and picnic area, hike to Henwallow Falls or Mount Cammerer, or join up with the Appalachian Trail.

COURTESY OF WILDERNESS AT THE SMOKIES RESORT

The Wild Vortex waterslide at the Wilderness at the Smokies Resort is big fun on a hot day.

Historically, Cosby was known as a moonshiners' town. Today, it is home to artists and craftspeople. Near Cosby, the town of Hartford is noted for white-water rafting, and Newport is a center for commerce in the area.

Arts and Crafts

Holloway's Country Home Quilts (3892 Cosby Hwy./Hwy. 321, 423/487-3866) is a quilter's studio, quilting supply store, and place to purchase finished quilts and other mountain handicrafts. Holloway's is a cozy, welcoming place, jam-packed with goodies of interest to quilters and nonquilters alike. Pop in next door at the studio to see a quilter at work.

Look for the barn board building where the Cosby Highway intersects with Wilton Springs Road to find **Santa Cruz Woodworks** (2776 Cosby Hwy./Hwy. 321, 423/623-7856). Bob and Cindy Evans make solid wood cabinets, rocking chairs, birdhouses, trunks, and much more. Browse the shop or put in your custom order.

River Rafting

Near the town of Hartford, the Pigeon River is a popular venue for **white-water rafting.** The Upper Pigeon offers fast-paced class III and IV rapids while the Lower Pigeon is placid and peaceful. Outfitters offer trips on both sections of river, but not every day. Since the Pigeon is a dam-controlled river, as are most in the state, trips are offered only when there is water on which to raft. Make your reservations in advance.

Outfitters including **Wildwater Ltd.** (866/319-8870, www.wildwaterrafting.com) and the **Nantahala Outdoor Center** (NOC) (888/905-7238, www.noc.com) offer journeys on both parts of the river. All outfitters are located along Old Hartford Road, at exit 477 off I-40. NOC also offers stand-up paddling classes and a number of other water-based activities for all ages and ability levels. NOC is one of the country's top water-education centers. If you're the kind of traveler who plans

GREAT SMOKY MOUNTAINS

vacations around access to white water, check out their offerings in advance.

Llama Trekking

For a truly upscale day hike or a luxurious backpacking expedition, consider llama trekking. Let the llamas carry your picnic or overnight gear while you walk comfortably to destinations in the Cherokee National Forest and Nantahala National Forest (llamas aren't permitted in the Great Smoky Mountains National Park). **English Mountain Llama Treks** (828/622-9686) in Newport offers day trips for $75–100 a person. A two-day trip costs $280 per person, and a three-day trip is $380; all gear and food are provided. The owner also operates horse trail rides.

Accommodations

The nine-room **Christopher Place** (1500 Pinnacles Way, Newport, 423/623-6555, www.christopherplace.com, $150–330) is an intimate and elegant bed-and-breakfast. Located near Newport, atop English Mountain, this colonial-style resort with a European atmosphere is perfect for a romantic getaway. Guests may walk the extensive grounds, play tennis, work out in the fitness room, swim in the pool, or relax in the billiards room or library. You may also simply want to retreat to your suite, which is appointed with luxurious furnishings and private bath. Some rooms also have private balconies overlooking the mountains. Christopher Place guests enjoy a full breakfast as part of their room rate. Dinner is served nightly at the Mountain View Dining Room for an additional $40 per person. Reservations are required 24 hours in advance.

Not just a place to stay, the **French Broad Outpost Ranch** (461 Old River Rd., Del Rio, 423/487-3147, www.frenchbroadriver.com, $200–250) is a place to go. This dude ranch offers overnight accommodations in the Rough Cut, a Western-style lodge, and daily horseback riding, ranching, and white-water rafting excursions. Meals are included in the rates, which are $250 per adult per night during the high season and $200 in the low season. Slightly lower prices are offered for children, and week-long packages are available. Prices include all of the activities in which you'll partake at the ranch. Rooms are rustic and designed to sleep families or groups. Meals are served family-style and feature hearty meat-and-potatoes fare.

Food

C Carver's Applehouse Restaurant (3460 Cosby Hwy./Hwy. 321, 423/487-2710, daily 8 A.M.–8 P.M., $6–16) is country dining the way it ought to be. The dining room overlooks the Carver apple orchard, and the home-style fare is comforting and tasty. Each meal—breakfast, lunch, or dinner—comes with sweet-savory apple fritters and a glass of homemade apple cider. The apple-smoked barbecue is a standout, as is the chicken potpie. Other choices include steaks, chicken, and fresh mountain trout—grilled or fried. The breakfast menu is extensive, with eggs, pancakes, fried potatoes, and more.

Next door to the restaurant is a farmers market that sells fresh apples and other local specialties.

The folks in Cosby know that as strange as it may seem, homemade Mexican food goes well with homegrown mountain music. The **C Front Porch Mexican Restaurant** (2912 Cosby Hwy./Hwy. 321, 423/487-2875, Fri.–Sat. 5–10:30 P.M., Sun. 5–9:30 P.M., $10–20) serves real homemade food—it's not your run-of-the-mill Mexican restaurant. The enchiladas, burritos, and chiles rellenos are made from scratch with fresh ingredients. On Friday and Saturday at 7 and 9 P.M., local musicians take the stage to play bluegrass and folk music. Overall, it's a dining experience not to be missed. The Front Porch is closed in December and January.

For fine dining, make reservations at least 24 hours in advance at the **Mountain View**

Restaurant (1500 Pinnacles Way, 423/623-6555, Tues.–Sat. 7–9 P.M., $40), the restaurant at upscale Christopher Place resort on English Mountain, near Newport. Dinner is served at 7 P.M., and diners must choose their entrée when they make their reservation the day before. The food is excellent, and the refined ambience perfect for that special occasion. For something decidedly more casual, go to Christopher Place's **Marston's Library Pub** (1500 Pinnacles Way, 423/623-6555, Sun.–Mon. 5:30–8 P.M., $12–15), which serves casual English-style food without advance reservations. Menu options are bangers and mash, fish-and-chips, or a ploughman's lunch of sliced meats, bread, cheese, and mixed greens.

TOWNSEND

Located in the broad flat plain of Tuckaleechee Cove, Townsend is a world apart from Pigeon Forge and Gatlinburg. This park gateway, which provides quick access to Cades Cove and the Little River Road, seems to have the proportions just right: There is still a lot of undisturbed green space surrounding a few hotels, restaurants, and the only heritage center this side of the Smokies. Outfitters rent tubes for floating down the Little River, and Tuckaleechee Caverns are nearby for underground exploring.

Recent archaeological digs found evidence of human settlement in the Tuckaleechee Cove as many as 10,000 years ago. During the early 20th century, Townsend was the end of the railroad line; timber cut from forests inside what is now the national park was floated down the river and loaded onto railcars here in Townsend.

Sights

For an introduction to the history and culture of Townsend and the surrounding park area, visit the **Great Smoky Mountains Heritage Center** (123 Cromwell Dr., 865/448-0044, www.gsmheritagecenter.org, Mon.–Sat. 10 A.M.–5 P.M.,

adults $6, seniors and children 6–17 $4). Exhibits here describe the remarkable archaeological finds made in Townsend and explain what scientists have learned from their discoveries. There are interactive exhibits about the lifestyles and culture of Native Americans who lived in the mountains, as well as the white settlers who carved out a life here beginning in the 1700s. Another exhibit, "Tennessee on the Move," describes just how hard it was to get around the mountains before paved roads and advanced automobiles. Outside, you can tour replicas of mountain cabins, a gristmill, cantilever barn, and smokehouse. There is an outdoor amphitheater and indoor auditorium for special events. The street address does not work well on a GPS. To get to the center from Townsend, drive toward the Smoky Mountains, through the stoplight, for 0.75 mile. The center will be on the right.

The **Little River Railroad and Lumber Museum** (Hwy. 321, 865/448-2211, June–Aug. and Oct. Mon.–Sat. 10 A.M.–5 P.M., Sun. 1–5 P.M., Apr.–May, Sept., and Nov. Sat. 10 A.M.–5 P.M., Sun. 1–5 P.M., call for an appointment Dec.–Mar., free) is more than another railroad museum. It is also a place to learn about the extensive logging that took place in the Smokies during the early 20th century. Originally called Tuckaleechee Cove, Townsend got its name from the founder of the Little River Railroad and Lumber Company, Col. W. B. Townsend. Exhibits here include antique railroad equipment and photographs from the era of railroads and logging in the Smokies.

Tuckaleechee Caverns (825 Cavern Rd., 865/448-2274, daily 10 A.M.–6 P.M., adults $15, children 5–11 $7) is the oldest tourist attraction in these parts. The caverns were known to Native Americans and early white settlers who would travel to the mouth of the caves on hot summer days to cool off. In the early 1950s, local residents W. E. Vananda and Harry Myers invested their savings into making the caves a tourist attraction, because no bank would loan to them. A year after the caverns first opened to the public, its greatest attraction—its underground Big Room—was discovered. The Big Room, part of the one-mile underground tour, is 300 feet by 400 feet, with ceilings of up to 150 feet high. The cave maintains a constant 58°F temperature, and it's open rain or shine.

Watch dulcimers and other mountain instruments being made at **Wood-n-Strings Dulcimer Shop** (7645 E. Lamar Alexander Pkwy., 865/448-6647, www.clemmerdulcimer. com, hours vary, call ahead). This music shop also hosts a free "Pickin' Porch" on Saturday at 7 P.M. during the summer. Call or check their website for a schedule.

Tubing

Tubing may be the lazy man's version of river rafting, but, boy, is it fun! Plunk your behind down in the middle of an inner tube and float on down the river. It's that simple.

Tubing is great for the whole family and the perfect way to cool off on a hot day (and there are plenty of hot days in Tennessee). Be sure to wear shoes and sunscreen; a pair of sturdy-bottomed shorts is also recommended.

There are several tubing outfitters in Townsend, including **Smoky Mountain River Rat** (205 Wears Valley Rd., 865/448-8888, www.smokymtnriverrat.com, May–Sept. daily 10 A.M.–6 P.M., $13). Outfitters transport you a mile or so up the river and let you float back down to the starting point.

Festivals and Events

During the summer and fall, the **Sunset Concert Series** (Great Smoky Mountains Heritage Center, 123 Cromwell Dr., 865/448-0044, www.gsmheritagecenter.org) offers live music in a lovely outdoor amphitheater. The heritage center also puts on the **Spring Festival Day** in May.

Accommodations

Located right on the main highway in Townsend, **Highland Manor Inn** (7766 E. Lamar Alexander Pkwy., 800/213-9462, www. highlandmanor.com, $60–100) is a respectable motor inn with king- and queen-size rooms. All rooms have refrigerators, and guests receive free continental breakfast and use of the outdoor swimming pool and playground.

The 10-room **Richmont Inn** (220 Winterberry Ln., 865/448-6751, www.rich-montinn.com, $160–275) offers guest rooms and suites, all named for notable Smoky Mountains people and decorated in a tasteful yet rustic style. Guests enjoy a full breakfast featuring homemade breads, plus healthy and hearty options. Evening dessert is served by candlelight with gourmet coffee. Both are served in the inn's dining room, with panoramic views of the mountains.

Dancing Bear Lodge (137 Apple Valley Way, 865/448-6000, www.dancingbearlodge.com, $139–339) offers both guest rooms and one- and two-bedroom cabins with a pronounced upscale edge. The lodge has a rustic feel—afforded by lots of wood finishes and botanical artwork—with refined touches like feather beds and hot tubs. Cabins feature full kitchens, wood-burning fireplaces, and private porches. Guests are invited to a top-notch continental breakfast each morning, and they may make reservations for dinner in the lodge restaurant, which features the only full bar in Townsend. Guests are also invited to lounge in front of the lodge fireplace in the lobby or on the porch overlooking the mountains.

The Smokies' most luxurious accommodations are, without a doubt, at **◖ Blackberry Farm** (1471 W. Millers Cove Rd., Walland, 865/380-2260, www.blackberryfarm.com, $745–2,000). A 4,200-acre working farm located in unblemished seclusion not far from Townsend, Blackberry Farm is a true upscale resort. A member of the Relais and Chateaux group of resorts and perennial member of the elite circle of top U.S. resorts, Blackberry Farm is a remarkable place to stay. While the refined elegance of meals and atmosphere seems far removed from the rustic, down-home character of the Smokies, the closeness to the land and unspoiled nature of the property bring guests straight to the marvelous beauty of this corner of the world.

Blackberry Farm has 63 guest accommodations, including rooms, suites, cottages, and houses. All rooms are carefully appointed and leave nothing to be desired. Rates include three meals a day, many of which are prepared with organic meats and produce raised right on the farm. The food served at Blackberry Farm is simply unparalleled in these parts and combines the best of regional ingredients with sophisticated culinary techniques.

Blackberry Farm may not be for most of us, but hats are off to those who can afford this special type of Smoky Mountains luxury.

Food

Coming to ◖ **Sister Cats Cafe** (7327 E. Lamar Alexander Pkwy., 865/438-4435, Mon. Tues. and Thurs.–Sat. 11 A.M.–3 P.M., $9) is a highlight of any trip to Townsend. This casual yet sophisticated restaurant offers refreshingly creative fare. Entrées include smoked chicken salad and an array of panini—including a vegetarian smoked portobello. A changing daily special may be spinach enchiladas or Italian-sausage lasagna roll. Sides are creative and unexpected: grape salad, mandarin muffins, and corn-bread salad are a few favorites. A unique feature of Sister Cats' menu is that all lunches cost $9 and include one entrée and one side. Every other Friday evening, Sister Cats puts on a special romantic dinner by reservation only.

Miss Lily's Cafe (122 Depot St., 865/448-1924, Mon.–Sat. 11 A.M.–9 P.M., Sun. 10 A.M.–2 P.M., $11–20) serves Southern food, but with a freshness unknown at many country-cooking-style restaurants. Try the Yankee pot roast or fish and grits. Salads are fresh and filling. The pulled-pork sandwich is a favorite at lunch or dinner.

Miss Lily's Cafe is next door to the Lily Barn, a venue for weddings and other special events. The barn also sells daylilies, and the gardens are ideal for a picturesque stroll after dinner.

You can catch your own supper at the **Tuckaleechee Trout Farm and Restaurant** (142 Tipton Rd., 865/448-2290, Apr.–Oct. Tues.–Sun. 4–8 P.M.). Spring-fed trout ponds teem with fish. Catch your own, or let the staff catch one for you. Either way, the capable staff will clean and cook your dinner. It doesn't get any fresher, or more fun, than this. Call ahead to confirm hours.

GREAT SMOKY MOUNTAINS

THE FIRST FRONTIER

The mountains and valleys of Tennessee's northeastern tip were the first frontier of settlement during the 18th century. Old towns and historic sites—including the birthplace of Davy Crockett, the tailor shop of an American president, and Tennessee's first capitol—are the legacy of this rich history. Modern-day cities including Jonesborough and Elizabethton have preserved their historic buildings and are now among the best places to soak in the atmosphere of early Tennessee.

The easternmost band of land in Tennessee is the Cherokee National Forest, and it is some of the most beautiful landscape in the state, with rhododendron gardens, cranberry bogs, and high mountain vistas. The Appalachian Trail and other hiking paths are ideal for exploring on foot; winding blacktop roads invite auto touring. Friendly mountain towns like Mountain City, Erwin, and Unicoi provide the essentials for exploring this still-wild part of Tennessee.

West of the mountains lie the Tri-Cities: Bristol, Kingsport, and Johnson City, each with its own unique character. Bristol straddles the state line with Virginia and is known as the place where the first country music stars were discovered (not to mention a big NASCAR track). Johnson City is home to East Tennessee State University and a state-of-the-art fossil museum. Kingsport, a leader in downtown revitalization, has a pleasant, walkable downtown district. Together, the Tri-Cities serve as the unofficial

HIGHLIGHTS

LOOK FOR ◖ TO FIND RECOMMENDED SIGHTS, ACTIVITIES, DINING, AND LODGING.

◖ **Bristol Motor Speedway:** This modern-day temple to speed and adrenaline is a popular stop on the NASCAR circuit (page 450).

◖ **Gray Fossil Site:** Road crews discovered this major fossil site near Johnson City in 2000; now it's home to an interactive and educational museum of prehistoric Tennessee (page 457).

◖ **Roan Mountain:** With dramatic mountain peaks, mysterious balds, and the beauty of rhododendron gardens, Roan Mountain lets you experience the natural beauty and the majesty of the Southern mountains (page 466).

◖ **National Storytelling Festival:** Be enter-tained by the world's best storytellers from African, European, Native American, and Appalachian traditions at this annual event (page 472).

◖ **Andrew Johnson National Historic Site:** The home and tailor shop of Andrew Johnson in Greeneville are a memorial to one of the most controversial commanders in chief in this country's history (page 475).

◖ **Kyles Ford:** This small town on the Clinch River is representative of the rural, remote communities of the Appalachian region. A top-notch country restaurant and ecovillage make it a worthy destination (page 481).

capital cities of the rugged mountain region of upper East Tennessee and southwest Virginia.

West of the Tri-Cities the landscape becomes a series of long valleys divided by steep ridges. Tucked into this ridge-and-valley landscape is the city of Greeneville, hometown of U.S. president Andrew Johnson. A staunch Unionist in a secessionist state, Johnson's story evinces the complexity of Civil War history in this border state. Rogersville is home to the oldest newspaper press in Tennessee. As you leave the cities

and strike out over the countryside of this isolated and enchanting landscape, you realize that Tennessee's first frontier is also quite likely its last.

PLANNING YOUR TIME

If you want to see all of northeastern Tennessee, plan on at least a week. This is dense territory: It may look compact on a map, but narrow, windy roads and steep mountains and ridges make travel slow.

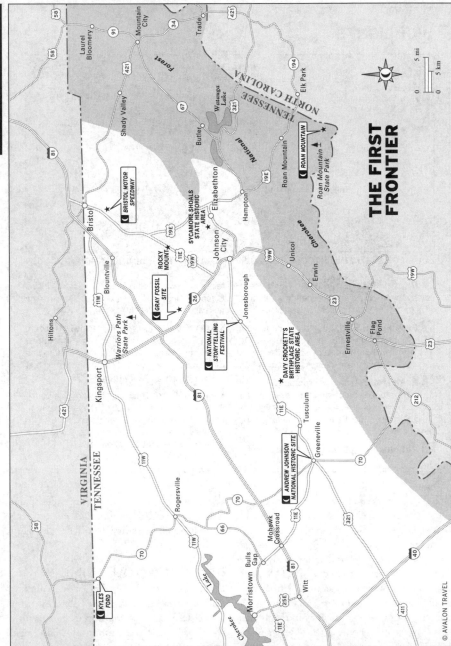

THE FIRST FRONTIER

© AVALON TRAVEL

If you have less than a week, choose a sub-region as your focus. The Tri-Cities offer the greatest diversity of attractions: motor speed-ways, historic sites, fossils, and live music. If you enjoy the outdoors, focus on the north-ern Cherokee National Forest; spend your time auto touring, hiking, and rafting along the Nolichucky River. The remote ridges and valleys in the western area of this region are an ideal destination if you want to leave the hustle and bustle behind and see some of the most re-mote territory in the state.

The Tri-Cities

It was an accident of history that three midsize cities grew up so close to one another. Bristol and Johnson City were small hamlets until the railroads came through these parts; Kingsport was a quiet river port until it became a planned industrial city at the turn of the 20th century.

The Tri-Cities region has a total population of about 500,000. Johnson City is the largest of the three, closely followed by Bristol and then Kingsport. They are separated by no more than 30 miles each and form a triangle of urban and suburban sprawl.

Because of their proximity to each other, you can stay in one Tri-City and tour all three. They are also convenient to the northern Cherokee National Forest, Jonesborough, and Elizabethton. If you come for general sightsee-ing, be sure not to plan your trip to coincide with a major event at Bristol Motor Speedway, when hotels are full and the roads are clogged.

Getting There

Tri-Cities Regional Airport (TRI or TCRA, 2525 Hwy. 75, 423/325-6000, www.triflight.com) is lo-cated equidistant from each of the Tri Cities. This small airport offers general aviation services as well as commercial flights to hub airports in the region.

Three airlines serve the Tri-Cities. Allegiant Air has nonstop service from Orlando and Tampa Bay; Delta Connection flies from Atlanta and Cincinnati; and US Airways Express flies from Charlotte to the Tri-Cities.

Getting Around

Getting around the Tri-Cities is easy, although

a little confusing thanks to the sheer number of roads. I-26 connects Kingsport and Johnson City, and I-81 connects Bristol with points south. U.S. 11E/19W, also called the Bristol Highway, connects Bristol and Johnson City. U.S. 11W connects Kingsport and Bristol.

BRISTOL

Long before the U.S. Congress declared Bristol the birthplace of country music, this city was closely associated with traditional mountain music. It was here in 1927 that a record pro-ducer named Ralph Peer came to record local musicians. During these now-famous Bristol Sessions, Peer recorded the Carter Family and Jimmie Rodgers, who have been credited as the first popular country music stars.

Bristol was first named Sapling Grove, and from its founding in 1771 until the late 19th century it was nothing more than a rural country hamlet. But then the railroads came to town—Southern Railway and the Norfolk and Western Railroad—and a modern, indus-trial city was born.

Bristol famously straddles two states, and its main drag, appropriately called State Street, follows the state line between Tennessee and Virginia. South of the city is Bristol's biggest attraction, the Bristol Motor Speedway, which draws a quarter million people on major race days twice annually.

Sights

State Street is a pleasant four-block row of

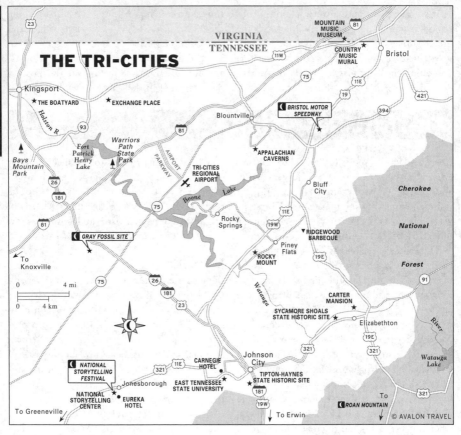

retail shops and professional offices, with a few restaurants and bars along the way. The city's most famous landmark is the **Bristol VA-TENN Sign,** which spans the eastern end of the street. Erected in 1910, the first city slogan to appear was "Push—That's Bristol." In 1921, after a citywide contest was held, the slogan was changed to today's "A Good Place to Live." If you drive down State Street headed east, it is fun to watch the sign come into clearer and clearer focus as you approach.

Another Bristol landmark is the *Country Music Mural,* painted in 1987, which depicts heroes of the city's country music story. The mural features the Carter Family, Jimmie

Rodgers, and Ralph Peer, the record producer who orchestrated the 1927 Bristol Sessions. The park at the foot of the mural is a venue for public concerts and the weekly State Street Farmers Market, which takes place May–October.

The **Bristol Depot** (corner of E. State St. and Martin Luther King Blvd., 276/644-1573) was built in 1902 for less than $80,000. This handsome brick two-story train station was a busy passenger and freight depot from its construction until the 1970s. It was restored for Bristol's 150th anniversary in 2006. About 12 freight trains continue to pass through each day.

The 1902 redbrick home of Bristol

THE BRISTOL SESSIONS

By the mid-1920s, a genre of music variously called "old-time music," "old Southern tunes," "hill-country tunes," and "hillbilly music" was gaining popularity. The first fiddle record was made in 1922 and the first country vocal record made a year later. Early recording artists like Charley Oaks, Uncle Am Stuart, George Reneau, and Uncle Dave Macon made records that were distributed on a small scale by a Knoxville music promoter named Gus Nennsteil.

Soon major-label record executives sensed that something was happening down South. Beginning in 1926, record companies began to organize "field sessions" so artists could be recorded without having to make an expensive trip to New York. The sessions that took place in Bristol in July and August 1927 proved that country music—as it eventually came to be called—both sounded good and could be a commercial success.

It was Victor Talking Machine Company talent scout Ralph Peer who ran the Bristol sessions. He chose Bristol because it was the largest urban center in the Appalachian region. Peer, who had run previous field sessions for Victor and other music labels, set up his studio in a hat warehouse on State Street. Advertisements in the newspaper initially generated limited response, but when news emerged that artists were being paid up to $100 in cash on the spot and could earn more in royalties, Peer had to schedule night sessions to accommodate everyone.

By the end of the sessions, Peer had recorded 19 performers and 76 songs, including A. P., Sara, and Maybelle Carter singing "Bury Me Under the Weeping Willow," "Little Log Cabin By the Sea," "The Storms Are on the Ocean," "Single Girl, Married Girl," and "The Wandering Boy." Jimmie Rodgers, who heard about the sessions only because he was staying in a boardinghouse in town, recorded "The Soldier's Sweetheart" and "Sleep, Baby, Sleep." Other artists included a gospel quartet from Alcoa, Bristol's Tenneva Ramblers string band, and a Kentucky holiness preacher and his congregation.

As a result of the Bristol sessions, Jimmie Rodgers and the Carter Family became overnight commercial successes. Musicologists who look back on the sessions also note that Peer made little attempt to coach or influence the artists who came to record in 1927, so the entire session is a valuable portrayal of traditional American music of the period. In addition, the business model that Peer established, where performers were paid cash up front for recording and then earned royalties for each record sold, formed the basis of the modern recording industry.

Record labels continued to schedule field sessions around Tennessee in the succeeding years, hoping to replicate the success of Bristol in 1927. Victor returned to Bristol in 1928 and went to Nashville the same year; Columbia had sessions in Johnson City and Memphis in 1929, and Vocalion recorded in Knoxville in 1929 and 1930. The sessions led to a rich trove of recordings by diverse Tennessee artists.

The Great Depression and other economic and social forces put a close on field sessions by the early 1930s. But the genre that had been born in Bristol in 1927 was established, and music has never been the same.

---

industrialist E. W. King was acquired by the Bristol Historical Association, but at press time it was up for sale. You can walk by and see the exterior of the **E. W. King Home** (www.bristol historicalassociation.com), which is located at the corner of Anderson and 7th Streets.

There is a detailed self-guided walking tour of downtown Bristol available from the convention and visitors bureau. You can also rent an audio version of the tour, or listen to it on the chamber of commerce website.

MOUNTAIN MUSIC MUSEUM

In 1998, Bristol opened its first museum dedicated to the city's place in musical history. The Mountain Music Museum (500 Gate City Hwy., Bristol Mall, 276/645-0035, www.mountain-musicmuseum.org, Mon.–Sat. 10 A.M.–9 P.M.,

A racer competes at the Bristol Motor Speedway.

U.S. NAVY PHOTO BY MASS COMMUNICATIONS SPECIALIST 2ND CLASS KRISTOPHER WILSON

Sun. 1–6 P.M., free) is located in a shopping mall a few miles away from downtown Bristol.

The exhibits include memorabilia from the Carter Family, hometown boy Tennessee Ernie Ford, Jimmie Rodgers, bluegrass legend Bill Monroe, the Stanley Brothers, Flatt & Scruggs, and several lesser-known Bristol artists and groups. Its gift shop has the town's best selection of traditional, bluegrass, and old-time music CDs.

TENNESSEE ERNIE FORD'S HOME
Bristol native Ernest Jennings Ford was a country and gospel star during the 1950s and '60s. Ford got his start as a radio announcer in California after World War II, where he adopted the nickname "Tennessee Ernie" and the country character the Pea Picker. Ford recorded his first album in 1949 and made his Grand Ole Opry debut in 1950. He is known for his gravelly, deep voice and his rendition of "Sixteen Tons," a song about the hardships of coal mining. The chorus goes:

You load 16 tons, and what do you get /
Another day older and deeper in debt /
St. Peter don't you call me, cause I can't
go / I owe my soul to the company store

Ford was born and grew up in a small white house on Anderson Street, a few blocks away from downtown Bristol. His home was purchased and restored by the Bristol Historical Association (www.bristolhistoricalassociation.com), which now uses the building (1223 Anderson St.) for storage and meetings. Ford died in 1991 of liver disease, but the musician knew about plans to restore his home and was pleased by the honor.

◖ BRISTOL MOTOR SPEEDWAY
The Bristol Motor Speedway (151 Speedway Blvd., 423/989-6933, www.bristolmotorspeedway.com) looks like a spaceship that has landed on the countryside southeast of Bristol. The speedway is a massive building, arguably one of the largest arenas in the United States. It

seats 160,000 people, and on major race days as many as 100,000 more crowd the grounds around the track to tailgate.

Bristol's race track was first developed in the early 1960s, and it would have been in nearby Piney Flats if the town hadn't banned alcohol sales on Sunday. The first race was the Volunteer 500, run in July 1961. Today Bristol is one of NASCAR's most beloved tracks, renowned for its 36-degree banking on both ends. It was sold to its current owner, Bruton Smith, for $26 million in 1996.

Going to the races is one of the most popular, and iconic, things to do while in Bristol. The track's main events take place in the spring and late summer, and attract a quarter million race fans. These events sell out in a matter of days and are a major commitment: Ticket prices start at $100, and you'll also need a place to stay. The best accommodations are in your own RV or trailer at one of the campgrounds immediately around the track. You can also get a hotel room around Bristol, but if you do so, be prepared to fight the traffic to and from the track every day.

If you can't make it to one of the major events, check out the schedule at the Bristol Dragway, also called **Thunder Valley.** Weekend events are held here March–September, and most will set you back a mere $5. Events include street fights, drag-bike events, and the NHRA-rated Thunder Valley Nationals, usually in May. For a current schedule, contact the Dragway at 423/989-6933 or www.bristoldragway.com.

Even if you can't make a race event, it is worth your time to take a tour of the massive racetrack. Even non–race fans will enjoy seeing such a major racetrack up close. During the hour-long tour of the facility, you will see the area where drivers stay when they come to Bristol, take a cruise down the drag strip, and circle the track itself. You'll also get a bird's-eye view of the track from track owner Bruton Smith's own suite.

Tours begin at the souvenir shop in the Bruton Smith building, a large white building next to the track. They depart every hour on the hour. Tours are offered Monday–Saturday, with the first tour at 9 A.M. and the last starting at 4 P.M. On Sunday, the tours start at noon and end at 4 P.M. No tours are given during the week preceding a major race event. A tour will run an adult $5 (much less than the $100 or $200 price tag for a seat at the main events). Call 423/989-6960 for tour information.

APPALACHIAN CAVERNS
Tour a cave and learn about the people who used it during the settlement period and the Civil War at Appalachian Caverns (420 Cave Hill Rd., Blountville, 423/323-2337, www.appacaverns. com, Mon.–Sat. 9 A.M.–6 P.M., Sun. 1–5 P.M., adults $12, seniors 55 and older $10, children 4–12 $7.50, children 3 and under free). The hour-long regular tour is good for all audiences. Wild tours, where you get dirty, are also available and cost more than the regular admission.

Entertainment and Events
NIGHTLIFE
O'Mainnin's Pub and Grille (712 State St., 423/844-0049) has open-mic nights on Tuesday and live entertainment on weekends. **State Line Bar and Grill** (644 State St., 423/652-0792) has happy hour, ladies' nights, and DJ music for the dance floor.

THE ARTS
Bristol's historic **Paramount Center for the Arts** (518 State St., 423/274-8920, www.the-paramountcenter.com) is city's first venue for theater and concerts. Built in 1931 and restored in 1991, the Paramount is a historic site and a great venue for entertainment. The stage hosts concerts, plays, musicals, and more.

The Appalachian Cultural Music Association puts on free concerts most Thursdays 7–9 P.M. at the **Pickin' Porch** (500 Gate City Hwy.,

MOUNTAIN MUSIC IN THE FOLD

While technically it's located across the state line in Virginia, it's impossible to talk about this part of Tennessee without mentioning **The Carter Family Fold** (A.P. Carter Hwy., Hiltons VA, 276/386-6054, www.carterfamilyfold.org), a music center and memorial to the music created by the Carter family. Established in the 1970s by Janette Carter, a daughter of A.P. and Sara Carter, the center's mission is to preserve old-time music.

The Carter Fold is in Poor Valley, north of Clinch Mountain in southwest Virginia. This humble, yet lovely, corner of the world is where Carters have lived for generations. The music center consists of the Carter Family Museum, which houses exhibits about the first family of country music; the one-room log cabin where A.P. Carter was born; and an outdoor amphitheater where live concerts are held on Saturday nights.

Action at the Carter Fold revolves around the Saturday-night concerts. You may not hear big names, but you will hear big sounds. This is mountain music the way it really is, without interference from slick record producers and music executives. There is lots of room up front for dancing. No alcohol is permitted; these are family-friendly affairs. Tickets are $7-10 for adults and $1 for children 6-11. Make sure you come early enough to tour the museum and the A.P. Carter Cabin.

Camping is allowed on the grounds of the music center. The closest hotels are in Bristol and Kingsport.

The Carter Fold is located just a few miles over the border, but getting there involves a 20-minute drive over winding back roads (as so much in this part of the state does). To get there, go to Gate City and then head east on Highway 58. Follow the green highway signs to the Carter Fold.

Bristol Mall, 276/645-0035, free, but a $4 donation is appreciated). Few things connect you to the legacy of this area more than listening to its music. Call for a schedule.

FESTIVALS AND EVENTS

Bristol's headline event of the year is the **Rhythm and Roots Reunion** (www.bristol-rhythm.com, three-day pass $35–60), held in late September. Stages are set up along State Street, inside the Paramount Center, and in other venues downtown for the three-day weekend festival that draws fans from around the country. Musical styles include alternative country, bluegrass, roots, and blues. Headliners have included Ralph Stanley, Sam Bush, Doc Watson, and the Carolina Chocolate Drops.

Reserve your hotel room early since this is an increasingly popular event. Organizers offer shuttle buses to and from area hotels, so you can skip the driving once you get to town.

The **State Street Farmers Market** (www.statestreetfarmersmarket.com) convenes in front of the *Country Music Mural* in downtown Bristol on Saturday mornings May–October, and on Saturday and Wednesday June–September. In addition to local produce, the farmers market often has musicians performing live music.

Recreation

The **Bristol White Sox** (1501 Euclid Ave., 276/206-9946, www.bristolsox.com), a farm team for the Chicago team with the same name, play at DeVault Memorial Stadium June–August. Tickets are a bargain at $4 for adults ($3 for kids). Box seats are just $6.

Accommodations

Bristol is the land of chain motels. Partly because I-81 passes right through town, and partly because of the heavy demand for rooms caused by the Bristol Motor Speedway, Bristol seems to have more than its share of standard-issue motels.

BRISTOL VISITORS BUREAU

The crowds love the sounds at Bristol's annual Rhythm and Roots Reunion.

Be aware that while room rates around Bristol are generally low, during the weekends of the big race events, in March and August, hotels hike their prices by as much as 1,000 percent. On one trip, a nondescript Econo Lodge that was charging $38 on other days raised its price to more than $350 per night.

The **Holiday Inn** (3005 Linden Dr., 276/466-7725, $95–120) is located at the Bristol Convention Center and offers more amenities than most Bristol motels, including a fitness room, business center, and airport shuttle. Nearby is the **Courtyard by Marriott** (3169 Linden Dr., 276/591-4400, $110–200), whose guests enjoy an indoor pool, on-site restaurant, fitness and business centers, and airport shuttle.

Over on the Tennessee side of the state line, **Hampton Inn** (3299 W. State St., 423/764-3600, $139–200) is located along Highway 11W, near the Bristol Regional Medical Center.

Food

Bristol's finest restaurant is **The Troutdale**
Dining Room (412 6th St., 423/968-9099, www.thetroutdale.com, Tues.–Sat. 5 P.M.–close, $25–60). Located in an 1850 Victorian town house, the Troutdale has a superb menu that changes with the seasons. Dishes like veal scaloppine and pan-seared Hawaiian sea bass are impressive and well executed. The restaurant offers an array of trout dishes made with seafood from the Troutdale's own 600-gallon fish tank. There's no batter-fried fish here, though—it's more in the vein of trout roulade and Akashi poached trout. There are daily and monthly specials, as well as a glorious six-course tasting menu ($100-plus) that is like heaven for your taste buds. Other features you can expect: exquisite service, a superior wine list, delectable desserts, and an unquestionable upscale atmosphere.

There are several restaurants downtown. Pick up a cup of coffee or a sandwich from **Java J's** (501 State St., 276/466-8882, Mon.–Fri. 7 A.M.–9 P.M., Sat. 8 A.M.–9 P.M., $5–9), a relaxing and comfortable place for a pick-me-up,

Fill up with panini and designer salads, or just sip hot, cold, or blended coffee beverages.

Just a few steps from State Street you can dine in an authentic burger bar, straight from the 1950s. **Burger Bar** (8 Piedmont Ave., 276/466-6200, Mon.–Thurs. 8 A.M.–4 P.M., Fri.–Sat. 8 A.M.–6 P.M., $3–8) may be where the legendary Hank Williams passed up his last meal (or so the story goes), but you won't go hungry here. Burgers are what they're famous for, but their plate lunches and homemade desserts are also worth the trip. This is the type of place that is worth getting out of the big cities to experience.

For Italian food, choose **Valentino's** (1501 King College Rd., 423/968-7655, Mon.–Fri. 11 A.M.–10 P.M., Sun. 11 A.M.–9:30 P.M., $6–16), which serves pasta, pizza, calzones, subs, gyros, and salads.

If you're up for an adventure, or if barbecue is your calling, then make a detour to **❰ Ridgewood Barbeque** (900 Elizabethton Hwy./Old 19E, 423/538-7543, Mon.–Thurs. 11 A.M.–7:30 P.M., Fri.–Sat. 11 A.M.–2:30 P.M. and 4:30–8:30 P.M., $7–12). Here the beef and pork barbecue is made the old-fashioned way—slowly—and the result is the most sublime barbecue within at least 100 miles. At the Ridgewood, there's no pork shoulder, only hams, which are smoked over hickory embers for nine hours before being cooled, thin sliced, and then heated on the grill and sauced with the Ridgewood's own sweet and tangy barbecue sauce. Pork and beef (barbecue aficionados scoff at beef) platters come smothered with hand-cut, home-fried french fries. Sandwiches are served on white-bread sandwich buns. Side dishes of tangy coleslaw and smoky baked beans are advisable, although not because you need added sustenance. Portion control is not something that is practiced at the Ridgewood.

The Ridgewood is well off the beaten track, but that hasn't limited its popularity, so expect to wait if you arrive at peak mealtimes. (Seating is also limited, so that contributes to the wait.)

To find the Ridgewood, drive southeast from Bristol toward Blountville and Bluff City. From Bluff City, take Highway 19E/37 toward Elizabethton. Shortly after crossing the railroad tracks, look on your right for the nondescript two-lane Elizabethton Highway, also called Old 19E. It's easy to miss. Once you're on the Elizabethton Highway, the Ridgewood is located on your right in a low-slung strip mall with a red awning. Look for the cars in the parking lot.

Information

The **Bristol Convention and Visitors Bureau** (20 Volunteer Pkwy., 423/989-4850, www.bristolchamber.org, Mon.–Fri. 8:30 A.M.–5 P.M.) publishes maps, guides, and a walking tour of the downtown. The office also serves as a visitors center.

The **Birthplace of Country Music Alliance** (www.birthplaceofcountrymusic.org) is the driving force behind a lot of the good things that are happening in Bristol. This organization is working on the establishment of a downtown museum, and they promote local musical events. In addition, they are an excellent resource for information about Bristol's musical heritage.

JOHNSON CITY

The largest city in Washington County, Johnson City was once an industrial city. It was founded in 1856 by Henry Johnson as a railroad depot called Johnson's Station. After the Civil War, iron ore furnaces here processed ore from the Cranberry Mines in North Carolina. Three railroads—including the Carolina, Clinchfield, and Ohio—passed through the city.

In 1903 a U.S. Veterans Administration rest home was built in Johnson City for Union Civil War veterans, and 10 years later a normal school was established. The Quillen College of Medicine, named for State Representative James Quillen, was founded in 1974.

Downtown Johnson City still has a gritty, postindustrial feel, with lots of boarded-up buildings and empty streets. The city is enlivened by the presence of East Tennessee State University (ETSU), a state school with total enrollment of about 14,000. It includes the Quillen College of Medicine and also a College of Pharmacy that opened in 2007. ETSU's Appalachian Studies program is also of note. Its journal *Now and Then* is a biannual magazine devoted to the history and culture of Appalachia. The university campus lies southwest of the city center and provides several attractions for visitors.

archives are an important depository of documents and primary source material related to the culture, economics, and history of the Appalachian region.

ETSU has an arboretum, and you can take a tour of its giant trees, including a 200-year-old white oak in front of Sherrod Library. Collect a map of the giant trees from the Reece Museum, or contact the ETSU Arboretum (www.etsu.edu/arboretum).

If you visit ETSU, stop at the public safety office at the main entrance for a visitor's parking pass.

East Tennessee State University

The **Carroll Reece Museum** (ETSU, 423/439-4392, www.etsu.edu/reece), a regional art and history museum, was named for the late congressman B. Carroll Reece. The museum's permanent exhibit includes a feature on music of the Tri-Cities. An interactive computer kiosk allows you to see archival video footage of early performances by stars such as Jimmie Rodgers and the Carter Family. Other exhibit halls feature student work and changing exhibits. As of press time, the museum was under a $1.5 million capital improvement project, so call ahead.

Congressman James Quillen hailed from upper East Tennessee, and he represented the area for more than 30 years in Congress. A noted conservative, Quillen introduced the first law outlawing desecration of the U.S. flag in 1968. The late congressman's papers and memorabilia are housed on the 4th floor of the Sherrod Library. The **Quillen Gallery** (Lake St. and Seehorn Rd., 423/439-1000, Mon. Fri. 8 A.M.–4:30 P.M., free) includes dozens of cases of photographs, plaques, and other memorabilia of the Republican's career in politics, including his collection of elephant statues. There is a room that has been furnished to look like the congressman's Washington office.

Also on the 4th floor of the library is the **Archives of Appalachia** (423/439-4338), a project of the Appalachian Studies Department. While not much to see, the

Quillen Veterans Administration Medical Center

The massive medical school and health center located adjacent to ETSU has an interesting history. In 1903, it was established as a residential home for ailing Union Army veterans. Later it evolved into a facility for all veterans of war. At the time of the writing of the 1939 *WPA Guide to Tennessee,* Mountain Home, as the facility came to be known, was home to 3,500 patients, including 400 hospital cases and 2,000 permanently disabled residents. Mountain Home had its own post office, theater, and chapel, and residents here were trained in handicrafts.

In the 1960s, civic leaders in upper East Tennessee first started to discuss the need for a regional health center in the area. It took almost 20 years to make this dream a reality, and in 1978 the first class of students at the Quillen College of Medicine began courses. Today, the university's medical school is a leading healthcare provider in the region.

Tipton-Haynes Historic Site

The Tipton-Haynes Historic Site (2620 S. Roan St., 423/926-3631, www.tipton-haynes. org, Apr.–Nov. Tues.–Sat. 9 A.M.–3 P.M., adults $4, children 12 and under $2) consists of 11 historic buildings, a cave, and a wooded area. It represents several areas of early Tennessee history. Woodland Indians and Cherokee hunted buffalo that were drawn to the spring here.

Later, the buffalo trail became an early stage road, and long hunters camped in the cave.

The home on the property began in 1784 when John Tipton, a Maryland native, built a log cabin here. Tipton is remembered in history because he was an outspoken opponent of the State of Franklin, the unofficial state established by overmountain settlers in 1783. When North Carolina authorities seized some of State of Franklin proponent John Sevier's slaves in 1788, they took them to Tipton's home. When Sevier tried to recover his slaves, a skirmish erupted. This so-called Battle of the Lost State of Franklin marked the end of the State of Franklin movement.

In 1837 the property changed hands from the Tipton to the Haynes family. Landon Carter Haynes, who added a Greek Revival portico, was a farmer, lawyer, newspaper editor, and a three-term member of the Tennessee General Assembly. Haynes was also a secessionist who departed to West Tennessee after the Civil War.

The Tipton-Haynes property was conveyed to the state in 1944–1945. It is maintained by the Tipton-Haynes Historical Association. Call ahead to arrange an appointment during the winter.

Hands On! Regional Museum

Travelers with children should take note of the Hands On! Regional Museum (315 E. Main St., 423/434-4263, www.handsonmuseum.org, Tues.–Fri. 9 A.M.–5 P.M., Sat. 10 A.M.–5 P.M., Sun. 1–5 P.M., adults and children three years and up $8). This is an interactive museum of arts and sciences where children can fly an airplane, visit a coal mine, and walk through an ancient ark filled with exotic animals from around the world. In addition to its regular hours, the museum is also open 9 A.M.–5 P.M. Mondays June–August.

Entertainment

There are two live-music venues that you shouldn't miss in Johnson City. The first, the

Down Home (300 W. Main St., 423/929-9822, www.downhome.com), is this region's best venue for rock, folk, blues, and other roots-style music. Founded in 1976, the Down Home has now nurtured at least two generations of music lovers in upper East Tennessee.

The inside is polished wood on the floor and walls. There are about 160 seats—most of them in straight-back wooden chairs—so the atmosphere is intimate. There are shows here most every Thursday–Sunday night and open mics on Wednesday. The kitchen serves bar food and Tex-Mex Thursday–Sunday nights.

The Down Home is located on a nondescript block a short drive from downtown. A small marquee is about all you'll see from the road, so it's easy to miss it.

The second venue for live music in Johnson City is the **Acoustic Coffeehouse** (415 W. Walnut St., 423/434-9872, www.acousticcoffeehouse.net), which has live acts most nights of the week. The patio out front is a popular place to sit in nice weather, and this is also a good place to grab a cup of joe day or night.

Accommodations

Carnegie Hotel (1216 W. State of Franklin Rd., 423/979-6400, www.carnegiehotel.com, $135–260) is Johnson City's finest hotel. Located next door to ETSU, the hotel offers standard amenities plus special high-end touches like separate soaking tubs, daily newspapers, bathroom scales, and dry-cleaning service. An on-site restaurant, spa, and fitness room mean you may not ever have to leave the grounds if you don't want to. The Carnegie first opened in the 1890s and reopened in 2000.

Food

Quite possibly the most popular restaurant in Johnson City, **The Firehouse** (627 W. Walnut St., 423/929-7377, Mon.–Sat. 11 A.M.–9:30 P.M., $7–18) serves hickory-smoked barbecue with traditional accompaniments like corn bread, coleslaw, and baked beans. You can also order nonbarbecue items such as fish and sandwiches.

A popular choice for decent Italian food is **Alta Cucina** (1200 N. Roan St., 423/928-2092, www.altacucinajc.com, Mon.–Sat. 11 A.M.–2 P.M. and 5–10 P.M., Sun. 11:30 A.M.–2 P.M. and 5–10 P.M., lunch $6–13, dinner $12–30). The lunch menu includes hot and cold sandwiches, salads, pasta, pizza, calzone, stromboli, and other Italian favorites. Dinner specialties include fresh grilled seafood and steak, plus pastas. There is a full bar, and takeout is available.

Information

The **Johnson City Chamber of Commerce** (603 E. Market St., 423/461-8000, www.johnsoncitytnchamber.com) provides visitor information.

AROUND JOHNSON CITY
Rocky Mount

The first territorial capitol of Tennessee, **Rocky Mount** (200 Hyder Hill Rd., Piney Flats, 423/538-7396, www.rockymountmuseum.com, Mar.–mid-Dec. Tues.–Sat. 11 A.M.–5 P.M., other times by appointment, adults $8, seniors $7, children 5–17 $5) sits about five miles outside of Johnson City, on the road to Bristol. It was in this frontier homestead—the home of land surveyor William Cobb—that the governor of the Southwest Territory, William Blount, lived from October 1790 to March 1792. In a spare office here Blount organized the territory's first census and elections. In 1792 he moved to Blount Mansion in Knoxville, and the capitol moved with him.

Although the home seems rustic to us today, it was luxurious by the standards of the early Tennessee frontier. Glass windows, abundant provisions, and feather beds were some of the comforts Blount enjoyed at Rocky Mount.

Today, the home is primarily a living-history museum. Staff dress in period costumes and play Mr. and Mrs. Cobb, Governor Blount, and other members of the Cobb household and extended family. They also tend to farm animals, toil in the kitchen garden, and perform other daily tasks of frontier life. Inside, there is a museum and video that look at frontier life and the early political history of Tennessee.

◀ Gray Fossil Site

Crews cutting a new road near Gray, Tennessee, in 2000 discovered fossilized animal bones, setting off a sequence of events that led to the opening in 2007 of the **Natural History Museum at the Gray Fossil Site** (1212 Suncrest Dr., 866/202-6223, www.grayfossilmuseum.org, Tues.–Sat. 8:30 A.M.–5 P.M., adults $5, seniors $4, children 5–12 $3). The fossil find spawned the creation of a paleontology program at East Tennessee State University, which now leads the scientific investigation of the Gray site. So far, two new ancient animal species, a red panda and badger, have been discovered.

The Gray site is more than five acres, and the best estimate is that it will take more than 100 years to fully excavate and study the fossils that lie here. It is so rich in fossil remains because 4.5–7 million years ago it was a water hole where beasts large and small came to drink and, in some cases, die.

The museum and outdoor displays are designed for children, but adults enjoy them, too. The museum describes the animal and plant life that surrounded the water hole. It also takes visitors through the tedious yet exciting process of discovery and analysis that scientists follow. Overall, the exhibits are captivating and creative.

Upstairs, you join a guide who takes you out to the site itself. Inside, you can peer into the laboratory where each bone fragment that is found is carefully cleaned, analyzed, preserved, and stored.

KINGSPORT

A city with industrial roots and a unique history, Kingsport is perhaps the most culturally sophisticated of the Tri-Cities. Located

THE FIRST FRONTIER

© CINDY CARLTON

Examine the evidence of a different era at the Gray Fossil Site.

on the Holston River, Kingsport was an important shipping port for years before the city was born. The Long Island of the Holston, a large island that lies in the Holston River, was a site of political and spiritual importance to Cherokee Indians.

Downtown Kingsport is being revived, and it is a pleasant place to stroll. Attractions around the city include historic homes and one of the largest city parks in the state.

History

Kingsport is located along the route of a historic trail used by Indians, hunters, and early settlers. The Long Island of the Holston, a 3,000-plus-acre island in the Holston River, was important to Cherokee Indians, and it served as a neutral meeting ground for Indians and settlers. The Long Island of the Holston Treaty was negotiated here in 1777. By 1809 Cherokee had ceded the island and nearby lands to settlers, and the settlement on the

Holston became known as Ross's Landing. The city of Kingsport was first chartered in 1822.

Kingsport was destined to remain a quiet river community until the early 20th century, when industrialists and city planners joined to establish a new, model city. This self-proclaimed "All-American City" was born around 1915 with the establishment of the Kingsport Improvement Corporation. The corporation, founded by the owners of the Carolina, Clinchfield & Ohio Railway, had the job of planning and building a new industrial city.

Different experts were hired to plan the city, design housing, make landscape designs, develop a school system, and install sewerage and sanitation facilities. Corporation lawyers drew up articles of incorporation in 1917.

But what really made Kingsport a success was the industry that it attracted. Tennessee Eastman was and is Kingsport's largest employer. Over the years, Eastman has produced photographic chemicals, war explosives, acetate yarn, polypropylene for outdoor signs, and polyester plastic for use in beverage bottles, among many other things. During World War II and beyond, Eastman was responsible for managing the Y-12 National Security Complex at Oak Ridge.

Like other small and midsize American cities, Kingsport has wrangled with problems like sprawl and the decline of its downtown over the years.

Sights

Central Kingsport is the city that was laid out by town planners and industrialists in the early 20th century. The oldest attractions in Kingsport are located slightly west of downtown, along the Holston River. A lovely nine-mile greenway connects the Holston River area with Historic Exchange Place on the east side of town.

HISTORIC DOWNTOWN

The planned nature of Kingsport is evident downtown. Broad Street is a wide, divided two-lane road with four blocks of storefronts, many of which still sport notable art deco architecture. The old depots for the Carolina, Clinchfield & Ohio railway stand along Main Street; the passenger depot is now a bank, and the freight depot houses the visitors bureau. At the other end of Broad Street is the **Church Circle,** a traffic circle that houses four churches. At the corner of Center and Commerce Streets is a mural that represents Kingsport's history. Students of architecture should follow the 1.8-mile walking tour developed by the Downtown Kingsport Association.

It has taken a lot of effort to make Kingsport's downtown what it is today. Like other towns of its size in Tennessee, Kingsport suffered during the 1970s and '80s as businesses moved out of downtown and economic activity spread to the outlying areas, starting with the first shopping malls. But in 1974 a downtown association was formed, and over the past 30-plus years they have led the way in Kingsport's resurgence. They have been involved with projects ranging from the improvement of sidewalks to annual arts events.

THE BOATYARD

The oldest part of Kingsport is the Boatyard, located along the Holston River on the west side of town. The **Netherland Inn** (2144 Netherland Inn Rd., 423/335-5552, www.netherlandinn.com, May–Oct. Sat.–Sun. 2–4 P.M., free) was a stagecoach stop, inn, and boatyard catering to travelers who came through this country by land or river. The inn, first built between 1802 and 1808 by William King, is named after Richard Netherland, who bought the property in 1818 and expanded it. Group tours may be arranged by appointment.

At the rear of the inn are several log homes, including a Daniel Boone cabin, which was moved here in order to preserve it. This is the symbolic beginning of the Daniel Boone Heritage Trail, which celebrates the wilderness trail that Boone and thousands of other early settlers used to enter the Tennessee frontier.

Across the road from the Netherland Inn is one end of Kingsport's greenway system. You can walk or bike nine miles from here to Exchange Place, on the other side of town.

The greenway passes the **Long Island of the Holston.** A site of political and spiritual importance to the Cherokee, and a place for meetings between the Cherokee and white settlers, the Long Island is now home to **Heritage Park,** which has walking trails, picnic tables, and historical markers. Parts of the island are residential, while a coal gasification plant belonging to Tennessee Eastman sits on the southern end of the island.

EXCHANGE PLACE

This 1850s homestead is a living-history museum and center for workshops, festivals, and other special events that celebrate traditional arts, crafts, and ways of life. Exchange Place (4812 Orebank Rd., 423/288-6071, www.exchangeplace.info, May–Oct. Sat.–Sun.

2–4:30 P.M., adults $1, children under 12 $0.50) consists of about a dozen period buildings, most of them original to the property. They include the "saddlebag"-style log house, kitchen, springhouse, schoolroom, blacksmith shop, and barn. Across the road is an early-20th-century home that serves as the visitors center. Exchange Place got its name because its owner, John Preston, exchanged money for travelers who passed by on the stagecoach road from Virginia into Tennessee. He also exchanged goods.

Exchange Place is operated by a private nonprofit organization. Some of the funds needed to maintain the old buildings come from the proceeds of selling works completed by the Exchange Place Quilters and Overmountain Weavers, volunteers who weave and quilt.

Several special events are held here every year. They include the Spring Garden Fair at the end of April, the Fall Folk Arts Festival at the end of September, and Christmas activities in December.

Festivals and Events

The **Spring Garden Fair** (www.exchangeplace. info) kicks off the season in April at Exchange Place, a working farm and living-history museum. The Garden Fair features local and regional craftspeople, food, and music. The bookend to the fair is the **Fall Folk Arts Festival** in September, also held at Exchange Place.

In July, Kingsport celebrates **Fun Fest** (www.funfest.net), a weeklong series of concerts, sports competitions, fireworks, and a hot-air balloon rally.

Recreation

Kingsport has an extraordinary city park. **Bays Mountain Park** (853 Bays Mountain Park Rd., 423/229-9447, www.baysmountain.com, June–Aug. Mon.–Sat. 8:30 A.M.–8 P.M., Sun. noon–8 P.M., March–May and Sept.–Oct. Mon.–Fri. 8:30 A.M.–5 P.M., Sat. 8:30 A.M.–8 P.M., Sun. noon–8 P.M., Nov.–Feb. Mon.–Sat. 8:30 A.M.–5 P.M., Sun. noon–5 P.M., $4 per car) is a 3,300-acre nature preserve that lies between Bays Mountain and the Holston River Mountain, southwest of downtown Kingsport. It takes about 15 minutes to drive to Bays Mountain from downtown. The park's attractions include a **nature center** (June–Aug. Mon.–Fri. 8:30 A.M.–6 P.M., Sat.–Sun. noon–7 P.M., Mar.–May and Sept.–Oct. Mon.–Fri. 8:30 A.M.–5 P.M., Sat.–Sun. 8:30 A.M.–7 P.M., Nov.–Feb. Mon.–Fri. 8:30 A.M.–5 P.M., Sat.–Sun. noon–5 P.M.) with exhibits on plants, weather, space, and animals; a planetarium with regularly scheduled shows; star observatory; deer, wolf, bobcat, otter, and raptor habitats; farmstead cabin; and 25 miles of hiking trails. There are also service roads open to mountain bikers after they have paid a $2 registration fee. A barge cruises the Bays Mountain Reservoir on weekends year-round and daily June–August. Bays Mountain offers special naturalist-led programs nearly every day, ranging from wolf howls to moonlight barge rides. Check their website for current programs and schedules.

Warriors' Path State Park (490 Hemlock Rd., 423/239-8531) is located on the shores of Fort Patrick Henry Lake, as the Holston River is called south of the Fort Patrick Henry Dam. There are 12 miles of hiking trails, mountain bike paths, an Olympic-size swimming pool, an 18-hole golf course, and a 22-hole disc golf course in this 950-acre park. Boaters enjoy cruising and fishing on the lake; paddle- and fishing boats are available for rent from the marina office. In addition, there is a 135-site campground with modern hot-water bathhouses and water and electrical hookups. Warriors' Path State Park is located southeast of downtown Kingsport, just a quick 15-minute drive from the city.

Accommodations

Located near the civic auditorium and close to

SUDDEN SERVICE

For once, it is not the Golden Arches that define fast food. At least not here. In the Tri-Cities, look for the large, turquoise, and garishly decorated fast-food chain known locally simply as **Pal's.**

Fred "Pal" Barger opened his first fast-food restaurant in Kingsport in 1956, after meeting Ray Kroc (of McDonald's fame) at a restaurant convention. The second Pal's opened in 1958. The chain expanded again in the 1990s and at the same time adopted its present slogan, "Great Food in a Flash." Now there are 20 Pal's from Morristown to Lebanon, Virginia. Many are drive-ins only.

Don't worry about driving past Pal's; you can't miss them! The restaurants are painted a blinding shade of blue and come with a humongous wiener, drink, french fries, and burger as outdoor decorations. Pal's is beloved for its quart-size iced tea (sweetened, of course; this is the South), called the Big Tea, as well as for fast and accurate service. The Sauceburger, chipped ham, and Frenchie Fries are also well loved. In 2002, President George W. Bush gave Pal's Sudden Service the Baldridge National Quality Award.

dryers, microwaves, and refrigerators. There is an outdoor pool.

Located about midway between downtown and Exchange Place is a **Comfort Inn** (100 Indian Center Ct., 423/378-4418, $80–90), a 122-room hotel with standard amenities and an above-average hot breakfast bar, plus an outdoor pool for those hot Tennessee summer days.

Food

The **Café N'Orleans** (161 E. Main St., 423/245-5400, Mon. 11 A.M.–3 P.M., Tues.–Thurs. 11 A.M.–8 P.M., Fri. 11 A.M.–9 P.M., Sat. 5–9 P.M., $5–11) downtown offers gumbo, jambalaya, po'boys, and other Louisiana favorites.

Jan Mar Restaurant (114 Broad St., 423/245-0731, Mon.–Fri. 6:30 A.M.–3 P.M., Sat. 6:30 A.M.–2 P.M., $5–9) is a cozy, comfortable place for breakfast or lunch. Biscuits and gravy are the morning favorite, and at lunch choose between a hearty burger or one of the daily plate-lunch specials.

Sandwiches are the specialty at **Deli Sandwich Factory** (1308 E. Stone Dr., 423/246-3354, www.delisandwichfactory.com, Mon.–Sat. 10 A.M.–7 P.M., $3–7). The house specialty is the Kitchen Sink Sandwich, which features ham, smoked turkey, salami, corned beef, roast beef, and swiss cheese.

For home-style Southern fare, head to **Mama's House Buffet** (2608 N. John B. Dennis Hwy., 423/247-5691, Mon.–Sat. 11 A.M.–8:30 P.M., Sun. 11 A.M.–6:30 P.M., $6–10), which offers lunch and dinner daily, and breakfast on Wednesday and Saturday. The buffet features different meats and sides daily, but expect choices like sweet potatoes, meat loaf, bread dressing, pork loin, sliced ham, brown beans, and spaghetti and meatballs.

Broad Street BBQ (2921 E. Center St., 423/247-8646, daily 11 A.M.–8 P.M., $5–7) is one of Kingsport's most popular barbecue joints. Check out the full menu of barbecue choices, including hickory-smoked ribs, pulled pork, and barbecue chicken.

downtown Kingsport, **Fox Manor B&B** (1612 Watauga St., 423/378-3844 or 888/200-5879, www.foxmanor.com, $110–150) is a 19th-century town home that has been converted into a luxurious bed-and-breakfast. The five guest rooms are decorated with rich fabrics, deep woods, and top-notch furnishings. High-quality linens, fireplaces, ceiling fans, and private baths add to the appeal. Start the morning off right with breakfast served in an elegant dining room. Other common rooms include the library, with an English-style bar, and the cozy verandah.

Chain hotels in Kingsport include the **Days Inn Kingsport** (805 Lynn Garden Dr., 423/246-7126, $70–80), located very close to downtown. There is free continental breakfast, in-room coffeemakers, hair

Kingsport's favorite seafood restaurant is **Riverfront Seafood Company** (1777 Netherland Inn Rd., 423/245-3474, Mon.–Sat. 11 A.M.–close, $7–20). Casual food here includes oyster, shrimp, white fish, and smoked turkey po'boys. At least a dozen types of fish are available, fried, grilled, or prepared specially according to house recipes. Crab legs and Maine lobster are also on the menu.

Information

Downtown Kingsport (140 W. Main St., 423/246-6550) promotes the city center and publishes a walking tour to historic sites. The **Kingsport Convention and Visitors Bureau** (400 Clinchfield St., Ste. 100, 423/392-8820, www.visitkingsport.com) has maps and brochures, and can help you organize tours and group events.

Northern Cherokee National Forest

The northern Cherokee National Forest covers 327,000 acres from the northern boundary of the Great Smoky Mountains National Park to the Virginia state line. It encompasses wilderness regions, state parks, and towns. Because it is a national forest and not a national park, commercial enterprises, including logging, are allowed.

The Appalachian Trail passes through this part of the Cherokee National Forest, giving you abundant opportunities for hiking, biking, camping, and other outdoor pursuits. The Nolichucky River is popular with white-water rafters, and the Watauga Lake offers boating and fishing prospects.

Sights include Roan Mountain's verdant rhododendron gardens, Shady Valley's cranberry bogs, and dramatic Backbone Rock. Thanks to the smattering of towns, including Erwin and Mountain City, there is enough "civilization" to make this countryside accessible and easy to explore. While it's outside of the bounds of the national forest, Elizabethton shares the characteristics of the region and offers a quaint downtown experience with shopping, restaurants, and historic homes.

Visitor Information

For information about the northern Cherokee National Forest, visit one of two ranger stations. The **Watauga Ranger District** (4400 Unicoi Dr., Unicoi, 423/735-1500, Mon.–Fri.

8 A.M.–4:30 P.M.) is in the town of Unicoi and is the headquarters for the northernmost portion of the forest. The **Unaka/Nolichucky Ranger District** (4900 Asheville Hwy./Hwy. 70, Greeneville, 423/638-4109, Mon.–Fri. 8 A.M.–4:30 P.M.) is headquartered outside of the bounds of the forest, in Greeneville. Both ranger stations offer maps, guides, and other helpful information about the forest.

LAUREL BLOOMERY

Laurel Bloomery is located in the extreme northeastern corner of Tennessee, the first town you will meet after crossing over the Virginia state line. Named for the mountain laurel that grows here and the iron smelters, or bloomers, that once raged here, Laurel Bloomery is now a peaceful mountain village. Every August, on the weekend before Labor Day, the town hosts an **Old Time Fiddlers' Convention** (423/727-9595, www.oldfiddlersconvention.com) at the Old Mill Music Park on Highway 91. The tradition of an annual music convention began here back in 1925, and this is one of the best places to come to hear real old-time music. The music usually gets started around 6 P.M. and keeps rolling well into the night. Many conventioneers set up camp along the river for the weekend. Ticket prices range $6–12; camping is $80.

Gentry Creek Falls

Chain-effect waterfalls—one 30 and one 40

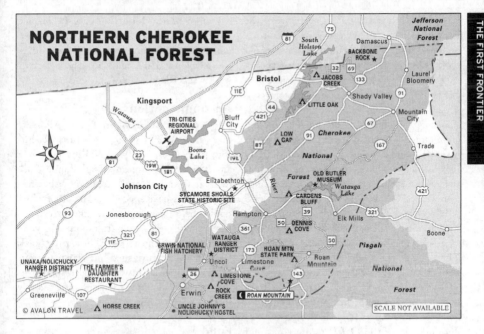

NORTHERN CHEROKEE NATIONAL FOREST

© AVALON TRAVEL

SCALE NOT AVAILABLE

feet high—are located along Gentry Creek near Laurel Bloomery. It is a 2.5-mile hike to the falls from the trailhead, which is located on Gentry Creek Road a short ways off Highway 91. To get there, turn on Gentry Creek Road and drive for 0.7 mile. Turn right, following Gentry Creek Road, for another 1.8 miles. At this point the road becomes unpaved. Drive for 0.2 mile and turn right again, and follow the road another 1.8 miles to the trailhead. There is limited parking. For information, contact the Watauga Ranger District of the Cherokee National Forest at 423/735-1500.

BACKBONE ROCK

A remarkable natural and man-made landmark west of Laurel Bloomery, on the road between Damascus, Virginia, and Shady Valley, Tennessee, Backbone Rock is a rock formation that developed where the Beaverdam Creek flows past a spur of Holston Mountain. The rock is almost 100 feet tall in places and about 50 feet thick; it is called Backbone Rock because it resembles a spine. In 1901 a tunnel was drilled through the rock to make way for the railroad. Today, the road passes through this gap, known locally as the shortest tunnel in the world.

Get out of your car and hike the short path up and over the rock. The trail is steep and rocky, and children should be closely supervised along it. Another hike takes you to Backbone Falls.

There is a lovely creekside picnic area here, and the Beaverdam Creek invites you to wade or swim in its clear waters.

Facilities include a picnic area and a primitive campground.

SHADY VALLEY

Located at 2,800 feet and surrounded by mountains is Shady Valley, a high-mountain cove that is best known for its wetlands. Bogs and white pine/hemlock forests once covered most of the valley; they flourished here due to the higher elevation and the influence of the last ice age. With human settlement, many of the bogs were drained to make way for agriculture.

Today, Shady Valley is a quiet collection of old and new homes on rolling farmland. The winding rural roads leading to the valley attract motorcyclists. The four-way intersection of highways constitutes the commercial center—there are three gas station/delis but little else. The town has erected an information board near the intersection, and here you'll find a map to at least four of Shady Grove's cranberry bogs. The easiest one to find is **Schoolyard Springs,** located a few hundred yards from the Shady Valley Elementary School. Local residents have built a boardwalk over and around the bog. Here you can watch the bog bubble up from below and listen to a symphony of birdsong. The effort to preserve Shady Valley's bogs has been led by the Nature Conservancy.

Shady Valley celebrates its cranberry bogs and much more with the annual **Cranberry Festival** (423/739-2131), held during the second full weekend in October. You could not imagine a more picturesque setting, what with the glorious fall leaves surrounding the valley like a giant-size stadium. The festival includes various cranberry-themed events, a parade, an arts-and-crafts auction, and other amusements. Shady Valley also holds an all-you-can-eat **Soup Supper** each March.

MOUNTAIN CITY

This small town of about 3,000 is the seat of Johnson County and a commercial hub for the northernmost mountains in Tennessee. The **Johnson County Welcome Center and Museum** (716 S. Shady St./Hwy. 421, 423/727-5800, www.johnsoncountychamber.org, Mon.–Sat. 9 A.M.–5 P.M.) is a good stop for information and orientation. The museum houses local historical relics, and there are brochures, maps, and helpful people to offer assistance.

Recreation

Redtail Mountain is a high-end residential

development near Mountain City. Its 18-hole, par 72 **golf course** (423/727-7931) is open to nonresidents. Greens fees are $45 Monday–Thursday and $50 Friday–Sunday. Check for weekly specials like ladies' day and men's day.

Accommodations

The **Prospect Hill B&B Inn** (801 W. Main St./Hwy. 67, 423/727-0139, www.prospect-hill.com, $109–180) is a five-room inn housed in an 1889 brick Victorian-shingle home. Fully renovated and carefully restored, the inn's guest rooms have special features like whirlpool tubs, private balconies, and private entrances. All guests enjoy the mountain views from the porch and a hearty homemade breakfast. Rooms are furnished in a classic, tasteful style, with original artwork hanging in many of them. If you're looking for a romantic getaway, this is a good choice.

Food

For a cup of coffee, light lunch, or slice of homemade cheesecake, come by **Craig's Coffee House** (122 Murphy St., 423/727-0567, Mon.–Wed. 7 A.M.–3 P.M., Thurs.–Fri. 7 A.M.–2 P.M. and 5–8 P.M., Sat. 8 A.M.–2 P.M., $4–15). Serving fresh-roasted coffee, daily lunch specials, and home-cooked dinners twice a week, Craig's is a popular meeting place for the citizens of Mountain City. It is located in a cozy white building across the street from the Mountain City Primary School.

TRADE

Considered the oldest community in Tennessee, this mountain hamlet is located within spitting distance of the North Carolina state line. Named Trade because it was where settlers and Indians once met to trade, the town is now a quiet, rural settlement with lovely scenery all around. Highway 421, which connects Trade with Mountain City, is a winding, scenic route through the mountains. It is said that North

CAMPING IN THE NORTHERN CHEROKEE NATIONAL FOREST

Campgrounds are located throughout the Unaka and Watauga Districts of the Cherokee National Forest and are a great way to really experience these great outdoors. All forest service campgrounds are available on a first-come, first-served basis only. They have potable water and toilets; some have warm-water showers.

- **Backbone Rock Recreation Area** is located near the Virginia state line. Its 11 campsites accommodate tents or trailers; only a few accommodate RVs. There are flush toilets and drinking water, but no showers or electrical hookups.

- **Cardens Bluff Campground** is a 43-site campground on Watauga Lake, which can accommodate tent and trailer campers, plus a few RVs. Amenities include showers, drinking water, and flush toilets. There are no electrical hookups.

- **Jacobs Creek Recreation Area** is located near the Virginia state line on the banks of South Holston Lake. Its 27 sites can accommodate tents or RVs. There are showers, drinking water, flush toilets, and a dump station.

- **Little Oak Campground,** also located on South Holston Lake, is a large campground with 70 tent and RV sites. It has showers, flush toilets, dump station, and drinking water.

- **Rock Creek Recreation Area** near Erwin sits at the foot of Unaka Mountain. It has 37 campsites, 14 with electrical hookups. Day-use facilities include a swimming hole, bike trail, hiking paths, and picnic tables. Fees are $10 a day for tent sites with no electricity, $15 a day for single site with electric hookups, $30 a day for a double site with electric hookups; day-use fee is $2 a day per car. To find Rock Creek, take Rock Creek Road from Main Street in Erwin. It is three miles to the campground.

- **Dennis Cove Campground** near Hampton has 16 campsites, flush toilets, no hookups, and no showers. It is along Laurel Fork Creek, making it popular among anglers. To get here, take U.S. 19E through Hampton and turn right onto Dennis Cove Road. Drive up the mountain 4.5 miles; the campground is on your right.

Carolina fugitive Tom Dula, made famous by the folk song "Tom Dooley," hid out in Trade until a posse found him and arrested him for murdering his fiancée.

For a bite of food in Trade, stop at **Sharpie's Restaurant** (11888 Hwy. 421, 423/727-0079, Mon.–Thurs. and Sat. 6 A.M.–8 P.M., Fri. 6 A.M.–9 P.M., Sun. 11 A.M.–2 P.M., $5–12). This friendly little diner-style restaurant has burgers, steaks, roasted chicken, and sandwiches.

WATAUGA LAKE

The Tennessee Valley Authority was at work in this part of Tennessee, too. In 1949, TVA completed the Watauga Dam and created Watauga Lake, the highest-elevation lake in Tennessee. Even today, it is surprising to find a placid lake amid the Unaka mountain peaks in this landscape. The lake is picturesque, with clear, cool waters ideal for swimming and fishing.

Pontoon boats, fishing boats, and sailboats are available for rent from **Fish Springs Marina** (191 Fish Springs Rd., Hampton, 423/768-2336). An all-day rental will cost $180–215, plus fuel. Reservations are recommended, particularly on weekends.

When the lake was formed, the town of Butler was covered with water. "Old Butler" lies at the bottom of the lake, but "New Butler" remains on the shore. The **Old Butler Museum** (23 Selma Curtis Rd., 423/768-3880, Sat.–Sun. 1–4 P.M. and other times by appointment, adults $3, seniors/students $2) houses community artifacts taken from the post office, barber

© DANNA LYNN

You can't beat the views from atop Roan Mountain.

kitchens, and plenty of space to relax and unwind. Weekly rates are available.

Iron Mountain Inn (268 Moreland Dr., Butler, 423/768-2446, www.ironmountaininn. com, $350) is a four-room bed-and-breakfast located in a log cabin. The innkeepers offer a variety of special packages that focus on pastimes including hiking, golf, fishing, and biking. There are also romantic getaways, holiday specials, and special midweek or off-season rates.

◖ ROAN MOUNTAIN

Quite possibly the most lovely natural site in northeastern Tennessee, Roan Mountain is a high mountain ridge noted for its open balds and rhododendron gardens. Part of the Cherokee National Forest, Roan Mountain is a five-mile stretch of ridge that straddles the North Carolina–Tennessee state line and ranges from 6,286 feet at its peak to 5,500 feet at Carver's Gap. The 10-mile stretch of the Appalachian Trail that follows the crest of Roan Mountain is believed by some to be the most beautiful of the entire trail. Treeless mountain balds, including Jane's Bald, Grassy Bald, and Round Bald, open up sweeping views of the Blue Ridge Mountains. During June, the tall, bushy Catawba rhododendron bloom, creating a blanket of pink, white, and yellow flowers.

Visitors to the top of Roan Mountain can stop at the National Park Service information cabin for maps and directions. From the cabin you can take an easy, short walk along a paved track through the rhododendron gardens to an overlook. The Cloudland Trail is a 1.2-mile moderate hike to the Roan High Bluff Overlook.

Also nearby is **Dave Miller Homestead** (Memorial Day–Labor Day Wed.–Sun. 9 A.M.–5 P.M., Oct. Sat.–Sun. 9 A.M.–5 P.M., free), a 1909 farmhouse that has been restored to show traditional mountain life. On summer weekends, special storytelling, music, and arts-and-crafts programs keep it alive.

If you wish to make Roan Mountain your

shop, and people's homes before it was flooded, and it records the way of life of more than 400 families in the Watauga River valley who were forced to move when the lake was made.

Downstream from Watauga Lake is Wilbur Lake, also called Horseshoe Lake. Wilbur Lake was created in 1912 when the Watauga Power Company dammed the Watauga River. The dam has been owned by TVA since 1945.

There are public canoe launches on Wilbur Lake, but no commercial recreation facilities. Because the water is so cold, only rainbow and brown trout are found in the waters. Both are stocked.

Accommodations

You can rent your own cabin overlooking the lake from **Cherokee Forest Mountain Cabins** (798 Grindstaff Rd., Butler, www.cabin4me. com, $170–210). These fully furnished homes away from home have fireplaces, hot tubs, full destination, then there is no better home base than **Roan Mountain State Park** (1015 Hwy. 143, 423/772-0190), located eight miles down the mountain. Park facilities include a museum, cabins, campground, swimming pool, and tennis courts. Even if you don't stay at the park, the **museum** (daily 8 A.M.–4:30 P.M., free) in the visitors center is well worth a stop for its detailed look at the natural and human history of the nearby mountains.

The 30 fully equipped cabins ($70–170) are open year-round and provide kitchens, woodstoves, and outdoor grills. A campground ($20–70) has 107 sites, including 87 with RV water/electricity hookups.

ELIZABETHTON

The seat of Carter County, Elizabethton is one of the oldest incorporated towns in Tennessee. Its downtown is vibrant, and the important historic site of Sycamore Shoals is on the outskirts of town. The Doe River, which passes through the city, makes it a scenic spot.

Historic Downtown

Spanning the Doe River in downtown Elizabethton is the **Doe River Covered Bridge,** which crosses the Doe River at Hattie Avenue. This 1882 wooden bridge spans some 134 feet and rests on earth and limestone abutments. It was high enough to withstand floods, including the Great May Flood of 1901. It is now closed to vehicular traffic—a new concrete bridge spans the river at Elk Avenue but remains open to foot and bike traffic. There is a pleasant park on the east bank of the river from which you can enjoy views of the bridge.

On the west bank, you can see a piece of early Tennessee history. It was in the early 1770s that the very first overmountain settlers began to establish farms in what is now northeastern Tennessee. The wilderness still belonged to the Cherokee Indians, but the settlers could not resist the promise that it represented.

By 1772, an estimated 80 farms were located along the Holston and Watauga Rivers.

The settlers soon realized they needed some form of local government. They were outside the bounds of the closest state—North Carolina—and far away from the nearest courthouse. In 1772 the settlers formed the Watauga Association, which allowed them to prosecute criminals and settle disputes. A part of the sycamore tree under which this association was formed is on display a few steps from the Doe River Covered Bridge.

Elizabethton has a number of historic homes, old businesses, and landmarks, including the tallest Fraser fir in the state of Tennessee. Get a copy of the brochure *Elizabethton Walking Tour* from the visitors bureau or the public library to explore further.

Carter Mansion

One of the first settlers in this area was John Carter, a trader who first moved into

The Carter Mansion was one of finest homes on the Tennessee frontier.

modern-day Tennessee in 1770. In 1772 he moved near the Watauga River, in present-day Elizabethton. John Carter was one of the signers of the Watauga Association agreement. John Carter's son, Landon, was also a political leader and businessman. Landon Carter's wife, Elizabeth, was Elizabethton's namesake, and Carter County was named for him. The family home has been preserved and is now called the Carter Mansion (1013 Broad St., 423/543-6140 or 423/543-5808, tours May 15–Aug. 15 Wed.–Sun. at 2 P.M., other times by appointment, free). The simple white frame home may look homely, but it was luxury on the frontier. Its hand-carved crown molding, chair rail, and mantels are evidence of this. The home is managed by the Sycamore Shoals State Historic Site.

Port Rayon

As you drive into Elizabethton from the west, you cannot miss the large factory that sits along the banks of the Watauga River. This is the remains of the **Bemberg and Glanzstoff rayon factories,** which opened in the 1920s. In their heyday, these factories had their own rail depot, called Port Rayon, which brought members of their workforce to the factory every day. The factories experienced ups and downs throughout the Great Depression, World War II, and during the postwar years. At their peak in 1949, the factories employed some 6,000 people. Economic fluctuations, the cost of new environmental protection measures, and changing corporate structures caused the factories to downsize during the 1970s, '80s, and '90s. By 1998, there were just 250 people employed at the factory, now called North American Rayon Corporation. A massive fire broke out at North American Rayon in 2000. It took firefighters a week to fully put out the blaze, which led to the final closure and demolition of the factory.

Sycamore Shoals

Many of the most important events in early Tennessee history took place in the area of Sycamore Shoals State Historic Site (1651 Elk Ave., 423/543-5808) along the Watauga River, just a few miles outside of Elizabethton. It was near here in 1775 that the Cherokee agreed to sell 20 million acres of land to Richard Henderson in what is now known as the Transylvania Purchase. Fort Watauga, built as a defensive fort for early settlers along the Watauga River, was near here. And in an open glade next to the river, hundreds of overmountain men mustered in 1780 as they began their march to King's Mountain to fight the British during the Revolutionary War.

The historic site consists of a replica of Fort Watauga and a walking trail that takes you along the Watauga River to the areas where some of these momentous events are believed to have taken place. Inside the **visitors center** (Mon.–Sat. 8 A.M.–4:30 P.M., Sun. 1–4:30 P.M., free) there is a museum and video.

Annual events at Sycamore Shoals include the staging of *The Wataugans* in July, the Muster at Fort Watauga in May, the Native American Festival in June, the Overmountain Victory Trail Celebration in September, and the Fort Watauga Knap-In in October.

Accommodations

The Doe River Inn (217 Academy St., 423/292-2848, up to $75) is set in an 1894 home near where early settlers forded the Doe River. There are two guest rooms in the house, or you can rent the two-bedroom cottage or one-bedroom carriage house, also on the property.

Food

The Coffee Company (444 E. Elk Ave., 423/542-3438, Mon.–Sat. 7 A.M.–5 P.M. for coffee and desserts, kitchen is open 11 A.M.–3 P.M.) is a coffee shop and bakery that also offers the best salads and sandwiches in town. Sandwiches include a grilled panini with meat or veggies, French dip, or pesto turkey. Salads feature fruit, meat, and vegetables.

Information

The best guide to Elizabethton is the walking tour, a substantial brochure available from the local tourism council and some downtown businesses. Pick up a copy at the **Elizabethton-Carter County Chamber of Commerce and Tourism Council** (Hwy. 19 E., 423/547-3850, www.tourelizabethton.com) or the **Elizabethton Public Library** (201 N. Sycamore St., 423/547-6360).

ERWIN

Gateway to the Cherokee wilderness and commercial center for largely rural Unicoi County, Erwin is a friendly and unpretentious town located along both I-26 and an active railroad line, Erwin is a place where things and people are on the move. A smattering of restaurants, hotels, and the only bona fide hostel in these parts make it a good home base for exploring the forest.

Erwin had a succession of names during its early history. First known as Unaka, it was changed to Longmire in 1840. Then it became Vanderbilt. In 1879 town officials agreed to name the city after D. J. N. Ervin, who donated 15 acres of land to establish a county seat. Unfortunately for Mr. Ervin, a mistake by post office officials caused the name to be recorded as Erwin. Finally, a name stuck.

Unlikely industries keep Erwin afloat: State and federal fish hatcheries produce broodstock and fish, and National Fuel Services prepares enriched uranium for nuclear-powered navy ships. CSX Rail also has a depot and car repair center in Erwin.

For 40 years starting in 1917, Erwin was home to one of America's largest and most well-known manufacturers of hand-painted pottery. Southern Pottery, located a few miles outside of town, created dinnerware that was sold under the name Blue Ridge. Men shaped, finished,

and fired the dishes while a decorating department of more than 500 area women painted designs on by hand. Blue Ridge pottery is now highly collectable.

The appeal of Blue Ridge pottery is the individual flair left behind by the painters. While the women worked from patterns, they painted by hand, and so each plate turned out just a little different from the next.

Sights

Erwin is home to two fish hatcheries, one operated by the state and one by the federal government. The **Erwin National Fish Hatchery** (520 Federal Hatchery Rd., 423/743-4712, Mon.–Fri. 7:30 A.M.–4:30 P.M., free) produces 10–12 million rainbow trout eggs annually, which are shipped to federal, state, and tribal fish hatcheries around the country. It is one of two federal rainbow trout broodstock facilities in the country. There is a small exhibit and display raceway for visitors. If you visit outside of working hours, there is an outdoor kiosk next to the display raceway.

The **Erwin State Trout Hatchery** (475 Banner Springs Rd., 423/743-4842, Mon.–Fri. 7:30 A.M.–4:30 P.M., free) is one of the facilities that receives Erwin's trout eggs. This hatchery keeps the trout until they are big enough to be released into area streams and lakes. Visitors can walk up and down the raceways and look at the fish.

On the grounds of the Erwin National Fish Hatchery, in a building that once housed the fishery superintendent, is the **Unicoi County Heritage Museum** (529 Federal Hatchery Rd., 423/743-9449, May–Oct. 31 daily 1–5 P.M., adults $2, children $1). The museum houses exhibits about Erwin and Unicoi County; it has a nice collection of Blue Ridge pottery from the old Southern Pottery plant in Erwin and displays about the Clinchfield Railroad, which is closely tied to the history of Erwin. At the rear of the museum is a nature trail with marked trees and other plants. A 30-minute cassette narrative is available to accompany the walk.

The heritage museum is housed in a white Victorian farmhouse built in 1903 as accommodation for the fish hatchery superintendent. In 1982, instead of demolishing the old house as ordered by the federal government, the local chamber of commerce petitioned for the old building to be saved and turned into a local history museum.

Erwin is surrounded by good **apple-growing country.** Farms in this area produce sweet, crisp apples that are sold in the fall. The **Unicoi County Chamber of Commerce** (100 Main St., 423/743-3000, www.unicoicounty.org) can provide you with a list of area farms that are open to the public.

Festivals and Events

The **Unicoi County Apple Festival** (www.unicoicounty.org) takes place in October and includes a gospel music showcase, apple contests, a show of Blue Ridge pottery, and free shuttle buses to the Unicoi County Heritage Museum.

Shopping

Alan Stegall keeps the tradition of pottery alive in Erwin. His shop, **Stegall's Pottery** (200 Nolichucky Ave., 423/743-3227), across from the public library, produces beautiful mugs, platters, and other stoneware.

Recreation

The Nolichucky River makes for an exciting, beautiful, and unpredictable rafting trip. River outfitters in Erwin offer trips along the Upper and Lower Nolichucky. With Class II–IV rapids, the river trip is exciting. It also offers a lovely journey down an otherwise inaccessible 3,000-foot river gorge. Due to the rapids, no one under 12 is allowed on the river. On average, a full-day river trip costs $60–80 per person.

Erwin-based outfitters include **Cherokee Adventures** (2000 Jonesborough Rd., 423/743-7733, www.cherokeeadventures.com) and **USA Raft** (1002 Jones Branch Rd., 423/743-7111, www.usaraft.com), also known as Mountain Adventure Guides.

Accommodations

Hikers and budget travelers love **Uncle Johnny's Nolichucky Hostel** (151 River Rd., 423/735-0548, www.unclejohnnys.net, $17.50–40). Located just two miles outside of Erwin along the Nolichucky River, the hostel is about 60 feet from the Appalachian Trail. Through-hikers fill up the hostel during the early spring months, but outdoor folks with lesser ambitions love it year-round. Guests at Uncle Johnny's choose from accommodations ranging from private cabins to communal bunkhouses. Rooms are heated, and there is a bathhouse with hot water, showers, and a sink for washing dishes. There is a definite outdoors feel here; the front desk sells just about every piece of gear a hiker might need, and the accommodations are rustic. But for a hiker, particularly one who is trying to complete the 2,170-mile Appalachian Trail, the digs are downright palatial.

There is a bike path into town and a fleet of bikes available to borrow. Uncle Johnny will also shuttle you into town. Most hikers head first for food—Erwin has its share of chain restaurants—and then to do a load of laundry and check their email at the local library. The Nolichucky Hostel is a good base even if you are not hiking the whole Appalachian Trail. Section hikers use it as a base, and others fashion great day hikes that end at the doorstep. Talk to Uncle Johnny for help planning your itinerary.

In addition to the hostel, there is a **Holiday Inn Express** (2002 Temple Hill Rd., 423/743-4100, $80–100) and a **Super 8** (1101 N. Buffalo St., 423/743-0200, $50–99).

Food

J. D.'s Market (1313 Jackson Love Hwy., 423/743-4035, daily 6 A.M.–11 P.M., $5–9), a low-slung circular building that is also a gas station, is a popular pit stop for a working-man's breakfast of eggs, toast, hash browns, and coffee. At lunch, grilled sandwiches, burgers, and hot dogs are on the menu, along with specials—burrito casserole, for example. Sit at the lunch counter or at a booth in the small dining room.

Located on Highway 107, midway between Erwin and Greeneville, is ☾ **The Farmer's Daughter Restaurant** (7700 Erwin Hwy./Hwy. 107, 423/257-4650, Fri.–Sat. 11:30 A.M.–8:30 P.M., Sun. 11:30 A.M.–5 P.M., $12). This wood-paneled eatery is well worth the drive, particularly for those who relish home-style country cooking. The menu features a changing selection of main entrées, which are served with a smorgasbord of family-style side dishes: mashed potatoes, corn-bread salad, carrot soufflé, fried okra, creamed corn, and coleslaw. Entrées include dishes like fried chicken livers, fried chicken, chicken and dumplings, barbecue ribs, and country ham. Adult plates are $12.75, and plates for children (6–11 years) are $6.38. Children five years and younger eat free. Each table gets to choose two main dish entrées. The day's vegetables come with the meal, along with drinks.

Ridges and Valleys

West of the Cherokee National Forest, the high mountains are replaced with a series of ridges and valleys. These ridges run parallel to the mountains—at a northeasterly keel—and cause roads and railways to follow a similar slantways track.

Some of these valleys are home to relatively large towns and busy roads. But as you head westward and push north toward the Kentucky state line, you enter into countryside that remains largely unblemished by widespread development.

JONESBOROUGH

If this region of Tennessee is the state's first frontier, then Jonesborough is its first town. Established in 1779 while the frontier was still part of North Carolina, Jonesborough was named for Willie Jones, a North Carolina legislator who supported westward expansion. Jonesborough was the capital of the erstwhile State of Franklin and an important commercial and political hub in the years before Tennessee became a state. Other interesting historical connections are that Andrew Jackson practiced law in Jonesborough for several months in 1788, and that the first regularly published abolitionist newspaper was published in Jonesborough by Quaker Elihu Embree starting in 1820.

The best thing about Jonesborough today is that its history has been preserved. Way back in the 1970s, when other cities were building strip malls and highways, Jonesborough started to preserve its historic downtown. It was the first downtown district in Tennessee to be placed on the National Register of Historic Places. In 1973, the first National Storytelling Festival was held, and it continues to be one of Tennessee's most popular annual events.

Today, historic Jonesborough is one of the most vibrant small towns in the region for shopping and dining. Its downtown district is inviting and a pleasant place for a stroll. And since the National Storytelling Center opened here in 2002, visitors who miss the storytelling festival may still hear some great tales.

Sights

The **Historic Jonesborough Visitors Center** and the **Jonesborough-Washington County History Museum** (117 Boone St., 423/753-1010, Mon.–Fri. 8 A.M.–5 P.M., Sat.–Sun. 10 A.M.–5 P.M., free) share a building about one block from Main Street. Together, they make a good first stop for visitors to the town. The visitors center has maps and other information,

THE LOST STATE OF FRANKLIN

For about five years in the 1780s, settlers in what is now upper East Tennessee tried to establish a new American state called Franklin. The movement was spurred mostly by the feeling among many of these overmountain families that they were too far away from the government of North Carolina, and that North Carolina was not providing the law and order that they needed.

The State of Franklin movement met with opposition in North Carolina, which viewed it as an act of rebellion. More important, however, was the fact that many wealthy North Carolina land speculators held title to land over the mountains, and that the existence of a separate state could invalidate their claims.

Despite the opposition from North Carolina and a few local settlers, the State of Franklin enjoyed some success. In December 1784 a convention met in Jonesborough and agreed that the North Carolina constitution would form the basis of Franklin's government, with a few minor alterations. A second convention a year later led to the adoption of the Holston Constitution, which provided for a unicameral legislature. At a third convention in March 1786, John Sevier was elected the governor of Franklin.

North Carolina continued to oppose the statehood movement in its western territories. Overmountain settlers themselves had mixed feelings about Franklin. North Carolina improved its government services in the frontier as conciliation, so some settlers no longer saw the need for a separate state government. But in the area south of the French Broad, the frontier of the day, residents appreciated the strong anti-Indian stance taken by Sevier and the Franklin government.

Support for the State of Franklin dwindled by early 1789. By this time the Cherokee had been pushed south of the Little Tennessee River, providing, at least for the time being, peace. John Sevier became a member of the North Carolina legislature from Greene County and retreated as an outspoken proponent of separate statehood.

No leader emerged to succeed Sevier, and the movement faded into history. Less than 10 years later, the lands over the mountain, now called Tennessee, were admitted as the 16th state.

while the museum houses artifacts and memorabilia about Tennessee's oldest town, including the oldest known photo of Jonesborough, which dates to 1850.

HISTORIC DOWNTOWN

Jonesborough's oldest frame building is the **Chester Inn** (116 W. Main St.). The Chester Inn was constructed in the late 1790s by William Chester, a medical doctor who capitalized on the new stage road that passed through town. Now owned by the state, the Chester Inn houses the offices of the National Storytelling Festival.

The **Christopher Taylor House** (124 W. Main St.) appears a bit out of place among Jonesborough's handsome frame and brick buildings. This log cabin, which once housed Andrew Jackson, was moved to Main Street and restored. It was built around 1778. Some say Andrew Jackson's ghost still haunts this house.

◖ National Storytelling Festival

The National Storytelling Festival (800/952-8392, www.storytellingcenter.net) is Jonesborough's premier event. Taking place during the first weekend in October, the festival features multiple tents with storytellers from a diverse range of traditions and styles. Traditional mountain tellers share the stage with world performers from Africa, Asia, Europe, and South America. Native American, Irish, and African American storytelling traditions are showcased. Indeed, if you thought that storytelling was a dying art, you will be pleasantly surprised by the depth and relevance of the artists who perform at the festival.

Folks flock to Jonesborough to hear tall tales at the National Storytelling Festival.

The storytelling festival began in 1973, and today it attracts some 10,000 people each year. Weekend passes cost $165 for adults and $145 for children; single-day passes are also available. Registered attendees receive a detailed schedule for each tent, and you can simply choose which tellers you want to hear. Food is served in a food court and at area restaurants, or you can pack a picnic. The storytelling festival is a good experience for people of just about every walk of life, and it's considered to be one of Tennessee's best and most distinctive events.

Book a room very, very early if you hope to stay in Jonesborough proper during the festival (and be prepared to pay premium rates). The closest motel accommodations are in Johnson City. Erwin and Greeneville are not far away, and camping is available at Davy Crockett State Park.

If you can't make it to the national festival, you can still hear stories in Jonesborough. The **National Storytelling Center** (116 W. Main St., 423/753-2171, www.storytellingcenter.net, Tues.–Sat. 10 A.M.–5 P.M., matinees: adults $12, seniors, students, and children under 18 $11, evening tickets: adults $15, not recommended for children under 12) offers storytelling from the storyteller in residence June–October. While it lacks the electricity and excitement of the large-scale festival, it is still a wonderful way to pass some time and rediscover this classic art form. During the rest of the year, the center houses exhibits about storytelling. It also has a nice gift shop.

Recreation

For something a little different, take the family to **The Wetlands** (1523 Persimmon Ridge Rd., 423/753-1550, May–mid-Aug. Mon.–Sat. 10 A.M.–6 P.M., Sun. noon–6 P.M., mid-Aug.–Sept. weekends only, adults $12, seniors and children 4–12 $9), a water park that includes flume rides, boardwalks, a wave pool, and much more. Check for exact opening dates, which normally coincide with local school calendars.

Accommodations

There are bed-and-breakfast-style inns and guesthouses in Jonesborough. On the highways leading to town you will find major chain motels.

The historic **Eureka Hotel** (127 W. Main St., 423/913-6100 or 877/734-6100, www.eurekajonesborough.com, $119–139) is your best choice for accommodations in Jonesborough. Built in 1797 and expanded 100 years later, this handsome hotel offers 16 guest rooms that blend old-fashioned atmosphere with modern comforts. Amenities include soundproof insulation, voice mail and dataports, private telephone lines, individual climate control, and cable TV. Private baths, high-speed wireless Internet, and a continental breakfast round out the offerings. The Eureka Inn is centrally located, and guests will enjoy use of the back garden, plus off-street private parking.

Many of Jonesborough's other bed-and-breakfasts are located in historic homes that line quiet side streets in town. Distinctive bed-and-breakfast-style accommodations are found at the **Blair-Moore House** (201 W. Main St., 423/753-0044, $150–185). This Greek Revival–style brick home has been fully restored and an English-style garden built in the rear. The two guest rooms and one suite have high ceilings, four-poster beds, and fine linens. Rooms also each have a private balcony, and bathroom with antique claw-foot tubs. The suite also has a walk-in shower. The homemade breakfast prepared by hostess Tami Moore is a real winner.

The **Fiddler's Glen Bed 'n' Breakfast** (104 S. 3rd Ave., 423/913-3259, www.fiddlersglenbnb.com, $120–130) is an 1854 Carpenter Gothic home with two guest rooms, friendly cats, and a hostess who plays the fiddle. The music room holds a large collection of musical instruments, and the library upstairs will keep you occupied if Jonesborough fails to. Rooms have private bathrooms, and guests will enjoy a filling breakfast in the morning.

Housed in an elegant 1832 home on four acres, the **Febuary Hill Bed and Breakfast** (102 W. College St., 423/737-6501, $150–200) is named for a local family, not the month. This large and upscale home sits just a block from Main Street atop a hill overlooking the town. Each room has a private bathroom.

Food

Jonesborough has a pleasing array of eateries. Located a few blocks from the historic downtown, the **Olde Town Pancake House** (142 Boone St., 423/913-8111, Mon.–Thurs. and Sat. 7 A.M.–2 P.M., Fri. 7 A.M.–9 P.M., Sun. 8:30 A.M.–2 P.M., $8–12) is a classic breakfast eatery. There are dozens of varieties of pancakes, including buttermilk, buckwheat, and apple stack. In addition, choose from omelets, biscuits and gravy, or classic breakfasts of eggs, toast, and bacon. At lunch you can also order grilled sandwiches or burgers, and dinner specials include fried catfish and rib-eye steak.

Jonesborough's "it" restaurant is **The Bistro** (105 E. Main St., 423/788-0244, Tues.–Sat. 11 A.M.–4 P.M. and 5–9 P.M., $8–23), which serves dishes like pecan-encrusted salmon, filet mignon, and even a Black Angus hot dog.

Information

The **Historic Jonesborough Visitors Center** (117 Boone St., 866/401-4223, www.historicjonesborough.com, Mon.–Fri. 8 A.M.–5 P.M., Sat.–Sun. 10 A.M.–5 P.M.) provides free maps, a walking tour, and other information about the town.

GREENEVILLE

Founded in 1783 and named after Nathanial Greene, a Revolutionary War hero, Greeneville is the seat of Greene County. Two American heroes, Davy Crockett and U.S. president Andrew Johnson, are affiliated with the city and the county.

© JOSEPH T. RICHARDSON

The Andrew Johnson National Historic Site showcases the work of our 17th president.

◖ Andrew Johnson National Historic Site

America's 17th president called Greeneville home. Andrew Johnson was born in Raleigh, North Carolina, in 1808, but he spent the better part of his life in this Tennessee city. It was here that Johnson, a self-educated tailor, first showed promise as a debater and political leader. Three Johnson buildings remain in Greeneville, and together they make up the Andrew Johnson National Historic Site (121 Monument Ave., 423/638-3551, www.nps.gov/anjo, daily 9 A.M.–5 P.M., free). Johnson's Early Home is where he and his wife, Eliza McCardle, lived during the early years of their marriage. Next door is Johnson's old Tailor Shop, fully enclosed by the present-day visitors center, where Johnson sewed clothes and debated local politics with his customers and friends. About

three blocks away is the Johnson Homestead, the grander home to which the Johnsons moved in 1851, and where they returned in 1869 after his term as president ended.

Inside the Early Home are displays about Johnson's early life and family. The visitors center contains a museum about Johnson's political career, and inside the Tailor Shop you can see some of the tools Johnson would have used to sew clothes. Guided tours of the Homestead include several family bedrooms and the parlor, arranged as it would have been during Johnson's postpresidential years. As evidence of the unpopularity of Johnson's pro-Union views, the tour includes a section of unflattering graffiti on an interior wall, just some of what the Johnsons found upon their return to Greeneville in 1869.

In addition to these buildings, there

HUNTING FOR QUILTS

As you drive through Tennessee, look for quilt squares on the sides of barns and other buildings. These aren't spontaneous displays of artwork; they are part of the Appalachian Quilt Trail (AQT), a program designed to encourage visitors to get off the interstate and explore the smaller roads and communities; i.e., "the scenic route."

The program began in 2004 when the first quilt panel was hung on a barn in Grainger County. Over the succeeding years, almost 800 quilt patterns have been hung. Though the program started in rural East Tennessee, it has grown to span across the entire state. In East Tennessee, however, the trail is most developed. The squares are designed to highlight something unique to travelers who are drawn to take the path off the highway. The architecture of the rural South is something they aim to preserve. The squares also highlight artists, craftspeople, galleries, and farms with homemade wares for sale. Some of these goods are available at River Place on the Clinch and at local craft fairs across the state. AQT attempts to bring rural craftsmanship to a larger audience and encourage sustainable tourism and growth.

Download a guide from the AQT website at www.vacationaqt.com or pick one up at a Tennessee visitors center. The trail is diverse enough that you can choose a minitrail that highlights a certain area, county, art form, or even quilt pattern.

is also a replica of the Raleigh, North Carolina, building where Johnson was born. This is located across the street from the Early Home and was erected in 1999. On a hill overlooking the town is Johnson's grave, over which are the words, "His Faith In the People Never Wavered."

The visitors center is open daily except holidays. Tours of the Homestead are offered hourly on the half hour; tours are free, but tickets for this tour must be obtained from the visitors center in advance.

Other Sights

Revolutionary War hero Nathanael Greene is not only the namesake of the county and town, but also the local history museum. Come to the **Nathanael Greene Museum** (101 W. McKee St., 423/636-1558, www.nathanaelgreenemuseum.com, Tues.–Sat. 10 A.M.–5 P.M., open Mon. in the summer, free) for a closer look at the town's history, its notable buildings, and its hometown hero, Andrew Johnson.

Greeneville's most prominent home was built between 1815 and 1821 by Irish and enslaved African artisans. The **Dickson-Williams**

Mansion (108 N. Irish St., reservations and information 423/787-0500, Mon.–Sat. 10 A.M.–2 P.M.) was owned first by William Dickson, a wealthy landowner, merchant, and Greeneville's first postmaster. His daughter, Catherine Dickson Williams, was well known for entertaining esteemed guests, including the Marquis de Lafayette, Davy Crockett, and three presidents: Andrew Johnson, Andrew Jackson, and James K. Polk. Tours of the home are given Monday–Saturday at 1 P.M. and cost $10 for adults and $5 for children 6–18.

Tours

Main Street Tours (310 S. Main St., 423/787-0500) offers a guided walking tour of Greeneville, which stops at historically and architecturally significant buildings, including the oldest jail in Tennessee and sites important to Andrew Johnson's history. The tours are offered April–October Monday–Saturday at 9:30 A.M. Tickets, which cost $5, may be purchased at the General Morgan Inn.

In addition to these guided tours, local officials have developed two self-guided tours for visitors. One, titled "A Walk with the President," is a walking tour of Greeneville.

The second includes 40 different auto tours of Greene County. Copies of either are available from Greene County Partnership (115 Academy St., 423/638-4111, www.greenecountypartnership.com).

Recreation

Kinser Park (650 Kinser Park Ln., 423/639-5912, www.kinserpark.com, Apr.–Oct., hours vary, call ahead) is a public park with a swimming pool; waterslide; putt-putt golf course; 18-hole golf course; volleyball, basketball, tennis, and other ball fields; and a 157-site campground.

Accommodations

Named for the Confederate outlaw and hero Gen. John Hunt Morgan, nicknamed "The Thunderbolt of the Confederacy," who was killed in Greeneville, the **C General Morgan Inn** (111 N. Main St., 423/787-1000, www.generalmorganinn.com, $105–159) is Greeneville's most distinctive hotel. First opened as the Grand Central Hotel in 1884, the General Morgan was restored and re-opened in 1996. Its lobby has a high ceiling and elegant chandeliers; the refinement continues in the 52 guest rooms and suites, where you'll find luxury linens, marble vanities, wireless Internet, and iPod-compatible radios. Guests can also take advantage of business services and passes to a local gym.

Food

The denizens of Greeneville meet for lunch of club sandwiches and chicken salad at the **Tannery Downtown** (117 E. Depot St., 423/638-2772, Mon.–Fri. 10:30 A.M.–2 P.M., $5–6), located a few doors down from the Andrew Johnson visitors center.

For something more elegant, choose **Brumley's** (111 N. Main St., 423/787-1000, Mon.–Fri. 7–9 A.M., 11 A.M.–2 P.M., 5–9 P.M., Sat. 10 A.M.–2 P.M., 5–9 P.M., Sun. 10 A.M.–2 P.M., lunch $7–10, dinner $18–30) in the General Morgan Inn. The weekday soup and salad bar is popular with lunchtime diners,

along with the smothered black beans and rice, roasted pork, and crab cakes. Dinner choices include baked sea bass and filet mignon.

Information

The **Greene County Partnership Tourism Council** (115 Academy St., 423/638-4111, www.greene-countypartnership.com) has maps and other guides to Greeneville and the rest of Greene County.

AROUND GREENEVILLE
Tusculum

About 10 miles east of Greeneville is Tusculum, a small college town. Tusculum College was chartered in 1794 and is the oldest college in Tennessee. In 1872 it admitted women, making it one of the first coeducational colleges in the United States. Nine buildings on the Tusculum campus have been placed on the National Register of Historic Places, including the **Andrew Johnson Presidential Library and Museum** (Tusculum College, 423/636-7348, www.tusculum.edu/pages/ajohnson, Mon.–Fri. 9 A.M.–5 P.M., free). This is the official museum and library dedicated to Johnson, a Tusculum trustee, as designated by Congress. The museum houses political memorabilia, artifacts, and photographs emphasizing the daily life of the Johnson family, including the bed in which he died. His papers are also here and are used by researchers and historians.

The **Samuel Doak Museum** (Tusculum College, 423/636-8554, http://doakhouse.tusculum.edu, Mon.–Fri. 9 A.M.–5 P.M., adults $5, children $2), owned by the college, is the home that the Reverend Samuel Witherspoon Doak built beginning in 1818 for his father, Dr. Samuel Doak. Dr. Doak had been one of the first ministers on the Tennessee frontier. He preached to the overmountain men before they left on their journey to Kings Mountain in 1780. Dr. Doak moved to Washington County and established Salem Church and school in the early 1780s. The school became Washington College, a day and boarding school for young men. Boys from far and near traveled for the opportunity to learn Latin, mathematics, and other subjects.

The Samuel Doak House is where both Samuel Doaks lived from 1818 until 1829, when Dr. Doak died. The museum features a few articles of furniture original to the Doak home. The handsome redbrick building was lived in by members of the Doak family until the 1950s. There is also a replica of Doak's original schoolhouse on the property.

For food in this area, head to **Tusculum Eatery** (905 Erwin Hwy., 423/638-9210, Mon.–Fri. 10:30 A.M.–2:30 P.M., $4–7), a pleasant place to pass the time while you munch on fresh-made sandwiches, salads, and daily specials like lasagna and chicken potpie. Artwork by local artists adorns the walls.

Limestone

Davy Crockett was not born on a mountaintop in Tennessee, as the song goes (guess it was a better rhyme); he was born in the rolling foothills, near where the Limestone River flows into the Nolichucky. His birthplace is near the present-day settlement of Limestone, about 15 minutes' drive from Greeneville. The cabin where Crockett was born is long gone, but a replica sits on the banks of the Nolichucky at the **Davy Crockett Birthplace State Park** (1245 Davy Crockett Park Rd., 423/257-2167), also home to a museum about this most famous Tennessean.

Crockett lived on the banks of the river with his parents for 10 years before the family decamped to Morristown to open a tavern. After he became a man, Crockett continued to move gradually westward, seemingly following the ever-migrating frontier of America. He is known to have lived in Greene, Hamblen, Lincoln, Franklin, Lawrence, and Obion Counties in Tennessee before he moved to Texas, where he was killed at the Alamo.

Crockett's folksy language and boasting stories turned him into one of the most enduring symbols of the frontiersman. A museum at the state park includes copies of all the known portraits of Crockett, memorabilia he inspired, plus information about what is known about this remarkable man. Crockett's most famous sayings include, "Let your tongue speak what your heart thinks," and "Be always sure you're right, then go ahead."

In addition to the sights related to all things Crockett, the state park has a campground with 88 sites, which are available on a first-come, first-served basis; about 2.5 miles of hiking trails; and a swimming pool, which is open Memorial Day–Labor Day.

ROGERSVILLE

A town of many firsts, Rogersville is a worthwhile destination. Tennessee's first newspaper was published here, and the city is home of the oldest courthouse, inn, and post office still in operation in Tennessee.

Rogersville was settled in about 1775. According to legend, some of those early settlers were Davy Crockett's grandparents. It was named after Joseph Rogers, an Irishman who received the land on which Rogersville sits as a wedding present from his father-in-law, Col. Thomas Amis.

Rogersville was on the Wilderness Road, the route that traveled from Bean Station to Cumberland Gap and into Kentucky. Beginning in the 1840s, the city was a transportation hub for native pink and red marble, which was used in construction of the Washington Monument in Washington DC, the South Carolina State Capitol, and the municipal buildings in Baltimore.

Today, Rogersville is a quiet yet relatively happening place. A handful of attractions, an inviting downtown district, and the nearby countryside, which is beautiful and rural, make this a small town worth remembering.

Historic Downtown

Take a few minutes to explore Rogersville's

THE MELUNGEON MYSTERY

Hancock County was one of the first parts of Tennessee to be settled by Europeans. A 1673 letter by early explorer Abraham Wood described his visit to the area: "Eight dayes jorny down this river lives a white people which have long beards and whiskers and weares clothing . . ." These white people were also described by John Sevier in 1784, who reported that they seemed to have been living in the area for some time.

The word that came to be used to describe these mysterious early settlers was *Melungeon*. Even the origin of the word is unclear; it was initially thought to have derived from the French word *mélange* (mixture). Other research suggests it may be an Afro-Portuguese word meaning white person, and still other scholars believe it is from the Turkish language and means cursed soul.

When Anglo-European settlers arrived in the area, they conveniently decided that the Melungeons, who had olive complexions and dark hair, were people of color and promptly took their land. Discrimination and prejudice caused Melungeons and their descendants to retreat to some of the most rural and remote territory of the county.

Despite ongoing efforts to determine exactly how and when Melungeons arrived in Appalachia, there are still many questions about the origins of these very early Tennesseans. In the 1990s, a 30-member panel put together by Clinch Valley College of the University of Virginia spent four years researching Melungeons. The consensus, by no means definitive, was that they are of Middle Eastern or Mediterranean heritage. It is still debated how they came to Appalachia and whether they intermarried with Native Americans.

Despite the passage of time and increasing interest in Melungeon heritage, the story of the Melungeons remains one that is often told in whispers. A good source of information is the Melungeon Heritage Association (www.melungeon.org).

---

historic district. The **Hawkins County Courthouse** is the oldest original courthouse still in use in Tennessee. It was built in 1836 and was fashioned after Independence Hall in Philadelphia. Across the road from the courthouse is **Overton Lodge,** the oldest Masonic lodge in continuous operation in Tennessee. The lodge was chartered in 1805. The present building was constructed in 1839 as the first branch of the Bank of the State of Tennessee.

Also on the town square is the **Hale Springs Inn** (110 W. Main St.). Built in 1824, it is the oldest continually operating inn in Tennessee.

A few blocks north is the **Swift College Campus** (200 N. Depot St.). Swift College was a Northern Presbyterian college for African Americans and operated from 1883 to 1955. It was founded by Dr. William Henderson Franklin of Knoxville, who was the first black graduate of Maryville College. From 1955 to 1963 it was Hawkins County's African American high school. After integration, the lovely administration building was torn down. Remaining buildings are used by the Hawkins County Department of Education.

Price Public School (203 Spring St., 423/921-3888, Mon.–Fri. 10 A.M.–2 P.M., Sat. noon–2 P.M.) is a community center that was once Rogersville's African American school. Established in 1868, Price Public School educated blacks from 1870 until desegregation. The present building was constructed in 1922. If you go inside, you can view a room dedicated to Swift College and Price Public School.

A printed guide to historic Rogersville is available from the Rogersville Heritage Association (415 S. Depot St.) and the Rogersville–Hawkins County Chamber of Commerce (107 E. Main St.).

Tennessee Newspaper and Printing Museum

The *Knoxville Gazette* was first published in Rogersville in November 1791, before it was moved to Knoxville. George Roulstone and Robert Ferguson arrived in Rogersville on the invitation of governor William Blount, and they named their newspaper in anticipation of the establishment of the new city to the south. But while Knoxville was getting off the ground, Roulstone and Ferguson published for about one year from Rogersville. When the time came to move, they moved the presses to Knoxville on a flatboat down the Holston River.

Rogersville's first newspaper is recalled at the Tennessee Newspaper and Printing Museum (415 S. Depot St., 423/272-1961, Mon.–Thurs. 10 A.M.–3 P.M., free), located in the town's old train depot. It is best to call ahead and confirm hours.

The museum contains a re-created 19th-century print shop, original copies of more than two dozen newspapers that were printed here, and artifacts from the Pressman's Home. You can also see the last linotype machine used to set type for a Tennessee newspaper; the machine was used by the *Rogersville Review* until 1982.

Pressman's Home

Located about 12 miles north of Rogersville are the abandoned remains of Pressman's Home, a once-thriving community affiliated with the 125,000-member International Printing Pressmen and Assistants' Union (IPPAU). Rogersville native George Berry headed the union from 1907 until 1948, and it was due to his efforts that the substantial facility was built in remote upper East Tennessee.

Pressman's Home covered 2,700 acres. It had its own phone and electrical system, post office, and farm. In addition to being the administrative headquarters of the IPPAU, Pressman's Home was a retirement home, sanatorium, and printing trade school. For a time, Pressman's Home was the largest training school of its kind in the world. New and experienced pressmen came here to learn offset printing methods. They also offered a correspondence school.

Pressman's Home operated from 1911 until 1966, when union officials decided they needed to return to a more cosmopolitan place. In 1967 the IPPAU headquarters moved to Washington DC. Not 10 years later the IPPAU merged with another union and disappeared from the union registry.

Today, Pressman's Home is abandoned, and the community has been renamed Camelot. It is not a very inviting place. A former country club and golf course on the property failed, and plans to turn it into a state prison and an environmental education center did not reach fruition. In 2008, fire destroyed what was left of the hotel. But if you drive north on Highway 70, and then turn left on Highway 94, you will soon see the still-imposing edifices of the remaining buildings.

Shopping

The **Local Artists Gallery** (124 E. Main St., 423/921-7656, www.rogersvillegallery.com) has a wide selection of arts and crafts, including paintings and prints, woodwork, pottery, textiles, and candles.

Accommodations

The **Hale Springs Inn** (110 E. Main St., 423/272-5171, www.halespringsinn.com, $125–165) was built in 1824 and reopened in 2009 following extensive renovations. The inn balances modern comfort with ambience befitting such a historic structure. This should be your first choice for accommodations in Rogersville.

Food

Rogersville has several casual coffee shops that double as cafés. **Miss Bea's Perks and Pies** (109 S. Church St., 423/272-6555, Mon.–Thurs. 7 A.M.–3 P.M., Fri. 7 A.M.–5 P.M., Sat. 8 A.M.–3 P.M., $4–5) has a wide repertoire of sandwiches, panini, wraps, and soups. Each day, they offer two soups and sandwiches to choose from. Popular favorites are the turkey and artichoke panini, chicken and grape salad sandwich, and the stuffed-pepper soup. For breakfast, Miss Bea offers stratas and biscuits, plus a variety of pastries. They also serve fresh-brewed specialty coffees.

Offering lunch-counter fare, daily lunch specials, and hearty breakfast platters, **Oh Henry's** (201 E. Main St., 423/272-0980, Mon.–Sat. 6 A.M.–11 P.M., $4–12) is an institution in Rogersville. It's a down-home, no-frills, friendly type of place.

Information

The **Rogersville Heritage Association** (415 S. Depot St., 423/272-1961, www.rogersville-heritage.org) does an admirable job of promoting the town and sharing its history with the world. You can also contact the **Rogersville-Hawkins County Chamber of Commerce** (107 E. Main St., 423/272-2186, www.rogersville-tn.com).

◖ KYLES FORD

The countryside north of Rogersville, in Hawkins and Hancock Counties, is some of the most rural and isolated in this region. If the northeastern tip of Tennessee is its first frontier, then this is the last.

It is the rugged landscape that keeps this area from changing. Long, steep valleys lie between Clinch and Powell Mountains. The Clinch River flows unimpeded from Virginia, cutting a wide valley, which is prone to flood. And narrow, two-lane roads wind around hills and over mountains. This is beautiful countryside, but only if you're willing to slow down and enjoy it.

As for a destination, head north along Highway 70 to Kyles Ford, a small settlement along the Clinch just a few miles from Virginia. In 2007, an exciting development project led by the Clinch River RC&D, a rural development organization serving Claiborne, Grainger, Hancock, Hawkins, and Union Counties, gave visitors a good reason to make the trip.

◖ **River Place** (2788 Hwy. 70, 423/733-4400, www.clinchriverecotourism.com,

Freshwater mussels are among the unique wildlife found in the water at Kyles Ford.

© STEPHANI RICHARDSON

River Place in Kyles Ford

Mon.–Sat. 6:30 A.M.–9 P.M., Sun. 9 A.M.–6 P.M., $4–9), a general store and restaurant, is the cornerstone of the development project. This handsome riverfront building is a small grocery and the best restaurant in these parts. The food here is actually made from scratch (not just claimed to be the case); homemade biscuits, comfort casseroles, and sides like real mashed potatoes will please your palate. The matter-of-fact friendliness of the folks here will please your spirit. The slogan is: "Nothing fancy. Just food you want to eat."

Behind the café are ◖ **River Place Cabins** (423/733-4400, www.clinchriverecotourism. com, $80–95 or $575 per week), four vacation cabins and an 1800s cottage now restored for guests. The vacation cabins were constructed in 2007 but look like they've been settled into the hillside for years. Interior wood paneling, quilts, and simple decor ease your mind and invite relaxation. The cabins overlook the Clinch

River and have fully functioning kitchens, telephones, and central heat and air. There's no cell phone service, and you have to drive to the local library to check your email.

A few hundred yards down the road, on the other side of the river, the **Clinch River Conservation and Retreat Center** (3225 Hwy. 70, 423/733-4400) is an old farmhouse has been restored and renovated to become an environmental retreat center and venue for reunions, meetings, and other gatherings.

SNEEDVILLE

A small town deep in the rural landscape, Sneedville suffers from an unfairly unflattering name. It is named for Knoxville lawyer W. H. Sneed, who represented Hancock County in its 1840s struggle to become a county. Sneedville is the commercial and government center for a mostly rural and largely undeveloped part of the state.

Sneedville is the headquarters of a regional artisans cooperative. **Clinch Appalachian Artisans Cooperative** (Jubilee Center, 197 N. Jockey St., 423/733-4195, http://jubileeproject.holston.org/business.htm) appears at area festivals and art shows. Inside this Sneedville gift shop you'll find locally made jewelry, woodwork, brooms, stained glass, gourd art, and more great ideas for souvenirs for those back home.

Located in the same building as the artisans cooperative is a retail outlet of **Jubilee Country Store and Eatery** (423/733-4007, www.countrystoreandeatery.weebly.com), an innovative project that allows farmers use of a commercial kitchen to bottle or package their goods. The retail outlet is an excellent place to stock up on locally produced jams, salsas, vegetable preserves, and other goods that support local farmers and the local economy. They also deliver and serve meals to the hungry in the community for a suggested donation of $5.

BACKGROUND

The Land

Tennessee is a long, narrow state. Shaped roughly like a parallelogram, it is 500 miles from east to west and 110 miles from north to south. Partly due to its unusual shape, Tennessee, along with Missouri, borders more states than any other in the country. Its neighbors are North Carolina, Virginia, Kentucky, Missouri, Arkansas, Mississippi, Alabama, and Georgia. Tennessee is the 36th-largest state in the United States, with a land mass of 44,169 square miles.

Like the rest of the United States, Tennessee was covered by a large shallow sea approximately 500 million years ago. As the sea dried up, the land that is now Tennessee turned swampy and eventually dry. The sea creatures that once lived in the sea died, their skeletons forming limestone. The plants and animals that lived in the swampy landscape died, eventually forming coal.

Beginning about 600 million years ago, the Appalachian Mountains were formed through plate movement. Once sharp and rocky, the Appalachians have been worn down over million of years to the gentle, rounded slopes that now characterize the range.

GEOGRAPHY

If you ask a Tennessean where they are from, the answer is never as simple as "Tennessee." Tennessee is divided by the Tennessee River into three "Grand Divisions": East Tennessee, Middle Tennessee, and West Tennessee.

East Tennessee

East Tennessee is defined by the Appalachian Mountains and their foothills. This region was historically small farms and isolated mountain communities.

Within East Tennessee are two geographic regions. The Unaka Mountains are part of the Appalachian Mountain chain, which peak along the state's border with North Carolina. This zone includes the Great Smoky Mountains National Park. It is also where you will find Clingmans Dome, which at 6,643 feet above sea level is the highest point in Tennessee.

West of the Unaka Mountains is the Great Valley of East Tennessee, home to Knoxville and Chattanooga. This region is characterized by picturesque low ridges and a wide, fertile valley.

Middle Tennessee

Middle Tennessee is home to Tennessee's capital city, Nashville, and some of its most fertile farmland. Before the Civil War, great plantation mansions dotted the countryside south of Nashville.

Geographically, Middle Tennessee begins with the Cumberland Plateau, which rises to about 2,000 feet above sea level and lies west of East Tennessee's Great Valley. Despite its name, the plateau is not flat; there are a number of steep valleys in the plateau, the largest being the Sequatchie Valley.

The Highland Rim is a region of hills, valleys, and fertile farmland that lies west of the plateau. The largest physical region of Tennessee, the Highland Rim contains 10,650 square miles of land, or almost 25 percent of the state. Almost entirely surrounded by the Highland Rim is the Central Basin, a low, flat, and fertile region in north-central Tennessee. Nashville is located in the Central Basin.

West Tennessee

West Tennessee is more like the Deep South than the rest of the state. Mostly flat and rural, this was the epicenter of the state's cotton industry both before and after the Civil War. The Gulf Coastal Plain, an area of 9,000 square miles, is drained by the Mississippi River and its tributaries. Memphis lies in the southwestern corner of this area.

RIVERS AND LAKES

The largest river in Tennessee is the Mississippi River, which forms the western border of the state. The Hatchie River is among the smaller tributaries that drain West Tennessee and flow into the Mississippi.

The state's two most important rivers are the Cumberland and Tennessee Rivers. The Cumberland River flows through Nashville and along the north-central portion of the state. The Tennessee River flows in a U shape, first flowing south through East Tennessee, through Knoxville and Chattanooga, and then northward, defining the boundary between Middle and West Tennessee. Both the Cumberland and the Tennessee Rivers empty into the Ohio River, which flows to the Mississippi.

All but one of Tennessee's major lakes are artificial, having been created by the Tennessee Valley Authority during the last century. The lone exception to this is Reelfoot Lake in northeastern Tennessee, which was formed from the 1811 New Madrid earthquake when the mouth of what had been Reelfoot Creek was closed off and the creek's water spread out to cover the surrounding land.

CLIMATE

Tennessee has a mild climate. The average temperature is 58°F; in winter, temperatures generally hover 30–40°F, and summer temperatures

Cotton ready for harvest is still a common sight in parts of West Tennessee.

are 70–80°F. Summer days can feel very hot, however, particularly in Middle and West Tennessee. Of the state's three major cities, Memphis temperatures rise slightly higher than the others during the summer, and the city stays warmest in winter. Knoxville is the coolest city.

The state receives an average of 50 inches of rain per year, and only a few places in the Appalachian Mountains receive more than 10 inches of snow per year. Most parts of Tennessee receive little, if any, snow or ice precipitation annually. When they do, schools and streets close, as few cities own snow-removal equipment.

Heavy rains associated with tropical weather systems can sometimes affect the state, and winter weather can close roads in the higher elevations along the Cumberland Plateau and the Smoky Mountains.

A historic drought in the summer of 2007 raised concerns about water supply throughout Tennessee.

Tornadoes

The Mid-South, including western and central Tennessee, is prone to tornadoes. The tornado season runs November–April. The danger of tornadoes is compounded by the fact that they may strike after dark and that in many areas of the state, visibility is limited by hills and trees.

On Super Tuesday, February 5, 2008, a series of tornadoes struck Tennessee, killing 32 people, most of them in Sumner and Macon Counties north of Nashville. Of those who died, 20 were in mobile homes when the storm struck. The event, one of the most deadly natural disasters in Tennessee history, led to calls for better education and awareness.

The best way to avoid injury in a tornado is to monitor a weather radio and move quickly to a cellar, basement, or windowless interior room if a tornado is on the way.

Floods

The devastating flood in Nashville and Middle Tennessee in May 2010 brought the issue of global climate changes, combined

the Mississippi River and downtown Memphis

© HENRYK SADURA/123RF

with man-made development and water management, to the forefront of the minds of city planners and residents. The flood caused more than $1.5 billion of damage to the Music City. At press time, most of the commercial public repairs to the city had been made, but residential redevelopment continues. Floods were also a concern in 2011 when the Mississippi threatened to cover parts of Memphis with water.

FLORA AND FAUNA

Encyclopedias are written about Tennessee's rich and diverse menagerie of animals and plants. The eastern mountains are one of the most biologically diverse areas in the United States, and whole volumes are devoted to their flora and fauna.

Middle and West Tennessee share the more typical plants and animals of the Deep South. Western Tennessee's cypress swamps are rich depositories of plant and animal life, while the plains are important for agriculture.

Wildflowers

In the spring and summer, wildflowers spring up along roadsides, mountain streams, and pastures. Look for the small yellow blooms of **St. John's wort** and the bushy purple crowns of **ironweed.** Delicate purple **bluebells** and white, pink, or purple **phlox** blanket cool stream banks and coves. Placid lakes and ponds come alive with the white-pink blooms of **water lily.**

Fields and gardens are decorated with the bracing yellow blooms of **sunflowers** and the bright-orange colors of **butterfly weed.** Cultivated lawns and gardens showcase delicate **roses** and elegant **irises,** the state flower of Tennessee.

Trees

Tennessee's official state tree is the **tulip poplar,** a fast-growing tree often used for timber. It blooms in May. **Flowering dogwoods** are celebrated with a springtime festival in Knoxville. The dogwood's vibrant flowers are actually white-colored leaves that surround a tight

TENNESSEE PEARLS

The fast-running rivers of Tennessee are great for recreation, but they also are home to freshwater mussels, and these mussels sometimes create surprises: beautiful pearls.

Native Americans were the first to discover Tennessee's pearls; Indians harvested mussels for food and used the pearls in jewelry. Tennessee history knows many stories of simple folks who stumbled upon a pearl, getting an unexpected payday in the process. In one such story, Charles Bradford and James Johnson were looking for bait to go fishing in the Caney Fork River in the early 1880s. They had pulled up several mussels and found a large white pearl inside one of them. The boys sent the pearl to Tiffany's in New York and received a check for $83.

Stories such as this one fueled the Tennessee pearl industry for many years. The industry peaked between 1882 and 1914, when special musseling boats would ply the Tennessee and other rivers, dragging a "brail" (resembling an underwater rake) that captured river mussels. In more modern times, diving is the most popular way to harvest wild mussels from the watery depths.

Tennessee pearls were a variety of colors and shapes, and the mother-of-pearl from the mussel shells was used in button manufacturing during the early part of the 20th century, before plastic buttons became common.

Tennessee pearls declined following the establishment of the Tennessee Valley Authority and the damming of many rivers in the state. This is because dams caused rivers to flow more slowly, thus eliminating the fast-moving water habitat required by freshwater mussels. Pollution also hurt wild mussels, as did overfishing and the rise of pearl cultivation in Asia.

The Tennessee River Pearl Farm, near Camden, Tennessee, still harvests pearls from the river, although they are cultivated. Some of the pearls harvested here are fashioned into jewelry, but most are exported to Asia, where they are used in the cultivation of high-grade pearls.

The pearl was named the Tennessee state gem in 1979.

---

cluster of flowers in the center. Some dogwood "blooms" are pink. Throughout the state you will see **magnolia** trees, notable for their thick, heavy green leaves and large white blooms, as well as their sweet scent. The Vanderbilt University campus in Nashville is particularly fragrant when magnolias are in bloom.

In West Tennessee's wetlands and at Reelfoot Lake, look for **cypress** trees, easily identifiable by their rough, bumpy knees.

Birds

Field, swamp, house, chipping, and song **sparrows,** as they flit about and perch on tree limbs, are ubiquitous in the Volunteer State. Look for the red **cardinal,** the black-and-white **junco,** and the yellow **goldfinch.**

The **Carolina chickadee** puffs out its breast in winter, and the **blue jay** patrols bird feeders. The **mockingbird** is Tennessee's state bird; it mimics the calls of other birds and has a gray body and dark wings.

Unless you are unusually patient or light of foot, you're unlikely to see the nocturnal **Eastern screech owl** or its cousins, the great horned owl and barred owl, in the wild. Keep your eyes pinned on the sky for **hawks,** red-tailed, sharp-shinned, and Cooper's. **Bald eagles** winter at Reelfoot Lake and other protected locations in the state.

Wild turkeys are making a comeback; groups may be seen patrolling many state parks and natural areas. Look for the male's impressive feathers. Listen for the knocking of the **woodpeckers**—hairy, redheaded, downy, and pileated varieties.

Bodies of water are some of the best places to seek feathered friends. **Sandhill cranes** winter on the Hiwassee River in East Tennessee. Float down a river, and you may see a statuesque

HEMLOCKS UNDER THREAT

First the American chestnut, then the Fraser fir, and now the hemlock: Nonnative insects have taken a terrible toll on the native trees of the Smokies. The dead trees visible throughout the spruce-fir forests at high elevations are testament to the loss of Fraser firs. Now park scientists and others are racing against time to protect hemlock trees.

The hemlock woolly adelgid is the culprit. Native to Asia, the adelgid feeds at the base of the hemlock needles, disrupting nutrient flow and eventually causing the tree to starve to death. Hemlock woolly adelgids were first discovered near Richmond, Virginia, in 1951. To date, they have spread through the eastern regions of the hemlock's native range. As of 2010, they were found in North Carolina, Georgia, Tennessee, Kentucky, Virginia, and South Carolina.

Hemlocks are beautiful, big trees. They can live to be more than 600 years old and can grow to heights of more than 165 feet. Hemlock trees grow in a variety of habitats and serve myriad purposes in the Smokies' ecosystem. By blocking out the sunlight, hemlocks keep mountain streams cool. Migratory birds such as the Blackburnian warbler and the wood thrush shelter in hemlock groves. Loss of hemlocks will have a negative effect on rivers and streams. Scientists are already seeing higher acidity in some streams where dead hemlock trees have fallen.

Scientists are using insecticidal soap to spray infested trees, but this method is labor intensive and works only for trees that are near roadsides or otherwise easily accessible. Insecticides applied around the soil of the trees is also an effective method, but it's prohibitively expensive for a park with millions of hemlock trees to protect.

Biological control—the introduction of a natural predator beetle to the woolly adelgid—is the most promising long-term preventative. Scientists have pinned their hopes on a poppy-seed-size predator beetle that, in its native Japan, eats only hemlock adelgids. Since 2002 the park has been releasing the predator beetle in the Smokies, and more than 350,000 have been released to date. The predator program got a boost in 2004 when the University of Tennessee opened a new beetle-rearing facility. However, the cost and limited supply of the beetles is the greatest hurdle.

A large number of hemlocks have already been lost, and park officials warn that the consequences of their deaths are only beginning to show. In addition to efforts to stop the spread of the adelgid, scientists are intent on saving enough hemlocks at different elevations in the park in order to save a representative gene pool, which could be used to repopulate the forest if the adelgid threat is ever fully contained.

great blue heron hunting for food. **Wood ducks** and **mallards,** whose males have a striking green head, live around ponds and lakes.

Large Mammals

Many of the large, wild creatures of Tennessee are threatened. **Elk** and **bison,** which ranged here before settlement by Europeans, have been reintroduced at Land Between the Lakes and the Great Smoky Mountains National Park. Scruffy **feral pigs** live in scattered populations in East Tennessee. **Black bears,** the icon of the Smoky Mountains, have a shaggy black coat and sharp sense of smell. They can run and climb trees. **Coyotes** and **red fox** are lovely, quick, and adaptable. **Bobcats** are stealthy and elusive hunters that prefer the hours right before sunrise and right after sunset.

Small Mammals

Raccoons, with their bandit's mask and striped tail, are adorable until one has ruined your bird feeder or gotten into your garbage (or even bitten you, which has been known to happen). **Eastern cottontail** is the most common type of rabbit, and they prefer grasslands and cultivated areas. Look for the white of their stubby tail. **Eastern chipmunks** are small creatures that scurry along forest floors, pastureland, and city parks. **Eastern gray squirrels** are easier to see—they are larger and more ubiquitous.

Amphibians and Reptiles

Listen for the "harumph" of the **bullfrog** or the night song of the **Cope's gray tree frog** near water. Salamanders and newts flourish in the damp, cool forests of the eastern mountains: look for the lizard-like **Eastern newt** and the **spotted salamander,** which can grow up to 10 inches. The largest of the salamanders is the **Eastern tiger salamander,** which comes in a rainbow of colors and patterns best left to your imagination. They grow up to 13 inches.

Snapping turtles live in rivers and streams, rarely coming on land. The **Eastern box turtle** prefers moist forests and grasslands. Most Tennessee snakes are harmless. The **garter snake** is the most common. It prefers areas that are cool and moist. **Green snakes** like bushes and low-hanging branches near the water.

© BRIAN LASENBY/123RF

goldfinch

ENVIRONMENTAL ISSUES
Forestry

Beginning in the 1980s, the number of paper and wood chip mills in Tennessee grew dramatically. With no legislation regulating the clearing of forested land, some parts of Tennessee experienced widespread clear-cutting of old forests. Over the years, local environmental groups have fought for an overarching law that would insist on responsible forestry practices. While no such law has been passed, some stop-gap measures have been put in place.

Strip Mining

Strip mines have a devastating environmental impact. In a strip mine, the surface of the earth above a seam of coal is removed, leaving scarred and bare earth. The most devastating type of strip mining is mountaintop removal, when the whole mountain is destroyed by explosives to get to the coal, which can lie as many as 800 feet below the surface.

Mountaintop removal and other types of strip mining have terrible consequences for drinking-water quality, animal and plant life, and the native culture of places that are affected. Dumping of debris from the removal process buries streams and fills valleys. When the coal companies are done, they pile dirt back up on the exposed mountains and drop exotic grass seed from above. In this way, they say, the mountain is restored. But while they may be able to approximate the shape of the old mountain, they cannot re-create the intricate web of life that once existed there.

Strip mining is most common in parts of Virginia, West Virginia, and Kentucky, but it takes place in Tennessee, too. Mining operations exist in Scott, Campbell, and Claiborne Counties in the northern Cumberland Plateau region. Residents and environmental activists fought to prevent mountaintop removal at Zeb Mountain in Scott and Campbell Counties but were unsuccessful.

In 2004, the last year for which statistics are available, Tennessee had 43 coal mines and produced 2.8 million short tons of coal.

Air Pollution

Car emissions, industrial pollution, and other activities cause air pollution. In Tennessee, exhaust from cars and trucks, plus the toxic emissions from coal-fired generating plants, are the biggest contributors to air pollution.

The air quality in the Great Smoky Mountains National Park is a serious concern for scientists. This is because so many people drive to this car-friendly national park. According to the park, the average visibility is 25 miles, compared to the national average of 93 miles. Some days, haze causes visibility to diminish to less than one mile. Some days, the level of ground-level ozone exceeds what is recommended for human exposure.

Air quality is typically worst during the hot summer months of July and August.

Land Use

According to the Tennessee Environmental Council, the state has the seventh-highest rate of development in the United States. In fact, 80,000 acres of rural land are developed in Tennessee each year. The areas around Nashville and Knoxville have seen the greatest sprawl.

Urban and suburban sprawl leads to long driving times, increased air pollution, strain on scarce water resources, and the elimination of farmland, rural landscapes, and natural habitats. Smart growth policies, zoning issues, and better transportation solutions are some of the biggest challenges facing Tennessee at the moment.

Water Pollution

The cleanliness of Tennessee's rivers, lakes, and streams is monitored according to the standards of the Clean Water Act. The Tennessee Department of Environment and Conservation monitors the health of the state's rivers. In its last report, the agency reported that 25 percent of the state's river miles were category one, the cleanest, and 31 percent were in the dirtiest category. As for lakes and reservoirs, 21 percent of lake acres were classified as "impaired."

Most water pollution is caused by sedimentation and silt runoff from construction and agriculture. Habitat alteration, pathogens found in wastewater, and nutrients from fertilizers are also problems. Some pollution can be readily cleaned up, but so-called legacy pollutants, such as PCBs (polychlorinated biphenyl) and chlordane from old industrial sites, can remain present for years and can poison fish and other marine animals.

According to the state government, 41 percent of pollution in streams and rivers in 2006 came from agriculture, 19 percent from hydrologic modification, and 18 percent from municipal sources. For lakes, 72 percent of contaminants were legacy pollutants.

The state is supposed to post a warning when a river or stream is deemed too polluted for fishing, swimming, or other forms of use. For a listing of such bodies of water, contact the Water Pollution Control division of the Department of Environment and Conservation (615/532-0625), or in Middle Tennessee check with the Cumberland River Compact (www.cumberlandrivercompact.org).

History

THE FIRST TENNESSEANS

The first humans settled in what is now Tennessee 12,000–15,000 years ago. Descended from people who crossed into North America during the last ice age, these Paleo-Indians were nomads who hunted large game animals, including mammoth, mastodon, and caribou. Remains of these extinct mammals have been found in West Tennessee, and the Indians' arrowheads and spear points have been found all over the state. The ice age hunters camped in caves and under rock shelters but remained predominantly nomadic.

About 10,000 years ago, the climate and vegetation of the region changed. The deciduous forest that still covers large parts of the state replaced the evergreen forest of the fading ice age. Large game animals disappeared, and deer and elk arrived, attracted by the forests of hickory, chestnut, and beech. Descendants of the Paleo-Indians gradually abandoned the nomadic lifestyle of their ancestors and established settlements, often near rivers. They hunted deer, bear, and turkey; gathered nuts and wild fruit; and harvested freshwater fish and mussels. They also took a few tentative steps toward cultivation by growing squash and gourds.

This Archaic Period was replaced by the Woodland Period about 3,000 years ago. The Woodland Indians adopted the bow and arrow for hunting and—at the end of their predominance—began cultivating maize and beans as staple crops. Ceramic pottery appeared, and ritualism took on a greater importance in the society. Pinson Mounds, burial mounds near Jackson in West Tennessee, date from this period, as does the wrongly named Old Stone Fort near Manchester, believed to have been built and used for ceremonies by the Woodland Indians of the area.

The development of a more complex culture continued, and at about A.D. 900 the Woodland culture gave way to the Mississippian Period, an era marked by population growth, an increase in trade and warfare, the rise of the chieftain, and cultural accomplishments. The Mississippian era is best known for the impressive large pyramid mounds that were left behind in places such as Etowah and Toqua in Tennessee and Moundville in Alabama. Mississippian Indians also created beautiful ornaments and symbolic objects including combs, pipes, and jewelry.

Europeans Arrive

Having conquered Peru, the Spanish nobleman Hernando de Soto embarked on a search for gold in the American southeast in 1539. De Soto's band wandered through Florida, Georgia, and the Carolinas before crossing into what is now Tennessee, probably in June 1540. His exact route is a source of controversy, but historians believe he made his way through parts of East Tennessee before heading back into Georgia. The popular myth that he camped on the Chickasaw Bluff—the site of Memphis today—in 1541 remains unproven.

It was more than 100 years until another European was reported in the Tennessee wilderness, although life for the natives was already changing. De Soto and his men brought firearms and disease, and there was news of other whites living to the east. Disease and warfare led to a decline in population for Tennessee's Indians during the presettlement period. As a result, Indian communities formed new tribes with each other: The Creek Confederacy and Choctaws were among the tribes that were formed. In Tennessee, the Shawnee moved south into the Cumberland River country—land previously claimed as hunting ground by the Chickasaw Nation. Also at this time, a new tribe came over the Smoky Mountains from North Carolina, possibly to escape encroachment of European settlers, to form what would become the most important Indian group in modern Tennessee: the Overhill Cherokees.

In 1673 European scouts entered Tennessee at its eastern and western ends. Englishmen James Needham, Gabriel Arthur, and eight hired Indian guides were the first European party to enter East Tennessee. Needham did not last long; he was killed by his Indian guides early in the outing. Arthur won over his traveling companions and joined them on war trips and hunts before returning to Virginia in 1674. Meanwhile, on the western end of the state, French explorers Father Jacques Marquette and trader Louis Joliet came down the Mississippi River and claimed the surrounding valley for the French.

Nine years later, Robert Cavelier de La Salle paused at the Chickasaw Bluff near present-day Memphis and built Fort Prudhomme as a temporary base. The fort was short-lived, but the site would be used by the French in years to come in their war against the Chickasaws and later in the French and Indian War.

The Long Hunters

The first Europeans to carve out a foothold in the unknown frontier of Tennessee were traders who made journeys into Indian territory to hunt and trade. These men disappeared for months at a time into the wilderness and were therefore known as long hunters. They left with European-made goods and returned with animal skins. They led pack trains of horses and donkeys over narrow, steep, and crooked mountain trails and through sometimes-hostile territory. It was a lonely, hard life, full of uncertainty. Some of the long hunters were no better than crooks; others were respected by both the Indians and Europeans.

The long hunters included men like Elisha Walden, Kasper Mansker, and Abraham Bledsoe. Daniel Boone, born in North Carolina, was in present-day Washington County in northeastern Tennessee when, in 1760, he carved on a beech tree that he had "cilled" a "bar" nearby. Thomas Sharp Spencer became known as Big Foot and is said to have spent the winter in a hollowed-out sycamore tree. Another trader, a Scotch-Irish man named James Adair, traded with the Indians for years and eventually wrote *A History of the American Indian,* published in London in 1775 and one of the first such accounts.

The animal skins and furs that were the aim of these men's exploits were eventually sold in Charleston and exported to Europe. In 1748 alone, South Carolina merchants exported more than 160,000 skins worth $250,000. The trade was profitable for merchants and, to a lesser extent, the traders themselves. But it was rarely profitable for the Indians, and it helped to wipe out much of Tennessee's native animal life.

The French and Indian War

In 1754 the contest between the French and the British for control of the New World boiled over into war. Indian alliances were seen as critical to success, and so the British set out to win the support of the Cherokee. They did this by agreeing to build a fort in the land over the mountain from North Carolina—territory that came to be known as the Overhill country. The Cherokee wanted the fort to protect their women and children from French or hostile Indian attack while the men were away. The fort was begun in 1756 near the fork of the Little Tennessee and Tellico Rivers, and it was named Fort Loudoun after the commander of British forces in America. Twelve cannons were transported over the rough mountain terrain by horse to defend the fort from enemy attack.

The construction of Fort Loudoun did not prove to be the glue to hold the Cherokee and British together. In fact, it was not long before relations deteriorated to the point where the Cherokee chief Standing Turkey directed an attack on the fort. A siege ensued. Reinforcements were called for and dispatched, but the British colonel and 1,300 men turned back before reaching the fort. The English inside the fort were weakened by lack of food and surrendered. On August 9, 1760, 180 men, 60 women, and a few children marched out of Fort Loudoun, the first steps of a 140-mile journey to the nearest British fort. The group had been promised to be allowed to retreat peacefully, but on the first night of the journey the group was ambushed: killed were 3 officers, 23 privates, 3 women. The rest were taken prisoner. The Indians said they were inspired to violence upon finding that the British had failed to surrender all of their firepower as promised.

The Cherokee's action was soon avenged. A year later, Col. James Grant led a party into the Lower Cherokee territory, where they destroyed villages, burnt homes, and cut down fields of corn.

The French and Indian War ended in 1763, and in the Treaty of Paris the French withdrew any claims to lands east of the Mississippi. This result emboldened European settlers and land speculators who were drawn to the land of the Overhill country. The fact that the land still belonged to the Indians did not stop the movement west.

EARLY SETTLERS
The First Settlements

With the issue of French possession resolved, settlers began to filter into the Overhill country. Early settlers included William Bean, on the Holston River; Evan Shelby, at Sapling Grove (later Bristol); John Carter, in the Carter Valley; and Jacob Brown, on the Nolichucky River. By 1771 the settlers at Watauga and Nolichucky won a lease from the Cherokee, and the next year, they formed the Watauga Association, a quasi government and the first such in Tennessee territory.

The settlers' success in obtaining land concessions from the Indians was eclipsed in 1775 when the Transylvania Company, led by Richard Henderson of North Carolina, traded £10,000 of goods for 20 million acres of land in Kentucky and Tennessee. The agreement, negotiated at a treaty conference at Sycamore Shoals, was opposed by the Cherokee Indian chief Dragging Canoe, who warned that the Cherokee were paving the way for their own extinction. Despite his warning, the treaty was signed.

Dragging Canoe remained the leader of the Cherokee's resistance to European settlement. In 1776 he orchestrated assaults on the white settlements of Watauga, Nolichucky, Long Island, and Carter's Valley. The offensive, called by some the Cherokee War, had limited success at first, but it ended in defeat for the natives. In 1777 the Cherokee signed a peace treaty with the settlers that ceded more land to the Europeans.

Dragging Canoe and others did not accept the treaty and left the Cherokee as a result. He and his followers moved south, near Chickamauga Creek, where they became known as the Chickamauga tribe. Over time, this tribe attracted other Indians whose common purpose was opposition to white settlement.

The Indians could not, however, overpower the increasing tide of European settlers, who brought superior firepower and greater numbers. Pressure on political leaders to free up more and more land for settlement made relations with the Indians and land agreements with them one of the most important features of political life on the frontier.

In the end, these leaders delivered. Europeans obtained Indian land in Tennessee through a series of treaties and purchases, beginning with the Sycamore Shoals purchase in 1775 and continuing until 1818 when the Chickasaw ceded all control to land west of the Mississippi. Negotiating on behalf of the settlers were leaders including William Blount, the territorial governor, and Andrew Jackson, the first U.S. president from Tennessee.

Indian Removal

Contact with Europeans had a significant

© SUSANNA HENIGHAN POTTER

Fort Nashborough, the first settlement in Nashville, was founded on Christmas Day, 1779. A re-creation of the original fort remains on the riverfront in Nashville.

impact on the Cherokee's way of life. Christian missionaries introduced education, and in the 1820s Sequoyah developed a Cherokee alphabet, allowing the Indians to read and write in their own language. The Cherokee adopted some of the Europeans' farming practices, as well as some of their social practices, including slavery. Adoption of the European lifestyle was most common among the significant number of mixed-race Cherokee. In 1827 the Cherokee Nation was established, complete with a constitutional system of government and a capital in New Echota, Georgia. From 1828 until 1832, its newspaper, the *Cherokee Phoenix,* was published in both English and Cherokee.

The census of 1828 counted 15,000 Cherokee remaining in Tennessee. They owned 1,000 slaves, 22,400 head of cattle, 7,600 horses, 1,800 spinning wheels, 700 looms, 12 sawmills, 55 blacksmith shops, and 6 cotton gins.

Despite these beginnings of assimilation, or because of them, the Cherokee were not welcome to remain in the new territory. Settlers pushed for a strong policy that would lead to the Cherokee's removal, and they looked over the border to Georgia to see that it could be done. There, in 1832, authorities surveyed lands owned by Cherokee and disposed of them by lottery. Laws were passed to prohibit Indian assemblies and bar Indians from bringing suit in the state. The majority of Tennessee settlers, as well as Georgia officials, pushed for similar measures to be adopted in Tennessee.

The Cherokee were divided in their response: Some felt that moving west represented the best future for their tribe, while others wanted to stay and fight for their land and the Cherokee Nation. In the end, the Cherokee leaders lost hope of remaining, and on December 29, 1835, they signed the removal treaty. Under the agreement, the Cherokee were paid $5 million for all their lands east of the Mississippi, and they were required to move west within two years. When that time expired in 1838 and only a small number of the Cherokee had moved, the U.S. army evicted the rest by force.

Thousands of Cherokee died along the ensuing Trail of Tears, which followed four different routes through Tennessee and eventually into Oklahoma: A southern route extended from Chattanooga to Memphis, two northern routes headed into Kentucky and Missouri before turning southward into Oklahoma, and the fourth was a water route along the Tennessee and Mississippi Rivers. Harsh weather, food shortages, and the brutality of the journey cost thousands of Cherokee lives. In the end, out of the estimated 14,000 Cherokee who began the journey, more than 4,000 are believed to have died along the way.

Some Cherokee remained by hiding deep in the Great Smoky Mountains. Later, they were given land that became the Cherokee Reservation in North Carolina.

STATEHOOD

Almost as soon as settlers began living on the Tennessee frontier there were movements to form government. Dissatisfied with the protection offered by North Carolina's distant government, settlers drew up their own governments as early as the 1780s. The Watauga Association and Cumberland Compact were early forms of government. In 1785, settlers in northeastern Tennessee seceded from North Carolina and established the State of Franklin. The experiment was short-lived but foretold that in the future the lands west of the Smoky Mountains would be their own state.

Before Tennessee could become a state, however, it was a territory of the United States. In 1789 North Carolina ratified its own constitution and in doing so ceded its western lands, the Tennessee country, to the U.S. government. These lands eventually became known as the Southwest Territory, and in 1790 President

George Washington appointed William Blount its territorial governor.

Blount was a 41-year-old land speculator and businessman who had campaigned actively for the position. A veteran of the War for Independence, Blount knew George Washington and was one of the signers of the U.S. Constitution in 1787.

At the time of its establishment, the Southwest Territory was 43,000 square miles in area. The population of 35,000 was centered in two main areas: the northeastern corner and the Cumberland settlements near present-day Nashville.

Governor Blount moved quickly to establish a territorial government. In October 1790 he arrived in Washington County and established the state's first capitol in the home of William Cobb. This simple wood frame house, known as Rocky Mount, would be the territory's capitol for the next 18 months before it moved to James White's Fort in Knoxville.

The territory's first election was held in 1793, and the resulting council met a year later. They established the town of Knoxville, created a tax rate, and chartered Greeneville and Blount Colleges. They also ordered a census in 1795, which showed a population of more than 77,000 people and support for statehood.

The territory had met the federal requirements for statehood, and so Blount and other territorial leaders set out to make Tennessee a state. They called a constitutional convention, and delegates spent three weeks writing Tennessee's first constitution. The first statewide poll elected John Sevier governor of the new state. Meanwhile, Tennessee's request to become a state was being debated in Washington, where finally, on June 1, 1796, President Washington signed the statehood bill and Tennessee became the 16th state in the Union.

Frontier Life

The new state of Tennessee attracted settlers who were drawn by cheap land and the opportunity it represented. Between 1790 and 1800 the state's population tripled, and by 1810 Tennessee's population had grown to 250,000. The expansion caused a shift in power as the middle and western parts of the state became more populated. The capital moved from Knoxville to Nashville in 1812.

Life during the early 19th century in Tennessee was largely rural. For the subsistence farmers who made up the majority of the state's population, life was a relentless cycle of hard work. Many families lived in one- or two-room cabins and spent their days growing food and the fibers needed to make their own clothes; raising animals that supplied farm power, meat, and hides; building or repairing buildings and tools; and cutting firewood in prodigious quantities.

Small-hold farmers often owned no slaves. Those who did only owned one or two and worked alongside them.

Children provided valuable labor on the Tennessee farm. Boys often plowed their first furrow at age nine, and girls of that age were expected to mind younger children, help cook, and learn the skills of midwifery, sewing, and gardening. While women's time was often consumed with child rearing, cooking, and sewing, the housewife worked in the field alongside her husband when she was needed.

Education and Religion

There were no public schools on the frontier, and the few private schools that existed were not accessible to the farming class. Religious missionaries were often the only people who could read and write in a community, and the first schools were established by churches. Presbyterian, Methodist, and Baptist ministers were the first to reach many settlements in Tennessee.

Settlements were spread out, and few had established churches. As a result, the camp meeting became entrenched in Tennessee culture. The homegrown spirituality of the camp meeting appealed to Tennesseans' independent spirit, which looked suspiciously at official religion and embraced the informal and deeply personal religion of the camp meeting.

The meetings were major events drawing between a few hundred and thousands of people. Wilma Dykeman writes:

> From distances as far as 40, 50 and more miles, they came in wagons, carriages, a wide array of vehicles, and raised their tents...They spent the summer days and nights surrounded by seemingly endless expanse of green forest, supplied with a bounty of cold pure water, breathing that acrid blue wood smoke from rows of campfires and the rich smells of food cooking over glowing red coals, listening to the greetings of old friends, the voices of children playing, crying, growing drowsy, a stamping of the horses, and the bedlam of the meeting itself once the services had begun.

Camp services were passionate and emotional, reaching a feverish pitch as men and women were overtaken by the spirit. Many camp meetings attracted both black and white participants.

The War of 1812

Tennesseans were among the "War Hawks" in Congress who advocated for war with Great Britain in 1812. The conflict was seen by many as an opportunity to rid their borders once and for all of all Indians. The government asked for 2,800 volunteers, and 30,000 Tennesseans offered to enlist. This is when Tennessee's nickname as the Volunteer State was born.

Nashville lawyer, politician, and businessman Andrew Jackson was chosen as the leader of the Tennessee volunteers. Despite their shortage of supplies and lack of support from the War Department, Jackson's militia prevailed in a series of lopsided victories. Given command of the southern military district, Andrew Jackson led U.S. forces at the Battle of New Orleans on January 8, 1815. The ragtag group inflicted a crushing defeat on the British, and despite having occurred after the signing of the peace treaty with Great Britain, the battle was a victory that launched Jackson onto the road to the presidency.

Growth of Slavery

The state's first settlers planted the seed of slavery in Tennessee, and the state's westward expansion cemented the institution. In 1791 there were 3,400 blacks in Tennessee—about 10 percent of the general population. By 1810, blacks were more than 20 percent of Tennessee's people. The invention of the cotton gin and subsequent rise of King Cotton after the turn of the 19th century also caused a rapid expansion of slavery.

Slavery was most important in West Tennessee; eastern Tennessee, with its mountainous landscape and small farms, had the fewest slaves. In Middle Tennessee the slave population was concentrated in the central basin, in the counties of Davidson, Maury, Rutherford, and Williamson. By 1860, 40 percent of the state's slave population was in West Tennessee, with the greatest concentration in Shelby, Fayette, and Haywood Counties, where cotton was grown on plantations somewhat similar to those of the Deep South.

As slavery grew, slave markets were established in Nashville and Memphis. The ban on the interstate sale of slaves was virtually ignored.

From 1790, when the state was founded, until 1831 Tennessee's slave code was relatively lenient. The law recognized a slave as both a chattel and a person, and slaves were entitled to expect protection against the elements and other people. Owners could free their slaves for any reason, and many did, causing growth in Tennessee's free black population in the first half of the 1800s. These free blacks concentrated in eastern and Middle Tennessee, and particularly the cities of Nashville, Memphis, and Knoxville, where they worked as laborers and artisans.

There were vocal opponents to slavery in Tennessee, particularly in the eastern part of the state. The first newspaper in the United States devoted to emancipation was established in 1819 in Jonesborough by Elihu Embree. Charles Osborne, a Quaker minister, preached against slavery shortly after the turn of the 19th century in Tennessee. Emancipationists formed societies in counties including Washington, Sullivan, Blount, Grainger, and Cocke. Many of these early abolitionists opposed slavery on religious grounds, arguing that it was incompatible with the spirit of Christianity.

These abolitionists often argued for the gradual end of slavery and sometimes advocated for the removal of freed slaves to Africa.

Slave Experiences

There was no single slave experience for Tennessee's slaves. On the farm, a slave's experience depended on the size of the farm, the type of crops that were grown, and the number of slaves on the farm.

Most Tennessee slaves lived on small- or medium-size farms. The 1860 census showed that only one person in the state owned more than 300 slaves, and 47 owned more than 100. More than 75 percent of all slave owners had fewer than 10 slaves. Work assignments varied, but almost all slaves were expected to contribute to their own subsistence by keeping a vegetable garden. Slaves with special skills in areas like carpentry, masonry, blacksmithing, or weaving were hired out.

Urban slaves were domestics, coachmen, house painters, laundresses, and midwives. In cities, many families owned just one or two slaves, and it was common for slaves to be hired out to others in order to provide a source of income for the slave owner. It became customary in some cities for a market day to be held on New Year's Day, where employers bargained for slave labor over the coming year.

Slaves sought to overcome their circumstances by building close-knit communities. These communities acted as surrogate families for slaves whose own spouse, parents, siblings, and children were often sold, causing lifelong separation.

Religion also served as a survival mechanism for Tennessee's slaves. Methodist and Baptist churches opened their doors to slaves, providing a space were slaves could be together. The musical tradition that resulted is today's gospel music. Religion also provided a vehicle for some slaves to learn how to read and write.

THE CIVIL WAR

In the 1830s, Tennessee's position on slavery hardened. The Virginia slave uprising led by Nat Turner frightened slave owners, who instituted patrols to search for runaway slaves and tightened codes on slave conduct. In 1834, the state constitution was amended to bar free blacks from voting, a sign of whites' increasing fear of the black people living in their midst.

The division between East and West Tennessee widened as many in the east were sympathetic with the antislavery forces that were growing in Northern states. In the west, the support for slavery was unrelenting.

Despite several strident secessionists, including Tennessee governor Isham Harris, Tennessee remained uncertain about secession. In February 1861, the state voted against a convention on secession. But with the attack on Fort Sumter two months later, followed by President Abraham Lincoln's call for volunteers to coerce the seceded states back to the Union, public opinion shifted. On June 8, 1861, Tennesseans voted 105,000 to 47,000 to secede.

A Border State

Tennessee was of great strategic importance during the Civil War. It sent an estimated 186,000 men to fight for the Confederacy, more than any other state. Another 31,000 are credited with having joined the Union army.

Tennessee had resources that both Union and Confederacy deemed important for victory, including agricultural and manufacturing industries, railroads, and rivers. And its geographic position as a long-border state made it nearly unavoidable.

Tennessee Battles

Some 454 battles and skirmishes were fought in Tennessee during the war. Most were small, but several key battles took place on Tennessee soil.

The first of these was the Union victory at Forts Henry and Donelson in January 1862. Gen. Ulysses S. Grant and 15,000 Union troops steamed up the Tennessee River and quickly captured Fort Henry. They then marched overland to Fort Donelson, and, 10 days later, this Confederate fort fell as well. The battle of Fort Donelson is where U. S. Grant earned his sobriquet: He was asked by the Confederate general the terms of capitulation, and he replied, "unconditional surrender."

The Battle of Shiloh was the bloodiest and largest to take place in Tennessee. The battle took place near Pittsburgh Landing (the Federal name for the struggle), on the Mississippi River about 20 miles north of the Mississippi state line. More than 100,000 men took part in this battle, and there were more than 24,000 casualties.

The battle began with a surprise Confederate attack at dawn on April 6, 1862, a Sunday. For several hours, victory seemed in reach for the Southern troops, but the Union rallied and held. They built a strong defensive line covering Pittsburgh Landing, and on April 7 they took the offensive and swept the Confederates from the field. The Confederates' loss was devastating, and Shiloh represents a harbinger of the future bloodletting between Blue and Gray.

Another important Tennessee battle was at Stones River, near Murfreesboro, on December 31, 1862. Like at Shiloh, the early momentum here was with the Confederates, but victory belonged to the Union. The Battle of Chickamauga Creek, fought a few miles over the state line in Georgia, was a rare Confederate victory. It did not come cheaply, however, with 21,000 members of the Army of Tennessee killed.

view of the state capitol near the end of the Civil War, circa 1862-1865

Federal forces retreated and dug in near Chattanooga, while Confederates occupied the heights above the town. Union reinforcements led by General Grant drove the Confederates back into Georgia at Battle of Lookout Mountain, also known as the "Battle Above the Clouds," on November 25, 1863.

Wartime Occupation

Battles were only part of the wartime experience in Tennessee. The Civil War caused hardship for ordinary residents on a scale that many had never before seen. There was famine and poverty. Schools and churches were closed. Harassment and recrimination plagued the state, and fear was widespread.

In February 1863, one observer described the population of Memphis as "11,000 original whites, 5,000 slaves, and 19,000 newcomers of all kinds, including traders, fugitives, hangers-on, and negroes."

Memphis fell to the Union on June 6, 1862,

and it was occupied for the remainder of the war. The city's experience during this wartime occupation reversed decades of growth and left a city that would struggle for years.

Those who could fled the city. Many of those who remained stopped doing business (some of these because they refused to pledge allegiance to the Union and were not permitted). Northern traders entered the city and took over many industries, while blacks who abandoned nearby plantations flooded into the city.

While the military focused on punishing Confederate sympathizers, conditions in Memphis deteriorated. Crime and disorder abounded, and guerrilla bands developed to fight the Union occupation. The Federal commander responsible for the city was Maj. Gen. William T. Sherman, and he adopted a policy of collective responsibility, which held civilians responsible for guerrilla attacks in their neighborhoods. Sherman destroyed hundreds of homes, farms, and towns in the exercise of this policy.

The war was equally damaging in other parts

of Tennessee. In Middle Tennessee, retreating Confederate soldiers after the fall of Fort Donelson demolished railroads and burned bridges so as not to leave them for the Union. Union troops also destroyed and appropriated the region's resources. Federals took horses, pigs, cows, corn, hay, cotton, fence rails, firearms, and tools. Sometimes this was carried out through official requisitions, but at other times it amounted to little more than pillaging.

Criminals took advantage of the loss of public order, and bands of thieves and bandits began roaming the countryside.

The experience in East Tennessee was different. Because of the region's widespread Union sympathies, it was the Confederacy that first occupied the eastern territory. During this time hundreds of alleged Unionists were charged with treason and jailed. When the Confederates began conscripting men into military service in 1862, tensions in East Tennessee grew. Many East Tennesseans fled to Kentucky, and distrust, bitterness, and violence escalated. In September 1863 the tables turned, however, and the Confederates were replaced by the Federals, whose victories elsewhere enabled them to now focus on occupying friendly East Tennessee.

The Effects of the War

Tennessee lost most of a generation of young men to the Civil War. Infrastructure was destroyed, and thousands of farms, homes, and other properties were razed. The state's reputation on the national stage had been tarnished, and it would be decades until Tennessee had the political power that it enjoyed during the Age of Jackson. But while the war caused tremendous hardships for the state, it also led to the freeing of 275,000 black Tennesseans from slavery.

RECONSTRUCTION

Tennessee was no less divided during the years following the Civil War than it was during the conflict. The end to the war ushered in a period where former Unionists—now allied with the Radical Republicans in Congress—disenfranchised and otherwise marginalized former Confederates and others who had been sympathetic with the Southern cause.

They also pushed through laws that extended voting and other rights to the newly freed blacks, changes that led to a powerful backlash and the establishment of such shadowy groups as the Ku Klux Klan.

William G. "Parson" Brownlow of Knoxville, a vocal supporter of the Union, was elected governor of Tennessee in 1865. During the same year, the voters approved a constitutional amendment abolishing slavery, making Tennessee the only seceded state to abolish slavery by its own act. Brownlow and his supporters bent laws and manipulated loyalties in order to secure ratification of the 14th and 15th Amendments to the constitution, paving the way for Tennessee to be admitted back to the Union, the first Southern state to be readmitted following the war. Brownlow's success ensured that Tennessee would not experience the Congressionally mandated Reconstruction that other former Confederate states did.

Recognizing that the unpopularity of his positions among Tennessee's numerous former Confederates placed his political future in jeopardy, Brownlow and his supporters extended the right to vote to thousands of freedmen in February 1867. During the statewide vote a few months later, Brownlow and his followers were swept to victory, largely due to the support of black voters.

The quick rise to power of former enemies and the social changes caused by the end of slavery led some former Confederates to bitterness and frustration. In the summer of 1867, the Ku Klux Klan emerged as a political and terrorist movement to keep freedmen in their traditional place. Klan members initially concerned themselves principally with supporting former Confederates and their families, but they were soon known more for their attacks

AUTHOR UNKNOWN, MCCLURE'S MAGAZINE/WIKIMEDIA

General Ulysses S. Grant (lower left-hand corner) visits Missionary Ridge, scene of a Civil War battle.

on black men and women. The KKK was strongest in Middle and West Tennessee, except for a small pocket near Bristol in East Tennessee.

Governor Brownlow responded strongly to the KKK's activities, and in 1869 he declared martial law in nine counties where the organization was most active. But when Brownlow left Tennessee shortly thereafter to fill a seat in the U.S. Senate, the KKK's grand wizard, former Confederate general Nathan Bedford Forrest, declared the group's mission accomplished and encouraged members to burn their robes. The KKK's influence quickly faded, only to reemerge 50 years later at Stone Mountain, Georgia.

Brownlow was replaced by Senate Speaker Dewitt C. Senter, who quickly struck a more moderate position than his predecessor by setting aside the law that had barred Confederate veterans from voting.

The greatest legacy of the Civil War was the emancipation of Tennessee's slaves. Following the war, many freed blacks left the countryside and moved to cities, including Memphis, Nashville, Chattanooga, and Knoxville, where they worked as skilled laborers, domestics, and more. Other blacks remained in the countryside, working as wage laborers on farms or sharecropping in exchange for occupancy on part of a former large-scale plantation.

The Freedmen's Bureau worked in Tennessee for a short period after the end of the war, and it succeeded in establishing schools for blacks. During this period the state's first black colleges were established: Fisk, Tennessee Central, LeMoyne, Roger Williams, Lane, and Knoxville.

As in other states, blacks in Tennessee enjoyed short-lived political power during Reconstruction. The right to vote and the concentration of blacks in certain urban areas paved the way for blacks to be elected to the Tennessee House of Representatives, beginning with Sampson Keeble of Nashville in 1872. In all, 13 blacks were elected as representatives between 1872 and 1887, including James C. Napier, Edward Shaw, and William Yardley, who also ran for governor.

Initially, these pioneers met mild acceptance from whites, but as time progressed whites became uncomfortable sharing political power with black people. By the 1890s, racist Jim Crow policies of segregation, poll taxes, secret ballots, literacy tests, and intimidation prevented blacks from holding elected office—and in many cases, voting—in Tennessee again until after the civil rights movement of the 1960s.

The Republican party saw the end of its influence with the end of the Brownlow governorship. Democrats rejected the divisive policies of the Radical Republicans, sought to protect the racial order that set blacks at a disadvantage to whites, and were less concerned about the state's mounting debt than the Republicans.

Economic Recovery

The social and political upheaval caused by the Civil War was matched or exceeded by the economic catastrophe that it represented for the state. Farms and industry were damaged or destroyed, public infrastructure was razed, schools were closed, and the system of slavery that underpinned most of the state's economy was gone.

The economic setback was seen as an opportunity by proponents of the "New South," who advocated for an industrial and economic revival that would catapult the South to prosperity impossible under the agrarian and slavery-based antebellum economy. The New South movement was personified by carpetbagging Northern capitalists who moved to Tennessee and set up industries that would benefit from cheap labor and abundant natural resources. Many Tennesseans welcomed these newcomers and advocated for their fellow Tennesseans to put aside regional differences and welcome the Northern investors.

The result was an array of industries that were chartered during the years following the Civil War. Mining, foundries, machine shops, sawmills, gristmills, furniture factories, and textile and other manufacturing industries were established. Knoxville and Chattanooga improved quickly. Over the 10-year period from 1860 to 1870, Chattanooga's industrial works grew from employing 214 men to more than 2,000.

Memphis and Nashville also worked to attract industries. Memphis was on the cusp of a commercial and industrial boom in 1873 when yellow fever hit the city; the epidemic caused widespread death and hurt Memphis's economic recovery. In Nashville, new distilleries, sawmills, paper mills, stove factories, and an oil refinery led the way to industrialization.

Industry also settled in the small towns and countryside. The coal-rich region of the Cumberland Mountains were the site of major coal mining operations. Copper mines were opened in Cleveland, flouring mills in Jackson, and textile factories in Tullahoma and other parts of the state.

Agriculture

A revolution was brewing in agriculture, too. Civil War veterans returned to small farms all over the state and resumed farming with implements largely unchanged for hundreds of years. Every task was achieved by hand, with the lone help of one or two farm animals.

But farm technology was beginning to change. Thirty years after the war, new labor-saving devices began to be put to use. These included early cotton pickers, reapers, and planters. Seed cleaners, corn shellers, and improved plows were made available. In 1871 the state formed the Bureau of Agriculture, whose employees prepared soil maps and studied the state's climate, population, and the prices of land. New methods such as crop diversification, crop rotation, cover crops, and the use of commercial fertilizers were introduced, and farmers were encouraged to use them.

Meanwhile, farmers themselves established a strong grassroots movement in the state. The Patrons of Husbandry, or the Grange, was organized shortly after the war to encourage members to improve farming methods and enhance their economic influence. Government encouraged county fair associations, which organized fairs where farmers could be awarded for their crops and encouraged to use new farming methods. The Farmers' Alliance and the Agricultural Wheel, both national organizations, grew in prominence in the 1880s and advocated currency reform, empowerment of farmers, and control of communication and transportation systems. The Alliance gave low-interest loans to farmers and encouraged cooperative selling.

While the Alliance and the Wheel were not political organizations as such, they supported candidates who adopted their views on agricultural matters. In 1890 the Alliance supported Democrat John P. Buchanan for governor, and he was successful. For their part, political elites did not take the farming movement or its leaders very seriously, ridiculing them as "hayseeds," "clodhoppers," and "wool-hat boys." In other places, rural and small-town residents resisted the Wheel and the Alliance, in part because they feared challenge of the status quo. As the Alliance became more radical in its views, the support in Tennessee dwindled, and by 1892 it had faded in many parts of the state.

While some blacks remained on farms as wage laborers or sharecroppers, many left for the cities, causing a labor shortage. Attempts to attract foreign or Northern immigrants to the state were unsuccessful. Tennessee's poor whites filled this labor shortage, now able to own or rent land for the first time.

Education

Despite popular attempts and pleas by some politicians for a sound education system, Tennessee lagged behind in public education during the postwar years. In 1873 the legislature passed a school law that set up a basic framework of school administration, but the state's debt and financial problems crippled the new system. Private funds stepped in—the Peabody Fund contributed to Tennessee's schools, including the old University of Nashville, renamed Peabody after its benefactor. Meanwhile, teachers' institutes were established during the 1880s in order to raise the level of instruction at Tennessee's public schools.

PROHIBITION

Prohibition was the first major issue Tennesseans faced in the new century. An 1877 law that forbade the sale of alcohol within four miles of a rural school had been used to great effect by Prohibitionists to restrict the sale and traffic of alcohol in towns all over the countryside. As the century turned, pressure mounted to extend the law, and public opinion in support of temperance grew, although it was never without contest from the powerful distillery industry. Finally, in 1909, the legislature passed the Manufacturer's Bill, which would halt the production of intoxicants in the state and overrode Governor Patterson's veto. When the United States followed suit with the 18th Amendment in 1920, Prohibition was old news in Tennessee.

WORLD WAR I

True to its nickname, Tennessee sent a large number of volunteer troops to fight in World War I. Most became part of the 30th "Old Hickory" Division, which entered the war on August 17, 1918. The most famous Tennessee veteran of World War I was Alvin C. York, a farm boy from the Cumberland Mountains who staged a one-man offensive against the German army after becoming separated from his own detachment. Reports say that York killed 20 German soldiers and persuaded 131 more to surrender.

WOMEN'S SUFFRAGE

The movement for women's suffrage had been established in Tennessee prior to the turn of the 20th century, and it gained influence as the century progressed. The Southern Woman Suffrage Conference was held in Memphis in 1906, and a statewide suffrage organization was established. State bills to give women the right to vote failed in 1913 and 1917, but support was gradually growing. In the summer of 1920, the 19th Amendment had been ratified by 35 states, and one more ratification was needed to make it law. Tennessee was one of five states yet to vote on the measure, and on August 9, Governor Roberts called a special sitting of the legislature to consider the amendment.

Furious campaigning and public debate led up to the special sitting. The Senate easily ratified the amendment 25 to 4, but in the House of Representatives the vote was much closer: 49 to 47. Governor Roberts certified the result and notified the secretary of state: Tennessee had cast the deciding vote for women's suffrage.

AUSTIN PEAY

The 1920s were years of growth and development in Tennessee, thanks in part to the able leadership of Austin Peay, elected governor in 1922. He reformed the state government, cut waste, and set out to improve the state's roads and schools. The improvements won Peay support from the state's rural residents, who benefited from better transportation and education. Spending on schools doubled during Peay's three terms as governor, and the school term increased from 127 to 155 days per year.

Peay also saw the importance of establishing parks: Reelfoot Lake State Park was established during his third term, finally ending fears of development in the area. Peay also supported establishment of the Great Smoky Mountains National Park, and he raised $1.5 million in a bond issue as the state's part toward the purchase of the land. Peay was dead by the time the park was opened in 1940, but it is largely to his credit that it was created.

THE DEPRESSION

The progress and hope of the 1920s was soon forgotten with the Great Depression. Tennessee's economic hard times started before the 1929 stock market crash. Farming in the state was hobbled by low prices and low returns during the 1920s. Farmers and laborers displaced by this trend sought work in new industries like the Dupont plant in Old Hickory, Eastman-Kodak in Kingsport, or the Aluminum Company of America in Blount County. But others, including many African Americans, left Tennessee for northern cities such as Chicago.

The Depression made bad things worse. Farmers tried to survive, turning to subsistence farming. In cities unemployed workers lined up for relief. Major bank failures in 1930 brought most financial business in the state to a halt.

President Roosevelt's New Deal provided some relief for Tennesseans. The Civilian Conservation Corps, Public Works Administration, and Civil Works Administration were established in Tennessee. Through the CCC, more than 7,000 Tennesseans planted millions of pine seedlings, developed parks, and built fire towers. Through the PWA more than 500 projects were undertaken, including bridges, housing, water systems, and roads. Hundreds of Tennesseans were employed by the CWA to clean public buildings, landscape roads, and do other work.

But no New Deal institution had more impact on Tennessee than the Tennessee Valley Authority. Architects of TVA saw it as a way to improve agriculture along the Tennessee River, alleviate poverty, and produce electrical power. The dam system would also improve navigation along what was then an often dangerous river. The law establishing TVA was introduced by Senator George W. Norris of Nebraska and passed in 1933. Soon after, dams were under construction, and trade on the river increased due to improved navigability. Even more importantly, electric power was now so cheap that even Tennesseans in remote parts of the state could afford it. By 1945, TVA was the largest electrical utility in the nation, and new industries were attracted by cheap energy and improved transportation. Tourists also came to enjoy the so-called Great Lakes of the South.

The TVA story is not without its losers, however. TVA purchased or condemned more than one million acres of land and flooded 300,000 acres more, forcing 14,000 families to be displaced.

THE CRUMP MACHINE

The 1930s in Tennessee was the age of Ed Crump, Memphis's longtime mayor and political boss. The son of a former Confederate, Crump was born in Mississippi in 1874 and moved to Memphis when he was 17 years old. First elected in 1909 as a city councilman, Crump was a genius of human nature and organization. Able to assure statewide candidates the support of influential Shelby County, Crump's power extended beyond Memphis. His political power often required corruption, patronage, and the loss of individual freedoms. To get ahead, you had to pay homage to Boss Crump. He was particularly popular during the Depression, when constituents and others looked to Crump for much-needed relief.

Crump manipulated the votes in his home Shelby County by paying the $2 poll tax for cooperative voters. He allied with black leaders such as Robert Church Jr. to win support in the black community of Memphis.

WORLD WAR II

Tennessee, like the rest of the country, was changed by World War II. The war effort transformed the state's economy and led to a migration to the cities unprecedented in Tennessee's

history. The tiny mountain town of Oak Ridge became the state's fifth-largest city almost overnight, and it is synonymous with the atomic bomb that was dropped on Hiroshima at the final stage of the war.

More than 300,000 Tennesseans served in World War II and just under 6,000 died. During the war, Camps Forrest, Campbell, and Tyson served as prisoner-of-war camps. Several hundred war refugees settled in Tennessee, many in the Nashville area.

The war also sped up Tennessee's industrialization. Industrial centers in Memphis, Chattanooga, and Knoxville converted to war production, while new industries were established in smaller cities such as Kingsport. Agriculture was no longer Tennessee's most important economic activity. The industrial growth was a catalyst for urbanization. Nashville's population grew by 25 percent during the war, and Shelby County's by 35 percent. The war also finally saw the end of the Great Depression.

The war also brought women into the workplace in numbers that were then unprecedented; approximately one-third of the state's workers were female by the end of the war.

Tennesseans supported the war not only by volunteering to serve overseas, but on the home front as well. Families planted victory gardens, invested in war bonds, and supported soldiers.

Tennesseans served with distinction during the war. Cordell Hull, a native of Pickett County, was U.S. secretary of state for 12 years and is known as the Father of the United Nations for his role in drawing up the foundation of that institution.

Oak Ridge

No community was more transformed by the war than Oak Ridge. A remote area of countryside west of Knoxville in East Tennessee, Oak Ridge was home to 4,000 people, most of them farmers. The army was searching for a place to build the facilities to construct an atom bomb, and this 52,000-acre area fit the bill. In 1942 residents of Oak Ridge began to receive notices that they would have to leave because the government was taking their land. Clinton Laboratories, named after the nearest town, was built seemingly overnight. Housing was provided in dormitories, trailers, and "victory cottages." Scientists, engineers, and researchers moved in, together with blue-collar workers who were needed to labor at the facility, later named Oak Ridge National Laboratory.

Work proceeded on schedule inside the laboratory, and on August 6, 1945, shortly after 9 A.M., the first atomic bomb was dropped over Hiroshima. Three days later the second bomb exploded over Nagasaki, and on August 14 Japan surrendered.

Oak Ridge, nicknamed the Secret City, remains today a key part of the United States' nuclear system. While some degree of integration has taken place, Oak Ridge still has a different feel than most Tennessee towns, due in large part to the thousands of scientists and professionals who live there.

POSTWAR TENNESSEE

Tennessee's industrialization continued after the war. By 1960 there were more city dwellers than rural dwellers in the state, and Tennessee was ranked the 16th most industrialized state in the United States. Industry that had developed during the war transformed to peacetime operation.

Ex-servicemen were not content with the political machines that had controlled Tennessee politics for decades. In 1948 congressman Estes Kefauver won a U.S. Senate seat, defeating the candidate chosen by Memphis mayor Ed Crump. The defeat signaled an end to Crump's substantial influence in statewide elections. In 1953 Tennessee repealed the state poll tax, again limiting politicians' ability to manipulate the vote. The tide of change also swept in Senator Albert Gore Sr. and Governor Frank Clement in 1952. Kefauver, Gore, and Clement were moderate Democrats of the New South.

CIVIL RIGHTS

The early gains for blacks during Reconstruction were lost during the decades that followed. Segregation, the threat of violence, poll taxes, and literacy tests discriminated against blacks in all spheres of life: economic, social, political, and educational. The fight to right these wrongs was waged by many brave Tennesseans.

Early civil rights victories in Tennessee included the 1905 successful boycott of Nashville's segregated streetcars and the creation of a competing black-owned streetcar company. In the 1920s in Chattanooga, blacks successfully defeated the Ku Klux Klan at the polls. Black institutions of learning persevered in educating young African Americans and developing a generation of leaders.

Following World War II, there was newfound energy in the fight for civil rights. Returning black servicemen who had fought for their country demanded greater equality, and the opportunities of the age raised the stakes of economic equality. In 1946, racially based violence targeted at a returned black serviceman in Columbia brought national attention to violence against black citizens and raised awareness of the need to protect blacks' civil rights.

The Highlander Folk School, founded in Grundy County and later moved to Cocke County, was an important training center for community activists and civil rights leaders in the 1950s. Founder Miles Horton believed in popular education and sought to bring black and white activists together to share experiences. Many leaders in the national civil rights movement, including Rev. Martin Luther King and Rosa Parks, attended the folk school.

In the 1950s, the first steps toward public school desegregation took place in Tennessee. Following a lawsuit filed by black parents, Clinton desegregated its schools in 1956 on order of a federal court judge. The integration began peacefully, but outside agitators arrived to organize resistance, and in the end Governor

Clement was forced to call in 600 National Guardsmen to diffuse the violent atmosphere. But the first black students were allowed to stay, and in May 1957 Bobby Cain became the first African American to graduate from an integrated public high school in the South.

In the fall of 1957 Nashville's public schools were desegregated. As many as half of the white students stayed home in protest, and one integrated school, Hattie Cotton School, was dynamited and partially destroyed. Other Tennessee cities desegregated at a slower pace, and by 1960 only 169 of Tennessee's almost 150,000 black children of school age attended integrated schools.

The Nashville lunch counter sit-ins of 1960 were an important milestone in both the local and national civil rights movements. Led by students from the city's black universities, the sit-ins eventually forced an end to racial segregation of the city's public services. Over two months hundreds of black students were arrested for sitting at white-only downtown lunch counters. Black consumers' boycott of downtown stores put additional pressure on the business community. On April 19 thousands of protesters marched in silence to the courthouse to confront city officials, and the next day Rev. Martin Luther King Jr. addressed Fisk University. On May 10, 1960, several downtown stores integrated their lunch counters, and Nashville became the first major city in the South to begin desegregating its public facilities.

As the civil rights movement continued, Tennesseans played an important part.

Tennesseans were involved with organizing the Student Nonviolent Coordinating Committee and participated in the Freedom Rides, which sought to integrate buses across the south. In 1965 A. W. Willis Jr. of Memphis became the first African American representative elected to the state's General Assembly in more than 60 years. Three years later, Memphis's sanitation workers went on strike to protest discriminatory pay and work rules. Dr. King came to Memphis to support the striking workers. On April 4, 1968, King was assassinated by a sniper as he stood on the balcony of the Lorraine Motel in downtown Memphis.

MODERN TENNESSEE

The industrialization that began during World War II has continued in modern-day Tennessee. In 1980 Nissan built what was then the largest truck assembly plant in the world at Smyrna, Tennessee. In 1987 Saturn Corporation chose Spring Hill as the site for its $2.1 billion automobile plant.

At the same time, however, the state's older industries—including textiles and manufacturing—have suffered losses over the past three decades, due in part to the movement of industry outside of the United States.

During the 1950s and beyond, Tennessee developed a reputation as a hotbed of musical talent. Memphis's Elvis Presley may have invented rock 'n' roll, and his Graceland mansion remains one of the state's most enduring tourist attractions. The Grand Ole Opry in Nashville was representative of a second musical genre that came to call Tennessee home: country music.

Government and Economy

GOVERNMENT

Tennessee is governed by its constitution, unchanged since 1870 when it was revised in light of emancipation, the Civil War, and Reconstruction.

Tennessee has a governor who is elected to four-year terms, a legislature, and court system. The lieutenant governor is not elected statewide; he or she is chosen by the Senate and also serves as its speaker.

The legislature, or General Assembly, is made up of the 99-member House of Representatives and the 33-member Senate. The Tennessee State Supreme Court is made of five members, no two of whom can be from the same Grand Division. The Supreme Court chooses the state's attorney general.

The executive branch consists of 21 cabinet-level departments, which employ 39,000 state workers. Departments are led by a commissioner who is appointed by the governor and serves as a member of his cabinet.

Tennessee has 95 counties; the largest is Shelby County, which contains Memphis. The smallest county by size is Trousdale, with 113 square miles; the smallest population is in Pickett County.

The state has 11 electoral college votes in U.S. presidential elections.

Modern Politics

Like other Southern states, Tennessee has seen a gradual shift to the political right since the 1960s. The shift began in 1966 with Howard Baker's election to the U.S. Senate, and it continued with Tennessee's support for Republican presidential candidate Richard Nixon in 1968 and 1972. Despite a few exceptions, the shift

Tennessee State Capitol and the downtown skyline in Nashville

© BRUCE PATTEN/123RF

has continued into the 21st century, although Nashville, Memphis, and other parts of Middle and West Tennessee remain Democratic territory.

East Tennessee holds the distinction as one of a handful of Southern territories that has consistently supported the Republican party since the Civil War. Today, Republicans outpoll Democrats in this region by as much as three to one.

The statewide trend toward the Republican party continued in 2008, with Tennessee being one of only a handful of states where Democrat Barack Obama received a lesser proportion of votes than did Senator John Kerry four years earlier. State Republicans also succeeded in gaining control of both houses of the state legislature. The general shift to the right has continued in the governor's office. Previous governor Phil Bredesen is a Democrat, but he was succeeded by Republican Bill Haslam. Since 1967, no party has been able to keep the governor's seat for two terms.

Andrew Jackson may still be the most prominent Tennessean in American political history, but Tennessee politicians continue to play a role on the national stage. Albert Gore Jr., elected to the U.S. House of Representatives in 1976, served as vice president under President Bill Clinton from 1992 until 2000, and he lost the highly contested 2000 presidential contest to George W. Bush. Gore famously lost his home state to Bush, further evidence of Tennessee's move to the right. Gore went on to champion global climate change and win the Nobel Peace Prize, and he is often seen around Nashville.

Lamar Alexander, a former governor of Tennessee, was appointed secretary of education by the first President Bush in 1990. Alexander—famous for his flannel shirts—ran unsuccessfully for president and was later elected senator from Tennessee. Bill Frist, a doctor, was also elected senator and rose to be the Republican majority leader during the presidency of George W. Bush, before quitting politics for medical philanthropy.

The most recent Tennessean to seek the Oval Office was former senator and *Law and Order* star Fred Thompson, from Lewisburg in Middle Tennessee.

One of the most persistent political issues for Tennesseans in modern times has been the state's tax structure. The state first established a 2 percent sales tax in 1947, and it was increased incrementally over the years, eventually reaching 7 percent today. With local options, it is one of the highest sales tax rates in the country. (The state sales tax on food is 5.5 percent.) At the same time, the state has failed on more than one occasion—most recently during the second term of Republican governor Donald Sundquist in the late 1990s—to establish an income tax that would provide greater stability to the state's revenues.

Like much of the country, in 2008 Tennessee faced a serious budget crunch that led to the elimination of thousands of state jobs, cutbacks at state-funded universities, and the scaling back of the state health insurance program.

ECONOMY

Tennessee has the 18th-largest economy in the United States. Important industries include health care, education, farming, electrical power, and tourism. In the past few years, most job growth has been recorded in the areas of leisure, hospitality, education, and health care. Manufacturing, mining, and construction jobs have declined. Despite the overall decline in manufacturing, there was good news in 2008 when Volkswagen announced that it chose Chattanooga as home for a new, $1 billion plant, expected to bring 2,000 jobs to the state in the coming years.

Tennessee's unemployment rate fluctuates but generally sits a half point above the national average. In 2010, the jobless rate was about 9.4 percent.

About 16.5 percent of Tennessee families live in poverty, roughly 3 percent higher than the nationwide average. The median household

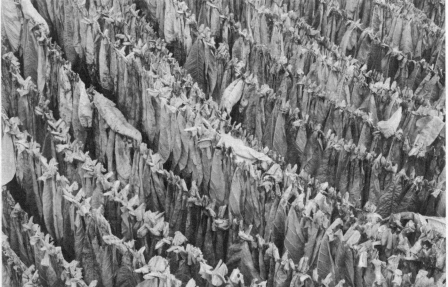

© ZORAN SIMIN/123RF

the traditional drying of tobacco

income in 2011 was $38,686—75 percent of the U.S. median income.

All of Tennessee's cities have poverty rates higher than the state or national average. Memphis's poverty rate is the state's highest: 19 percent of Memphis families are poor. The U.S. Census calls Memphis one of the poorest cities in the nation. Knoxville's family poverty rate is 8.73 percent.

Agriculture

Farming accounts for 14.2 percent, or $38.5 billion, of the Tennessee economy. More than 42 percent of the state's land is used in farming; 63.6 percent of this is cropland.

Soybeans, tobacco, corn, and hay are among Tennessee's most important agricultural crops. Cattle and calf production, chicken farming, and cotton cultivation are also important parts of the farm economy.

Greene County, in northeastern Tennessee, is the leading county for all types of cow farming;

Giles and Lincoln Counties, in the south-central part of the state, rank second and third. The leading cotton producer is Haywood County, followed by Crockett and Gibson, all three of which are located in West Tennessee. Other counties where agriculture figures largely into the economy are Obion, Dyer, Rutherford, and Robertson.

Tennessee ranks sixth among U.S. states for equine production, and walking or quarter horses account for more than half of the state's estimated 210,000 head of equine. The state ranks third for tomatoes, fourth for tobacco, and seventh for cotton.

Some farmers have begun converting to corn production in anticipation of a biofuel boom.

Tourism

According to the state tourism department, the industry generated $14.1 billion in economic activity in 2010. More than 170,000 Tennessee jobs are linked to tourism. The state credits the industry with generating more than $1 billion in state and local tax revenue.

People and Culture

DEMOGRAPHICS

Tennessee is home to 6.4 million people. Almost one quarter of these are 18 years and younger; about 13 percent are older than 65. Tennessee is 77 percent white and 16 percent black. Eighty percent of Tennesseans have a high school diploma, and 23 percent have at least a bachelor's degree.

Memphis counts 663,000 residents and is the state's largest city. More than 60 percent of Memphians are African American, a greater proportion than is found in any other American city. Memphis has the youngest average age of the four major Tennessee cities.

Nashville's population is 605,473. Approximately 60 percent of these are white, 27 percent are African American, and 8 percent are Latino or Hispanic. Nashville's foreign-born population tripled during the decade between 1990 and 2000, and 11 percent of the city's population was born outside of the United States. This includes large populations from Mexico, Vietnam, Laos, and Somalia. Nashville is also home to more than 11,000 Iraqi Kurds.

Knoxville, Tennessee's third-largest city, has a population of about 178,000. More than 168,000 people live in Chattanooga.

RELIGION

Tennessee is unquestionably part of the U.S. Bible Belt; the conservative Christian faith is both prevalent and prominent all over the state. Eighty-two percent of Tennesseans call themselves Christians, and 40 percent of these identify as Baptist. The second-largest Christian denomination is Methodist. Nashville is the headquarters of the Southern Baptist Convention, the National Baptist Convention, and the United Methodist Church. Memphis is the headquarters of the mostly African American Church of God in Christ. However, the state's major cities do have growing populations that practice Judaism and Islam.

While Tennessee's urban centers are the home of church headquarters, religious fervor is strongest in the rural communities. Pentecostal churches have been known for rites such as speaking in tongues and snake handling, although these activities are not as widespread as they once were.

Non-Christians will feel most comfortable in urban areas, where numbers of religious minorities have grown in recent years and where the influence of the local churches is not as great.

One practical effect of Tennessee's Christian bent is that many counties and even cities are totally dry, while most bar the sale of alcohol on Sunday.

LANGUAGE

Tennesseans speak English, of a kind. The Tennessee drawl varies from the language of the upper South, spoken in East Tennessee and closely associated with the region's Scotch-Irish roots, and the language of West Tennessee, more akin to that of Mississippi and the lower South.

Little in Tennesseans' speech is distinct to the state itself. Speech patterns heard in Tennessee are also heard in other states in the region.

Speech patterns that have been documented throughout the state, but that may be more prevalent in the east, include the following, outlined by Michael Montgomery of the University of South Carolina in the *Tennessee Encyclopedia of History and Culture.* Montgomery writes that Tennesseans tend to pronounce vowels in the words *pen* and *hem* as *pin* and *him;* they shift the accent to the beginning of words, so *Tennessee* becomes *TIN-isee;* they clip or reduce the vowel in words like *ride* so it sounds more like *rad;* and vowels in other words are stretched, so that a single-syllable word like *bed* becomes *buy-ud.*

"Beale Street Blues" by W. C. Handy, cover of 1919 sheet music republication (first published 3 years earlier), with singer Teddy Tappin on the cover

Tennessee speech patterns are not limited to word pronunciation. Tennesseans also speak with folksy and down-home language. Speakers often use colorful metaphors, and greater value is placed on the quality of expression than the perfection of grammar.

THE ARTS
Crafts

Many Tennessee craft traditions have their roots in the handmade housewares that rural families had to make for themselves, including things like quilts and coverlets, baskets, candles, and furniture. These items were fashioned out of materials that could be raised or harvested nearby, and colors were derived from natural dyes such as walnut hulls and indigo.

Many of the same crafts were produced by African Americans, who developed their own craft traditions, often with even fewer raw materials than their white counterparts. For example, African American quilts often used patterns and colors reflective of African culture. Blacksmiths were often African American, and these skilled artisans developed both practical and decorative pieces for white and black households.

As the lifestyles of Tennesseans changed and more household items were available in stores and by mail order, crafts were produced for sale. In 1929, the Southern Highland Handicraft Guild was formed and held its first meeting in Knoxville. In 1950 the guild merged with Southern Highlanders Inc., an organization established by the Tennessee Valley Authority, and the group's marketing and promotion efforts pushed westward toward the Cumberland Plateau and Nashville.

Today, artists from around the United States have settled in Tennessee to practice modern forms of traditional crafts of quilting, weaving, pottery, furniture making, and basket making, among others. While market forces have promoted a certain false folksiness among some artists, a great many of today's practicing artisans remain true to the mountain heritage that gave birth to the craft tradition in the first place.

Music

Tennessee may be more famous for its music than for anything else. The blues was born on Beale Street; the Grand Ole Opry popularized old-time mountain music; and the Fisk Jubilee singers of Nashville introduced African American spirituals to the world. Rock 'n' roll traces its roots to Elvis Presley, Carl Perkins, Jerry Lee Lewis, and the city of Memphis.

The blues became popular in cities from New Orleans to St. Louis at the turn of the 20th century. But thanks in large part to composer and performer W. C. Handy, the musical form will be forever associated with Memphis and Beale Street. Early blues greats like Walter "Furry" Lewis, Booker T. Washington "Bukka"

White, "Little Laura" Dukes, and Ma Rainey started in Memphis.

Sun Studio recorded some of the first commercial blues records in the 1950s, but the label is most famous for discovering Elvis Presley. Stax Records created a new sound, soul, in the late 1950s and early 1960s.

Country music was born in Bristol, Tennessee, where the earliest recordings of Jimmie Rodgers and the Carter Family were made in the 1920s. In the decades that followed, Nashville became the capital of country music, beginning thanks to radio station WSM and dozens of rural musicians who trekked to town to play on the radio. America was hungry for a type of music to call its own, and country music was it. First called "hillbilly music," country was popularized by barn-dance radio shows, including the Grand Ole Opry. Over the years, country music mellowed out, adopting the Nashville sound that softened its edges and made it palatable to a wider audience. Today, the city is second only to New York as a center for recorded music, and many country music stars still live in and around the city.

Dance

Clogging, or buck dancing, is a style of folk dance that originated with the Scotch-Irish settlers in the eastern mountains of Tennessee. Characterized by an erect upper body and a fast-paced toe-heel movement with the feet, traditional clogging is improvisational. Performers move at a very fast pace to the music of string bands.

Clogging was popularized during the 1940s and '50s on television and radio shows that showcased country music. Modern clogging is often choreographed and performed with a partner.

Clogging can trace influences from Native American and African American styles of dance, as well as the traditional dance of the British Isles.

Literature

The first literature inspired by Tennessee is not well known. *The Tennessean; A Novel, Founded on Facts* is a melodramatic novel written by Anne Newport Royall and published in 1827. Its plot brings readers along on a three-day journey from Nashville to Knoxville, and it is the first novel set in Tennessee. The first novel written by a Tennessean was *Woodville; or, The Anchoret Reclaimed. A Descriptive Tale,* written by Charles W. Todd and published in Knoxville in 1832.

Later Tennessee literature is better known. English novelist **Frances Hodgson Burnett** lived in New Market and then Knoxville in the 1860s and 1870s. While best known for her tales *Little Lord Fauntleroy* and *The Secret Garden,* Burnett penned several works set in Tennessee. In the 1920s, a group of writers at Vanderbilt University emerged under the leadership of John Crowe Ransom. The group's magazine, *The Fugitive,* was published 1922–1925. The Fugitives were succeeded by the Agrarians, who published their manifesto, *I'll Take My Stand,* in 1930. Writer **Robert Penn Warren** was a member of both the Fugitives and the Agrarians, and he went on to win the Pulitzer Prize for *All the King's Men,* about governor Huey Long of Louisiana. Warren's novels *The Cave, Flood,* and *Meet Me in the Green Glen* are set in Tennessee.

Another award-winning Tennessee writer is **Peter Taylor,** who studied at Rhodes College and Vanderbilt University before moving to North Carolina and writing the Pulitzer Prize–winning *A Summons to Memphis* in 1986 and *In Tennessee Country* in 1994.

James Agee is another Pulitzer Prize winner. Raised in Knoxville, Agee wrote poetry, journalism, and screenplays before his winning *A Death in the Family* was published. Agee is also known for his singular work *Let Us Now Praise Famous Men,* with photographer Walker Evans, which documented the lives of poor whites during the Great Depression.

Few people knew Memphis-born writer and

historian **Shelby Foote** until Ken Burns's landmark Civil War documentary. In addition to his seminal trilogy on the war, Foote wrote the novel *Shiloh* in 1952.

Women have also excelled as writers in Tennessee. **Anne Armstrong** published *The Seas of God* in 1915 and *This Day and Time* in 1930, both of which were set in her native East Tennessee. **Evelyn Scott** wrote *The Wave,* set during the Civil War, as well as an autobiography, *Escapade,* depicting the six years she and her common-law husband spent living in Brazil.

Perhaps the best-known female Tennessee writer is **Nikki Giovanni,** of Knoxville, who established herself as a poet of international importance with her 1968 *Black Feeling, Black Talk.* In recent years author Ann Patchett has built a national reputation, thanks to her articles about living in Nashville, covering everything from the real estate to the 2010 floods. Patchett, who wrote the acclaimed *State of Wonder* and *Bel Canto,* opened Parnassus Books, an independent bookstore, in Nashville in 2011.

No Tennessee writer is better known or more widely acclaimed than **Alex Haley,** whose *Roots* won the Pulitzer Prize and inspired a landmark film and television series. Haley's other works include *Queen,* which is based on the story of his grandmother, who worked and lived in Savannah, Tennessee, on the Tennessee River.

Knoxville native **Cormac McCarthy** is widely known for his works, including *All the Pretty Horses* and *The Road,* which were both made into films. But McCarthy had started out writing about his native East Tennessee in works such as *The Orchard Keeper* and *Suttree.*

ESSENTIALS

Getting There and Around

Most visitors to Tennessee drive their own cars, and for good reason. The highways are good, distances are manageable, and many, if not most, destinations in the state are not accessible by public transportation. Plus, the state is less than a day's drive from a large percentage of the population of the United States.

If you're coming to Nashville or Memphis for a short stay (a weekend getaway or a conference), you likely can manage without a car. Otherwise, you will need your own wheels to get around.

AIR

International airports in Tennessee include Nashville International Airport (BNA) and Memphis International Airport (MEM). McGhee Tyson Airport (TYS) in Knoxville, Chattanooga Metropolitan Airport (CHA), and the Tri-Cities Regional Airport (TRI) in Blountville offer domestic service to hubs in the eastern United States.

RAIL

Only western Tennessee is easily accessible by passenger rail. Amtrak runs from Chicago

to New Orleans, with stops in Memphis, Newbern-Dyersburg in West Tennessee, and Fulton on the border with Kentucky. The route, called The City of New Orleans, runs daily.

BUS

Greyhound fully serves Tennessee, with daily routes that crisscross the state in nearly every direction.

CAR

Tennessee is within one day's drive of 75 percent of the U.S. population, and most visitors to the state get here in their own cars. There are seven interstates that run into the state, from just about every direction you might want to come.

While urban centers, pit-stop motels, and population centers are all found along or very near interstates, some of Tennessee's most lovely landscapes are far from the stretches of multilane pavement (and worth the drive to get there).

Road Rules

Tennessee recognizes other states' driver's licenses and learner's permits. New residents are required to obtain a Tennessee license within 30 days of establishing residency, however.

Speed limits vary. On interstates limits range 55–75 miles per hour. Limits on primary and secondary routes vary based on local conditions. Travelers should pay special attention to slow zones around schools; speeding tickets in these areas often attract high penalties.

It is required by law that all drivers and passengers in a moving vehicle wear their seatbelts. Infants less than one year old must be restrained in a rear-facing car seat; children 1–3 years must be restrained in a front-facing car seat. A child of 4–8 years who is less than four feet, nine inches tall must have a booster seat.

Drunk driving is dangerous and against the law. It is illegal to drive in Tennessee with a blood alcohol concentration of 0.08 percent or more.

Car Rentals

Rental cars are widely available throughout Tennessee. The greatest concentration of rental agencies are found at major airports, but there are also neighborhood and downtown locations. Most rental agencies require the renter to be at least 24 years old; some have an even higher age requirement.

Before renting a car, call you credit card company and primary car insurance provider to find out what kind of insurance you have on a rental. You can likely forego the expensive insurance packages offered by rental companies.

For the best rates on car rentals, book early. Most companies allow you to reserve a car in advance without paying a deposit.

Taxis

Taxis are available in major cities, including Memphis, Nashville, Knoxville, Chattanooga, and Clarksville. Taxi service in other parts of the state will be spotty and expensive.

Taxi stands are found in just a few locations, including airports and major tourist sites, such as Beale Street in Memphis. Otherwise you will have to call to summon a taxi.

Traffic Reports

For current traffic and road reports, including weather-related closures, construction closures, and traffic jams, dial 511 from any mobile or landline. You can also log on to www.tn511.com.

RECREATIONAL VEHICLES

Recreational vehicles are an increasingly popular way to see Tennessee due to the prevalence of good campgrounds and the beautiful landscape of the state.

All state park campgrounds welcome RVs and provide utilities such as water, electricity, and a dump station. For people who enjoy the outdoors but do not want to forgo the basic comforts of home, RVs provide some real advantages. RVs range from little trailers that pop up to provide space for sleeping to monstrous homes on wheels. Gas mileage ranges 7–13 miles per gallon, depending on the size and age of the RV.

All RVers should have mercy on other drivers and pull over from time to time so that traffic can pass, especially on mountain roads that are steep and difficult for RVs to climb.

RV Rentals

You can rent an RV for a one-way or local trip from **Cruise America** (www.cruiseamerica.com), which has locations in Knoxville (6100 Western Ave., 865/450-5009), Nashville (201 Donelson Pk., 615/885-4281), and Memphis (10230 Hwy. 70, Lakeland, 901/867-0039). Renters should be 25 years or older. Rental rates vary depending on the size of the vehicle and other factors. They also charge for mileage, and you can buy kits that include sheets, towels, dishes, and other basic necessities.

Recreation

NATIONAL PARKS

Tennessee's most significant national park is the Great Smoky Mountains National Park, the most visited national park in the United States. This is the crown jewel of the state's natural areas and a major draw for visitors.

Other federal lands are more wild and less visited. The Big South Fork and Land Between the Lakes are uncrowded recreation areas along the northern border with Kentucky. The Cherokee National Forest flanks the Smokies on the north and south, creating an uninterrupted buffer of federally protected lands along the entire eastern mountain range.

STATE PARKS

Tennessee's state parks are glorious and one of the state's best calling cards. The state has 54 parks and 77 state natural areas, stretching from the Appalachian Mountains in the east to the banks of the Mississippi River in the west. State parks and natural areas encompass 185,000 acres throughout the state. In 2007, Tennessee's parks were judged the best in the nation by the National Recreation and Park Association. The commendation came after a long and bitter fight over user fees and state budget woes that led to the closure of 14 parks and the imposition of user fees at 23 parks

between 2002 and 2006. The fight over the future of the state parks illustrated how valuable they are indeed.

Each state park includes basic amenities such as picnic facilities and day-use areas with public restrooms, water, and a park office of some kind. Most parks also have campgrounds, hiking trails, playgrounds, and facilities for sports such as volleyball, basketball, and baseball. A number of parks have swimming beaches, bicycle trails, areas for fishing or hunting, and backcountry campsites.

The park system includes 6 parks with inns, 12 with golf courses, 8 with restaurants, and 4 with marinas. A number of parks also have cabins, ideal for families or other groups.

For travelers who enjoy the out-of-doors, the state parks are some of the best places in the state to visit. Despite persistent budget problems, the parks are generally well maintained. Accommodations are not luxurious, but they are clean and comfortable, and the natural beauty that exists in many of the parks is unparalleled. Camping in a state park sure beats the KOA any day.

Detailed information about fees, amenities, and services may be found on the state park website (http://state.tn.us/environment/parks). You can also request a published map

© BARRY BEARD

Deer graze in a field at Cades Cove in Great Smoky Mountains National Park.

and brochure. Enthusiasts may also want to subscribe to the *Tennessee Conservationist,* a magazine published by the State Department of Environment and Conservation.

HIKING

Opportunities to hike are abundant in Tennessee. State parks, national forests, national parks, and wildlife refuges are just a few of the areas where you will find places for a walk in the woods.

High-profile hiking trails such as the Appalachian Trail in the eastern mountains are indeed special. But lesser-known walks are often equally spectacular, and the best hike may well be the one closest to where you are right now.

Day hikes require just a few pieces of gear: comfortable and sturdy shoes; a day pack with water, food, and a map; and several layers of clothing, especially during volatile spring and fall months. In the winter, it's a good idea to bring a change of socks and extra layers of warm clothes.

Other gear is optional: A walking stick makes rough or steep terrain a bit easier, and a camera is always a nice idea.

Whenever you go hiking, tell someone where you're going and when you expect to be back. Do not expect cell phones to work on the trail.

Many state parks and the national parks in the eastern mountains welcome overnight hikers. Backpackers must carry lightweight tents, sleeping bags, food, and extra gear on their backs. They must also register in advance. You can sometimes reserve backcountry campsites. These campsites offer little more than a clearing for your tent and a ring of stones for your fire. Some are built near sources of water. Some trails have overnight shelters, especially nice in winter.

Hiking is one of the best ways to experience Tennessee's nature, and there are few better ways to spend a day or two.

BICYCLING

Bicycling is an increasingly popular pastime in Tennessee. Only in a handful of urban areas, and on some college campuses, is bicycling a form of regular transportation. But mountain and road biking is popular for staying fit and having fun. Many area parks offer BMX tracks.

Of course you can bicycle just about anywhere (but not on the interstates). Cities such as Nashville, Chattanooga, Knoxville, and Murfreesboro have greenways especially for bikers (and walkers). Dedicated mountain bike trails are popping up in parks across the state, including at Montgomery Bell State Park, Big Ridge State Park, and Meeman-Shelby Forest State Park. City parks in Memphis and Nashville also welcome bikers.

The Tennessee Bicycle Racing Association (www.tbra.org) promotes biking and is an umbrella organization for several local bike groups. The Tennessee Mountain Biking Alliance (www.mtbtn.org) promotes mountain biking and can put you in touch with mountain bikers in your neck of the woods. Local bike shops are also a good place to find out about good bike routes, local safety issues, and upcoming events.

FISHING

Fishing is tremendously popular in Tennessee. The lakes created by the Tennessee Valley Authority produced many opportunities to fish. Smaller rivers and streams in all parts of the state are also good for fishing.

Some of the most common types of fish caught in Tennessee rivers and lakes are bass, trout, crappie, perch, pike, catfish, and carp. Various rivers and lakes are stocked regularly with fish.

Subject to a few exceptions, everyone who is 13 and older and who attempts to take fish from a body of water should have a valid Tennessee fishing license. License fees vary by type and duration: A one-day fishing license for a Tennessee state resident is $5.50; an annual fish-hunt license for a state resident is $28. Out-of-staters pay more: An annual license for all types of fish costs $81.

Annual licenses go on sale every year on February 18 and are good until the last day of February the next year.

You can buy a fishing license from county clerks, sporting goods stores, boat docks, and offices of the Tennessee Wildlife Resources Agency. You can buy a license online at http://wildlifelicense.com; licenses processed online are subject to a $3 or $4.25 processing fee depending on how the license is printed and fulfilled. You can also buy licenses by mail or over the phone by calling 888/814 8972.

Rules about limits, minimum sizes, and seasons are detailed and depend on the lake or stream. The Tennessee Wildlife Resources Agency publishes a comprehensive guide to fishing regulations every year. This guide includes fish stocking schedules, dam release timetables, detailed information about limits, and warnings about contaminants in certain types of Tennessee fish. You can request a copy of the guide from any TWRA office or download a copy online from www.tnwildlife.org

TWRA offices are located in Crossville (931/484 9571 or 800/262 6704), Nashville (Ellington Agricultural Center, 615/781-6500 or 800/781-6622), Morristown (423/587-7037 or 800/332 0900), and Jackson (731/423 5725 or 800/372-3928).

PADDLING

The Volunteer State has some of the best paddling—kayaking, white-water rafting, canoeing, and stand-up paddling—in the country. Chattanooga and the eastern part of the state, near the Ocoee, are most well known for their water-sports access. But, in truth, all of the state's major cities and many rural areas have opportunities for guide-led and independent paddling adventures.

Paddlers are required to have a U.S. Coast Guard approved life preserver and whistle with them while on the water. In addition to the safety reasons for wearing one, there are fines for not complying with these regulations.

The Tennessee Scenic Rivers Association (TSRA) has been working to build more paddler access points across the state. Visit www.paddletsra.org for more details on their work.

Other good resources include the Cumberland River Compact (www.cumberlandrivercompact.org) and the Tennessee Clean Water Network (www.tcwn.org).

Accommodations

Accommodations in Tennessee fall into three main categories, with little gray area in between.

HOTELS AND MOTELS

Chain motels are ubiquitous, particularly along interstates. These properties are entirely predictable; their amenities depend on the price tag and location. Most motel chains allow you to make reservations in advance by telephone or on the Internet. Most motels require a credit card number at the time of reservation, but they don't usually charge your card until you arrive. Always ask about the cancellation policy to avoid paying for a room that you do not ultimately need or use.

Savvy shoppers can save money on their hotel room. Shop around, and pay attention to price differentials based on location; if you're willing to be a few miles up the interstate from the city, you'll realize some significant savings. You may also be amazed by the power of the words "That rate seems high to me. Do you have anything better?" Employed regularly, this approach will usually save you a few bucks each night, at least.

Chain motels do not offer unique accommodations, and only the rarest among them is situated somewhere more charming than an asphalt parking lot. But for travelers who are looking for flexibility, familiarity, and a good deal, chain motels can fit the bill.

Independent motels and hotels range from no-brand roadside motels to upscale boutique hotels in urban centers. By their very nature, these properties are each a little different. Boutique hotels tend to be more expensive than chain hotels, but they also allow you to feel as if you are staying in a place with a history and character of its own. They may also offer personalized service that is not available at cookie-cutter motels.

BED-AND-BREAKFASTS

Bed-and-breakfasts are about as far from a chain motel as one can get. Usually located in small towns, rural areas, and quiet residential neighborhoods of major cities, bed-and-breakfasts are independent guesthouses. The quality of the offering depends entirely on the hosts, and the entire bed-and-breakfast experience often takes on the character and tone of the person in whose home you are sleeping. Good bed-and-breakfast hosts can sense the line between being welcoming and overly chatty, but some seem to struggle with this.

Bed-and-breakfasts offer a number of advantages over the typical motel. Their locations are often superior, the guest rooms have lots of character and charm, and a full and often homemade breakfast is included. Some bed-and-breakfasts are located in historic buildings, and many are furnished with antiques.

Reservations for bed-and-breakfasts are not as flexible as most motels. Many bed-and-breakfasts require a deposit, and many require payment in full before you arrive. Making payments can be a challenge, too; while some are equipped with credit card facilities, others accept only checks and cash. Cancellation policies are also more stringent than most motels. All of this can make it hard for travelers who like to be flexible and leave things till the last minute. Additionally, if you're bringing children with you, be sure to check that your bed-and-breakfast allows children; some don't. If your travel plans are certain and you just can't bear another night in a bland hotel room, a bed-and-breakfast is the ideal alternative.

Bed-and-breakfast rates vary but generally range $90–150 per night based on double occupancy.

Bed and Breakfast Inns Online (www.bbonline.com) is a national listing service that includes a number of Tennessee bed-and-breakfasts.

HOSTELS

At this writing, there are youth hostels in Nashville, Knoxville, and upper East Tennessee. Hostels provide dormitory-style accommodations at a fraction of the cost of a standard motel room. Bathroom and kitchen facilities are usually shared, and there are common rooms with couches, televisions, and Internet access. Hostels are usually favored by young and international travelers, and they are a good place to meet people.

Food

Throughout Tennessee, you will find restaurants that specialize in local and regional dishes. In urban centers, there is a wide variety of dining available, from international eateries to fine-dining restaurants.

Chain restaurants, including fast-food joints, are all over the state. But travelers owe it to themselves to eat in local restaurants for a taste of something more authentic.

MEAT-AND-THREES

Meat-and-threes, also called plate-lunch diners, are found throughout Tennessee, with the greatest concentration in Memphis and Nashville. The name is used to refer to the type of restaurant and the meal itself. These eateries serve the type of food that Tennesseans once cooked at home: main dish meats like baked chicken, meat loaf, fried catfish, and chicken and dumplings; side dishes (also called "vegetables") including macaroni and cheese, mashed potatoes, greens, creamed corn, squash, and fried okra; breads including corn bread, biscuits, and yeast rolls; and desserts like peach cobbler, Jell-O, and cream pies. Hands down, these diners are the best places to become acquainted, or renew your relationship, with Southern home cooking.

Plate-lunch diners focus on the midday meal. Most offer a different menu of meats and sides daily. Large restaurants may have as many as eight different main dishes to choose from; smaller diners may offer two or three. Some are set up cafeteria-style, and others employ servers. All offer a good value for the money and generally speedy food service.

Meat-and-threes exist in rural and urban communities, although in the countryside there's less fuss attached. They are simply where people go to eat.

The food served in these restaurants is generally hearty; health-conscious eaters should be careful. Vegetarians should also note that most vegetable dishes, like greens, are often cooked with meat.

REGIONAL SPECIALTIES
Barbecue

Memphis is the epicenter of Tennessee's barbecue culture. Here they host an annual festival dedicated to barbecue, and bona fide barbecue pits burn daily. In Memphis, they'll douse anything with barbecue sauce, hence the city's specialty: barbecue spaghetti.

Barbecue restaurants are usually humble places by appearances, with characters behind the counter and in the kitchen. Most swear by their own special barbecue recipe and guard it jealously. Nearly all good barbecue, however, requires time and patience, as the meat—usually pork—is smoked for hours and sometimes days over a fire. After the meat is cooked, it is tender and juicy and doused with barbecue sauce, which is tangy and sweet.

Pork barbecue is the most common, and it's often served pulled next to soft white bread. Barbecue chicken, turkey, ribs, bologna, and beef can also be found on many menus.

The Southern Foodways Alliance, part of the University of Mississippi's Center for the Study of Southern Culture, conducted an oral history project about Memphis and West Tennessee barbecue in the early 2000s. You can read transcripts of the interviews and see photos on the SFA website at www.southernfoodways.com.

Hot Chicken

Pan-fried "hot chicken" is one of Nashville's truly distinct culinary specialties. Breasts of spicy chicken are individually pan fried in cast-iron skillets at several holes-in-the-wall around Music City. They are traditionally served on white bread with a pickle. Don't come in a hurry; hot chicken takes time to prepare, and don't be overconfident with your tolerance for spice. Start with "mild" or "medium."

Catfish

Fried catfish is a food tradition that started along Tennessee's rivers, where river catfish are caught. Today, fried catfish served in restaurants is just as likely to come from a catfish farm. For real river catfish, look for restaurants located near rivers and lakes, such as those near Reelfoot Lake in northwestern Tennessee, or the City Fish Market in Brownsville.

Fried catfish (it's rarely served any way besides fried) is normally coated with a thin dusting of cornmeal, seasonings, and flour. On its own, the fish is relatively bland. Tangy tartar sauce, vinegar-based hot sauce, and traditional sides like coleslaw and baked beans enliven the flavor. Hush puppies are the traditional accompaniment.

FARMERS MARKETS

Farmers markets are popping up in more and more Tennessee communities. Knoxville, Nashville, and Memphis have large markets every Saturday (Nashville's operates daily). Dozens of small towns have their own weekly, seasonal markets.

There is a great deal of variety when it comes to the types of markets that exist. Some markets take place under tents, provide entertainment, and invite artisans to sell arts and crafts as well as food products. Other markets consist of little more than a bunch of farmers who have arranged the week's harvest on the back of their tailgates.

Regardless of the style, farmers markets are a great place to meet people and buy wholesome food.

The State Department of Agriculture (www.agriculture.state.tn.us) maintains a listing of all registered farmers markets, including locations and contact information.

Tips for Travelers

OPPORTUNITIES FOR STUDY

Tennessee is home to almost 50 colleges and universities, plus 13 public community colleges. The University of Tennessee, with campuses in Knoxville, Chattanooga, and Martin, is the largest. Other public colleges and universities include East Tennessee State University in Johnson City, Middle Tennessee State University in Murfreesboro, Tennessee State University in Nashville, and the University of Memphis. Private colleges include the historically black Fisk University in Nashville and Lemoyne-Owen College in Memphis; the University of the South at Sewanee, which is affiliated with the Episcopal Church; Memphis College of Art and Rhodes College in Memphis; and Vanderbilt University in Nashville. Each of these, plus the 31 other private institutions of higher learning, offer myriad short- and long-term education programs in fields as various as religious studies and medicine.

Several institutions of note offer workshops in arts and crafts. **The Appalachian Center for Craft** (Smithville, 931/372-3051, www.tntech.edu/craftcenter) is an affiliate of Tennessee Tech University and specializes in instruction in decorative arts and crafts. Full-time students can pursue a bachelor's degree in fine arts or a certificate in clay, fiber, glass, metal, or woodwork. The center also offers more than 100 different workshops each year. The school is set in scenic countryside on the Cumberland Plateau.

Perhaps one of the best-known craft schools in the entire United States, Gatlinburg's **Arrowmont** (865/436-5860, www.arrowmont.org) offers dozens of short courses and weekend

the Arrowmont School of Arts and Crafts

workshops annually. Arrowmont began as a settlement school for mountain folks, but today it is a center that combines traditional crafts with modern techniques and themes.

WOMEN TRAVELING ALONE

Women traveling alone in Tennessee may encounter a few people who don't understand, but most people will simply leave you alone. Solo women might find themselves the object of unwanted attention, especially at bars and restaurants at night. But usually a firm "I'm not interested" will do the trick.

Anyone—man or woman—traveling alone in the outdoors should take special precautions. Backpackers and campers should always tell someone where they will be and when they expect to be back. Ideally, establish a check-in routine with someone back home, and beware of overly friendly strangers on the trail.

GAY AND LESBIAN TRAVELERS

Tennessee's gay, lesbian, bisexual, and transgender people have a mixed bag. On one hand, this is the Bible Belt, a state where not long ago a bill was introduced that would have banned teachers from even saying the word *gay* in the classroom. (This is often referred to as the "Don't Say Gay" bill.) On the other hand, there has been no better time to be gay in Tennessee. More and more social, civic, and political organizations are waking up to the gay community, and there are vibrant gay scenes in many Tennessee cities.

For gay travelers, this means that the experience on the road can vary tremendously. You may or may not be able to expect a warm welcome at the mom-and-pop diner out in the country, but you can find good gay nightlife and gay-friendly lodging in many cities.

The decision about how out to be on the road is entirely up to you, but be prepared for some harassment if you are open everywhere you go. The farther off the beaten track you travel, the less likely it is that the people you encounter have had many opportunities to get to know openly gay people. Some may be downright mean, but others probably won't even notice.

Several specific guidebooks and websites give helpful listings of gay-friendly hotels, restaurants, and bars. The Damron guides (www.damron.com) offer Tennessee listings; the International Gay and Lesbian Travel Association (IGLTA, www.iglta.org) is a trade organization with listings of gay-friendly hotels, tour operators, and much more. San Francisco–based Now, Voyager (www.nowvoyager.com) is a gay-owned and gay-operated travel agency that specializes in gay tours, vacation packages, and cruises.

You should also check out local gay and lesbian organizations and newspapers.

Nashville

Three different publications cover the gay, lesbian, bisexual, and transgender community in Nashville. *InsideOut Nashville* (www.insideoutnashville.com) is a free weekly; *Out and About* (www.outandaboutnewspaper.com) is a free monthly newsmagazine.

In Nashville, the **Doubletree Downtown** welcomes lesbian and gay guests. They also offer commitment ceremonies. **International Travel Inc.** (4004 Hillsboro Rd., 615/385-1222) is a Nashville-based gay-friendly travel agency.

Memphis

The **Memphis Gay and Lesbian Community Center** (892 S. Cooper St., 901/278-6422, www.mglcc.org) is a clearinghouse of information for the gay and lesbian community. They have a directory of gay-friendly businesses, host social events, and promote tolerance and equality.

Mid-South Pride (www.midsouthpride.org) organizes Memphis Pride in June.

SENIOR TRAVELERS

Elderhostel (800/454-5768, www.elderhostel.org), which organizes educational tours for people over 55, offers tours in Memphis and Nashville.

For discounts and help with trip planning, try the **AARP** (800/687-2277, www.aarp.org), which offers a full-service travel agency, trip insurance, a motor club, and AARP Passport program, which provides you with senior discounts for hotels, car rentals, and other things.

Persons over 55 should always check for a senior citizen discount. Most attractions and some hotels and restaurants have special pricing for senior citizens.

TRAVELERS WITH DISABILITIES

More people with disabilities are traveling than ever before. The Americans with Disabilities Act requires most public buildings to make provisions for disabled people, although in practice accessibility may be spotty.

When you make your hotel reservations, always check that the hotel is prepared to accommodate you. Airlines will also make special arrangements for you if you request help in advance. To reduce stress, try to travel during off-peak times.

Several national organizations have information and advice about traveling with disabilities. The Society for Accessible Travel and Hospitality (www.sath.org) publishes links to major airlines' accessibility policies and publishes travel tips for people with all types of disabilities, including blindness, deafness, mobility disorders, diabetes, kidney disease, and arthritis. The society publishes *Open World*, a magazine about accessible travel.

Wheelchair Getaways (800/642-2042, www.wheelchairgetaways.com) is a national chain specializing in renting vans that are wheelchair accessible or otherwise designed for disabled drivers and travelers. Wheelchair Getaways has locations in Memphis (901/795-6533 or 866/762-165), Knoxville (865/622-6550 or 888/340-8267), and Nashville (615/451-2900 or 866/762-1656), and they will deliver to other locations in the state.

Avis offers **Avis Access,** a program for travelers with disabilities. Call the dedicated 24-hour toll-free number (888/879-4273) for help renting a car with features such as transfer boards, hand controls, spinner knobs, and swivel seats.

TRAVELING WITH CHILDREN

It is hard to imagine a state better for family vacations than Tennessee. The state parks provide numerous places to camp, hike, swim, fish, and explore, and cities have attractions like zoos, children's museums, aquariums, and trains.

Many hotels and inns offer special discounts for families, and casual restaurants almost always have a children's menu with lower-priced, kid-friendly choices.

FOREIGN TRAVELERS

Tennessee attracts a fair number of foreign visitors. Elvis, the international popularity of blues and country music, and the beauty of the eastern mountains bring people to the state from all over the globe.

Communication

Foreign travelers will find a warm welcome. Those in the tourist trade are used to dealing with all sorts of people and will be pleased that you have come from so far away to visit their home. If you are not a native English speaker, it may be difficult to understand the local accent at first. Just smile and ask the person to say it again, a bit slower. Good humor and a positive attitude will help at all times.

Visas and Officialdom

Most citizens of a foreign country require a visa to enter the United States. There are many types of visas, issued according to the purpose of your visit. Business and pleasure travelers apply for B-1 and B-2 visas respectively. When you apply for your visa, you will be required to prove that the purpose of you trip is business, pleasure, or for medical treatment; that you plan to remain in the United States for a limited period; and that you have a place of residence outside the United States. Apply for your visa at the nearest U.S. embassy. For more information, contact the U.S. Citizenship and Immigration Service (www.uscis.gov).

Nationals of 36 countries may be able to use the Visa Waiver Program, operated by Customs and Border Protection. Presently, these 36 countries are: Andorra, Australia, Austria, Belgium, Brunei, Czech Republic, Denmark (including Greenland and Faroe Islands), Estonia, Finland, France, Germany, Greece, Hungary, Iceland, Ireland, Italy, Japan, Latvia, Liechtenstein, Lithuania, Luxembourg, Malta, Monaco, the Netherlands (including Aruba, Bonaire, Curacao, Saba, and Sint Maarten), New Zealand, Norway, Portugal (including Azores and Madeira), San Marino, South Korea, Singapore, Slovenia, Spain, Sweden, Switzerland, and the United Kingdom.

Take note that in recent years the United States has begun to require visa-waiver participants to have upgraded passports with digital photographs and machine-readable information. They have also introduced requirements that even visa-waiver citizens register in advance before arriving in the United States. For more information about the Visa Waiver Program, contact the Customs and Border Protection Agency (www.travel.state.gov).

All foreign travelers are now required to participate in U.S. Visit, a program operated by the Department of Homeland Security. Under the program, your fingerprints and photograph are taken—digitally and without ink—as you are being screened by the immigration officer.

Arrival

Nashville and Memphis are international airports with daily international flights. At the Nashville International Airport, you can exchange currency at SunTrust Bank near A/B concourse or at the Business Service Center (Wright Travel, 615/275-2658) near C/D concourse.

The Memphis airport is well equipped for foreign travelers. The lone international airline, Northwest/KLM Royal Dutch Airlines, provides interpreters for the Customs Clearance Facility and the boarding areas for international flights. They can accommodate Dutch-, German-, Arabic-, Spanish-, and French-speaking passengers.

International travel services are provided at the Business Service Center (Ticket Lobby B, 901/922-8090, Mon.–Fri. 7 A.M.–7:30 P.M., Sat. 10 A.M.–7:30 P.M., Sun. 11 A.M.–7:30 P.M.). Here you can exchange currency, buy travel insurance, make telephone calls and send faxes, wire money, and buy traveler's checks. An additional kiosk is located in Concourse B near the international gates (gate B-36). Here you can buy travel insurance and exchange currency. The hours are daily 4:30–7:30 P.M.

Memphis International Airport is a "Transit Without Visa" port of entry. This means that foreign travelers whose flight will connect through Memphis on the way to another foreign destination beyond the United States no longer need a U.S. transit visa just to connect.

Health and Safety

DISEASES
West Nile Virus

West Nile virus was first recorded in humans in the United States in the early 2000s, and by 2007 nearly every state, including Tennessee, had reported confirmed cases of the disease. West Nile is spread by mosquitoes.

Summer is mosquito season in Tennessee. You can prevent mosquito breeding by eliminating standing water around your property. You can prevent mosquito bites by wearing an insect repellant containing 30–50 percent DEET. An alternative to DEET, picaridin is available in 7 and 15 percent concentrations and would need to be applied more frequently. Wearing long-sleeved pants and shirts and avoiding being outdoors during dusk and dawn are also ways to avoid exposure to mosquitoes.

Fever, chills, weakness, drowsiness, and fatigue are some of the symptoms of West Nile virus.

Lyme Disease

Lyme disease is a bacterial infection spread by deer ticks. The first indication you might have Lyme disease is the appearance of a red rash where you have been bitten by a tick. Following that, symptoms are flu-like. During late-stage Lyme disease, neurological effects are reported.

Ticks are external parasites that attach themselves to warm-blooded creatures like dogs, deer, and humans. Ticks suck blood from their host.

Tick bites are unpleasant enough, even if there is no infection of Lyme disease. After coming in from the woods, especially if you were walking off-trail, carefully inspect your body for ticks. If one has attached itself to you, remove it by carefully "unscrewing" it from your body with tweezers.

You can avoid ticks by wearing long sleeves and pants, tucking in your shirt, and wearing a hat. You can minimize your exposure to ticks

by staying on trails and walking paths where you don't brush up against trees and branches.

White-Nose Syndrome

In 2006 in upstate New York a caver noticed a substance on the noses of hibernating bats, as well as a few dead bats. The next year, more of both were found. Now bats dying of a fungus called "white-nose syndrome" have been found as far south as Tennessee.

Researchers are still trying to find out what causes the deadly (to bats, not people) fungus. Until then, certain caves may be closed to prevent the disease from spreading. Check individual cave listings before heading out.

POISON IVY

If there is one plant that you should learn to identify, it is poison ivy. This woody vine grows in woods all around Tennessee. Touching it can leave you with a painful and terribly uncomfortable reaction.

Poison ivy is green, and the leaves grow in clusters of three. There are no thorns. Its berries are a gray-white color, and if the vine is climbing, you will notice root "hairs" on the vine. The following mnemonic might help: "Leaves of three, let it be; berries white, danger in sight."

An estimated 15–35 percent of people are not allergic to poison ivy. But after repeated exposure this protection is worn down. People who are allergic will experience more and more severe reactions with each episode of exposure.

Poison ivy is easily spread over your body by your hands, or from person to person through skin-to-skin contact. Never touch your eyes or face if you think you may have touched poison ivy, and always wash yourself with hot soapy water if you think you may have come into contact with the vine.

Treat poison ivy rashes with over-the-counter

itch creams. In severe cases, you may need to go to the doctor.

VENOMOUS SNAKES

The vast majority of snakes in Tennessee are nonvenomous. Only four species of venomous snakes exist here. Copperheads (northern and southern) live throughout the state, along with the timber rattlesnake. The pygmy rattlesnake lives in the Kentucky Lake region, and the cottonmouth water moccasin is found in wet areas in the western part of the state.

Venomous snakes of Tennessee can usually by identified by their elliptical (cat-eye) shaped pupils (not that you really want to get close enough to see that). Most also have thick bodies, blunt tails, and triangular-shaped heads.

MEDICAL SERVICES

Hospitals, medical centers, and doctors' offices are located throughout the state. Walk-in medical centers may be found in the yellow pages and are the best bet for minor needs while you're on vacation. In an emergency, proceed to the closest hospital or call 911.

The single most important thing you can have if you get sick while traveling is health insurance. Before you leave, check with your insurance provider about in-network doctors and medical facilities in the area where you'll be traveling.

Prescriptions

Always travel with your prescription drugs in their original container and with a copy of the prescription issued by your doctor. If you can, get refills before you leave. National chains of many drugstores exist across the state.

DRUGS

Tennessee's greatest drug problem is with methamphetamine, the highly addictive stimulant sometimes called "speed," "crank," and "ice," among other names. During the 1990s and 2000s, meth use spread quickly through rural America, including Tennessee. In 2004, Tennessee passed comprehensive legislation to combat meth. A year later, some 60 percent of Tennessee counties reported that meth remained their most serious drug problem.

The state's antimeth strategy has been to aggressively seek out illegal meth labs, increase public education about meth use, and promote recovery programs. Despite the efforts, it is still difficult to eliminate meth use, partly because meth is relatively easy to manufacture in so-called labs, which can be built in homes, hotel rooms, trailers, and even vehicles.

Meth is a dangerous and highly addictive drug. It takes a terrible toll on the health of users, creates myriad family and social problems, and is among one of the most addictive drugs out there.

CRIME

Crime is a part of life anywhere, and travelers should take precautions to avoid being a victim of crime. Leave valuables at home and secure your hotel room and car at all times (including GPS devices, iPads, and other car-friendly technology). Always be aware of your surroundings, and don't allow yourself to be drawn into conversations with strangers in deserted, dark, or otherwise sketchy areas. Single travelers, especially women, should take special care to stay in well-lit and highly populated areas, especially at night.

Information and Services

MONEY
Banks
Dozens of local and regional banks are found throughout Tennessee. Most banks will cash traveler's checks, exchange currency, and send wire transfers. Banks are generally open weekdays 9 A.M.–4 P.M., although some are open later and on Saturday. Automatic Teller Machines (ATMs) are ubiquitous at grocery stores, live-music venues, and elsewhere, and many are compatible with bank cards bearing the Plus or Cirrus icons. Between fees charged by your own bank and the bank that owns the ATM you are using, expect to pay $2–5 extra to get cash from an ATM that does not belong to your own bank.

Sales Tax
Sales tax is charged on all goods, including food and groceries.

The sales tax you pay is split between the state and local governments. Tennessee's sales tax is 5.25 percent on food and groceries and 7 percent on all other goods. Cities and towns add an additional "local use tax" of 1.5–2.75 percent.

Hotel Tax
There is no statewide tax on hotel rooms, but 45 different cities have established their own hotel tax, ranging 5–7 percent.

Cost
Tennessee routinely ranks favorably on cost-of-living indexes. Visitors can comfortably eat their fill in casual restaurants and coffee shops for $30 a day, although it is possible to spend much more if you prefer to eat in upscale restaurants.

The cost of accommodations varies widely, depending on the area you are visiting, the type of accommodations you are seeking, and when you are traveling. The most expensive hotel rooms are in urban centers. Rates go up during major events, on weekends, and during peak travel months in the summer. Cheaper accommodations will be found on the outskirts of town and along rural interstate routes. Budget travelers should consider camping.

If you are not coming in your own car, one of your most substantial expenses will be a rental car. Most rentals bottom out at $35 a day, and rates can be much higher if you don't reserve in advance or if you are renting only for a day or two.

Discounts
Most historic sites, museums, and attractions offer special discounts for senior citizens and children under 12. Some attractions also have discounts for students and members of the military. Even if you don't see any discount posted, it is worth asking if one exists.

Many chain hotels offer discounts for AAA members.

Bargaining
Consumer Reports magazine reported that you can often get a better hotel rate simply by asking for one. If the rate you are quoted sounds a little high, simply say that it is more than you were planning to spend and ask if they can offer a better rate. Many times, especially if it is out of season, the answer will be yes. Your negotiations will be more successful if you are willing to walk away if the answer is no.

Tipping
You should tip waiters and waitresses 15–20 percent in a sit-down restaurant. You can tip 5–10 percent in a cafeteria or restaurant where you collect your own food from the counter.

Tip a bellhop or bag handler $1 per bag, or more if they went out of their way to help you.

TOURIST INFORMATION

The **Tennessee Department of Tourism Development** (615/741-2159, www.tnvacation.com) is a source of visitor information about Tennessee. They publish an annual guide that contains hotel and attraction listings. The website has lots of links to local attractions and chambers of commerce.

Many cities have their own tourist organizations: Memphis, Nashville, Knoxville, Chattanooga, and Clarksville are among the Tennessee cities with a visitors bureau. In some rural areas, counties have teamed up to develop visitor information for the region. Other organizations, such as the National Park Service, Army Corps of Engineers, and the Tennessee State Parks, publish visitor information for certain attractions. Specific listings for visitor information are found throughout this book.

Several regional tourism organizations provide useful information and publications.

In West Tennessee there is the **Southwest Tennessee Tourism Association** (www.tast.tn.org) and the **Northwest Tennessee Tourism Association** (www.reelfootlakeoutdoors.com).

Middle Tennessee has the **Middle Tennessee Tourism Council** (www.middletennesseetourism.com), which covers the counties around Nashville; the **Upper Cumberland Tourism Association** (www.uppercumberland.org), which promotes the region surrounding the Cumberland River and the northern plateau; and the **South Central Tennessee Tourism Association** (www.sctta.net).

East Tennessee has several regional organizations. In southeast Tennessee, contact the **Tennessee Overhill Heritage Association** (www.tennesseeoverhill.com) or the **Southeast Tennessee Tourism Association** (www.southeasttennessee.com). Northeast Tennessee is represented by the **Northeast Tennessee Tourism Association** (www.netta.com). The area surrounding Knoxville and including the Smoky Mountains is served by the **Middle East**

Tennessee Tourism Council (www.vacationeasttennessee.org).

If all else fails, contact the chamber of commerce for the county you will be visiting. Chambers of commerce will willingly mail you a sheaf of brochures and any visitor information that may exist. If you are already in town, stop by in person. You are sure to find someone who will be glad to help you.

Maps

Rand McNally publishes the best maps of Tennessee. In addition to the statewide map, Rand McNally publishes maps of Memphis, Nashville, Knoxville, Chattanooga, the Great Smoky Mountains National Park, Clarksville, Murfreesboro-Smyrna, and Gatlinburg–Pigeon Forge. You can buy Rand McNally maps from bookstores and through online sales outlets like Amazon.com. Rand McNally also sells downloadable PDF maps that you can view on your computer or print out.

For trail maps or topographical maps of parks and other natural areas, look for National Geographic's Trails Illustrated series.

The State Department of Transportation updates its official transportation map annually. Request a free copy at www.tdot.state.tn.us or by calling 615/741-2848. The official map is also available from many Tennessee welcome centers, chambers of commerce, and other tourism-related offices.

The state also creates maps of dozens of Tennessee cities and towns. All these maps are available for free download from the department of transportation website.

Hubbard Scientific (www.amep.com) produces beautiful raised-relief maps of Tennessee, the Great Smoky Mountains National Park, and other regions of the state. Found on display in some visitors centers, these maps make great wall art. They are also useful reference, especially for the eastern parts of Tennessee where the landscape is mountainous.

Many GPS apps are now available for iPhones and other smart devices.

COMMUNICATION
Area Codes

At this writing, Tennessee has six different area codes. Memphis and vicinity use 901; the western plains are 731. The Heartland, including Clarksville, uses 931, while Nashville and the counties immediately north of the city are in 615. East Tennessee uses 423, except for Knoxville and eight surrounding counties, which are in 865.

Cell Phones

Cell phone signals are powerful and reliable in cities and along the interstates. In rural parts of the state you should not count on your cell phone, and in mountainous areas such as the Cumberland Plateau and the Great Smoky Mountains National Park, forget about it altogether.

TIME ZONES

The eastern third of Tennessee lies in the Eastern time zone; Middle and West Tennessee are in the Central time zone, one hour earlier. The time zone line runs a slanted course from Signal Mountain in the south to the Big South Fork National River and Recreation Area in the north. The time zone line falls at mile marker 340 along I-40, just west of Rockwood and a few miles east of Crossville. Chattanooga, Dayton, Rockwood, Crossville, Rugby, Fall Creek Falls State Park, the Catoosa Wildlife Management Area, and Big South Fork lie close to or on the time zone line, and visitors to these areas should take special care to ensure they are on the right clock.

RESOURCES

Suggested Reading

PHOTOGRAPHY AND ART

Escott, Colin. *The Grand Ole Opry: The Making of an American Icon.* Nashville: Center Street, 2006. An authorized (and somewhat sanitized) look at the Grand Ole Opry. Lots of pictures, reminiscences, and short sidebars make it an attractive coffee-table book.

McGuire, Jim. *Nashville Portraits: Legends of Country Music.* Guilford CT: The Lyons Press, 2007. Sixty stunning photographs of country music legends including Johnny Cash, Waylon Jennings, Doc Watson, and Dolly Parton. The companion book to an eponymous traveling exhibit that debuted in 2007.

Sherraden, Jim, Paul Kingsbury, and Elek Horvath. *Hatch Show Print: The History of a Great American Poster Shop.* San Francisco: Chronicle Books, 2001. A fully illustrated, beautiful book about Hatch Show Print, the Nashville advertising and letterpress founded in 1897.

Wood, Nicki Pendleton. *Nashville Yesterday and Today.* Lincolnwood, IL: West Side Publishing, 2010. This is an illustrated guide of what makes Music City tick, written by a local former newspaper writer, restaurant critic, and cookbook author.

GUIDES

Brandt, Robert. *Touring the Middle Tennessee Backroads.* Winston-Salem, NC: John F. Blair Publisher, 1995. Robert Brandt is a Nashville judge and self-professed "zealot" for Middle Tennessee. His guidebook details 15 driving tours through back roads in the heartland of Tennessee. Brandt's knowledge of local history and architecture cannot be surpassed, and his enthusiasm for his subject shines through the prose. While some of the entries are now dated, the guide remains an invaluable source of information about small towns in the region.

Hiking Trails of the Smokies. Gatlinburg TN: Great Smoky Mountains Natural History Association, 2001. The most comprehensive guide to hiking trails of the Smokies is small enough to fit in the glove compartment of your car. Descriptions give details of elevation, distance, and difficulty. They also describe the natural and historical features along the trail. The same publishers produce related guides of day hikes and history hikes.

Van West, Carroll. *Tennessee's Historical Landscapes: A Traveler's Guide.* Knoxville: University of Tennessee Press, 1995. The editor of the *Tennessee Historical Quarterly* and a professor of history at Middle Tennessee State University, Carroll Van West guides readers along highways and byways, pointing out historical structures and other signs of history along the way. A good traveling companion, especially for students of architecture and landscape.

The WPA Guide to Tennessee. Knoxville: University of Tennessee Press, 1986. The Works Progress Administration guide to Tennessee, written in 1939 and originally published by Viking Press, is a fascinating portrait of Depression-era Tennessee. Published as part of a New Deal project to employ writers and document the culture and character of the nation, the guide contains visitor information, historical sketches, and profiles of the state's literature, culture, agriculture, industry, and more. The guide, republished as part of Tennessee's "Homecoming '86," is a delightful traveling companion.

GENERAL HISTORY

Bergeron, Paul H. *Paths of the Past: Tennessee, 1770–1970.* Knoxville: University of Tennessee Press, 1979. This is a concise, straight-up history of Tennessee with a few illustrations and maps.

Corlew, Robert E. *Tennessee: A Short History.* Knoxville: University of Tennessee Press, 1990. The definitive survey of Tennessee history, this text was first written in 1969 and has been updated several times by writers including Stanley J. Folmsbee and Enoch Mitchell. This is a useful reference guide for a serious reader.

Dykeman, Wilma. *Tennessee.* New York: W. W. Norton & Company and the American Association for State and Local History, 1984. Novelist and essayist Wilma Dykeman says more about the people of Tennessee and the events that shaped the modern state in this slim and highly readable volume than you would find in the most detailed and plodding historical account. It becomes a companion

and a means through which to understand the Tennessee spirit and character.

SPECIALIZED HISTORY

Beifuss, Joan Turner. *At the River I Stand.* Brooklyn NY: Carlson Pub., 1985. This account of the Memphis garbage men's strike of 1968 is told from the ground up. It places the assassination of Dr. Martin Luther King in its immediate, if not historical, context.

Bond, Beverley G., and Janann Sherman. *Memphis: In Black and White.* Mount Pleasant SC: Arcadia Publishing, 2003. This lively history of Memphis pays special attention to the dynamics of race and class. The slim and easy-to-read volume contains interesting anecdotes and lots of illustrations. It is an excellent introduction to the city.

Branch, Taylor. *Parting the Waters: America in the King Years 1954–63.* New York: Simon and Schuster, 1989. The most authoritative account of the civil rights movement, told through the life of Dr. Martin Luther King. The first in a three-volume account of the movement, *Parting the Waters* includes descriptions of the Nashville sit-ins of 1960. The final volume, *At Canaan's Edge,* includes King's assassination in Memphis.

Egerton, John. *Speak Now Against the Day: The Generation Before the Civil Rights Movement in the South.* Chapel Hill: University of North Carolina Press, 1995. Nashville native John Egerton tells the relatively unacknowledged story of Southerners, white and black, who stood up against segregation and racial hatred during the years before the civil rights movement.

Egerton, John. *Visions of Utopia.* Knoxville: University of Tennessee Press, 1977. An accessible and fascinating portrait of three intentional Tennessee communities: Ruskin in

Middle Tennessee, Nashoba in West Tennessee, and Rugby in East Tennessee. Egerton's usual sterling prose and sensitive observations make this volume well worth reading.

Honey, Michael. *Going Down Jericho Road: The Memphis Strike, Martin Luther King's Last Campaign.* New York: W. W. Norton & Co., 2007. Labor historian Michael Honey depicts with academic detail and novelistic drama the Memphis Sanitation Strike of 1968. He documents Memphis of the late 1960s and the quest for economic justice that brought Dr. King to the city. King's assassination and its aftermath are depicted in devastating detail.

Irwin, John Rice. *The Museum of Appalachia Story.* Atglen, PA: Schiffer Publishing, 1978. An illustrated look at how one man's garage collection of ephemera became a Smithsonian affiliate.

Potter, Jerry O. *Sultana Tragedy: America's Greatest Maritime Disaster.* Gretna LA: Pelican Publishing Company, Inc., 1992. The definitive account of American's worst maritime disaster. The end of the Civil War and the assassination of Abraham Lincoln grabbed the headlines in April 1864, so much so that the sinking of the *Sultana* and the death of more than 1,800 men in the Mississippi River near Memphis went almost unnoticed. This book tells a tale more poignant and moving than the loss of the *Titanic.*

Sides, Hampton. *Hellhound on His Trail: The Stalking of Martin Luther King, Jr. and the International Hunt for his Assassin.* New York: Doubleday, 2004. A well-written, captivating account of MLK's murder and the efforts to nab his killer. Sides provides perspective on Memphis's troubled history.

Sword, Wiley. *The Confederacy's Last Hurrah: Spring Hill, Franklin and Nashville.* Lawrence: University Press of Kansas, 2004. This is a well-written and devastating account of John Bell Hood's disastrous campaign through Middle Tennessee during the waning months of the Confederacy. It was a campaign that cost the South more than 23,000 men. With unflinching honesty, Sword describes the opportunities lost and poor decisions made by General Hood.

BIOGRAPHY

James, Marquis. *The Raven: A Biography of Sam Houston.* Indianapolis: The Bobbs-Merrill Company, 1929. Possibly the most remarkable Tennessean in history, Sam Houston was raised by the Cherokee, memorized Homer's *Iliad,* and was twice elected governor of Tennessee before he headed west to the new American frontier to become president of the Texas Republic.

Leeming, David. *Amazing Grace: A Life of Beauford Delaney.* New York: Oxford University Press (USA), 1998. Beauford Delaney was a brilliant but often overlooked modernist painter who was born in Knoxville in 1901. African American and gay, Delaney later moved to New York, where he worked as an artist and moved in circles that included James Baldwin and Henry Miller.

Moore, Carmen. *Somebody's Angel Child: The Story of Bessie Smith.* New York: Thomas Cromwell Company, 1969. The illustrated story of Chattanooga native Bessie Smith's remarkable rise to, then fall from, the top of the music world.

MUSIC

Carlin, Richard. *Country Music.* New York: Black Dog and Leventhal Publishers, 2006. This is a highly illustrated, well-written, and useful reference for fans of country music. It profiles the people, places, and events that contributed to country's evolution. With lots of graphic elements and photographs, it is a good book to dip into.

Chapman, Marshall. *They Came to Nashville.* Nashville: Vanderbilt University Press, 2010. Singer-songwriter Chapman tells her tales, as well as those of many others, as they came to Music City and set about hitting the big time.

Escott, Colin. *Hank Williams: The Biography.* Boston: Back Bay Books, 2004. No country star had a bigger impact on Nashville's evolution to Music City than Hank Williams. This detailed history shares his failings, downfall, and remarkable legacy.

Gordon, Robert. *It Came from Memphis.* Boston: Faber and Faber, 1994. Memphis resident Robert Gordon takes the back roads to tell the remarkable musical story that emerged from Memphis during the 1950s and '60s. He paints a textured picture of the milieu from which rock 'n' roll eventually rose.

Guralnick, Peter. *Careless Love: The Unmaking of Elvis Presley.* Boston: Little, Brown and Company, 1999. Volume two of Peter Guralnick's definitive biography of Elvis Presley. Guralnick writes in the introduction that he "knows of no sadder story" than Presley's life from 1958 until his death in 1977. The book unflinchingly examines the gradual unraveling of America's greatest pop star.

Guralnick, Peter. *Last Train to Memphis: The Rise of Elvis Presley.* Boston: Little, Brown and Company, 1994. Quite possibly the definitive biography of the King. In volume one, Guralnick re-creates Presley's first 24 years, including his childhood in Mississippi and Tennessee, his remarkable rise to fame, and the pivotal events of 1958, when he was drafted into the army and buried his beloved mother.

Handy, W. C. *Father of the Blues.* New York: The Macmillan Company, 1941. This memoir by Memphis's most famous blues man depicts the city during the first quarter of the 20th century. It is an entertaining and endearing read.

Kingsbury, Paul, ed. *Will the Circle Be Unbroken: Country Music in America.* London: DK Adult, 2006. An illustrated collection of articles by 43 writers, including several performing artists, this book is a useful reference on the genre's development from 1920 until the present.

Kossner, Michael. *How Nashville Became Music City: 50 Years of Music Row.* Milwaukee: Hal Leonard, 2006. Forget about the stars and the singers; this profile of country music focuses on the people you've never heard of: the executives, songwriters, and behind-the-scenes technicians who really make the music happen. It's an interesting read for fans who don't mind seeing how the sausage is made and a good introduction for people aspiring to be a part of it.

Raichelson, Richard M. *Beale Street Talks: A Walking Tour Down the Home of the Blues.* Memphis: Arcadia Records, 1999. A slim, well-written book that describes Beale Street as it was and Beale Street as it is. This is a handy companion for exploring the street.

Sharp, Tim. *Memphis Music: Before the Blues.* Mount Pleasant SC: Arcadia Publishing, 2007. Part of the Images of America series, this work includes rare and evocative photographs of Memphis people. The result is a painting of the backdrop on which the Memphis blues were born in the early 20th century.

Wolfe, Charles K. *Tennessee Strings.* Knoxville: University of Tennessee Press, 1977. The definitive survey of Tennessee musical history. This slim volume is easy to read.

Zimmerman, Peter Coats. *Tennessee Music: Its People and Places.* San Francisco: Miller

Freeman Books, 1998. Tries, and succeeds, to do the impossible: tell the varied stories of Tennessee music all the way from Bristol to Memphis. Nicely illustrated.

REFERENCE

Abramson, Rudy, and Jean Haskell, eds. *Encyclopedia of Appalachia*. Knoxville: University of Tennessee Press, 2006. From language to food to history, this tome has 2,000 entries that will force readers to expand their conception of just what "Appalachia" is.

Van West, Carroll, ed. *The Tennessee Encyclopedia of History and Culture*. Nashville: Tennessee Historical Society and Rutledge Hill Press, 1998. Perhaps the most valuable tome on Tennessee, this 1,200-page encyclopedia covers the people, places, events, and movements that defined Tennessee history and the culture of its people. Dip in frequently, and you will be all the wiser.

FICTION

Agee, James. *A Death in the Family*. New York: Vintage, 1998. First published in 1958, this is the story of a Knoxville family whose domestic happiness is disrupted by the sudden death of the father. The story is largely autobiographical and features evocative descriptions of Knoxville in 1915. Winner of the Pulitzer Prize for fiction.

Burton, Linda, ed. *Stories from Tennessee*. Knoxville: University of Tennessee Press, 1983. An anthology of Tennessee literature, the volume begins with a story by David Crockett on hunting in Tennessee and concludes with works by 20th-century authors such as Shelby Foote, Cormac McCarthy, and Robert Drake.

Cawood, Chris. *Tennessee's Coal Creek War: Another Fight for Freedom*. Kingston TN:

Magnolia Hill Press, 1995. For 18 months in the late 19th century, the National Guard occupied Coal Creek, now known as Lake City, to prevent labor unrest among coal miners. This historical novel is set during this so-called coal war of 1891.

Grisham, John. *The Firm*. Boston: G. K. Hall, 1992. Probably the most celebrated Memphis-set novel in recent years, especially following the success of the eponymous film. Mitchell McDeere takes on corrupt and criminal mob lawyers. It includes references to many city landmarks.

Haun, Mildred. *The Hawk's Done Gone and Other Stories*. Nashville: Vanderbilt University Press, 1968. A collection of stories set in the Smoky Mountains and told using dialect. This volume comes closer than any other to capturing the authentic language, culture, and way of life of East Tennessee's mountain residents during the early 20th century.

Hicks, Robert. *Widow of the South*. New York: Grand Central Publishing, 2006. Tour guides at Carton Plantation gripe about the poetic license taken with some facts in this fictional tale, but it offers a moving story of the Battle of Franklin and the high emotional costs of the Civil War.

Marshall, Catherine. *Christy*. New York: McGraw Hill, 1967. The fictional story of a young teacher, Christy Huddleston, who moves to the Smoky Mountains in 1912 to teach. The story is based on Catherine Marshall's own experience in the mountains. It was adapted into a drama and spawned a television miniseries.

McCarthy, Cormac. *Suttree*. New York: Random House, 1979. Cornelius Suttree is a fisherman who lives in a houseboat in Knoxville during the 1950s. This novel possesses Mc-Carthy's typically clear language and robust characters, and tells a tale punctuated by violence and shocking events.

Neely, Jack. *From the Shadow Side and Other Stories of Knoxville.* Oak Ridge TN: Tellico Books, 2003. Columnist for the Knoxville *Metropulse,* historian, and master storyteller Jack Neely has done more to preserve Knoxville history than any other. This work builds on his previous volumes, *Secret History* and *Secret History II,* both of which are also worth seeking out.

Taylor, Peter. *Summons to Memphis.* New York: Knopf Publishing Group, 1986. Celebrated and award-winning Tennessee writer Peter Taylor won the Pulitzer Prize for fiction for this novel in 1986. Phillip Carver returns home to Tennessee at the request of his three older sisters to talk his father out of remarrying. In so doing, he is forced to confront a troubling family history. This is a classic of American literature, set in a South that is fading away.

Wright, Richard. *Black Boy.* New York: Chelsea House, 2006. The 1945 memoir of African American writer Richard Wright recounts several years of residency in Memphis. His portrayal of segregation and racism in Memphis and Mississippi are still powerful today.

FOOD

Lewis, Edna, and Scott Peacock. *The Gift of Southern Cooking: Recipes and Revelations from Two Great American Cooks.* New York: Knopf Publishing Group, 2003. Grande dame of Southern food Edna Lewis and son-of-the-soil chef Scott Peacock joined forces on this seminal text of Southern cuisine. It demystifies, documents, and inspires. Ideal for those who really care about Southern foodways.

Lundy, Ronnie, ed. *Cornbread Nation 3.* Chapel Hill: University of North Carolina Press, 2006. The third in a series of collections on Southern food and cooking. Published in collaboration with the Southern Foodways Alliance, which is dedicated to preserving and celebrating Southern food traditions, the Cornbread Nation collection is an ode to food traditions large and small. Topics include paw-paws, corn, and pork. *Cornbread Nation 2* focused on barbecue. *Cornbread Nation 1* was edited by restaurateur and Southern food celebrant John Egerton.

Stern, Jane, and Michael Stern. *Southern Country Cooking from the Loveless Cafe: Biscuits, Hams, and Jams from Nashville's Favorite Café.* Nashville: Rutledge Hill Press, 2005. Road-food aficionados wrote the cookbook on Nashville's most famous pit stop: the Loveless Cafe. Located at the northern terminus of the Natchez Trace Parkway, the Loveless is quintessential Southern cooking: delectable biscuits, country ham, and homemade preserves. Now you can take some of that down-home flavor home with you.

Internet and Digital Resources

TOURIST INFORMATION

Chattanooga Convention and Visitors Bureau
www.chattanoogafun.com
The official tourism website for the Scenic City, this resource offers suggestions for where to stay, eat, and visit, with lots of tips on Chattanooga's outdoor activities.

Knoxville Tourism & Sports Corporation
www.knoxville.org
The official travel website for Knoxville features current news, a calendar of events, and links to the live stream of radio station WDVX, East Tennessee's finest. You can request visitor information through the site.

Memphis Convention and Visitors Bureau
www.memphistravel.com
The official travel website for Memphis has listings of hotels, attractions, and events. You can also download coupons, request a visitors guide, or book hotels. The bureau also offers a free iPhone app called Memphis Travel Guide.

Nashville Convention and Visitors Bureau
www.visitmusiccity.com
The official tourism website for Nashville, this site offers concert listings, hotel booking services, and useful visitor information. You can also order a visitors guide and money-saving coupons.

Oak Ridge
http://oakridgevisitor.com
Get the lowdown on visiting the Secret City from the official tourism website.

Tennessee Department of Tourism Development
www.tnvacation.com
On Tennessee's official tourism website you can request a visitors guide, search for upcoming events, or look up details about hundreds of attractions, hotels, and restaurants. This is a great resource for suggested scenic drives.

NEWS AND CULTURE

Eat Drink Smile
www.eat-drink-smile.com
A fun blog about what to eat (and drink) in Music City.

The Memphis Flyer
www.memphisflyer.com
Memphis's alternative weekly newspaper publishes entertainment listings and article archives on its website.

Memphis Magazine
www.memphismagazine.com
Good restaurant reviews and useful event listings. Subscriptions available online ($15 annual).

Metropulse
www.metropulse.com
The finest alternative weekly in the state, Knoxville's *Metropulse* offers the usual entertainment listings, restaurant reviews, and political analysis, plus special features like Jack Neely's *Secret History* column.

Nashville Essential Guide
www.sutromedia.com/apps/Nashville_Essential_Guide
A digital iPhone app from the author of this book, Nashville Essential Guide includes regularly updated Nashville highlights, plus links to where to listen to live music and where to hang out downtown, Twitter and Facebook information for key sites, and more.

The Nashville Scene
www.nashvillescene.com
Nashville's alternative weekly has a great

website. The dining guide is fabulous, the stories are interesting and archived, and the entertainment calendar is the best in town. Go to "Our Critics' Picks" for a rundown of the best shows in town. The annual manual, reader's choice awards, and other special editions are useful for newcomers and old-timers alike.

Nooga.com
www.nooga.com
Launched in 2011, this site offers local news and lifestyle happenings for Chattanooga.

Stuck Inside of Knoxville
www.stuckinsideofknoxville.com
This blog provides a quirky look at what's going on in downtown Knoxville.

The Tennessean
www.tennessean.com
Nashville's major newspaper posts news, entertainment, sports, and business stories online. Sign up for a daily newsletter of headlines from Music City or search the archives.

Visit Sevierville
Take virtual tours of Sevierville, or plan your own in real life, through this free iPhone and iPad app.

VisitSouth
http://visitsouth.com
Weekly blog postings on what to do in Southern cities, including Nashville, Memphis, Chattanooga, Knoxville, and the Smoky Mountains.

PARKS AND RECREATION
Outdoor Chattanooga
www.outdoorchattanooga.com
If your main reason for coming to Chattanooga is to bike, run, climb, paddle, or kayak, this is the website for you.

Tennessee State Parks
www.state.tn.us/environment/parks
An online directory of all Tennessee state parks, this site provides useful details, including campground descriptions, cabin rental information, and the lowdown on activities.

TVA Lake Info
This free iPad and iPhone app lists recreational dam release schedules for across the state.

HISTORY
Tennessee Civil War 150
A free app for iPhones and iPads provides quick-hit history lessons about Civil War battle sites, plus information about visiting them.

Tennessee Encyclopedia of History and Culture
www.tennesseeencyclopedia.net
The online edition of an excellent reference book, this website is a great starting point on all topics Tennessee. Articles about people, places, and events are written by hundreds of different experts. Online entries are updated regularly.

Index

List of Maps

Acknowledgments

Even in the face of approaching deadlines, stacks of photo-filled jump drives on the desk, and marked-up maps littering the floor, I'm convinced I have the world's best job. I have a legitimate, work-related excuse to throw my tent in the station wagon, strap the paddleboard to the top, and head to Land Between the Lakes for a weekend. Or to call a few friends and ask them to help me check out Nashville's honky-tonks. Or taste-test the newest variety of Moon Pie.

I'm grateful to many people who helped me synthesize what I've heard, seen, and experienced into something coherent that others could share. First and foremost, thanks go to DG Strong, who encouraged me to move back to Tennessee after many years away and who indulges (if not enables) my whims to drive for miles to see a new boat launch or try a new hot chicken place. Joy Lusk showed me much to love in her hometown of Chattanooga, as did friends in Memphis, Knoxville, Oak Ridge, and other spots across the state.

Perhaps no one loves Music City more than I do except for Jenny Steuber of the Nashville Convention and Visitors Bureau. She's always available for brainstorming and, of course, providing photos. Convention and Visitor Bureau staffs across the state, including Wendy Bishop, Candace Davis, Kim Davis, Jim Davis, Bob Hazlitt, Katherine Roberts, Cindy Dupree, and Melanie Beauchamp, were instrumental in helping me get up-to-date information and photographs that best illustrated the gems I experienced.

Other invaluable photographers were Sarah Blackburn, Hannah L. Coffey, DG Strong, and Liz Littman.

Emily Moe jumped in as an excellent editorial assistant when I needed one most, verifying the alphabet soup of phone numbers and URLs and tracking down better photos than the ones I took.

I first worked with the crackerjack staff of Avalon Travel on *The Dog Lover's Companion to Chicago* and while other authors complain about their publishers, I've never felt like mine were anything less than essential partners in this process. Particular thanks this time around to Grace Fujimoto, Leah Gordon, Domini Dragoone, and Albert Angulo. Many thanks to those who worked on previous editions of *Moon Tennessee*, including Susanna Henighan Potter and Jeff Bradley.

As always, I am grateful for the help and support of my family and friends, who tolerate my working long hours on "vacation" and dragging them to sightsee wherever we are, not to mention my soundtrack of bluegrass and country music and the wardrobe of cowboy hats.

www.moon.com

DESTINATIONS | ACTIVITIES | BLOGS | MAPS | BOOKS

MOON.COM is ready to help plan your next trip! Filled with fresh trip ideas and strategies, author interviews, informative travel blogs, a detailed map library, and descriptions of all the Moon guidebooks, Moon.com is all you need to get out and explore the world—or even places in your own backyard. While at Moon.com, sign up for our monthly e-newsletter for updates on new releases, travel tips, and expert advice from our on-the-go Moon authors. As always, when you travel with Moon, expect an experience that is uncommon and truly unique.

KEEP UP WITH MOON ON FACEBOOK AND TWITTER
JOIN THE MOON PHOTO GROUP ON FLICKR

MAP SYMBOLS

▦	Expressway	◖	Highlight	✕	Airfield	⚲	Golf Course
▦	Primary Road	○	City/Town	✕	Airport	🅿	Parking Area
▦	Secondary Road	◉	State Capital	▲	Mountain	◢	Archaeological Site
----	Unpaved Road	⊛	National Capital	✚	Unique Natural Feature	🍶	Church
------	Trail	★	Point of Interest			🛢	Gas Station
....	Ferry	•	Accommodation	🗟	Waterfall		Glacier
▬▬	Railroad	▾	Restaurant/Bar	▲	Park		Mangrove
▦	Pedestrian Walkway	▪	Other Location	🛑	Trailhead		Reef
▦	Stairs	∧	Campground	🎿	Skiing Area		Swamp

CONVERSION TABLES

$°C = (°F - 32) / 1.8$
$°F = (°C × 1.8) + 32$
1 inch = 2.54 centimeters (cm)
1 foot = 0.304 meters (m)
1 yard = 0.914 meters
1 mile = 1.6093 kilometers (km)
1 km = 0.6214 miles
1 fathom = 1.8288 m
1 chain = 20.1168 m
1 furlong = 201.168 m
1 acre = 0.4047 hectares
1 sq km = 100 hectares
1 sq mile = 2.59 square km
1 ounce = 28.35 grams
1 pound = 0.4536 kilograms
1 short ton = 0.90718 metric ton
1 short ton = 2,000 pounds
1 long ton = 1.016 metric tons
1 long ton = 2,240 pounds
1 metric ton = 1,000 kilograms
1 quart = 0.94635 liters
1 US gallon = 3.7854 liters
1 Imperial gallon = 4.5459 liters
1 nautical mile = 1.852 km

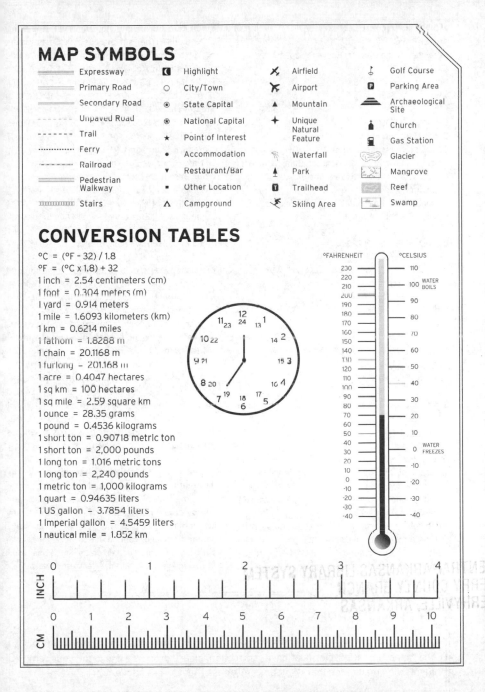

MOON TENNESSEE

Avalon Travel
a member of the Perseus Books Group
1700 Fourth Street
Berkeley, CA 94710, USA
www.moon.com

Editor: Leah Gordon
Series Manager: Kathryn Ettinger
Copy Editor: Justine Rathbun
Graphics & Production Coordinator: Domini Dragoone
Cover Designer: Domini Dragoone
Map Editor: Albert Angulo
Cartographers: Kaitlin Jaffe, Heather Sparks
Indexer: Rachel Kuhn

ISBN-13: 978-1-61238-150-3
ISSN: 1091-3343

Printing History
1st Edition – 1997
6th Edition – March 2013
5 4 3 2 1

Front cover photo: Hernando DeSoto Bridge on the
Mississippi River in Memphis, © Amie Vanderford
Photography - www.amie.org/Flick/Getty Images
Title page photo: sunset in the Smoky Mountains, ©
Timothy Mainiero/123RF
Front color photos: pg. 6 & 8 (bottom) © Brian
Stansberry/CreativeCommons; pg. 7, 11 (top
left), & 22 © Susanna Henighan Potter; pg. 8
(top) & 10 © Margaret Littman; pg. 9 (top left) ©

Sarah Blackburn, pg. 9 (top right) & 11 (top right)
© Knoxville Tourism and Sports Corporation;
pg. 9 (bottom left) © Timothy Mainiero/123RF;
pg. 9 (bottom right) & 20 (both) © Dave Allen
Photo/123RF; pg. 12 © Hannah L. Coffey; pg.
13 (top) © Don Fink/123RF; pg. 13 (bottom) ©
Steve Prorak/123RF; pg. 14 © DN Davis/123RF;
pg. 15 © Doug Force/123RF; pg. 16 (left) © James
Cullen/123RF; pg. 16 (right) © Wayne Hsieh; pg. 17
© Henryk Sadura; pg. 18 © Nevena Kozekova; pg.
19 (left) Courtesy of The Peep Holes/Wikimedia
Commons; pg. 19 (right) Courtesy of Telling History/
Wikimedia Commons; pg. 21 © Matthew Howard; pg.
23 Courtesy of Nashville Convention and Visitors
Bureau; pg. 24 Courtesy of Ryman Auditorium.

Printed in Canada by Friesens

KEEPING CURRENT

If you have a favorite gem you'd like to see included in the next edition, or see anything
that needs updating, clarification, or correction, please drop us a line. Send your comments via email to feedback@moon.com, or use the address above.

THE GOLDEN ASS

APULEIUS was born in the mid-120s AD in Madauros (modern Mdaurusch in Algeria). His father was a *duumvir*, one of the two chief magistrates in the Roman colony, and Apuleius received a superior education at Carthage and then at Athens. He lived in Athens for several years and travelled widely in Greece. Later he lived long enough in Rome to obtain recognition as a literary figure amongst men of social standing. In 155 Apuleius began a journey to Alexandria, but fell ill and had to rest with the family of his friend Pontianus in Oea (modern Tripoli). After his marriage to Pontianus' widowed mother he was indicted on a charge of magic, and in a famous speech, his *Apologia*, he secured his acquittal. He returned to Carthage and there became famous as a writer and lecturer. It is clear that he was still in Carthage during the 160s, but nothing can be established about his life after that date.

P. G. WALSH is Emeritus Professor of Humanity at the University of Glasgow. His publications include *The Roman Novel* (1970, 1995). He has also edited Petronius' *Satyricon* for Oxford World's Classics.

OXFORD WORLD'S CLASSICS

For almost 100 years Oxford World's Classics have brought readers closer to the world's great literature. Now with over 700 titles—from the 4,000-year-old myths of Mesopotamia to the twentieth century's greatest novels—the series makes available lesser-known as well as celebrated writing.

The pocket-sized hardbacks of the early years contained introductions by Virginia Woolf, T. S. Eliot, Graham Greene, and other literary figures which enriched the experience of reading. Today the series is recognized for its fine scholarship and reliability in texts that span world literature, drama and poetry, religion, philosophy and politics. Each edition includes perceptive commentary and essential background information to meet the changing needs of readers.

OXFORD WORLD'S CLASSICS

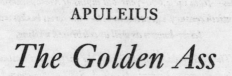

APULEIUS

The Golden Ass

Translated with an Introduction and Notes by
P. G. WALSH

OXFORD
UNIVERSITY PRESS

Oxford University Press, Great Clarendon Street, Oxford OX2 6DP

Oxford New York

Athens Auckland Bangkok Bogotá Buenos Aires Calcutta
Cape Town Chennai Dar es Salaam Delhi Florence Hong Kong Istanbul
Karachi Kuala Lumpur Madrid Melbourne Mexico City Mumbai
Nairobi Paris São Paulo Singapore Taipei Tokyo Toronto Warsaw
and associated companies in Berlin Ibadan

Oxford is a registered trade mark of Oxford University Press

Published in the United States
by Oxford University Press Inc., New York

First published as a World's Classics paperback 1995
Reissued as an Oxford World's Classics paperback 1999

British Library Cataloguing in Publication Data

Data available

Library of Congress Cataloging in Publication Data

The golden ass / Apuleius: translated with introduction
and explanatory notes by P. G. Walsh.
Includes bibliographical references and index.
1. Mythology, Classical—Fiction. 2. Metamorphosis—Fiction.
I. Walsh, P. G. (Patrick Gerard).
PS6209.M3W35 1994 873'.01—dc20 93-37772
ISBN 0-19-283888-1 (pbk.)

1 3 5 7 9 10 8 6 4 2

Printed in Great Britain by
Cox & Wyman Ltd.
Reading, Berkshire

For
John

ACKNOWLEDGEMENTS

This translation was begun and ended in Glasgow, but the greater part of it was completed at Pomona College, at which I spent a pleasant and profitable semester of teaching in 1992. I should like to thank the members of the academic and administrative staff who made our stay a happy one, and who so willingly put the necessary facilities for congenial study at my disposal.

Professor E. J. Kenney offered usefully trenchant criticism of a first draft of a section of Book 4; I hope that his suggestions will be seen to have borne fruit. I have benefited too from the encouraging observations made by the anonymous reader who scrutinized the same specimen translation on behalf of the Press. During our stay in California, Professor Ellen Finkelpearl of Scripps College cast a friendly and expert eye over another section of the translation. Members of my family have also offered useful criticism. None of these helpful adjutants has seen the final version.

It is now more than thirty years since my admiration for *The Golden Ass* induced me to embark on preparatory study for publication of *The Roman Novel* (1970), and later for the chapter on Apuleius in *The Cambridge History of Classical Literature*. In composing this Introduction, I have tried to take account of the more important studies which have subsequently appeared, but the diligent reader will note without surprise some repetition incorporated from those earlier analyses. *The Roman Novel* has now been reissued under the auspices of the Bristol Classical Press (1995), and can serve as a useful companion-volume for this translation.

P. G. W.

CONTENTS

ABBREVIATIONS

AJP	*American Journal of Philology*
ANRW	*Aufstieg und Niedergang der römischen Welt*
APA	*American Philological Association*
Apol.	*Apology*
CJ	*Classical Journal*
CQ	*Classical Quarterly*
CR	*Classical Review*
CW	*Classical Weekly*
GLK	*Grammatici Latini*, ed. Keil
Flor.	*Florida*
G&R	*Greece and Rome*
JHS	*Journal of Hellenic Studies*
Mnem.	*Mnemosyne*
OCD	*Oxford Classical Dictionary*
Onos	*Lucius or the Ass*
PCPS	*Proceedings of the Cambridge Philological Society*
Philol.	*Philologus*
PP	*Parola del Passato*
RÉA	*Revue des Études Anciennes*
RÉL	*Revue des Études Latines*
RhM	*Rheinisches Museum*
RHR	*Revue de l'histoire des religions*
SHA	*Scriptores Historiae Augustae*
TAPA	*Transactions and Proceedings of the American Philological Association*

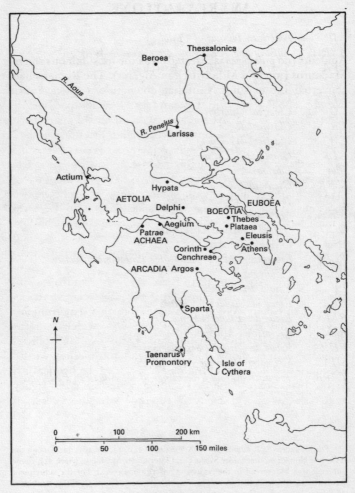

Map of Greece

INTRODUCTION

I

Apuleius (no *praenomen* is attested) was the most famous son of Madauros (modern Mdaurusch in Algeria). The Romans had converted the existing Numidian town into a *splendidissima colonia*, probably in the Flavian era a generation before Apuleius was born. His memory was preserved there by a statue which bore the inscription 'To the Platonist Philosopher', the role in which he was chiefly celebrated. When Augustine two centuries after Apuleius journeyed south from Thagaste to attend this pleasant university town in the furtherance of his education, Apuleius' name there was a byword. On two occasions Augustine associates him specifically with the town; it must have been during his brief studies there that he first gained acquaintance with Apuleius' philosophical works and with *The Golden Ass*, which was to play so large a part in shaping the *Confessions*.[1]

The date of Apuleius' birth there was in the mid-120s AD. His father was a *duumvir*, one of the two chief magistrates in the Roman colony. We may assume from this that Apuleius was bilingual from boyhood; Punic was widely current throughout his native region, but Latin was the official language of the colony. His father had the modest wealth appropriate to his social prominence; at death he bequeathed to his two sons almost two million sesterces. This legacy enabled Apuleius to enjoy a superior education, first at

---

[1] For Madauros as Apuleius' *patria*, Augustine, *CD* 8. 14, *Ep.* 102. 32. Though the town was Numidian, first under Syphax and later under Masinissa (*Apol.* 24), Punic influence was widespread in the region, as inscriptions reveal. For the subsequent Romanization ('splendidissima colonia', *Apol.* 24), see J. Gwyn Griffiths, *Apuleius of Madauros: The Isis Book* (Leiden, 1975), 60 f. For the statue and inscription, J. Tatum, *Apuleius and The Golden Ass* (Cornell, 1979), 106 ff. For *The Golden Ass* and the *Confessions*, Nancy J. Shumate, *Phoenix* (1988), 35 ff.; Walsh, *G&R* (1988), 73 ff. For the prominence of Apuleius' philosophical writings in the *Civ. Dei*, see 4. 2, 8. 14 ff., 9. 3, 7 ff.

Carthage and later at Athens. He boasts that already at Carthage he had embarked on the study of philosophy, though this must have been subsidiary to his rhetorical studies. At Athens, in his own words, he cultivated 'all nine Muses with equal enthusiasm', though his chief love was philosophy 'of which no one can ever drink enough'. He resided for several years at Athens; his literary studies imparted a wide familiarity with Greek culture. At Carthage in later life he lectured in both Latin and Greek.[2]

While resident in Greece he travelled widely, not only on the mainland but also across the Aegean to Samos and to Hierapolis in Phrygia. Later he lived long enough in Rome to obtain recognition as a literary figure amongst men of social standing.[3]

Shortly afterwards in 155, at the age of about 30, Apuleius decided to extend his travels with a journey to Egypt; doubtless his enthusiasm for the Isiac religion, a dominant theme in *The Golden Ass*, was a leading motive in this decision. As he was *en route* to Alexandria, he fell ill, and decided to relieve his indisposition by resting with friends at Oea (modern Tripoli). There he resumed acquaintance with Pontianus, with whom he had been on friendly terms as a fellow-student at Athens. His friend persuaded him to prolong his stay at Oea, and to take up residence in the family home, where his brother and his mother, a wealthy widow, shared his studies. The acquaintance ripened, fostered by Pontianus. Apuleius stresses that she was no beauty ('non formosa pupilla, sed mediocri facie mater liberorum'), and indeed she was about seven years older than he. Discreetly avoiding mention of money, he claims that he came to love her for her

---

[2] For the date of birth, see Walsh, *The Roman Novel* (Cambridge: CUP, 1970), App. 2. For Punic widespread in the region, n. 1 above, and Gwyn Griffiths, *Apuleius of Madauros*, 60 ff.; Apuleius' condescending attitude towards the language, *Apol.* 98. Education at Carthage, *Flor.* 18. 15; at Athens, *Flor.* 20. 4. Lengthy residence at Athens, *Apol.* 23. 2; still there shortly before 155, *Apol.* 72. 3. Lecturing in Greek and Latin, *Flor.* 18. 38 f.

[3] Wide travels, *Apol.* 23. 2; Samos, *Flor.* 15. 4; Hierapolis, *De mundo*, 17; Rome, *Flor.* 17. 4 (in the circle of Scipio Orfitus, proconsul of Africa, 163–4).

sterling qualities. But relations become soured when Pontianus took a wife. Her father, Herennius Rufus, orchestrated opposition to Apuleius' projected union with Pudentilla, and after the marriage he persuaded Sicinius Aemilianus, brother of Pudentilla's first husband, to indict Apuleius on a charge of magic. The charge was that he had bewitched the rich widow with love-philtres to induce her to marry him; in addition, Pontianus had met with a sudden death, and an additional accusation of murder was initially made though rapidly dropped. The trial was held at Sabrata in 158-9 before the proconsul Claudius Maximus. Conviction for magic under the *lex Cornelia de sicariis et veneficiis*, promulgated in the days of Sulla, was punishable by death. Apuleius defended himself against the charge; his speech, which has survived and is conventionally known as the *Apologia*, secured his acquittal.[4]

Thereafter he returned to his native province and took up residence at Carthage, determining to spend the rest of his life there. His fame as writer and lecturer was so widespread that he was honoured in various cities and at Carthage itself with a public statue. The ex-consul Aemilianus Strabo made the formal proposal in the Carthaginian senate, promising to meet the cost himself. Apuleius' eminence in the city is further attested by his tenure of a select priesthood, and by his being chosen to deliver the parting panegyric to two retiring proconsuls. Public lectures and orations which have survived in part under the title *Florida* document his social prominence; one of them states that his distinction as orator has been celebrated at Carthage for six years. It is therefore clear that he still flourished there in the late 160s, but nothing can be established about his life after that date.[5]

---

[4] Date of arrival at Oea, *Apol.* 55. 10 ('abhinc ferme triennium'); circumstances of encounter with Pontianus, *Apol.* 72. Pontianus' encouragement of the match, and Apuleius' appraisal of Pudentilla's charms, *Apol.* 73. Herennius Rufus as villain, inducing Sicinius Aemilianus to lodge an indictment, *Apol.* 74. For the charges, *Apol.* 2. 2–4.

[5] Decision to reside at Carthage, *Flor.* 16. 3. Statue at Carthage, *Flor.* 16. 39; elsewhere, 16. 37. Priesthood, 16. 38. Panegyrics to departing proconsuls, *Flor.* 9. 17. Six years at Carthage, *Flor.* 18. 16.

II

As a writer, Apuleius has two main claims to fame. As a philosopher without original genius he is important for his transmission of the seminal ideas of Middle Platonism into the increasingly Greekless world of Western Europe from the fourth century to the thirteenth. As a writer of romance, he is the author of the one Latin novel to have survived whole and entire from the Classical period. Its later influence on the vernacular literatures of Europe has been immense. The student of the romance cannot afford to ignore the philosophical works, since its Platonist stance is prominent. Apuleius' other surviving writings, in themselves of subsidiary importance, also contribute to a fuller appreciation of *The Golden Ass*, for there is no doubt that the author in important ways identifies himself with his hero Lucius, and both his speech of self-defence at Sabrata, and his orations at Carthage, provide important elements of autobiography.

Our author's claim that at Athens he cultivated 'all nine Muses' is borne out by the extraordinary range of his subsequent writings, most of them unfortunately lost. It is hardly surprising to find a man of such literary leanings boasting in the *Apology* and the *Florida* that he has composed Catullan love-lyrics, hymns, satirical epigrams, and other forms of poetry; that already at Oea he had published a literary lecture; and that he had written a variety of works of fiction, including an anthology of love-anecdotes, symposium-literature, and a second romance in addition to *The Golden Ass*. What is surprising is that he complemented this literary output with technical treatises which reflect the curiosity of the practical scientist. He wrote treatises on dendrology, agriculture, and medicines. He wrote a work on natural history, and for good measure composed it in Greek. Other monographs deriving from his education in the seven liberal arts were devoted to astronomy, music, and arithmetic.[6]

---

[6] Love-lyrics and satirical epigrams, *Apol.* 6. 3, 9. 12 ff.; hymns, *Flor.* 17. 18, 18. 37 ff.; other poetry, *Flor.* 9. 27 f., 20. 6; published speeches, *Apol.* 55. 10, Augustine,

These multifarious compositions were, however, incidental
to his central passion for philosophy. Just as he proclaimed
himself a second Seneca by entitling his work on nature
Quaestiones naturales, so he followed the footsteps of Cicero in
composing a treatise on political philosophy under the
heading *De republica*, and in translating Plato's *Phaedo*.[7] These
two works are lost, but five others traditionally ascribed to
him have survived.

These five treatises are *De deo Socratis*, *De Platone et eius
dogmate*, *De mundo*, Περὶ ἑρμηνείας, and *Asclepius*.
There is little dispute about the authenticity of the first, and
though the second and third are composed in a less exuberant
style, the manuscripts and Augustine ascribe them to
Apuleius, and the content further encourages the attribution.
The fourth, 'On interpretation', appears in a separate
manuscript-tradition, and is more jejune in content; the fifth
appears to be a Latin translation of a lost Greek hermetic
work. These last two works can be safely disregarded in any
consideration of Apuleius as novelist dominated by Platonist
preconceptions; the content of the first three has an important
bearing on *The Golden Ass*.[8]

De deo Socratis ('On the god of Socrates') is more general in
its approach than the title suggests; the treatise is devoted to
the existence and nature of demons, and is the most
systematic exposition of the subject to have emerged from the
Graeco-Roman world. After first surveying the separated
world of gods (visible stars and invisible members of the
Pantheon), Apuleius describes the place of demons in the

Ep. 138. 19; love-anecdotes, Lydus, *Mag.* 3. 64; second romance (*Hermagoras*),
Priscian in *GLK* 2. 85; dendrology, Servius, *ad Georg.* 2. 126; agriculture, Palladius,
1. 35. 9; medicines, Priscian in *GLK* 2. 203; natural history, *Apol.* 36 ff.; liberal arts,
Cassiodorus, *Inst.* 2. 4. 7.

[7] *De rep.*, Fulgentius, p. 122 Helm; *Phaedo*, Sid. Apoll. 2. 9. 5.

[8] On these three treatises, J. Beaujeu's excellent edition (Paris, Budé 1973). On *De
mundo*, F. Regen, *Apuleius Philosophus Platonicus* (Berlin, 1971), arguing for Apuleian
authorship; on *De interpretatione*, M. W. Sullivan, *Apuleian Logic* (North Holland,
1967), again claiming Apuleius as author. There is a good survey of Apuleius as
philosopher by B. L. Hijmans, 'Apuleius, Philosophus Platonicus', *ANRW* II. 36. 1
(Berlin, 1987), 395 ff.

hierarchy of rational beings as intermediaries between gods and men; they approximate to angels in the Hebraic tradition. Apuleius divides them into three classes. The first are souls within human bodies (hence the title *De deo Socratis*). The second have quitted human bodies to become Lemures, Lares, Larvae, and Manes. The third group are wholly free of bodily connections, and are endowed with special powers and special duties. Somnus and Amor are cited as examples; the story of Cupid and Psyche at the heart of the romance should be read with this in mind. The baroque Latinity of the treatise suggests that it was composed, like *The Golden Ass*, to be recited in the literary salon, and at a date not too distant from that of the novel.

By contrast, the second of the three works, *Plato and his Doctrines*, is a summary of the master's philosophical teaching composed in a more restrained style for a reading public; it outlines in two books Plato's physics and ethics. These summaries are preceded by a hagiographical life on lines similar to the later biography of Diogenes Laertius. While the treatment of physics adheres faithfully to Plato's *Timaeus* and *Republic*, the section on ethics owes more to Middle Platonism with its incorporation of Peripatetic and Stoic elements. The brief appendix on politics reverts more faithfully to the fundamentals of Plato's *Republic* and *Laws*. This precious evidence of the teachings of Middle Platonism provides the reader of *The Golden Ass* with the necessary indications of Apuleius' philosophical and religious preoccupations.

The third of the philosophical disquisitions, *On the World*, is a close adaptation of ps.-Aristotle's Περὶ Κόσμου, which was composed a century or two earlier. The work is divided into two sections on cosmology and theology. It begins with an account of the aether and the various aspects of life on earth. Following a bridging discussion on the harmony between the earth's constituent parts, the second part describes how God, known to mankind under different names, animates and preserves all things; the aretalogy in the final book of the romance swings sharply into focus here. It is instructive to observe how the Greek original has been lent a

Roman flavour for a Roman audience. There is abundant citation of Roman as well as Greek poetry; aspects of city-life at Rome are adduced to exemplify the harmony existent in the larger world, just as in his romance Apuleius adds jocose touches to the Greek story to lend it a Roman flavour. More important, the distinction in the Greek treatise between God's transcendent existence beyond the world and his immanent power within it is adapted to accommodate the demons of *De deo Socratis*. The style in which this treatise is written is more akin to *Plato and his Doctrines* than to *The God of Socrates*, though there are occasional literary evocations and rhythmical riots. It is tempting to suggest that *Plato and his Doctrines* and *On the World* are earlier compositions, written before Apuleius' career as sophist at Carthage, while *The God of Socrates* like *The Golden Ass* itself was composed for declamation in the literary salons of the African capital.[9]

Apuleius' speech of self-defence against the charge of magic, the *Apology*, exhibits remarkable contrasts with the forensic orations of Cicero delivered two centuries earlier. The speech is enclosed within the conventional frame of exordium and peroration, but the heart of the speech, divided into three sections, begins with a leisurely rebuttal of attacks on the manner of his private life. So far from pleading urgently for his very life, Apuleius adopts the manner of the public lecturer, regaling the court and its president with disquisitions on such themes as 'The private innocence of the lascivious versifier', 'The enlightened master', 'The true nature of poverty', and interlarding these themes with a host of quotations from Greek and Latin poetry. His purpose is clearly to establish himself as a man of superior culture whom it would be absurd to accuse of such a degrading activity as magic. In his second section, he reinforces the impression that he is a lofty intellectual by demonstrating that the alleged magical malpractices were the zoological studies befitting a second

---

[9] On the importance of the Platonist treatises, C. C. Schlam, *The Metamorphoses of Apuleius* (Chapel Hill: NC, 1992), 11 ff. Middle Platonism is discussed in detail by J. Dillon, *The Middle Platonists* (Ithaca: NY, 1977).

Aristotle, the medical researches of an aspiring Hippocrates, and the religious devotions befitting a Middle Platonist. The distinction which he draws here between the devotee of magic and the genuine searcher after philosophical truth is an important consideration in the message of *The Golden Ass*. In the final section he adopts a more urgent tone as he delineates the history of his arrival and marriage at Oea. Although the outcome of the trial is not recorded, the issue was clearly in no doubt; Apuleius secured his acquittal.[10]

The speech at many points records incidents similar to those experienced by Lucius in the romance; in particular, the reader must wonder how far the comic account of the trial at the Festival of Laughter, of which there is no sign in the Greek version of the story of Lucius and which has almost certainly been inserted by Apuleius himself, was inspired by the author's own experience.

The *Florida*, the other surviving work, is a collection of twenty-three extracts from the published lectures and speeches of Apuleius after his return to Carthage in the early 160s. These extracts are all taken from the exordia of lectures and speeches; often prefaced by modest disclaimers of his own merits and abilities, they frequently exploit anecdotes which find an echo in some of the inserted stories in *The Golden Ass*. Thus, for example, the story of Asclepiades chancing upon a funeral and discovering that the man to be buried was still alive, recalls the tale of the buried youth and the wise physician at 10.12. The description of the crowds thronging the theatre at the Festival of Laughter at 3.2 is markedly similar to that at *Florida* 16. 11 ff. When the citizens of Hypata propose to erect a public statue in honour of Lucius (3.11), we recall that Apuleius was similarly honoured (*Florida* 16. 41 and 46). These extracts are often not dissimilar in their flowery Latin from the narrative passages of the *Metamorphoses*, suggesting that the romance may have been composed during the same period of Apuleius' residence at Carthage.[11]

[10] For the relevance of the *Apology* to *The Golden Ass*, see Tatum, *Apuleius and the Golden Ass*, ch. 4. [11] Ibid. 123 ff.

III

Reference is frequently made to our romance by the alternative titles of *Metamorphoses* and *The Golden Ass*. The former is the title found in the manuscripts; the latter is attested by Augustine, who claims that Apuleius himself entitled his work *Asinus aureus* (*CD* 18. 18). In that same passage, however, Augustine states that Apuleius is describing *his own* experience of being transformed into an ass; he is clearly speaking from memory, rather than citing a manuscript before him, which detracts from the reliability of his witness. We have noted our author's fondness for appropriating titles used by Cicero (*De republica*) and Seneca (*Quaestiones naturales*); here we seem to have 'an inescapable reminiscence of Ovid's *Metamorphoses*'.[12] The plural is appropriate: it covers more than Lucius' becoming an ass and reverting to human shape. In his introductory chapter Apuleius describes his theme as the transformation of 'shapes and fortunes', so that Aristomenes' experience in the role of tortoise with his bed over him, and Thelyphron's disfigurement, and Psyche's apotheosis can qualify for inclusion. *Metamorphoses*, then is the correct title of the romance, but *The Golden Ass* has become so familiar that it seems pedantic to dispense with it.[13]

The date of the work has been a source of controversy. Many scholars (e.g. Rohde, Purser, Haight) incline to the earlier period of Apuleius' life when he was at Rome, because of the topographical references, the legal jokes, the references to senatorial procedures; it has been further suggested that the racy content and ebullient style befit a younger man.[14] Such arguments are clearly subjective, and can be countered by the claim that the older Apuleius, a man young in heart, was

[12] So E. J. Kenney, *Cupid and Psyche* (Cambridge, 1990), 2.

[13] For a friendlier view of the evidence of Augustine, J. J. Winkler, *Auctor and Actor* (Berkeley, Calif., 1985), 292 ff.

[14] See most recently K. Dowden in J. Tatum and G. Vernazza (eds.), *The Ancient Novel* (Proceedings of the Dartmouth ICAN Conference, Hanover, 1989), 147; on the allegedly youthful style, M. Bernhard, *Der Stil des Apuleius von Madaura*[2] (Amsterdam, 1965), 360.

writing with a Roman audience in mind. Arguments favouring a later date include legal references in the *Cupid and Psyche* story, and the significance of Lucius' claim that the philosopher Sextus as well as Plutarch was an elder relative. Plutarch had probably died about the time Apuleius was born, but Sextus as tutor to the emperor Verus was probably still alive when Apuleius visited Rome. It is unlikely that in a work of fiction such a reference would be made to an eminent author still living. So far as the ebullient style is concerned, we have noted similarly baroque passages to be found in the *Florida*, dating to the 160s. The crucial argument, however, supporting the later date, when Apuleius was in Carthage, is the apparent presence of autobiographical elements in the story such as the offer of a statue to Lucius after the trial at Hypata and to Apuleius likewise at Oea, and the journey to Rome of both hero and author. On balance, the arguments for a date in or after the 160s are overwhelming.[15]

In his prologue, Apuleius informs us that the romance on which he is embarking is the adaptation of a Greek story ('fabulam Graecanicam incipimus'). The original, whose author the ninth-century patriarch Photius calls 'Lucius of Patrae', is now lost, but an abridged version of it appears in the works of Lucian, who is a likely candidate as author of the original.[16] Dispute rages about the length of the original story compared with the abridged version, which bears the title *Lucius or the Ass*, and in which in half-a-dozen places there is evidence of unskilful epitomizing. The most systematic investigation has concluded that *Lucius or the Ass* is at most only five Teubner pages shorter than the original.[17] (If Lucian

[15] For the legal passages, see 6.2, 4, 7, and G. W. Bowersock, *RhM* (1965), 282 n. 31. For Sextus 1, 2 and *SHA, Verus* 2. 5. On the statutes, 3.11, and 'Augustine *Ep.* 138. 19; see also 6.9, 6 with Kenney's note.

[16] So B. E. Perry, *The Ancient Romances* (Berkeley, Calif., 1967), ch. 4; G. Anderson, *Studies in Lucian's Comic Fiction* (Leiden, 1976), 34 ff.

[17] The text of *Lucius or the Ass* can be consulted in M. D. McLeod's Loeb edn. of Lucian vol. 8. The calculation of length is made by P. Junghanns, *Die Erzählungstechnik von Apuleius Metamorphosen und ihrer Vorlage* (Leipzig, 1932), 118; Perry, *Ancient Romances*, 216, suggests ten pages longer. There is a good discussion of the problem by H. J. Mason in B. L. Hijmans and R. Th. van der Paardt (eds.), *Aspects of Apuleius' Golden Ass* (Groningen, 1978), ch. 1.

were the author, the criterion of the length of his other works
would support this judgement.)

This controversy is of some importance for *The Golden Ass*. It
is clear from *Lucius or the Ass* that Apuleius followed the main
lines of the original as far as the climax of the transformation
back into human shape, but that he has inserted additional
incidents and anecdotes to point the moral and adorn the tale.
Estimates of the extent of these additions have varied. The
'minimalist' position is that the additions are confined to the
central *conte* of Cupid and Psyche, the Isis-book at the close of
the novel, and the occasional sentimental story, notably the
tragic end of Charite. The 'inclusive' thesis, supported by the
greater number of scholars, is that virtually all the extended
sections not appearing in *Lucius or the Ass* have been added by
Apuleius.[18]

A thematic comparison between the abridged Greek version
and *The Golden Ass* is helpful as an indication of the insertions
(denoted here in italics) made by Apuleius.[19]

	Apuleius	Lucius or the Ass
Bk	Theme	Theme (nos. refer to sections)
1	*Aristomenes and Socrates*	
	Hypata; house of Milo	1–3 Hypata; house of Hipparchus
2	Byrrhena; Photis	3–11 *init.* Abroea; Palaestra
	Thelyphron	
3	*The spoof trial*	
	Metamorphosis and departure	11–17 *init.* Metamorphosis and departure
4	Journey to robbers' cave	17–23 *init.* Journey to robbers' cave
	Three robbers' stories	
	Cupid and Psyche i	
5	*Cupid and Psyche ii*	

---

[18] See my review of H. van Thiel, *Der Eselsroman*, vol. 1 (Munich, 1971, taking the
minimalist view) and of G. Bianco, *La fonte greca delle Metamorfosi di Apuleio* (Brescia,
1971) in *CR* (1974), 215 ff. More recent assessments by Mason in *Aspects*, and
Schlam, *Metamorphoses*, 22 ff.

[19] I reproduce this table from Walsh, *Roman Novel*, 147.

Though some scholars demur at such a radical restriction of the content of the original, even van Thiel would concede that the lost Greek work can have been no more than twice as long as *Lucius or the Ass*.[20] It is accordingly clear that Apuleius has converted a Greek short story into an extended romance with a tripartite structure. The first three books recount the undisciplined curiosity of the hero Lucius, which results in his transformation into an ass; the ensuing seven unfold the saga of bizarre experiences of his human intellect enclosed in the

[20] Van Thiel, *Der Eselsroman*, ch. 3; Schlam, *Metamorphoses*, 22 f. adopts an intermediate position.

animal frame, and the final book describes his redemption by the gratuitous grace of Isis and the hero's subsequent submission to the service of the Isiac religion. The curious length of eleven books, unique in works of ancient fiction as in Roman creative literature generally, is worthy of note. It has been reasonably suggested that Book 11 is designed to stand out apart from the rest, to draw attention to the radical difference of its content, and perhaps to underline the significance of the number eleven in Pythagorean and Platonist thought.[21] It is even possible that Augustine acknowledged and imitated this contrast at the close of the novel, for in his *Confessions* he shifts abruptly from autobiography at the close of Book 9 to philosophical and theological reflection in the final books.[22]

IV

The central problem which confronts the interpreter of the romance is to decide whether Apuleius intended it merely as ribald entertainment, or whether he shaped it to be a fable, a story with a moral. The programmatic first chapter seems deliberately designed to beguile; it has rightly been observed that whereas *Lucius or the Ass* plunges directly into I-narrative ('I was once visiting Thessaly . . .'), Apuleius' exordium reads like the prologue of a Latin comedy. He opens the proceedings in the persona of the author, in the spirit of a Terence; he then teasingly combines the promise of risqué narrative of incidents and anecdotes ('the Milesian mode') with hints of a sober connection with Egypt, the implications of which will become clear only in the final book. (This is the initial justification for Winkler's analogy of an Agatha Christie detective story, the suggestion that clues are planted but fully understood only retrospectively at Book 11.) Apuleius as author then slips on the stage-outfit, so to say, and identity of Lucius his hero, and

---

[21] See Kenney, *Cupid and Psyche*, 3; S. Heller, *AJP* (1983), 321 ff. R. Heine, in *Aspects*, 37, speculates on Book 11 as a later addition.

[22] See R. McMahon, *Augustine's Prayerful Ascent* (Athens, Ga., 1989), ch. 4.

proceeds to play the part with relish;[23] thus the potted biography that follows in the first-person narrative belongs to Lucius. It includes a visit to Rome, an experience which has given the Greek youth sufficient Latin to tell the story in that language. When he speaks of himself as a circus-performer leaping from one horse to another, he may obliquely refer to the alternation of fidelity to the Greek source and insertion of additional episodes and anecdotes. The final sentence of the chapter, it should be noted, promises the reader no more than enjoyable entertainment in reading this mélange: 'lector, intende; laetaberis.' There is no hint here of any ulterior motive in the adaptation of the Greek story.

Many perceptive readers from Macrobius onward have thus strong justification for proclaiming that the work is in essence an entertainment. For Winkler it is 'a philosophical comedy about religious knowledge', in which 'all answers to cosmic questions are non-authorised'; 'Book 11 is designed to be not a statement of faith for the reader to accept, but an experience that reproduces the original surprise and wonder of a religious revelation.' G. N. Sandy finds himself in substantial agreement with Farquharson's withering judgement that *The Golden Ass* is 'a mere adventure story, a kind of horrid nightmare, with stories of the Decameron kind but infinitely worse told'; Sandy draws particular attention to the lubricious episodes in the second part of the novel, which appear to be designed 'purely for comic entertainment rather than to put into relief the moral degradation' of Lucius. For B. E. Perry, the *Metamorphoses* is 'a series of mundane stories exploited on their own account as such for the reader's entertainment', and the final book is merely a note of edification employed as 'ballast to offset the prevailing levity

---

[23] In this controversy concerning the spokesman in the first chapter, I agree with Rohde and many successors. For a useful outline of the dispute and various solutions offered, see K. Dowden, *CQ* (1982), 419 ff. Two further suggestions have been made subsequently: S. J. Harrison, *CQ* (1990), 507 ff., argues that the prologue is an address by the book itself; Winkler, *Auctor and Actor*, 203, that the spokesman is 'an itinerant Greek now working as a storyteller in Rome'. I find Rohde's thesis more persuasive than these.

of the preceding ten books', so that Apuleius can 'bow deeply and reverently to his audience'. A critic of similar views, Frances Norwood, describes the final book as 'the climax of *Pilgrim's Progress* tacked on to the end of *Tom Jones*', and suggests that Apuleius exploits the Isiac religion as 'a juggler keeps his best trick for the climax of the performance'.[24]

For those who are content to restrict Apuleius' purposes to those of a literary juggler or entertainer, three lines of enquiry are especially profitable. The first is to study his narrative skills against the presentation of the compendious *Lucius or the Ass*. His careful attention to structure becomes immediately apparent.[25] *Cupid and Psyche* occupies the centre of the novel; as we shall note, it is the projection into myth of the sin, sufferings, and redemption of Lucius. On each side of this central episode, each book is a confluence of contrasting themes, carefully achieved by inserted episodes. In the first book, the comic detail of Lucius' first encounter with his miserly host Milo, adapted from the Greek, is complemented by the insertion of a dramatic story of the death of Socrates by magic; in the second, the social and sexual encounters with his relative and with the maidservant (the Greek continuation of the tale) is offset by the chilling story of the disfigurement of Thelyphron; in the third, the reverse pattern is notable, for here the Greek original has the dramatic content of the metamorphosis of Lucius, and Apuleius prefaces it with an episode of comedy, the Festival of Laughter. Thus throughout the first section of the romance there is a characteristic combination of the comic and the magical. In the second section, following the tale of Cupid and Psyche, this planned variation is continued between the comic on the one hand and the romantic or tragic on the other. Thus in the seventh book

---

[24] Macrobius, *In Somn. Scip.* 1. 2. 8, 'solas aurium delicias profitetur'. Winkler, *Auctor and Actor*, 124 f.; G. Sandy in Hijmans and van der Paardt, *Aspects* 123 ff., citing Farquharson's *Marcus Aurelius* (Oxford, 1951), 99; Perry, *Ancient Romances* 243; F. Norwood, *Phoenix* (1956), 5. Similar views are expressed by E. H. Haight, *Apuleius and his Influence* (NY, 1927), 57.

[25] For more detailed considerations of structure, A. Scobie, in Hijmans and van der Paardt *Aspects*, 43 ff.

the romantic rescue of Charite is juxtaposed with Lucius' privations at the farm; in the eighth, Charite's tragic death, a long episode inserted by Apuleius, is followed by the adventures with the priests, a comic episode derived from the Greek story. Thereafter Apuleius' structure comes under more strain as the Greek version relates Lucius' treatment at the hands of three owners, but the adept balance of themes is still observable: thus in Book 10 two tragic episodes alternate with two jocular accounts.

In addition to such refinements of plot and structure, comparison with *Lucius or the Ass* reveals Apuleius' careful attention to the development of the characters. Thus in the first book Milo the host is a much more miserly skinflint than in the Greek account, and all else is subordinated to this enhanced characterization. In the second book the portrait of the maidservant is more romantically drawn; Photis enchants Lucius with her beauty, whereas in *Lucius or the Ass* her counterpart Palaestra merely lives up to her name as a wrestling-partner. The witch Pamphile in the third book is depicted more horrifically than in the Greek version. Similarly in Lucius' later encounters Charite is a more romantic and ultimately a more tragic figure, the boy to whom he is consigned at the farm is more cruel, the priests of Atargatis are more degenerately effeminate and mendacious, and the baker's wife is more sadistic as well as unfaithful.[26]

The second line of enquiry is to be directed at the inserted episodes and anecdotes, which reveal Apuleius' talents and limitations as a story-teller. These insertions, as we have suggested, successfully integrate comic and dramatic scenes; their underlying purpose is to reflect in different ways the situation of the hero Lucius. In this aim, the stories in the first section of the novel (notably the death of Socrates and the disfigurement of Thelyphron) are closely relevant, and *Cupid and Psyche* has an important bearing on the main theme; the later insertions, however, though illustrative in a general sense

---

[26] For fuller discussion of characterization, see Walsh, *Roman Novel*, 150 ff.

of the degenerate and hazardous world into which the hero has sunk, are less closely articulated to the fortunes of Lucius, and indeed Apuleius at some points recounts them with such lubricious zest that his moralizing purposes all but disappear.

In several of the insertions, Apuleius seeks to demonstrate his skill at combining different tales (presumably known to his readers), but not always with conspicuous success; loose ends are left trailing. Thus in Aristomenes' story in Book 1, where the point is that Socrates died through his entanglement with magic, the attempted suicide adds a comic and distracting element extraneous to the main theme. In the story of Thelyphron in Book 2, Apuleius is not content to recount the disfigurement of this character after his rash undertaking to guard a corpse; he appends a sequel in which the corpse is reanimated to condemn his widow as a murderess. This addition allows him to introduce an Isiac priest with magical powers, but it distracts the reader (some may think intentionally) from the relevance of the anecdote, which is the danger of involvement with magic. The long account in Book 8 of the deaths of Tlepolemus (at the hands of Thrasyllus) and of Charite knits together different literary forbears, as we shall note later. Further examples of such patchwork stories are seen in Book 10. In the anecdote of the lovesick stepmother and her reluctant stepson, the story is introduced as a tragedy on the lines of Euripides' *Hippolytus* and Seneca's *Phaedra*; but after the stepmother's natural son has drunk the 'poison' intended for the stepson, it becomes a comedy, for the 'poison' turns out to be a mere soporific. Most glaring of all these patchwork creations in its improbabilities is the history of the female criminal with whom Lucius-turned-ass is to copulate at the public show in Book 10. She first appears as a jealous wife who falsely suspects her husband's sister of alienating his affections, and kills her; but she then transforms herself into an avaricious shrew who poisons her husband and the apothecary who furnished the drug, her own daughter and the apothecary's wife. The ostensible purpose of the story, the demonstration of the infidelity which stalks through Lucius' degenerate world, loses all impact because of its inconse-quentialities.[27]

The third feature worthy of note in this analysis of the romance as entertainment is the literary texture. In the Roman system of mandarin education, those who graduated to the enjoyment of such literature as this were few but well-read, and the fiction of Petronius and Apuleius could be enjoyed at two levels; the narrative-content (comic, romantic, and tragic) provides the running entertainment of an interest-ing story, and superimposed on this is the more sophisticated amusement of repeated evocation of earlier masterpieces of literature. In some episodes, notably *Cupid and Psyche*, the long inserted narrative of Charite, Tlepolemus, and Thrasyllus (in which Herodotus, Sophocles, Virgil, Ovid, and Plutarch are all brought into play), and the Phaedra-story in Book 10 (where Virgil and Seneca are brought continually before our minds), the literary evocations are prominent in establishing the structural frame. In other places Apuleius exploits these familiar texts for glancing parody. For example, when the sight of Photis in the kitchen excites Lucius to sexual arousal ('obstipui et mirabundus steti, steterunt et membra quae iacebant ante'), the evocation of the *Aeneid*, 'obstipui, steteruntque comae', disarms possible puritanical reactions from the reader. Or again, when in *Cupid and Psyche* Venus begs Jupiter for the loan of his messenger Mercury and Jupiter graciously accedes, the phrase which indicates his approval ('nec rennuit Iouis caerulum supercilium') comically echoes a response of Zeus to Thetis in Homer's *Iliad*.[28]

Like Petronius, Apuleius on occasion burlesques the pre-

---

[27] On the narrative technique in the inserted episodes, see Perry, *Ancient Romances*, ch. 7, and his earlier articles cited there; E. Paratore, *La novella in Apuleio*[2] (Messina, 1942); J. Tatum, *TAPA* (1969), 487 ff. On the Aristomenes and Thelyphron stories, see also C. Meyrhofer, *Antichthon* (1975), 8 ff.; on Thelyphron also G. Drake, *Papers in Language and Literature* (1977), 3 ff. On the story of Charite, W. Anderson, *Philol.* (1909), 537 ff.; C. Forbes, *CW* (1943), 39 f.; R. van der Paardt, *Symp. Apul. Gronignanum* (1981), 19 ff. On the stories in Bk. 10, S. Hammer, *Eos* (1923), 6 ff.

[28] See 8.14, 10.3, 2.7, 6.7 with nn.

sentation of Roman historians like Sallust and Livy. When the members of the robber-band drive Lucius-turned-ass to their mountain-lair, Apuleius commences his narrative of events there with the time-honoured formula: 'Res ac tempus ipsum locorum speluncaeque illius ... descriptionem flagitant.' Later in the romance, the calamities of an estate-owner are prefigured with exotic prodigies; the catalogue of them reminds us of similar prodigy-lists in Livy foretelling, for example, the disasters of Trasimene and Cannae.[29]

Further opportunities for such literary parody are exploited with lawcourt scenes, which figure prominently also in the Greek love-romances. The Festival of Laughter provides the most extended example, with its speeches for the prosecution and defence constructed according to the rules tabulated by Quintilian. The court-scene in the Phaedra episode in Book 10 offers a second example; here the litigants are warned to observe the rules laid down on the Areopagus, and the decision is reached by dropping pebbles in the urn according to the regular Roman procedure. More amusingly, Roman oratory is parodied in a scene outside the courts: when Lucius-turned-ass abandons the cruel boy to be mangled to death by a rampant bear, the boy's rustic mother becomes a veritable Cicero as she assails Lucius in his stall with a splendid parody of a prosecuting counsel's attack.[30]

Beyond purely literary parody, Apuleius introduces Roman legal and procedural motifs for humorous effect, aware that his cultured readers would appreciate the technicalities. It is not only the Greek protagonists who are bound by Roman law; the very gods and goddesses on Olympus respect Roman edicts in matters of inheritance, or marriage, or adultery, or runaway slaves.[31] The deities likewise organize their

---

[29] 4.6 and Sallust, *BJ* 17. 1, 95. 2; 9.33 f. and Livy 21. 62, 22. 1. 8 ff.

[30] 3.3 f. and Quintilian 3. 9; 10. 7 ff.; 7. 27. On Apuleius' literary texture in general I have benefited greatly from discussion with Prof. Ellen Finkelpearl of Scripps College, who hopes eventually to publish a monograph on the subject.

[31] 5.991 6.9, RR, 4, cf. P. Norden, *Apuleius von Madaura und das römische Privatrecht* (Leipzig, 1912).

assemblies according to Roman convention, with threats of fines for non-attendance and rules of procedure; here Apuleius exploits a comic motif prominent earlier in Ovid and in Seneca's *Apocolocyntosis*.[32]

It is clear beyond doubt, then, that the romance is a literary entertainment, and commentators who wholly reject the notion of an underlying moral purpose are content to explain the final book as Apuleius' exploitation of exotic religious practices solely for the diversion of readers. The rescue of Lucius from his plight through the acknowledgement of the saving power of Isis is visualized as having been inspired by similar *dénouements* in the Greek romances, where hapless lovers are similarly delivered from their privations by the intervention of a kindly deity. In Chariton's novel Aphrodite is the rescuer, in Longus it is Pan; most piquantly of all, in Xenophon of Ephesus the lovers Anthia and Habrocomes address their thanks to Isis, whose role as protector of chastity is emphasized earlier in this novel. Apuleius' entire romance is thus envisaged as literary entertainment in which Apuleius merges the disparate Greek genres of comic short story and extended 'ideal' romance into a novel unity for the pleasurable relaxation of his readers.

V

Yet there is no doubt that designation of the romance merely as entertainment leaves many readers dissatisfied. From the time of Beroaldus and Adlington, the first commentator and the first translator of the novel into English respectively, there was virtual unanimity until the later nineteenth century that it is presented not merely as a moral fable but also as an allegory of the human condition. In his Introductory Address and his Epistle Dedicatory, delivered from University College, Oxford on 18 September 1566, Adlington claims: 'Although the matter therein seeme very light and merry, yet the effect thereof tendeth to a good and vertuous moral . . .'; 'Under the

---

[32] See 6.23. 1 with Kenney, *Cupid and Psyche*, n. ad loc.

wrap of this transformation is taxed the life of mortall men,
when as we suffer our mindes so to bee drowned in the
sensuall lusts of the flesh, and the beastly pleasure thereof . . .
so can we never be restored to the right figure of ourselves
except we taste and eat the sweet Rose of reason and vertue,
which rather by the mediation of praier we may assuredly
attaine.'[33]

It is an absorbing question to ask why many modern critics
have earlier poured scorn on this interpretation, and why
more recently there has been an increasing tendency to
acccept the romance as fable as well as entertainment. One
important factor has been the recent rehabilitation of the
philosophus Platonicus and the greater attention paid to the
dominant ideas of Middle Platonism. The contemporaries of
Apuleius approached the novel with a greater awareness of
the resonances of second-century philosophy in this theme of
the deliverance of Lucius-turned-ass by the grace of Isis. A
crucial figure in this connection is Plutarch, whose *Moralia* can
enlighten us on many aspects of *The Golden Ass*. It is notable
that at two important junctures early in the novel, Lucius'
descent from Plutarch is stressed; there is no mention of this
provenance in *Lucius or the Ass*, and we may assume that
Apuleius has added this characterizing detail to suggest that
Lucius' family connections should have enabled him to avoid
the hazards of curiosity for magic by way of sex. This is the
lesson impressed upon him by the priest of Isis in the final
book: 'Nec tibi natales . . . uel ipsa qua flores usquam doctrina
praefuit.'[34]

The familiar title of the romance, *Asinus aureus*, is conventionally rendered as 'The Prince of Ass-stories', but there may be
a purposeful ambiguity here. It has been suggested that the
Latin translates the Greek *onos purros*, the 'tawny ass' of

[33] *The Eleven Bookes of The Golden Asse* (London, 1566). R. Heine in Hijmans and
van der Paardt, *Aspects*, takes the allegorical interpretation back to Fulgentius in the
6th cent., and reminds us that Boccaccio treats the *Cupid and Psyche* episode similarly
in his *De genealogiis deorum gentilium libri*. Beroaldus' comm. was pub. in 1500 at
Bologna.
[34] Mention of Plutarch at 1. 2. 1, 2. 3. 2. The lesson from the priest, 11. 15. 1.

Typhon which in Plutarch's *De Iside et Osiride* symbolizes the forces of evil. This treatise is of vital importance for a fuller understanding of the romance, since it offers a full explanation of how the Isiac religion is reconciled with the dualist philosophy of Plato. Osiris and Isis represent order and reason; over against them stands Typhon, the principle of irrationality and disorder. We should assign to Isis all that is well-ordered and beautiful in the world, and to Typhon all that lacks measure and order. Isis and Osiris have been transformed from demons into gods, with power above and below the earth.[35]

The ass, 'the most stupid of domestic animals', is assigned to Typhon, the malevolent demon whom it resembles in stupidity and lust. Hence Lucius' transformation into a donkey, and his eventual resumption of human shape, pregnantly signify a relapse into bestial living and re-emergence into authentic humanity. It seems beyond doubt that when Apuleius transformed the climax of the ass-story (which in the Greek version ends on the same note of lubricious comedy which characterizes it throughout) into an apologia for the Isiac religion, he was inspired by Plutarch's *De Iside*. It is true that Plutarch's treatment is the more philosophical, whereas Apuleius emphasizes salient detail of ritual and religious practice; but these variations are attributable to the differing purposes of philosopher and novelist. Even so there are numerous correspondences of detail.[36]

The moral of the *Metamorphoses* is that Lucius' avid curiosity to explore the realm of magic, attained by way of sexual encounter with Photis, was punished because it was a perverted path to universal knowledge. This lesson was already present in the Greek version, but the *curiositas*-motif is

---

[35] For *onos purros*, *Moralia* 362 F; cf. R. Martin, *RÉL* (1970), 332 ff. For the reconciliation of the Isiac religion with Platonism, see *Moralia*, 371 ff., 376–7A. For Isis and Orisis as gods, *Moralia* 361 D.

[36] For the ass and Typhon, *Moralia* 362 F, 371 C. For the parallels, see my 'Apuleius and Plutarch', in H. J. Blumenthal and R. A. Markus (eds.), *Neoplatonism and Early Christian Thought* (London, 1981), 31 n., 25.

much more pervasive and exemplary in Apuleius, who seeks
in the *Apology* to establish a distinction between healthy
curiosity, which seeks knowledge of the true reality by
intellectual effort and religious experience, and the debased
curiosity which seeks a false reality by way of magic and
sensuality. It is not without significance that this issue is
earlier treated in Plutarch's treatise *De curiositate*.[37]

A further important treatise of Plutarch is the *De genio
Socratis*. We have already noted that Apuleius' monograph
called *De deo Socratis* is of considerable significance for *The
Golden Ass* as indicating the preoccupation of Middle Platonism with demons as intermediaries between gods and men.
The close similarity between the titles is no coincidence;
Apuleius, as we have seen, deliberately selects titles which
connect his studies with those of famed forebears. In the first
two books of his romance, the stories of the death of Socrates
and the disfigurement of Thelyphron underline the malevolent
power of witches; they are to be regarded as demons inimical
to the human race. The same inference is to be made about
the old man in Book 8 who entices one of Lucius' cortege to be
devoured by a dragon, and likewise about the witch in Book
10 who is hired by the baker's wife to dispose of her
husband.[38]

It will be clear that the reader who approaches *The Golden
Ass* with an awareness of Apuleius' philosophical and religious
suppositions will suspect from the outset that there is more to
the story than mere entertainment. Those without such
knowledge, however, are led by the author up the garden path
of 'entertainment' until they are suddenly confronted with the
moralizing in the final book. But a retrospective survey of

[37] For the two contrasting forms of curiosity, see C. C. Schlam, *CJ* (1968), 120 ff.;
G. Sandy, *Latomus* (1972), 179 ff.; J. L. Penwill, *Ramus* (1975), 49 ff. For Plutarch's
treatise, *Moralia*, 517 c ff.

[38] The *De genio Socratis* complements *De deo Socratis* on the tenets of Middle
Platonism concerning demons. They lodge on the moon; unjust demons commit
crimes, while good demons participate in the mysteries, and punish evil deeds. They
can rescue individuals from danger if the souls of such persons pay heed to
them.

Lucius' experiences must then convince them that Apuleius
has created a pattern of events which is summarized in the
condemnation by the Isiac priest: 'In the green years of youth,
you tumbled on the slippery slope into slavish pleasures, and
gained the ill-omened reward of your unhappy curiosity.' The
'slavish pleasures' (*seruiles uoluptates*) are the sexual prelude
with Photis, and the 'unhappy curiosity' (*curiositas improspera*)
the obsession with magic.[39]

In the first three books which document Lucius' fall from
grace, he is given warning after warning of the hazards that
attend his fixation on magic, but in spite of his upbringing and
learning he remains impervious to them. Aristomenes' story of
the death of Socrates posts the initial warning: Socrates
forsook his family responsibilities, bound himself by sexual
ties to the witch Meroë, and suffered the consequences. But
Lucius fails to grasp that *fabula de eo narratur*. A little later at
the house of his kinswoman Byrrhena, he examines statuary
depicting the myth of Actaeon spying on Diana's naked form,
and being turned into a stag to be mangled by his own
hunting-dogs; Lucius fails to heed the dangers of such
peeping-Tom curiosity (*curioso optutu*) and is to be turned into
an ass to be the butt of similar attacks. Byrrhena reinforces the
warning by explicit advice about his hostess Pamphile, who
enchains handsome youths with the fetters of love, and
transforms them to other shapes; Lucius' response is to form a
close love-compact with the maid Photis to enable him to gain
access to the witch's magical practices. Photis reinforces the
warning: 'The honey that tastes so sweet may bring on an
attack of bitter bile.' In spite of his superior philosophical
knowledge, which he demonstrates in the conversation with
his host Milo following the flickering lamp, and in spite of the
horrendous warning of the mutilation of Thelyphron (like
himself a youthful visitor to Thessaly, land of witches), he tells
Photis: 'I am aflame to observe magic with my own eyes.' He
adds to this confession of *curiositas* an explicit rejection of
family ties in his enslavement to sensual pleasures: 'Now I do

[39] 11.15.

not desire home or hearth; this night with you I count above all that.'[40]

This patterning in the first three books is so crystal-clear, especially on a second reading following awareness of the Isiac priest's condemnation in Book 11, that Apuleius' purpose of converting his entertainment into a fable cannot reasonably be doubted. Difficulty does, however, arise in the second part of the story (Books 4–10), in which the author's task was to portray the punishment incurred by Lucius for his sins. Apuleius' decision to follow the main lines of the Greek story, with its aim no more than comic entertainment, results in his recounting Lucius' good times as well as bad; for example, the favoured treatment which he receives from Charite following her rescue and return home, or again, during the brief interlude with the cooks and their master Thiasus, when with his 'human' tricks he becomes a social attraction. Even so, the main emphases are on his sufferings as an ass in a degenerate world, as in his grisly experiences with the bandits, his privations at the mill, his ordeal at the hands of the sadistic boy, and the degrading nature of his life with the eunuch-priests. The role of Fortune throughout these unhappy experiences should be noted: this victimizing Fortune represents the arbitrary and irrational course of events in a fallen world, and it is significant that the priest of Isis in the final book contrasts her with 'the Fortune with eyes'. Implicit here is the contrasting dominion of Typhon with that of Isis.[41]

Interpenetrating these harsh experiences, earlier recounted by the Greek source, are the insertions and changes introduced by Apuleius himself. In sum they depict a world dominated by deceit, cruelty, and infidelity. The trinity of bandits' exploits, though recounted in a mock-serious tone, none the less reflects

[40] The lesson of Aristomenes, 1.7–8; the statuary, 2.4; Byrrhena's warning, 2.5; Photis' ambivalent rebuke, 2.10; Thelyphron, 2.21 ff. Lucius' abandonment of kin for sensual pleasure, 3.19. The Festival of Laughter, as Photis explains, was the result of Pamphile's magical practices, and posted a further warning.

[41] Favourite of Charite, 7.14; with the cooks and Thiasus, 10.13 ff. For the hostility of Fortune, see 7.2, 3, 16, 17, 25; 8.24; for blind Fortune contrasted with the Fortune with eyes, 11.15.

the world of violence encompassing Lucius. The story of
Charite undergoes a total transformation in Apuleius; in the
Greek version she and her husband Tlepolemus accidentally
perish by drowning, whereas Apuleius composes a story of
cruelty and lust in which Thrasyllus wantonly kills Tlepolemus
in his attempt to obtain Charite's hand in marriage. In the
wanderings of Lucius and his ménage that ensue, Apuleius in
a trinity of episodes depicts a hostile, hateful world of spirits,
nature, and men. The anecdotes that follow repeatedly advert
to sexual lust and magical practices. Four stories centre on
deceiving wives, in one of which the baker's wife engineered
the murder of her husband through the magical arts of a
witch; later Lucius tells the stories of the stepmother's
destructive passion for her stepson, and of the wife whose
jealousy impelled her to mass murder.[42] All these narratives
depict the various facets of the corrupt world into which
Lucius has descended.

VI

It is accordingly clear that Apuleius has artfully converted his
entertainment into a fable. This does not, however, foreclose
his surprises, for in the final book his fable, his story with a
moral, becomes his testament. As *Lucius or the Ass* reveals, the
Greek source reached its climax with a public show mounted
at Thessalonica; there Lucius-turned-ass gulped down some
roses carried by an attendant, was restored to human shape,
and explained his history to the governor, who by a mind-
stretching coincidence happened to know his family, and
facilitated his departure. He then hopefully revisited the lady
who had enjoyed his sexual services when he was an ass, but
he was scornfully rejected by her, whereupon he returned
home. There is dispute about whether the fuller Greek version
ended in precisely this way, but clearly the final book in

---

[42] Bandits' stories, 4.9 ff.; Charite and Thrasyllus, 8.1 ff.; trinity of episodes, 8.
17–22; adulterous wives, 9.5, 16 ff. The baker murdered by magic, 9.30; the
stepmother and the mass-murderess, 10.2 ff., 23 ff.

Apuleius' romance presents a wholly original climax to the tale.[43]

If Apuleius had wished merely to edify his readers by appending a moralizing close, it would have been sufficient to describe how Lucius recovered his human shape by eating the roses proffered to him by the priest of Isis, and how the remonstration of the priest pointed the moral. Instead of this, Apuleius transfers the *mise-en-scène* from Thessalonica in the Greek original to Corinth and its suburb Cenchreae, presumably because he had personal acquaintance with its importance as a centre of Isiac worship. On the shore at Cenchreae Lucius addresses despairing prayers to Isis, and when by her aid he has resumed his human shape, he becomes her votary. The lyrical prayers, the rapt meditation before her statue, the account of the cult-initiation, and the description of other ceremonials make this book the most detailed account of the Isis-liturgy that we possess from antiquity. Apuleius is not content even with this; he records how Lucius upon the advice of Isis travelled to Rome, and there underwent two further initiations. Prior to the first of these, the priest who was to initiate him received a divine message that *a man from Madauros*, the native city of Apuleius, was to be admitted as a votary. The author therefore identifies himself at this point with his hero, so that there is a clear case for calling Book 11 a personal testament. The propaganda elements in his account are conspicuous. There is emphasis on the number of initiates of all ranks and ages; the antiquity of the cult is stressed; the bystanders who have witnessed Lucius' recovery of his human form are urged to amend their lives. 'Let unbelievers observe you, and . . . recognize the errors of their ways.'[44]

Elsewhere I have speculated that this fervid recommendation of the religion of Isis may represent a counterblast to the

[43] The various theories about the ending of the Greek *Metamorphoses* are helpfully summarized by Schlam, *Metamorphoses*, 24 ff.

[44] For Cenchreae as a centre of Isiac worship, Gwyn Griffiths, *Apuleius of Madauros*, 14 ff. A man from Madauros, 11,27; initiates, 11.10; antiquity, 11.5; unbelievers, 11.15.

meteoric spread of Christianity in Africa in the later second century. This suggestion has been sceptically received, but it is worth summarizing the arguments here, which depend on the thesis that the romance was written in Carthage in the later second century, after earlier residence in Athens and Rome. It seems probable that in Rome he encountered Christian apologies proliferating there; that composed by Marcianus Aristides contains a scathing attack on Isis, who by this date had been accepted as an honoured inmate in the *curia deorum*. His return to Carthage coincided with the extraordinary flowering of Christianity in North Africa. Madauros, Apuleius' own birthplace, is mentioned as the first focal point of Christian witness; more important, however, is the evidence of Tertullian's *Apology*, which claims that the whole province of Africa was in ferment in the 190s because of the inroads made by Christianity.[45]

If this were the sum of evidence, and the speculation rested merely on the vague claim that 'Genuine conversion to paganism will appear . . . only when Christianity had become so powerful that its rival was, so to speak, made an entity by opposition and contrast', the thesis would lack substance. Two further factors, however, must be taken into account. The first is a remarkable statement by Tertullian that at least some fellow-Africans believed that Christians worshipped *an ass's head* (*somniastis caput asininum esse deum nostrum*), and that a condemned man in the amphitheatre aped the Christian god by equipping himself with ass's ears and a hoof, and by carrying the inscription 'The God of the Christians, Offspring of an Ass'. Tertullian explains this strange notion by suggesting that it was a distortion of Tacitus' excursus on Jewish practices in his *Histories* (5. 3 ff.). This popular belief that Christians worshipped the ass is also retailed by

---

[45] On this theory that Apuleius was reacting to Christian inroads, see *Phoenix* (1968), 151 ff.; Walsh, *Roman Novel*, 186 ff. Marcianus Aristides, *Apol.* 12. 3: 'If Isis is a goddess, and could not help her own brother and husband, how can she help anyone else?' Madauros as a Christian centre, Augustine, *Ep.* 16. 2. Tertullian's evidence, *Apol.* 37 (date AD 197).

Minucius Felix, and it is accordingly possible to interpret Lucius' metamorphosis into an ass, and his restoration to human shape, as the adoption and later renunciation of Christian beliefs.[46]

The second factor worthy of consideration relates to the condemnation of the baker's wife in Book 9: 'Instead of adhering to a sure faith, she sacrilegiously feigned bold awareness of a deity whom she proclaimed to be the only God.' This condemnation must obviously be directed at either Jewish or Christian beliefs and practices, and given the increased Christian presence in Africa, Christianity is the likelier target. The claims made for the Isiac religion certainly swing into sharper focus if considered against the competing claims of Christianity. The emphasis on the *numen unicum multiformi specie* of Isis, the consecration of Lucius' entire lifespan to her, the prominence lent to contemplation, the preoccupation with sexual chastity all gain greater significance when considered in this defensive light against the external challenge.[47]

VII

At the centre of this unprecedented synthesis of entertainment, fable, and testament is the inserted story of Cupid and Psyche.[48] The purpose of this story within a story (a technique familiar to educated readers from both Alexandrian and

---

[46] For the quotation on conversion to paganism, see A. D. Nock, *Conversion* (Oxford, 1933), 14. The Tertullian passage is at *Apol.* 16; cf. Minucius Felix, *Oct.* 9. 4, 28. 8.

[47] The baker's wife, 9.14; cf. L. Herrmann, *Latomus* (1953), 188 ff. For Isis' *numen unicum* and compassionate care, 11.1–2; consecration of Lucius' life-span, 11.6; cf. A. J. Festugière, *Personal Religion among the Greeks* (Berkeley, Calif., 1960), 80; contemplation, 11–17 ff.; sexual chastity, 11.6, 19, 23 (for Christian emphasis on this virtue, Hermas, 29. 1 ff.; Justin, *1 Apol.* 15; Tertullian, *Apol.* 9).

[48] The *conte* of Cupid and Psyche has been recently ed. by E. J. Kenney with a comprehensive introduction and bibliography. L. C. Purser's edn. (London, 1910) is still serviceable; P. Grimal has published a French edn. (Paris, 1963). G. Binder and R. Merkelbach have assembled a collection of essays in *Amor und Psyche* (Wege der Forschung, 126, Darmstadt, 1968).

Roman literature) is to illuminate the larger whole; Apuleius has projected into the wider world of myth the central thread of *The Golden Ass*. Like the romance proper, the *conte* is introduced with the beguiling promise of an elegant narration, a programmatic parallel. Like Lucius, Psyche indulges her curiosity, in spite of repeated warnings; as punishment she wanders like Lucius-turned-ass forlornly through the world; her deliverance is preceded by a series of trials which correspond with the initiation of Lucius into the Isiac mysteries in the final book. The correspondence is especially marked in the final trial, in which Psyche is required to visit the realm of the dead; Lucius likewise in his initiation treads 'the threshold of Persephone'. After successfully performing these tasks, Psyche is rescued by Cupid from the suspended death brought on by her curiosity; she is transported to heaven, and bears a child who is called Pleasure, just as Lucius' intimate relationship with Isis brings him pleasure beyond telling (*inexplicabilis uoluptas*).[49]

This striking series of connections led Merkelbach to argue that the entire romance was a *roman-à-clef* rooted in the Isiac mystery-religion, and meaningful only to the initiates. This view has, however, failed to win wide acceptance.[50]

The source or sources on which Apuleius drew for his story cannot be definitely established. The basic themes of the beautiful girl with two jealous sisters, her courtship by an enchanted suitor reputed to be a monster, the enforced separation from him because of the breaking of a taboo, the oppression by a witch who imposes impossible trials upon her, and the ultimate reconciliation with her lover, can all be paralleled in widespread versions of folklore tales; the existence of a North African version is of particular interest. It was Apuleius' brilliant achievement to convert this *Märchen*

[49] For the technique of a story within a story, see esp. Catullus, 64 (and Kenney, *Cupid and Psyche*, 12 f.). The culminating trial of Psyche and the initiation of Lucius, 6. 20 and 11.21, 23. Birth of Voluptas and *inexplicabilis uoluptas*, 6.24 and 11.24.

[50] The notion of *The Golden Ass* as sacral myth was earlier propounded by R. Reitzenstein and K. Kerényi. Merkelbach has argued that all the extant Greek romances except Chariton's, as well as that of Apuleius, are coded documents in this sense.

into a *Kunstmärchen* for his special purpose of illuminating the career of Lucius.[51]

In this adaptation of a traditional story, our author's Platonist preoccupations are especially prominent; he has grafted on to his source the names of the protagonists to indicate that Psyche's separation from, and ultimate reunion with, Cupid is an allegory for the soul's restless aspiration to attain the divine, as Plato depicts it in his *Phaedrus*. Beyond this, it has been suggested that the Platonist doctrine of the two Venuses, as first recounted by Pausanias in the *Symposium* and reproduced by Apuleius in his *Apology*, is central to the story. Just as the higher Venus ('recommending virtues by beauty of character to those who love her') and the lower Venus ('binding in her embrace enslaved bodies') contend for mastery over Lucius, so in *Cupid and Psyche*, it is suggested, the two Venuses (and the two Cupids or forms of love) compete for the soul of Psyche. The thesis is clearly valid in the case of Lucius, for the higher Venus prevails when Isis replaces Photis as the object of his affections. It seems, however, less relevant in the career of Psyche, for though the character of Cupid is schizoid, his less reputable persona is never revealed to her, and her sexual role as *matrona* is clearly different from Lucius' random sensuality. Nor does Apuleius characterize Venus in deliberately contrasted philosophical roles; she is a many-sided literary creation.[52]

Apuleius did not invent the story of the love between Cupid and Psyche; that relationship, stemming from the influence of Plato, was already celebrated in the art and literature of the

---

[51] For the folk-tale and its diffusion see J. O. Swähn, *The Tale of Cupid and Psyche* (Lund, 1955); J. R. G. Wright, *CQ* (1971), 273 ff. For the N. African version, see O. Weinreich in Binder and Merkelbach, *Amor und Psyche*, 293 ff., with earlier bibliography. It seems perverse to argue that Apuleius created rather than adapted the basic tale, as suggested by D. Fehling, *Amor und Psyche* (Wiesbaden, 1977).

[52] For Psyche (the soul) and her aspiration to the divine in Plato, see esp. *Phaedrus* 248c and compare 5.24 here. For the two Venuses, *Symp.* 180d 181b and Apuleius, *Apol.* 12; see E. J. Kenney, 'Psyche and her mysterious Husband', in D. A. Russell (ed.), *Antonine Literature* (Oxford, 1990), 175 ff., and his *Cupid and Psyche* at 5.6. 9, where he suggests that 'Psyche tempts Cupid physically as Photis had tempted Lucius'. But the two situations (marital bliss and random sensuality) are wholly different.

Hellenistic age. Erōs, the wanton boy who inflames with passion both deities and human beings, frequently appears in the poems of the Palatine Anthology, on occasion suffering the love-torments which he inflicts on others; Psyche by name is more fugitive, but in Hellenistic statuary the love-relationship of Cupid with a winged maiden is a frequent theme, and must relate to the Platonist myth as depicted in the *Phaedrus* and *Symposium*.[53]

The schizoid character of Cupid—now the sober husband, now the wanton boy of Hellenistic literature—is best explained as the combination of the traditional portrayal of the enchanted suitor with the literary stereotype. It is notable that throughout his relationship with Psyche—except when she breaks the taboo by gazing on him in his sleep—the wanton boy with his torch and arrows is wholly absent; on the other hand, in his dealings with his mother Venus and with other deities, including Jupiter, he is invariably depicted as the mischievous ne'er-do-well. Venus is a composite of a purely literary kind, depicted with affectionate ribaldry now as the irascible Juno of the *Aeneid*, now as the self-inflating creator of all new life as in Lucretius, now as the prickly Aphrodite in Apollonius Rhodius.[54]

Psyche's portrayal is even more diverse. Initially she is cast in the role of Chariton's Callirhoe, the sweet heroine of the Greek love-romance. When her father exposes her as bidden on a deserted rock, she becomes the tragic heroine like an Iphigenia or a Polyxena. After her sisters have persuaded her that she must behead her monstrous husband, she acts the irresolute heroine as depicted in the dramas of Euripides and Seneca, and (more directly) in the *Metamorphoses* of Ovid. When, now pregnant, she embarks on her journey of pilgrimage through the world, she becomes a second Io, the

---

[53] For the texts in the *Palatine Anthology* see Walsh, *Roman Novel*, 195 f. For the representations in art, C. C. Schlam, *Cupid and Psyche: Apuleius and the Monuments* (*APA*, University Park, 1976), esp. 4 ff.

[54] For Venus playing the role of Juno and of Lucretius' Venus, see 4.29–30; for the reincarnation of Aphrodite in Apollonius Rhodius, 5.29; see also the endnotes on those sections.

mortal maiden pursued by a goddess's spite in Aeschylus and
Ovid. In the final trial imposed by Venus, when she must visit
Hades, she becomes a second Aeneas. These are the more
sustained evocations, but throughout the story Apuleius the
literary opportunist (to exploit the phrase without denigra-
tion) entertains his learned readers with a host of poetic
reminiscences from Greek and Latin predecessors.[55]

VIII

It is salutary to recall that the influential *Nachleben* of *The
Golden Ass* from the time of the Italian Renaissance onwards
depended on the precarious survival of a single manuscript **F**
(Florence Laur. 68.2), copied at Monte Cassino in the late
eleventh century. This manuscript derives ultimately from a
double recension made by a certain Sallustius, first at Rome in
395 and then at Constantinople in 397. At that date the
pagan Macrobius and the Christian Augustine attest their
knowledge of the romance; a century later Fulgentius, bishop
of Ruspe in North Africa, indicates that it was still being read
in that province. But it is hardly surprising that Apuleius'
philosophical works were more in evidence in the ensuing
Christian centuries.[56]

The eleventh-century Manuscript **F**, illegible at some
points, was happily copied a century or two later, probably
also at Monte Cassino. This copy, identified by the siglum φ,
usefully supplements the readings of **F**, though the scribe was
negligent. During the Italian Renaissance of the fourteenth
and fifteenth centuries further copies were made, not from **F**
or φ, but from another copy of **F** subsequently lost; the text as

[55] Most recently gathered in Kenney's excellent commentary. For Psyche as a
second Callirhoe, 4.28 and Chariton 1. 1. 2; for the irresolute heroine in Ovid,
Kenney on 5.21. For Psyche as a second Io (cf. Ovid, *Met.* 1. 588 ff.), see Walsh,
Roman Novel, 52 f. On Psyche and Aeneas, Ellen Finkelpearl, *TAPA* (1990), 333 ff.
On Apuleius' exploitation of Virgil in general, C. Lazzarini, *Studi Classici e Orientali*
(Pisa, 1985), 131 ff.

[56] For Macrobius and Augustine, nn. 24 and 1 above. For Fulgentius' allegorical
interpretation of *Cupid and Psyche*, see *Mitologiae* 3. 6 (ed. Helm, the text is reproduced
in Binder and Merkelbach, *Amor und Psyche*, 435 ff.)

now established is based primarily on **F** and φ, and to a minor degree on readings from these Renaissance copies. The autograph copy of Boccaccio (Florence Laur. 54. 32) survives as a literary curiosity, but is of no importance for the establishment of the text.[57]

A textual curiosity worthy of note is the *spurcum additamentum* inserted in φ after the first sentence of 10.21 but omitted from all modern editions and accordingly not included in this translation. The hand has been identified as that of Zanobi da Strada (d. 1361), who may have been responsible for conveying this and other manuscripts from Monte Cassino to Florence.[58]

Following the pioneering commentary of Beroaldus published at Bologna in 1500, other notable annotated editions were produced by Oudendorp (Leiden, 1786) and Hildebrand (Leipzig, 1842). These established the scholarly base for a trinity of notable modern editions, those of Helm (Leipzig, 1909, rev. 1955), Giarratano-Frassinetti (Turin, 1960), and Robertson (Paris, 1940; repr. 1956), on the last of which this translation is based.[59]

IX

In the half-century following publication of the *editio princeps* by Bussi in 1469, further imprints of all Apuleius' works appeared at Vicenza, Venice, Milan, and Florence, and separate editions of *The Golden Ass* at Bologna and Venice. (Even a century before 1469, Petrarch and Boccaccio had possessed their own copies; Boccaccio not only offered an allegorized interpretation of *Cupid and Psyche*, but also

---

[57] For the history of the text, see D. S. Robertson's introduction to the Budé edn. of the *Met.* (Paris, 1940); and earlier in *CQ* (1924), 27 ff., 85 ff. There are briefer accounts by P. K. Marshall in L. D. Reynolds (ed.), *Texts and Transmission* (Oxford, 1983), and in Kenney, *Cupid and Psyche*, 38.

[58] On the *spurcum additamentum*, E. Fraenkel, *Eranos* (1953), 151 ff. On Zanobi's role in conveying the MSS to Florence, G. Billanovich, *I primi umanisti* (Fribourg, 1953), 31 ff.

[59] For a useful tabulation of editions and commentaries, see Hijmans and van der Paardt, *Aspects*, 247.

incorporated three of the adultery-stories from Book 9 into his
Decameron.) The romance gained an even wider circulation in
1518, when following the influential commentary of
Beroaldus (1500), Boiardo's celebrated translation was
published in 1518, to be followed thirty years later by
Firenzuola's free version, which through numerous reprints
became one of the most widely read books in Western Europe.
The book promoted an explosion of social satire on the central
theme of *asinità*, in which Giordano Bruno was especially
prominent.[60]

Meanwhile in Spain López de Cortegana, archdeacon of
Seville, had exploited Beroaldus' commentary to produce his
Spanish translation, probably in 1525. This was to exercise
considerable influence on the birth of the picaresque in Spain.
Lazarillo de Tormes (1554) contains no direct verbal
reminiscences, but the general similarities of the I-narrative,
the emphasis on the role of Fortune, the satire directed against
men of religion, and the characterization of the hero all
suggest Apuleian influence. Aleman's *Guzmán de Alfarache*
(1599) more obviously reflects the influence of *The Golden Ass*;
not only is Guzmán repeatedly described as an ass, but the
novel contains a description of a festival of Isis. In other
Spanish novels of the period, such as Úbeda's *La picara Justina*
(1605) and Vincente Espinel's *Vida del escudero Marcos de
Obregon* (1618), the debt to Apuleius is either acknowledged or
clearly implicit. Whether Cervantes was directly evoking
Apuleius in his *Don Quixote* is controverted, but certain scenes,
especially Lucius' engagement with the wineskins, reappear
in the Spanish novel.[61]

---

[60] For the early edns. of Apuleius, see J. E. Sandys, *A History of Classical Scholarship*
(Cambridge, 1903–8), ii. 96. For Boccaccio's allegorization of *Cupid and Psyche*, *De
genealogiis* (op. cit. n. 33 above), 5.22; the adultery-tales, see endnotes on 9.4 and 9.
22. For the translations by Boiardo and Firenzuola, see A. Scobie in Hijmans and van
der Paardt, *Aspects*, 214 ff. For the subsequent explosion of *asinità*, see E. H. Haight,
Apuleius and his Influence (London, 1927), 117 ff., underlining the importance of
Bruno.

[61] See Walsh, *Roman Novel*, 235 ff., for discussion of such Apuleian influence; more
cautious estimates in A. Scobie, *Aspects of the Ancient Romance* (Meisenheim, 1969),
91 ff., and Hijmans and van der Paardt, *Aspects*, 218 ff.

In Germany the Latin romance was translated by Johann Sieder (1538), in France by Michel (1522) and again by Louveau (1586), and in England by William Adlington, Fellow of University College Oxford (1566). Adlington's version, heavily indebted to his Continental predecessors, was immediately 'ransacked to furnish the playhouses of London'; it went through five editions by 1600. Aside from dramatic performances, 'almost every one of the major English writers of the period . . . made use of *The Golden Asse*, sometimes along with the Latin original'. Sidney's *Arcadia*, Spenser's *The Faerie Queene*, Marlowe's *Hero and Leander*, Milton's *Comus* and *Paradise Regained* exemplify this adaptation of Apuleian themes in non-dramatic works. Shakespeare among dramatists is the exemplar *par excellence* of those who repeatedly evoke episodes, and indeed the language, of Adlington's rendering of the romance.[62]

Of the Shakespearian plays *A Midsummer Night's Dream* reflects the clearest influence; it is true that works such as Reginald Scot's *Discovery of Witchcraft* (1584) may also have been influential, but the two features of Bottom's transformation into an ass, and Titania's obsessive attachment to his animal form, make the thesis of direct borrowing from Apuleius persuasive. In *Much Ado About Nothing*, in which Dogberry on six occasions describes himself as an ass, there are several scenes and incidents which recall the privations of Lucius. Even more obvious is the parallel between Othello and Psyche, as both plan the execution of their spouses. Both victims awake as the assassins address the light ('Put out the light, and then put out the light.'). Just as a drop of burning oil from Psyche's lamp falls on the recumbent Cupid, so a tear from Othello's eye awakens Desdemona. Similarities of

---

[62] For the later influence of *The Golden Ass* in Germany, see A. Rode and E. Burck, *Metamorphosen oder Der goldene Esel* (Hamburg, 1961), 256 ff., for the French translations, R. R. Bolgar, *The Classical Heritage and its Beneficiaries* (Cambridge, 1954), 526. The quotations (the first reproduced from Stephen Gosson (1582)) are to be found in J. J.M. Tobin, *Shakespeare's Favorite Novel* (University Press of America, Lanham, Md., 1984), p. xiii. I have derived the substance of this and the next paragraph from Tobin's book.

language in this scene make the inspiration from *The Golden Asse* clear-cut. *Hamlet*, too, with similarities of episodes (poisoned husband, widow warned by husband's ghost, sexual tension between stepmother and stepson as in Apuleius' inserted stories), contains striking verbal expressions unique in the Shakespearian canon and occurring in Adlington. This is a mere selection of the more obvious parallels; less conspicuous echoes from Apuleius can be cited from other plays of Shakespeare.[63]

The influence of *Cupid and Psyche* on the art and literature of post-Renaissance Europe is even more pervasive. The reflection in art begins with Raphael's famous frescos in the Villa Farnesina, which portray twelve facets of the love-relationship. Raphael's pupil, Pierino del Vaga, similarly painted nine panels on the theme in the Castel Sant' Angelo. Giulio Romano in the Palazzo del Tè at Mantua depicted a running sequence of episodes from the story. From this period onward many of the greatest painters of Europe, including Titian, Caravaggio, Rubens, Velasquez, and Van Dyck, pay their tribute to the love-theme. The subject is prominent in the history of tapestry, as Boucher's eighteenth-century sets demonstrate. In sculpture perhaps the most famous representations are those of Canova and Rodin.[64]

We have already noted some of the creative writers on whom *Cupid and Psyche* exercised a potent spell, including Boccaccio and Spenser, whose *Faerie Queene* contains a poetic summary of the story. Heywood's *Love's Mistris*, a dramatic exposition of the *conte*, was staged by Inigo Jones before King James I in 1636. In his Preface, Heywood says: 'The Argument is taken from Apuleius, an excellent Morall if truely understood . . .'. A year later his friend Marmion published,

---

[63] On *A Midsummer Night's Dream*, J. Dover Wilson, *Shakespeare's Happy Comedies* (Evanston, Ill., 1963), points to seven close similarities with *The Golden Ass*. For the ass-references in *Much Ado About Nothing*, see esp. IV. ii and V. i. *Othello* reflects Apuleian influence esp. in V. ii. *Hamlet* reveals 'the pervasive use of *The Golden Ass*' (so Tobin, *Shakespeare's Favorite Novel*, 86). Tobin analyses the plays of Shakespeare in chronological order to demonstrate the extraordinary influence which Adlington's translation exercised on him throughout his composition of them.

[64] See Haight, *Apuleius and his Influence*, 171 ff.

in heroic couplets, 'a Morall Poem intituled the Legend of Cupid and Psyche', an allegorical epic in two books. Another celebrated seventeenth-century production was Joseph Beaumont's *Psyche, or Love's Mystery* in which the author exploits the story to 'represent a soul led by divine Grace'.

The romantics of the nineteenth century revived the interest of English readers in the tale. John Keats before composing his *Ode to Psyche* had identified with the creative impulse of Apuleius ('So felt he, who first told how Psyche went | On the smooth winds to realms of wonderment'), and he prefaced the Ode with a letter which underlines the reverence with which he regarded the story. Later, William Morris in his *Earthly Paradise*, and Robert Bridges in *Eros and Psyche*, wrote poetic versions of the story, Bridges patronizingly claiming that Psyche 'deserves more care in handling the motives of her conduct than was perhaps felt in Apuleius' time and country'. Perhaps the outstanding tribute to the *conte* in the nineteenth century was the creative translation which Walter Pater enclosed in his novel *Marius the Epicurean* (1885).[65]

X

Several modern translations of Apuleius' romance have been issued. The Bohn translator (1853) claims that '*The Golden Ass* has been several times presented to the English public, but, it is believed, never so completely or faithfully';[66] like other volumes in the Bohn series, its aim is primarily to assist readers struggling with the Latin rather than to present a version to be read independently. The translation of F. D. Byrne (London, 1905) is praiseworthy; B. E. Perry considered it the best of the modern renderings. H. E. Butler's two volumes (Oxford, 1910) suffer from the squeamishness of his day; he omits passages which he regards as sexually

---

[65] Ibid. 138 ff.; see also L. C. Purser's edn. of *Cupid and Psyche* (London, 1910), pp. lxvi ff. For Apuleius and Pater, see E. J. Brenk in Hijmans and van der Paardt, *Aspects*, 231 ff.

[66] Doubtless with reference to the versions of Thomas Taylor (London, 1822), and of Sir George Head (London, 1851), as well as to that of Adlington.

indelicate without offering any indication of where his axe falls. Moreover, he is out of sympathy with Apuleius' flamboyant presentation, simplistically condemning 'a style which, by whatever canons it be judged, was intrinsically bad'. In North America, Jack Lindsay's racy version (New York, 1932) is widely popular, but it contains many errors and some infelicities.

Finally comes Robert Graves's Penguin version (1950), recently reissued with a foreword and some tactful revision by Michael Grant. The poet-craftsman's enviably supple use of the English language makes this translation attractive to read independently of the Latin, but it is by no means always faithful to the original, and in places seems merely to offer a paraphrase of Adlington. Of Graves a similar judgement can be passed as of Adlington; literary skill and versatility, not exact scholarship, is the primary requirement for the popular success of a translation. There is a disastrous exordium with 'Apuleius' address to the reader', in which the miniature biography which belongs to the hero Lucius is attached to the author; the translation misleads at some points and condenses at others. But the jocose spirit of the original is well captured, and one may confidently predict an extended life for this version.

Any justification of a new translation rests largely on the claim that greater understanding of the Latinity of Apuleius has been achieved over the past half-century. Robertson's text has provided a more satisfactory base. The new critical editions of individual books, notably those produced at Groningen and the two British contributions of Kenney (*Cupid and Psyche*) and Gwyn Griffiths (Book 11) are particularly useful in this respect. The new Loeb version of J. A. Hanson (1989), which has replaced that of Gaselee, is admirable in every respect. I have constantly consulted it. Kenney's facing translation in his edition of *Cupid and Psyche* has also furnished valuable aid.

SELECT BIBLIOGRAPHY

This is a selection of the more important publications of recent years. For fuller bibliographies, consult from the list below Scobie, *Comm. on Met. I*, 6 ff.; Gwyn Griffiths, 360 ff.; Hijmans-van der Paardt, *Aspects*, 247 ff.; Schlam, *The Metamorphoses*, 157 ff.; Kenney, *Cupid and Psyche*, 226 ff. See also G. N. Sandy, *CW* (1974), 321 ff. (*ANRW* announces that in its forthcoming volume, II. 34. 2 (?1994), the following contributions will appear: G. Sandy, 'Apuleius' *Metamorphoses* and the Ancient Novel'; W. S. Smith, 'Style and Character in *The Golden Ass*: "Suddenly an Opposite Appearance" '; L. Callebat, 'Traditions formelles et création de langage dans l'œuvre d'Apulée'; H. J. Mason, 'Greek and Latin Versions of the Ass Story'; B. L. Hijmans, 'Apuleius Orator: *Pro se de magia* (*Apologia*) and *Florida*'; M. G. Bajoni, 'Il linguaggio filosofico di Apuleio: aspetti linguistici e letterari del *De mundo*'.)

1. *Editions and Commentaries*

R. HELM, *Apulei opera quae supersunt* (Leipzig, 1907; repr. with additions, 1955).

C. GIARRATANO and P. FRASSINETTI, *Apulei Metamorphoses Libri XI* (Turin, 1960).

D. S. ROBERTSON and P. VALLETTE, *Apulée: Les Métamorphoses* (Paris, Budé, 1940–5).

A. SCOBIE, *Apuleius: Metamorphoses I* (Meisenheim am Glan, 1975).

R. T. VAN DER PAARDT, *A Commentary on Book III* (Amsterdam, 1971).

B. L. HIJMANS *et al.*, *Metamorphoses IX* Groningen, 1995).

B. L. HIJMANS Jun., A. TH. VAN DER PAARDT, *et al.*, *Book IV. 1–27* (Groningen, 1977).

P. GRIMAL, *Apulei Metamorphoseis IV. 28–VI. 24* (Paris, 1963).

E. J. KENNEY, *Cupid and Psyche* (Cambridge, 1990).

B. L. HIJMANS *et al.*, *Books VI. 25–VII* (Groningen, 1981).

—— *Book VIII* (Groningen, 1985).

J. GWYN GRIFFITHS, *Apuleius of Madauros: The Isis-Book* (Leiden, 1975).

J. C. FREDOUILLE, *Apulée: Métamorphoses Liber XI* (Paris, 1975).

Philosophical Works

J. BEAUJEU, *Apulée: Opuscules philosophiques* (Paris, Budé, 1973).

Apology and Florida

P. VALLETTE, *Apulée: Apologie, Florides*[2] (Paris, Budé, 1960).
B. MOSCA, *Apuleio: La Magia* (Florence, 1974).

Lucius or the Ass

M. D. MACLEOD, *Lucian VIII* (London, Loeb, 1967).

2. *Translations*

(Eng.) F. D. BYRNE, *The Golden Ass of Apuleius* (London, 1905).
H. E. BUTLER, *The Metamorphoses or Golden Ass of Apuleius of Madaura* (Oxford, 1910).
J. LINDSAY, *The Golden Ass of Apuleius* (New York, 1932).
R. GRAVES, *The Transformations of Lucius* (Harmondsworth, 1950).
J. A. HANSON, *Apuleius, Metamorphoses* (new Loeb edn. London, 1989).
E. J. KENNEY, *Apuleius, The Golden Ass* (Harmondsworth, 1998).
(Fr.) P. GRIMAL, *Romans grecs et latins* (Paris, 1958).
(Ger.) A. RODE and E. BURCK, *Metamorfosen oder Der goldene Esel* (Hamburg, 1961).
(Ital.) Q. CATAUDELLA (ed.), *Il romanzo antico greco e latino* (Florence, 1973).

3. *General*

ANDERSON, G. *Eros Sophistes: Ancient Novelists at Play* (APA, Chico, Calif., 1982).
—— *The Novel in the Graeco-Roman World* (Beckenham, 1984).
BERNHARD, M., *Der Stil des Apuleius von Madaura* (repr. Amsterdam, 1965).
BIANCO, G., *La fonte greca delle Metamorfosi di Apuleio* (Brescia, 1971).
BINDER, G., and MERKELBACH, R. (eds.), *Amor und Psyche* (Wege der Forschung 126, Darmstadt, 1968. Incl. essays by P. Grimal, L. Friedländer, F. Liebrecht, G. Heinrici, R. Reitzenstein, R. Helm, D. Weinreich, H. Jeanmaire, L. Bieler, H. Erbse, H. Wagenfoort, R. Merkelbach, S. Lancel).
CALLEBAT, L., *Sermo Cotidianus dans les Métamorphoses d'Apulée* (Caen, 1968).
CIAFFI, V., *Petronio in Apuleio* (Turin, 1960).
DERCHAIN, P., and HUBEAUX, J., 'L'affaire du marché à Hypata dans la Mét. d'Apulée', *AC* (1958), 100 ff.
DILLON, J., *The Middle Platonists* (Ithaca, NY, 1977).

DOWDEN, K., 'Apuleius and the Art of Narration', *CQ* (1982), 419 ff.

—— 'Psyche on the Rock', *Latomus* (1982), 336 ff.

DRAKE, G., 'Candidus. A Unifying Theme in Apuleius' *Met.*', *CJ* (1968/9), 102 ff.

—— 'Lucius' "Business" in the *Met.* of Apuleius', *PLL* (1969), 339 ff.

—— 'The Ghost Story in The Golden Ass by Apuleius', *PLL* (1977), 3 ff.

ENGLERT, J., and LONG, T., 'Functions of Hair in Apuleius' *Met.*', *CJ* (1972/3), 236 ff.

FEHLING, D., *Amor und Psyche* (Wiesbaden, 1977).

FERGUSON, J., 'Apuleius', *G&R* (1961), 61 ff.

FESTUGIÈRE, A. J., *Personal Religion among the Greeks* (Berkeley, Calif., 1960).

FINKELPEARL, E., 'Psyche, Aeneas and an Ass: *Met.* 6. 10–21', *TAPA* (1990), 333 ff.

—— 'The Judgment of Lucius: *Met.* 10. 29–34', *CA* (1990), 221 ff.

FLIEDNER, H., *Amor und Cupido* (Meisenheim, 1974)

FORBES, C., 'Charite and Dido', *CW* (1943), 39 f.

GRIMAL, P., 'Le calame égyptien d'Apulée', *REA* (1971), 343 ff.

Groningen Colloquia 1981 (ed. B. L. Hijmans and V. Schmidt), 1988 (ed. H. Hofmann).

HÄGG, T., *The Novel in Antiquity* (Oxford, 1983).

HAIGHT, E. H., *Apuleius and his Influence* (London, 1927).

—— 'Apuleius and Boccaccio', in *More Essays on Greek Romances* (New York, 1945), 113 ff.

HANI, J., 'L'âne d'or et l'Égypte', *RP* (1973), 274 ff.

HEISERMAN, A., *The Novel before the Novel* (Chicago, 1977).

HELLER, S., 'Apuleius, Platonic Dualism, and Eleven', *AJP* (1983), 321 ff.

HERRMANN, L., L'Ane d'Or et le Christianisme', *Latomus* (1953), 188 ff.

HICTER, M., *Apulée, Conteur Fantastique* (Brussels, 1942).

—— 'L'autobiographie dans l'âne d'or d'Apulée'. *AC* (1944), 95 ff., (1945), 61 ff.

HIJMANS, B. L., and VAN DER PAARDT, R. TH. (eds.), *Aspects of Apuleius' Golden Ass* (Groningen, 1978). Incl: H. J. Mason, 'Fabula Graecanica: Apuleius and his Greek Sources'; P. G. Walsh, 'Petronius and Apuleius'; R. Heine, 'Picaresque Novel versus Allegory'; A. Scobie, 'The Structure of Apuleius' Met.';

A. G. Westerbrink, 'Some parodies in Apuleius' Met.'; R. Th. van der Paardt, 'Various Aspects of Narrative Technique in Apuleius' *Met.*'; C. C. Schlam, 'Sex and Sanctity: the Relationship of Male and Female in Apuleius' *Met.*'; B. L. Hijmans, 'Significant Names and their Function in Apuleius' *Met.*'; G. N. Sandy, 'Book 11; Ballast or Anchor?'; J. Cwyn Griffiths, 'Isis in the *Met.* of Apuleius'; A. Scobie, 'The Influence of Apuleius' *Met.* in Renaissance Italy and Spain'; E. J. Brenk, 'Apuleius, Pater, and the Bildungsroman'; (also papers by L. Callebat and B. L. Hijmans on prose-style, and by E. Visser on Coupcrus and Apuleius)).

JAMES, P. *Unity in Diversity* (Hildesheim, 1987).

JONES, C. P., 'Apuleius' *Met.* and Lollianus' Phoinikika', *Phoenix* (1980), 243 ff.

JUNGHANNS, P., *Die Erzählungstechnik von Apuleius' Met. und ihrer Vorlage* (Leipzig, 1932).

KENNEY, F. J., 'Psyche and her Mysterious Husband', in D. A. Russell (ed.), *Antonine Literature* (Oxford, 1990), 175 ff.

KENNY, B., 'The Reader's Role in The Golden Ass', *Arethusa* (1974), 187 ff.

KRABBE, J. K., *The Metamorphoses of Apuleius* (New York, 1989).

LABHARDT, A., '*Curiositas*: notes sur l'histoire d'un mot et d'une notion', *Mus. Helv.* (1960), 206 ff.

LANCEL, S., '*Curiositas* et préoccupations spirituelles chez Apulée', *RHR* (1961), 25 ff.

LAZZARINI, C., 'Il modello Virgiliano nel lessico delle *Met.* di Apuleio', *Studi Classici e Orientali* (Pisa, 1985), 131 ff.

LESKY, A., 'Apuleius von Madaura und Lukios von Patrai', *Hermes* (1941), 43 ff.

MACKAY, L. A., 'The Sin of the Golden Ass', *Arion* (1965), 474 ff.

MARTIN, R., 'Le sens de l'expression Asinus Aureus et la signification du roman apuléen', *RÉL* (1970), 332 ff.

MASON, H. J., 'Lucius at Corinth', *Phoenix* (1971), 160 ff.

—— 'The distinction of Lucius in Apuleius' *Met.*', Phoenix (1983), 135 ff.

MAZZARINO, A., *La Milesia e Apuleio* (Turin, 1950).

MERKELBACH, R., *Roman und Mysterium in der Antike* (Munich, 1962).

METTE, H. J., 'Curiositas', in H. Erbse, (ed.), *Festschr. Bruno Snell* (Munich, 1956), 227 ff.

MEYRHOFER, C., 'On Two Stories in Apuleius', *Antichthon* (1975), 8 ff.

MILLAR, F., 'The World of the Golden Ass', *JRS* (1981), 63 ff.

MORESCHINI, C., 'La demonologia medioplatonica et le *Met.* di Apuleio', *Maia* (1965), 30 ff.

—— *Apuleio e il Platonismo* (Florence, 1978).

NETHERCUT, W., 'Apuleius' Literary Art; Resonance and Depth in the Met.', *CJ* (1968), 110 ff.

NEUMANN, E., *Amor and Psyche* (New York, 1962).

NOCK, A. D., *Conversion* (Oxford, 1933).

NORDEN, F., *Apulejus von Madaura und das römische Privatrecht* (Leipzig, 1912).

NORWOOD, F., 'The Magic Pilgrimage of Apuleius', *Phoenix* (1956), 1 ff.

PARATORE, E., *La novella in Apuleio*[2] (Messina, 1942).

PENWILL, J. L., 'Slavish Pleasures and Profitless Curiosity', *Ramus* (1975), 49 ff.

PERRY, B. E., *The Ancient Romances* (Berkeley, Calif., 1967) (cf. *CP* (1923), 229 ff., (1929), 231 ff.; *TAPA* (1923), 196 ff., (1926), 238 ff.); *CJ* (1968/9), 97 ff.)

REGEN, F., *Apuleius Philosophus Platonicus* (Berlin, 1971).

REITZENSTEIN, R., *Hellenistische Wunderezählungen* (Stuttgart, 1963)

RIEFSTAHL, H., *Der Roman des Apuleius* (Frankfurt, 1938).

SANDY, G., *The Greek World of Apuleius* (Leiden, 1997).

SANDY, G. N., 'Knowledge and Curiosity in Apuleius' *Met.*', *Latomus* (1972), 179 ff.

—— 'Foreshadowing and Suspense in Apuleius' *Met.*', *CJ* (1973), 232 ff.

—— '*Serviles voluptates* in Apuleius' *Met.*', *Phoenix* (1974), 234 ff.

SCAZZOSO, P., *Le Metamorfosi di Apuleio* (Milan, 1951).

SCHLAM, C. C., 'The Curiosity of the Golden Ass', *CJ* (1968), 120 ff.

—— 'Platonica in the *Metamorphoses* of Apuleius', *TAPA* (1970), 477 ff.

—— *Cupid and Psyche: Apuleius and the Monuments* (*APA*, Penn., 1976).

—— 'Apuleius and the Middle Ages', in Bernardo and Levin (eds.), *The Classics in the Middle Ages* (Binghampton, NY, 1990), 363 ff.

—— *The Metamorphoses of Apuleius* (Chapel Hill, NC, 1992).

SCOBIE, A., *Aspects of the Ancient Romance and its Heritage* (Meisenheim, 1969).

—— *More Essays on the Ancient Romance and its Heritage* (Meisenheim, 1973).

—— *Apuleius and Folklore* (London, 1983).

SHUMATE, N., 'The Augustinian Pursuit of False Values as a Conversion Motif in Apuleius' *Met.*', *Phoenix* (1988), 35 ff.

SHUMATE, N., *Crisis and Conversion in Apuleius' Metamorphoses* (Ann Arbor, 1996).

SMET, R. DE 'The Erotic Adventures of Lucius and Photis in Apuleius' *Met.*', *Latomus* (1987), 613 ff.

SMITH, W. S., 'The Narrative Voice in Apuleius' *Met.*', *TAPA* (1972), 513 ff.

STABRYLA, S., 'The Functions of the Tale of Cupid and Psyche in the Structure of the *Met.* of Apuleius', *Eos* (1973), 261 ff.

STEPHENS, S. A., and WINKLER, J. J., *Ancient Greek Novels* (Princeton, 1995).

STEPHENSON, W. E., 'The Comedy of Evil' in Apuleius', *Arion* (1964), 87 ff.

SUMMERS, R. G., 'Apuleius Juridicus', *Historia* (1972), 120 ff.

—— 'A Note on the date of the Golden Ass', *AJP* (1973), 375 ff.

SWAHN, J. Ö., *The Tale of Cupid and Psyche* (Lund, 1955).

TATUM, J., 'The Tales in Apuleius' Metamorphoses', *TAPA* (1969), 487 ff.

—— 'Apuleius and Metamorphosis', *AJP* (1972), 306 ff.

—— *Apuleius and The Golden Ass* (Ithaca, NY, 1979).

THIBAU, R., 'Les Mét. d'Apulée et la théorie Platonicienne de l'Eros', *Stud. Phil. Gand.* (1965), 89 ff.

TOBIN, J. J. M., *Shakespeare's Favorite Novel* (New York, 1984) (cf. also *Shakespeare Survey* (1978), 33 ff.; *English Studies* (1978), 199 ff.; *Studia Neophilologica* (1979), 225 ff.; *Notes and Queries* (1978), 120 f.

VAN DER PAARDT, R. 'The Unmasked "I"; Apuleius, *Met.* XI 27', *Mnem.* (1981), 96 ff.

VAN THIEL, H., *Der Eselsroman* (2 vols. Munich, 1971).

VEYNE, P., 'Apulée a Cenchrées', *RP* (1965), 241 ff.

WALSH, P. G., 'Was Lucius a Roman?' *CJ* (1968), 264 ff.

—— *The Roman Novel* (Cambridge, 1970).

—— 'Apuleius and Plutarch', in H. J. Blumenthal and R. A. Markus (eds.), *Neoplatonism and Early Christian Thought* (London, 1981), 20 ff.

—— 'Apuleius', in E. J. Kenney and W. K. Clausen (eds.), *The Cambridge History of Classical Literature* (Cambridge, 1982), 774 ff.

—— 'The Rights and Wrongs of Curiosity', *G&R* (1988), 73 ff.

WINKLER, J. J., *Auctor & Actor* (Berkeley, Calif., 1985).

WLOSOK, A., 'Zur Einheit der *Met.* des Apuleius'. *Philol.* (1969), 68 ff.

WRIGHT, C. S., 'No Art at all. A Note on the Procmium of Apuleius' *Met.*', *CP* (1973), 217 ff.

WRIGHT, J. R. G., 'Folk-Tale and Literary Technique in *Cupid and Psyche*, *CQ* (1971), 273 ff.

BOOK I

Journey to Hypata: The Exemplar of Socrates

1 What I should like to do is to weave together different tales
in this Milesian mode of story-telling and to stroke your
approving ears with some elegant whispers, as long as you
don't disdain to run your eye over Egyptian paper inscribed
with the sharpened point of a reed from the Nile. I want you
to feel wonder at the transformations of men's shapes and
destinies into alien forms, and their reversion by a chain of
interconnection to their own. So let me begin! Who is the
narrator? Let me briefly explain: my antique stock is from
Attic Hymettus, the Ephyrean Isthmus, and Spartan Taenarus,
fertile territories established for ever in yet more fertile works
of literature. In those regions, in the initial campaigns of
boyhood, I became a veteran in Attic speech. Later in Rome,
as a stranger to the literary pursuits of the citizens there, I
tackled and cultivated the native language without the
guidance of a teacher, and with excruciating difficulty. So at
the outset I beg your indulgence for any mistakes which I
make as a novice in the foreign language in use at the Roman
bar. This switch of languages in fact accords with the
technique of composition which I have adopted, much as a
circus-rider leaps from one horse to another, for the romance
on which I am embarking is adapted from the Greek. Give it
your attention, dear reader, and it will delight you.

2 I was on my way to Thessaly to transact some business. My
family on my mother's side hails from that region, and the
prominence lent to it by the famous philosopher Plutarch, and
later by his nephew Sextus, lends us esteem. I was riding on
my home-bred horse, which is pure white in colour. After we
had crossed high mountain tracks, slippery paths in the
valleys, dew-laden pastures, and churned-up ploughlands, I
dismounted, for the horse was now tired, and I too needed to
invigorate myself by walking, for I was saddle-sore. I

attentively wiped the sweat from the horse's brow, fondled his
ears, loosened the reins, and took him along at a slow and
gentle pace until nature in its usual protective way could
relieve the strain of his tiredness. With his head bent low and
his mouth turned sideways, he took a walking breakfast from
the fields through which he passed. In the course of the walk,
I made myself a third to two companions who happened to be
journeying a little way ahead. I overheard what they were
saying. One of them guffawed, and said: 'Spare me this tissue
of crazy and monstrous lies.' Now I am always interested in
unusual stories, so on hearing this I demurred, and said: 'Do
tell me all about it. I am not inquisitive, but am the type
which likes to know about everything, or at least about most
things. And your elegant and amusing tales will lighten the
rigours of the hill which we are beginning to climb.'

3   But the man who had spoken earlier said: 'Surely this lying
tale of yours is only as true as the claim that when magic
formulae are whispered, running rivers go backward, the sea
is stopped and becomes idle, the winds die down and cease to
blow, the course of the sun is halted, the moon runs dry of
dew, the stars are plucked from the sky, daylight is blotted
out, and darkness prevails.' At this I broke in with some
assurance. 'Come on,' I urged the story-teller, 'don't be
ashamed or reluctant to spin out the rest of the story, now that
you have recounted the earlier part.' Then I addressed the
other man. 'Because your ears are deadened and your mind is
closed, you are contemptuous of reports that may well be true.
Heavens, man, you aren't too bright in your quite perverse
belief that all that seems unfamiliar to the ear, or unprecedented to the eye, or even too hard for our thoughts to
grasp, is to be accounted lies. Investigate such features a little
more carefully, and you will find that they are not merely
open to discovery, but are also easily performed.

4   'For example, yesterday evening I was trying to compete
with fellow-guests in greedily bolting down a largish portion
of cheesecake. Because the stuff was so soft and sticky, it stuck
in my throat and impeded my breathing so that I very nearly
choked. Yet recently at Athens I saw with my own two eyes a

contortionist performing in front of the Painted Porch; he swallowed a razor-sharp cavalry-sword with a lethal point. Then he was offered a small coin, and this encouraged him to thrust a hunting-spear deep into his gizzard, with the mortally dangerous end going in first. Then to my astonishment a handsome nancy-boy climbed up above the metal section, where the upturned shaft protruded from the man's throat up towards his head. With sinuous movements he performed a ballet-routine as though there was not a single sinew or bone in his body. Everyone watching was amazed; you would have said that it was the noble serpent which coils itself in slippery embraces round the staff of the god of healing, that knotted club with half-sheared branches which the god carries round with him. So do, please, now run through the story again which you had begun. I'll believe it, if this man won't, and I'll stand you lunch at the first inn we reach on our journey. That is the reward that I have in store for you.'

5 The man replied: 'There is no need for your fair and kind offer. I'll certainly embark on the story I began earlier, but first I'll swear to you by the sun-god who gazes down on us that what I'm telling you is true. You will harbour no further doubts once you reach the next town in Thessaly, because what happened for the world to see is common gossip there. But first let me tell you where I'm from: I'm a native of Aegium. You should hear as well how I make a living: I trade in honey, cheese, and the like with the women who run hostelries, and I journey to and fro throughout Thessaly, Aetolia, and Boeotia. So when I heard that some fresh and succulent cheese was on the market for a modest price at Hypata, the leading city in all Thessaly, I made my way quickly there to buy the lot. But I got off on the wrong foot, as often happens, and was disappointed in my hope of profit, because a wholesale merchant called Lupus had bought it all up the previous day. I was exhausted by this fruitless dash, so I made my way to the baths just as the evening star came up.

6 'Whom should I spy there but my old friend Socrates? He was sitting on the ground, only half-covered by a torn and dingy cloak, so pale as to be almost unrecognizable, and

shrunk to a mere shadow, like one of Fortune's outcasts who often beg for pennies at street-corners. I approached him because he was a close and intimate friend, but with some reluctance because of his appearance. "Good Lord, Socrates, whatever is the matter? How ghastly you look! What a scandal this is! They are weeping and mourning your death at home. Guardians have been appointed for your children by decree of the provincial judge. Your wife has performed the routine of mourning; she is ravaged after months of grief and sorrow, her eyes almost blind with weeping. Her parents are urging her to lighten the unhappiness of the household with the joys of a new marriage. And here you are, looking like a ghost, and bringing down the utmost shame on us!"

' "Aristomenes," said Socrates, "it is clear that you are innocent of the treacherous twists and turns, the unsteady assaults and see-sawing changes our fortunes bring." As he spoke, he drew his patched cloak over his face, which had been blushing with embarrassment all this time, with the result that he uncovered the rest of his body from the navel to his private parts. At that moment I could bear the wretched sight of his hardships no longer. I took his hand, and tried to bring him to his feet.

7   'But he would not budge, and kept his head covered. "Leave me, let me be!" he cried, "Let Fortune feast her eyes longer on me as the token of her victory!" But I induced him to accompany me, and at the same time I slipped off one of my two shirts, and hastily clothed him, or rather covered him up. There and then I hauled him off to the baths, coughed up for the oil and towels, and vigorously scrubbed off a huge deposit of filth. Once he was well cleaned up, I took him to an inn, supporting his exhausted body with great difficulty, for I too was tired out. I made him lie down to recover, gave him a good meal and a relieving drink, and chatted with him to enable him to relax. In no time he showed an eager desire to talk; he joked, even indulging in some clever repartee and unassuming wit. But then he heaved a tortured sigh from the depths of his heart, and beat his forehead repeatedly and savagely with his hand.

' "What a mess I'm in!" he began. "I have fallen into this misfortune through seeking a diversion at a celebrated gladiatorial show. You will remember that I made for Macedonia on a business-trip. I was busy there for nine months and more, and was making my way home with a good bit of money in my pocket. Shortly before reaching Larissa, where I intended to take in the show as I was passing through, I was making my way along a trackless, pitted valley when I was held up by some brigands of massive physique who robbed me of all my money. When I finally got away I stopped at an inn, because I was badly shaken up. It was run by a woman called Meroë, who was getting on in years, but was still quite attractive. I explained to her the circumstances of my long period away from home, my eagerness to get back, and the robbery that I had suffered. Her reaction was to treat me with extraordinary sympathy. She set me down without payment in front of a welcome supper, and then as she was feeling sexy she took me to her bed. From the moment I slept with her my misery began. The scourge of a long and baneful association sprang from that one act of sexual intercourse. Even the shabby clothes which those generous brigands had left me to cover my body I surrendered to her, and every penny I earned as a porter, as long as I still had my strength. So the combination of such a kind wife as this and malevolent Fortune has brought me to the condition which you have just witnessed."

8   ' "Good Lord!" I exclaimed. "You certainly deserve to suffer the worst possible fate, if there is anything worse than your recent experiences, because you put the pleasures of sex and a leather-skinned whore before your home and children." Socrates put his index-finger to his lips, registering shocked alarm. "Hush!" he said, looking round to see if it was safe to speak. "Don't mention the prophetess in case your loose tongue brings you harm."

' "Really?" I replied. "What sort of woman is this mighty queen of inn-keepers?"

' "She's a witch", he said, "with supernatural powers. She can bring down the sky, raise the earth, freeze running waters,

melt mountains, raise ghosts, dispatch gods to the world
below, black out the stars, and light up hell itself!"

'"Come, come," I said, "ring down the tragic curtain, fold
up the backcloth, and do please use the language of every
day."

'"Would you care to hear one or two of her magic feats, or
still better, a whole string of them? She makes not only the
locals fall madly in love with her, but also Indians, both lots of
Ethiopians, and even Antipodeans, but such things as these
are trivial aspects of her art, mere play. Just hear what she
brought about with dozens of people watching.

9   '"A lover of hers went after another woman. With one word
the witch transformed him into a beaver. Why a beaver?
Because that animal in fear of captivity escapes its pursuers by
biting off its own genitals, and she wanted the same fate to
befall him likewise for having made love to this other woman.
Then there was a neighbouring innkeeper competing for
custom with her; she changed him into a frog, and now the old
man swims in a barrel of his own wine, and as he squats in the
lees he greets his former customers with dutiful croaks.
Another man she changed into a ram because he was a
barrister who prosecuted her, and now it's as a ram that he
pleads his cases. Then there was the wife of a lover of hers who
was heavy with child. Because she made witty and disparaging
remarks about the witch, Meroë has condemned her to an
indefinite pregnancy by sealing up her womb and postponing
the birth. The general estimate is that the poor woman has
now been carrying her burden for eight years, and is so
misshapen it's as though she were giving birth to an elephant.

10   '"Because of these periodic outrages that brought harm to
many there was a general swell of indignation, and the
community decreed that on the following day she should
suffer the extreme punishment of stoning. But she anticipated
this plan by the potency of her spells. You remember the case
of Medea, who won a respite of a single short day from Creon,
and ignited his whole house and daughter and the old man
himself with flames which burst out from the bridal crown?
Well, Meroë confided to me recently, when she was drunk,

that she dug a trench and performed rites of black magic in it by invoking the spirits of the dead. By this means she locked the entire community in their houses by the silent powers of supernatural spirits, so that for two whole days they could not break the bars, force open the doors, or even tunnel through the walls. Eventually the citizens bolstered each other and made a united appeal to her, swearing by all that was holy that they would not lay a finger on her, and that if anyone had ideas to the contrary, they would rescue her. Once they had appeased her in this way, she set the whole town free. As for the man who had summoned the public gathering, she shifted him and his entire barred dwelling—walls, floor and foundations—to another community at dead of night. This town was a hundred miles away, perched on the tip of a rugged mountain, and waterless owing to its position. But the houses of the residents there were so closely packed that they allowed no room for a new arrival, so the witch just dumped the house in front of the town gate, and made off."

11   ' "This account of your experience", I rejoined, "is remarkable, and as harrowing as it is strange. Indeed, it has pricked me with no small anxiety or rather fear; I feel not so much niggling doubt as sharp apprehension that the old hag may exploit the aid of her supernatural power in the same way to learn of this conversation of ours. So we must retire to bed quite early, and once our tiredness is relieved by sleep, we must hasten away before dawn, and put the greatest possible distance between ourselves and this place."

'While I was still urging this course, my good friend Socrates was overcome by the unaccustomed drinking and by protracted exhaustion. He fell asleep, and began to snore quite heavily. So I closed and bolted the door, pushed my bed up against the hinges to fasten them securely, and then lay down. At first my fear kept me awake for a while, but then about half way through the night I began to nod off. I had just fallen asleep when the doors were suddenly flung open, with a violence greater than you would associate with robbers; indeed, the hinges were smashed and torn from their sockets, and the doors sent crashing to the ground. My bed was small and decrepit, and had a broken leg; it was overturned by the savage force of the assault. I myself was thrown out, and as the bed landed upside down, it covered and concealed me.

12   'At that moment I recognized that certain feelings naturally give birth to their opposites, for just as tears often flow as the result of joy, so even at that moment of extreme fear I could not restrain my laughter at being transformed from Aristomenes into a tortoise. As I lay sprawled on the ground hidden by my wise old bed, I squinted out to see what was happening, and caught sight of two elderly women. One was carrying a blazing lamp, and the other a sponge and an unsheathed sword. With these objects in their hands they stood on each side of Socrates, who was sleeping soundly. The woman with the sword spoke first: "This, sister Panthia, is my dear Endymion, my Ganymede who has abused my tender years day and night, but now considers my love beneath him. Not only does he malign me with his insults, but he is also planning his escape. I suppose I am to play the role of Calypso abandoned by the guileful Ulysses and doomed to lament my loneliness for ever!" Then she extended her finger, and pointed me out to her dear Panthia: "This good fellow", she said, "is Aristomenes the counsellor. He proposed the escape, and now he lies close to death. He is lying on the ground, stretched out beneath the bed, watching all that is going on, and thinking that he will get away scot-free with insulting me. I'll make him sorry one day—in fact I'll do it now, at this very moment—for his earlier facetiousness and his insistent curiosity."

13   'In my desperate plight as I heard this, I broke out in a cold sweat, and my stomach turned over with fright, so that my shaking even disturbed the bed, which bounded up and down in spasms on my back. Then the kindly Panthia said: "Wouldn't it be a good idea, then, sister, to deal with him first, to tear him to pieces as the frenzied Bacchants did, or to tie his legs together and cut off his manhood?" Meroë answered her; I recognized who she was, as the name accorded so well with the stories Socrates had told about her. What she said was: "No; he shall live at least long enough to

bury this wretch's body in a shallow grave." She then drew
Socrates' head to one side, and plunged the sword right down
to the handle through the left side of his neck. As the blood
spurted out, she caught it in a leather bottle which she applied
to the wound, so that not a single drop was visible anywhere. I
witnessed this with my own eyes. Then the good lady stuck her
right hand deep into the wound, probed around for my poor
friend's heart, and drew it out. No doubt she wished to
observe the proprieties of a sacrifice. When the impact of the
weapon had cut his throat, Socrates uttered a sound or rather
an inarticulate gurgle through the wound, as he breathed out
his life's breath. Panthia then applied the sponge to seal the
wide expanse of the wound, and addressed it: "Listen, sea-
born sponge; be sure not to float away in the following
stream." After these words, they departed. On their way they
both pushed aside the bed, sat astride me, and voided their
bladders over my face until they had doused me in their
noisome urine.

14   'As soon as they left the premises, the doors reverted
undamaged to their previous position. The hinges settled back
in their sockets, the bars were restored to the doorposts, the
bolts jumped back into the locks. I remained still stretched out
on the ground, lifeless and naked, shivering and soaked in
urine. I was like a new-born baby just out of its mother's
womb, or like someone on the point of death; or more
precisely, like someone who has survived death and been born
posthumously—at any rate, like someone doomed to the
inevitable gibbet. "What will become of me", I asked myself,
"when Socrates here is seen in daylight with his throat cut?
Who will believe that my story is at all plausible, though I
recount the truth? What people will say is: 'You could at least
have clamoured for help, even if a man of your size couldn't
withstand a mere woman. What, you watched a man have his
throat cut, and you kept quiet? And how did you escape from
that murderous incursion? How was it that the perpetrators of
such bestial cruelty spared you, when you were clearly a
witness and could denounce the crime? Because you managed
to avoid death, death is now your point of return.' "

'These were the thoughts which repeatedly preoccupied my mind as night began to advance towards day. My best course of action therefore seemed to be to steal away before daybreak and take to the road, however fearful my progress would be. I collected my haversack, inserted the door-key, and drew back the bars. But those honest and faithful doors, which had sprung ajar of their own accord during the night, opened only with the greatest reluctance and after repeated turning of the key.

15   ' "Hullo, there!" I cried. "Where are you? Open the inn-gate. I want to leave before daybreak." The doorman, who was lying behind the inn-gate and who was still half-asleep, replied: "What, setting out at this time of night? Don't you know that the roads are infested with robbers? You may be keen to die because you have some crime on your conscience, but I'm not such a blockhead as to perish on your behalf." "But daylight isn't far off", I rejoined. "Besides, what can robbers take from a wholly indigent traveller? You dolt, you must surely know the saying that as many as ten wrestlers can't strip a man when he's already naked." The janitor's reaction in his fragile and somnolent state was to turn over on his other side. "How do I know", he asked, "that you haven't cut the throat of that fellow-traveller with whom you booked in late yesterday, and that you aren't now covering yourself by running away?" At that moment, as I recall, the earth yawned open. I caught a glimpse of Tartarus deep below, and of Cerberus waiting to make a meal of me to relieve his hunger. I realized that the good Meroë's clear intention had been not to spare my throat out of pity, but to preserve me for the gibbet out of savage spite.

16   'So I went back into the dormitory, and began to ponder my quickest mode of death. Fortune, however, afforded me no death-dealing weapon other than my little bed. "My dear little bed," I said to it, "so dear to my heart! You have endured with me so many trials, and you observed the events of last night. You are the sole witness I can adduce at my trial to declare my innocence. As I hasten on the path to join the shades below, furnish me with some weapon which will

extricate me." Saying this, I began to unwind the rope with
which the bed was corded. I threw and attached one end of it
over a beam which jutted out beneath the window on the
inside. The other end I knotted firmly into a noose. I then got
off the floor and mounted the bed to kill myself, inserting my
head into the noose. But just as I was kicking away with one
foot the support of the bed, so as to allow the rope to tighten
on my throat, and by taking the weight of my body to deprive
it of its function of breathing, the rope which was old and
rotten suddenly broke. I fell headlong, right on top of Socrates
whose bed was next to mine, and we rolled down together on
the ground.

17   'At that very moment the janitor burst in, yelling at the top
of his voice. "Where have you got to? You were straining at
the leash while it was still dark, and now you are snoring in
your blankets!" Socrates was first on his feet before me,
wakened either by my fall or by the janitor's tuneless bellow.
"It's not surprising", he remarked, "that guests hate the sight
of all these janitors. This nosy character has burst cheekily in,
doubtless trying to lay his hands on some possession of ours,
and with his loud bawling he has wakened me when I was fast
asleep from utter exhaustion."

      'At this I shot up, alight with enthusiasm and in a transport
of unexpected joy. "Take a look, honest doorman. This is my
companion, my father and brother, whom you wrongly
accused me of killing during the night when you were in your
cups." Even as I spoke, I embraced and kissed Socrates, but
he was put off by the odour of that foulest of liquids which
those witches had deposited on me, and he pushed me
violently away. "Keep your distance," he said. "You stink like
a filthy urinal!" and he began to enquire genially about the
reasons for the foul smell. In my depression I made some
ridiculous joke on the spur of the moment, and then diverted
his thoughts to another topic. I laid my hand in his, and said:
"Let's go and enjoy the pleasures of an early-morning
journey." I seized my haversack, and paid the innkeeper the
bill for our stay. Then we set out.

18   'After we had travelled a fair distance, the sun came up and

brought light to the world. I kept a careful and watchful eye on the patch of my friend's throat where I had seen the sword make its entry, and I said to myself: "You fool! You had too much wine to drink, and you had a terrible nightmare. You can see that Socrates is untouched and healthy and unharmed. There is no sign of the wound or the sponge, or indeed of that deep and fresh incision." Then I said to Socrates: "Reliable doctors are quite right in their belief that when people have stuffed themselves with food and too much wine, they have harsh and disturbing dreams. I myself drank too much last evening, and had a bad night which brought such dreadful and troublesome dreams that I still feel as if I'm spattered and polluted with human blood."

'Socrates grinned, and countered: "It's not blood that spattered you; you merely wet yourself. Mind you, I too had a dream in which I seemed to get my throat cut. I felt a sharp pain in my neck here, and I thought that my heart was being torn out. Even now I feel out of breath; my knees are knocking, and my progress is unsteady. I need a bite of food to restore myself." "Here you are," I said, "breakfast is served." With that I took my haversack off my shoulder, and hastily handed him some bread and cheese. "Let's sit by that plane tree," I added.

19   'We did this, and I got myself something to eat from my pack. As he greedily wolfed the food, I paid closer attention to him, and I noted that he was fainting; his face was gaunt and as pale as boxwood. In a word, his deathly pallor had so altered his appearance that I was terrified, picturing again those Furies of the night, so much so that the first crust of bread that I had taken, small though it was, got stuck in my throat, and I could neither swallow nor regurgitate it. An additional cause of my panic was the absence of other travellers, for who was likely to believe that when one of a pair of companions had been killed, the other was innocent?

'Once Socrates had had enough to eat, he began to feel an intolerable thirst, for he had greedily wolfed a large slice of excellent cheese. Not far from the roots of the plane-tree was a quiet stream, glistening like silver or glass, its motion as gentle as a tranquil pond. "There you are," I said. "You can quench your thirst from the milky waters of the stream." He stood up, and for a moment sought out a more level section of the bank. Then he got down on his knees, and bent greedily over the water to take a drink. He had not quite touched the surface of the water with parted lips than the wound in his neck yawned deep and wide. The sponge suddenly tumbled out, and with it only a drop or two of blood. Then his lifeless body almost keeled over into the stream, but I managed to grab one foot, and after a hard struggle I dragged the corpse to the top of the bank. There I mourned my unhappy companion as much as time allowed, and then buried him in sandy soil to dwell for ever close to the stream. I fled for my life in fear and trembling through remote and trackless wastes, and now, like a man obsessed with human blood on his hands, I have quitted my native region and home, and have embraced voluntary exile. I now live in Aetolia, and have married again there.'

20   This was what Aristomenes told us. His companion from the very beginning had shown stubborn disbelief and contempt for his account. 'I've never heard a taller story than this, nor a more stupid one than this tissue of lies', he said. Then he turned to me, and said: 'Your clothes and deportment show that you are a man of culture; can you believe that the story is true?' 'I consider nothing impossible,' I replied, 'for I believe that people undergo all that their fates decree. My view is that you and I and the whole world experience many strange, almost impossible happenings which lose their credibility when recounted to one who is unaware of them. Not only do I believe our friend—indeed I do—but I am most grateful to him for distracting us with such an amusing and elegant tale, so that I have completed this rough and extensive lap of my journey without strain or boredom. I suspect that my mount too is grateful for the favour, since I have not tired him out, and have ridden all the way to the city gate not on his back, but on my ears.'

21   This made an end to our conversation and joint journey, for my companions both went off to a small farmhouse on the left of the road, while I made for the first inn that I saw, and at

once made enquiries of the old woman who kept the tavern. 'Is this town Hypata?' I asked. She nodded. 'Do you know of a man named Milo, one of the outstanding citizens?' She smiled, and said: 'He is rightly labelled an outstanding citizen of this district, for he stands outside the city boundary; in fact, he lives outside the town.' 'Now joking apart, dear mother, would you please tell me something of his background, and which house he lives in?' 'Do you see the last set of windows looking out on the town, with the entrance on the other side facing the nearest alley-way? Mister Moneybags Milo lives there. Though he is extremely wealthy, he is notorious for being an absolute miser, living in utter squalor. He is a money-lender on a large scale, charging high interest and taking gold and silver as security. Yet he lives in that tiny house, spending all his time counting his mildewed coins. He has a wife who shares his run-down life. The only servant he feeds is one young girl. He walks about dressed like a beggar.'

On hearing this I let out a laugh. 'My friend Demeas has certainly been kind and far-seeing in attending to my interests! So this is the kind of man to whom he introduces me at the outset of my travels, so I need have no fear of kitchen-smoke or foul-smelling fumes in his lodging.'

22   After making this observation, I walked on a little further, and reached the entrance to the house. The door was close-barred, and I began to shout and hammer on it. Eventually a young girl emerged. 'Hello there!' she said. 'You've certainly given the door a good wallop! What security do you intend to offer for a loan? You surely can't be the only one who is unaware that the only pledge we accept is gold or silver.' 'This is hardly a promising start,' I remarked. 'I'd much rather you tell me whether I find your master at home.' 'Yes, he is' she said. 'Why do you ask?' 'I have a letter addressed to him from Demeas of Corinth.' 'Just wait for me here', she replied, 'until I tell him.' With that she barred the door again, and vanished inside. After a while she returned, and held open the door. 'He asks you to come in,' she said.

When I made my way in, I found Milo reclining on quite a small couch, and on the point of starting his dinner. His wife

out by his feet, and there was a table before them with nothing
on it. He pointed to it, and said, 'Share our board.' 'That's
kind!', I said, at once passing across the letter from Demeas.
He hastily scanned it, and said: 'I'm grateful to my friend
Demeas for introducing me to such an important guest.'

23   With that he ordered his wife to quit the couch, and bade
me take her place. When I still demurred out of good manners,
he grabbed me by the shirt and pulled me down. 'Sit here,' he
said, 'we're so afraid of robbers that we can't buy chairs or
even enough table-ware.'

I sat down. 'I could rightly have guessed from your civilized
appearance and your quite innocent modesty that you come
from a good family, and Demeas confirms this in his letter.
I beg you not to look with contempt on our small and
unpretentious dwelling. You will have the adjoining bedroom
here, to afford you decent privacy. Do have a pleasant stay
with us. You will add dignity to our house by consenting to
stay here, and if you rest content with our small abode, you
will bring great credit on yourself, for you will be imitating the
virtues of your father's namesake Theseus, who did not spurn
the tiny lodging of the aged Hecale.' Milo then summoned the
young maid. 'Photis,' he said, 'take our guest's baggage, and
store it carefully in the bedroom over there. Then go quickly
to the store-cupboard, and bring oil, towels, and whatever else
he requires for oiling and rubbing-down. After that, escort my
guest to the baths close by, for he is tired after his long and
quite taxing journey.'

24   On hearing these words I reflected on Milo's parsimony,
and sought to instal myself more closely in his affections. 'I
have no need of any of those things,' I said, 'for they
accompany me everywhere on my travels, and I can easily ask
the way to the baths. My chief concern is for my horse, which
has had a hard time getting me here. Take these coins,
Photis, and buy him some hay and barley.'

After these exchanges my luggage was deposited in the
bedroom, and I set out for the baths. But first I made for the
market, to obtain some food for supper, and I saw there some
fish of good quality on sale. I enquired about the cost, turned

down the asking price of a hundred sesterces, and got them for twenty denarii. I was just leaving the market when I encountered one Pythias, formerly a fellow-student of mine at Athens in Attica. He greeted me with affectionate signs of recognition after such a long time, and embraced and kissed me jovially. 'My dear Lucius,' he said, 'it's quite a long time since I saw you last. Heavens, the last time was when we said farewell to our master Clytius. What business brings you this way?' 'You'll find out tomorrow,' I said. 'But what's all this? Congratulations are in order, for I see you now have the attendants and rods and dress befitting a magistrate.' 'That's right,' he said, 'I'm charged with the corn-supply, and I have the rank of aedile. If you wish to buy provisions, I'm most ready to help you.' I refused the offer, because I had already provided myself with plenty of fish for supper. But then Pythias noticed my basket, and he shook the fish about to get a better view of them. 'How much have you paid for this load of rubbish?' he asked. 'I had difficulty getting the fishmonger to reduce the price to twenty denarii for them,' I replied.

25   On hearing this he at once seized my arm and took me back into the market. 'From which of these traders did you buy that trash?' he enquired. I pointed out an elderly man sitting in a corner. Pythias at once invoked his aedile's authority to rebuke him in the harshest terms. 'So', he said, 'you have no compunction in exploiting friends of mine, or indeed any strangers whatsoever. By putting such high prices on your wretched fish you are turning this desirable region of Thessaly into nothing but a rocky desert. But you won't get away with it. I'll make you realize how unscrupulous traders are to be kept in check while I'm in charge.' With that he threw the parcel of fish on the ground in front of us, and ordered his attendant to jump on the fish, and crush them all underfoot. Dear Pythias was pleased with this stern demonstration of righteousness, and he urged me to leave, saying: 'I'm well pleased, Lucius, with the dressing-down which we've handed out to the old man.' I was bowled over and struck utterly dumb by this performance. I retired to the baths, robbed of both my money and my supper by this stern sermon from my

wise fellow-student. After taking my bath, I turned back to
Milo's lodging and made for my bedroom.

26   The maid Photis then appeared. 'Your host is asking for
you,' she said. I was already au fait with Milo's niggardliness,
so I made the courteous excuse that I had decided to dispel
the trials of travelling with sleep rather than with food. On
hearing this, he came in person, placed his arm in mine, and
began gently to constrain me to accompany him. As I
hesitantly and meekly demurred, he said: 'I refuse to leave
until you come with me'. He swore an oath on this, and when
I reluctantly acceded to his insistence, he led me to that little
couch of his. When I was seated on it, he asked: 'How is our
friend Demeas? And his wife? And his children? And the
family-slaves?' I answered the queries one by one. He
questioned me also in some detail about the reasons for my
journey. I conscientiously explained. He then conducted an
exhaustive enquiry about my native region, its prominent
citizens, and finally the governor himself. At last he realized
that in addition to the upset of such a taxing journey, I was
further exhausted by this continuing patter, for I kept nodding
off midway through a conversation, and I was now so weary
that I was slurring out meaningless comments in my replies.
So finally he allowed me to go to bed, enabling me to escape
from the noisome old man's feast, which was long on words
but short on victuals. So, heavy with sleep but not with food
(for I had dined on nothing but gossip), I retired to my
bedroom, and sought the rest for which I longed.

BOOK 2

Further Warnings at Byrrhena's: The Exemplar of Thelyphron

1 As soon as the darkness was dispelled and a new sun ushered in the day, I rose from my couch the moment I awoke from sleep, for I was generally buoyed up, and most eager to discover the weird and wonderful features of the place. I recalled that I was in the heart of Thessaly, the source of those spells of the magic art which are famed by common consent through the entire world. I remembered too that the tale recounted by Aristomenes, that best of companions, had its origin in this city. So in expectation and enthusiasm alike I was quite alert, and I studied each feature with some care. I did not believe that anything which I gazed on in the city was merely what it was, but that every single object had been transformed into a different shape by some muttered and deadly incantation. I thought that the stones which caused me to trip were petrified persons, that the birds which I could hear were feathered humans, that the trees enclosing the city-limits were people who had likewise sprouted foliage, that the waters of the fountains were issuing from human bodies. I imagined that at any moment the statues and portraits would parade about, that the walls would speak, that oxen and other cattle would prophesy, that the very sky and the sun's orb would suddenly proclaim an oracular message.

2 In this trance, or rather hypnosis, induced by such tortured longing, I went round examining everything, but without finding a suggestion or even a trace of what I passionately sought. I wandered from door to door like a man seeking some extravagant and dissolute diversion, and all unknowing I suddenly found myself at the food-market. I caught sight of a woman walking through it, surrounded by a sizeable retinue, and I quickened my step and overtook her. Her jewellery was gold-inlaid and her clothes gold-

embroidered, undoubtedly signalling that she was an upper-class matron. Walking close to her side was a man of advanced years. As soon as he set eyes on me he exclaimed: 'Heavens, it's Lucius!' and he gave me a kiss of greeting. At once he whispered something in the lady's ear which I could not overhear. 'This is your aunt,' he said. 'You must approach her yourself, and greet her.' 'I'm shy of doing that', I said, 'for I do not know her.' Whereupon I blushed all over, and kept my distance with my head bowed.

The lady then turned to stare at me. 'My goodness,' she said, 'he has the manners of a gentleman. He gets them from his mother Salvia who is a model of goodness. And damn me if his appearance generally isn't just right! He is tall, but not lofty; he's slim, but there is spunk there; his colour is moderately ruddy, his hair is blonde but not foppish; his green eyes have a watchful look, quick to focus, sharp as an eagle's. His face looks healthy from every angle, and his walk is pleasing and natural.'

3   Then she added: 'Lucius, these hands of mine reared you. That was as it should be, for not only am I your mother's blood relation, but we were brought up together. We are both descended from Plutarch's household, we had the same wet-nurse, and we grew up together as inseparable sisters. The one thing that distinguishes us is our social standing. She contracted marriage with a prominent public figure, whereas I married a private citizen. I'm called Byrrhena; you may recall the name through mention of it among those who brought you up. So don't be shy of accepting our hospitality; in fact our house is yours.'

These remarks of hers had given me time to disguise my blushes, and I spoke up in reply. 'Dear aunt,' I said, 'I could hardly bid my host Milo goodbye without his feeling aggrieved. I shall make every effort to do what I can, short of breaching my obligation to him. Whenever any occasion for a journey this way arises in future, I shall always lodge with you.' In the course of these and similar exchanges, the short journey we had made on foot brought us to Byrrhena's house.

4   The reception-area was very fine. Pillars stood at each

corner, supporting statues representing the goddess Victory. In these representations, her wings were outspread but motionless, and her dewy feet stood on tiptoe on the slippery surface of a revolving sphere, momentarily joined to it but giving the impression of imminent flight. But the notable feature was Parian marble chiselled into the likeness of Diana, which occupied the centre of the whole atrium, and was raised off the ground. The statue gleamed spectacularly; with her garment breeze-blown, her lively figure was hastening forward as if to confront the incomer with the august majesty of her godhead. Hounds, likewise executed in marble, escorted the goddess on both flanks. Their eyes were threatening, their ears pricked up, their nostrils flaring, their maws savage. If barking sounded loudly from anywhere near at hand, you would think that it issued from those mouths of marble. But the highest feat of craftsmanship achieved by that genius of a sculptor was that the hounds were rearing breast-high, and their hind legs were braking while their forelegs were in rapid motion.

To the rear of the goddess rose a rock forming a cave. Out of the stone sprouted moss, green plants, foliage and brushwood; vines on one side were set off against miniature trees on the other. Within the cave the reflection of the statue shone out because of the smooth brightness of the marble. Apples and grapes hung from the lower edge of the rock; their highly artistic finish, depicted with a skill rivalling nature's, made them lifelike, so that you could imagine that some of them could be plucked for eating once the maturing autumn endowed them with the colour of ripeness. If you bent low and gazed into the water which skirted the goddess's feet as it lapped in gentle waves, you would think that the bunches of grapes hanging from the rock possessed the faculty of movement as well as other lifelike qualities. In the middle of the marble foliage a statue of Actaeon was visible, fashioned in marble and reflected in the water; his neck craned forward as he gazed with curiosity towards the goddess. He was already animal-like, on the point of becoming a stag as he waited for Diana to take her bath.

5   As I repeatedly ran my eye over this scene with intense
delight, Byrrhena remarked: 'All that you see is yours.' After
saying this, she had a private word with all the others, and
asked them to leave us. When they had all been sent away, she
said to me: 'Dearest Lucius, I swear by the goddess here; I am
troubled and fearful for you. Since you are my cherished son, I
should like to give you warning well in advance. Watch out for
yourself. Take stringent precautions against the wicked arts
and evil enticements of the notorious Pamphile, the wife of
Milo, who you say is your host. She is reputed to be a witch of
the first rank, a specialist in all forms of necromancy. She has
only to breathe on twigs, pebbles, and common objects of that
kind, and she can plunge all this light of day which descends
from the starry heavens into the lowest depths of Tartarus,
reducing it to the chaos of old. Then as soon as she catches
sight of any handsome young man, she is captivated by his
charms, and at once focuses her eyes and her attention on
him. She sows the seeds of allurements, dominates his will,
and proceeds to imprison him in eternal bonds of deep love. If
those who are less amenable prove worthless to her because
they scorn her, she transforms them in a trice into stones or
cattle or any animal you can think of, while others she utterly
destroys. These are the fears I have for you, and I think that
you should be on your guard against them, for she is
constantly ablaze with desire, and your youth and handsome
bearing make you a suitable target for her.' These were the
troubled thoughts which Byrrhena shared with me.

6   But I was already disposed to curiosity, and as soon as I
heard mention of the art of magic which I had always prayed
for, so far from taking precautions against Pamphile, I was
eager even without compulsion to undergo such schooling
willingly, and to pay a heavy price for it. In short, I was all for
taking a running jump and landing myself headlong in those
murky depths. So with lunatic haste I freed myself from
Byrrhena's detaining hand as if from a confining chain, and
bade her a hasty farewell. I then flew off at top speed to Milo's
lodging. As I redoubled my steps like one demented, I said to
myself: 'Lucius, look alive, and keep your wits about you.

This is the chance you were praying for. You will be able to achieve that long-standing ambition of yours, and obtain your heart's content of wonderful stories. Dismiss your childish fears, come to grips with the issue at close quarters and without cowardice. You must steer clear of any love-relationship with your hostess, and scrupulously respect the good Milo's marriage-bed. Make a bee-line instead for the maidservant Photis. She is attractive, she has amusing ways, and she is quite sharp. Last night when you retired to sleep, she genially escorted you to your room, fussed over you in getting you to your bed, tucked you in quite affectionately, kissed your forehead, and showed by her face her unwillingness to leave. In fact she kept halting and looking back. So even though it has its hazards, Photis must be your target. The best of luck in your endeavours.'

7   These were the arguments occupying my mind as I made for Milo's door. I voted with my feet, as the expression goes. I found neither Milo nor his wife at home, but only my dear Photis. She was cooking minced pork for stuffing, and slices of meat, and some very spicy sausage of which I had already caught a whiff. She was wearing an elegant linen dress, with a bright red belt fastened up supporting her breasts. As she turned the casserole-dish round and round with her petal-like fingers, and shook it repeatedly in its circular motion, she simultaneously rotated her body. Her hips moved lightly in rhythm, and as she wiggled her supple spine, her person rippled most attractively. I was spellbound at the sight, and stood there lost in admiration. The parts of me that were asleep before now stood to attention. Finally I managed to speak to her; 'My dear Photis,' I said, 'how lusciously and attractively you wiggle that wee pot, and your bottom with it! That's a succulent dish you have in readiness there! How lucky a fellow would be if you let him stick his finger in—he'd be on top of the world!'

That pert and witty girl at once replied: 'Keep clear, poor boy, keep clear as far as possible from this stove of mine. If once my little flame shoots out and as much as sears you, you will be all ablaze inside, and I'll be the only one who can put your fire out. The spices which I incorporate are sweet. I'm an expert at pleasurably shaking a bed as well as a pot.'

8   With these words she looked me in the eye, and grinned. I did not leave her presence until I had carefully studied all the features of her appearance. Of her other charms I need say nothing, for it has always been my one obsession first to examine a person's head of hair thoroughly and openly outside, and then to take pleasure in it privately indoors. I have a secure and well-established justification for preferring this criterion of beauty. First comes the fact that the head is the outstanding part of the body; it is exposed and prominent, and is the first feature to meet the eye. Secondly, whereas the other physical parts are made attractive by the gay colour of bright clothing, it is the head's own natural sheen which achieves this. Lastly, most women when they wish to demonstrate their personal attractions disrobe and remove all their clothes in their eagerness to show off their naked beauty, seeking to please the eye more with the rosy blush of their skin than with the golden colour of their dress. But if you were to scalp some lady of outstanding beauty, and thus rob her face of its natural adornment—this is a sacrilegious suggestion, and I pray that so grisly an illustration of my point may never materialize—it would not matter if she came down from heaven, or rose from the sea, or was sprung from the waves. In other words, it would not matter if she were Venus herself, flanked by a whole choir of Graces, accompanied by the entire body of Cupids, wearing that belt of hers around her waist, diffusing the scent of cinnamon and bedewing the air with balsam; if she appeared without her hair, she would not give pleasure even to her Vulcan.

9   How enchanting is a woman's hair when its pleasing colour and glossy sheen shines out! When it faces the sun's rays, it is enlivened and flashes fire, or gently reflects the sunlight. Sometimes it offers contrasting pleasures by varying its appearance. Hair with a golden glow subsides into the soft shaded colour of honey. Hair which is raven-black seeks to rival the ultramarine necks of doves. Hair oiled with drops of Arabian perfume, parted with the fine teeth of a sharp comb,

and gathered at the back, serves as a mirror when it confronts the lover's eyes, and affords him a more flattering reflection. Sometimes numerous strands are combined to form a thick wedge on top of the head, or they flow down the back, extending in a long plait. Such in fact is the lofty status of a woman's hair that she can appear before us adorned with gold, fine clothes, jewellery and the rest of her finery, but unless she has ordered her hair she cannot be regarded as well-groomed.

My Photis, however, had not fussed over hers, and yet its tousled arrangement lent her added charm. Her abundant hair had been let hang soft and free down from her head over her neck, and having rested briefly on the golden border of her dress, it had finally been gathered and fastened in a knot on top of her head.

10   I could no longer endure the fierce torture of my extreme pleasure. I leaned over her, and implanted the sweetest of honeyed kisses where her hair reached the crown of her head. She then twisted her neck to face me, and gave me a sidelong look with devouring eyes. 'Hey there, schoolboy,' she said, 'the savoury dish you're sampling is bitter as well as sweet. Just watch out; that honey which tastes so sweet may bring on a lengthy attack of bitter bile.'

'How can you say that, light of my life?' I asked. 'I am ready to be laid and grilled on this fire of yours, once you have roused me with one little kiss.' As I spoke I grasped her tightly in my arms, and started to kiss her. In a moment she was as abandoned as I was, as she rose to the same heat of passion. With unrestrained desire she showed her longing for me; the breath from her open lips was like cinnamon, and the thrust of her tongue was like nectar as it met mine. I said to her: 'This is killing me! Indeed, I'm already dead unless you take pity on me.' She gave me another long kiss, and answered: 'Don't worry. That longing which we share makes me your slave, and our pleasure will be postponed no longer. As soon as the first lamp is lit, I'll be in your bedroom. So be off with you, and make your preparations. I shall engage you in an all-night battle with the strength of passion.'

11   After this genial exchange and others of a similar kind, we
parted. Just after midday Byrrhena sent over to me some
guest-presents: a fat pig, five chickens, and a cask of vintage
wine. I summoned Photis then, and said to her: 'Look at this!
Bacchus, the spokesman and squire of Venus, has turned up
without prompting. All this wine we must drink today so as to
dispel the cowardice induced by embarrassment, and instil
into ourselves the onset of sexual pleasure. These are the only
provisions needed on Venus' barque to ensure that throughout the night-watch we have plenty of oil in the lamp and
plenty of wine in the cup.'

We devoted the rest of the day to the baths and then to
supper, for I had been invited to that elegant little board of
Milo. I took my place on the couch as safely remote from his
wife's eye as I could, for I had Byrrhena's warning in mind,
and I watched her face with as much apprehension as if I were
gazing into Lake Avernus. But repeated glances at Photis as
she served at table restored my spirits. As darkness closed in,
Pamphile peered at the lamp, and remarked: 'We are to have
quite a storm tomorrow.' When her husband asked her how
she knew, she replied that the lamp foretold it to her. Milo
greeted this reply with a laugh. 'What a splendid Sibyl we are
nurturing in the lamp here! From her observatory on the
lampstand she observes all the activities in the sky, and the
sun as well.'

12   At this point I interposed. 'I have had experience of this
kind of prophecy, but there is nothing surprising about it. It is
true that this tiny flame is insignificant and fashioned by
human hands, but it is mindful of the greater fire in the
heavens, which is, so to say, its progenitor. So by a divine
foreknowledge it is itself aware, and communicates to us, what
the sun intends to bring forth in the height of the heavens. At
this very time in the city of Corinth where I live there is
a Chaldaean visitor who with his remarkable responses is
causing absolute mayhem. For a small fee he makes public the
secret decrees of the fates. He advises on a day for a wedding
which will make the marriage stable, or the day on which to
lay wall-foundations to ensure that they last, or a day which

will profit the business-man, or which will be auspicious for a traveller, or suitable for vessels to commence their voyage. When I questioned him on how this journey of mine would turn out, his lengthy reply was quite surprising and varied. He said that at one time my fame would blossom considerably, and at another I would be the subject of a lengthy story, an unbelievable tale spread over several books.'

13   Milo grinned at this. 'This Chaldaean of yours—what sort of appearance has he, and what is his name?' 'He's tall', I said, 'and on the dark side. His name is Diophanes.' 'The very one,' said Milo. 'He's been here as well, making many similar forecasts to many people. His takings were not just in pennies; in fact he had already made a fortune. But then the poor chap found Lady Luck capricious, or it would be truer to say, vicious.

'One day he was hemmed in by a large crowd gathered round him, and he was predicting futures for the circle of bystanders when a business-man called Cerdo approached him. He wanted to know the right day for starting a journey. Diophanes selected and apportioned a day, and Cerdo laid down his purse, poured out the coins, and counted out a hundred denarii as Diophanes' fee for the prophecy. At this moment a young nobleman crept up in Diophanes' rear, seized him by the cloak, and pulled him round. He then embraced and kissed him with great warmth. Diophanes returned the kiss, and made the young man sit down beside him. In his surprise at his sudden appearance, he forgot the transaction which he was conducting. "How long is it since you got here?" he asked. "I have been so looking forward to your arrival." The other man replied: "It was just before dark yesterday. But tell me about yourself, brother. When you sailed in some haste from the island of Euboea, how did the rest of your voyage and the journey overland go?"

14   'That distinguished astrologer Diophanes was still distracted, and had not yet recovered his wits. "I only pray", he said, "that all our enemies public and private may experience so grim a journey; it was as bad as that of Ulysses. The ship in which we were sailing was battered by competing storm-

winds. We lost both rudders, and just managed to run aground on the fringe of the opposite shore. There the ship went straight down, and we barely managed to swim ashore, with the loss of all our possessions. Such things as we managed to gather through the compassion of strangers or the kindness of friends were all purloined by a band of brigands, and to crown it all my only brother Arignotus tried to resist their violent attack, and the poor man had his throat cut before my very eyes."

'Diophanes was still sadly recounting these experiences when Cerdo the business-man grabbed the coins which he had laid out as payment for his forecast, and at once took to his heels. It was only then that Diophanes awoke to the situation, and realized his foolish mistake, once he saw that every single one of us had collapsed in gales of laughter. But doubtless the Chaldaean foretold the truth for you, Master Lucius, if for no one else in the world. Good luck to you, and have a prosperous journey!'

15 While Milo was giving us this long rigmarole, I was silently seething, hugely annoyed with myself for having precipitated needlessly one unseasonable anecdote after another, with the result that I was losing a large part of the evening, and the most welcome pleasure which it would yield. Eventually I swallowed all feelings of decency, and I said to Milo: 'Well, then, let Diophanes bear with his fortune, and once again consign to sea and land alike the spoils which he has gained from my countrymen. You will have to pardon me, but I am still feeling the effects of yesterday's exhausting journey, and I should like to retire to bed early.'

I made off even as I was speaking, and hastened to my bedroom. There I found that the arrangements for the celebration were quite as they should have been. The slaves had their floor-space arranged as far as possible away from the door; I imagine that this was so that they would not be near enough to overhear our chat during the night. Close to my bed stood a small table on which were laid acceptable leftovers from all the courses of the dinner. There were generous cups already half-filled with wine, awaiting only the necessary dilution, and by them was a flagon, its neck already smoothly cut so that it lay open for easy pouring. These, then, were the apposite preliminaries for our gladiatorial combat of love.

16   I had just climbed into bed when my Photis, having tucked her mistress in, made her smiling entrance. She wore a garland of roses, and had a rose-blossom tucked between her breasts. She kissed me hard, put garlands round my neck, and sprinkled petals over me. Then she seized a cup, poured hot water into the wine, and gave it to me to drink. Just before I downed the lot, she took gentle possession of the cup, and with her eyes fixed on me, she charmingly sipped the rest, allowing it slowly to vanish between her lips. A second and third cup was shared between us as we passed it quickly from hand to hand. By now the wine had gone to my head, and I felt restless and randy physically as well as in mind. For some little time now I had felt my wound swelling. I pushed my clothes clear of the groin, and showed Photis that I could not delay the love-encounter any longer. 'Take pity,' I said, 'come to my aid with all speed. As you can see, the war which you declared on me without employing the services of the fetials, is now imminent, and I am extended in readiness. Once I felt the impact of cruel Cupid's first arrow in the depth of my heart, I stretched my bow strongly likewise, and I am mortally afraid that the string may break through being drawn too tightly. Now indulge me a little further; let your hair run free and flow over me in waves as you offer me your love-embrace.'

17   At once she hastily removed all the food-dishes. She stripped off her clothes, and let her hair flow loose. Then with a show of genial wantonness she adopted the charming pose of Venus treading the ocean waves. She even for a moment covered her hairless parts with her rosy little hand, a deliberate gesture rather than modest concealment. 'Engage,' she said, 'and do so bravely. I shall not yield before you, nor turn my back on you. Direct your aim frontally, if you are a man, and at close quarters. Let your onslaught be fierce; kill before you die. Our battle this day allows no respite.' As she spoke she mounted the bed, and eased herself slowly down on

top of me. She bounced up and down repeatedly, manœuvring her back in supple movements, and gorged me with the delight of this rhythmical intercourse. Eventually our spirits palled as our bodies lost their zest; we collapsed simultaneously in a state of exhaustion as we breathlessly embraced each other. Engaged in these and similar grapplings we remained awake almost until dawn. From time to time we refreshed our weary bodies with wine, which fired our sexual urges and renewed our pleasure. Several other nights we spent similarly, taking that first night as our model.

18   One day it chanced that Byrrhena pressed me strongly to have dinner at her house, and though I made valiant excuses, she would have none of them. So I had to approach Photis and seek her advice—taking the auspices, so to say, to discover her will. Though she was reluctant to let me go more than a nail's breadth from her, she genially allowed me a short furlough from our love-campaign. But she added this proviso: 'Be sure to come back from your dinner reasonably early, because there is a lunatic band of upper-class youths disturbing the peace of the streets. You will see the corpses of murdered people lying in various places on the public highways. The provincial governor's forces cannot rid the city of all this killing, because they are so far away; and your conspicuous status, together with their lack of respect for a stranger travelling abroad, may cause them to lie in wait for you.'

'Photis, my dear,' I said, 'let me reassure you. In the first place I should much prefer my own pleasures here to dining with strangers. Secondly, I shall dispel this fear of yours by returning early, and I shall not be unattended, because with my short sword buckled by my side I shall be bearing the guarantee of my safety.' I duly took this precaution, and made my way to the dinner.

19   There was quite a crowd of guests. The hostess was a leading figure locally, so the élite of the town was there. The expensive tables gleamed with citrus-wood and ivory, the couches were draped with golden coverlets, the large cups though not a matching set were equally costly as each other.

One was of glass skilfully inlaid, a second of unblemished crystal; others were of bright silver, gleaming gold, amber marvellously hollowed out, precious stones shaped into drinking-vessels. There were cups there which you would have said were impossible to fashion. Several waiters strikingly dressed were expertly serving heaped-up dishes, while curly-haired boys in splendid uniforms regularly circulated with jewelled cups of vintage wine. Once the lamps were brought in, conversation at table became animated. Laughter was rife, wit ran free, and repartee was exchanged.

Byrrhena then began to speak to me. 'How pleasant is your stay in our region turning out?' she asked. 'My information is that our temples, baths, and other public buildings are much superior to those of all other towns, and that we are also plentifully equipped with the practical requirements for living. Here at any rate the man of leisure is free to roam, the business-man from abroad finds a population similar to that at Rome, and the guest of modest means can relax in a country house. In short, we serve as the holiday centre in this entire province for the pleasure-seeker.'

20   I acknowledged this claim. 'What you say is true. My belief is that nowhere in the world have I been so free as here. But I am quite apprehensive of the dark dens where magic is practised, and which cannot be sidestepped. People say that not even the tombs of the dead are safe, and that human remains, parts of human bodies, are extracted from graves and funeral-pyres to encompass deadly disaster for the living. At the very moment when a body is being borne out to burial, there are aged sorceresses who move at high speed and reach the burial plots of strangers before anyone else.'

Another guest took up the topic and carried it further. 'Why,' he said, 'in this place they don't even spare the living. There was some fellow or other who had just such an experience, for he had his face completely disfigured and mutilated.' At these words the entire table exploded into ribald laughter, and all turned their heads and eyes towards a man reclining by himself in a corner. He was embarrassed by this general attention paid to him, and made as if to rise, muttering at this unkind treatment. But Byrrhena interjected. 'No, don't go, dear Thelyphron. Stay for a little while, and in your civilized fashion tell us again that tale of yours, so that my son Lucius here may enjoy your genial and elegant account.' Thelyphron responded: 'You, my lady, continue to show your unimpeachable good manners, but there are some people here whose arrogance is intolerable.' His words reflected his annoyance, but Byrrhena swore on her own life that he must stay, and so overcame his reluctance that she finally induced him to consent to speak.

21 So then Thelyphron piled up the couch-coverlets, and raised himself partly upwards on the couch by leaning on them with his elbow. He then stretched out his right hand, deploying an arm as orators do, with the two smaller fingers bent and the others extended, and with the thumb gently but accusingly pointed upward. This was how he began.

'As a young lad I set out from Miletus to attend the Olympic games, and as I was eager to visit this region of the celebrated province as well, I travelled the length and breadth of Thessaly, and arrived at Larissa in an evil hour. My travel-funds were now running low, so as I wandered about viewing all the sights, I was looking out for some means of relieving my poverty. I saw in the middle of the market-place a tall old man standing on a stone. He was making a public announcement that if any person was willing to guard a corpse, the fee could be negotiated. I remarked to one of the passers-by: "Whatever is this all about? Do corpses often take to their heels in these parts?" "Hush!" he replied. "You are just a boy and a mere stranger, so naturally you are unaware that the Thessaly in which you are lodging contains witches who in different localities bite morsels off dead men's faces, and use them as additional materials for their practice of magic."

22 ' "Do please tell me," I replied, "What does this protection of a corpse involve?" "To begin with", he said, "you must keep intensive watch all night through, keeping your eyes trained unblinkingly and continuously on the body. Your gaze must not be distracted in the slightest, not even so much as by a swivelling of the eyes. Those most repellent hags change

their outward appearance by transforming themselves into any creature, and they creep in so surreptitiously that they easily escape the eyes even of the sun-god himself and of the goddess Justice, for they take on the shape of birds, or again of dogs, or mice, or even flies. Then by their dread spells they shroud the watchers in sleep. No individual could properly assess the number of hidden tricks which those most wicked women devise to attain their lustful desires. Yet the payment offered for this mortally dangerous task is no more than about four or six gold pieces. Oh yes, and there is a further point which I had almost forgotten. If the watcher does not hand over the body intact in the morning, he is forced to make good any feature which has been prised off, wholly or partly, with the equivalent feature cut off from his own face."

23   'On hearing this, I exhibited a manly spirit, and at once approached the man making the announcement. "You can stop shouting now," I said, "I'm ready to stand guard. Tell me the fee." "A thousand sesterces will be credited to you", he said. "But look here, young man; you must be scrupulously careful to guard with care the son of leading citizens of this town from those wicked Harpies." "What you tell me is stuff and nonsense," I rejoined. "The person you see before you is a man of steel, whose eyes never close and whose sight is certainly keener than that of Lynceus himself, or of Argus. In fact he is eyes personified."

'He barely heard me out, but at once led me to a house whose entrance was barred. He ushered me inside through a tiny rear door, and opened up a room deep in shadow, since the windows were shuttered. He pointed out a tearful matron clothed in black, and he approached her side. "This man has commissioned himself to guard your husband, and has arrived full of confidence." The lady pushed her overhanging hair to each side, revealing a face which was attractive even in grief. She turned her eyes on me, and said: "Do please ensure that you perform the task with the greatest vigilance." "Have no worries on that score," I replied, "as long as you have ready the appropriate payment."

24   'When this was agreed, she rose and led me to another

retiring-room. There in the presence of seven witnesses who were brought in, she uncovered with her own hand the body, which was shrouded by gleaming linen sheets. For some time she wept over it, and then she tremblingly pointed out each feature of the corpse, asking those present to witness them. One of them committed to tablets the formal inventory: "Observe", she said, "the nose intact, the eyes undamaged, the ears unharmed, the lips untouched, the chin entire. Good citizens, solemnly witness to this." After these words the tablets were sealed up, and she rose to withdraw. I said to her: "Give instructions that everything I need is made available to me." "What is it you need?" she asked. "An outsize lamp," I said, "enough oil to keep it alight till daylight, hot water with jars of wine and a cup, and a plate bearing the left-overs from your dinner." "Away with you, you silly man," she said, tossing her head. "The house is in mourning, and yet you ask for dinners and courses? In this house not a whiff of smoke has been visible for days on end. Do you think that you have come here to a drinking-party? The proper fare for you here is grief and tears." As she said this, she looked round at a little maid-servant, and said: "Myrrhine, bring a lamp and some oil quickly. Lock the guard in this room, and then leave at once."

25   'So I was left alone to console the corpse. I massaged my eyes, and prepared them for the night-watch. As I sought to soothe my spirits by singing songs, dusk fell, and night came on. Soon it got darker, and then as bedtime came, darker still, until finally it was dead of night. I began to get more and more jittery, when suddenly a weasel crept in and halted facing me, fixing me with the sharpest gaze imaginable. It showed such extraordinary self-assurance for such a tiny animal that it quite upset me. Finally I said to it: "Clear off, you filthy creature. Go and hide with your mates in the garden, before you feel the force of my arm here and now. Be off!"

'It retreated, and scuttled out of the room at once. A minute later I was overpowered by a deep sleep which plunged me suddenly into a bottomless gulf. Even the god of Delphi could not easily have decided which of the two of us there was more dead than the other. I lay there lifeless, needing a second guard to watch over me. It was almost as if I were not present.

26 'The crowing of crested cocks was just proclaiming a truce to the invasion of night when I finally awoke. I was absolutely aghast, and I rushed over to the corpse. I held the lamp up to it, and uncovered the dead man's face, peering at each feature, but all were unharmed. The wretched wife now came bursting in, tearful and troubled, accompanied by the witnesses of the previous day. She at once descended on the corpse. After kissing it long and hard, she examined all its features under the revealing witness of the lamp. She then turned away, and called for her steward Philodespotus, instructing him to pay the faithful guard his reward at once. There and then the money was handed over. "Young man", she said "we are most grateful to you. I swear that from now on we will regard you as one of our intimate friends, because of this conscientious service which you have performed."

'I was ecstatic with joy at this turn of events, and at the profit which I had obtained against all expectation. Those gleaming gold coins I jangled repeatedly in my hand, gazing in wonder at them. "My lady," I said, "think of me not as a friend, but as one of your servants. Whenever you need my assistance you can call on me with assurance." No sooner were the words out of my mouth than the whole ménage at once attacked me, grabbing any weapon to hand and cursing this outrageous suggestion of future misfortune. One battered my face with his fists, another elbowed me betwen the shoulder-blades, a third pummelled my ribs violently with his hands. They kicked me, pulled my hair, ripped my clothes. I was ejected from the house, lacerated and torn apart like the arrogant Aonian, or the Pipleian poet who sang his poems.

27 'Out in the street close by I recovered my breath. I realized all too late that my words had been ill-omened and thoughtless, and I ruefully acknowledged that I had deserved a worse beating than I had sustained. But by now the corpse had emerged and was being greeted with tears and the final lamentations. Since the dead man was from the upper class, he was being conducted through the forum in a public funeral-procession according to ancestral ritual. Then an old

man clad in black confronted the cortège; he showed his
distress by weeping and tearing at his noble white hair. He
laid hold of the coffin with both hands, and spoke in strained
tones, punctuated by frequent sobbing. "Citizens," he said, "I
beg you by your sense of honour and devotion to the state to
avenge this murdered citizen, and to punish harshly this
wicked and criminal woman for her most pernicious crime.
She and no other has poisoned this wretched young man, the
son of my sister, to win the favour of her adulterous lover, and
to lay hands on the spoil of his inheritance."

'These were the tearful complaints loudly voiced by the old
man to one and all. The crowd meanwhile was becoming
aggressive, for the plausibility of the accusation inclined them
to lend credence to the charge. They called for torches,
demanded stones, encouraged urchins to finish off the woman.
She confronted the attack with crocodile tears, and swore by
all the gods as reverently as she could that she was guiltless of
such a dread crime.

28   'In consequence the old man said: "Then let us refer
judgement of the truth to the foresight of the gods. Zatchlas, a
leading Egyptian prophet, is here. Some time ago he promised
on payment of a large fee to bring back for a short time this
spirit from the dead, and to instil into this body the life which
it enjoyed before death." As he spoke, he introduced a young
man clad in linen garments, with palm-leaf sandals on his
feet. His head was wholly shaven. For some time the old man
kissed the prophet's hands and clasped his knees, saying:
"Have pity, O priest, have pity! By the stars of heaven, by the
powers of hell, by the elements of the universe, by the silences
of the night, by the sacred shrines of Coptus, by the floods of
the Nile, by the mysteries of Memphis and the rattles of
Pharos, grant a momentary loan from the sun and inject some
modest light into these eyes which are forever closed. We do
not seek to defy fate, or to deny to the earth its possession, but
we implore a brief moment of life to obtain the consolation of
vengeance."

'The prophet was won over by these words, and placed one
small herb on the corpse's mouth, and another on the heart.

Then he turned to the east, and silently prayed to the nascent rising of the venerable sun. The sight of this awesome drama roused those present to vie in eagerness to witness so great a miracle.

29   'I slipped into the midst of the crowd of the dead man's associates, and perched on a rock behind the bier. The rock was a little higher, and I surveyed the whole scene with inquisitive eyes. The dead man's chest first began to swell, his life-giving veins began to throb, and his body filled with breath. Then the corpse sat up, and the young man spoke. "Why, I implore you, now that I have drunk of the cups of Lethe and am swimming in the marshy waters of the Styx, why do you haul me back to life's duties for a brief moment? Cease to summon me, cease, I beg you; allow me to return to my rest." These were the words heard from the corpse, but the prophet addressed him rather sharply: "Why do you not recount the details and reveal to the citizens the secrets of your death? Are you not aware that the Furies can be summoned by my curses on you, and that your weary limbs can be subjected to torture?" The dead man raised himself from the bier, and uttering the hollowest of groans he addressed the people in these words: "I was destroyed by the evil arts of my new bride. I was sentenced to drink a cup of poison, and I surrendered my bed while it was still warm to an adulterer."

'Then that most worthy wife adopted a bold stratagem suited to the moment, and with sacrilegious spirit confronted her husband, and argued with him as he condemned her. The citizens were fired up, but took opposite stances. Some claimed that this was the worst woman alive, and that she should be buried with her husband's body, while others argued that no credence should be lent to the lying words of the corpse.

30   'But the next words of the young man removed this hesitation. Once again he uttered a hollow groan, and said: "Very well, I shall offer you, yes, offer you, clear proofs of the untainted truth. I will reveal what no person whosoever other than myself will know or prophesy." He then pointed me out

with his finger. "When this most prudent guardian of my corpse was keeping a careful watch over me, some aged sorceresses were hovering close to my remains. They transformed themselves several times to get at me, but in vain, because they failed to beguile his conscientious diligence. Finally they invested him in a cloud of sleep, and immured him in deep slumber. Then they never ceased summoning me by name until my immobile joints and cold limbs made sluggish attempts to render obedience to their magic art. This fellow here was actually alive, and merely dead to the world in sleep. He bears the same name as I, and at the calling of his name he rose up all unknowing, and stepped out of his own accord like the ghost of a dead man. Though the doors of the chamber had been barred carefully, there was a hole in them, and through it the witches cut off first his nose and then his ears. In this way he took my place in undergoing such surgery. Then, to ensure that their deceit would pass unnoticed in what followed, they shaped wax to represent the ears which they had cut off, and gave him a perfect fit. Likewise they fashioned a nose like his own. The poor man now standing here gained a reward not for being diligent, but for being mutilated."

'At these words I was panic-stricken, and proceeded to investigate my face. I clapped my hand to my nose; it came away. I pulled at my ears, and they too fell off. The bystanders identified me by pointing me out with their fingers, and turning their heads towards me, and they broke out into shrieks of laughter. I was in a cold sweat, and I slipped away, threading my path between their feet. Because of my mutilated appearance I am a risible figure, and I have been subsequently unable to return to my ancestral home. I have concealed the loss of my ears by letting my hair grow on both sides of my face, and the unsightly appearance of my lost nose I have made respectable by covering it with this linen bandage which is tightly wrapped over it.'

31   As soon as Thelyphron had finished this story, the drinkers, who were now well into their cups, renewed their guffaws. As they demanded their customary toast to the god Laughter,

Byrrhena explained to me: 'Tomorrow is a feast-day which was established in the early days of this city. We are the only people who on this day seek the benevolence of the god Laughter in an amusing and joyful ritual. Your presence will make the day more pleasant for us. My wish is that you may devise some happy entertainment from your store of wit to honour the god, so that in this way our offering to the great deity may be enlarged and enhanced.'

'That is a good suggestion', I replied, 'and I will follow your instruction. I only hope that I can think of some material to enable the great god to deck himself out in a flowing mantle.' Then, at the prompting of my slave, who warned me that darkness had fallen, I hastily rose from the table. By now I was as bloated with drink as the rest, and with an abrupt farewell to Byrrhena I started to weave my way homeward.

32   But as soon as we reached the nearest street, the torch on which we depended was blown out by a sudden gust of wind. We could scarcely escape the grip of the blinding darkness, and as we wearily made our way back to the lodging, we bruised our toes on the cobble-stones. As we held on to each other, we were now nearing our goal when suddenly three lusty figures with massive frames pushed against our doors with all their weight. They showed not the slightest concern at our arrival, but battered the doors with greater violence, vying with each other in their assaults. We both, and I myself in particular, reasonably assumed that they were ruffians of the most violent kind, so I at once extricated and gripped my sword which I had concealed beneath my clothing, and had carried abroad for just such an occasion as this. Without hesitation I flew into the band of robbers, and drove my sword up to the hilt into each one that I encountered in the struggle. Eventually they lay before my feet, punctured by numerous gaping wounds, and they gasped out their last breath.

The din of this engagement had roused Photis, and she opened the door. I crept in, panting and bathed in sweat. I at once retired to bed and sleep, for I was wearied with this battle against three brigands, which had been a re-enactment of the slaughter of Geryon.

BOOK 3

The Festival of Laughter: Lucius Becomes an Ass

1 Just as Aurora with her crimson trappings brandished her rosy arm and began to drive her chariot across the sky, I was wrenched out of untroubled sleep as the night restored to me the light of day. Anxiety assailed my mind as I recalled the incident of the previous evening. With my feet tucked beneath me and my hands clasped over my knees with fingers interlocked, I sat squatting on my bed and wept floods of tears, picturing before my mind now the forum as the scene of the trial, now the sentence, and finally the very executioner. 'Will any juror', I asked myself, 'show himself so merciful and well-disposed to me as to be able to declare me innocent, gore-stained as I am after that triple slaughter, and steeped in the blood of so many citizens? Was this the journeying which the Chaldaean Diophanes proclaimed with such assurance would bring me fame?' As I turned these thoughts over repeatedly in my mind, I lamented my misfortune.

2 Meanwhile there was a banging on the door, and our portals echoed with the shouting of a crowd outside. At once the house was thrown open, and a great number burst in. The whole place was jammed with magistrates, their officials, and an assorted mob. Two attendants proceeded to lay hands on me on the instruction of the magistrates, and began to drag me off as I offered no resistance. As soon as we reached the nearest street, the whole township poured out and followed us in astounding numbers. As I walked along dejectedly with head bowed towards the ground (or rather, towards the denizens of hell), I observed from the corner of my eye a most surprising sight. Of the thousands of people milling about, there was not a single one who was not splitting his sides with laughter. After being paraded through all the streets—for they led me round from one corner to another, as if they were expiating the threat of portents by driving round sacrificial

victims in ceremonies of purification—I was dragged before the tribunal in the forum.

The magistrates now took their seats on the raised platform, and the city-herald loudly demanded silence. Suddenly from all present there was a concerted demand that since the huge crowd was in danger of being crushed because of the excessive numbers, this important case should be tried in the theatre. At once from every side the people darted off and with astonishing speed packed the auditorium. They even jammed the aisles and the concourse at the top. Several wound their legs round columns, others hung from statues, a few were partly visible through the windows and ornamental trellis-work. All were indifferent to the hazards threatening their physical safety in this curious eagerness to observe the proceedings. Then the city officials escorted me like a sacrificial victim across the stage, and made me stand in the orchestra.

3   The prosecutor, an elderly man, was then summoned by a further loud cry from the herald. As he rose, water was poured into a small vessel, which was finely perforated like a colander to allow it to run out drop by drop; this was to regulate the time allowed for speaking. The man addressed the assembly as follows:

'The case before us, august citizens, is no trivial one. It has a bearing on the peace of the whole community, and will be valuable for the stern example it sets. Hence it is all the more fitting that one and all here present, in the interests of the dignity of this our city, should carefully ensure that this impious killer may not escape punishment for the multiple butchery which he has bloodily perpetrated. Pray do not believe that I am fired by private enmity, or that I am indulging savage hatred of a personal kind. My job is as commander of the night-patrol, and I believe that my sleepless supervision can be censured by no one up to this very day.

'I shall now turn to the matter in hand, and scrupulously recount the events of last night. Just after midnight I patrolled the city, scrutinizing in careful detail every area door by door.

I caught sight of this most savage youth with his dagger
drawn, wreaking slaughter all around, and before his feet I
observed three victims slain by his savagery. They were still
breathing, their bodies suffering convulsions in pools of blood.
This man was justly apprehensive because he knew that he
had committed this great outrage, and so he at once fled,
slipping away under cover of darkness into some house where
he lay hidden throughout the night. But the gods' foresight
allows no respite to evildoers, and early this morning I waited
for him before he could escape by unobserved paths, and I
ensured that he was haled before this most austere court
which exacts sacred oaths. Here, then, you have a defendant
sullied by numerous murders, a defendant caught in the act, a
defendant who is a stranger to our city. So cast your votes
responsibly against this foreigner, who is charged with an
offence for which you would heavily punish even a fellow-
citizen.'

4   With these words that most incisive prosecutor ended his
monstrous indictment. The herald bade me at once to embark
upon whatever response I wished to make. But at that
moment I could come out with nothing but tears, caused by
contemplating not so much that remorseless indictment as my
own afflicted conscience. But then I felt the accession of
heaven-sent courage, so I made this response to the charges.

'I am well aware how difficult it is for a man accused of
murder to persuade this large crowd of his innocence when
the bodies of three citizens lie here before your eyes. This
would be the case even if he speaks the truth and acknow-
ledges the deed without prompting. But if with collective
good-will you consent to grant me a cursory hearing, I shall
readily persuade you that it is through no fault of mine that I
am burdened with this capital charge. Rather, the considerable odium of the accusation is baselessly imposed on me
through the chance outcome of my reasonable indignation.

5   'I was making my way back from dinner at a rather late
hour. Admittedly I had taken too much to drink, and I shall
not deny the truth of that. But as I turned in at the house of
your fellow-citizen, the honest Milo, I saw before the very

entrance to the lodging some most ruthless robbers seeking to force their way in. They were trying to wrench the house-doors off their hinges; all the bars which had been most securely installed had been violently torn away. The robbers were plotting with each other the murder of those within. Then one of them, more eager for action and of more imposing physique than the others, began to rouse them to the same pitch with exhortations like these: "Come on, lads, let's attack them, while they sleep, with all our manly spirit and ready vigour. Away with all feelings of hesitation and cowardice! Let slaughter stalk with drawn sword throughout the house. Let's cut down those who lie sleeping, and run through those who try to resist. We shall make good our retreat unscathed only if we leave no one in the house unscathed."

'I freely confess, citizens, that I sought to frighten off and rout these desperadoes. I was armed with a short sword which accompanied me in case of dangers of this kind, and I thought such action the duty of a good citizen. I was also extremely apprehensive for the safety of my hosts and myself. But those utterly savage and monstrous men did not take to their heels, and though they saw that I was armed, they none the less boldly confronted me.

6   'Their battle-line was now assembled. The leader and standard-bearer of the gang promptly assailed me with brute force. He seized me by the hair with both hands, bent my head backward, and intended to batter me with a stone. But while he was urging that one be handed to him, my sword-thrust was true, and I successfully laid him low. A second robber was hanging on to my legs with his teeth; I killed him with a well-directed blow between the shoulder-blades. A third who rushed blindly at me I finished off with a thrust to the heart.

'This was how I maintained the peace, and defended the house of my hosts and the safety of the townsfolk. I believed that I would not merely escape punishment, but would also win public praise. I had never been indicted before on even the most trivial charge. As one highly respected in my community, I had always placed unblemished behaviour

before any advantage. I can see no justification for now
having to stand trial here on account of the just vengeance
which impelled me to take action against these despicable
criminals. No one can point to any previous enmity between
them and myself, or indeed to any previous acquaintance
whatsoever with these robbers. If it is believed that a desire
for ill-gotten gains was the incentive for so great a crime, at
least let such gains be produced.'

7   Tears again rose to my eyes at the close of this utterance. I
stretched out my hands in doleful entreaty to one section of
the audience after another, appealing to their common
humanity and to the love which they bore for their dear ones.
Once I was satisfied that the compassion of all was roused,
and that my tears had stirred their pity, I called to witness the
eyes of the Sun and of Justice, and recommended my
immediate plight to the gods' future care. But when I raised
my gaze a little higher, I saw that the whole gathering without
exception was splitting its sides with loud laughter, and that
even my kind host and patron Milo was unable to contain
himself, and was laughing loudest of all. At that moment I
reflected: 'So this is the nature of good faith and awareness of
right conduct! Here am I, a killer indicted on a capital charge
through ensuring the safety of my host, and he is not satisfied
with refusing me his consoling support; he laughs aloud at my
undoing as well!'

8   At this moment a woman, sobbing and tear-stained,
wearing mourning black and carrying a baby in her lap, came
running down through the theatre. Behind her came a second
figure, an old hag clad in repulsive rags, and equally tearful.
Both brandished olive-branches. They stationed themselves
on each side of the bier on which the corpses of the slain were
shrouded, and they raised a din of lamentation dismally
bewailing their fate: 'We entreat you by the sense of
compassion which you share, and in the name of the universal
rights of mankind. Show pity for these young men un-
deservedly slain. By taking vengeance afford some consolation
to the one of us now widowed, and to the other left forlorn, or
at any rate lend support to the fortunes of this little child

orphaned in his infancy, and do justice to your laws and to public order with the blood of this ruffian.'

Next the senior magistrate rose and addressed the people: 'Not even the perpetrator himself can deny this crime which deserves stern punishment. Only one problem remains for us to deal with: we must seek out the associates in this dreadful deed, for it is unlikely that one man on his own took the lives of three such vigorous young men. So the truth must be extracted from this man by torture. The slave who supported him has escaped unnoticed. We have now reached the stage at which the defendant under interrogation must reveal his accomplices in this crime, so that we may once and for all dispel all our fear of this grim band.'

9   In accordance with Greek custom, fire and a wheel were brought in, together with every variety of whip. My consternation certainly grew; in fact it was redoubled at the prospect of my not being allowed to die unmutilated. But the old woman whose weeping had roused general indignation said: 'Good citizens, before you nail to the cross this ruffian who has murdered the wretched victims who are my dear ones, allow the corpses of the slaughtered men to be uncovered. By gazing on their youthful and handsome bodies you may be further roused to just indignation, and inflict harsh punishment which fits the crime.'

Applause greeted these words, and at once the magistrate ordered me to uncover with my own hands the bodies laid out on the bier. In spite of my struggles and lengthy refusal to revive the memory of my earlier crime by displaying the bodies afresh, at the command of the magistrates the attendants exerted the greatest physical pressure on me to compel me to do so. In short, they forced my hand from where it was dangling at my side to wreak its own doom by guiding it on to the corpses. I was finally compelled to yield; I drew back the pall with the greatest reluctance, and uncovered the bodies.

Heavens, what a sight met my eyes! What an extraordinary thing! What a sudden reversal of my fortunes! A moment before I had been consigned as a slave to the household of

Proserpina and Orcus, but now I was stopped in my tracks
and dumbfounded at this transformation. I have no adequate
words to explain the nature of that strange sight: those corpses
of the slain turned out to be three inflated wineskins which
had been slit open in various places. The gaping holes
appeared where, as I cast my mind back to the battle of
the previous night, I recalled having wounded those
brigands.

10   At that moment the laughter which some had guilefully
repressed for a short time now burst out without restraint to
engulf the entire crowd. Some cackled in paroxysms of mirth,
others pressed their hands to their stomachs to relieve the
pain. In one way or another the entire audience was overcome
with hilarity, and as they quitted the theatre, they kept
looking back at me. From the moment when I seized the
coverlet I myself stood rooted there, frozen into stone like one
of the statues or pillars in the theatre. I did not return to life
until my host Milo came up. As I held back, and sobbed
repeatedly with the tears again welling in my eyes, he laid his
hand on me, and with gentle force drew me along with him.
He took me home by a circuitous route wherever he spotted
deserted streets, and he sought to console me in my
despondency and my continuing apprehension by discoursing
on various matters. But he could not succeed in mitigating in
any way my anger at the insult which had struck me to my
heart's depths.

11   Now, however, the magistrates in person clad in their robes
of office entered our residence and sought to mollify me with
an explanation on these lines. 'Master Lucius, we are well
aware of your high rank, and also of your family's pedigree,
for the nobility of your famous house is known to the whole
province. We assure you that the humiliation which you so
bitterly resent was not intended as an insult, and so you must
banish all the melancholy which at present fills your heart,
and dispel your mental anguish. This festival, which we
regularly celebrate in public as each year comes round, in
honour of Laughter, the most welcome of the gods, always
owes its success to some novel subterfuge. This deity will

favourably and affectionately accompany everywhere the person who arouses and enacts his laughter, and he will never allow you to grieve in mind, but will implant continual joy on your countenance with his sunny elegance. The whole community has now bestowed outstanding honours on you for the pleasure you have given them; for they have enrolled you as patron, and have decreed that your statue be set up in bronze.' To this address I replied: 'The gratitude that I accord to this most glorious and unique city of Thessaly matches the distinctions which you offer me, but I urge you to reserve your statues and portraits for worthier and greater persons than myself.'

12   With this modest response I raised a fleeting smile, pretending as best I could to be cheerful, and as the magistrates departed I bade them a friendly farewell. Suddenly a servant came hastening in. 'Your aunt Byrrhena summons you,' he said. 'She wishes to remind you of the dinner-party which late last night you promised to attend and which will shortly begin.' But I was apprehensive, and even at a distance I shuddered at the thought of her house. So I made the following reply: 'How I wish, dear aunt, that I could obey your bidding, if only I could do so in good faith. But my host Milo has made me promise to have dinner with him today, invoking the deity who is in close attendance on us. He does not leave my side, and does not permit me to leave his, so we must postpone that promise of dinner.'

While I was still dictating this, Milo put his arm firmly in mine, and conducted me to the baths close by, giving instructions that the toiletries should accompany us. I sought to avoid everyone's eyes and made myself inconspicuous as I walked along at his side, avoiding the laughter of passers-by which I had myself promoted. My embarrassment was such that I do not recall how I bathed and towelled and returned to the house again, for I was distraught and paralysed as the eyes and nods and fingers of all present marked me down.

13   The outcome was that having enjoyed a hasty and extremely modest supper at Milo's table, I pleaded as excuse a sharp headache brought on by my continual weeping

carlier, and I readily obtained leave to retire to bed. I threw myself down on my little couch, and in my depression I recalled every detail of what had happened. Eventually my Photis came in, after having seen her mistress to bed. Her demeanour was quite different from before, for she did not look cheerful, nor was her conversation spiced with wit. She wore a sombre look, wrinkling her face into a frown.

At last she spoke hesitantly and timidly. 'I have to confess', she said, 'that I caused this discomfiture of yours.' As she spoke, she produced a strap from under her dress, and handed it to me. 'Take your revenge, I beg you,' she said, 'on a woman who has betrayed you, or exact some punishment even greater than this. But I implore you not to imagine that I deliberately planned this painful treatment for you. God forbid that you should suffer even the slightest vexation on my account. If anything untoward threatens you, I pray that my life-blood may avert it. It was because of a mischance that befell me, when ordered to perform a different task, that the damage was inflicted on you.'

14   Impelled by my habitual curiosity and eager to have the hidden cause of the incident of the previous night revealed, I then replied: 'This is a wicked and most presumptuous strap, since you have allotted it the task of beating you. I shall destroy it by cutting it up or by slashing it to pieces rather than have it touch your skin, which is soft as down and white as milk. But tell me truthfully: what action of yours was attended by the perversity of savage Fortune, and resulted in my downfall? I swear by that head of yours which is so dear to me that I can believe no one, and you least of all, in the suggestion that you laid any plan for my undoing. In any case, a chance happening, or even a detrimental occurrence, cannot convert innocent intentions into guilty deeds.' As I finished speaking, I thirstily applied my mouth to the moist and trembling eyes of my Photis, which were languid with uncontrolled desire, and were now half-closed as I pressed hungry kisses upon them.

15   Her high spirits now restored, 'Please wait a moment', she said, 'until I carefully close the bedroom door. I don't wish to

commit a grievous error by carelessly and sacrilegiously letting my tongue run free.' As she spoke, she thrust home the bolts and fastened the hook securely. Then she came back to me, and took my neck in both her hands. In a low and quite restrained voice, she said: 'I am fearful and mortally terrified of revealing the secrets of this house, and of exposing the hidden mysteries wrought by my mistress. But I have considerable trust in you and your learning. In addition to the noble distinction of your birth and your outstanding intellect, you have been initiated into several sacred cults, and you are certainly aware of the need for the sacred confidentiality of silence. So all that I entrust to the sanctuary of your pious heart you must for ever enclose and guard within its confines, and thus repay the ingenuous trust of my revelations with the steadfast security of your silence. The love which holds me fast to you compels me to reveal to you things which I alone know. You are now to gain acquaintance with the entire nature of our household, with the wondrous and secret spells of my mistress. To these the spirits hearken and the elements are enslaved, and by them the stars are dislocated and the divine powers harnessed. But for no purpose does my mistress have recourse to the power of this art so much as when she eyes with pleasure some young man of elegant appearance, and indeed this is a frequent practice of hers.

16   'At the moment she is passionately obsessed with a young and extremely handsome Boeotian, and she eagerly deploys every device and every technique of her art. Only this evening I heard her with my own ears threatening the sun itself with cloud cover and unbroken darkness because it had not retired from the sky quickly enough, and had yielded to nightfall too late for her to practise the enticements of magic. Yesterday, when she was on her way back from the baths, she happened to catch sight of the young man sitting in the barber's, and she ordered me to remove secretly his hair which had been snipped off by the scissors and was lying on the floor. As I was carefully and unobtrusively gathering it, the barber caught me at it. Now we in this city have a bad name for practising the art of sorcery, so he grabbed me brusquely and rebuked

me. "You brazen hussy, is there no end to your repeatedly stealing the hair of eligible young men? If you don't finally stop this criminal practice, I'll have you up at once before the magistrates." He followed up his words with action; he thrust his hands between my breasts, felt around, and angrily extracted some hair which I had already hidden there. I was extremely concerned at this turn of events, remembering my mistress's usual temper. She often gets quite annoyed if she is frustrated in this way, and she takes it out on me most savagely. I actually thought of running away from her, but the thought of you at once caused me to reject the idea.

17   'I was just returning dispirited and afraid to go back empty-handed from the barber's, when I saw a man paring some goatskins with scissors. Once I watched the skins inflated, tightly tied, and hanging up, and the hair from them lying on the ground and of the same blonde colour as that of the young Boeotian, I abstracted a quantity of it and passed it to my mistress, concealing its true provenance. So it was that in the first hours of darkness, before you returned from your dinner, my mistress Pamphile in a fit of ecstatic madness climbed up towards the overlapping roof. On the far side of the house there is an area which is uncovered and exposed to the elements. It commands every view on the eastern side, as well as those in other directions. So it is especially convenient for those magical arts of hers, and she practises them there in secret. First of all she fitted out her infernal laboratory with the usual supplies, including every kind of aromatic plant, metal strips inscribed with unintelligible letters, the surviving remains of ill-omened birds, and a fairly large collection of corpses' limbs, earlier mourned over by relatives and in some cases even buried. Noses and fingers were in a heap in one place, and in another, nails from the gibbet to which there still clung flesh from the men hanged there. In yet another place the blood of slaughtered men was kept, and also gnawed skulls, torn from the fangs of wild beasts.

18   'Then, after chanting spells over quivering entrails, she poured propitiating offerings of various liquids —now spring water, now cow's milk, now mountain-honey; she also poured

out mead. She twisted and entwined the locks of hair with each other, and placed them on live coals to be burnt with a variety of fragrant plants. Immediately, through this combination of the irresistible power of her magic lore and the hidden energy of the harnessed deities, the bodies from which the hair was crackling and smoking acquired human breath, and were able to feel and walk. They headed for the place to which the stench from the hair they had shed led them, and thus they took the place of the Boeotian youth in barging at the doors, in their attempt to gain entrance. At that moment you appeared on the scene, drunk with wine and deceived by the darkness of the sightless night. You drew your short sword, and armed yourself for the role of the mad Ajax. But whereas he inflicted violence on living cattle and lacerated whole herds, you much more courageously dealt the death-blow to three inflated goatskins. Thus you laid low the enemy without shedding a drop of blood, so that I can embrace not a homicide but an utricide.'

19   This elegant remark of Photis made me smile, and I responded in the same joking spirit. 'Well then,' I said, 'I can regard this as the first trophy won by my valour, in the tradition of Hercules' twelve labours, for I can equate the body of Geryon which was in triplicate, or the three-formed shape of Cerberus, with the like number of skins that I slew. But to obtain as you desire my forgiveness willingly for the entire error by which you involved me in such great distress, you must grant me the favour which is my dearest wish. Let me watch your mistress when she sets in train some application of her supernatural art. Let me see her when she summons the gods, or at any rate when she changes her shape. I am all agog to witness magic from close up. Mind you, you yourself do not seem to be a novice wholly innocent of such things. I have come to be quite convinced of this, for your flashing eyes and rosy cheeks, your shining hair, your kisses with parted lips, and your fragrant breasts hold me fast as your willing slave and bondsman, whereas previously I always spurned the embraces of matrons. So now I have no thought of returning home or planning my departure there;

there is nothing which I count better than spending a night with you.'

20   'Lucius,' she replied, 'I should dearly love to grant your wish, but her surly disposition aside, Pamphile invariably seeks solitude and likes to perform such secret rites when no one else is present. However, I shall put your wish before my personal danger. I shall watch out for a favourable occasion, and carefully arrange what you seek. My only stipulation, as I said at the beginning, is that you must promise to maintain silence in this momentous matter.'

As we chatted away, our desire for each other roused the minds and bodies of both of us. We threw off the clothes we wore until we were wholly naked, and enjoyed a wild love-orgy. When I was wearied with her feminine generosity, Photis offered me a boy's pleasure. Finally this period of wakefulness caused our eyes to droop; sleep invaded them, and held us fast until it was broad daylight.

21   After we had spent a few nights in such pleasurable pursuits, one day Photis came hurrying to me trembling with excitement. Her mistress, she said, was having no success in her love-affair by other means, and so she intended on the following night to invest herself with a bird's plumage, and to join her beloved by taking wing. I should accordingly be ready to observe with due circumspection this astonishing feat. So just as darkness fell, Photis led me silently on tiptoe to that upper chamber, and instructed me to witness what was happening there through a chink in the door.

Pamphile first divested herself of all her clothing. She then opened a small casket and took from it several small boxes. She removed the lid from one of these, and extracted ointment from it. This she rubbed for some time between her hands, and then smeared it all over herself from the tips of her toes to the crown of her head. She next held a long and private conversation with the lamp, and proceeded to flap her arms and legs with a trembling motion. As she gently moved them up and down, soft feathers began to sprout on them, and sturdy wings began to grow. Her nose became curved and hard, and her nails became talons. In this way Pamphile became an owl; she uttered a plaintive squawk as she tried out her new identity by gradually forsaking the ground. Soon she rose aloft, and with the full power of her wings quitted the house.

22   This was how Pamphile deliberately changed her shape by employing techniques of magic. I too was spellbound, but not through any incantation. I was rooted to the ground with astonishment at this event, and I seemed to have become something other than Lucius. In this state of ecstasy and riveted mindlessness, I was acting out a waking dream, and accordingly I rubbed my eyes repeatedly in an effort to discover whether I was awake. Finally I returned to awareness of my surroundings, and seizing Photis' hand I placed it on my eyes. 'While the chance allows', I begged her, 'do please allow me one great and unprecedented boon bestowed by your affection. Get me, my honey-sweet, a little ointment from that same box—by those dear breasts of yours I beg you. Bind me as your slave for ever by a favour which I can never repay, and in this way ensure that I shall become a winged Cupid, drawing close to my Venus.'

'Is that what you're after, my foxy lover?' she asked. 'Are you trying to force me to apply an axe to my own limbs? When you are in that vulnerable state, I can scarcely keep you safe from those two-legged Thessalian wolves! And where shall I seek you, when shall I see you, once you become a bird?'

23   'The gods preserve me from perpetrating such an outrage,' I replied. 'Even if I were to fly through the entire heavens on the soaring wings of an eagle, as the appointed messenger or happy squire of highest Jove, would I not sweep down from time to time from the enjoyment of such distinction on the wing to this fond nest of mine? I swear by this sweet knot that binds your hair and has enmeshed my heart, there is no other girl I prefer to my dear Photis. A second thought comes to my mind: once I have smeared myself and have become a bird like that, I shall have to keep a safe distance from all habitations. What a handsome and amusing lover I should make for matrons to enjoy when I'm an owl! If those night-

birds do get inside a house, the residents, as we see, take care to catch them and nail them to their doors, to expiate by their sufferings the threatened destruction to the household occasioned by their ill-omened flight. But I almost forgot to ask: what word or action do I need to discard those feathers and to return to my being Lucius?' 'You have no worries in ensuring that,' she answered, 'for my mistress has shown me each and every substance that can restore to human form those who have adopted such shapes. Do not imagine that she did this out of mere goodwill; it was so that I could aid her with an efficacious remedy on her return. Observe with what cheap and everyday herbs such a great transformation is achieved. You wash yourself with water in which a sprig of dill and some bay-leaves have been steeped, and drink some of it.'

24   She made this claim repeatedly, and then with great apprehension she crept into the chamber, and took a box from the casket. First I hugged and kissed it, and prayed that it would bring me happy flying hours. Then I hastily tore off all my clothes, dipped my hands eagerly into the box, drew out a good quantity of the ointment, and rubbed all my limbs with it. I then flapped my arms up and down, imitating the movements of a bird. But no down and no sign of feathers appeared. Instead, the hair on my body was becoming coarse bristles, and my tender skin was hardening into hide. There were no longer five fingers at the extremities of my hands, for each was compressed into one hoof. From the base of my spine protruded an enormous tail. My face became misshapen, my mouth widened, my nostrils flared open, my lips became pendulous, and my ears huge and bristly. The sole consolation I could see in this wretched transformation was the swelling of my penis—though now I could not embrace Photis.

25   As I helplessly surveyed the entire length of my body, and came to the realization that I was not a bird but an ass, I tried to complain at what Photis had done to me. But I was now deprived of the human faculties of gesture and speech; all I could do by way of silent reproach was to droop my lower lip,

and with tearful eyes give her a sidelong look. As soon as she saw what I had become, she beat her brow with remorseful hands and cried: 'That's the end of poor me! In my panic and haste I made a mistake; those look-alike boxes deceived me. But the saving grace is that the remedy for this transformation is quite easy and available. Just chew some roses, and you will stop being an ass and at once become my Lucius again. I only wish that I had plaited some garlands this evening as I usually do, and then you would not have had the inconvenience of even one night's delay. But as soon as dawn breaks, the remedy will be set before you with all speed.'

26   She kept wailing on like this. Though I was now a perfect ass, a Lucius-turned-beast, I still preserved my human faculties, and I gave long and serious thought to whether I should end the life of that most nefarious and abominable woman by kicking her repeatedly with my hooves and by tearing her apart with my teeth. But second thoughts deterred me from that rash course, for I feared that if Photis suffered the punishment of death, I should lose all my prospects of saving help. So angrily shaking my drooping head from side to side, I swallowed the indignity for the time being, and submitted to this most bitter of misfortunes. I retired to the stable to join the horse which had served as my trusty mount. I found another ass stabled there, which belonged to Milo my former host. I imagined that if dumb animals shared a silent comradeship bestowed by nature, that horse of mine would register some acknowledgement and pity for me, and would offer me hospitality and a decent lodging. But Jupiter, god of hospitality, and Faith, who has withdrawn her divinity from men, can testify how differently things turned out. That reputable mount of mine and the ass put their heads together and at once plotted my destruction. I can only assume that their concern was for their provender. Scarcely had they spotted me approaching the stall when they laid back their ears, and with flying hooves launched a frenzied attack on me. I was forced back as far as possible from the barley which earlier in the evening I had set down with my own hands in front of that most grateful serving-animal of mine.

27   Such treatment forced me to seek my own company, and I
retired to a corner of the stable. There I reflected on the
arrogance of my fellow-beasts, and I planned revenge on my
disloyal horse next day, when with the aid of roses I would
return to being Lucius. These thoughts were interrupted by
my catching sight of a statue of the goddess Epona seated in a
small shrine centrally placed, where a pillar supported the
roof-beams in the middle of the stable. The statue had been
devotedly garlanded with freshly picked roses. So in an
ecstasy of hope on identifying this assurance of salvation, I
stretched out my forelegs and with all the strength I could
muster, I rose energetically on my hind legs. I craned my neck
forward, and pushed out my lips to their full extent, making
every possible effort to reach the garlands. My attempt was
frustrated by what seemed to be the worst of luck: my own
dear servant, who always had the task of looking after my
horse, suddenly saw what was going on, and jumped up in a
rage 'For how long', he cried, 'are we to endure this clapped-
out beast? A minute ago his target was the animals' rations,
and now he is attacking even the statues of deities! See if
I don't maim and lame this sacrilegious brute!' At once he
looked around for a weapon, and chanced upon a bundle of
wood which happened to be lying there. In it he spotted a
cudgel with its leaves still attached which was bigger than the
rest. He did not lay off beating my wretched body until there
was a loud explosion. The doors were staved in with an
almighty din, and there were fearful shouts from close
at hand of 'Robbers!' At this my slave took to his heels in
panic.

28   At that very moment the doors were violently forced open,
and a band of robbers burst into the whole house. Each area
of it was ringed by an armed contingent, and as people rushed
from every side to lend help, the marauders swiftly positioned
themselves to block their progress. All the robbers were
equipped with swords and torches which brightened the
darkness, for the flames and weapons gleamed like the rising
sun. They then attacked and split open with heavy axes the
treasure-store, which was situated in the middle of the house,

and was secured and bolted with bars of considerable strength; it was packed with Milo's precious stones. When they had forced their way in from every side, they bore off the entire store of treasures, each taking his share in hastily accumulated bundles. But these when assembled proved too many for those who were to carry them, for the extraordinary abundance of their rich haul caused them quite a headache. So they then led the two asses and my horse out of the stable, and loaded us as far as they could with the heavier bundles. They then drove us off from the plundered house with threats from their cudgels, leaving behind one of their comrades to report on the enquiry into the outrage. With repeated beatings they drove us pell-mell over the trackless expanse of mountain.

29 By this time I was as good as dead from the weight of all the baggage, the steep climb over the mountain-top, and the quite lengthy trek. Then—better late than never—the idea occurred to me to appeal to the civil authority, and to free myself from all these hardships by appealing to the august name of the emperor. So when we were now passing in full daylight through a crowded village with a busy market, as I made my way through knots of people I tried to call out Caesar's venerable name in my native Greek tongue. I repeatedly declaimed the 'O' eloquently and loudly enough, but nothing further; the rest of the appeal, the name of Caesar, I could not articulate. The robbers took badly to my unmusical recital, and cut my wretched hide on both sides so severely that they left it useless even as a straining-cloth.

Finally, however, the Jupiter whom we all know handed me an unexpected prospect of salvation. After we had passed many farmhouses and large estates, I sighted a quite pleasing little garden, in which among other attractive plants some virgin roses were in full flower in the morning dew. I drew nearer, with my eyes glued on them. Hope of deliverance made me eager and cheerful. My lips were already working up and down as I made for them. But then a much more salutary plan occurred to me. Undoubtedly, if I shrugged off my ass-identity and returned to being Lucius, I should meet a sticky end at the hands of the robbers, whether because they might suspect me of magical arts, or allege that I would lay evidence against them. So necessity compelled me to steer clear of the roses. I continued to bear with my present plight, and I champed at the bit as though I were an ass.

BOOK 4

At the Bandits' Hideout. Cupid and Psyche (i)

1   At about midday, when the heat was already intense from the
blazing sun, we took lodgings in some village with elderly
acquaintances whom the bandits knew well. This intimacy
became clear to me, even though I was an ass, from their
initial encounter, their torrent of talk, and their exchange of
kisses. Moreover, the robbers presented their hosts with some
gifts unloaded from my back, and they were evidently
explaining in whispered chatter that they were stolen goods.
Next they relieved us of all the baggage, and let us out into the
nearest meadow to graze at will. But having an ass and my
own horse as grazing-companions could hold no pleasures for
me, unused as I yet was to a normal diet of grass. However, I
caught sight of an allotment behind the stable, and as I was
now desperate with hunger I broke boldly into it, and stuffed
myself liberally with the vegetables, raw though they were.
Then with a prayer to the entire company of gods I ran my
eye over the whole expanse in the hope of finding a rose-bed
standing out with its colour from the neighbouring allotments.
The fact that I was now alone made me optimistic; being out
of the way, under cover and well hidden, I thought that I
could gulp down the antidote, and while unobserved could
renounce the bent gait of a four-footed beast, and resume the
upright stance of a man.

2   So as my mind tossed on this sea of thought, I saw at some
distance a valley shaded by a leafy wood. Glinting among
diverse smaller plants and the most luxuriant shrubbery were
some bright roses of ruddy hue. Since my finer feelings were
not wholly bestial, that grove seemed to me to be the abode of
Venus and the Graces; in its shady recesses that delightful
blossom shone out with its brightness of royal crimson. At
once I bounded forward at a gallop, with a prayer to the
smiling deity Success on my lips; and heaven help me, that

swift burst of speed made me feel like a racehorse rather than
an ass. But alas, that superlatively nimble performance failed
to outpace my Fortune's perverse hostility. On drawing near
to the spot, I saw no soft and enticing roses, all moist with the
dew and nectar of heaven, sprouting from their luxuriant
bushes and blessed thorns; there was not even a valley
anywhere. Instead there was merely the lip of a river-bank
enclosed by thickly intertwining trees. These trees with their
abundant foliage look like laurels, and bear pale red, cup-
shaped blossoms opening out like the scented flower. Indeed,
though they have virtually no smell, uneducated folk call
them by their country-name of laurel-roses. If eaten they are
deadly to all grazing animals.

3   Caught fast in this net of fate, I disregarded my personal
safety, and was ready and eager to swallow those poisoned
roses. But as I hesitantly drew near to crop them, a young
man (I presumed him to be the allotment-holder whose entire
crop of vegetables I had plundered) on observing the extent of
his losses came rushing at me in a rage with a huge stick. He
grabbed me, and rained blows all over my body; he would
have put my very life in danger if I had not finally used my
brains, and become my own helper. I raised my rear end high,
kicked out at him repeatedly with my hind legs, and made
good my escape, leaving him badly bruised on the nearby hill
slope. But at that moment a woman (doubtless the man's
wife) looked down from the summit, and on seeing him
stretched out lifeless she at once came bounding down to him,
shrieking and bawling. The pity she meant to arouse was sure
to spell my imminent end, for all the villagers, roused by her
crying, at once together called out their dogs, and set them on
me from every side to charge me in a mad frenzy and rend me
to pieces. At that moment I was undoubtedly on the threshold
of death, for I could see that the dogs, massive in size and
many in number, a match for bears and lions, were
marshalled and being roused against me. So I adapted my
plan to the situation, abandoned my flight, and at full gallop
retired to the stable where our lodgings were. The villagers
held off the dogs with some difficulty, laid hold of me, and

fastened me to a ring with a most secure strap. Once again I would certainly have been finished off by their beatings, but my belly became constricted by the pain from their blows. It was crammed with the raw vegetables, and caused me to be afflicted with diarrhoea. The shit shot out in a stream; some of them were forced back from my now battered haunches when sprayed with this most putrid of fluids, and others with the stench of the stinking fumes.

4   As the sun's bright orb bent low towards the south, the bandits immediately loaded us, and especially myself, with much heavier burdens, and led us out of the stable. We had now travelled most of the way. I was exhausted by the long journey, sagging under the weight of the baggage, wearied by the blows from the cudgels, and now lame and tottering as well, since my hooves were worn out. So I halted by a small stream of gently winding water, and seized with alacrity this splendid opportunity, planning to flex my legs adroitly and to throw my body headlong in. I had made up my mind that no beatings would cause me to rise and continue the journey; I was even ready to die, not merely under the cudgel but also at the point of a sword. I reasoned that in my utter exhaustion and weakness I deserved a compassionate discharge, or at any rate that the bandits, both impatient at delay and eager to hasten their flight, would allot the burden on my back between the two other beasts, and abandon me as prey to the wolves and vultures rather than exact a heavier vengeance.

5   But this splendid plan was nipped in the bud by the most grievous misfortune, for the other ass guessed and forestalled my intention. He at once collapsed, baggage and all, with feigned exhaustion. He lay there like one dead, and made no attempt to rise, in spite of cudgels, goads, and hauling on his tail, ears and legs from every side. Finally the bandits grew weary and abandoned hope of him. They held a parley, and to avoid postponing their flight by tending for so long a dead or rather petrified ass, they divided his load between the horse and myself. They then drew a sword, cut his hamstrings right through, dragged him a little way off the road, and hurled him still breathing over the top of the cliff headlong into the

nearest valley below. As I reflected on the fate of my wretched comrade-in-arms, I decided to renounce guile and deceit, and to show myself a good ass to my masters, especially as I had heard them telling each other that we were about to lodge close by, and that this would form a peaceful end to our entire journey, for it was the base where they lived. We then climbed over a gentle hill, and reached the appointed spot. There all the baggage was unloaded from us, and stowed inside. Freed from my burdens, in place of a bath I sought to relieve my weariness by rolling in the dust.

6   Both subject and occasion demand that I offer an account of the region and of the cave which was the bandits' abode, for at one and the same time I shall stretch my mind and also enable you to measure carefully whether I was an ass in thought and feeling as well as in body. A bristling mountain rose up, shadowy with its woodland foliage, to a towering height. Its slanting and precipitous slopes, girt with rocks which were razor sharp and therefore insurmountable, were flanked by valleys full of hollows and cavities, from which thorn-bushes rose like gigantic ramparts; they formed a natural defence since they faced every side. From the summit a spring gushed out, forming huge bubbles. As it tumbled headlong down, it disgorged its silvery waters, opening out into several rivulets, watering the valleys with a succession of pools, and enclosing the whole area like an encompassing sea or a slow-moving river. A high tower rose over the cavern where the mountain's edges ended. There was a sturdy pen with a strong fence suitable for housing sheep; its sides extended all ways, and served in place of a regular wall before the tiny path which formed the entrance. You could call it— pardon the joke—the bandits' reception room. There was nothing else nearby except a small hut carelessly roofed with reeds, in which as I later discovered look-outs chosen by lot from the complement of bandits kept watch at night.

7   The robbers crouched and crept down into the cave one by one, having tied us with strong straps just outside the entrance. Inside was an old hag doubled up with age, the single individual to whom the safety and care of this

numerous and youthful band seemed to be entrusted. They accosted her with these unfriendly words: 'Hey, you body overdue for burning, you prime insult to the human species, hell's unique reject, are you going to go on sitting at home like this, enjoying yourself? Aren't you going to give us a long-delayed meal to comfort and restore us after our great and dangerous trials? Here you are as usual, doing nothing whatever day and night except greedily pouring strong wine into that demanding belly!' The old woman trembled at this, and fearfully replied in a hoarse whisper: 'My most gallant and faithful protectors, everything is ready, and plenty of it. The stew is cooked and tastes delicious; there's lots of bread, and generous helpings of wine in spotless cups; and the usual hot water is ready for a quick wash-down.' As she finished speaking, they at once stripped off. The heat of the roaring fire gave new life to their naked bodies; they sluiced themselves with hot water, and rubbed oil on themselves. Then they sat at the tables which were generously laden with food.

8   They had just reclined at table when another, much larger group of young men arrived, at once equally recognizable as bandits, for they too brought in their loot of gold and silver coin and vessels, as well as silk garments interwoven with gold thread. Like the others, they too had a wash to revive themselves, and then they took their places on the couches among their comrades. Next they drew lots to act as waiters. Their eating and drinking was uncouth; they devoured pounds of stew, mounds of bread, and buckets of wine. They sported noisily, sang lustily, joked contentiously; their behaviour generally resembled nothing so much as that of the semi-bestial Lapiths and Centaurs at table. Then the strongest of them all said: 'We for our part stoutly and successfully stormed the house of Milo at Hypata, and not only have we acquired this mass of riches by our courage, but we have returned to base without casualties, and if it's worth mention-ing, we have come back eight feet richer. Whereas you who made Boeotian cities your target have lost your most valiant leader Lamachus, and have returned with a reduced force. I should rightly put Lamachus' safety higher than all these

bundles which you have brought back. However it was that his outstanding courage caused his death, the memory of that great man will be famed as much as that of glorious kings and battle-leaders, whereas you, model robbers that you are, in your mean and despicable thieving carry on your rag-and-bone trade by creeping fearfully through baths and old women's lodgings.'

9   One of the later arrivals took up the cudgels. 'Surely everyone knows that larger houses are much easier to storm? Why? Because even if there is a considerable household living in a grand manor, they all take more thought for their own skins than for their master's property. But people who live alone on a modest scale, whether they have a small fortune or, come to that, a large one, hide it away as if it didn't exist, keep a sharper eye on it, and defend it to the point of endangering their life's blood. What happened to us will bear me out. As soon as we reached Thebes with its seven gates, we carefully investigated the inhabitants' finances. We became aware that a certain money-changer called Chryseros had a large fortune, but concealed his wealth by elaborate ruses for fear of having to shoulder public services and shows. In short, he lived alone without a companion, quite happy in his small but well-guarded shack, generally shabby and unkempt, but sitting on his bags of gold. So we decided to make him our first target, thinking nothing of a struggle with one man, and imagining that we could make off with all his riches without trouble and at leisure.

10   'So as soon as night fell we waited at the entrance to his house. We decided not to lift the outer door off its hinges, or to force it, or even to break it down in case the din from the doors roused the entire neighbourhood, and made an end of us. So then Lamachus, our splendid standard-bearer, showing all the confidence of his proven courage, gingerly pushed his hand through the opening made for the key, and tried to dislodge the bar. But Chryseros, that most worthless specimen of all who walk on two feet, had been spying on us all the time, and was watching our every move. On tiptoe and in dead silence he gradually edged his way to the door. Then

suddenly with the utmost force he impaled our leader's hand on the door-panel with a massive nail. He left him there to his fate, with his hand pinned as to a gibbet, and climbed on to the roof of his shack, from where he kept shouting at the top of his voice, imploring the help of his neighbours. He called on each of them by name, warning them of the danger they all faced, giving it out that his house was suddenly engulfed by fire. So one and all panicked at the imminent danger so close at hand, and anxiously rushed to lend help.

11 'This put us on the horns of a dilemma; either we would be overpowered or our comrade abandoned. So with his consent we contrived a drastic solution dictated by the circumstances. With a nicely judged blow right through the joint where the arm is attached to the shoulder, we hacked our leader's arm right off and abandoned it there. We staunched the wound with a bundle of rags so that the drops of blood should not betray our tracks, and we hastily made off, taking with us the rest of Lamachus. We were agitated by our sense of obligation to him, and this afflicted and greatly confused us; but fear of pressing danger frightened us into flight. Our magnanimous, lion-hearted leader could neither make haste to follow us, nor find safety in staying behind. He plaintively urged us with re-peated appeals and repeated prayers by Mars' right hand and by the sacred trust of our oath to deliver our goodly comrade from both pain and capture. Why, he demanded, should a brave bandit live on without the hand which alone could rob and strangle? He would be quite happy at the prospect of self-sought death at a comrade's hand. But when none of us could be induced to accede to his eager plea that we slay our father, with his remaining hand he drew his sword, planted a lingering kiss upon it, and with the fiercest of thrusts plunged it into his heart. We then paid our respects to the brave spirit of our stout-hearted leader. We carefully wrapped his body's remains in a linen cloth, and entrusted him to the safe anonymity of the sea. Our Lamachus now lies buried with an entire element for his grave.

12 'Lamachus, then, appended to his life an end worthy of his virtues. But Alcimus could not distract Fortune's savage will

from his ingenious plan. He broke into the tiny hut of an old woman as she slept, and climbed to her room above. But instead of throttling the life out of her as he ought to have done, he decided first to sling out her possessions one by one through the window, which was quite broad, so that we could bear them off. He heaved them all out enthusiastically, and he was disinclined to forgo even the couch on which the poor old thing was sleeping, so he rolled her off her little bed. He was about to throw down with it the rest of the bedclothes which he pulled from under her, when that shameless creature grovelled at his knees and pleaded with him: "Tell me, son, why are you presenting these measly, bedraggled possessions of a wretched old lady to my rich neighbours whose house is overlooked by this window?" Alcimus was taken in by the crafty guile of these words. Thinking that she was telling the truth, he feared that all that he had earlier dropped down, as well as what he was about to throw out, would be directed not to his comrades but into the house of strangers. He was now convinced of his mistake, so he hung out of the window to take a careful look all around, and in particular to assess the wealth of the neighbouring house which the old woman had mentioned. While concentrating on trying to do this, he was off his guard, and that wicked old woman gave him a push. It wasn't violent, but it was sudden and unexpected. He was balanced precariously, and focusing too on the scene outside. So she sent him flying down. Not only did he tumble from a great height, but he also landed on a huge boulder lying near the house. His rib-cage was shattered and burst open, and he spewed out streams of blood from deep down inside. After he had told us what had happened, he died without suffering much longer. We buried him as we did his predecessor, so Lamachus gained from our hands a good second-in-command.

13   'Under the blow of this double bereavement, we then abandoned our operations in Thebes, and moved up to Plataea, the nearest town. There we heard some common gossip about a certain Demochares who was soon to mount a gladiatorial show. This leading noble was fabulously wealthy and outstandingly generous, and he was laying on a public

entertainment matching the splendour of his fortune. I doubt if anyone has the talent or eloquence to describe properly the individual features of his diverse preparations. On one side were gladiators of celebrated prowess, on another hunters of renowned fleetness of foot, on another criminals whose prospects of reprieve were bleak; these last were the means by which the wild beasts would feast and fatten themselves. As part of a complex contraption there were gaily painted wooden towers assembled in stories to form a mobile house, and handsome animal-cages intended for the hunting-entertainment soon to be enacted. And then the number of beasts, and the different species! Why, in his boundless enthusiasm, Demochares had also imported from abroad the noble beasts which were to entomb the condemned criminals. In addition to the other furnishings of this splendid show, he had used every penny he inherited on purchasing a large number of huge she-bears; besides those he had trapped in local hunts and those he had bought at great expense, there were those which his friends had vied in bestowing on him on various occasions, and he had the costly business of upkeep and of careful feeding on them.

14   'But this bright and arresting provision of public entertainment did not escape Envy's baleful eyes. The bears, wearied by their long captivity, emaciated by the summer heat, and enervated by idle inactivity, succumbed to a sudden epidemic, so that scarcely one remained. You could see the hulks of half-dead beasts cast up like wrecks in street after street. Thereupon the common herd, compelled by sordid poverty and monotony of diet to seek any disgusting addition of free food for their shrunken bellies, fell on this feast which lay everywhere. This inspired Eubulus here and myself to devise a crafty plan. We carried off one of the bears, the biggest of the lot, to our hide-out as if to prepare it for eating. We carefully separated the flesh from the skin, adroitly keeping the claws whole and undamaged, and leaving the beast's head in place down to the neck-joint. We then carefully thinned out the skin by scraping it, sprinkled it with fine ash, and left it in the sun to dry. While the blazing heat of

heaven was absorbing the moisture, we stuffed ourselves
manfully with the bear-meat, and allotted duties for the
forthcoming operation. One of our number (it would be the
person who excelled the rest in mental resolve rather than in
physical strength, and who above all must be a volunteer) was
to cover himself in the skin, and assume the appearance of a
bear. He would be led into Demochares' house, and would
exploit the quiet of the night to give us ready access through
the gate.

15   'This crafty idea had induced quite a number of our most
valiant brotherhood to volunteer for the role. Thrasyleon was
chosen in preference to the rest by the vote of the band, and he
submitted to the hazard of this uncertain contrivance. With
untroubled face he enclosed himself in the skin, now supple
and easily adjusted. We then sewed the edges of it together
with tiny stitches, and we covered the slight slit, where we had
joined the skin together, with the thick surrounding bristles.
Then we forced Thrasyleon's head into the narrow confines of
the throat where the animal's neck had been cut out. We
made small holes around the nose and eyes to allow him to
breathe and to see, and then we guided our most intrepid of
comrades, now a hundred per cent beast, to a cage which we
had bought quite cheaply for the job. Of his own accord he
crept hastily in, bravely and eagerly. After thus making the
initial preparations, we proceeded to complete the deception.

16   'We elicited the name of a certain Nicanor, a Thracian by
origin who cultivated the closest ties of friendship with
Demochares, and then we composed a letter purporting to
convey that this good friend had devoted the first fruits of his
hunting to adorn the show. By now evening had come on, so
we exploited the cover of darkness to consign to Demochares
the cage containing Thrasyleon, together with the forged
letter. He marvelled at the size of the beast, and showed
delight at his friend's timely munificence. Generous fellow
that he was, he ordered ten gold pieces to be counted out of his
money-box and presented to us as the agents of his joy. The
novelty of such a sight usually draws people's attention, and
hordes of folk gathered to admire the beast. Our comrade

Thrasyleon was clever enough to keep their nosy inspection at bay by repeatedly and threateningly advancing on them. The citizens with one voice kept hymning Demochares as a quite god-favoured, blessed man, for after the great disaster which had befallen the bears, he was somehow managing to challenge Fortune by obtaining a new supply. He ordered the beast to be taken at once to his country estate, and later brought back again with the utmost care.

17   'But I broke in: "This bear, sir, is exhausted by the sun's heat and the long journey. You should be chary about putting her amongst a great herd of animals which I hear are unwell. Better instead to look for an open, airy space in your residence here, if possible somewhere cool close to a pond. You surely know that this kind of animal usually makes its home in wooded groves, moist caves, and by pleasant streams?" Demochares was chastened by these warnings, recalling the number of beasts which he had lost. He agreed without reluctance, and readily allowed us to position the cage where we thought best. "We are also quite ready", I said to him, "to stay here and keep watch on the cage overnight. The animal is exhausted by the trials of the heat and the upheaval, and we can be more careful in giving him his meals on time, and his usual drink." "There is no need for us to put you to this trouble", answered Demochares, "as virtually the whole household is used to feeding bears through long practice."

18   'We then said our goodbyes and departed. After emerging from the city gate, we caught sight of a tomb in a remote and hidden spot well away from the road. In it were scattered about some coffins, occupied by the dust and ashes of the departed, their lids only half-fastened through time's decay. These we opened so that they could serve as storage for our prospective loot. Then, following the routine of our school, we waited for the time of night when the moon has set, when sleep launches its initial attack on men's minds, and then invades them in greater force and subdues them. We positioned our detachment, armed with swords, at the very entrance to Demochares' house to demonstrate our intention to plunder it. Thrasyleon, no less active, crept out of his cage

at the precise hour of night which robbers favour. With his sword he at once disposed of every single guard heavily asleep nearby, and then killed the doorman himself. He abstracted the key, opened the doors, and as we rushed in eagerly and made for the inside of the house, he pointed out to us the strongroom where he had smartly observed a quantity of silver being stored the evening before. By a combined assault we at once forced our way in. I ordered each of the comrades to pick up all the gold and silver they could carry, hide it with haste in that abode of our faithful friends the dead, and run back at top speed for another load. In the interests of all of us I would wait alone at the door and keep a careful eye on the proceedings until they returned. And the sight of the bear charging at large through the middle of the house seemed enough to deter any of the household who might happen to be awake. However valiant and fearless any of them was, on sighting the monstrous shape of the huge beast, and especially at night, he would surely take to his heels at once, and shut himself in with fear and trembling, barring the door of his room behind him.

19   'But after we had duly organized all this with meticulous planning, a sinister incident befell us. While I was waiting on tenterhooks for my comrades to return, a slave-boy was roused by the noise; doubtless it was the will of heaven. He crept softly out, and sighted the beast charging around at large all over the house. Maintaining complete silence, he turned in his tracks and managed to inform everyone in the house of what he had seen. The whole place was at once overflowing with the teeming hordes of the household. The darkness was brightened with torches, lamps, tapers, candles, and other means of nocturnal illumination. Not one of that great crowd emerged unarmed; each and all stood guard over the doorways armed with cudgels, lances, and even drawn swords. There were hunting-dogs too, long-eared, shaggy creatures, being egged on to pin down the beast.

20   'While the confusion was still mounting, I imperceptibly stole away, retreating backwards, but as I lurked behind the door I could clearly see Thrasyleon putting up a marvellous

struggle against the dogs. Though heading close to life's finishing-post, he did not forget his honour or ours, nor his long-standing courage, but he continued to fight in the very jaws of the gaping Cerberus. In short, as long as life lasted he continued in the role which he had willingly undertaken. Now retreating, now holding fast, with various postures and body-movements he finally slipped out of the house. Yet though he had escaped into the open, he could not flee to safety, for all the fierce dogs from the next alley-way formed a column in great numbers and attached themselves to the hunting-dogs, which had likewise at that moment come pouring out of the house in pursuit. It was a grim and deadly sight to see; our Thrasyleon encircled and besieged by packs of savage dogs, and ripped apart by repeated bites. Finally, I could not bear the great strain. I joined myself to the milling crowd, and sought to lend a hidden hand to my good comrade by the only means I could, and to deter the leaders of the chase. "What a monstrous, unforgivable scandal!" I said, "we are destroying a great and truly precious beast!"

21   'But my artful words did not avail that most ill-starred young man, for a tall, strong fellow burst out of the house, and without hesitation plunged his lance into the beast's heart. A second man did the same, and a crowd of them, their fear now dispelled, vied with each other in plunging their swords also into him from close at hand. But Thrasyleon, that matchless glory of our band, did not betray the sanctity of his oath by any cry, let alone an exclamation of pain. It was not his endurance, but rather the breath of life in him which was finally overcome, though it deserved immortality. Now ripped apart by the hounds' teeth and slashed by swords, with resolute roaring and bestial howling he bore his imminent fate with noble animation, surrendering his life to its due end, but gaining glory for himself. He had thrown the mob into such panic-stricken and terrified confusion that until dawn broke, and in fact until it was fully daylight, not one man dared to lay so much as a finger on the beast, though it lay prostrate. But at last a butcher who was somewhat bolder than the rest gingerly and fearfully slit open the beast's belly, and stripped

our noble bandit of his bear. This was how Thrasyleon joined the ranks of our dead, but his fame will never die. We rapidly fastened up the baggage which the faithful corpses had preserved for us, and left the confines of Plataea at top speed. We repeatedly reflected how true it was that in this life of ours Lady Loyalty is not to be found, for in loathing at our treachery she has taken herself off to the world of the spirits and the dead below. So utterly exhausted by the weight of our baggage and the rigours of the journey, we have carted back this booty which lies before your eyes, mourning the loss of three of our comrades.'

22   Following the close of this speech, they poured libations of unmixed wine from golden cups in memory of their dead comrades. Then they appeased the god Mars with some hymns, and took a short nap. As for us, the old woman provided fresh barley in such unstinted abundance that my horse on receiving such a large allowance all to himself thought that he must be tucking into a dinner for the Salian priests. But I had never dined on raw barley previously, having always eaten it chopped up and softened from prolonged boiling. So when my eyes lit on the corner where the loaves surviving from the whole mob's depredations had been stacked, I vigorously exercised my jaws, which were weak from long hunger, and covered with cobwebs from long disuse. Then suddenly later in the night the bandits roused themselves, and packed up. They prepared themselves in various ways, some arming themselves with swords, some disguising themselves as ghosts, and rushed out at full speed. But even beckoning sleep could not restrain my urgent and overpowering appetite. Earlier, when I was Lucius, I would be satisfied with one or two bread-rolls and would then quit the table, but on this occasion I chewed through almost three basketfuls, for the belly I had to minister to was bottomless. Daylight broke as I devoted myself single-mindedly to this task.

23   Finally, my donkey's sense of decency induced me to abandon the bread with the greatest reluctance, and I quenched my thirst at the stream close by. At that moment

the bandits returned, wearing deeply worried and serious
frowns. They had no bags of loot to show, not so much as an
old rag. For all their swords, all their hands, all the combined
force of their gang, all that they brought with them was one
young girl. Her appearance proclaimed her to be free-born;
her ladylike outfit showed that she was one of the local
aristocracy. Heavens, she could have put ideas into the head
of even an ass like me! She was crying, and tearing at her hair
and clothes. They escorted her into the cave, and spoke to her
to temper her distress. 'Your life and virtue are in no danger.
Be patient with us for a short time until we get our cut. The
pressures of poverty have driven us to this occupation. Your
parents are rather grasping, but they will be prompt in paying
the proper ransom out of their large money-bags on behalf of
their own flesh and blood.'

24   But blarney such as this totally failed to soothe the girl's
distress, and no wonder. She put her head between her knees,
and wept uncontrollably. Whereupon the bandits called the
old woman in, and told her to sit by the girl and talk to her as
best she could in soft and consoling words. They then reverted
to the routine of their profession. But no words of the old hag
could distract the girl from her tears now in spate. Her
laments rose higher, and she sobbed her heart out unceasingly,
so that she forced the tears out of my eyes as well. She said;
'Here am I, as wretched as can be, deprived of my nice home
and large household and affectionate slaves and respected
parents, a mere chattel, the unhappy loot of a smash-and-grab
raid, shut up like a slave in this rock-walled prison, stripped of
all the comforts of my birth and upbringing, unsure of my
safety, exposed to an executioner's torture, among all these
dreadful bandits, this mob of horrid gangsters. How can I
stop weeping, or even go on living?' After this outburst of
crying, she was worn out with mental grief, constriction of the
throat and mental weariness, and she let her languid eyes
droop in sleep.

25   She had merely dropped off for a moment, when suddenly
she jerked out of sleep like a madwoman, and began to
maltreat herself much more severely. She started to beat her

breast with heavy blows and to belabour that bright face of hers, and though the old woman most pressingly sought the reasons for this fresh renewal of grief, her sighs grew deeper. Then she began: 'Now it's all up with me for sure, now I'm utterly finished, now I've lost all hope of being saved. The noose or the sword must be my only recourse, or at any rate I must throw myself off a cliff, no doubt about that.' The old woman's response was rather sharp. With a sterner face she told the girl to explain why the deuce she was crying, or what had suddenly caused her to renew her wild wailing after being sound asleep. 'I suppose you're trying to deprive my young men of their sizeable reward from ransoming you. If you go on like this, I'll have you burnt alive! I'll just ignore these tears of yours; bandits don't take much account of them.'

26 The girl was brought up short by these words. She kissed the old woman's hand, and said: 'Dear mother, forgive me. Call to mind the milk of human kindness, and give me some little support in this grimmest of misfortunes. Surely at your advanced age with its venerable grey hairs your sense of pity has not withered. Just contemplate the tragedy that has befallen me. I have a handsome young man, outstanding among his peers. The entire city voted him "favourite son of the community". He is in fact my cousin, just three years older than myself. From babyhood he was reared with me, and now that he's grown up we have been inseparable, sharing the same dear house, in fact the same room and bed. We are pledged to each other with fond feelings of sacred love, and for some time he has been bound by nuptial vows to marry me. With my parents' consent he has actually been registered as my husband. Just prior to the wedding he was sacrificing victims in the temples and public shrines, dutifully attended by a crowd of kith and kin. Our whole house was adorned with laurels and bright with torches as it re-echoed the marriage-hymn. At that moment my unhappy mother was holding me in her arms, and clothing me in the wedding-dress for the occasion. She was showering me with honeyed kisses, and murmuring anxious prayers to foster the hope of children to come. But then there was a sudden incursion as footpads

burst in; it was a scene of savage battle as they flashed their naked weapons menacingly. But they did not turn their hands to slaughter or plunder, but at once in close-packed formation they rushed into the bedroom. None of our household fought them off or so much as raised a finger to oppose them as they grabbed me, distressed and fainting with cruel fear, from my mother's fearful grasp. This was how they broke up and ruined my wedding; it was like the experience of Attis or of Protesilaus over again.

27   'Just now I had a terrible dream; the whole of my misfortune has been renewed or rather redoubled. I seemed to be forcibly dragged from my house, apartment, chamber, from my very couch, and to be calling on my most wretched husband's name through a trackless waste. Just torn from my embraces, still drenched in perfume and adorned with garlands of flowers, he chased after me as I fled on feet which did not belong to me. Then with piercing cry he complained that his lovely wife had been kidnapped, and called for the people's help. But one of the bandits was enraged by being hounded in this troublesome way. He grabbed a big stone lying by his feet, struck my unhappy young bridegroom with it, and killed him. I was fearstruck at this dreadful vision, and in panic was jerked out of that lethal sleep.'

The old woman sighed in sympathy with the girl's tears, and began to speak. 'Cheer up, my lady; don't be frightened by the baseless fancies of dreams. For one thing, dreams in daylight hours are held to be false, and for another, even night-dreams sometimes tell of untruthful happenings. So tears, beatings, even murders sometimes portend a profitable and favourable outcome, while on the other hand, smiles, bellyfuls of honey-cakes and pleasurable love-encounters foretell future affliction with melancholy, physical illness, and all such hardships. Come then, here and now I'll divert you with the pretty story of an old wife's tale.' This is how she began.

The Tale of Cupid and Psyche

28 In a certain city there lived a king and queen with three notably beautiful daughters. The two elder ones were very attractive, yet praise appropriate to humans was thought sufficient for their fame. But the beauty of the youngest girl was so special and distinguished that our poverty of human language could not describe or even adequately praise it. In consequence, many of her fellow-citizens and hordes of foreigners, on hearing the report of this matchless prodigy, gathered in ecstatic crowds. They were dumbstruck with admiration at her peerless beauty. They would press their hands to their lips with the forefinger resting on the upright thumb, and revere her with devoted worship as if she were none other than Venus herself. Rumour had already spread through the nearest cities and bordering territories that the goddess who was sprung from the dark-blue depths of the sea and was nurtured by the foam from the frothing waves was now bestowing the favour of her divinity among random gatherings of common folk; or at any rate, that the earth rather than the sea was newly impregnated by heavenly seed, and had sprouted forth a second Venus invested with the bloom of virginity.

29 This belief grew every day beyond measure. The story now became widespread; it swept through the neighbouring islands, through tracts of the mainland and numerous provinces. Many made long overland journeys and travelled over the deepest courses of the sea as they flocked to set eyes on this famed cynosure of their age. No one took ship for Paphos, Cnidos, or even Cythera to catch sight of the goddess Venus. Sacrifices in those places were postponed, shrines grew unsightly, couches become threadbare, rites went unperformed; the statues were not garlanded, and the altars were bare and grimy with cold ashes. It was the girl who was entreated in prayer. People gazed on that girl's human countenance when appeasing the divine will of the mighty goddess. When the maiden emerged in the mornings, they

sought from her the favour of the absent Venus with sacrificial victims and sacred feasts. The people crowded round her with wreaths and flowers to address their prayers, as she made her way through the streets. Since divine honours were being diverted in this excessive way to the worship of a mortal girl, the anger of the true Venus was fiercely kindled. She could not control her irritation. She tossed her head, let out a deep growl, and spoke in soliloquy:

30   'Here am I, the ancient mother of the universe, the founding creator of the elements, the Venus that tends the entire world, compelled to share the glory of my majesty with a mortal maiden, so that my name which has its niche in heaven is degraded by the foulness of the earth below! Am I then to share with another the supplications to my divine power, am I to endure vague adoration by proxy, allowing a mortal girl to strut around posing as my double? What a waste of effort it was for the shepherd whose justice and honesty won the approval of the great Jupiter to reckon my matchless beauty superior to that of those great goddesses! But this girl, whoever she is, is not going to enjoy appropriating the honours that are mine; I shall soon ensure that she rues the beauty which is not hers by rights!'

She at once summoned her son, that winged, most indiscreet youth whose own bad habits show his disregard for public morality. He goes rampaging through people's houses at night armed with his torch and arrows, undermining the marriages of all. He gets away scot-free with this disgraceful behaviour, and nothing that he does is worthwhile. His own nature made him excessively wanton, but he was further roused by his mother's words. She took him along to that city, and showed him Psyche in the flesh (that was the girl's name). She told him the whole story of their rivalry in beauty, and grumbling and growling with displeasure she added:

31   'I beg you by the bond of a mother's affection, by the sweet wounds which your darts inflict and the honeyed blisters left by this torch of yours: ensure that your mother gets her full revenge, and punish harshly this girl's arrogant beauty. Be willing to perform this single service which will compensate

for all that has gone before. See that the girl is seized with consuming passion for the lowest possible specimen of humanity, for one who as the victim of Fortune has lost status, inheritance and security, a man so disreputable that nowhere in the world can he find an equal in wretchedness.'

With these words she kissed her son long and hungrily with parted lips. Then she made for the nearest shore lapped by the waves. With rosy feet she mounted the surface of the rippling waters, and lo and behold, the bright surface of the sea-depths was becalmed. At her first intimation, her retinue in the deep performed her wishes, so promptly indeed that she seemed to have issued instructions long before. Nereus' daughters appeared in singing chorus, and shaggy Portunus sporting his blue-green beard, and Salacia, the folds of her garment sagging with fish, and Palaemon, the elf-charioteer on his dolphin. Bands of Tritons sported here and there on the waters, one softly blowing on his echoing shell, another fending off with silk parasol the heat of the hostile sun, a third holding a mirror before his mistress's face, while others, yoked in pairs to her chariot, swam below. This was the host of Venus' companions as she made for the Ocean.

32   Meanwhile, Psyche for all her striking beauty gained no reward for her ravishing looks. She was the object of all eyes, and her praise was on everyone's lips, but no king or prince or even commoner courted her to seek her hand. All admired her godlike appearance, but the admiration was such as is accorded to an exquisitely carved statue. For some time now her two elder sisters had been betrothed to royal suitors and had contracted splendid marriages, though their more modest beauty had won no widespread acclaim. But Psyche remained at home unattached, lamenting her isolated loneliness. Sick in body and wounded at heart, she loathed her beauty which the whole world admired. For this reason the father of that ill-starred girl was a picture of misery, for he suspected that the gods were hostile, and he feared their anger. He sought the advice of the most ancient oracle of the Milesian god, and with prayers and sacrificial victims begged from that mighty deity a marriage and a husband for that slighted maiden.

Apollo, an Ionian Greek, framed his response in Latin to accommodate the author of this Milesian tale:

33
    Adorn this girl, O king, for wedlock dread,
    And set her on a lofty mountain-rock.
    Renounce all hope that one of mortal stock
    Can be your son-in-law, for she shall wed
    A fierce, barbaric, snake-like monster. He,
    Flitting on wings aloft, makes all things smart,
    Plaguing each moving thing with torch and dart.
    Why, Jupiter himself must fearful be.
    The other gods for him their terror show,
    And rivers shudder, and the dark realms below.

The king had formerly enjoyed a happy life, but on hearing this venerable prophecy he returned home reluctant and mournful. He unfolded to his wife the injunctions of that ominous oracle, and grief, tears and lamentation prevailed for several days. But now the grim fulfilment of the dread oracle loomed over them. Now they laid out the trappings for the marriage of that ill-starred girl with death; now the flames of the nuptial torch flickered dimly beneath the sooty ashes, the high note of the wedding-flute sank into the plaintive Lydian mode, and the joyous marriage-hymn tailed away into mournful wailing. That bride-to-be dried her tears on her very bridal-veil. Lamentation for the harsh fate of that anguished household spread throughout the city, and a cessation of business was announced which reflected the public grief.

34
But the warnings of heaven were to be obeyed, and unhappy Psyche's presence was demanded for her appointed punishment. So amidst intense grief the ritual of that marriage with death was solemnized, and the entire populace escorted her living corpse as Psyche tearfully attended not her marriage but her funeral. But when her sad parents, prostrated by their monstrous misfortune, drew back from the performance of their monstrous task, their daughter herself admonished them with these words:

'Why do you rack your sad old age with protracted weeping? Or why do you weary your life's breath, which is dearer to me than to yourselves, with repeated lamentations?

Why do you disfigure those features, which I adore, with
ineffectual tears? Why do you grieve my eyes by torturing
your own? Why do you tear at your grey locks? Why do you
beat those breasts so sacred to me? What fine rewards my
peerless beauty will bring you! All too late you experience the
mortal wounds inflicted by impious envy. That grief, those
tears, that lamentation for me as one already lost should have
been awakened when nations and communities brought me
fame with divine honours, when with one voice they greeted
me as the new Venus. Only now do I realize and see that my
one undoing has been the title of Venus bestowed on me.
Escort me and set me on the rock to which fate has consigned
me. I hasten to embark on this blessed marriage, I hasten to
behold this noble husband of mine. Why should I postpone or
shrink from the arrival of the person born for the destruction
of the whole world?'

35   After this utterance the maiden fell silent, and with resolute
step she now attached herself to the escorting procession of
citizens. They made their way to the appointed rock set on a
lofty mountain, and when they had installed the girl on its
peak, they all abandoned her there. They left behind the
marriage-torches which had lighted their way but were now
doused with their tears, and with bent heads made their way
homeward. The girl's unhappy parents, worn out by this
signal calamity, enclosed themselves in the gloom of their
shuttered house, and surrendered themselves to a life of
perpetual darkness.

      But as Psyche wept in fear and trembling on that rocky
eminence, the Zephyr's kindly breeze with its soft stirring
wafted the hem of her dress this way and that, and made its
folds billow out. He gradually drew her aloft, and with
tranquil breath bore her slowly downward. She glided down
over the sloping side of that high cliff, and he laid her down in
the bosom of the flower decked turf in the valley below.

BOOK 5

Cupid and Psyche (continued)

1 In that soft and grassy arbour Psyche reclined gratefully on the
couch of the dew-laden turf. The great upheaval oppressing
her mind had subsided, and she enjoyed pleasant repose.
After sleeping long enough to feel refreshed, she got up with
carefree heart. Before her eyes was a grove planted with
towering, spreading trees, and a rill glistening with glassy
waters.

At the centre of the grove close to the gliding stream was a
royal palace, the work not of human hands but of divine
craftsmanship. You would know as soon as you entered that
you were viewing the bright and attractive retreat of some
god. The high ceiling, artistically panelled with citron-wood
and ivory, was supported on golden columns. The entire walls
were worked in silver in relief; beasts and wild cattle met the
gaze of those who entered there. The one who shaped all this
silver into animal-forms was certainly a genius, or rather he
must have been a demigod or even a god. The floors too
extended with different pictures formed by mosaics of
precious stones; twice blessed indeed, and more than twice
blessed are those whose feet walk on gems and jewels! The
other areas of the dwelling, too, in all its length and breadth,
were incalculably costly. All the walls shimmered with their
native gleam of solid gold, so that if the sun refused to shine,
the house created its own daylight. The rooms, the colonnade,
the very doors also shone brilliantly. The other riches likewise
reflected the splendour of the mansion. You would be justified
in thinking that this was a heavenly palace fashioned for
mighty Jupiter when he was engaged in dealings with
men.

2 Psyche, enticed by the charming appearance of these
surroundings, drew nearer, and as her assurance grew she
crossed the threshold. Delight at the surpassing beauty of the

scene encouraged her to examine every detail. Her eyes lit upon store-rooms built high on the other side of the house; they were crammed with abundance of treasures. Nothing imaginable was missing, and what was especially startling, apart from the breath-taking abundance of such riches, was the fact that this treasure-house had no protection whatever by way of chain or bar or guard.

As she gazed on all this with the greatest rapture, a disembodied voice addressed her: 'Why, my lady, do you gaze open-mouthed at this parade of wealth? All these things are yours. So retire to your room, relieve your weariness on your bed, and take a bath at your leisure. The voices you hear are those of your handmaidens, and we will diligently attend to your needs. Once you have completed your toilet a royal feast will at once be laid before you.'

3   Psyche felt a blessed assurance being bestowed upon her by heaven's provision. She heeded the suggestions of the dis-embodied voice, and after first taking a nap and then a bath to dispel her fatigue, she at once noted a semicircular couch and table close at hand. The dishes laid for dinner gave her to understand that all was set for her refreshment, so she gladly reclined there. Immediately wine as delicious as nectar and various plates of food were placed before her, brought not by human hands but unsupported on a gust of wind. She could see no living soul, and merely heard words emerging from thin air: her serving-maids were merely voices. When she had enjoyed the rich feast, a singer entered and performed unseen, while another musician strummed a lyre which was likewise invisible. Then the harmonious voices of a tuneful choir struck her ears, so that it was clear that a choral group was in attendance, though no person could be seen.

4   The pleasant entertainment came to an end, and the advent of darkness induced Psyche to retire to bed. When the night was well advanced, a genial sound met her ears. Since she was utterly alone, she trembled and shuddered in fear for her virginity, and she dreaded the unknown presence more than any other menace. But now her unknown bridegroom arrived and climbed into the bed. He made Psyche his wife, and

swiftly departed before dawn broke. At once the voices in attendance at her bed-chamber tended the new bride's violated virginity. These visits continued over a long period, and this new life in the course of nature became delightful to Psyche as she grew accustomed to it. Hearing that unidentified voice consoled her loneliness.

Meanwhile her parents were aging in unceasing grief and melancholy. As the news spread wider, her elder sisters learnt the whole story. In their sadness and grief they vied with each other in hastily leaving home and making straight for their parents, to see them and discuss the matter with them.

5   That night Psyche's husband (he was invisible to her, but she could touch and hear him) said to her: 'Sweetest Psyche, fond wife that you are, Fortune grows more savage, and threatens you with mortal danger. I charge you: show greater circumspection. Your sisters are worried at the rumour that you are dead, and presently they will come to this rock to search for traces of you. Should you chance to hear their cries of grief, you are not to respond, or even to set eyes on them. Otherwise you will cause me the most painful affliction, and bring utter destruction on yourself.'

Psyche consented and promised to follow her husband's guidance. But when he had vanished in company with the darkness, the poor girl spent the whole day crying and beating her breast. She kept repeating that now all was up with her, for here she was, confined and enclosed in that blessed prison, bereft of conversation with human beings for company, unable even to offer consoling relief to her sisters as they grieved for her, and not allowed even to catch a glimpse of them. No ablutions, food, or other relaxation made her feel better, and she retired to sleep in floods of tears.

6   At that moment her husband came to bed somewhat earlier than usual. She was still weeping, and as he embraced her, he remonstrated with her: 'Is this how the promise you made to me has turned out, Psyche my dear? What is your husband to expect or to hope from you? You never stop torturing yourself night and day, even when we embrace each other as husband and wife. Very well, have it your own way, follow your own

hell-bound inclination. But when you begin to repent at leisure, remember the sober warning which I gave you.'

Then Psyche with prayers and threats of her impending death forced her husband to yield to her longing to see her sisters, to relieve their grief, and he also allowed her to present them with whatever pieces of gold or jewellery she chose. But he kept deterring her with repeated warnings from being ever induced by the baleful prompting of her sisters to discover her husband's appearance. She must not through sacrilegious curiosity tumble headlong from the lofty height of her happy fortune, and forfeit thereafter his embrace.

She thanked her husband, and with spirits soaring she said: 'But I would rather die a hundred times than forgo the supreme joy of my marriage with you. For I love and cherish you passionately, whoever you are, as much as my own life, and I value you higher than Cupid himself. But one further concession I beg for my prayers: bid your servant the Zephyr spirit my sisters down to me, as he earlier wafted me down.' She pressed seductive kisses on him, whispered honeyed words, and snuggled close to soften him. She added endearments to her charms: 'O my honey-sweet, darling husband, light of your Psyche's life!' Her husband unwillingly gave way before the forceful pressure of these impassioned whispers, and promised to do all she asked. Then, as dawn drew near, he vanished from his wife's embrace.

7   Psyche's sisters enquired about the location of the rock on which she had been abandoned, and they quickly made their way to it. There they cried their eyes out and beat their breasts until the rocks and crags echoed equally loudly with their repeated lamentations. Then they sought to conjure up their sister by summoning her by name, until the piercing notes of their wailing voices permeated down the mountainside, and Psyche rushed frantically and fearfully from the house. 'Why', she asked, 'do you torture yourselves to no purpose with your unhappy cries of grief? Here I am, the object of your mourning. So cease your doleful cries, and now at last dry those cheeks which are wet with prolonged tears, for you can now hug close the sister for whom you grieved.'

She then summoned the Zephyr, and reminded him of her husband's instruction. He speedily obeyed the command, and at once whisked them down safely on the gentlest of breezes. The sisters embraced each other, and delightedly exchanged eager kisses. The tears which had been dried welled forth again, prompted by their joy. 'Now that you are in good spirits', said Psyche, 'you must enter my hearth and home, and let the company of your Psyche gladden your hearts that were troubled.'

8   Following these words, she showed them the magnificent riches of the golden house, and let them hear the voices of her large retinue. She then allowed them the rich pleasure of a luxurious bath and an elegant meal served by her ghostly maids. But when they had had their fill of the copious abundance of riches clearly bestowed by heaven, they began to harbour deep-seated envy in their hearts. So one of them kept asking with nagging curiosity about the owner of those divine possessions, about the identity and status of her husband. Psyche in her heart's depths did not in any way disobey or disregard her husband's instructions. She invented an impromptu story that he was a handsome young man whose cheeks were just darkening with a soft beard, and who spent most of his day hunting in the hills of the countryside. But she was anxious not to betray through a slip of the tongue her silent resolve by continuing the conversation, so she weighed her sisters down with gold artefacts and precious jewels, hastily summoned the Zephyr, and entrusted them to him for the return journey.

9   This was carried out at once, and those splendid sisters then made their way home. They were now gnawed with the bile of growing envy, and repeatedly exchanged loud-voiced complaints. One of them began: 'Fortune, how blind and harsh and unjust you are! Was it your pleasure that we, daughters of the same parents, should endure so different a fate? Here we are, her elder sisters, nothing better than maidservants to foreign husbands, banished from home and even from our native land, living like exiles far from our parents, while Psyche, the youngest and last offspring of our

mother's weary womb, has obtained all this wealth, and a god for a husband! She has not even a notion of how to enjoy such abundant blessings. Did you notice, sister, the quantity and quality of the precious stones lying in the house, the gleaming garments, the sparkling jewels, the gold lying beneath our feet all over the house? If she also has as handsome a husband as she claims, no woman living in the whole world is more blessed. Perhaps as their intimacy continues and their love grows stronger, her god-husband will make her divine as well. That's how things are, mark my words; she was putting on such airs and graces! She's now so high and mighty, behaving like a goddess, with those voices serving her needs, and winds obeying her commands! Whereas my life's a hell; to begin with, I have a husband older than my father. He's balder than an onion as well, and he hasn't the virility of an infant. And he keeps our house barricaded with bars and chains.'

10   The other took up the grumbling. 'I have to put up with a husband crippled and bent with rheumatism, so that he can succumb to my charms only once in a blue moon. I spend almost all my day rubbing his fingers, which are twisted and hard as flint, and burning these soft hands of mine on reeking poultices, filthy bandages, and smelly plasters. I'm a slaving nursing attendant, not a dutiful wife. You must decide for yourself, sister, how patiently or—let me express myself frankly—how menially you intend to bear the situation; I can't brook any longer the thought of this undeserving girl falling on her feet like this. Just recall how disdainfully and haughtily she treated us, how swollen-headed she'd become with her boasting and her immodest and vulgar display, how she reluctantly threw at us a few trinkets from that mass of riches, and then at once ordered us to be thrown out, whisked away, sent off with the wind because she found our presence tedious! As sure as I'm a woman, as sure as I'm standing here, I'm going to propel her headlong off that heap of riches!

'If the insulting way she's treated us has needled you as well, as it certainly should have, we must work out an effective plan together. We must not show the gifts in our possession to our parents or anyone else. We must not even betray the slightest awareness that she's alive. It's bad enough that we've witnessed the sorry situation ourselves, without our having to spread the glad news to our parents and the world at large. People aren't really fortunate if no one knows of their riches. She'll realize that she's got elder sisters, not maid-servants. So let us now go back to our husbands and homes, which may be poor but are honest. Then, when we have given the matter deeper thought, we must go back more determined to punish her arrogance.'

11   The two wicked sisters approved this wicked plan. So they hid away all those most valuable gifts. They tore their hair, gave their cheeks the scratching they deserved, and feigned renewed grief. Their hastily summoned tears depressed their parents, reawakening their sorrow to match that of their daughters, and then swollen with lunatic rage they rushed off to their homes, planning their wicked wiles—or rather the assassination of their innocent sister.

Meanwhile Psyche's unknown husband in their nightly conversation again counselled her with these words: 'Are you aware what immense danger overhangs you? Fortune is aiming her darts at you from long range and, unless you take the most stringent precautions, she will soon engage with you hand to hand. Those traitorous bitches are straining every nerve to lay wicked traps for you. Above all, they are seeking to persuade you to pry into my appearance, and as I have often warned you, a single glimpse of it will be your last. So if those depraved witches turn up later, ready with their destructive designs, and I am sure they will, you must not exchange a single word with them, or at any rate if your native innocence and soft-heartedness cannot bear that, you are not to listen to or utter a single word about your husband. Soon we shall be starting a family, for this as yet tiny womb of yours is carrying for us another child like yourself. If you conceal our secret in silence, that child will be a god; but if you disclose it, he will be mortal.'

12   Psyche was aglow with delight at the news. She gloried in the comforting prospect of a divine child, she exulted in the fame that such a dear one would bring her, and she rejoiced at

the thought of the respected status of mother. She eagerly counted the mounting days and departing months, and as a novice bearing an unknown burden, she marvelled that the pinprick of a moment could cause such a lovely swelling in her fecund womb.

But now those baneful, most abhorrent Furies were hastening on their impious way aboard ship, exhaling their snakelike poison. It was then that Psyche's husband on his brief visit again warned her: 'This is the day of crisis, the moment of worst hazard. Those troublesome members of your sex, those hostile blood-relations of yours have now seized their arms, struck camp, drawn their battle-line, and sounded the trumpet-note. Your impious sisters have drawn their swords, and are aiming for your jugular. The calamities that oppress us are indeed direful, dearest Psyche. Take pity on yourself and on me; show dutiful self-control to deliver your house and your husband, your person and this tiny child of ours from the unhappy disaster that looms over us. Do not set eyes on, or open your ears to, these female criminals, whom you cannot call your sisters because of their deadly hatred, and because of the way in which they have trodden underfoot their own flesh and blood, when like Sirens they lean out over the crag, and make the rocks resound with their death-dealing cries!'

13 Psyche's response was muffled with tearful sobs. 'Some time ago, I think, you had proof of my trustworthiness and discretion, and on this occasion too my resolution will likewise win your approval. Only tell our Zephyr to provide his services again, and allow me at least a glimpse of my sisters as consolation for your unwillingness to let me gaze on your sacred face. I beg you by these locks of yours which with their scent of cinnamon dangle all round your head, by your cheeks as soft and smooth as my own, by your breast which diffuses its hidden heat, as I hope to observe your features as reflected at least in this our tiny child: accede to the devoted prayers of this careworn suppliant, and grant me the blessing of my sisters' embraces. Then you will give fresh life and joy to your Psyche, your own devoted and dedicated dear one. I no longer

seek to see your face; the very darkness of the night is not oppressive to me, for you are my light to which I cling.' Her husband was bewitched by these words and soft embraces. He wiped away her tears with his curls, promised to do her bidding, and at once departed before dawn broke.

14   The conspiratorial pair of sisters did not even call on their parents. At breakneck speed they made straight from the ships to the familiar rock, and without waiting for the presence of the wafting wind, launched themselves down with impudent rashness into the depths below. The Zephyr, somewhat unwillingly recalling his king's command, enfolded them in the bosom of his favouring breeze and set them down on solid earth. Without hesitation they at once marched with measured step into the house, and counterfeiting the name of sisters they embraced their prey. With joyful expressions they cloaked the deeply hidden deceit which they treasured within them, and flattered their sister with these words: 'Psyche, you are no longer the little girl of old; you are now a mother. Just imagine what a blessing you bear in that purse of yours! What pleasures you will bring to our whole family! How lucky we are at the prospect of rearing this prince of infants! If he is as handsome as his parents—and why not?—he is sure to be a thorough Cupid!'

15   With this pretence of affection they gradually wormed their way into their sister's heart. As soon as they had rested their feet to recover from the weariness of the journey, and had steeped their bodies in a steaming bath, Psyche served them in the dining-room with a most handsome and delightful meal of meats and savouries. She ordered a lyre to play, and string-music came forth; she ordered pipes to start up, and their notes were heard; she bade choirs to sing, and they duly did. All this music soothed their spirits with the sweetest tunes as they listened, though no human person stood before them. But those baleful sisters were not softened or lulled even by that music so honey-sweet. They guided the conversation towards the deceitful snare which they had laid, and they began to enquire innocently about the status, family background, and walk of life of her husband. Then Psyche's

excessive naïvety made her forget her earlier version, and she
concocted a fresh story. She said that her husband was a
business-man from an adjoining region, and that he was
middled-aged, with streaks of grey in his hair. But she did not
linger a moment longer in such talk, but again loaded her
sisters with rich gifts, and ushered them back to their carriage
of the wind.

16   But as they returned home, after the Zephyr with his serene
breath had borne them aloft, they exchanged abusive
comments about Psyche. 'There are no words, sister, to
describe the outrageous lie of that idiotic girl. Previously her
husband was a young fellow whose beard was beginning to
sprout with woolly growth, but now he's in middle age with
spruce and shining grey hair: What a prodigy he must be!
This short interval has brought on old age abruptly, and has
changed his appearance! You can be sure, sister, that this
noxious female is either telling a pack of lies or does not know
what her husband is like. Whatever the truth of the matter,
she must be parted from those riches of hers without delay. If
she does not know what her husband looks like, she must
certainly be married to a god, and it is a god she's got for us in
that womb of hers. Be sure of this, that if she becomes a
celebrity as the mother of a divine child—which God forbid—
I'll put a rope round my neck and hang myself. For the
moment, then, let us go back to our parents and spin a fairy
story to match the one we concocted at first.'

17   In this impassioned state they greeted their parents
disdainfully, and after a restless night those despicable sisters
sped to the rock at break of day. They threw themselves down
through the air, and the wind afforded them his usual
protection. They squeezed their eyelids to force out some
tears, and greeted the girl with these guileful words: 'While
you sit here, content and in happy ignorance of your grim
situation, giving no thought to your danger, we in our
watchful zeal for your welfare lie awake at night, racked with
sadness for your misfortunes. We know for a fact—and as we
share your painful plight we cannot hide it from you—that a
monstrous dragon lies unseen with you at night. It creeps

along with its numerous knotted coils; its neck is blood-stained, and oozes deadly poison; its monstrous jaws lie gaping open. You must surely remember the Pythian oracle, and its chant that you were doomed to wed a wild beast. Then, too, many farmers, local huntsmen, and a number of inhabitants have seen the dragon returning to its lair at night after seeking its food, or swimming in the shallows of a river close by.

18   'All of them maintain that the beast will not continue to fatten you for long by providing you with enticing food, and that as soon as your womb has filled out and your pregnancy comes to term, it will devour the richer fare which you will then offer. In view of this, you must now decide whether you are willing to side with your sisters, who are anxious for your welfare which is so dear to their hearts, and to live in their company once you escape from death, or whether you prefer to be interred in the stomach of that fiercest of beasts. However, if you opt for the isolation of this rustic haunt inhabited only by voices, preferring the foul and hazardous intimacy of furtive love in the embrace of this venomous dragon, at any rate we as your devoted sisters will have done our duty.'

Poor Psyche, simple and innocent as she was, at once felt apprehension at these grim tidings. She lost her head, and completely banished her recollection of all her husband's warnings and her own promises. She launched herself into the abyss of disaster. Trembling and pale as the blood drained from her face, she barely opened her mouth as she gasped and stammered out this reply to them.

19   'Dearest sisters, you have acted rightly in continuing to observe your devoted duty, and as for those who make these assertions to you, I do not think that they are telling lies. It is true that I have never seen my husband's face, and I have no knowledge whatsoever of where he hails from. I merely attend at night to the words of a husband to whom I submit with no knowledge of what he is like, for he certainly shuns the light of day. Your judgement is just that he is some beast, and I rightly agree with you. He constantly and emphatically warns

me against seeing what he looks like, and threatens me with great disaster if I show curiosity about his features. So if at this moment you can offer saving help to your sister in her hour of danger, you must come to my rescue now. Otherwise your indifference to the future will tarnish the benefits of your previous concern.'

Those female criminals had now made their way through the open gates, and had occupied the mind of their sister thus exposed. They emerged from beneath the mantlet of their battering-ram, drew their swords, and advanced on the terrified thoughts of that simple girl.

20   So it was that one of them said to her: 'Our family ties compel us, in the interests of your safety, to disregard any danger whatsoever which lies before us, so we shall inform you of the one way by which you will attain the safety which has exercised us for so long. You must whet a razor by running it over your softening palm, and when it is quite sharp hide it secretly by the bed where you usually lie. Then fill a well-trimmed lamp with oil, and when it is shining brightly, conceal it beneath the cover of an enclosing jar. Once you have purposefully secreted this equipment, you must wait until your husband ploughs his furrow, and enters and climbs as usual into bed. Then, when he has stretched out and sleep has begun to oppress and enfold him, as soon as he starts the steady breathing which denotes deep sleep, you must slip off the couch. In your bare feet and on tiptoe take mincing steps forward, and remove the lamp from its protective cover of darkness. Then take your cue from the lamp, and seize the moment to perform your own shining deed. Grasp the two-edged weapon boldly, first raise high your right hand, and then with all the force you can muster sever the knot which joins the neck and head of that venomous serpent. You will not act without our help, for we shall be hovering anxiously in attendance, and as soon as you have ensured your safety by his death, we shall fly to your side. All these riches here we shall bear off with you with all speed, and then we shall arrange an enviable marriage for you, human being with human being.'

21   Their sister was already quite feverish with agitation, but
these fiery words set her heart ablaze. At once they left her, for
their proximity to this most wicked crime made them fear
greatly for themselves. So the customary thrust of the winged
breeze bore them up to the rock, and they at once fled in
precipitate haste. Without delay they embarked on their ships
and cast off.

But Psyche, now left alone, except that being harried by the
hostile Furies was no solitude, tossed in her grief like the
waves of the sea. Though her plan was formed and her
determination fixed, she still faltered in uncertainty of
purpose as she set her hands to action, and was torn between
the many impulses of her unhappy plight. She made haste,
she temporized; her daring turned to fear, her diffidence to
anger, and to cap everything she loathed the beast but loved
the husband, though they were one and the same. But now
evening brought on darkness, so with headlong haste she
prepared the instruments for the heinous crime. Night fell,
and her husband arrived, and having first skirmished in the
warfare of love, he fell into a heavy sleep.

22   Then Psyche, though enfeebled in both body and mind,
gained the strength lent her by fate's harsh decree. She
uncovered the lamp, seized the razor, and showed a boldness
that belied her sex. But as soon as the lamp was brought near,
and the secrets of the couch were revealed, she beheld of all
beasts the gentlest and sweetest, Cupid himself, a handsome
god lying in a handsome posture. Even the lamplight was
cheered and brightened on sighting him, and the razor felt
suitably abashed at its sacrilegious sharpness. As for Psyche,
she was awe-struck at this wonderful vision, and she lost all
her self-control. She swooned and paled with enervation; her
knees buckled, and she sought to hide the steel by plunging it
into her own breast. Indeed, she would have perpetrated this,
but the steel showed its fear of committing so serious a crime
by plunging out of her rash grasp. But as in her weariness and
giddiness she gazed repeatedly on the beauty of that divine
countenance, her mental balance was restored. She beheld on
his golden head his luxuriant hair steeped in ambrosia; his

neatly pinned ringlets strayed over his milk-white neck and
rosy cheeks, some dangling in front and some behind, and
their surpassing sheen made even the lamplight flicker. On
the winged god's shoulders his dewy wings gleamed white
with flashing brilliance; though they lay motionless, the soft
and fragile feathers at their tips fluttered in quivering motion
and sported restlessly. The rest of his body, hairless and rosy,
was such that Venus would not have been ashamed to
acknowledge him as her son. At the foot of the bed lay his
bow, quiver, and arrows, the kindly weapons of that great god.

23   As Psyche trained her gaze insatiably and with no little
curiosity on these her husband's weapons, in the course of
handling and admiring them she drew out an arrow from the
quiver, and tested its point on the tip of her thumb. But
because her arm was still trembling she pressed too hard, with
the result that it pricked too deeply, and tiny drops of rose-red
blood bedewed the surface of the skin. So all unknowing and
without prompting Psyche fell in love with Love, being fired
more and more with desire for the god of desire. She gazed
down on him in distraction, and as she passionately smothered
him with wanton kisses from parted lips, she feared that he
might stir in his sleep. But while her wounded heart pounded
on being roused by such striking beauty, the lamp disgorged a
drop of burning oil from the tip of its flame upon the god's
right shoulder; it could have been nefarious treachery, or
malicious jealousy, or the desire, so to say, to touch and kiss
that glorious body. O you rash, reckless lamp, Love's
worthless servant, do you burn the very god who possesses all
fire, though doubtless you were invented by some lover to
ensure that he might possess for longer and even at night the
object of his desire? The god started up on being burnt; he saw
that he was exposed, and that his trust was defiled. Without a
word he at once flew away from the kisses and embrace of his
most unhappy wife.

24   But Psyche seized his right leg with both hands just as he
rose above her. She made a pitiable appendage as he soared
aloft, following in his wake and dangling in company with him
as they flew through the clouds. But finally she slipped down

to earth exhausted. As she lay there on the ground, her divine lover did not leave her, but flew to the nearest cypress-tree, and from its summit spoke in considerable indignation to her.

'Poor, ingenuous Psyche, I disregarded my mother Venus' instructions when she commanded that you be yoked in passionate desire to the meanest of men, and that you be then subjected to the most degrading of marriages. Instead, I preferred to swoop down to become your lover. I admit that my behaviour was not judicious; I, the famed archer, wounded myself with my own weapon, and made you my wife—and all so that you should regard me as a wild beast, and cut off my head with the steel, and with it the eyes that dote on you! I urged you repeatedly, I warned you devotedly always to be on your guard against what has now happened. But before long those fine counsellors of yours will make satisfaction to me for their heinous instructions, whereas for you the punishment will be merely my departure.' As he finished speaking, he soared aloft on his wings.

25   From her prostrate position on the ground Psyche watched her husband's flight as far as her eyes allowed, and she tortured her heart with the bitterest lamentations. But once the sculling of his wings had removed him from her sight and he had disappeared into the distance, she hurled herself headlong down from the bank of a river close by. But that kindly stream was doubtless keen to pay homage to the god who often scorches even the waters, and in fear for his person he at once cast her ashore on his current without injuring her, and set her on its grassy bank. The rustic god Pan chanced to be sitting at that moment on the brow of the stream, holding the mountain deity Echo in his arms, and teaching her to repeat after him all kinds of songs. Close by the bank nanny-goats were sporting as they grazed and cropped the river-foliage here and there. The goat-shaped god was well aware of the calamity that had befallen Psyche. He called her gently to him, lovesick and weary as she was, and soothed her with these consoling words.

'You are an elegant girl, and I am a rustic herdsman, but my advanced years give me the benefit of considerable experience. If my hazard is correct—sages actually call such guesswork divine insight—I infer from your stumbling and frequently wandering steps, from your excessively pale complexion and continual sighs, and not least from your mournful gaze, that you are suffering grievous love-pains. On that account you must hearken to me: do not seek again to destroy yourself by throwing yourself headlong or by seeking any other means of death. Cease your sorrowing, lay aside your sadness, and instead direct prayers of adoration to Cupid, greatest of gods, and by your caressing attentions win the favour of that wanton and extravagant youth.'

26   Psyche made no reply to this advice from the shepherd-god. She merely paid reverential homage to his divine person, and proceeded on her way. After wandering with weary steps for a considerable distance, as night fell a certain path led her all unknowing to a city where the husband of one of her sisters had his realm. Psyche recognized it, and asked that her arrival be announced to her sister. She was then ushered in, and after they had greeted and embraced each other, her sister enquired why she had come.

Psyche began to explain. 'You recall that plan of yours, by which you both persuaded me to take a two-edged razor and slay the beast who used to lie with me falsely claiming to be my husband, with the intention of later devouring my poor self with his greedy maw? I fell in with your proposal, but when the lamp which conspired with me allowed me to gaze on his face, the vision I beheld was astonishing and utterly divine: it was the son of the goddess Venus, I mean Cupid himself, who lay peacefully sleeping there. I exulted at the sight of such beauty, and was confused by the sense of overwhelming delight, and as I experienced frustration at being unable to enjoy relations with him, the lamp by a dreadful mischance shed a drop of burning oil on his shoulder. At once the pain caused him to start from his sleep, and when he saw me wielding the steel and the flame, he said: "This is a dreadful deed you have done. Leave my bed this instant, and take your goods and chattels with you. I shall now take your sister"—at this point he cited your name specifically—"in solemn marriage." At once he then ordered the Zephyr to waft me outside the bounds of his estate.'

27   Psyche had not yet finished speaking when her sister, goaded by mad lust and destructive envy, swung into action. She devised a lying excuse to deceive her husband, pretending that she had learnt of her parents' death; she at once boarded ship, and then made hot-foot for the rock. Although the wrong wind was blowing, her eagerness was fired by blind hope, and she said: 'Take me, Cupid, as your worthy wife; Zephyr, take your mistress aboard!' She then took a prodigious leap downward. But not even in death could she reach that abode, for her limbs bounced on the rocky crags, and were fragmented. Her insides were torn out, and in her fitting death she offered a ready meal to birds and beasts.

The second punitive vengeance was not long delayed. Psyche resumed her wanderings, and reached a second city where her other sister similarly dwelt. She too was taken in by her sister's deception, and in her eagerness to supplant Psyche in the marriage which they had befouled, she hastened to the rock, and fell to her deadly doom in the same way.

28   While Psyche was at this time visiting one community after another in her concentrated search for Cupid, he was lying groaning in his mother's chamber, racked by the pain of the wound from the lamp. But then the tern, the white bird which wings her way over the sea-waves, plunged swiftly into the deep bosom of ocean. She came upon Venus conveniently there as the goddess bathed and swam; she perched beside her, and told her that her son had suffered burning, and was lying in considerable pain from the wound, with his life in danger. As a result the entire household of Venus was in bad odour, the object of gossip and rebuke on the lips of people everywhere. They were claiming that Cupid was relaxing with a lady of easy virtue in the mountains, and that Venus herself was idly swimming in the ocean, with the result that pleasure and favour and elegance had departed from the world; all was unkempt, rustic, uncouth. There were no weddings, no cameraderie between friends, none of the love which children inspire; all was a scene of boundless squalor, of unsavoury

tedium in sordid alliances. Such was the gossip which that garrulous and prying bird whispered in Venus' ear, tearing her son's reputation to shreds.

Venus was absolutely livid. She burst out: 'So now that fine son of mine has a girl-friend, has he? Come on, then, tell me her name, since you are the only one who serves me with affection. Who is it who has tempted my innocent, beardless boy? Is it one of that crowd of nymphs, or one of the Hours, or one of the band of Muses, or one of my servant-Graces?' The garrulous bird did not withhold a reply. She said: 'I do not know, mistress; I think the story goes that he is head over heels in love with a girl by the name of Psyche, if my memory serves me rightly.' Then Venus in a rage bawled out at the top of her voice: 'Can it really be true that he is in love with that Psyche who lays claim to my beauty and pretends to my name? That son of mine must surely have regarded me as a procuress, when I pointed the girl out to him so that he could win her acquaintance.'

29   As she grumbled she made haste to quit the sea, and at once made for her golden chamber. There she found her son lying ill as she had heard, and from the doorway she bellowed out as loudly as she could: 'This is a fine state of affairs, just what one would expect from a child of mine, from a decent man like you! First of all you trampled underfoot the instructions of your mother—or I should say your employer—and you refused to humble my personal enemy with a vile love-liaison; and then, mark you, a mere boy of tender years, you hugged her close in your wanton, stunted embraces! You wanted me to have to cope with my enemy as a daughter-in-law! You take too much for granted, you good-for-nothing, loathsome seducer! You think of yourself as my only noble heir, and you imagine that I'm now too old to bear another. Just realize that I'll get another son, one far better than you. In fact I'll rub your nose in it further. I'll adopt one of my young slaves, and make him a present of these wings and torches of yours, the bow and arrows, and all the rest of my paraphernalia which I did not entrust to you to be misused like this. None of the cost of kitting you out came from your father's estate.

30   'Ever since you were a baby you have been badly brought
up, too ready with your hands. You show no respect to your
elders, pounding them time after time. Even me your own
mother you strip naked every day, and many's the time you've
cuffed me. You show me total contempt as though I were a
widow, and you haven't an ounce of fear for your stepfather,
the bravest and greatest of warriors. And why should you?
You are in the habit of supplying him with girls, to cause me
the pain of having to compete with rivals. But now I'll make
you sorry for this sport of yours. I'll ensure that you find your
marriage sour and bitter.

'But what am I to do, now that I'm becoming a laughing-
stock? Where shall I go, how shall I curb in this scoundrel?
Should I beg the assistance of my enemy Sobriety, so often
alienated from me through this fellow's loose living? The
prospect of having to talk with that unsophisticated, hideous
female gives me the creeps. Still I must not despise the
consolation of gaining revenge from any quarter. She is
absolutely the only one to be given the job of imposing the
harshest discipline on this rascal. She must empty his quiver,
immobilize his arrows, unstring his bow, extinguish his torch,
and restrain his person with sharper correction. Only when
she has sheared off his locks—how often I have brushed them
shining like gold with my own hands!—and clipped those
wings, which I have steeped in my own breast's liquid nectar,
shall I regard the insult dealt to me as expiated.'

31   These were her words. Then she bustled out, glowering and
incensed with passionate rage. At that moment Ceres and
Juno came up with her. When they observed her resentful
face, they asked her why she was cloaking the rich charm of
her radiant eyes with a sullen frown. 'You have come, she
answered, 'at a timely moment to fulfil my wishes, for I am
seething inside. I ask you to search with might and main for
that fickle runaway of mine called Psyche. I'm sure that the
scandalous gossip concerning my household, and the
behaviour of that unspeakable son of mine, have not passed
you by.' They knew quite well what had happened, and they
sought to assuage Venus' raging temper. 'My lady, how is it

that your son's peccadillo has caused you to war on his
pleasures in this unrelenting way, and also to desire to destroy
the girl that he loves? What harm is there, we should like to
know, in his giving the glad eye to a nicely turned-out girl?
Don't you realize that he is in the prime of manhood, or are
you forgetting his age? Just because he carries his years well,
does he strike you as a perpetual Peter Pan? You are a mother,
and a sensible one at that. Are you always going to pry nosily
into your son's diversions, and condemn his wanton ways,
censure his love-life, and vilify your own skills and pleasures
as practised by your handsome son? What god or what person
on earth will bear with your scattering sensual pleasures
throughout the world, when you sourly refuse to allow love-
liaisons in your own house, and you close down the
manufacture of women's weaknesses which is made available
to all?'

This was how the two goddesses sucked up to Cupid,
seeking to win his favour, though he was absent, by taking his
part, for they feared his arrows. But Venus was affronted that
the insults which she sustained were treated so lightly. She cut
the two of them short, turned on her heel, and stalked quickly
off to the sea.

BOOK 6

Cupid and Psyche (continued):
The Frustrated Escape

1 Meanwhile Psyche in her random wanderings was suffering
torment, as she sought day and night to trace her husband.
She was restless in mind, but all the more eager, in spite of his
anger, to soften him with a wife's endearments, or at any
rate to appease him with a servant's entreaties. She spied a
temple perched on the peak of a high mountain, and she said:
'Perhaps this is where my lord dwells?' She made her way
quickly there, and though her feet were utterly weary from her
unremitting labours, her hope and aspiration quickened
them. She mounted the higher ridges with stout heart, and
drew close to the sacred shrine. There she saw ears of wheat in
a heap, and others woven into a garland, and ears of barley as
well. There were sickles lying there, and a whole array of
harvesting implements, but they were in a jumbled and
neglected heap, thrown carelessly down by workmen's hands,
as happens in summer-time. Psyche carefully sorted them out
and ordered them in separate piles; no doubt she reflected
that she should not neglect the shrines and rites of any deity,
but rather implore the kindly pity of each and all.

2 Kindly Ceres sighted her as she carefully and diligently
ordered these offerings, and at once she cried out from afar:
'Why, you poor Psyche! Venus is in a rage, mounting a
feverish search for your traces all over the globe. She has
marked you down for the sternest punishment, and is using all
the resources of her divinity to demand vengeance. And here
you are, looking to my interests, with your mind intent on
anything but your own safety!'

Then Psyche grovelled at the goddess's feet, and watered
them with a stream of tears. She swept the ground with her
hair, and begged Ceres' favour with a litany of prayers. 'By
your fruitful right hand, by the harvest ceremonies which

assure plenty, by the silent mysteries of your baskets and the winged courses of your attendant dragons, by the furrows in your Sicilian soil, by the car which snatched and the earth which has latched, by Proserpina's descent to a lightless marriage, and by your daughter's return to rediscovered light, and by all else which the shrine of Attic Eleusis shrouds in silence—I beg you, lend aid to this soul of Psyche which is deserving of pity, and now entreats you. Allow me to lurk hidden here among these heaps of grain if only for a few days, until the great goddess's raging fury softens with the passage of time, or at any rate till my strength, which is now exhausted by protracted toil, is assuaged by a period of rest.'

3   Ceres answered her: 'Your tearful entreaties certainly affect me and I am keen to help you, but I cannot incur Venus's displeasure, for I maintain long-standing ties of friendship with her—and besides being my relative, she is also a fine woman. So you must quit this dwelling at once, and count it a blessing that I have not apprehended and imprisoned you.' So Psyche, in suffering this reverse to her hopes, was now beset by a double grief. As she retraced her steps, she noticed in a glimmering grove in the valley below an elegantly built shrine. Not wishing to disregard any means, however uncertain, which gave promise of brighter hope, and in her eagerness to seek the favour of any divinity whatsoever, she drew close to its sacred portals. There she observed valuable offerings, and ribbons inscribed with gold letters pinned to the branches of trees and to the doorposts. These attested the name of the goddess to whom they were dedicated, together with thanks for favours received. She sank to her knees, and with her hands she grasped the altar still warm from a sacrifice. She wiped away her tears, and then uttered this prayer.

4   'Sister and spouse of mighty Jupiter, whether you reside in your ancient shrine at Samos, which alone can pride itself on your birth, your infant cries, and your nurture; or whether you occupy your blessed abode in lofty Carthage, which worships you as the maiden who tours the sky on a lion's back; or whether you guard the famed walls of the Argives, by

the banks of the river-god Inachus, who now hymns you as bride of the Thunderer and as queen of all goddesses; you, whom all the East reveres as the yoking goddess, and whom all the West addresses as Lucina, be for me in my most acute misfortunes Juno the Saviour, and free me from looming dangers in my weariness from exhausting toils. I am told that it is your practice to lend unsolicited aid to pregnant women in danger.'

As she prayed like this, Juno at once appeared before her in all the venerable majesty of her divinity. There and then the goddess said: 'Believe me, I only wish that I could crown your prayers with my consent. But shame prevents me from opposing the will of Venus, my daughter-in-law whom I have always loved as my own daughter. There is a second obstacle—the legislation which forbids sanctuary for runaway slaves belonging to others, if their owners forbid it.'

5   Psyche was aghast at this second shipwreck devised by Fortune. Unable to meet up with her elusive husband, she abandoned all hope of salvation, and had recourse to her own counsel. 'What other assistance can I seek or harness to meet my desperate plight? Even the goodwill of goddesses however well-disposed has been of no avail to me. Now that I am trapped in a noose as tight as this, where can I make for, under what roof or in what dark corner can I hide, to escape the unwinking eyes of mighty Venus? Why don't you show a manly spirit, and the strength to renounce idle hope? Why don't you surrender yourself voluntarily to your mistress, and soften her savage onslaught by showing a humble demeanour, however late in the day? You never know, you may find the object of your long search in her house.' This was how she steeled herself for the uncertain outcome of showing obedience, or rather for her certain destruction, as she mentally rehearsed the opening lines of the plea she was to utter.

6   Venus now despaired of a successful search for her by earthly means, and she made for heaven. She ordered her carriage to be prepared; Vulcan had lovingly applied the finishing touches to it with elaborate workmanship, and had given it to her as a wedding-present before her initiation into

marriage. The thinning motion of his file had made the metal gleam; the coach's value was measured by the gold it had lost. Four white doves emerged from the large herd stabled close to their mistress's chamber. As they strutted gaily forward, turning their dappled necks from side to side, they submitted to the jewelled yoke. They took their mistress aboard and delightedly mounted upwards. Sparrows sported with the combined din of their chatter as they escorted the carriage of the goddess, and the other birds, habitually sweet songsters, announced the goddess's approach with the pleasurable sound of their honeyed tunes. The clouds parted, and heaven admitted his daughter; the topmost region delightedly welcomed the goddess, and the tuneful retinue of mighty Venus had no fear of encounter with eagles or of plundering hawks.

7   She at once made for the royal citadel of Jupiter, and in arrogant tones sought the urgent use of the services of the spokesman god Mercury. Jupiter's lowering brow did not refuse her. Venus happily quitted heaven at once with Mercury accompanying her, and she spoke seriously to him: 'My brother from Arcadia, you surely know that your sister Venus has never had any success without Mercury's attendance, and you are well aware for how long I have been unable to trace my maid who lies in hiding. So I have no recourse other than that you as herald make public proclamation of a reward for tracking her down. So you must hasten to do my bidding, and clearly indicate the marks by which she can be recognized, so that if someone is charged with unlawfully concealing her, he cannot defend himself on the plea of ignorance.' With these words she handed him a sheet containing Psyche's name and other details. Then she at once retired home.

8   Mercury did not fail to obey her. He sped here and there, appearing before gatherings of every community, and as instructed performed the duty of making proclamation: 'If anyone can retrieve from her flight the runaway daughter of the king, the maidservant of Venus called Psyche, or indicate her hidden whereabouts, he should meet the herald Mercury

behind the *metae Murciae*. Whoever does so will obtain as reward from Venus herself seven sweet kisses, and a particularly honeyed one imparted with the thrust of her caressing tongue.'

Longing for this great reward aroused eager competition between men everywhere when Mercury made the proclamation on these lines, and this above all ended Psyche's hesitation. As she drew near to her mistress's door, a member of Venus's household called Habit confronted her, and at once cried out at the top of her voice: 'Most wicked of all servants, have you at last begun to realize that you have a mistress? Or are you, in keeping with the general run of your insolent behaviour, still pretending to be unaware of the exhausting efforts we have endured in searching for you? How appropriate it is that you have fallen into my hands rather than anyone else's. You are now caught fast in the claws of Orcus, and believe me, you will suffer the penalty for your gross impudence without delay.'

9   She then laid a presumptuous hand on Psyche's hair, and dragged the girl in unresisting. As soon as she was ushered in and presented before Venus' gaze, the goddess uttered the sort of explosive cackle typical of people in a furious rage. She wagged her head, scratched her right ear, and said: 'Oh, so you have finally condescended to greet your mother-in-law, have you? Or is the purpose of this visit rather to see your husband, whose life is in danger from the wound which you inflicted? You can rest assured that I shall welcome you as a good mother-in-law should.' Then she added: 'Where are my maids Melancholy and Sorrow?'

They were called in, and the goddess consigned Psyche to them for torture. They obeyed their mistress's instruction, laid into poor Psyche with whips and tortured her with other implements, and then restored her to their mistress's presence. Venus renewed her laughter. 'Just look at her,' she said. 'With that appealing swelling in her belly, she makes me feel quite sorry for her. I suppose she intends to make me a happy grandmother of that famed offspring; how lucky I am, in the bloom of my young days, at the prospect of being hailed as a grandma, and having the son of a cheap maidservant called Venus's grandson! But what a fool I am, mistakenly calling him a son, for the wedding was not between a couple of equal status. Besides, it took place in a country house, without witnesses and without a father's consent, so it cannot be pronounced legal. The child will therefore be born a bastard— if we allow you to reach full term with him at all!'

10   Saying this, she flew at Psyche, ripped her dress to shreds, tore her hair, made her brains rattle, and pummelled her severely. She then brought some wheat, barley, millet, poppy-seed, chickpeas, lentils and beans. She mingled them together in an indiscriminate heap, and said to her: 'You are such an ugly maidservant that I think the only way you win your lovers is by devoted attendance, so I'll see myself how good you are. Separate out this mixed heap of seeds, and arrange the different kinds in their proper piles. Finish the work before tonight, and show it to me to my satisfaction.' Having set before her this enormous pile of seeds, she went off to a wedding-dinner. Psyche did not lay a finger on this confused heap, which was impossible to separate. She was dismayed by this massive task imposed on her, and stood in stupefied silence. Then the little country-ant familiar to us all got wind of her great problem. It took pity on the great god's consort, and cursed the vindictive behaviour of her mother-in-law. Then it scurried about, energetically summoning and assembling a whole army of resident ants: 'Have pity, noble protegées of Earth, our universal mother; have pity, and with eager haste lend your aid to this refined girl, who is Cupid's wife.' Wave after wave of the sespedalian tribe swept in; with the utmost enthusiasm each and all divided out the heap grain by grain, and when they had sorted them into their different kinds, they swiftly vanished from sight.

11   As night fell, Venus returned from the wedding-feast flushed with wine and perfumed with balsam, her whole body wreathed with glowing roses. When she observed the astonishing care with which the task had been executed, she said: 'This is not your work, you foul creature; the hands that accomplished it are not yours, but his whose favour you

gained, though little good it's done you, or him either!' The goddess then threw her a crust of bread, and cleared off to bed.

Meanwhile Cupid was alone, closely guarded and confined in a single room at the back of the house. This was partly to ensure that he did not aggravate his wound by wanton misbehaviour, and partly so that he would not meet his dear one. So the lovers though under the one roof were kept apart from each other, and were made to endure a wretched night. But as soon as Dawn's chariot appeared, Venus summoned Psyche, and spoke to her like this: 'Do you see the grove there, flanked by the river which flows by it, its banks extending into the distance and its low-lying bushes abutting on the stream? There are sheep in it wandering and grazing unguarded, and their fleeces sprout with the glory of pure gold, I order you to go there at once, and somehow or other obtain and bring back to me a tuft of wool from a precious fleece.'

12　　Psyche made her way there without reluctance, but with no intention of carrying out this task. She wanted to seek the cessation of her ills by throwing herself headlong from a cliff above the river. But from that stretch of stream one of the green reeds which foster sweet music was divinely inspired by the gentle sound of a caressing breeze, and uttered this prophecy: 'Psyche, even though you are harrowed by great trials, do not pollute my waters by a most wretched death. You must not approach the fearsome sheep at this hour of the day, when they tend to be fired by the burning heat of the sun and charge about in ferocious rage; with their sharp horns, their rock-hard heads, and sometimes their poisonous bites, they wreak savage destruction on human folk. But once the hours past noon have quelled the sun's heat, and the flocks have quietened down under the calming influence of the river-breeze, you will be able to conceal yourself under that very tall plane-tree, which sucks in the river-water as I do myself. Then, as soon as the sheep relax their fury and their disposition grows gentle, you must shake the foliage in the neighbouring grove, and you will find golden wool clinging here and there to the curved stems.'

13   This was how the reed, endowed with human qualities of
openness and kindness, told Psyche in her extremity how to
gain safety. She did not disregard this careful instruction and
suffer accordingly; she followed out every detail, and the theft
was easily accomplished. She gathered the soft substance of
yellow gold in her dress, and brought it back to Venus. But
the hazard endured in this second trial won her no favourable
acknowledgement from her mistress at least, for Venus
frowned heavily, smiled harshly, and said: 'I know quite well
that this too is the work of that adulterer. But now I shall try
you out in earnest, to see if you are indeed endowed with
brave spirit and unique circumspection. Do you see that lofty
mountain-peak, perched above a dizzily high cliff, from where
the livid waters of a dark spring come tumbling down, and
when enclosed in the basin of the neighbouring valley, water
the marshes of the Styx and feed the hoarse streams of the
Cocytus? I want you to hurry and bring me back in this small
jug some icy water drawn from the stream's highest point,
where it gushes out from within.' Handing Psyche a vessel
shaped from crystal, she backed this instruction with still
harsher threats.

14   Psyche made for the topmost peak with swift and eager
step, for she was determined there at least to put an end to
her intolerable existence. But the moment she neared the
vicinity of the specified mountain-range, she became aware of
the lethal difficulty posed by her daunting task. A rock of huge
size towered above her, hard to negotiate and treacherous
because of its rugged surface. From its stony jaws it belched
forth repulsive waters which issued directly from a vertical
cleft. The stream then glided downward, and being concealed
in the course of the narrow channel which it had carved out, it
made its hidden way into a neighbouring valley. From the
hollow rocks on the right and left fierce snakes crept out,
extending their long necks, their eyes unblinkingly watchful
and maintaining unceasing vigil. The waters themselves
formed an additional defence, for they had the power of
speech, and from time to time would cry out 'Clear off!' or
'Watch what you're doing!', or 'What's your game? Look

out!', or 'Cut and run!', or 'You won't make it!' The hopelessness of the situation turned Psyche to stone. She was physically present, but her senses deserted her. She was utterly downcast by the weight of inescapable danger; she could not even summon the ultimate consolation of tears.

15   But the privations of this innocent soul did not escape the steady gaze of benevolent Providence. Suddenly highest Jupiter's royal bird appeared with both wings outstretched: this is the eagle, the bird of prey who recalled his service of long ago, when following Cupid's guidance he had borne the Phrygian cupbearer up to Jupiter. The bird now lent timely aid, and directed his veneration for Cupid's power to aid his wife in her ordeal. He quitted the shining paths of high heaven, flew down before the girl's gaze, and broke into speech: 'You are in all respects an ingenuous soul without experience in things such as this, so how can you hope to be able to steal the merest drop from this most sacred and unfriendly stream, or even apply your hand to it? Rumour at any rate, as you know, has it that these Stygian waters are an object of fear to the gods and to Jupiter himself, that just as you mortals swear by the gods' divine power, so those gods frequently swear by the majesty of the Styx. So here, hand me that jug of yours.' At once he grabbed it, and hastened to fill it with water. Balancing the weight of his drooping wings, he used them as oars on right and left to steer a course between the serpents' jaws with their menacing teeth and the triple-forked darting of their tongues. He gathered some water in the face of its reluctance and its warning to him to depart before he suffered harm; he falsely claimed that Venus had ordered him to collect it, and that he was acting in her service, which made it a little easier for him to approach.

16   So Psyche joyously took the filled jug and hastened to return it to Venus. Even so, she was unable to conciliate the harsh goddess's resolve. Venus flashed a menacing smile as she addressed her with threats of yet more monstrous ill-treatment: 'Now indeed I regard you as a witch with great and lofty powers, for you have carried out so efficiently commands of mine such as these. But you will have to

undertake one further task for me, my girl. Take this box' (she handed it over) 'and make straight for Hades, for the funereal dwelling of Orcus himself. Give the box to Proserpina, and say: "Venus asks you to send her a small supply of your beauty-preparation, enough for just one day, because she has been tending her sick son, and has used hers all up by rubbing it on him." Make your way back with it as early as you can, because I need it to doll myself up so as to attend the Deities' Theatre.'

17   Then Psyche came to the full realization that this was the end of the road for her. All pretence was at an end; she saw clearly that she was being driven to her immediate doom. It could not be otherwise, for she was being forced to journey on foot of her own accord to Tartarus and the shades below. She lingered no longer, but made for a very high tower, intending to throw herself headlong from it, for she thought that this was the direct and most glorious possible route down to the world below. But the tower suddenly burst into speech, and said: 'Poor girl, why do you seek to put an end to yourself by throwing yourself down? What is the point of rash surrender before this, your final hazardous labour? Once your spirit is sundered from your body, you will certainly descend to the depths of Tartarus without the possibility of a return journey.

18   'Listen to me. Sparta, the famed Achaean city, lies not far from here. On its borders you must look for Taenarus, which lies hidden in a trackless region. Dis has his breathing-vent there, and a sign-post points through open gates to a track which none should tread. Once you have crossed the threshold and committed yourself to that path, the track will lead you directly to Orcus' very palace. But you are not to advance through that dark region altogether empty-handed, but carry in both hands barley-cakes baked in sweet wine, and have between your lips twin coins. When you are well advanced on your infernal journey, you will meet a lame ass carrying a load of logs, with a driver likewise lame; he will ask you to hand him some sticks which have slipped from his load, but you must pass by in silence without uttering a word. Immediately after that you will reach the lifeless river over

which Charon presides. He peremptorily demands the fare, and when he receives it he transports travellers on his stitched-up craft over to the further shore. (So even among the dead, greed enjoys its life; even that great god Charon, who gathers taxes for Dis, does not do anything for nothing. A poor man on the point of death must find his fare, and no one will let him breathe his last until he has his copper ready.) You must allow this squalid elder to take for your fare one of the coins you are to carry, but he must remove it from your mouth with his own hand. Then again, as you cross the sluggish stream, an old man now dead will float up to you, and raising his decaying hands will beg you to drag him into the boat; but you must not be moved by a sense of pity, for that is not permitted.

19   'When you have crossed the river and have advanced a little further, some aged women weaving at the loom will beg you to lend a hand for a short time. But you are not permitted to touch that either, for all these and many other distractions are part of the ambush which Venus will set to induce you to release one of the cakes from your hands. Do not imagine that the loss of a mere barley-cake is a trivial matter, for if you relinquish either of them, the daylight of this world above will be totally denied you. Posted there is a massive hound with a huge, triple-formed head. This monstrous, fearsome brute confronts the dead with thunderous barking, though his menaces are futile since he can do them no harm. He keeps constant guard before the very threshold and the dark hall of Proserpina, protecting that deserted abode of Dis. You must disarm him by offering him a cake as his spoils. Then you can easily pass him, and gain immediate access to Proserpina herself. She will welcome you in genial and kindly fashion, and she will try to induce you to sit on a cushioned seat beside her and enjoy a rich repast. But you must settle on the ground, ask for coarse bread, and eat it. Then you must tell her why you have come. When you have obtained what she gives you, you must make your way back, using the remaining cake to neutralize the dog's savagery. Then you must give the greedy mariner the one coin which you have held back, and

once across the river you must retrace your earlier steps and return to the harmony of heaven's stars. Of all these injunctions I urge you particularly to observe this: do not seek to open or to pry into the box that you will carry, nor be in any way inquisitive about the treasure of divine beauty hidden within it.'

20   This was how that far-sighted tower performed its prophetic role. Psyche immediately sped to Taenarus, and having duly obtained the coins and cakes she hastened down the path to Hades. She passed the lame ass-driver without a word, handed the fare to the ferryman for the river crossing, ignored the entreaty of the dead man floating on the surface, disregarded the crafty pleas of the weavers, fed the cake to the dog to quell his fearsome rage, and gained access to the house of Proserpina. Psyche declined the soft cushion and the rich food offered by her hostess; she perched on the ground at her feet, and was content with plain bread. She then reported her mission from Venus. The box was at once filled and closed out of her sight, and Psyche took it. She quietened the dog's barking by disarming it with the second cake, offered her remaining coin to the ferryman, and quite animatedly hastened out of Hades. But once she was back in the light of this world and had reverently hailed it, her mind was dominated by rash curiosity, in spite of her eagerness to see the end of her service. She said: 'How stupid I am to be carrying this beauty-lotion fit for deities, and not to take a single drop of it for myself, for with this at any rate I can be pleasing to my beautiful lover.'

21   The words were scarcely out of her mouth when she opened the box. But inside there was no beauty-lotion or anything other than the sleep of Hades, a truly Stygian sleep. As soon as the lid was removed and it was laid bare, it attacked her and pervaded all her limbs in a thick cloud. It laid hold of her, so that she fell prostrate on the path where she had stood. She lay there motionless, no more animate than a corpse at rest.

But Cupid was now recovering, for his wound had healed. He could no longer bear Psyche's long separation from him, so he glided out of the high-set window of the chamber which was his prison. His wings were refreshed after their period of rest, so he progressed much more swiftly to reach his Psyche. Carefully wiping the sleep from her, he restored it to its former lodging in the box. Then he roused Psyche with an innocuous prick of his arrow. 'Poor, dear Psyche,' he exclaimed, 'see how as before your curiosity might have been your undoing! But now hurry to complete the task imposed on you by my mother's command; I shall see to the rest.' After saying this, her lover rose lightly on his wings, while Psyche hurried to bear Proserpina's gift back to Venus.

22   Meanwhile Cupid, devoured by overpowering desire and with lovelorn face, feared the sudden arrival of his mother's sobering presence, so he reverted to his former role and rose to heaven's peak on swift wings. With suppliant posture he laid his case before the great Jupiter, who took Cupid's little cheek between his finger and thumb, raised the boy's hand to his lips and kissed it, and then said to him: 'Honoured son, you have never shown me the deference granted me by the gods' decree. You keep piercing this heart of mine, which regulates the elements and orders the changing motion of the stars, with countless wounds. You have blackened it with repeated impulses of earthly lust, damaging my prestige and reputation by involving me in despicable adulteries which contravene the laws—the *lex Iulia* itself—and public order. You have transformed my smiling countenance into grisly shapes of snakes, fires, beasts, birds, and cattle. Yet in spite of all this, I shall observe my usual moderation, recalling that you were reared in these arms of mine. So I will comply with all that you ask, as long as you know how to cope with your rivals in love; and if at this moment there is on earth any girl of outstanding beauty, as long as you can recompense me with her.'

23   After saying this, he ordered Mercury to summon all the gods at once to an assembly, and to declare that any absentee from the convocation of heavenly citizens would be liable to a fine of ten thousand sesterces. The theatre of heaven at once filled up through fear of this sanction. Towering Jupiter, seated on his lofty throne, made this proclamation: 'You gods whose names are inscribed on the register of the Muses, you

all surely know this young fellow who was reared by my own hands. I have decided that the hot-headed impulses of his early youth need to be reined in; he has been the subject of enough notoriety in day-to-day gossip on account of his adulteries and all manner of improprieties. We must deprive him of all opportunities; his juvenile behaviour must be shackled with the chains of marriage. He has chosen the girl, and robbed her of her virginity, so he must have and hold her. Let him take Psyche in his embrace and enjoy his dear one ever after.'

Then he turned to address Venus. 'My daughter,' he said, 'do not harbour any resentment. Have no fear for your high lineage and distinction in this marriage to a mortal, for I shall declare the union lawful and in keeping with the civil law, and not one between persons of differing social status.' There and then he ordered that Psyche be detained and brought to heaven through Mercury's agency. He gave her a cup of ambrosia, and said: 'Take this, Psyche, and become immortal. Cupid will never part from your embrace; this marriage of yours will be eternal.'

24   At once a lavish wedding-feast was laid. The bridegroom reclined on the couch of honour, with Psyche in his lap. Jupiter likewise was paired with Juno, and all the other deities sat in order of precedence. Then a cup of nectar, the gods' wine, was served to Jupiter by his personal cup-bearer, that well-known country lad, and to the others by Bacchus. Vulcan cooked the dinner, the Hours brightened the scene with roses and the other flowers, the Graces diffused balsam, and the Muses, also present, sang in harmony. Apollo sang to the lyre, and Venus took to the floor to the strains of sweet music, and danced prettily. She had organized the performance so that the Muses sang in chorus, a Satyr played the flute, and one of Pan's people sang to the shepherd's pipes. This was how with due ceremony Psyche was wed to Cupid, and at full term a daughter was born to them. We call her Pleasure.

25 This was the tale told to the captive maiden by that crazy, drunken old hag. I was standing close by, and God only

knows how sorry I was not to have writing-tablets and a stilus
to set down such a pretty story! Then suddenly the robbers
turned up, heavily laden; they had been involved in some
hard fighting, but several of the livelier spirits were keen to
leave the wounded at home tending their wounds, and to take
off again. They said they wanted to collect the remaining
bundles hidden in a cave. So they quickly gobbled down their
dinner, and then led my horse and myself out on to the road,
beating us with sticks all the while; we were to carry back
their spoils. After an exhausting journey over many hills and
winding paths, as night came on they brought us to a cave.
There they loaded us with heaps of baggage, and without
giving us a minute to recover our breath they swiftly got us
back on the road. They were in such agitated haste that in
driving me forward and belabouring me with repeated blows,
they caused me to tumble over a rock at the roadside. They
kept raining blows on me, and forced me to get up again, but
only with difficulty because my right leg and left hoof were
injured.

26   One of them said: 'How long are we to waste our time
feeding this broken-down ass now that he is lame as well?' A
second added: 'And what's more, he has brought bad luck on
our house. We haven't made a penny profit since his arrival—
just wounds and the slaughter of our bravest men.' A third
chipped in: 'What I intend to do, as soon as the unwilling
beast has finished carrying these sacks, is to push him over the
cliff at once to make a welcome meal for the vultures.' Whilst
these gentlest of souls were arguing with each other about how
to finish me off, we had now returned home, for fear had lent
wings to my hooves. They hurried to remove our loads, and
without thought for our welfare or indeed for my execution,
they took with them their comrades, who all this time had
stayed behind nursing their wounds, and they rushed back to
pick up the rest of the loot themselves, saying that they were
tired of our delaying tactics.

Even so I was consumed with considerable anxiety at the
thought of the death in store for me. I said to myself: 'Why are
you standing here, Lucius, waiting for the worst? The robbers

have passed sentence of death, death most painful, on you. It
won't require much of an effort from them. You see these
clefts close at hand with sharp rocks protruding from them;
before you have tumbled all the way down they will impale
you, and your limbs will be scattered in pieces, for that fine
magic of yours has given you merely the appearance and the
labours of an ass, and not an ass's thick hide but a leech's thin
skin. Why not pluck up a man's courage, and give thought to
your safety while you can? You have a perfect chance to
escape while the robbers are away. You're surely not afraid of
that hag with one foot in the grave who is guarding you? You
could finish her off with one kick even of your wounded foot.
But where in the world shall I take refuge, and who will give
me shelter? Yet that is a foolish thought, quite worthy of an
ass, for what traveller would not be delighted to make off with
a mount to carry him?

27   So there and then I yanked hard at the tether by which I
had been secured. I split it and plunged forward on my four
feet. But I failed to evade the vigilance of that old hag, for she
had eyes like a kite's. When she saw that I had broken free,
she seized the tether with a daring that belied her sex and age,
and she tried to pull me round and force me back. But that
murderous intention of the robbers was in my mind, so I felt
no tenderness towards her. I kicked out at her with my rear
hooves and sent her flying to the ground. But though she was
sprawled out there, she still clung grimly to the halter, and as
I galloped forward she was dragged along with me for a fair
distance. At once she let out noisy shrieks, begging the aid of
stronger hands. But the din that she raised with her crying
was futile, for the only person near who could come to help
was the imprisoned girl. The shouting roused her, and she
came racing out. Heavens, what a dramatic and memorable
scene she witnessed! There was the old woman playing Dirce,
but clinging to an ass and not a bull. With a man's resolution
the girl performed the noblest deed of daring: she tugged the
halter from the old hag's hands, whispered soothing words to
draw me back from bolting, nimbly leapt on my back, and
spurred me into a renewed gallop.

28   The desire to flee on my own account and my eagerness to free the girl were reinforced by the encouraging slaps which she gave me as a frequent reminder of our plight. So I sped along like a horse, hammering the ground at a four-footed gallop. I whinnied in response to the girl's honeyed words, and while pretending to scratch my back I kept bending my neck round and kissing the girl's dainty feet. Then she gave a deep sigh, turning her troubled face skywards. 'You gods in heaven,' she said, 'now at last lend me your aid in my desperate peril; and Fortune, now that you have shown your grimmer face, relent from your savage rage. These wretched torments of mine have appeased you enough. As for you, guardian of my freedom and my safety, if you deliver me home safe and sound, and restore me to my parents and my handsome suitor, what thanks I shall render you, what distinctions I shall confer on you, what dishes I shall serve up to you! First I shall lovingly comb this mane of yours, and adorn it with my childhood trinkets. After curling the hair on your brow, I shall part it neatly. Your tail, which is all matted and spiky because no one has washed it, I shall spruce up and make it glossy. You will be decked with lots of gold medals, so that you will shine like the stars of heaven as you celebrate your triumph in a joyous procession of the people. I shall stuff you every day with nuts and softer delicacies carried in the folds of my silk apron, hailing you as my saviour!

29   'As you enjoy your choice food, abundant leisure, and lifelong happiness, you will be accorded also the prestige of fame, for I intend to commemorate with an enduring memorial the fortune which divine providence has bestowed on me today. I shall have a picture painted of this flight of mine, and consecrate it in the atrium of my house. This unprecedented theme, "A noble maiden escaping captivity on an ass's back", will be on view, will be heard in common gossip, and will be immortalized by the pens of learned men. You too will have your place among the wonder-tales of old, cited as an example from real life to inspire our belief that Phrixus swam across the sea on a ram, that Arion piloted a dolphin, that Europe straddled a bull. If it is true that it was

Jupiter who bellowed in the form of a bull, there may lurk within my donkey some human identity or divine personality.'

Such were the words which the girl repeatedly uttered as she mingled repeated sighs with her prayers. We now reached the intersection of three roads. The girl grabbed the halter, and struggled hard to direct me to the right, doubtless because that was the road which led to her parents. But I knew that the robbers had taken that route to gather the rest of the loot, so I resisted stubbornly, and remonstrated with her in the silence of my heart. 'Wretched girl, what have you in mind? What are you doing? Why are you hell-bound so fast, and why use my feet to try to get there? You will be the death not only of yourself, but of me as well.' As we pulled in opposite directions, engaged in a boundary-dispute about land-rights or rather about rights of way, the robbers laden with their spoils caught us red-handed. In the bright moonlight they recognized us from a distance, and hailed us with waspish laughter.

30   One of the party greeted us like this: 'Where are you off to, moonlighting in such a hurry along this road? Aren't you afraid of ghosts and spirits abroad at dead of night? I suppose that as the most dutiful of girls you were hastening to visit your parents? Well, now, we shall escort you, since you are alone, and we shall show you a short-cut to your family.' Suiting the action to the word, he laid hold of the halter and turned me back the other way. He was carrying a knotted club, and did not spare me my customary beating. Since I was now on my way back to face an unwelcome and immediate death, I recalled the pain in my hoof, and I began to limp and let my head sag. 'So,' said the one who had pulled me round, 'are you stumbling and staggering again? Those worthless feet of yours can take off well enough, but now they cannot walk! Only a minute ago you were flying faster than the winged Pegasus!'

While my friendly companion was making these jokes at my expense and brandishing his cudgel, we had reached the outer enclosure of their base. The sight that greeted us was of the old hag with a rope round her neck, hanging from a branch of a tall cypress. They dragged her down, and unceremoniously trussed her up with her own rope, and threw her headlong over the cliff. At once they bound the girl tightly with ropes, and then they ravenously attacked the dinner which the poor old woman had prepared with devotion which survived her death.

31   As they tucked into the entire spread with gluttonous greed, they now began to discuss with each other the punishment to be meted out to us as their revenge. Opinions varied, as you would expect in such a discordant mob. The first man proposed that the girl be burnt alive, the second recommended that she be thrown to the beasts, the third urged that she be nailed to a gibbet, and the fourth suggested that her body be mangled by torture. They agreed unanimously on the one thing, that she be put to death. When the hubbub had died down, one of them said dispassionately:

'It is not in keeping with the philosophy of our brotherhood, with the civilized attitude of each of us, or indeed with my own moderation to allow you to indulge in barbaric excesses beyond what her crime demands. Wild beasts, the gibbet, firebrands, torture, even the precipitate darkness of a speedy death are inappropriate suggestions. So if you listen to my advice, you will grant the girl her life, but the life that she deserves. Doubtless you have not forgotten your earlier resolution about the ass here, which is always bone-idle, eats us out of house and home, and now falsely pretends to be lame, though he was the agent and minister of the girl's flight. You should accordingly vote to slit his throat tomorrow, and to sew the girl naked inside his belly, since he would rather have her than us. Leave only her face protruding, and let him enclose the rest of her body in his bestial embrace. Then you must expose him stuffed and fattened on some jagged rock, leaving him to the sun's blazing heat.

32   'In this way both of them will endure your righteous decree. The ass will meet his death, long and justly deserved; the girl will experience the teeth of wild animals as the worms draw his limbs apart, and fiery burning when the sun roasts his belly with excessive heat, and the tortures of the gibbet when

dogs and vultures drag out her inmost entrails. Consider too the aggregate of her other agonies and tortures. While she is still alive, her dwelling-place will be a dead beast's belly; the oppressive stench will scorch her nostrils; the deadly hunger of continued fasting will cause her to waste away; and she will not be able to contrive her death, for her hands will not be free.'

On hearing these words, the robbers voted for the proposal with acclamation, but as I took it in with my long ears, I could only shed tears for the corpse that I would be tomorrow.

BOOK 7

Charite (and Lucius) Rescued: Further Ordeals of Lucius

1 As soon as day dawned to dispel the darkness, and the sun's gleaming chariot brought brightness to the world, there was a fresh arrival. He belonged to the gang of robbers, as their ritual greeting to each other revealed. He was panting as he took his seat by the entrance to the cave. Once he had recovered his breath, this was the message that he brought to the company. 'We can stop worrying and breathe easily so far as Milo's house at Hypata is concerned, the house which we plundered the other day. After you had valiantly carried everything off and returned to base here, I mingled with the crowd of citizens, pretending to be indignant and outraged. I took note of the plans being laid to investigate the crime, whether they would decide to track down the robbers and to what extent this would be carried out, so that I could report everything to you according to your instructions. The whole crowd had reasonable grounds rather than doubtful arguments for accusing a certain Lucius as the clear culprit of the crime. A few days earlier he had brought a forged letter of introduction. He passed himself off to Milo as an honest man, winning his confidence so intimately that he was even welcomed as a guest and treated as a close friend. He had stayed a few days in the house, and had inveigled himself into the affections of Milo's maidservant by pretending to be in love with her. By this means he had carefully reconnoitred the bars on the gate, and the very rooms in which all the family wealth was usually kept.

2 'The evidence pointing to his being the miscreant was not slight, for he had made off at the very time when the crime was committed, and had not been seen anywhere since. His means of escape had been ready at hand, enabling him to outstrip his pursuers and to go to ground further and further

away, for he had kept with him the conspicuous white horse on which to make a getaway. The assumption was that his slave, who was discovered in his lodging there, would reveal his master's crimes and future intentions, but though the magistrates had taken him into state custody, and next day had inflicted sundry tortures on him, almost squeezing the life out of him, he had not made any such declaration. However, several investigators had been dispatched to the native region of this Lucius in order to search out the culprit, and make him pay the penalty for the crime.'

As the man recounted his tale, I was mentally contrasting the earlier condition of the happy Lucius I had been with the immediate hardships of the wretched ass I had become. I groaned in the depths of my heart, acknowledging that learned men of old had good grounds for envisaging and describing Fortune as blind and utterly sightless. That goddess, I mused, ever bestows her riches on the wicked and the unworthy, never favouring anyone by discerning choice, but on the contrary preferring to lodge with precisely the people to whom she should have given a wide berth, if she had had eyes to see. Worst of all, she foists on us reputations at odds with and contrary to the truth, so that the evil man boasts in the glory of being honest, while by contrast the transparently innocent man is afflicted with a damaging reputation.

3   In my case, Fortune by launching her most savage attack had transformed me into a four-footed beast of the most menial condition. Though my predicament seemed deserving of the distress and compassion of even the bitterest enemy, here I was being indicted for robbing a host who was most dear to me, a charge more truly deserving the label of parricide and not merely robbery. Yet I was unable to plead my case, or even to say one word to refute the charge. So I tried to avoid giving the impression that through a guilty conscience I was admitting to so wicked a crime by remaining silent. Unable to restrain myself, I sought merely to say 'Non feci', 'Not guilty'. I got the first word out repeatedly, but the second I wholly failed to articulate. I got stuck on the first

word, and kept braying 'Non, non', however much I waggled
my drooping lips to form as round a circle with them as I
could. But why do I go on lamenting Fortune's hostility? She
had not even baulked at my becoming the fellow-slave and
mate of my own serving mount, my horse.

4   This was the sea of troubles on which I tossed, but then a
more pressing anxiety took hold of me: I recalled the robbers'
decision that I be sacrificed to the shades of the maiden. I kept
eyeing my belly, feeling the sensation of having already given
birth to that poor girl. Then the robber who had just made the
lying allegation about me produced a thousand gold coins
which he had sewn in the lining of his coat. He explained that
he had relieved various travellers of them, and was now
demonstrating his probity by donating them to the common
chest. He further began to enquire with concern about the
safety of his comrades. On being told that some of them, in
fact the bravest, had met their deaths on active service
through various misfortunes, he recommended that for the
moment they should concentrate on enrolling fresh comrades,
making peaceful trips and pronouncing a truce on all
conflicts. By recruiting fresh blood they could bring up the
complement of their fighting-force to its earlier strength.
Reluctant individuals could be press-ganged by intimidation,
and volunteers enticed by rewards; and quite a number would
prefer to renounce the degradation of slavery, and to enhance
their way of life to that enjoyed by princes. He personally had
already met a candidate who was tall, young, well-built and
powerful. He had worked on him, and finally persuaded him
to turn his hands, which were flaccid from long idleness, to
better account, so that he might enjoy the blessings of rude
health as long as he could, and instead of holding out his
powerful hand to beg for pennies, he could use it for raking in
gold.

5   All the robbers applauded these words, and voted to enrol
the candidate who seemed already to have passed muster, and
to search out others to complement their number. The
speaker then went out, and only minutes later brought in a
young man as huge as had been promised. None of the present

company could apparently match him, for in addition to his powerful physique he was a whole head higher than all of them. A soft beard was spreading over his cheeks. His body was only half-covered with a patchwork cloak which was ill-fitting and roughly stitched together, and between the gaps in it his chest and belly rippled with close-packed muscles.

On making this entrance the newcomer spoke. 'Greetings, followers of Mars most valiant of gods, henceforth to be my trusty comrades. Give a warm welcome to a willing warrior of valorous vigour, one readier to sustain wounds in body than to gain gold in hand, and one who despises the death which others fear. Do not count me destitute or mean, nor judge my merits by the rags I wear. I was the leader of a most mighty band with which I despoiled the entire land of Macedonia. I am that celebrated brigand Haemus the Thracian, a man at whose name whole provinces tremble, son of Theron who was likewise a famous bandit. Human blood served as my milk, and I was reared among the platoons of my father's gang, to be his heir and rival in valour.

6   'But within a short time I lost that entire complement of brave comrades of old, and the great resources which we possessed. The cause was my having misguidedly attacked the emperor's financial agent as he was passing through. After earning a salary of 200,000 sesterces, he had lost his job through a stroke of bad luck. But to acquaint you with what happened I'll describe it from the beginning.

'This man had become a prominent celebrity at Caesar's court, and the emperor himself thought a lot of him. But he was falsely accused by certain deceitful persons, and harsh envy consigned him to exile. Now his wife Plotina was a woman of unique loyalty and matchless chastity, and she had established a firm family-foundation for her husband by ten terms of child-bearing. She rejected and disdained the pleasures of high life at Rome to accompany her exiled husband and to share his privations. Her hair was cropped, and her appearance mannish. All her valuable jewellery and gold coins she carried in bulging belts fastened round her, and she passed fearlessly among the bands of military guards as they brandished their unsheathed swords. She shared all her husband's dangers and kept ceaseless watch over his safety, facing unbroken hardships with the spirit of a man. At this time he had endured the many difficulties of the land-journey and the terrors of the sea, and he was making for Zacynthus, which the decree of fate had assigned to him as his temporary abode.

7   'He had just disembarked on the coast at Actium, at a time when we had slipped down from Macedonia and were prowling in the neighbourhood. Late at night we invaded a little inn lying close in to the shore and the ship; they were sleeping there to avoid being tossed on the ocean-waves. We plundered everything in it, but before we got away we faced considerable danger, for as soon as Plotina heard the door being forced open, she rushed into the dormitory and with agitated cries created wholesale disturbance as she summoned the soldiers, and her servants by name, and the entire neighbourhood as well, to lend help. However, we succeeded in escaping unharmed because they all took fright and hid out of fear for their own skins. But I must give the lady her due. That greatest integrity and matchless loyalty which she showed gained favour through such virtuous conduct, for there and then she sent a petition to the divine person of the emperor. This won a swift recall for her husband, and utter revenge on us for the attack we made on them. In short, Caesar refused to allow Haemus' brotherhood to exist any longer, and it was at once dissolved, for even a nod from the mighty emperor achieves this result. So military units hunted down our whole gang, which was suppressed and hacked to pieces. I managed with some difficulty to steal away unaccompanied, and to escape from the enveloping jaws of Orcus. I'll tell you how it happened.

8   'I put on a lady's dress with a floral pattern which spread out in billowing folds, and a woven turban to cover my head, and the kind of neat white shoes which women wear. In this way I disguised myself, passing myself off as a member of the other sex. I seated myself on an ass laden with ears of barley, and rode through the ranks of enemy troops which allowed me

free passage, for they thought that I was a woman mounted on
an ass, since my cheeks at the time were hairless and glowing
with the smooth sheen of boyhood. Though I trembled a bit at
being within range of these weapons of war, I was not untrue
to my father's fame or to my own valour, but under cover of
my strange disguise I launched attacks single-handed on
farm-houses and villages, thus scraping together the expenses
of my journey.'

He then ripped open his ragged outfit, and poured out
before them two thousand gold pieces. 'Here is my contribution,' he said, 'or rather my dowry, which I gladly present to
your brotherhood. I further offer myself to you as a most
trusty leader, and if you do not reject me, it will not be long
before I turn this stone dwelling of yours into a house of gold.'

9   The robbers without hesitation or delay voted unanimously
to appoint him as leader. They dug out a respectable outfit for
him to wear, in place of the patchwork cloak which had
proved so rich. In this new guise he kissed each of them, took
his place at the head of the table, and made his debut as
leader over dinner and some heavy drinking. In the ensuing
conversation he learned of the maiden's flight on my back and
of the hideous death appointed for both of us. He asked where
she was, and they led him to her. When he saw her weighed
down with chains, he turned up his nose in disgust, and
withdrew.

'I am not so ignorant, or at least not so rash, as to veto your
decision,' he said, 'but I shall have a guilty conscience if I
conceal my own attitude. But you must first trust in my
concern for your welfare, especially as you can revert to the
ass-plan if my suggestion does not find favour. My view is that
robbers with good sense should put no consideration before
their own profit, not even revenge, which often brings harm to
others as well as to its victims. So if you plant the girl in the
ass and finish her off, you will merely vent your annoyance on
her, and gain no profit. My alternative proposal is that she be
taken to some town and sold there; a young girl like this one
will fetch quite a high price. I myself have a long acquaintance with some brothel-keepers, and I imagine that one or

other of them will be willing to pay quite a few talents for this girl to be employed in a brothel, a suitable price for one of such high birth. She won't make her getaway from there as she did before, and her service in the bordello will give you adequate revenge. In my view this is an advantageous proposal, but you yourselves have discretion over the planning of your affairs.'

10   With these words the secretary of the robbers' chest had been pleading our case, becoming the noble saviour of both the girl and the ass. The other robbers held a lengthy discussion; their delay in reaching a decision tore at my innards and made me hold my breath anxiously. But finally they consented to the new bandit's proposal, and at once loosed the girl from her bonds. As soon as she had set eyes on that young man, and had heard mention of the brothel and its keeper, she began to perk up and to smile all over her face. My natural reaction was to criticize the whole sex when I observed that this girl, who had pretended to be in love with her young suitor and to long for a chaste marriage, welcomed the prospect of a foul and filthy brothel. At that moment the whole female sex and its morals lay perilously poised on the judgement of an ass.

The young man then spoke up again. 'So should we not address a prayer to Comrade Mars, and depart to sell the girl and search out fresh comrades? But I see that we have not a single beast to sacrifice, nor even abundance or sufficiency of wine to drink. So appoint ten representatives to accompany me; that will suffice to attack the nearest village, and enable me to bring back a meal fit for Salian priests.' So he set out; the rest laid a huge fire, and set up an altar to Mars on the green turf.

11   A little later they arrived back carrying wine-skins and driving a whole flock of farm-animals before them. From it they selected a huge billy-goat, old and shaggy, and sacrificed it to Mars, Follower and Comrade. At once they prepared a lavish spread, and then the presiding host said: 'You should regard me as your energetic leader not merely in your looting campaigns, but also in your entertainments.' He set to with

remarkable efficiency, organizing everything in lively fashion. He swept the floor, laid the table, cooked the meat, stuffed the sausages. He deftly served out the food, and above all he drowned them in huge goblets of wine, which he repeatedly replenished. From time to time he would pretend to take from the store-cupboard what the company needed; this allowed him to keep approaching the girl, and with a smile to offer her tit-bits which he had surreptitiously removed, and cups of wine which he had sampled. She would eagerly swallow them, and several times she readily assented to give him the kisses which he sought.

I was quite put out by this. 'Dear me, young lady, have you forgotten your marriage and your groom who shares your passion? Are you now preferring this blood-stained, murderous outsider to your newly-wed husband, whoever he is, to whom your parents have joined you in marriage? Isn't your conscience pricking you? Have you trodden your affection underfoot, that you like to play the wanton here among these spears and swords? Suppose the other bandits spot what is going on? I hope that you won't make a beeline for the ass again, and cause my downfall once more! It's another's hide that you are certainly putting at risk, and not your own!'

12   As I continued berating her and making these accusations with the liveliest displeasure, I became aware from some ambivalent remarks of theirs, which were not hard for a wise ass to fathom, that this fellow was not Haemus the notorious bandit but Tlepolemus the girl's bridegroom; for as the exchanges between them proceeded, he spoke in a louder voice, ignoring my presence as if I were actually dead. 'Take heart, dearest Charite,' he said, 'for all these enemies will soon be your prisoners.' All the time and with greater insistence he kept plying the wine, now undiluted and slightly warmed, upon the bandits, while he himself was not touching a drop. And bless me if it didn't strike me that he was mixing some soporific drug in with their cups. In the end every man jack of them lay out for the count with the wine; they were all as good as dead. It was no trouble then to shackle them very tightly

with chains, and when he had trussed them up to his liking, he put the girl on my back and made for their home town.

13   As soon as we got there, the whole town turned out to see the one they had been praying for. Parents, relatives, dependants, young wards, and slaves came dashing out, delight on their faces, ecstatic with joy. What a parade was on view—men and women, young and old, and a truly unforgettable sight, the girl riding in triumph on an ass! Then I too felt all the elation proper for a man to feel. Not wishing to be excluded as one detached from the celebrations, I pricked up my ears, flared my nostrils, and brayed enthusiastically; indeed, I sounded forth like a thunderclap. The girl's parents took her to her room, and fussed over her affectionately. Tlepolemus at once took me back to the cave with a great crowd of mules and citizens. I was not unwilling to go; apart from my habitual nosiness, I was keen at that moment to see the bandits under lock and key. We found them still in the grip of the wine more than of their bonds. So the citizens uncovered and brought out all the loot, and loaded us up with the gold, silver, and the rest of the booty. Some of the bandits still in their chains they then rolled headlong over into the nearest gorges; others they slew with their own swords, and left them exposed there. We then returned to the town, elated and in good spirits, having taken our revenge. The treasures they committed to public keeping, and they gave Tlepolemus legal rights over the girl whom he had rescued.

14   From then on Charite, now a married lady, addressed me as her saviour and tended me devotedly. On her wedding-day she ordered my manger to be stocked with heaps of barley, and enough hay left there to feed a Bactrian camel. But what grim curses pronounced on Photis would have been adequate for me? She had transformed me into an ass, not a dog; and there was I, watching the dogs, all of them stuffed and swollen with the left-overs and pickings from that magnificent banquet!

After that special night when she was initiated into love-making, the new bride never stopped recalling her gratitude to me in the presence of her parents and her husband, until she induced them to grant me the highest honours. So they met in council with their more reflective friends to decide how I could be most suitably rewarded. One proposal had been that I be granted a life of leisure indoors, stuffed with choice barley, beans, and vetch. But the second suggestion won the day; this envisaged giving me unrestricted freedom in country pastures, where I could sport at will among the herds of horses, and present the owners with a crowd of mule-foals by my superior services in mounting the mares.

15   So the groom in charge of the horses was at once summoned. After some lengthy words of explanation, I was put in his charge to be led away. I was naturally in good spirits and elated as I trotted ahead. I now had the prospect of release from lugging baggage and other burdens, and having gained my freedom I was sure to find some roses, since with the advent of spring the fields were sprouting. Then a second thought struck me as well; since so much gratitude and so many distinctions had been showered on me as an ass, I would be the recipient of many more generous awards once I regained my human shape.

But as soon as the groom drove me well away from the city, no luxuries and not even freedom awaited me. His wife, a greedy, utterly unscrupulous woman, at once harnessed me to the grinding-mill, punishing me from time to time with a leafy stick, as at the expense of my hide she prepared to make bread for her household and herself. She was not satisfied with wearing me out merely to provide herself with food; she hired me out to grind her neighbours' corn as I pounded round and round, and she did not give my wretched body even the standard rations for such heavy labours. For she would sell my barley, which I had crushed and ground under the same millstone by my own circling movements, to neighbouring farmers, while she would put before me, after a day harnessed to the exhausting contraption, some husks of bran, unsifted and grimy, with lots of rough gravel permeating it.

16   My head was already down because of these hardships, but cruel Fortune consigned me to fresh tortures, doubtless to enable me to take pride in my high renown through the

proverbial 'deeds of valour done at home and abroad'. At long last that exemplary herdsman followed his master's instructions, finally allowing me admission to the herds of horses. In my joy at being free at last, I pranced and capered gently around, and began to mark down the mares which would make the most suitable bed-mates for me. But even this happier prospect led to disastrous ruin. The stallions, well fed and long fattened from their lengthy period at stud, scared me stiff anyway, being certainly too powerful for any ass, but in addition they felt challenged by me, and were bent on preventing any adultery with an inferior breed. So they failed to observe the compact of hospitality laid down by Jupiter; they regarded me as a rival, and attacked me with rage and utter hatred. One raised his massive chest aloft, and with brow held high and rearing head, pummelled me with his front hooves. A second turned his ample, muscle-bound rump upon me, and launched a long-range attack with his hind legs. A third whinnied in threatening and hostile fashion; laying back his ears and baring white teeth like axes, he bit me all over. I had read of a similar happening in the story of a king of Thrace, who would throw his wretched guests to wild horses to be torn to pieces and devoured; that most powerful of all tyrants was so economical with his barley that he sated the hunger of his gluttonous beasts by generous provision of human bodies.

17   I too was similarly lacerated by these varied attacks of the horses, so that I longed to be back doing the rounds with the millstone. But Fortune, never satisfied with the tortures she inflicted on me, devised yet a further plague against me. I was given the job of carting timber down from a mountain, and the boy in charge of me was the most abominable youth in creation. Climbing the high ridge of the mountain exhausted me, and my hooves were chafed through collision with sharp rocks; this was bad enough, but I was also so savagely beaten by repeated blows from cudgels that the pain from the beatings penetrated deep down into my marrow. The boy kept raining blows on the one spot on my right hip, so that the skin was broken, and the huge sore beneath formed into a

cavity; I say a cavity, but it was more like a well or a window. He never stopped thumping the blood-smeared wound over and over again. Moreover, he weighed me down with such a load of timber that you would have thought that the pile of logs had been assembled for an elephant rather than an ass to carry. Then, whenever the load became top-heavy and slid over to one side, instead of removing some of the faggots from the side where it had shifted over, and thus giving me momentary relief by lessening the pressure, or at any rate equalizing the weight by transferring them to the other flank, instead he would pile up some stones on top, and seek to balance the uneven weight by that means.

18   Even then, following those very painful experiences of mine, he was not satisfied with burdening me with this monstrous load; for when we were crossing the stream which happened to flow alongside the road, he wanted to prevent the water soaking his boots, so he would jump on my hind-quarters and perch there, though I suppose this made only a slightly additional weight to that massive load. If I chanced to slip on the ridge of the river-bank, which was treacherous with slimy mud, and I collapsed through inability to maintain the weight, that peerless groom lent me no help in my exhaustion. He might have given me a hand, pulled me upright by the halter, raised me by the tail, or at any rate removed a part of the heavy load until I could stand up again. But instead he would seize his huge stick, and starting with my head or rather with my very ears, he would beat me all over until the blows themselves served as a sort of poultice and brought me to my feet. The boy then thought up a further torture for me. He fastened together some very sharp thorns, which had a lethally effective sting, into a bundle joined with a twisted knot, and he then attached them to my tail as a dangling weapon of torture. They came into play and became effective when I started walking, and with their deadly points they pierced me savagely.

19   So my suffering was twofold. If I galloped forward to avoid the boy's most painful beatings, I was smitten more sharply by the impact of the thorns, and if on the other hand I halted

for a moment to relieve the agony, his blows forced me to break into a trot. That criminal youth seemed to have nothing in mind except to finish me off one way or another, and in fact several times he threatened with an oath to do so. Then an incident occurred which clearly fired his unspeakable malice to more despicable action. One day my endurance snapped because of his extreme impudence, and I lashed out at him strongly with my hooves. The result was that he contrived this wicked design against me: he loaded a fair-sized bundle of tow on to my back, secured it carefully with ropes, and led me out on to the road. Then he stole a glowing coal from the nearest farm-house, and inserted it into the middle of the bundle. Once the fire grew hot as it was nourished by the thin tow, it burst into flame, and I was engulfed with the heat that spelt death. No escape was in sight from this most ghastly of afflictions, no consoling prospect of salvation. Such a conflagration admits of no delay; it moves too fast for well-considered remedies.

20   But in this grim plight Fortune smiled on me with kindlier eye. Perhaps she was preserving me to face future hazards, but at any rate she freed me from the immediate sentence of death. I chanced to observe close by a pool of muddy water caused by the previous day's rain. Without a thought and at one bound I hurtled headlong into it. The flames were completely doused, and eventually I emerged, both lightened of my load and delivered from destruction. But that most depraved, inconsiderate youth pinned the blame on myself for that dastardly trick of his. He assured all the herdsmen that when roaming of my own accord among braziers belonging to our neighbours, I had staggered and slipped, and wilfully brought the fire down over me. Then he added with a grin, 'How much longer, then, shall we go on feeding this fire-raiser to no effect?'

Not many days elapsed before he sought me out with a far more reprehensible ruse. He had sold the wood on my back to the next-door cottage, and as he led me along without a load, he bawled out that he could no longer cope with my evil ways. He said that he was giving up the impossible, wholly wretched job of looking after me, and he fabricated complaints on these lines:

21   'Do you see this lazy brute, this utterly slow, wholly asinine creature? To crown all his other villainies, he now causes further trouble by exposing me to fresh dangers. Whenever he spies a traveller—it could be an elegant lady, a grown-up girl, or an innocent young boy—he hastily shrugs off his load, sometimes throwing off his saddle as well, and makes a wild dash towards them; ass though he is, he aspires to be a lover of humans. He knocks them to the ground, eyes them fondly, and seeks to indulge his bestial urges with love-making at which Venus frowns. He even makes pretence of kissing, as with his filthy features he nuzzles and bites. This is a practice which will land us in fierce exchanges and disputes, perhaps even in criminal charges. Just now, for example, he caught sight of a splendid young woman. The wood he was carrying went flying off in all directions, and he made a mad dive at her. Jolly gallant that he is, he had her down on the filthy ground, for all the world as if he were going to mount her there and then before everyone's eyes. If her weeping and wailing hadn't roused some travellers to rush to her defence, to snatch her from between his hooves and free her, the poor woman would have been trampled on and torn apart. Her fate would have been agonizing, and for us the upshot would have been the penalty of death.'

22   He combined other allegations with lies like this to afflict my modest silence even more sorely, and to effect my destruction he pitilessly inflamed the anger of the herdsmen against me. Then one of them said: 'So why don't we solemnly sacrifice this marriage-partner who performs in public—or to put it better, this adulterer who offers his services to all? These unnatural love-liaisons would make him a suitable victim.' He added: 'So come on, boy, butcher him on the spot, throw his guts to our dogs, and then keep the rest of the meat for the workmen's dinner. We can stiffen his hide with a sprinkling of ashes, take it back to our masters, and easily invent a story that the ass was killed by a wolf.' My accuser was himself the guilty party, but now that he was appointed to carry out the

shepherds' sentence, he gleefully jeered at my predicament, and recalled the kicking which I bitterly regretted had not achieved its aim. Without delay he began there and then to sharpen his sword on a whetstone.

23   But then one of the gang of countrymen spoke up. 'It would be wrong', he said, 'to slaughter this fine ass like that, and to forgo such vital help and service just because we have charged him with immorality and sexual misbehaviour. An alternative is to hack off his genitals so that love-making is out for him; that way he can relieve you of all fear of danger. That's one advantage, and in addition he can become much stouter and heavier. I know of a number of animals, not just idle asses but also the most fiery horses, which suffered from excessive lust for coupling, and for that reason became recalcitrant and wild. But once they were castrated they at once became tame and manageable, quite ready to carry loads and submitting to their other duties. So as long as my advice doesn't meet with your disapproval, I can pick up the proper instruments from home and be back here shortly; I've been planning to visit the nearest market, so it will take me a little time. But then I can force this obstinate and unpleasant gallant's thighs apart, rob him of his manhood, and make him gentler than any wether in the flock.'

24   This proposal delivered me from the grasping clutches of Orcus, but I was most unhappy at this highly barbaric punishment in prospect. The thought that my body's rear end was to lose all its life made me weep. At that moment my idea was to dispose of myself by hunger-strike or by jumping off a height; I would die surely enough, but I would die with all my parts secure. While I was preoccupied with choosing my mode of death, that youthful executioner of mine led me out again early in the morning up the usual mountain track. He then tethered me to a branch dangling from a massive oak, climbed a little higher off the path, and began to wield his axe to chop wood to take down into the plain. All at once a deadly she-bear poked her monstrous head out of a nearby cave and sidled forth. As soon as I saw her, I was panic-stricken and aghast at her sudden appearance. I shifted the whole weight

of my body on to my back legs, raised my neck high in the air, broke the halter which tethered me, and took off promptly at high speed. It wasn't a matter of first feet forward; I threw my whole body hurtling pell-mell downward to the fields below, fleeing with the utmost urgency from that monstrous bear, and from the boy who was worse than the bear.

25   At that moment a traveller spotted me wandering without an owner. He took possession of me, quickly mounted, and beating me with the stick which he carried, he guided me along a byway which was new to me. I willingly co-operated with this course, as I was escaping from that most repulsive scheme of butchering my manhood. The beating I did not greatly mind, for I was used to such ritual assaults with the cudgel.

But Lady Fortune whom I knew well was bent on my undoing. With a speed which spelt misery for me, she pre-empted the timely prospect of concealment, and laid a fresh ambush. The herdsmen who had charge of me were hunting a lost heifer. After combing different areas, they chanced on us and recognized me at once. They seized me by the halter, and started to drag me off. But the traveller offered strong and bold resistance, appealing to the faith of men and gods: 'Why are you using force to drag me away? Why attack me?' 'What?' they responded. 'Are you saying that we are being rough with you when you have stolen our ass and are making off with him? You'd better tell us instead where you have hidden the beast's groom; presumably you've killed the boy.' They then pulled him to the ground, clobbered him with their fists, and put the boot in. He reacted with an oath, swearing that he had seen no rider; he had taken the ass when it was roaming free and unattended so as to obtain the reward for retrieving it, and he intended to restore it to its owner. 'I just wish', he added, 'that the ass himself—I wish to God that I'd never set eyes on him—could break into human speech and attest my innocence. If he did, you would certainly be ashamed of manhandling me like this.' But his protests were ineffectual; the herdsmen grabbed him by the neck and angrily dragged him back to the woodland glades of the mountain, where the boy usually gathered his wood.

26   There was no sign of the boy anywhere on the horizon, but a body was visible, torn limb from limb and scattered about, and it was obviously his. I knew beyond doubt that the bear's teeth were the perpetrators, and I would certainly have divulged this knowledge if the faculty of speech had been granted me. I did all that I could do; I silently welcomed this vengeance, delayed though it was. Eventually the herdsmen recovered the whole corpse, fitted the scattered parts together with some difficulty, and buried it in the earth there and then. As for my Bellerophon, they charged him with being caught red-handed as a thief and blood-stained assassin, and led him in chains to temporary confinement in their huts, so that as they said he could be turned over to the magistrates for punishment next day.

Meanwhile, as the boy's parents were beating their breasts in tearful lamentation, who should appear but the countryman, true to his promise and demanding to carry out the surgery as arranged. One of the mourning party said: 'The pernicious ass is not to blame for our present bereavement, but tomorrow you can certainly lop off not only his manhood but his head as well, and you can count on the help of these herdsmen.'

27   So my ordeal was postponed until next day, and I offered my thanks to that kind boy because at least in death he had granted me a stay of execution for one short day. But even this small respite afforded no chance of thanksgiving or rest, because the boy's mother burst into my stable, lamenting her son's bitter death. She was sobbing tearfully, dressed in sombre black, tugging her grey hair coated in ashes with both hands, moaning and bawling incessantly, beating and tearing violently at her breasts.

Then she broke into speech: 'Here he is, happily reclining in his manger, a slave to gluttony, perpetually stuffing and expanding that greedy, bloated belly, showing no pity for my distress, without a thought for the gruesome ill-fortune of his dead master! Doubtless he spurns and despises the infirmity of my old age, and imagines that he will survive this abominable crime without paying for it. But then, I suppose, he considers himself innocent; it is the usual way when people behave atrociously to expect no repercussions, in spite of a guilty conscience. You utterly worthless four-footed creature, God knows that even if you could acquire a human voice to plead your case, you could not persuade the dimmest fool that you are innocent of this horrible deed! You could have defended my poor little boy with your feet, and shielded him with your teeth. O yes, you could lash out at him time and time again with your hooves, so why couldn't you show the same readiness to prevent his death? The least you could have done was to hoist him on your back and clear off at once, saving him from that violent brigand's blood-stained hands! Above all, you should not have forsaken and abandoned your fellow-slave and master, your comrade and herdsman, to escape yourself. Do you not know that those who have failed to lend help to save people in danger of death are often punished for acting in such a despicable manner? But you will not laugh at my misfortunes any longer, you murderer. You will find that my wretched grief has a strength all its own—I'll see to that!'

28   As she spoke, she thrust her hands beneath her dress, loosened her breast-band, wound it round each of my feet separately, and lashed them together as tightly as she could, so that I would have no resource with which to seek revenge. She seized the bar used to reinforce the stable-doors, and proceeded to beat me with it until her strength was sapped with exhaustion, and the stick slipped from her grasp, borne down with its own weight. Then, grumbling at how quickly her arms grew tired, she ran to the hearth, seized a burning brand, and thrust it between my buttocks. This continued till I had recourse to my sole remaining means of defence. I unleashed at close quarters a stream of excrement, and covered her face and eyes with the foul liquid. That menace was at last forced back from me by that blinding and malodorous substance; otherwise this ass would have been a second Meleager, consigned to death by the firebrand of a maddened Althea.

BOOK 8

Charite's Revenge and Death: Lucius with the Catamite Priests

1 As cockcrow signalled the end of night, a young man arrived from the neighbouring city. I assumed that he was one of the servants of Charite, the girl who had endured hardships as trying as mine at the hands of the brigands. As he sat by the fire in the company of his fellow-slaves, he reported the strange and sacrilegious saga of the girl's death and the disaster which had struck her whole house. This was what he told them.

'Grooms, shepherds and herdsmen, our Charite is dead. Poor thing, she has departed to the shades below through the harshest of fates, but she has not gone alone. So that you may know the whole story, I shall tell you what happened from the beginning. It is a sequence of events which persons more learned than I, writers whom Fortune has invested with fluency of the pen, can appropriately commit to paper as an example of historical narrative.

'In a nearby town lived a young man of high birth, his nobility matched by his wealth. But he spent his time in the degenerate pursuits of the tavern, the brothel, and day-long drinking. This had led him to evil association with gangs of robbers, so that his hands were even stained with human blood. His name was Thrasyllus. Rumour circulating about him was matched by the reality.

2 'As soon as Charite had reached marrying-age, he had become one of her chief suitors. He devoted the greatest energy to the task of courting her; but though he was the leading contender among all those of his social rank, and sought to obtain her parents' consent with lavish gifts, his character as a reprobate led to the ignominy of rejection. Our young mistress was then joined in marriage to the worthy Tlepolemus, but Thrasyllus continued to nurture intensely

the love for which he had been utterly rejected, and with it he
mingled his resentment at having been refused marriage. He
then sought an opportunity to commit a bloodstained crime.
Eventually he gained a suitable pretext for attendance on the
couple, and he made preparations for the outrage which he
had long planned.

'On the day when the girl was delivered from the
threatening daggers of the robbers by the crafty and courageous deeds of her bridegroom, Thrasyllus mingled with the
crowd of those who felicitated her, and he made a show of his
delight. He expressed joy at the recent deliverance of the
newly-weds, and at the prospect of children to be born to
them. Their acknowledgment of the distinction of his glittering parentage led them to admit him to our household as one
of our most honoured guests. He concealed his wicked design,
and falsely played the role of the truest of friends. Soon by
regular conversation, continual association, and occasional
dinners and drinks together, he grew closer and closer to
them, until gradually and without realizing it he had fallen
headlong into the destructive depths of lust for Charite. This
was inevitable, for the flame of fierce love when it burns low
gives pleasure with its initial warmth, but once fed by
familiarity it becomes a fierce fire, scorching our whole bodies
with uncontrollable heat.

3   'It had long preoccupied Thrasyllus that he could find no
suitable opportunity for secret conversation with Charite. He
now saw that the possibilities of adulterous love were
increasingly barred by the number of retainers guarding her,
and he realized that the bond of the couple's new and growing
affection was so strong that it could not be severed. Moreover,
even if the girl showed willing, an impossible supposition, her
inexperience of conjugal deceit was an obstacle. Yet he was
driven on towards the impossible goal by the destructive
striving which made it seem attainable. When love strengthens
day by day, what at first is regarded as difficult to achieve
seems easy to accomplish. So now observe—I ask you to pay
attention closely here—the violent outcome of the onset of his
mad lust.

4   'One day Tlepolemus went hunting in company with
Thrasyllus. His quarry was wild animals, but only in the
sense that mountain-goats are wild, for Charite did not allow
her husband to hunt beasts armed with tusks or horns. Soon
the hunt reached a leafy eminence, where the thick cover of
branches cast its shadow. There were goats enclosed there,
hidden from the view of the trackers. The pedigree hounds,
trained for their tracking faculties in the hunt, were released
with the command to attack the animals crouching in their
lairs. Without hesitation they recalled the smart training they
had received, and they spread out to cover all the means of
entry. At first they confined themselves to low growls, but
then on receipt of a sudden signal they caused all hell to be let
loose with their fierce and discordant barking. But what
emerged was no she-goat, no fearful young deer, no hind (that
gentlest of all creatures in the wild), but a monstrous boar of
unprecedented size. His coarse flesh bulged with muscle; his
hide was disfigured with spiky hair; his back was shaggy with
bristles standing erect. He foamed at the mouth as he loudly
ground his tusks; fire flashed from his menacing eyes; the
savage onset of his ranting jaws moved like a bolt of lightning.
At first he lunged with his tusks this way and that, to slash
and slaughter the more adventurous hounds which had
ventured to close quarters. Then he trampled underfoot the
flimsy net which had held up his first attacks, and then made
his escape over it.

5   'While all the rest of us in panic took cover behind foliage or
tree-trunks (for usually our hunting expeditions were not
dangerous, and on this occasion we had no weapons or means
of defence), Thrasyllus exploited an opportune trick to
achieve his treachery. He craftily said to Tlepolemus: "Why
are we so thunderstruck, showing the same sort of idle fear as
our grovelling slaves here, or the lack of spirit of terrified
women, in letting such a splendid prize slip from our grasp?
Why don't we mount and chase after him at full speed? Here,
you take a hunting-spear and I shall grab a lance."

'They did not delay for a moment, but at once leapt on their
horses and pursued the beast with the greatest vigour. The

boar, still conscious of its native strength, wheeled round to attack. Aglow with the savage fire of rage, it whetted its tusks as it peered at them, in doubt whom to attack first. Tlepolemus was first to hurl the spear which he carried, and he pierced the animal's back from above. Thrasyllus, however, did not attack the beast, but with a blow of his lance cut the rear hamstrings of Tlepolemus' mount. The horse collapsed in a pool of its own blood, fell full length on its back, and unintentionally threw its master to the ground. The boar lost no time in savagely attacking his prostrate form. With repeated lunges of its tusks, it tore first at his clothing and then at Tlepolemus himself as he sought to rise. His good friend showed no compunction for his criminal deed, and could not even find full satisfaction in observing the sacrificial victim of his cruelty in such mortal danger. In fact he plunged his lance through his comrade's right thigh, as Tlepolemus in panic vainly sought to protect his crippled limbs and pitiably implored the other's help. Thrasyllus assailed him all the more confidently in his belief that wounds inflicted by the steel would resemble those ripped open by the tusks. He also ran through the beast itself with practised hand.

6   'After the youthful Tlepolemus had been dispatched in this way, the members of his retinue were all roused from our various hiding-places, and hastily gathered with downcast faces. Thrasyllus was delighted at having achieved his wish by bringing his enemy low, but he wiped the joy from his face, wore a troubled look, feigned sorrow, and affectionately embraced the corpse which he himself had slain. Indeed, he made practised pretence of performing all observances of mourners except for his tears alone, which refused to flow. In this way he modelled his actions on the rest of us who were genuinely mourning, and he kept blaming the beast for the foul deed inflicted by his own hand.

'The crime had scarcely been fully perpetrated when Rumour slipped from the scene and guided her twisted course first to the house of Tlepolemus, where she smote the ears of the hapless bride. As soon as Charite took in the message, the like of which she will never hear again, she became deranged and fired by madness. She rushed wildly about in a frenzy, coursing through crowded streets and the fields of the countryside, bewailing with demented cries her husband's misfortune. Sad bands of citizens gathered; they followed and drew up with her to share her grief. The entire city was deserted in the citizens' desire to look on her. What a scene it was as she rushed towards her husband's remains, and with gasping breath threw her whole body on the corpse! There and then she virtually surrendered to her dead husband the life that she had pledged to him. With some difficulty she was torn away from him by the hands of her kinsfolk, and she unwillingly survived. The dead body was conducted to burial with the whole citizen-body attending the funeral-train.

7 'Thrasyllus made a show of crying out and beating his breast all too vehemently. Doubtless under the stimulus of mounting joy, he now shed the tears which he could not summon when he first expressed grief. He beguiled Truth herself with his many expressions of affection, as he called on his friend, his contemporary, his comrade, and to crown all his brother, citing him by name as well. From time to time he would also draw Charite's hands back from beating her breasts, quieten her grief, restrain her lamentation, dull the sharp pain of her sorrow with soothing words, and weave a web of consolations by adducing various instances of wide-ranging misfortunes. Yet while performing all these observances of feigned devotion, he was indulging his eagerness to fondle the lady, and nurturing his own hateful love by seeking to arouse a perverse pleasure in her.

'But as soon as the funeral observances were over, the girl at once made haste to join her husband below. She tried every possible avenue, or at any rate the route that is non-violent and leisurely and needs no weapon to accomplish it, but is akin to peaceful rest. In short, she wretchedly starved herself, and foully neglected her person. She hid herself in the deepest darkness, and no longer had dealings with the light of day. But Thrasyllus applied constant pressure partly by his own efforts, partly through her other friends and relatives, and finally through the girl's very parents. He finally constrained

her to tend her body, now almost lifeless in its pallid and filthy
state, by washing and later by eating. She was a girl who in
general respected her parents, and though reluctant, she
yielded to the dictates of her sense of duty. So she performed
as bidden the routine tasks of the living, not smilingly but with
a calmer countenance than before. But in her heart, indeed in
the depths of her being, grief and sadness were gnawing at her
mind. All her days, all her nights she now spent in the grief of
longing. She had statues of her dead husband made in the
likeness of the god Liber; she made herself his votary, and
paid him divine honours in worship, thus torturing herself in
the very act which consoled her.

8   'Thrasyllus, however, was temperamentally impulsive and
rash, living up to his name. Tears had not yet sated Charite's
grief; the uncontrolled emotions of her disturbed mind had
not yet subsided; her sorrow had not worn itself out through
its protracted vehemence. She was still weeping after her
husband, still rending her garments, still tearing her hair. Yet
he did not hesitate to broach the possibility of marriage. The
lapse of an unguarded moment led him to disclose his
unspeakable treachery, which in silence and secrecy he had
hugged to his heart. Charite was appalled at this sacrilegious
disclosure, and she abominated it. It hit her like a thunderclap, or an explosive downpour in the rainy season, or a bolt
of lightning from heaven. It shattered her physically, and
made her mind a blur. Gradually, however, her spirit revived.
Over and over again she moaned like an animal. She now saw
through the unspeakable Thrasyllus' pretence, but in order to
refine a plan of action she sought a delay to the aspiration of
her suitor.

       'During this moratorium the shade of Tlepolemus, so
wretchedly slain, disturbed his wife's chaste sleep. He raised
his face, gore-stained and unsightly in its pallor, before her. "I
greet you as my wife", he said, "though no other will be able
to call you mine. Even if remembrance of me is now firm in
your heart, and the calamity of my bitter death does not sever
the bond of our love, you must find greater happiness in
marriage to another, provided that you do not accept the

sacrilegious hand of Thrasyllus. Do not speak with him, or recline at table with him, or share his bed; shun the bloodstained hand of my assassin. Do not embark upon a marriage initiated by the murder of your kin. Those wounds whose blood your tears washed away are not all the work of tusks; it was the lance of the wicked Thrasyllus which has set me apart from you." Further words which he spoke revealed the nefarious plot in its entirety.

9   'Charite slumbered on, her face sunk into the couch as it had been when sleep first overtook her in her melancholy. Her tears streamed forth and bedewed her cheeks. Then she was roused from sleep as if some weapon of torture had jolted her, and her grief was renewed. She uttered prolonged wailing, tore her nightgown, and with merciless hands beat her pretty arms. But she did not divulge the vision of that night to anyone; the revelation of the crime she kept wholly secret. She silently decided both to punish the iniquitous assassin and to detach herself from a life which had become intolerable.

'The abominable Thrasyllus now made a further appearance. In pursuit of his thoughtless pleasure, he assailed with talk of marriage the ears which she kept firmly barred. But her rejection of his address was gentle, and her role-playing was performed with admirable guile. In response to his insistent chatter and obsequious pleading, she said: "The handsome face of your fraternal friend, my dearest husband, is still vivid before my eyes; the cinnamon-like fragrance of his body with its scent of ambrosia still pervades my nostrils; handsome Tlepolemus is still alive in my heart's depths. So you will show proper and exemplary prudence if you grant the required period of lawful mourning to this woman in her great misery, until the remainder of the year is completed by the months still to elapse. This delay is in the interests of both my modesty and the good of your health; otherwise, by marrying too early we may fire my husband's ghost to bitterness and justified anger, and he may bring about your death."

10   'These words of hers did not induce sobriety in Thrasyllus, or even hearten him with their distant promise. He continued to press her repeatedly with suggestive whispers from his

wearying tongue. Finally Charite pretended to yield, and
answered him. "Very well, Thrasyllus, but at least grant me
this pressing request: our intimate relations must in the
meantime be conducted silently and in secrecy. No member of
the household must become privy until the remaining days of
mourning are past."

'Thrasyllus bowed in defeat to this deceitful promise of the
lady, and he enthusiastically endorsed the suggestion of secret
love-encounters, for his own unprompted longing aspired to
the night and the cover of darkness. He relegated all else to
the single desire to possess her. "But be sure", added Charite,
"to come well concealed by a cloak, and with no companion.
Make your way silently, just after dark, to my gate. A single
whistle will suffice; wait for this nurse of mine here, who will
have her hand on the bolt, watching out for your arrival. She
will likewise open the house, let you in, and guide you to my
bedroom without the conspiratorial help of a lamp."

11   'This staging of a marriage with death appealed to
Thrasyllus. With no suspicion of anything amiss, he was in a
turmoil of expectation, and his only complaint was that the
day was long and the night slow in coming. But when the sun
finally yielded to darkness, he clothed himself as Charite
demanded. The sight of the nurse astutely posted on watch
deceived him; he crept into the bedroom hell-bent on gaining
his desire. The old nurse had received her instructions from
her mistress. She fawned on him, and then unobtrusively
brought out goblets and a wine-jar containing a sleeping-
draught mixed with the wine. Greedily and without suspicion
he drained his cup several times; the nurse had lyingly
excused her mistress's late arrival by claiming that she was at
the bedside of her sick father. Without difficulty she soon had
him sleeping like the dead; once he was laid out and
vulnerable to any assault, Charite was summoned in. She was
animated by a man's courage as she strode to the assassin
with steely aggression and fierce rage. She stood over him,
and said:

12   ' "Here he is, my husband's faithful comrade, a huntsman
beyond compare, my own dear spouse! Here is the hand that

shed my blood, here is the breast that devised a deceitful fraud
to encompass my destruction! These are the eyes which found
perverted pleasure in gazing on me. But already here they
anticipate the darkness which is to descend on them, and they
have foresight of the punishment to visit them. Take your
untroubled rest, enjoy your blessed dreams! I shall not assault
you with sword or steel, for I would not have you ranked with
my husband by your sharing the nature of his death. You will
live, but your eyes will perish; only when you sleep will you
exercise your sight. I shall ensure that you regard your
enemy's death as more blessed than your life. What is certain
is that you will not see the light of day, and that you will need
a companion's guiding hand. You will not embrace Charite or
enjoy marriage with her. You will neither gain renewed vigour
by the tranquillity of death, nor take joys in the pleasures of
life. Instead you will wander between the regions of hell and of
the sun, a dubious image of a living man. You will spend long
days seeking the hand that stormed your eyesight, and your
suffering will be compounded by your wretched ignorance of
whom to blame. The blood from your eyes will be the libation
which I shall pour on the tomb of my Tlepolemus; those eyes
will constitute the sacrifice which I shall make to his sacred
shade.

' "But why do I grant you the boon of a respite from the
torture you deserve, and perhaps allow you to dream of
baneful embraces with me? Emerge from the shadows of sleep,
awake to that other darkness which will be your punishment.
Lift up your eyeless face, acknowledge this my vengeance,
apprehend your misery, take stock of your sufferings. This is
how your eyes have gained the favour of a chaste woman; this
is how the marriage-torches have lit your bridal chamber.
Your bridesmaids will be the avenging Furies; blindness will
be your groomsman, and the prick of undying guilt."

13   'This was how she prophesied his future. She then took a
pin from her hair, and pierced his eyeballs through, leaving
him totally sightless. As he shook off his drunken sleep
through the pain which he could not identify, she seized the
unsheathed sword which Tlepolemus had been accustomed to

buckle on, and she burst out at a frenzied pace through the middle of the city. It was clear that she had some criminal deed in mind as she made straight for her husband's tomb. We and the entire citizen-body quitted all our houses and anxiously overtook her, urging each other to wrest the sword from her crazed hands. But Charite took her stand by Tlepolemus's coffin, and drove each of us back with the gleaming sword. As she surveyed the copious tears which we were all shedding, and our discordant wailing, she said: "Dry your untimely tears, renounce the grief which is out of keeping with my valorous deeds. I have exacted vengeance from the bloodstained murderer of my husband; I have punished the plunderer who brought death to my marriage. It is now time for me to seek through this sword the downward path to Tlepolemus."

14   'She then recounted in sequence all that her husband had told her in her dream, and the trickery she had employed to deceive and to lay hands on Thrasyllus. She then drove the sword below her right breast, and slid to the ground. As she writhed in her own blood, she stuttered some last incoherent words, and died like a man. Her kinsfolk then hastened to wash poor Charite's body with devoted care, and restored her to her husband in their common burial-place to be his spouse for ever.

'When Thrasyllus heard all that had happened, he found himself unable to bring this present tragedy to its appropriate close, for he was convinced that not even death by the sword was meet for such a foul crime. At his request he was led to the tomb, where he repeatedly cried out: "Hostile shades, here is your willing victim!" He then deliberately closed the doors of the tomb over himself, and by self-starvation opted to expel from his body the life that he had condemned by his own sentencing.'

15   This was the news that the slave brought, punctuated with extended sighs and occasional tears; his audience of country-workers was deeply moved. But they felt apprehensive at being under new ownership, and their sympathy ran deeper for the disaster which had struck their former master's house.

Accordingly they planned to run away. The head groom, who was charged with the horses and who upon Charite's strong recommendation had undertaken to look after me, loaded on my back and on those of the other beasts all the valuables that he kept stored in his cottage. He then carried them away, and abandoned his former abode. We carried on our backs young children, women, chickens, sparrows, kids, pups; and all those who had difficulty in walking and who hindered our swift departure exploited our feet to make the journey. The weight of my load was prodigious, but it did not dishearten me, for in joyful flight I was leaving behind the abominable fellow who sought to slice off my manhood.

We made our way over the rough ridges of a wooded mountain, and then journeyed through the plains extending beyond. As evening overshadowed our path, we came to a crowded and prosperous village. The inhabitants there tried to deter us from leaving in darkness or even in the early morning. They said that there were hordes of gigantic wolves plaguing all that district; they were burly and big-bodied, exceedingly fierce and savage, and were constantly hunting plunder in many areas. At that time they were blockading the very roads, and like highwaymen they attacked travellers as they passed by. Indeed, their mad hunger made them so savage that they stormed neighbouring farmhouses, and the fate suffered by unresisting cattle now overhung the human occupants themselves. They claimed that the road on which we were to travel was littered with half-devoured bodies, all gleaming white because the bones had been stripped of their flesh. Hence it was vital that we observe the greatest caution in resuming our journey, and take the most stringent care to travel in broad daylight, when the hour was well advanced and the sun was at its zenith. We should avoid the traps lurking round us on all sides, and negotiate the hazards at a time when the aggression of those foul beasts was tempered by the sun's rays. We should proceed not strung out in isolation, but in compact wedge-formation.

16   But our most negligent runaway leaders were rash in their blind haste, and fearful that we might be followed. They

disregarded this salutary advice, and without awaiting the
morning light they drove us with full loads on to the road just
after midnight. I was fearful of the danger of which we had
been forewarned, so I then sought the innermost possible
position, hiding myself to lurk unnoticed in the crowd of
closely-packed beasts, and thus protecting my haunches
against the attacks of those wild animals. There was general
astonishment at the turn of speed with which I outpaced the
horses accompanying us. Such acceleration was a mark of
apprehension rather than eagerness on my part; indeed, I
reflected that it was panic more than anything which had
induced the celebrated Pegasus to take to the air, and that the
tradition that he had wings was justified because he leapt
upward as high as heaven in his fear of being bitten by the
fire-breathing Chimaera. An additional reason for apprehension was that the shepherds who were herding us had
equipped themselves as if for battle. One wielded a lance,
another a hunting-spear, a third darts, a fourth a club; they
also carried stones which the rugged path supplied in
abundance. Some of them had sharp stakes, but most deterred
the beasts with flaming torches. The only thing they lacked for
a formal battle-line was a bugle.

However, our fears on this score were wholly groundless
and superfluous, but we landed ourselves in a much stickier
trap. The wolves were doubtless frightened off by the din
raised by our close-knit group of young men, or at any rate by
the glaring light of the torches, or they may have been
plundering elsewhere. None of them attacked us, or were even
in evidence some way off.

17 But we chanced to pass by an estate in which the
farmhands mistook our large band for robbers. They were
considerably exercised for their property as well as extremely
frightened, so they set their dogs on us with the usual halloos
and shouts of every kind. These animals were wild, huge, and
more ferocious than any wolves or bears, and had been
carefully reared as guard-dogs. Their native savagery was
intensified by the din which their masters made. They
charged at us, surrounded us on all sides, and leapt at us from

every angle, making no distinction between man and beast as they mangled us. Their sustained attacks left many of us lying on the ground. I swear that the sight you would have beheld there was worthier of pity than of the pen: that large pack of dogs was fiercely intent on tugging at those who fled, clinging to those who stood their ground, mounting on some who were prostrate, and in their progress through our entire column, sinking their teeth into everything and everyone.

18   This hazard was bad enough, but worse was to follow. Those countrymen posted themselves on rooftops and on the nearest hill, and sent rocks rolling full tilt on us. We were utterly at a loss to decide whether to take cover more against the dogs at close quarters or the rocks at long range. One of the rocks suddenly struck the head of a woman astride my back; she reacted to the pain by weeping and wailing, and by shouting to her husband the head-groom to come to her aid. He kept calling on the gods to witness what was happening, and as he wiped the blood from his wife, he raised his voice in complaint. 'Why are you attacking and oppressing us so cruelly? We are poor people struggling on our way. What booty do you cast your eyes on? What losses are you seeking to avenge? I cannot believe that you are beasts dwelling in caves, or barbarian rock-dwellers, that you take pleasure in shedding human blood!'

The words were scarcely out of his mouth when the heavy shower of stones ceased, and the storming attack of the dogs was quietened as they were called off. Then one of the estate-workers called out from the top of a cypress-tree: 'We are not brigands eager to plunder you. Our aim has been to avoid that same harsh treatment at your hands. You can now proceed untroubled and without interference.'

These were his words. But we embarked on the rest of our journey bearing the marks of many wounds. Some had been struck by stones, others bitten by the dogs; all of us were injured. After we had travelled a fair distance on the road, we reached a grove planted with tall trees and with delightful patches of green meadow. Our leaders decided to refresh themselves here with a brief rest, and to give more careful

treatment to their bodies which had suffered various lacera-
tions. So they sprawled out at various places on the ground,
and hastened first to restore their wearied spirits, and then to
apply different remedies to their wounds. One washed off the
blood in the waters of a stream which flowed by; another
reduced the swellings with sponges soaked in vinegar; a third
bound his gaping wounds with bandages. This was how each
looked after his own well-being.

19   While this was going on, an old man surveyed the scene
from the top of a hill. Nanny-goats cropping the grass all
around plainly showed that he was a herdsman. One of our
number asked him if he had milk for sale, either still liquid or
newly curdled into cheese. He shook his head over and over
again. 'What?' he asked. 'Are your minds at this moment on
food or drink or any sort of refreshment? Do none of you know
about this place where you have taken rest?' With these words
he rounded up his devoted sheep, turned on his heel, and
retired to a distance. His comment and his precipitate
departure considerably agitated our herdsmen. In their
disquiet they were eager to enquire about the nature of the
place, but there was no one to inform them. But then another
old man, tall but weighed down with age, leaning with his
whole weight on his stick and dragging his feet wearily along,
approached in floods of tears along the road. When he sighted
us, he wept copiously, touched the knees of each of the young
men, and pleaded with them in these words:

20   'I implore you by your personal Fortunes and your
guardian spirits to come to the aid of this destitute old man. If
you do, I pray that you may reach my time of old age still
strong and happy. Rescue my little one from death, and
restore him to these grey hairs of mine. My grandson, my
engaging companion on this journey, chanced to be trying to
catch hold of a sparrow chirruping in a hedgerow, and he has
fallen into a pit close by which lies open beneath the
brambles. He is now in the greatest danger of his life. I know
that he is alive, for I can hear him crying and repeatedly
calling for his grandfather, but I cannot go to his rescue
because of my poor bodily health, as you can see. But it would

be easy for you with the resource of your youth and strength to come to the aid of this most unhappy old man, and to save the life of that boy, who is the last of my descendants and the only one of my stock still surviving.'

21   As he pleaded in this way and tore at his grey hairs, the whole of our company pitied him. One in particular, more stout-hearted, younger, and physically stronger than the rest, had emerged unscathed from the earlier fracas. He jumped up smartly, and asked where the boy had tumbled in. When the old man pointed with his finger at some prickly brambles not far away, the young man briskly accompanied him there. Meanwhile we had restored ourselves, the beasts by eating our fodder and the humans by tending their needs, and we all took up our baggage and set out. To begin with the men repeatedly shouted after the young fellow, loudly calling on him by name, but then the long delay caused them disquiet, and they sent one of their number to summon him, to search out their comrade, to tell him it was time to leave, and to escort him back. The messenger returned after a short time, trembling and pale as boxwood. He had an extraordinary tale to tell about his fellow-slave: he had seen him lying prostrate, with a monstrous snake perched on top of him gnawing his flesh, so that the youth was now almost entirely gobbled up. There was not a sign anywhere of that unhappy old man. When they heard this, they connected it with the words of the shepherd, who had clearly been warning them against that inmate of this desolate region who was as old as himself. So they abandoned that baneful spot, and took to their heels in headlong flight, driving us along with frequent blows of their cudgels.

22   We finally reached a village after completing a long journey at top speed, and we rested there for the entire night. A quite noteworthy outrage had been committed there, and I am eager to recount it.

The extensive estate where we lodged was managed by a slave whose master had entrusted him with the entire supervision of the household. This bailiff was married to a fellow-slave in the same retinue, but was inflamed with passion for a free woman who lived beyond the estate. His wife burned with resentment at this adulterous liaison. She set fire to all her husband's account-books, and all that was stored in the granary. Still not satisfied at having avenged the slight to her marriage-bed by inflicting such damage, she next took drastic steps against the fruit of her own womb. She lassooed herself, and then wound the same rope round the baby whom she had borne some time before to that same husband. She then threw herself down into the deepest of wells, taking the small child with her. Their master took her death very badly. He seized the wretched slave whose licentious behaviour had been responsible for this appalling outrage, stripped him and smeared his whole body with honey. Then he bound him tightly to a fig-tree, in the rotting trunk of which resident ants were busy building their nests and scurrying to and fro in a continuous stream. Once they smelt the honey-sweet odour of his body, they clung fast to it, taking tiny but regular and continual bites from it. This torture continued over a long period, until his flesh and inner organs were gnawed away. So the bailiff was devoured, and the ants stripped his limbs bare, so that nothing but the bones were left adhering to that tree of death. They hung there, stripped of the flesh, gleaming starkly white.

23   So we abandoned this accursed resting place as well, leaving the villagers to their heartfelt grief. We took to the road again, and for a whole day we travelled on routes which straddled a plain. We finally arrived exhausted at a populous and famous town. The shepherds escorting us decided to make this their permanent abode, for it seemed a safe place to hide from those who might be searching for them at some distance away; in addition, the plentiful abundance of grain was enticing. So for three days the pack-animals were rested and fed, to ensure that our appearance would fetch a better price, and then we were led to market. The auctioneer loudly announced the price of each beast, and the horses and other asses were bought by wealthy buyers, most of whom turned up their noses at me and passed by, leaving me forlorn and isolated. I became so irritated with people mauling me and

trying to assess my age from my teeth that I fastened my grinders into the foul-smelling hand of one individual who kept massaging my gums with his filthy fingers, and completely crushed it. This incident cooled the enthusiasm of prospective buyers among the crowd, for they thought me over-aggressive. Then the auctioneer, now hoarse from straining his tonsils and exercising his raucous voice, began to concoct amusing jokes about my prospects: 'For how long are we to try in vain to sell this nag? The poor old thing is feeble, his hooves are worn down, and the painful treatment he has suffered has made him unsightly. He is vicious too, for all his stupidity and lethargy. He is nothing better than a braying, worn-out sieve. So let us at any rate make a present of him, if we can find someone who does not object to wasting his fodder.'

24   With words like these the auctioneer raised guffaws from the bystanders. But that most malevolent Fortune of mine, whom I had failed to shake off in my flight through numerous regions, or to placate through the ills I had already suffered, turned her blind eyes on me again. Remarkably, she found me a buyer most suited to my grim misfortunes, and thrust him upon me. Let me outline his type: he was a catamite, and an old one at that, bald on top, with ringlets streaked with grey dangling round his head. He was representative of the meanest dregs of society, those people who parade through the streets of towns banging cymbals, shaking castanets, and carrying round the Syrian goddess whom they adduce to solicit alms. In his eagerness to purchase me, he asked the auctioneer where I hailed from; the man declared that I was a Cappadocian, and quite virile. When the other in turn asked my age, the auctioneer flippantly replied: 'The astrologer who drew his horoscope claimed that he was in his fifth year, but doubtless the ass is a better authority for his own age, since he registered for the census. I know that I am with forethought risking indictment under the Cornelian law if I sell you a Roman citizen as a slave, but why don't you buy this worthy and honest piece of goods? He will be able to offer you satisfaction both outdoors and indoors.' The loathsome purchaser, however, kept on posing one question after another

incessantly, finally asking with furrowed brow whether I was
meek and mild.

25   The auctioneer replied: 'This is no ass you see; he's gelded,
compliant in any service. He doesn't bite or lash out. You
could believe that in this ass's skin there lurks an unassuming
human being. You can readily observe this; just push your
head between his thighs, and you'll easily establish what a
massive length of endurance he has on offer!'

This was how the auctioneer exercised his wit at the
expense of the greedy priest. But the other detected the tone of
mockery, and with a show of indignation said: 'You lifeless
deaf and dumb creature! You crazed auctioneer! I pray that
the Syrian goddess our all-powerful universal mother, and
holy Sabazius, and Bellona, and the Idaean mother and her
Attis, and the lady Venus and her Adonis may blind you for
making me the butt of your coarse witticisms! You surely do
not imagine, you fool, that I can entrust the goddess to an
untamed animal? Why, he might suddenly throw a fit and
dislodge the statue of the goddess, and then I, poor queen,
would have to rush around with my hair flying loose, seeking
a doctor for my goddess as she lies prostrate on the ground!'

When I heard words like these, my first thought was to
bound suddenly into the air as though crazed, so that he
would lose interest in buying me, once he saw that I had a
furious temper when roused. But the purchaser was keen, and
forestalled my intention by at once forking out the price of
seventeen denarii. My master readily accepted it, and gladly,
for he had had enough of me. There and then he fastened a
bridle of flax round my mouth, and consigned me to Philebus,
the name of my new owner.

26   The priest took over his untrained servant, and dragged me
off home. As soon as he reached the threshold, he shouted out:
'Look, girls, what a handsome wee slave I've brought for you!'
The 'girls' were in fact a bunch of catamites. Their joy was
immediate and ecstatic; they cried out discordantly in their
cracked, hoarse, girlish voices, doubtless under the impression
that some slave-boy had been procured to serve them. But
when they saw that an ass was there in place of a man—and

not a hind for a maiden!—they turned up their noses, and taunted their master with various comments to the effect that it wasn't a slave which he'd brought, but a marriage-partner for himself. 'Just be sure not to devour this lovely little chick yourself!' they said. 'You must share him from time to time with your lovey-doveys.'

Whilst babbling to each other with remarks such as these, they secured me close to the manger. There was a quite well-built young man there, an expert piper; they had bought him at a slave-stand with the coins which they had collected. When they were carrying the goddess around outside, he would walk beside them playing the horn, but indoors his role was that of communal bedfellow, spreading his services around. As soon as he set eyes on me inside, he delightedly set lots of fodder before me, and said to me in happy tones: 'At last you have come to deputize for me in my most pitiable toil. I wish you long life. May you win the approval of our masters, and relieve the pressure on my now wearied loins.' As I heard these words, I now began to give thought to the fresh trials in store for me.

27   Next day the priests set out, clad in multicoloured garments and with features hideously made up; their faces were smeared with clay pigment, and their eyes were daubed with mascara. They had put on conical caps and saffron garments of linen and silk. Some wore white shirts decorated with purple stripes in spear-motifs pointing in different directions, and gathered up at the waist; they had yellow sandals on their feet. The goddess, who was attired in a garment of silk, they consigned to me to carry. Their arms were bared to the shoulder; they carried fearsome swords and axes; and they leapt about uttering ecstatic cries, for the pipe-music fired them to frenzied dancing.

After visiting several cottages in the course of their wanderings, they reached an estate belonging to a wealthy owner. As soon as they entered it they dashed forward frantically, making the place resound with their discordant wailing. For some time they bent their heads low and twisted their necks in supple movements, making their dangling locks rotate. Occasionally they would sink their teeth into their own flesh, and as a finale they each slashed their arms with the two-edged swords which they brandished. In the course of this performance, one of them behaved even more frenziedly. Drawing frequent breaths from deep within as though filled with the heaven-sent inspiration of a deity, he would pretend to be struck with madness—as if men visited by a divine presence are usually rendered feeble or sick, rather than raised to higher things!

28　　　But now observe how divine providence repaid him as he deserved. In loud, oracular tones he began lyingly to reproach and charge himself with having committed some wicked sin against the sacred tenets of his holy religion, and he proceeded to demand due punishment at his own hands for his sinful deed. He then seized the whip which these effeminates carry around as their distinctive possession. It is fringed with long, twisted tassels of wool, inset with several knuckle-bones from sheep. Wielding it, he scourged himself with lashes from this heavily knotted weapon, withstanding the pain of the blows in remarkable fashion by gritting his teeth. You could see the ground getting soaked with the filthy blood of the catamites as a result of the incisions of the swords and the blows of the whips. The sight made me considerably anxious, when I saw the blood gushing out in torrents from all these wounds, in case the stomach of the foreign goddess craved the taste of ass's blood, just as some people like to drink ass's milk.

Eventually exhaustion overtook them with this self-laceration, or at any rate they felt that they had had enough, so they called a halt to the torture. Many of those watching vied with each other in contributing coppers and even silver coins which the priests caught in the open folds of their garments. They also obtained a cask of wine, milk, cheeses, and a quantity of spelt and fine flour. Some people presented barley for the goddess's mount. All of this the priests raked in with greedy eagerness, stuffing it into sacks purposely brought for this windfall. They then heaped the sacks on my back, so that I doubled as a walking larder and a walking temple, for I was bowed down under the weight of the double burden.

29   During such wanderings as this they plundered the entire region. In one hill-village they felt so pleased with the size of their unusually large haul that they organized a celebratory banquet. By citing a false oracular utterance they extracted from some farmer the fattest of rams, so that when sacrificed it could fill the belly of the starving Syrian goddess. When their supper was elegantly laid, they visited the baths and returned from there spick and span, bringing with them as a dinner-guest a peasant of powerful physique, especially chosen for the capacity of his loins and lower parts. Those most filthy reprobates had no more than tasted a few greens prior to the meal proper when they were fired with unspeakable longing to perform the most despicable outrages of unnatural lust. They surrounded the young fellow on every side, stripped off his clothes, laid him on his back, and kept smothering him with their abominable kisses. My eyes could not long endure such evil conduct. I longed to cry out: 'O citizens, to the rescue!' but the only sound that came out was 'O!', without being supplemented by the other syllables and consonants. The 'O' was quite clear and strong, an apt expression for an ass, but the timing was inopportune.

The trouble was that several young men from a neighbour-ing village were searching for an ass stolen from them during the night. They were conducting a most thorough search of all the inns, and when they heard my braying coming from within our lodging, they thought that their plundered beast had been secreted in some remote corner of the dwelling. They burst suddenly in with a concerted rush to seize their property on the spot, and caught the priests red-handed engaged in those obscenely foul practices. They at once summoned the locals from all quarters, and pointed out to them this most degrading display, adding their sardonic praise of the priests' wholly unblemished chastity.

30   The priests were shattered by this notoriety, which was avidly circulated by word of mouth among the common folk, and which made them deservedly hated and loathed by all. So about midnight they gathered up all their belongings and furtively quitted the village. Before sunrise they had completed

a good part of their journey, and by daylight reached a
trackless, desolate region. There, after considerable discussion
among themselves, they made preparations to kill me. The
goddess whom I had carried was lifted off my back, and set on
the ground. They stripped me of all my blankets, tied me to an
oak-tree, and then flogged me with the whip strung with
sheep's knuckle-bones, until they all but finished me off. One
of them threatened to cut my hamstrings with his axe, because
my triumph over their lily-white virtue had so humiliated
them. But the rest, with an eye not to my welfare but to the
statue lying before them, decided that I must be kept alive. So
they loaded me up again with the baggage, and kept
threatening me with the flat of their swords until they reached
a famous town. There was a leading citizen there who was in
general a scrupulous person and who held the gods in especial
awe. He was roused by the clashing of the cymbals, the
beating of the drums, and the soothing measures of the
Phrygian chant. He came running to meet us, welcomed the
goddess with the hospitality of a votary, and installed us in the
precincts of his very spacious house. There he hastened to
appease the deity with most devout worship and with rich
sacrificial victims.

31   It was here, as I recall, that my life was exposed to the
greatest danger. One of the estate-workers had been out
hunting, and had sent in part of the bag, the plumpest haunch
of a huge stag, to his master as a gift. It had been carelessly
hung at a modest height behind the kitchen-door, and some
dog—as good a hunter as the estate-worker!—had stealthily
seized it and made off in haste, pleased with his prize and
escaping the eyes of those looking after it. When the loss was
discovered, the cook blamed his own carelessness, and shed
long and futile tears of lamentation. His master was pressingly
demanding his dinner. The unhappy cook, in a state of abject
fear, kissed his little son goodbye and seized a length of rope to
fashion a noose and encompass his own death. But his trusty
wife observed her husband's desperate danger. She fiercely
grabbed the deadly halter with both hands, and said to him:
'Has your panic in your present plight driven you out of your

mind? Haven't you noted that the gods with their foresight have provided you with a chance remedy to hand? If you have retained an atom of sense in this harshest of hurricanes imposed by Fortune, listen carefully to me. Take this ass, this new arrival, to some remote spot, and slit its throat. Tear off its haunch to make it resemble the one you have lost, cook it with due care, adding plenty of spicy flavours, and set it before the master in place of the venison.'

That most depraved scoundrel decided to save his skin at the price of my death. He lavishly praised the wit of his fellow-slave, and proceeded to sharpen his knives for the butchery which he was contemplating.

BOOK 9

With the Priests, the Baker, the Market-Gardener:
Four Tales of Cuckolding

1 This was how that foulest of executioners was equipping his
sacrilegious hands to slaughter me. But the onset of such
pressing danger prompted me to a plan of action, and without
indulging in lengthy reflection I decided to bolt and thus
avoid the threat of the butcher's knife. So I snapped the rope
which secured me, and at once charged out at full speed to
gain sanctuary, bursting along with rapid hoof-beats. I
negotiated the adjacent colonnade at speed, and propelled
myself without hesitation into the dining-room; where the
master of the house in company with the goddess's priests was
dining on the sacrificial meat. My unceremonious entry upset
several of the dinner-dishes, tables and lamps as I collided
with them. The master was annoyed at this unsightly havoc
wreaked on his furniture. He put me in the close charge of one
of his servants, regarding me as an ill-mannered, licentious
beast, and ordered him to confine me in some securely barred
place to ensure that I could not disrupt their peaceful feasting
with similarly wanton behaviour a second time. Having
cleverly protected myself by this smart trick so that I was
delivered from the clutches of the butcher, I was delighted at
being confined in a prison which guaranteed my safety. But
the truth is that if Fortune is hostile, nothing can turn out
auspiciously for any person alive. The economy of divine
providence is foreordained, and cannot be undermined or
changed by any wise plan or sage remedy. So that very
stratagem which seemed to have gained me safety for the time
being, now unleashed a further great hazard —indeed, it spelt
instant destruction.

2   Suddenly a slave burst into the dining-room as the guests
chatted amiably. His face was contorted with fear as he
reported to his master that a mad bitch had just burst in from

the nearest lane through the rear gate with incredible violence. She had attacked the hunting-hounds with the most flaming fury, and had then made for the stable close by and assaulted several of the pack-animals equally savagely. To crown all, she had not left even the men unscathed: Myrtilus the muleteer, Hephaestio the cook, Hypnophilus the chamberlain, Apollonius the physician, and indeed several other members of the household had all been mangled and bitten in various places as they tried to fend the animal off. A number of the pack-animals had been affected by her poisonous bites and were turning rabid like the dog.

This news at once struck the diners with dismay, for they thought that I was likewise infected and out of control. They seized any weapons that came to hand, and encouraged each other to ward off such a destructive menace to the community. So they came after me, though they rather than I myself were in the grip of that diseased madness. They would undoubtedly have butchered me limb from limb with the lances or hunting-spears and with the double-edged axes which the servants had urgently provided, but I got wind of this sudden storm of danger, and at once burst into the sleeping-quarters allotted to my owners as their lodging. They then closed and barred the doors behind me and blockaded the place, intending to wait until I was dead after being gripped and consumed by the tenacious fury of the deadly plague. This turn of events had at last liberated me, and I welcomed the boon of my isolation. I threw myself on a made-up bed, and enjoyed what I had lacked for many a day, the sleep of a human being.

3   My weariness was dispelled by the soft bed, and it was broad daylight when I arose fully refreshed. The men had remained awake all night keeping watch on me, and I could hear them exchanging views such as these about my condition: 'Are we to believe that the poor ass is still violently possessed by continuing madness?' 'No, he must be quite dead, now that the savage effect of the poison has intensified.' They suspended these differing opinions by exploring the situation. When they put their eyes to a crack in the door, they saw me standing at my ease, sound and self-possessed. So then they seized the

initiative and opened the doors to investigate more fully whether I was now docile. One of them proved to be my heaven-sent redeemer; he pointed out to the rest that the way of proving my sound health would be to offer me a full dish of fresh water to drink. If I drank the water without concern in the normal way, they would know that I was healthy and free of all disease. On the other hand, if on sighting and tasting the water I showed revulsion and sought to avoid it, they would realize that the baneful madness still persisted. This, he said, was the usual diagnostic technique, also recommended in ancient books.

4   The suggestion met with their approval, and a large vessel of clear water was hastily fetched from a nearby stream. With continuing hesitation they set it before me. I did not linger in advancing to meet them; I bent to it quite thirstily, plunged in my entire head, and proceeded to drain the water which was truly my salvation. I then endured with equanimity the clapping of their hands, the twisting of my ears, the tugging at my muzzle, and such other tests as they sought to apply until I could clearly give proof to them all of my controlled behaviour, which was the polar opposite of their lunatic assumptions.

In this way I had avoided a double danger. Next day I was again burdened with the temple-spoils, and led on to the road with the rattles and cymbals to form a peripatetic begging-outfit. After we had wandered round to several cottages and hill-villages, we halted at a hamlet which according to the residents' account was built among the tumbling relics of a once wealthy city. We were accommodated at the nearest inn, and there we heard a witty story which I should like you too to hear. It concerns the cuckolding of an indigent man.

5   This fellow lived a hard life in grinding poverty. What little pay he obtained to keep body and soul together was gained by performing manual work. He had a slip of a wife who was likewise poverty-stricken, but she had a bad name for being extremely promiscuous. One day, after her husband had left early for a job which he had undertaken, her barefaced lover at once crept stealthily into her lodging. He and the wife were

quite untroubled as they practised love's wrestling-holds. But then the husband, blissfully ignorant and entertaining no suspicions of his wife's conduct even at that stage of their marriage, unexpectedly returned to the house. Finding the entrance already closed and barred, he thought highly of his wife's chaste behaviour. He hammered on the door and whistled to announce his arrival. Then that clever woman, who was quite resourceful in such unsavoury circumstances, freed the lover from her close embraces, and craftily hid him in a corn-jar lying half-buried in a corner, with nothing else in it. Then she opened the door, and greeted her husband as he entered by speaking to him sharply.

'Is this how I find you,' she asked, 'strolling about idly at leisure? Why are you not attending to your usual work to ensure our livelihood and to make provision for our daily bread? Here am I, working desperately night and day, spinning wool till my arms ache, to see that our hovel has a lamp to light it if nothing more. How much happier my neighbour Daphne is! There she is, roistering with her lovers, flushed with wine and food from early morning!'

6   This rattled her husband. 'Whatever do you mean?' he asked. 'It's true that our foreman has a lawsuit on his hands and has given us the day off, but I've still made provision for our supper today. Just take a look at that corn-jar. It's for ever empty, occupying all that space to no purpose. The only contribution it makes is to get in the way of our daily round. I have sold it to a buyer for six denarii, and he is on the point of stumping up for it and taking it with him as his property. So why not buckle to and lend me a hand to dig it out and pass it over at once to the buyer?'

That guileful woman improvised, and with a shameless guffaw replied: 'What a splendid husband, what a keen man of business I have here! I'm merely a house-bound woman, but I've already sold for seven denarii what he has disposed of for less!' The husband was delighted at this raised bid. 'Who', he asked, 'has offered so much for it?' She answered: 'You silly man, he has already climbed down into the jar to take a good look and ensure that it is in good shape.'

7   The lover, duly prompted by the woman's words, emerged
smartly. 'Do you want the candid truth, ma'am?' he asked.
'This jar of yours is very old. It's been knocked about and has
gaping cracks in several places.' He then turned to her
husband, pretending not to know who he was. 'I don't know
you, little man,' he said, 'but why don't you look sharp and
hand me a lamp? Then, when I've scraped off the dirt inside, I
can take a careful look at the jar to see if it is serviceable. Or
do you think that my money grows on fruit-trees?' That
sharp-witted, admirable husband, as gullible as ever, lit a
lamp without delay, and said: 'Step out, brother; stand here
and relax till I clean it out properly, and then I'll show it to
you.' As he spoke, he stripped off, took the lamp down inside,
and began to scrape the long-standing grime from the
mouldering jar.

Then that handsome lover-boy the adulterer laid the
workman's wife face down over the jar, bent over her, and
screwed her without fear of interruption. Meanwhile she
thrust her hand into the jar, and with the wit of a lady of easy
virtue made a fool of her husband. With her finger she pointed
out various places that needed cleaning, until the job was
completed both above and below. She took the seven denarii,
while the hapless workman had to put the jar on his shoulders
and carry it to the adulterer's lodging.

8   Those priests, veritable models of chastity, lingered in that
place for a few days, growing fat on the citizens' generosity,
and stuffing themselves with the abundant profits from their
prophecies. There they devised a novel source of gain. They
composed one oracular response to cover a number of
situations, and in this way made fools of several people who
consulted them on diverse matters. This was the response:

> Why do the harnessed oxen cleave the field?
> To make the seeds a luxuriant harvest yield.

Then, if questioned by people who happened to be arranging
a marriage, their answer was that this response accorded with
their situation: the couple should be 'harnessed' for marriage
and for begetting the 'seeds' of children. If a potential buyer of

property made enquiry of them, the reply was that 'oxen', 'harnessing', and flourishing fields of seedlings were being aptly prophesied for them. If a person was troubled about departing on a journey and consulted the divine auspices, the priests claimed that the most docile of all four-footed beasts were now 'harnessed' and standing ready, and that gain was being promised him by the 'yield' from the 'field'. If a man about to engage in battle or to pursue a gang of robbers enquired whether his foray would be successful, they would claim that the efficacious prophecy made his victory secure, for the necks of the enemy would be 'harnessed' beneath the yoke, and most abundant and 'luxuriant' profit would be forthcoming from depredations from the foe. By such crafty, guileful prophecy they had raked in quite a sum of money.

9 However, the non-stop enquiries they received made them weary, and they grew tired of offering explanations. So they took to the road again. The journey was considerably worse than the night-long travelling which we had earlier completed, for the road was deeply pitted with steep ruts, awash with stagnant marsh-water in some places, and in others slippery with foul mud. The result was that my legs were bruised through numerous collisions and constant tumbles before I succeeded finally in emerging on to level paths in an exhausted state.

But suddenly a band of horsemen descended on us from the rear. With great difficulty they halted the mad gallop of their horses. Then they set about Philebus and the rest of his comrades with a will. They grabbed them by the throat, called them impious and obscene, and from time to time gave them a good pummelling with their fists. They then hand-cuffed them all, and in menacing tones repeatedly demanded that they produce without delay a golden goblet which was the ill-gotten gain of the crime which they had committed. They claimed that the priests had furtively abstracted it from the very shrine of the Mother of the Gods, under the pretence of performing solemn ceremonies conducted in secret; and that then before it was broad daylight they had quitted the city-limits, blithely imagining that they could evade punish-

ment for such a monstrous crime by their stealthy departure.
10   One of them did not fail to lay his hand on my back, and
after groping around in the very bosom of the goddess whom I
was carrying, he uncovered and extracted the golden goblet
before the eyes of all. But those most depraved creatures were
not to be confounded or abashed even when confronted with
their most impious crime. Instead they indulged in forced
laughter and joking, saying: 'What harsh, unworthy treatment we are getting! So often innocent people find their heads
in a noose! To think that for the sake of one mere cup, which
the Mother of the Gods bestowed on her sister the Syrian
goddess as a guest-present, we ministers of religion are being
tried for our lives as if we were criminals!' But this and
similarly stupid blusterings were of no avail, for the villagers
escorted them back, and at once tied them up and locked
them in the local Bridewell. The goblet and indeed the statue
which I had been carrying were deposited in the temple-
treasury, and consecrated there.

    Next day they brought me out, and the auctioneer
announced that I was for sale once more. A baker from a
neighbouring hill-town purchased me for seven sesterces more
than Philebus had earlier paid for me. He also bought some
corn, and at once loaded me up with it in heavy quantity. He
then led me up a steep path, which sharp stones and assorted
brushwood made hazardous to negotiate, to the mill which he
used for grinding the corn.

11   In the mill there were several pack-animals turning
millstones of varying dimensions by repeatedly circling them.
They worked not only during the day but also throughout the
night, sleeplessly producing flour by incessant rotation of the
machinery. My new master, however, doubtless fearing that
I would baulk at my first apprenticeship to slavery, made
generous provision for me; he gave me a holiday on that first
day, and filled my manger to the brim with fodder. But that
blessed period of leisure and abundant food did not extend
longer, for early next day I was appointed to what seemed the
largest of the millstones. I was blindfolded, and at once
pushed on the curving course of the circular track, so that I

was to retrace my steps over the identical path within the orbit of the circumscribed limits, and thus go a-wandering but without deviating. But I had not so far forgotten my native wit and wisdom as to lend myself readily to this apprenticeship to the trade. Though in my earlier life among men I had often watched millstones being rotated in this way, I stood rooted to the spot in feigned astonishment, as if I were without experience and knowledge of their working. My thinking was that I would be regarded as unsuitable and quite useless for duties of this kind, and would at worst be deputed to some lighter labour, or even left to forage at leisure. But the cunning which I deployed was vain and damaging. Several men armed with sticks at once surrounded me; being blindfolded I was still unsuspecting. Suddenly, at a given signal and with concerted shouts they rained a shower of blows on me, and the din they made so confused me that I abandoned my entire tactic, and at once showed the greatest skill in applying my whole weight to the rope round my neck, and in making the rounds with alacrity.

12   This sudden improvement in my attitude roused the whole crowd of workmen to laughter. Once the greater part of the day was over (by then I was reduced to exhaustion), they unhooked me from the grinding-machine, removed the horse-collar from my neck, and set me in front of the manger. Though I was extremely tired, urgently in need of restoring my strength and on the point of collapse through hunger, my habitual curiosity and my considerable apprehension kept me rooted there. So I deferred my meal of abundant fodder, and took some pleasure in observing how this unprepossessing bakery was run.

Great heavens, what poor specimens of humanity the men were! Their entire bodies formed a pattern of livid bruises. Their backs, which bore the marks of the whip, were not so much covered as shaded by torn shirts of patchwork cloth. Some wore nothing except a thin covering over their private parts; all were clad in such a fashion that their bodies were visible through the rags they wore. They had letters branded on their foreheads, half-shaved heads, and chains round their ankles. Their faces were a ghastly yellow, and their eyes had contracted in the smoke-filled gloom of that steaming, dank atmosphere, making them half-blind. They resembled boxers who coat themselves with dust when they fight, for their bodies were a dirty white from the oven-baked flour.

13   As for my fellow-beasts, what can I say, what words can I use to describe those superannuated mules and enfeebled geldings surrounding the manger with their heads bent low as they munched the piled-up straw? Their necks, pockmarked with running sores, were twitching; their limp nostrils gaped wide from constant bouts of coughing; their chests were a mass of raw patches from the continual rubbing of their rope-harnesses; their flanks were exposed to the bone from constant beatings; their hooves were distended and misshapen through their incessant circling of the millstones; their entire skins were coarse with age and scurvy emaciation.

Such were the members of the baker's establishment, and I feared that I too would be emulating their grisly example. As I recalled the happy state of the Lucius of old, now reduced to a most precarious level of existence, I dropped my head in depression. Nowhere at hand was there any consolation for my pain-wracked existence, except that my innate curiosity did something to restore me, for no one took any account of my presence; they all did and said whatever they liked without inhibitions. That godlike creator of ancient poetry among the Greeks, when seeking to depict a man of the greatest circumspection, was justified in singing of him who had attained the highest virtues by visiting many cities and gaining acquaintance with various peoples. Indeed, I myself now gratefully recall my existence as an ass, for when I was concealed in the ass's covering and was tried by varying fortunes, I gained a knowledge of many things, though admittedly I was less wise.

14   From that experience I have decided to let you in on an outstandingly good and attractively elegant story, on which I now embark.

The baker who had bought me was in all respects a decent and quite sober fellow, but the luck of the draw had given him the most evil wife, easily the worst woman in the world. So he had to endure the most excruciating torments affecting his bed and his home. I swear that even I constantly grieved in silence for his lot. There was not a single vice which that most despicable woman did not possess; every conceivable wickedness had accumulated in her mind as in some filthy cesspool. She was crabbed and crotchety, libidinous and bibulous, obdurate and obstinate. Her greed was evident in her base thieving, her prodigality in her unsightly extravagance. She was a foe to fidelity, and made war on chastity. In addition, she despised and ground beneath her heel the powers of heaven; instead of adhering to a sure faith, she sacrilegiously feigned bold awareness of a deity whom she proclaimed to be the only God. By devising empty ceremonies she misled the people at large, and deceived her hapless husband by devoting herself to early-morning drinking and day-long debauchery.

15   This was the nature of the woman, and the rancour with which she victimized me was amazing. Even before daylight, while she still lay in bed, she would loudly order the novice-ass to be harnessed to the mill-wheel. As soon as she quitted her bedroom, she would insistently designate me for repeated whipping before her eyes. When the other pack-animals were turned loose to enjoy their meal at the proper time, on her instruction I was allowed access to the manger only much later. This harsh treatment had greatly intensified my native curiosity about her behaviour. I divined that a young man was visiting her chamber with some regularity, and I was extremely keen to set eyes on his face, if only the covering over my head allowed my eyes a glimpse of him at some moment, for I would have had sufficient wit one way or another to expose the immoral activities of that most disgusting female.

There was an old woman who attended her in her sexual escapades and acted as go-between in her extra-marital affairs. All day and every day she was her inseparable companion. First thing at breakfast, and then as they poured out undiluted wine for each other, the old hag and her mistress would launch preliminary attacks and devise deceitful plots with cunning intrigues to achieve the undoing of the wretched husband. Though I was utterly furious with Photis for the error she made in changing me into an ass when intending to turn me into a bird, I was nevertheless heartened by one consolation at least in my hideous deformity: I was endowed with massive ears, and even at a distance I could very easily overhear all that was going on.

16   So it was that one day my ears caught these words of that audacious old hag: 'Mistress, you must yourself come to a decision about this lazy, fear-ridden boyfriend whom you acquired without my approval. He shrinks like a coward from the wrinkled frown of that boorish and loathsome husband of yours, and because of this he frustrates your eager embraces through a lack of urgency in his limp love-making. How much better is the young Philesitherus! He is handsome, generous, energetic; he never rests in challenging the precautions which husbands vainly take. I swear that he is the only man who deserves to enjoy the favours of every married woman. He alone merits a golden crown on his head, if for no other reason than that of late he showed outstanding resource in cuckolding a jealous husband. Listen to this, and then contrast the differing temperaments of the two lovers.

17   'You know, I think, a man called Barbarus, one of our town-councillors, the man they call Scorpion because of his needling ways? His wife comes of a good family and is outstandingly beautiful. He has taken the most stringent measures to confine her in his house under elaborate supervision.' The baker's wife answered this last query. 'Of course,' she said. 'I know them well. You are speaking of my friend Arete. I was at school with her.' 'Well, then,' said the hag, 'do you know the full story about her and Philesitherus?' 'I haven't heard a word of it,' replied her mistress. 'I'm most eager to know about it, so please, mother, reveal all the details in order.' So without delay that garrulous old gossip began her tale.

'This man Barbarus was preparing to go on a journey he had to make, and was anxious to ensure his dear wife's chaste behaviour by taking the most careful precautions. So he gave secret instructions to his confidential slave Myrmex, who was

a byword for his outstanding loyalty, and entrusted him with
the entire supervision of his mistress. He threatened to clap
the slave in irons and imprison him for life, and finally said he
would have him put to death violently and shamefully, if any
man so much as touched Arete with his finger in passing. He
backed this threat with an oath sworn by all the gods in
heaven. He accordingly set out on his journey with his mind
at rest, leaving Myrmex at home neurotic and frantic with
anxiety as he shadowed the wife with the utmost vigilance.

'Myrmex was on tenterhooks, his attention riveted on his
task. He refused to allow his mistress to go out anywhere, and
when she busied herself spinning wool at home, he would sit
close by her, refusing to leave her side. Equally when she had
to go out late in the day to take her bath, he would stick close
to her, clutching the hem of her cloak. So he performed his
duty and maintained the trust reposed in him with exemplary
prudence.

18   'But the dazzling beauty of that married lady could not be
kept hidden from the eager and watchful eye of Philesitherus.
The very challenge of her reputation for chastity, and of the
excessive and extraordinary precautions taken to guard her,
acted as a spur and kindled his excitement. He was ready to
perform or to endure anything, and he harnessed all his
powers to overcome the strict routine of the household. He
was convinced of the frailty of human loyalties, believing that
all obstacles could be surmounted by money, and that even
doors of adamant are often breached by gold. He seized the
opportunity of finding Myrmex alone, confided his love-
feelings to him, and imploringly sought from him the remedy
for his harsh pain. He claimed that unless he gained the object
of his desire with all speed, he was resolved and ready to
embrace imminent death. The meeting could easily be
arranged, so Myrmex should have no fears; for when evening
fell, he could rely on the darkness and creep in alone, heavily
cloaked and muffled, and be away again in no time. After
pressing these and other similarly persuasive arguments, he
finally inserted a solid wedge to prise violently open the
extremely stiff resistance mounted by the slave. He extended

his hand and showed him some spanking new gleaming gold pieces; twenty of them he would like Myrmex to pass on to the girl, and ten he was delighted to offer to Myrmex himself.

19   'Myrmex bridled at this unprecedentedly shameful proposal. He put his fingers to his ears and bolted. Yet the glowing gleam of gold was ever before his eyes. Though he put a distance between himself and Philesitherus, and winged his way homeward at full speed, he could still visualize those beautiful, gleaming coins, and in his mind he already possessed that rich haul. The poor slave had the strange sensation of tossing mentally on a sea of troubles, his thoughts tearing him apart; he was pulled one way and dragged the other towards opposing resolutions. Loyalty lay on one side, profit on the other; torture lay with the one, and gratification with the other. In the end gold prevailed over fear of death. His longing for the lovely lucre did not diminish with time; baneful greed preoccupied him even in the night-hours, with the result that though his master's threats confined him to the house, the gold summoned him outside. Finally he swallowed his shame and brooked no further delay, and accordingly he presented the suitor's proposal to the ears of his mistress.

'The lady was fickle by nature. She followed her inclinations, and at once put her chastity at the service of the accursed metal. Myrmex was overjoyed, and rushed off to the man who had subverted his loyalty, eager not only to obtain but merely to handle the money, the sight of which had caused his downfall. In a paroxysm of joy he informed Philesitherus that his own great exertions had brought the suitor's longings to fruition, and he at once demanded the promised reward. Myrmex clutched the golden currency with a hand which had never known the feel even of copper.

20   'When the night was well advanced, he led that lively lover unaccompanied to the house, and escorted him with head well covered to his mistress's bedroom. With unfamiliar embraces they were just seeking favourable omens for their untried love, and as naked combatants were embarking on their first campaign under Venus, when to the general surprise the husband unexpectedly appeared at the gate of his house; he

had exploited the cover of darkness to arrive unobserved. He banged and shouted and battered the doors with a stone. The delay in answering made him suspicious, and he threatened Myrmex with dire punishment. The slave was panic-stricken at this unexpected reverse; in his craven fear he felt utterly resourceless, and the only excuse which he could offer was that the darkness of night was hindering him from finding the key which he had carefully hidden away. Meanwhile Philesitherus had heard the commotion, and hastily put on his shirt, but in the confusion he raced from the bedroom without his slippers. Finally, Myrmex inserted the key in the lock and opened the door to his master who was still calling the gods to witness. While Barbarus rushed to the bedroom, the slave sent Philesitherus hastily and stealthily on his way, and felt reassured once he was safely beyond the threshold. He locked up the house, and returned to bed.

21   'But when dawn broke and Barbarus was leaving the bedroom, he noticed the unfamiliar slippers under the bed; Philesitherus had been wearing them when he crept in. The material evidence made Barbarus suspect what had occurred, but he did not reveal to his wife or to any of his household the resentment he felt. He removed the slippers and stealthily hid them under his clothes. He brusquely ordered Myrmex to be put in chains by his fellow-slaves, and dragged to the forum. He then made his way swiftly there, grumbling repeatedly under his breath. He was sure that the evidence of the slippers could easily put him on the track of the adulterer. With face livid and eyebrows furiously raised, he strode angrily along the street. Behind him followed Myrmex, burdened with chains; though his guilt had not been clearly established, he was having a bad attack of conscience, and was weeping and howling desperately in a vain attempt to elicit pity. Suddenly at this vital moment Philesitherus confronted them. Though he was pursuing some other business, this sudden sight gave him pause. But he was not apprehensive. He recalled the gaffe which he had made in his hurried exit, and inferring all that had happened thereafter, his brain at once summoned all its habitual resourcefulness. He brushed the slaves aside, and

made for Myrmex, shouting at the top of his voice. He rained his fists on the slave's cheeks, but pulled his punches as he cried: "You dissolute, lying blackguard! I only pray that your master here, and all the powers of heaven which you have been summoning with rash oaths, may bring you to a sticky end as your evil character deserves! You stole my slippers from me yesterday at the baths. By God, you thoroughly deserve to keep those chains about you till they wear out, and to endure the darkness of a dungeon as well."

'Barbarus was taken in by the timely trick of that forceful young man; indeed, as his spirits rose, he was lulled into gullibility. So when he got back home, he summoned Myrmex, forgave him with his whole heart, handed over the slippers, and advised him to return them to their owner from whom he had stolen them.'

22   The old woman had got as far as this in her prattling when her mistress interrupted: 'She's a lucky lady to enjoy the uninhibited approaches of such a determined companion! Just think of poor me; the friend I've met up with jumps even at the noise of the mill, and at the sight of that scurvy ass over there.' The old woman replied: 'I'll soon win that eager lover over completely, and strengthen his resolve; I'll have him here for you, true to his pledge.' She then promised also to return in the evening, and hurried out of the chamber. That chaste wife at once prepared a meal fit for a Salian priest, decanted a vintage wine, and seasoned fresh meat with sausages. Finally, when the table was groaning with food, she awaited the adulterer's coming as if he were some god. Luckily for her, her husband was dining out at the house of the laundryman near by.

As the day was now reaching its close, I was at last freed from my collar, and restored to the relaxation of the manger. But to tell the truth, I was thankful not so much for this relief from toil as for the uncovering of my eyes, which enabled me to watch all the manœuvres of that criminal woman without hindrance. By now the sun had glided down beneath the ocean, and was giving light to the regions of the world below the earth. At this moment that rash adulterer arrived, cleaving to the side of that most depraved old hag. He was still a mere boy; his cheeks shone smooth and bright, and he was himself still a source of pleasure to male lovers. The woman welcomed him with a flood of kisses, and bade him recline at the board laid before him.

23   But just as the young man was raising his preliminary glass of wine and his first mouthful of food to his lips, the husband approached, returning much earlier than expected. That model wife uttered savage curses against him, praying that he might break both his legs. The lover turned pale, and trembled with fright. A wooden tub chanced to be lying upended there; its usual purpose was for holding sifted flour. She pushed him out of sight under it. Then with her native guile she affected innocence of her base behaviour, and assumed an untroubled countenance. She asked her husband whatever was the reason for his leaving his closest friend's dining-table and returning home at that early hour. He was depressed, and sighed repeatedly. 'I just could not bear the disgraceful, outrageous behaviour of that wicked wife of his, so I cleared off. Ye gods! A married woman like her, so trustworthy and sober, and yet she has blackened her reputation with a most unholy scandal. I swear by holy Ceres here that even now I can scarcely believe my eyes when I consider the sort of woman she is.'

That most shameless woman's interest was roused by these words of her husband, and in her eagerness to know what had happened, she kept loudly demanding that he reveal the entire story from the beginning. She did not stop pressing him until her husband complied with her wish, and recounted the disgrace attending the household of another, all unaware of the situation in his own.

24   'My friend the laundryman has a wife who has always seemed a highly moral woman, priding herself on her good reputation and managing her husband's domestic affairs with due modesty. But then she threw herself into the arms of some adulterer, for whom she conceived a secret passion. She has often been meeting him for stealthy embraces, and at the very time when the two of us were arriving from the baths for dinner, she was having it off with that same young fellow. So

our arrival caused her sudden panic, and she had to improvise a plan. She hid him in the bottom of a wicker cage; it was built upright with wooden slats intertwined, and clothes were hanging round it to be bleached with the white sulphur fumes coming from the cage. Since she thought that he was now quite safely hidden there, she stopped worrying, and joined us at table. But meanwhile the young man was being choked and enveloped by that most acrid and oppressive smell of sulphur. He couldn't get his breath, and began to feel dizzy, and the natural effect of the powerful sulphur was to make him sneeze repeatedly.

25   'The first time the husband heard a sneeze coming from behind his wife's back, he thought it came from her, and he uttered the conventional "Bless you" over her. The same thing happened again, and was repeated several times until he was alerted by the excessive sneezing and finally tumbled to the truth. He at once shifted the table, lifted off the cage, and dragged out the young fellow, who was gasping repeatedly and could scarcely breathe. The laundryman was seething with anger at the dishonour done to him; he called for his sword, and gave every sign that he would have killed the youth by slitting his throat, if I had not given thought to the danger which we both faced, and with difficulty restrained him from launching a wild attack. I maintained that this enemy of his would shortly die from the severe effects of the sulphur alone, without our incurring responsibility for his death. The laundryman cooled down, not at my persuasion but through the force of circumstances, for the adulterer was now barely alive. He dragged him out into the nearest alley. I then exercised some quiet persuasion with the wife, and finally induced her to go away for a little while and to lodge in the meantime with some female friend away from the shop, until in due course her husband's blazing anger had subsided. He was so inflamed and furious that he undoubtedly planned to inflict some more damaging harm on his wife and himself. So I have come back home; revulsion drove me from my friend's table.'

26   As the baker recounted these details, the woman with her

long history of wantonness and shamelessness kept cursing
the laundryman's wife, uttering oaths of condemnation; she
called her disloyal, shameless, and in short a disgrace to her
entire sex for having banished her modesty, ground beneath
her heel the contract of the marriage-bed, and begrimed her
husband's home with the notoriety of the brothel. She said
that the woman had dispensed with the worthy role of wife,
and won for herself the title of prostitute; such women should
be burnt alive.

But she herself was mindful of her own secret vulnerability
and sullied conscience; and so that she could more speedily
free her adulterer from his cramped position in his hiding-
place, she repeatedly urged her husband to retire to bed
earlier than usual. But since his abrupt departure had
interfered with his dinner and he was extremely hungry, in
courteous tones he demanded a dinner at home instead. The
woman hastily if unwillingly placed before him the food which
she had intended for another.

As I reflected on this dreadful woman's earlier misbehaviour
and her present persistence in it, I was seething inwardly, and
pondered carefully within myself whether I could somehow
uncover and expose her deceit, and render help to my master
by kicking away the cover and revealing to the eyes of all the
lover who was crouching under the tub like a tortoise.

27   In the end divine Providence looked kindly on my
anguished concern for the insult dealt to my master. All the
beasts of burden had been put in the charge of a lame old
man, who began to herd us to the nearest pool to drink, as the
hour of day now prescribed. This routine provided me with
the opportunity for which I had devoutly prayed, for as I
passed the tub I noticed the tips of the adulterer's fingers
protruding through a narrow opening in his hollow cover.
With a fierce sideways thrust of my hoof I stamped on them
until they were thoroughly squashed, and the unbearable pain
finally forced him to raise a tearful shout. He pushed the bin
off him, and cast it aside; being thus restored to the gaze of the
uninitiated, he revealed the character of that infamous
woman.

The baker, however, was not greatly concerned at his wife's loss of her chastity. To calm the boy, who had turned deathly pale and was trembling, he assumed a benevolent and kindly look as he began to talk to him. 'Have no fear, son, of any grim retribution from me. I am no barbarian with unsightly, rustic manners; I shall not finish you off with deadly sulphur-fumes, like the vindictive laundryman. I shall not invoke the rigour of the law, and indict you on a capital charge of adulterous behaviour, for you are such a charming and beautiful wee boy; instead, I shall share you with my wife. I shall not contest ownership so as to partition our estate, but rather seek to divide you between us, so that without any argument or dispute the three of us may agree to share the one bed. I have always lived in such harmony with my wife that following the guidance of the philosophers, our tastes are identical. But equity does not permit a wife to exercise more authority than a husband.'

28   With caressing words like these he led the way to bed. The boy followed, though reluctantly. While that most chaste of wives was locked in another room, the baker had the boy to himself in bed, where he enjoyed the sweetest possible revenge for the damage done to his marriage. But as soon as the sun's bright wheel ushered in the day, he summoned two of his strongest slaves, and when they had hoisted the boy high, he beat his buttocks with a rod, and questioned him: 'What? Do you, still a boy so soft and tender, seek to deprive lovers of the bloom of your youth, and instead make free-born women your target? Do you pollute lawfully joined marriages, and at your early age claim the title of adulterer?'

Following these and other rebukes, and after giving him a good hiding as well, he kicked him out of the house. So that stoutest of all adulterers unexpectedly got away in one piece, but his swift departure was painful because those white buttocks of his got a pounding both during the night and by day. The baker punished his wife too; he gave her notice of separation, and at once drove her out of his house.

29   That lady's natural propensity for wickedness was re-inforced by deeper anger at this contemptuous treatment,

however much she deserved it. In her annoyance, she reverted
to her old tricks, and was fired to have recourse to practices
naturally favoured by women. She took great pains to seek out
an old woman who was believed able to achieve any purpose
by spells and witchcraft. She implored her with many prayers,
and showered her with numerous gifts, as she sought one or
other of two requests: either that her husband relent and she
be reconciled to him, or if the witch could not achieve this,
that he should meet a violent end through the agency of a
spectre or some dread power. Then the witch, who was
endowed with supernatural faculties, made a preliminary
assault, as yet deploying only the rudimentary weapons of her
art; by these she tried to divert the deeply resentful spirit of
the husband, and to direct him towards feelings of love. But
when this attempt on him turned out differently from her
expectation, she grew irritated with the divine powers which
she had invoked. She was goaded by the scorn which the
baker displayed, as well as by the profitable reward promised,
so she began to threaten the very life of that most wretched
husband, to bring about his death by rousing the ghost of a
woman slain by violence.

30   But perhaps, diligent reader, you will censure my version of
events with an argument of this kind; how could you, clever
ass though you were, ascertain as you claim what these women
were secretly hatching, when you were enclosed within the
confines of the bakery? Listen, then, and I will explain to you
how this inquisitive fellow disguised as a beast discovered all
that was done to achieve the destruction of my master the
baker.

Suddenly about noon a woman made her appearance in the
bakery. She was dishevelled as if she were on trial and deeply
distressed. Her body was only half-covered by a pitiable
patchwork garment; her feet were bare and unshod; her
unsightly complexion was drawn, and pale as boxwood; her
greying hair was disordered, blackened by ashes sprinkled
over it and hanging low to cover most of her face. In this guise
she laid her hand gently on the baker, and led him off to his
bedroom as if she wished to converse with him in private. She

closed the door, and remained there for a considerable time.
But by now the workmen had finished grinding all the grain
which they had been handling, and they needed to obtain a
fresh supply. The favoured slaves on duty outside the
bedroom called to their master, and asked for a fresh supply to
grind, but when he made no response to their loud and
repeated shouts, they began to hammer harder on the door.
The fact that it was so securely barred made them suspect
that something was very seriously wrong, so they bent back or
broke off the hinges by powerful thrusts of their shoulders,
and finally forced their way in. The woman was nowhere to be
found, and they saw their master strung up on a beam,
hanging there already dead. They freed him from the noose
round his neck, and lowered his body. They then tended it
with the final washing, brutally beating their breasts and
keening loudly; once these rites to the dead were completed,
they accompanied the hearse in large numbers, and consigned
him to the grave.

31   Next day his daughter came running from the nearest hill-
village, where she had resided for some time following her
marriage. In her grief she tugged at her unbound hair, and
repeatedly beat her breasts with her fists. Though no member
of the household had told her of the tragedy, she had learnt all
that had happened. The sorrowing image of her father had
appeared to her in sleep, his neck still encircled with the
noose, and had revealed to her all the details of her
stepmother's criminal behaviour—the adultery, the witchcraft, and his descent to the realm of the dead when
constrained by the ghost. After the daughter had abused her
person with lengthy demonstrations of grief, she was finally
checked by the concerted action of the household, and
suspended her mourning. On the ninth day after death, the
formal ritual at the tomb was duly completed, and as heiress
she then sold by auction the household slaves, the furniture,
and all the beasts. Thus unbridled Fortune, operating
through the uncertainties of an auction, distributed the
possessions of one household into various hands. So it
happened that I was purchased for fifty sesterces by a poor

and insignificant market-gardener. As he remarked, the price was high, but he intended to make a living by making me share his labours with him.

32   The situation seems to demand of me an explanation of the routine of this new form of my slavery. My master was accustomed to load me up early in the morning with a consignment of vegetables, and to drive me to the nearest town; when he had delivered the produce to those who bought it, he would return to the allotment riding on my back. While he was bent over the servile tasks of digging, watering, and his other jobs, I restored my strength with untroubled rest. But now the stars were advancing on their ordered paths, and the year on its returning journey through the allotted days and months had bent its course beyond the pleasant autumn harvest towards the wintry frosts of Capricorn. During this time of unceasing rain and dew-laden nights, I was housed in an unroofed stall beneath the open sky, and was in agony with the constant cold; for my master was extremely poor, and could not buy a blanket or thin coverlet for himself, let alone for me. He resigned himself to lodging within the leafy enclosure of his tiny hut. Moreover, when in the early morning I stepped out with no shoes on my feet, and trod on extremely cold mud and on sharp patches of ice, I suffered torment. I could not fill my belly even with the usual fodder, for my master and I ate equal amounts of similar food, which was far from filling. It consisted of mouldering, bitter lettuces which had gone to seed so long ago that they looked like brooms, and because they were long past their best, they had a rotting and bitter taste, exuding a muddy juice.

33   One night an estate-owner from a neighbouring village was finding it hard to find his way through the darkness of a black, moonless night, and he was drenched with heavy rain. So he was prevented from journeying straight home, and turned aside into our modest allotment, for his horse was now exhausted. He was welcomed in friendly fashion as the circumstances demanded, and though the refreshment was Spartan rather than luxurious, he was anxious to repay the generosity of his host. So he promised to give him from his

lands some grain and olive-oil, and two casks of wine as well. My master promptly mounted my bare back, taking with him a sack and some empty wineskins, and embarked on a journey of about seven miles. On completing this distance, we reached the estate I mentioned, where the genial host at once allowed my master to share a handsome meal.

As they chatted with each other and passed the winecups to and fro, a quite astonishing portent occurred. One of the flock of hens came running through the middle of the yard, cackling with the characteristic squawk which indicated her eagerness to lay an egg. Her master eyed her, and said: 'What a good, productive servant you are! For quite a time now you have laid an egg every day to fatten us up, and I see that it is your intention to provide our first course today as well.' Then he turned to a slave. 'Come on, boy,' he said, 'put the basket in which the hens lay their eggs in its usual corner.' But when the slave had seen to this as ordered, the hen ignored the usual bed for laying, and deposited its load before the very feet of the master. The egg was premature, and to be the cause of the greatest anxiety, for she did not lay it in the form familiar to us. It was a fully grown chicken, with feathers, claws, eyes; it was even cheeping, and at once began to shadow its mother.

34   But a similar, much more sinister portent then appeared, such as would rightly cause any person to shudder. Under the very table which bore the remains of the supper, the earth yawned open, and from its depths gushed a towering fountain of blood. Great showers of drops flew out from it, and spattered the table with gore. Then, at the very moment when the company was stupefied with astonishment and terror at these warnings from heaven, a servant came running from the wine-cellar to report that the wine, which had earlier been apportioned out after fermenting, was bubbling up again with boiling heat in all the casks, exactly as if a roaring fire had been lit beneath them. In the meantime a weasel was also seen dragging a dead snake in its mouth out into the open, and a green frog leapt out of the mouth of a sheepdog. Then that very dog was attacked by a ram close by, and had its throat

severed by a single bite. All these portents, and others like
them, caused the master and his whole household the greatest
consternation, and totally paralysed their minds. They could
not decide what to do first and what next, with what number
and what kind of sacrificial victims to seek to conciliate the
heavenly powers.

35   In this stupor as they awaited some grisly and fearful
outcome, a young slave came rushing in, and reported to the
estate-owner calamities so great that they could not have been
worse. This master boasted three grown-up sons, all well
educated and endowed with modest manners. They had long
been friendly with a poor man living in a small cottage. Now
this tiny residence abutted upon a huge, rich estate owned by
a powerful neighbour. He was a rich young man of illustrious
descent, who however exploited for evil purposes the fame of
his ancestors. He had a powerful band of dependants, and was
able to do in the community whatever he wished. He kept
treating his needy neighbour like an enemy, launching attacks
on his humble property by slaughtering his cattle, driving off
his oxen, and trampling down his crops when they were still
ripening. Having by then stripped him of all his modest
possessions, he was attempting even to force him off his poor
holding. He raised a groundless suit over boundaries, and
claimed for himself the other's entire property. The peasant
was in general an inoffensive person, but now that he had
been stripped bare by the greed of this rich neighbour, he
sought to keep his ancestral soil if only for his own grave. So
with considerable apprehension he invited a large gathering of
friends so that they could witness the demarcation of the
boundaries. Among the rest were the three brothers, anxious
to afford such little help as they could to their friend in his
grievous plight.

36   But that crazed estate-owner was not in the least frightened
or even troubled by the presence of many citizens. He had not
restrained his plunderings, and now he did not seek even to
restrain his language. When those friends made gentle
representations and sought to soften his hot temper with
soothing words, he suddenly uttered a most solemn oath by

his own life and that of his dear ones: he swore that he
regarded the presence of all those intermediaries as of trifling
importance, and finally claimed that his slaves would hoist
that neighbour of his up by the ears, and at once sling him out
of the cottage into the furthest distance. These words induced
impassioned anger to seize the hearts of all the listeners. Then
one of the brothers made a prompt and somewhat franker
response: it was no use the magnate's relying on his wealth
and making threats with despotic arrogance, for even poor
people were in general accustomed to enjoy protection from
the haughty treatment of the rich through that defence of the
laws accorded to free men.

These words fed the man's vile temper as oil feeds a flame,
as sulphur feeds a fire, as a whip goads a Fury. His madness
now advanced to the furthest pitch. He shouted that he bade
them all be hanged, their laws as well, and then he
commanded his sheepdogs to be released. These guardians of
the estate were fierce and huge; they were in the habit of
devouring carcases left lying in the fields, and were trained to
bite passing travellers without discrimination. He ordered
them to be set upon the peasant's supporters and egged on to
kill them. No sooner were they roused and fired by the
customary signal from the shepherds than they were goaded
to ungovernable madness; their discordant barking inspired
terror as they made for the men, inflicting all kinds of wounds
as they tore and mauled them. Even those who bolted they did
not spare, but pursued them all the more viciously.

37   In the course of this mêlée as the panicking crowd was
being butchered, the youngest of the three brothers stubbed
his toes and tripped over a rock. As he fell headlong to the
ground, he provided a shameful feast for those savage and
most fierce dogs, for they at once took possession of their
prostrate prey, and tore the poor young fellow to pieces. When
the other brothers heard his dying cries, they were appalled,
and rushed to rescue him. They covered their left arms with
their cloaks, and sought to defend their brother and to drive
off the dogs by showering them with stones. But they could
neither wear down nor overcome their ferocity, with the result

that the most wretched youth was mangled and died on the spot. The last words which he uttered were a plea that they should exact revenge from that most depraved man of wealth for the death of their younger brother.

Then I swear that the surviving brothers did not so much abandon hope of their safety as totally disregard it. They made a rush at the rich proprietor, and blazing with anger they assaulted him wildly, pelting him with a shower of stones. Though covered in blood, he was experienced in the role of assassin from many such despicable deeds in the past. He hurled his spear and pierced one of the pair clean through the breast. Though he was mortally wounded with no breath of life left in him, the young man did not sink to the ground; as the spear passed right through him, the greater part of it emerged through his back, and the force of the impact made it stick in the earth, so that it kept his body upright, stiff and in balance. Meanwhile one of the rich man's slaves, a tall, strong individual, came to the aid of his murderous master. He fired a stone at long range, aiming at the right arm of the third youth, but without success; to the general surprise the stone fell harmlessly by, merely grazing the tips of his fingers.

38   That happier outcome gave the most resourceful youth some slight hope of revenge. He pretended that his hand was disabled, and he cried to that most cruel young proprietor: 'Enjoy, then, the destruction of our entire family, feed your insatiable cruelty on the blood of three brothers, celebrate a splendid triumph over your fellow-citizens stretched out here. But realize that though you deprive this poor man of his possessions, and extend your boundaries without limit, you will none the less have to live with a neighbour. As for this right hand of mine, which would gladly have severed your head, it too hangs useless, shattered by the malevolence of fate.'

That crazed thief was already provoked, but these words drove him wild. He grabbed his sword and eagerly advanced to slaughter with his own hand that most unhappy youth. But the man he challenged was no more of a coward than himself. Quite contrary to the aggressor's anticipation, the young man put up unexpected resistance. He seized the other's right arm in a terrier-like grip, raised his weapon high, and with great force struck the rich man repeatedly until he squeezed the wicked life out of him. Then, to escape the violence of the slaves who rushed on him, he at once boldly cut his own throat with the dagger which was still dripping with the enemy's blood.

These were the events foreshadowed by those portentous prodigies and reported to that most wretched master. Encompassed by all these disasters, the old man could not utter a word, or even shed a silent tear. He seized the knife with which he had just divided the cheese and the other dishes of the meal among his guests, and following the example of his most unfortunate son he too slashed his throat repeatedly, until he slumped with bent head over the table, and with a stream of fresh blood washed away the stains left by the gore of that earlier portent.

39   The market-gardener expressed his sorrow for this extremely sudden collapse of the family's prosperity, and also bitterly lamented his own misfortunes. Having paid for his meal with his tears, and repeatedly wrung empty hands, he at once mounted me, and made his way back on the road by which we had come. But even that return journey proved disastrous for him, for a tall fellow accosted us. His uniform and his behaviour showed that he was a legionary soldier. In a haughty, supercilious voice he demanded to know where the gardener was taking the unladen ass. My master was still distracted with grief, and in any case did not understand Latin, so he tried to pass without replying. The soldier could not control his habitual arrogance; he angrily interpreted the other's silence as an insult, struck him with the vine-staff that he carried, and knocked him off my back. The gardener then grovellingly replied that through ignorance of the language he could not understand what the centurion was saying. So the soldier questioned him in Greek: 'Where are you taking this ass of yours?' The gardener replied that he was making for the nearest town. 'Well, I need this beast's help,' said the soldier. 'He must take his place with the other beasts, and transport

the baggage of my commanding officer from that fortress near by.'

Then he at once laid hands on me, seized the halter with which I was led, and began to drag me off. The gardener wiped his head clean of the blood which poured from the wound caused by the previous blow, and spoke submissively a second time. He pleaded with that comrade-in-arms to behave more courteously and temperately, and swore that such behaviour would crown his hopes with success. 'In any case,' he added, 'this ass is a lazy beast, and he bites as well; and then he has a nasty malady that makes him tumble, so that he can barely carry a few handfuls of vegetables from my allotment near by. He gets tired, and his breath is laboured, so still less would he be able to cope with carrying heavier loads.'

40   But he then realized that the soldier, impervious to all his pleas, was even more determined to put an end to his life, for he had now turned the vine-rod round, intending to split the gardener's head with the knob at the thicker end. So my master had recourse to hasty measures of defence. He pretended that he was trying to grasp his opponent's knees to arouse his pity, so he bent low in suppliant fashion. But he then seized both his feet, raised him high, and brought him down heavily to earth. He then proceeded to assault his entire face, hands and ribs with his fists, elbows, teeth, and a stone which he grabbed from the road. From the moment that he lay prostrate on the ground the centurion could not fight back or offer any resistance. He had to content himself with repeated threats that if he got back on his feet, he would cut him into little pieces with his sword. The gardener took note of his words, snatched the sword from him, threw it as far away as he could, and resumed the attack on him with still fiercer blows. The soldier was flat on his back, and hindered by his wounds; he could devise no means of ensuring his survival, so he took the only course available to him, and pretended to be dead.

The gardener then took the sword with him, mounted my back, and headed directly for the town. Without even a thought of visiting his allotment, he went to lodge with a close

friend of his, to whom he told the whole story. He begged this
friend's help in his hour of danger, asking that he should
conceal his ass and himself long enough for him to keep out of
sight for two or three days, and thus escape indictment on a
capital charge. His host was not unmindful of their long-
standing friendship, and readily took us in. My feet were
roped together, and I was dragged upstairs into the attic. The
gardener stayed in the shop downstairs, where he crept into a
chest and hid there, with the lid closed over his head.

41   I later learnt that after some time the soldier arrived in
town looking as if he were the worse for a heavy bout of
drinking. He was tottering along, incapacitated by the pain of
his many wounds, and just managing to support himself on
his staff. He was too embarrassed to say a word to any of the
townsfolk about his sluggish inability to defend himself, but
he silently nursed his grievance, and when he encountered
some fellow-soldiers he divulged to them his unhappy
experience. They agreed that he should lie low for a time in
his quarters, for apart from the indignity which he had
suffered, the loss of his sword made him fear the implications
of his oath as a soldier. Meanwhile they said that now that
they had obtained particulars of how to identify us, they
would take pains to seek us out and exact revenge.

    Inevitably there was a traitorous neighbour to lay informa-
tion that we were hidden in that place. The soldiers then sent
for the magistrates. They falsely claimed that on the road they
had lost a very valuable silver vessel belonging to their
commanding officer, that a gardener had found it and refused
to give it back, and that he was holed up in the house of a
friend of his. The magistrates, on hearing of this loss and its
association with the commander's name, came to the door of
the lodging where we were staying. They loudly ordered our
host to surrender us—for, they said, it was beyond dispute
that he was concealing us—or else face the danger of a capital
indictment. But in his zeal for the safety of his friend whom he
had promised to help, he was not in the least deterred. He laid
no information about us, and maintained that he had not even
set eyes on the gardener for several days. The soldiers swore

oaths to the contrary by the emperor's life-spirit, claiming that he was hiding there and in no other place. The magistrates eventually decided to put the man's resolute denial to the test by mounting a search. So they sent in lictors and other state-officials, and ordered them to give the whole premises a rigorous examination, probing one corner after another. They reported back that there was no sign of any man or indeed of the ass within the threshold of the dwelling.

42   A more contentious argument then broke out on both sides. The soldiers kept calling on Caesar to witness that their assertions about us were well grounded, while the home-owner denied the charge, and supported his stance by repeated oaths invoking the majesty of the gods. This argument conducted with noisy altercations reached my ears, and being a naturally inquisitive ass imbued with restless impulses, I craned my neck and tried to peer out through the small window to see what all the noise was about. It so chanced that one of the soldiers caught a glimpse of my shadow, and called all of them to witness it on the spot. At once a great hubbub arose. Some of them immediately mounted the stairs, laid their hands on me, and dragged me down as though I were under arrest. All their doubts were now banished, and they searched in every nook and cranny. On opening the chest, they found the wretched gardener. They hauled him out and consigned him to the magistrates; then they escorted him to the city gaol, where he was doubtless to suffer execution. They could not stop laughing and joking at my peering out; this is the origin of the much-quoted proverb about the peeping ass and its shadow.

BOOK 10

*Tales of Wicked Women: Pleasant Life with the Cooks
Leads to Public Humiliation*

1 I have no knowledge of what befell my master the gardener
next day. But the soldier, who had endured at his hands such
a gratifying beating for his excessive aggression, unharnessed
me and led me out of the stable without encountering any
opposition. He then loaded me with his luggage from what I
assumed were his quarters, and led me out on the road, duly
adorned and equipped in military fashion, for I carried a
helmet which gleamed brightly, a shield which glittered still
further afield, and also a lance with a notably long shaft. He
had carefully set these on top of his high-piled baggage as
though he were serving with the army on campaign; not, I
imagine, because this conformed with battle-orders at the
time, but in order to terrorize wretched travellers. Once we
had made a fairly easy journey through the plain, we reached
a small town where we lodged at the house of a town-
councillor rather than at an inn. The soldier at once put me in
charge of a slave, and dutifully left to report to his superior,
who commanded a thousand armed troops.

2 It was there a few days later, as I recall, that a wicked and
appalling crime was committed. I record it in this book so that
you can read of it as well.

The master of the house had a son, whose good education
had made him a model of filial devotion and decent
behaviour; he was the kind of son you would have wished to
have for yourself. His mother had died many years before, and
his father had married again. By this second wife he had
another son who had just celebrated his twelfth birthday. This
stepmother became dominant in her husband's house through
her beauty rather than her good character. Because she was
either libidinous by nature or was drawn to the most heinous
wickedness as the victim of fate, she cast her eyes on her

stepson. You should know, gentle reader, that you are now to read a tragedy and no mere anecdote; you are to rise from the comic sock to the tragic buskin.

As long as the love which that woman nurtured was in its first stages and undeveloped, she was able to suppress her slight blushes, and to resist in silence Cupid's as yet mild onset. But once her whole heart was filled with the fire of madness, that love grew wild and boiled up out of control, so that she now caved in before the god's fierce onslaught. She made a pretence of illness, falsely claiming that her heart's wound was a physical malady. We all know that sick people and lovers suffer precisely the same impairment of health and appearance; they are alike hideously pale, their eyes droop, their knees are unsteady, their sleep is disturbed, and their sighs grow stronger as the torture lingers on. You might have thought that the storm-tossed symptoms of this lady too were the effect merely of the heat of fever, except that she kept weeping as well. Alas, how ignorant are the minds of physicians! What do throbbings of the veins denote, or changes of colour, or laboured breathing, or frequent tossing and turning from one side to the other? Great heavens, how easy it is to diagnose! You need not be a practising physician as long as you have experience of love's longings, when you observe someone who is not running a temperature yet is all aflame.

3   So it was that in her inability to contain her madness, the wound struck deeper. So she broke her long silence, and ordered that her son be summoned to her presence. She would gladly have expunged that title of son had she been able, so as not to be reminded of her shame. The young man did not defer his obedience to his sick parent's command. He made *for her chamber with a brow puckered with an old man's* concern, for this was an obedience which in a sense he owed to his father's wife and his brother's mother. She, however, was exhausted by the tortured silence which she had endured for so long; she was, so to say, aground on the shallows of doubt, so that every greeting which she thought apt for conversation at that moment she would in turn dismiss. Even now, as her

sense of shame faded, she was hesitant about how best to begin. The young man for his part even at that moment had no suspicion that anything was amiss; with modest demeanour and without prompting he asked her the causes of her present illness. She then seized the baneful chance of their being alone together to become reckless. She burst into floods of tears, covered her face with the hem of her robe, and addressed a few words to him in a trembling voice.

'You yourself are the entire cause and source of my present suffering, but you are also the remedy and my sole chance of salvation. Those eyes of yours have inveigled themselves through my own eyes into the depths of my heart, and are kindling in my marrow the keenest of flames. So have pity on me, because I am wasting away because of you. Do not let reverence for your father hold you back in any way, for you will be the very means of keeping alive his wife now on the point of death. It is because I see his likeness in your face that my love for you is fitting. You can rest fully assured that we are by ourselves; you have sufficient leisure to perform what you must do. The deed that goes unseen is as if it's never been.'

4   The youth was thrown into confusion by this sudden, outrageous proposal. But though he felt immediate abhorrence at such evil behaviour, he thought it best not to make things worse by a harsh and untimely repudiation, but rather to soften the blow and put her off with a guarded promise. This he accordingly wrapped in many words. He vehemently urged her to be of good heart, and to devote herself to the recovery of her health until some journey of his father granted them free scope for their pleasure. He then at once retired from his stepmother's sight which he found abhorrent. He reflected that this great calamity to his house needed further counsel, so he at once referred the matter to his aged tutor, a man of acknowledged sobriety. The outcome of their lengthy discussion was that the safest course seemed to lie in avoiding raging Fortune's storm by precipitate flight.

But the woman could not endure even slight delay. With remarkable cunning she at once invented some pretext to induce her husband to make an immediate and pressing journey to widely scattered estates. Thereupon her mad hope, which had now reached its height, impelled her boldly to demand the lustful encounter which the youth had pledged. But by pleading various pretexts he avoided the sight of her which he had come to abhor. Finally, the variety of excuses which he sent made her realize clearly that he was reneging on his promise to her, and with inconstant fickleness she translated her impious love into a hatred far more impious. She at once took aboard a favourite slave who had accompanied her as part of her dowry. He was a most wicked fellow, free of all scruples in performing any crime. She shared with him her treacherous designs; the course which seemed best to them was to rob the wretched youth of his life. So the scoundrel was at once dispatched to obtain poison taking instant effect, which he carefully diluted with wine to encompass the death of that blameless stepson.

5   While the guilty pair were conferring about the apt moment for offering him the poisoned drink, it chanced that the younger boy, that most debased woman's own son, arrived home after a morning devoted to his studies. After eating his lunch, he felt thirsty, and when he came upon the glass of wine in which the poison lurked, he at once drained it in his ignorance of the secret conspiracy. No sooner had he drunk the deadly draught prepared for his brother than he fell lifeless to the ground. The boy's escort was devastated by this sudden collapse of the boy, and at once with cries of distress summoned the mother and the whole household. Once the poisoned drink was identified as the cause of the misfortune, those present variously assigned the responsibility for the outrageous crime. But that cruel woman, whose vindictiveness as a stepmother was beyond compare, remained untroubled by the bitter death of her son, by guilt at the murder of her kin, by the disaster to the family, by the grief of her husband, or by the harrowing funeral rites. Instead she exploited the disaster of the household to gain revenge. She at once sent a runner to report to her husband on his journey the disaster which had befallen his house; then, when he returned

from his journey with all speed, she put on the boldest of faces, and pretended that her son had been cut off by poison administered by her stepson. In a sense this was not a lie, since the boy had pre-empted the death intended for the young man. But the fiction she told was that the younger brother had been wickedly murdered by her stepson because she had refused to yield to the immoral lust in which he had tried to have his way with her. Even this monstrous lying did not satisfy her, for she added that he had also threatened her with his sword for exposing his evil deed.

That unhappy father was then devastated by the double death of his two sons, and was bitterly storm-tossed on a sea of troubles. He had to watch his younger son being buried before his eyes, and was totally convinced that the other would be condemned on charges of incest and murder of kin. To crown all, the feigned mourning of the wife he loved so much was driving him to utter hatred of his own child.

6   The funeral procession and burial of his son had scarcely been completed when straight from his funeral-pyre the old man burst frantically into the market-place. He was still staining his cheeks with fresh tears, and tugging at his grey hairs, now grimy with ashes. In ignorance of that wicked woman's deceit, with tears and prayers—even grasping the knees of the city-councillors—he there indulged the full gamut of his emotions to encompass the destruction of his remaining son. He claimed that the youth had committed incest in his father's chamber, that he was a murderer of kin by causing a brother's death, and that in threatening the murder of his stepmother he was an assassin. In his grief the father had roused the council and the common folk to such feelings of pity and anger that they sought to waive the tedium of a formal trial with its clear proofs provided by the prosecution and its studied evasions offered by the defence. Instead they all loudly demanded that this public scandal be publicly punished and buried under a hail of stones.

The magistrates meanwhile were apprehensive of danger to themselves, in case from these small evidences of indignation, disaffection should develop into the collapse of public order.

So in part by pleas to the councillors and in part by restraining the common folk, they sought to have judgment duly done in the traditional manner, with the claims of both sides scrutinized before proclamation of the sentence, in accord with the civil law. No person, they said, should be condemned unheard, as happened among savage barbarians or in an arbitrary tyranny; so grim a precedent should not be bequeathed to posterity in time of peace.

7   This healthy advice prevailed, and the herald as instructed immediately announced that the councillors should assemble in the council-chamber. They at once took their usual places according to the order of precedence. On a further proclamation from the herald the prosecuting counsel entered first; finally the defendant too was summoned and escorted in. Following the procedures of Attic law observed on the Areopagus, the herald forbade the advocates in the case either to utter preambles or to arouse pity.

That this was the procedure I gathered from overhearing several conversations, but since I was in my manger away from the scene, I cannot know of or report to you the pressing arguments of the prosecutor, or the points on which the defendant sought acquittal—in short, the speeches and exchanges. What I did discover for certain I shall record in writing here.

Once the opposing statements of the speakers were concluded, it was decided to establish the truth and reliability of the charges by definite proofs rather than to allow inferences in so important a case to rest on suspicions. Above all, it was necessary at all costs to put in the witness-box the slave who alone was said to know that events had occurred as claimed. That gallows-bird was not a whit disconcerted by the uncertain outcome of such an important case, or by the sight of the crowded chamber, or even by personal feelings of guilt. He began to claim and proclaim as truth the story which he had invented: that the youth in anger at being rejected by his stepmother had summoned him; that in seeking to avenge that slight, he had bidden the slave kill her son; that he had promised a huge reward for his silence; that he had threatened

him with death if he refused; that the youth had mixed the
poison with his own hand, and had then given it to the slave to
administer to his brother; that he then suspected that the
slave had withheld the cup as proof of the crime, and had not
played his part; and that in the end the youth had
administered it to the boy with his own hand. Once the rascal
had recounted all this without the slightest apprehension as
though it were the gospel truth, the case was concluded.

8   Not one councillor had remained so fair-minded towards
the young man as not to find him clearly guilty and to
condemn him to be sewn in the sack. All their pens alike
inscribed the one word 'guilty', and following the invariable
custom, their identical votes were about to be consigned to the
bronze urn. Once the voting-pebbles had been lodged there,
and the affair (and the defendant's fate) was decided, nothing
could be subsequently changed, for power over his life passed
into the hands of the executioner. But then one of the
councillors, a physician whose known honesty and outstanding authority excelled that of the rest, covered the mouth of
the urn with his hand to prevent anyone idly dropping in his
pebble. Then he addressed these words to the council:

'My happy boast is that my past life has met with your
approval, and I refuse to countenance what would be a clear
case of murder, since the defendant has been arraigned on
false charges. You are under oath as you pass judgment, and I
will not let you perjure yourselves through being deceived by
the lies of a cheap slave. Nor can I trample underfoot my own
obligation to the gods by beguiling my conscience and
pronouncing a wrong sentence. So learn from me the facts of
the case.

9   'Not long ago this gallows-bird made an approach to me.
He was anxious to procure some swift-acting poison, and
offered me a hundred gold pieces for it. He said that it was
required for a sick person who was in the painful throes of a
wasting and incurable disease, and was eager to withdraw
himself from the torture of a continuing existence. I saw
through the wicked scoundrel as he blustered and offered his
implausible explanation. I was convinced that he was plotting

some crime, yet I did give him a potion. Yes, I gave him a potion, but I did not there and then accept the price which he offered, for I was guarding against a future enquiry. I said to him: "In the event that any of these gold pieces which you offer me turns out to be counterfeit or not one hundred per cent gold, kindly put them in this wallet, and seal them up with your ring. Then tomorrow they can be verified in the presence of a dealer." This pretext persuaded him to put his seal on the bag of money. When he was brought before the court, I at once ordered one of my servants to pick up the bag from my shop and to bring it here at the double. See, it has been brought here, and I now display it to you. The slave can examine it and identify his seal. So how can the brother be accused of procuring this poison when the slave purchased it?'

10   The scoundrel was then gripped by violent trembling, and his natural complexion turned deathly pale. A cold sweat seeped over all his limbs. Then he began to shift uncertainly from one foot to the other. First he scratched the front of his head, and then the back; with his mouth half-closed he stammered and muttered such ridiculous nonsense that not a single person could reasonably regard him as innocent. But then his native cunning reasserted itself, and with great insistence he kept denying the truth of the physician's account, and accused him of lying. When the physician realized that not only the sanctity of the law but also his own honesty was being openly damaged, he redoubled his efforts and strove to rebut the scoundrel, until on the magistrate's instructions the city-officials seized the hands of that vilest of slaves, pulled off his iron ring, and compared it with the seal on the wallet. They matched, and this confirmed earlier suspicions. The wheel and rack were then wielded in the Greek manner to torture the slave, but he remained steadfast with remarkable obstinacy, and yielded neither to blows nor even to fire.

11   Then the physician exclaimed 'By heaven, I will certainly not allow you to exact punishment from this innocent youth, for it would be impious. Nor will I permit this slave to make sport of our legal processes, and escape punishment for this

criminal outrage. I shall offer you clear proof of the actual facts. When this blackguard was eager to procure this deadly poison, I did not regard it as appropriate to my profession to provide anyone with the means of death, for my apprenticeship had taught me that the purpose of medicine was to restore people to health. However, I feared that if I refused to give it to him, my untimely rejection would minister to his crime, for he would purchase the deadly potion from some other person, or in the final extremity perform the impious deed with a sword or some other weapon. So I gave him mandragora, which is a mere soporific; the drug is well known for its reliable knock-out effect, for it induces sleep almost indistinguishable from death. It is hardly surprising that this scoundrel, in his utter desperation and awareness of the final punishment which ancestral custom has appointed for him, should readily endure these tortures which are light by comparison. But if the boy did indeed drink the potion mixed by my hands, he is still alive. He is peacefully sleeping, and as soon as he has shaken off his torpid sleep, he will return to the bright light of day. But if he has been killed, or if death has overtaken him, you can investigate other causes of his demise.'

12   Following the old man's speech delivered on these lines, it was decided to investigate. They made their way to the tomb at once with great urgency, where the boy's body had been laid. There was no city-councillor, no member of the ruling class, no individual even from the common folk whose curiosity did not impel him to flock there. Then the father removed the lid of the coffin with his own hands. Just then his son shook off the deadly sleep, and rose from the realms of the dead. His father hugged him close; the joy of the moment deprived him of speech. He led the boy out before the people's eyes; still tightly bound and wrapped in his funeral garments, he was brought to the courtroom. So now the crimes of that most villainous slave and that still more villainous woman were out in the open; the bare truth was visible for all to see. The stepmother was condemned to exile for life, and the slave was hoisted on the gallows. By general accord the gold pieces

were awarded to the good apothecary as a reward for that
timely soporific. As for the aged father, the celebrated and
famed stresses of Fortune ended in a manner worthy of the
divine Providence that shaped them; in a short period of time,
in fact in one brief moment, he suddenly became the father of
two grown sons, after enduring the perils of childlessness.

13   I myself at that time was adrift on the waves of my destined
fate. The soldier had procured me and laid claim to me
without payment, for no one had sold me to him. But now in
due obedience to the command of his commanding officer, he
was to convey a letter written to the great emperor at Rome.
So he sold me for eleven denarii to two brothers in the locality
who were slaves, and whose master was quite rich. One of
them was a confectioner who baked bread and honey-buns,
and the other a cook, who would braise the meat until it was
tender, and spice it with especially tasty sauces. The brothers
lived together, sharing a common lodging. Their purpose in
buying me had been to have me carry the numerous vessels
necessary for the various needs of their master as he travelled
over different regions. So I was adopted as a third lodger
accompanying the two brothers, and at no time did I find
Fortune so accommodating; for in the evening, after luscious
dinners had been served on most exquisite dishes, my masters
would bring back numerous left-overs to their modest abode.
One of them would carry the sizeable remains of pork,
chicken, fish, and all sorts of meat, while the other brought
bread, cakes, pastries, tarts, biscuits, and several other
honeyed sweetmeats. Once they had locked up their lodging
and departed to the baths to freshen themselves up, I used to
stuff myself to repletion on these god-given feasts, for I was
not such a fool or complete ass as to dine on prickly hay and
leave all that delicious food untouched.

14   For quite a time I got away handsomely with my crafty
pilfering, for up to that point my thieving was cautious and
quite modest. I contented myself with rather few delicacies
from so many, and the brothers had no suspicion that an ass
was playing tricks on them. But then my confidence at being
unobserved grew greater. I began to dispose of all the choicest

left-overs, and to select and lick clean the more luscious sweets. Nagging suspicion pricked the minds of the brothers, but even at that stage they did not suspect me of such behaviour, but began systematically to seek out the person guilty of these daily thefts. In the end they even started to blame each other for this disgraceful thieving. They took more diligent note, instituted closer watch, and kept careful count of the left-overs. Finally, one of them threw restraint to the winds and accosted the other.

'It is unfair and indeed uncivilized of you to steal the choicer left-overs every day, to sell them secretly to increase your savings, and then to demand an equal division of what is left. So if our joint association is not to your liking, we can continue to live as brothers in all other ways, but abandon this link by which we share and share alike; for I see that the cause of my complaint is subjecting me to heavy losses and is engendering considerable antipathy between us,' The other interjected. 'Heavens, I like this brazen cheek of yours! Every day you have been quietly stealing the left-overs, and now you have got your grumble in before mine, which all this time I have been nursing and bemoaning in secret so as not to appear to accuse my own brother of mean thieving. But it is good that we have both spoken out, and that we are seeking a means of stemming our losses, for if this silent resentment between us continued, it would result in the strife that befell Eteocles.'

15   Having exchanged these and similar rebukes, they both swore that they were wholly guiltless of any deceit or pilfering, and agreed that they must use every means of detecting the thief who was causing their joint loss. They assured each other that the ass in the lodging by himself could not be attracted to such foodstuffs, yet every day the choicest morsels were nowhere to be found. Nor was it possible that their room was being invaded by monster flies like those Harpies of old which used to plunder the banquets of Phineus.

Meanwhile I was feasting on this generous fare, and waxing fat on this abundance of human food. My body had now filled out to a generous plumpness, my hide had become juicily soft and greasy, and my coat was well nourished, with a handsome sheen. However, my enhanced physical beauty was the cause of a signal blot on my reputation. The brothers' interest was aroused by my enlarged frame, for they noted that the hay remained wholly untouched day by day. So they concentrated their attention wholly on me. They pretended to depart to the baths at the normal hour, and as usual closed the doors behind them. But then they spied on me through a tiny hole, and saw me tucking into the feast which was spread around. They no longer worried about the losses they were sustaining; they were astonished at the portentous spectacle of an ass as gourmet, and they split their sides with uncontrollable laughter. They summoned a fellow-slave, and then a second, and then several more, and let them observe the indescribable gluttony of the slow-witted ass. In the end they were all overcome by such loud and unrestrained laughter that it reached the ears of their master as well, as he was passing by.

16   He then asked what was so funny as to rouse the laughter of the household, and when he was told the reason, he also took a look through the same crack and was extremely diverted. He too began to laugh so loudly that he got the belly-ache. He then opened the door, stood beside me, and watched me openly. Now that at last I was finding Fortune's face smiling more benevolently on me, my confidence was boosted by the pleasure I was giving to the present company. So with total unconcern I continued happily eating. Eventually the master of the house was so pleased by this unusual sight that he ordered me to be led—in fact, he guided me with his own hands—to his dining-room. There he ordered the table to be laid, and every variety of freshly-prepared foodstuffs and untouched dishes to be set before me. I had already had an elegant sufficiency, but I wished to ingratiate myself and make myself more acceptable to him, so I attacked the food placed before me as if I were famished. They gave detailed thought to the food which would be particularly repugnant to an ass, and then set this before me to test my docility. There were meats spread with silphium, fowl sprinkled with pepper,

and fish swimming in some foreign sauce. Meanwhile the dining-room reverberated with the loudest laughter.

Then some wit present said: 'Give this dining-guest of ours a drop of wine.' The master responded to this witticism: 'That joke of yours, you scallywag, is not such a mad idea. It's quite possible that our fellow-guest will be glad to take a cup of sweet wine as well. Hey, boy, take this gold beaker, and wash it well. Then mix in some wine and honey, and offer it to this self-invited guest of mine. Tell him too that I've already drunk his health.' The guests were roused to intense expectation. I was not in the least perturbed; with a leisurely and quite good-humoured gesture, I screwed the edges of my lips into a ladle-shape, and drained the large cup at a single gulp. A din broke out as they all bade me good health.

17   The master of the house was so overjoyed that he summoned his slaves who had bought me, and gave instructions to pay them the purchase-price four times over. Then he put me in the care of a freedman of his, of whom he greatly approved and who had a fair sum of money tucked away, and instructed him to look after me carefully. The freedman fed me up in a quite civilized and friendly fashion, and to win the greater esteem of his patron, he took great pains to divert him with the tricks which I had performed. First he taught me to recline at table, leaning on my elbow, and then to wrestle and also to dance with my forefeet off the ground; and most wonderful of all, to respond to words with a sign, for I would indicate refusal by tossing back my head, and acceptance by a nod. If I was thirsty, I would demand a drink by turning to the wine-steward and winking with each eye successively. All these promptings I obeyed with the greatest ease; in fact I could have performed them without instruction, but I was afraid that if I did a number of tricks without coaching as if I were human, they might think that this presaged something sinister, slaughter me as a monstrous prodigy, and throw me as rich fare to the vultures.

By now the story had circulated widely, and my marvellous tricks had brought my master fame and renown. 'That's the man', people would say of him, 'who keeps an ass as a companion and guest at table. The creature wrestles, and dances, and understands human language, and indicates its feelings by motions of the head.'

18   I must first tell you—in fact I should have mentioned it at the outset, but I'll do it now—who the man was, and where he came from. My master's name was Thiasus, and his native city was Corinth, the capital of the entire province of Achaea. His ancestry and social rank had entitled him to rise step by step up the ladder of offices, and he was now in line for the quinquennial magistracy. To show that he was worthy of receiving these badges of office, he extended his generosity more widely, with the promise of a gladiatorial show affording a three-day spectacle. In his eagerness for public fame, he had at that time even visited Thessaly to obtain there the most notable beasts and gladiators of renown, and now that he had made all his arrangements and purchases to his satisfaction, he was preparing to return home. He rejected his gleaming coaches and relegated his handsome four-wheelers, some of which were covered and some open; they were drawn along unoccupied at the rear of his column. He also disdained the Thessalian horses and his other Gallic beasts, though their noble stock attaches high monetary value to them. Instead, he decked me out with gold trappings, purple housings, crimson covers, silver bridle, embroidered belt and tinkling bells; then he mounted me, and from time to time would address me with most affectionate words. Among several other remarks, he claimed that he was absolutely charmed at having in me both a dinner-companion and a means of transportation.

19   After completing our journey, partly by land and partly by water, we reached Corinth, where great crowds of citizens gathered. My impression was that they were not so much anxious to honour Thiasus as to take a good look at me; for there too I had become so celebrated that I was a source of considerable profit to the man in charge of me. When he realized that so many were eager and extremely enthusiastic to view my tricks, he locked the door and let them in one at a time. By charging admission, he routinely raked in quite a bit each day.

Among the crowd that gathered was a married lady of position and wealth. Like the rest, she paid to watch me, and as a result was diverted by my various tricks. Gradually constant admiration developed into a strange longing for my person. She could devise no remedy for her insane lust; she burningly desired my embraces like some asinine Pasiphaë. The outcome was that she bargained with the keeper, offering a large sum for the right to sleep with me for a single night. The keeper was not in the least concerned whether I could be the source of any pleasure to her. He was merely concerned with his own profit, so he agreed.

20   When we had finished dinner and had retired from the master's dining-room, we found the married lady already in attendance; she had been waiting in my room for some time. Heavens, what splendid preparations she had made! Four eunuchs were busily laying a bed for us on the ground, with pillows bulging with soft feathers making an airy base. Over these they carefully spread coverlets of gold braid adorned with Tyrian purple, and on top they laid other pillows; these were quite tiny, but there were several of them, the kind that refined women usually rest their chins and necks on. They did not postpone the pleasures of their mistress by lingering long, but closed the doors of the chamber and made off. Within, candles gleamed brightly, and illumined for us the darkness of the night.

21   The lady then stripped herself stark naked, removing even the band which confined her lovely breasts. She stood close to the light, and from a pewter jar anointed herself with large quantities of oil of balsam. She then rubbed generous measures of it with much more enthusiasm on me; she also applied frankincense to my nostrils. Then she kissed me hard—not the sort of kisses casually offered in the brothel, whether by harlots demanding money or customers refusing it, but those sincerely offered from the heart. She also addressed me most affectionately, with 'I love you', 'I want you', 'You are my only love', 'I can't live without you', and the other phrases with which women both rouse their partners and attest their own feelings. She then grabbed my halter, and

made me lie as I had learnt to do; it was readily done, for I envisaged nothing new or difficult in prospect, especially as I was to enjoy the embraces of so beautiful and passionate a woman, and this after so long a time. My zeal was enhanced by the fact that I had soused myself with a bellyful of the finest wine, and the perfume with its heady scent had roused in me a longing to copulate.

22   But I was sorely exercised and considerably fearful, wondering how I could mount such a fragile lady with my four hulking legs; how I could embrace such soft and shining limbs fashioned of milk and honey with my hard hooves; how I could kiss such small red lips steeped in the liquid of ambrosia with my huge mouth, which was so misshapen and ugly with its teeth like rocks; finally, how that woman could admit my massive penis, however much she yearned for it from the tips of her toes. I felt sorry for myself, for if I split that noble woman apart I should be thrown to the beasts and incidentally grace my master's show. Meanwhile she was repeatedly whispering gentle endearments, pressing constant kisses, and uttering rapturous sounds with devouring eyes; and as climax she murmured 'I have you, I have you, my fond dove, my sparrow.' As she spoke, she showed that my reservations were needless, and my fear unfounded; for she hugged me as closely as she could, and admitted me absolutely all the way. Whenever I withdrew my buttocks in an attempt to spare her, she would lunge madly towards me, seize my back, and cling to me in a still closer grip. Ye gods, I began to think that I had not the strength to satisfy her, and to believe that the mother of the Minotaur had succeeded in extracting pleasure from her lowing lover! After that sleepless night of activity, the woman shrank from being seen in daylight and retired, having agreed on the same fee for the next night.

23   My keeper was not reluctant to bestow these pleasures as the lady ordained, in part because of the large payment he was receiving, and partly to set up a new diversion for his master. Without delay he informed him of our sexual performance. The master rewarded his freedman lavishly,

and booked me in for his public show. But that worthy bed-
mate of mine could not be hired because of her high rank, and
no other lady could be induced to participate in spite of the
considerable reward. So he obtained a woman of low repute
who by decree of the governor had been condemned to be
thrown to the beasts. She was to appear in company with me
in the theatre before the people, and publicly demonstrate her
chaste behaviour there. The story that I heard of how she
merited this punishment was as follows.

This woman had a husband whose father was to travel
abroad. On his departure he instructed his wife, who was
carrying the burden of pregnancy and was the mother of the
young husband, that if she gave birth to a child of the weaker
sex, the baby was to be killed at once. But when a baby girl
was born in the absence of her husband, she was induced by
the innate love which mothers have for their offspring to
disobey her husband. She gave the girl to neighbours to rear,
and when her husband returned she told him that the baby
was a girl and had been disposed of. But when the girl
matured to her full womanhood, making it necessary that a
date be set for her marriage, the mother could not bestow on
her daughter the dowry appropriate to her birth without the
knowledge of her husband. So she did the only possible thing:
she revealed the hidden secret to her son, for she greatly
feared that by some mischance he might succumb to the
pressures of youthful ardour, and fall in love with his sister in
the blissful ignorance which she shared. The young man was
a model of family devotion; he scrupulously observed both
obedience to his mother and his duty to his sister, and by
hiding his motives behind an apparent display of common
kindness, he discharged the duty demanded by the blood-
relationship. He admitted the girl into the protection of his
home as if she were a neighbour abandoned and orphaned of
the support of her parents, and later he entrusted her in
marriage to a very close and much loved friend, bestowing on
her a dowry most generously from his own pocket.

24   However, these most suitable arrangements so religiously
made could not escape Fortune's deadly intent, for at her

prompting, savage jealousy at once guided its course to the young man's house. For there and then this wife of his—she was the one now to be exposed to the beasts as a result of these events—first began to suspect this girl to be a rival for her bed, and her supplanter; and then her suspicion turned to hatred, and hatred thereafter led to her ambushing the girl in the most cruel of death-traps.

The foul deed which she eventually devised was this: she secretly commandeered her husband's ring, and set off to the country. She then dispatched a favourite slave, one faithful to her but deserving ill of the goddess Good Faith, to report to the girl that the young man had gone to his country house, and was summoning her to join him; she should come with all speed, he added, alone and unaccompanied. To ensure that the sister would not hesitate to come, she gave the slave the ring which she had secretly taken from her husband, and which when displayed would authenticate the message. The girl obeyed the instruction of her brother (this relationship with him was known to her alone), and having also identified the seal shown to her, she made lively haste, journeying alone as ordered. But once the girl had tumbled into the trap laid with such deep deceit, and was caught in the snare in which she had been ambushed, that worthy wife lost all control under the pricks of lustful fury. First she stripped her husband's sister naked, and gave her a severe whipping. Then, as the girl cried out the truth, that the wife's boiling rage at having a rival in love was unjustified, and repeatedly screamed that the young man was her brother, the wife assumed that her whole story was a tissue of lies, and she killed her most cruelly by thrusting a white-hot brand between her thighs.

25   Then the girl's brother and husband both hastened there, roused by the tidings of this cruel death. In their different ways they mourned and wept over the girl, and consigned her to burial. Her youthful brother could not endure with equanimity the wretched and wholly unjustified death of his sister. He was stricken to the heart with grief, and flushed with the baleful fury of the keenest resentment. In consequence he was fired with such fiercely flaming fever that he

now seemed to require medical treatment as well. His wife, who had long since forfeited the title as well as the loyalty of a wife, made an assignment with a physician whose lack of integrity was notorious; he was well known for the battles which he had fought, and the many palms of victory which he had won, for he could number many trophies as the work of his right hand. She at once promised him fifty thousand sesterces if he would sell her a quick-acting poison, so that she could procure her husband's death. When the bargain was struck between them, he made a pretence of dispensing the celebrated potion called by more learned people 'The Health-offering', a drug necessary for easing gastric pains and dissolving bile; but in its place he substituted another draught, 'The Proserpina-offering'. Then, in the presence of the household and of several friends and relatives, the physician handed the cup, carefully mixed with his own hand, to the sick man.

26   But that shameless woman now sought both to remove her associate in crime, and to recoup the money which she had promised him, so she placed a restraining hand openly on the cup. 'You are the best of physicians,' she said, 'but you must not offer this draught to my dearest husband until you yourself have taken a good drink of it, for how can I be sure that there is no harmful poison secreted in it? As a man of circumspection and learning, you above all can scarcely be offended if I, as a scrupulous wife concerned for my husband's health, show such necessary devotion to him.'

The physician, thrown into sudden turmoil by the un-expected and desperate boldness of this ruthless woman, was put totally out of his stride, and because of shortage of time was deprived of the leisure for a measured reply. So rather than incur suspicion of a guilty conscience by displaying any fear or hesitation, he took a good drink of that same potion. The young man was reassured by this, and he too took the cup and drank the proffered medicine. The physician, after concluding his immediate business in this way, made to return home with all speed, in his haste to counteract the harmful effect of the poison he had taken by means of a potion which would save his life. But that ruthless woman continued with the same impious determination with which she had begun, and refused to allow him to move an inch from her sight until, as she put it, the potion had been absorbed, and the effects of the medicine were patent. Finally, wearied with his numerous lengthy appeals and protestations, she reluctantly let him leave. Meanwhile that hidden and destructive poison was raging all through his internal organs, and had penetrated deep into his marrow. By this time he was grievously affected, and he reached home only with the greatest difficulty, plunged into a comatose stupor. He had just time to recount the entire circumstances to his wife, and to instruct her at least to demand the promised payment for the twin deaths, before that most responsible of physicians after violent convulsions yielded up his life.

27   The young man likewise failed to hold on to life, and met his death from the same mortal causes while his wife shed crocodile tears. Following his burial, and after the few days during which funeral services are offered to the dead had elapsed, the physician's wife arrived to demand payment for the two deaths. The woman continued true to her nature; she expunged the true face of honesty, but superimposed its outward appearance, and she answered the doctor's wife with soothing words. She promised everything lavishly and abundantly, and stated that she would pay the appointed price without delay if only the other agreed to give her a little of the potion to carry through the job which she had begun.

I need say no more. The physician's wife was trapped in the noose of this most wicked deceit, and she readily consented. To ingratiate herself still further with that woman of wealth, she hastened to collect the entire box of poison from her home, and gave it to her. The murderess had now obtained ample means of committing her crimes, and she extended her bloodstained hands far and wide.

28   She had a young daughter by the husband whom she had recently murdered, and she was intensely irritated by the fact that the laws bestowed the requisite right of inheritance upon this little girl. In her avid desire for the daughter's entire

patrimony, she began to threaten her life as well. In her awareness that unscrupulous mothers obtain inheritances when their children die, she showed herself to be the same sort of mother as she had proved a wife. She contrived a meal suited to the occasion, and with the same poison prostrated both the physician's wife and her own daughter. The baleful drug made short work of the little girl's soft and tender internal organs, and put an end to her frail life. But the physician's wife first began to suspect the truth when that abominable potion began to storm around her lungs on its destructive journey. Her suspicions were confirmed when her breathing became laboured, so she made straight for the governor's house. There with loud cries she invoked the good faith of the governor, and raised an outcry among the citizens, since she intended to expose such monstrous crimes. She at once succeeded in opening both the house and the ears of the governor to listen to her. Then, after carefully recounting from the very beginning all the heinous deeds of that most cruel woman, she was suddenly gripped by a dizziness that clouded her mind. Her lips which had been half-open she locked tightly together; a continued whistling sound was heard as her teeth clamped upon each other, and then she fell lifeless before the governor's very feet.

This governor was a man of experience, and he did not permit such manifold outrages committed by that venomous serpent to fester through passive delay. He at once had the woman's personal servants arrested, and by applying torture he extracted the truth from them. He then decreed that she be exposed to the wild beasts, a punishment less than she deserved, but no other fitting mode of torture could be devised.

29   This, then, was the woman with whom I was to be joined publicly in marriage. It was with great anguish and considerable anxiety that I awaited the day of the show. I repeatedly felt the urge to contrive my own death rather than be defiled by the contagion of that female criminal, and feel the ignominy of disgrace at a public show. But without the resource of a human hand or fingers, I was quite unable to

draw a sword with the round stump of my hoof. In this extreme calamity I sought consolation in one slight and extremely slender hope: spring now dawning was adorning all nature with blossoming buds, clothing the fields in bright crimson. Roses were bursting out from their thorny clothing, exuding a fragrance like cinnamon, and gleaming brightly. They could transform me back to the Lucius of old.

The day appointed for the show was now at hand. As I was led to the theatre, a crowd of people cheering in procession attended me. During the preliminaries of the show, devoted to mimic dances by performers on the stage, I was posted before the gate. There I found it pleasant to munch the luxuriant grass sprouting at the very entrance to the theatre. From time to time I refreshed my inquisitive eyes by gazing through the open gate at the highly pleasing spectacle afforded by the show. Boys and girls in the first flower of blossoming youth were embarking on the Greek Pyrrhic dance. They looked strikingly beautiful in their gleaming garments as they made their expressive entry. They were marshalled in lines, and moved round beautifully in their circling steps. At one moment they would glide sinuously round to form a circle, at another they would link with each other in slanting column; next they would wedge themselves into a hollow square, and then open out into separate groups. But when the closing note of the trumpet brought their complex manœuvres to an end as they danced to and fro, the curtain was raised, the backcloths were folded away, and the stage was set.

30   A mountain of wood had been constructed with consummate workmanship to represent the famous mountain which the poet Homer in his song called Mount Ida. It was planted with thickets and live trees, and from its summit it disgorged river-water from a flowing fountain installed by the craftsman's hands. One or two she-goats were cropping blades of grass, and a youth was acting out control of the flock. He was handsomely dressed to represent the Phrygian shepherd Paris, with exotic garments flowing from his shoulders, and his head crowned with a tiara of gold. Standing by him appeared a radiant boy, naked except for a youth's cloak

draped over his left shoulder; his blonde hair made him the cynosure of all eyes. Tiny wings of gold were projecting from his locks, in which they had been fastened symmetrically on both sides. The herald's staff and the wand which he carried identified him as Mercury. He danced briskly forward, holding in his right hand an apple gilded with gold leaf, which he handed to the boy playing the part of Paris. After conveying Jupiter's command with a motion of the head, he at once gracefully withdrew and disappeared from the scene. Next appeared a worthy-looking girl, similar in appearance to the goddess Juno, for her hair was ordered with a white diadem, and she carried a sceptre. A second girl then burst in, whom you would have recognized as Minerva. Her head was covered with a gleaming helmet which was itself crowned with an olive-wreath; she bore a shield and brandished a spear, simulating the goddess's fighting-role.

31   After them a third girl entered, her beauty visibly unsurpassed. Her charming, ambrosia-like complexion intimated that she represented the earlier Venus when that goddess was still a maiden. She vaunted her unblemished beauty by appearing naked and unclothed except for a thin silken garment veiling her entrancing lower parts. An inquisitive gust of air would at one moment with quite lubricious affection blow this garment aside, so that when wafted away it revealed her virgin bloom; at another moment it would wantonly breathe directly upon it, clinging tightly and vividly outlining the pleasurable prospect of her lower limbs. The goddess's appearance offered contrasting colours to the eye, for her body was dazzling white, intimating her descent from heaven, and her robe was dark blue, denoting her emergence from the sea.

Each maiden representing a goddess was accompanied by her own escort. Juno was attended by Castor and Pollux, their heads covered by egg-shaped helmets prominently topped with stars; these Castors were represented by boys on stage. The maiden playing this role advanced with restrained and unpretentious movements to the music of an Ionian flute playing a range of tunes; with dignified motions she promised

the shepherd to bestow on him the kingship of all Asia if he
awarded her the prize for beauty. The girl whose appearance
in arms had revealed her as Minerva was protected by two
boys who were the comrades in arms of the battle-goddess,
Terror and Fear; they pranced about with swords unsheathed, and behind her back a flutist played a battle-tune in
the Dorian mode. He mingled shrill whistling notes with deep,
droning chords like a trumpet-blast, stirring the performers to
lively and supple dancing. Minerva with motions of the head,
menacing gaze, and writhing movements incisively informed
Paris that if he awarded her the victory for beauty, her aid
would make him a doughty fighter, famed for the trophies
gained in wars.

32   But now Venus becomingly took the centre of the stage to
the great acclamation of the theatre, and smiled sweetly. She
was surrounded by a throng of the happiest children; you
would have sworn that those litle boys whose skins were
smooth and milk-white were genuine Cupids who had just
flown in from sky or sea. They looked just the part with their
tiny wings, miniature arrows, and the rest of their get-up, as
with gleaming torches they lit the way for their mistress as
though she were *en route* to a wedding-banquet. Next floated
in charming children, unmarried girls, representing on one
side the Graces at their most graceful, and on the other the
Hours in all their beauty. They were appeasing their goddess
by strewing wreaths and single blossoms before her, and they
formed a most elegant chorus-line as they sought to please the
Mistress of pleasures with the foliage of spring. The flutes
with their many stops were now rendering in sweet harmony
melodies in the Lydian mode. As they affectingly softened the
hearts of the onlookers, Venus still more affectingly began
gently to stir herself; with gradual, lingering steps, restrained
swaying of the hips, and slow inclination of the head she
began to advance, her refined movements matching the soft
sounds of the flutes. Occasionally her eyes alone would dance,
as at one moment she gently lowered her lids, and at another
imperiously signalled with threatening glances. At the moment
when she met the gaze of the judge, the beckoning of her arms

seemed to hold the promise that if he preferred her over the other goddesses, she would present Paris with a bride of unmatched beauty, one like herself. There and then the Phrygian youth spontaneously awarded the girl the golden apple in his hand, which signalled the vote for victory.

33   You individuals who are the lowest form of life—I should call you rather sheep of the courts, or more aptly still, vultures in togas—why are you amazed that all jurymen nowadays trade their verdicts for money, seeing that when the world began, this suit conducted between deities and men was corrupted by grace and favour? This country bumpkin, chosen as judge in the plans laid by Jupiter, sold that first verdict for lustful gain, and thereby destroyed the whole of his race. And heavens, it was no different in the notorious dispute that followed between famed Greek leaders: Palamedes, who excelled in learning and knowledge, was condemned for treason on false charges, and again the mediocre Odysseus was given the verdict over Ajax, greatest of warriors and a man unsurpassed in martial bravery. Again, what sort of trial was that conducted before those shrewd Athenian legislators who were teachers of every form of knowledge? That old man possessed divine foresight; the god of Delphi pronounced him pre-eminent in wisdom before all other mortals. Yet was he not encompassed by the deceit and envy of a most wicked clique on the grounds that he was corrupting the youth, when in fact he was bridling and restraining them? And was he not executed by the juice of that baleful plant, stamping on his fellow-citizens the stigma of enduring disgrace? For even today outstanding philosophers prefer his most sacred school to all others, and in the loftiest pursuit of happiness they swear by his name.

But I would not wish any of you to censure this onset of my indignation with the unspoken reflection: 'What? Shall we now endure that ass making pronouncements to us on philosophy?' So I shall return to the story at the point where I left it.

34   Once Paris had completed that judgement of his, Juno and Minerva retired from the stage, downcast and apparently

resentful, indicating by gestures their anger at being rejected. Venus on the other hand was elated and smiling, and registered her joy by dancing in company with the entire chorus. At that moment a stream of saffron mixed with wine shot high in the air from the peak of the mountain. It issued from a hidden pipe, and as it coursed downward, it spread in a fragrant shower over the she-goats grazing all around, until the dye improved their colour by transforming their native grey into yellow. Then, as the entire theatre was permeated by the delightful scent, an abyss in the earth opened up and swallowed the wooden mountain.

A soldier now made his hasty way up the centre aisle to procure the woman from the state prison, as the crowd was now demanding her; she was the one who I mentioned had been condemned to the beasts for her manifold crimes, and assigned to the distinction of a wedding with me. A bed was being meticulously laid, doubtless to serve as our nuptial couch; it gleamed with Indian tortoiseshell, was stuffed with masses of feathers, and adorned with a coverlet of silk. Shame at the prospect of public copulation, and disgust at being besmirched by this foul female criminal, afflicted me, but I was in an agony of torment also through fear of death. I reflected that when we were joined close in sexual embraces, any beast dispatched to kill the woman could not prove to be so wisely discriminating, so skilfully trained, or so moderately self-denying as to tear to pieces the woman lying at my side, and to spare me because I had not been condemned and was innocent.

35   By now my anxiety was aroused not by a sense of shame but by regard for my very safety. So while my keeper was preoccupied and busy as he carefully arranged the couch, and the entire slave-retinue was concentrating on provision of the hunting-scene to follow, or wholly diverted by the pleasurable scene on stage, I was granted free scope for my deliberations, for no one considered that a tame ass like me needed very much watching. I edged unobtrusively forward until I reached the nearest gate; then I took off at full gallop. I covered a good six miles at top speed, and reached Cenchreae.

This is a town celebrated as part of the notable colony of the Corinthians, and is lapped by the Aegean sea and the Saronic gulf; there is also a harbour there which affords the safest refuge for ships, and great crowds of people throng there. So I gave these gatherings a wide berth, and chose a secluded beach where I stretched out and rested my weary body in the bosom of softest sand, close to the spray thrown up by the waves. The sun's chariot had by now bent its way past the last turning-point of the day; I surrendered myself to the silence of the evening, and sweet sleep descended on me.

BOOK 11

Salvation, and Conversion to Isis

1 A sudden fear aroused me at about the first watch of the night. At that moment I beheld the full moon rising from the sea-waves, and gleaming with special brightness. In my enjoyment of the hushed isolation of the shadowy night, I became aware that the supreme goddess wielded her power with exceeding majesty, that human affairs were controlled wholly by her providence, that the world of cattle and wild beasts and even things inanimate were lent vigour by the divine impulse of her light and power; that the bodies of earth, sea, and sky now increased at her waxing, and now diminished in deference to her waning. It seemed that Fate had now had her fill of my grievous misfortunes, and was offering hope of deliverance, however delayed. So I decided to address a prayer to the venerable image of the goddess appearing before my eyes. I hastily shook off my torpid drowsiness, and sprang up, exultant and eager. I was keen to purify myself at once, so I bathed myself in the sea-waters, plunging my head seven times beneath the waves, for Pythagoras of godlike fame proclaimed that number to be especially efficacious in sacred rites. Then with tears in my eyes I addressed this prayer to the supremely powerful goddess:

2 'Queen of heaven, at one time you appear in the guise of Ceres, bountiful and primeval bearer of crops. In your delight at recovering your daughter, you dispensed with the ancient, barbaric diet of acorns and schooled us in civilized fare; now you dwell in the fields of Eleusis. At another time you are heavenly Venus; in giving birth to Love when the world was first begun, you united the opposing sexes and multiplied the human race by producing ever abundant offspring; now you are venerated at the wave-lapped shrine of Paphos. At another time you are Phoebus' sister; by applying soothing remedies you relieve the pain of childbirth, and have brought

teeming numbers to birth; now you are worshipped in the
famed shrines of Ephesus. At another time you are Proserpina,
whose howls at night inspire dread, and whose triple form
restrains the emergence of ghosts as you keep the entrance to
earth above firmly barred. You wander through diverse
groves, and are appeased by varying rites. With this feminine
light of yours you brighten every city and nourish the
luxuriant seeds with your moist fire, bestowing your light
intermittently according to the wandering paths of the sun.
But by whatever name or rite or image it is right to invoke
you, come to my aid at this time of extreme privation, lend
stability to my disintegrating fortunes, grant respite and peace
to the harsh afflictions which I have endured. Let this be the
full measure of my toils and hazards; rid me of this grisly,
four-footed form. Restore me to the sight of my kin; make me
again the Lucius that I was. But if I have offended some deity
who continues to oppress me with implacable savagery, at
least allow me to die, since I cannot continue to live.'

3   These were the prayers which I poured out, supporting
them with cries of lamentation. But then sleep enveloped and
overpowered my wasting spirit as I lay on that couch of sand.
But scarcely had I closed my eyes when suddenly from the
midst of the sea a divine figure arose, revealing features
worthy of veneration even by the gods. Then gradually the
gleaming form seemed to stand before me in full figure as she
shook off the sea-water. I shall try to acquaint you too with
the detail of her wondrous appearance, if only the poverty of
human speech grants me powers of description, or the deity
herself endows me with a rich feast of eloquent utterance.

To begin with, she had a full head of hair which hung
down, gradually curling as it spread loosely and flowed gently
over her divine neck. Her lofty head was encircled by a
garland interwoven with diverse blossoms, at the centre of
which above her brow was a flat disk resembling a mirror, or
rather the orb of the moon, which emitted a glittering light.
The crown was held in place by coils of rearing snakes on
right and left, and it was adorned above with waving ears of
corn. She wore a multicoloured dress woven from fine linen,

one part of which shone radiantly white, a second glowed yellow with saffron blossom, and a third blazed rosy red. But what riveted my eyes above all else was her jet-black cloak, which gleamed with a dark sheen as it enveloped her. It ran beneath her right arm across to her left shoulder, its fringe partially descending in the form of a knot. The garment hung down in layers of successive folds, its lower edge gracefully undulating with tasselled fringes.

4   Stars glittered here and there along its woven border and on its flat surface, and in their midst a full moon exhaled fiery flames. Wherever the hem of that magnificent cloak billowed out, a garland composed of every flower and every fruit was inseparably attached to it. The goddess's appurtenances were extremely diverse. In her right hand she carried a bronze rattle; it consisted of a narrow metal strip curved like a belt, through the middle of which were passed a few rods; when she shook the rattle vigorously three times with her arm, the rods gave out a shrill sound. From her left hand dangled a boat-shaped vessel, on the handle of which was the figure of a serpent in relief, rearing high its head and swelling its broad neck. Her feet, divinely white, were shod in sandals fashioned from the leaves of the palm of victory. Such, then, was the appearance of the mighty goddess. She breathed forth the fertile fragrance of Arabia as she deigned to address me in words divine:

5   'Here I am, Lucius, roused by your prayers. I am the mother of the world of nature, mistress of all the elements, first-born in this realm of time. I am the loftiest of deities, queen of departed spirits, foremost of heavenly dwellers, the single embodiment of all gods and goddesses. I order with my nod the luminous heights of heaven, the healthy sea-breezes, the sad silences of the infernal dwellers. The whole world worships this single godhead under a variety of shapes and liturgies and titles. In one land the Phrygians, first-born of men, hail me as the Pessinuntian mother of the gods; elsewhere the native dwellers of Attica call me Cecropian Minerva; in other climes the wave-tossed Cypriots name me Paphian Venus; the Cretan archers, Dictynna Diana; the

trilingual Sicilians, Ortygian Proserpina; the Eleusinians, the ancient goddess Ceres; some call me Juno, others Bellona, others Hecate, and others still Rhamnusia. But the peoples on whom the rising sun-god shines with his first rays—eastern and western Ethiopians, and the Egyptians who flourish with their time-honoured learning—worship me with the liturgy that is my own, and call me by my true name, which is queen Isis.

'I am here out of pity for your misfortunes; I am here to lend you kindly support. End now your weeping, abandon your lamentation, set aside your grief, for through my providence your day of salvation is now dawning. So pay careful attention to my commands. The day to be born of this night has been dedicated to me in religious observance from time immemorial. Now that the storms of winter are stilled, and the tempestuous waves of the ocean are calmed, the sea is now safe for shipping, and my priests entrust to it a newly built vessel dedicated as the first fruits of our journeys by sea. You are to await this rite with an untroubled and reverent mind.

6   'As the procession forms up, a priest at my prompting will be carrying a garland of roses tied to the rattle in his right hand. So without hesitation part the crowd and join the procession, relying on my kindly care. Then, when you have drawn near, make as if you intend to kiss the priest's hand, and gently detach the roses; at once then shrug off the skin of this most hateful of animals, which has long been abominable in my sight. Do not be fearful and regard any of these commands of mine as difficult, for at this moment as I stand before you I am also appearing to my priest as he sleeps, and am instructing him what to do following this. At my command the close-packed crowds will give way before you. In the midst of the joyous ritual and the jolly sights, no one will recoil from your ugly shape, nor put a malicious complexion on your sudden metamorphosis, and lay spiteful charges against you.

'What you must carefully remember and keep ever locked deep in your heart is that the remaining course of your life until the moment of your last breath is pledged to me, for it is only right that all your future days should be devoted to the one whose kindness has restored you to the company of men. Your future life will be blessed, and under my protection will bring you fame; and when you have lived out your life's span and you journey to the realm of the dead, even there in the hemisphere beneath the earth you will constantly adore me, for I shall be gracious to you. You will dwell in the Elysian fields, while I, whom you now behold, shine brightly in the darkness of Acheron and reign in the inner Stygian depths. But if you deserve to win my divine approval by diligent service, you will come to know that I alone can prolong your life even here on earth beyond the years appointed by your destiny.'

7   When she had reached the close of her sacred prophecy, that invincible deity retired to keep her own company. Without delay I was at once released from sleep. With mingled emotions of fear and joy I arose, bathed in sweat, utterly bemused by so vivid an epiphany of the powerful goddess. I sprinkled myself with sea-water, and as I meditated on her important commands, I reviewed the sequence of her instructions. At that moment the clouds of dark night were dispersed, and a golden sun arose. There and then groups of people filled the entire streets, darting here and there in quite exultant devotion. My personal sense of well-being seemed to be compounded by a general atmosphere of joy, which was so pervasive that I sensed that every kind of domestic beast, and entire households, and the very weather seemed to present a smiling face to the world. For a sunny, windless day had suddenly succeeded the previous day's frost, so that even the birds were enticed by the spring warmth to burst tunefully into sweet harmonies, as with their charming address they soothed the mother of the stars, the parent of the seasons, the mistress of the entire world. Why, even the trees, both those fertile with their produce of fruit, and the barren ones content with the provision of mere shade, expanded under the southerly breezes, and smiled with the budding of their foliage; they whispered sweetly with the gentle motion of

their branches. Now that the great din of the storms was stilled, and the waves' angry swell had subsided, the sea quietened and controlled its floods, while the sky dispersed the dark rain-clouds and shone with the cloudless and bright brilliance of its light.

8   And now the outrunners of the great procession formed up to lead the way, each most handsomely adorned in the garb of his choice. One had buckled on a belt, and was playing the soldier; a second had tucked up his cloak, and his high boots and spears identified him as a huntsman; a third was wearing gilded shoes, a silk gown, costly jewellery, and a wig, and was mincing along impersonating a woman; a fourth was conspicuous with greaves, shield, helmet, and sword; you would have thought that he was emerging from a school of gladiators. A fifth who made his appearance was guying a magistrate, with the rods of office and a purple toga; a sixth was pretending to be a philosopher with his cloak and staff, sandals, and a goatee beard. Two others were carrying different types of rod, the one playing the fowler with bird-lime, the other the angler with his hooks. I saw also a tame she-bear dressed up as a matron, being carried along in a chair, and a monkey in the woven cap and saffron garment that Phrygians wear, carrying a golden cup to ape the shepherd-boy Ganymede; and an ass with wings stuck to its shoulders ambling along beside a feeble old man, so that you might have labelled the one Pegasus and the other Bellerophon, and enjoyed a hearty laugh at both.

9   While the participants in these comic diversions for the townsfolk were prancing about here and there, the special procession in honour of the saviour goddess was being set in motion. Some women, sparkling in white dresses, delighting in their diverse adornments and garlanded with spring flowers, were strewing the ground with blossoms stored in their dresses along the route on which the sacred company was to pass. Others had gleaming mirrors attached to their backs to render homage to the goddess as she drew near them, and others with ivory combs gestured with their arms and twirled their fingers as if adorning and combing their queen's

tresses. Others again sprinkled the streets with all manner of perfumes, including the pleasing balsam-scent which they shook out in drops. Besides these there was a numerous crowd of both sexes who sought the favour of the creator of the celestial stars by carrying lamps, torches, tapers and other kinds of artificial light. Behind them came musical instruments, pipes and flutes which sounded forth the sweetest melodies. There followed a delightful choir of specially chosen youths clad in expensive white tunics, who kept hymning a charming song composed to music by a talented poet with the aid of the Muses; the theme incorporated chants leading up to the greater votive prayers to follow. In the procession too were flautists dedicated to the great god Sarapis; the pipes in their hands extended sideways to their right ears, and on them they repeatedly played the tune regularly associated with their temple and its god. There were also several officials loudly insisting that a path be cleared for the sacred procession.

10 Next, crowds of those initiated into the divine rites came surging along, men and women of every rank and age, gleaming with linen garments spotlessly white. The women had sprayed their hair with perfume, and covered it with diaphanous veils; the men had shaved their heads completely, so that their bald pates shone. With their rattles of bronze, silver, and even gold, they made a shrill, tinkling sound. Accompanying them were the stars of the great world-religion, the priests of the cult who were drawn from the ranks of famed nobility; they wore white linen garments which fitted tightly across their chests and extended to their feet, and they carried striking attributes of most powerful deities. Their leader held out a lamp gleaming with brilliant light; it did not much resemble those lanterns of ours which illumine our banquets at night, but it was a golden, boat-shaped vessel feeding quite a large flame from an opening at its centre. The second priest was similarly garbed; he carried in both hands the altar which they call the 'altar of help', a name specifically bestowed on it by the providential help of the highest goddess. A third priest advanced, bearing a palm-branch, its leaves finely worked in gold; he carried also the staff of Mercury. A

fourth priest exhibited a deformed left hand with palm outstretched, symbolizing justice; since it was impaired by nature and endowed with no guile or cunning, it was thought more suited to represent justice than the right hand. He also carried a small golden vessel rounded like a woman's breast, from which he poured libations of milk. A fifth priest bore a winnowing-fan of gold, fashioned from laurel-twigs, and a sixth carried an amphora.

11   Immediately behind marched gods who deigned to advance on human feet. Here was Anubis, the awesome go-between of gods above and subterranean dwellers; with face part-black, part-golden, tall and holding his dog's neck high, he carried a herald's staff in his left hand, and brandished a green palm-branch in his right. Hard on his heels followed a cow rearing upright, the fertile representation of the goddess who is mother of all; a member of the priesthood held it resting on his shoulders, and he bore it with a flourish and with proud gait. Another carried the box containing the mysteries and concealing deep within it the hidden objects of that august religion. Yet another priest bore in exultant arms the venerable image of the supreme deity. It was not in the shape of a farm-animal or bird or wild beast or the human form itself, but in its ingenious originality it inspired veneration by its very strangeness, for it expressed in a manner beyond description the higher religious faith which has to be cloaked in boundless silence. Fashioned from gleaming gold, this was a small vase skilfully hollowed out on a perfectly rounded base, with remarkable Egyptian figures fashioned on its outer surface; it had not a high neck, but it projected into a long spout extending into a beak. On its other side a handle was set well back in a broad curve, and above it was an asp coiled in a knot, the striped swelling of its scaly neck rearing high.

12   Suddenly the blessings promised by that most supportive deity came near. A priest approached bearing with him my future fortune and my very salvation. Exactly in keeping with the divine promise, his right hand held an adorned rattle for the goddess and a crown of flowers for me; the crown was fittingly, God knows, a crown of victory, for after enduring

countless exhausting toils and after surviving numerous hazards, I was now through the providence of the highest goddess overcoming Fortune, who had grappled with me so fiercely. But though seized with sudden joy, I did not bound forward at an uncontrolled gallop, for obviously I feared that the tranquil course of the ritual would be disturbed by the sudden charge of a four-footed beast. Hesitantly and with subdued steps such as a man might make, I gradually worked my body sideways, and crept slowly nearer as the crowd parted, doubtless at the command of the goddess.

13   What happened next made me realize that the priest recalled the divine message which he had received the previous night. He registered astonishment at how the task laid upon him had materialized; he halted abruptly, stretched out his right hand unprompted, and dangled the garland before my very face. Then in trembling haste (for my heart was beating wildly), I seized with greedy mouth the garland which gleamed with its texture of beautiful roses. I was eager to see the promise fulfilled, so with even greater eagerness I bolted it down. Nor was I cheated of that promise from heaven, for my ugly animal form at once deserted me. First my unsightly bristles disappeared, and then my thick skin thinned out; my fat belly contracted; the soles of my feet extended into toes where the hooves had been; my forefeet became hands equipped for two-footed tasks; my long neck shrank, my face and head became round, my projecting ears resumed their earlier modest shape; my rocklike teeth were restored to human size, and my tail, earlier the chief cause of my distress, totally disappeared.

The crowd stood amazed, and the devotees paid homage to the demonstrable power of the greatest deity and to this wonder-working which corresponded with the visions of the night; aloud and in unison as they raised their hands to heaven they acclaimed this notable kindness of the goddess.

14   As for me, total astonishment rendered me speechless. My mind was unable to contain so sudden and boundless a joy, and I dithered, wondering what it would be best for me to say first, and how I could make first use of my new-found voice;

what words I should use to launch auspiciously my tongue
reborn, and how and at what length I should express my
thanks to the great goddess. But the priest, who by some
divine inspiration was aware of all my calamities from the
start, took the initiative, though he too was deeply moved by
the extraordinary miracle. With a nod he signalled an
instruction to hand me a linen cloth to cover my nakedness,
for as soon as the ass had stripped me of his accursed skin, I
had jammed my thighs tightly together and placed my hands
discreetly over them. So far as a naked man could, I had used
nature's resources to cover myself decently. Thereupon one of
the consecrated band quickly tore off his upper garment and
hastily threw it over me. Then the priest, eyeing my
appearance with astonishment, gazed on me indulgently
with what I swear was a godlike look, and spoke these
words.

15   'Lucius, the troubles which you have endured have been
many and diverse. You have been driven before the heavy
storms and the heaviest gales of Fortune, but you have finally
reached the harbour of peace and the altar of mercy. Your
high birth, and what is more, your rank and your accomplished
learning have been of no avail to you whatever. In the green
years of youth, you tumbled on the slippery slope into slavish
pleasures, and gained the ill-omened reward of your unhappy
curiosity. Yet somehow Fortune in her blind course, while
torturing you with the most severe dangers, has in her random
persecution guided you to this state of religious blessedness.
So she can now head off and muster her most savage rage in
search of some other victim for her cruelty, for hostile chance
has no influence over those whose lives our majestic goddess
has adopted into her service. Have brigands, or wild beasts, or
slavery, or those winding, wholly crippling journeys to and
fro, or the daily fear of death been of any avail to Fortune's
malice? You have now been taken under the protection of
Fortune with eyes, who with the brilliance of her light lends
lustre even to the other gods. Show now a happier face in
keeping with your white garment, and join the procession of
the saviour goddess with triumphal step. Let unbelievers see

you, and as they see you let them recognize the error of their
ways; for behold, Lucius is delivered from his earlier
privations, and as he rejoices in the providence of the great
Isis, he triumphs over his Fortune. But to ensure your greater
safety under closer protection, enrol in this sacred army to
which you were invited to swear allegiance not long ago.
Consecrate yourself from this moment to the obedience of our
religion, and of your own accord submit to the yoke of service.
Once you have begun to serve the goddess, you will then
better appreciate the reward of your freedom.'

16   This was how that remarkable priest phrased his prophecy.
Then he fell silent, showing signs of weariness as he recovered
his breath. I then took my place in the sacred procession and
walked along, keeping close attendance on the sacred shrine. I
was recognized, indeed I was the cynosure of all eyes; the
whole community singled me out with pointing fingers and
nods, and gossiped about me: 'Today the venerable power of
the almighty goddess has restored him to the ranks of men.
How happy, how blessed three times over he is! Doubtless
through the purity and faith of his former life he has deserved
such sovereign protection from heaven, and in consequence he
had been in a manner reborn, and has at once pledged himself
to the service of her cult.'

Meanwhile amid the din of joyous prayers we edged our
way slowly forward and drew near to the sea-shore, at that
very place where as Lucius-turned-ass I had bivouacked the
previous day. There the gods' statues were duly set in place,
and the chief priest named and consecrated to the goddess a
ship which had been built with splendid craftsmanship, and
which was adorned on all its timbers with wonderful Egyptian
pictures. Holding a flaming torch, he first pronounced most
solemn prayers from his chaste lips, and then with an egg and
sulphur he performed over it an elaborate ceremony of
purification. The bright sail of this blessed craft carried upon
it woven letters in gold, bearing those same petitions for
trouble-free sailing on its first journeys. The mast was of
rounded pine, gloriously tall and easily recognized with its
striking masthead. The stern was curved in the shape of a

goose, and gleamed with its covering of gold leaf. In fact the whole ship shone, polished as it was in clear citrus-wood.

Then the entire population, devotees and uninitiated alike, vied in piling the ship high with baskets laden with spices and similar offerings, and they poured on the waves libations of meal soaked in milk. Eventually the ship, filled with generous gifts and propitious offerings, was loosed from its anchor-ropes and launched on the sea before a friendly, specially appointed breeze. Once its progress had caused it to fade from our sight, the bearers of the sacred objects took up again those which each had brought, and they made their eager way back to the temple, following in tidy order the same detail of procession as before.

17   Once we reached the temple itself, the chief priest, those who carried the gods' images, and those previously initiated into the august inner sanctuary were admitted into the chamber of the goddess, where they duly set in place the living statues. Then one of the company, whom they all termed the scribe, stood before the entrance and summoned an assembly of the *pastophori*; this is the name of the sacred college. There from a high dais he first recited from a book formulaic prayers for the prosperity of the great emperor, the senate, the knights, and the entire Roman people; then for sea-travellers and for ships journeying within the bounds of our imperial world. Next he announced in the Greek language and according to Greek ritual the ceremony of the launching of the ships. The applause of the people that followed showed that this speech was well received by all. Then the folk, ecstatic with joy, brought up boughs, branches and garlands, and having kissed the feet of the goddess (her statue, wrought from silver, was attached to the temple-steps), they departed to their homes. But my enthusiasm did not permit me to separate myself by more than a nail's breadth from that spot, and I gazed intently on the image of the goddess as I pondered my earlier misfortunes.

18   Meanwhile, however, swift Rumour had not been idle or slow in winging her way. She had been prompt in recounting throughout my native region that blessing of the provident

goddess which was so worthy of veneration, as well as my own remarkable history. As a result, family friends, household slaves, and my closest blood-relatives dispelled the grief which had afflicted them at the false report of my death, and in raptures of sudden joy they all hastened with various gifts, wishing to set eyes on me at once as one returned from the dead to the light of day. I had despaired of ever seeing them again, so I was likewise restored by their presence. I accepted their kind offerings with gratitude, for my friends had considerately ensured that I had a generous allowance to cover clothes and living expenses.

19   So I dutifully spoke to each of them, and briefly recounted my earlier hardships and my present joys. But then I made my way back to feast my eyes on the goddess, for this gave me the greatest delight. I rented a dwelling within the temple-precinct, and made a temporary home for myself there, devoting myself to the goddess in service as yet unofficial, but associating closely with the priests and constantly worshipping that great deity. No single night, no siesta passed which was not haunted with the vision and advice of the goddess. By numerous sacred commands she decreed that since I had been so inclined for some time, I should now at last undergo initiation. Though I was eager and willing, a kind of religious fear held me back, for I had carefully enquired about the difficulties of such religious service—the quite demanding abstinence prescribed by the rules of chastity, and the need to control with careful circumspection a life subject to many chance events. So through pondering these problems repeatedly I somehow kept postponing a decision, in spite of my enthusiasm.

20   One night the chief priest appeared to me in a dream, offering me an armful of gifts. When I asked the meaning of this, he replied that they had been sent to me as my belongings from Thessaly, and that there had also arrived from the same region a slave of mine by the name of Candidus. On awakening I pondered this vision long and repeatedly, wondering what it meant, especially as I was convinced that I had never had a slave of that name. But

whatever the prophetic dream portended, I thought that in
any case this offering of belongings gave promise of un-
doubted gain. So I was on tenterhooks, beguiled by this
prospect of greater profit as I awaited the morning opening of
the temple. The gleaming curtains were parted, and we
addressed our prayers to the august image of the goddess. The
priest made his rounds of the altars positioned there,
performing the liturgy with the customary prayers, and
pouring from a sacred vessel the libation-water obtained from
the sanctuary of the goddess. With the ceremony duly
completed, the initiates greeted the dawning of the day, and
loudly proclaimed the hour of Prime. Then suddenly the
slaves whom I had left at Hypata, when Photis had involved
me in those notorious wanderings, appeared on the scene. I
suppose that they had heard the stories about me; they also
brought back that horse of mine which had been sold to
various owners, but which they had recovered after recognizing
the mark on its back. This caused me to marvel more than
anything else at the perspicacity of my dream, for quite apart
from getting confirmation of its promise of profit, by its mention
of a slave Candidus it had restored to me my white horse.

21   This event made me perform my diligent service of worship
more conscientiously, for these present blessings offered a
pledge of hope for the future. Every day my longing to be
admitted to the mysteries grew more and more, and I
repeatedly greeted the chief priest with the most ardent
requests that he should at last initiate me into the secret rites
of the sanctified night. But he was in general a sober
character, well known for his adhesion to a strict religious
routine, and he treated me in the same way as parents often
restrain their children's untimely desires. In a gentle and kind
way he postponed my pressing request, whilst at the same
time calming my agitation with the comforting expectation of
a rosier future. He explained that the day on which a person
could be initiated was indicated by the will of the goddess,
that the priest who was to perform the sacred ritual was
chosen by the foresight of that same goddess, and in addition
the expenses necessary for the ceremonies were indicated in

the same instruction. His advice was that I, like the others, should observe all these rules with reverent patience. It was my duty to take stringent precautions against both over-enthusiasm and obstinacy, avoiding both faults so as not to hang back when summoned, nor to push forward unbidden. Not one individual in his community was so depraved in mind, or so enamoured of death as to undertake that ministry in a rash and sacrilegious spirit, without having received the call individually from his mistress; for that would incur a guilt that spelt death. Both the gates of hell and the guarantee of salvation lay in the control of the goddess. The act of initiation itself was performed as a rite of voluntary death and of salvation attained by prayer; indeed, it was the will of the goddess to select persons when their span of life was complete and they were poised on the very threshold of their final days. Such people could be safely entrusted with the profound mysteries of the sect. By her providence they were in some sense reborn, for she set them back on the course of renewed health. So I too was to submit to heaven's command, even though I had for long been named and designated for that blessed ministry by the notable and manifest favour of the great deity. Like the other worshippers, I should meanwhile abstain from profane and unlawful foods, to allow myself worthier access to the hidden secrets of that most hallowed religion.

22   Once the priest had pronounced on the issue, I did not mar my allegiance by impatience, but in humble peace and praiseworthy silence I concentrated on performing the service of the sacred cult with diligence for several days. The saving kindness of the powerful goddess did not fail or torture me with lengthy delay, but in the darkness of the night by commands by no means dark she clearly warned me that the day I had always desired had arrived, on which she would bestow on me my greatest ambition. She also explained how much I needed to contribute to pay for the ceremonies; and she appointed Mithras himself, her own high priest, to carry out the ritual, since she said that he was joined to me by some divine conjunction of our stars.

I was invigorated by these and the other kindly commands of the supreme goddess. Before it was fully daylight, I abandoned my bed and hurried straight to the priest's lodging. I met him with a greeting just as he was leaving his chamber. I had decided that I would demand initiation into the sacred rites more insistently than usual because it was now apparently my due. But as soon as he set eyes on me, he anticipated me with the words: 'Lucius, how lucky and blessed you are! The worshipful deity honours you so greatly with her kindly favour!' He added: 'So why now stand idle there, the cause of your own delay? The day for which you longed in your constant prayers has dawned, when at the divine commands of the goddess with many names you are to be admitted through my agency to the most holy mysteries of our sacred rites.' That most genial old man then put his hand in mine, and led me to the portals of that most splendid temple. He performed the task of opening the temple in accord with the solemn ritual, and performed the morning sacrifice. Then from a hidden recess in the shrine he extracted some books headed with unfamiliar characters. Some were in the shapes of every kind of animal, and served as summaries of formulaic phrases. Others were knotted and twisted into wheel-shapes, or intertwined like vine-tendrils at the top, to prevent their being read by inquisitive non-initiates. From these books the priest recited to me the preparations necessary for conducting the initiation.

23   At once I energetically made the necessary preparations regardless of expense. Some I purchased personally, and others through my friends. The priest now told me that the required moment had come, so he led me to the baths close by in company with a group of initiates. First I was ushered into the normal bath. Then the priest first asked for the gods' blessing, and cleansed me by sprinkling water all over me until I was wholly purified. I was then escorted back to the temple. Two-thirds of the day had now elapsed; the priest set me before the very feet of the goddess, and gave me certain secret instructions too sacred to divulge. Then he commanded me openly, for all to witness, to discipline my pleasures in

eating for the ensuing ten days, taking no animal flesh and drinking no wine.

I duly observed these commands with respectful self-discipline. The day now came which was appointed for my promise to the gods, and as the sun bent its course and ushered in the evening, suddenly crowds of initiates gathered from every side, and in accord with ancient custom they each paid me honour with a variety of gifts. Then all the non-initiates were removed to a distance. I was shrouded in a new linen garment, and the priest took my hand and led me into the heart of the sanctuary.

Perhaps the reader's interest is roused, and you are keen to enquire about the ensuing words and actions. I would tell you if it were permitted to reveal them; you would be told if you were allowed to hear. But both your ears and my tongue would incur equal guilt; my tongue for its impious garrulity, and your ears for their rash curiosity. I will not keep you long on tenterhooks, since your anxiety is perhaps motivated by religious longing. So listen, and be sure to believe that what you hear is true. I drew near to the confines of death and trod the threshold of Proserpina, and before returning I journeyed through all the elements. At dead of night I saw the sun gleaming with bright brilliance. I stood in the presence of the gods below and the gods above, and worshipped them from close at hand. Notice, then, that I have referred to things which you are not permitted to know, though you have heard about them. So I shall recount only what can be communicated without sacrilege to the understanding of non-initiates.

24   Morning came, and the rites were completed. I emerged sacramentally clothed in twelve garments. Though the clothing is quite germane to the ritual, there is no bar to my mentioning it, because at the time there were numerous persons present to see it. I took my stand as bidden on a wooden dais set before the statue of the goddess at the very heart of the sacred shrine. The linen garment that I wore made me conspicuous, for it was elaborately embroidered; the expensive cloak hung down my back from the shoulders to the heels, and from whatever angle you studied it, I was adorned

all round with multicoloured animals. On one side were Indian snakes, and on the other Arctic gryphons begotten by a world beyond this in the shape of winged birds. This garment the initiates call 'Olympian'. In my right hand I wielded a torch well alight; a garland of glinting palm-leaves projecting like the sun's rays encircled my head. When I was thus adorned to represent the sun and set there like a statue, the curtains were suddenly drawn back, and the people wandered in to gaze on me. Subsequently I celebrated a most happy birthday into the sacred mysteries; there was a pleasant banquet and a gathering of witty guests. There was also a third day of celebration with a similar programme of ceremonies, including a sacred breakfast and the official conclusion to the initiation.

For a few days I lingered on there, for I enjoyed the indescribable pleasure of gazing on the divine statue. I had pledged myself to Isis for the kindness which I could not repay. Finally, however, at the behest of the goddess I wound up my thanks, admittedly not expressed fully, but humbly and as far as my poor abilities allowed, and I prepared my long-delayed journey home. Even then the bonds of my most ardent yearning were hard to break. So finally I crouched before the image of the goddess, and for long rubbed her feet with my cheeks. With rising tears and frequent sobs I addressed her, choking on and swallowing my words.

25   'O holy, perennial saviour of the human race, you are ever generous in your care for mortals, and you bestow a mother's sweet affection upon wretched people in misfortune. No day, no period of sleep, no trivial moment hastens by which is not endowed with your kind deeds. You do not refrain from protecting mortals on sea and land, or from extending your saving hand to disperse the storms of life. With that hand you even wind back the threads of the Fates, however irretrievably twisted. You appease the storms raised by Fortune, and restrain the harmful courses of the stars. The gods above cultivate you, the spirits below court you. You rotate the world, lend the sun its light, govern the universe, crush Tartarus beneath your heel. The stars are accountable to you,

the seasons return at your behest, the deities rejoice before you, the elements serve you. At your nod breezes blow, clouds nurture the earth, seeds sprout, and buds swell. The birds coursing through the sky, the beasts wandering on the mountains, the snakes lurking in the undergrowth, the monsters that swim in the deep all tremble at your majesty. But my talent is too puny to sing your praises, and my patrimony is too meagre to offer you sacrificial victims; I have neither the richness of speech, nor a thousand mouths and as many tongues, nor an endless and uninhibited flow of words to express my feelings about your majesty. Therefore I shall be sure to perform the one thing that a pious but poor person can do: I shall preserve your divine countenance and your most holy godhead in the recess of my heart, and there I shall for ever guard it and gaze on it with the eyes of the mind.'

This was the sense of my prayer to the highest deity. I then embraced Mithras, the priest who was now my father. I clung to his neck and kissed him repeatedly; I begged him to pardon me for being unable to offer him worthy recompense for such great kindnesses.

26   After remaining for some time prolonging my words of thanks, I eventually parted from him. I hastened by the shortest route to set eyes once more after this long lapse of time on my ancestral home. A few days later the powerful goddess moved me to pack my bags in haste, and to board ship. I set out for Rome, and very quickly arrived safe and sound through the favour of a following wind at the harbour of Augustus. From there I speeded along by carriage, and on the evening of 12 December I reached the sacred city. After that there was no task which I undertook with greater enthusiasm than my daily prayers addressed to the supreme godhead of queen Isis, who is appeased with the utmost reverence under the title of Campensis, which is adapted from the location of her temple. In short, I became a regular worshipper there, a stranger to the shrine but an adherent of the cult. By now the great sun had completed his year's course through the circle of the zodiac, when the watchful care of the beneficent deity again broke into my sleep to advise me a second time of the

need for initiation and sacred ritual. I wondered what she was putting in hand, what coming event she was proclaiming. My surprise was natural, for I believed that my full initiation had been performed long ago.

27   As I debated this religious difficulty in my own mind, and further scrutinized it with the advice of initiates, I became aware of a new and surprising aspect: I had been initiated merely into the rites of the goddess, but had not as yet been enlightened by the sacred mysteries of that great god and highest father of the gods, the unconquered Osiris. The nature of this deity and his cult was closely aligned to, and in fact united with, hers, but there was the greatest difference in the mode of initiation. Hence I ought to consider that I was being asked to become the servant of this great god as well.

The issue did not for long remain undecided, for next night one of the initiates appeared in a dream before me clad in linen garments. He was bearing thyrsus-rods and ivy, and certain objects which must not be revealed. These he set before my household gods, and then settled himself on my chair, and gave notice of a sumptuous religious banquet. To allow me to recognize him by a clear identification-mark, he walked gingerly with hesitant step, for his left heel was slightly misshapen. In view of this clear intimation of the gods' will, the entire cloud of my uncertainty was dispelled. As soon as my early-morning respects to the goddess had been paid, I began to ask each and everyone with the greatest animation whether anyone had a walk as in my dream. Confirmation was forthcoming, for I at once set eyes on one of the *pastophori* who coincided exactly with the vision of the night, not only by the evidence of his foot, but also by the rest of his build and by his dress. I later discovered that he was called Asinius Marcellus, a name quite relevant to my transformation. I approached him there and then; he was well aware of what I was about to say, for he had been already similarly instructed to conduct the initiation. The previous night he had had a vision: while he was adorning the great god with garlands, he had heard from the statue's mouth (this is the means by which Osiris proclaims the future of individuals) that a man from

Madauros who was quite poor was being sent to him, and that he must at once initiate him into his divine rites. By the god's providence this man would gain fame in his studies, and the priest himself would obtain a rich reward.

28   This was how I pledged myself to the rite of initiation, but my slender means with which to meet expenses delayed my aspiration. The expense of travel had reduced my modest capital, and the cost of living in Rome greatly exceeded my outgoings in the province. Harsh poverty was therefore the stumbling-block; as the old proverb has it, I was trapped and tortured 'twixt axe and altar'. None the less, the god continued to put repeated pressure on me. To my great embarrassment there were frequent attempts to cajole me, and finally came the command direct. So I scraped up just enough money by parting with my paltry wardrobe. This had been the specific instruction I received: 'If you were embarking on some activity for pleasure, you would certainly not hesitate to part with your shabby clothes; so now that you are embarking on these noble rites, do you hesitate to resign yourself to a poverty which you can never regret?'

Therefore I made the detailed preparations; for a second time I happily confined myself to a meatless diet for ten days, and I also shaved my head. I gained enlightenment in the nocturnal mysteries of the highest god, and now with full assurance I regularly attended the divine services of this kindred religion. It brought the greatest consolation to me during my time abroad, and equally important, it furnished me with a more opulent standard of living. This was not surprising, for I made a little money in the courts by pleading in the Latin language, and was attended by the wind of favouring Success.

29   Only a short time elapsed when I was again confronted by unexpected and quite remarkable commands from the deities, compelling me to undergo yet a third initiation. At this point the concern that gripped me was not trivial; I was quite troubled in mind as with some anxiety I pondered these issues: what was the point of this strange, unprecedented instruction of the gods? I had now undergone initiation a

second time, so what was lacking to make it complete? 'I suppose', I reflected, 'that the two priests performed the ceremony in my case incorrectly or incompletely.' I swear that I even began to take a jaundiced view of their good faith. But while I tossed on the tide of such speculation, and was being driven to the point of madness, a kindly apparition of the god in a prophetic utterance at night explained the situation to me.

'You should not be apprehensive at this long series of initiations, or believe that some element has been previously omitted. On the contrary, you should be delighted and overjoyed at this continual favour of the deities. You should glory in the fact that on three occasions you will have a role scarcely granted once to any other mortal, and you can rightly believe that you will be ever blessed as a result of your three inductions. A further sacred initiation is necessary in your case, for as you must now reflect, the garb of the goddess which you donned in the province continues to rest in the temple there. The result is that here at Rome you cannot wear it for worship on feast days; when bidden you cannot appear in the radiance of those blessed vestments. So with joyful heart and at the prompting of the great gods you must be initiated once more, and I pray that this induction may be blessed and auspicious for you, and bring you saving help.'

30   In this way the majestic persuasion of the god-sent dream declared what I must do. So without relegating or idly deferring the business, I at once reported the gist of my vision to my priest. Without delay I submitted to the abstemious and meatless diet, and by voluntary abstinence I exceeded the period of ten days laid down by the eternal law. I made generous provision for the initiation, providing all that was required with religious zeal rather than by calculation of my possessions. I swear that I had no regrets whatever about the hardship and expense; there was no reason for such regrets, since the bountiful provision of the gods had now made me comfortably off through the legal fees I was receiving.

Only a few days later Osiris, the god preferred before great gods, highest of the greater deities, greatest of the highest, ruler of the greatest, seemed to bid me welcome during the hours of sleep. He had not transformed himself into any other human shape, but deigned to address me in person with his own august words. He told me not to hesitate to continue as now with my celebrated advocacy in the lawcourts, and not to fear the aspersions of malignant men nettled by the expertise in my legal activities which was attained by strenuous application. So that I should not be one of the rank and file attending to his rites, he appointed me to the college of the *pastophori* and also one of the quinquennial administrators. So I had my head completely shaved once more, and gladly performed the duties of that most ancient college, founded as long ago as the days of Sulla. I did not cover or conceal my bald head, but sported it openly wherever I went.

EXPLANATORY NOTES

BOOK 1

1.1   *Milesian mode*: Hanson persuasively suggests that the story opens 'as if in the middle of a literary discussion'. The epithet 'Milesian' connotes entertaining anecdote of a risqué kind. See further, S. Trenkner, *The Greek Novella in the Classical Period* (Cambridge, 1958), 172 ff.; T. Hägg, *The Novel in Antiquity* (Oxford, 1983), 186 ff. Apuleius lulls the reader into the belief that the romance is to be an entertainment and nothing more.

Egyptian paper . . . Nile: a teasing hint is being offered about Egyptian connections with the romance, which do not become fully explicit until the final book.

my antique stock: Apuleius now assumes the persona of Lucius, as if on stage (see Introd. § IV). The claim to wholly Greek blood, and to ancestral connections with the leading Greek cities of Athens, Corinth, and Sparta, is to be referred to Lucius the I-narrator, not to Apuleius. It is not until 11. 27 that Apuleius of Madauros merges himself with his hero Lucius.

circus-rider: the image of the circus-rider leaping from one horse to another may signify the technique of inserting anecdotes or additional episodes into the frame of the Greek story. See Introd. §§ III–IV.

it will delight you: for the problems of identifying the spokesman in this introductory chapter, see n. 23 to the Introduction.

1.2   *Sextus*: the apparently casual reference to Sextus, tutor of Verus (co-emperor, 161–9), and to his uncle Plutarch, who in his *De Iside* reconciles Isiac worship with the philosophy of Plato, is important in the development of the fable; see Introd., p. xxxi.

1.4   *Painted Porch*: this was the covered colonnade adorned with paintings which was situated by the Athenian agora, and was the site of the Stoic school. There is an additional hint here of the philosophical connections of the hero Lucius.

the god carries round with him: the god of healing, Asclepius, is conventionally represented in art with a staff round which a serpent is entwined.

1.5 *sun-god*: for the oath by the sun, cf. Homer, *Il.* 3. 277.

Aegium: this city, one of the leaders of the Achaean League, lay in the Peloponnese immediately south of the Corinthian Gulf. Some modern translators confuse it with Aegina.

Lupus: 'Mr Wolfe', a name suggesting the business predator.

1.6 *Socrates*: doubtless the name is intended to be ironical, in view of the lack of practical wisdom which he demonstrates.

Aristomenes: the name, reserved for the heart of the story, has again an ironical ring, since it means 'One of heroic strength'.

1.7 *Larissa*: an ancient town on the river Peneius, lying directly on the route southward from Macedonia.

Meroë: the significance of the name is disputed. Some suggest a connection with the word for unmixed wine (*merum*), because of the traditional association of witches with drinking. Others less cogently see a coded reference to Isiac worship, because the island of Meroë in the Nile had a temple to Isis (Juvenal, 6. 527, 13. 163).

1.8 *She can . . . light up hell itself*: with this catalogue of disorders in nature achieved by witchcraft, compare Lucan 6. 461 ff.

Ethiopians . . . Antipodeans: 'Both lots of Ethiopians' connote dwellers at the eastern and western bounds of the world. Cf. Homer, *Od.* 1. 23 f.; J. Y. Nadeau, *CQ* (1970), 339 ff., esp. 347. The reference to Antipodeans may have been awakened by Plato, *Timaeus*, 63a and Plutarch 869c.

1.9 *elephant*: elephants take 22 months to bring forth their young, but popular belief extended the pregnancy to ten years; cf. Pliny, *NH* 8. 28.

1.10 *Medea*: in Euripides' *Medea*, Jason decided to desert Medea in favour of Creon's daughter. In revenge Medea sent the bride a present of a cloak which fastened on her flesh, and a crown from which issued a stream of devouring fire (line 1186).

1.12 *Panthia*: the name connotes 'All-divine'.

Endymion: the young hunter solicited nightly by Selene (the moon; cf. Plato, *Phaedo* 72c, Cicero, *Tusc.* 1. 92, etc.).

Ganymede was plucked from Mt. Ida by an eagle to become Jupiter's cup-bearer (Ovid, *Met.* 10. 155 ff. etc.).

Ulysses: for the classic account of Odysseus' departure from Calypso, see Homer, *Od.* 5.

1.13 *be sure not to float away*: others render *caue . . . transeas* in the positive sense ('Take care to travel back to the sea'). My translation regards it as an instruction to stop the flow of blood and not to float away upon it.

urine: in addition to the humiliation which the gesture imposes on Aristomenes, such urination could be a magical practice to prevent him making his escape; cf. Petronius, *Sat.* 57.

1.16 *my dear little bed*: it has frequently been noted that the address to the bed parodies a Roman prayer (see e.g. Scobie's edition of Book I). Evocation of Sallust, *Jug.* 14. 22 has also been suggested.

1.18 *disturbing dreams*: cf. Cicero, *Div.* 1. 60.

1.20 *elegant tale*: this story of Aristomenes and Socrates does not appear in *Lucius or the Ass* (henceforward *Onos*); it is part of the patterning of the fable introduced by Apuleius himself. Ironically, Lucius accepts the truth of the story but fails to apply the lessons of Socrates' sexual submission and Aristomenes' curiosity (see 1. 12 above) to his own circumstances.

1.21 *Milo*: in the *Onos* the host is named Hipparchus. He is by no means as miserly as Milo; Apuleius has developed the comic characterization considerably.

Demeas: the man's name in the *Onos* is Decrius Decrianos. Apuleius may have chosen the name Demeas to evoke Demea, the stern parent in Terence's *Adelphi* who closely superintends his son's behaviour.

1.22 *Corinth*: Lucius here specifies his native region; cf. also 2. 12. In the *Onos*, he hails from Patrae. H. J. Mason, *Phoenix* (1971), 165, suggests that Apuleius designates Corinth to evoke the permissive society which Lucius finally renounces.

1.23 *Hecale*: King Theseus was entertained by the aged Hecale before he joined combat with the bull of Marathon (cf. Plutarch, *Theseus*, 14). The fact that Lucius' father bears the same name perhaps suggests that he is an Athenian.

Photis: in the *Onos* the maid's name is Palaestra ('Miss Wrestling-ground'), a title associated with prostitutes. Photis evokes the Greek word for light, not so much connoting 'the dangerous light of eroticism and magic' (so Lancel, *AHR* (1961), 146) as identifying her as the counterpart of Lucius, whose name evokes *lux* in Latin.

1.24 *twenty denarii*: there are 4 sesterces to the denarius, so that the price was reduced to 80 sesterces.

tomorrow: no such intimation is made next day to Pythias; this is one of the many loose ends in the romance.

aedile: the aedile's duty included supervision of the market.

1.25 *this performance*: this episode at the market does not appear in the *Onos*, and has almost certainly been inserted by Apuleius himself. Some scholars (G. Drake, *Papers in Language and Literature* (1969), 356; P. Grimal, *RÉA* (1971), 343 ff.) see it as a coded reference to Isiac ritual, but it is better regarded as literary entertainment, recalling satirical treatments of the lordly behaviour of municipal magistrates (cf. Horace, *Sat*, 1. 5. 34 ff., Juvenal, 10. 100 ff.).

BOOK 2

2.3 *Plutarch's household*: n. on 1.2 above, *Sextus*.

Byrrhena: in the *Onos*, the lady is called Abroea.

2.4 *rock*: reading *rupe* for *rure* in *F* and Robertson.

Actaeon . . . Diana: the significance of this description of the statuary (absent from the *Onos*) now becomes clear. Actaeon was changed into a stag because he gazed with curiosity on Diana's naked form; this is a warning to Lucius about the dangers of curiosity, which he disregards with the catastrophic result of transformation into an ass. Byrrhena's next remark, 'All that you see is yours', is therefore charged with irony.

2.5 *the goddess*: Diana, represented in the statuary, is identified with Hecate, goddess of witchcraft.

Pamphile: the name means 'lover of all'; in the *Onos* the witch is not named. The parallel between the *libido* of Pamphile and that of Meroë in Aristomenes' story in Book I should be noted.

2.7 *slices of meat*: a further dish is mentioned here, but the Latin is hopelessly corrupt.

stood to attention: there is a joking reminiscence of Virgil, *Aen.* 2. 774 here: 'obstipui, steteruntque comae.'

2.8 *criterion of beauty*: an autobiographical element may intrude here. In his *Apology* 4. 11, Apuleius defends himself against the charge of playing the dandy with his long hair. His obsessive interest in hair emerges again at 5. 22 and 11. 3 in descriptions of the hair of Cupid and Isis. See J. Englert and T. Long, *CJ* (1972–3), 236 ff.

that belt of hers: for the belt of Aphrodite/Venus, see Homer, *Il.* 14. 215 ff., where its effect is detailed when Hera borrows it to have her way with Zeus.

Vulcan: Venus' marital relations with Vulcan are not always idyllic, but doubtless Apuleius has in mind Virgil, *Aen.* 8. 369 ff., where Vulcan is a slave to her charms.

2.11 *Lake Avernus*: the entry-point to Hades on the Bay of Naples (Virgil, *Aen.* 6. 237 ff.).

2.12 *Corinth*: see n. on 1.22 above, *Corinth*.

Chaldaean visitor: the Chaldaeans, dwelling close to the Persian Gulf, had such fame as astrologers that their name became synonymous with the profession; hence this visitor need not have been a foreigner.

several books: Apuleius sports with the reader, who is enjoying the 'unbelievable tale'.

2.13 *Diophanes*: the name suggests 'prophesying through Jupiter'.

Cerdo: 'Mr Profit'.

fee for the prophecy: the fee is high when we recall that Lucius paid only 20 denarii for his fish at 1. 24.

2.16 *hot water*: for this regular practice in antiquity, cf. e.g. Horace, *Odes* 3. 19. 6.

fetials: the college of fetials, 20 in number, had the formal task of declaring war on behalf of the Roman state; see *OCD*, 'Fetiales'.

2.17 *She even ... concealment*: she skittishly imitates the pose of Venus rising from the waves, a favourite subject in ancient art.

2.18 *taking the auspices*: Lucius describes the love-engagement in the language of military metaphor, as the Roman love-elegists do. Just as a Roman commander consulted the gods before battle by taking the auspices, so Lucius consults Photis before departure.

2.20 *Thelyphron*: the point of the name ('With a Woman's Mind') becomes clear in 2. 23, where Thelyphron depicts himself as a manly figure, but the bubble is later pricked.

2.21 *Miletus*: the city is chosen as the provenance of the story-teller because of its association with the Milesian tale; see n. on 1.1 above, *Milesian mode*.

celebrated province: the phrase suggests that Thessaly was still part of Achaea (it was joined to Macedonia in the Antonine period). But this is no index either to the date of composition or indeed to the date of the *mise-en-scène* at Larissa, since Thelyphron is recounting an incident of some years earlier.

2.22 *sun-god . . . Justice*: the sun (Apollo) and Justice (Themis or Dike) were associated at Delphi; see Pausanias, 10. 5.

gold pieces: the *aureus* was worth 25 denarii or 100 sesterces; see n. on 2.13 above, *fee for the prophecy*, to evaluate the comparative value of the proposed fee.

2.23 *Harpies*: these grisly creatures, half-bird half-woman, symbolically describe the rapacious witches of Thessaly.

Lynceus . . . Argus: Lynceus was an Argonaut famed for his keen sight (cf. e.g. Horace, *Epistles*, 1. 1. 28). Hundred-eyed Argus was commissioned by Juno to keep watch on Io, whom she had spitefully changed into a heifer when Jupiter impregnated her (Ovid, *Met.* 1. 625 ff.).

2.25 *in the garden*: reading *in hortulos* (Helm; *mosculos F*; *musculos* Robertson).

god of Delphi: Apollo, famed for his prophetic powers.

2.26 *Philodespotus*: 'Master-lover'.

future misfortune: Thelyphron's friendly offer was interpreted as a suggestion that there would be further corpses to guard.

Aonian: 'Aonian' is a learned term for 'Boeotian'; the reference is to Pentheus of Thebes, who in Euripides' *Bacchae* was torn to pieces for showing contempt to Dionysus. The Pipleian poet Orpheus (the adjective refers to his haunt near

Pieria, the Macedonian spring sacred to the Muses) suffered a similar fate.

2.28 *Zatchlas*: the introduction of the Isiac priest, the meaning of whose name is obscure (for possible interpretations, see Gwyn Griffiths, *Apuleius of Madauros*, 39 and 351; G. Drake, *Papers in Language and Literature*, 12), explains why Apuleius has incongruously stitched this surprise ending on to the tale of Thelyphron's mutilation. That main story is clearly a further warning to Lucius not to dabble in the occult; Zatchlas' raising of the corpse is to be visualized as contrapuntal to the vicious practices of the witches (so J. Tatum, *TAPA* (1969), 501) and a demonstration of the proper application of magical powers.

Coptus . . . Memphis . . . Pharos: the shrine of Coptus in upper Egypt had a god Min sometimes regarded as the son of Isis (Gwyn Griffiths, *Apuleius of Madauros*, 211). Isis herself had a shrine at Memphis. For the connection of Isis with Pharos, the island off Alexandria with the famous lighthouse, see Gwyn Griffiths, 43 (with bibliography). The rattle formed part of the appurtenances of Isis.

2.29 *Furies*: Apuleius perhaps evokes Lucan, 6. 719 ff. There the witch Erichtho recalls to life a soldier slain at Pharsalus; when he is as reluctant as the husband here. Erichtho summons the Furies Tisiphone and Megaera.

2.31 *joyful ritual*: though links have been suggested with the cult of Gelōs at Sparta mentioned by Plutarch (*Lys.* 25. 4; *Cleom.* 30. 1), or with the Roman festival of the Hilaria (D. S. Robertson, *JHS* (1919), 114) this Festival of Laughter is probably a purely imaginary one, invented to serve the purpose of his story by Apuleius; it further underlines the dangers of magic which Lucius continues to disregard.

flowing mantle: the joke reads lamely in English. It was the custom to deck out statues of the gods on feast-days; Lucius proposes to adorn the god Laughter with a literary tribute.

2.32 *Geryon*: the three-formed Spanish giant, slain by Hercules as one of his twelve labours; see n. on 3.19 below. When Apuleius makes Byrrhena claim that the Festival of Laughter was inaugurated 'in the early days of the city' (ch. 31) he is perhaps evoking Evander's account of the festival of Hercules at Pallanteum in Virgil, *Aen.* 8.

BOOK 3

3.1 *Aurora*: parody of epic descriptions of daybreak ('Rosy-fingered Dawn' appears more than twenty times in Homer; cf. Virgil, *Aen.* 12. 77) is one of Apuleius' amusing literary pleasantries. The technique reappears in the eighteenth-century novels of Fielding and others.

fame: see 2.12 above.

3.2 *ceremonies of purifications*: in the ceremony of lustration preceding a sacrifice (*Amburbium*, round the city, *Ambarualia* round the fields; see R. M. Ogilvie, *The Romans and their Gods* (London, 1969), 88 f.), the victims were led round in procession.

They even . . . to observe the proceedings: compare Apuleius' description of the crowds thronging the theatre at Carthage (*Flor.* 16. 11 ff.).

3.3 *time allowed for speaking*: the clepsydra, a regular feature in Roman courts from the first century BC (see e.g. Cicero, *Brutus*, 324, *Fin.* 4. 1; Pliny, *Ep.* 2. 11. 14), is described to lend comic verisimilitude to the trial.

addressed the assembly: as part of this literary entertainment, Apuleius presents two high-flown forensic utterances. For analysis of them, see van der Paardt's Commentary, ad loc.

3.7 *Sun . . . Justice*: see 2.22 and n. ad loc., *sun-god . . . Justice*.

3.9 *a wheel*: for the wheel as a Greek mode of torture, cf. Cicero, *Tusc.* 5. 24.

Proserpina and Orcus: the deities of the underworld.

3.11 *in honour of Laughter*: see n. on 2.31 above, *joyful ritual*.

statue: throughout his romance, Apuleius playfully incorporates autobiographical touches into Lucius' portrayal; for similar distinctions of statues granted to him, see *Flor.* 16; Augustine, *Ep.* 138. 19.

3.12 *the deity*: this is Risus, god of laughter.

3.15 *sacred cults*: there is more autobiographical intrusion here; Apuleius boasts of being initiated into Greek cults at *Apol.* 55, whereas Lucius elsewhere makes no such claim until he is initiated as Isis' votary in the final book.

3.17 *eastern side*: the eastern side, facing the rising sun, is especially important in magic; cf. 2.28 above.

unintelligible letters: these are the *tabellae defixionum*, tablets inscribed with *carmina* to entice a lover; cf. Virgil, *Ecl.* 8. 66 ff.

3.18 *mad Ajax*: in the *Ajax* of Sophocles, the hero is demented by the award of the arms of Achilles to Odysseus, and he slaughters a flock of sheep under the delusion that they are the Greek leaders.

utricide: 'A Skin-slayer'.

3.19 *Hercules' twelve labours*: for the twelve labours of Hercules, including the slaughter of the three-formed giant Geryon and the bringing up to the upper world of the three-headed Cerberus, see Ovid, *Met.* 9. 182 ff.

the embraces of matrons: Lucius' claim that he has previously spurned the embraces of matrons indicates a descent into sensuality in succumbing to the charms of Photis. In the patterning of his sinning, the 'servile pleasures' of sex precede his witnessing of magic; both are condemned by the priest of Isis at 11.15 as the cause of his sufferings.

3.21 *an owl*: for similar transformations by magic into birds, cf. Ovid. *Met.* 14. 388 ff., *Amores* 1. 8. 13.

3.22 *axe my own limbs*: this proverbial expression is equivalent to 'cutting one's own throat'; cf. Petronius, *Sat.* 74.

two-legged Thessalian wolves: the *lupulae* are the nymphomaniac witches who could gain control over Lucius if he became a bird.

3.26 *nefarious and abominable woman*: it is important to note that Photis the sex-object is responsible for Lucius' fall from grace; Apuleius stresses that Lucius has no regard for the girl beyond the sexual satisfaction she affords him.

hospitality and a decent lodging: the Latin (*loca lautia* are the hospitable lodgings afforded to visiting ambassadors at Rome) registers a mild joke impossible to reproduce in English.

Jupiter . . . Faith: for Jupiter as god of hospitality, see Ovid, *Met.* 10. 224; also 7.16 below. Faith (Fides) his companion is said to have quitted the earth with other deities at Juvenal, 6. 1 ff.

3.27 *Epona*: for this goddess, cf. Juvenal, 8. 157; she was prominent in Africa, where she was connected especially with beasts and their grooms (cf. Tertullian, *Apol.* 16; Minucius Felix, *Oct.* 28. 7).

For how long: apparently in parody of the exordium to Cicero's First Catilinarian.

3.29 *Jupiter whom we all know*: Robertson (*PCPS* 1926, 133 ff.) suggests that this refers to Caesar just invoked, but this is not borne out by what follows.

the bit: reading *frena* with Puteanus in preference to *faena* (Robertson; *foena F*) which is rarely found in the plural.

BOOK 4

4.2 *Success*: the Romans deified many abstract concepts. Apuleius may have had in mind Varro's invocation to the gods of country life in the exordium to his *Res Rusticae* (1. 1. 6), where Bonus Euentus is hymned—'without whom there is frustration, not cultivation'. Cf. also the statue of the goddess mentioned by Pliny, *NH* 34. 77.

laurel-roses: probably *nerium oleander* rather than the modern rhododendron; for its noxious effect on cattle, cf. Pliny, *NH* 16. 79, 24. 90.

4.4 *compassionate discharge*: Apuleius uses the Latin term (*causaria missio*) humorously to amuse his Roman audience. The *causarii* were soldiers invalided out of the army (Livy 6. 6. 14).

4.6 *subject and occasion demand*: this is parody of the conventional exordium used by historians when describing the location of an operation; cf. Sallust, *Jug.* 17. 1; Livy 26. 42. 7.

reception room: the atrium of a Roman house was the reception-room into which a guest first entered. Apuleius humorously suggests that the sheep-pen served this purpose for the robbers' cave.

4.8 *Centaurs at table*: reading *Centaurisque cenantibus* (Helm; *tebcinibus Centaurisque F, Centaurisque semihominibus* Robertson). For the feast of Perithous, king of the Lapiths, a Thessalian tribe, see Homer, *Od.* 21. 295 ff., Ovid, *Met.* 12. 210 ff.

eight feet richer: a comic formulation for the acquisition of Lucius-turned-ass and his horse.

Lamachus: a famous Athenian general of this name fought in the Sicilian expedition during the Peloponnesian War (cf. Thucydides, 6. 8. 2, 6. 101. 6). The name is jokingly attached to the bandit-leader.

4.9 *seven gates*: 'Seven-gated' was the traditional epithet for Thebes in epic (Homer, *Il.* 4. 406, *Od.* 11. 263, etc.), another literary pleasantry.

Chryseros: 'Mr Gold-lover.'

public services and shows: for this duty imposed on wealthy Greek citizens, cf. *OCD*, 'Liturgy'.

4.11 *the sea*: in burying Lamachus at sea, Apuleius appears to have forgotten that the bandits' operation was inland at Thebes; in addition, he may be evoking Thucydides 2. 43. The 'entire element' is water, one of the four elements.

4.12 *Alcimus*: 'Mr Valiant'.

rib-cage . . .: parody of Virgil, *Aen.* 12. 508 is evident here.

4.13 *Demochares*: 'Mr People-pleaser'.

4.14 *Eubulus*: emending *Babulus* (*F*; 'Mr Babbler') to Eubulus ('Mr Good-Counsellor') with Bursian and Robertson. Some scholars suggest that the episode of the bear-impersonation that follows parodies Virgil's account of the Wooden Horse in *Aen.* 2; see most recently S. A. Frangoulidis, *PP* (1991), 95 ff.

4.15 *Thrasyleon*: 'Mr Bold-Lyon'.

4.16 *Nicanor*: the name ('Victorious') is not significant, as Nicanor's role is minor.

4.20 *Cerberus*: the three-headed dog guarding the entrance to the underworld represents by metonymy Hades itself.

4.21 *We repeatedly reflected*: such laments for the departure of deities from the world are a frequent feature in earlier literature. See Hesiod, *WD* 200 (the departure of Aidos); Catullus, 64. 384 ff.; Juvenal, 6. 1 ff.

4.22 *Salian priests*: the luxurious feasts enjoyed by these priests of Mars were proverbial; cf. Cicero, *Att.* 5. 9. 1; Horace, *Odes*, 1. 37. 2, etc.

4.26 *Attis or Protesilaus*: Attis, votary of the goddess Cybele, was prevented from marrying by being castrated by the goddess;

see Ovid, *Fasti*, 4. 221 ff. with Frazer's note. Protesilaus' marriage to Laodamia was cut short when he was summoned to fight at Troy, where he was the first Greek to die (Ovid, *Met.* 12. 68).

4.28 *They would . . . upright thumb*: this was the gesture of adoration known as *proskunēsis* (cf. Apuleius, *Apol.* 56).

sprung from . . . frothing waves: for the myth of the birth of Venus, see Hesiod, *Theog.* 195 ff. There is a play on the name Aphrodite and the Greek word for foam (*aphros*).

4.29 *Paphos, Cnidos . . . Cythera*: these were centres of traditional worship of Aphrodite in Cyprus, Asia Minor, and off the coast of the Peloponnese respectively. At this point Apuleius visualizes the locale of the story as mainland Greece.

soliloquy: the physical manifestations of Venus' anger are described with evocations of Poseidon's fury in the *Odyssey* (5. 285) and Juno's in the *Aeneid* (7. 292).

4.30 *Here am I . . .*: the angry soliloquy is a composite of Lucretius, 1. 2 and Virgil, *Aen.* 7. 308 ff.

shepherd: this was Paris, who in the contest on Mt. Ida preferred the beauty of Aphrodite to that of Hera and Athena (cf. Paus. 5. 19. 1). He received Helen as his reward, and thereby brought on Troy the hostility of the spurned goddesses.

4.31 *the host of Venus' companions*: for the Nereids, Homer, *Il.* 18. 37 ff., Virgil, *Aen.* 5. 285 f.; Portunus, the old god of harbours, Cicero, *ND* 2. 26, Ovid, *Fasti*, 6. 547 (equating him with Palaemon); Salacia, Roman goddess of the sea-waves, Varro, *LL* 5. 72; Palaemon, the Greek sea-god, Cicero, *ND* 3. 39, Virgil, *Aen.* 5. 283; Tritons, attendants of Neptune, Virgil, *Aen*, 5. 824, etc.

4.32 *Milesian tale*: though the old hag is depicted as telling the story, Apuleius destroys the dramatic illusion with this genial reference to himself. Mention of the Milesian Tale, echoing the introductory chapter to the romance, preserves the mask of entertainment over the hidden purpose of edification; see Introduction p. xxiv ff.

4.33 *Lydian mode*: see 10.32 and n.

BOOK 5

5.6   *sacrilegious curiosity*: this key-phrase in the *conte* (and in the romance as a whole) made a deep impression on Apuleius' fellow-countryman Augustine; see my paper in *G&R* (1988), 73 ff.

5.8   *golden house*: perhaps evoking the celebrated palace of Nero at Rome.

5.9   *bars and chains*: at the outset of the story, the sisters had contracted 'splendid marriages' (4.32). Such inconsistencies reflect the author's tendency to write for the moment, here to underline the sisters' jealousy.

5.11 *he will be mortal*: the child when born proves to be female (6.24), another inconsistency.

5.17 *monstrous dragon*: this is a highly Virgilian snake; see especially *Georg.* 3. 425 ff.
      Pythian oracle: here referring to the oracle at Miletus (see 4.32), not at Delphi. Apollo ('Pythian' because he slew the dragon Python) was the god common to both.

5.24 *slipped down to earth exhausted*: the Platonist flavour of the *conte* is at its most pronounced here, when Psyche (the soul) aspires to union with the divine but is weighed down by the body (*Phaedrus*, 248c is close).

5.26 *take your goods and chattels with you*: Apuleius here uses the formal terms for divorce ('tibi res tuas habeto'; cf. Gaius, 24. 2. 2) and for the solemn form of marriage (*confarreatae nuptiae*) to divert his Roman readers.

5.27 *fell ... in the same way*: the deaths of the sisters can be visualized in the Platonist sense as the sloughing-off of bodily attachments, as Psyche seeks to attain union with the divine.

5.29 *your father's estate*: these are further technical pleasantries with which Apuleius regales his learned Roman readers. It was perfectly possible in Roman law for a mistress to adopt a slave; cf. F. Norden, *Apuleius und das römische Privatrecht* (Leipzig, 1912), 74.

5.30 *stepfather*: Apuleius makes humorous play with Venus' marital problems. Though married to the lame Vulcan, she had a liaison with Mars during which the couple were caught red-handed by the angry husband (cf. Ovid, *Met.* 4. 171 ff., *AA* 2. 561 ff.).

insult . . . expiated: the abusive comments heaped by Venus on Cupid here, and the ensuing conversation with Ceres and Juno, evoke the scene in Apollonius Rhodius, 3. 93 ff., where Hera and Athena are the participants.

BOOK 6

6.2   *begged Ceres' favour*: Demeter/Ceres was the deity at the centre of the Eleusinian mystery-religion. Psyche's litany here incorporates references to the myth of Proserpina, daughter of Ceres, who was borne off by Dis in his chariot ('the car which snatched') and imprisoned in Hades ('the earth which latched') during each winter, but was allowed to return to earth each summer. The myth symbolizes the death and rebirth also enacted in the case of Lucius in the liturgy of Isis in the final book.

6.4   *Sister and spouse . . .*: the litany to Juno envisages her syncretistically. Her Greek counterpart Hera has ancient connections with Samos and Argos (see *OCD*, Hera), and she is identified with the Carthaginian tutelary goddess Tanit. The river-god at Argos, Inachus, was the father of Io, whose myth was enacted in the liturgy of Isis. Juno's Greek title ('Yoking Goddess') and her Latin name 'Lucina' signal her roles as goddess of marriage and of childbirth respectively.

legislation: again the learned joke. Such legislation was enshrined in Roman law; see Introduction, n. 15.

6.6   *Heaven admitted his daughter*: Venus is the daughter of the sky-god Ouranos/Jupiter; in Apuleius' philosophical vision, as a lesser deity she lives on a lower level than her father.

6.7   *Jupiter . . . did not refuse her*: the sportive evocation of Homer, *Il.* 1. 528 is noteworthy here.

6.8   *metae Murciae*: this was the 'Murcian turning-point' in the Circus Maximus at Rome, so called because it was close to the temple of Venus Murcia. The indifference to geographical coherence (hitherto the action has centred on Greece and the Aegean) in the interests of momentary joking for a Roman audience is characteristic.

Habit: so called because 'Habit furthers love' (Lucretius, 4. 1283),

Orcus: see 3.9 and n. ad loc.

6.13 *Cocytus*: the house of Venus, where this instruction is given, is situated close to Taenarus (see 6.18); this is the modern Cape Matapan at the southernmost point of the Peloponnese. Psyche enters the region of the dead from there. The waterfall feeds into the Stygian world below. The language here is Virgilian, drawing on *Aeneid*, 6 to evoke the *katabasis* of Aeneas (*Aen.* 6. 323, 327). The motif of drawing water is from Hesiod, *Theog.* 782 ff., where Zeus sends Iris for the water which seals the oaths taken by the gods.

6.15 *cupbearer to Jupiter*: for the eagle's rape of Ganymede from Mt. Ida, see Ovid, *Met.* 10. 155 ff.

6.19 throughout this section there are verbal evocations of Aeneas' journey through the underworld in *Aeneid* 6.

6.22 *former role*: Cupid is a schizoid character, now sober lover and now wanton boy. He reverts to this second persona to win Jupiter's support against Venus.

lex Iulia: this law, passed under Augustus in 18 BC, made adultery a criminal offence for the first time. See Jane F. Gardner, *Women in Roman Law and Society* (London, 1986), 127 ff.

You have transformed my . . . countenance: see Ovid, *Met.* 6. 103 ff. for these various shapes adopted by Jupiter as depicted on Arachne's tapestry.

6.23 *liable to a fine*: another playful touch: such fines for non-attendance were imposed in the senate at Rome and increased in the Augustan age; cf. Cassius Dio, 54. 18. 3, 55. 3. 2.

6.24 *his personal cup-bearer*: for Ganymede, see n. on 6.15 above.

Pleasure: for the connection implicit here with Lucius' 'pleasure beyond telling' in his mystical union with Isis, see 11.24 and Introduction, p. xl.

6.25 *I was standing close by*: in *Onos* 22, the bandits make only two journeys, and Lucius goes with them on the first. Apuleius describes three journeys, on the first of which Lucius does not go. This allows him to overhear the story of Cupid and Psyche, grafted by Apuleius on to the main story.

6.26 *fear had lent wings*: an evocation of Virgil, *Aen.* 8. 224.

6.27 *Dirce*: wife of the Theban king Lycus, was tied to the horns of a bull by Amphion and Zethus, sons of Antiope, because she had planned a similar punishment against their mother; see Hyginus, 7 f.

6.28 *four-footed gallop*: a reminiscence of Virgil, *Aen.* 11. 875.

6.29 *Phrixus etc.*: for the flight of Phrixus, who sought to escape from his stepmother on the back of a ram, see Hyginus, 2 f. For Arion on the dolphin, Herodotus, 1. 24; for Europa and the bull, Ovid, *Met.* 2. 833 ff. etc.

6.30 *Pegasus*: the winged horse, born from Medusa's blood when the Gorgon's head was severed by Perseus, and later ridden by Bellerophon to slay the Chimaera, is the theme of Ovid, *Met.* 4. 785 ff.

6.31 *The first ... second ... third*: these are the punishments prescribed in the *Digest* (48. 19, 16, 10) for captured bandits. The speakers propose punishments which they themselves would suffer if captured. See T. N. Habinek, 'Lucius' Rite of Passage', in *Materiali e discussioni per l'analisi dei testi classici* (Pisa, 1990), 66.

BOOK 7

7.5 *Haemus ... Theron*: the names are a play on Mt. Haemus, the Thracian mountain expressive of the brigand's height, and on the Greek verb to hunt, reflecting the father's profession.

7.6 *Plotina*: Apuleius may have chosen the name because of Hadrian's virtuous wife Pompeia Plotina (see Pliny, *Paneg.* 83 f.). Her childlessness, in contrast to the fecundity of this lady, could be interpreted as Apuleian humour. Others note the similarity to Hypsicratea, wife of Mithridates of Pontus in Val. Max. 6. 5.

Zacynthus: he was to spend his exile in this island off the west coast of Greece.

7.7 *Orcus*: see 3.9 and n. ad loc.

7.8 : in the abbreviated Greek version (*Onos* 26), there is no trace of this story of Plotina and the escape of 'Haemus', who is later to be revealed as Charite's bridegroom Tlepolemus. Apuleius may have inserted the story so that the reader can interpret it as a coded message to Charite that her ordeal with the bandits would soon be ended. Haemus' description of his escape on an ass is a possible pointer to Charite's later departure on the back of Lucius.

dowry: the word has ironical implications. The true commitment of 'Haemus' is to his bride Charite, not to the bandits.

7.10 *secretary of the robbers' chest*: the Latin phrase wittily evokes the imperial office of finance established by Hadrian; cf. *SHA*, Hadrian, 20, 6.

Salian priests: see 4.22 and n. ad loc.

7.11 *wine he had sampled*: for this as erotic practice, see Ovid, *Amores*, 1. 4. 33 f.

7.12 *Tlepolemus . . . Charite*: the names of the bridal couple, Tlepolemus ('Enduring Warrior') and Charite ('Grace') do not appear in the *Onos* and have probably been invented by Apuleius.

7.14 *Bactrian camel*: since the Bactrian camel has two humps, it was able to store more food than the Arabian species; see Aristotle, *Hist. Anim.* 498b–499a; Pliny, *NH* 8. 67.

7.16 *Jupiter*: see 3.26 and n. ad loc.

king of Thrace: this refers to Diomedes of Thrace, later fed to his own horses by Hercules; see Diodorus Siculus 4. 15. 3 f.

7.26 *Bellerophon*: by equating the traveller with Bellerophon, the ass comically identifies himself with Pegasus; see 6.30 and n. ad loc.

7.27 *the boy's mother burst into my stable*: Apuleius sets the scene for the incongruous Ciceronian oration to follow; see Introduction, p. xxix.

despicable manner: a reference to the *senatus consultum Silanianum* (AD 10), by which a slave was required to aid an endangered master (*Digest* 29. 5).

7.28 *Althea*: Ovid, *Met.* 8. 425 ff., describes how Meleager slew his mother's brothers, and how in revenge his mother Althea caused his death. The Fates had decreed that his life would end when a firebrand was burnt, and she thrust it into the fire.

BOOK 8

8.1 *historical narrative*: Apuleius deliberately undercuts the dramatic impact of his narrative with this preliminary announcement of the literary genre. For the sources of the story, see n. on 8.14 below.

Thrasyllus: 'Mr Desperado'. He is modelled on Sallust's Catiline; cf. *Cat.* 5 and 14 f.

8.6 *The crime . . . misfortune*: this description is virtually a mosaic of Virgilian phrases. Note especially the Virgilian Fama (Rumour) (cf. *Aen.* 4. 172 f., 195 f., 9. 474 f., 11. 139 ff.) and Charite's wild behaviour which evokes that of Dido (4. 298 ff.).

8.7 *Liber*: the Latin god Liber (equated with Dionysus/Bacchus) was the youthful deity of the vintage. Charite's choice of the god closest in appearance to her dead husband allows her to indulge in devotions to Tlepolemus which might otherwise scandalize her family and friends. Virgil's Dido likewise commemorates her husband Sychaeus in his own shrine (*Aen.* 4. 457 f.); perhaps Apuleius has also in mind the story of Protesilaus and Laodamia; see B. L. Hijmans, *Mnem.* (1986), 358 f.

8.8 *his name*: see n. on 8.1 above, *Thrasyllus*.

disclose his unspeakable treachery: there is no need to assume that Thrasyllus divulges his role as assassin. It is merely the proposal of marriage that disquiets her; his part in the death of her husband is revealed to her later in her dream.

the shade of Tlepolemus: the Virgilian evocation continues; compare Sychaeus' appearance in a dream to Dido at *Aen.* 1. 353 ff.

8.9 *months still to elapse*: the period of mourning prescribed for a husband's death varied between ten months and a year; see the Groningen commentary (ed. Hijmans etc.) on this book.

8.13 *Dry your untimely tears . . .*: compare Dido's farewell speech at *Aen.* 4. 653 ff.

8.14 : this tragic story of Charite has been introduced by Apuleius, for in the Greek version she and her husband are accidentally drowned (*Onos* 34). Several themes from earlier literature have been stitched together to compose the story.

The hunting episode evokes the Atys story in Herodotus 1. 34 ff., and the Adonis story in Ovid, *Met.* 10. 710 ff. Charite's reactions are modelled on those of the demented Dido (see nn. on 8.6, 7, 13 above). Plutarch, *Mul. Virt.* 257 e–f has the similar story of the murdered husband and the wife Camma's revenge. The scene at the tomb is reminiscent of Haemon's behaviour in Sophocles, *Antigone* 1231 ff. (note the Haemus–Haemon coincidence). Apuleius exhibits his literary virtuosity.

8.16 *Pegasus*: see 6.30 and n. ad loc.

8.17–18 : neither this nor the following anecdote appears in the *Onos*; Apuleius, it seems, has inserted them to depict the hostile world into which Lucius has fallen as punishment for his sin.

8.22 *I am eager to recount it:* this story too bears all the marks of an Apuleian insertion; the intermingled themes of marital infidelity and magic recall the twin failings of Lucius.

8.23 *famous town*: in the *Onos*, the town is Beroia in Macedonia, but Apuleius leaves the itinerary vague since he is to diverge from the Greek version at the forthcoming climax.

jokes about my prospects: for Apuleius' literate readers the joking includes parody of Cicero's exordium in his First Catilinarian.

braying, worn-out sieve: *ruderarium cribrum*: *ruderarium* ('rubbishy') has the punning connotation of 'braying' (from *rudere*); the two meanings are impossible to combine in one word in English. The sieve would be made from the ass's hide.

8.24 *Syrian goddess*: this is Atargatis, whose cult was widespread in Greece from the third century BC onward. An inscription to her has been found at Beroia (see note on 8.23, *famous town*, above). By the first century AD the cult had reached Rome, for Nero became a follower (Suetonius, *Nero*, 56).

virile: Cappadocia was renowned for virile men (Petronius, 63. 5). There is sexual innuendo in this remark to the catamite priest.

census: Roman citizens were required to register for tax purposes.

Cornelian law: no such *lex Cornelia* forbidding the sale of citizens as slaves is known; it is probably 'un nom de fantaisie' (Vallette in the Budé edition, ad loc.)

8.25 *Syrian goddess . . . Adonis*: for the Syrian goddess, see note on 8.24 above. Sabazius was a Phrygian–Thracian deity with functions similar to those of Dionysus (Cicero, *ND* 3. 58 with Pease's note). Bellona was the Roman goddess of war. The Idaean Mother is Cybele, the Magna Mater whose priest Attis castrated himself in ecstasy (Catullus, 63). For Adonis beloved by Venus, see Ovid, *Met.* 10. 710 ff.

poor queen . . . hair flying loose: the catamite makes himself feminine, comically investing his baldness with hair.

seventeen denarii: compare the prices later paid for the ass: to the baker (9.10), 'seven sesterces more' (= 18¾ denarii in all); to the market-gardener (9.31), 50 sesterces (= 12½ denarii); to the cooks (10.13), 11 denarii (allegedly a hasty sale; in the *Onos* the price was 25 drachmas/denarii).

Philebus: 'The rev. Love-Boyes' (McLeod).

8.26 *a hind for a maiden*: the literary touch is Apuleius' addition; substitution of a hind for a maiden in propitiatory sacrifice evokes the spurious close of Euripides' *Iphigenia in Aulide*. The phrase became proverbial for unexpected substitution (Achilles Tatius, 6. 3. 3).

At last you have come: this may be a take-off of Anchises' greeting to Aeneas in the Elysian Fields (Virgil, *Aen.* 6. 687 f.).

8.27–8: Lucretius 2.614 ff. has clearly inspired this lengthy description of the wild behaviour of the catamite priests.

8.28 *ass's milk*: taken as a remedy for various illnesses; cf. Pliny, *NH* 28. 125.

8.30 *Phrygian chant*: this mode of music was associated especially with the flute, played in orgiastic ritual in honour of Bacchus or Cybele.

BOOK 9

9.1 *divine providence*: it is clear that Fortune is represented as that aspect of divine Providence which brings trials and reverses in its train; see 11.15 n.

9.2 *Myrtilus etc.*: this episode of the mad dog does not appear in the *Onos*, and these comically apt names have been coined by

Apuleius himself. Myrtilus is the name of a mythological charioteer (Hyginus, 224); Hephaestio evokes Hephaestus, god of fire; Hypnophilus in Greek means 'sleep lover', an apt name for a chamberlain; and Apollonius derives from Apollo, god of healing.

9.4 *temple spoils*: this reference to temple-spoils is puzzling until we reach 9.9, where it becomes clear that Apuleius has omitted from the Greek story an episode in which the priests stole a golden bowl from a shrine; see *Onos* 41.

cuckolding: the succession of stories about cuckolded husbands which now follows is inserted by Apuleius to demonstrate the infidelities of the unregenerate world in which he now roams. The first story was appropriated by Boccaccio in the *Decameron*, where it becomes the second story of the seventh day (Peronella and the lover in the tub).

9.8 *oracular response*: this, and the jocular interpretations of it, do not appear in the *Onos*; they read like a characteristic Apuleian insertion.

9.9 *Mother of the Gods*: Cybele, the Magna Mater.

9.10 *Bridewell*: Apuleius uses the term 'Tullianum' for the gaol. This was the Roman dungeon allegedly built by Servius Tullius in the Regal period. Apuleius cites it to amuse the Roman reader.

consecrated there: in *Onos* 41, the statue of Atargate is more aptly lodged in another temple, presumably one consecrated to Atargate rather than to Cybele.

Philebus . . . paid for me: see 8.25 and n. ad loc., *seventeen denarii*.

9.13 *godlike creator*: Homer, whom Lucius paraphrases (cf. *Od.* 1. 1 ff.) in singing Odysseus' praises.

9.14 *the only God*: clearly the jibe of worshipping 'the only God' and the other practices mentioned here are directed against an adherent of either Judaism or Christianity. Given the hectic growth of Christianity in North Africa in the late second century (see Introduction, p. xxxix), Christianity seems the likelier target.

9.16 *audacious*: reading *intimidae* (Helm; *timidae F*, Robertson).

Philesitherus: 'Master Love-chaser'.

9.17 *Arete*: 'Mrs Virtue', an ironical title.

Myrmex: the word means 'ant' in Greek, an apt name for the busy servant.

9.18 *breached by gold*: in this moralizing story of the power of gold, Apuleius flaunts his knowledge of Horace, *Odes*, 3. 16. 9 ff., where gold is said to make its way through ministers and stone walls. The image of the wedge a little later also evokes this ode.

9.22 *Salian priest*: see note on 4.22.

laundryman: the interrelated stories of the baker's wife and the laundryman's wife which follow are, like the earlier story in 9.5, incorporated into the *Decameron*, where they become Novella 10 of the fifth day (Pietro di Vinciolo and Ercolano).

mere boy: note the inconsistency in the character of Philesitherus, a more mature and adventurous figure in the earlier tale. Apuleius always writes for the moment, and a changed persona is necessary in this new anecdote.

9.23 *Ceres here*: since this episode takes place at the baker's, it is fitting that a statue of Ceres, goddess of corn, has a place there.

9.25 *we both faced*: a charge of collusion in the murder would have implicated the baker.

9.26 *eyes of all*: Apuleius seems to be so carried away with the mimic nature of this drama that here and at the end of the next paragraph he appears to forget that the sole persons present, other than Lucius, are the baker and his wife.

9.27 *vindictive laundryman*: thus the three stories of cuckolded husbands are drawn together. 'I am no barbarian' puns on the name of Barbarus, the husband in 9.17.

equity: these legal quips, as we note in the Introduction (pp. xxix f), are a frequent means of amusing sophisticated Roman readers, well acquainted with the laws of property.

9.31 *on the ninth day*: the *novendiale sacrificium* took place at the tomb on the ninth day after death, and a funeral banquet followed; cf. Tacitus, *Ann.* 6. 5.

price was high: but lower than that paid for Lucius earlier (note on 8.25, *seventeen denarii*).

9.32 *Capricorn*: the sun enters Capricorn at the winter solstice in December.

9.33 *One night*: no trace of the following episode appears in the *Onos*; we can be reasonably certain that it is Apuleius' own insertion, since the citation of the horrific prodigies adds a further Roman touch of a literary nature to the narrative.

9.39 *his own misfortunes*: the gardener no longer had any prospect of receiving the produce promised him by the bereaved proprietor.

vine-staff: this was the symbol of the centurion's rank and authority; see Tacitus, *Ann.* 1. 23.

9.42 *The peeping ass and its shadow*: the proverb is found in Menander's fragmentary play *The Priestess* (fr. 246 K). It seems to have developed from two earlier expressions, 'Because of an ass's gaze', and 'Concerning an ass's shadow'; for conjectural explanations of these, see Gaselee's note in the earlier Loeb edn. of *The Golden Ass* (tr. Adlington), ad loc. The incident is found in the Greek story (*Onos*, 49), but Apuleius exploits it to lay further emphasis on the curiosity of the hero.

BOOK 10

10.2 *I record it in this book*: this long anecdote, not in the *Onos*, appears to have been inserted by Apuleius as a further depiction of the fallen world into which the hero is plunged.

sock . . . buskin: the promise of high tragedy (the sock is the low shoe of the comic actor, the buskin the high boot of the tragic player) is not fulfilled, for the episode ends happily. Apuleius merely announces that the theme of the stepmother infatuated with her stepson is inspired by Euripides' *Hippolytus* and Seneca's *Phaedra*.

undeveloped: the Latin (*Cupido paruulus*) recalls Virgil, *Aen.* 1. 715. The lady's subsequent behaviour contains further evocations of Virgil's Dido, and of the Phaedra of Seneca and Ovid, *Heroides*, 4.

Alas . . . physicians: echoing Virgil's 'heu uatum ignarae mentes!' (*Aen.* 4. 65), in the apt context of Dido's love-sickness; cf. also Petronius, 42. 5.

colour: retaining *coloris* with *F*, Robertson against *caloris*, in view of 'not running a temperature' in the following sentence.

10.3   *It is because . . . fitting*: cf. Seneca, *Phaedra*, 646 f.

10.7   *the Areopagus*: at Athens, the ancient court for trying homicide. For the procedure, see D. M. MacDowell, *The Law in Classical Athens* (London, 1978), 116 ff. For the injunction against irrelevance, cf. Lysias 3. 34; Aristotle, *Rhet.* 1354ª; and other references in MacDowell, 43.

10.8   *sewn in the sack*: this was the traditional penalty prescribed by the Twelve Tables. The convicted parricide was enclosed in a sack with a dog, a cock, a snake, and an ape, and drowned. This method of execution had long been abandoned. See *OCD*, *parricidium*.

10.10   *Greek manner*: cf. note on 3.9, *a wheel*.

10.11   *purpose of medicine*: Hippocrates, 1. 299: 'Neither will I administer a poison to anyone when asked to do so, nor will I suggest such a course.'

Mandragora: (or mandrake) was commonly used as a narcotic in surgical operations. For the ancient texts, see C. B. Randolph, *Proc. American Acad. of Arts and Sciences* (1905), 487 ff.

10.13   *eleven denarii*: in the *Onos*, 46, the price was 25 drachmas/denarii; Apuleius freely changes the sums paid for the transaction.

master was quite rich: the owner is from Thessalonica in the *Onos*, but Apuleius makes him a Corinthian (see 10.18 below) for the purposes of the climax of the story.

10.14   *savings*: a slave at his master's discretion could purchase his freedom by accumulating his *peculium*; see T. Wiedmann, *Greek and Roman Slavery* (Beckenham, 1981), 52.

Eteocles: the fratricidal strife between Eteocles and Polynices, sons of Oedipus, at Thebes is prominent in Aeschylus, *Seven Against Thebes*, and Sophocles, *Antigone*.

10.15   *Phineus*: the blind Phineus was constantly robbed of his meal by the Harpies, a theme appearing on vase-paintings and in Apollonius Rhodius, 2. 180 ff.

10.16   *silphium*: this plant associated with Cyrene (Catullus, 7. 4; Pliny, *NH* 19. 38) was used for both culinary and medicinal purposes.

10.17 *four times over*: at *Onos*, 48, the master pays only twice as much; Apuleius' underlines the lavish spending of his new master.

on my elbow: Adlington thoughtfully misrenders 'on my tail'; the absurdity of 'elbow' seems not to have occurred to the author of the *Onos* or to Apuleius.

10.18 *Thiasus*: the name suggests 'The Reveller', befitting the man who mounts the show; the *Onos* calls him Menecles.

quinquennial magistracy: the two principal officers of the municipality (*duouiri*) received this honorific title every fifth year.

10.19 *Pasiphaë*: wife of king Minos of Crete; she conceived a passion for a bull, and the fruit of their union was the Minotaur.

10.22 *lowing lover*: see the previous note.

10.23 *The story . . .*: this anecdote too has apparently been inserted by Apuleius; see note on 10.2 above.

killed at once: in Roman law a father had the right to rear or to expose a child (*Digest*, 28. 2. 11; see Jane F. Gardner, *Women in Roman Law and Society* (London, 1986), 155).

10.27 *funeral services*: see note on 9.31, *on the ninth day*.

10.29 *Pyrrhic dance*: initially a war-dance in armour, this became a more general choral performance, it is apt here, for the contest on Mt. Ida precipitated the Trojan War in which Pyrrhus was prominent (Virgil, *Aen.* 2. 469 ff.).

10.30 : The pageant that follows, described in Apuleius' most florid style, does not appear in the *Onos*. The theme of Venus' victory is the ironical prelude to the bestial copulation scheduled to follow.

10.31 *Castor and Pollux*: Juno's stepsons; Leda after being visited by Jupiter in the form of a swan gave birth to them in an egg; they were known as the Castors.

the Dorian mode: considered manly, and thus apt for Minerva, whereas the Ionian was thought effeminate; cf. Plato, *Rep.* 399a, *Laches*, 188d.

10.32 *the Lydian mode*: likewise rejected by Plato as effeminate (*Rep.* 398e).

10.33 *vultures in togas*: Apuleius amuses his readers with this disparaging address to Roman lawyers.

Palamedes: condemned on the evidence of a forged letter planted by Odysseus (Virgil, *Aen.* 2. 82 with Williams's note; Ovid, *Met.* 13. 308 ff.). The contest between Odysseus and Ajax for the arms of Achilles, Ovid, *Met.* 13. 1 ff. These examples may have occurred to Apuleius because they appear in Plato's account of the trial of Socrates (*Apol.* 41b), which is mentioned next here.

That old man: for Socrates' execution in 399 BC, and the judgement of the Delphic oracle that 'no man was wiser', cf. Plato, *Apol.* 24b ff. and 21a.

they swear by his name: Apuleius has himself in mind as a prominent Middle Platonist; Introd. pp. xv ff.

10.35 *took off at full gallop*: at this point Apuleius departs radically from the Greek story to incorporate the novel climax of conversion to Isis. In the Greek version, Lucius gulps down roses carried by the attendant at the Thessalonican games, is restored to manhood, and retires home after being humiliatingly rejected by the matron who was obsessed with him as an ass.

Cenchreae: excavations at Cenchreae have uncovered a shrine with Egyptian motifs which must be one of the temples mentioned by Pausanias 2. 4. 6 (see Gwyn Griffiths's edn. of Book 11, 18 ff.).

BOOK 11

11.1 *seven times*: for such importance attached by Pythagoreans (and subsequently by Platonists) to the number seven, see W. K. C. Guthrie, *A History of Greek Philosophy*, vol. (Cambridge, 1962), 303 f.

supremely powerful goddess: Lucius recognizes the moon as the one deity in various guises, but does not make the specific identification with Isis until 11.5 below.

11.2 *Ephesus*: this is Diana/Artemis, who in her role as Lucina presides over childbirth.

Proserpina: Hecate/Proserpina is depicted in Greek art with three bodies or heads; she is identified as 'the three-formed goddess' with Diana and Luna at Horace, *Odes* 3. 22. 3, and Virgil speaks of the 'Virgin's triple countenance' (*Aen.* 4.

511). Here her roles as Proserpina and Luna are acknowledged.

11.3–4: this description of the robes and accessories of the goddess is modelled on the statuary of Isis; virtually all the details recorded here can be paralleled from the statues. See Gwyn Griffiths's edn. of Book 11, ad loc.

11.5 *variety of . . . titles*: like the prayer of Lucius in 11.2 above, this aretalogy falls into four sections of three phrases each. The syncretism is characteristic of second-century Isiac worship. The Phrygians ('first-born' according to Herodotus, 2. 2) worshipped Cybele at Pessinus. Athena/Minerva is called 'Cecropian' because Cecrops was the legendary first king of Athens. Paphos in Cyprus had a celebrated shrine of Aphrodite/Venus. Cretan Dictynna is identified with Artemis/Diana in the Greek dramatists (see Guthrie, *The Greeks and their Gods* (London, 1950), 105). The Sicilians ('trilingual' because of the successive incursions of Carthaginians, Greeks, and Romans) worshipped 'Ortygian' Proserpina because Ortygia is the island off Syracuse, and the goddess was carried off to Hades from Sicilian fields. The Rhamnusian goddess is Nemesis, worshipped at Rhamnus near Marathon. 'Eastern and western Ethiopians' translates *utrique* (so Robertson; *arique F*); for the sense see note on 1.8, *Ethiopians . . . Antipodeans*.

this rite: the *nauigium Isidis*, celebrated on 5 March and hence inaugurating the sailing-season, is described in 11.16.

11.6 *spiteful charges*: Lucius might have feared that those observing his change of shape would charge him with the capital offence of magic.

Elysian fields: like Anchises, father of Aeneas, Lucius is to enjoy the state of natural bliss attained in this region of Hades.

11.8 *Ganymede*: see note on 1.12, *Endymion*.

Pegasus and Bellerophon: see note on 6.30.

11.9 *votive prayers*: presumably those uttered at 11.17.

Sarapis: (or Serapis) frequently replaces Osiris as husband of Isis in the Hellenistic period, but is mentioned in the romance only here, whereas Osiris appears at 11.27 and 30. Osiris is considered by some as the 'Greek' title, Sarapis as the 'foreign' name, but they are regarded as the same god.

11.10 *staff of Mercury*: Anubis bears similar objects in the next chapter, so this must be a priest of his; like Mercury, he is the guide of souls to Hades. (Apuleius carried round a statue of Mercury, and sacrificed in private to it; see *Apol.* 63. 3.)

11.15 *Fortune with eyes*: here Apuleius evokes the composite figure of Isis-Fortuna, who in her Hellenistic guise is accompanied by the cornucopia and rudder as symbols of her provision and guidance. The Fortune of the Greek novels, who has so unremittingly persecuted Lucius, is blind and malignant, equated with Typhon; Isis-Fortuna by contrast is the saving power with sight and foresight.

11.16 *sacred shrine*: presumably the altar described in 11.10.

egg and sulphur: for their use in purification ceremonies, see Ovid, *AA* 2. 330.

11.17 *living statues*: perhaps 'living' because represented by humans (as is the case with Lucius when initiated at 11.24). But the Latin *spirantia* can mean 'lifelike'.

sacred college: Lucius himself is admitted to the college of 'shrine-bearers' (11. 30), a lower order 'on the borderline between priests and temple-servants' (Gwyn Griffiths).

entire Roman people: unlike Christianity, the Isiac religion is now comfortably established at Rome.

11.18 *my native region*: at 2.12, Lucius stated that his home was in Corinth where he now is; cf. 1.22.

11.20 *Candidus*: 'white'. The 'belongings' promised are presumably the slaves.

11.22 *Mithras*: the name suggests a connection between the ritual of Mithras and that of Isis; 'an atmosphere of friendly syncretism' (Gwyn Griffiths). Winkler, 245, is unnecessarily taken aback, regarding it as 'like introducing the Pope, and calling him Martin Luther'. But the cult-figures of paganism unite in the face of the emergent Christian threat.

unfamiliar characters: the Egyptian hieroglyphs would be unfamiliar to a Greek.

11.24 *Olympian*: presumably so-called because the initiates have a rapport with the Olympian gods. The Arctic or Hyperborean epithet attached to the gryphons reflects the tradition that they came from the far north (Herodotus, 4. 13, 32; Pliny, *NH* 10. 70. 136). On the garb, see Gwyn Griffiths, ad loc.

11.26 *the harbour of Augustus*: constructed close to Ostia, had been built under Augustus; see R. Meiggs, *Roman Ostia* (Oxford, 1960), 54 ff., 153 ff.

Campensis: the temple was called Campensis because it lay on the Campus Martius; see Josephus, *Ant.* 18. 65 ff.; S. B. Platner and T. Ashby, *Topographical Dictionary of Ancient Rome* (Oxford, 1929), 283 ff.

11.27 *Osiris*: as Isis' husband, he was closely associated with her ritual. The epithet 'unconquered' commemorates his victory over Seth-Typhon, and may have been influenced by Mithras' title *Sol invictus*.

pastophori: see note on 11.17, *sacred college*.

a name quite relevant: Asinius is cognate with *asinus*, an ass.

Madauros: Apuleius' native city (Introd. p. xi); thus at the climax of his novel the author identifies himself with his hero.

11.28 *twixt axe and altar*: for the saying, reflecting the plight of the sacrificial victim, cf. Plautus, *Captiui*, 617.

11.30 *pastophori*: see note on 11.17, *sacred college*.

quinquennial administrators: for this honorific title awarded to the chief officials of the municipality every fifth year, see note on. 10.18. Presumably the usage was extended to temple-wardens.

days of Sulla: scholars speculatively connect Sulla's cult of Fortune with worship of Isis, but there is no other evidence than this for his establishment of the college.

INDEX AND GLOSSARY OF NAMES

The Oxford World's Classics Website

www.worldsclassics.co.uk

- Information about new titles
- Explore the full range of Oxford World's Classics
- Links to other literary sites and the main OUP webpage
- Imaginative competitions, with bookish prizes
- Peruse *Compass*, the Oxford World's Classics magazine
- Articles by editors
- Extracts from Introductions
- A forum for discussion and feedback on the series
- Special information for teachers and lecturers

www.worldsclassics.co.uk

American Literature

British and Irish Literature

Children's Literature

Classics and Ancient Literature

Colonial Literature

Eastern Literature

European Literature

History

Medieval Literature

Oxford English Drama

Poetry

Philosophy

Politics

Religion

The Oxford Shakespeare

A complete list of Oxford Paperbacks, including Oxford World's Classics, OPUS, Past Masters, Oxford Authors, Oxford Shakespeare, Oxford Drama, and Oxford Paperback Reference, is available in the UK from the Academic Division Publicity Department, Oxford University Press, Great Clarendon Street, Oxford OX2 6DP.

In the USA, complete lists are available from the Paperbacks Marketing Manager, Oxford University Press, 198 Madison Avenue, New York, NY 10016.

Oxford Paperbacks are available from all good bookshops. In case of difficulty, customers in the UK can order direct from Oxford University Press Bookshop, Freepost, 116 High Street, Oxford OX1 4BR, enclosing full payment. Please add 10 per cent of published price for postage and packing.